1908.

THE

COMMONWEALTH LAW REPORTS

CASES DETERMINED IN THE

HIGH COURT OF AUSTRALIA.

Editor—JAMES C. ANDERSON, LL.B., Barrister-at-Law.

REPORTERS :

New South Wales . C. A. WHITE, B.A. (Oxon.), *Barrister-at-Law.*

Victoria . . . . .
South Australia . . } BENNET LANGTON, B.A., LL.B., *Barrister-at-Law.*
Tasmania . . . .

Queensland . . . .
} H. V. JAQUES, B.A., LL.B., *Barrister-at-Law.*
West Australia . .

VOL. 5.

1907-8—7 & 8 EDWARD VII.

THE LAW BOOK COMPANY OF AUSTRALASIA, LIMITED.
72 CASTLEREAGH STREET, | 41 & 43 ADELAIDE STREET,
SYDNEY. | BRISBANE.

1908.

Melbourne:
Harston, Partridge & Co., Printers,
452-454 *Chancery Lane.*

JUSTICES OF THE HIGH COURT
OF AUSTRALIA

DURING THE CURRENCY OF THIS VOLUME (1907-8).

THE RIGHT HONOURABLE SIR SAMUEL WALKER GRIFFITH, P.C.,
G.C.M.G., CHIEF JUSTICE.

THE RIGHT HONOURABLE SIR EDMUND BARTON, P.C., G.C.M.G.

THE HONOURABLE RICHARD EDWARD O'CONNOR.

THE HONOURABLE ISAAC ALFRED ISAACS.

THE HONOURABLE HENRY BOURNES HIGGINS.

ATTORNEY-GENERAL:

THE HONOURABLE LITTLETON E. GROOM, M.P.

THE mode of citation of this volume of the COMMONWEALTH LAW REPORTS will be as follows:—

5 C.L.R.

A TABLE

OF THE

NAMES OF THE CASES REPORTED

IN THIS VOLUME.

TABLE OF CASES CITED.

A

L

M

N

ERRATA.

Page.	Line.	For.	Read.
200	Solicitors	Chambers & Macnab ..	Atthow & McGregor.
222	5 from bottom.. ..	48 Vict. No. 18	53 Vict. No. 21.
487	1 of Headnote	1887	1877.
491	8 from bottom.. ..	1887	1877.
861	9 ,, ,, ...	transmuted into.. .	*transit in.*
864	1 ,, ,, ...	removed	renewed.

REPORTS OF CASES

DETERMINED IN THE

HIGH COURT OF AUSTRALIA

1907-1908.

[HIGH COURT OF AUSTRALIA.]

KELLY . . . . APPELLANT;
DEFENDANT,

AND

TUCKER . . . . RESPONDENT.
PLAINTIFF,

ON APPEAL FROM THE SUPREME COURT OF VICTORIA.

Partnership—Dissolution—At will or for single venture—Unequal contribution of capital—Repayment—Partnership Act 1891 (Vict.) (No. 1222), secs. 28, 30, 36, 39, 48.

H. C. OF A.
1907.

MELBOURNE,
June 21, 24, 25;
Sept. 12.

Griffith C.J.,
Barton,
Isaacs and
Higgins JJ.

A. and B. made a verbal contract whereby they agreed to enter into partnership in the business of buying racehorses in Australia, shipping them to South Africa, and there selling them; that A. should provide £800 as capital for the business; and that the profits should be equally divided between A. and B. A. provided the £800, and racehorses were bought and raced in Australia, but no horses were sent to South Africa. A. gave notice of dissolution of the partnership. In an action by A. for winding up the partnership he claimed a declaration that the £800 should be paid to him out of the assets of the partnership in priority to any payment to B. in respect of profits. Judgment was given declaring that the partnership was dissolved, and that A. was entitled to be allowed the whole of the £800, and ordering that, in the taking of the accounts, the sum of £800 should be allowed to A. as capital of the partnership business.

Held, that there was evidence to justify a finding that there was an implied agreement that the £800 should be repaid to A. before there was any division of profits.

Held also (Higgins J. dissenting), that there was evidence to justify a finding that the adventure to South Africa was abandoned, and, therefore, that the partnership became one for an indefinite term and was determined by the notice.

Judgment of *Hood* J. affirmed.

APPEAL from the Supreme Court of Victoria.

An action was brought in the Supreme Court of Victoria by George Edward Tucker against John Joseph Kelly, the writ in which was issued on 29th September 1906 and served on 4th October 1906. By the statement of claim the plaintiff alleged as follows :—That, in November 1905, it was verbally agreed between the plaintiff and the defendant that they should enter into partnership in the business of buying some racehorses in Australia and shipping them to South Africa and there selling them, and that the plaintiff should provide £800 as the capital for the said business, and that the plaintiff and the defendant should both go to South Africa with the said horses for the purpose of so selling them, and that the profits should be divided equally between them ; that no agreement was made as to the length of time during which the partnership business was to be carried on ; that in pursuance of such agreement the defendant bought certain racehorses on account of the partnership, and the plaintiff paid to the defendant the sum of £800 ; that in December 1905 the defendant received £240 for and on behalf of the plaintiff in respect of a bet made and won by the defendant on behalf of the plaintiff, and the defendant paid the said sum into the partnership banking account which was in fact in the defendant's name ; that about January 1906 it was verbally agreed between the plaintiff and the defendant that the said racehorses should not be shipped to South Africa and there sold, and the said racehorses had since been raced on account of the partnership ; that in September 1906 the plaintiff became desirous of terminating the said partnership, and that disputes arose between the plaintiff and the defendant as to the basis upon which the affairs of the partnership should be wound up, the plaintiff affirming that the said

H. C. of A.
1907.

KELLY
v.
TUCKER.

sums of £800 and £240 should be repaid to the plaintiff out of the assets of the partnership in priority to any payment to the defendant in respect of the profits, the defendant denying that the said sum of £800 should be so repaid, and at first admitting and afterwards denying that the said sum of £240 should be so repaid ; that on the 24th September 1906, written notice was given to the defendant on behalf of the plaintiff dissolving the partnership as from the date of such notice, that the plaintiff by writing ratified and confirmed such notice, and that such writing was on 4th October 1906 served upon the defendant.

The plaintiff claimed :—

(a) A declaration that the partnership was dissolved on the 24th September 1906 or on the 4th October 1906, or alternatively an order for the dissolution of the partnership.

(b) An order that the affairs of the partnership be wound up.

(c) A declaration that the two sums of £800 and £240 should be paid to the plaintiff out of the assets of the partnership in priority to any payment to the defendant in respect of profits.

(d) All necessary accounts and inquiries.

(e) An order for the appointment of a receiver and manager.

(f) Such further order as may be necessary.

It is not necessary for this report to set out the defence.

The evidence, so far as is material, is set out in the judgments hereunder.

Hood J., who heard the action, gave a judgment declaring that the partnership was dissolved on 4th October 1906, that, on the taking of the accounts in the judgment directed, the plaintiff was entitled to be allowed the whole of the £800 mentioned in the statement of claim, but that the sum of £240 mentioned in the statement of claim should be deemed assets of the partnership. The judgment then went on to order accounts of the partnership dealings to be taken on that basis. On a subsequent day *Hood* J. appointed a receiver and manager of the partnership assets and property. The defendant appealed to the High Court from the judgment in the action, except so far as it applied to the £240, and from the order appointing a receiver and manager.

Hayes, for the appellant. Primâ facie, the £800 is capital of

H. C. of A.   the partnership, and belongs equally to the partners.   The £800
1907.   was not a loan to the partnership.   *Hood* J. must have found
KELLY   that the partnership was one at will, but the evidence shows that
v.   it was a partnership for a single adventure to last until one visit
TUCKER.   had been paid to South Africa, when it would be dissolved : Sec.
36 of the *Partnership Act* 1891.   That being so, a dissolution
could not have been decreed until that event happened, unless the
relations between the parties had become such that the partnership could not be carried on : See sec. 39 of the *Partnership Act*
1891.   No case was made for a decree for dissolution, and if an
amendment had been asked for, it would only have been on terms
of the respondent paying all the costs.   Secs. 28 (1) and 48 of the
Partnership Act 1891 must be read together, and the effect is that
on a winding up of the partnership the partners are entitled to
share equally in the capital unless some other agreement is
proved.

[HIGGINS J. referred to *Lindley on Partnership*, 7th ed., p. 385.
ISAACS J. referred to *Pollock on Partnership*, 6th ed., p. 131.]

The fact that the partners have contributed towards capital
unequally does not affect the matter.   *Story on Partnership*, 5th
ed., par. 47.   Here the effect of the respondent paying in £800
and the appellant nothing is that the respondent pays £400 for
the appellant's skill.

[ISAACS J. referred to *Binney* v. *Mutrie* (1), and *Wilson* v.
Kircaldie (2).]

It is admitted that if this was a partnership at will it was
terminated by the first notice given.

[Counsel also referred to *Reade* v. *Bentley* (3).]

McArthur, for the respondent.   The statement of claim does
not allege that the partnership was for a single venture.   Even
if it was, there is abundant evidence to justify the Judge in
saying that the trip to South Africa was abandoned, and that the
partnership became one at will.   As to what is reasonable notice
to determine, see *Featherstonhaugh* v. *Fenwick* (4).   The burden
of showing there was more than a partnership at will is on the

(1) 12 App. Cas., 160.   (3) 4 Kay & J., 656.
(2) 13 N.Z.L.R., 286.   (4) 17 Ves., 298, at p. 308.

appellant : *Burdon* v. *Barkus* (1). Sec. 28 of the *Partnership Act* 1891 applies to a partnership while it exists, and regulates the duties and position of the partners during that time; while sec. 48 applies after the partnership is wound up. The skill of the partners or of one partner cannot be regarded as capital of the partnership. The position is the same as if £800 had been advanced to the partnership by the respondent, and it must be' repaid to the respondent before there is any other distribution.

[HIGGINS J. referred to *Reid* v. *Hollinshead* (2), and *Kilpatrick* v. *Mackay* (3).]

In *Garner* v. *Murray* (4), it was assumed that, where there were unequal contributions of capital, the capital should be returned according to the amount contributed. See also *Nowell* v. *Nowell* (5) ; *Ross* v. *White* (6). According to the evidence the bargain was to share profits and not to share losses, although it may be implied that the losses were to be shared.

Hayes, in reply, referred to *Syers* v. *Syers* (7).

Cur. adv. vult.

GRIFFITH C.J. This action was brought by the respondent for a declaration that a partnership between him and the appellant had been dissolved in September 1906, or, alternatively, for a dissolution of the partnership, and for a declaration that two sums of £800 and £240 respectively should be paid to the respondent out of the assets of the partnership in priority to any claim made by the appellant in respect of profits, with consequential relief. The agreement for partnership, which was verbal only, was made in November 1905. As alleged by the plaintiff in the statement of claim, the agreement was that the parties should enter into partnership in the business of buying some racehorses in Australia and shipping them to South Africa and there selling them, that the plaintiff (the respondent) should provide £800 as the capital for the business, that both partners should go to South Africa with the horses for the purpose of so

Sept. 12.

(1) 4 DeG. F. & J., 42.
(2) 4 B. & C., 867.
(3) 4 V.L.R. (Eq.), 28.
(4) (1904) 1 Ch., 57.

(5) L.R. 7 Eq., 538, at p. 541.
(6) (1894) 3 Ch., 326.
(7) 1 App. Cas., 174.

H. C. of A.
1907.
KELLY
v.
TUCKER.
Griffith C.J.

selling them, and that the profits should be equally divided. He alleged that no agreement was made as to the duration of the partnership. He also alleged that about January 1906, it was verbally agreed that the horses (which had then been bought) should not be shipped to South Africa, and that the horses had since been raced in Australia on account of the partnership. The appellant, who was a trainer, alleged in his defence that the objects of the partnership were to consist of buying racehorses in Australia, training and running them on race-courses for stakes, and in earning profits for the partnership by winning stakes and wagers by means of the partnership horses, and, if necessary or desirable, in shipping racehorses to South Africa and elsewhere for the purposes of sale. He also alleged that, in consideration of the respondent's contribution of £800 to the partnership, he was not to be bound to give any of his time to the partnership business, and that the appellant, in place of a money contribution, was to devote his whole time and attention to the partnership business, and that the capital, assets and profits of the partnership were to belong to the partners in equal shares. He further alleged that the partnership was not to be determinable at will, but was to continue for a reasonable time, or until reasonable notice had been given to determine it. On 24th September 1906 the respondent, treating the partnership as a partnership at will, gave notice of dissolution, and on 29th September he began his action. The writ was served on 4th October.

If the partnership was a partnership at will, or a partnership for an indefinite time, it is not disputed that the bringing of the action was a sufficient notice of intention to dissolve it within sec. 36 of the *Partnership Act* 1891 (No. 1222).

The action was tried before *Hood* J. without a jury. He declared that the partnership was dissolved on 4th October, *i.e.*, from the date of service of the writ, that the £800 should be allowed to the plaintiff, " as the capital for the said business," and that the other sum of £240 should be deemed partnership assets. This appeal was then brought. We have not been favoured with any statement of the reasons of the learned Judge. This is much to be regretted, especially as the evidence, which, so far as we can

H. C. or A.
1907.

KELLY
v.
TUCKER.

Griffith C.J.

judge from the notes, was very meagre and unsatisfactory, was conflicting.

But, since the learned Judge declared that the partnership was dissolved as from the date of service of the writ, he must, I think, be taken to have found as a fact that the partnership was one for an indefinite time. It is contended that this finding, as well as his finding as to the £800, was not supported by the evidence, to which I will briefly refer.

Both parties agreed that the original intention was to buy racehorses and take them to South Africa, and sell them there. It is common ground that, after the horses were bought, they were for some time raced in Australia by mutual consent. The departure to South Africa appears to have been delayed in consequence of a difficulty in obtaining a jockey to go with them, and that part of the project does not seem to have been revived up to September 1906, when the plaintiff gave his notice of dissolution. On these facts the first question is whether the learned Judge could find that there was an implied agreement which excluded the general rule laid down in sec. 28, sub-sec. (1) of the *Partnership Act* 1891 (assuming it to be *primâ facie* applicable) that " all the partners are entitled to share equally in the capital and profits of the business." Having regard to the original intention of the parties, which related mainly to a single adventure to terminate with the sale of the horses in South Africa, I think it is not unreasonable to infer that it was an implied term of the partnership agreement that the £800 should be repaid to the plaintiff before the profits of the joint adventure were divided. The plaintiff in his evidence said that the agreement was that they were to share the " profits." The sense in which spoken words are used is a question of fact for the tribunal which is the judge of fact. The word " profits " is certainly capable of bearing the meaning put on it by the plaintiff. I think, therefore, that a verdict by a jury, that there was an implied agreement that the £800 should not form part of the assets of the partnership so as to be divisible without repayment to the plaintiff, could not be impeached as being one which reasonable men could not have found. The learned Judge saw the witnesses and their demeanour, and I am not prepared to differ from his conclusion. If sec. 28 does not apply, *cadit quæstio.*

In this view, the other question—whether the partnership was in September 1906 a partnership for an indefinite time—is of only academical interest, for I have no doubt that, under the circumstances of this case, it was at the time of the trial "just and equitable that the partnership should be dissolved" (*Partnership Act* 1891, sec. 39 (*f*)), and the pleadings should, if necessary, be taken to have been amended accordingly. It is, however, contended for the plaintiff that, in the events that had happened, the adventure to South Africa ought to be considered as having been tacitly abandoned by mutual consent. In that view the partnership would clearly have become one for an indefinite time. On this point I think that it was open to a jury on the evidence to find either way. I am not, therefore, able to say that the learned Judge was wrong in the finding on which the judgment for dissolution was based. The appellant has therefore failed to show that the judgment was erroneous, and the appeal must be dismissed.

BARTON J. I concur, and I do not think it necessary to add anything.

ISAACS J. I agree that this appeal should be dismissed. The parties by their conduct had, in my opinion, quite abandoned all intention to persevere with the South African part of their undertaking. Whatever its original duration may have been, the partnership was on 4th October 1906, when the notice of dissolution was served, a partnership for an undefined term, and by force of sec. 36 of the *Partnership Act* 1891 was dissolved by the notice.

The only other question, and really the one substantial question as the facts now appear, is whether the appellant is entitled to share equally with the respondent in the assets of the firm without first crediting the respondent with £800 he provided in the first instance; or whether the respondent is entitled to be considered as having a claim against the firm of £800 advanced, which must be satisfied before the ultimately divisible residue is arrived at.

It is not necessary to determine the effect of secs. 28 and 48 of the *Partnership Act* upon each other or their operation upon the case, although considerable argument was addressed to us on this subject. The facts are clearly susceptible to the view that the £800 found wholly by the respondent was, on the true meaning of the original agreement, an advance to be accounted for before arriving at the profits to be divided. Apparently this was the opinion of Mr. Justice *Hood*, and I see no reason to differ from that conclusion.

With regard to the argument that a finding of the learned Primary Judge should not be reversed unless demonstrably wrong, I do not agree with it. That would improperly narrow the duty of the Court of Appeal. The proper rule is stated by the learned Chief Justice in *McLaughlin* v. *Daily Telegraph Newspaper Co. Ltd.* (1).

HIGGINS J. On the main matter in contest—the rights of the parties in respect of the £800 contributed by Tucker—I concur with my learned colleagues. I think that there was sufficient evidence to justify the learned Judge below in coming to the conclusion that there was an agreement to give Kelly a share of the profits, and no more. It is, no doubt, our duty to " rehear " the case, and to reconsider the materials, as is laid down in *Coghlan* v. *Cumberland* (2); but, after performing this duty, I see no ground for holding that the learned Judge was wrong. I confess, however, that I have been somewhat puzzled by sec. 28 (1) of the *Partnership Act* 1891. It prescribes that, subject to any agreement expressed or implied, all the parties are entitled to share equally in the capital and profits of the business. No doubt, this is an Act to " amend " as well as to " declare " the law of partnership; but was it intended to amend the law in this respect ? The text writers show that, in the ordinary course of accounting as between partners, each partner takes out his contributed capital before any distribution of the surplus. (*Pollock, Partnership*, 4th ed., pp. 69-70; *Collyer, Partnership*, 2nd ed., pp. 105-106; *Lindley, Partnership*, 6th ed., pp. 399-404; and see *Garner* v. *Murray* (3); *Kilpatrick* v. *Mackay* (4), and *Partnership Act* 1891, sec. 48 (b) (3).)

H. C. OF A.
1907.

KELLY
v.
TUCKER.

Isaacs J.

(1) 1 C.L.R., 243, at pp. 261, 277.   (3) (1904) 1 Ch., 57.
(2) (1898) 1 Ch., 704.   (4) 4 V.L.R. (Eq.), 28.

H. C. of A.
1907.

KELLY
v.
TUCKER.

Higgins J.

In the treatise of Lord *Lindley*, this sec. 28 is not treated as
obliterating, for purposes of distribution, inequalities in capital
contributed (*Lindley on Partnership*, 6th ed., p. 356 ; 7th ed., pp.
385, 450.) *Primâ facie*, where one partner has skill, and the
other has money, when the one departs with his skill, the other
—one would think—should be able to depart with his money.
But the difficulty occasioned by sec. 28 does not really arise for
settlement in this case, as an agreement is found, express or
implied, to the effect that Kelly should share profits only.

On the other point—the dissolution of the partnership by the
plaintiff's notice, or else dissolution by the Court—I am unable to
find any sufficient ground existing for dissolution at the date of the
writ (29th September 1906). According to Tucker's own case as
put in his statement of claim, there was a partnership agreement
in November 1905 to buy racehorses in Australia and ship them
to South Africa, and there sell them ; about January 1906, it was
verbally agreed that the racehorses should not be shipped to South
Africa, and then sold; and, in September 1906, the plaintiff became
desirous of terminating the partnership, disputes arose and the
plaintiff gave written notice of dissolution on the 24th of September, and confirmed it by writing dated 28th September and
served on 4th October. It was admitted by Mr. *McArthur* for
the plaintiff—as, indeed, appeared from the statement of claim—
that originally the partnership was to be for one trip at least to
South Africa, and that, unless this stipulation were varied by
agreement, the partnership could not be dissolved at an earlier
stage at the will of one partner : *Reade* v. *Bentley* (1); *Partnership Act* 1891, secs. 4 (2), 36. But the plaintiff sought to meet
this position by alleging a verbal agreement in January 1906 not
to ship to South Africa. Now, such an agreement has not been
proved, either as to January or to any other time ; and, as it is
the only ground on which the prayer for declaration of dissolution, or, in the alternative, for dissolution by the Court, is based,
it seems to me that the prayer ought not to have been granted.
I shall take the plaintiff's own evidence on the subject. We have
not the advantage of His Honor's reasons for his judgment, but
treating the plaintiff as entitled to the assumption that His

(1) 4 Kay & J., 656.

Honor found such facts in his favour as are necessary for the judgment pronounced, is there any evidence of the alleged agreement not to ship to South Africa ? The plaintiff says :—

"On 27th January at Williamstown was the first race run by Mereworth. Kenny rode him. Kenny had no jockey's licence. Kelly got a permit for him for that day pending his application for a licence to the committee. Kenny applied for a licence and it was refused. Kelly and I spoke about going to South Africa, but we could not go till Kenny got a licence, and this was the sole reason why we waited before going to South Africa. We were waiting for a boy all the time and drifted on."

"Waiting" or "drifting on" does not involve an agreement not to ship for South Africa. I cannot see any evidence on which one could find that the idea of shipping to South Africa was abandoned at any time before the writ; and, if it was not abandoned, the partnership was not dissolved before the writ, and there was no ground for invoking the jurisdiction of the Court to dissolve it. As for the suggestion that the statement of claim might be amended by stating, under sec. 39, that circumstances have arisen which render it just and equitable that the partnership be dissolved, the case has not been fought on that issue, and there has been no opportunity to tender evidence thereon ; and I cannot think it fair to the defendant to let the plaintiff shift his ground at this stage. Nor, indeed—even if I ignore the pleadings, and the conduct of the case up to the present—can I point to any fact which, at the time of the writ, rendered it "just and equitable" that the partnership should be dissolved.

Appeal dismissed with costs.

Solicitor, for appellant, *W. J. Woolcott*, Melbourne.
Solicitors, for respondent, *Ellison & Hewison*, Melbourne.

B. L.

[HIGH COURT OF AUSTRALIA.]

PHILLIPS . . . . APPELLANT;

AND

LYNCH, AND THE MINISTER FOR LANDS . RESPONDENTS.

ON APPEAL FROM THE SUPREME COURT OF NEW SOUTH WALES.

H. C. OF A.
1907.

SYDNEY,
Aug. 14, 15,
16.

Barton,
O'Connor,
Isaacs and
Higgins JJ.

Crown Lands Act 1889 *(N.S.W.)* (53 *Vict. No.* 21), *sec.* 47—*Married Women's Property Act* 1901 *(N.S.W.)—Crown Lands Act Amendment Act* 1903 *(N.S.W.)* (*No.* 15 *of* 1903), *secs.* 3, 17—*Right of married woman to acquire additional conditional purchase—"Original application"—Construction.*

Under the Crown Lands Acts conditional purchases of Crown lands may be made by application to the Crown in the prescribed manner. By sec. 47 of the *Crown Lands Act* 1889 a married woman living with her husband is prohibited from conditionally purchasing Crown lands under the Crown Lands Acts, but under the decision of the Supreme Court in *Ex parte Luke*, (1901) 1 S.R. (N.S.W.), 322, she may out of moneys belonging to her separate estate acquire a conditional purchase by transfer from the holder.

Held, affirming the decision of the Supreme Court, that the general enabling words of sec. 3 of the *Crown Lands Act Amendment Act* 1903, which provides, *inter alia*, that "the holder of any conditional purchase" may apply for additional Crown land to be held as an additional conditional purchase, do not repeal the special prohibition as to married women contained in sec. 47 of the Act of 1889 ; and that nothing in the provisions of the *Married Women's Property Act* 1901 has that effect.

But *held*, reversing the decision of the Supreme Court, that sec. 17 of the *Crown Lands Act Amendment Act* 1903, confers upon a married woman, living with her husband, who has become the holder of a conditional purchase by transfer from the holder, and has obtained the consent of the Minister to her application, the right to apply to the Crown for an additional conditional purchase in virtue of her holding, and to acquire it, out of moneys belonging to her separate estate.

Hall v. *Costello*, (1905) 5 S.R. (N.S.W.), 573, overruled.

Decision of the Supreme Court : *Phillips* v. *Lynch*, (1906) 6 S.R. (N.S.W.), 645, reversed in part.

H. C. of A.
1907.
PHILLIPS
v.
LYNCH.

APPEAL from a decision of the Supreme Court of New South Wales on a special case stated by the Land Appeal Court.

The appellant, a married woman living with her husband, purchased at a sheriff's sale out of moneys belonging to her separate estate an original conditional purchase on 16th June 1903, and from that date continuously resided upon the holding.

On 12th February 1904 she applied to the Minister for Lands under the provisions of sec. 17 of the *Crown Lands Act Amendment Act* 1903 for his consent to her acquiring an additional conditional purchase of 59 acres in virtue of her holding of the original conditional purchase, and the Minister gave his consent. She then applied for an additional conditional purchase of the area mentioned. The deposit and the fees and expenses in connection with the application were paid by her out of her separate estate. At the same time the respondent Lynch applied for an additional conditional purchase including the area applied for by the appellant, and the local Land Board disallowed the appellant's application. She appealed to the Land Appeal Court, and the appeal was dismissed. That Court stated a special case for the decision of the Supreme Court under the provisions of the Crown Lands Acts, the following questions being submitted : whether under sec. 3 of the *Crown Lands Act Amendment Act* 1903 the appellant, having fulfilled the conditions as to residence on her original holding, was entitled to make application for an additional conditional purchase ; whether under sec. 17 of that Act, having fulfilled the conditions required by that section, she was entitled to apply for and acquire such an additional holding with moneys belonging to her separate estate ; and whether under the *Married Women's Property Act* 1901 she was capable of acquiring and holding such an area in the same manner as if she were a *feme sole.*

The Supreme Court answered the three questions in the negative and dismissed the appeal. The first question was the only one argued, it being considered that the second question had

H. C. of A. already been determined by the Supreme Court in *Hall* v.
1907.   *Costello* (1), and the third in *Ex parte Luke* (2). *Phillips* v.
PHILLIPS   *Lynch* (3).
v.
LYNCH.   From this decision the present appeal was brought.

Whitfeld (*Pike* with him), for the appellant. The general
scheme of the Act of 1903 was to extend the rights of persons
holding under tenures created by the previous Acts; and to give a
wider discretion to the Land Board in dealing with applications
for Crown Lands. There was therefore no longer any reason to
restrict the rights of a married woman living with her husband
to apply for land. The Board could take into consideration the
area already held by her and her husband. See sec. 3 (*d*) of the
Crown Lands Act Amendment Act 1903. Under the Act of
1884 there was no restriction upon the right of a married woman
to take up land whether as an original or as an additional holding.
The first restriction appeared in sec. 47 of the Act 53 Vict. No. 21,
the effect of which, so far as it is material to this case, was to
prevent a married woman living with her husband from applying
to the Crown for an original conditional purchase. [He referred to
In re Ousby (4).] It was held in *Ex parte Luke* (2) that there is
nothing in that section to prevent a married woman living with her
husband from acquiring by purchase from the holder a conditional
purchase out of the moneys belonging to her separate estate. She
may thus become a holder. Subsequent legislation must be taken to
have adopted that construction, and to have used the word "holder"
in the sense in which it had been interpreted by the Courts, especially in view of the fact that titles have been acquired upon the
basis of that decision. [He referred to sec. 4 of the *Appraisement
Act* 1902 (No. 109 of 1902).] Assuming that, at the time of the
passing of the Act of 1903 such married women were debarred
from taking up an additional holding by virtue of any holding
which they might have acquired by purchase, and bearing in
mind the purpose of the Act of 1903, *i.e.* to extend the rights of
holders, there is nothing *a priori* improbable in the legislature
including married women holders amongst those to receive benefit
from the Act. Sec. 3 gives "the holder" of any conditional pur-

(1) (1905) 5 S.R. (N.S.W.), 573.   (3) (1906) 6 S R. (N.S.W.), 645.
(2) (1901) 1 S.R. (N.S.W.), 322.   (4) 14 N.S.W. L.R., 506.

chase the right to take up an additional area subject to the conditions specified. *Primâ facie*, that includes married women who are holders, whether living with their husbands or not, and that is the construction put upon the words, by a long course of practice and legal decision. The old presumption against the inclusion of married women, in legislation as to rights of property in land, had disappeared with the *Married Women's Property Act* 1893 (consolidated in 1901, No. 45, secs. 3, 8, 9). The construction of sec. 3 of the Act of 1903 should not be cut down by reference to prior legislation. If the meaning is to be so limited, sec. 47 of the Act of 1884 would make the exception of non-residential conditional purchases unnecessary.

Sec. 17, at any rate, confers upon married women in the position of the appellant the right to acquire, *inter alia*, a conditional purchase in any way except by an "original application," provided that they have fulfilled the other requirements of the section. The words "the provisions of the principal Acts to the contrary notwithstanding" suggest that something is to be granted which might conflict or appear to conflict with earlier enactments. "Conditional purchase" would include additional as well as original, and the only exception is that the holding may not be acquired by "original application." That may mean either an application for an original holding of a series, or an application direct to the Crown for any holding. If the latter construction is adopted, no new right is conferred by the section, because under the previously existing law a married woman could become a holder by purchase from a holder or by devolution or devise, &c. If the former construction is adopted a new right of a kind in conformity with the scope of the Act is conferred, and that construction is consistent with the use of the word original throughout the Crown Lands Acts in connection with applications for holdings.

Canaway, for the respondent Lynch. The prohibition in sec. 47 of the 53 Vict. No. 21 against a married woman "conditionally purchasing" extends to the holding of a conditional purchase as well as to making. *Ex parte Luke* (1) was wrongly decided, but as

(1) (1901) 1 S.R. (N.S.W.), 322.

titles have been established under its authority this Court may
refuse to review it. The legislature indicated in that section
the persons who are to be deemed holders of conditional purchases, and has excluded married women living with their
husbands. Sec. 23 of the 48 Vict. No. 18 would exclude married
women without separate estate, because their disabilities had not
then been removed. See also sec. 124 of that Act. The policy
of the legislature, as shown by the 48 Vict. No. 18, was to restrict
the area to be enjoyed by one man, and with that view a married
woman living with her husband was prohibited from acquiring
an area which would, in effect, be added to that held by the
husband. This restriction was held not to apply to married
women with separate estate : *In re Melvil* (1). The Act 53 Vict.
No. 21, sec. 47 was intended to get rid of the effect of that decision,
except as to a married woman judicially separated from her
husband, who from the nature of the case might require a holding
of her own to support herself and family. That section clearly
barred a married woman living with her husband from applying
for a conditional lease, and there is no reason why it should not
apply equally to an additional conditional purchase. Both are
holdings appurtenant to an original conditional purchase. The
natural meaning of the words should not be cut down unless a
strong reason is shown for doing so. "Crown land" includes
land held under conditional purchase until a grant has been
made, and it would therefore seem that the prohibition extends
to the acquisition of an area by purchase from the holder. The
appellant must go to the length of contending that that section
is repealed, as regards applications for additional holdings, by sec.
3 of the Act of 1903. But the general rule of construction is that
a particular enactment of a negative character, such as sec. 47, is
not impliedly repealed by an affirmative enactment in general
terms. If sec. 3 is not to be read in the light of the earlier Acts
on the same subject, "holder" would include lunatics and all
persons debarred under those Acts, although, by sec. 1, the Act of
1903 is to be read and construed with the Principal Acts. Those
Acts should be applied except so far as expressly repealed. [He
referred to sec. 3, sub-sec. (f) of No. 15 of 1903; *In re Smith's*

(1) 10 N.S.W.L.R., 286.

Estate; *Clements* v. *Ward* (1); *Kutner* v. *Phillips* (2); *Healey* v. *Egan* (3).]

In sec. 17 " original application " means the application from which the particular holding in question originates, that is to say, the application to the Crown for that area, whether the holding is the first of a series or an additional one. The parenthesis ending with the word " *notwithstanding* " may be attributed to a doubt in the minds of the legislature as to the correctness of the statement of the law in *Ex parte Luke* (4). Original application must be something which can be predicated of all the forms of tenure referred to in the section. But it can have no sensible reference to a conditional lease, if construed in the way contended for by the appellant, because such a holding can only be taken up by virtue of a conditional purchase. But if it means the application to the Crown, in contradistinction to the application for a transfer, the expression can be applied to all the tenures referred to. [He referred to *Ex parte Bone* (5); secs. 13, 25, 26 of the 53 Vict. No. 21 ; sec. 27 of 58 Vict. No. 18; sec. 14 of the *Crown Lands Act* 1905.]

[ISAACS J. referred to *Tearle* v. *Edols* (6), and sec. 48 of 48 Vict. No. 18.]

If the matter is in doubt, the onus is on the appellant to establish that the policy of the earlier Acts has been departed from. The Act of 1903 is not merely an enabling Act. It may have the effect of curtailing the rights of applicants, in that the Board has a discretion to disallow upon grounds not previously open to it. The cross headings in the printed Act cannot control the interpretation. They are merely for convenience of reference : *Hardcastle on Statutory Law*, 2nd ed., p. 229 ; 3rd ed., pp. 214, 217.

[BARTON J. referred to *Eastern Counties and London and Blackwall Railway Companies* v. *Marriage* (7).

ISAACS J. referred to *Inglis* v. *Robertson* (8).]

Bethune (*Hanbury Davies* with him), for the Minister. The

(1) 35 Ch. D., 589.
(2) (1891) 2 Q.B., 267.
(3) (1905) 5 S.R. (N.S.W.), 107.
(4) (1901) 1 S.R. (N.S.W.), 322.
(5) 9 N.S.W.L.R., 363.
(6) 13 App. Cas., 183.
(7) 9 H.L.C., 32 ; 31 L.J. Ex., 73.
(8) (1898) A.C., 616.

H. C. of A.
1907.

PHILLIPS
v.
LYNCH.

Barton J.

general policy of the legislature, as revealed in the Crown Lands
Acts from 1889 to 1905, having been to exclude a married woman
living with her husband from acquiring land direct from the
Crown, it will not be presumed that an intervening Act in 1903
has a contrary effect unless very clear words are used. The *Crown
Lands Act* 1905 in secs. 14 and 23 manifests the same policy as the
Acts before 1903. The rights conferred by sec. 3 of the Act of
1903 should be taken as subject to the limitations in sec. 47 of
the 53 Vict. No. 21. In *Ex parte Luke* (1) a judicial interpretation
had been placed on the words "original application." Sec. 17
should be construed in the light of that case. It appears to be a
declaration of the law, which may have been considered doubtful
on the wording of the earlier Acts, in view of the decisions of the
Supreme Court in *Ex parte Luke* (1), and *In re Melvil* (2).

Whitfeld in reply, referred to *Hack* v. *Minister for Lands* (3);
Fielding v. *Morley Corporation* (4).

Cur. adv. vult.

BARTON J. I have had the advantage of reading the judgment which *O'Connor* J. is about to read, and it so clearly
expresses my views upon the matter that I need only say that I
concur in it. The first question will be answered in the negative,
the second question in the affirmative, and as to the third question, which has not really been brought before us, it may be
taken that we agree with the Supreme Court in giving a negative
answer to it.

O'CONNOR J. read the following judgment. The appellant, a
married woman living with her husband, purchased out of her
separate estate, at a sheriff's sale in 1903, an original conditional
purchase upon which she has since resided. In the following year,
having obtained the consent of the Minister under sec. 17 of the
Crown Lands Act Amendment Act of 1903, she applied for an
additional conditional purchase in virtue of the original conditional purchase. The matter for determination is whether she
could legally do so.

(1) (1901) 1 S.R. (N.S.W.), 322.   (3) 3 C.L.R.. 10.
(2) 10 N.S.W.L.R., 286.   (4) (1899) 1 Ch., 1 ; (1900) A.C., 133.

H. C. of A.
1907.

PHILLIPS
v.
LYNCH.

O'Connor J.

It may be taken as established by *Ex parte Luke* (1) that, notwithstanding the provisions of sec. 47 of the *Crown Lands Act* of 1889, a married woman may legally become the holder of a conditional purchase which she has bought from the sheriff out of her separate estate. The correctness of that decision was not impeached by the respondent's counsel, and if it had been I see no reason to differ from it.

It was claimed on behalf of the appellant that, being the lawful holder of a conditional purchase, she was entitled under sec. 3 of the *Crown Lands Act Amendment Act* of 1903 to make application for an additional conditional purchase irrespective of sec. 17 of that Act. The Supreme Court decided that she was not so entitled, and that, although she was the lawful holder of the conditional purchase which she had purchased from the sheriff, she was subject to the disabilities in respect of acquiring any conditional purchase by her own application direct from the Crown which sec. 47 of the *Crown Lands Act* of 1889 imposes on all married women who do not come within the exceptions mentioned in that section. That decision is so plainly right that I do not think it necessary to add anything upon that portion of the subject to what was said by the learned Chief Justice in the Court below.

The real difficulty in the case is to determine what are the rights of a married woman living with her husband who has, in accordance with sec. 17 of the Act of 1903, obtained the consent of the Minister to acquire an additional holding. In the Supreme Court no argument was heard on that question, the Court considering itself bound by its judgment in *Hall* v. *Costello* (2) which decided that sec. 17 did not so far remove the disability imposed by sec. 47 of the Act of 1889 on a married woman living with her husband as to enable her even with the consent of the Minister to make an application for a conditional lease in respect of a conditional purchase of which she was then the lawful holder. It becomes necessary for us therefore to consider whether that case was rightly decided.

The whole controversy turns upon the interpretation of the words " original application " as used in sec. 17. The Supreme Court adjudged them to mean any application by which a person

(1) (1901) 1 S.R. (N.S.W.), 322.   (2) (1905) 5 S.R. (N.S.W.), 573.

acquires land direct from the Crown as contrasted with the acquisition of land before then purchased by another person directly from the Crown. The appellant asks us to read the words as meaning the application to the Crown for the foundation holding of a series, in virtue of which additional holdings have been or may be applied for. If the former is the correct interpretation the appeal must fail, if the latter is the correct interpretation it must succeed.

The expression "original application" as it stands in the context is very indefinite whichever meaning is to be attached to it. But there is no doubt that it is capable of either meaning. The well recognized rule in such cases is to endeavour by examination of the context, and a consideration of other provisions of the Act and of other enactments *in pari materia*, to ascertain the real intention of the legislature, and then to give the expression that meaning which will best carry out that intention.

Before entering upon such an investigation it will be useful to consider the sense in which the words have been used in the various Lands Acts and in the judgments of the Supreme Court.

Mr. *Canaway*, in an argument which evidenced careful research, has put before us several instances from the Lands Acts and the Supreme Court judgments in which the expression has been used in the sense for which he contends. I shall briefly refer to them. By sec. 13 of the Act of 1889 the Land Board is empowered to allot lands not included in the application for conditional purchase or conditional lease. They are alluded to as "allotted lands not described in the original application." The meaning in that connection is obviously "allotted lands not originally described in the application." In sec. 34 of the same Act the expression is used in the same connection, and evidently with the same meaning. In the Act of 1895, sec. 47, which deals with exchanges of land between pastoral lessees and the Crown, preserves "the right of an applicant to complete an exchange where the lease by virtue of which it was made has expired pending its being dealt with, the rights preserved are described as rights under the "original application." In *Ex parte Bone* (1), sec. 47 (2) of the Act of 1884 was under consideration. It declared that

(1) 9 N.S.W. L.R., 363.

no person who had made a conditional purchase under the section should be permitted to make or hold any other conditional purchase under the Lands Acts, and the question was whether a person who had become a transferee of a conditional purchase made under the section came within the prohibition. *Windeyer* J., in delivering judgment, says (1):—"The sub-section, in my opinion, applies only to persons who have made an *original application for a conditional purchase*, and the language of the Act prevents our extending it to transferees." There the phrase was used to distinguish the person who first obtained land from the Crown from the person who afterwards by transfer became the holder of the same land. In *Ex parte Luke* (2) before referred to, *G. B. Simpson* J., in the course of his judgment, expresses the opinion that "the intention of the legislature was to take away the right of a married woman to make an *original application* for Crown land," thus using the expression as *Windeyer* J. used it in the previous case to distinguish the person whose application first acquired the land from the Crown from the person who afterwards obtained it by transfer. The illustrations from the two sections of the Act of 1889, and from the section of the Act of 1895, throw no light on the matter, because in none of them is the expression used in the sense which Mr. *Canaway* seeks to attach to it in sec. 17. In the judgments referred to no doubt the phrase is used with the meaning for which he is contending. But from both of them it is evident that the words are used, not as having acquired any definite recognized legal signification, but merely as being a concise convenient form of expression for describing the conditional purchase application by which the land is acquired from the Crown in the first instance.

Except in the instances to which I have referred, the phrase "original application" is not used in any of the Lands Acts so far as I have been able to find, but all through the Acts the expression "original conditional purchase" is used to describe the first conditional purchase of a series to distinguish it from those which the holder acquires later, and by virtue of it, and which are called additional conditional purchases. Throughout

H. C. of A.
1907.

PHILLIPS
v.
LYNCH.

O'Connor J.

(1) 9 N.S.W. L.R., 363, at p. 365.
(2) (1901) 1 S.R. (N.S.W.), 322, at p. 334.

H. C. of A.
1907.

PHILLIPS
v.
LYNCH.

O'Connor J.

the Act of 1903 this nomenclature is preserved. By sec. 3, for
instance, the holder of any " original conditional purchase "
(non-residential conditional purchases excepted) may make
application for additional land to be held as by the section
provided. In sub-sec. (c) of that section the expressions " original
conditional purchase of the series," " original homestead selection,"
and " original settlement lease," are used in distinction from the
" additional conditional purchase, homestead lease, and settlement
lease," to be applied for in virtue of the original holdings.
Sub-sec. (e) of the same section gives to the applicant for an
additional holding a preferent right, pending the disposal of his
application, over a person who is applying for the same land as
an " original holding "—the phrase there covers applications for
original conditional purchases, original homestead selections, and
original settlement leases. By sec. 4 the Minister is empowered
to set apart areas for " additional holdings" to the exclusion of
" original holdings," and for "original holdings " to the exclusion
of " additional holdings." Without further multiplying instances,
it may be affirmed generally that throughout the Act the word
" original " prefixed to any class of holding signifies the first
holding of the series, the holding by virtue of which all subsequent holdings of the series have been applied for.

Turning now to sec. 17, it appears to me that it is at least as
permissible a use of language to describe the application for an
original conditional purchase by the expression " original application," as it is to use that expression for describing the application
by virtue of which a piece of land is in the first instance acquired
from the Crown. The words " original application " as they stand
in the section are thus ambiguous, and the Court must attach that
meaning which will most effectually carry out the purpose of the
legislature as indicated by the whole Statute.

One of the main objects of the Act of 1903 was, as its title
declares, " to provide for granting increased areas to present
holders." It is full of provisions conferring on different classes
of holders the right of enlarging their holdings. That right can
be effectively exercised only by the acquisition of additional
land from the Crown. The Act of 1889 had placed a married
woman living with her husband under a disability in regard to

the acquisition of land direct from the Crown by conditional purchase, and that disability had been again enacted in regard to homestead selections and settlement leases by the Statute creating these new tenures. *Ex parte Luke* (1) had decided that a married woman living with her husband might lawfully become the holder of a conditional purchase by purchase from the sheriff. The provisions of sec. 47 of the Act of 1889, however, still prohibited her from becoming the applicant for either an original or an additional conditional purchase. Unless, therefore, she was to be shut out from the benefits which the Act of 1903 was conferring on other lawful holders of Crown lands, it became necessary to deal with her case specially. Sec. 17 was evidently enacted for that purpose, and in the first few words of it the expression is used "the provisions of the Principal Acts to the contrary notwithstanding." From all which I think it is plain that the legislature intended to confer on a married woman living with her husband some new and substantial right to increase her holding.

It is here that Mr. *Canaway's* suggested interpretation fails. If the meaning which he suggests is to be adopted, no right is conferred on her to extend her holding by the acquisition of any additional land from the Crown. She may, it is true, convert one kind of holding into another, she may make her title more indefeasible and thus make her holding more valuable, but she can acquire no additional area of land from the Crown. Such an interpretation would fail to give any substantial effect to the plain object of the section.

The interpretation suggested by the appellant's counsel would read the words "original application" as meaning original conditional purchase, original conditional lease, original homestead selection, and original settlement lease—the effect of which would be to give a married woman living with her husband the same rights of acquiring additional lands by virtue of her present holding as other lawful holders have, but with the limitation that the consent of the Minister must be obtained before she makes any application, and that the application must not be for an original conditional purchase, original conditional lease,

(1) 1901) S. R. (N.S.W.), 322.

original homestead selection, or original settlement lease. The necessity for obtaining the Minister's consent, and the large discretionary powers vested under the Act of 1903 in the Land Board in allotting the area of additional land in accordance with the reasonable requirements of an applicant and his or her family, were no doubt considered by the legislature to be adequate safeguards against the abuse of these new rights in the interest of the husband.

It was argued against that interpretation that the expression "original application," in the sense of application for an original holding, could not apply to a conditional lease, that there could not from the nature of the holding be an original conditional lease. But, in my opinion, that criticism is not sound. The conditional lease which is taken up by virtue of and at the same time as the original conditional purchase may fairly be described as an original conditional lease. The original conditional purchase and conditional lease together would in such a case constitute an original holding in contradistinction to the additional holdings which the Act of 1903 authorizes. This view has legislative sanction in the provisions of sec. 4 of the *Crown Lands Act Amendment Act* of 1905, No. 42, which, in providing for the setting apart of Crown lands for original and conditional holdings respectively, defines original holdings (sub-sec. 1 (*b*)) as including "original conditional purchases and conditional leases to be taken up in virtue of and at the same time as the original conditional purchases within the said area." I can see no ground for objection to the interpretation contended for by the appellant, which is strictly reasonable, and is indeed the only interpretation which gives effective meaning to the words of the legislature.

I am therefore of opinion that the appellant, having obtained the Minister's consent under sec. 17, was lawfully entitled to apply for an additional conditional purchase in virtue of the conditional purchase of which she was then the lawful holder. It follows that the second question must be answered in the affirmative and the appeal, in so far as that question is concerned, must be upheld.

ISAACS J. read the following judgment. This case depends

H. C. of A.
1907.

Phillips
v.
Lynch.

Isaacs J.

upon the construction to be placed upon secs. 3 and 17 of the *Crown Lands Act Amendment Act* 1903 (No. 15 of 1903.)

I was very much impressed by the arguments of Mr. *Canaway*, and if the matter were *res integra* I am not at all sure what conclusion I should arrive at as to the proper interpretation of the sections mentioned. But there is a distinct starting point in the case of *Ex parte Luke* (1).

That case, whatever were the grounds for the decision, determined that " a married woman living with her husband may out of her separate estate purchase a conditional purchase from the sheriff and hold the same ": *Per G. B. Simpson* J. (2). This view of the decision is recognized by *Darley* C.J. in the case now under appeal, where His Honor after stating the effect of *Ex parte Luke* adds (3): "I assume that if she bought from any persons other than the sheriff the same law would have been laid down."

It is too late now to question *Ex parte Luke* (1). Parliament has legislated twice since that case was decided, and has not overridden the law there declared. Titles have doubtless been based upon it, and in those circumstances a Court would have to find very clear words to reverse a decision of that nature.

Approaching the consideration of sec. 17 of the Act of 1903 from that starting point, two positions may be predicated. One is that some change in the law was intended, and the other is that the section is evidently an enabling and not a disabling enactment.

The words " the provisions of the Principal Act to the contrary notwithstanding" preclude the argument that the section is merely declaratory ; while it is abundantly plain from several circumstances, some of which I shall presently refer to, that the object of the section is not. to place a married woman in any worse position than she previously occupied.

If then, as necessarily follows, sec. 17 was to confer new rights, what are these rights ? It includes " any married woman," that is whether judicially separated from her husband or not. Already by sec. 47 of the Act of 1889 as interpreted by *Ex parte Luke* (1) a married woman though living with her husband could, out of

---

(1) (1901) 1 S.R. (N.S.W.), 322.   (3) (1906) 6 S.R. (N.S.W.) 645, at p.
(2) (1901) 1 S.R. (N.S.W.), 322, at   647.
p. 334.

H. C. or A. her separate estate, purchase from a subject his rights already
1907.   granted by the Crown under an original purchase or a conditional
PHILLIPS   lease, and therefore sec. 17 could have no relation to the grant of
v.   such a power. It was not needed for that purpose, and if con-
LYNCH.   fined to acquisition from a subject it would have no effect what-
Isaacs J. ever. It is proper to notice that Mr. Justice *Cohen* in the case
           under appeal says (1):—"Looking, too, at sec. 17, we see that
           while it apparently recognizes the decision in *Luke's Case*, it adds
           to it the obligation that before a married woman can acquire
           land, *i.e.*, Crown lands, otherwise than by original application, she
           must have the Minister's consent."

But it is difficult to adopt this reasoning, because sec. 17 speaks
of " any married woman," and therefore applies equally whether
she is living with her husband, or is judicially separated from
him, and I cannot think the legislature meant to require a woman
judicially separated to also obtain the Minister's consent to purchase from a subject.

Upon a review of the whole situation I am driven to the
conclusion that the married woman was enabled by sec. 17 to
acquire in some instances from the Crown direct. This construction is aided, not merely by the considerations already adverted
to, but also by the position and surroundings of the enacting
words of the section. Looking at sec. 16 we find it headed
" Parents may assist children to acquire land." The acquisition
there referred to refers exclusively to an application direct to the
Crown, and is enabling.

Then sec. 17 is similarly preceded by the heading " Married
women may acquire land." There is no incongruity to begin
with in the word " acquire " including the acquiring by means of
an application to the Crown.

One would naturally *primá facie* assume from such a heading
in a Crown Lands Act, particularly in such close connection with
the subject already dealt with in sec. 16, that when Parliament
is proposing to enact that " married women may acquire land " it
intends to enable them in some way and to some extent to acquire
land from the Crown. That meaning is frequently attached to
the words in the Lands Acts, for instance, in sec. 11 of the Act

(1) (1906) 6 S.R. (N.S W.), 645, at p. 652.

of 1903 and sec. 23 of the Act of 1905. This assumption is strengthened too by the somewhat significant fact of the departure in expression in sec. 17 from that employed in the immediately preceding section. Sec. 16 speaks of " an application," which of course refers to any application. Sec. 17, however, uses the term " an original application." The change of language is not decisive, but in a case of doubt it is important. There are extraneous circumstances relative to the matter which are urged to be of some weight on either side. The expression "original application" was used in two cases: *Ex parte Bone* (1), and *Ex parte Luke* (2), as contradistinguished from acquiring as a transferee.

On the other hand the same expression " original application " has been sometimes used in previous legislation, as in sec. 13 of the Act of 1889, and sec. 47 of the Act of 1895, No. 18, to contrast one application with another actual or presumed. But I do not think reliance can be placed on either set of references, because on the one hand to attribute to the phrase "original application" the meaning of all applications to the Crown direct would reduce the section to a nullity, or, if the section were regarded as disabling, would restrict existing powers of judicially separated married women who were quite outside *Luke's Case* (3). The looseness of expression in this section is only what *Darley* C.J. in *In re Charles Baldwin* (4) aptly described as " the inexactitude of language which is so characteristic of the Land Acts." *Hall* v. *Costello* (5) decided that the expression "original application " meant any application for a conditional purchase, &c. But no reasons for the decision were given by the Court, nor does it appear from the report of the case that any reasons in support of that view were advanced by learned counsel. The difficulties that press upon us were apparently not presented to the Supreme Court.

In face of those difficulties we are thrown back upon general principles. Courts are not at liberty to speculate as to the intention of Parliament. The only safe and legitimate guide to the legislative intention is the language of the legislature itself

H. C. or A.
1907.

PHILLIPS
v.
LYNCH.

Isaacs J.

(1) 9 N.S.W. L.R., 363, at p. 365.
(2) (1901) 1 S.R. (N.S.W.), 322, at p. 334.
(3) (1901) 1 S.R. (N.S.W.), 322.
(4) 12 N.S.W. L.R. 128, at p. 133.
(5) (1905) 5 S.R. (N.S.W.), 573.

fairly interpreted. Some effect must be given to that language
if possible, and, therefore, laying aside the view that the section
is merely declaratory or a nullity, and the view that it is a
purely disabling section, striking alike at judicially separated
women and women living with their husbands, the necessary
result is that it enlarges the previous rights of married women
not judicially separated. It can only do this by permitting them
in some cases to obtain additional land from the Crown, while
not enabling them to start the series by an original application.

Sec. 3 must be read with the rest of the Crown Lands Acts.
It is a general enactment but subject always to the provisions of
the Lands Acts making specific provision for particular cases as in
the case of married women.

As to sec. 47 of the Act 1889 it is only necessary to say that
the prohibition extends quite clearly to additional as well as to
original holdings.

In the result the appeal substantially succeeds. The first
question resting the claim solely on sec. 3 should be answered in
the negative; the second question should be answered in the affirmative, and the third relying on the *Married Women's Property
Act* alone is properly answered in the negative.

HIGGINS J. read the following judgment. I have come to the
same conclusion. The Land Appeal Court has stated three
questions for the Supreme Court; but the only question argued
before the Supreme Court was the first—as the second and third
had been the subject of previous decisions. The first question is,
whether under sec. 3, taken by itself, of the Act of 1903, the
appellant was entitled to acquire the land. The Supreme Court
has held that she was not; and I concur with this view. The Act
of 1903 (sec. 1) provides that the Act is to be read and construed
with the Act of 1889 as well as with other Acts; and under the
Act of 1889 (sec. 47), a married woman was not entitled to conditionally purchase Crown land. This prohibition applies, in my
opinion, to an additional conditional purchase as well as to an
original conditional purchase. It is true that the words of sec. 3
of the Act of 1903 are general, and do not expressly exclude
married women—"The holder of any original conditional purchase

H. C. of A.
1907.

PHILLIPS
v.
LYNCH.

Higgins J.

may make application . . . for additional land to be held by him as an additional holding under the same class of tenure "—; but the general words cannot be treated as repealing the special prohibition contained as to married women in sec. 47 of the Act of 1889. The principle is well summed up in the old formula— *generalia specialibus non derogant*: see *Seward* v. " *Vera Cruz* " (1).

The third question is whether the *Married Women's Property Act* of 1901 enables the applicant to acquire the land. I see no reason for differing from the view taken by the Supreme Court on this point in *Ex parte Luke* (2).

The second question is much more difficult. It involves the interpretation of sec. 17 of the Act of 1903. Does that section enable a married woman, who already holds an original conditional purchase by purchase from the sheriff, or from some party other than the Crown, to acquire an additional conditional purchase from the Crown? With the assistance of counsel on both sides, and of my colleagues familiar with the New South Wales Acts, I have found my way to the light, I think, after struggling through the jungle of the Lands Acts. The only reading of sec. 17 that will give meaning to all its words seems to be that pressed upon us by the appellant. For I take it that that section was clearly meant to enlarge the powers of married women, and to clear away some obstructions created by the earlier Acts. The section is headed " Married women may acquire land "; the section itself is enabling in form; and the powers are conferred, " the provisions of the Principal Acts to the contrary notwithstanding." Now, at the time of the passing of this Act, sec. 47 of the Act of 1889 had provided (*inter alia*), " Except as aforesaid a married woman shall not be entitled to lease or conditionally purchase Crown land under the Principal Act or this Act "; and it had been decided in *Ex parte Luke* (2) that a married woman might, notwithstanding that section, purchase an original conditional purchase from the sheriff, or, indeed, by parity of reasoning, from any private holder. To read sec. 17, therefore, as the respondent reads it, as merely allowing a married woman to purchase from another holder, would be to treat the section as

(1) 10 App. Cas., 59, at p. 68.   (2) (1901) 1 S.R. (N.S.W.), 322.

conferring no privilege further than the married woman already enjoyed. Judging from the form and substance of the section, it was drawn by one who had sec. 47 of the Act of 1889 before his mind, in all its lengthy obscurity; and, with sec. 47 in view, he provided that a married woman may, notwithstanding the provisions of the previous Acts, "acquire by purchase or otherwise than by an original application a conditional purchase, conditional lease, homestead selection, or settlement lease."

The question is, what is the meaning of "original application" in sec. 17. Does it involve, as the respondent argues, that a married women may not apply to the Crown for land at all; or does it mean that she may not be an applicant for an original conditional purchase? If the respondent is right, there is no force in the word "original." The only authority to which an "application" can be made, in the sense of the Lands Acts, is the Crown. As the only thing prohibited to the married woman by the section is an "original" application, it seems to follow that she can acquire land by application (to the Crown), provided it be not an "original" application. Therefore, *primâ facie*, she may apply for an additional conditional purchase. The original application is for the original conditional purchase; the secondary, or ancillary, application is for the additional conditional purchase. The words "acquire by purchase or otherwise" are not happily chosen, on either view of the clause; but, as the Act is a Crown Lands Act, and as a married woman could already acquire by purchase from a private person, they must mean acquire from the Crown. What the draftsman seems to have had in his mind was the phrase used in sec. 47 of the Act of 1889—"purchase or lease land conditionally or otherwise"; but inasmuch as new provisions for acquiring lands had been devised since that Act, (*Homestead Selections Act* of 1895, secs. 13 to 23; settlement leases, *ib.* sec. 25), provisions to which the word "purchase" and the word "lease" might not be deemed strictly applicable, he uses the general words "by purchase or otherwise"; and a married woman is thereby enabled to acquire, not only a conditional purchase (otherwise than by an original application), but also a "conditional lease, homestead selection or settlement lease."

It seems to me that the key to the provisions of sec. 17 is to be

H. C. OF A.
1907.

PHILLIPS
v.
LYNCH.

Higgins J.

found in sec. 3. The first object of the Act, as stated in its title, is " to provide for granting increased areas to present holders." Accordingly, sec. 3 enabled the holder of any homestead selection, any settlement lease, any original conditional purchase, to apply for additional land to be held by him as an additional holding under the same class of tenure. Also, the holder of an original or additional conditional purchase was enabled to apply for a conditional lease. These new privileges, as well as certain old privileges, the legislature intended to extend to married women, by sec. 17. If she has acquired by purchase from another person a homestead selection, she may now acquire an additional homestead selection. If she has acquired, by such purchase, a settlement lease, she may now acquire an additional settlement lease. If she has acquired, by such purchase, an original conditional purchase, she may now acquire an additional conditional purchase, or additional conditional lease. Secs. 3 and 4 use the words " original " and " additional " as applicable to all these tenures. It is probable that sec. 17 also allows a married woman to exercise such powers as that of converting part of land held under a settlement lease into a homestead selection ; and this may explain the omission of the word " additional " before the words " conditional purchaser, homestead selection or settlement lease " in sec. 17. But it is not necessary, in the present case, to decide what are the limits of the powers conferred by the section. It is enough to say, generally, that if a married woman has already become, by virtue of a transaction with some party other than the Crown, the holder of land on which a secondary application to the Crown might, if the land were not held by a married woman, be based, for some further or other holding, she may make that secondary application, and acquire land thereby. But the prohibitions as to application for original holdings still apply (sec. 14 of the Act of 1895 ; sec. 24 (v.) of the Act of 1895 ; sec. 47 of the Act of 1889). It is true that there is some difficulty in applying this theory to the case of a conditional lease. Conditional leases are not granted except in connection with conditional purchases ; and it is asked, what can be meant by an " original " application for a conditional lease ? But even if the word " original " in this sense cannot be applied to a conditional

H. C. of A.
1907.

PHILLIPS
v.
LYNCH.

Higgins J.

lease, it does not follow that the meaning suggested is wrong. The word is clearly applicable to the three other tenures mentioned; and, if it cannot be applied to conditional leases, it simply follows that the married woman's right to acquire conditional leases, under the same circumstances as other persons, is unrestricted. It may be, however, as suggested by some of my colleagues, that in the case of conditional leases, "original" has a reference to the conditional lease which may be taken up at the time of taking up a conditional purchase, as distinguished from that which can be taken up subsequently. But it is not necessary to decide this question.

This view of sec. 17 is strongly confirmed on a consideration of the title and scope of the Act of 1903. The title is unusually lengthy and exhaustive, setting out, apparently, all the objects of the Act; but the primary and dominant object is "to provide for granting increased areas to present holders." All the other objects can be assigned to specific sections of the Act. But unless this sec. 17 can be treated as coming under the primary and dominant object, "to provide for granting increased areas to present holders," it cannot be brought under any specific objects. Mr. *Canaway* urges that the section was meant to clear away doubts as to the validity of the decision in *Ex parte Luke* (1) as to the right of the married woman to purchase from the sheriff, &c.; but there is nothing in the section, or in the heading, to show any intention to clear away doubts, or even to declare existing rights. The section applies to the future, not to the past: "*may* acquire." The Act is mainly one to enable present holders to get increased areas; and as a married woman could already be a holder of an original conditional purchase by purchase from the sheriff or a private person, I think that the legislature meant that she also should have the privilege of getting an increased area, and probably, the privilege of converting her tenure into some other tenure.

> *Appeal allowed. Questions 1 and 3 answered in the negative, and question 2 in the affirmative.*

(1) (1901) 1 S.R. (N.S.W.), 322.

Solicitor, for the appellant, *F. Crommelin* by *Ellis & Button.*
Solicitors, for the respondents, *J. N. Moffitt*, by *McDonnell & Moffitt*; *The Crown Solicitor for New South Wales.* ·

C. A. W.

[HIGH COURT OF AUSTRALIA.]

AMALGAMATED SOCIETY OF CAR-
PENTERS AND JOINERS, AUS- $\left.\right\}$. APPELLANTS ;
TRALIAN DISTRICT . . .
> PROSECUTORS,

AND

THE HABERFIELD PROPRIETARY $\left.\right\}$. RESPONDENTS.
LIMITED . . . . . .
> DEFENDANTS,

ON APPEAL FROM THE SUPREME COURT OF
NEW SOUTH WALES.

Industrial Arbitration Act 1901 (*N.S. W.*), (*No.* 59 *of* 1901), *sec.* 37—*Jurisdiction of Court of Arbitration—Breach of common rule— Question for determination by Court—Relationship of employer and employé—Element of offence charged— Effect of erroneous decision—Prohibition.*

H. C. of A.
1907.

SYDNEY,
Aug. 22, 23,
26, 30.

Griffith C.J.,
O'Connor and
Isaacs JJ.

Although a Court of limited statutory jurisdiction, from which there is no appeal, cannot give itself jurisdiction by an erroneous decision upon a preliminary question upon the answer to which its jurisdiction depends, an erroneous decision upon a point which, however essential to the validity of its order, it is competent to try is not a ground for prohibition.

Sec. 37 of the *Industrial Arbitration Act* 1901 provides that the Arbitration Court may declare that any term of agreement or condition of employment shall be a common rule of an industry, fix the limits of the operation of the rule, and impose penalties for its breach, and that the penalties may be recovered either in the Court of Arbitration by a person entitled to sue, or before a stipendiary or police magistrate in Petty Sessions, subject to an appeal in the latter case to the Arbitration Court instead of to the Supreme Court. There is no appeal from any decision of the Arbitration Court.

In a proceeding before it the Arbitration Court made an award fixing a minimum daily wage for carpenters, and subsequently made the award a

H. C. OF A.
1907.

AMALGAM-
ATED SOCIETY
OF CARPEN-
TERS AND
JOINERS
v.
HABERFIELD
PROPRIETARY
LTD.

common rule binding upon all master builders and other persons engaged in the building industry within a certain area. The respondents were summoned before the Arbitration Court, and convicted of having committed a breach of the award in paying certain carpenters less than the minimum wage for certain work. It appeared that the work in question was done under written contracts, and the respondents contended that the Arbitration Court had no jurisdiction over them inasmuch as, upon the proper construction of the contracts, they were not employers, and, therefore, not bound by the common rule, the workmen being independent contractors. It was not disputed that the respondents would have been within the common rule if they were employers.

The Supreme Court having granted a prohibition on the ground that the Arbitration Court had exceeded its jurisdiction :

Held, that one element of the offence with which the respondents were charged was that they had employed the carpenters in question, and that the Arbitration Court was bound to inquire into that as well as the other elements of the offence charged, and, however erroneous their decision on the point might be in law or in fact, prohibition would not lie in respect of it.

The Queen v. *Bolton*, 1 Q.B., 66, and *Colonial Bank of Australasia* v. *Willan*, L.R. 5 P.C., 417, considered and applied. *Clancy* v. *Butchers' Shop Employés Union*, 1 C.L.R., 181, distinguished.

Decision of the Supreme Court : *Ex parte Haberfield Proprietary Limited*, (1907) 7 S.R. (N.S.W.), 247, reversed.

APPEAL from a decision of the Supreme Court of New South Wales.

The respondents were proceeded against by summons before the Court of Arbitration for breach of an award, which had been made a common rule under sec. 37 of the *Industrial Arbitration Act* 1901. At the hearing the respondents took the objection that on the admitted facts they were not employers, and therefore were not bound by the award, and the Court had no jurisdiction to entertain the summons. The Court held that the relationship of employer and employé existed, and convicted the respondents.

On the motion of the respondents the Supreme Court made absolute a rule *nisi* for a prohibition restraining the Arbitration Court and the prosecutors from proceeding upon the conviction : *Ex parte Haberfield Proprietary Limited* (1).

From this decision the present appeal was brought.

(1) (1907) 7 S.R. (N.S.W.), 247.

The facts are sufficiently stated in the judgment.

H. C. of A.
1907.

AMALGAM-
ATED SOCIETY
OF CARPEN-
TERS AND
JOINERS
v.
HABERFIELD
PROPRIETARY
LTD.

G. S. Beeby, solicitor, for the appellants. Even if the contract between the respondents and the persons in respect of whom the breach was alleged to have been committed, was not such an employment as at common law would have established the relationship of master and servant, there was an employment within the meaning of the *Industrial Arbitration Act* 1901. The writing did not conclude the matter. There was other evidence from which the Court might have concluded that the relationship of master and servant existed. The Supreme Court misinterpreted the decision in *Clancy* v. *Butchers' Shop Employés Union* (1). That decision was based on the fact that there was no industrial matter involved, and the jurisdiction of the Court was restricted to such matters. But it was shown here that the carpenters were engaged in work in the industry, and that the work was being paid for by the respondents. There was in fact an employment in the industry. [He referred to *Beath, Schiess & Co.* v. *Martin* (2), and the definitions of " industrial matter," " employer," and " employé " in sec. 2 of the Act No. 59 of 1901.] If this was not an employment, then any industry may be taken out of the operation of the Act.

[GRIFFITH C.J.—That does not follow. That is only a sort of bogey.

ISAACS J.—Even if it were a possible consequence, it might nevertheless not be contrary to the Act. Acts of Parliament can sometimes be evaded.]

Even if the Court of Arbitration was wrong on this point it is not a ground for prohibition. It is a matter which it has jurisdiction to decide. If the Court's decisions were subject to an appeal this would perhaps be a matter for appeal, but there is no appeal: sec. 32 ; and prohibition will not lie unless the Court exceeds its jurisdiction. The existence of the relationship of employer and employé was not a fact upon which the jurisdiction of the Court depended. It was not the subject of an independent or preliminary inquiry, but was one of the elements of the offence charged. The Court had necessarily to decide

(1) 1 C.L.R., 181.   (2) 2 C.L.R., 716.

H. C. of A.
1907.

AMALGAM-
ATED SOCIETY
OF CARPEN-
TERS AND
JOINERS
v.
HABERFIELD
PROPRIETARY
LTD.

whether the respondents were employers in order to determine
the matter before them. If the question is one without determining which the matter cannot be decided, and the subject
matter of the charge is within the Court's jurisdiction, and the
defendant is within its territorial jurisdiction, a wrong decision
is not a ground for prohibition. Here the question went to the
merits of the case. [He referred to sec. 37 of the Act 59 of 1901 ;
Brittain v. *Kinnaird* (1); *Thompson* v. *Ingham* (2); *The Queen*
v. *Bolton* (3); *Holburd* v. *Burwood Extended Coal Mining Co.*
(4); *Ex parte Scandritt* (5); *Joseph* v. *Henry* (6).]

[ISAACS J. referred to *Colonial Bank of Australasia* v. *Willan*
(7); *The Queen* v. *Farmer* (8).]

Even if the question of the construction of the contract was
one affecting the jurisdiction, the decision of the Court of Arbitration was right, and the prohibition was wrongly granted.

[GRIFFITH C.J.—We are not called upon to express an opinion
on that point. We are not a Court of Appeal from the Arbitration Court, and will not decide whether that Court was right
unless we are obliged to do so. The general principle is of much
greater consequence than the merits of the particular dispute
between these parties.]

Knox K.C. and *J. L. Campbell*, for the respondents. The jurisdiction of the Arbitration Court is strictly limited to matters
arising between employer and employé. Persons who are not
employers are not within the jurisdiction of the Court, and
could not be summoned before it. The fact that the respondents
are not employers is not the subject of a plea of not guilty, but
of a plea to the jurisdiction. Being an employer is not an
element of the offence, though it may be necessary for the Court
to decide whether a person charged is or is not an employer. By
deciding wrongly that he is, it cannot extend its jurisdiction:
Bunbury v. *Fuller* (9); *Reg.* v. *Yaldwin* (10). There are two
stages in the inquiry, (1) whether the defendant is a person

(1) 1 Brod. & B., 432.
(2) 14 Q.B., 710 ; 19 L.J.Q.B., 189.
(3) 1 Q.B., 66, at p. 72.
(4) 11 N.S.W. L.R., 365.
(5) 15 N.S.W. W.N., 244.
(6) 1 L. M. & P., 388 ; 19 L.J.Q.B.,
369.
(7) L.R. 5 P.C., 417, at p. 442.
(8) (1892) 1 Q.B., 637.
(9) 9 Ex., 111, at p. 140 ; 23 L.J.,
Ex., 29.
(10) 9 Q.L.J., 242.

H. C. of A.
1907.

AMALGAM-
ATED SOCIETY
OF CARPEN-
TERS AND
JOINERS
v.
HABERFIELD
PROPRIETARY
LTD.

within the Court's jurisdiction, (2) whether he has committed the offence charged. The first is an independent inquiry, similar to the inquiry whether title to land is in dispute in a case before a Court which may not try such question, and if the Court wrongly decides that question and tries the case, prohibition will lie. The question always is whether the Act conferring jurisdiction has given jurisdiction to decide the preliminary questions upon which the jurisdiction to adjudicate depends. There is nothing in the *Arbitration Act* giving such a jurisdiction. If such a power is conferred upon a Court, and the jurisdiction depends merely upon facts as to which there is a conflict, the Court's decision will not be reviewed if there is any evidence to support it; but where it is a matter of law, as here, depending upon the construction of a document, the decision is reviewable by prohibition, and the Court will be restrained from dealing with persons who are in law not amenable to its jurisdiction. There is no difference in principle between limiting the jurisdiction territorially and limiting it to persons of a certain description. [They referred to *Liverpool United Gaslight Company* v. *Everton* (1); *The Queen* v. *Justices of Surrey* (2).]

If the respondents were not employers, they were never subject to the common rule. The fact that the evidence on the point would not come out until the hearing of the case generally does not alter the position. As soon as it appears, the Court is bound to refuse to deal with the case. Cases in which the Court has jurisdiction over the person and in which the only questions that can arise are as to the subject matter do not apply. [They referred to *Colonial Bank of Australasia* v. *Willan* (3); *Thompson* v. *Ingham* (4); *Elston* v. *Rose* (5); *Clancy* v. *Butchers' Shop Employés Union* (6); *Trolly, Draymen and Carters Union of Sydney and Suburbs* v. *Master Carriers Association of New South Wales* (7).]

[GRIFFITH C.J. referred to *The Queen* v. *Special Commissioners of Income Tax* (8).]

(1) L.R. 6 C.P., 414.
(2) 6 Q.B.D., 100, at p. 107.
(3) L.R. 5 P.C., 417, at p. 442.
(4) 14 Q.B., 710; 19 L.J.Q.B., 189.
(5) L.R. 4 Q.B., 4, at p. 8.
(6) 1 C.L.R., 181.
(7) 2 C.L.R., 509.
(8) 21 Q.B.D., 313, at p. 319, *per* Lord *Esher* M.R.

H. C. of A.
1907.

AMALGAM-
ATED SOCIETY
OF CARPEN-
TERS AND
JOINERS
v.
HABERFIELD
PROPRIETARY
LTD.

ISAACS J. referred to *Barraclough* v. *Brown* (1), and *The Queen* v. *St. Olave District Board* (2).]

The respondents were neither in law nor in fact employers. The relationship contemplated by the Act as constituting employment is that of master and servant. The workmen in this case were independent contractors. That is a matter of law upon the construction of the contract, and there was no evidence *aliunde* that the work was actually done under different conditions. The fact that the respondents exercised some control over the order of the work does not make the workmen their servants in the legal sense. [They referred to *Hardaker* v. *Idle District Council* (3); *Riley* v. *Warden* (4); *Hardy* v. *Ryle* (5); *Marrow* v. *Flimby and Broughton Moor Coal and Fire-Brick Company Ltd.* (6); secs. 34 and 35 of the *Industrial Arbitration Act* 1901.]

G. S. Beeby, in reply.

Cur. adv. vult.

GRIFFITH C.J. This case arises out of a prosecution of the respondent company before the Arbitration Court for an alleged breach of a common rule made on 13th February 1906 relating to the industry of builders. By the order of the Court making the common rule it was directed that the terms and conditions of employment set out in the award of the Court in a dispute between the appellant Society and a firm called Porter & Green should be a common rule of the industry of building, and binding upon all master builders and other persons engaged in the industry of building, and all persons employing carpenters and joiners within a certain area. It was further ordered that any employer bound by the order of the Court who committed a breach of it should be liable to a penalty of £100.

On 28th August 1906 a summons was taken out in the Arbitration Court against the respondent company, calling upon them to show cause why they should not be ordered to pay to the secretary of the appellant society certain sums as penalties for breaches of the award. In substance the prosecution was for

(1) (1897) A.C., 615.	(4) 2 Ex., 59; 18 L.J. Ex., 120.
(2) 8 El. & Bl., 529.	(5) 9 B. & C., 603.
(3) (1896) 1 Q.B., 335.	(6) (1898) 2 Q.B., 588.

breaches of the common rule, four breaches being alleged in H. C. of A.
respect of four different persons. The proceedings in the 1907.
Arbitration Court are informal, and the summons did not form- AMALGAM-
ally set out the offence, but in substance the charge amounted to ATED SOCIETY OF CARPEN-
this, that the defendants, the present respondents, being persons TERS AND JOINERS
engaged in the industry of building, employed the persons v.
specified in the summons contrary to the terms of the award. HABERFIELD PROPRIETARY
The elements of the alleged offence were that the defendants LTD.
were persons engaged in the industry of building, and that, being Griffith C.J.
such persons, they had committed breaches of the common rule.

When the case came before the Arbitration Court the objection
was taken by the defendants that the case was not within the
jurisdiction of the Court, because the relationship of employer and
employé did not subsist between the defendants to the summons
and the persons in respect of whom the breach was alleged to
have been committed. We have been favoured with the judgment delivered by the learned president, from which it appears
that he directed his attention mainly to the question whether such
a relationship had subsisted or not, because, if it did, the breaches
were not disputed. The nature of the relationship between the
respondents and the persons named in the summons was expressed in written contracts, and the question discussed in the
Arbitration Court was whether under the terms of those contracts
the relationship of employer and employé subsisted. The learned
president apparently thought that that was substantially the
same question as whether the relationship of master and servant
subsisted ; and I am strongly disposed to think that the correct
view. It was necessary for the Arbitration Court to inquire into
the question whether this relationship did or did not subsist, and
the Court came to the conclusion that it did, and found that the
defendants had committed the breach alleged, and fined them.
The respondents applied to the Supreme Court for a prohibition
on the ground that the Court of Arbitration ought to have held
that they had no jurisdiction, that upon the evidence admissible
the relationship of employer and employé did not subsist, and
therefore that the defendants were not guilty of any breach of
the common rule. The Supreme Court after argument made the
rule absolute for a prohibition. They were of opinion that the

H. C. of A.
1907.

AMALGAM-
ATED SOCIETY
OF CARPEN-
TERS AND
JOINERS
v.
HABERFIELD
PROPRIETARY
LTD.

Griffith C.J.

case was not within the jurisdiction of the Court, because, as they thought, it was a case only of ordinary contract, by which I understand the learned Judges to mean a contract of a different kind from that establishing the relationship of employer and employé. On that point they thought that the conclusion of the Arbitration Court was wrong, and that that Court consequently had no jurisdiction. But in my judgment the question whether the conclusion of the Court was wrong on that point, and the question whether it had jurisdiction to hear the charge, are quite different questions.

It has been held by this Court on more than one occasion that the jurisdiction of the Arbitration Court is limited, and that if it exceeds its jurisdiction it may be restrained by prohibition from the Supreme Court. But those decisions have all been decisions as to the subject matter of the jurisdiction. The jurisdiction of the Arbitration Court to decide between employer and employé and to make common rules governing the relations between them is limited in the way indicated in those cases. This Court has held that the Arbitration Court cannot, under the guise of making an award in a matter within its jurisdiction, deal with something that is not an industrial matter. Nor can they make an award unless there is a dispute between persons standing to one another in the relationship of employer and employé. It is necessary however, to remember that the jurisdiction of the Arbitration Court under the Act is not limited to making awards or common rules. The jurisdiction of the Court is conferred by sec. 37, and incidentally by other sections. Section 37 relates particularly to the common rule. Under it the Court has jurisdiction to do eight different things. Amongst them are to declare that any term of agreement or condition of employment shall be a common rule of an industry, and to fix the limits of its operation, and impose penalties for its breach, and so on. But the second part of the section provides that all fines and penalties for any breach of an award may be sued for and recovered either in the Court by a person entitled to sue or before a stipendiary or police magistrate sitting as a Court of Petty Sessions, with a proviso that, if the proceeding for the recovery of the fine is taken before a stipendiary or police magistrate sitting as a Court of Petty

Sessions, the appeal shall be to the Arbitration Court instead of to the Supreme Court as in ordinary cases.   The jurisdiction conferred by the Act is therefore twofold.   There is, first, an arbitral jurisdiction, to determine disputes between employer and employé for the purpose of laying down the terms upon which the industry is to be carried on, and, secondly, a punitive or correctional jurisdiction, conferred upon it in common with stipendiary or police magistrates.

This Court has held that the arbitral jurisdiction can only be exercised with respect to matters which are actually within the limits of the jurisdiction conferred by the Act ; but it has never determined that when exercising the punitive jurisdiction the Arbitration Court is bound by the limits which define the arbitral jurisdiction.   Of course in that case also the Arbitration Court must keep within its jurisdiction.   It has, for instance, no jurisdiction to summon before it a person who is not within New South Wales.   But, in considering the extent of a punitive jurisdiction of this sort, very different considerations apply from those applicable to the consideration of the arbitral jurisdiction of the Court.

The rules as to the jurisdiction of inferior Courts or Courts of limited jurisdiction and the extent to which they will be restrained by the superior Courts are well established.   I will refer only to two of the authorities on that subject.   The first is *The Queen* v. *Bolton* (1) which was decided by the Court of Queen's Bench in 1841, and has been cited many times since and always with approval, has been very often applied, and never dissented from. Its authority is recognized by the Court of Appeal in England, by the Privy Council, and also, I think, by the House of Lords.   In that case Lord *Denman* C.J. delivered the judgment of the Court, and laid down so clearly the principles applicable to these cases that I will read at length the material parts of the judgment. He said (2):—"Two points were made in support of the order ; the first, that, the proceedings all being regular on the face of them, and disclosing a case within the jurisdiction of the magistrates, this Court could not look at affidavits for the purpose of impeaching their decision ; the second, that, even if those affidavits were

H. C. OF A
1907.

AMALGAM-
ATED SOCIETY
OF CARPEN-
TERS AND
JOINERS
v.
HABERFIELD
PROPRIETARY
LTD.

Griffith C.J.

(1) 1 Q.B., 66.   (2) 1 Q.B., 66, at p. 71.

looked at, the case would be found to be one of conflicting evidence, in which there was much to support the conclusion to which the magistrates had come ; and that this Court would not disturb that conclusion, even if it might have been disposed to have decided differently had the matter originally come before it.

"The first of these is a point of very much importance, because of very general application ; but the principle upon which it turns is very simple : the difficulty is always found in applying it. The case to be supposed is one like the present, in which the legislature has trusted the original, it may be (as here) the final, jurisdiction *on the merits* to the magistrates below, in which this Court has no jurisdiction as to the merits either originally or on appeal. All that we can then do, when their decision is complained of, is to see that the case was one within their jurisdiction, and that their proceedings on the face of them are regular and according to law.

"Even if their decision should upon the merits be unwise or unjust, on these grounds we cannot reverse it. So far, we believe, was not disputed ; but, as the inquiry is open, *ex concessis*, to see whether the case was within the jurisdiction of the magistrates, it is contended that affidavits are receivable for the purpose of showing that they acted without jurisdiction ; and this is, no doubt, true, taken literally : the magistrates cannot, as it is often said, give themselves jurisdiction merely by their own affirmation of it. But it is obvious that this may have two senses : in the one it is true ; in the other, on sound principle and on the best considered authority, it will be found untrue. Where the charge laid before the magistrate, as stated in the information, does not amount in law to the offence over which the Statute gives him jurisdiction, his finding the other party guilty by his conviction in the very terms of the Statute would not give him jurisdiction ; the conviction would be bad on the face of the proceedings, all being returned before us. Or if, the charges being really insufficient, he had mis-stated it in drawing up the proceedings, so that they would appear to be regular, it would be clearly competent to the defendant to show to us by affidavits what the real charge was, and, that appearing to have been insufficient, we should quash the conviction. In both these cases a charge has

H. C. of A.
1907.

AMALGAM-
ATED SOCIETY
OF CARPEN-
TERS AND
JOINERS
v.

HABERFIELD
PROPRIETARY
LTD.

Griffith C.J.

been presented to the magistrate over which he had no jurisdiction; he had no right to entertain the question, or commence
an inquiry into the merits; and his proceeding to a conclusion
will not give him jurisdiction. But, as in this latter case we
cannot get at the want of jurisdiction but by affidavits, of
necessity we must receive them. It will be observed, however,
that here we receive them, not to show that the magistrate has
come to a wrong conclusion, but that he never ought to have
begun the inquiry. In this sense, therefore, and for this purpose,
it is true that affidavits are receivable."

I pause here to point out that in the present case there is no
doubt that the charge made against the present respondents was
a charge which it was apparently within the jurisdiction of the
Arbitration Court to determine. It alleged a breach of a common
rule, and that common rule, being an order laid down by a Court
having statutory authority to do so, had the effect of the law of
the land, so far as regards the matter dealt with by it, in the
same way as a by-law of a municipal authority, when promul-
gated in a proclamation by the Governor in Council.

Lord *Denman* C.J. went on:—" But, where a charge has been
well laid before a magistrate, on its face bringing itself within his
jurisdiction, he is bound to commence the inquiry: in so doing he
undoubtedly acts within his jurisdiction: but in the course of the
inquiry, evidence being offered for and against the charge, the
proper, or it may be the irresistible, conclusion to be drawn may be
that the offence has not been committed, and so that the case in
one sense was not within the jurisdiction. Now to receive affidavits for the purpose of showing this is clearly in effect to show
that the magistrate's decision was wrong if he affirms the charge,
and not to show that he acted without jurisdiction: for they would
admit that, in every stage of the inquiry up to the conclusion, he
could not but have proceeded, and that, if he had come to a
different conclusion his judgment of acquittal would have been
a binding judgment, and barred another proceeding for the same
offence. Upon principle, therefore, affidavits cannot be received
under such circumstances. The question of jurisdiction does not
depend on the truth or falsehood of the charge, but upon its
nature: it is determinable on the commencement, not at the con-

H. C. of A
1907.

AMALGAM-
ATED SOCIETY
OF CARPEN-
TERS AND
JOINERS
c.
HABERFIELD
PROPRIETARY
LTD.

Griffith C.J.

clusion, of the inquiry: and affidavits, to be receivable, must be
directed to what appears at the former stage, and not to the facts
disclosed in the progress of the inquiry.

" We will cite only two authorities in support of this reasoning.
The former, that of *Brittain* v. *Kinnaird* (1), and the admirable
judgment of *Richardson* J. (2) are too well known to make it necessary to state them at length. There, in the case of a conviction
under the *Bum-boat Act*, it was asked, shall the magistrate, by
calling a seventy-four-gun ship a boat, give himself jurisdiction
and preclude inquiry ? The learned Judge gave the answer:—
' Whether the vessel were a boat or no, was a fact on which the
magistrate was to decide ; and the fallacy lies in assuming that
the *fact*, which the magistrate has to decide, is that which constitutes the jurisdiction'."   He quoted then another case in the
Common Pleas to the same effect: *Cave* v. *Mountain* (3).   In
conclusion he said this :—" It is of much more importance to hold
the rule of law straight than, from a feeling of the supposed
hardship of any particular decision, to interpose relief at the
expense of introducing a precedent full of inconvenience and
uncertainty in the decision of future cases."

The only other case I think it necessary to mention is *The
Queen* v. *Special Commissioners of Income Tax* (4) which has
been often cited in this Court. Lord *Esher* M.R., with whom
Lindley L.J. entirely agreed, after pointing out that there may
be cases in which a tribunal has not jurisdiction to determine
whether the state of facts exists necessary to give it jurisdiction,
said (5):—" The legislature may entrust the tribunal or body
with a jurisdiction, which includes the jurisdiction to determine
whether the preliminary state of facts exists as well as the jurisdiction, on finding that it does exist, to proceed further or do
something more. When the legislature are establishing such a
tribunal or body with limited jurisdiction, they also have to
consider, whatever jurisdiction they give them, whether there
shall be any appeal from their decision, for otherwise there will
be none. In the second of the two cases I have mentioned it is
an erroneous application of the formula to say that the tribunal

(1) 1 Brod. & B., 432.   (4) 21 Q.B.D., 313.
(2) 1 Brod. & B., 432, at p. 442.   (5) 21 Q.B.D., 313, at p. 319.
(3) 1 Man. & G., 257.

H. C. OF A.
1907.

AMALGAM-
ATED SOCIETY
OF CARPEN-
TERS AND
JOINERS
v.
HABERFIELD
PROPRIETARY
LTD.

Griffith C.J.

cannot give themselves jurisdiction by wrongly deciding certain facts to exist, because the legislature gave them jurisdiction to determine all the facts, including the existence of the preliminary facts on which the further exercise of their jurisdiction depends ; and if they were given jurisdiction so to decide, without any appeal being given, there is no appeal from such exercise of their jurisdiction."

Under which class of cases then does the jurisdiction of the Arbitration Court, or the police magistrate, to inquire into a charge of a breach of the common rule, fall ?

In the case of a charge of this sort all that it is necessary for the prosecutor to prove is that the defendant is a person of the class engaged in the industry to which the common rule applies, and that he has committed the particular breach alleged. In answer to that charge the defendant may set up various defences. It is not necessary to mention every possible defence, but I will point out four. (1) He may set up that he is not within the operation of the rule at all, never having been engaged in the industry. (2) He may contend that, though he is within the operation of the common rule, he did not make the alleged contract of service, in fact or in law, that is he may say that, though made in his name, it was not made with his authority. Or (3) he may say that the alleged contract was not a contract of service, and therefore there was no breach of the award. Or (4) he may set up that, assuming he is within the common rule, he did not commit any breach of it, that he paid all the wages required by the award. It is clear that in all these cases the Court must have jurisdiction to inquire into the facts. But it is said that, unless a man is in fact and in law an employer, the Court has no jurisdiction over him. In the second of the cases I have put, it clearly must have jurisdiction to inquire whether the defendant in fact and in law made any, and, if any, what, contract. This may involve questions of construction of the rule and the Court must have jurisdiction to inquire into that as well as into the other elements of the offence. The same principle must apply if any of the other suggested defences are set up. It is impossible to limit the authority of the Court to inquire into any of these matters. The functions of the Court being to inquire whether the

H. C. of A.
1907.

Amalgam-
ated Society
of Carpen-
ters and
Joiners
v.
Haberfield
Proprietary
Ltd.

Griffith C.J.

person charged has broken the law, it has of necessity jurisdiction to determine any questions of fact or law on which the guilt or innocence of the defendant depends, and, if no appeal is given from its decision, no Court can review it. In the present case it is not disputed that no appeal lies from the Arbitration Court; and, therefore, if the case is within its jurisdiction, no matter how erroneous its decision may be, there is no remedy. If the legislature chooses to set up a Court of that kind it is perfectly free to do so. Legislatures have very often done so. In the present case it is provided by the Act that if the proceedings are taken before a magistrate the appeal is to the Arbitration Court. When the Act was passed the Arbitration Court was presided over by a Judge of the Supreme Court, so that the only difference made in that respect was that before the Act was passed there was an appeal from the magistrate in all cases to any Judge of the Supreme Court, whose decision was final, and after the Act was passed the appeal in these cases was to a Court presided over by a particular Judge of the Supreme Court, and the decision of that Court was final. There is, therefore, nothing suspicious in the finality of the decision of the Court if it sits as a Court of first instance.

I am of opinion that this case cannot be taken out of the ordinary rule that the duty of the Court is to examine the charge in order to see whether it discloses a matter that is within its jurisdiction, and, if it does, to proceed to determine it. If it does proceed to determine the matter, and determines it wrongly, there is no remedy. If the legislature desires to provide a remedy it is open to it to do so. As the law stands at present the decision of the Arbitration Court, being on a matter within its jurisdiction, is not examinable by the Supreme Court.

It may be right to add, in view of the opinion expressed by the learned president of the Arbitration Court on the question which he thought it necessary to decide, and of the general importance of the matter, that I am at present disposed to the opinion that the conclusion at which he arrived was wrong, and there was no contract between the parties creating the relationship of employer and employé. That was, however, a question for the Arbitration Court to determine, and this Court cannot review its decision.

No point was raised before us as to the person to whom the penalty is payable. It may be that the common rule is defective in that respect. But, no objection having been taken as to that point, we express no opinion upon it.

I think that the appeal must be allowed.

H. C. of A.
1907.

AMALGAM-
ATED SOCIETY
OF CARPEN-
TERS AND
JOINERS
v.
HABERFIELD
PROPRIETARY
LTD.

O'Connor J.

O'CONNOR J. The Supreme Court, after an inquiry into the evidence and documents, determined that the Arbitration Court had erroneously decided that the relation between the respondent company and the carpenters, whose cases were considered, was that of employer and employé within the meaning of the *Industrial Arbitration Act* 1901. Upon that ground they held that that Court had exceeded its jurisdiction and granted a prohibition. On behalf of the appellants, the objection was taken that the Supreme Court could not lawfully enter upon that inquiry. In the view that I take of the objection, it becomes unnecessary for this Court to determine whether the Supreme Court arrived at a correct conclusion upon the matter which it actually decided, though if it were necessary to do so, I am of opinion that their conclusion was correct. I base my judgment, however, solely on the ground that the Supreme Court had no jurisdiction to inquire whether on the matters mentioned the Arbitration Court had, or had not, come to a right conclusion.

The Court constituted under the *Industrial Arbitration Act* is a Court of limited jurisdiction. Its powers extend only to dealing with disputes on " industrial matters " within the meaning of the Act. To constitute such a dispute there must exist the relationship of employer and employé between the disputant employer or the Union which represents him and some member or members of the disputant Union of employés. That has been established by *Clancy v. Butchers' Shop Employés Union* (1). The Court is endowed with very wide powers for the making of awards in settlement of industrial disputes, for the fixing of penalties to enforce their observance, and for the punishment of breaches by the infliction of penalties. The observance of awards may also be enforced by order of a stipendiary or police magistrate. In respect of that part of their jurisdiction, therefore, the

(1) 1 C.L.R., 181.

H. C. of A.
1907.

AMALGAM-
ATED SOCIETY
OF CARPEN-
TERS AND
JOINERS
v.
HABERFIELD
PROPRIETARY
LTD.

O'Connor J.

powers of the Arbitration Court and of the stipendiary and police magistrate are co-extensive; the Supreme Court has no wider jurisdiction in reviewing an award of the Arbitration Court inflicting penalties for breach of an award than it has in reviewing a conviction of a stipendiary or police magistrate inflicting penalties for breach of the same award.

On behalf of the appellants sec. 32 of the Act was to a certain extent relied on. It enacts amongst other things that "no award, order, or proceeding of the Court shall be vitiated by reason only of any informality or want of form or be liable to be challenged, appealed against, reviewed, quashed, or called in question by any Court of Judicature on any account whatsoever." But this Court in *Clancy's Case* (1), following the English decisions on similar provisions, held that the section must be construed as not extending to cases in which a Court with limited jurisdiction has exceeded its jurisdiction. Notwithstanding that section, therefore, the question still remains whether the Arbitration Court has exceeded its jurisdiction in such a way as to entitle the Supreme Court to interfere.

It is important to consider the form in which the question arises. The original award, dated 15th December 1905, settling a dispute between the Carpenters and Joiners Union and a firm of employers, fixed a minimum daily rate of pay for carpenters. By order of the Court, dated 13th February 1906, the award was made a common rule of the building trade within certain geographical limits, and its terms were thereby made binding on all persons engaged in the industry of building within the area limited. A summons was issued against the respondent company, which was engaged in building within that area, for breach of the award in paying certain carpenters less than the minimum rate. On that summons the Arbitration Court, having heard the evidence, found that the breach complained of had been committed, and made an award adjudging that the respondent company should pay certain penalties. It is in respect of the award inflicting these penalties that the Supreme Court has made the order now under appeal.

The original award, the common rule, the summons and the

(1) 1 C.L.R., 181.

award thereon admittedly disclose no want of jurisdiction. But it is contended that the Arbitration Court, having found, on evidence from which that inference could not legally be drawn, that the relation of employer and employé between the respondent company and its carpenters did exist, has exceeded its jurisdiction, and its award, based on that finding, is open to prohibition.

H. C. OF A.
1907.

AMALGAM-
ATED SOCIETY
OF CARPEN-
TERS AND
JOINERS
v.
HABERFIELD
PROPRIETARY
LTD.

O'Connor J.

The law is well settled that superior Courts will not interfere by way of prohibition with the decisions of inferior Courts of limited jurisdiction unless want of jurisdiction is clearly established. But as is pointed out by *Sir James Colvile*, delivering the judgment of the Privy Council in the *Colonial Bank of Australasia* v. *Willan* (1), it is necessary before applying that principle to have a clear apprehension of what is meant by the term "want of jurisdiction." He then proceeds :—"There must, of course, be certain conditions on which the right of every tribunal of limited jurisdiction to exercise that jurisdiction depends. But those conditions may be founded either on the character and constitution of the tribunal, or upon the nature of the subject-matter of the inquiry, or upon certain proceedings which have been made essential preliminaries to the inquiry, or upon facts or a fact to be adjudicated upon in the course of the inquiry. It is obvious that conditions of the last differ materially from those of the three other classes. Objections founded on the personal incompetency of the Judge, or on the nature of the subject-matter, or on the absence of some essential preliminary, must obviously, in most cases, depend upon matters which, whether apparent on the face of the proceedings or brought before the superior Court by affidavit, are extrinsic to the adjudication impeached. But an objection that the Judge has erroneously found a fact which, though essential to the validity of his order, he was competent to try, assumes that, having general jurisdiction over the subject-matter, he properly entered upon the inquiry, but miscarried in the course of it. The superior Court cannot quash an adjudication upon such an objection without assuming the functions of a Court of Appeal, and the power to re-try a question which the Judge was competent to decide.

"Accordingly, the authorities, of which *Reg.* v. *Bolton* (2) and

(1) L.R. 5 P.C., 417, at p. 442.   (2) 1 Q.B., 66.

H. C. of A.
1907.

AMALGAM-
ATED SOCIETY
OF CARPEN-
TERS AND
JOINERS
v.
HABERFIELD
PROPRIETARY
LTD.

O'Connor J.

Reg. v. *St. Olave's District Board* (1), may be taken as examples, establish that an adjudication by a Judge having jurisdiction over the subject-matter is, if no defects appear on the face of it, to be taken as conclusive of the facts stated therein; and that the Court of Queen's Bench will not on certiorari quash such an adjudication on the ground that any such fact, however essential, has been erroneously found."

It was urged by Mr. *Knox* in the course of his argument that the question whether the relation of employer and employé existed was a matter "extrinsic to the adjudication impeached," and stood upon the same footing as those questions which may be raised in the County Courts regarding the residence of a defendant, or the existence of a *bonâ fide* dispute as to title to land. In such cases no doubt a County Court could not by a wrong decision on such a question give itself jurisdiction. On such matters, which are extrinsic to the adjudication impeached, the decision of the inferior Court is always open to inquiry.

In support of that contention the respondents' counsel argued that the jurisdiction of the Arbitration Court was restricted by the Act to one class of persons—those persons between whom the relation of employer and employé existed—and that it was necessary to establish as a collateral, extrinsic, or preliminary fact that the disputants came within that class before the Court could have jurisdiction over them. I can see in the Act no foundation for that contention. The jurisdiction of the Court is general over every person in New South Wales as to whom is established before the Court that state of facts which the Statute has authorized it to deal with. There is indeed nothing to distinguish in principle the facts to be established before the Arbitration Court has jurisdiction to make its order from the facts which had to be established in *R.* v. *Bolton* (2); *Brittain* v. *Kinnaird* (3); and *R.* v. *St. Olave's District Board* (1). In *R.* v. *Bolton* (2) the decision under consideration was a conviction by magistrates, but the principle laid down by Lord *Denman* C.J. in his judgment is equally applicable to the conviction of the Arbitration Court (4). "But," he says, " where a charge has been

(1) 8 El. & Bl., 529.   (3) 1 Brod. & B., 432.
(2) 1 Q.B., 66.   (4) 1 Q.B., 66, at p. 73.

well laid before a magistrate, on its face bringing itself within his
jurisdiction, he is bound to commence the inquiry : in so doing he
undoubtedly acts within his jurisdiction : but in the course of the
inquiry, evidence being offered for and against the charge, the
proper, or it may be the irresistible, conclusion to be drawn may
be that the offence has not been committed, and so that the case
in one sense was not within the jurisdiction.   Now to receive
affidavits for the purpose of showing this is clearly in effect to
show that the magistrate's decision was wrong if he affirms the
charge, and not to show that he acted without jurisdiction : for
they would admit that, in every stage of the inquiry up to the conclusion, he could not but have proceeded, and that if he had come
to a different conclusion his judgment of acquittal would have
been a binding judgment, and barred another proceeding for the
same offence.   Upon principle, therefore, affidavits cannot be
received under such circumstances.   The question of jurisdiction
does not depend on the truth or falsehood of the charge, but upon
its nature : it is determinable on the commencement, not at the
conclusion, of the inquiry : and affidavits, to be receivable, must
be directed to what appears at the former stage, and not to the
facts disclosed in the progress of the inquiry."

To apply these principles to the matter before us—the Court
has jurisdiction in disputes as to industrial matters within the
meaning of the Act where the relation of employer and employé
is involved—in the hearing of the dispute which it is empowered
to settle it must necessarily determine whether that relation does
or does not exist, and it is empowered to decide every question of
fact or law necessary for that determination.   Its determination
of that question may be right or may be erroneous.   If its error
is shown on the face of its proceedings as in *Clancy's Case* (1), the
superior Court will have power to grant a prohibition.   But if
the error is not shown on the face of its proceedings, there is no
way by which the correctness of the determination can on a
motion for prohibition be questioned.   In the proceedings before
the Court the original award was made binding only on employers
and employés.   The common rule similarly in its terms extended
only to employers and employés—the summons by reference

(1) 1 C.L.R., 181.

H. C. of A.
1907.

AMALGAM-
ATED SOCIETY
OF CARPEN-
TERS AND
JOINERS
v.
HABERFIELD
PROPRIETARY
LTD.

O'Connor J.

H. C. of A.
1907.

AMALGAM-
ATED SOCIETY
OF CARPEN-
TERS AND
JOINERS
v.
HABERFIELD
PROPRIETARY
LTD.

O'Connor J.

embodied the award. The matter for determination by the Court
was, first, whether there existed between the respondent company
and the carpenters the relation of employer and employé necessary to bring them within the terms of the common rule; second,
whether there had been a breach of the award.

It was clearly within the jurisdiction of the Court to enter
upon that inquiry, and, having determined that the relation of
employer and employé did exist, the order inflicting penalties was
founded on that determination. It discloses no want of jurisdiction on the face of it. Under the circumstances the decision of
the Court, whether right or wrong in fact or in law, is conclusive,
and beyond reach of inquiry by the Supreme Court or any other
Court.

In my opinion, therefore, the Supreme Court had no jurisdiction
to make the order appealed against, and the appeal must be
allowed.

ISAACS J. Prohibition at common law to restrain an inferior
Court from proceeding in respect of its order rests upon the
assumption that the Court had no jurisdiction whatever to make
the order. If it had jurisdiction to entertain and determine the
application in which the order is made, error, either of fact or law,
will not justify prohibition. The question, therefore, is whether
the Arbitration Court had jurisdiction to entertain and determine,
one way or the other, the application in which the order of the
14th November 1906 was made. It is said for the respondents
that no such jurisdiction existed, because the relation between
the respondents on the one hand and Roberts and Fry on the other
was not that of employers and employés, and that consequently the
respondents were not subject to the common rule. It was argued
that the Supreme Court had power to review the finding of the
Arbitration Court with regard to that relation, because that was
a collateral or preliminary matter, and having arrived at the
conclusion that the Arbitration Court was wrong in that respect,
the Supreme Court was right in issuing the prohibition. Reliance was placed upon the well known rule in *Bunbury* v.
Fuller (1):—" That no Court of limited jurisdiction can give

(1) 9 Ex., 111, at p. 140.

itself jurisdiction by a wrong decision on a point collateral to the merits of the case upon which the limit to its jurisdiction depends; and however its decision may be final on all particulars making up together that subject-matter which, if true, is within its jurisdiction, and, however necessary in many cases it may be for it to make a preliminary inquiry, whether some collateral matter be or be not within the limits, yet, upon this preliminary question, its decision must always be open to inquiry in the superior Court."

This rule is beyond question, but everything depends upon ascertaining in any particular case whether the matter in contention is collateral or preliminary, or is part of the subject matter, which, if true, is within the Court's jurisdiction.

In the *Colonial Bank of Australasia* v. *Willan* (1) it is pointed out that conditions of jurisdiction which depend upon facts or a fact to be adjudicated upon in the course of an inquiry differ from other classes of conditions of jurisdiction. Their Lordships say, as to the class referred to :—" But an objection that the Judge erroneously found a fact which, though essential to the validity of his order, he was competent to try, assumes that, having general jurisdiction over the subject-matter, he properly entered upon the inquiry, but miscarried in the course of it. The superior Court cannot quash an adjudication upon such an objection without assuming the functions of a Court of Appeal, and the power to re-try a question which the Judge was competent to decide."

What, then, is the subject matter which, in such an application as the Arbitration Court had before it, that tribunal is empowered and required by law to determine ? The application was in respect of an alleged breach by the respondents of a common rule in the building industry. The order directed that the common rule should be binding upon certain classes of persons within a designated area. The effect of the common rule and of sec. 37 (2) of the Act is that all persons comprised within these classes are bound by law to observe the obligations declared by the common rule, and in case of breach are liable to the prescribed penalties. The individuals who fall within those classes may vary from day to day, and whether a specified individual answers

H. C. of A.
1907.

AMALGAM-
ATED SOCIETY
OF CARPEN-
TERS AND
JOINERS
v.
HABERFIELD
PROPRIETARY
LTD.

Isaacs J.

(1) L.R. 5 P.C., 417, at p. 443.

H. C. of A. to the general description at any given moment is a question of
1907.   fact, and one perhaps depending upon circumstances which the

AMALGAM-   Arbitration Court from its special constitution is better fitted to
ATED SOCIETY
OF CARPEN- determine than the ordinary Court of law.   But the determina-
TERS AND   tion of that fact is absolutely essential to the ascertainment of
JOINERS
v.   whether a breach of the common rule has or has not been
HABERFIELD committed by the individual charged; and unless the Court finds
PROPRIETARY
LTD.   that he is an employer, and that the person alleged to have been

Isaacs J.   underpaid is his employé, within the meaning of the Act, there
            could be no breach of a common rule to pay the minimum wage.
            The question of whether the defendants fall within the specified
            class is not an element which is merely essential to jurisdiction but
            it is essential to an adverse adjudication; because it is an ingredient
            in the breach alleged.   It is therefore not a preliminary matter,
            nor a collateral point within the rule of *Bunbury* v. *Fuller* (1),
            but is part of the subject matter, and necessarily comes within the
            purview of the Court, which cannot possibly arrive at a decision
            against the defendants without determining this point. The Arbi-
            tration Court has to judge of this in the course of the case, just as
            much as of the amount of remuneration paid. It was in the
            present instance dealing with a class of questions plainly within
            its jurisdiction ; it was competent and bound to commence the
            inquiry, and to proceed to ascertain the facts, including the
            relations of the respondents to the men; there was no point at
            which it was bound or authorized to stop short of a final adjudi-
            cation on the truth or otherwise of the charge laid; there was
            evidence upon which the Court was as a tribunal entitled to rest,
            and did rest its conclusions of fact and law, whether those con-
            clusions were accurate or not; and consequently it cannot be said
            to have acted without jurisdiction. The reasoning of the Privy
            Council in the *Colonial Bank of Australasia* v. *Willan* (2),
            entirely supports the appellants' contention.

               This case resembles in principle *The Queen* v. *Dayman* (3)
            where the magistrate had no power to make an order for paving
            expenses except in the case of a " new street." The question
            whether the street was a new street or not was therefore one of

(1) 9 Ex., 111.   (2) L. R. 5 P.C., 417.
                         (3) 7 El. & Bl., 672, at p. 678.

the issues he had to try. He held it was not a new street and refused to make an order. The Court of Queen's Bench by a majority discharged the rule for a mandamus to compel him to hear and adjudicate. *Crompton* J. said that the magistrate had already heard and determined, and the learned Judge observed :—
"It is not a case in which the existence of a fact determines whether the inferior tribunal had jurisdiction or not, as when title to land comes into controversy in a County Court. Had this Act said that, as soon as there was a dispute as to whether the place was a new street, the jurisdiction should cease, it might give rise to different considerations. But in every cause that comes before any Court there are matters of law and fact, and matters of mixed law and fact, which the prosecutor must establish, or else he fails. On such matters, under this Act, the magistrate finally decides. If he were to step wholly out of his jurisdiction, then, though the certiorari is taken away, we could bring up and quash his order."

Every word of that quotation applies to the present case. In *R. v. Nunneley* (1) *Crompton* J. again differentiates the cases where, if a particular circumstance occurs, the jurisdiction is entirely gone, from those where the fact which gives jurisdiction is itself an ingredient in the judgment which is to be given if there be jurisdiction.

The case of *The Queen v. St. Olave's District Board* (2) was based on the same grounds, and appears to me to be an authority covering the present case. The Arbitration Court here had as much jurisdiction to determine the question as to whether Roberts was an employé of the respondents, as in that case the Metropolitan Board or, as *Coleridge* J. thought, the District Board, had to decide that Defree was an officer.

As the Arbitration Court possessed power to decide this controverted point, as part of the matter in dispute, jurisdiction was established, and prohibition cannot issue.

I may add that, so far as I am concerned, having regard to the whole of the evidence, I am by no means convinced that the decision of the Arbitration Court as to the real relationship of the respondents to the workmen was wrong.

(1) El. B. & E., 861.   (2) 8 El. & Bl., 529.

H. C. of A.
1907.

AMALGAM-
ATED SOCIETY
OF CARPEN-
TERS AND
JOINERS
v.
HABERFIELD
PROPRIETARY
LTD.

Isaacs J.

H. C. of A.
1907.

AMALGAM-
ATED SOCIETY
OF CARPEN-
TERS AND
JOINERS
v.
HABERFIELD
PROPRIETARY
LTD.

Appeal allowed. Order appealed from
discharged. Rule nisi for prohibition
discharged with costs. Respondents to
pay the costs of the appeal.

Solicitors, for the appellants, *Brown & Beeby.*
Solicitors, for the respondents, *Dawson, Waldron & Glover.*

C. A. W.

[HIGH COURT OF AUSTRALIA.]

MOY　　　.　　　.　　.　　.　　.　　.　　APPELLANT;

AND

BRISCOE & COMPANY LIMITED　　.　　.　RESPONDENTS.

ON APPEAL FROM THE SUPREME COURT OF
NEW SOUTH WALES.

H. C. of A.
1907.

SYDNEY,

Aug. 26, 27.

Griffith C.J.,
Barton,
O'Connor and
Isaacs JJ.

Bankruptcy Act 1898 *(N.S. W.),* (*No.* 25 *of* 1898), *secs.* 133, 137—*Supreme Court*
and Circuit Courts Act 1900 *(N.S. W.),* (*No.* 35 *of* 1900), *sec.* 15—*Vacancy in*
office of Judge in Bankruptcy—Delegation of powers of Judge to Registrar in
Bankruptcy.

Act of bankruptcy—Notice of intention to suspend payment of debts—Bankruptcy
Act 1898 *(N.S. W.),* (*No.* 25 *of* 1898), *sec.* 4.

The *Bankruptcy Act* 1898, sec. 133, provides that the bankruptcy jurisdiction of the Supreme Court shall be exercised by the Judge of that Court duly
appointed under the title of Judge in Bankruptcy. The *Supreme Court and
Circuit Courts Act* 1900, sec. 15, provides that where under any Act any
jurisdiction, power or authority of the Supreme Court is to be exercised by
any one Judge, any other Judge may for any reasonable cause exercise such
jurisdiction, power or authority in all respects as the Judge designated might
have exercised it.

During a short interval which elapsed between the resignation of the titular
Judge in Bankruptcy and the appointment of his successor, one of the other
Judges of the Supreme Court purported to exercise the power of delegation

conferred by sec. 137 of the *Bankruptcy Act*, which provides that the Judge (defined in sec. 1 as the Judge having jurisdiction in Bankruptcy or any Judge acting as such) may delegate to the Registrar such of the powers vested in the Court as may be expedient.

Held, that the delegation was valid, notwithstanding that there was at the time no titular Judge in Bankruptcy.

A statement by a debtor to the agent of a creditor, in answer to a demand by the creditor for the payment of a debt, that he has placed his affairs in the hands of accountants to prepare a statement of his accounts for him, and that in the meantime he had been advised not to pay any accounts, amounts to a notice that the debtor has suspended or is about to suspend payment of his debts, within the meaning of sec. 2 of the *Bankruptcy Act* 1898, and is therefore an available act of bankruptcy.

Rule laid down by *Bowen* L.J. in *In re Lamb* ; *Ex parte Gibson*, 4 Morr., 25, at p. 32, applied.

Decision of *Street* J. : *Re Moy* ; *Ex parte Briscoe & Co. Ltd.*, (1907) 7 S.R. (N.S.W.), 164, affirmed.

APPEAL from a decision of *Street* J., Judge in Bankruptcy of the Supreme Court of New South Wales.

Walker J., the Judge in Bankruptcy appointed under the *Bankruptcy Act* 1898, resigned on 29th January 1907, and his successor, *Street* J., was appointed a few days later.   In the interval the respondents presented a petition for the sequestration of the appellant's estate, and *A. H. Simpson*, C.J. in Eq., for the purpose of enabling the Registrar in Bankruptcy to deal with the petition, purported to delegate to him the power to do so, under sec. 15 of the *Supreme Court and Circuit Courts Act* (No. 35 of 1900), and sec. 137 of the *Bankruptcy Act* (No. 25 of 1898).   The Registrar heard the petition and made an order for the sequestration of the appellant's estate.   The act of bankruptcy was notice of suspension of payment of debts.

The appellant appealed to *Street* J., who dismissed the appeal with costs : *Re Moy* ; *Ex parte Briscoe & Co. Ltd.* (1).

From that decision the present appeal was brought, the amount involved being over the appealable amount.

The facts, and the sections of the Acts referred to, appear in the judgment of *Griffith* C.J.

(1) (1907) 7 S.R. (N.S.W.), 164.

Bradburn (*Perry* with him), for the appellant. The terms of sec. 15 show that the legislature presumed the existence of a Judge in Bankruptcy at the time when the section was to be applied. No other Judge can exercise the power of the Judge in Bankruptcy when there is no such Judge. *A. H. Simpson* C.J. in Eq., could not under the circumstances have sat as Judge in Bankruptcy, and therefore he could not delegate the powers of that Judge. Judge, in the definition sec. 2, means the Judge duly appointed, either in the first instance or by virtue of sec. 15 of the *Supreme Court and Circuit Courts Act.* Under the latter section there must be a Judge in whom the jurisdiction " is vested," and a reasonable cause. The words do not naturally cover the case of a vacancy in the office. If that had been intended it would have been expressly stated. The Executive could have got over any difficulty by appointing an acting Judge in Bankruptcy, who could have exercised all the powers of that Judge. The power of delegation under sec. 137 (2) of the *Bankruptcy Act* is given to the Judge personally, and can only be exercised by him : *Re Home* ; *Ex parte Edwards*(1). Sec. 15 was intended to provide for the temporary inability of the Judge in a special jurisdiction to sit, owing to some temporary cause such as illness or being engaged in another Court.

Notice of intention to suspend payment, in order to constitute an available act of bankruptcy within sec. 4 (1) (*h*), must be made to the creditor direct. In the present case the statement was made to another person, and was merely tentative, not intended to be acted upon, and was made on an occasion when the debtor would not have reasonably supposed that it would be acted upon. Under the circumstances it was natural for the debtor to suppose that he would be allowed time to refer his books to an accountant in order that he might ascertain how he stood, and in the meantime he would preserve the *status quo.* Nobody but the petitioning creditor was pressing him, and he was issuing a writ. There was no suspension in the sense in which it is used in the Act, and there was no formal and deliberate statement of intention as regards suspension. Where the question is what effect the notice would naturally have on the

(1) 54 L.J.Q.B., 447 ; 2 Morr., 203.

mind of the creditor, the Court should be strict in examining whether it was given to the creditor and intended as a notice: *Ex parte Blanchett*; *In re Keeling* (1). It should be given to a person authorized to receive it either expressly or by virtue of his employment, and with a clear intention to convey a definite meaning, not a mere casual statement of what the debtor contemplates doing for the present. [He referred to *Companies Act*, No. 40 of 1899, sec. 223; *Re Bacon*; *Ex parte Foley* (2); *In re Reis*; *Ex parte Clough*; *Clough* v. *Samuel* (3); *Ex parte Oastler*; *In re Friedlander* (4); *Trustee of Lord Hill* v. *Rowlands* (5).]

[GRIFFITH C.J. referred to *In re Reis*; *Ex parte Clough* (6).

O'CONNOR J. referred to *In re Pike* (7); *In re Fischer* (8).

ISAACS J. referred to *In re Scott*; *Ex parte Scott* (9); *In re Dagnall*; *Ex parte Soan and Morley* (10).]

H. C. OF A.
1907.

MOY
v.
BRISCOE &
Co. LTD.

Knox K.C. (*Clive Teece* with him), for the respondents. Sec. 15 applies whenever it is necessary that some Judge should exercise the jurisdiction in Bankruptcy and it is expedient for any reasonable cause that a Judge other than the titular Judge in Bankruptcy should do so. It gets rid of the difficulty that would arise in a case of urgency owing to the absence or illness of the Judge, and applies *à fortiori* where there is no titular Judge at all. The jurisdiction is vested permanently in the Supreme Court, not in any particular person, and may be exercised by any person who comes within the provisions for that purpose in the Acts dealing with the subject. The definition of Judge in Bankruptcy includes any Judge acting as such. For the time being he holds the office, to which the exercise of jurisdiction is attached. The non-existence of a Judge in Bankruptcy duly appointed is very different from the non-existence of the office. Sec. 15 is an enabling section, and will be read *ut res magis valeat quam pereat*. [He was not called upon on the question whether there had been an act of bankruptcy or not.]

GRIFFITH C.J. The *Bankruptcy Act* 1898 confers jurisdiction

(1) 17 Q.B.D., 303.
(2) 6 N.S.W. Bkptcy. Cas., 85.
(3) (1905) A.C., 442.
(4) 13 Q.B.D., 471, at p. 475.
(5) (1896) 2 Q.B., 124.

(6) (1904) 2 K.B., 769.
(7) 6 N.S.W. Bkptcy. Cas., 87.
(8) 1 N.S.W. Bkptcy. Cas., 84.
(9) (1896) 1 Q.B., 619.
(10) (1896) 2 Q.B., 407.

H. C. OF A.
1907.

MOY
v.
BRISCOE &
CO. LTD.

Griffith C.J.

upon the Supreme Court. All the judicial acts necessary to be done to give effect to that Act are to be done by the Supreme Court, and they collectively make up the jurisdiction of the Supreme Court. Sec. 133 provides that the jurisdiction in insolvency under the earlier Act and the jurisdiction under this Act "shall . . . be the bankruptcy jurisdiction of the Supreme Court." The section goes on to provide that "the bankruptcy jurisdiction of the Supreme Court shall, except as herein otherwise provided, be exercised by such Judge of the Supreme Court as may from time to time be duly appointed in that behalf by the Governor under the title of Judge in Bankruptcy."

For a few days in January last there was no titular Judge in Bankruptcy. *Walker* J. had resigned, and his successor had not been appointed. During that interval one of the other Judges of the Supreme Court, *A. H. Simpson* C.J. in Eq.—purporting to exercise the authority conferred by sec. 137 of the *Bankruptcy Act*, which provides that: "The Judge may delegate to the Registrar such of the powers vested in the Court as it may be expedient for the Judge to delegate to him"—made an order of delegation under which the Registrar acted in making the order of sequestration.

It is suggested that, as there was no titular Judge in Bankruptcy at that time, this power of delegation could not be exercised. Whether it could or could not depends upon the provisions of sec. 15 of the *Supreme Court and Circuit Courts Act* 1900, which enacts that:—"Where under any Act any jurisdiction, power, or authority is vested in the Chief Judge in Equity, the Judge exercising the Matrimonial Causes Jurisdiction of the Court, the Judge in Bankruptcy, or the Probate Judge, then"—in certain specified cases of which one is—"for any reasonable cause any other Judge may exercise such jurisdiction, power, or authority in all respects as such Judge in whom the same is so vested might have done, and shall while so acting have co-ordinate jurisdiction with and all the powers and authority of, such Judge, subject to the same right of appeal."

It is contended that that section only applies in cases where there is in existence a titular Judge of one of the classes mentioned. Strictly speaking, no doubt, sec. 15 is not quite accurate. The *Bankruptcy Act* does not vest the jurisdiction in the Judge,

H. C. of A.
1907.

Moy
v.
Briscok &
Co. Ltd.

Griffith C.J.

but in the Supreme Court, and directs that jurisdiction to be exercised by the Judge. Sec. 15, therefore, must be read as meaning that, where under any Act, any jurisdiction, power, or authority of the Court is to be exercised by a particular Judge, any other Judge may in the specified cases exercise that jurisdiction as fully as the Judge designated might have done.

In other words, any other Judge may exercise any jurisdiction, power, or authority which attaches to the office of the designated Judge. In this view it makes no difference whether the office of the Judge is for the moment vacant or not. The jurisdiction is the jurisdiction of the Court, and may be exercised by any Judge.

There is another argument which perhaps would be sufficient to dispose of the objection. The *Bankruptcy Act* provides by sec. 3 that the term "The Judge" means "the Judge having jurisdiction in bankruptcy under this Act"—that must mean the Judge by whom jurisdiction ought to be exercised—"or any Judge acting as such." I think it would be difficult to contend successfully that the word as so defined does not include any Judge of the Supreme Court acting *de facto* as Judge in Bankruptcy. It may be a case for the application of the maxim *Quod fieri non debuit factum valet.*

For these reasons I think that the objection to the authority of the Registrar fails.

As to the merits, I agree with the conclusions arrived at on the question of fact by the learned Judge from whose judgment the appeal is brought. All that can be said in the appellant's favour has been said by Mr. *Bradburn.* The question is really one of fact. There was a conflict in the oral evidence given before the Registrar, who believed the evidence of the agent for the petitioning creditor as to an interview between him and the debtor. The learned Judge was not prepared to dissent in this respect from the Registrar. He referred to that evidence and, accepting it as true, thought there was clear proof of the commission of the act of bankruptcy relied on, which was that the debtor had given notice to one of his creditors that he had suspended, or was about to suspend, payment of his debts.

The rule of law to be applied in construing that provision is

H. C. of A.
1907.

Moy
v.
Briscoe &
Co. Ltd.

Griffith C.J.

stated in the passage from the judgment of *Bowen* L.J. in *In
re Lamb*; *Ex parte Gibson* (1) cited by *Street* J. :—" We have
in each case to ask ourselves, and in each case to answer the
question, what is the reasonable construction which those who
receive this statement of the debtor would have a right, under
the circumstances of the debtor's case, to assume, and would
assume, to be his meaning as to what he intends to do with
respect to paying, or suspending payment of, his debts."

Street J. also referred to the speech of Lord *Macnaghten* in
the case of *Clough* v. *Samuel* (2). In that case Lord *Macnaghten*
was the dissenting Lord, so that his opinion is not binding, but
there can be no doubt of the accuracy of the passage quoted :—
" The notice need not be in writing. It is enough if notice is
given to any one of the creditors. No particular form is
required. There is nothing said in the Act about the debtor's
intention. The question is what effect would the communication
have on the minds of the persons to whom it is addressed.
That is the test laid down by this House. It is only a matter
of common sense. . . . All that is required is that a communication proceeding from the debtor, made seriously, should
give the creditors or any of the creditors to understand from
the state of circumstances as disclosed at the time that the
debtor has suspended or that he is about to suspend payment."

For myself I do not think there is any substantial conflict in
the evidence between the debtor's and the creditors' witnesses.
The facts were that the debtor had a demand made upon him by
the petitioning creditors for a debt amounting to £1,200. Demand
had been made for payment, and an action at law was threatened.
The agent of the petitioning creditors went to the debtor and had
a conversation with him. The debtor told him that he had placed
his affairs in the hands of Messrs. Starkey & Starkey, accountants,
as he put it, " to prepare a statement of my accounts for me, and
that in the meantime I had been advised not to pay any accounts."

Although, as Lord *Macnaghten* said, there is nothing in the Act
about the intention of the debtor, yet, if you know what his
intention is, you are in some way advanced on the inquiry. In
this case, there is no doubt that the debtor formed the intention

(1) 4 Morr., 25, at p. 32.   (2) (1905) A.C., 442, at p. 446.

H. C. of A.
1907.

Moy
v.
Briscoe &
Co. Ltd.

Griffith C.J.

that he would not pay his creditors until he had ascertained the result of the examination into his affairs by a firm of accountants. That was his state of mind. He had made up his mind that he would not pay, that is to say, that he would suspend payment, for a certain time. When asked by the petitioning creditors' agent why he would not pay, he said, " I have been advised not to pay until I have ascertained certain facts." That, it seems to me, would convey to any ordinary person that the debtor did not intend to pay his debts in the meantime, in other words, that he had suspended or was about to suspend payment for a time. The term "suspension" implies that the stoppage is not intended to be permanent. It is suggested that, even so, that was not a notice of suspension. I agree that the notice must be a deliberate statement, but when a man is asked why he does not pay a debt and he replies, " Well, I won't pay you because I have made up my mind not to pay anybody at present," I think that is a deliberate communication of intention to the creditor. The notice need not be anything more than such a deliberate communication of intention. Therefore, all the elements involved in an act of bankruptcy were proved, and the learned Judge was right in his conclusion.

* O'Connor J. and Isaacs J. concurred.

Knox K.C. asked for an order declaring that the costs of the appeal be petitioning creditors' costs. The Supreme Court could make such an order. There is no rule of Court giving him these costs. [He referred to In re Bright; Ex parte Wingfield and Blew (1).]

Griffith C.J. The costs of the appeal will be petitioning creditors' costs. We cannot order costs out of the estate unless the estate is before the Court.

Appeal dismissed with costs, to be costs of the petitioning creditors.

(1) (1903) 1 K.B., 735.

* *Barton* J. owing to illness was unable to be present during the second day of the hearing of the appeal.

H. C. of A.
1907.

Moy
v.
Brisook &
Co. Ltd.

Solicitor, for the appellant, *A. H. Jones.*

Solicitors, for the respondents, *Perkins, Stevenson & Co.*

C. A. W.

[HIGH COURT OF AUSTRALIA.]

LILA ELIZABETH BAYNE . . . . . Appellant;

AND

BAILLIEU AND OTHERS . . . . . Respondents.

ON APPEAL FROM THE SUPREME COURT OF
VICTORIA.

H. C. of A.
1907.

MELBOURNE,
Sept. 9.

Griffith C.J.,
Barton and
O'Connor JJ.

*Insolvency—Order nisi for sequestration based on judgment for costs of prior action
—Appeal pending to High Court from prior judgment—Adjournment of insolvency proceedings.*

After notice of appeal to the High Court from a judgment dismissing an
action with costs, the defendants in the action, having in a subsequent action
recovered judgment for the costs, presented a petition for sequestration of
the plaintiff's estate, the act of insolvency being failure to comply with a
debtor's summons founded on the judgment and to satisfy a writ of *fieri facias*
issued upon it.

It was not suggested that the debtor had any estate, or that the judgment
creditor would obtain any advantage from the sequestration other than putting
difficulties in the way of prosecuting the appeal.

Held, that an order of sequestration ought not to have been made, but that
the petition should have been either adjourned until after the hearing of the
appeal or dismissed.

An order absolute for sequestration having been made under these circumstances, and the prior judgment having, on appeal to the High Court, been
discharged, an application was made to the Supreme Court to annul the
sequestration.

Held, that the application ought to have been granted, notwithstanding
that the judgment for the costs was still standing.

Judgments of *Hood* J. and of *Hodges* J. reversed.

APPEAL by special leave from two orders of the Supreme Court.

An action having been brought by Lila Elizabeth Bayne and her sister Mary Bayne against Arthur Palmer Blake and William Riggall for certain breaches of trust, judgment was on 6th December 1905 given by *Holroyd* J. for the defendants with costs. The costs were afterwards taxed and allowed at £628 14s. 4d., and on the 20th December a debtor's summons was issued against the two plaintiffs for these costs.

On 21st December 1905, Miss L. E. Bayne duly gave notice of appeal to the High Court from the judgment of 6th December 1905. On 23rd December 1905 a writ was issued by Messrs. Blake & Riggall against the two Misses Bayne for the taxed costs above referred to. On 4th January 1906 the debtor's summons of 20th December 1905 was served on Miss L. E. Bayne. On 26th January 1906 final judgment was signed for the amount of the taxed costs. A writ of *fieri facias* issued on this judgment was on 5th February 1906 returned wholly unsatisfied.

On 6th February 1906 an order *nisi* was obtained by Messrs. Blake & Riggall for the sequestration of the estate of Miss L. E. Bayne, based on the judgment of 26th January 1906 and the writ of *fieri facias* issued thereon, and the debtor's summons of 20th December 1905 and on failure to comply therewith. This order *nisi* was on 22nd February 1906 made absolute by *Hood* J., and Arthur Sydney Baillieu was appointed assignee. No creditors other than Messrs. Blake & Riggall proved in the estate of Miss L. E. Bayne.

On 8th March 1906 the sum of £50 was paid into the High Court by Miss L. E. Bayne as security for the costs of the appeal from the judgment of 6th December 1905. On the hearing of that appeal on 17th June 1906, the appeal was allowed, and the judgment of 6th December 1905 was ordered to be discharged: *Bayne* v. *Blake* (1). From that judgment of the High Court Messrs. Blake & Riggall subsequently obtained leave to appeal to the Privy Council.

On 30th May 1907 a motion was made by Miss L. E. Bayne to the Supreme Court to set aside or annul the order absolute for sequestration of 22nd February 1906, notice of the motion having

(1) 4 C.L.R., 1.

been given to A. S. Baillieu. *Hodges* J., who heard the motion, refused to set aside or annul the order absolute, but, with the assent of A. S. Baillieu, he stayed all proceedings under the order absolute until further order.

On 10th June 1907 Miss L. E. Bayne obtained special leave to appeal to the High Court from the order absolute of 22nd February 1906, and from the judgment of *Hodges* J. of 30th May 1907. The respondents to the appeal were the assignee in insolvency, A. S. Baillieu, and Messrs. Blake & Riggall.

Agg (with him *Ah Ket*), for the appellant. Notice of appeal to this Court from the judgment of 6th December 1905 having been given, and that appeal being *bonâ fide*, the order *nisi* for sequestration should not have been made absolute, but should at least have been adjourned until after the hearing of the appeal : *Ex parte Heyworth; In re Rhodes* (1) ; *In re Bayne* (2). The real object of the insolvency proceedings was, not to obtain a distribution of the appellant's assets, but to prevent her proceeding with the appeal, and therefore the order for sequestration should not have been made absolute: *In re Smart & Walker* ; *Ex parte Hill* (3) ; *Ex parte Bourne; In re Bourne* (4).

Mann, for the respondent, A. S. Baillieu.

McArthur, for the respondents, Messrs. Blake & Riggall, did not oppose the setting aside of the orders appealed from on grounds which did not reflect on the conduct of his clients.

GRIFFITH C.J. The proceedings for the sequestration of the estate of the appellant were begun after she and her sister had given notice of appeal to this Court from a judgment of the Supreme Court adverse to them, and were founded upon that judgment. While that notice of appeal was still pending, but before the appellant had given security for the costs of the appeal, the insolvency proceedings were pressed on, with the result that the order of sequestration—one of the orders now appealed from—was made by *Hood* J., but, as Mr. *McArthur* tells us, nothing was done under that sequestration after the

(1) 14 Q.B.D., 49.	(3) 20 V.L.R., 97.
(2) 25 A.L.T., 176.	(4) 2 G. & J., 137.

appeal to this Court was completely instituted. Subsequently an application was made to *Hodges* J. to annul the order of sequestration, based practically on the circumstances I have pointed out. He refused to do so. Without saying that under all circumstances proceedings for sequestration founded upon a judgment, from which notice of appeal to this Court has been given must fail, it is sufficient in this case to say that, in the absence of any evidence that the appellant had an estate which the respondents desired to have administered in the Insolvency Court, they must fail. There is no evidence on that point at all. Upon the facts I have stated it appears to me, and I think to my brothers, that the order for sequestration ought not to have been made, but the motion should properly have been adjourned or perhaps dismissed. That being so, this Court on appeal can reverse the order for sequestration. Again, on the application to *Hodges* J., the same materials having been brought before him, he ought to have annulled the sequestration, but he did not.

Another point was suggested by Mr. *McArthur*, which might raise a formal objection to the second appeal, but has nothing in it of substance, viz., that his clients were not formally made parties to the motion to annul the sequestration. It is very arguable whether they were necessary parties. The official assignee was the only formal party, but it is not denied that Mr. *McArthur's* clients were the only creditors, and their solicitor represented the official assignee. Under all the circumstances I think the appeal should be allowed and the orders appealed from reversed.

BARTON J. I concur.

O'CONNOR J. I concur.

> *Appeal allowed.   Orders appealed from reversed.   Respondents Blake & Riggall to pay costs of appeal.*

Solicitor, for appellant, *Frank S. Stephen.*
Solicitors, for respondents, *Rigby & Fielding* ; *Blake & Riggall.*

                                                B. L.

H. C. OF A.
1907.

BAYNE
v.
BAILLIEU.

Griffith C.J.

[HIGH COURT OF AUSTRALIA.]

HOWARD SMITH AND COMPANY ⎫   .   APPELLANTS;
LIMITED .   .   .   .   . ⎬
PLAINTIFFS,

AND

VARAWA .   .   .   .   RESPONDENT.
DEFENDANT,

ON APPEAL FROM THE SUPREME COURT OF
NEW SOUTH WALES.

H. C. OF A.   *Contract—Statute of Frauds—Negotiations in code cablegrams—Offer and accept-*
1907.   *ance—Ambiguity—Extrinsic evidence—Subsequent correspondence.*
               Principal and agent—Undisclosed principal—Ratification.
SYDNEY,
Aug. 27, 28,   Where the documents relied upon to prove a contract consisted of transla-
29, 30.   tions and expansions of a number of cablegrams in code which passed between
               the parties :
Griffith C.J.,
O'Connor and   *Held,* that the Court, in considering whether there was a concluded
Isaacs JJ.   agreement at a certain date should look at all the surrounding circumstances
               for the purpose of ascertaining the sense in which abbreviated communica-
               tions, capable of more than one meaning, were likely to have been understood
               by the recipients, and that, although the documents of that date were capable
               of being read so as to constitute a complete contract, evidence was admissible
               of communications between the parties before and subsequent to that date
               which tended to negative that conclusion.

               Hussey v. *Horne-Payne,* 4 App. Cas., 311, applied.

               Although as a general rule it is not necessary, in order to satisfy the
               requirements of the *Statute of Frauds,* that the acceptance of an offer in
               writing should also be in writing, yet if the facts show that the party making
               the offer did not intend to be bound unless the other party accepted it in
               writing, there is no contract without such acceptance.

               So, where the parties were in places far apart and all the negotiations were
               necessarily conducted by cable :

H. C. OF A.
1907.

HOWARD
SMITH & CO.
LTD.
v.
VARAWA.

Held, that the inference was irresistible that a party making a cabled offer did not intend to be bound by it until he was informed in like manner that the offer was accepted.

Moore v. *Campbell*, 10 Ex., 323, applied.

Where in an action upon a contract of sale, involving a number of special terms and conditions, subsidiary to the main transaction, the owners, as plaintiffs, rely upon ratification of a contract made by their agent, they must establish that the agent professed to be acting as an authorized agent for the owners with respect to the whole bargain.

Keighley, Maxsted & Co. v. *Durant*, (1901) A.C., 240, applied.

Decision of the Supreme Court, 15th February 1907, affirmed.

APPEAL from a decision of the Supreme Court of New South Wales.

The following statement of the proceedings in the case is taken from the judgment of *Griffith* C.J.:—

"This was an action brought by the appellants (plaintiffs) against the respondent (defendant) for damages for breach of an alleged contract for the sale of the s.s. *Peregrine* by the plaintiffs to the defendant for the sum of £28,000. The defendant denied the making of the alleged contract, and also set up the *Statute of Frauds*. The documents relied upon to prove the contract were cablegrams which passed between one Moller, who was the defendant's agent, and who was a ship broker at Shanghai in China, and one Miles, who was alleged to be the plaintiffs' agent, and who was at Manila in the Philippine Islands. The contract set up by the plaintiffs at the trial was alleged to have been made on 1st December 1904. A nonsuit moved for on the ground that this contract was not proved was refused, and the defendant entered upon his case and put in evidence several cablegrams of later date, on which the plaintiffs then relied as proving a completed contract. The learned Judge who tried the case directed the jury that there was a concluded contract between the parties on 3rd December 1904, and, as the refusal to accept was not in dispute, the jury had only to assess damages, which they fixed at £10,000. It appeared that the defendant acted in the transactions in question as an agent for the Russian Government, the Russo-Japanese war

H. C. of A.
1907.

HOWARD
SMITH & Co.
LTD.
v.
VARAWA.

being then in progress.   On an application by the defendant to
the Full Court for judgment or a new trial on the ground of the
wrongful rejection of evidence, the Court directed a verdict to be
entered for him, and from that decision this appeal is brought."

The correspondence, so far as is material to this report, is fully
set out in the judgment of *Griffith* C.J.

Knox K.C. (*J. L. Campbell* with him), for the appellants. The
cablegram of 1st December was an unconditional acceptance of
the offer by the defendant's agent.   It does not matter when it
was received.   Sending an acceptance in the channel indicated
by the offeror concludes the contract: *Household Fire and
Carriage Accident Insurance Company* v. *Grant* (1); *Pollock on
Contracts*, 6th ed., p. 31. Any subsequent revocation or qualification of that was inoperative : *Henthorn* v. *Fraser* (2); *Harris'
Case*; *In re Imperial Land Co. of Marseilles* (3); *Byrne* v. *Van
Tienhoven* (4).

[ISAACS J. referred to *Bruner* v. *Moore* (5).]

When there has been an unconditional acceptance, subsequent
correspondence cannot be looked at in order to qualify it or cut
it down. On the correspondence up to 1st December there was
clear evidence of an offer and acceptance. The fact that the
acceptance leaves the details to be arranged does not impair its
efficacy. The subsequent correspondence was merely negotiation
as to particular terms and conditions. *Hussey* v. *Horne-Payne*
(6), on which the Supreme Court relied, is merely a decision that
on the particular facts of that case there was no concluded contract at a certain point; it does not decide that a definitely concluded contract can be re-opened by subsequent correspondence.

[He referred to *Bristol, Cardiff, and Swansea Aerated Bread
Co.* v. *Maggs* (7); *Bellamy* v. *Debenham* (8).

ISAACS J. referred to *Brauer* v. *Shaw* (9).]

Although it is always a question of the intention of the parties,
and that is a question of fact, the written statements of the

(1) 4 Ex. D., 216.
(2) (1892) 2 Ch., 27.
(3) L.R. 7 Ch., 587.
(4) 5 C.P.D., 344.
(5) (1904) 1 Ch., 305.

(6) 4 App. Cas., 311.
(7) 44 Ch. D., 616.
(8) 45 Ch. D., 481.
(9) 168 Mass., 198.

H. C. of A.
1907.

HOWARD
SMITH & CO.
LTD.
v.
VARAWA.

parties are the best evidence of intention, and where their meaning is clear, the writer cannot afterwards say that he meant something else. Even if there was no completed contract on 1st December there was on 3rd December, and the jury found that the defendant by his conduct had assented to the new terms: *Brogden v. Metropolitan Railway Company* (1). If the subsequent conduct of the parties is evidence of their intention at that date, it shows clearly that they were acting on the basis of a concluded contract.

Though the agent did not disclose his principals' name at the time of making the contract, he showed that he was acting for the owners whoever they might be, and the owners were therefore entitled to ratify: *Keighley, Maxsted & Co.* v. *Durant* (2).

Cullen K.C. (*Mitchell* with him), for the respondent. There can be no ratification unless the alleged agent represented to the other party that he was acting for some principal, though he had no authority in fact: *Keighley, Maxsted & Co.* v. *Durant* (2); and the ratification must extend to the whole of the matters in negotiation. The whole transaction was never really communicated to the appellants, and therefore they could not ratify. It was not sufficient for them to merely ratify the sale. All through, Miles was in fact acting to a certain extent on his own behalf. Part of the transaction was incompatible with agency for the appellants. The contract, if there was one, concluded on 1st December, was never ratified, and, if it was concluded on 3rd December, the appellants were never ready and willing to perform it. [He referred to *Managers of Metropolitan Asylums Board* v. *Kingham & Sons* (3); *Bolton Partners* v. *Lambert* (4); *In re Portuguese Consolidated Copper Mines Limited*; *Ex parte Badman*; *Ex parte Bosanquet* (5); *In re Tiedemann and Ledermann Frères* (6); *Fleming* v. *Bank of New Zealand* (7).]

There was no evidence to support the finding that the respondent authorized the cablegram of 1st December from Moller to Miles. Even if there was such evidence, it is clear that the

(1) 2 App. Cas., 666.
(2) (1901) A.C., 240.
(3) 6 T.L.R., 217.
(4) 41 Ch. D., 295.

(5) 45 Ch. D., 16.
(6) (1899) 2 Q.B., 66, at p. 71.
(7) (1900) A.C., 577, at p. 587.

H. C. of A.
1907.

HOWARD
SMITH & Co.
LTD.
v.
VARAWA.

parties regarded the longer cablegram of that date as a step in the negotiations. That is inconsistent with the completion of a contract on that date. The contract was either not concluded or it was re-opened by the parties. [He referred to *Bellamy* v. *Debenham* (1).] If on the evidence it is impossible to say which cablegram was first received by Miles, the plaintiffs failed to establish their case. If there was no concluded contract on 1st December, it was never completed afterwards. New terms were discussed, but were never finally settled. Where parties negotiate by code telegrams, the plaintiff must show clearly that an agreement was concluded. If the cables are capable of more than one meaning, one of which is inconsistent with a concluded contract, the defendant must succeed: *Falck* v. *Williams* (2).

Even if the respondent is not entitled to a verdict, there should be a new trial. Fresh evidence is available since the first trial, relevant to the question whether the appellants were ready and willing to deliver. That is ground for a new trial, even though the evidence is not conclusive on the point: *Broadhead* v. *Marshall* (3). Moreover, evidence of cablegrams was wrongly rejected, and the special findings were against evidence. The jury were wrongly directed as to what it was that the appellants were bound to deliver. The damages were assessed on a wrong basis. The proper measure was, not the difference between the contract price and what the ship would have brought in Australasia where there was no market, but in the Pacific. [He referred to *Dunkirk Colliery Company* v. *Lever* (4).]

Knox K.C., in reply, referred to *Sutton & Co.* v. *Ciceri & Co.* (5); *Hagedorn* v. *Oliverson* (6); *In re Tiedemann and Ledermann Frères* (7).

Cur. adv. vult.

The following judgments were read.

GRIFFITH C.J., [after referring to the proceedings, as already reported, continued:] Several points are made for the respondent.

(1) 45 Ch. D., 481; (1891) 1 Ch., 412.   (5) 15 App. Cas., 144, at p. 153.
(2) (1900) A.C., 176.   (6) 2 M. & S., 485.
(3) 2 W. Bl., 955.   (7) (1899) 2 Q.B., 66.
(4) 9 Ch. D., 20, at p. 25.

He contends that there was no concluded contract, either on 1st
December or on 3rd December, or at any later date, and that, if
there was, the contract was not between the plaintiffs and the
defendant, but between Miles and the defendant, and that Miles,
who, it is admitted, had no actual authority from the plaintiffs
to make it, did not at the time of making it profess to be acting
on behalf of a principal, so that it could not, under the doctrine
of *Keighley, Maxsted & Co.* v. *Durant* (1), be ratified by the
plaintiffs. The evidence rejected was said to have an important
bearing on this last question.

The case depends entirely upon the construction to be put upon
the cablegrams, which were in code, and of which translations or
expansions only were in evidence. These documents are often
ambiguous, or at least difficult of interpretation. The onus is
upon the plaintiffs to establish their case. In my opinion the
case is not one in which the Court is called upon merely to interpret the meaning of a written contract of which the words are
certain and unambiguous, but involves a consideration of all the
surrounding circumstances for the purpose of ascertaining the
sense in which abbreviated communications, capable of more than
one meaning, were likely to be understood by the recipients.

I will first deal with the question whether any contract was
proved to have been made on 1st December. This question is
presented in three different aspects : (1) whether the documents
relied upon disclose a contract upon their face ; (2) whether the
relation between Miles and Moller was that of intending vendor
and purchaser at all ; and (3) whether, if the relation was that
of intending vendor and purchaser, and if the documents purport
to show on their face a completed contract, they were intended
to have the effect of a present contract. I will deal with these
questions separately.

Before referring to the terms of the cablegrams it is necessary
to say a few words as to the relation of Miles and Moller as
shown by extrinsic evidence. Their acquaintance appears to have
been of a very slight character. Miles was not called as a
witness. Moller who was examined on commission as a witness
for the plaintiffs deposed as follows :—

(1) (1901) A.C., 240.

H. C. of A.
1907.

HOWARD
SMITH & Co.
LTD.
v.
VARAWA.

Griffith C.J.

H. C. of A.
1907.

HOWARD
SMITH & Co.
LTD.
v.
VARAWA.

Griffith C.J.

" Q. Did you know Captain Miles ?   A. Yes.

" Q. Had he any business relations with you ?   A. He tried to have, but he did not have any before that.

" Q. What did you know him as ?   A. I knew him as a wealthy man from Tasmania.   He told me he was.

" Q. What did he tell you at Manila ?   A. He came to Shanghai, and told me he was one of the wealthiest men in Tasmania.

" Q. Did you know him as a shipbroker, that is what I mean ?

" A. He told me he was travelling around with a certain number of ships for sale.   He said he had them for the owners, and he was doing it for a pastime."

There was no more evidence on the subject, and it is difficult to draw any definite conclusion from that which I have read.

The *Peregrine*, the subject of the alleged contract, was a steamship then employed in the passenger and goods trade on the Australian coast.

The first cablegram, which was sent by Moller to Miles on 22nd November, was as follows : " Telegraph whether you can purchase two steamers not less than seventeen knots 2000 tons dead weight delivery Hongkong as soon as possible."   Miles replied on the same day in these words : " *Mararoa Peregrine Moura.*"   On 23rd November Moller wired as follows ; " *Mararoa Peregrine Moura* if you guarantee 17 knots we can buy : telegraph lowest possible price delivery Sydney also Singapore : what deposit is required : telegraph immediately : there is every prospect of business."   On the following day, 24th November, Miles replied : " *Peregrine* £28,000 Sydney : *Mararoa* £45,000 New Zealand : Singapore will be extra £2,000 : Highest speed 17 knots 10 p.c. deposit."   On the same day, apparently in reply to this message, Moller wired as follows : " *Peregrine Mararoa* : Telegraph the lowest firm offer Singapore delivery minus 5 p.c. : If vessels not suitable £2,000 stg. each will be paid to pay expenses : Deposit arranged : When will you be ready for delivery : How many hours can steamer maintain seventeen : Also name speed for ordinary fast voyage : Name lowest price."   On 25th November Miles replied :—" Has been given the lowest price and no reduction can be made : Cannot give the option of pur-

H. C. of A.
1907.

HOWARD
SMITH & Co.
LTD.
v.
VARAWA.

Griffith C.J.

chase: Must be accepted Australia: Speed can be tested." On 28th November Miles again wired as follows:—" *Mararoa* has been withdrawn: *Peregrine* very cheap: Everything has been arranged trial trip Government inspection 2nd December Sydney: As soon as surveying has been finished if satisfactory payment against inspector's certificate on final delivery: Speed will be guaranteed: Can only give refusal until Thursday." Thursday was the 1st of December. On the same day Moller telegraphed: —" *Mararoa*: We are authorized will accept £45,000 delivery Australia: £12,000 in our hands: In whose name shall we deposit Chartered Bank: Will you send vessel Singapore at our expense: Balance of purchase money paid when ready to leave Australia: Telegraph expected delivery Singapore: Make as soon as possible: Do your utmost: Do not disappoint." This cablegram related only to the *Mararoa*. On 29th November Miles telegraphed:— " Afraid cannot sell for immediate delivery: Have telegraphed: Will communicate with you as soon as we have a reply: Will send either or both Singapore." Although this message was no doubt an answer to Moller's of the 28th, there is nothing on the face of it to connect it with any previous document. I am, however, disposed to think that it might be shown by evidence that the words "either or both" mean the *Mararoa* and *Peregrine*.

On the same day Moller telegraphed:—" *Mararoa*: Confirm the sale as soon as possible: If everything in order there is every prospect of buying *Peregrine*: Keep offer open as long as possible," and again on the 30th:—" Please answer as soon as possible."

This document contains a reference to an offer, and it may, I think, be shown by extrinsic evidence what that offer was. That appears by Miles's messages of 24th and 28th. It was an offer to sell the *Peregrine* for £28,000 delivered at Sydney, which offer was to be open until 1st December. The words " will send either or both to Singapore " in Miles's message of the 29th appear to relate to an intended subsidiary arrangement as to the expenses of the voyage from Sydney to Singapore. It is at least doubtful whether they should be regarded as referring to a term of the bargain which Moller desired to make with the owners of the ship, or to a private understanding between Miles and Moller. The latter

H. C. of A.
1907.

Howard
Smith & Co.
Ltd.
v.
Varawa.

Griffith C.J.

view is favoured by the first message of the series, in which Miles is asked if he can "purchase," not whether he can "sell." On 30th November Miles telegraphed: "*Mararoa*: Cannot give a definite answer until Friday (i.e., 2nd December) what is the matter with *Peregrine*: Fastest: a much better purchase: if there is nothing definite to-morrow (i.e., 1st December) cannot guarantee delivery before (some date which is unintelligible): Subject to immediate acceptance will arrive on 16th Singapore." This message to some extent answered the two queries contained in Moller's telegram of the 29th, and may, I think, be expanded to mean:—"If acceptance is immediate the ship will be despatched so as to arrive at Singapore on 16th December." Many details would, however, be still left uncertain, such as the financial arrangements to be made for the expenses of the voyage, and the manner in which the purchase money was to be paid.

On 1st December Moller sent an urgent cablegram as follows: "*Peregrine* accepted."

At this point the plaintiffs closed their case, contending that they had proved a complete contract in writing. If there was such a contract, it was to buy the *Peregrine*, *simpliciter*, for £28,000 to be delivered at Sydney. No doubt a contract for the purchase of a named ship for a lump sum without more may be a good and complete contract. But it is highly improbable that it would be made unless both parties were familiar with the subject matter, and were *ad idem* as to what was intended to be included by the name of the ship, and it seems to me still more improbable when one of the parties had no acquaintance with the subject matter which was at a distance of several thousand miles. Was it intended to include the apparel and furniture of the ship, which was a passenger ship, or not? Was the delivery to be immediate or deferred, and to whom and where was it to be made? On the whole, I am of opinion that, if the correspondence between the parties had ended at this point, it would have been incomplete, inasmuch as the writing did not express all the terms of it. The mere name of the ship is itself ambiguous. Upon the sale of a ship certain matters must be provided for, either expressly or by implication. In this case there is no express provision, and the circumstances do not afford grounds for any definite implication.

I proceed to consider the further correspondence on which the plaintiffs rely alternatively. The cablegram "*Peregrine* accepted" was sent as an urgent message from Shanghai at 4 p.m. on 1st December. At 3.40 Moller had sent to Miles a message as follows:— "*Peregrine* : Have accepted : Confirm the purchase : A complete inventory must be taken : Must be held responsible until we take charge Singapore : Subject to survey by Lloyds Sydney on condition that passes first class with 17 knots in light cargo : Apply for payment to Chartered Bank here to-morrow : *Mararoa* reply." The meaning of the word " to-morrow " is not explained, but it is quite clear that, if this message is to be taken as part of the correspondence, there was not on 1st December an acceptance by Moller of Miles's offer, but a counter offer on terms materially different. The telegram of 3.40 appears to have arrived at Manila at 5.30 p.m. There was no evidence to show when that of 4 p.m. arrived there.   An interesting argument was addressed to us to the effect that the telegram of 3.40 operated from the time of its despatch, and had the effect of a refusal which could not be followed by an acceptance of the original offer, even if an acceptance of that offer were in fact received before it, and *à fortiori* if the acceptance were received after the refusal.   It is not necessary to decide the point, for, if the plaintiffs' case rests upon the receipt of the message of 4 p.m. before that of 3.40, they have failed to discharge the onus of showing that it was so received. If the messages were received together, or that of 3.40 was received first, the question at once arises whether the message of 4 p.m. was sent as part of the negotiations, and as intended to supersede the message of 3.40, or as a mere notification that the bargaining as to the *Peregrine* was to continue.   Having regard to the subsequent conduct of the parties, to which I will directly call attention, I have no doubt that the message of 4 p.m. was not intended to have a contractual operation at all, but was merely a notification to Miles of the intention of Moller's principals.

The case of *Hussey* v. *Horne-Payne* (1) was referred to and relied upon by the learned Judges of the Full Court. In that case it was held that, although two letters of a correspondence

(1) 4 App. Cas., 311.

H. C. of A.
1907.

HOWARD
SMITH & Co.
LTD.
v.
VARAWA.

Griffith C.J.

H. C. of A.
1907.

HOWARD
SMITH & Co.
LTD.
v.
VARAWA.

Griffith C.J.

seemed on their face to constitute a complete contract, it was open to show by other documents and oral evidence that no complete and concluded contract had in fact been made. In the present case we have nothing but written documents, to which I will now refer. It is plain that, the question being whether the parties had in fact concluded an agreement on 1st December, any statements or conduct on their part after that date inconsistent with the existence of a concluded contract are relevant for this purpose.

In reply to Moller's message of 3.40 p.m. of 1st December, Miles wired as follows :—" Agree to all conditions except owners will accept no responsibility whatever after delivering Sydney : If they approve will arrange Dalgety's accept delivery for account of : Provide everything that is needed coal provisions insurance crew : Will not guarantee payment purchasers on final delivery Singapore." The last sentence is not intelligible. It may mean that payment by the purchasers is to be made on final delivery Singapore, and in view of a later telegram of 10th December, by which Miles informed Moller that delivery could not be made until a credit was opened in favour of the owners for £2,000 for the expenses to Singapore, this would appear to be the meaning. It is important to bear in mind that Miles had in fact no authority from the owners to sell the ship, so that this concession by him would not be so surprising as it might seem at first sight. On the same day (2nd December) Moller replied as follows :—" Purchasers require condition of vessel on arrival Singapore to be same as surveyor's report Sydney : therefore to ensure good delivery as guaranteed keep present crew on board : expenses insurance wages to be paid by us guaranteed by Comptoir Nationale : Reply before noon to-morrow : If accepted meet Moller Hong Kong further business." This communication again imports a new term into the conditions of the bargain. On the same day Miles telegraphed to Moller as follows :—" You must distinctly understand owners cannot accept any responsibility during the voyage Singapore : In case of accident collisions it is impossible guarantee delivery in the same condition." This may or may not have been sent in reply to Moller's message of the same day. Whether it was or no, it is clear that on 2nd Decem-

H. C. of A.
1907.

HOWARD
SMITH & Co.
LTD.
v.
VARAWA.

Griffith C.J.

ber Miles and Moller were still negotiating the terms of the sale of the *Peregrine*, and that the parties were not *ad idem*. Under these circumstances it is, in my opinion, equally clear that Moller's telegram of 4 p.m. of 1st December was not intended to have a contractual operation.

The next question is whether a concluded contract was completed on 3rd December. On the 2nd the position was that Moller had asked for terms which Miles had refused. On 3rd December Moller wired as follows: "Purchasers fully understand owners cannot accept any responsibility force majeur collisions: but you must take immediate steps to protect us if there is anything wrong with carelessness machinery boilers inventory &c.: . . . Cover insurance Australia Singapore against all risks £32,000 at our expense."

The plaintiffs contend that this communication operated as a withdrawal of all the terms on which Moller had insisted in his telegrams of the 1st and 2nd. They say that the words "force majeur collisions" are equivalent to "accident collisions" in Miles's second telegram of the 2nd. Assuming that this is so, there still remains a difficulty. If the message of 3rd December is regarded as a single message addressed to Miles as the agent of the owners, and as expressing terms to be included in the contract of sale, there would be no contract until the new terms as to protecting the purchasers were accepted by the vendors. It is said that the acceptance need not be in writing. In one sense that is no doubt true: *Reuss* v. *Picksley* (1). But, if the facts show that the party making the offer in writing did not intend to be bound unless the other party accepted it in writing, there is no contract without such acceptance: *Moore* v. *Campbell* (2). This is a question of fact. But when the parties are in different places far apart, and all the correspondence is conducted by cable, I think the inference is irresistible that the purchasers did not intend to be bound until they were informed in like manner that the terms offered were accepted. There was no evidence of the acceptance of the new terms by Miles, unless it is to be found in a message sent by him to Moller on 8th December, which is as follows:—"Owners require vessel registered in the name of

(1) L.R. 1 Ex., 342.   (2) 10 Ex., 323.

H. C. of A.
1907.

Howard
Smith & Co.
Ltd.
v.
Varawa.

Griffith C.J.

purchasers before delivery : to whom will transfer be made ?" If the telegram of 3rd December is regarded as addressed to Miles as agent for the owners, I do not think that any assent by the owners to the new terms expressed in it can be inferred from the telegram of the 8th. If, on the other hand, it is suggested that the telegram of the 3rd should be treated as divisible, the first sentence being read as an acceptance of the owners' final terms, and the rest of it being regarded as addressed to Miles in the capacity of agent for Moller, other questions arise. It is true that the first sentence uses the words " owners " while the second says " You must" &c. Nevertheless the treatment of the message as two distinct messages addressed to Moller in two distinct capacities seems to be based on pure conjecture. *Primâ facie*, the whole of the communications from Moller to Miles were addressed to the latter in the same capacity, whether that was as agent for the owners of the *Peregrine* or as an independent adventurer.

The plaintiffs do not set up any document of later date than 3rd December as a sufficient note or memorandum of the contract, although Miles and Moller seem to have regarded the purchase as then practically settled. On the whole I am unable to dissent from the conclusion of the Full Court that no complete contract in writing had been shown to have existed on 3rd December.

This conclusion is to some extent confirmed by the terms of a message sent by Moller to Miles on 7th December, in which he said : "*Peregrine*: when is arrival expected Singapore: any small difficulties can easily be overcome : buyer's representative will pass rather than lose the business: telegraph definite information as soon as possible." This seems to indicate that at that date Moller did not regard the bargain as finally concluded with the owners. On 26th December Moller telegraphed for the first time to the plaintiffs. His message was as follows : " Are buyers of *Peregrine*: are ready to take delivery: you are running no risk by sending Singapore according to terms of telegrams and guarantee Comptoir Nationale D'Escompte : forward an immediate answer by telegraph date of sailing." This message incorporates by reference the terms of previous telegrams,

H. C. of A.
1907.

HOWARD
SMITH & Co.
LTD.
v.
VARAWA.

Griffith C.J.

but does not supply the want of any acceptance by plaintiffs or their agent of the stipulations of the telegram of 3rd December. The telegram was not answered by plaintiffs.

Assuming, however, that there was a completed contract on 3rd December, the question still remains—Who were the parties to it? Up to this time the plaintiffs had given Miles no authority to sell the ship for them.

It will be convenient to consider this question together with the question whether Miles professed to be making the contract on behalf of the owners. It is now necessary to refer to the evidence which was rejected by *Pring* J., which consisted of two cablegrams from Moller to Miles. The first, dated 23rd November, was as follows :—"Add 10 p.c. for outside commissions clear beside our 2½ : cannot be helped : keep confidential." The second, dated the following day, was as follows :—" Keep us fully protected : Commission and brokerage as per our telegram of 23rd : Will hold us responsible : Will probably lead to business." This telegram, read in conjunction with Moller's first inquiry, " Can you purchase " &c. suggests that Miles was asked to obtain an option of purchase of ships, and that he was to add to the price at which he might obtain the option an additional 10 per cent. for purposes which it is easy to read between the lines. They also show that, if Miles was expected to act as agent for the owners, the price at which he was to agree to sell the ships to Moller's principals was not to be the price which the owners were to receive, but a larger sum. In my opinion these messages were relevant both to the question whether the supposed contract was in fact made with Miles as an individual or with him as a person purporting to act as the authorized agent of the owners of the ship, and also to the question of the proper meaning to be attributed to Moller's message of 3rd December. There would therefore, in any event, have to be a new trial, if the defendant is not entitled to a nonsuit or verdict. But, apart from these telegrams, I think that the documents relied upon do not show upon their face that in making any contract which could be deduced from them Miles professed to be acting on behalf of the owners of the ship. If the contract had been for the sale of the ship *simpliciter* for a fixed sum it might perhaps be inferred that he did so pro-

H. C. of A.
1907.

HOWARD
SMITH & Co.
LTD.
v.
VARAWA.

Griffith C.J.

fess. But the question is whether in making the whole of the bargain between himself and Moller he professed to be acting for the owners. I think that, if there were no more in the case, the message of 3rd December must be read as a stipulation insisted upon by the purchasers, but as one intended to be performed by Miles personally under some understanding between him and Moller. The bargain was, however, a single bargain.

Some additional light is thrown upon this part of this case by messages which passed between Miles and the plaintiffs. On 1st December he telegraphed to them that he had a firm offer of £26,000 for the *Peregrine*. On the 6th he telegraphed that he would do his utmost to "keep the offer open." This is difficult to reconcile with the notion that there was a concluded contract on the 3rd. On 7th December plaintiffs telegraphed to him that they would accept " £26,000 nett free of commission, cash on delivery, napery crockery plateware excluded : vessel to be transferred in the name of new owners before delivery."

It may be that Miles was playing a double part as representing himself to Moller as agent for the owners and to them as agent for the purchasers. But, on the whole, I do not think that the plaintiffs have established that with respect to the whole of the bargain, which, as I have said, was a single bargain, Miles professed to be acting as an authorized agent for the owners. And, in my opinion, this is a necessary condition of the existence of any right of ratification in the plaintiffs within the rule laid down in *Keighley, Maxsted & Co.* v. *Durant* (1). The onus of proof that he did so profess is on the plaintiffs, and they have failed to discharge it. Moreover, the contract now sought to be ratified is a contract under which the vendors were to receive £26,000, while that made, if any, was one under which the purchasers were to pay £28,000. If there were no more in the case, this discrepancy would be fatal. For these reasons I think that the appeal must be dismissed.

O'CONNOR J. I have had the opportunity of reading the judgment of my learned brother the Chief Justice, and I entirely concur in the conclusion at which he has arrived and in the

(1) (1901) A.C., 240.

reasoning by which it is supported. Having regard to the pleadings the plaintiffs cannot succeed without proving a contract in
writing. The contract, if any there is, must, therefore, be made
out from the cablegrams which passed between Miles and Moller.
From those cables it is necessary to establish : first, that the parties
were *ad idem*, that they arrived at a concluded contract; secondly,
that the contract was made between Miles, acting as the plaintiffs'
agent, and Moller, acting as the defendant's agent. The Court is
entitled, in reading the cables, to any assistance which evidence
of the subject matter and surrounding circumstances may afford.
But the facts and circumstances of which there is evidence do not
afford much assistance. The cables themselves are, as is to be
expected in that species of communication, in some instances
obscure and confused. However, a Court must do the best it can
to arrive at the meaning of the communications by which the
parties have chosen to negotiate their contract. To my mind it
is quite clear that on the 1st December 1904 there was no concluded agreement. I was at first disposed to think that the
parties were in agreement on the 3rd December 1904. But
further consideration of the cables of that and subsequent dates
satisfies me that there was one matter at least as to which the
parties were never *ad idem*, that is, which party was to bear the
responsibility of any difference between the condition of the *Peregrine* as she arrived at Singapore and as she was passed for
delivery in Sydney. Proposals and counter proposals were made,
but that question was never settled by the cables. Indeed, the
evidence appears to show that it was because of the difficulty of
coming to any agreement on that matter that Moller and Varawa
came on to Sydney. I am also of opinion that there was no evidence in the cables or letters to show that Miles contracted or
purported to contract as the plaintiffs' agent. The cables not
admitted in evidence furnish strong evidence that he was not
acting as their agent. Leaving those out of consideration and
taking only the cables and letters in evidence, a strong light is
thrown on Miles's position by the cables which were passing
between him and the plaintiffs at the time he was negotiating
the alleged contract with Moller. The latter set of cables appears
to be entirely inconsistent with the position that he made the

H. C. of A.
1907.

HOWARD
SMITH & Co.
LTD.
v.
VARAWA.

O'Connor J.

H. C. of A.
1907.

HOWARD
SMITH & Co.
LTD.
v.
VARAWA.

Isaacs J.

contract with Miller as their agent. The Supreme Court, in my opinion, therefore came to a right conclusion in the matter submitted for their consideration and rightly directed the verdict to be entered for the defendant. I agree that the appeal must be dismissed.

ISAACS J. The plaintiffs cannot succeed unless they establish a ratification of a concluded contract entered into between Moller acting for the defendant and Miles professing to act for the plaintiffs.

The telegram of 1st December cannot be relied on as closing the bargain. It was despatched twenty minutes later than the other telegram of the same date and, in the absence of any evidence to the contrary, the earlier cable may be assumed to have reached its destination earlier than the second cable sent. But it is unnecessary to decide whether in view of this assumption the bargain was closed when the later cable came to hand, because the matter did not rest there. The subsequent correspondence shows conclusively that, even if a contractual obligation had been technically created, the parties mutually abandoned it, re-opened the transaction, and continued negotiations. Then as to the telegram of 3rd December, did this of itself close the bargaining? Clearly not. It contains a new requirement, viz. :—" You must protect us," &c. If Miles is to be considered as acting for the plaintiffs this is a stipulation demanded of him as agent, and unless assented to by or on behalf of the plaintiffs, prevents a conclusion of the contract. If it had been expressly refused, no question could have arisen; there would obviously have been a failure to agree.

Then silence is relied on as assent to this new stipulation. That depends on the circumstances. Here the known circumstances of the two negotiating parties, the distance of Miles from the owners, and the nature of the intervening cables, entirely preclude any such assumption in this case. There is no indication that Miles ever agreed to this stipulation; he was certainly hovering a good deal, neither he nor Moller wanted the affair to slip out of their hands. Moller knew that Miles would do all that was possible to secure the owners' acquiescence to assure the

good condition of the vessel at Singapore—which was the view
point of the purchasers—but there is nothing to show that Moller
ever believed or had reason to believe that Miles, as representing
the owners, did accede to that requirement.

H. C. of A
1907.

HOWARD
SMITH & Co.
LTD.
v.
VARAWA.

Isaacs J.

There appears to have been no recession from the unequivocal
statement on 2nd December that the "Owners will accept no
responsibility whatever after delivery Sydney."

In my opinion there was not a concluded bargain between
Moller and Miles in whatever character we may regard the latter
as acting.

But, on the supposition of a binding contract, in what capacity
did Miles profess to enter into it ?　I pass by any question of the
Statute of Frauds for this purpose, and consider the question
purely as one of fact.

I shall state the general result of the evidence as it appears to
me to be the undeniable story told by the documents and
admitted circumstances of the case. Particular references to the
cables will be few.

Captain Miles, a Tasmanian gentleman, went to the East in 1904
during the Russo-Japanese war.　He went with the design of
trafficking in ships, then owned by other persons, that is to say
shipping companies in Australia and New Zealand.　He took up
his temporary abode in Manila, and got into communication
with the firm of Moller Bros., shipbrokers of Shanghai, from
whom he ascertained that some fast sailing steamers were
required for their principal.　The defendant Varawa was their
immediate principal, and legally the only one that could be looked
to, though he was in fact purchasing for the Russian Government.
Miles went to Shanghai and had an interview with Moller of
which some account is given by Moller.　Miles gave no evidence
at the trial.　It is evident from the documentary evidence that
the oral testimony of the conversation between Miles and Moller
is far from complete.　When he returned to Manila a series of
telegrams passed between him and Moller, which alone or with
conduct constitute the alleged contract relied on.

They prove beyond doubt that the inquiry made by Moller of
Miles was whether Miles could *purchase* two steamers for him,
and that Miles was told to add, that is to the price he would

H. C. of A.
1907.

HOWARD
SMITH & Co.
LTD.
v.
VARAWA.

Isaacs J.

otherwise ask, ten per cent. for outside commissions, and 2½ per cent for Moller & Co. So that Miles was not to receive net the price he nominally asked but only that sum less 12½ per cent. of the net price.

Moller of course knew Miles had to get the ships from others ; that is why "purchase" was used ; and so on the basis of this knowledge and of the telegraphic arrangements already adverted to, two sets of cable negotiations took place. The first was between Miles and Moller, and the second between Miles and the plaintiffs.

These sets of negotiations were perfectly distinct and separate ; and as might be expected from a person in Miles's position, a buyer in one aspect and a seller in the other, they are often irreconcilable and apparently contradictory.

In the cables between Miles and Moller there is to be found in Ex. 10 (8th December) and afterwards some mention of the owners, not however expressly as contractors with Moller, but only as persons whose objection to a desired course was an insuperable obstacle to Miles agreeing to it, or whose insistence on a guarantee was a condition to the delivery of the ship to the purchaser. If those references stood alone and were capable of no other construction they might greatly assist the plaintiffs in this branch of the case, but they are altogether counterbalanced by the other written evidence. The opening cables of the Miles-Moller negotiations are decisive that Miles at all events did not enter upon his work as owner's agent, and was not intended to. He was first of all asked if he could *purchase* two steamers, which is quite inconsistent with the plaintiffs' theory to start with ; then this is followed by a cable to which I have already referred to and which should be quoted verbatim. It was part of the negotiations between Miles and Moller and clearly admissible. It runs thus : " Add ten per cent. for outside commissions clear besides our two half cannot be helped keep confidential."

Apart from the moral aspect of the scheme, upon which Moller and Miles were embarking, it is clear that this telegram is destructive of the suggestion that Miles was professedly bargaining for Howard Smith & Co. That would suppose that Howard Smith & Co. were to add the 12½ per cent. commission, that they

H. C. of A.
1907.

HOWARD
SMITH & Co.
LTD.
v.
VARAWA.

Isaacs J.

were to receive their price plus the padding, and were to delude the purchaser by giving a receipt to him for the whole gross sum as if for purchase money only, and then hand over the 12½ per cent. to the purchaser's agents for distribution to the intended recipients of the commission. This is a material circumstance when the question of ratification is considered. In succeeding telegrams expressions are used which taken literally point to Miles as the vendor to Moller, no mention being made to the owners till 8th December. Reference is also several times made to the *Mararoa* as well as the *Peregrine* in the same telegrams, and it fits in better with the view that Miles dealt with Moller in respect of both, than that he was acting in one line of a cable as agent for the owners of the *Mararoa* and in the next as agent for Howard Smith & Co. as owners of the *Peregrine*. On the whole I feel no doubt on the construction of this first set of telegrams that Miles professed and purported to act for himself and not for Howard Smith & Co. He, of course, depended for his ability to do this on his success with the second set of negotiations, namely with the plaintiffs, to which I shall now refer. I may state *in limine* that nowhere in these negotiations is there a direction or arrangement to sell for £28,000. The price asked is £26,000. On 23rd November he tells the plaintiffs that he is offered £25,000 for the *Peregrine* if he will guarantee 17 knots, and is informed in reply that plaintiffs will accept £27,500, and they add significantly " must have a guarantee from a responsible party." In other words, in response to his virtual question how much less than £25,000 they can take, they tell him they want more, and in addition cannot accept merely his responsibility. On 7th December plaintiffs cable that they will accept £26,000 nett free of commission, cash on delivery. Next day Miles cables the plaintiffs that on certain conditions the " National Bank will pay £28,000, £26,000 purchase money, £2,000 commission and brokerage, which they will receive. Fully expect £100 from you to pay expenses " &c. The plaintiffs reply the same day is " If you accept delivery " &c. Now the telegram sent by Miles does not say the £28,000 is to be paid to Howard Smith & Co., nor could they with any honesty receive it. They were plainly told the bank was to pay £28,000 evidently to Miles in the first place, and

H. C. of A.
1907.

HOWARD
SMITH & Co.
LTD.
v.
VARAWA.

Isaacs J.
of that only £26,000 was purchase money, that is for Howard Smith & Co., being the sum they asked. The remaining £2,000 was stated to be commission and brokerage, which according to the telegram the National Bank was to receive, it may be to receive back from Miles for the ultimate recipients whoever they might be. In other words, as far as the cable discloses Howard Smith & Co. were not to touch a penny of this £2,000. Under no possible interpretation of either set of cables could the plaintiffs claim to be entitled to £28,000. Under their own cables with Miles £26,000 was distinctly fixed as the price. If they ratified Miles's contract with Moller, they ratified the whole of his acts, including the arrangement by which the 12½ commission was to be secretly added to the real price. Naturally the plaintiffs would disclaim any such indefensible transaction. But without it how do they arrive at £28,000 ? That amount was fixed because of the confidential telegram of 23rd November, and Howard Smith & Co. were informed on 8th December that £26,000 was the purchase money, and that £2,000 was an addition. Their case, however, as pleaded and pressed is on a contract for the price of £28,000. If they succeeded they would have established their right to have had the whole of the £28,000 supposing the contract carried out ; and damages must be based on that supposition. But by what right would they receive the full £28,000 ? For them to retain the £2,000 commission would be quite contrary to either set of cables ; but, if not, how would they distribute it ?

To my mind the plaintiffs' claim, when the facts are carefully examined, breaks down at every point.

Some interesting questions of law raised relative to ratification were argued, but in the view I have taken their determination is not necessary.

Appeal dismissed with costs.

Solicitors, for the appellants, *Sly & Russell.*
Solicitors, for the respondents, *Minter, Simpson & Co.*

C. A. W.

[HIGH COURT OF AUSTRALIA.]

MILLER . . . . APPELLANT;
DEFENDANT,

AND

HAWEIS . . . . RESPONDENT.
COMPLAINANT,

ON APPEAL FROM A COURT OF PETTY SESSIONS OF VICTORIA

Appeal to High Court from State Court of Summary Jurisdiction—Court exercising federal jurisdiction—Decision of two questions either of which supports judgment—The Constitution (63 & 64 Vict. c. 12), sec. 31—Judiciary Act 1903 (No. 6 of 1903), sec. 39 (2) (d)—Constitution Act Amendment Act 1890 (Vict.) (No. 1075), sec. 282—Commonwealth Electoral Act 1902 (No. 19 of 1902).

A Court of Summary Jurisdiction of a State exercises federal jurisdiction within the meaning of sec. 32 (2) (d) of the *Judiciary Act* 1903, if it be necessary in the particular case for the Court to decide any question arising under the Constitution or involving its interpretation.

If, however, whether that question is answered rightly or wrongly, the Court answers another question, not arising under the Constitution or involving its interpretation, and their answer to that other question enables them to decide the case, the Court does not exercise federal jurisdiction, and therefore no appeal lies to the High Court from that decision.

On a complaint in a Court of Petty Sessions of Victoria for work and labour done concerning an election for the House of Representatives for the Commonwealth Parliament, the defence being that sec. 282 of the *Constitution Act Amendment Act* 1890 (Vict.) was a bar to the complaint, the Court held that that section was a "law relating to elections," and was consequently by sec. 31 of the Constitution adopted and applied to elections for the House of Representatives, and also held that, being so adopted and applied, it was repealed by the *Commonwealth Electoral Act* 1902, and therefore gave judgment for the complainant.

H. C. OF A.
1907.
⌣
MELBOURNE,
Sept. 11, 12,
19.

Griffith C.J.,
Barton,
Isaacs and
Higgins JJ.

Held, that in determining the second point the Court of Petty Sessions had not exercised federal jurisdiction, and therefore that no appeal lay to the High Court from their decision.

APPEAL from a Court of Petty Sessions of Victoria.

Thomas W. Haweis brought a complaint in the Court of Petty Sessions at Prahran against John Miller, who was a candidate for the Fawkner Electoral Division, at the election held on the 12th December 1906, for the House of Representatives of the Commonwealth Parliament. Haweis claimed £15 for work and labour done in issuing and distributing circulars in connection with Miller's candidature. The case was heard on 2nd May 1907, the Court of Petty Sessions being constituted by Mr. Keogh, Police Magistrate, and two honorary Justices of the Peace, and an order was made for the amount claimed.

An order *nisi* to review this decision was granted by *Barton* J., on the grounds :—

1. That the complaint was not maintainable having regard to sec. 31 of the Constitution and sec. 282 of the *Constitution Act Amendment Act* 1890 (Vict.).

2. That the jurisdiction exercised by the Court of Petty Sessions, being federal jurisdiction, was exercised in a manner contrary to the provisions of sec. 39 (2) (*d*) of the *Judiciary Act* 1903.

The order *nisi* now came on for argument.

Arthur, for the appellant. The question is whether the prohibition in the Victorian *Constitution Act Amendment Act* 1890, sec. 282, against the bringing of an action for work and labour done in and about an election, applies by virtue of sec. 31 of the Constitution to elections for the House of Representatives. The Commonwealth Parliament has not otherwise provided within the meaning of sec. 31 of the Constitution. The *Commonwealth Electoral Act* 1902 is not a complete code, and does not repeal all the State legislation, so far as by sec. 31 of the Constitution it was made applicable to federal elections, but only repeals those provisions of the State legislation which are inconsistent with it, or as to which an intention is shown that they should not apply : See *Quick and Garran's Constitution of the Australian Common-*

wealth, pp. 427, 467, 471; *State of Tasmania* v. *The Common-wealth and Victoria* (1); *Ex parte Siebold* (2). The Parliament of a State may go on making laws as to federal elections so long as they are not inconsistent with federal legislation. Sec. 282 of the *Constitution Act Amendment Act* 1890 is a law relating to elections within the meaning of sec. 31 of the Constitution: *Henningsen* v. *Williams* (3).

The determination of this question involves the construction of sec. 31 of the Constitution, and therefore was a matter of federal jurisdiction. For that reason a Court of Petty Sessions constituted of a Police Magistrate and two Justices had no jurisdiction to hear it: *Judiciary Act* 1903, sec. 39 (2) (*d*). For the same reason an appeal lies to this Court.

[He also referred to *Cope* v. *Cope* (4); *Garnett* v. *Bradley* (5).]

H. Barrett, for the respondent. This matter came before the Court of Petty Sessions as a State matter. The only defences stated were sec. 282 of the *Constitution Act Amendment Act* 1890, and that there was no debt. It was not objected that it was a matter of federal jurisdiction.

The matter does not involve the interpretation of the Consti-tution, but merely the interpretation of the *Commonwealth Electoral Act* 1902. That Act is a complete code, and from the time it was passed the State Acts no longer applied to federal elections. Sec. 282 of the *Constitution Act Amendment Act* 1890 is not a law relating to elections, but is a law relating to procedure and to the limitation of actions.

Arthur, in reply.

Cur. adv. vult.

The judgment of the Court was delivered by

GRIFFITH C.J. This is an appeal from a Court of Petty Ses-sions of Victoria which was constituted by a Police Magistrate and other justices. The appeal is brought to this Court on the assump-tion that the matter determined by the Court of Petty Sessions

Sept. 19.

(1) 1 C.L.R., 329.
(2) 100 U.S., 371.
(3) 27 V.L.R., 374; 23 A.L.T., 92.
(4) 137 U.S., 682, at p. 686.
(5) 3 App. Cas., 944, at p. 965.

H. C. of A.
1907.

MILLER
v.
HAWEIS.

was a matter of federal jurisdiction, and reliance is placed on sec. 39 (2) (d) of the *Judiciary Act* 1903, which provides that :—"The federal jurisdiction of a Court of summary jurisdiction of a State shall not be judicially exercised except by a Stipendiary or Police or Special Magistrate, or some Magistrate of the State who is specially authorized by the Governor-General to exercise such jurisdiction." If, therefore, the Court was exercising federal jurisdiction, it was improperly constituted ; if it was not exercising federal jurisdiction, this Court cannot entertain an appeal from it. It is necessary, therefore, first of all to inquire whether the Court of Petty Sessions was exercising federal jurisdiction or not.

The complaint was for work and labour alleged to have been done by the respondent for the appellant at an election for the House of Representatives. The appellant relied on the provisions of sec. 282 of the Victorian *Constitution Act Amendment Act* 1890 that :—"No action suit or other proceeding whatsoever shall be brought or maintained whereby to charge any person upon any contract or agreement for the loan of money or the doing of any work or service or the supply of any goods for or towards or concerning or in carrying on or prosecuting any election of a member under this Act or any Act hereby repealed." The appellant maintained before the Court of Petty Sessions that under the Constitution that section was applicable to federal elections, relying on sec. 31 of the Constitution, which provides that :— " Until the Parliament otherwise provides, but subject to this Constitution, the laws in force in each State for the time being relating to elections for the more numerous House of the Parliament of the State shall, as nearly as practicable, apply to elections in the State of members of the House of Representatives." He contended that this was a law " relating to elections" within the meaning of sec. 31, and therefore became the law of Victoria with regard to federal elections. The respondent in answer to that argument said that, supposing it to be so, the Parliament of the Commonwealth had " otherwise provided " by the *Commonwealth Electoral Act* 1902. There were, therefore, two questions to be determined

This Court has defined the meaning of federal jurisdiction

more than once. For the purpose of sec. 39 of the *Judiciary Act* 1903, it means all matters over which the High Court has, under the *Judiciary Act*, original jurisdiction. The matter in the present case is said to be one over which this Court has jurisdiction under sec. 30 of the *Judiciary Act* 1903, which confers jurisdiction "in all matters arising under the Constitution or involving its interpretation."

A question of federal jurisdiction may be raised upon the face of a plaintiff's claim, as in *Baxter* v. *Commissioners of Taxation* (*N.S.W.*) (1), or may be raised for the first time in the defence, but as soon as the question is raised, if the jurisdiction of the State Court has been taken away, it must stay its hand. As was pointed out in *Starin* v. *New York* (2) by Chief Justice *Waite*:—" The character of a case is determined by the questions involved: *Osborne* v. *Bank of the United States* (3). If from the questions it appears that some title, right, privilege, or immunity, on which the recovery depends, will be defeated by one construction of the Constitution or a law of the United States, or sustained by the opposite construction, the case will be one arising under the Constitution or laws of the United States, within the meaning of that term as used in the Act of 1875 ; otherwise not."

But, in order that the jurisdiction of a Court which starts with jurisdiction may be ousted, the case must be such that it is necessary to determine a question of federal jurisdiction in order to decide the case. A very similar rule is well settled in the United States with regard to a class of cases in which under the Judiciary Acts of that republic an appeal lies to the Supreme Court from the highest Court of State. The point is not quite the same as that now before us, but it is very analogous. I will refer to one of the later cases in which the rule has been stated. I read from the judgment in *Hale* v. *Akers* (4):—" In *Murdock* v. *City of Memphis* (5), this Court announced, as one of the propositions which flowed from the provisions of the second section of the Act of February 5th 1867, 14 Stat., 386," (the *Judiciary Act*) "embodied in sec. 709 of the Revised Statutes of 1874, and

(1) 4 C.L.R., 1087, at p. 1136.   (4) 132 U.S., 554, at p. 564.
(2) 115 U.S, 248., at p. 257.   (5) 20 Wall., 590, 636.
(3) 9 Wheat., 737, at p. 824.

still in force, that even assuming that a federal question was erroneously decided against the plaintiff in error, the Court must further inquire whether there was any other matter or issue adjudged by the State Court, which is sufficiently broad to maintain the judgment of that Court, notwithstanding the error in deciding the issue raised by the federal question; and that, if that is found to be the case, the judgment must be affirmed, without inquiring into the soundness of the decision on such other matter or issue. This principle has since been repeatedly applied. In *Jenkins* v. *Lowenthal* (1), where two defences were made in the State Court, either of which, if sustained, barred the action, and one involved a federal question and the other did not, and the State Court in its decree sustained them both, this Court said that, as the finding by the State Court of the fact which sustained the defence which did not involve a federal question was broad enough to maintain the decree, even though the federal question was wrongly decided, it would affirm the decree, without considering the federal question or expressing any opinion upon it, and that such practice was sustained by the case of *Murdock* v. *City of Memphis* (2)." After citing a number of cases in which the principle had been applied, the judgment continues :—" It appears clearly from the opinion of the Supreme Court " (*i.e.*, of the State) " that it was not necessary to the judgment it gave that the words 'taking the direction of the Arroyo Seco' should be construed at all. It is, therefore, of no consequence whether or not that Court was wrong in its conclusions as to the meaning of the Huichica grant." That doctrine is, as I said, not the same as this, but it is very similar.

We must, therefore, inquire in this case whether it was necessary for the Court of Petty Sessions, in order to give effect to the respondent's claim against the appellant, to decide any question arising under the Constitution or involving its interpretation. It was necessary to interpret sec. 31 of the Constitution to discover whether sec. 282 of the *Constitution Act Amendment Act* 1890 of Victoria was a law relating to elections, because only such laws were adopted by sec. 31. The Court of Petty Sessions appears to have thought that that law was adopted, following a

(1) 110 U.S., 222.   (2) 20 Wall., 590.

decision of *Hood* J. But, whether they decided that question rightly or wrongly, another question remained to be determined before judgment could be given against the appellant, viz., whether that provision, assuming it to have been adopted by sec. 31 of the Constitution, had been repealed by the *Commonwealth Electoral Act* 1902, that is to say, whether the Commonwealth Parliament had otherwise provided. But that was not a question of the interpretation of sec. 31 of the Constitution ; it was a question of the interpretation of the Act relied upon as repealing the Victorian Act. The Court of Petty Sessions thought that the *Commonwealth Electoral Act* 1902 repealed sec. 282 so far as it related to Commonwealth elections. The Court had jurisdiction to construe that Act, and they construed it in that way. Their conclusion may have been right or wrong, but it was not upon a matter of federal jurisdiction. The Court of Petty Sessions as a Court exercising State jurisdiction had authority to determine that question, and, having that authority, might determine the question rightly or wrongly, and we have no jurisdiction to review its decision. It follows also that the Court was not improperly constituted. The appeal must be dismissed.

Appeal dismissed with costs.

Solicitors, for appellant, *Maddock & Jamieson*, Melbourne.
Solicitor, for respondent, *Claude I. Lowe*, Melbourne.

B. L.

[HIGH COURT OF AUSTRALIA.]

COMMISSIONER OF INCOME TAX (QUEENS-
LAND) . . . . APPELLANT;

AND

THE BRISBANE GAS COMPANY . . RESPONDENTS.

ON APPEAL FROM THE SUPREME COURT OF
QUEENSLAND.

H. C. OF A. *Income tax—Dividend out of Reserved Funds—Capitalization of profits—Bonus—*
1907. *Consolidated Income Tax Acts 1902-4 (Qd.) (2 Edw. VII. Nos. 10 and 23; 4*
  Edw. VII. No. 9), secs. 7 (iv.), 12 (vii.), 20.

BRISBANE,
Oct. 2, 3, 4.

Griffith C.J.,
Barton and
Isaacs JJ.

The directors of a company which had power to declare and pay dividends only out of profits, reserved or unreserved, and to hold land as part of the capital of the company, declared dividends in 1905 out of an accumulated reserve fund, and out of a sum representing profits on the sale of a piece of land which had been held by the company.

Held.—Both dividends were liable to be assessed for income tax under sec. 7 (iv.) of the Queensland *Income Tax Acts* 1902-4.

No grounds for exemption from such liability are afforded by the fact that the dividend declared from reserve fund was not in fact paid in cash, but was applied, in the exercise of an option given to the shareholders, in payment for new shares issued to them *pro ratâ*; nor by the fact that such dividend was declared from a fund consisting of undistributed profits which had accumulated for some years previous to the *Income Tax Act* 1902, and had already paid income tax upon a lower scale as undistributed profits.

Bouch v. *Sproule* (12 App. Cas., 385), explained and distinguished.

Judgment of Full Court, *Commissioner of Income Tax* v. *Brisbane Gas Co.*, 1907 St. R. Qd., 57, reversed.

APPEAL from the decision of the Full Court of Queensland upholding, on a special case stated, the opinion of the Judge of the Court of Review. The Brisbane Gas Company, as constituted

H. C. of A.
1907.

COMMIS-
SIONER OF
INCOME TAX
(QUEENS-
LAND)
v.
BRISBANE
GAS CO.

under its deed of settlement in 1863, and incorporated by Act in 1864, was empowered, *inter alia*, to hold land as part of the capital of the Company, to declare dividends and/or bonuses out of the profits, whether in hand or placed to reserve ; and to create new shares, which might be offered to shareholders as fully or partly paid up in payment of the whole or part of any dividend or bonus then payable. In 1902 the company disposed of some land, which had stood in the books at £20,000, for £30,000 thus making a book profit of £10,000. On 1st January 1902 the general reserve fund, which did not include the profit on the land, stood at £15,000, and increased with undistributed profits to more than £20,000 in 1905. About £15,000 of this reserve fund was employed in the business and in extensions of plant and works. In August 1905 the directors of the company, on a special resolution of the shareholders, decided to increase the capital by creating 4,000 new shares at £5 each fully paid up, to be offered *pro ratâ* to the shareholders at their option, and £20,000 of the reserve fund was to be distributed " as a dividend," payable at the option of the shareholders in cash or as a set-off against shares. The company's shares being worth more than double par value, all the new shares were taken up against the dividend, none of which was paid in cash. An ordinary dividend of £16,100 out of the year's profits was also declared, and a bonus of £4,900, which was part of the £10,000 profit on the sale of land. The Commissioner of Income Tax claimed payment on the total amount of £41,000, being the dividends declared for 1905. The company disputed payment on the £20,000 dividend and the £4,900 bonus, and their objections were sustained by the Court of Review and the Full Court (*diss. Chubb* J.) (1).

The Commissioner now appealed to the High Court.

Lukin and *Macgregor*, for the appellant. The respondents, by declaring these sums of £20,000 and £4,900 as a " dividend " and a " bonus," conclusively bring themselves within the operation of sec. 7 (iv.) of the *Income Tax Acts* 1902-1904, in which the amount of dividends declared is adopted as the test of the minimum sum assessable for income tax. The

(1) 1907 St. R. Qd., 57.

H. C. of A.   assertions relied upon by respondents, that no amount per share
1907.   was declared as a dividend, and that no dividend was in fact
Commis-   distributed in money, are irrelevant to the question whether or
sioner of   not a dividend was declared, which is decisive: *R.* v. *Stevenson*
Income Tax
(Queens-   (1). This cannot be set up as a distribution of capitalized profits;
land)   the directors had power to declare and pay dividends solely out
· v.   of profits, whether reserved or not, and not out of capital. It is
Brisbane
Gas Co.   equally immaterial to inquire in what year the profits now
distributed as a dividend were earned.

The definition of "dividend" appeared in the *Dividend Duty
Act* 1890 (Qd.) (54 Vict. No. 10), secs. 2, 6 ; this Act was repealed
by the *Income Tax Act* 1904, but sec. 7 was adopted from the
1890 Act, and the word "dividend" used in that section must
therefore bear the meaning given to it by the 1890 Act : *Mayor
&c. of Portsmouth* v. *Smith* (2); *R.* v. *Atkinson* (3); *Parker* v.
Talbot (4). *Bouch* v. *Sproule* (5), upon which the Courts below
relied, is distinguishable, being a case of the construction of rights
between a tenant for life and remaindermen ; a will speaks of
"income" in a very different meaning to that used in a taxing
Statute. Also that case turned upon the shareholders having
been given no option between taking shares or cash, whereas in
the present case such an option was given. *In re Alsbury;
Sugden* v. *Alsbury* (6); *In re Northage; Ellis* v. *Barfield* (7);
In re Malam ; Malam v. *Hitchens* (8); *In re Piercy ; Whitwham*
v. *Piercy* (9); *In re Bridgewater Navigation Co.* (10); *In re
Armitage ; Armitage* v. *Garnett* (11).

Although the £4,900 may not have been a true profit of the
company's business, but an increase of capital assets, yet the
company has chosen to treat it as income and declare it as a
bonus or dividend.

Lilley, for the respondents. No tax was payable under the
Income Tax Act 1902 on profits earned before 1902, nor under
the *Income Tax Act* 1904 on profits earned before 1904; the

(1) 7 Q.L.J., 7.
(2) 10 App. Cas., 364, at p. 371.
(3) 3 C.L.R., 632, at p. 639.
(4) (1905) 2 Ch., 643.
(5) 12 App. Cas., 385.
(6) 45 Ch. D., 237.
(7) 60 L.J. Ch., 488.
(8) (1894) 3 Ch., 578.
(9) (1907) 1 Ch., 299.
(10) (1891) 2 Ch., 317.
(11) (1893) 3 Ch., 337.

question is not concluded by the distribution of these profits as a
" dividend," as these Acts are intended only to tax current profits
made and distributed or accumulated since their enactment: Commissioner of
Income Tax
(Queens-
land)
v.
Brisbane
Gas Co.
Income Tax Acts, 1902-4, secs. 7 (iv.), 39 (iii.). The 1904 Act
can only have retrospective action so far as is provided by sec. 2,
and then only as regards the years 1902-3-4.

Under sec. 12 (ii.) of the 1902 Act, the Commissioner, in
estimating the amount of income tax on profits of a company,
must deduct the amount paid by the company in dividend tax ;
he has the option of choosing between taxing on the dividend at
1s. in the £, or on the income at 6d. in the £. Dividend tax and
income tax were alternative to each other. Hence, since the
respondent company in 1902-3-4 paid in dividend tax amounts
greater than what they would have had to pay at the lower rate
in income tax on the whole of the profits made in any of those
years, the profits not distributed in those years have passed the
time when they would have been liable to income tax. That
liability having been compounded for, those profits cannot now
be again subjected to that liability. If the appellant is right,
undistributed profits must pay 6d. in the £ in the year when
earned, and 1s. in the £ when declared as a dividend, a total of
1s. 6d. in the £. The Income Tax Acts operate in annual fiscal
periods, and were not intended to follow up the profits in
continuous succession ; each year is cleared off when it is paid.

No dividend was actually declared at all, in form or in
substance ; there was only a special resolution, a circular to shareholders, and an allotment of shares, merely a book entry against
assets used as capital in the business ; it was never intended to
be " paid " as a real dividend would be ; and, as in *Bouch* v.
Sproule (1), although an option was held out, there was really no
option, because the dividend was not declared against any cash
assets : *Gilbertson* v. *Ferguson* (2) ; *Commissioners of Inland
Revenue* v. *Angus* (3) ; *R.* v. *Stevenson* (4).

The £4,900 was not declared out of profits of the company's
business undertakings ; it was merely an accretion to capital, an

(1) 12 App. Cas., 385, at p. 398.　　(3) 23 Q.B.D., 579.
(2) 7 Q.B.D., 562.　　　　　　　　(4) 7 Q.L.J., 7.

H. C. of A.
1907.

COMMIS-
SIONER OF
INCOME TAX
(QUEENS-
LAND)
v.
BRISBANE
GAS CO.

accession of value which was only a windfall, not taxable as profits: *Mooney* v. *Commissioners of Taxation* (N.S.W.) (1).

Lukin in reply. Until 1904 the *Dividend Duty Act* 1890 was separately administered from the *Income Tax Act* 1902; the combination of both Acts in 1904 did not operate to relieve accumulated profits from taxation when declared as a dividend. The 1904 Act did not impose a double burden; it afforded relief, by allowing the deduction of the 6d. in the £ paid on profits under the Income Tax Acts from the formerly additional amount payable at 1s. in the £ under the *Dividend Duty Act* 1890. Whether the dividend was a book entry or not, it was "paid" in substance and in fact; the unanimous choice of the shareholders proved that the allotment of shares was a payment more valuable than actual cash.

Cur. adv. vult.

GRIFFITH C.J. This is an appeal by the Commissioner of Income Tax from the judgment of the Supreme Court, on a special case stated by the Court of Review under the *Income Tax Act* 1902. The claim made is in respect of two sums of £20,000 and £4,900, which were distributed by the respondents amongst their shareholders in the year 1905, and which the Commissioner claims to have been dividends within the meaning of the 7th section of the Income Tax Acts as they now stand, and therefore dutiable as income whether the money was received during the year 1905 or not. Sec. 7 provides that there shall be charged, levied, collected and paid an income tax in respect of the annual amount of the incomes of all persons at the rates following, and then follows a table. Sub-sec. (iv.) of that section provides that the tax on the incomes of all companies shall be one shilling in each and every pound, and then follow two provisoes. The first is :—"Provided that the income subject to the tax of every company having its head office or chief place of business in Queensland shall be assessed at not less than the amount of the dividends declared by such company during the year in respect of which the assessment is made. Provided further that where any

(1) 3 C.L.R., 221.

H. C. of A.
1907.

Commis-
sioner of
Income Tax
(Queens-
land)
v.
Brisbane
Gas Co.

Griffith C.J.

of the profits of such company remain undistributed amongst the shareholders then upon such undistributed profits only sixpence in each pound shall be payable as income tax; and should any part of such undistributed profits be afterwards distributed as dividends, the amount already paid as tax shall be allowed for in computing the amount of tax payable on such dividend." On that proviso the Commissioner rests his case. He says that it is a fact that the respondents, who are a company, and have their head office in Queensland, declared in the year 1905 a dividend, or rather two dividends of the sums of £20,000 and £4,900, and that by the operation of this section they cannot be heard to say that their income in that year was less than that amount. He says they come within the literal words of the Act, and, in the case of a taxing Act, that is sufficient.

Now the facts with respect to the dividends may be briefly stated thus:—The company was formed in 1864 under a deed of settlement, which was afterwards incorporated in a Statute. By clause 64 of the deed of settlement the directors are authorized from time to time to declare out of the profits of the company— whether the profits have been from time to time placed to the reserved fund or not—a dividend or bonus, or a dividend and bonus; but no such dividend or bonus shall be payable except out of such profits. Before the year 1905 a reserve fund had been accumulated by the company, which in that year stood at a larger sum than £20,000. In that year the directors called a general meeting of the company, at which a resolution was passed that £20,000 of the reserve fund should be distributed amongst the members as a dividend, which dividend might be drawn in cash. It was part of the scheme under which that dividend was declared that 4,000 new shares of £5 each should be issued, and that the shareholders to whom this dividend was payable should have the option of taking up an aliquot number of the fully paid up new shares of the company. As a matter of fact they all agreed to do so—and naturally, because the shares stood at more than 100% premium. The other £4,900 assessed was part of a sum of £10,000 profits earned by the company or received by the company in the year 1902 or 1903, but which had not been treated as part of the current revenue. That was divided in the

H. C. of A.
1907.

Commis-
sioner of
Income Tax
(Queens-
land)
v.
Brisbane
Gas Co.

Griffith C.J.

form of a bonus in the year 1905. The sum of £20,000 was all earned before 1905. The respondents maintain, first of all, that these are not dividends at all within the meaning of the Act. The word dividend does not really require any interpretation, although there has been on the Statute Book in Queensland a *Dividend Duty Act*, to which I shall directly refer, in which there was a definition of a dividend. But, when the articles of association of a company provide that the accumulated profits, whether they have been placed to reserve fund or not, may be divided by way of dividend amongst the shareholders, and after that the shareholders by resolution resolve to distribute them, I think it is very hard to say that the amount then distributed is not a dividend. As to the £4,900, there can be no doubt that it was a dividend, called a bonus; but the respondents say, " even if these were dividends, yet this is an Income Tax Act, and the intention of the Act was only to tax income, and this money, although it was in one sense a dividend, and might *primâ facie* come within the meaning of sub-sec. (iv.) of sec. 7, cannot be brought within the true meaning of that section, because the ruling principle of the Act is to tax income." That is a plausible argument, and possibly if the words were ambiguous it might be capable of acceptation. Before doing so, however, it will be worth while to look a little further. That argument is based upon this : The Income Tax Acts, when they were brought in, were to tax future income. There was no intention to tax any previous income. It was further very unlikely, to begin with, that the legislature in an Act dealing with future income would use such a phrase, " shall be assessed at not less than the amount of the dividend declared by such company," if it intended the money earned in the past would be taxed as future income. That argument is very plausible, and if there were no more in the facts or the law, it might possibly be accepted, but I only say, possibly. I doubt whether it should, if the case falls within the literal meaning of the Statute. If we inquire a little further, we find that this section, which from that point of view looks like an unjust attempt to tax past earnings by calling them future income, was in reality not a clause imposing a new liability, but a clause diminishing existing liability—a clause passed in relief of the

company, and not for the purpose of imposing an additional
burden upon it.   Under the *Dividend Duty Act*, passed in 1890,
a tax of one shilling in the pound was imposed on all dividends
declared by a company, no matter from what source they came,
or when they were earned.   In 1902, when the *Income Tax Act*
was first introduced, an income tax of 6d. in the pound was
imposed on the profits of all companies, whether distributed or
not.   But the *Dividend Duty Act* 1890 still remained in force,
so that there were two taxes—6d. in the pound on the gross
income, and 1/- in the pound on all dividends—but there was a
proviso that credit should be given as against the tax on income
to the extent of the amount actually paid by way of dividend
duty.   If none of the profits were distributed the company paid
the whole 6d. in the pound, and when they came to be distributed,
the company paid 1/- in the pound, so that it might easily and
generally did happen that they paid 1/6 in the pound on part of
their profits.   Then in the year 1904 the legislature repealed the
Dividend Duty Act 1890, and substituted the provision as it now
stands, that is to say, the company was to pay 1/- in the pound on
all its profits, with a proviso that, " where any of the profits of
such company remain undistributed amongst the shareholders then
upon such undistributed profits only sixpence in each pound shall
be payable as income tax ; and should any part of such undistributed profits be afterwards distributed, as dividends, the
amount already paid as tax shall be allowed for, in computing
the amount of tax payable on such dividend."   The result was
that, instead of a company being liable to pay 1/6 in the pound,
it pays no more than 1/-.   It is still, as before, required to pay a
tax of 1/- in the pound on all its dividends.   That being the
change made in the law, a construction, which at first sight seems
plausible, becomes highly improbable, and there is no reason why
the literal meaning should not be given to the words " that the
income subject to the tax   .   .   .   shall be assessed at not less
than the amount of the dividends declared by such company
during the year in respect of which the assessment is made."
During the year 1905 the dividends declared by this company
included those two sums.   There were other dividends declared,
but in respect of them no question arises.   There is no reason

H. C. of A.
1907.

COMMIS-
SIONER OF
INCOME TAX
(QUEENS-
LAND)
v.
BRISBANE
GAS CO.

Griffith C.J.

H. C. of A.
1907.

Commis-
sioner of
Income Tax
(Queens-
land)
v.
Brisbane
Gas Co.

Griffith C.J.

why the literal words of the section should not be adopted—there is no escape from it.

It was contended as a subsidiary point, that with respect to the £4,900, the respondents are entitled to the benefit of the proviso I have just read, and that arises in this way: In 1902 the dividend declared was about £15,000, and the dividend duty on that was at the rate of 1/- in the pound. Now £10,000 were the profits earned in that year, of which the £4,900 formed a part, and it was argued that any income tax payable upon it would have been covered by the dividend duty actually paid, because the dividend duty paid would have been sufficient to defray the income tax on an income of £30,000, which was greater than the actual profits, with more than £10,000 added. But they cannot bring this within the proviso, because they did not pay any income tax. They paid dividend duty because they were bound to do it, but they did not in fact pay any income tax on that £10,000, so that they cannot bring it within the words of the proviso, and, for the reasons I have given, I do not think they bring it even within the spirit of it. The majority of the learned Judges of the Supreme Court, and the learned Judge of the Court of Review, thought the case was to a great extent governed by the principles laid down in *Bouch* v. *Sproule* (1), but that was a case between tenant for life and remainderman, under the terms of a will by which the income was given to the tenant for life. Very different questions arise in a case of that sort. There, what the Court had to do was to discover what was the meaning of the testator's words. When he said the tenant for life was to have the income, did he intend to cover a case of a division of past accumulated profits? The House of Lords held in that case that he did not. Here the question is the construction of a taxing Act. The distinction was drawn by *North* J. in the case of *In re Northage*; *Ellis* v. *Barfield* (2), where he adopted what seems to be a rule of common sense, that so much of the dividend as was really payable in cash went to the tenant for life, and anything that represented profits would be for the remainderman. It is quite unnecessary to deal with that subject in this case. All we are concerned with is the interpretation of the Statute. The respondents have been

(1) 12 App. Cas., 385.　　　　　　　(2) (1891) W.N., 84.

brought within the literal words of the Act, and there is nothing in the context or in the history of the law to show that these words should have any but their literal meaning. For these reasons I am of opinion that the appeal should be allowed, and that the respondents are liable to be taxed at the rate of 1/- in the pound on both sums. With respect to the £4,900, which represented profits on the sale of land, it was said that that was capital, or, at any rate, came out of the reserve fund. Perhaps it was—I doubt it. Suppose it was—the company declared a dividend of £4,900, and I do not think it lies in their mouth, or the Commissioner of Taxation, to say that that dividend was an unlawful one. They paid the dividend, and they must pay 1/- in the pound upon it. That is made the more clear by the provisions of section 31 (a) of the Act, which now imposes upon the company the duty of paying the tax before they pay the dividend.

H. C. of A.
1907.

Commis-
sioner of
Income Tax
(Queens-
land)
v.
Brisbane
Gas Co.

Griffith C.J.

BARTON J. I have nothing to add. I find myself unable to resist the conclusion that the defendant company has brought itself clearly within the terms of the Act, whatever hardship may appear to be entailed. I therefore concur with the judgment just delivered.

ISAACS J. read the following judgment. This case was in the first instance heard by Judge *Rutledge* sitting as a Court of Review under the *Income Tax Acts* 1902-1904.

In pursuance of sub-sec. 8 of sec. 55 of the Consolidated Acts His Honor stated a special case for the opinion of the Supreme Court, from whose judgment this appeal is brought. To the special case the learned Judge who stated it mentioned in one of the paragraphs that he annexed copies of the notes of evidence taken, the exhibits admitted, and his judgment. The annexures however form no part of the special case itself, and must simply be disregarded. Both the Supreme Court and this Court are confined to the special case for the purpose of ascertaining the facts, and although the reasons of the learned Judge may materially assist an Appellate Court in its deliberations, they are quite outside the statutory material on which the decision of the Court of Appeal must be founded.

H. C. of A.
1907.

COMMIS-
SIONER OF
INCOME TAX
(QUEENS-
LAND)
v.
BRISBANE
GAS Co.

Isaacs J.

Looking then to the special case, it appears that on 4th August 1905 the company passed resolutions to increase the capital of the company by creating 4,000 new shares of £5 each, the then members of the company to have the option of taking them up in certain proportions, and the sum of £5 to be immediately called up. The 4th resolution is as follows: (His Honor read the resolution and continued). Shares not taken up were to be sold by public auction and the proceeds, less £5 and certain other sums, were to be divided among members declining to take up their proportion of shares. The 6th and 7th resolutions are as follow: (His Honor read the resolutions, and continued).

The directors carried out the resolutions, and it must be assumed, there being no evidence to the contrary, that they acted formally and in accordance with the provisions of the deed of settlement.

Par. 15 of the special case is as follows: (His Honor read the paragraph, and continued).

The Commissioner of Income Tax claims that these facts render the company liable to pay income tax at the rate of 1s. in the pound on £19,730.

Mr. *Lilley* contended in the first place that his client was clear of the *Income Tax Act* 1902 as to these profits, assuming them to be profits, because they were earned before the passing of the *Income Tax Act*.

His argument I confess impressed me considerably. But the words of the Act are too strong to give effect to it, especially when sec. 7 (iv.) is read in conjunction with secs. 12(vii.) and 31 (*a*).

The legislature evidently had in its mind a deliberate intention to tax profits divided in any year by a company among its shareholders quite irrespective of the time when those profits were made by the company. Full protection is given by the 2nd proviso to sec. 7 (iv.) against taxing the same income twice by way of income tax. There is no reason therefore for departing from the primary meaning of the words in sec. 7 (iv.), " The dividends declared by such company during the year in respect of which the assessment is made."

Then a view was urged for the respondents, which has been accepted by both the Court of Review and the majority of the Supreme Court, that the company is at liberty, notwithstanding

H. C. or A.
1907.

COMMIS-
SIONER OF
INCOME TAX
(QUEENS-
LAND)
v.
BRISBANE
GAS CO.

Isaacs J.

the apparent declaration of a dividend, to go behind it, and to show—as it claims it has shown—that it is nevertheless free from the tax, because there never was any real intention to divide profits, or to pay a dividend in cash, but merely to increase capital, and that what the shareholders received, and were always intended to receive, was in fact capital. It is not denied that profits had been made which would certainly at one time have been properly applied to the payment of dividends, but it is said as they had been in fact employed in the business they had ceased to be divisible profits, and had become in some sense capital, and at least were not in such a condition as to justify the conclusion that they were ever intended to be paid over as dividends.

The case of *Bouch* v. *Sproule* (1), was relied on for this position. The decision of the House of Lords determined certain principles of law, which are summarised in *Lindley on Companies*, 6th ed., at p. 742, and then applied them to the facts, the ultimate determination turning entirely on the view their Lordships took of the facts before them.

In arriving at their conclusion of fact the learned Lords took into consideration many circumstances. They thought it important that the company had by its articles of association power to capitalize its profits, they interpreted the directors' annual report and balance sheet, they looked at the financial position of the company, the market value of the shares, the form of the document sent out to shareholders, and the way in which the books were kept, all of which had more or less weight in the minds of their Lordships.

A similar course has been adopted here to sustain the position of the respondents, and the Courts below have held that the view of the facts presented by the respondents is correct.

I lay aside the possible results of establishing that the resolutions did not mean what they plainly said, and that the scheme was to that extent misleading, and in substance a transgression of the provisions of the deed of settlement, and consider the argument solely in its relation to this revenue Statute. I do not think it at all permissible to embark on this elaborate investiga-

(1) 12 App. Cas., 385.

H. C. of A.
1907.

Commis-
sioner of
Income Tax
(Queens-
land)
v.
Brisbane
Gas Co.

Isaacs J.

tion for the purpose of ascertaining liability, or the extent of liability of a company under the *Income Tax Act* where the Commissioner is content to rest on the declaration of a dividend, and therefore I do not examine the facts with any such view. The language of the Statute lends no countenance to such an investigation in that case.

It lays a tax on the income of a company for a given year of 1/- in the pound. But the ascertainment of a company's profits is not always an easy process, the very cases relied on demonstrate that, and it seems to me the legislature by this Act, not only determined by the sections I have already quoted to tax all profits actually divided in any year, but provided also, in the case of a dividend declared, a simple and decisive means of establishing up to a certain limit that there was taxable income and the amount of it, and so of avoiding the complicated inquiry otherwise necessary.

When a company openly asserts that it has profits available for distribution among its shareholders, and formally announces that distribution, then to that extent there was thought to be no need to call for further evidence, for there really can be no better evidence against the company than its own public recognition of the fact, and that is made by the Act conclusive, and the Commissioner, if satisfied to accept that as proving the taxable income, may do so without question.

It would, in my opinion, be altogether reversing the manifest intention of Parliament if the simple and undeniable circumstance of a dividend actually declared were allowed to be controverted and turned into the subject of such difficult questions of law and complicated elements of fact as have been raised here. No such defence is possible, according to my reading of the Act, where the Commissioner relies on the mere declaration of a dividend of profits.

I hold, therefore, that *Bouch* v. *Sproule* (1) has no relevancy whatever to the present case.

With regard to the sum of £4,900, if it were permissible to enter upon an investigation of the items, I should feel some doubt. That doubt would not arise on account of the company

(1) 12 App. Cas., 385.

H. C. of A.
1907.

COMMIS-
SIONER OF
INCOME TAX
(QUEENS-
LAND)
v.
BRISBANE
GAS CO.

Isaacs J.

not carrying on a land business, because the land was held only in connection with the company's actual business. See sec. 11 of the Act and clause 29 of the articles. My hesitation would be occasioned by the provision in clause 29 that the land is to be regarded as part of the company's capital. However, as already stated, I do not think it open to a going company to controvert, either as to fact or amount, what would be ordinarily regarded as a declaration of dividend. This sum must therefore be included in the taxable amount. I agree that this appeal should be allowed.

GRIFFITH C.J. The formal order will be : Appeal allowed, order appealed from discharged, and case remitted with a declaration that the respondents are liable to assessment on the sums of £19.730 and £4,900 at the rate of 1/- in the pound. Respondents to pay the costs of the special case and of the appeal. I do not think we have anything to do with the costs in the Court of Review. The case is remitted and is still pending in the Court of Review. It will have to go back to that Court to dismiss the appeal.

Lukin. Since the appeal the District Court has entered judgment, notwithstanding there was an appeal pending to this Court.

GRIFFITH C.J. Where the appeal is allowed any order consequent upon it must be discharged. The case must go back to the District Court Judge, and he will then dismiss the appeal, and deal with the costs.

> *Appeal allowed. Order appealed from and*
> *consequent orders discharged. Case*
> *remitted to District Court.*

Solicitor, for the appellant, *Hellicar* (Crown Solicitor for Queensland).

Solicitor, for the respondents, *T. O. Cowlishaw.*

N. G. P.

[HIGH COURT OF AUSTRALIA.]

STEWART AND WALKER . . . . APPELLANTS;

AND

WHITE (TRUSTEE OF SPRINGALL, AN INSOLVENT)   RESPONDENT.

ON APPEAL FROM THE SUPREME COURT OF
QUEENSLAND.

H. C. OF A.   *Insolvency Act* 1874 (*Qd.*), (38 *Vict. No. 5*), *sec.* 107—*Fraudulent preference—*
1907.   *Pressure by creditor—" With a view to " prefer—Intention or motive.*

BRISBANE,   A debtor, who was unable to pay his debts as they became due out of his
Oct. 4, 7, 8.   own moneys, handed to creditors, who were aware of his financial position,
               and had for some time unsuccessfully used pressure, a series of small cheques
Griffith C.J., payable at extended dates and representing the amount of the debt. The
  Barton   debtor having been adjudicated insolvent within six months:
and Isaacs JJ.

                  Held, the payments were a fraudulent preference under the *Insolvency Act*
               1874, sec. 107. The words " with a view to prefer " in that section refer to
               the intention or purpose of the debtor, and not to his motive bringing
               about that result.

                  Dictum in *Russell Wilkins & Sons Ltd.* v. *Outridge Printing Co. Ltd.*, (1906
               St. R. Qd., 172), relating to the effect of pressure on the intention to prefer,
               overruled.

APPEAL from a judgment of *Cooper* C.J. sitting in the Insolvency jurisdiction of the Supreme Court of Queensland. The
insolvent, Springall, trading as the South Brisbane Butter Company, had transactions with the appellants, a firm of butter
merchants, during 1906. In April and May 1906 he bought
goods from the appellants to the value of £1,091, and gave in
part payment a cheque for £519 which was dishonoured. By
December 1906 under severe pressure his debt to them had been

reduced to £606.   At that date, while unable to pay his debts as they became due out of his own moneys, he gave the appellants a series of fifteen post-dated cheques, in all £661, which fell due and were paid at various times within two months.   The Court held upon the evidence that the appellants were aware that the probable effect of the transaction would be to give them a preference over other creditors.   On 5th June 1907 the debtor was on his own petition adjudged insolvent, with a deficiency of over £6,000, and the official trustee of his estate claimed the payments made to the appellants as fraudulent preferences.   *Cooper* C.J. declared the payments fraudulent and void against the trustee ; and he found as facts :—that the payments were made " with a view of giving" the appellants a preference over the other creditors " and under pressure by them," and that the payments were made " for valuable consideration but not in good faith within the meaning of sec. 107."

Lilley for the appellants.   *Cooper* C.J. based his judgment upon that of the Full Court in *Russell Wilkins & Sons Ltd.* v. *Outridge Printing Co. Ltd.* (1),' thinking that it bound him to interpolate " or by reason of pressure " after " with a view of giving such creditor a preference over the other creditors " in sec. 107.   The finding of fact made by *Cooper* C.J. as to preference in these payments was therefore due to his having misdirected himself, in reliance on the erroneous decision of the Full Court.

There was in fact no intention shown on the part of the debtor to prefer the appellants.   He was carrying on a lucrative butter contract with a certain firm, and his business was improving ; he made these payments to the appellants in order to save the business as a going concern from the severe and continuous pressure they were applying.   The cheques were payments of a recognized trade debt, made in the ordinary way of business, received honestly by the appellants, who were told by the debtor, and believed, that his only creditors were well secured by his assets, although in fact there were other larger creditors whose existence he concealed from them.

The elements of good faith and no pressure are immaterial

(1) 1906 St. R. Qd., 172.

H. C. of A.
1907.

STEWART &
WALKER
v.
WHITE.

under sec. 107 unless and until the essentials of the first part of the section are proved in full detail. It must be shown that the debtor made the payments with the intention of giving a preference; whereas the evidence is all the other way, that his intention was to save the business from forced realization and keep it going at a profit. Pressure cannot be interpolated in the middle of the section; it was put in at the end of the section in order to negative the English rule under which the existence of any pressure completely excluded any consideration of preference. The decision in *Russell Wilkins & Sons Ltd.* v. *Outridge Printing Co. Ltd.* (1) would make every payment without exception a preference, because, if made voluntarily without pressure, it would be a preference, and if made under pressure, it would equally be a preference under the rule of law there laid down. The necessary proof of intention to prefer is lacking where it is shown that the only desire in the debtor's mind was to keep the business going: *Kinross, Official Assignee of* v. *Robjohns* (2); *Bills* v. *Smith* (3); *Castendyck* v. *Official Assignee of McLellan* (4); *Mynott, Official Assignee of* v. *Moa Dairy Factory Co.* (5); *In re Reimer* (6); *Butcher* v. *Stead*; *In re Meldrum* (7).

[ISAACS J. referred to *Brown* v. *Kempton* (8).]

" With a view to prefer" essentially demands a wish or motive to desire: *Ex parte Hill*; *In re Bird* (9); *Ex parte Griffith*; *In re Wilcoxon* (10). If pressure was the dominant motive, sec. 107 does not apply.

[ISAACS J. referred to *In re Fletcher*; *Ex parte Suffolk* (11). Where the debtor knew that if insolvency were to supervene the distribution would be disturbed by the payments made, this is *primâ facie* evidence of intention to prefer.]

That presumption is rebutted by the evidence, and *Cooper* C.J. was led to find intention to prefer, as a fact, solely by the erroneous view taken by the Full Court with regard to the effect of pressure. The test is whether the pressure was the dominant cause or motive of the payment; *New, Prance, & Garrard's*

(1) 1906 St. R. Qd., 172.
(2) 8 N.Z.L.R., 224.
(3) 6 B. & S., 314 ; 34 L.J.Q.B., 68.
(4) 6 N.Z.L.R., 87.
(5) 6 N.Z.L.R., 177.
(6) 15 N.Z.L.R., 198.

(7) L.R. 7 H.L., 839.
(8) 19 L.J.C.P., 169.
(9) 23 Ch. D., 695.
(10) 23 Ch. D., 69.
(11) 9 Morr., 8.

Trustee v. *Hunting* (1); *Sharp* v. *Jackson* (2); *In re Tweedale*;
Ex parte Tweedale (3) ; *In re Arnott* ; *Ex parte Barnard* (4).

[ISAACS J. referred to *In re Bell* (5).]

Feez and *O'Sullivan*, for the respondent.   The debtor was
insolvent in December 1906 ; and at that time he was not carrying on a lucrative or improving business, because between then
and the date of filing his petition he went £5,000 more to the
bad.

It is immaterial, even if true, that *Cooper* C.J. found it necessary to base his findings on *Russell Wilkins & Sons Ltd.* v.
Outridge Printing Co. Ltd. (6).   Leaving the pressure out of
consideration, as sec. 107 directs, there is nothing left but a
voluntary payment which necessarily was made " with a view to
prefer."   Where a payment prefers a creditor, the onus is on the
person supporting the transaction to show that there was no
view to prefer : *In re Eaton & Co.* ; *Ex parte Viney* (7) ; *In re
Lake* ; *Ex parte Dyer* (8).

[*Lilley* referred to *In re Laurie* ; *Ex parte Green* (9).]

ISAACS J. referred to *Ex parte Lancaster* ; *Re Marsden* (10) ;
Williams' Bankruptcy Practice, 8th ed., p. 251.]

The burden of proving good faith is on the creditor : *Ex parte
Tate* (11).

If there is an onus on the trustee, he has satisfied it by showing an imminent insolvency, a payment which injures the other
creditors, not made in the ordinary course of business, not *bonâ
fide* on the debtor's part, and under the suspicious circumstances
of this series of post-dated cheques.   The prior English rule that
pressure cannot coexist with intention to prefer depended on the
doctrine of dominant motive ; this cannot apply to sec. 107,
which was expressly framed to do away with that doctrine and
its complications of motives upon motives : *Tomkins* v. *Saffery* ;
Ex parte Saffery ; *In re Cooke* (12) ; *Butcher* v. *Stead* ; *In re*

(1) (1897) 2 Q.B., 19.
(2) (1899) A.C., 419, at p. 426.
(3) (1892) 2 Q.B., 216.
(4) 6 Morr., 215.
(5) 10 Morr., 15.
(6) 1906 St. R. Qd., 172.

(7) (1897) 2 Q.B., 16.
(8) (1901) 1 Q.B., 710.
(9) 67 L.J.Q.B., 431 ; 5 Manson, 48.
(10) 25 Ch. D., 311
(11) 35 L.T., 531.
(12) 3 App. Cas., 213.

Meldrum (1). The true question under that section now is, not as to the motive or desire of the debtor, but as to his intention, and pressure is excluded from consideration as an immaterial fact. [They referred to New Zealand *Bankruptcy Acts*, 48 Vict. No. 29, s. 27, and 49 Vict. No. 22, s. 13.]

Lilley in reply.

Cur. adv. vult.

GRIFFITH C.J. This is an appeal from the decision of the learned Chief Justice of Queensland, made upon a motion by the respondent, who is trustee of the property of one Springall, an insolvent, for a declaration that certain payments amounting to about £660, made by the insolvent within six months of insolvency to the appellants, were fraudulent preferences within the meaning of sec. 107 of the *Insolvency Act* 1874. The case was heard partly orally, and partly upon affidavit. The learned Chief Justice found as a fact that at the time when the payments were made the insolvent was unable to pay his debts as they became due out of his own moneys; that the payments were made with a view to prefer the creditors; and that they were not received by the creditors in good faith. He also found that the payments were made under pressure. Reliance was placed by the appellants upon the decision of the Supreme Court of Queensland in the case of *Russell Wilkins & Sons Ltd.* v. *Outridge Printing Co.* (2), which was to the effect that the fact of pressure was itself sufficient to bring the case within sec. 107. (That is, I assume, in the absence of good faith.) They contend that that decision was wrong, and that the learned Chief Justice decided the present case only upon its authority. He, however, found certain facts specifically, at the request of the appellants' counsel, amongst which was that the payments were made with a view to prefer the appellants over the other creditors, and under pressure. Sec. 107 is in these words :—" Every conveyance assignment gift delivery or transfer of property or charge thereon made every payment made every obligation incurred and every judicial proceeding taken or suffered by any debtor unable to pay

(1) L.R. 7 H.L., 839.   (2) 1906 St. R. Qd., 172.

H. C. of A.
1907.

STEWART &
WALKER
v.
WHITE.

Griffith C.J.

his debts as they become due from his own moneys in favour of any creditor, or any person in trust for any creditor with a view of giving such creditor a preference over the other creditors shall if a petition for adjudication of insolvency be presented against such debtor within six months after the date of making taking paying or suffering the same and adjudication of insolvency be made on such petition be deemed fraudulent and void as against the trustee of the insolvent appointed under this Act but this section shall not affect the rights of a purchaser payee or incumbrancer in good faith and for a valuable consideration." The presumably relevant words in that provision are " payee in good faith." Then it proceeds :—" Provided that pressure by a creditor shall not be sufficient to exempt any transaction from the operation of this section."

Sec. 107 of the Queensland *Insolvency Act* is a transcript of sec. 92 of the English *Bankruptcy Act* 1869, with the addition of the proviso that pressure shall not be sufficient to exempt any transaction from the operation of the section.

Before the Act of 1869 the rule as to fraudulent preference was not expressed in any statutory provisions. Under the former law the elements of a fraudulent preference were that the transaction should be made by the debtor in contemplation of bankruptcy, and that it should be made voluntarily. The second element was sometimes expressed as being with a view of preferring the particular creditor. Under this law it became very material, in considering whether the payment was voluntary, to inquire whether it was made under pressure. For, if it was so made, the pressure might have been, and was generally held to be, sufficient to negative the existence of the element of voluntariness. The Act of 1869 substituted a definite rule for that to be collected from the decided cases. For the inquiry whether the act was done in contemplation of bankruptcy it substituted the inquiry whether the debtor was able to pay his debts as they became due out of his own moneys, and whether bankruptcy occurred within a prescribed period. For the inquiry whether the transaction was voluntary it substituted an inquiry whether it was made " with a view of giving" the creditors a preference over the other creditors. It was held in England that this sec-

H. C. of A.
1907.

Stewart &
Walker
v.
White.

Griffith C.J.

tion left the old rules as to pressure unaltered, so that, in determining with what " view " the act was done, it was still necessary to consider whether it was done voluntarily.

I pause to remark that the section contains two phrases open to different constructions. The words " with a view of giving " may mean " in order to effect the result of giving," or they may mean " actuated by a desire to give." In one sense the words refer to an intention, in the other to a motive. The word " prefer " also is capable of meaning either that one creditor is in fact put in a better position than others, or that the debtor likes one creditor better than another, and therefore desires to give him an advantage. In sec. 92 it is obviously used in the first sense, although in argument, and, I fear, in some of the cases, the latter sense has inadvertently crept in. This aspect, however, of the question really belongs to the word " view," and not to the word " preference."

I think that in many of the decided cases the word " view " has been used in both senses in the same judgment, and hence some confusion has arisen. The difference between the motive which induces an act and the end intended to be attained by the act is recognized by the statute law of Queensland, (see *Criminal Code*, sec. 23), and is very material in construing sec. 107 of the *Insolvency Act*.

The existence of pressure was material, not for the purpose of determining the result intended to be effected, but for determining the motive for effecting that result, *i.e.*, for determining whether the act was voluntary or not. When, therefore, it was declared by the Queensland Act that pressure should not be sufficient to exempt a transaction, the element of motive was in effect excluded from the new provisions. An act must either be voluntary or not voluntary, and if that fact is no longer material the word " view " can no longer refer to it.

It follows, I think, that the words " with a view of giving " in the Queensland section must be read as equivalent to " with an intention to give." In this regard I accept the reasoning of the learned Judges of the Supreme Court of New Zealand in the case of *Official Assignee of Kinross* v. *Robjohns* (1). I think that

(1) 8 N.Z. L.R., 224.

H. C. of A.
1907.

Stewart &
Walker
v.
White.

Griffith C.J.

when a debtor, knowing that he cannot pay all his creditors in full, deliberately pays one of them, he intends the necessary consequences of his action, *i.e.*, he intends to give him a preference. And I think that under such circumstances he makes the payment with a view of giving the creditor a preference within the meaning of sec. 107. Under the Statute, however, the intention of the debtor to prefer the creditor is not decisive as it was under the old law. If the payment is made in good faith the creditor is protected. But, if the payment is made out of the ordinary course of business, and under such circumstances as to show that the creditor knew or had reason to suspect that the effect of it would be to pay him in full and leave other creditors unpaid, it is not made in good faith: *Tomkins* v. *Saffery* (1).

From this point of view pressure may be very material, not however, as affording conclusive proof that the payment is made with a view to give a preference, (which was the view of the learned Judges in *Russell Wilkins & Sons Ltd* v. *Outridge Printing Co.* (2)), but as affording material evidence on the question whether the transaction was made in good faith. To this extent I am unable to agree with the judgment in that case, though I think it was rightly decided on the whole facts.

In my opinion a payment made by a debtor who is unable to pay his debts as they become due from his own moneys, and which is not made in the ordinary course of business, and is made under such circumstances that the creditor has good reason to suspect that he is obtaining a preference from an insolvent debtor, is void under sec. 107. That is to say, the case is brought within the first part of the section, and the creditor cannot bring himself within the protective proviso.

All these circumstances occur in the present case. The debtor was undoubtedly unable to pay his debts as they became due from his own moneys, and when he paid the money, he must have known that the effect would in all probability be to pay those creditors in full, and leave the others unpaid. The payments were not made in the ordinary course of business; they were made by giving a series of small cheques extending over a period of two months in respect of an old debt which the debtor

(1) 3 App. Cas., 213.   (2) 1906 St. R. Qd., 172.

H. C. of A.
1907.

Stewart &
Walker
v.
White.

Griffith C.J.

had been unable to pay for some months.   The creditors were aware of all these facts, and they must have had very good reasons for believing that they were getting an advantage over the other creditors.   I think that, whatever view is taken of the findings of the learned Chief Justice, he was not only justified in finding that the payments were made with an intention to prefer within the meaning of the Statute, but on the facts, could not have properly come to any other conclusion.   I think, therefore, that the appeal must be dismissed.

BARTON J.   While I agree in the view of the facts taken by the Chief Justice of this Court, and think that they amply sustain the findings of *Cooper* C.J., I wish to add a few words on the case of *Russell Wilkins & Sons Ltd.* v. *Outridge Printing Co.* (1) out of respect to the Court which decided that case.   I agree that this appeal must be dismissed on grounds which render it unnecessary to rely on the law there laid down, but I feel bound to go on to say that I cannot bring myself into accord with the conclusions there arrived at.   Sec. 107 of the *Insolvency Act* 1874 is, as *Real* J. points out, a transcript of sec. 92 of the English Act 1869 with the addition of the second proviso, and divesting it of words which have no relation to the case of payments, it reads as follows :—" Every payment made . . . . . by any debtor unable to pay his debts as they become due from his own moneys in favour of any creditor . . . . with a view of giving such creditor a preference over the other creditors shall . . . . . be deemed fraudulent and void as against the trustee of the insolvent appointed under this Act," if a petition for adjudication of insolvency be presented against such debtor within 6 months after the date of making or paying the same and adjudication of insolvency be made on such petition.   But " this section shall not affect the rights of a . . . . . payee . . . in good faith and for valuable consideration   Provided that pressure by a creditor shall not be sufficient to exempt any transaction from the operation of this section."

The Full Court of Queensland held (1) that the section must be read as if in lieu of the last proviso, the words " or by reason

(1) 1906 St. R. Qd., 172.

H. C. of A.
.1907.

STEWART &
WALKER
v.
WHITE.

Barton J.

of pressure by such creditor " had been inserted in the body of the section after the words, " with a view of giving such creditor a preference over the other creditors." In other words, they treated the proviso as if, standing where it does, it had said that " pressure by a creditor, in place of a view on the part of the debtor of giving such creditor a preference over the other creditors, shall itself, if the other conditions abovementioned exist, suffice to vitiate the transaction." It is impossible to determine what was in the mind of the legislature except by what it has said, and I cannot agree that by anything it has said it has shown that it had in its mind anything like the words suggested in the judgment of *Real* J., any more than it had in its mind the words I have just set out. If it has said the one set of words, it has in effect said the other. With all respect, I cannot see how it has said either. The words of the proviso, being on their face clear, must be read to mean just what they say, or a context as plain or plainer must be pointed out to show that they mean less, or more, or something quite different. For that position there is no need at this day to cite any of the numerous cases which sustain it. But if the words do, as I think they must, in the absence of some such context, mean what they say, then in saying that pressure is not enough to take a transaction out of the section so as to save it, they certainly cannot mean that pressure is of itself enough to bring a transaction within the section so as to vitiate it.

I am of opinion that the proviso means no more than this, that pressure is to be taken into consideration with the other circumstances of the case ; that where those circumstances disclose an intention to prefer, pressure is not to prevent their operating to bring a case within the section : that whether or not " a view to prefer " includes *only* an intention to prefer, it certainly does include such an intention. In my judgment it follows that where there is a payment which does in fact prefer the creditor paid to the other creditors, and such a payment is made intentionally by a debtor actually unable to pay his debts as they became due from his own moneys, and who evidently knows his position and the effect that the payment will have, he must be taken to have intended the preference that

H. C. or A. results, and therefore to have made the payment with a view to
   1907.   prefer; and the mere pressure of the creditor does not suffice to
Stewart & exempt the transaction. In other words, unless the payee has
 Walker   acted both for valuable consideration and in good faith, the
   v.
 White.   transaction is void as against the insolvent's trustee impeaching it.

Barton J.   In the present case all the elemental circumstances concur
upon the evidence and upon the findings of *Cooper* C.J., who had
the advantage of hearing oral evidence in addition to the
affidavits. These findings include one which negatives good
faith on the part of the appellant creditors. I should be loth to
interfere with them if I were in doubt, but I agree with them.

I am therefore of opinion that the appeal must be dismissed
with costs.

Isaacs J. I agree that this appeal should be dismissed. The
first question of law involved in this appeal is the construction of
sec. 107 of the *Insolvency Act*, having regard to the proviso. The
Act was passed in 1874 and the meaning attached to it then must
be its meaning now. It has been held in *Russell Wilkins & Sons
Ltd.* v. *Outridge Printing Co.* (1) that the effect of the proviso
is to so modify the whole section as to declare any payment to a
creditor, which is made by an insolvent debtor within six months
of his insolvency and solely as the result of pressure, and with no
desire in fact to prefer the creditor, a fraudulent preference. By
that decision pressure is either made conclusive evidence of
intention to prefer, or is erected into a separate or co-ordinate
ground of invalidity. The reasoning by which the Supreme
Court arrived at its conclusion may be thus stated. In England
the Act of 1869 was held to enact that pressure by a creditor was
sufficient in all cases to exempt a transaction from the operation
of the fraudulent preference section; therefore when the Queensland legislature added the proviso to sec. 107 in these words:—
" Provided that pressure by a creditor shall not be sufficient to
exempt any transaction from the operation of the section," it
meant to reverse the English rule; and lastly, reversal meant that
pressure should have exactly the opposite effect, or in other

(1) 1906 St. R. Qd., 172.

words, as pressure *ipso facto* preserved the transaction in England, therefore pressure *ipso facto* avoided it in Queensland.

H. C. OF A.
1907.
⏜
STEWART &
WALKER
v.
WHITE.
——
Isaacs J.

The words of the proviso read in their ordinary sense have no affirmative operation. They merely declare that pressure of itself shall not suffice to prevent a transaction from being a fraudulent preference.

Before the English Act of 1869 was passed the law on this subject was laid down in the leading case of *Brown* v. *Kempton* (1) decided in 1850 by a very strong Court. In that case *Parke* B., who delivered the judgment of the Court, laid down that pressure was immaterial unless it operated on the bankrupt's mind in inducing him to make the payment, and that if a payment were made under the influence of pressure, and also with a desire to give a preference in the event of bankruptcy, there was no fraudulent preference, because the payment was not voluntary.

In 1856 in *Hale* v. *Allnutt* (2) the case of *Brown* v. *Kempton* (1) was followed, *Jervis* C.J. saying :—" There is not, therefore, sufficient ground for coming to the conclusion that the pressure of the defendant exercised no influence upon the mind of the bankrupt ; and, if it did exercise any, there was no fraudulent preference." In 1859 in *Edwards* v. *Glyn* (3) the Court of Queen's Bench followed *Brown* v. *Kempton*.

Then came the Act of 1869, which used language different from that found in the older law. Still the cases upon that Act up to 1874—the material period for ascertaining the meaning of Parliament in this case—followed the rule in *Brown* v. *Kempton* (1). In *Ex parte Tempest* ; *In re Craven & Marshall* (4), it was expressly approved and followed by *James* and *Mellish* L.JJ., and its principle was made the basis of their decision in *Ex parte Bolland* ; *In re Cherry* (5). In the last mentioned case, *Sir G. Mellish* L.J. said :—" If there has been such a demand as partly influenced the bankrupt in making the payment so that he did not make it *entirely voluntarily*, the payment is not a fraudulent preference."

These cases show most clearly to my mind that in the first

.H. C. of A.
1907.

Stewart &
Walker
v.
White.

Isaacs J.

place to escape the consequences of what otherwise would be a fraudulent preference, it was always necessary, if pressure were relied on, to show that it exerted influence on the debtor's mind —some influence was sufficient—it need not be the dominating influence; but in order to operate as an exempting force, it had to be an effective element in the transaction to some extent, and that deprived the transaction of its voluntary character and prevented the preference being fraudulent. This is put very clearly by *Vaughan Williams* J. in *In re Bell; Ex parte the Official Receiver* (1) in 1892. He said:—" I cannot help feeling a sort of envy of those Judges who had to decide questions of fraudulent preference in days gone by, and in which one of the plainest and most simple of rules was laid down to guide them. The rule was laid down by Baron *Parke* in the case of *Brown* v. *Kempton* (2), which enabled one, the moment one had arrived at the conclusion that honest pressure had something to do with bringing about the payment, to hold that the payment in question was not a fraudulent preference."

The learned Judge goes on to say that later cases alter the test and says " that the law is well established now, and that one has to ascertain in each case what was the dominant motive which operated on the bankrupt's mind when he made the payment in question."

He uses the expression " dominant motive." I prefer to say " real view," that is, the real intention or purpose of the debtor, as far as interchange of words can express the idea. In *Ex parte Hill; In re Bird* (3), *Baggallay* L.J., says:—" The substantial object or view must be the giving of the creditor a preference." *Bowen* L.J. (4) adopts the expression " the real effectual, substantial view of giving a preference to the creditor." All the Lords Justices hold distinctly that it need not be the sole view. I am not sure however whether, having regard to the observations of Lord *Halsbury* and Lord *Macnaghten* as to *Butcher* v. *Stead* (5), the case of *Sharp* v. *Jackson* (6), does not establish that even now under English law where real pressure exists, and

(1) 10 Morr., 15, at p. 17.   (4) 23 Ch. D., 695, at p. 704.
(2) 19 L.J.C.P., 169.   (5) L.R. 7 H.L., 839.
(3) 23 Ch. D., 695, at p. 701.   (6) (1899) A.C., 419

H. C. of A.
1907.

Stewart &
Walker
v.
White.

Isaacs J.

exerts any influence on the debtor whereby he is induced to make the payment, the transaction is outside the fraudulent preference section. It is not necessary in this case to decide that.

But it is quite apparent that from the earliest case to the latest whenever pressure was proved the person relying upon it as an exculpatory fact, was called upon to show that it did in fact operate upon the mind of the debtor so as in some measure to coerce him. If so the payment was not voluntary and was protected.

Now *Real* J. seems to stop at this point, and assume that, because a payment was made by reason of pressure, there could be no intention to prefer—that, in other words, pressure was inherently inconsistent with an intention to prefer. Having once made this assumption he not unnaturally proceeded to seek for a construction that would give some effect to the proviso. As it was not necessary to call in aid the proviso to prevent the operation of something that could not exist simultaneously with pressure, he held that it must have the effect of invalidating the transaction.

But to begin with the assumption that pressure is inherently inconsistent with an intention to prefer is not well founded. Pressure is certainly consistent with an actual preference ; it may be the very cause of the debtor deliberately doing something which he knows will have the effect of preferring, and so may co-exist with actual intention to prefer, and then in one sense the preference is voluntary because the debtor is quite free, if he so chooses, to adopt the course of at once placing his insolvent estate in the hands of the law for equal distribution amongst his creditors. But because the act is not voluntary in the strict sense, the preference is not regarded in English law as fraudulent. We need only turn back for a moment to the English cases that were open to the Queensland Parliament in 1874 to see how the Courts recognized the possible co-existence of pressure and of intention or desire to prefer. In the passage I have already quoted from *Brown* v. *Kempton* (1), *Parke* B. in so many words adverted to the instance of a payment being made under the influence of pressure, and also with a desire to give a preference in the event of bankruptcy. So too in the cases in which that decision was

(1) 19 L.J.C.P., 169.

H. C. of A.
1907.

STEWART &
WALKER
v.
WHITE.

Isaacs J.

followed.   And though not material to ascertaining what the
legislature meant in 1874, it is not out of place in this connection,
to point out that in *Sharp* v. *Jackson* (1) Lord *Macnaghten's*
judgment shows that in his opinion there might, alongside the
intention to protect himself from pressure, be in the debtor's mind
a secondary view of preferring creditors.   The true position then
is this: That in 1874, prior to the passing of the Act, the law
was declared to be that a payment, where there was pressure in
fact, operating to some extent upon the debtor's mind, was exempt
from the fraudulent preference law, whether there was any other
view or purpose or not—even though that other view or purpose
was to prefer the creditor.   Now in 1874 the legislature declared
that pressure should not any longer be sufficient to exempt.   In
my opinion, the only effect of that was that the fact of there
being pressure was henceforth, for the purpose of determining
whether a preference was fraudulent, to be ignored and treated
as legally non-existent.   It was to be discarded from consideration as having any protective effect in law.   If, after treating the
mere fact as non-existent, the circumstances nevertheless disclose
any view or purpose to prefer, however it has arisen, whether as
the result of pressure or not, the transaction is obnoxious to the
Statute—if not, there is no fraudulent preference because no
intention to prefer.   There cannot be a fraudulent preference
without intention to prefer; and under the present law of
Queensland, such an intention is not overcome by the fact that it
has been caused by pressure, nor by the fact that there was
pressure which to some extent and together with the debtor's
desire to prefer independently existing actuated the payment.

Once a real intention to prefer is established, howsoever it has
come into existence, that is so far sufficient, and the law makes
no allowance for its having originated even in the pressure of
the creditor, and *a fortiori* if it is merely accompanied by such
pressure.   But without a view to prefer, an actual preference is
not fraudulent.   The law is not so inconsistent as to say that a
payment made without pressure may not be voluntary, but if
made under pressure must be regarded in all cases as voluntary.
I therefore think on principle that the rule of law laid down in

(1) (1899) A.C., 419.

Russell Wilkins & Sons Ltd. v. *Outridge Printing Co.* (1) cannot be supported.

H. C. OF A.
1907.

STEWART &
WALKER
v.
WHITE.

Isaacs J.

Some reliance was placed by the learned Judges who decided the *Russell Wilkins Case* and by counsel here on the New Zealand case of the *Official Assignee of Kinross* v. *Robjohns* (2) as supporting the Queensland decision. A careful examination of the New Zealand case leads me to the conclusion that, so far as it is an authority at all upon the Queensland Statute, it looks in quite the opposite direction. The Court in *Robjohns' Case* did not simply inquire whether the payment was induced by pressure, and so end the matter. They examined the evidence closely to ascertain whether in fact the bankrupt had a view to prefer his creditor. They found that he had, because he deliberately did what he knew would give a preference to that creditor. They also found that he was pressed to do it, that it was an enforced preference, but still it was a preference within the meaning of the New Zealand Act, which recognized that a payment with a view to prefer might be either voluntary or under pressure. The important point is that the New Zealand Court did not merely ask whether there was pressure causing payment, it thought it necessary to further inquire whether the payment was made in such circumstances as would lead to the inference that the debtor knew that the creditor would be preferred to other creditors, and therefore must be taken to have intended to prefer him; and then it applied the principle I have already adverted to, that, once given the intention, it matters not how it originated whether out of pressure or otherwise. This too is very strongly shown by the judgment in *Official Assignee of Mynott* v. *Moa Dairy Factory Co.* (3) cited and relied on in *Robjohns' Case*. In *Mynott's Case, Prendergast C.J.*, says (4):— "The law of New Zealand certainly recognises that there may be more than one operating cause; for though the act be done under pressure it may still be done within the meaning of the amended provision, with a view to give a preference." That, would of course depend upon the facts of the case, but the effect of *Russell Wilkins Case* is that if done under pressure, it must

(1) 1906 St. R. Qd., 172.   (3) 6 N.Z. L.R., 177.
(2) 8 N.Z. L.R., 224.   (4) 6 N.Z. L.R., 177, at p. 184.

H. C. OF A.
1907.

STEWART &
WALKER
v.
WHITE.

Isaacs J.

necessarily be done as a fraudulent preference, which is a conclusion quite beyond the New Zealand authorities as I read them.

With reference to the argument that the debtor here was moved by the hope of pulling through, I would refer to the case of *In re Vingoe*; *Ex parte Viney* (1), which shows that a hope of pulling through does not necessarily negative an intention to prefer. It may be coupled with a desire to make the creditor safe in any case, and then a payment to him is a fraudulent preference.

Appeal dismissed with costs.

Solicitors, for the appellants, *W. H. Wilson & Hemming.*
Solicitors, for the respondent, *Thynne & Macartney.*

N. G. P.

[HIGH COURT OF AUSTRALIA.]

JEREMIAH KELLY   .   .   .   .   .   APPELLANT;
COMPLAINANT,

AND

SYDNEY WIGZELL   .   .   .   .   RESPONDENT.
DEFENDANT,

ON APPEAL FROM THE SUPREME COURT OF
QUEENSLAND.

H. C. OF A.
1907.

BRISBANE,
Oct. 10.

Griffith C.J.,
Barton and
Isaacs JJ.

Brisbane Traffic Act 1905 (*Qd.*), (5 *Edw. VII. No.* 18), *sec.* 6—*Traffic Regulations*
—"*Permitting*" *passengers in excess of prescribed number to travel on tramcar*
—*Duty of tramway conductor*—*Variance between information and evidence as*
to place—*Justices Act* 1886 (*Qd.*), (50 *Vict. No.* 17), *sec.* 48.

In a prosecution for an offence against a by-law which prohibits a conductor from permitting any person in excess of the maximum number prescribed to travel on a tramcar, the fact that there are more than the

(1) 1 Manson, 416.

prescribed number actually travelling in a tramcar is sufficient evidence of such permission on the part of the conductor.

An information ought not to be dismissed on the ground of a merely technical variance between the information and the evidence with regard to the name of the place in which an offence is proved to have been committed.

Decision of the Full Court : *Kelly* v. *Wigzell*, 1907 Q. W. N., 1, reversed.

The Brisbane Tramway Company in 1906 ran tramcars in the streets of Brisbane and South Brisbane. One of their cars, running from South Brisbane towards Brisbane, drew up in Melbourne Street on the south bank of the river, entered Victoria Place (a short approach continuing Melbourne Street to the bridge), and was there boarded by police officers, who counted the passengers while going across the bridge, and found that several in excess of the regulation number fixed by the Traffic Regulations of 6th April 1906 (framed under the provisions of the *Brisbane Traffic Act* 1905,) were travelling in the car. The conductor was prosecuted for a breach of the Regulations, sec. XVIII. (5), which provides that " no conductor shall . . . permit any person in excess of the maximum number prescribed in clause 2," (which was 50 for that type of car), " to travel in or upon any tramcar." The information charged the offence as having been committed in Melbourne Street, South Brisbane. The magistrate dismissed the complaint on the ground that there was no evidence that any offence had been committed in Melbourne Street, as the passengers were not counted until after the car had left that place. This decision was affirmed by the Supreme Court (1), who added as an additional ground that the evidence did not establish any " permission " on the part of the conductor.

The complainant appealed by special leave to the High Court.

Power (with him *Macleod*), for the appellant. " Permitting to travel " is fully established by the evidence ; the conductor is the person in charge of the car, and knows when passengers get on the car, and has full power to exclude any in excess of the prescribed number from getting on.

(1) 1907 Q. W. N., 1.

H. C. OF A.
1907.

KELLY
v.
WIGZELL.

The evidence that an offence was committed being clear, it is immaterial that the information is at variance, if at all, with the evidence in its statement of the place where the offence occurred : *Justices Act* 1886, sec. 48. As a matter of fact, Melbourne Street and Victoria Place are the same street in a direct line ; the place where the offence occurred is known by both names. In any case the magistrate was bound to grant an amendment of such a detail ; and this Court may do so now: *Gabriel* v. *Rickards* (1) ; *Keliher* v. *Bleakley* (2).

Feez (with him *Shand* and *Lukin*), for the respondent. The special leave should be rescinded ; this is a trivial matter involving no substantial or important question: *Dalgarno* v. *Hannah* (3) ; *Connolly* v. *Meagher* (4). The Traffic Regulations have also been radically amended, so as to make the present regulation of no importance. If the new by-law—which enacts that if any person or persons in excess of the maximum number prescribed "are" upon any tramcar, the conductor shall be guilty of a breach of the preceding regulation (*i.e.* sec. XVIII. (5))—is invalid, the whole question is clear ; the only question therefore substantially in dispute is whether the new by-law is not invalid by reason of the Traffic Commissioners thus setting up, *ultra vires*, a new rule of evidence, and also making a conductor guilty of an offence even though forced upon him by other persons against his resistance. The only evidence relating to the *locus* of the offence was that the passengers were counted on the bridge. No amendment was asked for in the magistrate's Court, and it should not be granted now : *R.* v. *Justices of South Brisbane* ; *Ex parte Thornton* (5); *R.* v. *Justices of Clifton* ; *Ex parte McGovern* (6).

[GRIFFITH C.J.—Sec. 48 says that the amendment "shall" be made, and the Court will therefore regard the amendment as made.]

There was no evidence of "permission" by the conductor ; it was not shown that he had any knowledge of the excess of passengers ; he would only be guilty if he omitted to take action

(1) 10 Q.L.J., 143.   (4) 3 C.L.R., 682.
(2) 1902 St. R. Qd., 61.   (5) 1902 St. R. Qd., 152.
(3) 1 C.L.R., 1.   (6) 1902 St. R. Qd., 177.

when he knew of that excess.   By-laws cannot alter the rules of
evidence: *Somerset* v. *Wade* (1); *Sherras* v. *De Rutzen* (2). The
prosecution must show either guilty knowledge or else that the
conductor did not upon reasonable grounds believe that the car
was not overcrowded.   Passengers jump up on a car from all
sides, and at all times, when the conductor has no means of
knowing of the excessive number, or of excluding the last
comers from boarding the car.   Considering the harshness of the
by-law, and the fact that the respondent has defended the case
in the public interest, costs should be allowed to the respondent
against the Crown.

Power in reply.   An unsuccessful respondent, who has fought
the case through three Courts on untenable points, should not be
awarded costs.

GRIFFITH C.J.   The defendant, a tramway conductor, was
prosecuted for the breach of a regulation made under the
Brisbane Traffic Act 1905, which provides that:—"No conductor shall permit any person in excess of the maximum
prescribed in clause 2 to travel in or upon any tramcar."   The
number prescribed for the tramcar in question was 50.   There
was evidence that there were 65 persons travelling in the tramcar, and the defendant was the conductor of it.   It is said that
that was not sufficient evidence that the defendant permitted
them to travel in the car.   I confess I have had some difficulty
in grasping the argument.   When the law prescribes that the
person in charge of a vehicle shall not permit more than a
certain prescribed number to enter that vehicle, surely it imposes
on him the duty to count them to see that not more than that
number enter; otherwise the law would be absolutely futile.
The fact, therefore, that there are more persons than the law
permits in the car is evidence, not only that they entered the
car, but that the person in charge of it allowed them to enter it.
There was, therefore, sufficient evidence of permission.   Another
point was made incidentally that the place in which the car was
alleged to have been travelling was described as Melbourne

(1) (1894) 1 Q.B., 574.   (2) (1895) 1 Q.B., 918.

H. C. of A.
1907.

KELLY
v.
WIGZELL.

Griffith C.J.

Street, South Brisbane, whereas its true name is Victoria Place.
According to the case stated, it bears both names.   It is the end
of Melbourne Street, where that street joins Victoria Bridge, and
it is sometimes called Victoria Place.   If there were anything in
the point at all, it would be cured by sec. 48 of the *Justices Act*,
which declares that objections to variances of that sort shall not
be allowed.   I think, therefore, that on the evidence defendant
was manifestly guilty and ought to have been convicted.   The
Supreme Court took the contrary view, and this is an appeal by
special leave from their decision.   This Court gave leave to appeal,
regarding the matter as one of general importance, since if such
evidence is not sufficient to convict a conductor for a breach of
the regulations, the regulations would be futile.   The learned
Chief Justice said :—" A conductor cannot eject a person having
the right to travel from his car." Probably not.   " He cannot eject
any passenger unless he does so lawfully."   I quite agree.   He
goes on :—" And therefore the respondent could only have turned
those persons off this car who had entered it at a time when it
already contained the maximum number."   I agree again, but
because he had the right to turn them off, and it was his duty to
turn them off, and he failed to do so, he must take the consequences.   The appeal must be allowed, and the case remitted
to the Police Magistrate to convict.

BARTON J. I am of the same opinion. I think there was
ample evidence to justify a conviction, and that evidence was
wholly unanswered.   On the question of permission, the regulation on which the prosecution was instituted is positive in its
terms, it forbids the conductor to permit any person to enter the
tramcar after the number prescribed by clause 2 have entered.
The conductor enters upon his duties under the provisions of the
Act under which this prosecution was instituted, and he must be
taken to have known the regulation, or paragraph of the
regulation, immediately preceding that under which the charge
was laid.   By it he is forbidden to allow any person to enter his
car if the maximum number of persons—in this case fifty—are
already upon it.   It is therefore hard to see how he could fail to
know that there were more than the maximum number on his

car. The presence of more than the maximum number is *primâ fâcie* evidence that he knew there were more than the maximum number, and there was no answer given to that evidence. For those reasons I am of opinion that the appeal should be allowed.

ISAACS J.   I agree.

Power.   As to the costs of the motion to rescind ?   That was a separate motion and we were brought to answer it.

ISAACS J.   Was there no notice that the two motions would be heard together ?

Power.   No.   The motion to rescind was heard first on the first day of the sittings, and the case was low down in the list.

GRIFFITH C.J.   There can be only one taxation of course.   Have the costs been paid ?

Power.   No.   The costs were taxed, but not paid.

GRIFFITH C.J.   The respondent must pay the costs of the appeal and the motion to rescind, but of course there will be only one taxation.

> *Appeal allowed.   Order appealed from discharged, appeal from justices allowed with costs, case remitted to the Police Magistrate, with direction to convict. Respondent to pay the costs of the appeal and of the motion to rescind leave.*

Solicitor, for appellant, *Hellicar* (Crown Solicitor for Queensland).

Solicitors, for respondent, *Thynne & Macartney.*

N. G. P.

[HIGH COURT OF AUSTRALIA.]

SCOTT . . . . APPELLANT;
    DEFENDANT,

                              AND

CAWSEY . . . . RESPONDENT.
    PLAINTIFF,

ON APPEAL FROM THE SUPREME COURT OF
                    VICTORIA.

H. C. OF A.   *Sunday entertainment—Charge for admission—" Place "—Portion of room railed*
1907.   *off and charge for admission to it—Entrance to rest of room free—Advertising*
⌣   *entertainment—21 Geo. III. c. 49, secs.* 1, 3.
May 29, 31 ;
June 4, 5.   The Act 21 Geo. III. c. 49 is in force in Australia.

Griffith C.J.,   In a large room a public entertainment within the meaning of 21 Geo. III.
Isaacs and   c. 49 was given on a Sunday.   Portion of the room, containing about two-
Higgins JJ.   fifths of the sitting accommodation, was railed off, and in this portion the
            seats were more comfortable than those in the rest of the room, and it was
Sept. 3, 4, 13. the best part of the room for hearing and seeing the entertainment.   The
            only entrance to the railed off portion of the room was from the other portion.
Griffith C.J.,   There was only one entrance to the room from the outside, and any person
Barton,   might enter there without payment and participate in the entertainment, but
O'Connor,   a charge was made for entering the portion of the room which was railed off.
Isaacs and
Higgins JJ.
                  Held (Isaacs and *Higgins* JJ. dissenting) that neither the room itself nor
            the portion of it railed off was " a house, room, or other place, . . . opened
            or used for public entertainment or amusement " upon Sunday " and to
            which persons " were " admitted by the payment of money," within sec. 1 of
            21 Geo. III. c. 49, and, also, that the advertising of an entertainment to be
            given under such circumstances was not within sec. 3 of that Act.

                  Judgment of *Chomley* J.: *Cawsey* v. *Scott*, 28 A.L.T., 112, reversed.

APPEAL from the Supreme Court of Victoria.

An action was brought in the Supreme Court by Henry Cawsey against Ebenezer Erskine Scott to recover penalties under the Act 21 Geo. III. c. 49. The plaintiff alleged that the defendant was on three several Sundays " the keeper of a house, room, or place in Fitzgerald's Circus Building situate at South Melbourne which was then opened or used for public entertainment or amusement and to which persons were then admitted by the payment of money or by tickets sold for money." For this the plaintiff claimed a penalty of £200 in respect of each Sunday. Alternatively the plaintiff claimed a penalty of £100 from the defendant for managing or conducting such entertainment, or, alternatively, a penalty of £50 for receiving money or tickets sold for money for such entertainment. A further penalty of £50 was claimed for advertising such entertainment on two of the Sundays. The defence was a general denial.

In reference to the advertisements it was proved that at one of the entertainments a reflection was thrown by a lantern on a screen showing a notice stating that on the next Sunday a similar entertainment would be given.

The other facts are sufficiently set out in the judgments hereunder.

Chomley J., who heard the action, gave judgment for the plaintiff for £650, being £200 in respect of being the keeper of a place within the Act on each of the three Sundays, and £50 in respect of advertising, with costs: *Cawsey* v. *Scott* (1).

The defendant now appealed to the High Court.

Schutt, for the appellant. The plaintiff is limited by his pleading to the " reserve," or portion of the room which was railed off, as being the place which was kept or used, and he cannot be heard to say that the whole room is the place which the appellant was charged with keeping. The reserve does not constitute a place within the meaning of the Act. There must be a charge for admission to the entertainment. Here the entertainment was free to any one who chose to enter the building. The only charge made was after a person had been admitted to the entertainment, and it was a charge for extra comfort only. A charge for

(1) 28 A.L.T., 112.

H. C. of A.
1907.

SCOTT
v.
CAWSEY.

reserved seats does not bring the entertainment within the Act:
Encyclopædia of Law of England, tit. " Sunday " ; *Williams* v.
Wright (1). The terms of the Act are not applicable to a place
within a place.

[HIGGINS J.—*Baxter* v. *Langley* (2) seems to assume that
charging for reserved seats would bring the entertainment within
the Act.]

The Act only contemplates a charge for admission to the room
where the entertainment is held. The Act is not in force in Victoria. It is either a police law or an ecclesiastical law, or partly
one and partly the other, and comes within the exceptions to the
principle laid down in *Blackstone's Commentaries,* vol. I., p. 108,
which is quoted in *Jex* v. *McKinney* (3), and in *Quan Yick* v.
Hinds (4).

[HIGGINS J.—Was 9 Geo. IV. c. 83, sec. 24, intended to extend
that principle, and to introduce into Australia more laws than
would have been in force under the common law ?]

No. It only put into statutory form what was the common
law. The Act 21 Geo. III. c. 49 was not suitable or applicable to
Australia where there was no established church, and where all
creeds were equal. In *M'Hugh* v. *Robertson* (5), where it was held
by the Full Court that this Act was in force in Victoria, the question whether it was a police law was not argued, but *Williams* J.
in the Court below was inclined to think it was. There has been
subsequent legislation in Victoria dealing with Sunday observance
impliedly declaring that the English laws relating thereto are
not in force in Victoria. That amounts to an implied repeal of
21 Geo. III. c. 49. At any rate, " limitations and modifications "
of that Act, within the meaning of 9 Geo. IV. c. 83, have been
established. See 18 Vict. No. 14, sec. 24 ; *Police Offences Act*
1890, sec. 31, *et seq.* ; 6 Will. IV. No. 1 ; 5 Vict. No. 6. As to
repeal by implication, see *R.* v. *Hilaire* (6); *Attorney-General
for Victoria* v. *Moses* (7). [He also referred to *Raithby's Index
to the Statutes at Large,* vol. III., tit. " Sunday."]

(1) 13 T.L.R., 551 ; 41 Sol. Jo., 671.
(2) L.R. 4 C.P., 21.
(3) 14 App. Cas., 77, at p. 81.
(4) 2 C.L.R., 345, at p. 355.
(5) 11 V.L.R., 410.

(6) (1903) 3 S.R. (N.S.W.), 228, at
p. 229.
(7) (1907) V.L.R., 130 ; 28 A.L.T.,
125.

H. C. of A.
1907.

Scott
v.
Cawsey.

Pigott, for the respondent.   The Act 21 Geo. III. c. 49 has not been repealed by implication.   There is no inconsistency or repugnancy between its provisions and those of subsequent Victorian legislation.   *Hardcastle on Statutory Law*, 4th ed., p. 304. Sec. 2 of the *Theatres Act* 1896 recognizes that the disabilities created by 21 Geo. III. c. 49 still existed.   The latter Act is not an ecclesiastical Act, nor is it a police Act within the principle stated by *Blackstone*.   If the word "police" is there used as meaning "criminal" the principle must be corrected, for there is no doubt that the criminal law was introduced by the first settlers. *Bentham's Principles of Morals and Legislation*, Chap. XVIII. The Act 21 Geo. III. c. 49 is criminal law.   *Delohery* v. *Permanent Trustee Co. of New South Wales* (1); *Attorney-General for Ontario* v. *Hamilton Street Railway Co.* (2).   The Act may be held to apply to Victoria as being one to protect Sunday as a civil institution beneficial to the State, as expressed by *Williams* J. in *M'Hugh* v. *Robertson* (3).   It has for more than fifty years been held to be in force in Victoria : *Ronald* v. *Lawlor* (4).   See also *Walker* v. *Solomon* (5); *Ex parte Rogerson* (6).   A part of a room is a "place" within the meaning of the Act if it is substantially differentiated from the rest of a room.   *Prior* v. *Sherwood* (7).

[GRIFFITH C.J. referred to *Powell* v. *Kempton Park Racecourse Co.* (8), as to the meaning of "place."]

That is sufficiently done in this case by the wooden rail.   If the admission for which a charge is made must be admission to the whole hall, then, if a person is admitted free to a part of the hall and is then charged for admission to another part, he is charged for admission to the hall.   If the place has its own sufficient entity and the entertainment can be enjoyed there, that is sufficient.   Thus the charging for admission to a room in a house to hear music, which was being played in an adjoining public place, would be contrary to the Act.   There was here an advertising within the meaning of the Act.   Anything expressed in

(1) 1 C.L.R., 283, at p. 293, *per Griffith C.J.*
(2) (1903) A.C., 524.
(3) 11 V.L.R., 410 ; 6 A.L.T., 227.
(4) 3 A.J.R., 11, 87.

(5) 11 N.S.W. L.R., 88.
(6) 9 N.S.W. L.R., 30.
(7) 3 C.L.R., 1054, at p. 1070.
(8) (1899) A.C., 143.

the same way as a libel is required to be expressed in an advertisement.

[Isaacs J. referred to *Smith* v. *Mason & Co.* (1), as to the meaning of "advertisement."]

There must be knowledge on the part of the advertiser that a
charge is to be made to the entertainment.

Schutt in reply. The construction of the Act contended for by
the respondent requires the words "or part of a place" to be read
after the word "place." Such a construction will not be given to
a penal Act; *London County Council* v. *Aylesbury Dairy Co.* (2).

[Isaacs J. referred to *Dyke* v. *Elliott*; *The Gauntlet* (3).]

An advertisement must be a notification to the general public,
and not to those persons only who happen to be at one of these
entertainments.

Cur. adv. vult.

The case was subsequently directed to be re-argued before the
Full Bench.

Sept. 3. The case was re-argued when the following additional arguments were adduced.

Schutt, for the appellant. It is immaterial whether all the
people or none of them are within the reserve. As long as a
substantial portion of the hall is open without payment for
admission, the Act is not infringed. Part of a room cannot be a
"place" within the Act because the Act speaks of the "owner"
or "occupier" of the place. Sec. 3 of the Act means that the
advertisement must state that a charge was to be made for
admission, and it must also be shown that the entertainment was
held, and that a charge for admission was made. An advertisement must also be something printed and published. If there are
two reasonable constructions of a penal Act open, one of them
favourable to the defendant, he should have the benefit of that
interpretation which is favourable to him: *Hardcastle on Statutory Law*, 4th ed., p. 430; *Nicholson* v. *Fields* (4).

(1) (1894) 2 Q.B., 363. (3) L.R. 4 P.C., 184, at p. 191.
(2) (1898) 1 Q.B., 106. (4) 7 H. & N., 810.

[Isaacs J.—If both constructions are equally reasonable you have to look at the intent of the Statute. *Llewellyn* v. *Vale of Glamorgan Railway Co.* (1).]

Pigott, for the respondent. By the *Public Moneys Act* 1890, sec. 4, the Governor in Council may remit penalties for offences, so that the position here in that regard is the same as in England. On the construction contended for by the appellant the Act could be easily evaded, and the Court will construe the Act so as to prevent evasions of it: *Maxwell on Statutes*, 4th ed., p. 171; *Morris* v. *Blackman* (2); *Booth* v. *Bank of England* (3).

[Isaacs J. referred to *Bullivant* v. *Attorney-General for Victoria* (4).]

The word " place " should be interpreted *ejusdem generis* with "house" and "room," and, in its collocation, means part of a room: *Sandiman* v. *Breach* (5).

[Isaacs J. referred to *Plymouth, Stonehouse, and Devonport Tramways Co.* v. *General Tolls Co.* (6).

Schutt referred to *Anderson* v. *Anderson* (7).]

If on the evidence the judgment can be supported on any ground it should be supported, although it may not be for the same reason given by the Judge. The fact that the advertisement was produced by a means not known when the Act was passed does not affect the matter: *Graves* v. *Ashford* (8).

Schutt, in reply.

　　　　　　　　　　　　　　　Cur. adv. vult.

The following judgments were read :—

Griffith C.J. The Act 31 Geo. III. c. 49, provides (sec. 1) that "any house, room, or other place, which shall be opened or used for public entertainment or amusement, or for publicly debating on any subject whatsoever" on Sunday, "and to which persons shall be admitted by the payment of money, or by tickets sold for money, shall be deemed a disorderly house or place"; and that the keeper shall be liable to a penalty of £200 a day for every

(1) (1898) 1 Q.B., 473.
(2) 2 H. & C., 912.
(3) 7 Cl. & F., 509.
(4) (1901) A.C., 196.

(5) 7 B. & C., 96.
(6) 14 T.L.R., 531.
(7) (1895) 1 Q.B., 749.
(8) L.R. 2 C.P., 410.

day that the house, room, or place is so opened or used, to be recovered by any person suing for it, and be otherwise punishable as the law directs in cases of disorderly houses. The third section of the same Act imposes a penalty of £50 for advertising any public entertainment or amusement or public meeting for debating on any subject whatsoever on Sunday " to which persons are to be admitted by the payment of money, or by tickets sold for money." In this section the admission spoken of is to the entertainment or amusement or meeting, whereas in the first section the admission spoken of is to the house, room, or place. The term " admission," however, involves the idea of locality, and of the ability of the person who permits the admission to exclude others from the place of entertainment or amusement except with his consent.

The material words of both sections are " to which persons shall be (are to be) admitted," and what is made unlawful is opening or using for the specified purposes a house, room, or place to which persons are admitted on payment, and not the receipt of money from persons already admitted in consideration of some special privilege, such as the use of a seat.

It appears in the present case that the appellant was in possession of a large hall in Melbourne called Fitzgerald's Circus Building, in which musical entertainments were given on Sunday evenings. The hall, which had eight sides, may be described as an elongated octagon, two sides being much longer than the others. The entrance to the hall was at one end. The short side adjoining that end to the right was occupied by a stage for the performers, who faced obliquely across the length of the hall. Around all the rest of the hall were gallery seats, and there was a large vacant space in the middle available for promenade. Some of the gallery seats on the part of the left hand side nearest the door were covered with carpet, and were enclosed with a light handrail, inside of which there were also some chairs. This part of the hall was spoken of in the evidence as the " reserve," but there was no notice put up to the effect that it was reserved. The admission to the hall was free, and persons who had obtained admission were at liberty to go to any portion of the gallery seats at the right hand side or at the end, or to any part of the

H. C. of A.
1907.

Scott
v.
Cawsey.

Griffith C.J.

floor in the middle of the building, but, if they desired to use the part of the hall spoken of as the reserve, a small charge was made. According to the plan put in evidence the space to which there was free admission comprised at least three fourths of the total area.

The stage for the performers was, as already stated, on the opposite side of the hall from the reserve, so that the reserve was the best place for hearing, but all the persons in the hall could participate in the entertainment or amusement, with such difference only in point of amenity as arose from the point of view, the greater or less distance from the performers, and the degree of comfort afforded by the seats or absence of seats.

Under these circumstances this action was brought against the appellant claiming penalties for breaches of secs. 1 and 3 of the Act. The breaches alleged under sec. 1 were that he was on three specified Sundays the keeper of a house, room, or place which was then opened or used for public entertainment or amusement, and to which persons were then admitted by the payment of money or by tickets sold for money. The charge as originally framed was of keeping the whole building as a place of entertainment to which &c.; but at the trial the statement of claim was amended to charge the appellant with keeping a house, room, or place *in* the building, *i.e.*, the reserve, as such a place of entertainment. The respondent, in effect, claims that sec. 1 forbids admission by payment to any part of a room used for public entertainment or amusement, although free admission is granted to the room itself, and, alternatively, that, if a charge is made for admission to any part of the room which is in any way delimited from the rest, that part is a place within the meaning of the Statute.

In my opinion, the decision of the case depends upon the answer to two plain questions of fact. First, what was the house, room, or place which was in fact opened or used for public entertainment on the dates alleged ? Second, were persons admitted to that house, room, or place by the payment of money or by tickets sold for money ? The plain and obvious answer to the first question is that the house, room, or place opened or used was the large room or hall called Fitzgerald's Circus Building. The answer to the second must be in the negative. In my judgment this ends the matter.

It appears from the passage read by Mr. *Schutt* from the *Encylopædia of Law* that this is the accepted construction of the Statute in England.   In the case of *Williams* v. *Wright* (1) an attempt was made to set up the construction now contended for by the respondent.   That was an action against the publisher of the " Times " for a penalty under sec. 3 for publishing an advertisement of a Sunday entertainment.   The advertisement announced the place, time, and character of the entertainment and added " Tickets 1/- 2/- 3/- 5/-." At the trial it appeared that the plaintiff had bought a ticket marked " Admission free : Reserved Seat 1/- " for which he paid 1/-. *Collins* J. (now Lord *Collins*) appears to have construed sec. 3 as relating only to advertisements of entertainments which were actually unlawful as being in contravention of sec. 1. And he held that, as it appeared by the evidence that admission to the hall in question (a well known hall in London) in which the entertainment advertised was held was in fact free, the entertainment was not within the prohibition, and the publisher of the advertisement was not liable. He pointed out that the Statute spoke of admission, not to a seat, but to an entertainment.   The word " admission," as already pointed out, connotes a place from which persons can be excluded. So, sec. 1 speaks of admission, not to a seat, but to a place opened or used for entertainment. This view appears to have been followed ever since, and we are told that such entertainments have received the sanction of the Royal presence, and are regularly advertised.   I cannot doubt that any Court in England would follow that decision.

It is, however, contended that the reserve should be regarded as a separate place, distinct from the rest of the hall, or, in other words, that the appellant opened and used for public entertainment two distinct and separate places, (1) the reserve, and (2) the rest of the hall, to one of which persons were, and to the other were not, admitted on the payment of money. By parity of reasoning, if he had had separate reserves or compartments in the hall with seats at different prices, he would have been the

(1) 13 T.L.R., 551.

keeper of as many different places, each separately opened for public entertainment, and would have been liable to a separate penalty of £200 in respect of each. If the room were a theatre, he would be liable to a separate penalty of £200 in respect of each box for admission to which payment was demanded, whether occupied or not. The appellant, in truth, opened and used for public entertainment one room, and one room only, the hall.

The word " place " is not a word of art, and its meaning may be different in different Statutes. In the *Betting Act* 1853, for instance, as pointed out in the cases of *Powell* v. *Kempton Park Racecourse Co. Ltd.* (1) and *Prior* v. *Sherwood* (2), it means a place which can at least constructively be regarded as a common gaming house, and over which the alleged keeper has actual and exclusive dominion for the time being. But it does not follow that every small area of the earth's surface, of which these attributes can be predicated, is a place within the meaning of some other Statute. I agree that part of a room may be a place within the meaning of the Statute now under consideration, if it is separated from the rest of the room by some line of demarcation, and is used for some purpose for which the rest of the room is not being used. But, when a single entertainment is given in a room, it is, in my opinion, impossible to construe the words " house, room, or other place " in such a way as to treat the single room as subdivided into several distinct places. To do so would be, in effect, to interpolate the words " or to any part of which " after the words " to which " in the section. Such an interpolation is not justified unless without it the enactment would fail to have any effect. In my opinion, the Statute as it stands is not capable of that construction. It is not, therefore, a case of ambiguity, and, if it were, the construction in favour of liberty should be adopted.

The fallacy of the argument for the respondent becomes manifest when it is stated in the form of a syllogism :—" Admittance to part of a room is admittance to the room : Therefore, refusal of admittance to part of a room is refusal of admittance to the room." *Aliter*, all B is A: no C is B : Therefore, no C is A. There could hardly be a plainer instance of the undistributed middle. It was suggested that the provision in sec. 2 of the Act,

(1) (1899) A.C., 143,   (2) 3 C.L.R., 1052.

which makes the fact that refreshments are sold in the room at higher than ordinary prices sufficient evidence that persons are admitted to the room on payment, supports the respondent's view. In my opinion it has a contrary operation. The legislature thought fit to single out one set of circumstances as sufficient evidence of one element of the offence. The omission to say that a different set of circumstances should have the same effect indicates, if it indicates anything, that they did not intend that result, not that they did intend it.

Cases may be supposed in which the only part of a room to which admission is free is so small as to be illusory. That would raise a question of fact to be proved by evidence. It certainly does not arise in the present case.

In this view it is unnecessary to consider the subsidiary question raised under sec. 3.

I am myself unable to discover any provision in the Act showing an intention, or even any suggestion of a desire, to prohibit a charge for special comfort afforded to persons present at an entertainment to which admission is free. In my opinion, both upon principle and upon authority, the case is free from doubt.

On the question whether the Statute is in force in Australia I should be strongly disposed, if the matter were *res integra*, to adopt the view originally taken by *Molesworth* J. But, having regard to the fact that the English Acts relating to Sunday observance were held forty years ago to be in force in Victoria, I do not feel justified in disturbing the law as then laid down.

I think that the appeal should be allowed.

BARTON J. As to the main question in this case, that is whether the appellant is liable to be penalised as keeper of a disorderly house within the meaning of the *Sunday Observance Act* 1780, our duty, looking the Statute in the face, is to determine, (1) whether, at the time he is alleged to have incurred such a liability, he was the keeper of a "house, room, or other place" which was during any part of Sunday opened or used for public entertainment or amusement, and (2) whether persons were admitted to that "house, room, or other place" by "the payment

of money, or by tickets sold for money." Now, I have no doubt
on either of these queries, answering the first in the affirmative
and the second in the negative. The Statute clearly requires
that the "house, room, or other place, which shall be opened or
used" for the purposes described must be the same house, room,
or place to which the public were admitted (to be amused or
entertained) on "the payment of money, or by tickets sold for
money." That was not so in this instance. The entertainment
was beyond question carried on in the large hall, being Fitzgerald's
Circus Building, or being in the Circus Building; I do not care
which. No one was excluded—that is, all were admitted—to
that house or room free. But, as the appellant admitted to
Sergeant McManamny, there was a part reserved with chairs
(and carpet covered seats) and the tenants, one of whom is the
appellant, had men standing at the entrance for the purpose of
collecting a small sum from people to go in (i.e. to these chairs and
seats) and, as he phrased it, "have comfort." The rest of the
audience had to stand or to sit elsewhere. The part reserved was
within the large hall, and was reached through the same entrance
by which all were admitted, it was lightly railed off and had an
opening, but no gate or bar thereat. But the people who paid
for this extra privilege of a seat—this "comfort,"—had been
admitted to hear and see the whole entertainment without charge,
and, therefore, before they engaged seats they were on the same
footing as the rest of the audience. They could stand and see
and hear everything without paying anything. The place in
which the entertainment took place was the place of which the
appellant was undoubtedly a "keeper," but no charge was made
for admission to that place. That is the state of facts established
beyond all doubt by the evidence, and *Chomley* J. does not appear
to have found otherwise; but he has come to the conclusion that
the reserved portion was a "place" within the meaning of the
Act, and as money was charged for admission to it, he held the
defendant, now the appellant, liable.

The circumstances of this case cannot be distinguished in substance from those of *Williams* v. *Wright* (1). There *Collins* J.,
afterwards Master of the Rolls, and now Lord *Collins*, held that,

(1) 13 T.L.R., 551.

where persons could gain entrance to the building generally and hear and see the entertainment without being subjected to any charge, the fact that a portion only of the building in which the entertainment was held, was reserved, so that people who desired seats might have them on paying a charge for admission, or for a ticket which admitted them, to this comfort and privilege, did not render the last mentioned portion a "house, room, or other place" within the meaning of the Act.

On the other hand, *Hodges* J. in *Cawsey* v. *Davidson* (1), a case from which he said he was not sure he could distinguish that of *Williams* v. *Wright* (2), seems to have thought, though he had not to decide, that under circumstances such as exist in the present case the reserved seats were a place within the meaning of the Act.

To my mind the place "opened or used for public entertainment or amusement" was the large hall, and, though the reserved seats were within it, that did not make them another place. Therefore the reason of the matter, as well as the high authority of Lord *Collins*, leads me to the conclusion that the appellant ought to succeed.

In *Reid* v. *Wilson* (3) a case involving the construction of this Statute, but on another point, Lord *Esher* M.R. said of it:—" The Act imposes penalties, and therefore must be construed and applied strictly;" and *Lopes* L.J. said (4):—"This is a penal Statute, and it is a well-established rule that the person whom it is sought to make liable under such a Statute must be strictly brought within its words. The defendants must, therefore, be strictly brought within the description of the persons mentioned in this Act as intended to be made liable to penalties." These words are as applicable to facts and things as to persons in the process of ascertaining whether the person is liable.

But it is not pretended in these days that this rule should be so applied that cases, which would be ordinarily included within the meaning of the terms used, should be placed outside it by a forced or strained construction. To use the words of the Judicial

---

(1) (1906) V.L.R., 32 ; 27 A.L.T.,
121.

(2) 13 T.L.R., 551.

(3) (1895) 1 Q.B., 315, at p. 320.

(4) (1895) 1 Q.B., 315, at p. 322.

Committee of the Privy Council in *Dyke* v. *Elliott*; *The Gauntlet* (1):—"No doubt all penal Statutes are to be construed strictly, that is to say, the Court must see that the thing charged as an offence is within the plain meaning of the words used, and must not strain the words on any notion that there has been a slip or a *casus omissus*, that the thing is so clearly within the mischief that it must have been intended to be included and would have been included if thought of." To my thinking, the plain meaning of the words does not render the appellant liable. But if I had any real doubt as to them, I should be guided by the very plain sense of the words of Lord *Esher*, then *Brett* J., when in *Dickenson* v. *Fletcher* (2), he said :—" Those who contend that a penalty may be inflicted, must show that the words of the Act distinctly enact that it shall be incurred under the present circumstances. They must fail, if the words are merely equally capable of a construction that would, and one that would not, inflict the penalty." It is as true now as when *Blackstone* wrote it, that "The law of England does not allow of offences by construction." It has been urged that the interpretation endorsed by the high authority of Lord *Collins* leads or will lead to evasion of the Act. What then is meant by an evasion ? *Chitty* L.J. in *Attorney-General* v. *Beech* (3) said, in a judgment concurring with that of *A. L. Smith* L.J., *Collins* L.J. concurring with both :—" Much was said upon opening the door to evasion. Would these be cases of evasion ? Certainly not. Indeed, the whole argument on evasion of the Act is fallacious. *The case either falls within the Act or it does not. If it does not, there is no such thing as an evasion.*" That is much the same thing as *Jessel* M.R. said in *Yorkshire Railway Wagon Co.* v. *Maclure* (4) thirteen years earlier :—" It seems to me our decision in this case will by no means encourage people to evade the Act of Parliament, or enable them to evade it, *that is, to do anything which is either expressly or impliedly prohibited by the Act of Parliament.*"

On the question arising under sec. 3, as to the advertisements, I think the appellant is entitled to succeed. The word "admitted" in that section clearly implies locality, and means admitted to

(1) L.R. 4 P.C., 184, at p. 191.   (3) (1898) 2 Q.B., 147, at p. 157.
(2) L.R. 9 C.P., 1, at p. 7.   (4) 21 Ch. D., 309, at p. 316.

such an entertainment or public meeting on a Sunday as the Statute attacks, that is, one held in some "house, room, or other place," if the admission is on "payment of money, or by tickets sold for money." As I hold that in this case admission to the "house, room, or other place" for the entertainment was not charged for, I cannot think the appellant liable under the third section by reason of the advertisements.

For these reasons I am of opinion that the appeal ought to be allowed.

O'CONNOR J.   This is an appeal from a judgment of Mr. Justice *Chomley* awarding £650 penalties against the appellant under the *Sunday Observance Act*, 21 Geo. III., c. 49. That Act was passed by the British Parliament in 1781. It has been decided by the Supreme Court of Victoria to be in force here, and it must, I think, be taken as now settled that it is part of the law of Victoria. How far its provisions may be in accord with modern public opinion it is no part of the duty of this Court to inquire. If an offence under the Act has been committed, the Statute gives the plaintiff a right to recover these penalties, and he is entitled to have his right enforced. The sole matter therefore for our consideration is whether the facts proved in evidence and found by the Judge constitute an offence under the Act.

The charge upon which the plaintiff based his case is set out in the beginning of Mr. Justice *Chomley's* judgment as follows:—
" The plaintiff claims £200 for that the defendant was (stating date) the keeper of a house, room, or place in Fitzgerald's Circus Building situate at South Melbourne which was then opened or used for public entertainment or amusement and to which persons were then admitted by the payment of money or by tickets sold for money." That charge may be read as applying either to the whole room in which the entertainment was being held, or to the reserved portion only. It is clear that the learned Judge in the Court below regarded the charge as referring to the reserved portion only. His finding of fact is directed solely to that view. " . . . the evidence to my mind," he says, " shows clearly that persons who paid a small sum, a silver coin, were admitted within the reserved portion, but if they did not pay that sum

they were directed elsewhere.   Following the judgment of *Hodges* J. with whom I agree I hold that this reserved portion was a ' place,' and for the reasons already stated I think that money was charged for admission thereto " (See *Cawsey* v. *Scott* (1).)

Assuming, however, that the charge can be read either way, the question is whether the evidence and findings disclose any offence against the Act.   The Act follows a plan common enough in the criminal legislation of that time.   The first section declares that under certain stated circumstances a house, room, or place shall be deemed to be a disorderly house or place, thereby giving the house or place the criminal status of a gaming house, or an unlicensed place of entertainment.   It then proceeds to impose on the keeper of the house or place a fine of £200 for every day on which the house or place shall be opened or used under the circumstances stated ; it further directs him to be punished as the law directs in the case of disorderly houses, and follows by imposing fines of less and less amount on managers, conductors, and chairmen, door-keepers, and servants, according to the descending scale of responsibility.   The essence of the offence is concentrated in the circumstances which are declared by the section to constitute the house or place a disorderly house or place.

Leaving out the reference to Sunday public debates, consideration of which is not material in this case, the following circumstances must concur.   The " house, room, or other place " must be opened or used on Sunday for public entertainment or amusement, and there must be a charge for admission to the house, room, or place, either in the shape of direct payment of money or presentation of tickets sold for money.   The legislature might, if it thought fit, have declared that any charge for the viewing or listening to or being present at the entertainment would have constituted the house, room, or place a disorderly house or place, but they have not done that.   They have declared in very clear language that the circumstance which shall constitute a house, room, or place opened or used on Sunday for public entertainment or amusement a disorderly house or place is the charge for admission into the house, room, or place which is then so opened and used.   If it is once established that the public are admitted into the house, room,

(1) 28 A.L.T., 112.

or place free of charge the action must fail. There is nothing in the Act to prevent the managers of the entertainment from making a charge to any member of the public after his free admission into the house, room, or place for special advantages in the way of more comfortable or more exclusive seats or a better view of the performance. As to this, *Williams* v. *Wright* (1) is directly in point. That was an action against the printer and publisher of the "Times" for penalties under the same Act. The offence charged was under sec. 3 for advertising a Sunday evening concert in the Queen's Hall, London. The defendant pleaded that the advertisement was not the advertisement of a public entertainment or amusement within the meaning of the Act, alleging that it was not the advertisement of a public entertainment or amusement to which persons were admitted by the payment of money. It became necessary, therefore, to establish that there was a charge for admission to the entertainment. The plaintiff proved that he had gone to the concert and had paid 1/- for a ticket. The ticket had on it :—

"Admission free."

"Reserved Seat 1/-."

One of the grounds of defence was that on the ticket it was stated that admission was free, and that, unless the entertainment was illegal, the advertisement could not be illegal. Mr. Justice *Collins*, now Lord *Collins*, who tried the case, upheld that defence, and found for the defendant on the ground that on the ticket was printed "Admission Free." From the very condensed report of this judgment in the Times Law Reports he appears to have said (2) :—"The fact that 1/- was charged for a reserved seat was not incompatible with the admission being free. The Statute spoke of admission, not to a seat, but to an entertainment."

In that case the material question was whether the charge for a reserved seat to hear the entertainment was a charge for admission to the entertainment. It being established in this case that the public were admitted free into the room in which the entertainment was being held, the material question is whether the charge for a seat in the reserved portion of the room amounted to a charge for admission into the room itself. To my

(1) 13 T.L.R., 551.   (2) 13 T.L.R., 551, at p. 552.

mind the same principle is applicable to both cases, and therefore Mr. Justice *Collins'* decision is a direct authority, if such authority were needed, that, when the public are admitted free to a room then being used for public entertainment, a charge made for admission to some special accommodation provided in part of it is not a charge for admission to the room within the meaning of the first section.

In the view which the learned Judge in the Court below took of the facts it was not necessary for him to find, and he did not expressly find, that the public were admitted without charge into the room in which the entertainment was being held. But it is quite clear that no charge was made for entering into the room, and no payment was required or suggested to persons in the room except to those who required the special accommodation of the reserved area. Taking therefore the wider view of the plaintiff's complaint, namely, that it applies to the room in which the concert was being held, it is clear that the plaintiff has failed to prove that there was a charge for admission within the meaning of the first section.

I turn now to the more limited view of the complaint upon which Mr. Justice *Chomley's* judgment was based. He must be taken to have found that the reserved portion of the concert room was a "place" opened and used for public entertainment and amusement to which persons were admitted by payment within the meaning of the Act, and that the defendant was the keeper of that place. Circumstances no doubt may arise in which portion of a room, if sufficiently marked off from the rest of it, may be a place within the meaning of the section. But, in my opinion, that cannot be so on the facts established in this case.

The offence, leaving out words not applicable to the present case, may be thus stated. Any house, room, or place used on Sunday for public entertainment, and to which house, room, or place while so being used persons shall be admitted by the payment of money or by ticket sold for money, shall be deemed a disorderly house or place, and the keeper of such house, room, or place shall be liable to penalties. The respondent alleges that the reserved portion was used for public entertainment, that money was charged for admission to it while so being used, and

H. C. of A.
1907.

SCOTT
v.
CAWSEY.

O'Connor J.

that, as the appellant was the keeper of it, the offence is complete.

The difficulty I have in accepting that contention is that I cannot see any evidence that the reserved portion was " used for public entertainment " in the sense intended by the Act. The only evidence of user for public entertainment was that an entertainment, held in the room of which the reserved portion was part, was heard and seen by the occupants of that portion in common with the rest of the audience. Though the entertainment was seen and heard from the reserved portion, it by no means follows that the reserved portion was *used* for the entertainment. It was the one entertainment that was seen and heard from all parts of the room, and the whole room, not the reserved portion only, was used for holding it.

If the respondent's contention is right, then two parts of the same room were at the same time being used for the same entertainment, but with different consequences. The use of the reserved portion constituted that portion a disorderly place, and rendered the keeping of it a criminal offence. But the use of the rest of it was entirely legal. If we inquire what it was that could make the use of one portion of the room innocent, and the use of the other portion criminal, the answer must be—it was the fact that a charge was made for admission to one part of the room and not to the other. In other words, the offence of which the defendant has in reality, though not in form, been found guilty is being the keeper of a room used for Sunday entertainment, to a portion of which room money was charged for admission. There is no such offence under the Act. It is the charge for admission into the room or place used for entertainment, not the charge for admission to a portion of the room or place, which constitutes the room or place a disorderly house or place.

It has been urged that, unless the Act is read as the respondent contends, it can be easily evaded, and illustrations were given in which, if the appellant's contention were adopted, a concert hall, in which all but a small portion of the auditorium contained paying seats, could carry on a Sunday business with impunity. The answer to that is twofold. First, in cases where there is in reality a charge for admission to the room used for public Sunday entertainment the tribunal which tries the facts can so find, notwithstanding any fraudulent device to conceal the real nature of the transaction. Secondly, where a Statute constitutes the committing of certain acts a criminal offence, the commission of those acts must be proved before the defendant can be found guilty. It is not enough to prove that he has committed acts of the same kind and which would lead to the same result. Nor is it the duty of a Court to so add to the language of a Statute as to make it include the committing of acts of the same kind which lead to the same result, but which the legislature has not constituted an offence. To do so would be to make laws, not to interpret them.

For these reasons I am of opinion that, on the facts of this case, the reserved portion of the room in which the entertainment was held was not a "place" within the meaning of the Act, and that the evidence disclosed no offence under the first section.

It must follow that there was no offence in the publication of the advertisement. The advertisement which is prohibited by the Act is the advertisement of an entertainment which is contrary to the provisions of the Act.

On the whole case, therefore, I am of opinion that the appeal must be allowed, the judgment appealed from must be set aside, and judgment entered for the defendant.

Isaacs J. The *Sunday Observance Act* of 1780, under which this action was brought, enacts in the first section as follows:— "That any house, room, or other place, which shall be opened or used for public entertainment or amusement, or for publicly debating on any subject whatsoever, upon any part of the Lord's day called Sunday, and to which persons shall be admitted by the payment of money, or by tickets sold for money, shall be deemed a disorderly house or place." Then follow provisions for penalties.

The appellant has been adjudged to have contravened this law, and he contends that he has not done so. In the first place he argues that the Act is not in force. But as to this I agree with what has fallen from the learned Chief Justice. The application of this and similar Acts to Victoria has been the subject of decisions of various Full Courts going back to 1864. My own

H. C. of A.
1907.

Scott
v.
Cawsey.

Isaacs J.

view is that these decisions were right, and I agree with the reasons given by *Holroyd* J. in *M'Hugh* v. *Robertson* (1). But even if I entertained a doubt, I should be very slow to overrule the opinions of men who lived much nearer to the time and circumstances by which the applicability of the law must be tested.

It was also suggested that the local legislature had assumed to deal with the question of Sunday observance in various directions, and it was argued that this Act might be treated as impliedly repealed or as no longer in force. But no trace of any parliamentary reference to the Act can be found, and there is no local legislation touching the particular phase of Sunday observance dealt with by the Statute, nor is there any inconsistency between it and any later enactment. I am, therefore, not able to accede to the view that the Act is not in force in Victoria.

Then, dealing with the Act as it stands, I pass by for the moment the appellant's argument as to the way in which the complaint was framed. The facts are few and simple. At Fitzgerald's Circus there was a large building, the interior consisting of an octagonal room capable of holding about 3,500 people, and in which Sunday secular concerts were given by the appellant. There was one entrance to the room, which was called the main entrance. Immediately to the right of the main entrance was erected a stage for the performers, and all around the room were seats. About two-fifths of the seating accommodation was entirely separated from the rest by a railing and baize curtain about 3 feet high; this was called the reserve. There was, however, a special entrance into this reserve at which an attendant was stationed.

According to one of the witnesses, the reserve would hold 1,000 persons, according to another 2,000. The latter witness said that on one of the occasions the subject of the action, it held 1,500. Both witnesses agreed that the total capacity of the room was about 3,500.

The facts establish beyond doubt that nearly everybody who entered the reserve was compelled to pay, and did pay, for admission there.

The main entrance had no door or gate, but it was divided into

(1) 11 V.L.R., 410, at p. 430.

two passages by a rail 3 ft. or 3ft. 6in. high running inwards and having a passage of about 3ft. or 3ft. 6in. on either side of it. There at the very entrance stood 3 or 4 persons, namely the defendant, his partner and one or two attendants, with plates. When a person was in the act of entering a plate was presented. If no coin was put in the plate he was allowed to enter, but was directed to the unreserved portion. If a coin was put in the plate he was allowed to pass in, sometimes with and sometimes without a ticket, to the reserved portion. There he found another attendant with a plate at the entrance of the reserve who said "Collection Please." If no ticket were presented or coin put in the plate the visitor was sometimes allowed to enter the reserve, but nearly always directed to the unreserved portion. On one occasion the room was crowded both in the reserve and other portions. It was conceded that any person could, if he insisted, enter the unreserved portion without payment.

The only difference between the seating accommodation in the reserve and elsewhere was that some of the seats in the reserve were chairs, and others were covered with carpet, while in the rest of the auditorium the benches were bare. The evidence is clear that the charge was made, not merely for seating accommodation, but for bare admission to a particular part of the room which, besides being reserved, was in a very advantageous position from which to witness the performance.

The appellant's contention is that he has not contravened the Act. He says, first, that, so far as the whole room is concerned, it is true it was used for the entertainment, but everybody was allowed to enter the room free, and, once being in, a charge could lawfully be made for permission to occupy any special part of it, however extensive that part might be, always supposing some other substantial part of the room was not charged for.

I should notice that, it was said, the way in which the claim was ultimately framed enables the appellant to maintain that the respondent did not rely on the whole room being used for the concert, but only the reserve. He urges that by the use of the word " in " instead of the word " namely " the plaintiff deliberately abandoned all contention that the concert took place in the whole room, and proceeded merely on the assumption that the reserve was the only place where any part of the entertainment was held. Notwithstanding the complaint still alleges that the " defendant was the keeper of a house room or place in Fitzgerald's Circus Building situate in South Melbourne which was then opened or used for public entertainment or amusement and to which persons were then admitted by the payment of money &c," the defendant says, that by virtue of the word " in " the plaintiff was pinned down for all purposes to the reserve as the place used for entertainment, and could not call in aid the rest of the facts which have already been alluded to. I am unable to read the claim with such limitations. The word "room" still remaining in the claim ought not, I think, to be ignored. It is true the learned Judge below thought the plaintiff's case sufficiently established by treating the reserve as a " place " in law both as being used for entertainment and as being charged for. But if the learned Judge were wrong in this, that should not, in my opinion, defeat the plaintiff's case, if his claim be properly made and sufficiently supported by the evidence. If he can show that the Judge should have decided in his favour on any ground, the decision he has already obtained ought to be sustained.

I proceed, therefore, to consider whether the plaintiff has proved a breach of the law, on the assumption that the whole room was alleged to have been used, as indisputably it was in fact used, for the purpose of entertainment.

This leads us at once to the construction of the Act. It was urged that this Act being penal should receive a strict construction. If by that is meant that a Court should construe an Act of Parliament so as to exclude from it as much as an ingenious mind can by a possible interpretation contrive to exclude, I do not agree with the contention. If it means simply that the Court should not strain the words beyond their fair meaning, I do agree with it. As this contention is so frequently put forward it is desirable to deal with it fully.

When it is said that penal Acts or fiscal Acts should receive a strict construction I apprehend it amounts to nothing more than this. Where Parliament has in the public interest thought fit in the one case to restrain private action to a limited extent and penalise a contravention of its directions, and in the other to exact from individuals certain contributions to the general revenue, a Court should be specially careful, in the view of the consequences on both sides, to ascertain and enforce the actual commands of the legislature, not weakening them in favour of private persons to the detriment of the public welfare, nor enlarging them as against the individuals towards whom they are directed.

In *Attorney-General* v. *Sillem* (1), *Bramwell* B. quoted a passage from *Sedgwick on Statutory and Constitutional Law,* which he said was " a passage in which good sense, force and propriety of language are equally conspicuous; and which is amply borne out by the authorities, English and American," which he cites. The passage is as follows :—" But the rule that Statutes of this class are to be considered strictly, is far from being a rigid and unbending one ; or rather, it has in modern times been so modified and explained away, as to mean little more than that penal provisions, like all others, are to be fairly construed according to the legislative intent as expressed in the enactment ; the Courts refusing on the one hand to extend the punishment to cases which are not clearly embraced in them, and on the other, equally refusing by any mere verbal nicety, forced construction, or equitable interpretation, to exonerate parties plainly within their scope."

James L.J. in delivering the judgment of the Privy Council in *Dyke* v. *Elliott; The Gauntlet* (2), said :—" Where the thing is brought within the words and within the spirit, there a penal enactment is to be construed, like any other instrument, according to the fair common-sense meaning of the language used, and the Court is not to find or make any doubt or ambiguity in the language of a penal Statute, where such doubt or ambiguity would clearly not be found or made in the same language in any other instrument."

The views expressed by *Chitty* L.J. for the Court of Appeal in *Llewellyn* v. *Vale of Glamorgan Railway Co.*(3), when interpreting a penal Statute may be referred to as completing the statement of the rule. His Lordship said :—" When an Act is open to two constructions, that construction ought to be adopted which is the

(1) 2 H. & C., 431, at pp. 531, 532.   (3) (1898) 1 Q.B., 473, at p. 478.
(2) L.R. 4 P.C., 184, at p. 191.

H. C. of A.
1907.

SCOTT
v.
CAWSEY.

Isaacs J.
more reasonable, and the better calculated to give effect to the expressed intention."

Two further references of high authority may with advantage be made. In *Caledonian Railway Co.* v. *North British Railway Co.* (1), *Selborne* L.C. said :—" The more literal construction ought not to prevail if (as the Court below has thought) it is opposed to the intentions of the legislature, as apparent by the Statute ; and if the words are sufficiently flexible to admit of some other construction by which that intention will be better effectuated."

This is in perfect accordance with the statement of the Supreme Court of the United States in *Johnson* v. *Southern Pacific Co.* (2), which I cite because it so well represents my own views. One question was whether a locomotive engine was a "car" within the meaning of a penal Statute. *Fuller* C.J., in delivering the unanimous judgment of the Court, said :—" It is settled that ' though penal laws are to be construed strictly, yet the intention of the legislature must govern in the construction of penal as well as other Statutes; and they are not to be construed so strictly as to defeat the obvious intention of the legislature'. *United States* v. *Lacher* (3)." The learned Chief Justice quotes a passage from a judgment of Mr. Justice *Story* in *United States* v. *Winn* (4), referring to the rule that penal Statutes are to be construed strictly, in which that learned Judge said :—" I agree to that rule in its true and sober sense ; and that is, that penal Statutes are not to be enlarged by implication, or extended to cases not obviously within their words and purport. But where the words are general, and include various classes of persons, I know of no authority, which would justify the Court in restricting them to one class, or in giving them the narrowest interpretation, where the mischief to be redressed by the Statute is equally applicable to all of them. And where a word is used in a Statute, which has various known significations, I know of no rule, that requires the Court to adopt one in preference to another, simply because it is more restrained, if the objects of the Statute equally apply to the largest and broadest sense of the word. In short, it appears to me, that the proper course in all these cases, is to search out and follow the true intent of the legislature, and to adopt that sense of the words which harmonizes best with the context, and promotes in the fullest manner, the apparent policy and objects of the legislature." Applying those principles of interpretation to this Act, the defendant has, in my opinion, committed a breach of the first section, and the plaintiff is entitled to hold his judgment as to the penalties for the concert.

The statutory prohibition is against admitting persons to the room by payment of money or tickets sold for money. Can it not reasonably be said that persons who are admitted to a particular part of the room by payment of money are admitted to the room by payment of money? It seems to me that the part to which they are admitted by payment is no less for this purpose to be considered the room, than the portion to which they are admitted free. It is an irrelevant circumstance that some persons are admitted free to the whole room, if others are charged; and it appears equally irrelevant that the same person is admitted free to one half of the room if he is charged in respect of the other half. The admission to the room in the latter case is free up to a certain point, that is as to one portion of the room, and not free as regards the remainder of the room; and if, as regards the remainder, a charge is made, I am forced to the conclusion, if any substantial validity is to be preserved for the Statute, that there is then a contravention of its provisions. The Act looks to the whole room as a place where the entertainment is given, and forbids a breach by insisting on payment as to any part of it. The opposite view, which is not only possible, but commends itself to a majority of my learned colleagues, appears to me to have this overpowering defect, that it practically reduces the Act to a nullity. That is a result that a Court should always strive against, if the language permits.

If payment for admission to any specified portion of the room is not sufficient to constitute a breach, then there is never a breach, so long as mere ingress in permitted free, always provided it is real and actual ingress. But if once the public are admitted to enter clear within the doors, they are, on this assumption, admitted to the room within the meaning of the Act; and if no charge is made so far, the promoters of the entertainment can, despite the Act, charge whatever they like for either sitting accommodation or standing space anywhere else.

A concert manager may engage or build a vast hall, divide off a small portion near the entrance, to which gratuitous freedom of access is given, and whether a single person remains in or enters that free part or not, the management may with impunity charge whatever it pleases for the rest of the place.

The fallacy of the appellant's view as a matter of reasoning appears to me to consist in regarding admission as the mere passing the doors. It assumes that if up to a certain point of space —namely, the interior of the room—it is free, the admission continues free ever afterwards, whatever charge is insisted upon for other portions of the room. It regards admission as looking to nothing but bare entrance to the room, or rather to some part of it, and takes no account of the opportunity by presence in the room to share in the entertainment or amusement. A very probable case may be supposed which tests this position. A large hall is used for dancing. Admission through the doors is free in the first instance. On entering, you find a raised stage or platform on which the band is seated. At a distance of six feet from the walls and from the stage a barrier is constructed within which the dancing takes place. To this inner portion admission is charged for. The band is outside the barrier and beyond the free space. In the case supposed, the entertainment or amusement necessarily includes both the band, and the dancing within the inner portion ; no dancing taking place in the intermediate space. According to the appellant's argument, admission to the room being free, there is no contravention of the Act, and as we shall see presently, he also contends that, as the band is not within the dancing reserve, that reserve is not a " place " within the meaning of the Act ; and so he is altogether clear of the Statute.

Or the promoters might vary the situation by providing a part of the room, small, inconvenient and rough, as a free part for dancing, while charging for admission to a large, and prepared portion of the same room barricaded off.

They might even further extend their operations under the shelter of the word " house " in the Statute. If bare admission to any part of the room where an entertainment is proceeding is admission to the room, so admission to any part of the house must be admission to the house. And therefore if in several rooms in a house dancing is proceeding, so long as gratuitous admittance to them by the street door and into one of the rooms is permitted, the promoters of the amusement could without any breach of the Act charge for admission to all the other rooms. A room divided off into distinct compartments by barricades, is for this purpose no different from one house divided into several rooms.

I think the true position is that admission may be free up to a point, and cease to be free afterwards. The original admission is limited to a prescribed space, and it is just as if at the outer door the proprietor said :—" You can go in free to such a space, and you must pay to enter the rest of the room." If payment is made there and then for the rest of the room, it would seem an unanswerable case that admission, quâ the unfree portion, is admission by payment of money. And it appears to me to make no difference that the charge is made after entrance. It makes no more difference in my opinion than if admission were free for the first hour to the whole room, and permission to remain charged for during the remainder of the performance.

A striking instance of what can be done appears in the present case. On 1st April, as testified by Constable Bateman, the building was crowded, both the reserve and the other portions. Among those in the reserve there were probably many hundreds who could not have found space within the room at all had they not gone to the reserve itself and paid, and yet by the appellant's argument they are supposed to have been admitted to the place free. Indeed every theatre may, so far as this Act is concerned, be opened on Sunday, the ordinary performance given and the ordinary charges made, provided only some portion of the place, however inconvenient and insufficient to accommodate the whole audience, be allotted as a free portion.

It is said this is the intention of the legislature as gathered from the words of the Statute. I confess, however reluctant to differ from the weighty opinions of my learned brethren, I am unable to discover that intention.

On the contrary, as I read the Act, a different intention is dis-

H. C. of A.
1907.

Scott
v.
Cawsey.

Isaacs J.

coverable, not merely from the nature of the evil struck at, and the incompetency of the Statute to meet it if construed on the appellant's lines, but also from the express provisions of the enactment.

Sec. 2, which begins by referring to the many "subtle and crafty contrivances" of the keepers of the houses, rooms, or places dealt with, provides *inter alia* that any room at which persons are supplied with refreshments of eating or drinking on Sunday at more than usual prices on other days, shall be deemed a room to which persons are admitted by the payment of money, although money is not taken as for admittance, or when the persons enter or depart from the room. This is not the creation of a new offence, but it is guarding against a subtle contrivance to evade the consequences of the offence already provided against, and throws light upon what that offence comprehends. It clearly, to my mind, evinces that the legislature was not narrowly confining the word "admittance" to the mere original entry into the room, with permission to charge afterwards whatever the proprietor might desire, but was giving a larger meaning to it by including in admittance to the room of entertainment the providing for payment something which was part of the inducement to enter or remain in the room as being the entertainment or as a part of the entertainment, even though it was perfectly optional once the person was inside to take the refreshment or not. If this particular class of charge be included as a charge for admittance, still more must the legislature have regarded the compulsory payment for actual admission to the best part of the room to witness or participate in the entertainment as admittance to the room by the payment of money.

The case of *Williams* v. *Wright* (1) was pressed upon us. The view taken of that decision by three of my learned brethren certainly adds greatly to its force. I have closely examined it, but cannot say it is so clear and convincing to me as to dispel the views I have otherwise formed of the effect of sec. 1 of the Statute. It is to be observed that there was no railed off space deposed to in that case, and the learned Judge did not address himself to the meaning of the term "place." He treated the

(1) 13 T.L.R., 551.

Statute as speaking of admission to an entertainment, and went on the ground that there might be free admission to an entertainment consistently with a seat being charged for. If, however, the principle be the same, and if the view of *Collins* J. be correct, then the consequence follows that, without contravening the section, theatres could be open for Sunday entertainments, as I have mentioned, without infraction of this Statute, a result I regard as quite opposed to the fair intendment of the enactment. The case has not found its way into any of the regular reports.

The suggested signification of the term "admittance" seems to me to disappoint the intention of the legislature. I shall presently refer to the history of the Act and the position it occupies in the legislation of the period. But, whatever its history, if the words were so plain and precise as to be capable of one signification only so that the actual provision were its own expositor, leaving no room for construction, no Court could venture to alter its meaning. However absurd or unexpected the result might be, the legislature alone could in that case intervene to change the law it had plainly and unequivocally declared. But here the exoneration of the appellant is a matter at least open to grave doubt. The mere fact that up to the present case, which has been a mere experiment so far as Victoria is concerned, the whole of this community has constantly acted upon the assumption that the law prohibited what the appellant contends for as lawful, is sufficient to preclude the assertion that his contention is beyond the region of controversy. And, in passing, I think the general understanding in this country of the effect of the Act is as important as the asserted general understanding at the present day to the contrary in England.

If the words here, at all events capable as I think them of the interpretation I have put on them, are interpreted so as to give effect to the intention of the Act as apparent from its general provisions, the present case falls both within the words and the spirit of the Statute according to the rule in "*The Gauntlet*" (1), and the judgment ought to stand.

If, moreover, the charge of contravention be confined entirely

(1) L.R. 4 P.C., 184.

H. C. of A.
1907.

Scott
v.
Cawsey.

Isaacs J.

to the reserve, I think there is still enough to bring the appellant within the words of the Act.

After the best consideration I am able to give to the question, it appears to me that the railed off portion has received, by the very act of the appellant himself, a distinctive character as a place of entertainment, and is as much a separate locality, for the purpose of entertaining such of the audience as are willing to pay, as if a high partition had been erected. It was certainly " used " by the appellant for entertaining spectators as much as any other part of the room, and its use was distinct from the remainder of the building in this respect that it was fenced off and " reserved " for those who pay. If the appellant insists on treating it as a separate subdivision of his property for the purpose of charging for admission, I think he cannot complain if he be held to the legal consequences of its separate character. He cannot be heard to say it is separate from the rest so as to make free admission to the other part a free admission to the room, and yet that it is inseparable from the other part as to the holding of the concert. Nor do I think the absence of the entertainers from this portion of the building affects the position. The entertainment they afford reaches the audience seated in the reserve, and it seems to me obviously to be a place of entertainment. The spectators do not desire, and could not well have, the bodily presence of performers in the reserve, but find their pleasure in seeing and hearing them from a distance. The appellant procures the entertainers, provides the entertainment, and creates a distinct and quite defined place for the entertained for admission to which he demands money. He is certainly, as I have already said, within the spirit of the law. He is also, in my opinion, even as regards this railed off space, within the letter of it.

The expression " house, room, or place " is found in the *Gaming Act* 1745 (18 Geo. II. c. 34), which is still in force. With some variation it has appeared in various English Acts relating to gaming. In the Act 16 & 17 Vict. c. 119 (1853) the words are " house, office, room or other place," and they appear in conjunction with " opened, kept or used." In the Act 17 & 18 Vict. c. 38 (1854) the expression is " house, room or place." It was on the words of the Act of 1853 that the House of Lords decided the case of *Powell* v. *Kempton Park Racecourse Co. Ltd.* (1). The *Earl of Halsbury* L.C. said (2):—" any place which is sufficiently definite, and in which a betting establishment might be conducted, would satisfy the words of the Statute." Lord *James of Hereford* said (3):—" directly a definite localization of the business of betting is effected, be it made under a tent or even movable umbrella, it may be well held that a 'place' exists for the purposes of a conviction under the Act."

The analogue here of the betting establishment is the place of entertainment—that is where the public are entertained.

Turning now to the Georgian legislation as to entertainments, we find that about the same period, that is in 1751, an Act 25 George II. c. 36 was passed which is styled an Act for the better preventing thefts and robberies and for regulating places of public entertainment and punishing persons keeping disorderly houses. In that Act the phrase is " house, room, garden or other place." That Statute required licences for places of entertainment, otherwise they were to be disorderly houses and places.

In 1781 was passed the Act now under consideration which describes itself in the title as " An Act for preventing certain abuses and profanations on the Lord's Day, called Sunday." It recites that certain " houses, rooms, or places " had of late frequently been opened for public entertainment or amusement upon Sunday evening &c., and then forbids the taking of money for admission on Sunday.

Looking at the two lines of legislation, and the course of each, I feel no real doubt—except such as is naturally occasioned by the opinions of those of my learned brethren from whom I have the misfortune to differ—first, that the same method of interpretation must be applied to the Act we are now considering, to discover the meaning of the term " place," and next, that in each case there may be as many such places as the defendant chooses to segregate and localize for his own purposes.

I should observe that the manifest intention of the Act of 1781 was to put an additional check for the purposes of Sunday observance upon the same classes of entertainments as were

---

(1) (1899) A.C., 143.   (2) (1899) A.C., 143, at p. 162.
          (3) (1899) A.C., 143, at p. 194.

H. C. of A.
1907.

Scott
v.
Cawsey.

Isaacs J.

already partially dealt with by the Act of 1751. In the earlier Act, entertainments were included which were held in a " house, room, garden or other place " and for effective purposes it is only natural to suppose that the expression "house, room, or other place " in the later Act has a signification as extensive as that in the prior enactment. A licence under the earlier Act for the whole of a garden, for instance, would cover every part of the garden, no matter how it was sub-divided; and, if immediately the *Sunday Observance Act* were passed, a whole garden were used for Sunday entertainment or amusement, fireworks in one part, dancing in another, singing in a third, music in a fourth, with the usual connected and lighted paths and communications, though the whole of the garden were licensed, yet if the portion confined to fireworks were free, and those devoted to dancing, singing, and music were charged for, it would be difficult to say that the later Act was not contravened. The whole garden would, of course, be in its entirety one place of public amusement, of a varied nature, and admission through the outer gates could be said to be free admission to the garden with equal force to that of the appellant's argument here. But the case would, I consider, be obviously an infringement of the Act. And, if so, I am unable to perceive the difference between that case and the present.

The appellant argues that, if the reserve be itself a place of entertainment, there would be a separate " place," wherever a distinct reserve existed. Thus in a theatre, the dress circle, the reserved stalls, the unreserved stalls, the pit and the gallery would each be a place, and subject him to a separate penalty. And why not ? It is within his own absolute uncontrolled power to prevent it. No one can force him to incur penalties. All he has to do is to refrain from charging, or if he does charge, he may throw the whole of the seating accommodation open at the one price. Then he has only one place to be liable for. But if, while breaking the law, he chooses to increase his profits by creating several distinct places, even if he choose to carry it so far as to make different prices for different seats, what just cause of complaint can he have if the law takes him at his word ? If there are separate places for his profit, there is no injustice in considering them separate places for his responsibility. He might urge the same argument with equal force with respect to several rooms in one house, opened for dancing.

On every ground, therefore, in my opinion, the judgment of Mr. Justice *Chomley* was correct as to the first part of the claim, and should be sustained.

With regard to the advertisements, if the main judgment appealed from is right, I think that the respondent should succeed on this branch also. The appellant contended that the notice on the screen was not an advertisement. I think it was. There are many methods of advertising; insertion in newspapers, placards on hoardings and walls, sky signs, and notices published on screens are equally intimations to the public; these are advertisements. Then he argued that the advertisement did not state that admission was to be charged for. I agree that an advertisement is not of the nature struck at by the section, unless, on the face of it, it states directly or indirectly that the entertainment is one to which persons are to be admitted by the payment of money or tickets sold for money. It was not contemplated by the legislature that a printer, for instance, having no reason to suppose the entertainment to be of that nature, should be liable for these penalties.

But much depends on the circumstances in which the advertisement appears. Here the notice was given in the following terms:—"Our patrons are respectively notified that we shall continue these concerts every Sunday night with the same completeness as hitherto but no advertisement will be inserted in the papers. Kindly inform your friends."

The expression "these concerts," means, when there and then published to the persons present, concerts of the same class; if admission was charged for at the concert when the notice was given, then it conveys the intimation that admission was to be charged for in future.

Holding the views I have expressed on the main question, I think that on this branch also the decision appealed from was correct and should be upheld.

Higgins J. I should have been glad to think that the appellant is not liable to these penalties, not only because thereby my judgment would be in accord with that of the majority of the Court,

but because I cannot but feel that the Act 21 Geo. III., c. 49, is
not such an Act as public opinion in Victoria would permit at the
present day. But, after full consideration, I see no course open to
me but to say that the defendant has brought himself within the
provisions of the Act. It appears that the entertainment consisted
of some innocent songs and some innocent biograph pictures;
that the performances were well-conducted ; and that the public
appreciated them. There was no disorder : and yet, if persons are
admitted by the payment of money, the " house, room, or other
place " where they are entertained is, by the Act, to be deemed a
"disorderly house or place." Even if a place be used for public
debate on Sunday, with payment for admission, and if the discussion be limited to texts of holy scripture, it becomes, by the
Act, " a disorderly place," without further proof ; because, forsooth,
the Houses of Parliament in England, in 1781, conceived that such
debates were necessarily held " by persons unlearned and incompetent to explain " the holy scripture, " to the corruption of good
morals, and to the great encouragement of irreligion and pro-
faneness."

I concur with my colleagues that we have to treat the Act of
1781 as being in force in Victoria by virtue of the Act of 9 Geo.
IV., c. 83, sec. 24, if not by virtue of the principle that colonists
take with them all appropriate British laws. In face of the long
and consistent course of decisions in Victoria, enforcing Sunday
Acts such as this, and in view of the decisions to the same effect
in New South Wales, it is impossible for this Court to hold that
in 1829 the Act was not reasonably applicable to these Colonies.
Indeed, the *Theatres Act* 1896 of Victoria treats the Act as applicable. I also concur with my colleagues in thinking that this Act
has not been repealed as to Victoria by any legislation that has
been enacted since. If there has been a change in the fashion
of regarding such subjects, it is for the legislature to alter the
law, not for the Court. The only question that remains is, has
the defendant so acted as to come within the penalties of the
Act ? The difficulty which arises as to this point is owing to the
endeavour of the defendant to evade the Act—probably acting
under well-considered advice. I do not say " evade " in any
unpleasant sense. It is our duty to " evade " Acts, in the sense

of not disobeying them. But the defendant has tried how far
he can go in the direction of giving public entertainments on
Sunday, for payment, without violating the letter of the law.

Now the Act provides (sec. 1) that "any house, room, or other
place, which shall be opened or used for public entertainment or
amusement . . . upon any part of the Lord's day called Sunday,
and to which persons shall be admitted by the payment of money,
or by tickets sold for money, shall be deemed a disorderly house
or place ; and the keeper of such house, room, or place shall forfeit
the sum of £200 for every day that such house, room, or place
shall be opened or used as aforesaid." The hall is a large one.
People are admitted free of charge to all parts except the gallery
which faces the stage—the part which is obviously the best place
for seeing the biograph pictures, and for watching the performances; but as to this " reserve," as it is called, the learned Judge
who tried the case has found—and there is ample evidence to
support his finding—" that persons who paid a small sum, a silver
coin, were admitted within the reserved portion, but if they did
not pay that sum, they were directed elsewhere." The reserve
would hold from 1,000 to 2,000 people ; but people come into the
unreserved portion also. The reserve is railed off by a thin small
rail, about three feet high, with baize attached. There is a man
in charge of the reserve, standing at the entrance, and collecting
the money and the tickets. I am of opinion that this " reserve "
is a " place " within the meaning of the Act ; that it was "used "
for public entertainment or amusement; and that persons were
admitted to that " place " by the " paying of money, or by tickets
sold for money."

The differentiating fact which makes a lawful entertainment
unlawful, as regards any definite place, is payment for admission.
It is quite true that the entertainers are not in the reserve, but
on the stage ; but I cannot regard it as being any the less " used
for public entertainment " merely because the music is rendered,
and the biograph is worked, on the stage opposite ; or because
other people not in the reserve are also entertained (though not
so satisfactorily). The public are entertained in the reserve, and
for money ; and it makes no matter that others of the public are
entertained in other places in the hall without money. I quite

accept the position that the use of one place in this huge hall for entertainment is legal, and that the use of another place is illegal —the distinction lying in the payment for admission to the latter place. I might have had more difficulty in coming to this conclusion if the words of the Act were " used for a public entertainment," implying that the entertainment must be one and indivisible. But the phrasing is simply " used for public entertainment." Here I find the fallacy of the appellant's argument. He says there is no evidence that the reserve was used for " the " entertainment. Quite true, in one sense; but the Act does not require such a fact to be proved. It requires proof merely that the reserve was used for entertainment. If the defendant's contention is right, of course the Act becomes practically a dead letter without any action on the part of the Parliament. Halls and theatres may be opened for entertainments and amusements on Sundays; and those who hold the entertainment will escape penalties by simply leaving a portion of the hall or theatre free of charge. Mr. *Schutt*, for the defendant, admits that this is the result. If the defendant's contention succeed, a building such as a theatre may be opened, and a performance in the nature of a concert or a ballet-dance may take place on Sunday, provided only that no charge be made for admission (say) to a portion of the " gods."

Again—according to the defendant's argument—there may lawfully be a Sunday Christy Minstrel entertainment in the organ wing of the Melbourne Exhibition Building, and a charge made for admission to that wing, provided that the rest of the building be left open to all, free of payment. I do not say that the argument allows evasion of the Act. Every one is entitled to evade an Act by not disobeying its terms. What I say is that the argument involves that the Act was futile, and obviously futile, for its purposes; and I regard it as the duty of the Court so to construe the Act, if possible, as to avoid treating the legislature as making an utterly futile provision—to construe the Act *ut res magis valeat quam pereat*: *Curtis* v. *Stovin* (1); " *The Duke of Buccleuch* " (2); *Macleod* v. *Attorney-General for New*

(1) 22 Q.B.D., 513.   (2) 15 P.D., 86, at p. 96.

South Wales (1). There is nothing whatever in the Act to indicate that the " place " to which payment admits must be roofed in separately from all places in respect of which there is no payment.

I adopt the words of the *Earl of Halsbury* L.C., in an analogous case, *Powell* v. *Kempton Park Racecourse Co.* (2). In that case, the question was as to a " place　.　.　. open kept or used " for betting; but, paraphrasing his Lordship's words so as to meet the present case, I should say that, for the purposes of the Act now in question, every place which is sufficiently definite, and in which the public can be entertained, would satisfy the words of the Act. There is no need to introduce any refinement or subtlety into the crude language of this crude enactment. I feel strongly that men trained in law are ever under a tendency to over-subtlety in matters of verbal interpretation, and that it is necessary for us, again and again, to revert to the ordinary lay attitude. There are no technical associations with this Act. The word " place " is as wide as any word that could be used; and when it is used in the collocation " house, room, or other place　.　.　. used for public entertainment," any layman would, I think, conclude that for the purposes of the section it is sufficient if there be a house, or a room, or a part of a hall. Probably, the place *in a* room or hall would have to be of considerable size; for, otherwise, the *public* could not be entertained there, or *any* considerable number of people. Mr. *Pigott* has urged that the *only* meaning of " place " in this context is a part of a room. But, without adopting the argument in this extreme form, I think a portion of a room or hall was probably the thing primarily before the minds of those who framed the section. As for the contention that, on the plaintiff's view, every row of seats could be considered as a " place," and there could be a score of " places," some legal and some illegal, within the same room, it does not impress my mind. There may be more difficulty in dealing with the case of a charge for admission to very small portions of a room. But that difficulty does not apply where the reserve for which charge is made takes up, as here, about two-fifths of the room. It is an unpleasant thing to find that one's

(1) (1891) A.C., 455, at p. 457.　　　　(2) (1889) A.C., 143, at p. 162.

H. C. of A.
1907.
——
SCOTT
v.
CAWSEY.
——
Higgins J.
house or garden or enclosure may possibly be called " a disorderly
house or place "—with all the nasty associations which such an
expression evokes—but such is the language of the legislature,
and it is not for us to alter it.   There is nothing that I can find
in the Act to indicate that a place cannot be " used for public
entertainment" unless both entertainers and entertained are
present in that place. The stage of a theatre is usually excluded
to the audience ; and it could hardly be meant to allow tickets to
be issued for the stalls, for the dress circle, for the family circle,
for the " gods," simply because the entertainers are not in these
places, but on the stage. A man with the lease of a cricket
ground may use it for the entertainment of the public by sending
up fireworks outside the enclosure, and admitting the public
within the enclosure. It is unnecessary to consider the case of a
man allowing the public to enter his garden for payment, in
order to hear music provided by others outside the garden ; for
in this case before us the same man provides both the music and
the enclosure in which to hear it.

As for the case of *Williams* v. *Wright* (1) the report is
unsatisfactory. There is no report of it in the *Law Reports* or in
the *Law Journal* or in the *Law Times.*   But, so far as I can
gather from the report that we have, Mr. Justice *Collins* was not
asked to decide whether a reserved portion of a hall, for admittance
to which reserved portion a charge is made, could be treated as a
" place " within the meaning of the Act.   The charge was made
under a different section of the Act—sec. 3—against the publisher of the *Times* newspaper for publishing an advertisement of
a public entertainment " to which persons are to be admitted by
the payment of money."   The word " place " is not used in sec. 3 ;
and therefore no question could arise as to the meaning of the
word " place " in that case.   The ticket said " Admission free,
reserved seats 1/- ; " and *Collins* J. came to the conclusion of fact
that the charge was for the seat, not for the admission to the entertainment. " The Statute spoke of admission, not to a seat, but to
an entertainment." The learned Judge dealt only with two
alternatives—admission to a seat and admission to an entertainment. He had not to deal with the third case—admission to a

(1) 13 T.L.R., 551.

reserve. The plaintiff was not represented by counsel, and the decision turned on the charge being made merely for the seat—just as a charge might be made for the use of an opera glass. There was nothing, in the facts as found, to show any charge for a reserved area. I cannot attach much importance to the statement made in the *Encyclopædia of the Laws of England*, "Sunday" page 36. The statement is that the Act is usually evaded *e.g.*, at the Albert Hall, and Queen's Hall, by giving free admission, and charging for "reserved seats." There is not in these words, I think, any clear indication that a definite portion of the hall is set apart for those who pay; and, even if that is the practice, the practice has not been tested in the law Courts. It is also gravely urged that Royalty has been present at such entertainments. This alleged fact does not appear in evidence; and we should not, I presume, take judicial notice of it. Rather than admit the possibility of His Majesty doing even so much wrong as would be involved in helping people to break one of his own laws, it might be proper to presume that, as, in the drama of Euripides, the real Helen was not carried away to Troy, but some wraith or *simulacrum* of the lady, so the King himself was not present *in propriâ personâ* at the Queen's Hall on a Sunday. In any case, as Lord Coke informed His Majesty King James the First, the King does not expound the law personally, but through the mouths of his faithful servants the Judges (1). *Baxter* v. *Langley* (2) shows that the point raised by the defendant here, as to the meaning of "place," was raised by the defendant there, amongst other things; but the Court decided in defendant's favour merely on the ground that there was no "entertainment" within the Act, without saying anything against a reserve being a "place." The Judges in England enforce the penalties with regret, and do not hesitate to say so. (See *Terry* v. *Brighton Aquarium Co.*) (3); and immediately after, and probably in consequence of the *Brighton Aquarium Case*, the British Parliament specifically authorized the Government to remit the penalties under this Act (38 & 39 Vict. c. 80). The Government of Victoria has also general power to remit such penalties: *Public Moneys Act* 1890, sec. 4.

(1) 12 Rep., p. 64.   (2) 33 L.J.M.C., 1.   (3) L.R. 10 Q.B., 306.

H. C. of A.
1907.

Scott
v.
Cawsey.

Higgins J.

As for the penalty of £50 for advertising on a screen during the performance, I had much doubt; but I think that it was rightly imposed. Sec. 3 of the Act provides that "any person advertising . . . any public entertainment or amusement . . . on the Lord's day to which persons are to be admitted by the payment of money . . . shall . . . forfeit the sum of £50." During the performance, there were thrown on a screen these words :—" Our patrons are respectfully notified that we shall continue these concerts every Sunday night with the same completeness as hitherto but no advertisement will be inserted in the papers. Kindly inform your friends." It is urged that there is nothing in this notice to indicate that payment will be expected for admission. But I cannot find anything in the Act requiring that payment should be actually mentioned in the advertisements. The advertising may be, as in the present case, the act of the entertainer himself, and effected at an entertainment for which payment has been made; and when he announces to his " patrons" that he will " continue these concerts every Sunday night" the audience knows, without being told, that they are to come on the same terms. The words of sec. 3, " to which persons are to be admitted by the payment of money " mean, as in sec. 1, that *as a fact* persons are to be admitted by the payment of money. I am strongly opposed to improving or altering an Act by implying words that are not there, unless the words are *necessarily* implied ; and the Act does not say that the advertisements must state that there is to be a payment. It is enough that payment is in fact to be made ; and, as for the argument that on this construction a newspaper publisher would be rendered liable to the penalty, although he knew nothing about payment being required, I am of opinion that he would not be liable if he did not know about the payment. For criminal offences there must be guilty knowledge—knowledge here that payment will be required unless the Act clearly indicates the contrary. In *Reg.* v. *Sleep* (1) a Statute made it an offence to be found in the possession of naval stores marked with the broad arrow. The jury found that there was not sufficient evidence to show that the prisoner knew the stores to be so marked, and the

(1) 30 L.J.M.C., 170.

conviction was held bad.   (See also *Anonymous* (1); *Hearne* v.
Garton (2)).   Knowledge of the relevant fact is necessarily
implied in Acts creating crimes, unless expressly negatived.   I
see no reason for differing from the additional view put by
Isaacs J., to the effect that, if a charge be made for admission so
far as regards a prescribed portion of a room, it is made for
admission to the room.   But I prefer to rest on the simpler
aspect of the case.

I accept unreservedly the doctrine that in Statutes imposing
taxes or penalties the person sought to be charged has to be
brought within the letter of the law.   I do not suggest any
addition to or qualification of the words of the Act.   It seems to
me that the appellant here is within both the letter and the spirit
of the law, and, but for the contrary opinions of my colleagues,
I should regard the case as free from doubt.   I am therefore of
opinion that the judgment of Mr. Justice *Chomley* in this case,
and the judgment of Mr. Justice *Hodges*, so far as it relates to
the same points, in *Cawsey* v. *Davidson* (3) are right; and that
this appeal should be dismissed with costs.

H. C. of A.
1907.
Scott
v.
Cawsey.
———
Higgins J.

> *Appeal allowed.   Order appealed from dis-*
> *charged.   Judgment for defendant*
> *with costs.   Respondent to pay costs of*
> *appeal.*

Solicitor, for appellant, *W. E. Brunt.*
Solicitor, for respondent, *Guinness*, Crown Solicitor for Victoria.

                                                        B. L.

(1) Fost., 439.   (3) (1906) V.L.R., 32; 27 A.L.T.,
(2) 2 El. & E., 66.   121.

[HIGH COURT OF AUSTRALIA.]

WILLIAMSON   .   .   .   .   .   PLAINTIFF;

AND

THE COMMONWEALTH   .   .   .   .   DEFENDANT.

H. C. of A.   *Commonwealth Public Service Act 1902 (No. 5 of 1902), secs. 46, 78—Public Ser-*
1907.   *vant — Dismissal — Procedure — Suspension—Condition precedent— Wrongful*
        dismissal—Relief—Damages — Reinstatement—Defence—Money not voted by
MELBOURNE,   *Parliament.*
Nov. 18, 19,
20, 29.   On 30th January 1907 an officer of the Public Service of the Commonwealth
                was suspended from duty in reference to a shortage which had been dis-
Higgins J.   covered in his accounts. He was prosecuted criminally in connection with
                that shortage, was tried and was acquitted. Afterwards, on 2nd May, the
                officer was charged under the *Commonwealth Public Service Act* 1902 by the
                Chief Officer with three offences, one being in connection with the shortage
                in his accounts, and was required to admit, deny or explain these charges,
                but the original suspension had not been removed, nor was the officer
                suspended on the later charges. The officer having denied these charges, was
                on the 7th May further suspended, and, after proceedings which were in
                accordance with sec. 46, the Governor-General in Council "approved" of his
                dismissal, and the Government excluded him from the Department, and would
                not allow him to perform his duties.

                Held, that the officer was wrongfully dismissed and was entitled to recover
                damages from the Commonwealth for such wrongful dismissal.

                Sec. 78 of the *Commonwealth Public Service Act* 1902 is not an answer to a
                claim for damages for wrongful dismissal from the Commonwealth Public
                Service.

                There is no right to dismiss an officer at will or otherwise than in accord-
                ance with the procedure prescribed in that Act.

                The power of dismissal under sec. 46 of that Act must be exercised strictly,
                and suspension from duty of an officer on the charges for which he is subse-
                quently dismissed is a condition precedent to his rightful dismissal; but

although the power has been wrongfully exercised, if he has been in fact put out of the service, he is not entitled to a declaration that he remains in the service.   He has the same remedy as any other servant wrongfully dismissed.

In assessing damages for such a wrongful dismissal the Court will take into consideration the fact that the officer was liable to be forthwith dismissed rightfully under the process prescribed by the Act.

TRIAL OF ACTION.

The plaintiff, William Suckling Williamson, brought an action in the High Court against the Commonwealth claiming £3,000 damages for the wrongful and illegal dismissal of him from his office of Postmaster in the Public Service of the Commonwealth, and alternatively :—(a) A declaration that the plaintiff still was, or was entitled to be reinstated as, an officer in the Public Service of the Commonwealth ; (b) if necessary, an order for the reinstatement of the plaintiff in the Public Service of the Commonwealth ; (c) an order for payment to the plaintiff by the defendant of all arrears of salary at the date of such order for payment, or, alternatively, of a sum of money equivalent to the whole salary the plaintiff would have received, or would have been entitled to receive, up to the date of such order had he not been deprived of his salary ; (d) such other declaration or order as the Court might deem proper or necessary.

Prior to 1st March 1901 the plaintiff had been an officer in the Post and Telegraph Department of Victoria, and on that day, when that Department was transferred to the Commonwealth, the plaintiff was transferred to the Public Service of the Commonwealth, and thereafter remained an officer in the Department of the Postmaster-General.   At the beginning of the year 1907 the plaintiff was Postmaster at Dimboola, in Victoria, at a salary of £235 per annum.   On 29th January 1907 an inspector of the Department examined the Post Office books under the charge of the plaintiff and found a shortage of £50 6s. 7½d.   On 30th January 1907 a letter was written by F. L. Outtrim, Deputy Postmaster-General and Chief Officer of the Department, to the plaintiff as follows :—" With reference to the shortage of £50 6s. 7½d. discovered in your advances by the inspector who visited your office yesterday I have to inform you that, pending

H. C. of A. further action, you are suspended from duty under the provisions
   1907.   of sec. 46 of the *Commonwealth Public Service Act* 1902."

WILLIAMSON   On 20th February 1907 the plaintiff was at the Court of
    v.   Petty Sessions, Dimboola, charged on information with larceny
THE COM-
MONWEALTH. of £50 6s. 7½d. the property of His Majesty, and on the hearing
           of the information the plaintiff was discharged.

On 10th April 1907 the plaintiff was at the Court of Petty
Sessions, Dimboola, committed for trial on an information for
that on or about 29th January 1907 he being an accounting
officer within the meaning of the *Audit Acts* 1901 and 1906 did
improperly dispose of certain public moneys, to wit, £50 6s. 7½d.,
which sum had been received for or on account of the Commonwealth by the plaintiff. On this charge the plaintiff was on 26th
April 1907 tried at the Court of General Sessions at Ararat, and
was found not guilty.

On 2nd May 1907 a letter was written by W. B. Crosbie,
Acting Deputy Postmaster-General (F. L. Outtrim having ceased
to act as Chief Officer about 21st February 1907) to the plaintiff
as follows :—" Take notice that you are hereby charged under
sec. 46 of the *Commonwealth Public Service Act* 1902 with the
offences of

" (1) Improper conduct in that on 29th January 1907 you
failed to produce when called upon by Mr. H. S. Edgar, District
Inspector, the sum of £50 6s. 7½d., Government moneys held by
you as an officer of the Postmaster-General's Department.

" (2) Being negligent or careless in the discharge of your
duties.

" (3) Using intoxicating beverages to excess.

" You are required to forthwith state in writing whether you
admit or deny the truth of such charges and to give any written
explanation relative to such offences that you may consider
proper for my consideration."

The plaintiff having denied these charges, on 7th May 1907
he was further suspended from duty. A Board of Inquiry was
then appointed to consider the charges, and, having considered
them, the Board on 29th May 1907 found that all the charges
were proved.

On the same day, the Acting Deputy Postmaster-General

recommended that the plaintiff should be dismissed from the service. On 6th June 1907, R. Betheras, Deputy Public Service Commissioner, recommended the dismissal of the plaintiff, and that recommendation was on 22nd June approved by the Governor-General in Council, and his approval was notified in the *Gazette* of 29th June 1907.

The plaintiff then brought this action. The Commonwealth by its defence (*inter alia*) objected that the claim for salary could not be maintained inasmuch as it was not alleged that any greater sum than that received by the plaintiff by way of payment of salary had been appropriated by Parliament for the purpose, and they relied on sec. 78 of the *Commonwealth Public Service Act* 1902. They also, without admitting any liability, brought into Court the sum of £63 16s. 1d., and said that it was sufficient to satisfy any claim of the plaintiff for salary. The plaintiff accepted this sum in satisfaction of the claim in respect of which it was paid in.

W. Fink, for the plaintiff.

Duffy K.C. (with him *Lewers*), for the defendant. The proceedings taken against the plaintiff were perfectly regular. The word " forthwith " in sec. 46 (2) (b) of the *Commonwealth Public Service Act* 1902 means as soon as is reasonable under the circumstances : *Ex parte Lamb* ; *In re Southam* (1); *R.* v. *Justices of Worcester* (2). But sec. 66 (1) of the *Commonwealth Public Service Act* 1902, which provides that, if on indictment or presentment an officer is convicted of an offence he shall be deemed to have forfeited his office, contemplates that, where an officer is charged with an offence for which he should be tried by a judicial tribunal, further proceedings under sec. 46 should not be taken until that trial has been had. In such a case, therefore, the intention indicated by the word "forthwith" is satisfied if the proceedings which are to follow upon suspension are postponed until the result of the trial is known. That was the course taken here. The fact that the suspension was on a charge different from that subsequently made, and on which the plaintiff

(1) 19 Ch. D., 169.   (2) 7 Dowl. P.R., 789.

H. C. of A. was dismissed, is immaterial, for the suspension is not a condition
   1907.   precedent to the subsequent inquiry and the proceedings follow-
WILLIAMSON ing upon it : *Hardcastle on Statutory Law*, 3rd ed., p. 267.   If
    v.   the suspension is under any circumstances a condition precedent,
THE COM-
MONWEALTH. it is not so when the officer is already under suspension at the
           time the charge is made in respect of which he is subsequently
           dismissed. No claim for damages for wrongful dismissal can be
           maintained. The plaintiff was either rightly dismissed or else he is
           still in the service, and is entitled to a declaration to that effect.
           The power of dismissal is in the Governor-General : The Constitu-
           tion, sec. 67. And, even if he has acted illegally, no action will
           lie against the Commonwealth : *Mattingley* v. *The Queen* (1). If
           the plaintiff is entitled to damages, the Court in assessing them
           must take into account the fact that proceedings may at once be
           taken under sec. 46 to dismiss him : *French* v. *Brookes* (2). See
           also *McDade* v. *Hoskins* (3). So that the plaintiff has really
           suffered no damage. By virtue of sec. 78 of the *Commonwealth
           Public Service Act* 1902 no action for salary will lie here, for no
           money has been voted by Parliament for that purpose. *Bond* v.
           The Commonwealth (4) ; *Cousins* v. *The Commonwealth* (5) ;
           Miller v. *The King* (6) ; *Fisher* v. *The Queen* (7) ; *Bremner* v.
           Victorian Railways Commissioner (8).

           Proceedings under sec. 46 are quite independent of criminal
           proceedings, and there can be no question of election between them.

           Fink in reply. The word " forthwith " means " immediately,"
           the object being that there may be a speedy trial while the
           evidence is fresh. The defendant by prosecuting the plaintiff
           criminally made its election, and is not now entitled to pro-
           ceed against him under sec. 46 of the *Commonwealth Public
           Service Act* 1902. That section is a criminal code and must be
           followed strictly. In assessing damages it is to be assumed that
           the plaintiff is innocent of these charges, and that he will remain
           in the service until his death or until he reaches the age of
           retirement.

(1) 22 V.L.R., 80 ; 16 A.L.T., 171.   (6) 28 V.L.R., 530 ; 24 A.L.T., 150.
(2) 6 Bing., 354.   (7) 26 V.L.R., 781, at p. 796 ; 22
(3) 18 V.L.R., 417 ; 14 A.L.T., 56.   A.L.T., 217 ; (1903) A.C., 158.
(4) 1 C.L.R., 13.   (8) 27 V.L.R., 728 ; 23 A.L.T., 210.
(5) 3 C.L.R., 529.

[The following authorities also were cited : *In re Gavegan* (1) ; *Stockwell* v. *Rider* (2) ; *Grant* v. *Secretary of State for India* (3) ; *Smith's Master and Servant*, 5th ed. p. 157.]

Cur. adv. vult.

HIGGINS J. read the following judgment.

This is an action by a Postmaster for damages for wrongful dismissal by the defendant, or, in the alternative, for a declaration that he is still in the defendant's service, and payment of salary.

It seems to be beyond question that in the case of an officer under the *Commonwealth Public Service Act* 1902 there is no right to dismiss him at will, or otherwise than in accordance with the procedure prescribed in the Act : *Gould* v. *Stewart* (4). The procedure is set forth in sec. 46.

Under sec. 46, if an officer be charged with an offence, he may either be reprimanded or temporarily suspended. The person to suspend is either the Chief Officer, or some other officer authorized to suspend. "The *suspending* officer or the Chief Officer shall *forthwith* furnish the offending officer with a copy of *the charge on which he is suspended*, and require him to forthwith state in writing whether he admits or denies the truth of *such charge*, and to give any explanation," &c. (sec. 46 (2) (*b*)). Then the Chief Officer may either (*a*) remove *such suspension*, or (*b*) reprimand, and remove *the suspension*, or (*c*) fine the officer, or (*d*) *further suspend* him, and refer the charge to a Board of Inquiry ; and one of the Board must be a representative of the Division in the State in which "the *suspended officer* performed his duties." The Board must not include the person by whom the *officer was suspended*. If "such *suspended* officer" do not admit the truth of the charges, the Board inquires and reports (sec. 46 (3), (4)). If any of the charges is found to be proved, then, on the recommendation of the Chief Officer the Permanent Head may impose a penalty ; or the Public Service Commissioner may reduce the officer in rank ; or the Governor-General in Council may dismiss him from the service. In the event of dismissal, the officer shall not be entitled to any salary

(1) "Brisbane Courier" 1st Dec. 1905.
(2) 4 C.L.R., 469.
(3) 2 C.P.D., 445.
(4) (1896) A.C., 575.

or wages during the time of his *suspension*, unless the Governor-General otherwise order (sec. 46 (5)).

It will be noticed that the whole machinery is made to hinge on an initial suspension of the officer. There is no obligation to suspend; just as there is no obligation to adopt the other alternative—reprimand.   But unless there be a suspension, the rest of the machinery prescribed for removal is not applicable. The officer is to be given a copy of the charge " on which he is suspended "; and he is to state whether he admits or denies the truth of " such charge."   The Chief Officer, if he think that the offence has not been committed, may remove " such suspension." If there is to be a Board of Inquiry he may " further suspend " the officer.   The Board cannot inquire unless the " suspended officer " do not admit the truth of the charges.   In short, if there be no suspension for the charges, the officer cannot be furnished with a copy of the charges " on which he is suspended "; and unless he be furnished with such a copy, there is no power to appoint a Board of Inquiry ; and if there be no valid Board of Inquiry, the power of the Governor-General to dismiss does not arise.   It may be thought that the officer suffers no harm in not being suspended.   I am not sure that he is not prejudiced, especially if—as the parties assume—a suspended officer is entitled to pay during suspension, in the event of his not being dismissed.   But, prejudiced or not, suspension on the charges for which he is dismissed is made a condition precedent to dismissal. Powers of dismissal under this Act, like powers of expulsion under partnership and other agreements, must be exercised strictly as prescribed.

In the present case, the order of dismissal is based on the three charges contained in the letter of 2nd May 1907.   But the plaintiff was not suspended for these three charges.   He had been suspended on 30th January 1907 on a certain charge— one only ; and the suspension was wrongfully continued till 2nd of May.   I say wrongfully, because the section contemplates that the suspension shall be only temporary, and that a copy of the charge should be " forthwith " furnished to the officer ; and no such copy was furnished ; and the officer was not asked to admit or deny this first charge, but was prosecuted before the

Courts on two abortive informations. Perhaps the strict course for the Department to adopt was to remove the improper suspension, and then to suspend again on the three new charges. But, however that may be, I cannot see how I can say that the Governor-General's order, or "approval" of dismissal, was made in pursuance of the section, when I find that it was made on the basis of the charges other than the charge on which the plaintiff was suspended. In my opinion, the order of dismissal was not justified by the antecedent facts.

Looking at the facts more in detail, it appears that on 30th January 1907, after an inspector's visit to the plaintiff's post office at Dimboola, Mr. Outtrim, the Deputy Postmaster-General, and Chief Officer for Victoria, wrote to the plaintiff, a letter informing him, "with reference to the shortage of £50 6s. 7½d. discovered" in his "advances," that he is suspended from duty under sec. 46 of the Act. The plaintiff replied on 5th February, stating that he intended to make good the shortage, and asking to be allowed to hand it to the relieving officer; and further asking that the Board of Inquiry be held in Melbourne. But the Chief Officer, instead of following the procedure prescribed in sec. 46, on 11th February took out an information against the plaintiff, as a public servant, for stealing the said sum of money. This information was dismissed at Petty Sessions on 20th February. On 5th April 1907 another information was taken out against the plaintiff, under the Audit Acts, for improperly disposing of the said sum of public money. The plaintiff was committed for trial, and on 26th April was tried in General Sessions, and was found not guilty, and discharged. At this time, it will be noticed, the plaintiff was wrongfully under suspension. Even if the loose words of the recital in the letter of 30th January can be treated as stating a definite charge (which I doubt), the plaintiff was not asked to admit or deny or to explain, and the necessary consequential steps were not taken. Then the Department formulated three new charges against the plaintiff. On 2nd May the Acting Deputy Postmaster-General sent him notice that he was charged under sec. 46 with three offences :—
(1) improper conduct in failing to produce the said money to the inspector; (2) being negligent or careless in the discharge of his

H. C. of A.
1907.

WILLIAMSON
v.
THE COM-
MONWEALTH.

duties; and (3) using intoxicating beverages to excess. This notice also called on him, in pursuance of sec. 46, for admission or denial, and explanation. But the plaintiff was never suspended on these three charges; and what sec. 46 requires is that the officer shall be forthwith furnished with a copy of the charge *on which he is suspended*. The rest of the procedure seems to have been regular under sec. 46. On 29th May a so-called Board of Inquiry found against the plaintiff on all three charges. On 31st May the Acting Deputy Postmaster-General recommended that the plaintiff be dismissed from the service. On 6th June the Deputy Public Service Commissioner recommended to the Governor-General in Council that the plaintiff be dismissed; and on 22nd June—as appears by the *Gazette* of 29th June—the Governor-General " approved " of many departmental recommendations, including the dismissal of the plaintiff. On 5th July the plaintiff received from the Acting Deputy Postmaster-General a letter stating that the Governor-General in Council " has approved of your dismissal from the public service, and you have been dismissed accordingly."

It has been urged for the defendant that, if the dismissal was illegal, it was only a dismissal or pretended dismissal by the Governor-General in Council, and not by the defendant (see par. 2 statement of claim and defence). But this is, in my opinion, a curious misconception of the basis on which the Courts grant relief in cases of wrongful dismissal. I need not examine the logical puzzles which the position might suggest—a man dismissed by one who had no power to dismiss is not dismissed, &c. Nor is it necessary to enter into an elaborate examination of the legal and constitutional position of the Governor-General, and the responsibility of the Commonwealth for his acts. In my opinion, the plaintiff has proved the statements in par. 2, that the defendant—the Commonwealth—has refused and still refuses to allow him any longer to discharge his duties. If there were nothing else, the letter of the Acting Deputy Postmaster-General of 5th July shows that the Department adopted and acted on the Governor-General's order of dismissal, excluded the plaintiff from the Department, and prevented him from doing the work by which he could earn his salary. It is to be observed, also, that this objection to the action for wrongful dismissal was not even suggested in the similar Queensland case of *Stockwell* v. *Rider* before the Full High Court (1).

The defendant has, however, resisted this action on the ground, also, of sec. 78 of the Act. Sec. 78 provides that "nothing in this Act shall authorize the expenditure of any greater sum out of the Consolidated Revenue Fund by way of payment of any salary than is from time to time appropriated by the Parliament for the purpose." This section, however, in no way interferes with the power and the duties of the Court to declare rights and to pronounce judgments, leaving it to Parliament to find money for payment of the judgments against the Crown. It refers only to the process of drawing money out of the Consolidated Revenue Fund, forbidding (say) payment of £250 as salary when the sum of £200 only has been appropriated ; and it does not apply to the payment of damages at all. It was not meant to affect the substantive rights, created by the Act, of officers against the Crown (sec. 21). It was drawn in view of the *Audit Act* (cf. sec. 34 (4) &c.), and was intended to prevent any inference to the effect that the *Commonwealth Public Service Act* 1902 operated in any way of itself as an appropriation of a larger salary for any officer than that appearing in the *Appropriation Act*. Under the numerous Crown Remedies Acts, a successful petitioner got a certificate of the judgment ; and on receipt of the certificate the Governor in Council was authorized to pay the amount out of the Consolidated Revenue. If the Governor in Council refused, there was no legal remedy. The *Judiciary Act* 1903 (sec. 56) has allowed the Commonwealth to be sued instead of the King ; but there is no indication of any intention to make such a grave alteration of the legal position as is claimed on behalf of the defendant. A similar contention was raised for the Crown in *Fisher* v. *The Queen* (2) ; but it was rejected both by the Victorian Full Court, and by the Judicial Committee of the Privy Council. It is urged on me that the Full High Court has taken a different view of this section in *Cousins* v. *The Commonwealth* (3) but I do not think so. The Full Court there had to deal with the

(1) 4 C.L.R., 469.
(2) 26 V.L.R., 781 ; 22 A.L.T., 217 ;

(1903) A.C., 158, at p. 167.
(3) 3 C.L.R., 529, at p. 542.

H. C. of A.
1907.

Williamson
v.
The Com-
monwealth.
specific case pointed at in sec. 78—not a claim for damages, but
a claim for a salary greater than that appearing in the *Appropriation Act.* The subject does not appear to have been argued,
and the points of distinction were not discussed. But the Court
referred to the previous case of *Bond* v. *The Commonwealth* (1),
in which the long established practice is clearly stated; and it
showed no intention of overruling that case. At all events, sec.
78 has nothing to do with the claim for damages for wrongful
dismissal.

There were two points to which considerable attention was
given in the argument, but as to which I shall merely state my
conclusions. I cannot concur with Mr. *Fink* in his contention
that the defendant must be treated as having elected to prosecute
the plaintiff criminally, and thus to have precluded itself from
proceeding under sec. 46. I think also that Mr. Crosbie, the
Acting Deputy Postmaster-General, was competent to give to the
plaintiff the notices of May. Mr. *Duffy* seems to me to have
proved conclusively that Crosbie was duly appointed by the
Permanent Head to perform the duties of Chief Officer under
sec. 13 (3).

What, then, is the remedy ? My chief difficulties are owing to
the form of the pleadings, and the conduct of the case. The
parties ignore the fact that the suspension of 30th January has
no logical connection with the dismissal in June—that the
suspension from 30th January to May might be unauthorized,
even if the subsequent steps were proper (see defence, paragraphs
2, 3 and 4). There seem to have been at least two distinct
breaches of contract on the part of the defendant—one in the
suspension from work from 30th January to May, or perhaps
June; the other in the dismissal of June. Nor have the parties
noticed that under Order XVIII. of the High Court Rules any
payment of money into Court must be in respect of " a cause of
action "; that is to say, in respect of the entire set of facts that
give rise to an enforceable claim—" every fact which it would be
necessary for the plaintiff to prove, if traversed, in order to support his right to the judgment of the Court " : *Read* v. *Brown* (2).
But putting aside for the present the difficulty arising from the

(1) 1 C.L.R., 13.   (2) 22 Q.B.D., 128, at p. 131, *per Esher* M.R.

payment into Court, I think that I may fairly deal with the case
on the substantial merits—treating the case, as the parties have
treated it, as if the plaintiff were suspended on 30th January, as
the first step towards the dismissal which took place in June.
This course will involve no difference in the result. A suspension
under the Act seems to be a conditional or provisional dismissal;
if a dismissal follow, the officer is not entitled to pay during the
time of suspension (sec. 46 (5)).

Now, under the ordinary law, a servant dismissed has an option
between two remedies.   He cannot have both remedies; he must
elect between them.   One remedy is on the contract for the
wrongful dismissal; the other remedy is to treat the contract as
rescinded, and to sue for his actual service: *Goodman* v. *Pocock*
(1). There was for some time an impression that a servant could
wait till the end of his term, doing nothing, but remaining ready
and willing to work; and then sue for his wages for the balance
of the term.   This view seemed to rest on the theory of a status
in the servant, such as could not be affected by a wrongful act;
but the view has long since been exploded : 2 Sm. L.C., 11th ed.,
p. 48; *Goodman* v. *Pocock* (2).   The truth is, a servant cannot
claim wages unless he perform the condition precedent of doing
the work. If he have been prevented from doing the work, he has
an action for damages for breach of the contract; or he may accept
the position, rescind the contract which the master refuses to
perform, and sue for the work actually done. In the present case
the plaintiff claims, alternatively, for damages for wrongful dismissal. or for salary up to the order for payment thereof; and, in
the event of the latter order, he asks for a declaration that he
still is, or is entitled to be reinstated as, an officer in the service,
and for an order for reinstatement.   I know of no authority or
ground for any such order or declaration; and I certainly shall
not declare the plaintiff to be still in the Government service
when, according to his own allegation as well as my finding, he
has been put out of the service, and remains out.

As for the alternative remedy, damages for wrongful dismissal,
a servant dismissed would be entitled to recover the amount of

(1) 15 Q.B., 576, at p. 583, *per*   (2) 15 Q.B., 576, at pp. 581, 583,
Erle J.   *per Patteson* and *Erle* JJ.

H. C. of A.
1907.

WILLIAMSON
v.
THE COM-
MONWEALTH.

the loss which he has sustained by the breach of contract; and in assessing the damages it would be proper, and necessary, to take into account the wages attributable to the broken period, the time of actual service since last pay time till dismissal: *Goodman* v. *Pocock* (1). In this case, under the circumstances, I propose to take into account in assessing damages the amount of the plaintiff's salary until dismissal. I regard him as being unable, until dismissal, to get other employment. The plaintiff's case for damages was based on the theory that if he had not been dismissed he would have remained in the service till the age of 60, and would get a pension afterwards. But I have to take into account, not only the risk of death, and the risk of removal, but the probability—the extreme probability—of the plaintiff speedily losing his office by legal means, and even for the offences already charged against him (see *French* v. *Brookes* (2); *Maw* v. *Jones* (3).) If the defendant, instead of dismissing the plaintiff in June or July, had chosen to start anew, to suspend him, and to take proper proceedings for dismissal, the plaintiff's tenure of office would have been very short indeed; and the wages would cease at the suspension. In my opinion, such fresh proceedings would have been taken; and if the plaintiff were still in the service, they would now be taken; and a fresh Board of Inquiry would come to the same conclusions of fact as the former Board. As regards the possible earnings of the plaintiff from other sources, having seen him, and heard him, and ascertained his age and qualifications, I think that £78 per annum is as much as he could reasonably expect to earn, year in year out. On the whole, I assess the damages at £100.

But then I have to deal with the payment into Court. The defendant, without admitting any liability, brought into Court £63 16s. 1d., and said that this sum was "sufficient to satisfy any claim of the plaintiff for salary." The particulars showed this sum to be meant for the salary from 31st January to 7th May (the date of sending the three charges to a Board of Inquiry). The plaintiff, by his reply, accepted this sum "in satisfaction of his claim for salary." Now, the rule says that the money must be accepted "in satisfaction of the *cause of action*" (rule 6); and

(1) 15 Q.B., 576.   (2) 6 Bing., 354.   (3) 25 Q.B.D., 107.

in such a case the plaintiff cannot proceed with his action except
as to costs : *In re Earl of Stamford* ; *Savage* v. *Payne* (1). The
defendant's repudiation or breach of the contract is an essential part
of the cause of action, whichever remedy be pursued. The parties
treat the case as one breach, involving one of two remedies. But,
even if the action could proceed, notwithstanding the acceptance of
the money, I should have thought that the acceptance of the payment showed an election on the part of the plaintiff to treat the
contract as rescinded, and to sue for any past wages for services
rendered, and not to sue for damages. I should have thought
that the plaintiff could claim no more salary than that paid in,
could not claim any damages attributable to salary. But Mr.
Duffy, for the defendant, has admitted that notwithstanding
the withdrawal from Court of £63 16s. 1d., the plaintiff, if he has
been wrongfully dismissed, is entitled to have damages assessed
on the basis that he would get salary as an officer as from 7th May
1907. I shall not insist on the rigour of the pleadings where
neither party wishes me to do so. Both parties have acted on
the understanding that the acceptance of the money did not conclude the plaintiff's rights ; and I think that under the circumstances I shall best do justice by dealing with the merits of the
case unfettered, with regard to the money in Court, by the form
of the proceedings. Having found the plaintiff's loss, apart
from the money in Court, to be £100, I deduct the money
already taken out by the plaintiff, £63 16s. 1d. ; and I find his
net loss, the amount for which I shall give judgment, to be
£36 3s. 11d.

Judgment for the plaintiff for £36 3s. 11d.

Solicitor, for plaintiff, *Peers*.

Solicitor, for defendant, *Powers*, Commonwealth Crown
Solicitor.

                                                    B. L.

(1) 53 L.T., 512.

[HIGH COURT OF AUSTRALIA.]

LUCAS   .   .   .   .   APPELLANT;
DEFENDANT,

AND

GRAHAM .   .   .   .   RESPONDENT.
INFORMANT,

ON APPEAL FROM THE SUPREME COURT OF
VICTORIA.

H. C. OF A. *Licensing Act* 1906 (*Vict.*) (*No.* 2068), *secs.* 31, 32—*Licensing Act* 1890 (*Vict.*)
1907.   (*No.* 1111), *secs.* 5, 12—" *Australian* " *wine licence*—·" *Colonial* " *wine licence*—
            Rights and obligations of licensee—Permitting liquor other than wine &c. to be
MELBOURNE,   *brought on premises—Liquor purchased for customer.*
Sept. 25.
                 Sec. 32 (1) of the *Licensing Act* 1906 (Vict.) is not limited to liquor (other
Griffith C.J., than wines, &c.), brought on the licensed premises for the purpose of sale by
  Barton,   the licensee, or which is the property of the licensee.
  O'Connor,
  Isaacs and   The effect of sec. 31 (1) of the *Licensing Act* 1906 is to change the name of a
  Higgins JJ. colonial wine licence to an Australian wine licence. Sec. 32 imposes the same
               restrictions upon the holders of all such licences, whether they were originally
               granted as colonial wine licences or as Australian wine licences.

                 Held, therefore, that a person who, before the *Licensing Act* 1906 came
               into force, obtained pursuant to the *Licensing Act* 1890 a renewal of his
               colonial wine licence, and who in 1907 permitted stout bought on behalf of a
               customer to be brought on his licensed premises, was properly convicted of an
               offence under sec. 32 (1) of the *Licensing Act* 1906, which forbids the bringing
               of liquor other than Australian wine on premises for which an Australian wine
               licence is in force.

                 Judgment of Supreme Court (*Graham v. Lucas*, (1907) V.L.R., 478 ; 29
               A.L.T., 10), affirmed.

APPEAL from the Supreme Court of Victoria.

On 28th March 1907, at the Court of Petty Sessions at
Melbourne, an information was heard, whereby Thomas Graham,

inspector of the Latrobe Licensing District, charged Anthony Lucas that he, on 19th January 1907, then being the holder of an Australian wine licence within the meaning of the Licensing Acts, and then holding a licence for the licensed premises situate at 240 and 242 Collins Street, Melbourne, did permit certain liquor, to wit, stout, to be brought on the said licensed premises contrary to the said Acts.

It appeared from the evidence that, on 3rd December 1906, the defendant, who was the proprietor of a café, carrying on business in the above-mentioned premises, was granted a certificate of renewal of his colonial wine licence for the ensuing year by the Licensing Court sitting at Melbourne; and that, on 19th January 1907, one of his waiters went out from those premises and purchased at a neighbouring hotel on behalf of a customer, who had provided the money for the purpose, some stout to be consumed, as it was consumed, by the customer at the café with a meal supplied by Lucas. It was contended for the defence that sec. 32 (1) of the *Licensing Act* 1906 did not apply as Lucas was the holder of a colonial wine licence. The Court of Petty Sessions having dismissed the information, an order *nisi* to review their decision was obtained on the grounds that the holder of a colonial wine licence for the year 1907 was within the provisions of sec. 32 of the *Licensing Act* 1906, and that on the evidence the justices ought to have convicted the defendant.

On the return of the order *nisi*, the Full Court made the order absolute: *Graham* v. *Lucas* (1).

The defendant by special leave now appealed to the High Court.

On the appeal to the High Court the question was raised whether, where an information for an offence is dismissed by a Court of Petty Sessions, the informant is a "person who feels aggrieved" within the meaning of sec. 141 of the *Justices Act* 1890 so as to be entitled to appeal to the Supreme Court, but, as this question was not dealt with by the High Court, the arguments upon it are not reported.

Starke, for the appellant. In sec. 32 (1) of the *Licensing Act*

(1) (1907) V.L.R., 478; 29 A.L.T., 10.

1906 the prohibition against keeping, bringing or permitting to be brought liquor on the premises specified should be construed as limited to liquor kept or brought on the premises for the purpose of sale by the licensee. That is shown by sec. 32 (2), which provides that the finding of liquor other than wine &c. is to be *primâ facie* evidence of an unlawful sale of liquor. There was no evidence of a sale by the licensee: *Graves* v. *Panam* (1). See however *Graham* v. *Matoorekos* (2). The provisions of sec. 32 (1) do not apply to the holder of a colonial wine licence for the year 1907, but only apply to Australian wine licences, properly so called, and granted after the passing of the Act. See also secs. 34, 78 (2). The renewal of the appellant's licence was granted on 3rd December 1906, and the *Licensing Act* 1906 was not assented to until 28th December 1906. That Act did not affect any change in licences granted before it came into operation, nor did sec. 31 alter the name of those licences. The repeal of the section under which the licence was granted to the appellant, and its re-enactment with the words " Australian wine licence " substituted for " colonial wine licence," would not affect the appellant's rights which he had gained under the repealed section : *Acts Interpretation Act* 1890, sec. 27. Although no right which was conferred upon the holder of a colonial wine licence by his licence may be taken away by sec. 32 (1) of the *Licensing Act* 1906, yet a disability is imposed upon the holder of an Australian wine licence, and the section should not be interpreted to impose that disability on a person who is not in truth the holder of an Australian wine licence.

Duffy K.C. (with him *Meagher*), for the respondent, was not called upon.

GRIFFITH C.J. This case was taken out of its turn in order to decide a point which was said to be one of urgency. The question is raised upon the construction of secs. 31 and 32 of the *Licensing Act* 1906, which was assented to on 28th December 1906. Sec. 31 provides that :—" In the Licensing Acts for the words ' a colonial '

(1) (1905) V.L.R., 297 ; 26 A.L.T., 232.
(2) (1907) V.L.R., 270 ; 28 A.L.T., 173.

or the word 'colonial' wherever occurring before the words 'wine licence' or 'wine licences' there shall be substituted the words 'an Australian' or the word 'Australian' as the context may require." A wine licence was a well known form of licence under the old Licensing Acts in which they were called "colonial wine licences." That section provides that for the future they are to be called "Australian wine licences." Sec. 32 (1) provides that : —" The holder of an Australian wine licence shall not keep nor bring or permit to be brought any liquor other than wine cider or perry the produce of fruit grown in any Australian State on the premises specified in such licence."

The first point taken is that sec. 32 (1) only applies to liquor brought on to the premises for the purpose of sale by the licensee, or to liquor the property of the licensee. The words are perfectly general, and that point therefore fails.

The next point made is that the appellant had obtained last year, and before this Act was assented to, a colonial wine licence which was still in force, and that when he obtained that licence there was no law prohibiting the holder of a colonial wine licence from bringing liquor upon his premises. Consequently, it is argued, when the new Act came into force, it could not deprive him of the right which he had to bring liquor on his premises. But that was not a right which he acquired by virtue of the *Licensing Act* 1890 ; it was a right enjoyed by everybody else in the community. The Supreme Court thought there was nothing in the objection. *àBeckett* J. put the case thus (1) :—" It is clear, therefore, that where the old Act spoke of 'a colonial wine licence,' it is now to be read as speaking of 'an Australian wine licence.' The new Act contains no provision keeping alive the rights conferred by the colonial wine licence. They are at an end unless the licensee can exercise them by reason of his licence being treated as equivalent to an Australian wine licence. The document which he holds confers no rights by itself independently of the Act under which it issued. When the existing law ceases to give any rights to the holder of a colonial wine licence, the licence is a nullity unless it can operate as an Australian wine licence, to the holder

(1) (1907) V. L. R., 478, at p. 479 ; 29 A. L. R., 10, at p. 11.

H. C. of A.
1907.

Lucas
v.
Graham.

Griffith C.J.

of which the existing law gives the rights which the holder of a colonial wine licence previously possessed, qualified by the conditions added by the amending Act. It cannot have been the intention of the amending Act to destroy these rights. I think that by force of sec. 31, they are preserved by converting that which was theretofore called a colonial wine licence into a licence to be called an Australian wine licence. The holder cannot claim the rights without incurring the obligations which this change involved, or be considered an Australian wine licensee within the meaning of some section of the existing law, and not of others." I entirely adopt, if I may venture to say so, that reasoning of the learned Judge. It appears to me that all that section does is to change the name of the licence, leaving the substance exactly the same as before, and then sec. 32 goes on to impose certain restrictions upon the holder of such a licence. On the merits, therefore, I am of opinion that the judgment appealed from was right. The consideration of the other point, which is not urgent, will stand over.

BARTON J. I concur with the opinion of the Full Court on the questions raised as to secs. 31 and 32 of the *Licensing Act* 1906, and think it is the only conclusion they could reasonably have come to. The question as to the meaning of sec. 141 of the *Justices Act* 1890 is of the highest importance, and deserves further argument.

O'CONNOR J. I am of the same opinion, and have nothing to add.

ISAACS J. I concur. I would like to say that on the first point, as to whether it is necessary that the liquor should be brought on to the premises for the purpose of sale, the matter has been thoroughly and perfectly dealt with by *Madden* C.J. in *Graham* v. *Matookeros* (1). I think there is nothing to be added to His Honor's reasoning on that subject.

With regard to the other point, I agree that the reasons of *à Beckett* J. should govern the matter, and I should like to add

(1) (1907) V.L.R., 274 ; 28 A.L.T., 173.

that what *Hood* J. said was correct, viz., that the right to bring liquor on to his premises was not a right conferred on the licensee by the licence, but was a right which he possessed in common with all other persons, and therefore no statutory right was taken away from the licensee by upholding the conviction.

HIGGINS J. I concur.

Solicitor, for appellant, *Raynes W. S. Dickson*, Melbourne.

Solicitor, for respondent, *Guinness*, Crown Solicitor for Victoria.

B. L.

H. C. OF A.
1907.

LUCAS
v.
GRAHAM.

Isaacs J.

[HIGH COURT OF AUSTRALIA.]

IN RE DALEY.

ON APPEAL FROM THE SUPREME COURT OF NEW SOUTH WALES.

Appeals to High Court—Suspension of solicitor by Supreme Court for professional misconduct—Discretion of Supreme Court as to punishment of its officers—Special leave.

A solicitor of the Supreme Court of New South Wales was suspended from practice by that Court for having by a false representation induced a barrister to accept a brief which otherwise he might not have accepted.

The High Court, being of opinion that the Supreme Court clearly had jurisdiction to deal with one of its officers who had been guilty of such misconduct as was alleged, and seeing no reason to differ from them in the conclusion to which they had come on the facts, refused to grant special leave to appeal from their decision.

The nature of the punishment in cases of professional misconduct on the part of an attorney is entirely within the discretion of the Supreme Court.

In re Coleman, 2 C.L.R., 834, followed.

Special leave to appeal from the decision of the Supreme Court: *In re Daley*, (1907) 7 S.R. (N.S.W.), 561, refused.

H. C. OF A.
1907.

SYDNEY,
Aug. 13.

Barton,
Isaacs and
Higgins JJ.

H. C. of A. APPLICATION for special leave to appeal from a decision of the
1907.   Supreme Court of New South Wales.

In re Daley.   The applicant, a solicitor practising in Sydney, was called upon
by the Supreme Court to show cause why he should not be
struck off the rolls, or otherwise punished, for professional misconduct. The misconduct alleged was that, for the purpose of
inducing a barrister to accept a brief in a case to be tried in a
Circuit Court, he falsely represented that, although he had
not the money in hand at the time to pay the counsel's fees,
his client had certain produce for sale in the hands of a
wool selling firm in Sydney, and had given him an order to
collect the proceeds of the sale, and that the fees would be paid
out of those proceeds. Counsel, relying upon these representations, accepted the brief and did the work, but the fees were not
paid. The evidence before the Supreme Court was conflicting,
but they came to the conclusion that the charge had been made
out, and suspended the solicitor from practice for a period of
eighteen months: *In re Daley* (1).

The present application was for special leave to appeal from
that decision.

Delohery, for the applicant. The Supreme Court came to a
wrong conclusion as to the facts which were in dispute, and the
inference which they drew from the admitted facts cannot be
supported. There was no intent to defraud. This does not come
within the class of cases in which the disciplinary power of the
Court should be exercised.

[BARTON J.—Surely the Court was justified in punishing a
solicitor for gross misrepresentation to the prejudice of a member
of the other branch of the profession.

ISAACS J.—The Court disbelieved the applicant's version of
the facts. You must satisfy us that they were wrong.]

Assuming that the Court was right in its conclusion, it was
the duty of counsel to get his fees before accepting the brief.
There is no duty on a solicitor's part to pay the fees himself, and
there can be no " inducement," whatever he may say. There is

(1) (1907) 7 S.R. (N.S.W.), 561.

no capacity to contract. [He referred to *Kennedy* v. *Brown* (1); *Re Neville*; *Ex parte Pike* (2); *Angell* v *Oodeen* (3).]

[ISAACS J. referred to *Guilford* v. *Sims* (4).

HIGGINS J. referred to *In re Hall* (5).]

There was nothing in the nature of professional misconduct: *Re Four Solicitors* (6); *In re Stewart* (7).

The judgment of the Court was delivered by

BARTON J.   This appeal is on a matter affecting the professional conduct of one of the officers of the Supreme Court. It is not to be looked at with reference to the personal or legal relations between the counsel concerned and the solicitor whose conduct is called in question. If there is jurisdiction in the Supreme Court to deal with one of its officers in the circumstances here alleged, and believed by that Court to have existed, then it seems to us to be a case in which we certainly ought not to interfere.

A representation has been made by this solicitor to a barrister for the purpose and with the result of inducing him to accept a brief which otherwise he might not have accepted. That representation is believed by the Supreme Court—and we cordially agree with them in that respect—to have been false. As Mr. Daley has urged that there is nothing fraudulent in the transaction, we are bound to say that, in our opinion, the conduct of Mr. Daley was as nearly fraudulent in its essence as one can well conceive, whether it is conduct that is subject to a certain class of proceeding or not.

We have no doubt of the jurisdiction of the Supreme Court to deal with its officers when their conduct, considered in a purely professional aspect, is misconduct tending to uproot the confidence which should exist between solicitor and client.

In the case of *In re Coleman* (8) we used these expressions:—

" That Court " (that is the Supreme Court) " was of opinion that the applicant had been guilty of professional misconduct which merited punishment, and we see no reason to differ from them." We apply the same statement to this case.

(1) 13 C.B.N.S., 677.	(5) 2 Jur. N.S., 1076.
(2) 17 N.S.W. L.R. (B. & P.), 24.	(6) 7 T.L.R., 672.
(3) 29 L.J.C.P., 227	(7) L.R. 2 P.C., 88.
(4) 13 C.B., 370.	(8) 2 C.L.R., 834, at p. 836.

H. C. of A.   "That being so, it is difficult to see how we can properly inter-
   1907.   fere with the exercise of the Court's discretion in inflicting
In re Daley. punishment upon one of its own officers." We adhere to that
              opinion.

              "In such cases the nature of the punishment is a matter
              entirely within the discretion of the Supreme Court itself."

              Holding that opinion also, it seems to us that this is a case
              within the lines which the Court there laid down, and therefore
              that we ought not to grant special leave to interfere with the
              decision of the Supreme Court in any matter of such a character.

                                            Special leave refused.

Solicitors, for applicant, *Sullivan Bros.*

                                            C. A. W.

[HIGH COURT OF AUSTRALIA.]

MARGARET WALSH   .   .   .   .   .   APPELLANT;
    DEFENDANT,

                              AND

THOMAS DOHERTY   .   .   .   .   .   RESPONDENT.
    COMPLAINANT,

ON APPEAL FROM THE SUPREME COURT OF
QUEENSLAND.

H. C. of A.   *Notice of prosecution—" Institution of proceedings "—Notice given after lodging of*
   1907.   *complaint—Licensing Act* 1885 *(Qd.),* (49 *Vict. No.* 18), *sec.* 75 (2)*—Liquor*
              Act 1886 *(Qd.),* (50 *Vict. No.* 30), *sec.* 25*—Justices Act* 1886 *(Qd.),* (50 *Vict.*
BRISBANE,   *No.* 17), *secs.* 42, 52.
  Oct. 8.
                  In a prosecution under the Queensland *Liquor Act* 1886 for any of the
Griffith C.J., offences named in sec. 25 of that Act, the provisions of that section—that
Barton and   notice in writing of the intended prosecution shall be given to the person
Isaacs JJ.   intended to be prosecuted, specifying the section of the Act for breach of
              which the prosecution is intended to be instituted—are not satisfied by the

H. C. of A.
1907.

Walsh
v.
Doherty.

service of a notice of prosecution after the information for the offence in question had already been laid. A prosecution has been "instituted" as soon as the complaint is lodged and the summons issued.

Decision of the Full Court: (*Doherty v. Walsh*; *Ex parte Walsh*, 1907 St. R. Qd., 180), reversed.

APPEAL by special leave from a decision of the Supreme Court of Queensland.

The appellant, licensee of an hotel at Roma, was prosecuted by the respondent, the licensing inspector, for an offence against sec. 75 (2) of the *Licensing Act* (Qd.), (49 Vict. No. 18), in keeping her licensed premises open for the sale of liquor on a Sunday, and was convicted and fined. She appealed from the conviction to the Supreme Court on the ground that by sec. 25 of the *Liquor Act* 1886 (Qd.), (50 Vict. No. 30), no licensee should be convicted of any offence against sec. 75 of the *Licensing Act*, "unless within fourteen days after the day on which the offence is alleged to have been committed notice in writing of the intended prosecution is given to the person intended to be prosecuted, specifying the section of the Act for breach of which the prosecution is intended to be instituted;" whereas in fact the constable who lodged the complaint had not served such notice upon the appellant until after he had taken out a summons on the complaint, which he served upon her immediately after delivery of the notice. An order *nisi* was granted by *Real* J. to quash the conviction, but the Full Court (*Cooper* C.J. and *Power* J., *diss. Real* J.) discharged the rule, considering that the word "prosecution" was used in sec. 25 in its popular meaning, so as to denote merely the proceedings in the Police Court on the day of hearing before the magistrate, and not in the legal sense of the initiation of proceedings in the prosecution by the formal lodging of a complaint. From this decision (1) an appeal was brought to the High Court by special leave.

Power, for the appellant. The meaning of sec. 25 is that the notice of the intended institution of proceedings must be served on the defendant before the institution of the proceedings, which are instituted as soon as the complaint is lodged and a summons

(1) 1907 St. R. Qd., 180.

H. C. of A.   issued : *Thompson* v. *Harvey* (1); *Clarke* v. *Bradlaugh* (2);
1907.   *Thorpe* v. *Priestnall* (3); *Beardsley* v. *Giddings* (4); *Brooks* v.
WALSH   *Bagshaw* (5); *R.* v. *Jack* (6); *Justices Act* 1886 (Qd.). (50 Vict.
v.   No. 17), secs. 42, 52.
DOHERTY.

Henchman, for the respondent. Sec. 25 is only intended to
secure that the defendant shall have notice within fourteen days
of the alleged offence that a prosecution is being commenced, in
order that the evidence available for the defence may be preserved.
The facts in this case amply satisfy the intention of this section,
because the notice and the summons was served the very next
day after the offence, and the prosecution took place, with several
adjournments, at from ten to twenty-five days from the service of
the notice. Under these circumstances the present objection is a
pure technicality without any merits. This requirement of notice
before criminal proceedings was peculiar to this Act, until the
Motor Car Act 1903 (Eng.), (3 Edw. VII. c. 36), sec. 9 (2); and it
differs from the requirement of notice in some civil actions. In
the latter the defendant has to be given a certain time by notice
before the action in which to consider whether he will admit or
contest the claim, whereas in criminal cases no time at all need be
allowed before the institution of proceedings. Hence it is clear
that the notice is not a condition precedent to the lodging of the
complaint. Also it is immaterial that the notice should be literally of an "intended" prosecution, if it is only a matter of five
minutes between the time when the complaint was actually
lodged and the time when it could properly have been lodged ;
de minimis non curat lex. The clearest and most reasonable
meaning of sec. 25 is that the licensee must be given a notice
of the prosecution within fourteen days of the offence ; the
remaining words of the section are only ancillary, or descriptive
of the notice ; they cannot be treated as conditions precedent:
Hardcastle on Statutory Law, 3rd ed., 104. *Thorpe* v. *Priestnall*
(3), and that line of cases are distinguishable ; they turned upon
the words " no prosecution shall be instituted ; " whereas sec. 25
enacts that " no licensee shall be convicted."

(1) 4 H. & N., 254 ; 28 L.J.M.C., 163.   (4) (1904) 1 K.B., 847.
(2) 8 Q.B.D., 63.   (5) (1904) 2 K.B., 798.
(3) (1897) 1 Q.B., 159.   (6) 6 Q.L.J., 60.

No costs should be given against the respondent; this is a quasi-criminal matter in which the Crown appears in the public interest; and the appellant can only succeed, if at all, on a technical point.

Power in reply. Costs should only be refused for a technicality if it was an after-thought. But the appellant took the objection as soon as the evidence for the prosecution closed, and has relied throughout upon this point. When the Crown saw that the conviction was bad, it should have withdrawn the proceedings and had the conviction quashed under the powers given by sec. 215 of the *Justices Act* 1886. The Crown is answerable for costs if it supports the mistakes of others: *R.* v. *Whelan* (1), even though the successful appellant has been guilty of reprehensible conduct: *Fraser* v. *Graham* ; *Ex parte Graham* (2).

GRIFFITH C.J. The 25th section of the *Liquor Act* 1886 enacts that no licensee shall be convicted of any offence against certain provisions of the *Licensing Act* 1885, and of the *Liquor Act* 1886, " unless within fourteen days after the day on which the offence is alleged to have been committed notice in writing of the intended prosecution is given to the person intended to be prosecuted, specifying the section of the Act for breach of which the prosecution is intended to be instituted." Three times that section uses words importing futurity. It speaks of notice of an intended prosecution ; of a person intended to be prosecuted ; and of a prosecution intended to be instituted. It follows that the notice must be given before the prosecution is instituted. Now a prosecution is instituted by the laying of the complaint. In the present case no notice had been given when this complaint was laid, so that the case falls within the precise language of the Statute. There is no ambiguity, and there is no context to show that the plain words ought to receive some other construction. It follows, therefore, that the point taken by the appellant was a good one, and that the information ought to have been dismissed. I think the appeal should be allowed.

(1) 6 Q.L.J., 165.   (2) 1905 St. R. Qd., 137.

Barton J.   I agree; I think the case should have been dismissed.

Isaacs J.   I agree, and I would like only to add that in this case, whichever way you look at it, the prosecution must fail because the notice that was given was a notice that " an information will be laid against you."   That was attempted to be proved in aid, not of an information afterwards laid, but of an information then already laid.   The two things do not cohere; so, whatever interpretation is given to the section, there was absolutely no previous notice given at any time of the information that had been laid, and there was no summons afterwards issued in pursuance of the notice that was given.

Griffith C.J.   With regard to costs, we do not see any satisfactory reason for departing from the ordinary rule that the loser pays.

> *Appeal allowed; order appealed from discharged; order to quash made absolute with costs; respondent to pay the costs of the appeal.*

Solicitors, for appellant, *Chambers & Macnab.*

Solicitors, for respondent, *Hellicar* (Crown Solicitor).

N. G. P.

[HIGH COURT OF AUSTRALIA.]

JOSEPH VARDON   .   .   .   .   .   PETITIONER;

AND

JAMES VINCENT O'LOGHLIN .   .   .   RESPONDENT.

ON A REFERENCE BY THE SENATE OF THE COMMONWEALTH.

The Constitution (63 & 64 *Vict.* c. 12), *secs.* 13, 15, 47—*Election of senators—Void*   H. C. OF A.
as to return of one senator—Vacancy in Senate—Election of senator by State   1907.
Parliament—Validity of election disputed—Reference to High Court—Disputed   ⌇
Elections and Qualifications Act 1907 (*No.* 10 *of* 1907), *sec.* 2.   SYDNEY,

The Court of Disputed Returns having declared a periodical election of   Dec. 17, 18,
senators for the State of South Australia absolutely void as to the return of one   20.
senator, the Houses of Parliament of the State, sitting together, and assuming   ⎯⎯⎯
to act under sec. 15 of the Constitution, chose a senator to fill the vacancy.   Griffith C.J.,
          Barton,
On a petition to the Senate, removed into the High Court as the Court of   Isaacs and
Disputed Returns under sec. 2 of the *Disputed Elections and Qualifications*   Higgins JJ.
Act 1907 :

Held, that the vacancy existing after the declaration by the Court of
Disputed Returns was not a vacancy arising in the place of a senator before
the expiration of his term of office within the meaning of sec. 15 of the
Constitution, and, therefore, the choice or election of a senator by the State
Parliament was null and void.

PETITION removed from the Senate into the Court under sec. 2 of
the *Disputed Elections and Qualifications Act* 1907.

Joseph Vardon, the petitioner, was returned at the election of
1906 as one of the three senators elected to represent the State of
South Australia, but on a petition presented to the Court of
Disputed Returns the election of senators for that State was
declared absolutely void in respect of his return. Thereupon the
Houses of Parliament of the State, sitting together and assuming

to act under the provisions of sec. 15 of the Constitution, chose James Vincent O'Loghlin, the respondent, to hold the place then vacant in the representation of the State in the Senate.

The petitioner then presented this petition to the Senate, asking that the choice or election by the State Houses of Parliament of the respondent to hold the place of senator for the State might be declared null and void, that it be declared that the respondent had not been duly chosen or elected as a senator, or to hold the place of a senator, and had no right or title to sit vote, or act as a senator, and that the seat of one senator for the State be declared vacant, with a prayer for costs against the respondent.

The matter was then referred to the Court under the Act No. 10 of 1907.

The facts having been fully stated in the report of the case of *The King v. The Governor of the State of South Australia* (1), it is not necessary to make further reference to them here.

Piper, for the petitioner. Sec. 15 of the Constitution has no application to the facts of this case. From the date of the declaration by the Court of Disputed Returns that Vardon's election was absolutely void, the position is the same as if he never had been elected. Any other construction would be contrary to the spirit of the Constitution, which requires that, except where expressly otherwise provided, the senators shall be chosen by popular election.

[GRIFFITH C.J.—That appears to be the dominant principle. If so it should not be defeated by a mere accident or mistake.]

Sec. 7 states the guiding principle, and there is nothing in the Constitution which modifies its effect to the extent of providing that senators should not be so chosen whenever a breach of duty by some electoral officer or some act of corruption on the part of a candidate invalidates the election. The words of sec. 15, naturally construed, are apt to meet the contingencies contemplated in secs. 19, 20 and 45. To make the words of sec. 15 fit the present case involves straining them to a meaning quite different from that in which they fit the sections mentioned. They all con-

(1) 4 C. L. R., 1497.

template the case of a senator with title ceasing to hold the office, H. C. of A.
whereas in the present case there was never any title. It is not 1907.
a casual vacancy occurring before the expiration of a senator's VARDON
term of office, to be temporarily filled as provided by sec. 15, but v.
a normal vacancy occurring by rotation, which has not yet been O'LOGHLIN.
filled. This construction is in accordance with the common law of
elections as established by parliamentary practice. Ouster of a
member for want of title is not merely effective as causing a cesser
of possession by the member ousted, but as evidence that the
member was never in the office. *Haynes on Election of Senators*,
p. 60, cited in *Commonwealth Hansard*, 16th Oct. 1907, p. 4721.]

[GRIFFITH C.J.—The American authorities on the point, though
not exactly parallel, suggest that, where a primary or a secondary
mode of election is provided, the Courts have refused to allow
the second or alternative method to be adopted until the first has
been tried and has failed.

HIGGINS J. referred to *May, Law and Practice of Parliament*,
3rd ed., p. 453.]

To transfer the rights of the people to the Parliament would
open the door to grave abuses. It might at times be in the
interests of some local party, temporarily predominant, to contrive
that an election should be invalidated.

Rolin, for the respondent. No doubt the primary mode of
election of senators under the Constitution is by the people of
the State, but sec. 15 plainly provides other methods, which to
some extent deprive the people of their privilege, and the question
is whether the present is a case coming within that section. By
adopting the procedure under sec. 15 the direct popular choice is
not destroyed, it is merely postponed. For the purpose of
expedition, convenience, or economy the Constitution has provided that the people shall choose a senator through their representatives in Parliament. The section is really for the benefit of
the people, to prevent their being disfranchised through accident
or the fault of others.

[ISAACS J.—The last part of the section is most in your way,
" until the election of a successor." Can that language be used
with reference to a person whose election was bad from the
beginning ?]

H. C. of A.
1907.

VARDON
v.
O'LOGHLIN.

A senator *de facto* may have a successor, as well as a senator *de jure.* Vardon was *de facto* senator until his election was declared void. If there had been no petition within the time he would have still been there, however wrongly he was elected. The declaration by the Court did not make the election void from the beginning, but from the date of the declaration. Till then the election was valid.

[GRIFFITH C.J.—Yes, but only for certain purposes. He was a senator in the sense that nobody could impeach his acts as a senator while he sat.

HIGGINS J.—Does not sec. 15 only refer to changes in the personnel of the Senate taking place according to the normal course of things? Is there anything in the Constitution dealing with vacancies caused by an infringement of the law as to elections? Should it not be assumed that the Constitution deals only with cases in which its provisions have been observed?]

Possibly, but vacancies may arise through infringement of the law of election, and therefore, in providing for vacancies, the Constitution should be construed as having provided for vacancies so caused, just as for those caused by death. If Vardon's actions while in the Senate are treated as valid, he has filled the place, and has had a term of office, and his ceasing to be there causes a vacancy. [He referred to *May, Law and Practice of Parliament,* 11th ed., p. 631; *McDowell* v. *United States* (1).] The irregularity in the election did not create the vacancy, but the decision of the Court.

[BARTON J.—The Court found that there had been no election, that the original necessity to fill the place had not been fulfilled.]

Upon the construction contended for by the petitioner there is no provision in the Constitution for filling such a vacancy, but upon the other construction sec. 15 covers the case, and there is no necessity to strain sec. 13 so as to make it apply. The voidness intended by the Electoral Acts has no place in the Constitution at all, and cannot affect its construction.

The object of the Constitution is to have popular elections only at definite periods, not at odd times. It cannot have been intended that the expense of such an election should be incurred

(1) 159 U.S., 596.

for the election of a single member.   An election *nunc pro tunc* would be in opposition to the spirit of the Constitution, would involve straining the words of sec. 13, and would derange the calculation of the statutory periods for senatorial office.   Where a specific time is fixed by Statute for the election of officers, an election out of time will not satisfy the Statute: *Rochester, Mayor of* v. *The Queen* (1); *Bowman* v. *Blyth* (2); *In re Stafford, Coroner for* (3); *In re Delgado* (4); *Sutherland, Notes on the United States Constitution* (1904), p. 52, and cases cited.

[GRIFFITH C.J. referred to *The King* v. *Norwich, Mayor of* (5).

ISAACS J. referred to *The Queen* v. *Monmouth, Mayor of* (6); *The Queen* v. *Farquhar* (7).

HIGGINS J. referred to *The King* v. *Sparrow* (8).]

Piper in reply.   If it is necessary to strain either sec. 13 or sec. 15, it should not be in the direction of cutting down the rights of the people.   The respondent interprets sec. 13 literally so as to exclude a bye election, and then, to fit that construction, interprets sec. 15 in such a way as to put a strain upon every important word in it.   The Constitution could not be expected to go into details as to the machinery of bye elections, but secs. 9, 12 and 21 are comprehensive enough to include them.   If sec. 15 had been intended to cover all possible cases of election to fill vacancies, it would have said " whenever any vacancy occurs " without qualification.   " Election " under the Constitution includes the whole proceeding by which the people choose representatives, from the issue of a writ until the full number are validly elected.   [He referred to *The Dungarvan Case* (9).]

[GRIFFITH C.J. referred to *Rogers on Elections*, 13th ed., p. 241.]

It is immaterial at what time some parts of the election take place, provided that the process is begun in accordance with the Constitution.   A supplementary writ should be issued under sec. 108 of the *Commonwealth Electoral Act* 1902.   The duty to hold an election is the primary one ; the requirement that it should be

(1) 7 El. & Bl., 910 ; El. B. & E.,
1024.
(2) 7 El. & Bl., 26, at p. 47.
(3) 2 Russ., 475, at p. 483.
(4) 140 U.S., 586.

(5) 1 B. & Ad., 310.
(6) L.R. 5 Q.B., 251.
(7) L.R. 9 Q.B., 258.
(8) 2 Stra., 1123.
(9) 2 P. R. & D., 300.

H. C. of A.
1907.

VARDON
v.
O'LOGHLIN.

held at a particular time is subsidiary, and should not be used as a pretext to excuse omission to perform the main duty when the prescribed time has passed. [He referred to *The Queen* v. *Justices of County of London and London County Council* (1).]

Cur. adv. vult.

The judgment of GRIFFITH C.J., BARTON J., and HIGGINS J., was read by

GRIFFITH C.J. Sec. 7 of the Constitution, which introduces Part II. dealing with the Senate, is as follows :—

" The Senate shall be composed of senators from each State, directly chosen by the people of the State, voting, until Parliament otherwise provides, as one electorate."

This is the dominant provision. Those which follow, and which include provisions allowing the choice of a senator to be made in certain cases otherwise than by the people of the State, are ancillary.

At the election of senators appointed to be held in December 1906, three persons were returned as duly elected for the State of South Australia. Subsequently in May 1907 it was determined by the Court of Disputed Returns that the election of one of the persons so chosen was void. The question thereupon arose how the vacant place was to be filled.

Sec. 15 provides as follows :—" If the place of a senator becomes vacant before the expiration of his term of service, the Houses of Parliament of the State for which he was chosen shall, sitting and voting together, choose a person to hold the place until the expiration of the term, or until the election of a successor as hereinafter provided, whichever first happens."

The Houses of Parliament of South Australia, assuming and intending to act under the authority of this section, chose the respondent to fill the vacant place. The petitioner claims that they had no power to do so, but that the vacancy must be filled by a popular election. He maintains that sec. 15 is applicable only to cases in which a senator holding his place *de jure* as well as *de facto* vacates his seat by death, resignation (sec. 19), absence

(1) (1893) 2 Q.B., 476.

without leave (sec. 20), or disqualification (sec. 45), and he appeals
to what has been called the law of Parliament, under which the
resignation of a person who had been returned as elected, but
whose election was liable to be avoided, was not allowed to
prejudice the rights of another candidate who claimed to have
been elected. It was answered that the so-called law of Parliament had no application if the seat were not claimed by another.
Nor was there any reason for its application in such a case, since
a new election was equally necessary whether the first election
was void or valid. But in either case the election was by the
same body of electors. The petitioner contends that the same
rule should be applied in order to preserve the rights of the
people of the State to make a direct choice of the full number of
senators. Reference was also made to the *Dungarvan Case* (1)
(cited in *Rogers on Elections*, Part II., 16th ed., p. 263), in which
it was laid down—not, it is true, by a Court of law—that an
election which has been set aside by a competent authority as
null and void is considered in law as no election, since there has
never been a valid return according to the exigency of the first
writ; and that all the proceedings subsequent to the issue of
that writ until a valid return has been made according to its
exigency constitute in law but one election, because the original
vacancy remains until lawfully filled according to the exigency
of the first writ. The actual question for decision in the *Dungarvan Case* (1), was whether the whole proceedings should be
regarded as one election for the purpose of the law relating to
disqualification created by bribery committed at " the election."

This view appears to have been accepted by the Parliament
when they enacted sec. 108 of the *Commonwealth Electoral Act
1902*, which provides that:—" Whenever an election wholly or
partially fails a new writ shall forthwith be issued for a supplementary election." If this section is contrary to the Constitution
it has, of course, no validity. But, if the rule of the *Dungarvan
Case* (1) be adopted, sec. 108 merely provides the machinery for
giving effect to a right created by the Constitution itself.

The behest contained in sec. 7 may fail in effect in either of
three ways. It may happen (1) that no election is held at all ;

(1) 2 P.R. & D., 300.

(2) that an election is held in fact, but that a sufficient number of senators are not elected; (3) that the full number are returned as elected, but that the election of some or all of them is invalid. In the last case the return is regarded *ex necessitate* as valid for some purposes unless and until it is successfully impeached. Thus the proceedings of the Senate as a House of Parliament are not invalidated by the presence of a senator without title. But the application of this rule is co-extensive with the reason for it. It has no application as between the sitting senator and any other claimant for the place which he has taken, or as between him and the electors, by whom he was not in fact chosen. The question for our decision is whether, for the purpose of determining how the vacancy declared by the Court of Disputed Returns is to be filled, the choice, which has been declared by that Court to be invalid, is to be regarded as no choice at all, *i.e.*, as a failure to choose, or as a choice which is valid for all purposes until declared invalid, so that the same consequences follow as if the first election had been valid.

It is admitted that in some cases the adjudication of the Court of Disputed Returns must have a retrospective effect. If, for instance, a person who has been returned *de facto*, and against whose return a petition is presented claiming (as in the present case) that another person was duly elected, resigns his place under sec. 19, whether before or after presentation of the petition, the Court must proceed to hear it, and if the Court determines that the other person was duly elected that person will take his place in the Senate, and his term of service will run from the same period as if he had been originally returned. If in the meantime the Houses of Parliament of the State, acting upon his resignation, have assumed to choose a senator under sec. 15, it is conceded that that choice would be superseded by the adjudication. That is to say, all that happened consequent upon the election which is declared void would be disregarded as if it had never happened. The reason is that, as the election itself was void, nothing can be founded upon it, or upon any act of the person who wrongly assumed to act as a senator. The circumstance that the seat is claimed by another is an accident, and not the governing consideration. The election is either valid or

invalid. If invalid, the reason of the invalidity is not material
so far as regards its consequences. We think it follows that,
upon the avoidance of the election itself by the Court of Disputed Returns, the case is to be treated for all purposes, so far as
regards the mode of filling the vacancy, as if the first election
had never been completed, unless there is something in the
Constitution to lead to a contrary conclusion. This view is in
accordance with the general rule as to the effect of an adjudication of a competent tribunal on a question of status. If in a
suit of nullity of marriage the marriage is declared void, the
effect of the judgment is retrospective, and the children of the
marriage are illegitimate. So, a declaration of legitimacy in a
suit for that purpose, in England, is retrospective and takes effect
from the birth of the child. The operation of this rule can only
be excluded by the necessity of the case or by express legislation,
as in the well known instance of the validation of certain transactions entered into by debtors after acts of bankruptcy, or
transactions declared void on the ground of fraud.

It follows that the result of a declaration that the election of a
senator is void is the same as if he had not been originally
returned as elected, and that the three cases enumerated are in
principle identical. What then does the Constitution prescribe
in such a case ? It prescribes (sec. 13) that the Governor of a
State may cause writs to be issued for elections of senators for
the State. *Primâ facie*, this is to be done whenever the necessity
arises. Sec. 9 empowers the State Parliament to make laws for
determining times and places of elections of senators for the State.
In the absence of any express law the days of nomination and
polling must be fixed by the Governor in the writ. The Constitution does not make any express provision for such a case as a
failure to issue a writ at the prescribed time. If, however, a writ
were not issued at the prescribed time, or if, a writ having been
issued, no nominations were received, it would appear to follow
of necessity that a writ, or a second writ, as the case may be,
should be issued later, for otherwise the primary object of the
Constitution in this regard—to secure the representation of the
States in the Senate—would be frustrated (see *per* Lord *Tenterden*

H. C. of A.
1907.

VARDON
v.
O'LOGHLIN.

C.J. in *In re Stafford, Coroner for* (1)). In such a case the provisions of sec. 15 of the Constitution have no application, for
there was no senator whose place could become vacant. Since
then, in some cases, the issue of a writ or a second writ is necessary, and therefore authorized, there is no reason why it should
not be held to be authorized in all cases of necessity. As pointed
out by *Parke* J. in *R.* v. *Mayor of Norwich* (2) the same construction must be given to the Statute whether the failure to elect
extends to the whole number to be elected or to some of them
only.

But it is said that the context of the Constitution excludes this
construction.

Sec. 13 was relied on as showing that the term of service of an
elected senator must be counted from the first of January following the day of his election. This, it is said, would lead to
confusion, if a bye election could be held after the lapse of perhaps a year or more from the day originally appointed. It is
plain, however, that sec. 13 was framed *alio intuitu*, *i.e.*, for the
purpose of fixing the term of service of senators elected in
ordinary and regular rotation. The term "election" in that
section does not mean the day of nomination or the polling day
alone, but comprises the whole proceedings from the issue of the
writ to the valid return. And the election spoken of is the
periodical election prescribed to be held in the year at the expiration of which the places of elected senators become vacant. The
words "the first day of January following the day of his election '
in this view mean the day on which he was elected during that
election. For the purpose of determining his term of service any
accidental delay before that election is validly completed is quite
immaterial. This section therefore does not stand in the way of
the petitioner.

We pass to the arguments founded on sec. 15. Every system of
election of members of any collective body for a fixed term is
liable to have the regularity of rotation interrupted by accidental
circumstances, such as the death or resignation of a member or
his disqualification after election. Every system accordingly
makes provision for such emergencies. Secs. 19, 20, and 45 deal

(1) 2 Russ., 475, at p. 483.   (2) 1 B. & Ad., 310, at p. 317.

H. C. of A.
1907.

VARDON
v.
O'LOGHLIN.

with the events of resignation and disqualification by matter subsequent. It being then necessary, or at least desirable, to make express provision in the Constitution for filling vacancies so caused, sec. 15 was introduced, evidently as part of a complete scheme intended to secure a constant succession of senators for every State without undue multiplication of popular elections. On its face this section is, primarily at any rate, intended to deal with things occurring in the ordinary course of human events, and there is, *primâ facie*, nothing to suggest that it was intended to apply to such abnormal events as a failure to elect a senator or senators. Its language is all consistent with this view. The condition on which it comes into operation is that " the place of a senator becomes vacant before the expiration of his term of service." This assumes a previous election and the existence of a senator who has a " term of service." Those words obviously relate to sec. 13, which prescribes the term of service of senators chosen by the people, although they would, no doubt, also cover the case of a senator chosen by the Houses of Parliament in the place of such a senator. But if there is no senator who has a term of service, the section literally read does not come into operation at all. It was contended that, since the ousted senator had *de facto* a place in the Senate, that place could become vacant. That is, no doubt, true in one sense, but it appears to be irrelevant to the question whether he was a senator having a term of service.

It was further contended that the second paragraph of sec. 15, which is as follows :—" At the next general election of members of the House of Representatives, or at the next election of senators for the State, whichever first happens, a successor shall, if the term has not then expired, be chosen to hold the place from the date of his election until the expiration of the term," shows an intention that there should not be any bye elections for the Senate. It was no doubt intended to avoid them in the case specified. There was, however, nothing to require the polling for a senator to be held on the same day as the polling for members of the House of Representatives. We do not think that this general indication of a desire to avoid unnecessary bye elections is sufficient to control the plain meaning of the other provisions of the Constitution or to prevent effect from being given to the dominant provision of sec. 7, that the senators shall be directly chosen by the people of the State.

For these reasons we are of opinion that the Houses of Parliament had no power to choose a senator in the events that happened, and that the choice of the respondent was void. Sec. 108 of the *Commonwealth Electoral Act* 1902 affords the Governor sufficient authority, if any express authority be necessary, for the issue of a supplementary writ.

ISAACS J. read the following judgment.

I entirely concur with the judgment read by the learned Chief Justice. But as the legality of the action of the Parliament of South Australia is under consideration, I desire to state my reasons separately.

The petition states that the election of Mr. Vardon was declared by the Court of Disputed Returns to be absolutely void. In this case it must be taken that the declaration meant that the election was always void in law—a mere unsuccessful attempt to elect—and not that it was a good election until the decision, and only avoided by the declaration.

Taking that as a starting point, the question is whether the only condition under which sec. 15 of the Constitution can operate existed in this case. In other words did the declaration, that the election was void in respect of Mr. Vardon, give rise to the situation contemplated by the opening words of sec. 15, namely, that "the place of a senator becomes vacant before the expiration of his time of service."

Sec. 1 of the Constitution vests the legislative power of the Commonwealth in the Federal Parliament which is to consist of the Sovereign, a Senate and a House of Representatives.

Sec. 7 declares that "the Senate shall be comprised of senators for each State directly chosen by the people of the State, voting, until the Parliament otherwise provides, as one electorate."

Sec. 24 in like manner declares that "the House of Representatives shall be comprised of members directly chosen by the people of the Commonwealth," &c.

The requirement in each case that members of the Parliament

shall be "directly chosen by the people" is more than a mere
direction, more even than a simple mandate as to the mode of
election; it describes the composition of the Houses themselves,
so as to express the essential nature of these branches of the
Parliament.	Nothing could be more fundamental than the
directly elective character of the two Houses.

H. C. of A.
1907.

VARDON
v.
O'LOGHLIN.

Isaacs J.

Passing to sec. 13, the Constitution assumes the Senate is fully
constituted according to law, and accordingly provides for
rotation of senators by means of two classes of senators whose
places are to become vacant at different periods so as to maintain
the continuity of that House.	It provides in the second para-
graph as follows: "The election to fill vacant places shall be
made in the year at the expiration of which the places are to
become vacant." The recent constitutional amendment of sec. 13
does not affect this case.

I shall hereafter allude to an argument for the respondent
Mr. O'Loghlin based upon the words just quoted, but, for the
present, I wish to emphasize the fact that this paragraph gives a
direction regarding the filling of vacant places *at* the expiration
of the term.	In other words, senatorial succession upon the
normal ending of the term of service of a senator is provided for.
That necessarily connotes a valid election of the retiring senator
to begin with, and the undisturbed fulfilment of his service.

Then comes sec. 15 which, as I read it, is a provision in the
event of the abnormal ending of the same term of service, that is,
the term of service of a senator lawfully elected.	It begins with
the words already quoted :—" If the place of a senator becomes
vacant *before* the expiration of his term of service," &c.

That is clearly dealing with the same senators, the same places,
and the same terms of service as are already dealt with in sec. 13,
but providing for the mode of filling the places in case the vacancy
takes place *before* instead of *at the end of* the term.	That is the
natural and ordinary construction to which the words of the sec-
tion lend themselves.	If this be their true meaning, the section does
not include a case like the present because, by the decision of the
Court of Disputed Returns, Mr. Vardon was declared not to have
been elected, and from the moment of that decision he must be

considered in law never to have been a senator, never to have had a place, never to have had a term of service.

The validity of his public acts as a senator prior to the declaration is, of course, unaffected.

If then the effect of the declaration be as I have stated, sec. 15 never came into operation, and the action of the Parliament of South Australia was not authorized, and the prayer of the petition should be granted. It is, however, contended that sec. 15 does apply to the case for two reasons. The first is that Mr. Vardon was at all events *de facto* a senator, and had *de facto* a place and a term of service. The true answer is that, although it was honestly and reasonably, but, as it has since appeared, erroneously believed he was a senator, and in such belief he so acted, and occupied a place, and served for a time, yet that is not what the Constitution contemplates. It assumes legality of action, and when it speaks of a senator, it does not mean one who is already ascertained not to have been by law a senator.

Sec. 15 can only operate after the vacancy has occurred; and in this case that must be after the decision, and consequently after Mr. Vardon was removed as never having been legally elected. But in those circumstances how can the section intend to include him as a former senator?

Moreover sec. 15 refers to the election of a *successor* to the senator whose place becomes vacant. It would be incongruous to speak of a successor to a person who is declared by law to have been at all times improperly exercising senatorial functions. The word " successor " recognizes the rightfulness of the predecessor's occupancy of the place.

The second reason pressed for the application of sec. 15 is that the necessary construction of sec. 13 compels it.

It is said that the second paragraph of sec. 13 already quoted could not be complied with in view of such circumstances as have arisen here, with the result that no election of a third senator for South Australia could take place unless the means afforded by sec. 15 were resorted to.

But apart from the objections already stated to the inclusion of such a case as the present in sec. 15, the argument fails in assuming that the second paragraph of sec. 13 prohibits an election taking place after the expiration of the year. Such a deferred election might not strictly follow the direction in sec. 13 of the Constitution and, if so, would be opposed to the policy of preserving the continuity of complete State representation in the Senate by having new senators ready to take the place of retiring senators immediately their terms expire. But it by no means follows that because the minor benefit—continuity—is lost, the greater object —complete direct representation—is impossible.

H. C. OF A.
1907.

VARDON
v.
O'LOGHLIN.

Isaacs J.

It might as well be contended from the 12th section that, if by some mischance the State Governor were to omit to issue writs within 10 days of the proclamation of dissolution of the Senate, all right to State representation would be forfeited.

Mr. Justice *Story* in *Prigg* v. *Pennsylvania* (1) said of the American Constitution :—" Perhaps, the safest rule of interpretation after all will be found to be to look to the nature and objects of the particular powers, duties, and rights, with all the lights and aids of contemporary history ; and to give to the words of each just such operation and force, consistent with their legitimate meaning, as may fairly secure and attain the ends proposed."

And if, as I conceive, the same safe rule should be applied in interpreting our own Constitution, then the provisions of secs. 7, 9, and 12 are ample in themselves to provide by direct election for the filling of places of senators retiring at the expiration of their term, notwithstanding any failure to strictly comply with the second paragraph of sec. 13.

On the whole, therefore, it appears to me that the constitutional position, so far as it is material to the present case, may be thus stated. The only *title* to a place and to a term of service is by direct election by the people. If such a title has been once lawfully created for the constitutional term, then, if the senator elected runs his course of service regularly, sec. 13 makes normal provision for the period of election of his successor; if, however, his term of service ends abruptly, as by death, resignation, or disqualification, sec. 15 applies. In that event the State Parliament or the State Governor in Council as the case may be does not elect a *successor*,—there is created no new place and no new term ; there is merely the nomination of a temporary occupant of the place

(1) 16 Pet., 539, at p. 610.

H. C. OF A. already granted for the constitutional term by the people to the late
1907.   senator, and the new occupant so chosen holds the place, not as a
VARDON   successor, but rather as a substitute, and for no definite period.
v.   His occupancy ends, of course, at latest when the term ends; but
O'LOGHLIN. it may end sooner, that is, when at the next general election of
Isaacs J. the House of Representatives or at the next election of the
           senators for the State, the people re-grant the place definitely for
           the remainder of the original term to a true successor of the
           original senator.

Cases might be imagined which, upon the construction I have
placed on the 15th section, would give rise to considerable
inconvenience and expense, and so lend weight to the respondent's
contention—as if three several petitions were presented against
the three senators for a State, the decisions being given at varying dates, and requiring separate intervening elections. But such
instances, though conceivable, are not likely to arise, and the
truth is that sec. 15 of the Constitution was not framed with the
object of meeting numerous instances of irregular Senate elections,
but of providing for possible but rare contingencies of the
abnormal termination of the service of senators; so rare that
departures from the fundamental principle of representation
through popular election would be really inappreciable because
infrequent and possibly of short duration.

The respondent's argument, on the contrary, though not without considerable force, would yet lead to a serious inroad upon
the most vital of all the principles upon which the Federal system
of Parliamentary representation rests. Such a construction as
he contends for is, in my opinion, unsustained by the true reading
of the Constitution, and consequently I think the petition is well
founded, and a declaration should be made accordingly.

> *Election of the respondent by the Houses of*
> *Parliament of the State of South Aus-*
> *tralia declared absolutely void.*

Solicitors, for the petitioner, *Bakewell, Stow & Piper*, Adelaide ;
and *Minter, Simpson & Co.*, Sydney.
Solicitors, for the respondent, *Sly & Russell*, Sydney.

C. A. W.

[HIGH COURT OF AUSTRALIA.]

O'KEEFE AND OTHERS   .   .   .   .   APPELLANTS ;
PLAINTIFFS,

AND

WILLIAMS   .   .   .   .   RESPONDENT,
NOMINAL DEFENDANT.

ON APPEAL FROM THE SUPREME COURT OF
NEW SOUTH WALES.

Crown Lands Act 1884 *(N.S.W.)* (48 *Vict. No.* 18), *secs.* 5, 6—*Crown Lands Act*
1889 *(N.S.W.)* (53 *Vict. No.* 21), *sec.* 33—*Crown Lands Act* 1895 *(N.S.W.)* (58
Vict. No. 18), *sec.* 49—*Occupation licence—Relationship between Crown and
licensee—Agreement by Crown not to disturb licensee—Implication of covenant for
quiet enjoyment—Powers of Minister with respect to Crown lands—Estoppel—
Res judicata.*

H. C. OF A.
1907.
~
SYDNEY,
Nov. 29,
Dec. 2, 3, 9.

Griffith C.J.
Barton and
Isaacs JJ.

An occupation licence under the Crown Lands Acts is an annual tenure of
land, in respect of which the licensee pays fees subject to re-appraisement, and
which is renewable under certain conditions from year to year. The holder of
such a licence agreed with the Government that there should be a re-appraisement of the licence fees, but before the re-appraisement the Government
demanded payment at the original rates. The licensee failed to pay the
amounts claimed, and the Government published a notification in the *Government Gazette* that the licence had not been renewed. The result of the notification, if valid, was that the lands in question became Crown lands available
for occupation under annual lease.

In an action by the licensee against the Government for damages for breach
of contract the declaration alleged that the licensee then agreed with the
Government that, in consideration of his paying the fees demanded, the notification should be withdrawn and he should be permitted, subject to the
provisions of the Crown Lands Acts, to quietly enjoy the area so long as the
licence should be renewed, free from interference, disturbance, or eviction by
the Government or persons claiming under it by matter subsequent to the
payment of the fees in question. The fees were paid by the licensee, but the
notification was not revoked, and an annual lease was granted to another
person of portion of the area.

By the decision of the Privy Council in *O'Keefe* v. *Malone*, (1903) A.C., 365, the Crown was not entitled to the fees demanded in respect of the lands in question, and the licensee was, therefore, entitled to remain in possession under his licence.

Held, on demurrer to the declaration, that it disclosed a good cause of action. The agreement, regarded as an agreement by the Crown for valuable consideration not to do any act in violation of the rights of the licensee, was a valid exercise of the power of the Executive to make contracts with respect to the lands of the Crown within the limits imposed by Statute; and, if the rights of the parties had been doubtful, the contract would have been good as a compromise of a *bond fide* dispute. Even if the Crown had been entitled to the fees demanded, and the licence had therefore become liable to forfeiture for breach of the condition of payment of fees, the agreement on the part of the Crown would have been justifiable as an exercise by the Minister of the power of waiver conferred by sec. 6 of the *Crown Lands Act* 1891.

Quære, whether there is an implied covenant for quiet enjoyment in the tenure created by an occupation licence under the Crown Lands Acts.

The local Land Boards, subject to appeal to the Land Court, have jurisdiction to entertain applications for annual leases of Crown lands, and to make recommendations thereon to the Minister.

Held, that, where the lands, as to which an application for an annual lease was made, were lawfully held under an occupation licence, though the area was by the Crown Lands Acts liable to disposition by the Crown in certain ways adversely to the licensee, yet it was not Crown lands available for annual lease, and was consequently not subject to the jurisdiction of the Land Board for the purpose of such an application, and, therefore, an erroneous decision to the contrary by the Land Court did not create an estoppel as between the licensee and the Crown in any subsequent proceedings with respect to the same area.

Per Griffith C.J.—The Crown is not a party to the proceedings before a Land Board on such an application, and, therefore, in any case between a subject who had been a party and the Crown, estoppel could not arise, owing to want of mutuality.

Decision of the Supreme Court : *O'Keefe* v. *Williams*, (1907) 7 S.R. (N.S.W.), 304, reversed.

APPEAL from a decision of the Supreme Court of New South Wales.

The appellants, executors of the estate of Andrew O'Keefe, were plaintiffs in an action against the respondent, as nominal defendant on behalf of the Government. The declaration alleged that the testator had become the holder by assignment of an occupation licence and a preferential occupation licence under the

Crown Lands Acts 48 Vict. No. 18, sec. 81, and 53 Vict. No. 21, sec. 33; and that, in consideration of the testator making certain payments in respect of fees wrongfully demanded by the Government for the lands held under the licence, the Government agreed, *inter alia*, to permit him to quietly enjoy the lands during the year 1900 and any succeeding years in respect of which the licence might be renewed free of disturbance or eviction by the Government or any person claiming under it by matters subsequent to the payment mentioned, and that the Government in breach of this agreement gave annual leases of portions of the area to other persons, and put the testator to great expense &c. in consequence. The material portions of the declaration are more fully stated in the judgment of *Griffith* C.J. The defendant pleaded, *inter alia*, estoppel by a judgment of the Land Court that the lands in question were available for annual lease, in a proceeding at which the testator appeared as an objector. The plaintiffs demurred to the plea on the ground that the determination of a Land Board or Land Court in an application for an annual lease cannot work an estoppel, as their function is advisory only. Defendant joined in demurrer and gave notice of intention to object to the declaration as being bad in substance upon the ground that the agreement sued upon was void.

After argument the Supreme Court gave judgment for the defendant on the demurrer: *O'Keefe v. Williams* (1).

From this decision the present appeal was brought.

Canaway, for the appellants. An occupation licence is equivalent to a demise by parol; there is no real distinction between a lease and a licence in respect of their incidents under the Crown Lands Acts. [He referred to 48 Vict. No. 18, secs. 81, 128; 53 Vict. No. 21, sec. 33; 58 Vict. No. 18, sec. 4.] The Crown being in the position of landlord in respect of the Crown estate, its lessees or licensees have the rights and liabilities of tenants as against the Crown, except so far as it is expressly provided to the contrary by Statute. [He referred to *The Queen v. Mayor of City of Wellington* (2); *Kickham v. The Queen* (3); *McCulloch*

(1) (1907) 7 S.R. (N.S.W.), 304.   (2) 15 N.Z.L.R., 72.
(3) 8 V.L.R. (E.), 1.

v. *Abbott* (1); *Blackburn* v. *Flavelle* (2); *Blackwood* v. *London Chartered Bank of Australia* (3).] There being the relationship of landlord and tenant, the principles of law governing that relationship apply. Every demise by parol contains an implied covenant for quiet enjoyment. [He referred to *Bandy* v. *Cartwright* (4); *Hall* v. *City of London Brewery Co. Ltd.* (5); *Robinson* v. *Kilvert* (6); *Jones* v. *Lavington* (7); *Budd-Scott* v. *Daniell* (8); *Roberts* v. *Birkley* (9); *Lamb* v. *Evans* (10); *Amer. and Eng. Encyc. of Law*, 1st ed., vol. IX., p. 964. The Crown is in the same position as a private landlord in this respect: *Macdonald* v. *Tully* (11); *Ricketson* v. *Smith* (12); *Ricketson* v. *Cook* (13); *Farnell* v. *Bowman* (14).

[GRIFFITH C.J.—But the Crown can only deal with the land in the ways prescribed by the Statute. How can you say that a covenant is implied that it will not do what it cannot legally do?

BARTON J.—The covenant for quiet enjoyment is only as against persons lawfully claiming under the landlord.]

That is, lawfully claiming as between the landlord and the person claiming. Even though the Crown had no statutory right to effectively interfere with O'Keefe's possession, they might attempt to do so and cause him serious actual disturbance.

[GRIFFITH C.J.—But if the Crown attempted to do so, would it not be a trespass rather than a breach of covenant? Does not a breach of covenant for quiet enjoyment import an eviction by title paramount.]

It may be both a trespass and a breach of covenant.

[ISAACS J. referred to *Manchester, Sheffield and Lincolnshire Railway Co.* v. *Anderson* (15); *Long Eaton Recreation Grounds Co.* v. *Midland Railway Co.* (16); *Child* v. *Stenning* (17); *Brashier* v. *Jackson* (18).]

Apart from the implication of a covenant, there was an express agreement by the Crown not to disturb the licensee. Such an

(1) 6 N.S.W.L.R., 212.
(2) 1 N.S.W.L.R., 58.
(3) L.R. 5 P.C., 92.
(4) 8 Ex., 913; 22 L J. Ex., 285.
(5) 2 B. & S., 737; 31 L.J.Q.B., 257.
(6) 41 Ch. D., 88.
(7) (1903) 1 K.B., 253.
(8) (1902) 2 K.B., 351.
(9) 14 V.L.R., 819.

(10) (1893) 1 Ch., 218.
(11) 1 Q.L.J. (Supp.), 21.
(12) 16 N.S.W.L.R., 221.
(13) 20 N.S.W.L.R., 438.
(14) 12 App. Cas., 643.
(15) (1898) 2 Ch., 394.
(16) (1902) 2 K.B., 574.
(17) 11 Ch. D., 82.
(18) 6 M. & W., 549.

agreement is valid. It is ancillary to the kind of tenure created by the Crown Lands Acts, and effectuates the intention of the legislature. The power of the Crown to contract is limited only by Statute. There was valuable consideration for the Crown's promise. There was a *bonâ fide* dispute as to the Crown's right to the payments claimed, and the agreement made was a compromise. It in no way conflicted with the provisions of the Crown Lands Acts, and was not against public policy.

[Isaacs J. referred to *Callisher* v. *Bischoffsheim* (1); *Miles* v. *New Zealand Alford Estate Co.* (2).]

Piddington (*H. M. Stephen* with him), for the respondent. The declaration sets up an express agreement, not an implied covenant, to deal with Crown lands in a particular manner. That agreement is *ultra vires*. By secs. 5 and 6 of the 48 Vict. No. 18 the Crown may not deal with Crown lands except in accordance with the provisions of the Crown Lands Acts.

[Griffith C.J.—The second agreement alleged has nothing to do with the Crown Lands Acts. An agreement not to alienate lands in violation of the Act may or may not be nugatory, but it is not on that account unlawful.]

This agreement was to deal with the lands in a way contrary to the provisions of the Act. The Minister had no power to make a compromise. If he thought that under the Act the Crown had a right to the sums claimed, he was bound to insist upon the payment.

[Griffith C.J. referred to *Davenport* v. *The Queen* (3).]

The Executive are virtually trustees to deal with the Crown estate as the law requires. The effect of the agreement alleged is to dispose of Crown lands to the prejudice of other claimants, contrary to the Statute. 53 Vict. No. 21, sec. 33 gives the first applicant a right to the lease, and the Crown's agreement with O'Keefe would defeat that right. [He referred to *Martin* v. *Baker* (4); *King* v. *McIvor* (5).] The declaration merely shows an agreement to issue a licence, not a right to have a licence. It does not allege compliance with the provisions of sec. 81 of 48

(1) L.R. 5 Q.B., 449.
(2) 32 Ch. D., 266.
(3) 3 App. Cas., 115.
(4) 1 Knox, 418 (N.S.W.).
(5) 4 N.S.W. L.R., 43.

H. C. of A.   Vict. No. 18. The consideration offered by O'Keefe is an illegal
   1907.   consideration, and at the best the Crown simply agreed to do
O'KEEFE   what the law required, so that there was no consideration for
   v.   O'Keefe's promise.
WILLIAMS.
                  [ISAACS J.—Does it lie in the Minister's mouth to say that?]

In order to constitute a valid contract there must be mutuality.
If there was any consideration for the Crown's promise the Crown
was not entitled to accept it or to exact it. The grant of tenures
is not a matter of contract, but of statutory right on the one side
and duty on the other. Such a contract is contrary to public
policy. It is virtually an agreement not to treat the lands as
Crown lands.

[GRIFFITH C.J.—But they were not Crown lands as between
O'Keefe and the Crown until notification, and the Crown had no
right to lease them to another.]

As regards the implication of a covenant for quiet enjoyment,
the occupation licence is not a demise but a statutory tenure,
with statutory incidents, and such a covenant cannot be implied,
nor would it be in the power of the Crown to make it. [He
referred to *O'Keefe* v. *Malone* (1); *Edols* v. *Tearle* (2); 48 Vict.
No. 18, secs. 95, 126; 53 Vict. No. 21, sec. 10; 58 Vict. No. 18,
secs. 10, 49.] If the Statute authorizes interference with the
licensee no action will lie in respect of it, (see sec. 33 of 53 Vict.
No. 21), and if it does not authorize it the interference is a
trespass, not a breach of contract. [He referred to *Williams* v.
Gabriel (3).] This action cannot be treated as one of trespass,
and if it could, the person to whom the lease was granted was
not the agent of the Crown to commit a trespass.

The plea of estoppel is good. O'Keefe and the Crown were
parties to the proceedings before the Land Court, which decided
that the lands in question were available for annual leases. [He
referred to *Outram* v. *Morewood* (4); sec. 8. (3) of 48 Vict. No. 18.]

[GRIFFITH C.J.—In *O'Keefe* v. *Malone* (5) the Privy Council
held that the land was not available for lease when leased to
Malone. The Land Court therefore had no jurisdiction to decide
as they did.

(1) (1903) A.C., 365, at p. 377.   (3) (1906) 1 K.B., 155.
(2) 7 N.S.W. L.R., 374; 8 N.S.W.   (4) 3 East, 345.
L.R., 518.   (5) (1903) A.C., 365.

H. C. of A.
1907.

O'KEEFE
v.
WILLIAMS.

[ISAACS J. referred to *The Queen* v. *Hutchings* (1); *Wakefield Corporation* v. *Cooke* (2).]

It was a necessary ingredient in the matter which the Land Court had to decide, involving a question of fact, the decision of which was a condition precedent to the exercise of their jurisdiction. Their decision on such matters is final, between the present parties. [He referred to 48 Vict. No. 18, secs. 11, 13, 14, 17, 30, 31 ; *Attorney-General for Hong Kong* v. *Kwok-A-Sing* (3).] The decision of the Privy Council in *O'Keefe* v. *Malone* (4) does not affect the validity of this defence for the Crown in this case. The decision of the Land Court was that of a competent Court, binding the parties to it. [He referred to *The Queen* v. *Commissioners for Special Purposes of the Income Tax* (5).]

Canaway in reply. Estoppel does not extend to matters that are only incidentally or collaterally in question. Moreover the decision of the Land Court was erroneous, and the lands were not in fact or in law within their jurisdiction. Under such circumstances the appellants are not estopped : *Pearson* v. *Spence* (6).]

Cur. adv. vult.

GRIFFITH C.J. This is an action brought by the plaintiffs against a nominal defendant on behalf of the Government for the breach of an express contract set out in the declaration. Amongst other pleas defendant pleaded that the plaintiff was estopped from making certain allegations for the success of his case, and he demurred to the plea. The Supreme Court held that the declaration was bad.

The nature of the contract was that the Government would not interfere with the plaintiffs in the occupation of certain land, which was in one sense Crown land, but to the occupation of which as against the Crown the plaintiffs were entitled. The nature of the plaintiffs' title was what is called an occupation licence, and a preferential occupation licence under the *Crown Lands Act*, which is an annual tenure, and is renewable. The nature

1907
Dec. 9.

(1) 6 Q.B.D., 300.
(2) (1904) A.C., 31.
(3) L.R. 5 P.C., 179.
(4) (1903) A.C., 365.
(5) 21 Q.B.D., 313, at p. 319.
(6) 5 App. Cas., 70.

and incidents of that tenure were discussed in the case of *O'Keefe* v. *Malone* (1) in the Privy Council with respect to the same piece of land as to which the agreement now in question was made.

The declaration sets out facts showing that, according to the decision of the Privy Council in that case, the plaintiffs were entitled as against the Crown to undisputed occupation of the land in question. They then allege by way of inducement some subsidiary agreement as to re-appraisement of the rent of the land, and that in breach of that subsidiary agreement the Government had demanded from them payment of certain licence fees which, under the decision of the Privy Council, were not payable, and, those fees not having been paid, notified in the *Gazette* that the plaintiffs' licences were not renewed. If that notification had been valid the land had become available to be taken up under another tenure called an annual lease, as indeed was actually done, in the belief that the notification was valid. Having set out these facts by way of inducement, the plaintiffs allege that the Government and they entered into a further agreement that in consideration that the plaintiffs would forthwith pay the amount demanded by the Government, the notification in the *Government Gazette* should be revoked within a reasonable time after payment, and as from the date of the payment, and that the plaintiffs should be permitted, subject to the provisions of the Acts, to enjoy the land during the year 1900 and any succeeding year in respect of which the occupation licence and preferential occupation licence should be renewed, free from interference, disturbance, or eviction, on the part of the Government or any person claiming under it by matter subsequent to the said agreement. They then go on to allege that they accordingly performed the contract on their part by paying the amount demanded and then allege as a breach that the Government did not revoke the proclamation as agreed, and did not permit the plaintiffs, subject to the provisions of the Acts, to quietly enjoy the land in question during the term specified, but on the contrary allowed it to be treated as open for annual lease, and granted annual leases of the same land to other persons, and authorized them to enter upon it and dispossess the plaintiffs.

(1) (1903) A.C., 365.

It is to be noted that the agreement alleged is that the plaintiffs should be allowed to enjoy the land subject to the provisions of the Lands Acts. Now, under this particular tenure the occupation licence was good as between the Crown and the licensee, but land held under that tenure was liable to alienation under various provisions of the law. It was not liable to be alienated by annual lease. The agreement alleged, therefore, is, in effect, that the Government would not interfere with the occupation of the land by granting annual leases of it to other persons, that being the only form of alienation that was not permitted.

The Supreme Court held that the declaration was bad, on the ground, as I understand them, that it is not competent for the Minister to make any contract on behalf of the Crown with respect to Crown lands which is not expressly authorized by Statute. The learned Chief Justice gave a somewhat different reason for his decision.

On the argument before us it was contended for the plaintiffs that the declaration not only contained a statement of an express agreement with the Government, but also showed on its face an implied agreement in the nature of a covenant for quiet enjoyment, which, it was said, followed from the nature of the title which the plaintiffs had. Now, the implication of a covenant arises from necessity. What covenant, if any, it is necessary to imply in order to give effect to the relation between the Government and a subject in occupation of Crown land is an interesting question. It was argued at some length, and the contention raises a difficult point as to what would be a breach of such an implied covenant, but it is not necessary to answer it, as, in the view I take, the matter should be determined as a case of express contract. I entirely agree with the Supreme Court in the proposition that no Minister of the Crown has any authority to enter into any agreement for the disposition of an interest of the Crown in Crown lands which is not authorized by the law, and I agree that that applies to any interest which the Crown has power to dispose of; but it appears to me to have no relation at all to an agreement relating to the interest of a subject in land, which, although it is Crown land for certain purposes, is, as between the Crown and the subject, the property of the subject, and not of the Crown.

There is no reason why the Minister should not, for instance, agree with a subject as to the use and occupation of his lands, although they are for some purposes Crown lands, any more than if the lands were freehold. So it appears to me that the doctrine relied upon by the Supreme Court has no application to the case. The land in this instance, as between the Crown and the plaintiffs, was not Crown land; although for certain purposes it could be treated as Crown land, yet for certain other purposes it was not Crown land but the land of the plaintiffs, to which they had a good title. The subject matter of the title was therefore not Crown land within the meaning of the document in question. The question, therefore, is whether such an agreement as that alleged is within the general powers of the Executive Government. The question of the authority of the Minister does not arise under the *Crown Lands Act* at all, but depends upon the general authority of the officers of the Executive Government to make ordinary contracts relating to the administration of public affairs.

In substance, then, the case was this: The Crown claimed, wrongfully, to be entitled to dispossess a subject of his land in a particular manner. What they proposed to do would have been an unlawful, and, in one sense, an ineffectual act. He objected to their doing so, and thereupon an agreement was made for valuable consideration—because the money which he agreed to pay was not payable in point of law—that they would not do this unlawful act for a specified time. How can such an agreement as that be unlawful, or even invalid ?

From another point of view it is a lawful settlement of a *bonâ fide* dispute. In either point of view the promise is good, and a breach of it is admitted.

I have pointed out that on the face of the declaration it appears that the plaintiffs had a good title, and that what the Government proposed to do was unlawful. But suppose that the contention of the Government had been right and that the Government were entitled to dispossess the plaintiffs, though that, as I have pointed out, has been held by the Privy Council not to

be the law.   If it had been, then the agreement would have been
expressly authorized by the law.   The attention of the Judges of
the Supreme Court was not called to this point, but sec. 6 of the
Crown Lands Act Amendment Act 1891 provides that in any
case in which any licence " becomes liable to forfeiture by reason
of the non-fulfilment of any condition annexed by law to such
. . . licence, but in which the Minister shall be satisfied that
such non-fulfilment has been caused by accident, error, mistake,
inadvertence, or other innocent cause, and that such forfeiture
ought therefore to be waived, it shall be lawful for the Minister
to declare that such forfeiture is waived, either absolutely or
upon such conditions as he may see fit to declare, and the forfeiture shall thereupon be waived accordingly," and so on.   Now
the only condition in this licence was the payment of rent at a
prescribed time and in a prescribed manner.   If there had been
a default on the part of the plaintiffs, that would be a ground for
forfeiture which could have been waived by the Minister upon
such conditions as he might see fit to declare.   If he was entitled
to declare the conditions for the acceptance of the plaintiffs, it
was not unlawful to negotiate with the plaintiffs as to what conditions should be imposed.   So that if the Government's contention had been right and there was strictly speaking a right to
forfeit these lands, the agreement not to do so would have been
within the express powers of sec. 6.

I think, therefore, the declaration discloses a good cause of
action.

With respect to the plea, which set out that the Land Court had
decided that this was Crown land available for annual lease, and
that, therefore, the plaintiffs were estopped from suing, the foundation of that plea is that the Land Court had jurisdiction to determine whether the piece of land was Crown land.   There is no
provision of the law cited to us that in any way supports that
contention.   The plea alleges that the plaintiffs became a party
to some proceedings of the Land Court, and the Crown also
became a party.   The plaintiffs, it is true, appeared before the
Land Court and objected that it had no jurisdiction to entertain the matter because the land was the plaintiffs'.   That was
only as to a portion of the land, which in itself would have been

H. C. of A.
1907.

O'Keefe
v.
Williams.

Griffith C.J.

fatal to the plea. But, further, an estoppel must be between the same parties, and if the plaintiffs had made a mistake in litigating the matter in the Court below, that does not enable the Crown to set up the plea of estoppel as against them unless the Crown was a party. The Crown is not a party to proceedings in the Land Court. There is no proceeding between the Crown and its subjects in the Land Court, and therefore the Court has no jurisdiction to bind them. There is nothing in the Statutes to support the contention that a proceeding of the Land Appeal Court is in any way conclusive between the Crown and its subjects.

For these reasons I am of opinion that the plaintiffs are entitled to judgment on the demurrer.

Barton J. I am of the same opinion.

Isaacs J. read the following judgment. The plaintiffs' claim rests on breach of contract, and I think, moreover, the declaration aims, not at the breach of a contractual obligation to be implied from the original relation of the parties, but only at the breach of the alleged new and separate special contract, made upon fresh consideration.

The defendant impeaches the contract alleged as illegal or *ultra vires*.

In the first place the statutory right, which had passed from the Australian Mortgage Land and Finance Co. Ltd. to Andrew O'Keefe, and which must be taken to imply that all the conditions of the Act entitling the runholder to the occupation licences had been fulfilled, was in my opinion a contractual right. I agree with the observations on this point made by *Denniston* J. speaking for the Court of Appeal in *The Queen* v. *Mayor of the City of Wellington* (1). The learned Judge said :—" The Governor, on behalf of the Crown, deals with the lands of the Colony under the directions of the legislature, to which legislation the Crown is of course a party. If, therefore, the legislature creates an obligation on the Crown, with its assent, to convey land to a specified person or body, upon and in consideration of such person or body doing something on his or its part, it seems to us that

(1) 15 N.Z.L.R., 72, at p. 86.

H. C. of A.
1907.

O'Keefe
v.
Williams.

Isaacs J.

that constitutes an agreement or contract on the part of the Crown."

So in *Kettle* v. *The Queen* (1), *Sir Robert Molesworth* said:—" I think, when a Victorian Act, assented to by the Queen, authorizes persons of a certain description, having their rights authenticated by the Board of Land and Works, to proceed to the district land officer, and (subject to regulations as to competition) select defined lands, and pay him a year's rent for it, and thereby become entitled to a certain interest in the land, that the transaction completed by payment constitutes a claim or demand founded on and arising out of a contract entered into on behalf of Her Majesty, or by the authority of her local Government, within the meaning of the Act 241, sec. 7."

That Act was the *Crown Remedies Act* enabling a suit to be brought against the Crown if founded on contract.

The Attorney-General of Victoria v. *Ettershank* (2) was a case where the Privy Council dealt with an objection that a claim by a leaseholder to a grant in fee, to which a Statute entitled him, was not a claim founded on contract. Their Lordships said:—" It was said that the right to the grant of the fee was not given by contract but by Statute. It is true that the right is created by the Statute, but it is conferred upon the holder of a lease, and accrues to him by reason of such lease, and only upon payment of the full rent agreed to be paid under it. It is a statutory right annexed to the lease, and an implied term of the contract, and therefore may be properly said to be founded on and to arise out of it."

The principle of those observations conclusively establishes that the right which Andrew O'Keefe had to the licences was by contract with the Crown.

The Crown Lands Acts bear internal testimony to the fact that the legislature appreciated and recognized this principle. Not only have words of ordinary contractual connotation, such as sale, purchase, auction sale, conditional purchase, lease, and licence, been employed, but in various places the very word "contract" or "contracted" is used.

For example in the Act of 1884 by sec. 4 the expression "Crown

(1) 3 W.W. & àB. (E.), 50, at p. 59.   (2) L.R. 6 P.C., 354, at p. 372.

H. C. of A.
1907.

O'KEEFE
v.
WILLIAMS.

Isaacs J.

Lands " includes lands " lawfully *contracted* to be granted in fee simple." " Lease " means land not alienated by or held under any lease or *promise* of lease or licence from the Crown. Again in sec. 128 reference is made to " *any promise engagement or contract* from or with the Crown or its *agents* lawfully authorized in that behalf."

In the Act of 1891 sec. 2, " Forfeiture " includes the lapse or avoidance of any contract with the Crown, &c.

It may fairly be said that the whole frame of the *Crown Lands Act* shows that the legislature has merely enacted the method and conditions upon which the Crown may contract for the disposal of its interest in the public lands.

Now, it being the clear duty of the Crown to perform its obligation to O'Keefe, one other principle pertinent to the matter may with advantage be referred to. In every contract there is an obligation, implied where not expressed, that neither party shall do anything to destroy the efficacy of the bargain he has entered into. If authority were necessary for so obvious a proposition it is found in such cases as *Stirling* v. *Maitland* (1); *Hamlyn & Co.* v. *Wood & Co.* (2) ; *Hooper* v. *Herts* (3) ; and *Anning* v. *Anning* (4); and latest of all, *The Lyttelton Times Co. (Ltd.)* v. *Warners (Ltd.)* (5).

The Crown, however, according to the allegations in the declaration, insisting on certain payments which in law it had no right to demand, was about to break its obligations to O'Keefe, and he, in order to induce the Crown to forbear from committing an illegal act to his prejudice, consented to pay and did pay the sums demanded as the consideration for a special promise by the Government to desist from their intention. The Government took his money and have ever since retained it, but nevertheless persisted in granting to the persons permission to enter, in pursuance of which those persons entered and caused damage to the plaintiffs.

It is said that the agreement so set up is either illegal or *ultra vires.* In my opinion it is neither. It cannot be illegal to

(1) 5 B. & S., 840.
(2) (1891) 2 Q.B., 488.
(3) (1906) 1 Ch., 549.

(4) 4 C.L.R., 1049.
(5) 23 T.L.R., 751.

agree to refrain from illegality. The Lands Acts place restrictions on the disposal of Crown lands, but so long as the conditions imposed by the legislature are observed, and no unlawful course is entered upon, the Minister, to whom the Crown deputes the function of dealing with the public in connection with those lands, must surely have powers that are at least as wide as those impliedly possessed by the business manager of some private individual in the conduct of the business.

Whether we accept the situation as it actually was, namely, that the Government undertook for valuable consideration not to do what it would have been illegal to do and to do what it was already bound to do, or whether it be assumed that, contrary to what has been determined by the law, the Government was correct in demanding the higher rent on pain of forfeiture, and was exercising its power of waiver, for a consideration which was only one form of condition, the agreement set up was quite within the authority of the Government. Therefore, whether the basis of the agreement sued on be prior contractual obligation, or a merely statutory duty towards O'Keefe, or be the exercise of the power of waiver or compromise of the Crown's right of forfeiture, the same conclusion is reached. If the bargain was illegal, what law did it contravene? If *ultra vires*, it must be *ultra vires* of the Crown itself, and how is that to be established? How is the original and inherent right of the Crown to make contracts relative to its lands fettered except by the restriction of the Lands Acts, all of which were complied with here?

Section 6 of the Act of 1884 is in these terms :—" The Governor on behalf of Her Majesty may grant dedicate reserve lease or make any other disposition of Crown lands but only for some estate interest or purpose authorized by this Act and subject in every case to its provisions." The remainder of the section is immaterial. What is alleged here cannot be said to contravene that section. If not *ultra vires* of the Crown itself, who could exercise the power? Is it the King in person, or the Governor? By what means could the Crown delegate its authority better and more completely than by entrusting the power of bargaining with the public, as has been done, to the officers, political and permanent, who conduct the Lands Department of the State?

H. C. of A.
1907.

O'KEEFE
v.
WILLIAMS.

Isaacs J.

Subject to the provisions of the Crown Lands Acts, the Minister
of the Crown charged with the administration of those Acts
represents the Crown. It is not unworthy of notice that
the Privy Council in *Attorney General of Victoria* v. *Ettershank* (1), on the question of waiver and forfeiture, laid stress
on the fact that Ettershank on applying for his lease was led
to believe by the President of the Land Board that it would be
issued for an existing interest which he might safely purchase.

It is unnecessary at this stage of the case to pursue the investigation further with respect to the declaration, because it is
sufficient for the moment to determine that it discloses a good
cause of action.

With regard to the 5th plea, that can be very shortly dealt
with. The jurisdiction of the Land Board, and through it the
Land Appeal Court, depended entirely on the question whether
or not the land was Crown lands under lease and licence. If it
was, the Land Board's decision, and that of the Land Appeal
Court, were immaterial and may be disregarded. It was sought
to support the plea of estoppel on the ground that these
tribunals must have determined at the outset that the lands were
available, and therefore were not held under lease or licence, and
that this binds O'Keefe. In my opinion, the vice of that argument consists in this, that it overlooks the one fundamental and
decisive consideration, namely that, granting the tribunals would
for the purpose of the day form their own opinion on the point,
yet it is not a matter which has by the legislature been made
directly cognizable by them. The consequences of making the
determination of a Land Board or Land Appeal Court final and
conclusive as to whether any land in New South Wales, public
or private, was available or not available for annual lease so as
to affect existing titles, are too apparent to need extended
comment.

The principle upon which *Reg.* v. *Hutchings* (2), and its
converse case, *Wakefield Corporation* v. *Cooke* (3), were decided,
determines the point against the plea.

(1) L.R. 6 P.C., 351.   (2) 6 Q.B.D., 300.
              (3) (1904) A.C., 31.

The case of *Pearson v. Spence* (1), cited by Mr. *Canaway*, is quite in point in support of his contention.

H. C. of A.
1907.
O'Keefe
v.
Williams.

I agree that the appeal should be allowed, and that the demurrers to declaration and plea be decided in favour of the plaintiffs.

> *Appeal allowed. Judgment for defendant discharged and entered for plaintiffs. Respondent to pay costs of appeal.*

Solicitors, for the appellants, *Villeneuve-Smith & Dawes.*

Solicitor, for the respondent, *The Crown Solicitor for New South Wales.*

C. A. W.

[HIGH COURT OF AUSTRALIA.]

IRVING (COLLECTOR OF CUSTOMS FOR THE STATE OF QUEENSLAND) .   . } APPELLANT ;

COMPLAINANT,

AND

JENGORA NISHIMURA AND ANOTHER . RESPONDENTS.

DEFENDANTS,

ON APPEAL FROM THE DECISION OF A POLICE MAGISTRATE EXERCISING FEDERAL JURISDICTION.

Customs Act 1901 (*No.* 6 *of* 1901), *secs.* 233, 250, 255—*Unlawfully having possession of goods—Evidence of possession—Importation—Knowledge.*

The fact that a person has certain packages of goods in his possession, which he is in the act of importing into Australia, is evidence that he is aware of the contents of such packages and is in possession of such contents within the meaning of sec. 233 of the *Customs Act* 1901.

H. C. of A.
1907.

BRISBANE,
Oct. 4.

Griffith C.J.,
Barton and
Isaacs J.

(1) 5 App. Cas., 70.

H. C. OF A.   APPEAL from the decision of the Police Magistrate at Cairns,
1907.   sitting in federal jurisdiction, dismissing an information laid
IRVING   under sec. 233 of the *Customs Act* 1901. The facts and the
v.   decision of the magistrate are fully set out in the judgment
NISHIMURA.   of *Griffith* C.J. hereunder.
——

Power (with him *Macgregor*), for the appellant. The respondents were unlawfully in possession of goods subject to the
control of the Customs authorities, *i.e.* opium fit for smoking,
which had been absolutely prohibited from being imported
into the Commonwealth by a proclamation issued under sec. 255
of the *Customs Act* 1901. The evidence of possession was complete; the evidence that the goods were left overnight in the
Customs shed before being opened for inspection may have been
evidence upon which the magistrate could have found that the
goods had been tampered with, but was not, as the magistrate
erroneously thought, conclusive against his finding proof of
possession.

Lukin and *Walsh*, for the respondents. The information
should have been dismissed, as it disclosed no offence; this Court
may dismiss it now on that ground: *Prior* v. *Sherwood* (1).

Sec. 233 makes it an offence for any person to "have in his
possession any goods," which is outside the federal power to enact.

[GRIFFITH C.J.—If it is read literally; but it may be read as
limited to goods in the course of being imported, or perhaps to
imported goods: *Federal Amalgamated Government and Tramway Service Association* v. *New South Wales Railway Traffic
Employés Association* (2).]

The information does not, as it should, state how or in what
manner the respondents "unlawfully" had goods in their possession: *Paley on Summary Conviction*, 8th ed., p. 195.

[GRIFFITH C.J.—It goes on to specify the nature of the unlaw-
fulness, in having in their possession "goods, namely opium, the
importation of which was prohibited." That satisfies sec. 250,
being "set forth as nearly as may be in the words of this Act."]

(1) 3 C.L.R., 1054.   (2) 4 C.L.R., 488, at p. 546.

H. C. of A.
1907.

IRVING
v.
NISHIMURA.

Such words as those do not absolve the party from setting out the necessary elements of the offence: *Smith* v. *Moody* (1).

There was no proof of guilty knowledge ; merely having goods in one's possession is no proof of knowledge of what is hidden within them: *R.* v. *Colyer*; *Ex parte Colyer* (2) ; *Molloy* v. *Hallam* (3) ; *Walker* v. *Chapman* ; *Ex parte Chapman* (4).

Power was not called on to reply.

GRIFFITH C.J.   This is an appeal from a decision of a Police Magistrate dismissing a charge under sec. 233 of the Federal *Customs Act* 1901 that the defendants unlawfully had in their possession certain goods, namely, opium, the importation of which was prohibited. The facts were these :—On 8th February the s.s. *Chingtu* arrived in the roadstead at Cairns—it does not expressly appear from what port.   One of the respondents, who was a passenger by the ship, landed in a launch, taking with him two tubs purporting to contain Japanese Soy, which he claimed as his own.   The other respondent, who is a resident of Cairns, went out and returned in the launch, and on arrival at the wharf claimed the tubs as his.   The two respondents were then in company. The tubs were put in the Customs store for the night, and in the morning they were opened and found to contain opium suitable for smoking, an article the importation of which was absolutely prohibited by law at that time.   On these facts the Police Magistrate dismissed the complaint on the ground that there was no proof of possession by the defendants or either of them.   He adds in the case stated that he decided to dismiss the charge on that ground for the reason that he considered that the two tubs should have been examined on the wharf at the time of landing, or else sealed and locked up in the Customs bond, instead of being left in the Customs office on the wharf, where it was quite possible for them to be tampered with.   But the possibility of the tubs being tampered with is not conclusive of the question whether there was possession by the defendants.   There was ample evidence of joint possession of the

(1) (1903) 1 K.B., 56.
(2) 8 Q.L.J., 27.
(3) 1903 St. R. Qd., 282.
(4) 1904 St. R. Qd., 330.

tubs and their contents by both defendants, and also evidence of possession by each of them with the concurrence of the other, which is sufficient under the *Justices Act* to sustain a charge against both. The reason which the magistrate gives might have justified him in coming to the conclusion that the tubs had in fact been tampered with, but it was otherwise irrelevant to the question whether the opium was in the possession of the defendants. Mr. *Lukin* says that, even if the ground relied upon by the magistrate is wrong, yet the appeal should not be allowed if the magistrate was bound to dismiss the information in any event, and that is no doubt right. I will, therefore, refer briefly to the other objections taken. The first was that the complaint disclosed no offence. That is met by sec. 250 of the Act, which enacts that an information following the terms of the Statute is sufficient. The complaint in this case did so. Another objection was that there was no proof of importation. There was, at any rate, this evidence of importation : The goods arrived by the *Chingtu*, which was a ship to which Customs officers went for the purpose of granting a clearance, and the goods when landed were taken possession of by the Customs officers. I think that is sufficient *primâ facie* evidence that the goods were imported, and that both the defendants knew it. I pass over some other objections not relied upon by Mr. *Lukin.*

The important objection is that there was no evidence on which the justices could find that the defendants knew that these tubs, purporting to contain " Japanese Soy," really contained opium. It is said that the word "unlawfully" in the section of the Act imports knowledge, and in one sense I accept that contention. It was, indeed, boldly contended that the section was altogether invalid as exceeding the competency of the Commonwealth Parliament. It reads :—" No person shall smuggle or unlawfully import, export, convey or have in his possession any goods, and no master of a ship or boat shall use or suffer his ship or boat *to* be used in smuggling or in the unlawful importation, exportation, or conveyance of any goods." It is said that it would be absurd to interpret the words " have in his possession " in their plain literal meaning, because they would apply to all goods in all parts of the Commonwealth. No doubt they would, and therefore the

section must be construed as dealing only with matters within
the competency of the Commonwealth Parliament. The words
may, therefore, relate to any goods the subject of importation or
exportation, and whatever else they may mean, they certainly
include the case of goods imported. Whatever the section does
or does not include, it certainly includes the case of a person who
unlawfully has in his possession goods unlawfully imported.
These goods were undoubtedly unlawfully imported. That being
so, can it be said that the defendants had them unlawfully in their
possession ? It is said, and very properly, that a man, who does
not know that a thing is in his possession, cannot be convicted of
having it unlawfully in his possession. If a man has something
put into his pocket without his knowledge, he cannot be charged
with having it unlawfully in his possession, if that fact appears.
But in a case where goods are imported from abroad it is a difficult
thing for the importer to say that he does not know what is contained in the packages that are imported, and which he claims as
his own. It is open for him to show that, without his knowledge
or consent, some goods that he never desired to have imported
have been put in the package, but I think that when goods are
imported the fact of importation is sufficient *primâ facie* evidence
that the importer knows what is contained in the packages. It
is not conclusive evidence, and as this case must in any event go
back to the justice, it would not be proper to express any positive
opinion on the facts, but from what I have said it is sufficiently
obvious that the magistrate was not bound to dismiss the case.
The point which I understand him to have decided was wrongly
decided, and the case must be remitted to him for determination
on the merits.

BARTON J. I am quite of the same opinion.

ISAACS J. I shall say nothing about the questions of fact
because the case has to go back to the magistrate for him to consider, but I should like to say with regard to the construction of
sec. 233, and especially with regard to the argument that the words
" unlawfully having possession of any goods " was so wide as to
embrace the contravention of any law whatever relating to any
goods throughout Australia, and so make the section or that

H. C. of A.
1907.

IRVING
v.
NISHIMURA.

Griffith C.J.

H. C. of A.
1907.

IRVING
v.
NISHIMURA.

Isaacs J.

portion of it *ultra vires*, that we are not only not driven to that conclusion, but we ought not to adopt it. The general words in a Statute must always be construed in relation to the matter in hand—the subject matter of the enactment—and that principle was given effect to by the Privy Council in *Macleod* v. *Attorney-General for New South Wales* (1). Their Lordships there refused to adopt one possible construction of an Act which would have made it *ultra vires* of the New South Wales legislature, and adopted another construction, which the language permitted, and upon which the Act was clearly within the competency of the legislature. The principle is well stated by *Turner* L.J. in *In re Poland* (2), where the learned Judge says:—" There can be no doubt that the general words in an Act of Parliament must be construed in accordance with the circumstances to which the Act was intended to apply." That principle was applied by this Court very recently in the case of *Bank of Australasia* v. *Hall* (3) in relation to the words " creditor " and "debt," and when we apply it to this case, we see that the object of the Federal Parliament in sec. 233 was to prevent the evasion of its Statutes in relation to the importation and exportation of goods. The word " unlawfully," therefore, in that section gets full significance, and it is not left open to any imputation of being *ultra vires*, if it is understood in the sense that it means the contravening of some federal law relating to the matters that I have referred to. That is all I wish to say with regard to the case. The other matter has been fully dealt with by the learned Chief Justice, with whose observations I concur.

> *Appeal allowed. Case remitted to the Police Magistrate for determination. Respondent to pay the costs of the appeal.*

Solicitors, for appellant, *Chambers & McNab* for *Lilley & Murray*, Cairns.

Solicitors, for respondent, *Stephens & Tozer* for *Hartley*, Cairns.

N. G. P.

(1) (1891) A.C., 455.   (2) L.R. 1 Ch., 358.
                    (3) 4 C.L.R., 1514.

[HIGH COURT OF AUSTRALIA.]

SERMON . . . . APPELLANT;
　PLAINTIFF,

AND

THE COMMISSIONER OF RAILWAYS . RESPONDENT.
　DEFENDANT,

ON APPEAL FROM THE SUPREME COURT OF
WESTERN AUSTRALIA.

Fire caused by sparks from engine—Statutory authority—"Any kind of fuel"—
　Dangerous fuel—Reasonable precautions—Government Railways Act 1904
　(W.A.) (3 Edw. VII. No. 23), sec. 20—Statutory discretion, how to be exercised.

The *Government Railways Act* 1904 (W.A.) conferred upon railway
authorities a discretion to use in their engines "any kind of fuel."

Held, that an action could not be maintained against them for negligence
alleged to consist in the choice of a kind of fuel more likely to cause damage
by fire than other available kinds of fuel, provided that the best known safety
appliances and proper care were employed in its use.

Per Griffith C.J.—In order to determine the meaning of a statutory
authorization giving a discretion to carry out works by certain general means,
the circumstances of the country at the time of legislation may be considered.

Decision of the Supreme Court of Western Australia affirmed.

H. C. OF A.
1907.

PERTH,
Oct. 31 ; Nov.
1 ; Dec. 2.

Griffith C.J.,
Barton and
Isaacs JJ.

THE facts and the statutory enactments material to the case are
stated in the judgments hereunder.

Pilkington K.C. (with him *Stawell*), for the appellant. *Parker*
C.J. erroneously refused to draw the inference that the sparks
from the engine started the fire, because he felt suspicious of two

· H. C. of A.
1907.

SERMON
v.
THE COMMIS-
SIONER OF
RAILWAYS.

men who were on the spot when the fire started, and thought, without any evidence, that it might possibly have been caused by them. In this His Honor was properly overruled by the Full Court. The engine was burning a dangerous class of coal when there were other safe classes of coal available. The Commissioner is admittedly empowered by sec. 20 of the *Government Railways Act* 1904 to use any kind of fuel; but that does not exempt him from liability for the negligent exercise of that authority.

"Locomotive engines consuming any kind of fuel" is a phrase descriptive of steam engines which burn fuel; it does not authorize the indiscriminate use of all sorts of fuel, irrespective of dangerous circumstances, such as dry grass plains, and hot winds. For fuel in the engines wood or oil may be used, as well as coal, but the ordinary law of negligence still applies.

The use of the best and safest coal in an obsolete and dangerous engine would be negligent; similarly the use of the most dangerous coal, even in the best and safest engine, would be negligent, being an unreasonable use of a statutory power. Collie coal is dangerous by reason of its emitting sparks, even through the most improved spark arrester; and the Commissioner is authorized by the Act only to use such coal at his peril on a dangerous day such as that on which the fire arose. Such an authority is limited to reasonable user: *Roberts* v. *Charing Cross, Euston and Hamstead Railway Co.* (1); *Coats* v. *Clarence Railway Co.* (2); *Southwark and Vauxhall Water Co.* v. *Wandsworth District Board of Works* (3); *London, Brighton and South Coast Railway Co.* v. *Truman* (4); *Metropolitan Asylum District, Managers of* v. *Hill* (5); *Canadian Pacific Railway* v. *Roy* (6).

[ISAACS J.—*Canadian Pacific Railway* v. *Parke* (7) may draw the distinction you desire.]

The Statute must give a specific authority to make lawful the unreasonable or negligent exercise of the power given: *Vaughan* v. *Taff Vale Railway Co.* (8); *Gas Light and Coke Co.* v. *Vestry*

(1) (1903) W.N., 13 ; 87 L.T., 732.
(2) 1 Russ. & M., 181.
(3) (1898) 2 Ch., 603.
(4) 11 App. Cas., 45.

(5) 6 App. Cas., 193.
(6) (1902) A.C., 220.
(7) (1899) A.C., 535.
(8) 5 H. & N., 679, at p. 685.

H. C. OF A.
1907.

SERMON
v.
THE COMMIS-
SIONER OF
RAILWAYS.

of St. Mary Abbott's, Kensington (1); *Francis* v. *Maas* (2); *Geddis* v. *Proprietors of Bann Reservoir* (3); *Evans* v. *Manchester and Lincolnshire and Sheffield Railway Co.* (4); *Goldberg & Son Ltd.* v. *Mayor &c. of Liverpool* (5).

[GRIFFITH C.J.—You do not allow any weight to the fact that this is a Western Australian Statute, and that Collie coal is the only indigenous coal in Western Australia.]

No extraneous fact can make specific those words which are otherwise quite general.

The *Railways Act* 1897, sec. 2, enacted that the then Commissioners might " at all times " run locomotive engines consuming any kind of fuel. These words " at all times " were evidently omitted from sec. 20 of the 1904 Act in order to impose the duty of extraordinary care at dangerous times of the year. Where a power is given, the exercise of that power must be carried out with due regard for private rights, unless the enabling words expressly or necessarily authorize interference therewith : *Western Counties Railway Co.* v. *Windsor and Annapolis Railway Co.* (6).

Northmore, for the respondent. The finding of *Parker* C.J. upon the facts should not be disturbed; the inference was properly drawn, and was compatible with the evidence, that the fire was started by some agency other than the defendant's engine : *Smith* v. *London and South Western Railway Co.* (7).

Sec. 20 of the 1904 Act, or rather its prototype, sec. 2 of the 1897 Act, was passed under circumstances and at a time which show that it was intended to authorize the use of the Collie coal with the same impunity as the safest coal, so long as proper diligence was shown in installing the best safety appliances for spark arresting. This is apparent from contemporary legislation : *Collie Railway Act* 1895 (No. 33), which was passed to connect the Collie coal mines with the State railways. " Consuming any kind of fuel " is therefore not merely descriptive of engines.

[ISAACS J. referred to *Public Works Act* 1902 (W.A.) (1 Edw.

(1) 15 Q.B.D., 1.
(2) 3 Q.B.D., 341.
(3) 3 App. Cas., 430.
(4) 36 Ch. D., 626.

(5) 82 L.T., 362, at p. 367.
(6) 7 App. Cas., 178, at p. 189.
(7) L.R. 6 C.P., 14.

H. C. of A.
1907.

SERMON
v.
THE COMMIS-
SIONER OF
RAILWAYS.

VII., No. 47), sec. 99 (I.) (*a*). The Minister for Works may run locomotive engines over any land acquired for a railway "and any kind of fuel may be used" for such engines.]

The power given to the Commissioner will be liberally construed, as it is given to enable him to work the railways in the public interest, and not that of individuals. *Coats v. Clarence Railway Co.* (1); and *Roberts v. Charing Cross, Euston and Hamstead Railway Co.* (2) are distinguishable; they dealt only with the construction of railways, not the working of traffic: *Hood v. North Eastern Railway Co.* (3). There was actual negligence in the use of the statutory power in *Geddis v. Proprietors of Bann Reservoir* (4), and *London, Brighton and South Coast Railway Co. v. Truman* (5) turned on the same principle, *i.e.*, that the Commissioner would be answerable for negligence in the use of whatever kind of fuel he chose for the engines; but he would not be liable for choosing to use any one of a number of authorized kinds of fuel: *Vaughan v. Taff Vale Railway Co.* (6).

[ISAACS J. referred to *The Mayor of East Fremantle v. Annois* (7).]

If the Commissioner were *intra vires* in using Collie coal, he does not do so at his peril. He can use Collie coal wherever that use is reasonable; the evidence was that Collie coal is very nearly as safe as Newcastle coal, and the lower cost must also be considered in the question of what was reasonable. It had to be proved that it was so much more dangerous that it was negligence to use it with the best spark arresters: *Longman v. Grand Junction Canal Co.* (8).

Draper in reply. This Court can draw the inference that it was unreasonable to use dangerous coal under the circumstances when the fire was caused; this is open on the evidence. If this Court is not entitled to draw that inference, a new trial should be held to enable that fact to be established: *Dimmock v. North Staffordshire Railway* (9).

(1) 1 Russ. & M., 181.
(2) (1903) W.N., 13; 87 L.T., 732.
(3) L.R. 11 Eq., 116.
(4) 3 App. Cas., 430.
(5) 11 App. Cas., 45.

(6) 5 H. & N., 679.
(7) (1902) A.C., 213, at p. 217.
(8) 3 F. & F., 736.
(9) 4 F. & F., 1058.

No specific authority can be drawn from sec. 20 to use Collie coal; it authorizes the use of local or imported fuel, but still binds the Commissioner and his servants to use due care in consuming dangerous fuel at dangerous times and places. [He referred to *Western Counties Railway Co. v. Windsor and Annapolis Railway Co.* (1); *London County Council v. Great Eastern Railway Co.* (2); *Goldberg & Son Ltd. v. Mayor &c. of Liverpool* (3).]

H. C. of A.
1907.

SERMON
v.
THE COMMIS-
SIONER OF
RAILWAYS.

Cur. adv. vult.

The following judgments were read :—

GRIFFITH C.J. This is an action for damages alleged to have been sustained by the appellant by the negligence of the defendant in the use of a locomotive engine, in consequence of which the plaintiff's grass was burnt. The 6th paragraph of the statement of claim was as follows:—"The said fire was caused by the defendant's negligence in using a class of coal more likely to cause fires along the railway and upon adjoining lands than other coal in the possession of or reasonably procurable by the defendant for use upon the railway while passing through the said agricultural district, as the defendant was well aware, and in using the said coal during dry and hot weather when the grass and other growth were dry and easily set on fire, and in using the said coal upon an engine not fitted with a soft coal chimney, and in failing to take reasonable precaution to prevent damage by fire caused by sparks emitted from or dropped by his engine."

The allegations of negligence in using the coal upon an engine not fitted with a soft coal chimney and in failing to take reasonable precautions to prevent damage by fire caused by sparks, so far as such precautions depend upon matters of internal construction, were abandoned either at the trial or before the Full Court, so that the only negligence now to be considered consists in the use of the class of coal which was actually used at a time and under circumstances when that class of coal was likely to be dangerous, and not in the manner of its use if that use was lawful.

Dec. 2.

(1) 7 App. Cas., 178, at p. 189.   (2) (1906) 2 K.B., 312.
(3) 82 L.T., 362.

H. C. of A.
1907.

SERMON
v.
THE COMMIS-
SIONER OF
RAILWAYS.

Griffith C.J.

The case was tried before *Parker* C.J. without a jury. He was not satisfied that the plaintiff had established that the fire which occasioned the damage was caused by sparks emitted from the defendant's locomotive. But he was also of opinion that the use of the coal was authorized by law. He therefore on both grounds gave judgment for the defendant. The Full Court were of opinion that the evidence showed that the fire was caused by sparks emitted from the defendant's engine, but the majority of the Court (*McMillan* and *Burnside* JJ., *Rooth* J. diss.) agreed with the learned Chief Justice that the use of the coal was authorized by law. They therefore dismissed the appeal.

Numerous authorities were cited to us, but there is really no room for controversy as to the law. The defendant relies on sec. 20 of the *Government Railways Act* 1904 (3 Edw. VII. No. 23). By that Act the Commissioner for Railways is constituted a corporation sole, and is charged with the management, maintenance and control of the government railways. Section 20 enacts that the Commissioner " may use on any railway locomotive engines consuming any kind of fuel." The fuel in use when the damage complained of was occasioned consisted of a mixture of equal proportions of Collie coal, (the product of coal mines in the south western part of the State of Western Australia), and Newcastle coal (from New South Wales). It is conceded that this mixture was less likely to emit sparks than Collie coal alone. The respondent contends that authority to use " any kind of fuel " includes authority to use Collie coal as fuel, either alone or mixed with other coal, and that, the use being lawful, and there being no negligence in the manner of the use, an action will not lie. The appellant contends that the words " consuming any kind of fuel " are a mere description of the kinds of locomotives that may be used, and do not confer any authority which would not follow from the mere permission to use locomotives, and, further, that if they do authorize the use of any kind of fuel, still the Commissioner may be guilty of negligence in the choice or selection of the kind of fuel which he will use, so that, if he selects a kind which is more likely to emit sparks than another which he might reasonably have used, he is guilty of negligence,

H. C. of A.
1907.

SERMON
v.
THE COMMIS-
SIONER OF
RAILWAYS.

Griffith C.J.

which is established by the mere fact of the selection of such coal. I will deal first with the latter construction.

There is no doubt that the Commissioner is responsible for negligence in the exercise of his statutory authority, and it is not disputed that if, being authorized to use Collie coal, he used it negligently he would be liable. But no such case is made. The alleged negligence consists in the mere fact of use. It may be taken to be established by the evidence that Collie coal is more likely to emit sparks than some other coal which is also used by the Commissioner, such as Newcastle coal imported by sea from the other side of the continent of Australia. It is said that this is sufficient evidence of negligence, that is, of want of reasonable care. In this view of the case, however, there has been no finding of the necessary fact that under the circumstances it was not reasonable to use Collie coal, which is an inference of fact and not of law.

The respondent's case, on the other hand, is that the Statute entitles him to select what kind of fuel he will use, and that an action will not lie against him for the manner in which he exercises that power of selection. The distinction between liability for negligence in the use of an authorized instrument and negligence in the selection of one from among several authorized instruments is clearly pointed out in the case of *London, Brighton and South Coast Railway Co.* v. *Truman* (1). In that case a railway company, who were authorized by their Act to acquire land for cattle yards in such places as should be deemed eligible, bought land and used it for that purpose in a place where the noise occasioned by the use was a nuisance which, but for the Act, would have been actionable. *North* J. and the Court of Appeal held that the company could be restrained from using the land for the purpose, but this decision was reversed by the House of Lords. Lord *Halsbury* L.C., said (2):—" Neither the statement of claim nor any finding by the learned Judge suggests that the defendants were guilty of any negligence in the use of the cattle pens and dockyard, as distinguished from the selection of its site, and the whole question turns on the right of the railway company to select and use that

(1) 11 App. Cas., 45.　　　　(2) 11 App. Cas., 45, at p. 50.

H. C. of A.
1907.

Sermon
v.
The Commis-
sioner of
Railways.

Griffith C.J.

site, although its use may involve a nuisance to the neighbouring proprietors. That question must depend upon the authority which Parliament has granted to the railway company.

"The ground upon which *North* J. has proceeded in that respect, supported by the Court of Appeal, although for different reasons, has been, that it being competent to the company to select another site more convenient and less injurious to the plaintiffs, they have selected a site which has caused the injury of which the plaintiffs complain. It cannot now be doubted that a railway company constituted for the purpose of carrying passengers, or goods, or cattle, are protected in the use of the functions with which Parliament has entrusted them, if the use they make of these functions necessarily involves the creation of what would otherwise be a nuisance at common law. Ever since the decision of *Rex* v. *Pease* (1) in 1832, it has been established so firmly by repeated decisions that that proposition is no longer within the region of controversy, and if these cattle pens and dockyards had been within the original limits of deviation, or what was equivalent to the limits of deviation in modern Acts when the line was first authorized, and had been erected within those limits, I do not understand that any of the learned Judges would have doubted that the company were acting within their powers, and were protected upon the principle I have stated above."

The question for decision in the present case is, therefore, whether the Statute confers on the Commissioner an unqualified authority to select what kind of fuel he will use. This is a mere matter of construction.

It is not disputed that the words "any kind of fuel" have at least as extensive a meaning as if the words "coal, wood or oil" had been used in the place of them. It follows that on the principle stated in *Truman's Case* (2), the Commissioner would not be liable to an action merely because he selected and used wood as a fuel, although, as appears by the evidence in this case, wood is more likely to emit sparks than coal. But it is said that the permissible choice is only between what were called genera, such as coal, wood and oil, and not between species of the same

(1) 4 B. & Ad., 30.   (2) 11 App. Cas., 45.

H. C. OF A.
1907.

SERMON
v.
THE COMMIS-
SIONER OF
RAILWAYS.

Griffith C.J.

genus, such as anthracite coal, lignite, bituminous coal, and Collie coal, and that in making a choice between the different species the Commissioner must use reasonable care. There is no suggestion in any reported case that any such contention has ever been set up in Great Britain. It was, indeed, referred to by *Darling J.* in the *London County Council* v. *Great Eastern Railway Co.* (1), as an obviously impossible contention. Assuming, however, that the section is open to this construction, I proceed to inquire what is the real meaning. The duty of the Court is to ascertain the intention of the legislature, and in doing so regard must be had to the circumstances of the country at the time when the Act was passed.

It appears that coal had been discovered on the Collie coalfield at some time before 1895. In that year an Act was passed authorizing the construction by the Government of a line of railway to connect the coalfield with the government railways. In 1897 an Act (61 Vict. No. 32), entitled "An Act to further amend the Railways Act 1878" was passed, section 2 of which enacted that "The Commissioner may at all times run locomotive engines consuming any kind of fuel . . . . . . upon any railway," &c. The only other provisions in the Act related to gates at level crossings, and to an amendment of the provisions of the Principal Act as to arbitration. Section 2, therefore, appears to have been at least one of the chief objects of legislation, and it is *primâ facie* difficult to regard it as merely meaning that the Commissioner might run locomotives adapted to use either coal, wood or oil, which in fact were the only kinds of locomotives then known.

It appears in evidence that from a time very soon after the passing of this Act Collie coal has been used on the government railways.

In 1902 the legislature passed an Act called the *Public Works Act* 1902, (2 Edw. VII. No. 47), which consolidated the laws relating to the construction of public works, including railways, by the Government. Section 99 of that Act confers various powers upon the Minister in respect of any railways authorized by special Act. The first sub-paragraph authorizes entry upon any land necessary for the construction, and adds "and locomotive

(1) (1906) 2 K.B., 312.

H. C. of A.
1907.

SERMON
v.
THE COMMIS-
SIONER OF
RAILWAYS.

Griffith C.J.

engines, machines, carriages,   . . .   may be used upon and run
over any land entered upon or taken or acquired   . . .   and
any kind of fuel may be used for any such locomotive engines or
machines." It is, I think, impossible to read these last words
otherwise than as giving the Minister an absolute choice of the
fuel to be used on locomotive engines or other machines used in
the construction of railways.

Then in 1904 the Act now in force, which is a consolidating
Act, was passed, containing section 20 in its present form. At
this time Collie coal had been in use for at least four years. Its
use was, as I have shown, authorized on locomotives used in the
construction of railways, and I cannot bring myself to believe
that the legislature, by the use of a slightly different form of
words in an Act relating to maintenance and management of
railways, intended to effect a different result.

An additional fact, which, in my judgment, is very material in
the inquiry as to the intention of the legislature, is that coal of
the class of the Collie coal is the only coal which has yet been
found in Western Australia. To read the words "any kind of
fuel" as not including the only coal found within a distance of
some thousands of miles is, I think, to do violence to all
probabilities.

As to the argument that the choice given by the Statute is
only between genera and not between species, I can find no
foundation for it in reason or etymology. Why should it be said
that all coal, whether imported from Wales, from different
districts of New South Wales, where the quality of the coal
produced from different mines greatly varies, from Queensland,
where the qualities again differ, or from New Zealand, is the
same "kind of fuel" as local Western Australian coal? No
doubt in some contexts the word "kind" might bear that meaning. But in an enabling Act such as this I do not think that it
is the literal or the probable meaning.

As for the first construction contended for by the appellant, I
think that it gives no effect at all to the words "consuming any
kind of fuel." The words "locomotive engines," standing alone,
would have the same meaning as that contended for. It may be
observed, however, that it is a well known fact, and indeed,

H. C. OF A.
1907.

SERMON
v.
THE COMMIS-
SIONER OF
RAILWAYS.

Griffith C.J.

appears in evidence, that different kinds of coal require special adaptations to be made in the engine in which they are burnt, so that, if the word "consuming" is read "adapted to consume," as suggested, the right of choice of fuel is equally conferred.

For these reasons I am of opinion that the decision of the Full Court was right, and that this appeal must be dismissed.

BARTON J. The plaintiff's grass and feed had been set on fire by sparks from an engine under the defendant's control attached to a train. The cause of the emission of sparks from which the fire originated was alleged to be the defendant's "negligence in using a class of coal more likely to cause fires along the railway and upon adjoining lands than other coal in the possession of or reasonably procurable by the defendant." Negligence was also alleged in the failure of the defendant to take reasonable precaution to prevent damage by fire caused by sparks emitted from or dropped by his engine, and in the use by the defendant of the coal mentioned upon an engine not fitted with a soft coal chimney. The plaintiff failed at the trial. The learned Chief Justice of Western Australia, who tried the case without a jury, held against him on each of the grounds stated, being of opinion (1) that the coal used was a "kind of fuel" which the Commissioner was authorized by Statute to use, (2) that the Commissioner had taken all reasonable precaution to prevent damage by fire caused by sparks emitted from his locomotives, which in His Honor's view were suited for the consumption of the kind of fuel used, and (3) that the soft coal chimney was not as effective for the prevention of the emission of sparks as the appliances affixed to the engine on the date of the fire. On a fourth question His Honor found as a fact that the plaintiff had not satisfied him that the fire arose at all from sparks from the engine. In the last finding the Full Court did not support His Honor, and I take a view of this case which renders it unnecessary to consider which was right on that particular point, for, assuming the sparks from the engine to have kindled the fire, I still do not think the defendant liable. Now on the appeal to the Full Court the plaintiff abandoned his third ground, that the defendant should have used a soft coal chimney, and before this Court

H. C. of A.
1907.

SERMON
v.
THE COMMIS-
SIONER OF
RAILWAYS.

Barton J.

he has virtually abandoned the second ground, that the defendant failed to use all reasonable precautions. The only ground of negligence then that we have now to consider is the first mentioned, namely, that of negligence in the fact of the user of the particular coal burned on the day of the fire. I may at this stage say that I think that, in view of the strength of the evidence, the plaintiff has done wisely in virtually admitting that the soft coal chimney would not have been as good a preventive as the spark-arresters actually used, and that all reasonable precautions were taken by the Commissioner for the minimising of the sparks that must necessarily be emitted if steam is to be kept up. The sole ground of attack left is the choice of Collie coal, or, as will be seen, the choice of a mixture of Collie coal with Newcastle coal, for use in passing through an agricultural district in very dry hot weather. If the defendant Commissioner, the respondent, is protected by Statute, as he maintains that he is, in the choice of the fuel used, then he contends than he can-not be held liable for negligence because of the mere exercise of his right of selection in that regard, and that, as he has admittedly not been guilty of negligence in the manner in which he used the fuel chosen, he stands absolved altogether. What then was the fuel used on this occasion?

The *Collie Coalfields Railway Act* 1895 (59 Vict. No. 33) authorizes the construction of a railway from the South Western line to the Collie Coalfields (sec. 2), terminating at the Govern-ment Reserve for coal. From about March 1900, if not earlier, coal from these fields was, as the Chief Mechanical Engineer testified, used by the Commissioner's engines. To what extent, if at all, it was usually mixed with other coal we are not told. The witnesses speak of no other coal than that from Collie and that imported from Newcastle, about 2,500 miles from Fremantle. There may however be some difference between the products of Collie mines in the matter of "sparking." When the Commis-sioner began to use Collie coal he had the engines fitted to consume it, and their fitness to consume it without any reason-ably avoidable risk is no longer in controversy. On 20th Decem-ber 1904, the engine, after leaving Fremantle, burned only Collie coal until it reached Spencer's Brook. The unquestioned evidence

H. C. of A.
1907.

SERMON
v.
THE COMMIS-
SIONER OF
RAILWAYS.

Barton J.

of the engine-driver shows that after leaving that junction, and thence on to Beverley—that is, while traversing the length of road on which the fire occurred—the engine was burning a mixture of Collie and Newcastle coals in the proportion of about half of each. To sustain his case, therefore, the appellant has to argue that the use of such a mixture is not authorized by the Statute, and that its consumption by the respondent is therefore negligent on the ground that it was more dangerous than Newcastle coal alone, though less dangerous than Collie coal alone. In testing this contention it must be taken, and I think it has been shown, as a state of fact, that the Collie coal emits many more sparks than the Newcastle coal, and that the mixture used on the day of the fire between Spencer's Brook and Beverley was less dangerous than the first-named coal and more dangerous than the last-named.

The argument therefore amounts to this, that if there is a coal to be found which emits fewer sparks than another, then as between those two there is negligence actionable if damage be caused thereby in the mere fact of using the coal which emits the greater proportion of sparks, if the other is "reasonably procurable." That accessibility being postulated, the proposition probably expresses the position at common law. But if it remains true since the Statute law came, as the Commissioner thinks, to his rescue, then the Statute law has effected nothing in the authorization it is supposed to have given him. Let us see then what the Statute law is on which the respondent relies.

The *Railways Amendment Act* 1897 (61 Vict. No. 32), a short amending enactment, says (sec. 2) : " the Commissioner may at all times run locomotive engines consuming any kind of fuel, either with or without any carriages " on any railway or siding. This enactment, passed two years after the *Collie Coalfields Railway Act*, was probably passed by the legislature with keen recollections that it had practically opened the local coalfields by that piece of legislation, and with full consciousness that the Collie coal must sooner or later be largely used on the railways, if its use, as well as the use of other fuels, were sanctioned. Then the *Government Railways Act* 1904 (3 Edw. VII. No. 23), a consolidating and an amending Statute, authorizes the Commissioner

H. C. of A.
1907.

SERMON
v.
THE COMMIS-
SIONER OF
RAILWAYS.

Barton J.

by sec. 20 to "use on any railway locomotive engines consuming any kind of fuel," and to "draw or propel thereby carriages, wagons, machines, appliances and plant of every kind." It is contended for the appellant that the word "kind" means no more than genus, and that Collie coal is a species of the fuel generically called coal, and is therefore not authorized, because within the genus authorized it is still necessary to use care in the selection of the species, in the sense that the absence of such care will be actionable negligence if the species chosen, however carefully used, does cause damage that could have been avoided by the choice of another species within the same genus. Coal, it is said, is a kind of fuel, and Collie coal only a species of coal. The first is authorized, the second not so if it is reasonably possible to obtain a safer species of coal.

The argument is ingenious and was skilfully urged, but I am of opinion that it cannot prevail. It seems to me to have been the intention of the legislature to give the Commissioner complete liberty in the choice of the fuel for his engines, subject only to the duty of care in the use of the particular fuel chosen. I see no reason why in this connection the word "kind" should mean only genus. But there is a very strong reason, which McMillan J. has mentioned, why its meaning should not be restricted in that sense, for the result would be most anomalous. The Commissioner could burn wood for fuel, provided his engines were made reasonably fit for its consumption and he chose the least dangerous species of wood. But the least danger-ous wood will emit many more sparks, and consequently will cause much more risk than the most dangerous species of coal. Is it then possible that the Commissioner is to be scatheless when he burns the more dangerous fuel, and liable in damages when he chooses the less dangerous? I do not think we can possibly adopt a construction that would impute folly to the legislature, in face of the reasonable construction which is equally open to us. Accordingly I am of opinion that the law has authorized the Commissioner to choose Collie coal for fuel if he uses it with due care by adopting the best appliances procurable for minimis-ing the risk attendant on its use.

What effect the use of a mixture of Collie and Newcastle coals

H. C. of A.
1907.

SERMON
v.
THE COMMIS-
SIONER OF
RAILWAYS.

Barton J.

has on the argument which would restrict the Commissioner's authority to the choice of the genus, but not of the species, is a question which would provide an interesting subject of discussion. But the inquiry is not necessary in view of the fact that the Commissioner, had he chosen, might have used Collie coal by itself.

Reference was made during the argument to the *Public Works Act* 1902, sec. 99. That provision, in my opinion, relates to railways in course of construction by the constructing authority, the Minister, and not to railways constructed and handed over to the Commissioner, which are regulated by the *Government Railways Act*. Sec. 99 of the former Act gives the Minister in respect of the use of engines and fuel very wide powers. But though conveyed in more words, I doubt whether they are any ampler in practice than those conferred on the Commissioner by the provision now in question.

In my opinion, this case comes within the principle so clearly expressed by *Cockburn* C.J. in the case of *Vaughan* v. *Taff Vale Railway Co.* (1): "Although it may be true, that if a person keeps an animal of known dangerous propensities, or a dangerous instrument, he will be responsible to those who are thereby injured, independently of any negligence in the mode of dealing with the animal or using the instrument; yet when the legislature has sanctioned and authorized the use of a particular thing, and it is used for the purpose for which it was authorized, and every precaution has been observed to prevent injury, the sanction of the legislature carries with it this consequence, that if damage results from the use of such thing independently of negligence, the party using it is not responsible." So in this case, although in the absence of the statutory authorization the Commissioner, though he used all care, would be liable in an action of nuisance for damage done by his mere use of Collie coal, yet since the Statute that liability no longer exists, but his liability for damage caused by a negligent manner of use of the thing sanctioned still survives. In *London, Brighton and South Coast Ry. Co.* v. *Truman* (2), Lord *Halsbury* L.C. has stated the same principle in the words quoted by the Chief Justice.

(1) 5 H. & N., 679, at p. 685.　　　(2) 11 App. Cas., 45, at p. 50.

H. C. of A.
1907.

SERMON
v.
THE COMMIS-
SIONER OF
RAILWAYS.

Barton J.

And in the case of *The Mayor &c. of East Fremantle* v. *Annois*
(1), Lord *Macnaghten*, in delivering the judgment of the Judicial
Committee, said :—" The law has been settled for the last hundred
years. If persons in the position of the appellants," (who were
in the position of the Commissioner in the present case), " acting
in the execution of a public trust and for the public benefit, do an
act which they are authorized by law to do, and do it in a proper
manner, though the act so done works a special injury to a
particular individual, the individual injured cannot maintain an
action. He is without remedy unless a remedy is provided by
the Statute." And his Lordship went on to quote the words of
the then Master of the Rolls, now Lord *Collins*, in a recent
case (2):—" the only obligation on the defendants was to use
reasonable care to do no unnecessary damage to the plaintiff."

In the same judgment the Judicial Committee distinguished
two cases which in the present appeal have been cited in favour
of the plaintiff. It was pointed out that in *Geddis* v. *Proprietors
of Bann Reservoir* (3), the defendants had done the particular
act complained of without any statutory authority, and that the
same *discrimen* applied to the case of *Metropolitan Asylum
District, Managers of* v. *Hill* (4).

For the reasons given I am of opinion that this appeal must be
dismissed.

ISAACS J. With considerable reluctance I am forced to the
conclusion that the defendant must succeed.

The rule of law applicable to such a case as this is succinctly
and authoritatively stated by Lord *Macnaghten*, who delivered
the judgment of the Privy Council in *The Mayor &c. of East Fremantle* v. *Annois* (1). The passage has been already read by my
learned brother *Barton*, and I need not again quote it.

The defendant occupies the position described by Lord
Macnaghten, and the real question in controversy here is, what
has the Act authorized? Is it the use of Collie coal whenever
the Commissioner chooses, or is he only authorized to use it when
the circumstances do not render it more dangerous than other
coal which is then reasonably procurable?

(1) (1902) A.C., 213, at p. 217.   (3) 3 App. Cas., 430.
(2) (1902) A.C., 213, at p. 218.   (4) 6 App. Cas., 193.

H. C. of A.
1907.

Sermon
v.
The Commis-
sioner of
Railways.

Isaacs J.

The answer depends altogether on the intention of the legislature, and as Lord *Blackburn* said in *Metropolitan Asylum
District, Managers of* v. *Hill* (1):—" What was the intention of
the legislature in any particular Act is a question of the construction of the Act." I do not therefore stop to consider or
compare the construction given in other cases to other Acts, the
relevant rule of law deducible from the decisions having been
crystallized in the passage I have quoted from *The Mayor &c. of
East Fremantle* v. *Annois* (2).

Turning then to the Statute No. 23 of 1904, sec. 20 in its
primary signification appears to expressly authorize the Commissioner to use any kind of fuel he desires, without any limitation
of time, place, or circumstance, so long as there is no negligence
in the mode of using it. If it be used "in a proper manner," that
is taking reasonable care that in using it no unnecessary damage
is done, the Commissioner is not liable for whatever injury in
fact arises, even though less damage or none at all might have
resulted if other fuel had been used, and it is in this case
conceded that, unless the mere use of Collie coal was in the
circumstances negligent, there was no negligence.

The words "any kind of fuel" are inserted in the section, not
merely as descriptive of the locomotive engines, but as part of the
general authorization applying to the use of engines and the
nature of fuel. Reference to the rest of the Act in no way
weakens the primary meaning of the words. Besides the imperative nature of the authority created, its scope is so wide as to
rather strengthen the notion that the powers conferred on the
Commissioner with respect to the choice of fuel were intended to
be of the broadest character. Parliament has invested him as an
expert with the control and management of the great public
department, and in view apparently of the nature and situation
of the country, and taking into consideration its finances,
resources, and development, has reposed in the Commissioner the
right and the duty of selecting the fuel necessary or desirable to
work the railways, and accordingly has left him free to choose.
At all events there are no considerations I can discern which cut
down the primary meaning of the words relied on by the defendant.

(1) 6 App. Cas., 193, at p. 203.   (2) (1902) A.C., 213.

H. C. of A.
1907.

SERMON
v.
THE COMMIS-
SIONER OF
RAILWAYS.

Isaacs J.

If legislation *in pari materia* is looked at, the view I have taken is confirmed. In the *Public Works Act* 1902, sec. 99 dealing with railway construction, the words are " and any kind of fuel may be used for any such locomotive engine or machine." It would be difficult to contend that the constructing authority at all events had not full power to select Collie coal at any time. That Act was passed simultaneously with what I may call the *Commissioner's Act* 1902 No. 35, and these enactments separated construction and user. In Act 1902 No. 35, the Commissioner was given, *inter alia*, all the powers contained in sec. 2 of the *Railways Amendment Act* (No. 32 of 1897). That section began thus, " The Commissioner may at all times run locomotive engines consuming any kind of fuel." It is extremely improbable that Parliament intended to give a more limited meaning to the words " any kind of fuel " in one of these Statutes, than is attached to the same words in the other. Some argument was rested on the fact that in the *Government Railways Act* 1904 the words " at all times " have been omitted, but, as no qualifying words have been introduced, the meaning is the same. It would be an impossible construction of the Act to limit the times when the Commissioner could run locomotives, and yet that is what the contention would lead to.

The Commissioner, in my opinion, may at his discretion use at any time coal, wood, oil or any other kind of fuel he pleases, because he is expressly authorized to do so. Being authorized, and being under a duty to exercise his powers, it cannot be said that what is so authorized is unlawful. Wood is very much more dangerous in hot weather than any coal, and if he can with impunity use wood, it follows necessarily that he cannot be fixed with liability merely because he used Collie coal instead of Newcastle coal.

Upon the whole, therefore, I agree that the interpretation of sec. 20 adopted by the learned Chief Justice and the majority of the Full Court of Western Australia is correct, and that this appeal should be dismissed.

Appeal dismissed with costs.

Solicitors, for appellants, *Stone & Burt*, for *Kidston & Forbes*, Northam.

Solicitor, for respondent, *Barker* (Crown Solicitor).

N. G. P.

H. C. OF A.
1907.

SERMON
v.
THE COMMIS-
SIONER OF
RAILWAYS.

[PRIVY COUNCIL.]

THE ATTORNEY-GENERAL FOR THE STATE OF VICTORIA . . . } APPELLANT;

AND

THE MAYOR &c. OF THE CITY OF MELBOURNE . . . . . } RESPONDENTS.

ON APPEAL FROM THE HIGH COURT OF AUSTRALIA.

Electric Light and Power Act 1896 (*Vict.*) (*No.* 1413), *secs.* 13 (*d*), 38, 39, 52—Charge for supply of electricity—Preference—Uniform charge—Alternative rates—Option given to customer—"Flat rate"—"Maximum demand rate."

Undertakers under the *Electric Light and Power Act* 1896 had two scales under which they charged consumers for the supply of electricity, and all consumers had the option of which rate they would select. Under one scale, called the "flat rate," consumers were charged for the actual quantity of electricity supplied at the uniform rate of $4\frac{1}{2}$d. per unit. Under the other scale, called the "maximum demand rate," consumers were charged at the rate of 7d. per unit as to such portion of the electricity supplied to them as was equal to a consumption for a period of 45 hours per calendar month at the highest rate of consumption during the month, and, as to the remainder of the electricity so supplied during the month, at the rate of 2d. per unit.

Held: That the words "a supply on the same terms" in sec. 38 of the *Electric Light and Power Act* 1896 bear their natural meaning and include price; that the "preference" prohibited by sec. 39 is a preference between customers dealing under similar circumstances, and not between customers dealing under two different systems of supply, either of which they are free to select, and therefore dealing under entirely different circumstances; and that therefore the charges were lawful.

---

*Present.—The Lord Chancellor, Lord Macnaghten, Lord Atkinson, Lord Collins, Sir Arthur Wilson.

PRIVY
COUNCIL.
1907.

THE
ATTORNEY-
GENERAL FOR
THE STATE OF
VICTORIA
v.
THE MAYOR
&C. OF THE
CITY OF
MELBOURNE.

Decision of High Court (*The Mayor &c. of the City of Melbourne v. The Attorney-General for the State of Victoria*, 3 C.L.R., 467), affirmed.

APPEAL to His Majesty in Council from the decision of the High Court : *The Mayor &c. of the City of Melbourne* v. *The Attorney-General for the State of Victoria* (1).

The judgment of their Lordships was delivered by

LORD ATKINSON. The proceeding out of which the appeal in this case arose, was an information exhibited by the Attorney-General of the State of Victoria on the relation of the Metropolitan Gas Company against the Corporation of the City of Melbourne, who are by an Order of the Governor in Council, dated the 6th of September 1897, made under the authority of an Act of the Victorian legislature, entitled the *Electric Light and Power Act* 1896 (No. 1413), constituted undertakers for the supply of electricity within that City, to restrain them from continuing to charge their consumers for electricity supplied, rates which are not uniform per unit throughout the City.

There is no dispute as to the facts. It is admitted that the Corporation supply electricity under two different systems at rates appropriate to each, but not identical. Under the first, the quantity used is charged for at the rate of $4\frac{1}{2}$d. per unit. It is known as the "flat rate." Under the second a rate of 7d. per unit, known as the "maximum demand rate," is charged for such portion of the electricity supplied as is equal to a consumption for a period of 45 hours per calendar month at the highest rate of consumption during that month, and a rate of 2d. per unit is charged for the remainder of the electricity supplied during the month.

Both rates are less than the maximum rate authorized by the Act and Order. It is admitted that it is optional with every customer, or intending customers, to choose the system under which he shall be supplied, and that, as between the several customers under each system, no preference is given to one customer over the other, though under the operation of the second system different results work out in the case of different customers, as

(1) 3 C. L. R., 467.

must be the case where, as in this instance, the amount consumed is taken into consideration in fixing the price.

The counsel for the plaintiff contend that the mode of carrying on their business adopted by the defendants is illegal : that they cannot have two different systems of supply, and are only entitled to charge one uniform rate for all electricity supplied by them, irrespective of the quantity supplied, or the time when, or circumstances under which, it is supplied.

PRIVY
COUNCIL.
1907.

THE
ATTORNEY-
GENERAL FOR
THE STATE OF
VICTORIA
v.
THE MAYOR
&C. OF THE
CITY OF
MELBOURNE.

The question for decision turns on the construction of the 39th section of the above-mentioned Statute taken in connection, as it must be, with sec. 38 which immediately precedes it. The two sections are in the terms following :—

" Sec. 38.—(1) Where a supply of electricity is provided in any part of an area for private purposes, then, except in so far as is otherwise provided by the terms of the Order authorizing such supply, every council company or person within that part of the area shall on application be entitled to a supply on the same terms on which any other council company or person in such part of the area is entitled under similar circumstances to a corresponding supply.

" Sec. 39.—The undertakers shall not in making any agreements for a supply of electricity show any preference to any council company or person, and the charge for such supply shall be uniform throughout such area so that each council company or person shall be supplied at the same price and not less than any other council company or person, but such price shall not exceed the limits of price imposed by or in pursuance of the Order authorizing them to supply electricity."

The case came on for trial on the 26th September 1905 before the Chief Justice of Victoria, *Sir John Madden.* He referred the whole action on the pleadings and evidence to the Full Court of the Supreme Court of Victoria, who, considering that the case came within the principle of their previous decision in an action between the same parties : *The Attorney-General &c.* v. *The Mayor &c. of the City of Melbourne* (1), decided in favour of the plaintiff, and in effect granted the injunction prayed for, restraining the defendants from supplying throughout the area of supply

(1) 27 V.L.R., 568 ; 23 A.L.T., 123.

PRIVY
COUNCIL.
1907.

THE
ATTORNEY-
GENERAL FOR
THE STATE OF
VICTORIA
v.
THE MAYOR
&c. OF THE
CITY OF
MELBOURNE.

electricity at other than a uniform rate, except so far as is authorized by the *Electric Light and Power Act* 1901 (No. 1775).

By this previous decision the defendants had been restrained from supplying electricity for heating or power purposes, at a rate lower than the rate charged for lighting purposes. And in consequence of it the legislature of Victoria had passed the Act in the Order of the High Court mentioned, the third section of which runs as follows:—

"3. Notwithstanding anything in any other Act contained it shall be lawful for any undertaker within the meaning of the *Electric Light and Power Act* 1896 or for any gas company to charge for the supply of electricity or gas used for power or heating purposes respectively or both a lower uniform charge than that charged for the supply of electricity or gas used for lighting purposes."

On appeal to the High Court of Australia the decision in the present case was reversed, and an order made dismissing the plaintiff's action with costs. From this last-mentioned decision the present appeal has, by special leave, been brought.

It was in argument contended on behalf of the plaintiff on the authority of *The Attorney-General* v. *Clarkson* (1), that the above-mentioned Statute of 1901 amounted to a statutory declaration that according to the true meaning of the Act of 1896 only one uniform rate could be charged by the defendants for the electricity supplied by them throughout their district.

In *The Attorney-General* v. *Clarkson* (1), the Crown claimed payment of the further duty called "settlement estate duty" on a legacy bequeathed by a testator on a certain contingency which, at the date of his death, had not happened and might never happen. One of the questions for decision was whether this legacy could be held to be "settled property" within the meaning of sec. 5, sub-sec. 1, of the *Finance Act* 1894.

In a previous case of *The Attorney-General* v. *Fairley* (2), it had been decided that property, bequeathed by will on a contingency which had not arisen at the testator's death and might never arise, was under the provisions of the above-mentioned section liable to this higher duty.

(1) (1900) 1 Q.B., 156.   (2) (1897) 1 Q.B., 698.

PRIVY
COUNCIL.
1907.

THE
ATTORNEY-
GENERAL FOR
THE STATE OF
VICTORIA
v.
THE MAYOR
&C. OF THE
CITY OF
MELBOURNE.

By sec. 14 of the *Finance Act* 1898 (61 & 62 Vict. c. 10), it was provided that, "Where in the case of a death occurring after the commencement of this Act settlement estate duty is paid in respect of any property contingently settled, and it is thereafter shown that the contingency has not arisen, and cannot arise, the said duty paid in respect of such property shall be repaid." It is quite obvious that this enactment must have contemplated that the duty should continue to be paid on such a contingency, since it provided that, when so paid, it should, in certain cases, be returned, and was therefore an adoption of the construction put upon sec. 5, sub-sec. 1, of the *Finance Act* in *The Attorney-General v. Fairley* (1); but the Act of 1901 merely empowers the company to do that which they had insisted they had under the Act of 1896 the right to do, and by no means affirms expressly or impliedly that the Court, which held, on the construction of the latter Statute, that they had no right to do this thing, were justified in so deciding. Cases constantly occur where, if a Court, even of first instance, should put upon a Statute a construction which would defeat its obvious purpose, or cause great inconvenience, the speediest and most effective remedy is to pass an Act in a form similar to that of 1901, setting the matter right. Circumstances may not permit the delay necessarily involved in bringing the embarrassing decision before higher tribunals for reconsideration. The fact, however, that this remedy was at once applied by the legislature of Victoria does not, in the absence of express words or clear intendment, preclude those superior tribunals from reviewing the decision of the inferior when the occasion arises.

In the opinion of their Lordships the contention of the plaintiff on this point is entirely unsustainable.

Sec. 13 (*d*) of the *Electric Light and Power Act* 1896 provides that conditions and restrictions may be inserted in, or prescribed by, the Order in Council made under the Act with regard, amongst other things, to "the limitation of the *prices* to be charged in respect of the supply of electricity."

Sec. 38 is practically identical with the 19th section of the English Act, the *Electric Lighting Act* 1882 ; but sec. 39, dealing

(1) (1897) 1 Q.B., 698.

PRIVY
COUNCIL.
1907.

THE
ATTORNEY-
GENERAL FOR
THE STATE OF
VICTORIA
v.
THE MAYOR
&C. OF THE
CITY OF
MELBOURNE.

with preference, differs in its wording from sec. 20 of the English Act of 1882, relating to the same subject.

In *The Metropolitan Electric Supply Company Limited v. Ginder* (1), it was held by the present Lord Justice *Buckley* that the words "a supply on the same terms," used in sec. 19 of the English Act, bear their natural meaning and include price. Mr. *Danckwerts* contended, on behalf of the plaintiff, however, that the same words, contained in the corresponding section of the Victoria Act, namely, sec. 38, cannot, by reason of the provisions of sec. 39, which follows it, be held to include price. Their Lordships cannot concur in this view.

The 39th section is rather unskilfully drawn and clumsily worded, but their Lordships think that the "preference" prohibited in substance by it is "a preference" between customers dealing under similar circumstances, and not between customers dealing under two different systems of supply, either of which they are free to select, and therefore dealing under entirely different circumstances.

This construction reconciles the two secs. 38 and 39 one to the other, and makes them consistent; does no violence to any of the provisions of either; does not impose on the defendants, as would the construction contended for by the plaintiff, most embarrassing restrictions in the conduct of their undertaking; and at the same time promotes rather than hurts the interests of the consumers, while there is, in the view of their Lordships, nothing in sec. 52 of the Act which prevents its being adopted.

Their Lordships are therefore of opinion that the decision of the High Court of Australia was right and should be affirmed, and this appeal dismissed, and they will humbly advise His Majesty to that effect.

The appellant will pay the costs of the appeal.

(1) (1901) 2 Ch., 799, at p. 811.

[HIGH COURT OF AUSTRALIA.]

GOLDSBROUGH, MORT & COMPANY,
LIMITED . . . .} APPELLANTS ;

AND

LARCOMBE . . . . RESPONDENT.

ON APPEAL FROM THE SUPREME COURT OF NEW SOUTH WALES.

Pastures Protection Act 1902 *(N.S. W.), (No.* 111 *of* 1902*), sec.* 42—*Rabbit-proof fence on boundary of holding—Right of owner to contribution—Liability of adjoining owner —Time when liability arises—Effect of notice of demand—Construction of Statutes—Repeal and re-enactment with modifications.*

Sec. 42 of the *Pastures Protection Act* 1902 (N.S.W.) provides that the owner or occupier of a holding who erects rabbit-proof fencing on the boundary of his holding, or makes an existing fence rabbit-proof, may recover from the owner of adjoining land a contribution towards the cost of the work, "subject to the provisions of this section." The section then provides that no contribution shall be payable unless the fence has been erected or made rabbit-proof *bond fide* for the purpose of protection against rabbits and the owner who is called upon for contribution derives a benefit from the fence, and, further, that the right to contribution shall vest and the liability to pay it shall arise "when the then occupier or owner of the holding gives to the then owner of the land outside the holding the prescribed notice of demand," and from that time so much of the contribution as remains unpaid shall be a charge upon the land. It is immaterial whether the fencing was done before or after the commencement of the Act.

Held, that the right to contribution and the liability to pay it are not limited respectively to the owner who has actually incurred the expense of fencing and the person who was the owner of the adjoining land when the expense was incurred, but extend to subsequent owners, and, therefore, the owner for the time being of the holding in respect of which the expense was originally incurred is entitled, upon giving due notice of demand, to contribution from the holder for the time being of the adjoining land.

H. C. of A.
1907.

SYDNEY,
Nov. 25, 26,
27.

Griffith C.J.,
Barton and
Isaacs JJ.

H. C. of A.
1907.

GOLDS-
BROUGH,
MORT & Co.
LTD.
v.
LARCOMBE.

Where a provision in a Statute has been judicially interpreted, and the legislature subsequently, in a consolidating Statute, repeals that provision and substitutes for it a provision in substantially different language, it is to be presumed, *primâ facie*, that they intended to alter the law as declared by the previous decisions.

Decision of the Supreme Court: *Larcombe* v. *Goldsbrough, Mort & Co.*, (1907) 7 S.R. (N.S.W.), 123, reversed.

APPEAL from a decision of the Supreme Court on a special case stated by the Land Appeal Court.

This was a claim by the appellants under sec. 42 of the *Pastures Protection Act* 1902 before a local Land Board, for contribution by the respondent towards the cost of erecting a rabbit-proof fence on portion of the common boundary between their holdings. The holding of the respondent consisted of portions 102 and 95, but at the date of the erection of the fence in 1901 he was the owner of portion 95 only and had acquired portion 102 subsequently. Notice of demand was served by the appellants upon the respondent in August 1905, claiming a contribution in respect of the whole fence, including that bounding portion 102 as well as that bounding portion 95. The Land Board allowed the claim, and their decision was affirmed by the Land Appeal Court. A special case was then stated by the Land Appeal Court, the following questions being submitted for the opinion of the Full Court:—(*a*) Do the words "the then occupier or owner" and "the then owner" in the third paragraph of sec. 42 of the *Pastures Protection Act* 1902 (No. 111) mean the occupier or owner respectively at the date of notice of demand or such owner or occupier at the date of erection of the fence; (*b*) whether, the boundary fence between the land of the appellants and portion 102 having been made rabbit-proof when the respondent was not the owner, the claim for contribution in respect of that portion of the fence can be maintained against the respondent; (*c*) whether on the expiry of the annual lease of portion 102 held by the respondent's predecessor in title the half of the rabbit-proof fencing became the property of the Crown, so as to disentitle the appellants from bringing a claim in respect of it; and a fourth question which is not material to this appeal.

The Full Court answered these questions in favour of the

respondent: *Larcombe* v. *Goldsbrough, Mort & Co.* (1), and from that decision the present appeal was brought by special leave.

The material sections are set out in the judgments hereunder.

Windeyer (*Whitfeld* with him), for the appellants. The whole question turns on the word "then" in the third paragraph of sec. 42. The only reasonable construction is to make it relate to the giving of notice. That is the point at which the Act fixes the liability and the right to contribution. The person who is owner when the notice is given may claim contribution from the person who is holder of the adjoining land at that time. Reference to the previous provision, for which this has been substituted, and to the decisions upon it, makes the matter still clearer. [He referred to *Booth* v. *Bryce* (2); *Hill, Clark & Co.* v. *Dalgety & Co.* (3); *Goldsbrough, Mort & Co.* v. *Gow* (4).] The result of those cases was to establish the law under the *Rabbit Act* 1890, sec. 20 on the basis that the owner who actually erected the fence was the only person who could claim contribution, and the only person liable to contribute was the person who was the holder of the adjoining land at the date of the erection. The present section, which takes the place of sec. 20 of the *Rabbit Act*, contains the word "then" before owner in each instance, and it must be presumed that the legislature in so altering the language had in view the decisions on the construction of the original section, and intended to make a change in the law. This view is further strengthened by the middle part of the section, the proviso that there shall be no contribution unless the person from whom it is claimed derives benefit from the fence. It is possible that the adjoining holder might derive no benefit at the time of erection, but his successors in title may, and yet, on the respondent's construction, they would not be liable to pay for the benefit. [He referred also to section 43, as to annual contributions.]

Piddington (*Waddell* with him), for the respondent. Paragraph 1 of sec. 42 is the guiding portion of the enactment as to

H. C. of A.
1907.

GOLDS-
BROUGH,
MORT & Co.
LTD.
v.
LARCOMBE.

H. C. of A.
1907.

GOLDS-
BROUGH,
MORT & Co.
LTD.
v.
LARCOMBE.

the class of persons to pay and to be paid. It is the person who has incurred the expense who may make the claim, and the time within which the right can vest is limited to his tenure: *Mortimore* v. *Mortimore* (1); *Mortimer* v. *Slater* (2). This provision has reference only to personal rights and liabilities, and the corresponding provision in sec. 20 of the *Rabbit Act* is practically identical. The legislature must be presumed to have adopted the construction put upon that provision by the Courts: *Saunders* v. *Borthistle* (3). "Then owner" refers back to the time when the right to claim a contribution arises, that is to say, when the owner has erected a fence that is rabbit-proof and of benefit to the adjoining holder. The word "then" has been inserted for the purpose of pointing to the original owner as the person entitled, and the person who was "then" the holder of the adjoining land as the person liable to pay. Without that word the third paragraph would be possibly open to the construction contended for by the appellants. The vesting of the right and the arising of the liability are postponed until the notice of demand has been made, but the persons who may acquire the right or be made liable have been ascertained by the first paragraph. The third paragraph limits the right of the owner who has incurred the expense to enforce his claim by prescribing a notice of demand. The period of vesting is important for the purpose of sec. 43, which makes the contribution a charge upon the land. The proviso as to *bona fides* &c. was inserted to meet the case of *Goldsbrough, Mort & Co.* v. *Gow* (4). If the legislature had intended to impose upon subsequent adjoining holders the liability to contribute, they could have made it clear by using the words "or his transferee." The only transfer of liability that has been provided for is that incident to making the contribution a charge upon the land. [He referred to secs. 43, 48 (2) (e), and Form 25 of notice of demand, under Regulation 46; *Hill, Clark & Co.* v. *Dalgety & Co.* (5).]

Nov. 27th, 1907.   GRIFFITH C.J. This is an appeal from a judgment of the Supreme Court allowing an appeal from the Land Appeal Court

(1) 4 App. Cas., 448.   (4) (1901) 1 S.R. (N.S.W.), 36.
(2) 7 Ch. D., 322, at p. 330.   (5) 15 N.S.W. W.N., 50.
(3) 1 C.L.R., 379.

H. C. OF A.
1907.

GOLDS-
BROUGH,
MORT & Co.
LTD.
v.
LARCOMBE.

Griffith C.J.

on a case arising under the *Pastures Protection Act* 1902. The appellants and the respondent were owners of adjoining tracts of land. In 1901 the appellants, at their own expense, made an existing boundary fence between the two pieces of land rabbit-proof. At that time respondent was the owner in fee of a portion of the land of which he is now the owner, and he became the owner of the remainder by a special lease granted in 1904.

The appellants claim that under these circumstances they are entitled to obtain from him contribution in respect of the whole cost of the boundary fence. And so the Land Appeal Court thought. The Supreme Court held that they were not entitled to recover on the ground that the only person from whom contribution could be claimed was the person who was owner when the fence was made rabbit-proof.

The question arises under sec. 42 of the *Pastures Protection Act* 1902, which is a re-enactment of an Act passed earlier in the same year and called the *Rabbit Act* 1901. Sec. 42 provides:—
"Where the boundary, or any part thereof, of any holding is fenced with a rabbit-proof fence, or a fence of such boundary, or part thereof, has been made rabbit-proof at the expense of the occupier or owner of such holding, or of the occupier or the owner of any land included in the holding, a contribution towards the cost of the work shall, subject to the provisions of this section, be payable by the owner of any land outside the holding and adjoining the rabbit-proof fence to the occupier or owner who has incurred such expense:

"Provided that a contribution shall not be payable where the local Land Board is of opinion that the rabbit-proof fence has been erected, or the fence has been made rabbit-proof, otherwise than *bonâ fide* for the purpose of excluding or destroying rabbits, or unless or until in the opinion of the said Board the land from the owner whereof the contribution is demanded derives a benefit therefrom:

"The right to receive such contribution shall vest, and the liability to pay the same shall arise, when the then occupier or owner of the holding gives to the then owner of the land outside the holding the prescribed notice of demand; and from and after the date when such notice is given, the amount of the contribution,

H. C. of A.
1907.

GOLDS-
BROUGH,
MORT & Co.
LTD.
v.
LARCOMBE.

Griffith C.J.

or so much thereof as may for the time being be unpaid, shall, until payment, be and remain a charge upon the land in respect of which such contribution is payable."

Then follow some provisions to which it is not necessary to refer, except the last, which reads:—" It shall be immaterial whether the rabbit-proof fence was erected or the fence was made rabbit-proof before or after the commencement of the Act."

That last provision is very important, because it shows that the intention of the legislature was to give the right of contribution in respect of all rabbit-proof fencing, whether already existing or afterwards to be erected. It was to create a new right of recourse to the adjoining owner, no matter how old the fence might be, provided it was an effective fence. That is very important in consideration of the view taken by the learned Judges of the Supreme Court, who thought that the notice could only be given to the person who was the owner of the adjoining land when the fence was erected.

I will point out the extraordinary result that would follow. The owner of land who has erected a rabbit-proof fence before the passing of the Act, no matter how long before, is entitled to contribution. But according to the decision given, he cannot get that contribution until he has given notice to the owner of the adjoining land. In the meantime the land may have passed to a succession of owners, and he has to give notice to some person who has no longer any interest in the land, whom he may not be able to find, and a judgment against whom, if found, will bind his successor in title to the land. That is an extraordinary result.

For the appellants it is contended that the right of obligation to contribute is imposed on the person called the " then owner." Sec. 42 says " the right to receive such contribution shall vest, and the liability to pay the same shall arise, when the then occupier or owner of the holding gives to the then owner of the land outside the holding the prescribed notice of demand." It is said that that points clearly to the existing state of things. The person who for the time being is owner of the holding is to give notice to the person who is for the time being the owner of the adjoining land. That is the *primâ facie* meaning of the language of the section. The word " then " refers to some time.

The only time to which it can refer grammatically is to that of the verb " gives."

H. C. of A.
1907.

GOLDS-
BROUGH,
MORT & Co.
LTD.
v.
LARCOMBE.

Griffith C.J.

In my opinion the words of the section *primâ facie* mean that the owner for the time being may give the notice to the owner for the time being of the adjoining land. It is said that, although that may be the *primâ facie* meaning, it is not the true meaning, and that the context controls it.

There had been an earlier Act, the *Rabbit Act* 1890, by which also a right to contribution was given. Sec. 20 of that Act provided : —" When the boundaries of any holding or any portion of such boundaries shall have been made rabbit-proof, the owner of such holding shall be entitled to serve notice of demand and thereafter to enforce from the owner of any outside holding or lands (whether public or private) adjoining the rabbit-proof fence a contribution of one-half of the cost of making such boundaries rabbit-proof, and an annual contribution of one-half the cost of the mainten-ance and repair of the rabbit-proof fence, subject to the following provisions."

That also was intended to apply to fences erected before the passing of that Act, but the Supreme Court held in 1898 that that right could only be enforced against the person who was the owner of the adjoining land at the time when the fence was erected. It is unnecessary to consider whether that decision was correct or not, because in 1902 the legislature passed the section in the form now appearing.

It is contended that what the legislature intended was a mere re-enactment of the original Act. The *primâ facie* inference, however, is that they intended to change the then existing law. I have pointed out that the words " then owner," used twice in sec. 42, apparently mean the owner for the time being. I find two provisions which strongly confirm that view. The first paragraph of the section provides that a case for contribution has been made when a fence, or part of it, has been made rabbit-proof, at the expense of the occupier or owner, a contribution towards the cost shall be payable by the owner of any land outside the holding and adjoining the fence to the person who gives notice as owner of the holding. It follows, therefore, that, in the event of a present holding comprising land which previously formed two

H. C. of A.
1907.

Golds-
brough,
Mort & Co.
Ltd.
v.
Larcombe.

Griffith C.J.

or more holdings, the present holder may claim contribution in respect of the fencing erected by one of the previous separate owners, which clearly suggests that notice need not be given by the person who puts up the fence.

I find, again, the proviso that the contribution is not payable until the owner of the land derives a benefit from it. It may be, therefore—as is quite apparent to anyone familiar with the conditions of the country—that rabbit-proof fencing has not been of any value to the owners of the adjoining land for many years after erection, but as soon as it becomes of value, then the person who erected the fence can claim contribution.

The proviso also certainly suggests that the time referred to is not the time when the fence was erected, but the time when the owner becomes entitled to the benefit of the Act, which is not until he gives notice to the then owner of the adjoining land.

The only words which can be suggested to indicate a different meaning are, that the contribution shall be payable " to the occupier or owner who has incurred such expense." That, it is said, shows that the only person who can claim is the person who spends the money in putting up the fence ; but that is not consistent with the first part of the same sentence, which authorizes the owner of the holding to claim contribution in respect of a fence erected by the previous owner of part of it.

It may be that the present owner is to be regarded as a duly constituted agent of the previous owner to sue for that contribution, or the legislature may have taken the eminently common-sense view that, when a man has put up a rabbit-proof fence and afterwards sells the land, the person who purchased his land has in all probability paid for that fence, and is entitled to all the benefits arising from the ownership of it.

Such a construction gives a full and literal meaning to all parts of the section, with the exception of the few words, the " owner who has incurred such expense," &c.

For these reasons I am of opinion that the decision of the Land Appeal Court was right, and that the section must be read in its literal meaning, as giving the right to the present appellants to proceed against the present respondent for a contribution.

BARTON J.　There are two portions in question, 95 and 102. Liability as to portion 95 is apparently admitted, and it seems to be also admitted that, with regard to both portions, it was the appellants, who, acting as owners, incurred the expense of making a boundary fence rabbit-proof.

H. C. OF A.
1907.

GOLDS-
BROUGH,
MORT & Co.
LTD.
v.
LARCOMBE.

Barton J.

The sections now in question are purely consolidating sections taken from the *Rabbit Act* 1901 and passed in 1902. The claim is one for contribution for making rabbit-proof a fence situated on the common boundary of lands occupied by the claimant and appellant company, and that occupied by the respondent Larcombe, and the main contest in the case is as to the meaning of the words " the then occupier and owner of the holding " and "the then owner of the land outside the holding."

In the judgment of the Supreme Court the Chief Justice of New South Wales said (1) :—" Now, the then occupier or owner who is to give the notice is the occupier or owner who has incurred the expense ; it is he and he only who can claim contribution. The first adverb 'then' clearly refers to the occupier or owner who was the occupier or owner when the fence was made rabbit-proof ;　.　.　.　the second adverb 'then' has reference to the same time, and not, as has been contended, to the time when the notice of demand is given." If His Honor's opinion there stated is correct, of course that ends the case. But I have not been able to persuade myself that His Honor has correctly interpreted the section in the passage quoted. First let us read the last portion of the section by itself. " The right to receive such contribution shall vest, and the liability to pay the same shall arise, when the then occupier or owner of the holding gives to the then owner of the land outside the holding the prescribed notice of demand." So that it is the giving of the notice of demand which invests the claimant with the right to receive contribution, and imposes immediate liability to pay upon the adjoining owner. The then occupier or owner of the land, and the then owner of the land outside seem to me to be terms which require no explanation whatever as they stand. The time when the right of contribution vests and the liability arises is when the then occupier or owner gives to the then occupier or

(1) (1907) 7 S.R. (N.S.W.), 123, at p. 125.

H. C. of A.
1907.

Golds-
brough,
Mort & Co.
Ltd.
v.
Larcombe.

Barton J.

owner notice of demand. It seems to be a proposition for which it is difficult to find any plainer equivalent.

Primarily the words "then occupier or owner of the holding" plainly mean the existing occupier or owner of the holding, and the words "then owner of the land" mean the existing owner of the land outside. It is the meaning that persons in ordinary conversation would adopt, and unless there is something in the Statute to the contrary, it must control the Court.

As regards the judgment of the Full Court arising upon portion of the same section—the last part of the first paragraph —if that portion of the section were read in the way I am going to read it now, leaving out some of the words, it might be strongly contended that there was a context controlling the third paragraph, and affixing to it the meaning that the Full Court gave it. If it read:—"A contribution towards the cost of the work shall be payable by the owner of any land outside the holding and adjoining the rabbit-proof fence to the occupier or owner who has incurred such expense"—if, I say, that were the context, it might control the meaning of the third paragraph and form such a context to the word "then," as to give it a meaning which does not primarily appear. But that is not the first paragraph. The concluding words of the paragraph are these :—"A contribution towards the cost of the work shall, *subject to the provisions of this section*, be payable by the owner of any land outside the holding and adjoining the rabbit-proof fence to the occupier or owner who has incurred such expense." And it seems to me that by the insertion of the words "subject to the provisions of this section" the primary meaning of the words in the first paragraph, which might otherwise have been different, is subjected or controlled by the rest or the later part. Not to read the first paragraph in that manner is to deny the force and effect of the words "subject to the provisions of this section," which words subordinate that part of the section to the remainder of it.

It seems to me, therefore, that by the insertion of the words I have read—which do not appear to have impressed themselves upon their Honors—the legislature has intended to give a controlling force to the remaining provisions, so far as they are plain. And this provision in the third paragraph is, on its face, one that requires no definition. The right to receive vests, and the liability to pay arises, when the occupier for the time being gives the prescribed notice of demand to the person who owns the outside land at that time. I do not think that, in putting the words in this way, I have made them one jot clearer than they are in the section itself.

If there were any doubt as to the meaning of the section standing alone, that doubt is removed by the prior legislation of 1890, and the cases decided under it.

The *Rabbit Act* 1890, sec. 20, provided :—" When the boundaries of any holding or any portion of such boundaries shall have been made rabbit-proof, the owner of such holding shall be entitled to serve notice of demand and thereafter to enforce from the owner of any outside holding or lands (whether public or private) adjoining the rabbit-proof fence a contribution of one-half the cost of making such boundaries rabbit-proof, and an annual contribution of one-half the cost of the maintenance and repair of the rabbit-proof fence, subject to the following provisions : "

The 21st section provided :—" The provisions of the last preceding section shall extend and apply to rabbit-proof fences erected, and to fences made rabbit-proof, before the passing of this Act."

Now there are certain decisions under that Act, among them *Booth* v. *Bryce* (1) ; *Hill, Clark & Co.* v. *Dulgety & Co.* (2) ; and *Goldsbrough, Mort & Co.* v. *Gow* (3). The latter, I think, is not so important as the two earlier cases. Those decisions demonstrate that it was the opinion of the Full Court that under sec. 20 the word " owner " did not mean owner from time to time of the land, but the owner who had erected the fence or made it rabbit-proof. Whether sec. 20 really bears that meaning, or whether the word " owner " used in that section means " owner from time to time," it is not necessary now to inquire. It is enough to say that the decisions serve to show that their Honors put the interpretation I have mentioned on the express words of the *Rabbit Act* 1890, and therefore held that the word " owner "

H. C. of A.
1907.

GOLDS-
BROUGH,
MORT & Co.
LTD.
v.
LARCOMBE

Barton J.

(1) 13 N.S.W. W.N., 98.　　　　(2) 15 N.S.W. W.N., 50.
(3) (1901) 1 S.R. (N.S.W.), 36.

H. C. of A.
1907.

GOLDS-
BROUGH,
MORT & Co.
LTD.
v.
LARCOMBE.

Barton J.

was not the owner from time to time, in the signification I have attached to the words "then owner," in respect of the Act of 1902.

But what is important is that these decisions afford an aid to the construction of the Act of 1902. A judicial interpretation was placed upon portion of the *Rabbit Act* 1890, corresponding with that which we are now dealing with. The legislature, if they had found words judicially construed according to their own meaning and intention, might have been expected to leave these words as they stood. But the fact that they have altered the words substantially of course puts the duty upon the interpreter of the Statute to see whether the legislature has not altered the language in order to remove any doubt as to its meaning caused by intervening decisions. And I think that is what the legislature has done in this Act.

I mention at this stage that the sections which are of any importance are secs. 43 and 70 of the *Rabbit Act* 1901, passed in 1902, and then secs. 33, 34 and 62 respectively. It was in the *Rabbit Act* passed eleven years or so after the Act which has been judicially interpreted that these sections first occurred, and they are now transferred to the *Pastures Protection Act* 1902.

I have read the material portions of the 20th section of the *Rabbit Act* 1890, and it does appear that it was then doubtful whether or not the word "owner" bore the interpretation that the Court affixed to it. There was room for doubt whether the word in the Act of 1890 was not open to two constructions. Parliament has, to my mind, put a definite interpretation upon its meaning by the expression used in the *Rabbit Act* 1901, and copied into the Act of 1902. And so, if there were any doubt as to the meaning of the contested expressions in the Act of 1902, that doubt would be removed by contrasting them with the phrases of the Act of 1890; and, for the purpose of such contrast, it is enough to show that in the Act of 1890 there was an ambiguity as to the meaning of the word "owner." Then we turn, in the light of the intervening decisions, to the Act of 1902, and see the word "owner" qualified with another expression evidently intended to make clear the meaning of the words "occupier or owner of such holding" and "owner" of the holding

to be assessed. And when the word "then" is used in connection
with the endeavour, it seems to me to be a clear endeavour to
give a definite meaning to those two expressions for the purpose
of removing doubts which might have arisen under previous
legislation. Then the construction, that I have ventured to say
is to be put upon the 42nd section, is fortified by the change
made when Parliament had before it previous legislation, and the
interpretation that had been given it, and Parliament must be
assumed to have duly reconsidered its earlier work with the view
of making its intention clearer, and not of leaving things as they
were.

If the ordinary meaning of these words is just what they
say, and they cannot be controlled except by some such context
as has been pointed out in the first paragraph, then, unless they
are so controlled, the case for the appellants becomes amply clear.
I am of opinion that the words "subject to the provisions of this
section," in the first paragraph, were devised for the very purpose
of preventing that which had been held to be a controlling phrase
from being any longer a controlling phrase, and, indeed, of sub-
ordinating it to what follows ; and therefore that the words in
the last paragraph must be taken to mean what they say and to
govern the section.

There are other expressions in the 42nd section which
strengthen the construction this Court is placing on the words.
I need not refer to them. I rest my opinion upon the considerations I have already laid down, which seem to me to be sufficient.
I would add just one thing. The 70th section of the *Pastures
Protection Act* 1902 provides :—" Whenever by this Part, any sum
of money is expressed to be charged upon any private land, any
person thereafter becoming the owner of such land shall be taken
to have notice of such charge, and shall be liable to pay the sum
so charged or so much thereof as may for the time being remain
unpaid as if he were the person originally liable; but nothing
herein contained shall operate to discharge the liability of any
person originally or previously liable. Provided always such
charge shall be entered in the rate-book as against such land
at the date of transfer, and it shall be the duty of the board
when and so often as any land within the district becomes charge-

H. C. of A.
1907.

GOLDS-
BROUGH,
MORT & Co.
LTD.
v.
LARCOMBE.

Barton J.

H. C. of A.
1907.

GOLDS-
BROUGH,
MORT & Co.
LTD.
v.
LARCOMBE.

Barton J.

able with any sum under this Part to have an entry of the same made as aforesaid." That is a section copied from the 62nd section of the *Rabbit Act* 1902. It has been suggested that it refers only to rates, because the proviso declares that any charge upon the land shall be entered in the rate book. I cannot find that it requires any such interpretation. The section occurs in the same Part of the Act as sec. 42 and the connected sections.

There is thus imposed in connection with the charge, which the contribution forms upon the land of the outside holder, a distinct personal liability, and it would be impossible to contend that the owner of the land under that section does not mean the owner from time to time. That being so, it seems perfectly clear that there is running with the land a charge, and concurrently with that charge there is a liability.

I am therefore of opinion that the appeal should be allowed.

ISAACS J. read the following judgment. It is unnecessary to consider whether previous decisions under prior legislation were well founded or not, but I should like to state formally, as I indicated during the argument, what seems to me to be the connected and well settled plan devised by the legislature in secs. 42 and 43 of the Act.

Sec. 42 begins by providing that, where the owner (for brevity I leave out the occupier) of land provides a boundary rabbit-proof fence, a contribution towards the cost of the work shall "subject to the provisions of this section" be payable by the adjoining owner to the owner who incurred the expense. The respondent contends, and the Supreme Court has held, that the legislature means throughout the whole section to confine the right to receive the contribution, on the one hand, and the liability to pay it, on the other, to the two individuals who happen to be the fencing owner and the adjoining owner at the time the work is done. But that is not, in my opinion, the meaning of the section. The words "subject to the provisions of this section" are equivalent to saying "except as modified or otherwise provided by this section," and when the whole section is examined, it is found that the legislature has not only prescribed general conditions of liability for every case, but has also otherwise provided

H. C. of A.
1907.

Golds-
brough,
Mort & Co.
Ltd.
v.
Larcombe.

Isaacs J.

most carefully for what must be expected sometimes to happen, namely, transmission or transfer of ownership both of the fencing owner's land, and the adjoining owner's land, between the time when the fence, or portion of the fence as the case may be, is completed and the time when the demand is or can be lawfully and effectually made. The second paragraph of the first sub-section of sec. 42 insists on *bona fides*, and further enacts that no contribution shall be payable "unless or until in the opinion of the said board the land from the owner whereof the contribution is demanded derives a benefit therefrom." I may with advantage here read in connection with this provision the enactment later on in the section that the amount of contribution is not to exceed half the value at the date of the demand. Now the words "the land from the owner whereof the contribution is demanded" show clearly, to my mind, that the person from whom the demand is to be made must at the time of the demand be the owner of the adjoining land; the word "derives" shows that the benefit spoken of must be a present one, otherwise the demand is futile; and the later words quoted are decisive that the owner is not to be bound to pay for anything more than his share of the value of the fence at the moment of the demand. So far there is, at least, a strong implication that the operation of the section is not to be confined to the original parties.

But there are other words which make it absolutely necessary to imply the more extended meaning. Recollecting that what I may call the primary right to receive and the primary duty to pay in the first paragraph were made "subject to the provisions of this section," the third paragraph goes on to provide in whom and when the right to receive and the correlative duty to pay the contribution shall arise.

The words are "The right to receive such contribution shall vest"—the word "vest" is sufficient to confer the right—"and the liability to pay the same shall arise"—words equally potent to impose the obligation to pay—"when"—that is at the moment when—"the then occupier or owner of the holding gives to the then owner of the land outside the holding the prescribed notice of demand." Parliament has here marked out a specific moment of time, namely, the delivery of the demand; it has also marked

H. C. of A.
1907.

GOLDS-
BROUGH,
MORT & Co.
LTD.
v.
LARCOMBE.

Isaacs J.

out specific individuals, namely, the then owners—the word
"then" being referable only to the point of time just previously
specified—and it has declared that at that moment, on the one
hand, the right to receive shall vest—obviously for the benefit of
the person making the demand, because it meant the demand to
be complied with, and that could only be by paying the person
making it—and on the other hand, the liability to pay shall arise
just as obviously by the person of whom payment is demanded
—supposing, of course, all other conditions of the section are
satisfied.

This personal liability is followed up with the compelling
consequence that, until payment, the amount of the contribution
shall be a charge on the land, and that must, on all ordinary
principles, be the land of the person on whom the demand is
made, and who is bound to pay.

It is quite inconceivable to me that Parliament could have
intended a personal demand, made on A. for his own liability,
should have for its consequence a charge, not on any land of A.
however much he might have, but on the land of B. however
little he might possess, and yet this would be the inevitable
result if the view taken by the Supreme Court were upheld.
The matter does not stop even there. A fence when erected and
paid for must be maintained and repaired, and by sec. 43 the
fencing owner and the adjoining owner have to share the expense,
the adjoining owner being bound to make an annual contribution
for this purpose.

The second paragraph of sec. 43 follows exactly the same
scheme as sec. 42. The right to receive a contribution and the
duty to maintain and repair run with the fencing owner's land;
while the liability to pay the annual contribution is stated to
"run with the land whereof the owner was liable to pay the
aforesaid contribution towards the cost of the fence." The
words "liable to pay," like the phrase "right to receive," corres-
pond with the phraseology of the third paragraph of sec. 42, and
they refer to the obligation after demand, that is the obligation
of the "then owner" immediately on demand. Looked at,
therefore, either from the standpoint of literal construction or of
the reasonable working of the Act, I see no way of supporting

the view taken by the learned Judges of the Supreme Court of New South Wales, and therefore concur in thinking the appeal must be allowed. It may not be out of place to draw attention to what appears to be a slip in sec. 70 of the Act in the use of the word "Part." The wording of the proviso to the section indicates it was intended to apply to such a case as occurs in sec. 23, but the limitation of the section by the word "Part" excludes that application.

H. C. of A.

1907.

GOLDS-
BROUGH,
MORT & Co.
LTD.

v.

LARCOMBE.

Isaacs J.

> *Appeal allowed and order appealed from discharged. Questions answered: (a) At the date of notice; (b) Yes; (c) Not so as to disentitle respondent to pay costs of the Supreme Court and of this appeal. Case remitted to the Land Appeal Court.*

Solicitor, for the appellants, *W. A. Windeyer*, for *Alexander & Windeyer*.

Solicitors, for the respondent, *Ellis & Batton*.

C. A. W.

[HIGH COURT OF AUSTRALIA.]

THE TASMANIA GOLD MINING CO. LTD. APPELLANTS;
DEFENDANTS,

AND

ALICE MAUD CAIRNS . . . . . . RESPONDENT.
PLAINTIFF,

ON APPEAL FROM THE SUPREME COURT OF
TASMANIA.

H. C. OF A.
1908.

HOBART,
Feb. 17, 18,
19, 21.

Griffith C.J.,
Barton and
Isaacs JJ

Negligence—Evidence—Absence of direct evidence—Nonsuit—Mining shaft—Breach of regulations—Mining Act 1905 (Tas.), (5 Edw. VII. No. 23), sec. 182 ; First Schedule, Rules 17, 20.

In an action under sec. 182 of the *Mining Act* 1905 (Tas.), by the personal representative of a miner, who died from injuries sustained while working in the shaft of a mine in which he was employed by the mine owners, claiming damages for negligence against the mine owners, at the close of the plaintiff's case an application was made for a nonsuit which was refused, and, evidence having been called for the defendants, the jury found a verdict for the plaintiff. There was no direct evidence of the cause of the injuries, but a doctor said that, in his opinion, they were caused by a descending cage. There was other circumstantial evidence. Consistent with this view there was also evidence that the cage could only have descended in consequence of a signal given by the deceased, which would have been suicidal on his part, or in consequence of the breach of the Rules under the *Mining Act* 1905 to which the deceased was a party, or in consequence of negligence of the engine driver who was in charge of the winding engine at the time of the accident, but who, although an available witness, was not called by either party.

Held, that the case was properly left to the jury.

Judgment of the Supreme Court affirmed.

APPEAL from the Supreme Court of Tasmania.

H. C. of A.
1908.

TASMANIA
GOLD MINING
CO. LTD.
v.
CAIRNS.

An action was brought in the Supreme Court of Tasmania by Alice Maud Cairns, the personal representative of William James Cairns, deceased, against the Tasmania Gold Mining Co. Ltd., to recover £2,000 damages. By the declaration it was alleged that Cairns, the deceased, was employed by the defendant company in or about a certain mine of the defendant company, and that, in the course of his duty, he was lawfully and properly in a certain shaft in such mine in which a certain cage travelled upwards and downwards. The first count alleged that the defendant company by their servants negligently and wrongfully lowered the cage, or negligently caused it to be lowered, in consequence whereof the deceased was struck by the cage and sustained severe injuries, and was killed. The second count alleged that it was the duty of the defendant company to provide safe and proper appliances and machinery for the safety of their servants lawfully in the shaft, and that they altogether neglected to provide safe and proper appliances and machinery for that purpose, and in consequence thereof the deceased, whilst lawfully in the shaft, was struck by the cage, whereby he sustained severe injuries, and was killed. The third count alleged that the defendant company negligently and wrongfully omitted and failed to observe the provisions contained in certain Rules of the First Schedule to the *Mining Act* 1905, and in consequence thereof the deceased, whilst lawfully in the shaft, was struck by the cage and sustained severe injuries, and was killed.

After a first trial, at which the jury found a verdict for the plaintiff with £500 damages, which was set aside, the action was tried before *Clark* J. and a jury. At the close of the plaintiff's case counsel for the defendants applied for a nonsuit on the ground that there was no evidence to go to the jury.

The learned Judge refused the application, but reserved leave to the defendants to move the Full Court for a nonsuit. The defendants then called evidence, and the jury found a verdict for the plaintiff for £1,000. Subsequently a motion was made to the Full Court by the defendants to set aside the verdict and to enter a nonsuit or judgment for the defendants. That motion having been dismissed and judgment entered for the plaintiff for £1,000 with costs, the defendants now appealed to the High Court.

H. C. of A.
1908.

TASMANIA
GOLD MINING
Co. LTD.
v.
CAIRNS.

The evidence is sufficiently set out in the judgments hereunder.

Waterhouse and *Bryant,* for the appellants. The onus of proof was on the plaintiff of proving that Cairns received his injuries in consequence of the negligence of the defendant company. There was no direct evidence of, nor do the facts proved afford any reasonable inference as to, the cause of the injuries to Cairns. All that was proved is that he was injured in the mine at the 400ft. level. Everything else was left to conjecture. In these circumstances, even if there were evidence of negligence on the part of the defendant company, the case should not have been left to the jury: *Wakelin* v. *London and South Western Railway Co.* (1); *Avery* v. *Bowden* (2).

[ISAACS J. referred to *Pomfret* v. *Lancashire and Yorkshire Railway Co.* (3).]

The only state of facts which will support the plaintiff's case is that Cairns was struck by a descending cage, but there are other equally probable ways in which his injuries could have been caused, and, if he was injured in any one of those ways, it was primarily due to his own negligence. Even if there were evidence that Cairns was struck by a descending cage, there is no evidence of any negligence on the part of the defendant company. Assuming that the cage was lowered in accordance with the signals arranged between Bealey and the men working in the shaft—of which there is no evidence—that, under the circumstances, would not be a breach of Rule 20 of the Rules under the *Mining Act* 1905, so as to be evidence of negligence on the part of the defendant company; besides, it has never been suggested on the part of the plaintiff that such an arrangement would be in breach of the Rule. No conclusion adverse to the defendant company can be drawn from the fact that Bealey was not called as a witness. There was no evidence of negligence on his part, so that there was nothing for him to answer: *M'Kewen* v. *Cotching* (4).

[ISAACS J. referred to *Stephen's Digest of the Law of Evidence,*

(1) 12 App. Cas., 41 ; (1896) 1 Q.B.. 189 (*n*).
(2) 6 El. & Bl., 953, at p. 972.
(3) (1903) 2 K.B., 718.
(4) 27 L.J. Ex., 41.

5th ed., art. 96, p. 111 ; *Angus* v. *London, Tilbury and Southend Railway Co.* (1).]

H. C. of A.
1908.

TARMANIA
GOLD MINING
Co. LTD.
v.
CAIRNS.

Under sec. 182 of the *Mining Act* 1905, contributory negligence is an answer in an action for ordinary negligence, although it is not an answer to an action for negligence based on a breach of the Rules. The evidence of Dr. Graham is not evidence as to how the accident happened, but is merely an expression of his opinion that the injuries were such as could have been inflicted by a descending cage.

[Counsel also referred to *Cowie* v. *Berry Consols Extended Gold Mining Co.* (2); *Laurenson* v. *Count Bismarck Gold Mining Co.* (3); *Neville* v. *Lord Nelson Gold Mining Co. No Liability* (4).]

Lodge and *Crisp*, for the respondent. There was evidence to go to the jury both as to how the accident happened and as to negligence of the defendants. It was assumed throughout the whole conduct of the case in the State Court that, immediately before the happening of the accident, the cage was raised clear above the 400ft. level. There was evidence to support that assumption. That being so, there was evidence from which the jury might reasonably conclude that Cairns was injured by the descending cage, and Dr. Graham's evidence supports that conclusion. The question then is, was there evidence of negligence on the part of the defendant company ? The facts proved by the plaintiff were such that, without evidence being given by the defendant company to explain them, the jury could find that the accident was due to the negligence of the defendant company : *Byrne* v. *Boadle* (5).

[GRIFFITH C.J. referred to *Brown* v. *Great Western Railway Co.* (6).]

The defendant company having called evidence, the fact that they did not call Bealey, who alone could give evidence as to how the cage came to descend, affects the quantum of evidence necessary to allow the case to go to the jury. There were such breaches of the Rules, and they were so intimately connected with the accident, that the jury might reasonably infer negligence.

(1) 22 T.L.R., 222.
(2) 24 V.L.R., 319 ; 20 A.L.T., 124.
(3) 4 V.L.R. (L.), 83.
(4) (1905) V.L.R., 242 ; 26 A.L.T., 160.
(5) 2 H. & C., 722 ; 33 L.J. Ex., 13.
(6) 1 T.L.R., 406.

H. C. OF A.
1908.

TASMANIA
GOLD MINING
Co. LTD.
v.
CAIRNS.

[Counsel also referred to *O'Halloran* v. *Great Boulder Proprietary Mining Co.* (1).]

Bryant in reply referred to *Simson* v. *London General Omnibus Co.* (2); *Fenna* v. *Clare & Co.* (3); *East Indian Railway Co.* v. *Kalidas Mukerjee* (4).]

Cur. adv. vult.

The following judgments were read :—

Feb. 21.

GRIFFITH C.J. This was an action by the respondent, as personal representative of W. J. Cairns deceased, claiming damages for injuries which were sustained by him while in the employment of the appellants as a miner, and which resulted in his death. The first count of the declaration as finally amended was for negligence in lowering a cage in consequence of which Cairns was struck by it. The second count was for negligence in failing to provide proper appliances in the shaft, and the third for negligence in failing to observe the Rules contained in the *Mining Act* 1905. The action was twice tried. At the first trial the jury found a general verdict for the plaintiff with £500 damages. This verdict having been set aside, a new trial resulted in a verdict for £1,000. A rule *nisi* for a new trial or to enter a nonsuit was granted and discharged, and this appeal was brought from that decision.

The substantial ground of appeal is that upon the evidence it is quite uncertain whether the injuries which caused Cairns' death were due to some negligence for which the defendants were responsible, or to the negligence of Cairns himself, or were the result of pure accident, and it is contended that, there being nothing to incline the balance of probability either way, the defendants are entitled to judgment.

The accident—using that term in a neutral sense—occurred at the 400ft. level of the defendants' mine, where Cairns was employed alone. In compliance with a signal given by him, he was drawn up to the surface, when he was found to be suffering from the effects of a severe blow on the right lower jaw which

(1) 3 W. A. L. R., 41.   (3) (1895) 1 Q.B., 199.
(2) L. R. 8 C. P., 390, at p. 392.   (4) (1901) A.C., 396, at p. 401.

H. C. of A.
1908.

TASMANIA
GOLD MINING
CO. LTD.
v.
CAIRNS.

Griffith C.J.

had inflicted two incised wounds, apparently caused by a sharp-edged body, and had detached a portion of the jaw-bone containing four teeth. He was unable to speak, but muttered the word "cage," pointing to his mouth. On another occasion, in answer to an inquiry as to the cause of his injuries, he passed his hand over his head with a circular movement of his arm. He died two or three days afterwards. There was no other direct evidence as to the circumstances of the accident. But there was a good deal of circumstantial evidence, which was sufficient, if believed, to establish beyond reasonable doubt the actual circumstances.

A medical witness called by the defendants said that in his opinion Cairns received his injuries from a descent of the cage upon him while he was in a kneeling position and looking upwards. We are informed by counsel that this view was accepted by both sides at the trial. From the nature of the injuries themselves, and fortified by this opinion, the jury might reasonably conclude that they were so caused. It follows that immediately before the accident the cage must have been suspended above the 400ft. level. From this fact, with other facts to which I will call attention, several others may be inferred with such a high degree of probability as to amount almost to certainty.

At the time of the accident Cairns was, as already stated, employed alone at the 400ft. level. Two other men were employed at the 900ft. level in filling and loading trucks with material to be used in making concrete at the upper level. These they sent up to Cairns, whose duty it was to wheel the truck containing the material out of the cage, empty it, return it to the cage, and send it down to the lower level. One of the compartments of the shaft was exclusively used for this cage. The average time that elapsed between the successive despatches of the truck from the lower level to Cairns was about a quarter of an hour. In order to provide a resting place for the cage at the 400ft. level, so that the truck might be wheeled out of it, temporary appliances had been constructed in the shaft consisting of two pieces of railway iron described as bearers, resting and sliding upon fixed bars parallel to the sides of the compartment,

H. C. of A.
1908.

TASMANIA
GOLD MINING
Co. LTD.
v.
CAIRNS.

Griffith C.J.

and attached to a mechanism moved by a lever, by which the bearers could be brought out towards each other from the ends of the compartment towards the middle so as to form a support for a descending cage, or could be pushed apart and under the edges of the plats at either end, so as to leave a clear opening for the cage to pass, whether ascending or descending.

Unless they were in this position the cage could neither ascend nor descend past the level. The actual mode of working was as follows :—When the men at the 900ft. level had placed a full truck in the cage they gave the signal to hoist—one knock—which, by arrangement between them, Cairns and the engine driver, was to be taken to mean that the cage should be hoisted to a little above the 400ft. level, then stopped for a short time so as to enable Cairns to get the bearers in position, and then (after this short and indefinite time) lowered upon the bearers, which, as was assumed, would be in their proper places. During this short time Cairns would by a simple movement of the lever put them there. I pause to observe that this arrangement as to signalling was a plain violation of the statutory Rules.

On the day of the accident Cairns went down the mine at about 3.30 p.m. The miner who worked at the 400ft. level in the preceding shift said that, when he left, the mechanism was in good working order. After Cairns went down a truck was sent up to him from the 900ft. level, emptied, and returned. As this operation occupied about the usual time, it may be inferred that the lever apparatus was still in working order, but it is not, I think, material whether it was or not. A second truck was then filled and sent up, but it did not come back.

In fact it was not taken out of the cage by Cairns, and he was found lying upon it when taken to the surface as already stated, which was about an hour afterwards. But, since the ascending cage passed the 400ft. level and ultimately reached the surface, it follows that, when it went up, the shaft was free from obstructions at that level. There was, indeed, no reason why Cairns should have done anything to obstruct it, since, when he withdrew the bearers, as he must have done after the first load had been taken out, he expected another truck to come up in a few minutes. We thus arrive with certainty at another important

H. C. of A.
1908.

TASMANIA
GOLD MINING
Co. LTD.
v.
CAIRNS.

Griffith C.J.

fact, viz., that the cage had been hoisted from the 900ft. level to some (unknown) distance above the 400ft. level, whence it descended and struck Cairns. What, then, was he doing when it struck him? This question is also answered by circumstantial evidence. Shortly after Cairns had been brought to the surface, a party went down in the same cage (which still contained the truck load of material) to the 400ft. level, where they found that the mechanism already referred to had been partially dismantled. They also found that a strip of wrought iron, which had formed what was called the quadrant lever, and which worked on a central pin, being connected by bolts at its upper and lower ends to iron straps extending to the bearers at the eastern side of the shaft, had been forcibly bent upwards from below. The bolt at the top had been taken out, the straps had been disconnected from the lever but left attached to the bearers, and the bolt replaced. Similar straps on the western side had been also disconnected from the lever, but left attached to the bearers. This work must have been done by Cairns, and must have occupied some minutes of time. From the condition in which he arrived at the surface, it is a reasonable inference that he could not have done the work after receiving the blow.

It follows that the jury might find, as a fact, that he did the work after the cage had ascended past the level either on its first or second ascent.

Some argument was addressed to us as to the cause of the derangement of the mechanism, and it was contended that it must have occurred at the second ascent of the cage, and was probably caused by some part of the ascending body catching the lower end of the quadrant lever. It seems to me, however, to be immaterial whether the derangement was caused at the first or second ascent of the cage, and equally immaterial to determine how it was caused. The physical facts observed show that the mechanism had been disarranged, that this disarrangement was not such as to prevent the upward passage of the cage, and that Cairns endeavoured to disconnect the mechanism. His object was, apparently, to enable him to put the bearers in place without the aid of the lever mechanism, which would not work. This could be done with some little difficulty by hand, as was in

H. C. of A.
1908.

TASMANIA
GOLD MINING
CO. LTD.
r.
CAIRNS.

Griffith C.J.

fact done later in the day by the party who went down after the accident.

I have mentioned that the straps were not disconnected from the bearers. The free ends were placed so as to rest upon the centre pieces of the shaft, and by pulling upon them the bearers might be brought out from beneath the plats. In fact one end of one of them had been brought out for a short distance. If, then, the disarrangement occurred at the first ascent of the cage, it is probable that Cairns would have made the disconnection immediately after the cage went down, and in preparation for the next ascent. The cage having then ascended, and having stopped above the level in obedience to what was called the conventional signal, he would try to pull the bearers into position by means of the straps, and had in fact begun to pull one of them, when—again in obedience to the conventional signal—the cage without any further warning was lowered upon him.

If, on the other hand, the disarrangement occurred at the time of the second ascent, the cage must have been suspended above him for a sufficient time to enable him to make the disconnection described.

It was pointed out by the learned Judge who presided at the second trial (*Clark* J., whose lamented death has since deprived the State of the benefit of his learning and ability) that if the cage was lowered upon Cairns (as the jury might reasonably believe) it must have been lowered either

(1) in response to a signal from Cairns, or

(2) without a signal from him, or

(3) by being negligently allowed to drop by what was called a "creep" of the engine.

Evidence was adduced on both sides on the question whether, having regard to the construction of the engine in use, the cage, if suspended in the shaft, could have dropped without the active intervention of the engine driver, and upon this evidence the jury might reasonably infer that it was very likely to do so unless special care was taken.

The first hypothesis, that the cage was lowered in response to a signal from Cairns while he was engaged on a task which

H. C. of A.
1908.

TASMANIA
GOLD MINING
CO. LTD.
v.
CAIRNS.

Griffith C.J.

required him to be on his knees on the plat exposed to the risk of being struck, is highly improbable.

The only person who could give direct evidence on this point was the man in charge of the winding-engine. He was not called for the defendants, although he was available as a witness. Considering, then, that a signal by Cairns to lower the cage when he was either engaged in disconnecting the mechanism or in trying to pull out the bearers would have been almost suicidal, I think that the jury were justified, in the absence of any evidence to support this hypothesis—which evidence, if the hypothesis was true, was available—in rejecting it. If it is rejected, it is immaterial whether the second or third hypothesis is accepted. For, if the engine driver lowered the cage without a fresh signal, he was acting in clear violation of the Rules, which require that there shall be a definite code of signals posted up in the mine, and that any departure from them shall be an offence against the Act (Rule 20). Lowering the cage in obedience to what was called the conventional signal was not in accordance with the code, and was therefore (as already said) a non-observance of the Rules.

Sec. 182 of the Act provides that:—"If any person employed in or about any mine or works suffers injury in person or is killed— I. Owing to the negligence of the owner of such mine or works, or his agents or servants: or, II. Owing to the non-observance in any such mine or works of any of the provisions of this Act, such non-observance not being solely due to the negligence of the person so injured or killed, the person injured, or his personal representatives or the personal representatives of the person so killed, may, in any Court of competent jurisdiction, recover from the owner of such mine or works, as the case may be, compensation by way of damages, as for a tort committed by such owner: Provided that in estimating the damages due regard shall be had to the extent (if any) to which the person injured or killed contributed by any negligence on his own part to the injury or death."

If, therefore, the accident occurred from a non-observance of the Rules, the defendants have no defence to the action. No

H. C. of A.
1908.

TASMANIA
GOLD MINING
Co. LTD.
v.
CAIRNS.

Griffith C.J.

point was made as to any such negligence on the part of Cairns as should be taken into consideration in reduction of damages.

If the third hypothesis is accepted, the accident occurred through the negligence of the engine driver, for which it is not disputed that the defendants are liable.

It was suggested to us that it is probable that, after the cage had passed the 400ft. level on the second ascent, Cairns gave signals to hoist the cage and keep it hoisted, so as to give him time to prepare the bearers to receive it at the level, since, if the conventional signal had been observed, it would have probably caused a descent of the cage before he had time to finish his task. If he did not give such signals, the accident obviously arose from obedience to the conventional signal, which was a non-observance of the Rules for which the defendants are responsible. If he did give them, and the cage was hoisted, then its descent, whether without a further signal or by means of the carelessness of the driver, would, as already shown, be negligence for which the defendants are equally responsible. The only person who could give evidence on this point was not called by the defendants.

It follows, in my opinion, that, if Cairns was struck by the descending cage, there was evidence from which reasonable men might infer that that descent was due either to the negligence of the defendants' servants or to a non-observance of the Rules.

There is a further point deserving of mention. The winding gear in use had no indicator as required by the Rules to show to the engine driver the position of the cage in the shaft. He had, in fact, nothing to guide him but a piece of spunyarn (one of 20 pieces) on the rope to indicate that the cage was at the 400ft. level, so that he might very easily have misjudged the extent to which he lowered the cage. If this was the cause of the accident the defendants were clearly responsible.

It appears, as already stated, to have been assumed at the trial that the blow was struck by the descending cage. In the argument before us, however, some other possible causes of the accident were suggested. It was said that the blow might have been given by the top of the ascending cage while Cairns was stooping over the shaft. In this view the disarrangement of the mechanism must have occurred before the second ascent. But the hypothesis is rendered improbable by the nature of the wounds, since the part of the ascending cage which would have struck him would have been the rounded bonnet or cover of the cage which would be ascending slowly in anticipation of being stopped. It was also suggested that the ascending cage might have caught and lifted up one of the bearers, which might have fallen back and struck Cairns. In this event the bearer must have fallen upon the plat. It was, however, found in its proper place under the plat, where, in this view, it must have been replaced by Cairns after the blow, which is highly improbable, both from the weight of the bearer itself and from his condition.

In my opinion there was abundant evidence from which reasonable men might find that the injuries were caused by negligence or non-observance of Rules for which the defendants were responsible.

The appeal must therefore be dismissed.

BARTON J.   The real question in this case is whether the facts, as stated by the Chief Justice, furnish evidence on which a jury might reasonably affirm the issue to be proved.

I agree with His Honor in the conclusion at which he has arrived. In saying so I apply to the argument most strongly pressed for the appellants the words of *Kay* L.J. in the case of *Smith* v. *South Eastern Railway Co.* (1) :—" It was said that the facts were equally consistent with the accident having been due to want of care on the part of the deceased man himself as with its having been caused by the defendant's negligence, and, where that is so, the law is that the Judge ought to hold that there is no question for the jury to decide. I venture to say, with all respect for those who hold a different opinion, that as long as we have trial by jury and juries are judges of the facts, it should be a very exceptional case in which the Judge could so weigh the facts and say that their weight on the one side and the other was exactly equal. There may be such cases, and the House of Lords seems to have considered that there might be. I can only say that I think they must be very rare, and I certainly do not think that the present case is one of them."

(1) (1896) 1 Q.B., 178, at 188.

H. C. OF A.
1908.

TASMANIA
GOLD MINING
CO. LTD.
v.
CAIRNS.

Griffith C.J.

H. C. of A.
1908.

TASMANIA
GOLD MINING
Co. Ltd.
v.
CAIRNS.

Barton J.

I am of opinion that there was sufficient evidence to go to the jury, and sufficient evidence to support their verdict of negligence on the part of the appellant company causing the accident, whether on the 1st or the 3rd count of the declaration, although the negligence is to be inferred largely from circumstantial evidence. In saying this I do not forget the rule stated by *Willes* J. in the case of *Daniel* v. *Metropolitan Railway Co.* (1) approved of in the House of Lords (2), namely:—"It is necessary for the plaintiff to establish by evidence circumstances from which it may fairly be inferred that there is reasonable probability that the accident resulted from the want of some precaution which the defendants might and ought to have resorted to : and I go further, and say that the plaintiff should also show with reasonable certainty what particular precaution should have been taken." It has, I think, been shown in the judgment just delivered that the case proved warrants the inference that the blow which caused the death of Cairns was caused by the descent of the cage upon him, that descent at the particular time being caused by the negligence of the company, that is, by the cage having been either lowered or allowed to drop by the engine driver without any signal from Cairns. As *Clark* J. has said, the appellant company "is in either of these cases responsible for any consequence to Cairns which was not immediately produced by his own negligence." I do not find any evidence that the injuries were caused by any contributory negligence of Cairns, disentitling the plaintiff to succeed. There were, indeed, hypotheses to that effect, but the jury were entitled to disregard them, and they could within reason so connect the company's negligence with the accident as to say that the one was, on the whole, the cause of the other. Personally, I think the case is one of some difficulty, but I cannot say that it was not a proper case to leave to the jury, nor, if called on to decide whether the verdict was one which they could reasonably have found, can I say that it was not such a verdict. I am, therefore, of opinion that the appeal must be dismissed.

ISAACS J. This is a case really involving no question of law, but merely the application of a well established principle that,

(1) L.R. 3 C.P., 216, at p. 222.   (2) L.R. 5. H.L., 45.

H. C. of A.
1908.

TASMANIA
GOLD MINING
Co. LTD.
v.
CAIRNS.

Isaacs J.

before a plaintiff can succeed in maintaining a verdict for negligence, he must prove that the defendant was negligent and thereby caused him damage. He may do that by direct evidence which, if believed, at once completes his case; or he may do it by proving collateral facts which, being believed, lead to a reasonable inference of the ultimate fact sought to be established. The facts of different cases naturally vary, and whether in any particular case the collateral facts deposed to are sufficient for the purpose must depend upon a consideration of the whole circumstances. *Wakelin* v. *London and South Western Railway Co.* (1), which has been relied on here for the defendants, may be at once put aside, because it was bare of any evidence throwing light on the manner in which the deceased met his death, except that he was run over by a train which did not whistle when it should have whistled. As to whether he saw the train coming —and he could have seen it at a distance of at least nearly half a mile away—or whether he took his chances of getting across in time, nothing appeared, and the case was just as consistent with his death being unconnected with the defendant's absence of care as it was with being the result of the defendant's negligence.

But here there are a number of circumstances sworn to on one side or the other which, in my opinion, give a start to the plaintiff's case, that is to say, they are such as a jury of men of the world may fairly look at and draw from them a reasonable conclusion as to how Cairns met with the injuries that caused his death.

Now, the evidence of Dr. Graham, obviously based on the nature and position of the injuries, is very clear and distinct, and if believed, would lead the jury to a definite and certain commencing point.

He is called to refute Dr. Ramsay's theory as to the creep, and is supported by Dr. Clemons. He says:—"I believe that he received his injuries from a descent of the cage while he was in a kneeling position and looking upwards—his head was free— the mark of a bruise might be visible on the back of his neck on the next day to the extent of four or five inches but it would not represent a serious injury. I think that the injury was the

(1) 12 App. Cas., 41 ; (1896) 1 Q.B., 189 (n).

H. C. of A.
1908.

TASMANIA
GOLD MINING
Co. Ltd.
v.
CAIRNS.

Isaacs J.

result of direct violence and that the object that caused it came
quickly in contract with him ; the injuries he had received to his
jaw would be sufficient to produce pain all round his neck ; the
blow of the cage may have rolled him into the chamber behind
him; his mental condition was a slight indication that he had
received his injuries by a quick blow and not from a slow
pressure."

Now that evidence involves :—

(1) That the injury arose from impact with the cage.

(2) That Cairns was in a kneeling position looking upwards
when the injuries were received.

(3) That the cage was then descending quickly, that is, in
contra-distinction to the slow and comparatively speaking imperceptible movement of a creeping cage, which
would not directly wound but would crush.

There is nothing in the evidence inconsistent with this opinion,
and having been advanced as material testimony by the defendants' counsel, it cannot be regarded as unimportant.

Various theories have been urged by learned counsel as to the
mode in which the accident happened. Objections of more or
less weight present themselves to all these theories. But if it be
once supposed that, after the descent of the cage on the first
journey, Cairns saw that something was wrong with the catches,
occasioned possibly on the first upward journey, and then while
the cage was below, on the second journey, set to work to take
the catches to pieces, believing he could effect the necessary
changes in time to place the bearers in position to receive the
cage on its next trip—a not improbable supposition—the whole
difficulty disappears. Even the bending of the quadrant lever
may be thus explained ; but in any case this is only more or less
a matter of speculation under any one of the suggested theories,
and the ascertainment of its precise cause is not essential to the
real question at issue. If, then, in the second journey the cage
was raised and lowered in accordance with the concerted
arrangement, Cairns may have thought that by kneeling down he
could do sufficient to get the bearers into the requisite places to
hold the cage for that trip, and either complete the re-arrange-
ment of the catches before the third truck load came up or, if

H. C. or A.
1908.

TASMANIA
GOLD MINING
CO. LTD.
r.
CAIRNS.

Isaacs J.

necessary, report the matter. The cage, however, on this assumption descended while he was still engaged at the work, and
perhaps while he was turning his face upwards either to see if
he still had time, or when surprised by the descent of the cage,
and so was struck.

The theory of the creep has two great obstacles in the way of
its acceptance; it supposes a departure from the concerted plan,
and a consequent signalling by Cairns to lower, and of this there
is no evidence; and, next, it does not seem a probable way of
accounting for the injuries that Cairns received. It is, of course,
in opposition to Dr. Graham's evidence, already referred to, and
to that of Dr. Clemons, though favored by Dr. Ramsay.

The defendants have made the suggestion that Bealey the
driver may have had a signal from Cairns to lower. Now Bealey
was essentially in the defendants' camp both before and during
the trial. In these circumstances I can see no ground for
assuming the probability of a signal from Cairns which, if given,
Bealey alone could prove, and did not. The non-calling of Bealey
certainly weakens any suggestion of the defendants in support of
their case, or as an answer to the plaintiff's case, which is put
forward as a possible fact, the truth being known to Bealey, or to
him and the defendants to whom he may be supposed to have
communicated it.

The case then stands, so far, that it was quite open to the jury
to find, as apparently they have found, that by means of a cage,
which ought not to have been, but which was in fact, lowered
without a signal, Cairns was injured and so died.

If so, the cage descended, either slowly by means of a creep,
or more quickly in pursuance of the customary arrangement. In
the result, it is immaterial which of these alternatives was the
fact, because, in the first alternative, the jury had ample material
to find the defendants negligent, and there was no trace of contributory negligence on the part of Cairns; and in the second,
the complicity of Cairns in the non-observance of the signalling
Rules does not absolve the defendants from liability at least to
some extent, and no question is raised as to the quantum of
damages.

The creep, if it occurred, arose through the neglect of Bealey to keep the valve on the capstan engine in good order or to hold it securely, thus lowering the steam pressure, and permitting the cage to fall, as according to the evidence it would then do. In view of the testimony of Pope as to his practice to hold up the cage with steam and to keep his hand on the valve when he used steam, and that he showed Bealey how to work the engines, I think it was perfectly competent to the jury, seeing the cage did in fact come down, and no denial of the ordinary practice was deposed to, to infer that the usual course was followed on this occasion, and that a creep did take place, unless—and this is the other horn of the defendants' dilemma—the cage was deliberately lowered in accordance with the accustomed plan without a signal. The defendants are practically driven to one or other of these alternatives. If the second course was adopted, then, notwithstanding the arrangement made between Cairns, Collins, Cowie, and Bealey, it was an arrangement prohibited by the Act, and in violation of the signalling Rules. The capstan cage in that shaft, used as it was, ought not to have been lowered without a proper signal to lower, and I have no doubt that the evidence as to the arrangement taken in conjunction with the fact, which by this time must be assumed, of the descent of the cage, is ample to justify the conclusion that the lowering was in itself a distinct operation. The evidence as to the arrangement was thus deposed to by Collins:—"The signal of one knock was arranged by Cairns, Cowie and myself with the engine driver. It meant that the cage was to be hoisted to the 400ft. level and to be stopped there. The cage would be hoisted a short distance above the level and then lowered after the man working there had had time to arrange the catches."

Apparently it was a double operation that was to be performed upon receiving the one signal. The cage was to be hoisted to some distance above the 400ft. level, an indefinite distance to be roughly judged of by the driver, who had no indicator and therefore no means of precisely measuring the height of the cage, and he was to hold it there for an indeterminate period, sufficient in his opinion to allow the man working 400 feet below to arrange the catches if all went well. I am not resting my judgment upon the failure of an indicator or of hinged bearers, but the absence of these aids to safety are circumstances to bear in mind in considering how the arrangement to lower without a further signal would operate in fact. It would leave the miner below in a position of uncertainty unless everything worked smoothly; if, unhappily, the least thing went wrong his life would be in danger, and the lowering of the cage without a signal appropriate to that movement would be likely to do what it actually did in this case upon the jury's finding, inflict fatal injuries.

The legislature has expressly provided against such risks, and has enacted that in such a case a proper signal is essential. The legislative Rules, on the assumption of the second alternative, were disobeyed, and there was consequently a non-observance of one of the most important provisions of the Act. The fact that Cairns shared in the non-observance does not disentitle the plaintiff to succeed, because the non-observance was not solely due to Cairns's negligence.

These considerations are sufficient to show that the case could not possibly have been withdrawn from the jury, as being a mere case of conjecture, or as being a case in which the facts were so exactly balanced as not to be open to the jury as men of experience and common sense to arrive at a reasonable conclusion that the deceased met his death owing to the fault of the defendant company.

The appeal therefore should, in my opinion, be dismissed.

Appeal dismissed with costs.

Solicitors, for the appellants, *J. B. Walker, Wolfhagen & Walch*, Hobart, for *Ritchie & Parker*, Launceston.

Solicitor, for the respondent, *W. O. Hamilton*, Hobart, for *J. W. C. Hamilton*, Launceston.

B. L.

H. C. of A.
1908.

TASMANIA
GOLD MINING
CO. LTD.
v.
CAIRNS.

Isaacs J.

[HIGH COURT OF AUSTRALIA.]

MANUEL . . . . APPELLANT;
PLAINTIFF,

AND

PHILLIPS . . . .
DEFENDANT,

AND   RESPONDENTS.

MOSS (OFFICIAL RECEIVER, TRUSTEE OF THE
BANKRUPT ESTATE OF THE APPELLANT) .

ON APPEAL FROM THE SUPREME COURT OF
WESTERN AUSTRALIA.

H. C. OF A.   *Partnership—Dissolution—Agreement—Sale of Assets—Undervalue—Breach of*
1907.   *agreement to buy in—Release obtained by fraud—Rescission—Accounts—*
              Measure of damages—Costs.

PERTH,   A party to a deed of mutual indemnity and release sought rescission of a
Nov. 1, 4.   covenant of release made by him, without repudiating the whole of the deed;
              it further appeared that he had benefited considerably by the performance
Griffith C.J., of the covenants in the deed by the party resisting rescission, whom he could
Barton and   not restore to the same position as before, and the rescission was sought for
Isaacs JJ.
              the purpose of bringing an action for breach of contract in which the plaintiff
              could recover at most only nominal damages.

                  Held, that the rescission claimed could not be granted. A release con-
              tained in a deed cannot be severed from the rest of the document.

                  Urquhart v. Macpherson (3 App. Cas., 831), applied.

CROSS-APPEALS from the judgment of the Full Court setting aside
the judgment of *McMillan* J.

H. C. of A.
1907.

MANUEL
v.
PHILLIPS AND
MOSS.

The appellant Manuel and the respondent Phillips were partners since 1901 in a station property. In 1904 Dalgety & Co., being creditors for nearly £16,000, called for payment, and the partners then decided to sell the partnership assets and dissolve partnership. There were a few other creditors for small sums. An agreement, alleged by appellant, and found by the jury, was made that the respondent Phillips should at the auction sale buy in the property and stock at fixed prices totalling over £18,000, if those prices were not bid by other persons, and the property so bought in was to be disposed of again for the benefit of the partnership. At the sale, however, an agent for a firm of Forrest, Emanuel & Co., bought substantially all the assets for about £12,000; the respondent Phillips made no bids, although he was present, and the appellant protested against the continuance of the auction and against the respondent's failure to bid. Subsequently, and, as the jury found, on the faith of a false representation made by Phillips that Forrest, Emanuel & Co. were the *bond fide* purchasers of the property, the appellant executed a deed of indemnity and release, the other parties to the deed being the respondent Phillips and Dalgety & Co. Under this arrangement Manuel was released by Phillips and Dalgety & Co. from all the obligations of the partnership, and assigned to Phillips all his interest in the assets of the partnership, Phillips becoming solely answerable for all debts and liabilities. In April 1905 Manuel was adjudicated bankrupt, and the respondent Moss was appointed trustee of his estate. In realizing the estate Moss discovered that at the auction sale Forrest, Emanuel & Co.'s agent had in fact been acting on behalf of Phillips, who was the secret purchaser in his own interests. Manuel, having obtained his certificate of discharge in the bankruptcy, then obtained from Moss an assignment of the right of action of Moss, as trustee of the bankrupt estate, against Phillips arising out of the contract of partnership between Manuel and Phillips. As assignee of this right of action, Manuel, in conjunction with Moss, sued to have the deed of release set aside, and to have the property which was purchased at the auction declared partnership property, also for an account, and for damages for breach of the agreement to bid, and for the false

H. C. of A.
1907.

MANUEL
v.
PHILLIPS AND
MOSS.

representation. The action resulted in the release being set aside; but *McMillan* J., finding that the agreement to buy in, if carried out, would have resulted in involving Manuel in greater losses than if not carried out, gave judgment for the plaintiffs for a shilling damages, with costs of action. Manuel and Moss appealed to the Full Court to have the damages increased to half the difference between the price bid by Phillips at the auction and the price Phillips had agreed to bid. Phillips lodged a cross-appeal to the judgment of *McMillan* J., setting aside the deed of release. The Full Court dismissed the appeal, allowed the cross-appeal, and entered judgment in the action for Phillips with costs of the appeal, but made no order as to the costs of action. Manuel appealed to the High Court, Moss being joined as an appellant without his authority. He appeared in person to object to being joined as an appellant, and the Court then joined him as a respondent, with liberty to oppose Phillips' cross-appeal.

Villeneuve Smith and *F. S. Harney*, for the appellant. When the appellant was deceived into signing the deed of release, he was tricked out of a right to elect between rescinding the sale and affirming it. The right to rescind is not gone by reason of subsequent events, and he is relegated to his right to disaffirm the deed of release and sue for damages. It is immaterial for the respondent Phillips to urge that he ended by losing money on the manœuvre; he must be held bound by his agreement to bid the fixed prices for the partnership assets, which would have left a surplus over the total debts.

[GRIFFITH C.J.—You do not dispute the finding of fact by *McMillan* J. that the performance of the agreement must have ended in a loss; and you can hardly come into a Court of Equity to set aside a deed of release in order to enable you to recover 1/- damages: *Maturin* v. *Tredennick* (1).]

Burt K.C. and *Draper* (*F. Burt* with them), for the respondent Phillips. The appellant cannot claim rescission of the deed of release and an account, unless he is in a position to restore the respondent Phillips to his former position. The appellant has

(1) 12 W. R., 740.

enjoyed the full benefits of the deed of release, and circumstances have so altered that restitution cannot be made: *Urquhart* v. *Macpherson* (1); third parties have come in, whose interests would be affected: *Clough* v. *London and North Western Railway Co.* (2); and the appellant's bankruptcy, wherein he has obtained a discharge, stops all recourse against him, and third persons would also lose the right of proving in bankruptcy, examining the bankrupt as to assets, and opposing his discharge.

If the trustee in bankruptcy, knowing the facts of the case, recommended Manuel's discharge, he elected thereby to set up a claim for damages only, and abandoned any claim for an account.

The concealment by Phillips of the fact that he was the real purchaser was immaterial to the question of damages; at the time that Manuel signed the deed of release he was well aware that he had a right of action against Phillips for damages for breach of his contract to bid; the concealment had nothing to do with the release of that right of action; and Manuel ratified and acknowledged Phillips' dealings with the station as his own property, even making him an offer to purchase it.

On the 1/- damages that were awarded no costs should have been allowed, or at most only Local Court costs; there was no need to come to the Supreme Court: English *Judicature Act* (36 & 37 Vict. c. 66), sec. 89; *Local Courts Act* 1904 (W.A.) (4 Edw VII. No. 51), secs. 36, 39. If the judgment of the Full Court is upheld, the respondent Phillips should be allowed all costs of the action and the appeals; and if the judgment of *McMillan* J. is upheld, the respondent is equally entitled to costs, as the action was clearly unsubstantial. There is "good cause" why the appellant should be ordered to pay the costs: *Forster* v. *Farquhar* (3); Order LXI., r. 1 (W.A.); Order LXV., r. 1 (Eng.).

Villeneuve Smith in reply. The trustee in bankruptcy recommended the bankrupt's discharge on the sole ground of his conduct during the bankruptcy; and his recommendation was given a month before he learned of the respondent's false representations.

(1) 3 App. Cas., 831, at p. 838.   (2) L.R. 7 Ex., 26.
(3) (1893) 1 Q.B., 564.

The Local Court cannot deal with a suit for rescission. The finding of fraud still stands against Phillips, and the Full Court was therefore right in refusing him costs of trial: *Bostock* v. *Ramsey Urban Council* (1); *Scottish Gympie Gold Mines Ltd.* v. *Carroll* (2). The only question found against the appellant was the chance fact that the damages could only be nominal. The appellant was not a stranger or speculator in the action; the trustee in bankruptcy assigned the cause of action to him for the benefit of the creditors.

The following judgments were read:—

GRIFFITH C.J. This is an action brought by the purchaser from the Official Receiver in bankruptcy of a supposed asset in the estate of one Manuel, a bankrupt. The purchaser happens to be the bankrupt himself, but that circumstance is quite irrelevant. The local law allows an asset of that sort to be assigned, and, if the bankrupt himself after obtaining his discharge becomes the purchaser from the Official Receiver, he is in the same position as anyone else who purchases an asset in the bankrupt's estate. The cause of action as set up at the trial was twofold, for breach of an agreement, and for damages for fraudulent representation by which the bankrupt was induced to execute a release of any claim for damages for the breach. The bankrupt and the defendant had been partners in a pastoral property, and they desired to wind up that partnership. It was accordingly arranged that the partnership assets should be offered for sale at auction. The plaintiff alleges, and the jury have found, that the defendant agreed with the bankrupt that he would attend the sale and would bid certain specified sums for the various items of the property, if other intending purchasers did not bid so much. In the event of the defendant being the highest bidder his purchase was to be for the benefit of the partnership, and the property was to be disposed of in some other way. An auction was accordingly held, at which the bankrupt and the defendant both attended. The defendant did not bid according to the terms of the alleged agreement, and the property was knocked down nominally to the firm of Forrest, Emanuel & Co. Shortly afterwards, in

(1) (1900) 2 Q.B., 616.   (2) 1902 St. R. Qd., 311.

August 1904, a deed of mutual release was drawn up and executed, to which the bankrupt, the defendant, and their principal creditor were parties. The substantial effect of this deed was that the defendant should take over all the unsold assets of the partnership and assume all its liabilities, and that the creditor should release Manuel's liability to him. The deed included a mutual release of all claims. The defendant accordingly took over all the liabilities, and realized the unsold assets for his own benefit. Some months afterwards Manuel became bankrupt. In the meantime the terms of the deed of release had been carried out, and the defendant had discharged the liabilities of the partnership. In June 1905 an examination in bankruptcy disclosed the fact that at the auction sale the defendant had really bought the property for himself. The jury have found that Manuel was induced to execute his release by the false representation that Forrest, Emanuel & Co. were the purchasers. It is contended that the Official Receiver, on discovery of this fact, became entitled to elect to avoid the release and claim any rights to which he would have been entitled if it had not been executed. If the release had been out of the way, or could have been got out of the way, the Official Receiver might perhaps have been entitled when he discovered this fact to say that the property which the defendant bought under such circumstances continued to be partnership property for which he was liable to account. But he did not do so. In fact he did nothing. In December 1905 the bankrupt obtained his discharge, and in the same month was informed of the fact that defendant had bought for himself. On 8th January he brought this action, setting up the alternative claims which I have stated, and another to which it is not necessary to refer. It is plain that the action was wrongly brought, for, whatever the Official Receiver's rights were, they had not then been assigned to the plaintiff. The Official Receiver was subsequently joined as a co-plaintiff, and in July 1906 he executed an assignment to the plaintiff of "a certain cause of action arising out of a contract" between the bankrupt and the defendant. I will assume (without deciding) that this assignment comprised the two causes of action now set up, namely, for damages for breach of the promise he had made

H. C. of A.
1907.

MANUEL
v.
PHILLIPS AND
MOSS.

Griffith C.J.

H. C. of A.   to attend the sale and bid up to a certain amount for the
1907.   partnership property, and for damages for the fraudulent repre-
MANUEL   sentation.   To the first claim the release is an obvious answer,
v.   unless it can be got out of the way.   The jury have found the
PHILLIPS AND
Moss.   fact of fraud in the plaintiff's favour.   Supposing the release to

Griffith C.J. be out of the way, the relief to which the plaintiff would be
entitled in respect of the breach of contract would be such an
amount as would put him in the same position as if the contract
had been performed.   *McMillan* J., to whom the question of
damages was left, found that if the contract had been performed
the plaintiff would have been in a worse position than he was
when it was broken, since the property if bought in and resold
would have realized much less than the defendant gave for it.
He was, therefore, at most, only entitled to nominal damages, a
shilling.   The original competency of this appeal depended upon
an impeachment of this finding, but on that point the appellant
hopelessly failed.   It follows that he cannot succeed on his
alternative claim for damages for the fraud, since actual damage
must be established in order to support an action for fraud.   The
plaintiff, however, claims that, the appeal being competent, he is
entitled to have the deed of release set aside in order to enable
him to recover that one shilling for breach of contract.   His
counsel concedes that, unless this can be done, he cannot maintain
the action, even for the shilling.   I remark, in passing, that the
alleged fraudulent representation was absolutely irrelevant to the
release of that cause of action, because what the bankrupt lost by
his partner not bidding at the sale was the same whether the
property was sold to the defendant or to a stranger at the same
price.   It may therefore be contended that the fraud was not
fraus dans locum contractui.   It is not, however, necessary to
express any opinion as to the solidity of such a contention.
For, in order to avoid a contract for fraud, the plaintiff must
show both that he could repudiate and that he did repudiate
the fraudulent contract.   In this case there is no evidence whatever of any repudiation before the assignment of the cause of
action to the plaintiff.   It is not necessary to determine whether
a right of election to repudiate a contract for fraud can be
assigned and exercised by the assignee, but I must not be under-

stood to assent to the affirmative of that proposition. I think
further that it was not competent under the circumstances for
either the bankrupt or the Official Receiver to repudiate it. In
my opinion the case of *Urquhart* v. *Macpherson* (1), referred to
by the learned Judges of the Full Court, is exactly in point.
The deed of release in question in that case was very like that in
the present case. *Sir Montague Smith*, delivering the opinion of
the Judicial Committee, said (2):—" The general scheme of this
deed of dissolution is, that the plaintiff was to take over the
whole of the assets of the partnership, the stations, the stock,
and all the credits, and was to pay all the debts and liabilities of
it. It appears too by this deed that the tracts of land which had
belonged to the defendant were assigned by him absolutely to
the plaintiff, with the exception of the *Chintin* station, which
was to be retained by him. . . . Such being the general
nature of the deed, the release which it contains is found at the
end of it, and is in these terms : ' And this indenture lastly
witnesseth, that in consideration of the premises, each of them
the said *George Urquhart* and *Duncan Macpherson*, for himself,
his heirs, executors, and administrators, doth hereby remise and
release, and for ever quit claim unto the other of them, his
executors, administrators, and assigns, all actions, suits, accounts,
reckonings, claims, and demands whatsoever at law or in equity,
which either of them the said parties, his heirs, . . . now hath
or hereafter may have, claim or demand against the other of
them, his heirs, . . . for or by reason of any matter or thing
whatsoever touching or concerning the said joint trade or
partnership, subject and without prejudice nevertheless to the
covenants and agreements herein contained.' Therefore the object of this release, so far as the defendant was concerned, was to
release him from all matters and things whatever touching or
concerning the joint trade, without prejudice to the covenants
which he had entered into for the security of the plaintiff with
regard to certain matters.

"It seems to their Lordships impossible to sever this release
from the rest of the deed. There is but one contract for the
dissolution of partnership, though containing many terms, of

H. C. of A.
1907.

MANUEL
v.
PHILLIPS AND
MOSS.

Griffith C.J.

(1) 3 App. Cas., 831.   (2) 3 App. Cas., 831, at pp. 836-8.

H. C. of A. which this release is one. It is expressly said to be made ' in
1907.   consideration of the premises,' that is, in consideration of the
MANUEL   defendant having given up the whole of the partnership assets to
v.   the plaintiff, and his own runs, which at the end of the partner-
PHILLIPS AND
MOSS.   ship would otherwise have reverted to him.

Griffith C.J.   " Then, if the release cannot be separated from the rest of the
contract it falls within the ordinary principle. Contracts which
may be impeached on the ground of fraud are not void, but
voidable only at the option of the party who is or may be injured
by the fraud, subject to the condition that the other party, if the
contract be disaffirmed, can be remitted to his former state. The
plaintiff has taken the whole benefit of the deed so far as it was
beneficial to him, without at any time attempting to repudiate it,
and it now being impossible to restore the defendant to his
original position, he seems to destroy one particular part of the
contract, and that their Lordships think he cannot do."

So here the bankrupt took the whole benefit of the deed, so far
as it was beneficial to him, without attempting to repudiate it,
and it is impossible to restore the defendant to his former
position. I therefore agree with the learned Chief Justice,
although I do not attach so much importance to the mere fact of
Manuel having become bankrupt. Even without the bankruptcy
it would have been impossible to restore the parties to the same
position which they occupied before the release was executed.
In my opinion, therefore, the action cannot be maintained either
for breach of contract or for fraud.

With respect to the costs of the action, the Full Court ordered
judgment to be entered for the defendant without costs. We
have not had the opportunity of knowing the reasons for making
that order, but I think that in a purely speculative action which
is unsuccessful the defendant should not be deprived of his costs,
except so far as he may have been to blame for setting up untrue
defences. I think that the defendant should have the costs of
the action except so far as they were increased by issues upon
which he failed.

BARTON J. I concur, and have very little to add. With
respect to the agreement between the two parties, the position

H. C. of A.
1907.

MANUEL
v.
PHILLIPS AND
MOSS.

Barton J.

when they made it was that, unless the amount of debt were
realized from the money of an outside purchaser, there would be
a balance of debt to be discharged by Manuel and Phillips. This
they wished to avoid, and by an agreement between them,
separately from their principal creditor, Dalgety & Co., certain
sums were to be bid by Phillips as reserved prices, that is to say,
he was only to bid if an outsider did not bid them. Clearly they
were to be bid merely to protect the property and stock, and to
save them for future sale if a sale should thereafter be attempted.
That is the arrangement, and it is alleged that the defendant did
not keep it. If that was the case, and we have to look upon it in
that light, seeing that the jury have found that such an arrangement was made and broken, we then have to consider what are
the damages flowing as a natural consequence from that breach.
If the prices obtained were fair, and the learned Judge has so
found, and, I think, with reason, there was no loss by reason of
the non-bidding of a higher price by one who, by the terms
of the agreement, would not have become in truth a purchaser.
If value was obtained—and apparently it was—there was no
damage. Although it may have been a good speculation to buy
the property in upon a chance of getting a higher price in the
future, we have to remember that, as a matter of fact, if the
contract had been performed the plaintiff would have lost heavily.
As to the claim for a cancellation of the release, I am satisfied
that no Court of Equity would set aside that release to enable the
plaintiff Manuel to claim, under circumstances such as these, damages which, if they existed at all, could not be more than nominal
at best. As there were none, it would be merely *brutum fulmen*
to set the release aside. Finally, I agree with the Full Court of
this State that, in any event, it would have been impossible to
restore the parties to their original position even in substance.
Upon every ground the plaintiff has failed. The appeal should
therefore be dismissed.

ISAACS J. Even if the plaintiff had sued for damages for being
fraudulently led into this agreement of 8th August 1904 which
includes the release, he would have failed, because he benefited
by the transaction. If the contract to purchase at the auction

H. C. of A.
1907.

MANUEL
v.
PHILLIPS AND
MOSS.

Isaacs J.

sale, which is sued upon, had been carried out, and there had
been no purchase by Forrest, Emanuel & Co., and no release, the
property would have simply been bought in. It was only in
name that Phillips was to agree to give a sum of money for the
partnership property. If he had done so that would only have
been a payment to themselves, and consequently any breach of
that agreement would only entitle the plaintiff to, at the most,
one shilling damages unless he proved that substantial damage
had ensued, as by some other person getting the property for less
than its value. There is no claim here on the basis of a fiduciary
relation as between one partner and another in regard to partnership property. The plaintiff's claim is limited to the barest
technical point. He has shown no substantial damage at all,
and, in my opinion, he has failed in the action, although he might
be entitled to one shilling damages. The substance of his claim
was that by reason of the breach of agreement to purchase, he
suffered the loss set out in the 16th paragraph of the statement
of claim which alleges that, by reason of the matters stated, the
plaintiff was deprived of his share of the true net value of the
land and stock. He has altogether failed to prove that. He has
only succeeded in proving that in the result he has benefited by
any moral delinquency of which the defendant has been guilty.
As to setting aside the release for the purpose of getting the
nominal damage of one shilling, I fully concur in what has
been said by the Chief Justice. For the reasons stated in the case
of *Urquhart* v. *Macpherson* (1), I do not think this release could
be set aside at all. The substantial position here was that there
had been an agreement to sell the partnership property and
dissolve the partnership. A sale was held, but the final completion of the agreement is to be found in the indenture of 8th
August 1904. That was the act of final dissolution between the
partners, and the final settlement of their mutual rights. Reference is made in that document to a dissolution of partnership,
and, although in some parts it is referred to as "the late partnership," still there is a passage showing that the parties understood
that the dissolution was not absolutely complete until this document was executed. I find these words in that document, " And

(1) 3 App. Cas., 831.

H. C. of A.
1907.

MANUEL
v.
PHILLIPS AND
MOSS.

Isaacs J.

the company in consideration of the said Henry William Manuel relinquishing to the said Samuel James Phillips all the rights and claims of him the said Henry William Manuel in and to the assets of the partnership heretofore existing between the said Samuel James Phillips and Henry William Manuel doth hereby at the request of the said Samuel James Phillips release the said Henry William Manuel from all personal liability in respect to the mortgage and other debts due or owing by the said partnership firm to the company and from all claims and demands in respect thereof." I take it that that is a document finally concluding the partnership and mutually settling the rights of the partners on such dissolution; and, as I said before, under the authority of *Urquhart* v. *Macpherson* (1), you cannot sever the release from the rest of the document, nor can you, with the consequences of that document before you, by any means place those parties back in their former position. That would be to restore the partnership. Under these circumstances the release cannot be rescinded, and if so there is no power to give even one shilling damages. I do not think that the mere fact of a party having been defrauded and becoming insolvent is in itself sufficient to prevent his assignee in insolvency asking for the rescission of a contract induced by fraud. Rescission implies that the party wishing to avoid the contract is prepared to do equity, which means restoration to the former situation, and if that is so I cannot see that it is any answer in the mouth of the present plaintiff to say merely that insolvency has intervened.

> *Plaintiff's appeal dismissed. Judgment varied by directing the plaintiff to pay costs of the action, except so far as they were increased by the issues on which he succeeded, and to pay costs of the appeal.*

Solicitors, for the appellants, *Harney & Harney.*
Solicitors, for the respondent Phillips, *Parker & Parker.*

N. G. P.

(1) 3 App. Cas., 831.

[HIGH COURT OF AUSTRALIA.]

LEE FAN . . . . APPELLANT;
DEFENDANT,

AND

DEMPSEY . . . . RESPONDENT.
COMPLAINANT,

ON APPEAL FROM THE SUPREME COURT OF
WESTERN AUSTRALIA.

H. C. OF A. | *Vagrancy—Idle and disorderly person—" No visible lawful means of support "—*
1907. | *Police Act 1892 (W.A.) (55 Vict. No. 27), sec. 65 (1).*

PERTH,
Oct. 28, 31.

Griffith C.J.,
Barton and
Isaacs JJ.

The *Police Act* 1892 (W.A.), sec. 65 (1), provides that "every person who shall commit any of the next following offences shall be deemed an idle and disorderly person, . . . and shall on conviction be liable to imprisonment . . . (1) Every person having no visible lawful means of support . . . who being thereto required by any Justice, or who having been duly summoned for such purpose or brought before any Justice, shall not give a good account of his means of support to the satisfaction of such Justice."

Held, that the sub-section was intended to create an offence cognizable immediately by a Justice upon the accused person being brought before him and charged with the offence named, and that no preliminary or extra-judicial investigation by a Justice into the existence of lawful means of support is required before the formulation of the charge. Upon *primâ facie* proof of the absence of lawful means of support, the onus falls upon the accused to prove the existence of such means to the satisfaction of the Justice.

Wilson v. Benson ((1905) V.L.R., 229; 26 A.L.T., 144), and *Wilson v. Travers*, ((1906) V.L.R., 734; 28 A.L.T., 56), overruled.

THE appellant was brought before a magistrate and charged with being a person having no visible lawful means of support. Evidence was given for the prosecution that the appellant haunted gambling houses in the Chinese quarter of Perth, and lived on his pay as a fighting man hired by a certain Society to prevent evidence being given in gambling prosecutions. The defence also produced evidence of lawful means of support; but the magistrate found appellant guilty of the charge "and thereby deemed to be an idle and disorderly person," and sentenced him to four months' imprisonment with hard labour. He appealed to the General Quarter Sessions on questions of fact; but *Burnside* J. dismissed the appeal. From this decision an appeal was brought by special leave to the High Court.

H. C. of A.
1907.

Lee Fan
v.
Dempsey.

Penny, for the appellant. The requirements of sec. 65 (1) of *Police Act* 1892 were not complied with in the proceedings before the magistrate; no preliminary account of himself was required of appellant by any justice before his arrest, and no proof of the appellant's having failed to satisfy any such justice was given at the hearing: *Police Offences Act* 1890 (Vict. No. 1126), sec. 40 (1); *Wilson* v. *Benson* (1); *Wilson* v. *Travers* (2). The preliminary inquiry is an administrative proceeding, and he cannot be arrested and charged with an offence until the inquiry is decided against him.

Thomas, for the respondent. *Wilson* v. *Benson* (1), and *Wilson* v. *Travers* (2), were wrongly decided. Sec. 65 (1) of the Western Australian Act constitutes the offence of being an idle and disorderly person, consisting of the two elements of having no visible lawful means of support and of failing to give a good account of oneself to a magistrate. Both the elements of this offence must be the subject of judicial, not administrative, inquiry. The section would be rendered unworkable by the necessity for preliminary extra-judicial inquiry, which a magistrate has no jurisdiction to make, and the result of which there is no practicable way of proving. The ordinary procedure followed by the magistrate is plainly authorized by sec. 65 (1), and no other strained interpretation should be adopted to make it unworkable. [He referred to *Justices Act* 1902 (W.A.) (2

(1) (1905) V.L.R., 229; 26 A.L.T., 144.
(2) (1906) V.L.R., 734; 28 A.L.T., 56.

Edw. VII. No. 11), secs. 20, 42, 137, 140, 141; *Police Act* 1892 (W.A.) (55 Vict. No. 27), sec. 134).]

Penny in reply. The complaint did not charge the appellant with being an idle and disorderly person, but with having no visible lawful means of support; the whole proceedings are defective : *Reg.* v. *Scotton* (1).

Cur. adv. vult.

The following judgments were read :—

GRIFFITH C.J. The appellant was convicted under sec. 65 of the *Police Act* 1892 (W.A.) of being an idle and disorderly person. Special leave to appeal from the order of *Burnside* J. affirming the conviction was given on the suggestion that, according to the construction of a Victorian enactment in identical words, as declared by the Full Court of Victoria (*Wilson* v. *Travers* (2)), the proceedings against the appellant did not disclose any offence known to the law.

Sec. 65 enacts that " every person who shall commit any of the next following offences shall be deemed an idle and disorderly person within the meaning of this Act, and shall on conviction be liable to imprisonment for any term not exceeding six calendar months with or without hard labour." Then follows an enumeration of eight separate categories of persons, of which the first is (1) " Every person having no visible lawful means of support or insufficient lawful means of support, who being thereto required by any Justice, or who having been duly summoned for such purpose, or brought before any Justice, shall not give a good account of his means of support to the satisfaction of such Justice."

This category, like the others, is of a class of persons as to whom a state of facts can be predicated, and not of persons who do or omit to do some specific act.

It has been the practice in Western Australia, when it is sought to take advantage of this enactment, to bring the accused person before justices and offer evidence to show that he has no visible lawful means of support or insufficient lawful means of

(1) 5 Q.B., 493.   (2) (1906) V.L.R., 734; 28 A.L.T., 56.

support. It has been supposed that the burden was then cast upon him of giving a good account of his means of support to the satisfaction of the justices, and if he failed to do so a conviction has followed. The same practice had been followed in Victoria until the decision of the case of *Wilson* v. *Benson* (1) by *Hodges* J., and has also been followed in other States under similar enactments. The learned Judges of the Supreme Court of Victoria held that the failure to give a good account of his means of support must occur before any charge can be laid against a man under the Statute, so that the justice before whom he is called upon to give such account of his means of support cannot there and then convict him, but a new charge must be brought against him alleging the failure as an element of the offence. This point is one of great general importance, since similar provisions are in force all over the Commonwealth, and the provisions in question are much relied on by the police in the maintenance of order. Other objections to the conviction have been taken, but if they stood alone the leave to appeal should, I think, be rescinded.

The difficulty arises from the use in a somewhat loose and inaccurate sense of the word " offences " in the enacting sentence of sec. 65. In reality that section creates only one substantive offence, that of being an idle and disorderly person, and the eight categories of persons are not, properly speaking, definitions of offences, but of states of facts which, if proved, will establish that substantive offence. This is clearly shown by the following sec. (66) which is framed on the same lines as sec. 65, and provides that any person who shall commit any one of certain offences shall be deemed a rogue and vagabond. The first case is " Every person committing any of the offences in the next preceding section mentioned, ' having been previously convicted as an idle and disorderly person.' " The seventh case is " Every person apprehended as an idle and disorderly person, and violently resisting any constable or other officer so apprehending him," &c. In like manner sec. 68 speaks of a constable or other person apprehending " any person charged with being an idle and disorderly person." The Act 7 Geo. IV. c. 83, from which the scheme of sec. 65 is taken, gives a form of conviction of an idle and disorderly

(1) (1905) V.L.R., 229 ; 26 A.L.T., 144.

person. The form sets out that the defendant is convicted "of being an idle and disorderly person, for that" &c. setting out the terms of the particular category of idle and disorderly persons within which he falls.

In the case of the first category the accused cannot be convicted of the substantive offence until (1) it has been proved that he is without visible lawful means of support or has insufficient lawful means of support, and (2) he has failed to give a good account of his means of support to the satisfaction of the justices. But, in my opinion, this second condition is not an element of the charge to be made against the defendant, but a condition precedent to his conviction on the charge of being an idle and disorderly person, because he has no visible lawful means of support or has insufficient lawful means of support. If, on proof of this fact, and on being lawfully called upon, he fails to give a good account of his means of support, he may be convicted there and then. The section allows him to be so called upon in either of three ways: (1) on being thereto required by any justice; (2) on being duly summoned for such purpose; (3) on being brought before a justice. The first case appears to refer to a summary personal demand made by a justice out of Court in the exercise of his general authority, upon which, under the older Statutes, the justice under a practice now obsolete could have convicted upon view. In this case it might perhaps now be necessary to prefer a charge against the accused after he has failed to satisfy the demand, but I express no opinion on this point. In the second case a summons would be issued upon a complaint that the defendant is an idle and disorderly person being a person without visible lawful means, &c. The summons would be in the ordinary form, calling upon him to appear "to answer the said complaint and be further dealt with according to law." The third case assumes that the defendant is brought before the justice in custody and charged with being an idle and disorderly person for the same reason. The section itself says nothing as to the conditions under which a man may be apprehended on such a charge. Sec. 66 (7) and sec. 68, however, as already shown, contemplate that under some circumstances a man may be so apprehended. In

H. C. OF A.
1907.

LEE FAN
v.
DEMPSEY.

Griffith C.J.

my opinion the words " brought before any Justice " mean brought on warrant or without warrant as the case may be. Whether a constable has authority to apprehend a man without warrant as an idle and disorderly person on the ground that he is found offending must depend upon whether the category within which the man is alleged to fall is such that the guilt is capable of being ascertained upon view. Some of the cases mentioned in sec. 65 are clearly of such a kind, while others perhaps are not. In the latter case a personal demand by a justice or a summons would perhaps be necessary. The want of visible lawful means of support is certainly capable of being so ascertained.

But, for the reasons already given, I do not think that any of these matters are elements of the offence. They relate only to the procedure and not to the subject matter. Another instance of similar procedure is afforded by sec. 69, under which the charge on which a man is brought before a justice is " having on his person . . . . any thing which may be reasonably suspected of being stolen." If he then fails to give an account of the possession to the satisfaction of the justice he may be convicted. In this case it is clear that the giving of the account to the satisfaction of the justice must be after, and not before, the charge is laid. Other instances are afforded by the Statutes relating to offences committed by insolvent debtors, in which it is commonly provided that certain facts shall constitute an offence unless the jury are satisfied that there was no intent to defraud. The practical effect in all these cases is that the alleged offender is to be charged with the facts which *primâ facie* constitute an offence, that the onus to discharge himself is then cast upon him, and that if he fails to discharge that onus he may be convicted.

In my opinion, therefore, the procedure followed in the present case was right, and the view of the Statute taken by the learned Judges in Victoria was erroneous. The cases of *Wilson* v. *Benson* (1) and *Wilson* v. *Travers* (2) must be regarded as over-ruled so far as they are inconsistent with this judgment.

BARTON J. This Court is not concerned with the sufficiency of

(1) (1905) V.L.R., 229 ; 26 A.L.T., 14.   (2) (1906) V.L.R., 734 ; 28 A.L.T., 56.

the information, the quantum of the evidence, or the form of the conviction. The sole question on which special leave was granted was the meaning of sec. 65 (1) of the Western Australian *Police Act* 1892.

"Every person who shall commit any of the next following offences shall be deemed an idle and disorderly person within the meaning of this Act, and shall on conviction be liable to imprisonment," &c., namely :—

"(1) Every person having no visible lawful means of support or insufficient lawful means of support, who being thereto required by any Justice, or who having been duly summoned for such purpose, or brought before any Justice, shall not give a good account of his means of support to the satisfaction of such Justice."

It is contended for the appellant that justices who act under this provision are performing, not a judicial, but a ministerial or administrative duty, and that if a justice is not satisfied that the person before him has given a good account of his means of support, the justice is not entitled to convict, but that the person, before he can be found guilty, must be brought before another justice and the facts which constitute the offence must be proved over again before he can be called on for a defence. This is tantamount to saying that a second complaint must be laid against him (for it would be a strange thing to inquire whether he is an idle and disorderly person without a complaint in the first instance), and that unless this be done he is entitled to be acquitted or discharged, notwithstanding that he has had an opportunity of rebutting the inference which undeniably arises from the fact of his being without visible or sufficient lawful means of support. I cannot accede to that contention. It is, in effect, to say that in dealing with people, who in a vast number of cases cannot be dealt with at all unless summarily, the formalities are to be gone through which are necessitated upon magisterial inquiries into indictable offences, and that the justice is really called upon to perform a process equivalent to a committal for trial, with the result of a second investigation upon the same evidence for the prosecution which the accused person has already failed to rebut, and with the further grotesquerie that, if due effect be given to the final words of the sub-section,

guilt is only to be established finally by proving to the second
justice that the accused has failed to satisfy the mind of the
first. Obviously such a construction of the Act would lead to
absurd and futile results, and it should be avoided, according to
ordinary rules of interpretation, if there is another and a more
reasonable construction fairly open. Fortunately the position is
a safer one, and the practice sanctioned by usage, until recently
unbroken, rests upon the plain words of the enactment. The
conviction prescribed in sec. 65 is for the comprehensive offence
of "being an idle and disorderly person," and the section embraces
eight specific sets of facts any of which will prove the commission
of that offence, just as the next section (66) embraces twelve
separate sets which are each sufficient to prove a person to be a
"rogue and vagabond," and the 67th section includes three other
classifications, under any one of which a person may be brought
for proof that he is an "incorrigible rogue." Apart from procedure, there are in sub-sec. (1) of sec. 65 two things which
constitute the *probanda* : (*a*) that the person has no visible
lawful means of support or insufficient lawful means of support;
(*b*) that he fails to satisfy the justice by a "good," which means
a reasonably credible, account, and not what is commonly called a
"thin" one, that he has actual, that is, sufficient means of support.
Unless he can do that the *primâ facie* case arising by inference
from the absence or insufficiency of means, of which some evidence
must first be given (see *per Hood* J., *Appleby* v. *Armstrong* (1))
remains unrebutted, and the justice may and should convict and
punish, and there an end. Notwithstanding the rather incautious
application of the word "offence" to them in the opening words of
the section, instead of to the real offence of being an idle and disorderly person, to which the word "conviction" clearly applies,
the matters specified in the several sub-sections are just the
evidentiary ingredients of the offence in its eight phases. In
sub-sec. (1), indeed, the failure to satisfy the justice may be due
to entire absence of evidence of actual lawful means as well as
from unsatisfactory or insufficient evidence thereof, and there is
no compulsion upon the accused to give evidence personally, as
seems to be supposed. The person liable to conviction under

(1) 27 V.L.R., 136, at p. 138 ; 23 A.L.T., 35.

H. C. of A.
1907.

Lee Fan
v.
Dempsey.

Barton J.

sec. 65 (1) as an idle and disorderly person, in that he has no
lawful means of support, is, therefore, a person whose means
of support are non-apparent or insufficient, in the absence of
evidence either on his own part, or on that of others, or
both, giving an account of his means of support good enough
to satisfy the tribunal. If the man cannot satisfy the tribunal
he may be convicted, and I cannot imagine why the appellant
should conceive it necessary that he should be tried over again
before that tribunal or another one. In my view, with the
very greatest respect for the opinions of other Judges, it is as
unreasonable as to urge that a similar procedure is necessary
as to the proof, required by the seven remaining paragraphs
of sec. 65, the twelve paragraphs of sec. 66, and the three of
sec. 67, for I see no sound reason why this paragraph should
be thus distinguished from all the others, and held to require a
procedure so complex and elaborate. One would think the evidences of the offence of being an idle and disorderly person,
prescribed in that paragraph, were, alone among the means of
proving the same offence stated in the eight paragraphs, to be
treated as ingredients of an indictable offence until the matter
comes before a second justice.

. Some argument has been founded on the words "who being
thereto required by any Justice, or who having been duly summoned for such purpose, or brought before any Justice." I have
not found that their presence in the sub-section alters the otherwise plain meaning of the section as to its evidentiary requirements. The first phrase in all probability refers to cases where
the offender has come before the justice on another charge, or as
a witness, or as a bystander in Court, and is required to account
for his apparent lack of any means or of adequate means of
honest livelihood. At any rate the existence of such circumstances would satisfy the meaning of the phrase. The meaning
may include cases where the justice could at one time convict
"upon his own view," but does so no longer. Such a dealing
with the offender was sanctioned by 6 Wm. IV. No. 6, sec. 2.
" Duly summoned for such purpose " primarily means served with
a summons stating the nature of the complaint, and I see no
reason why another meaning should be sought. " Brought before

any Justice" seems to me clearly to mean, brought there in
lawful custody under the charge authorized by sec. 65, and on the
grounds stated in any of its paragraphs.

For the foregoing reasons I am of opinion that the Police
Magistrate of Perth, in treating the offence as proveable and
proved before him, acted upon the true view of the meaning of
the enactment, that *Burnside* J. was right in dismissing the
appeal under sec. 183 of the *Justices Act*, and that this appeal
should be dismissed.

H. C. of A.
1907.

Lee Fan
v.
Dempsey.

Barton J.

Isaacs J.   I am of the same opinion.   By secs. 65, 66 and 67
of the *Police Act* 1892 (55 Vict. No. 27) the legislature of Western
Australia has made provision for the punishment of three classes
of offenders, namely, (1) idle and disorderly persons, (2) rogues
and vagabonds, and (3) incorrigible rogues.

The first class is liable to six, the second to twelve, and the
third to eighteen months' imprisonment, the first two with or
without hard labour, and the last with hard labour.

A description is given in each section of the various persons
who fall within the class dealt with by that section.   Among
those who are deemed to be idle and disorderly persons is
(1) "Every person having no visible lawful means of support
. . . who being thereto required by any Justice, or who having
been duly summoned for such purpose, or brought before any
Justice, shall not give a good account of his means of support to
the satisfaction of such Justice."

Those who are to be deemed rogues and vagabonds include
every person who commits any of the offences, which make him
an idle and disorderly person if he has "been previously convicted as an idle and disorderly person," and also every person
"apprehended as an idle and disorderly person" if he violently
resists apprehension and is convicted of the offence for which he
was apprehended.

An incorrigible rogue includes every person committing an
offence subjecting him to be dealt with as a rogue and a vagabond,
if he has been "previously convicted as a rogue and a vagabond."

Sec. 68 speaks of a person being "charged with being an idle
and disorderly person, or a rogue and vagabond, or an incorrigible

H. C. of A.
1907.

Lee Fan
v.
Dempsey.

Isaacs J.

rogue." It refers to his being apprehended on that charge, and it gives power to take and convey him before a justice or justices, and it further enacts that the justice or justices by whom " any person shall be adjudged to be an idle and disorderly person, or a rogue and a vagabond, or an incorrigible rogue," may make certain orders.

The provisions referred to make it clear that the charge is that of being an idle and disorderly person, &c., and the conviction follows the charge.

The contention of learned counsel for the appellant rested entirely upon the Victorian case of *Wilson* v. *Travers* (1), the reasoning of which he simply presented to the Court as correct.

Wilson v. *Travers* (1) is largely based upon the reasoning which governed the case of *Wilson* v. *Benson* (2), a decision of *Hodges* J.

Without minutely dissecting the reasons given by the Full Court in *Wilson* v. *Travers* (1), it practically amounts to this : that if a person has no visible lawful means of support he may be questioned by a justice acting administratively and not judicially as to his means of support. This may be done either on the justice's own view, or when the person is summoned, in some unofficial way not provided for by law, to appear before the justice, or upon his being brought before the justice in some equally informal and undefined manner. If his account be then considered satisfactory by the justice there is an end to the matter ; but if the account be not satisfactory, or if he do not come, the person has committed an offence. Then, and then only, upon the reasoning of the Victorian Court, can a charge be formulated and the accused put upon his trial.

Passing by for the present the expression " who being thereto required by any Justice," which has an early origin, and at one time stood alone, and taking into consideration the two other branches of the latter portion of the sub-section, namely, " who having been duly summoned for such purpose, or brought before any Justice," they are, so far as the words themselves import, ordinary provisions commonly found in connection with the

(1) (1906) V.L.R., 734 ; 28 A.L.T., 56.   (2) (1905) V.L.R., 229 ; 26 A.L.T., 144.

H. C. of A.
1907.

Lee Fan
v.
Dempsey.

Isaacs J.

exercise of judicial functions by justices. A summons, or a warrant, or a summary arrest are well known methods of securing the attendance of an accused person. No instance has been brought before the Court where these expressions have been used to indicate the exercise of any administrative duties of a justice. It is a somewhat startling proposition that, although the officer, the procedure, and the determination are all *primâ facie* judicial, these are all, without any express statutory provision and by some exceptional implication, invested with an administrative character, and not for the purpose of simply ascertaining whether a person is already a criminal, but for the possible purpose of constituting that person by administrative process a criminal though otherwise he is not a criminal.

What is there in the Statute to justify, much less to require, this unique interpretation of what appears to me to be a very plain enactment? A person appears, suppose to a constable, to be going about at large without any visible lawful means of support, and therefore to be a menace to society. It is of importance to protect the public by means of preventive as well as punitive measures, and so the legislature has declared that such a person shall be deemed an idle and disorderly person, unless he can satisfy a justice, notwithstanding appearances, or what may be called the *primâ facie* conclusion which a fair-minded and careful observer would come to regarding his means, that he really has sufficient lawful means of support. The word "deemed" is significant; the person apparently without lawful means of support is in law considered dangerous, unless he shows the contrary. He may be charged with being an idle and disorderly person as having no lawful means of support; he may be summoned upon that charge for the "purpose" of giving a good account of his means if he can, it being essential, however, that the prosecution should first establish that he is without visible lawful means of support; or he may be brought before the justice by warrant or summary arrest as *primâ facie* an offender; and, assuming the onus of proof in the first instance is satisfied by the prosecution, he is then required to displace it, otherwise he may be convicted.

There is nothing new in this method of procedure, nothing

H. C. of A.
1907.

Lee Fan
v.
Dempsky.

Isaacs J.

unjust or out of harmony with the ordinary course of summary criminal procedure. The case is one requiring more prompt treatment than usual—rather than dilatory process; and, so far as I can ascertain, there is not, nor has there ever been in any State or Colony including New Zealand (see *Curran* v. *O'Connor* (1)), any difficulty in administering the law so interpreted with justice and efficacy.

This is sufficient to dispose of the case, and, if it were not that our decision is practically a reversal of the decisions in *Wilson* v. *Benson* (2), and *Wilson* v. *Travers* (3), I should not feel called upon to say anything further. But it is due to the learned Judges who determined these cases, to examine on its own basis the reasoning by which their judgments are supported. And before indicating what appears to me to be serious practical difficulties in the way of accepting their interpretation of the law, some of which were anticipated by their Honors, I would advert to the fact rightly pointed out by *àBeckett* A.C.J., that according to the practice previously followed, when a person having no visible means of support was brought before a Court of Petty Sessions, and evidence was given that he had no visible means, a *primá facie* case was made against him, which he could displace by proving that he had means, or by giving a good account to the satisfaction of the bench before whom he appeared. This interpretation of the law is very distinctly recognized by *Madden* C.J. in *Whitney* v. *Wilson* (4), and by *Hood* J. in *Appleby* v. *Armstrong* (5). The observations in the two last-mentioned cases on this point are of course not agreed with by the Full Court who decided *Wilson* v. *Travers* (3), and are at variance with the reasoning of *Hodges* J. in *Wilson* v. *Benson* (2); but the consistency of the practice referred to by *àBeckett* A.C.J. over a long period of considerably more than thirty years is undoubted. No inconvenience or injustice in following that practice has ever, so far as I am aware, been suggested, and the new construction introduced for the first time by *Wilson* v. *Travers* (3) and *Wilson* v. *Benson* (2), does, as *àBeckett* A.C.J. correctly points out, present

(1) 12 N.Z.L.R., 442.
(2) (1905) V.L.R., 229; 26 A.L.T.,
144.

(3) (1906) V.L.R., 734; 28 A.L.T., 56.
(4) 24 V.L.R., 574; 20 A.L.T., 157.
(5) 27 V.L.R., 136; 23 A.L.T., 35.

an unsatisfactory view of the sub-section under which the decision was given, and would leave the law ineffective as a working enactment. These are considerations which are very strong to lead a Court to inquire anxiously whether the former view of the enactment so long continued, so reasonable and effective and not unjust, is not after all the proper interpretation; in other words, whether the language of the legislature contained in that sub-section, when read in conjunction with other sections in the same part of the Act, is not reasonably capable of bearing that interpretation. If the history of the legislation be looked at the matter is beyond doubt. In 1835 an Act was passed in New South Wales, (6 Will. IV. No. 6), which is the Australian foundation of such legislation. By sec. 2 it was provided that "every person who having no visible lawful means of support or insufficient lawful means shall not being thereto required by a Justice of the Peace give a good account thereof to the satisfaction of such Justice" (then follows the enumeration of other descriptions of offenders) "shall be deemed an idle and disorderly person within the true intent and meaning of this Act, and it shall be lawful for any Justice of the Peace to commit such offender (being thereof convicted before him by his own view or by the confession of such offender or by the evidence on oath of one or more credible witness or witnesses) to His Majesty's nearest Gaol," &c. The form of conviction given by sec. 13 of the Act corresponded with the form under the English Act read by the learned Chief Justice.

It is manifest that, as under that enactment at least the justice might convict on his own view, the justice who had to be satisfied was the same justice who if not satisfied could on the same occasion convict. Further he might convict on the confession of the offender, and that confession could scarcely include a confession that some other justice, or the same justice on some other occasion, acting in another capacity, namely, in an administrative capacity, had not been satisfied with the account of his means.

In 1851 that Act was repealed in New South Wales and the enactment as to this description of persons was substantially repeated, except that the three alternatives as they have been called were inserted, namely, "required," "summoned," and "brought." Sec. 15 shows that the form of conviction should still be as before. The penal section in this later Act (15 Vict. No. 4) referring to disorderly persons, retained the same references to conviction on view, and confessions, as existed in the former Act. Those references are not now found in the Victorian Act of 1890, being matters of procedure, and procedure is otherwise provided for. But the meaning of the alternatives is the same as it was originally. If the view adopted by the Supreme Court of Victoria is correct, the working of the enactment would be not merely ineffective, but practically impossible, as well as out of harmony with the rest of the procedure relating to justices. That view supposes a person who to all appearance has no lawful means of support, and assumes that a justice may voluntarily visit him and require him to give an account of his means. No provision is made for recording or certifying the dissatisfaction of the justice, if he be not satisfied; and before he can lawfully put the inquiry at all, he must first, at least mentally, have satisfied himself that *primâ facie* the individual before him has no lawful means of support. If, however, the justice does not voluntarily go to the individual in question he is, according to the reasoning of the Supreme Court, to address some sort of notification to him to attend and be questioned. The further assumption of the Court is that so far no offence is possible, and no charge can be formulated, and consequently the notification cannot be more than a bare request to attend and give some explanation of his means without saying why. If there be nothing in the individual's outward appearance to justify the belief that he is without means, and if he do not admit it, I do not know by what process a justice can in the circumstances assumed obtain the right to require him to give any account of his means of support. It is by the express words of the sub-section a condition precedent to the right of the justice to make any inquiry that the person should have no visible lawful means or insufficient means of support, and if the justice is acting administratively merely and not judicially, I do not understand how, in the case I have supposed, he can get any evidence of the necessary fact. Nor do I understand how the individual

questioned can bring other persons to support his account and
corroborate his story.   He is, nevertheless, according to the
argument, concluded by the dissatisfaction of the justice.   But
let us carry the matter a stage further, and suppose that the
justice obtained an unsatisfactory account, or, after summons, none
at all; the next step is to charge the offender and bring him
before a justice in the ordinary criminal jurisdiction.   The fact
of his having no visible lawful means must be again proved, this
time before a justice acting judicially, and, on the assumption of
the Supreme Court, there must also be proved the necessary
dissatisfaction of the justice who acted administratively.   If it be
the same justice, I do not know how that essential fact will be
proved—it is impossible to imagine the same justice being both
Judge and witness or taking judicial notice of the fact—and even
if it were another justice who acted administratively, is he to be
called and to testify as to his dissatisfaction?   I can hardly
think the case is met by the suggestion of *Cussen* J., that some
person present who hears the justice openly express his dissatisfaction could be called to prove it.   Apart from this being a most
unusual mode of proving, in fact at secondhand so to speak,
what is assumed to be an essential element of an offence, one
can easily conceive of a conflict of evidence as to what the justice
actually said, and some difference of opinion as to what he meant.

Moreover the Court's reasoning involves the strange result,
adverted to by *à Beckett* A.C.J., that no matter what evidence the
accused may on his trial adduce to show that, notwithstanding
appearances, his means are in fact undeniable, it is unavailing,
because the administrative justice was previously dissatisfied, and
therefore on proof that the accused had no visible means the
judicial justice is bound to convict.   It seems to me that this
reasoning is by no means so well founded as that which has for
so many years supported the practice previously in force.   In
my opinion that practice was justified by the true construction
of the enactment.

Sec. 46 of the Victorian Act of 1890 and sec. 122 of the
Western Australian Act of 1892 strongly support the view I
have indicated : but independently of these sections the decision
upon which the appellant in this case relies cannot in my opinion

H. C. of A.
1907.

Lee Fan
v.
Dempsey.

Isaacs J.

H. C. of A. be supported, and if that decision be wrong the appellant's case
   1907.   must fall.*

  LEE FAN
     v.   *Appeal dismissed.*
  DEMPSEY.

  Isaacs J.   Solicitors, for the appellant, *Penny & Hill.*
            Solicitor, for the respondent, *Barker* (Crown Solicitor).

                                                        N. G. P.

[HIGH COURT OF AUSTRALIA.]

MOORE AND SCROOPE   .   .   .   .   APPELLANTS;
    SUPPLIANTS,

                              AND

THE STATE OF WESTERN AUSTRALIA   RESPONDENT.
    DEFENDANT,

        ON APPEAL FROM ·THE SUPREME COURT OF
                 WESTERN AUSTRALIA.

*Pastoral lease—Reservation of power to "sell"—Homestead and grazing leases—
    Conditional "sale"—Dispossession—Quiet enjoyment — Breach of covenant—*
H. C. of A. *Lease under regulations — Alteration of regulations and new legislation —*
   1907.   *Australian Waste Lands Act (18 & 19 Vict. c. 56)—Crown Lands Regulations*
            2nd March 1887 (W.A.)—Constitution Act 1890 (W.A.), (53 & 54 Vict. c.
  PERTH,   *26), sec. 4 (2)—Homesteads Act 1893 (W.A.), (57 Vict. No. 18)—Land Act 1898*
Oct. 28, 29, *(W.A.), (62 Vict. No. 17).*
   30;
 Nov. 4.   In pursuance of a power vested in the Crown to dispose of Crown lands in
            Western Australia under conditions prescribed by the Regulations then in
Griffith C.J., force "or by any Regulations amending or substituted for the same," a
 Barton and   pastoral lease was granted in 1887, containing a reservation to the Crown of
 Isaacs JJ.   a right to sell the land comprised in the lease ; and the Regulations also con-
            tained a similar reservation of a power to sell subject to the provisions of the

---

*NOTE :—Sec. 40 (1) of the *Police*   the *Police Offences Act* 1907 (Vict.)
Offences Act 1890 (Vict.), under which   and a new provision substituted. See
Wilson v. *Benson* and *Wilson* v. *Travers* secs. 3 and 4 of the amending Act.
were decided, has been repealed by   [ED.]

Regulations. By the Western Australian *Constitution Act* 1890, the right to dispose of Crown lands and to make regulations was transferred to the autonomous government then established; but all contracts made by the Crown and all vested rights already accrued relating to Crown lands prior to that Act were expressly saved from interference. In pursuance of the *Homesteads Act* 1893 and the *Land Act* 1898, which created new forms of conditional alienation of Crown lands not in use in 1887, the Government granted homestead and grazing leases to other persons, who by virtue thereof entered and took possession of the land of the pastoral lessees.

Held, that, assuming that a covenant for quiet enjoyment was implied in the pastoral lease, and that the homestead or grazing leases followed by dispossession would, if inconsistent with the rights of the pastoral lessee have been breaches of such a covenant (as to which *quære*), no breach had been committed by the Government of the covenant. The homestead and grazing leases were not infringements of the *Constitution Act* 1890, as they were "sales" within the meaning of the Crown's reservation of the power to sell contained in the pastoral lease and the Regulations. The pastoral lessee having no power under his lease to acquire the fee, his land remained "Crown lands," subject to be sold or otherwise disposed of under the Regulations, whether those in force in 1887 or as altered by subsequent amendments of the Regulations or by statutory enactments creating new forms of alienation. No covenant could be implied in the pastoral lease against the Crown, that it would not take advantage of such alterations of the Regulations as might take place subsequent to the granting of the lease.

Steere v. *The Minister for Lands*, 6 W.A.L.R., 178, over-ruled in part.

Decision of the Supreme Court varied.

The suppliants, pastoral lessees of Crown lands, sued the Government of Western Australia for damages for alleged breach of an implied covenant for quiet enjoyment, by granting homestead and grazing leases over land held by the suppliants, of which the new lessees dispossessed them. The Supreme Court of Western Australia, following their prior decision in *Steere* v. *The Minister for Lands* (1), held that the homestead and grazing leases were unlawfully granted and void; but that the Crown was not answerable for the dispossession by lessees claiming thereunder. The suppliants appealed to the High Court. The material facts and enactments relating to the case are set out in the judgment of *Griffith* C.J. hereunder.

Pilkington K.C. and *Stawell*, for the appellants. Assuming that *Steere* v. *The Minister for Lands* (1) is good law, the Crown is

(1) 6 W.A.L.R., 178.

H. C. of A.
1907.

MOORE AND
SCROOPE
v.
THE STATE OF
WESTERN
AUSTRALIA.

H. C. of A.
1907.

MOORE AND
SCROOPE
v.
THE STATE OF
WESTERN
AUSTRALIA.

liable for its unlawful conduct in giving authority to third persons to disturb the pastoral lessee's possession.

The pastoral lease granted in 1887, under 18 & 19 Vict. c. 56, sec. 7, embodied the Regulations in force at that time. It constituted the contract between the parties, and its terms could not be altered subsequently without liability for compensation. At the dates when the Regulations and the pastoral lease were drawn up, homestead and grazing leases were unknown forms of demise, and could not be granted in derogation of the pastoral lease before its expiration. The *Constitution Act* 1890 (W.A.) (53 & 54 Vict. c. 26), secs. 3 and 4, expressly save from alteration all rights arising from any land contracts previously made with the Crown; and under the existing law there is no power in the Government or Parliament to resume or take away land granted or leased before the *Constitution Act* 1890; the contracts under which these lands are held could only be varied by Imperial Act or other appropriate alteration of the *Constitution Act* 1890, not by any local Acts.

The *Homesteads Act* 1893 (57 Vict. No. 18), sec. 18, which gives power to grant homestead leases, and the *Land Act* 1898 (62 Vict. No. 37), sec. 68, which gives power to grant grazing leases, cannot be construed as a statutory authority to derogate from pastoral leases existing when the Act was passed. The granting of these homestead and grazing leases on the suppliants' land was a breach of the covenant for quiet enjoyment; even though such leases are invalid at law, they are a distinct authority to enter and dispossess, as the tenants are required by both the Acts to go into possession and make improvements on the land : *Budd-Scott* v. *Daniell* (1); *Williams* v. *Gabriel* (2); *Harrison, Ainslie & Co.* v. *Lord Muncaster* (3); *Sanderson* v. *Berwick-upon-Tweed (Corporation of)* (4); *Jenkins* v. *Jackson* (5); *Winter* v. *Baker* (6); *Norton on Deeds*, (1906 ed.), p. 485; *Windsor and Annapolis Railway. Co.* v. *The Queen* (7).

The contract contained in Scroope's pastoral lease included a reservation to the Crown of a right to " sell " any of the land

(1) (1902) 2 K.B., 351.
(2) (1906) 1 K.B., 155.
(3) (1891) 2 Q.B., 680, at p. 684.
(4) 13 Q.B.D., 547, at p. 551.

(5) 40 Ch. D., 71.
(6) 3 T.L.R., 569.
(7) 11 App. Cas., 607, at p. 613.

comprised therein.   The homestead and grazing leases were not H. C. OF A.
" sales " of the land ; they were, at most, leases with a right to 1907.
purchase the fee.   Such rights must, with respect to the pastoral MOORE AND
lease, be construed under the Regulations in force in 1887, which SCROOPE
did not recognize as sales such dealings as the homestead and THE STATE OF
grazing leases : *Johnson* v. *Thomson* (1). WESTERN AUSTRALIA.

The principle that Regulations are to be taken to be subject to
the power of amendment and substitution applies only in company law : *British Equitable Assurance Co.* v. *Baily* (2) ; such
power is not incorporated in any of the Regulations in force in
1887, and could never have been in the contemplation of the
parties at that time.   The *Homestead Act* 1893 can be construed
so as not to affect the pastoral leases granted before 1893, as there
are numbers since that date to work upon; it would only be
taken to authorize the present breach of contract if it specifically
did so.   The " right to sell " reserved in the pastoral lease contract and in the Regulations must mean a " right to sell under
the Regulations " as they then existed, otherwise the right of the
pastoral lessee to compensation under the Regulations for his
improvements would be gone.

" Conditional purchases " are not true sales ; much less are
homestead and grazing leases sales, within the meaning of the
reservation: *Bouvier's Law Dictionary*, " *Sale* " ; *Kansas Pacific
Railway Co.* v. *Dunmeyer* (3) ; these new special tenures, created
by local Statutes, are the very thing against which the *Constitution Act* 1890, sec. 4 (2) was enacted to protect the old tenures
held from the Crown : *Constitution Act* (N.S.W.) (18 & 19 Vict.
c. 54), Schedule sec. 58; *Australian Waste Lands Act* (18 & 19
Vict. c. 56), sec. 5.

Even if these homestead and grazing leases were lawfully
authorized, yet the Crown is liable for the breach of covenant for
quiet enjoyment ; the power to dispossess pastoral lessees, if
validly authorized, was still a general power, not compulsory, and
the individual breach is wrongful : *Brewster* v. *Kitchell* (4).

[GRIFFITH C.J.—But the legislature may have obliterated that
implied covenant.]

(1) 6 W. W. & aB. (M.), 18.   (3) 113 U.S., 629.
(2) (1906) A.C., 35.   (4) 1 Salk, 198.

H C. of A.   The Crown covenanted not to derogate from its grant "during
1907.   the term of the lease," not "while the law remains as it is"; a
MOORE AND covenant is only repealed by change of the law where breach of
SCROOPE   the covenant is made compulsory: *Western Counties Railway*
v.
THE STATE OF *Co.* v. *Windsor and Annapolis Railway Co.* (1). These Acts are
WESTERN
AUSTRALIA. not an authority to override existing titles subject to statutory
           compensation, if any ; private property can only be taken in that
           way if expressly so enacted by a plenary legislature: *Baker on
           United States Constitution*, 1891 ed., p. 184. If it is necessary
           to consider the Crown's power of legislation and revocation, the
           Crown must be taken to have covenanted not to exercise, in such
           a way as to derogate from its grant, any new powers of revoca-
           tion conferred by subsequent legislation. The pastoral lease
           was not a conveyance or executed contract, but an executory
           contract, with various active covenants and reservations continu-
           ing during the term. As to costs, *Parker* C.J. deprived the
           appellants of costs merely because they preferred to go to Court
           instead of to arbitration. That is not "good cause" under the
           Rules: *Huxley* v. *West London Extension Railway Co.* (2);
           Beckett v. *Styles* (3); *Forster* v. *Farquhar* (4).

           Draper and *Northmore*, for the respondent. The Crown did
           nothing unlawful or in breach of the pastoral lessee's rights in
           granting the homestead and grazing leases. The land scheme
           established under the Regulations was to grant a right to occupy
           land under pastoral lease so long as such land was not otherwise
           required for sale or other better tenures. Regulation 3 contained
           power to substitute other Regulations, so that pastoral leases were
           held subject to the Regulations from time to time in force : *British
           Equitable Assurance Co.* v. *Baily* (5). If the power to sell
           pastoral leased lands is only under the Regulations as existing in
           1887, then the subsequent repeal of the only Regulations on
           conditional sales, the conditional purchase Regulations, leaves these
           lands open only to direct sale for cash. But the contemplated
           alteration of the Regulations was effected by the *Homesteads Act*

           (1) 7 App. Cas., 178, at p. 188.   (4) (1893) 1 Q.B., 564.
           (2) 14 App. Cas., 26.   (5) (1906) A.C., 35.
           (3) 5 T.L.R., 88.

H. C. of A.
1907.

Moore and
Scroope
v.
The State of
Western
Australia.

1893 and the *Land Act* 1898. The reservation of power to sell in the pastoral lease covered these homestead and grazing leases, which were really conditional sales, under which the fee simple was in time acquired after performance of prescribed conditions: *Land Act* 1898 (62 Vict. No. 37), sec. 68 (7), (8); *Bennett* v. *Wyndham* (1); *Homesteads Act* 1893 (57 Vict. No. 18), secs. 19-29.

Even if these homestead and grazing leases were not " sales," yet there was nothing unlawful in granting them under the Acts which authorized them. Sec. 4 of the *Constitution Act* 1893 did not cut down the plenary power of legislation given by sec. 2 to make laws for the " peace, order, and good government " of the State: See *Powell* v. *Apollo Candle Co.* (2). The saving of existing contracts on Crown lands was only intended to prevent the change of Constitution from operating to invalidate existing titles; these still remained liable, as always, to alteration by the existing legislative authority. If the statutory alterations are valid, then the persons aggrieved must resort for compensation to the provisions, if any, contained in those enactments and no-where else: *Brand* v. *Hammersmith and City Railway Co.* (3). The Acts under which the homestead and grazing leases were granted clearly authorized the exercise of the leasing power over the pastoral lease as Crown lands; and the breach of the implied covenant being thus directly authorized, no action will lie.

Even if the leases were void, the Crown is still not liable in this action. The intruding lessees would be mere trespassers, whereas the covenant is only against intrusion by persons law-fully claiming under the lessor: *Sanderson* v. *Berwick-upon-Tweed (Corporation of)* (4).

[Isaacs J.—*Calvert* v. *Sebright* (5) shows also that the covenant refers to the future as well as the past.]

The Crown is not estopped, as an individual would be, from setting up that the leases were invalid.

If the *Constitution Act* 1890, sec. 4 (2) limits the Crown to non-interference with existing titles, any such interference is

(1) 23 Beav., 521.
(2) 10 App. Cas., 282.
(3) L.R. 4 H.L., 171, at p. 196.
(4) 13 Q.B.D., 547.
(5) 15 Beav., 156.

H. C. of A. outside the scope of the Crown's authority, and only the indi-
1907.   vidual agent of the Crown can be made responsible. Actions lie
Moore and   against the Crown for breach of covenant only where that breach
Scroope   was validly authorized: *Crown Suits Act* 1898 (62 Vict. No. 9),
v.   sec. 33; *Broom's Legal Maxims*, 7th ed., p. 38—" *Rex non potest*
The State of
Western
Australia. *peccare.*"

No covenant for quiet enjoyment can be implied against the
Crown: *Dart on Vendor and Purchaser*, 7th ed., p. 575; *Sugden
on Vendor and Purchaser*, 14th ed., p. 575. Any instrument
derogating from the Crown's grant will be supposed not to have
been intended, and will be treated as void; the true remedy is
against the intruding lessees, who are presumed to have "deceived"
the Crown: *Alton Woods' Case* (1); *Cumming v. Forrester* (2);
Staunford on the Prerogative, cited in *Clode on Petition of Rights*,
p. 105. *Western Counties Railway Co. v. Windsor and Annapolis Railway Co.* (3) is distinguishable; the Crown there was
bound at common law to respect a contract, but was not thereto
limited or compelled by the Constitution, and the Governor of
Canada was acting within his authority, although doing a wrongful act, in interfering with a contract which the Act in question
did not oblige him to affect.

Pilkington K.C., in reply. The Governor of Western Australia was exercising a general power of leasing conferred on him
by the *Homestead Act* 1893 and the *Land Act* 1898, in the same
way and to the same extent as in *Windsor and Annapolis
Railway Co. v. The Queen* (4).

The grazing leases were certainly not such "sales" as were in
the contemplation of the parties in 1887; and the purchase of the
lands was purely at the option of the lessees, who were never
even bound to pay the rents, as the leases were deeds poll
executed only by the Minister. The leases were merely occupation licences conditional on payment of the rents.

The idea that the pastoral lease was to be held subject to
by-laws variable from time to time was never within the contemplation of the parties; Regulation 59, under which the

(1) 1 Rep. 27a.   (3) 7 App. Cas., 178.
(2) 2 Jac. & W., 334, at p. 342.   (4) 11 App. Cas., 607.

pastoral lease was granted, contained nothing about alterations, and Regulation 3 was not meant to be incorporated into it.

H. C. of A.
1907.

MOORE AND
SCROOPE
v.
THE STATE OF
WESTERN
AUSTRALIA.

Griffith C.J.

Cur. adv. vult.

The following judgments were read :—

GRIFFITH C.J. In this case the suppliants (the appellants) claim damages against the Crown for breaches of an alleged contract in the nature of a covenant for quiet enjoyment, which, they contend, is contained in a pastoral lease of Crown lands in Western Australia issued under the law in force in the year 1887, before the grant of a Constitution to the Colony, the alleged breaches being the issue of certain homestead leases and grazing leases of part of the demised land to other persons under laws passed by the Parliament of Western Australia after the grant of the Constitution, followed by entry of the new lessees and dispossession of the suppliants. The Full Court, following a previous decision in the case of *Steere* v. *The Minister for Lands* (1), held that the homestead leases and grazing leases were void, on the ground that the latter leases were, if valid, infringements of the rights conferred by the pastoral leases, and that the local Parliament was incompetent to pass a law authorizing such dispositions of land in any way inconsistent with titles granted before the Constitution ; but they also held that, the leases being void, the Crown was not responsible in damages for the loss occasioned to the pastoral lessee by the entry of the homestead lessees and grazing lessees, and the consequent dispossession of the pastoral lessee. By the law of Western Australia a petition of right will not lie, nor can a suit be brought in any other form against the Crown, in respect of a tort except in a limited class of cases, which does not include such a dispossession as that complained of. The suppliants' case must therefore depend upon the existence and the breach of some contract. I have already said that the contract set up is in the nature of a covenant for quiet enjoyment. The pastoral lease uses the word " demise," and it is said that that word imports such a covenant. This is no doubt true in the case of ordinary leases. The covenant is, however, not express but implied. An

(1) 6 W.A.L.R., 178.

H. C. of A.   implied covenant or contract is held to arise, when, and only
   1907.   when, it appears that without it the intention of the parties with
MOORE AND   regard to the main object of the bargain would be frustrated.   A
SCROOPE   covenant by a lessor for quiet enjoyment is not the same thing
   v.   as a covenant that he will not grant a later lease to any other
THE STATE OF
WESTERN   person.   Since the lessor has already parted with the estate
AUSTRALIA.   demised, any attempt by him to dispose of it, or any part of it,
Griffith C.J. to another person would be futile.   There is, therefore, no neces-
             sity to imply a covenant not to do such a futile act.   Whether
             the entry of a person claiming under such an ineffectual attempt
             would operate as a breach of the implied covenant for quiet
             enjoyment or not is a different question.

             I proceed to examine the suppliants' title, with a view of
             discovering whether any and, if any, what covenant can be im-
             plied from its terms.   Before the grant of the Constitution the
             waste lands of the Crown in Western Australia were administered
             and disposed of under Regulations made by Order in Council
             under the authority of the Act 18 & 19 Vict. c. 56.   The Regula-
             tions material to the present case were proclaimed on 2nd March
             1887.   Regulation 3 authorized the Governor in the name and on
             behalf of Her Majesty to " dispose of the Crown lands within the
             Colony in the manner and upon the conditions prescribed by
             these Regulations or by any Regulations amending or substituted
             for the same."   The term " Crown lands " was defined by Regu-
             lation 2 to mean " the waste lands of the Crown within the
             Colony, that is to say, lands vested in Her Majesty and not for
             the time being dedicated to any public purpose or granted in fee
             simple or with a right of purchase under these or any previous
             Regulations."   Part V. deals with pastoral leases, which were to
             be for a term of years expiring on 31st December 1907.   Regu-
             lation 59 was as follows:—" A pastoral lease shall give no right
             to the soil or to the timber, and shall immediately determine over
             any land which may be reserved, sold, or otherwise disposed of
             under these Regulations."   Regulation 61 provided that "the
             right is reserved to the Commissioner with the approval of
             the Governor . . .   to sell any mineral land comprised
             within the limits of any pastoral lease whatever, and to sell
             any other portion of such lease, subject to the provisions of

H. C. of A.
1907.

Moore and
Scroope
v.
The State of
Western
Australia.

Griffith C.J.

these Regulations, at any time and with a right of immediate entry." Regulation 115 was as follows:—"In order to promote the construction of railways or other public works or the introduction and establishment of new industries and commercial undertakings of public utility, or for otherwise promoting the settlement of the Colony, the Governor in Council may grant special concessions of land in fee simple or otherwise, in any portion of the Colony, and may grant special concessions to cut and remove timber from Crown lands for any period, and such concessions may include special privileges, and shall be subject to any subsidy, rent, fees, conditions, or reservations as the Governor in Council may prescribe. Provided that any concession under this clause shall be subject to ·the approval of the Legislative Council." In my opinion this was a power which might have been exercised under the reservations in Regulation 61 with respect to lands comprised in a pastoral lease, and the exercise of which might have been dealt with by future Regulations.

Part IV. of the Regulations, which was headed "Alienation," included provisions for the sale of land by auction, and also for sale upon conditions of residence and improvement, to which I shall have occasion to call attention in more detail. It is sufficient for the present to say that the conditional purchaser became entitled to a grant in fee simple on payment of the prescribed price and on performance of the prescribed conditions. The holder of a pastoral lease acquired no such right. It follows that land held under a pastoral lease granted under these Regulations continued to be Crown lands within the definition in Regulation 2, and consequently continued to be land which the Governor was authorized to dispose of in the manner and upon the conditions "prescribed by these Regulations or any Regulation amending or substituted for them."

The form of pastoral lease was prescribed in a Schedule to the Regulations (Schedule 9), which may be referred to for the purpose of construing them. The lease, which is in the name of the Sovereign, witnesses that the Sovereign, in the exercise of the powers given by the Act of 18 & 19 Vict. c. 56, and the Regulations, "doth demise and lease" unto the lessee the land

H. C. of A.
1907.
~~~~
MOORE AND
SCROOPE
v.
THE STATE OF
WESTERN
AUSTRALIA.
——
Griffith C.J. described in the Schedule for the specified term, subject to certain reservations expressed in the following words :—" Except and always reserved to Us, Our Heirs and Successors, full power during the term hereby granted, from time to time to sell to any person or persons all or any unsold portion of the said demised premises, subject to any claim for improvements that may be lawfully made in pursuance of the said Regulations . . . and also to . . . resume and enter upon or dispose of in such other manner as for the public interest to Us, Our Heirs and Successors, may seem best, such part or parts of the said demised premises as may be required for . . . otherwise facilitating the improvement and settlement of the Colony . . . also to sell any mineral land comprised within the said demised premises, and, subject to the rights of the lessee aforesaid, to license to occupy, or to sell any other portion of the said premises at any time, and with a right of immediate entry." It is not disputed by the suppliants that under these reservations the Crown had power to sell any of the land comprised in the lease, but it is contended that the sale contemplated was an absolute immediate sale for cash only and not a conditional sale, and that, even if a conditional sale was included, the reservation only extended to a sale upon the particular conditions specified in Part IV., and would not authorize a sale on any conditions that might be prescribed by future Regulations.

If this view is correct, the lease created an estate in the land which could not be diminished by the Crown by means of any disposition of the land inconsistent with the continuance of the estate so created. A covenant not to make such an ineffectual disposition could not, because it need not, be implied. If, on the other hand, the reserved power of sale extended to any sale that might be made in pursuance of future Regulations, the implied covenant, to be of any service to the suppliants, must be that the Crown would not exercise to the prejudice of the lessee the power of making new Regulations for the sale of land on different terms, or, at least, that it would not dispose of the leased land under any such new Regulations. It is difficult, and I think impossible, to imply such a covenant against the Crown.

In the case of *British Equitable Assurance Co. Ltd.* v. *Baily* (1) H. C. of A.
1907.
the question was whether the appellants, a life assurance company, ought to be held to have entered into an implied contract Moore and
Scroope
v.
The State of
Western
Australia.
with the respondent, a policy holder, that they would not alter
their by-laws to his prejudice.   Lord *Macnaghten* said :—" Now
the whole question in the case is, did the appellant company
contract with the respondent to the effect of depriving themselves Griffith C.J.
of the right (which they had under their constitution) to make
this change ? "   So here the question would be, "did the Crown
·by the lease in* question contract with the lessee that it would
not exercise its right to alter the conditions of sale of land in
Western Australia so far as regards the demised premises ? "   As
I have said, it is impossible to answer this question in the affirmative.   It follows that the reservations included a power to sell
the land under any conditions that might be prescribed by future
Regulations, whatever the term " sell," as used in the reservations,
may mean.

I proceed to consider whether the homestead and grazing leases
in question were " sales " within the meaning of the Regulations
of 1887 and the reservations in the suppliants' lease.   By the Act
53 & 54 Vict. c. 26 Her Majesty was authorized to assent by
Order in Council to a Draft Bill conferring a Constitution on the
Colony of Western Australia as set out in the Schedule.   Sec. 3
of the Act was as follows :—" The entire management and control
of the waste lands of the Crown in the Colony of Western Australia, and of the proceeds of the sale, letting, and disposal thereof,
including all royalties, mines, and minerals, shall be vested in the
legislature of that Colony."   Sec. 4 repealed the 7th section of the
Act 18 & 19 Vict. c. 56 by which the power to make Regulations
for the disposition of Crown lands in Western Australia was
vested in Her Majesty, but provided that all Regulations made
under that section and in force at the commencement of the Act
should continue in force until altered or repealed in pursuance of
the powers conferred by it (*i.e.*, by sec. 3).   The second part of
sec. 4 is as follows :—" Nothing in this Act shall affect any contract or prevent the fulfilment of any promise or engagement
made before the time at which this Act takes effect in the Colony

(1) (1906) A.C., 35, at p. 39.

H. C. of A.   of Western Australia on behalf of Her Majesty with respect to
   1907.   any lands situate in that Colony, nor shall disturb or in any way
MOORE AND   interfere with or prejudice any vested or other rights which have
SCBOOPE   accrued or belong to the licensed occupants or lessees of any
   v.   Crown lands within that Colony."
THE STATE OF
WESTERN
AUSTRALIA.   The second section of the scheduled Bill provided that it should
Griffith C.J. be lawful for Her Majesty by and with the advice and consent of
             the Legislative Council and Legislative Assembly to make laws
             for the peace, order and good government of the Colony of
             Western Australia. These words confer a plenary power of
             legislation, except so far as their effect may be cut down by an
             enactment of equal authority. It is contended, however, by the
             appellants, and it was so held by the Supreme Court in *Steere's
             Case* (1), that they are cut down by the proviso to sec. 4 of the
             enabling Act, so that, with regard to land which was at the
             commencement of the *Constitution Act* the subject of any con-
             tract, promise or agreement made under the Regulations, the local
             legislature had no authority to pass any law which would pre-
             judicially affect any such contract, promise or agreement.

             The Royal Assent to the Constitution was proclaimed on 21st
             October 1890. In 1893 the legislature passed an Act, called the
             Homesteads Act (57 Vict. No. 18), by which certain of the
             Regulations of 1887 relating to the conditional sale of land were
             repealed and others substituted. The new conditions were
             framed on the same lines as the old, but were easier, and offered
             greater inducements to intending settlers. In 1898 a general
             Land Act (62 Vict. No. 37) was passed, under which a new mode
             of conditional sale of land called a grazing lease was established.
             The conditions differed from those under the *Homesteads Act*, but
             were framed on the same lines. In both cases, as under the
             Regulations, the title began with a lease, but, on performance of
             the prescribed conditions and payment of the full price, the pur-
             chaser or lessee became entitled to a grant in fee simple.

             The power to grant such leases was, by the Act, to extend to
             all Crown lands, which term was defined as bearing the same
             meaning as in the Regulations of 1887 with some exceptions not
             material to the present case. In execution of the powers thus

                          (1) 6 W.A.L.R., 178.

H. C. of A.
1907.

Moore and
Scroope
v.
The State of
Western
Australia.

Griffith C.J.

formally granted several homestead leases and grazing leases were issued in respect of land comprised in the suppliants' lease, and the new lessees entered and dispossessed the pastoral lessee. It is in respect of this dispossession that damages are claimed.

I proceed to consider the meaning of the term "sell" as used in the Regulations and in the reservations in the lease. Regulation 45 authorized the Governor in Council to define and set apart any Crown lands as an agricultural area, and to declare it open to selection under the provisions of the Regulations.

Regulation 46 provided that such areas should be "disposed of" under certain prescribed conditions, (*a*) to (*k*), which included residence. Condition (*a*) spoke of the "price" of the land. Condition (*h*) said that after a prescribed time "provided that an amount equal to the full 'purchase money' has been expended on the land in prescribed improvements, and further provided that the full 'purchase money' has been paid," a Crown Grant shall issue. Regulation 49 provided that land in the South Western Division of the Colony (in which the land in question is situated) might be "sold" without conditions of residence but subject to the other conditions "prescribed by Clause 46 of these Regulations." Regulation 52 restricted the alienation of land in certain other parts of the Colony except for specified purposes, or except within specially declared areas. It provided that within specially declared areas land might be "sold" under certain conditions. Condition (*a*) said that land within an area shall only be "disposed of" after survey under prescribed conditions of improvement. Condition (*b*) fixed the "price," which was to be payable in ten yearly instalments. A lease for ten years was to be issued to the applicant for the land. Condition (*i*) provided that at the expiration of the lease or at any time after its issue, provided that (amongst other things) an "amount equal to the full purchase money" had been expended on prescribed improvements, and further provided that the "full purchase money" had been paid, a Crown grant should issue. Regulation 53 provided that certain persons in certain districts might apply to "purchase" for a homestead an area of prescribed dimensions on the same terms and conditions as "prescribed for purchase" under Regulation 52. Regulation 54 authorized land within the South Western Division

H. C. OF A.
1907.

MOORE AND
SCROOPE
v.
THE STATE OF
WESTERN
AUSTRALIA.

Griffith C.J.

to be "sold" on certain other conditions of improvement, to be fulfilled within seven years.   Regulation 55 provided that land might be "disposed of" on other conditions.

I think that it clearly appears from the provisions to which I have referred that in the Regulations the words "sell" and "dispose of" are used, indiscriminately and interchangeably, to denote a contract for the alienation of Crown lands, whether for cash or on conditions, and I think that in the reservations in the pastoral lease the same words must have the same extended meaning.   I think, therefore, that in Regulation 61 the reserved right to "sell subject to the provisions of these Regulations" must be construed as meaning a right to sell in the same sense, subject to any rights reserved by the Regulations to the pastoral lessee on such a sale.   I think also that the word "sold" in Regulation 59 must receive the same construction, and that the words "under these Regulations" in the same Regulation include a reference to Regulation 3 which authorizes a sale under any amended Regulations.

It follows, in my opinion, that alienation under the provisions now contained in the *Homesteads Act* 1893, and the *Land Act* 1898, under which the homestead leases and grazing leases objected to were granted, would, if they had been issued under amended Regulations to the same effect, have been within the reservations in the suppliants' lease, and that, being in fact made under the powers conferred by the *Constitution Act* and the *Enabling Act*, they are equally within those reservations.

This conclusion is fortified by the historical fact that for more than a quarter of a century before the Regulations of 1887 were made the alienation of Crown lands upon conditions of residence and improvement had been a recognized mode of disposition in other Australian Colonies, and was always regarded as a sale.

It also follows, in my opinion, that *Steere's Case* (1) was wrongly decided on this point, and should, so far, be overruled.

I am therefore of opinion that the suppliants have failed to establish any breach of any implied contract on the part of the Crown.   It follows that so much of the judgment as declared that the homestead leases and grazing leases in question are void

(1) 6 W.A.L.R., 178.

was erroneous, and that the judgment should be varied by
omitting that declaration. I must not, however, be taken to
assent to the notion that such a declaration could in any event be
made in a suit to which the lessees are not parties.

In the view which I take of the construction of the lease it is
unnecessary to deal with the question of the competency of the
legislature of Western Australia to pass a law impairing the
rights of private persons under titles granted before the Constitution, or with the question whether the grant by a lessor of a
subsequent lease of the same land followed by dispossession of
the first lessee by the second under the supposed authority of his
lease would be a breach of a covenant for quiet enjoyment.

BARTON J. I have had the advantage of reading the judgment
of the Chief Justice, and consider its reasoning conclusive. I
am, therefore, of opinion with His Honor that the judgment
should be varied in favour of the Crown by omitting the
declaration as to the homestead leases and grazing leases, and
that the appeal should be dismissed.

ISAACS J. The homestead leases and the grazing leases
impeached by the suppliants were issued under the provisions
of the *Homesteads Act* 1893 and the *Land Act* 1898. Those
Acts authorize the grant of leases out of Crown lands. The
definition of Crown lands in the *Homesteads Act* is as they are
defined by the Land Regulations proclaimed on 2nd March
1887, unless the context otherwise requires. Those Regulations
defined Crown lands to be lands vested in the Crown, not
dedicated to any public purpose, or granted or lawfully contracted to be granted in fee simple, or with a right to purchase
under the Regulations. There is no context in the Act requiring
any other definition.

Crown lands are defined by the *Land Act* 1898, unless the
context necessarily requires, to be substantially as defined by the
Regulations, with the addition that they are not to be land held
under lease or licence under the *Goldfields Act* or *Mineral Lands
Act*.

The lands held by the suppliants under pastoral lease were

H. C. of A.
1907.

MOORE AND
SCROOPE
v.
THE STATE OF
WESTERN
AUSTRALIA.

Griffith C.J.

H. C. of A. therefore, *primâ facie*, clearly within the competency of the
1907.   Crown to grant as homestead or grazing leases.

Moore and   But the validity of these leases is challenged for the following
Scroope   reasons. First, it is said that lands held under the suppliants'
v.   pastoral lease must be excluded from the definition of Crown
The State of
Western   lands for this purpose, because to grant the leases in question
Australia. out of such lands would be a breach of an implied covenant for
Isaacs J.   quiet enjoyment, and therefore the legislature could not have
            intended the power to extend so far.

This contention turns out to be immaterial, because, on a
proper construction of the pastoral lease and the law relating to
the contested leases, the latter do not appear to conflict with the
former. But, apart from that, I could not accede to this argument, because the words of the legislature are too precise to
admit of hesitation ; and it is to be noticed that leased land
intended to be excepted, as for instance land leased under the
Goldfields Act, is expressly mentioned.

So far as the construction of the two Land Acts is concerned,
there cannot be a doubt that they purport to authorize the issue
of the leases. It was also urged in the same connection that,
assuming the bare power existed, the Crown must be taken to
have impliedly covenanted not to exercise it against the pastoral
lessee, as it would be inconsistent with the grant. It does not
seem to me very important whether this contention is rested on
the doctrine of an implied covenant for quiet enjoyment or on
the rule that a grantor cannot derogate from his own grant :
See *per Lindley* L.J. in *Robinson* v. *Kilvert* (1).

But this and the previous argument are met by the same
answer. If a Statute gives specific authority to do an act in
circumstances actually contemplated by Parliament, and which
if the act be done must necessarily constitute it a breach of
contract, it cannot be said to be unlawful ; and the remedy, if
any, must be found in some statutory provision. For this the
case of *Manchester, Sheffield and Lincolnshire Railway Co.* v.
Anderson (2) is a distinct authority with special relevance to
this case. The company were assignees of the reversion of land
of which their assignor had granted a lease to the defendant

(1) 41 Ch. D., 88, at p. 95.   (2) (1898) 2 Ch., 394.

with an express covenant for quiet enjoyment. In the exercise of their statutory powers the company executed some works which, it was assumed, would have been a breach of the covenant but for the Act of Parliament. It was held by the Court of Appeal that no action lay for the breach of the covenant, because the works were authorized by Statute. This principle was confirmed by another Court of Appeal in *Long Eaton Recreation Grounds Co. Ltd.* v. *Midland Railway Co* (1). In the first of these cases compensation might have been, and in the second it was successfully, claimed under the *Lands Clauses Consolidation Act* 1845, but no action lay as for a wrongful act.

But then it is said that, assuming so much against the appellants, if the acts were valid, the *Imperial Western Australia Constitution Act* 1890, forbids the issue of the leases as being a contravention of sec. 4 (2) of the State Constitution (53 & 54 Vict. c. 26). That depends upon two considerations: whether the issue of the leases was in breach of the suppliants' contract with the Crown, and whether if it was the Parliament of Western Australia had power nevertheless to authorize their issue. The State Court in the present case followed the case of *Steere* v. *The Minister for Lands* (2) in 1904, which decided that a grazing lease, granted out of lands held under a pastoral lease issued before 1890, would interfere with and prejudice the rights of the pastoral lessee, and that consequently the issue of such a grazing lease was prohibited by the Constitution. Of course, if the grazing lease is not a breach of the contract by the pastoral lease, there is no such prohibition. I am of opinion that the issue of grazing leases under the *Land Act* 1898, or of a homestead lease, is not a violation of that contract, and therefore it is not necessary to consider the very serious argument that, if it were such a violation, the State Parliament is incompetent to authorize it.

The ground upon which the Supreme Court in *Steere* v. *The Minister for Lands* (2) rested its opinion that the grazing lease violates the contract under the pastoral lease, was that the only sales of land comprised within the pastoral lease, permitted by the terms of the contract, were sales in accordance with the

(1) (1902) 2 K B., 574.　　　　(2) 6 W.A.L.R., 178.

H. C. OF A.
1907.

MOORE AND
SCROOPE
v.
THE STATE OF
WESTERN
AUSTRALIA.

Isaacs J.

H. C. of A.
1907.

Moore and
Scroope
v.
The State of
Western
Australia.

Isaacs J.

Regulations under which the lease was issued, and as a grazing lease was not issuable under the Regulations, but only by the Act of 1898, it fell outside the contract, and therefore outside the power of the Crown, and of the legislature.

With the greatest respect to the opinion of the learned Judges who came to that conclusion, I am unable to accept it.

The starting point from which to consider the question is sec. 7 of the Imperial Act 18 & 19 Vict. c. 56. That section provided that it should be lawful for Her Majesty " to regulate the sale, letting, disposal, and occupatian " of waste lands of the Crown, &c.

The Regulations of 2nd March 1887 provided in Part II., headed *Reserves*, for the disposal of lands in the public interest for certain enumerated objects; in Part IV. for *alienation*, including under that term sales by auction, free selection by conditional purchase by deferred payment and either with residence or without residence, or by conditional purchase by direct payment. Alienation is here evidently used as equivalent to sale, the consideration money being variously termed price or purchase money ; and if, instead of *alienation*, Part IV. were headed *sale*, the matter would to this extent be beyond argument.

In Part V. pastoral leases were permitted, this is "letting." In Part VI. mineral lands were dealt with. Part VII. provided for licences for timber cutting. Part VIII. was miscellaneous and dealt with rents, transfers, improvements, special occupation under previous Regulations, special leases, special concessions, &c.

I have referred to these various matters somewhat minutely in order to point to the care with which the Regulations followed the 7th section of the Imperial Act, in regard to the classification of sales, letting, disposal and occupation. It is plain too that, independently of the heading under which they are found, conditional purchases of themselves, when regarded from the standpoint of the Crown, fall naturally under the denomination of sales. The conditions upon which title was ultimately to pass were the means by which the sales were "regulated" within the meaning of the 7th section.

The Regulations prescribed the form of pastoral lease, which is that held by the suppliants. It declares that "We . . . do by these presents demise and lease unto the said lessees . . .

H. C. of A.
1907.

Moore and
Scroope
v.
The State of
Western
Australia.

Isaacs J.

except and always reserved to us . . . full power during the term hereby granted from time to time to sell to any person all or any unsold portion of the said demised premises, subject to any claim for improvements that may be lawfully made in pursuance of the said Regulations, . . . also to sell any mineral land comprised within the said demised premises ; and subject to any rights of the lessees as aforesaid to license to occupy, or to sell any other portion of the said premises at any time and with a right of immediate entry."

The habendum runs thus :—" To have and to hold the premises hereby demised, except as aforesaid, and subject to the powers, reservation and conditions herein, and in the said regulations contained, and with all the rights, powers and privileges conferred by such of the regulations as are applicable hereto unto the said lessees," &c., for 21 years.

The learned Judges of the Supreme Court in *Steere's Case* (1) thought that the words "subject to any claim for improvements that may be lawfully made in pursuance of the said Regulations" showed clearly that the only power of sale contemplated was a sale under the Regulations, and therefore there could be no other except such as would be a violation of the contract. In my opinion, at the moment and until the Regulations were altered, the only sales possible were those specified in the existing Regulations, yet the power to sell, which was reserved, was a power to sell by any means by which the Crown could at any given time lawfully sell as between the Crown and a purchaser : such sale might be under the then existing Regulations or any future Regulations which the third of the Regulations of 2nd March 1887 reserved power to make ; or to follow the concluding words of the 7th section of the Imperial Act as " Parliament shall otherwise provide." What concerned the pastoral lessee in that connection was not the method, or terms of sale by the Crown to another person, but the payment to him for improvements. What did it matter to the pastoral lessee if the land were sold outright by direct payment, or upon terms extending over twenty or fifty years, or by the medium of a transaction called a conditional purchase or a grazing lease ? So long as payment

(1) 6 W.A.L.R , 178.

H. C. of A.
1907.

MOORE AND
SCROOPE
v.
THE STATE OF
WESTERN
AUSTRALIA.

Isaacs J.

for improvements as provided by the Regulations was secured, the terms of the bargain between the Government and the purchaser could not possibly affect the pastoral lessee. I find it difficult to understand how the pastoral lessee could have any vested right in the method by which the Crown sold to a third person. That was no business of his. He must be taken to know that under sec. 7 of the Imperial Act the power always existed to make new Regulations regarding the sale of lands, which the Crown had power to sell at all, as well as the power of Parliament to otherwise provide which was in fact, though unnecessarily, expressly referred to. The words relied on by the Supreme Court have full operation to protect the pastoral lessee if limited to payment for improvements, and not extended to qualify the Crown's methods of selling Crown lands. The other extracts from the lease, already quoted, strongly support the view I have just expressed. So long as the Crown sells the land, it may, without any violation of the contract with the suppliants, sell it upon any terms and conditions which Parliament may authorize. No issue arises or could arise in this case as to payment for improvements. The only material question remaining is whether the homestead and grazing leases are properly to be termed sales. The *Homesteads Act* 1893 is intituled "An Act to provide facilities for permanent settlement by free grants of land for household farms and by homestead leases," &c. Homestead leases are for thirty years at a rent ranging from one penny to three pence per acre per annum; section 21 declares that "the said rents shall respectively be due and be paid in advance on the 1st day of March in every year." It is true that, in case of failure to pay regularly or with a fine if in arrear, his lease and the land and improvements shall be forfeited. But he is under a statutory obligation to pay, whatever may be the statutory remedy for non-payment. Section 23 requires him also to comply with conditions which obviously point to the intention of his permanently retaining the land as against the Crown. By sec. 25, if he has duly paid his rent and observed the conditions, he is entitled on payment of fees to a Crown grant of the lands. Section 26 permits him to accelerate the granting of title. Sec. 29 recognizes rights properly attributable to a virtual purchaser of the land. Broadly looked at, the issue of a homestead lease is only the first step in a continuous and connected process by which the Crown transfers for a fixed price its land to a permanent settler. A homestead lessee would undoubtedly regard the land as his, subject only to payment of the deferred price, and compliance with the conditions. There is no intention that his interest in the land shall terminate in thirty years; on the contrary the intention is that it shall then or sooner ripen by virtue of his contract into absolute ownership. It therefore answers more properly to a "sale" than to a "letting" within the meaning of the 7th section of the Act 18 & 19 Vict. c. 56, the Regulations, and the lease. To use the words of Lord *Herschell*, L.C. in *Helby* v. *Matthews* (1): "Unless there were a breach of contract by the party who engaged to make the payments the transactions necessarily resulted in a sale." Here the lessee applied for a lease on the basis of an Act of Parliament requiring him to pay the rent regularly during the whole period, and, unless there was a breach of that and other obligations, the transaction necessarily resulted in a sale.

In *McEntire* v. *Crossley Bros.* (2), there was an agreement by which the "owners and lessors" as they were called of a gas-engine agreed to let, and the "lessee" as he was called agreed to hire the engine at a rent to be paid by instalments amounting in all to £240; upon payment in full the agreement was to be at an end and the engine to become the property of the lessee, but until payment in full to remain the sole and absolute property of the lessors. It was also agreed that in case of failure to pay any of the instalments the lessors might elect either to recover the balance due, or instead resume possession of the engine and sell it, and, after retaining out of the purchase-money all expenses and the balance remaining due, pay the surplus to the lessee. It was held that looking at the substance of the agreement it was one of sale and purchase, though the property did not pass till full payment. Lord *Watson* said (3):—"Although the words 'lessors' and 'hirer' are used and the word 'rent' also occurs, it is perfectly plain that the agreement is one of sale and purchase, and nothing else."

H. C. of A.
1907.

MOORE AND SCROOPE
v.
THE STATE OF WESTERN AUSTRALIA.

Isaacs J.

(1) (1895) A.C., 471, at p. 478.   (2) (1895) A.C., 457.
                (3) (1895) A.C., 457, at p. 467.

H. C. of A.
1907.

MOORE AND
SCROOPE
v.
THE STATE OF
WESTERN
AUSTRALIA.

Isaacs J.

There are, of course, points of difference between that bargain and the bargain arising in a homestead lease, but there is also considerable resemblance, and, looking at the substance in either case, each seems to me alike in this that it amounts to an agreement to sell the property the subject matter of the transaction. The policy of the Land Acts requires some guarantee that a homestead lessee will permanently settle, and this guarantee is found by the legislature in his compliance with the conditions of sale.

As to the grazing lease, the statutory provisions in sec. 68 of the *Land Act* 1898 are, if anything, even stronger to show that the nature of the transaction is essentially a sale.

In the result, the issue of the challenged leases is no breach of agreement with the pastoral lessee, because, when regarded in their substance, they are a kind of conditional purchase and sale, differing only in form from the conditional purchases and sales provided for in the Regulations of March 1887, and therefore the appeal should be dismissed except to the extent mentioned.

It follows that the decision in the case of *Steere* v. *The Minister for Lands* (1) cannot be supported inasmuch as a grazing lease is not a breach of the Crown's contract in the pastoral lease—the other branch of that case being as I have said immaterial to consider. It is also, in the view I have taken, useless to discuss, and therefore I offer no opinion, how far an implied covenant for quiet enjoyment is broken by a subsequent grantee from the same lessor, entering the demised property under a claim of right by virtue of the grant. Such a question could not arise where, as here, the original lease expressly reserved to the lessor the right to make the grant and so empowered the act complained of.

> *Appeal dismissed. Judgment appealed from varied by omitting declaration of invalidity of homestead and grazing leases in question.*

Solicitors, for the appellants, *James & Darbyshire.*
Solicitor, for the respondent, *Barker* (Crown Solicitor).

N. G. P.

(1) 6 W.A.L.R., 178.

[HIGH COURT OF AUSTRALIA.]

PENNY AND ANOTHER　.　.　.　.　APPELLANTS;

AND

MILLIGAN AND OTHERS　.　.　.　.　RESPONDENTS.

ON APPEAL FROM THE SUPREME COURT OF
NEW SOUTH WALES.

Will—Construction—Provision for widow—" In lieu of dower and thirds "—Partial intestacy—Election—Absolute gift—Condition.

H. C. OF A.
1907.

Nov. 21, 22, 25; Dec. 4.

Griffith C.J., Barton and Isaacs JJ.

A testator by his will gave the residue of his personal estate to his wife for life, and after her death to his stepdaughter for life with remainder over to such of the stepdaughter's children as should survive her, and declared that the provision for his wife should be " in lieu of dower and thirds." The gift over in remainder having failed owing to the death of the children of the stepdaughter during the lifetime of the tenant for life, their interest fell into intestacy.

Held, that, inasmuch as it appeared from the terms of the will, that the events which happened and the consequent intestacy had never been contemplated by the testator, the declaration could not be construed as imposing a condition that the widow should only take the gift to her on the terms of renouncing any share on a possible partial intestacy, nor as a gift by implication of her share in the personalty to the next of kin, and that consequently she was entitled to both the provision and her share in the intestacy under the Statute of Distributions.

Lett v. *Randall*, 3 Sm. & G., 83; 24 L.J. Ch., 708, distinguished.

Naismith v. *Boyes*, (1899) A.C., 495, and *In re Williams; Williams* v. *Williams*, (1897) 2 Ch., 12, considered and applied.

Decision of *Street* J., *In re Eyers; McIntosh* v. *Milligan*, (1907) 7 S.R. (N.S.W.), 83, affirmed.

APPEAL from a decision of *Street* J. in Equity on an originating summons brought by executors for the determination of questions arising upon the construction of a will.

The testator, John Eyers, by his will, after providing for certain legacies, gave his real estate and the residue of his personal estate to his wife for life or so long as she should continue his widow and unmarried, and after her death or marriage to his step-daughter for life, and after her death to such of her children as should be then surviving. The will contained this provision:— "I declare that the provision hereby made for my said wife is in lieu of dower and thirds." The testator died in June 1888, leaving a large amount of personal property. The widow died in December 1895, and the stepdaughter in January 1906, having had five children, all of whom had died during the lifetime of the testator. The gift in remainder to the surviving children of the stepdaughter, therefore, failed. The testator left no issue.

The executors of the will took out an originating summons for the determination of the following among other questions:— Whether or not on the true construction of the will the sequels in title of the widow of the testator are entitled to any and what share in his intestate personal estate? *Street* J., before whom the questions were argued, held that the widow was entitled both to her provision under the will and to her distributive share under the intestacy, and declared that the sequels in title were therefore entitled to share in the testator's personal estate undisposed of in respect of the intestacy : *In re Eyers*; *McIntosh* v. *Milligan* (1).

From this decision the present appeal was brought.

Cullen K.C. (*R. K. Manning* with him), for the appellants. The declaration has the effect of preventing the representatives of the widow from sharing in the personal estate under the intestacy. The testator must be taken to have contemplated a possible partial intestacy, because the only provision for remainder was in favour of the surviving children of the second life tenant, and there was a strong possibility of a failure. The words "dower and thirds" can refer to nothing but an intestacy. It is not necessary that a partial intestacy should be shown on the face of

(1) (1907) 7 S.R. (N.S.W.), 83.

the will in order to exclude the widow in such an event, but, if it were necessary, it appears just as clearly in the present case as it appeared in *Lett* v. *Randall* (1), which is a direct authority in favour of the appellants. The testator made for his widow such provision as he thought reasonable, and did not intend her to have any more even if there should turn out to be an intestacy. No other reasonable construction can be put upon the words used. The declaration could not have been intended to protect other beneficiaries, because they are all fully protected by the rest of the will, and the *Dower Act* rendered it unnecessary to protect devisees. Although a mere declaration that the widow is not to share in an intestacy will not deprive her of her share (*Re Holmes*; *Holmes* v. *Holmes* (2)), yet if something else is given, as is the case here, she must elect between the two. *Pickering* v. *Lord Stamford* (3) is distinguishable. There was an absolute disposition of the remainder there, if it had been valid, whereas in the present case, as in *Lett* v. *Randall* (1), the remainder is contingent. *Re Benson* (4) is against the statement of principle in *Pickering* v. *Lord Stamford* (3), that such a bar as this is for the benefit of the devisees, and shows that its effect is to restrict the widow to the provision. To hold otherwise would be to render the declaration inoperative in the only contingency in which it could possibly have taken effect. *Lett* v. *Randall* (1) was referred to in *Sykes* v. *Sykes* (5) and was not disapproved, and the statement in the headnote of *Tavernor* v. *Grindley* (6), that *Lett* v. *Randall* (1) was distinguished is not accurate. *Vachell* v. *Breton* (7), and *Bund* v. *Green* (8) also support the appellants. The widow, by accepting the provision, accepts with it the condition that she is to get no more. The position of the widow is analogous to that under a contract to submit to the conditions attached to the bounty: *Gurly* v. *Gurly* (9); *Northumberland* (*Earl of*) v. *Aylesford* (*Earl of*) (10); *Naismith* v. *Boyes* (11).

(1) 3 Sm. & G., 83 ; 24 L.J. Ch., 708.
(2) 62 L.T., 383.
(3) 3 Ves., 332, 492.
(4) 96 N.Y., 499 ; 48 Amer. Rep., 646.
(5) L.R. 4 Eq., 200 ; s.c. on appeal, L.R. 3 Ch., 301.
(6) 32 L.T., 424.
(7) 5 Bro. P.C., 51.
(8) 12 Ch. D., 819.
(9) 8 Cl. & F., 743.
(10) Amb., 540, at p. 545.
(11) (1899) A.C., 495.

H. C. of A.
1907.
⁓
PENNY
v.
MILLIGAN.

[ISAACS J.—But the question is, does the condition conflict with the will, and to decide that we must look at the will: *Naismith* v. *Boyes* (1); *Hall* v. *Hill* (2).]

The former case dealt with Scottish law, and is not wholly applicable to the rights of a widow under our law. The *terce*, *jus relictæ*, and *legitim*, could be set up against any testamentary disposition. [He referred to *Rogers and Bell, Principles of Law of Scotland*, 1885 ed., p. 183.]

The exclusion of the widow is tantamount to a gift to the next of kin. The testator should be presumed to have made the will with knowledge of the legal consequences following upon a failure of any disposition in it: *Bickham* v. *Cruttwell* (3); *Collis* v. *Robins* (4); *In re March*; *Mander* v. *Harris* (5).

[ISAACS J. referred to *Garthshore* v. *Chalie* (6).]

The question whether this is a case of election and the question whether there is a gift to the next of kin are not mutually exclusive, but are to a certain extent bound up together. If the widow elects to accept the provisions on the terms imposed by the will, the result is, in effect, a gift to the next of kin to her exclusion. If she does not accept it, then there is no gift to the next of kin, but a partial intestacy in which she shares.

Owen K.C. (*Rich* with him), for the respondent Milligan. No doubt a widow may contract not to claim any share in intestacy, and a testator may so frame his will as to put her to her election, or may validly make a provision in such a way as to exclude the widow from a share in intestacy if he gives to someone else what the widow would otherwise have received. But there must be language implying that the next of kin are to get the widow's share. [He referred to *Williams on Executors*, 10th ed., p. 1234; *Naismith* v. *Boyes* (7); *Pickering* v. *Lord Stamford* (8); *Jarman on Wills*, 5th ed., p. 432; *Rogers on Legacies*, 4th ed., p. 1633.] There may be a contract to accept a condition imposed as in *Garthshore* v. *Chalie* (6). That is not the case here. There is no intestacy shown on the face of the will as there was in *Tavernor*

(1) (1899) A.C., 495.
(2) 1 Dr. & War., 94, at p. 105.
(3) 3 My. & Cr., 763, at p. 772.
(4) 1 De G. & Sm., 131, at p. 138.
(5) 27 Ch. D., 166, at p. 169.
(6) 10 Ves., 1.
(7) (1899) A.C., 495, at p. 505.
(8) 3 Ves., 332, 492.

v. *Grindley* (1) and *Lett* v. *Randall* (2). The testator plainly thought he was disposing of all his property. [He referred also to *Leake* v. *Robinson* (3); *Naismith* v. *Boyes* (4).] Mere words of exclusion will not make a gift to those not excluded: *Sympson* v. *Hornsby and Hutton* (5). Property not specifically disposed of will go to those who are by law entitled : *Re Holmes*; *Holmes* v. *Holmes* (6). To give something in lieu of dower does not exclude the widow from participation in such property.

[GRIFFITH C.J. referred to *Fitch* v. *Weber* (7).]

The testator may have meant to do what the appellants contend but he has not used words which have that effect : *Smidmore* v. *Smidmore* (8). He did not use the words in contemplation of the facts that resulted in failure of the gifts and gave rise to an intestacy ; he used them with the intention of benefiting the persons named as legatees.

Pickering v. *Lord Stamford* (9) is conclusive in favour of the respondents as to the effect of the words used here. Even if the testator made a mistake as to the law, the interpretation of the will is not affected thereby. [He referred also to *Waring* v. *Ward* (10); *Ramsay* v. *Shelmerdine* (11); *Sykes* v. *Sykes* (12).]

[GRIFFITH C.J. referred to *In re Williams*; *Williams* v. *Williams* (13).

ISAACS J. referred to *Birmingham* v. *Kirwan* (14).]

Harriott, for the other respondents, on the question of costs only.

Cullen K.C. in reply.

Cur. adv. vult.

The following judgments were read :—   Dec. 4.

GRIFFITH C.J. [having referred briefly to the facts and having read the material portions of the will already reported, continued.] The question is whether the final declaration just

(1) 32 L.T., 424.
(2) 38m. & G., 83 ; 24 L.J. Ch., 708.
(3) 2 Mer., 363, at p. 394.
(4) (1899) A.C., 495.
(5) 2 Eq. Ca. (Abr.), 439 ; 11 Viner's Abr., 185, Pre. Ch., 452.
(6) 62 L.T., 383.
(7) 6 Hare, 51, 145.

(8) 3 C.L.R., 344.
(9) 3 Ves., 332, 492.
(10) 5 Ves., 670, at p. 675.
(11) L.R. 1 Eq., 129.
(12) L.R. 4 Eq., 200.
(13) (1897) 2 Ch., 12.
(14) 2 Sch. & Lef., 444.

read has the effect of excluding the widow and her representatives from a share under the Statute of Distributions in the property, which, in the events that happened, was undisposed of by the will. The widow was not entitled to "dower or thirds" except in the event of intestacy. The general rule is thus stated in *Williams' Executors*, 10th ed., p. 1235, in a passage which was expressly approved by Lord *Shand* in *Naismith* v. *Boyes* (1). The learned authors, after referring to the case of a settlement by which the wife's claim to a share in the case of an intestacy may be excluded, proceed :—" But it is otherwise when a husband by will makes a provision for his wife, stating it to be in lieu and in bar of all her claims on his personal estate, and then subjects his personalty to a disposition which lapses, or is void, so that the latter fund is subject to distribution ; for then, notwithstanding the words of the will, the widow is entitled to a share under the Statute. The principle of this distinction is, that where a woman has before marriage agreed to accept a consideration for her widow's share, she is bound by her compact, whether her husband die testate or intestate ; but where there is no such contract, but the provision in bar of the distributive share arises upon the husband's will, it is presumed that the motive for the widow's exclusion originated in a particular design or purpose of the testator, viz., for the benefit of the person in favour of whom the property was bequeathed by him ; so that if the purpose be disappointed, there is no reason why the bar or exclusion should continue."

It is contended that the case of *Lett* v. *Randall* (2) established an exception to this rule. The foundation of the exception is said by the text writers to be the fact that there was in that case an intestacy on the face of the will. No doubt *Stuart* V.C. said so, but the actual intestacy arose, not from the testator leaving some of his property undisposed of, but from a failure of the objects of his bounty. In that respect the present case is not, I think, distinguishable. The learned Vice-Chancellor did not, however, I think, rely entirely on this ground. After pointing out that a mere exclusion of the heir or next of kin from a share in the

(1) (1899) A.C., 495, at p. 505.   (2) 3 Sm. & G., 83 ; 24 L.J. Ch., 708

H. C. of A.
1907.

PENNY
v.
MILLIGAN.

Griffith C.J.

estate is nugatory, he added (1) :—" But the exclusion by declaration of one only of the next of kin, if it be valid, would enure to the benefit of the rest, and has the same effect as a gift by implication to them of the share of the person excluded. It has been said that, if such a clause had occurred in a settlement, it would have an effect which it cannot have in a will, because a settlement would operate as a contract. But, if by will certain terms or a certain condition be annexed to a gift, those terms as much bind the object of a gift, who accepts it, as if he contracted to abide by the terms or conditions. This is an essential element in the law of election. As there is found in the present case an intestacy on the face of the will, with language excluding the widow, in absolute and comprehensive terms, from any further share of the testator's property, in whatever way it might accrue, I can find no authority to justify the Court in holding that, having enjoyed the annuity, she or her representatives are entitled to any share in the property now to be distributed."

The words of exclusion in that case were very full. " I do expressly . . . declare that the said . . . provision . . . for my said . . . wife . . . . are by me meant and intended to be, and shall by my said wife be accepted and taken, in full and entire . . . satisfaction of . . . all manner of claims . . . . which she at any time might or could have . . . into, or out of any part or parts of my real and personal estate or under . . . any settlement or other writing . . . . or as or for or on account of any dower or thirds which she . . . could . . . in any manner have, claim . . . out of . . . any part of my estate . . . in any manner howsoever." The learned Vice-Chancellor therefore, appears to have thought (1) that there was an intestacy on the face of the will; (2) that the testator contemplated the case of an intestacy; (3) that the exclusion of the wife had the effect of a gift by implication of her share to the next of kin; and (4) that the gift to the widow was conditional, so that by accepting the gift she accepted the condition of exclusion. He also thought that it was a case of election, as no doubt it was. On these grounds he decided that the widow was excluded. I cannot regard this case

(1) 24 L.J. Ch., 708, at p. 711.

H. C. of A.
1907.

Penny
v.
Milligan.

Griffith C.J.

as an authority governing the present case, even if the correctness of the learned Vice-Chancellor's conclusions as to the construction of that particular will be admitted.

In the present case there is no question of election, properly so called, since the testator did not purport to dispose of any thing which was not his own property. The clause relied upon cannot be read as a gift by implication to the other next of kin to the exclusion of the widow. The only way, therefore, in which the desired effect can be given to it is by treating it as imposing a condition upon the gift to the widow or an obligation upon her. The rule of construction applicable in such cases is thus stated by *Rigby* L.J. in the case of *In re Williams; Williams* v. *Williams* (1). (The learned Lord Justice in that case dissented from the opinion of the majority of the Court of Appeal on the construction of the particular will in question, but the accuracy of his statement of the rule was accepted by the Court of Appeal in *In re Oldfield; Oldfield* v. *Oldfield* (2).)   "In the present case the question is one of condition, or election, not of trust, as the testator could not declare a trust of his wife's property; but the cases as to trusts are so closely analogous that they must be examined, and it will be seen that the same doctrines have been laid down as to conditions and trusts. . . .   No authoritative case ever laid it down that there could be any other ground for deducing a trust or condition than the intention of the testator as shown by the will taken as a whole, though no doubt in older cases that intention was sometimes inferred on insufficient grounds. The general intention was always treated as the matter to be ascertained. . . .

"On these fundamental points there never has, in my opinion, been any real difference, though the application of them to particular instances has not always been satisfactory."

In the same case *Lindley* L.J. said (3):—"In each case the whole will must be looked at; and unless it appears from the whole will that an obligation was intended to be imposed, no obligation will be held to exist; yet, moreover, in some of the older cases obligations were inferred from language which in

(1) (1897) 2 Ch., 12, at p. 28.   (2) (1904) 1 Ch., 549.
(3) (1897) 2 Ch., 12, at p. 18.

modern times would be thought insufficient to justify such an
inference." And again (1):—"The whole equitable doctrine of
election, when a testator disposes of property not his own, is
based upon the principle that a Court of Equity will enforce
performance of implied conditions on which property is given and
accepted."

H. C. of A.
1907.

PENNY
v.
MILLIGAN.

Griffith C.J.

Can it then be inferred from the words of the will now before
us that the testator intended to impose as a condition that the
widow should not take anything under the will except on the
terms of renouncing any share in property as to which the other
dispositions of the will might fail? Looking at the matter apart
from authority, I cannot think that any such idea entered the
testator's mind. He dealt with the whole of his estate, and
thought that he had dealt with it effectually. It happened, as often
happens, that he had not provided for every event, but I do not
think that he contemplated such a contingency as a failure of his
intended bounty. If we have recourse to authority the appellants' case seems hopeless. In the case of *Sympson* v. *Hornsby
and Hutton* (2), decided by Lord *Cowper* in 1716, a testator gave
his daughter a legacy, and declared that it should be in discharge
of her "child's share" and anything she could claim out of his
estate. It was held that she was nevertheless entitled to a share
in property as to which, in the events that happened, the testator
died intestate. Without referring to the intermediate cases I
will pass to *Naismith* v. *Boyes* (3), which was the case of a
Scottish testamentary settlement. By the law of Scotland, a
widow and her children are absolutely entitled to shares in the
personalty of the husband, which cannot be disposed of by his
will to their prejudice. In that case the testator, who had been
twice married, gave the income of the residue of his estate to his
widow for life, with remainder to his children by her. He then
declared as follows:—"And I declare the provision hereby made
for my wife and the children of our present marriage and the
provisions previously made for the said Minnie Arthur Hamilton
(a child by the first marriage) to be in full of all that my said
wife can claim in name of *terce, jus relictæ,* or otherwise, and

(1) (1897) 2 Ch., 12, at p. 19.   (2) 2 Eq. Ca. (Abr.), 439 ; 11 Viner's Abr., 185.
(3) (1899) A.C., 495.

H. C. of A.   of all that my said children can claim in name of *legitim*,
1907.   portion natural, bairn's part of gear, or otherwise, in respect of
PENNY   my death." The gift over to the children failed. It was con-
v.   tended that it was a case of election (as no doubt it was), and
MILLIGAN.   that the widow having elected to take the life estate, her repre-
Griffith C.J. sentatives could not claim a share as on intestacy. But the
contrary was held. The *Earl of Halsbury* L.C. thought that
the provisions in question were intended to apply only to such
part of the estate as was disposed of by the testator, and could
not be intended to apply to any rights arising from intestacy
which were not contemplated by the terms of the settlement, and
that the law of intestacy took effect upon his property not
effectively disposed of. He added (1):—"This seems to me good
sense, and I am satisfied that it gives effect to the intentions of
the testator in the sense that he contemplated a state of things
by the clause in question which as a fact did not arise, and that
he never contemplated the clause as applying to intestacy at all."
Lord *Watson* said (2):—"I do not think it can be reasonably
assumed, in the absence of any provision to that effect either
express or implied, that he intended to regulate the disposal of
any part of his estate which might possibly lapse into intestacy."
Lord *Shand* thought that this was the law of England applicable
to such a case, as established by the case of *Pickering* v. *Lord
Stamford* (3) in which *Sir R. P. Arden* M.R. and Lord *Loughborough* L.C. followed *Sympson* v. *Hornsby and Hutton* (4).

The learned counsel for the appellants sought to distinguish
Naismith v. *Boyes* (5), on the ground that that was a true case
of election, in which the testator had in form disposed of property
not his own, namely, his wife's *jus relictæ.* But this difference
appears, if it has any bearing at all upon the point, to have a
contrary effect. If, in a case where a testator attempts to dispose
of property which belongs to the donee, such a direction as that
in question is insufficient to attach a condition to the gift of the
testator's property, it seems to me that *a fortiori* it cannot have
that effect when the testator disposes of nothing but his own

---

(1) (1899) A.C., 495, at p. 497.   (4) 2 Eq. Ca. (Abr.), 439; 11
(2) (1899) A.C., 495, at p. 501.   Viner's Abr., 185.
(3) 3 Ves., 332.   (5) (1899) A.C., 495.

property. In the present case I am of opinion that there is no
condition clearly and unequivocally attached to the gift of the
life estate. I am, therefore, of opinion that the decision appealed
from is correct, and should be affirmed.

BARTON J. *Sir Richard Arden* M.R., afterwards Lord *Alvanley*, gives, in his judgment in the case of *Pickering* v. *Lord
Stamford* (1), a statement of a case of *Sympson* v. *Hornsby and
Hutton* from the Register's book, explaining that as there
described, it seems to bear more upon the point he was there
considering than the reports in *Viner* and in *Equity Cases
Abridged*. The statement is shortly as follows:—Thomas Addi-
son gave his daughter Jane out of his real and personal estate
certain estates, leases, titles and money, and declared this provision to be in satisfaction of her child's part of whatsoever more
she might have expected from him or out of his personal estate.
He then devised to his wife, and gave her furniture and other
things; all which devises and bequests he declared to be in full
of her dower, thirds and other claims at law or in equity or by
any local custom to any other part of his real and personal estate.
He gave the residue to his other daughter, who died in his lifetime, leaving one child, who was the only person that could be
entitled under the *Statute of Distributions* besides the wife and
the excluded daughter. By a codicil he gave the residue to his
wife for life, with power to dispose of the same after her decease,
with the approbation of the trustees. Having this limited power,
she made a disposition without the consent of the trustees. The
decree of Lord *Cowper* declares, that Frances the widow, having
disposed without the consent of the trustees, had not pursued her
power, therefore the testator died intestate as to the residue,
which ought to go according to the *Statute of Distributions*, viz., in
thirds; one third to the plaintiff Sympson in right of his wife
Jane; one third to the child of the deceased daughter; and one
third to the devisee of the widow.

In the case of *Pickering* v. *Lord Stamford* (1) it was argued
that the widow was excluded from any share of so much of the
testator's personal estate as was invested in real securities, the

(1) 3 Ves., 332, 492.

H. C. of A.
1907.

PENNY
v.
MILLIGAN.

Barton J.

disposition of which to charitable purposes was void, and which was declared to be divisible among the next of kin. By the clause of the will drawn into question, the testator, after giving certain parts of his real and personal estate to his wife, declared the provision he had thereby made for her to be " in bar, full satisfaction, and recompense of all dower or thirds which his said wife can have or claim in, out of, or to all or any part of his real and personal estate, or either of them." The Master of the Rolls at first held in favour of the construction which excluded the widow from any share in the real securities in question, but after full consideration of the case of *Sympson* v. *Hornsby and Hutton*, as above described, he changed his mind, and said (1):—" I am now decided, by having found the very point determined by Lord *Cowper*; who was of opinion, in the case I have cited from the Register's book, that where a testator had given his wife that provision, which he meant to be a satisfaction for any claim she might have against the other objects of his bounty, if by any accident those objects should be unable to claim the benefit of that exclusion, no other person should set it up against the widow." After that, said *Sir Richard Arden*, "I cannot, upon such a point, set up my own judgment against Lord *Cowper's*. Therefore I think my former determination was wrong." This decision was affirmed on appeal by the Lord Chancellor, Lord *Loughborough* (2), who said:—" If the Master of the Rolls had not entertained different views of this case upon the two occasions, when it was before him, I should have thought there could be no doubt. If I look at the will, which I ought not, it is perfectly clear upon the will, the intention does not go in favour of the next of kin to prohibit the wife from taking any part of his personal estate; for the intention at the time was to guard, perhaps by unnecessary words, against any person setting up a claim to defeat the purpose of charity the testator had marked out: but neither an heir at law, nor by parity of reasoning next of kin, can be barred by anything but a disposition of the heritable subject or personal estate to some person capable of taking. . . . With regard to the two cases, the only two upon the subject, I perfectly approve Lord *Cowper's* decision. It is as

(1) 3 Ves., 332, at p. 337.　　　(2) 3 Ves., 492, at p. 493.

H. C. of A.
1907.

Penny
v.
Milligan.

Barton J.

exactly in point to this case, as two cases can well bear upon each other." And I venture to say of the two decisions, one of which the then Lord Chancellor was approving and the other of which he was affirming, that there cannot be found two cases more in point to any other than are these two to that which we have now to decide. If indeed a partial intestacy arose, not from the lapse or voidance of a disposition in a will, but appearing on the face of the will so clearly as to give rise to the inference that the testator contemplated it, and such an intestacy co-existed with words emphatically and comprehensively excluding the widow, an intention in favour of the next of kin would be disclosed. But in the present case, as was rightly argued in *Pickering* v. *Lord Stamford* (1), there is a clear disposition of every part of the property, and if as to any part that fails, *pro tanto* the testator's intention is removed entirely out of the way. Perhaps, indeed, it is more correct to say that, the intention in favour of the original objects of the testator's bounty being frustrated, the protection of their interests against those of the widow is no longer needed, and it cannot be turned into an intention to protect against her the next of kin, who were never intended to have the subject matter at all. In *Lett* v. *Randall* (2), *Stuart* V.C. was able to find a partial intestacy on the face of the will, though with all respect I should have thought, but for this decision, that the voidance of the gift to the children of the daughters scarcely gave foundation to the inference of a contemplated intestacy as to their part. Be that as it may, the law of *Sympson* v. *Hornsby and Hutton* (3), and *Pickering* v. *Lord Stamford* (1) was not questioned by the Vice-Chancellor in *Lett* v. *Randall* (2). It has never been challenged; and I cannot but hold it to apply to the present case, so strikingly similar in its features. *Lett* v. *Randall* (2) itself has been somewhat questioned, and has not, I think, been found exactly in point for any subsequent decision.

It is not necessary to traverse the field of the numerous cases which were cited in argument. In his judgment in this case (4), *Street* J. cites a passage from the 10th edition of *Williams*

(1) 3 Ves., 332, 492.
(2) 3 Sm. & G., 83 ; 24 L.J. Ch., 708.
(3) 2 Eq. Ca. (Abr.), 439 ; 11

Viner's Abr., 185.
(4) (1907) 7 S.R. (N.S.W.), 83.

H. C. of A.   *on Executors*, at p. 1235, in which it is stated that: "But it is
1907.   otherwise when the husband by will makes a provision for his
PENNY   wife, stating it to be in lieu and in bar of all her claims on his
v.   personal estate, and then subjects his personalty to a disposition
MILLIGAN.   which lapses, or is void, so that the latter fund is subject to dis-
Barton J.   tribution; for then, notwithstanding the words of the will, the
             widow is entitled to a share under the Statute. The principle of
             this distinction is, that where a woman has before marriage agreed
             to accept a consideration for her widow's share, she is bound by
             her compact, whether her husband die intestate or testate; but
             where there is no such contract, but the provision in bar of the
             distributive share arises upon the husband's will, it is presumed
             that the motive for the widow's exclusion originated in a
             particular design or purpose of the testator, viz., for the benefit
             of the person in favour of whom the property was bequeathed by
             him; so that if the purpose be disappointed, there is no reason
             why the bar or exclusion should continue." Coming to the recent
             case of *Naismith* v. *Boyes* (1), it was pointed out to us that Lord
             Shand there said of that passage that it "states the rule with
             accuracy and great clearness." It unmistakably states the
             doctrine of *Sympson* v. *Hornsby and Hutton* (2), and *Pickering*
             v. *Lord Stamford* (3), the latter decided 110 years ago, the former
             many years earlier; and with so recent and so valuable an
             endorsement, it is clear that the doctrine remains unshaken to-
             day. In *Naismith* v. *Boyes* (4) a Scottish testator, by his will,
             called a *mortis causa* settlement, made provision for his wife and
             declared it to be in full of all claims by her of *terce* and *jus
             relictæ* or otherwise. Certain devisees died before vesting took
             place, so that the residue fell into intestacy. It was held that
             the testator's declaration was to be construed as excluding the
             widow's claim in so far only as it conflicted with the will, and
             that, as the testator had never contemplated the event that had
             happened, the widow was not only entitled to her provision
             under the will, but also to *terce* and *jus relictæ* out of such
             heritables and movables as had fallen into intestacy. Lord

(1) (1899) A.C., 495, at p. 505.   (3) 3 Ves., 332, 492.
(2) 2 Eq. Cas. (Abr), 439; 11 Viner's   (4) (1899) A.C., 495.
Abr., 185; Pre Ch., 452.

H. C. of A.
1907.

Penny
v.
Milligan.

Barton J.

Watson said (1):—"In a case like the present, where the testator settled upon the members of his family all the property, both heritable and movable, of which he was possessed, I do not think it can be reasonably assumed, in the absence of any provision to that effect either express or implied, that he intended to regulate the disposal of any part of his estate which might possibly lapse into intestacy. In my opinion the testator, when he inserted a clause in his settlement barring the legal rights of the appellant and respondent, had no object in view except to protect the settlement, by preventing the enforcement of these claims to the disturbance of his will and to the detriment of the beneficiaries whom he had selected. When accordingly, by the premature decease of his children of the second marriage, the residue provided to them by his settlement became intestate, I do not think it can be held that the testator contemplated, or intended, that the exclusion of the legal rights of his widow and surviving child should any longer remain operative." It is true that Lord *Watson* said he had not thought it necessary to refer to *Pickering* v. *Lord Stamford* (2) or to any of the other English cases cited for the successful respondent. He thought they did not directly bear upon the question raised in that appeal, which related to the sense in which certain expressions were used by a Scottish testator, having due regard to the nature of the rights with which he was dealing as they existed in the law of Scotland. But in the same case Lord *Shand*, after stating the principle of *Pickering* v. *Lord Stamford* (2) and *Sympson* v. *Hornsby and Hutton* (3) in the words of Lord *Cowper* in the latter case, said (4):—"That seems to be exactly the principle to which the House is now giving effect," and added, "the question is not one as to the nature of the claim. . . In either case the purpose which the testator has in view is to exclude the claims, whatever may be their nature or origin and foundation, in order to benefit others. If the benefit to those others is entirely to fail, it is clear that in conformity with the English decisions and, as I think, with sound principle, the exclusion of the right, whatever

(1) (1899) A.C., 495, at p. 501.
(2) 3 Ves., 332. 492.
(3) 2 Eq. Ca. (Abr.), 439 ; 11 Viner's

Abr., 185 ; Pre. Ch., 452.
(4) (1899) A.C., 495, at p. 505.

be its character, also fails." And Lord *Halsbury* L.C. says of the
widow's claim (1) :—" On the other hand, it is said that the provisions made were intended to apply only to such part of the
estate as was disposed of by the settlor, and could not be intended
to apply to any rights arising from intestacy which was not contemplated by the terms of the settlement at all, and I think that
is a reasonable and sensible view of the matter. . . . As
regards all that remains over when the provisions of the will are
satisfied—in this case the whole residue—the law of intestacy
takes effect upon it. That seems to me good sense, and I am
satisfied that it gives effect to the intentions of the testator in the
sense that he contemplated a state of things by the clause in
question which as a fact did not arise, and that he never contemplated the clause as applying to intestacy at all."

That passage expresses to the letter my view of this will and
of the intention of its maker. I think the matter is concluded
alike by reason and by authority, that the decision of *Street* J. is
clearly right, and that this appeal should be dismissed.

ISAACS J. The appellants claim that in the distribution of
personal estate under the intestacy of John Eyers the widow
should be excluded. The burden of establishing the exclusion
rests upon them, and there are only two methods by which they
can maintain their position ; they must satisfy the Court, either
that John Eyers by his will gave them the widow's share, or that
he put the widow to her election whether she would retain her
ordinary right to share in the event of his intestacy—a right
which would then come into existence as her own against all the
world—or would accept the specific provision he made for her in
his will, and in consideration of that, surrender all claims to her
possible ordinary distributive share.

Both positions, though separate and distinct in principle, appear
to me in this case to depend on practically the same considerations.
Words of exclusion only are sufficient, of course, to prevent participation in benefits conferred by will; but are not enough of
themselves to deprive a person of rights given by law independently of the will ; and here the rights claimed by the widow are

(1) (1899) A.C., 495, at p. 497.

asserted as being independent of and outside the provisions of the will. Are the words relied on, namely, "I declare that the provision hereby made for my said wife is in lieu of dower and thirds" words of mere deprivation, or do they, on this branch of the case, amount, when considered with the rest of the instrument, to a gift by implication of the widow's share of personality to the next of kin, as in *Bund* v. *Green* (1)?

That amounts to a question of construction of the whole will, in order to discover the intention of the testator.

Similarly on the second point, did the testator's intention to exclude the widow extend to the case of his intestacy? Did he in such case require her to abandon her share to others? I may, before passing to the second point, advert to the circumstance, probably the governing circumstance, that in *Bund* v. *Green* (1), the testator expressly excluded the brother and sisters from any share in case he happened to die intestate.

As to *election*, I shall assume, without in any way so deciding, that the widow should be treated as having been put to an election, and that, on the facts so far as they appear, she should further be regarded as having elected. On that assumption, she elected to take what the will offered her, in return for giving up that of which the testator intended to deprive her? But still the question remains, of what did the testator intend to deprive her? And so the question arises does the declaration I have read refer to surrender or deprivation of dower and thirds even in case of intestacy, or only so far as was necessary to satisfy, or in consequence of, the testator's own scheme of distribution. There is nothing which expressly provides that in the event of intestacy the widow is not to participate. The appellants, therefore, are compelled to rely on implication. But implication to exclude her must be necessary, that is, the probability to do so must be so strong that a contrary intention cannot reasonably be supposed: *Crook* v. *Hill* (2).

Dr. Cullen has argued that this necessary implication arises from the mere use of the expression *dower and thirds*, because he contends the testator had, and must be taken to have known that he had, power by testamentary disposition to deprive his

(1) 12 Ch. D., 819.   (2) L.R. 6 Ch., 311.

H. C. of A.
1907.

PENNY
v.
MILLIGAN.

Isaacs J.

widow of any share in his estate, and, therefore, and more especially with respect to the word " thirds," the only reasonable meaning to attach to the excluding declaration is that of its application to intestacy. The argument has considerable force, but a testator's implied intention has to be gathered, not solely from any part of his will, not from any isolated passages, but from reading and weighing the will as a whole. To put the view concretely with reference to the present case; the argument is that the use of the word " thirds" demonstrates that the testator had in view the possible event of his intestacy. But when the rest of the instrument is looked at, is it a proper deduction that he had any such conception? And it is not always presumed that the testator had an accurate knowledge of his legal power of testamentary disposition: See per Lord *Alvanley* in *Pickering* v. *Lord Stamford* (1), and in *Whistler* v. *Webster* (2).

If upon the whole it appears he had no conception of his scheme failing, then he cannot have had any intention to use those comprehensive words of substitution with reference to the case of intestacy. In my opinion, and judging from the words he has used, when that will was executed there was no such conception in his mind. He was not thinking of providing for the case of intestacy at all, but he was in his own opinion finally and absolutely distributing his property, by means of specific legacies, and general and residuary gifts, and with considerable elaboration. He recognized that in that distribution, when carried into effect, there would be no room for dower and thirds, and so he declared that, having regard to his purpose to so distribute his property, there should and could be no dower and thirds. The widow, therefore, while put to her election as to whether she would take the benefits and bear the burdens of the will whatever they might be, or would reject both, is only bound, having taken the benefits, to bear those burdens which, on a fair construction of the will, it was the intention of the testator she should bear. It happens that by a series of accidents there has after all been an intestacy as to portion of the personal estate.

On the construction I give to the will there is nothing inconsistent in her accepting the benefits of the instrument and in her

(1) 3 Ves., 332.   (2) 2 Ves. Jun., 367.

representatives claiming under the intestacy, because upon that construction the distribution in the intestacy is entirely outside the terms of the instrument.

Why, on a fair interpretation of the will, may not the two positions stand together, the deprivation of dower and thirds as part of the testamentary scheme of distribution, and the enjoyment of thirds so far as the scheme failed? Where is there any manifest intention to the contrary? *James* V.C., in *Wollaston* v. *King* (1) adopted *Sir Richard Arden's* definition of election in *Whistler* v. *Webster* (2), which is in these terms "that no man shall claim any benefit under a will, without conforming so far as he is able, and giving effect, to everything contained in it, whereby any disposition is made, showing an intention that such a thing shall take place," and he adds—" without reference to the circumstance, whether the testator had any knowledge of the extent of his power or not." And *Cairns* L.C., in *Codrington* v. *Codrington* (3) said :—" By the well-settled doctrine, which is termed in the Scotch law the doctrine of 'approbate' and 'reprobate,' and in our Courts more commonly the doctrine of 'election,' where a deed or will professes to make a general disposition of property for the benefit of a person named in it, such person cannot accept a benefit under the instrument without at the same time conforming to all its provisions, and renouncing every right inconsistent with them." But where is the inconsistency which is necessary to maintain this defence of election?

The appellants rely on *Lett* v. *Randall* (4), in which it was held that general words of substitution and satisfaction deprived the widow of participation in intestate personalty.

That case, though challenged by learned counsel for the respondents, seems to me to be perfectly sound in principle, notwithstanding the case of *Tavernor* v. *Grindley* (5), the headnote of which, so far as it refers to *Lett* v. *Randall* (4), appears to go beyond the judgment. The learned Vice-Chancellor *Stuart*, having to ascertain in *Lett* v. *Randall* (4) whether the testator intended to exclude the widow from sharing in the intestacy, set himself to

H. C. or A.
1907.

PENNY
v.
MILLIGAN.

Isaacs J.

(1) L.R. 8 Eq., 165, at p. 174.
(2) 2 Ves. Jun., 367, at p. 370.
(3) L.R. 7 H.L., 854, at p. 861.

(4) 3 Sm. & G., 83 ; 24 L.J. Ch., 708.
(5) 32 L.T., 424.

H. C. OF A.
1907.

PENNY
v.
MILLIGAN.

Isaacs J.

construe the general clause referred to by the light of the whole disposition, and the circumstances appearing on the face of the will. Foremost among those circumstances he found what he termed an intestacy on the face of the will. I presume he was referring to the fact that, if the daughters remained unmarried, there was necessarily an intestacy. The Vice-Chancellor considered that the testator must be taken to have had in mind the possible, or even probable, case of intestacy when using the wide words of the clause under consideration. Taking that fact in conjunction with the comprehensiveness of the clause, he applied the words of exclusion to the intestacy. He did not take either the comprehensiveness of the clause, or the *ex facie* intestacy as in itself sufficient to determine his judgment. He did not regard either as a canon of construction. But, looking at them both as circumstances of importance, they helped to guide him to his conclusion as to the meaning of the will. I see no reason for finding any fault with the method followed by the learned Vice-Chancellor in gathering the intention of the testator. But how far is *Lett* v. *Randall* (1) a controlling authority in the present instance? It is trite law that, laying aside accepted specific canons of construction, each will must be read and construed independently of any construction that has been placed on other wills. See *per* Lord *Halsbury* L.C. in *Scalé* v. *Rawlins* (2), and in *MacCulloch* v. *Anderson* (3). In the last cited case his words were:—" I speak simply of the construction of this will. I decline absolutely, as in many other cases, to enter into the question of what would be the construction of other wills under other circumstances even if the same words occurred in them." And if reference to any authority be desirable that it is the whole will that must be considered, it is again supplied by the words of Lord *Halsbury* L.C. in *Inderwick* v. *Tatchell* (4). Consequently even if *Lett* v. *Randall* (1), resembled the present case more closely that it does, still it would not necessarily have a controlling effect. To my mind, however, there is one important difference between the two, which materially distinguishes this case from *Lett* v. *Randall* (1). In that case, unless a new event took place, namely, marriage of the daughters, or at least of one, and issue thereof, an intestacy was inevitable. The event was unforeseen, though doubtlessly much desired, but without it intestacy was obvious. In this case, however, unless an unforeseen event, certainly not desired, and apparently not expected, took place there was a complete testacy. This is, in my opinion, a weighty circumstance differentiating the two cases so far as relates to the question of whether the testator here was aiming at a future intestacy when inserting his declaration as to dower and thirds.

Tavernor v. *Grindley* (1), it was argued, was opposed to *Lett* v. *Randall* (2). But we have not the reasons of *Wood* V.C. for his construction of the will by which he held the widow not barred. It may have been that His Honor considered the omission of all mention of the consols from the will was a circumstance which, *inter alia*, enabled him to say that the words of exclusion were intended to apply only to such property as was covered by the will, so making it co-extensive with the scheme of distribution apparent on the face of the instrument, and thus leaving the consols entirely out of the whole will, including the clause of exclusion. The view is certainly borne out by the observations of *Bacon* V.C. And there is nothing reported as having fallen from either learned Vice-Chancellor which in anyway directly affects *Lett* v. *Randall* (2). *Stuart* V.C. distinguished that case from *Pickering* v. *Lord Stamford* (3), by pointing out that in the latter case all the property had been disposed of by the will, but had become distributable in intestacy through an unforeseen accident. "Unforeseen" must mean, unforeseen by the testator, because, although the law would not recognize the gift to the charity, yet he could not be supposed to have determined upon a scheme of distribution which he knew or intended to be futile, and it was his personal intention when using the words of exclusion that had to be ascertained.

Lord *Alvanley* M.R., in his ultimate opinion, rested, as I think, on election not to defeat the dispositions of the will, but interpreted the clause of substitution to go no further. He did so on

(1) 32 L.T., 424.   (2) 3 Sm. & G., 83 ; 24 L.T. Ch., 708.
                    (3) 3 Ves. 332, 492.

H. C. of A. the authority of *Sympson* v. *Hornsby and Hutton* from the
1907. Register's Book, and he says (1):—"I am now decided, by having
PENNY the very point determined by Lord *Cowper*; who was of opinion, in
v. the case I have cited from the Register's Book, that where a
MILLIGAN. testator had given to his wife that provision, which he meant to
Isaacs J. be a satisfaction for any claim she might have against the other
objects of his bounty, if by any accident those objects should be
unable to claim the benefit of that exclusion, no other person should
set it up against the widow. After that I cannot, upon such a point,
set up my own judgment against Lord *Cowper's.*" For myself I
think that the case of the daughter Jane in *Sympson* v. *Hornsby
and Hutton* (2) even more in support of the respondents' view
here than was that of the widow. When the case of *Pickering*
v. *Lord Stamford* (3) came before Lord *Loughborough* L.C., his
Lordship (as appears *in arguendo*) refused to treat the case on
the facts as one of actual election by the widow, and dealt with
it as arising purely in the *Statute of Distributions.* It was said
there in argument that it was an unusual thing to refuse to
consider the words of the will, but the explanation is not far to
seek. The Lord Chancellor had opened the will to ascertain how
far it could be construed as a gift to the next of kin, and found it
could not be so construed, and as there was in his view neither a
gift nor an act of election proved, he closed the will, and
declined to look at it to ascertain the testator's intentions. In
those circumstances he could, as it appears to me, do nothing else.
The case was then quite outside the will, and he says (4):—
"Being a legal intestacy, I am to control the *Statute of Distributions.* How can the Court possibly do that? I must close the
will; and cannot look at it."

He did approve of Lord *Cowper's* decision in *Sympson* v.
Hornsby and Hutton(2), and did not approve of *Vachell* v. *Breton*
(5). Possibly the latter case, if now to be looked upon as a guide
at all, comes more properly within the class of cases of election.

But however *Pickering* v. *Lord Stamford* (6) is regarded, it is
a powerful authority against the appellants. On the first branch

(1) 3 Ves., 322, at p. 337.   (4) 3 Ves., 492, at p. 494.
(2) 2 Eq. Ca. (Abr.) 439 ; 11 Viner's   (5) 5 Bro. P.C., 51.
Abr., 185 ; Pre. Ch., 452.   (6) 3 Ves., 332, 492.
(3) 3 Ves., 492.

of the case, namely, as to whether the words excluding the
widow amount to a gift to the next of kin, the Lord Chancellor's
view is against them ; and on the second branch, election, Lord
Alvanley's opinion—untouched on appeal—is also opposed to
them.   In this latter aspect, too, the observations of Lord *Eldon*
L.C. in *Garthshore* v. *Chalie* (1) are important, that learned Lord
Chancellor regarding *Pickering* v. *Lord Stamford* (2) as being
an authority that the widow is not barred in such a case, because
the intention is to bar her from thirds for the sake of persons
under that instrument to take the residue.

Naismith v. *Boyes* (3) is a case which, notwithstanding it
related to Scottish law, appears to me to be really a strong
authority for the respondents.   It is true the widow's claims to
terce and *jus relictæ* were inalienable without her consent, and
therefore arose either on the testacy or intestacy of her husband.
Dr. *Cullen* built an able argument up on this, and is certainly
supported by the facts in what he said regarding the difference
between a Scottish and an English widow's claims under the
general law.   But the answer is, I think, rightly given by Lord
Shand (4) in these words :—" It is true that in this case the
claims to *legitim* and *jus relictæ* are of a different character from
a mere beneficiary right, as my noble and learned friend Lord
Watson has pointed out ; but the question is not one as to the
nature of the claim, whether it is a right given by common law,
a right such as *jus relictæ* or *legitim* where there is a *jus crediti*,
or a right of succession under the *Statute of Distributions* or
otherwise.   In either case the purpose which the testator has in
view is to exclude the claims, whatever may be their nature or
origin and foundation, in order to benefit others.   If the benefit
to those others is entirely to fail, it is clear that in conformity
with the English decisions and, as I think, with sound principle,
the exclusion of the right, whatever be its character, also fails—
for the exclusion of the right was provided only to protect and
enlarge the purpose of the testator in making his testamentary
provisions, whereas these provisions have failed, and he has died
intestate."

H. C. of A.
1907.

PENNY
v.
MILLIGAN.

Isaacs J.

(1) 10 Ves., 1.   (3) (1899) A.C., 495.
(2) 3 Ves., 332, 492.   (4) (1899) A.C., 495, at p. 505.

H. C. of A.
1907.
⌣
PENNY
v.
MILLIGAN.
——
Isaacs J.

It is to be borne in mind that the case was dealt with as a matter of principle, there being no decisions governing the question in the Courts of Scotland. Lord *Halsbury* L.C. considered that the clause of exclusion could not be intended to apply to any rights arising from intestacy which was not contemplated by the terms of settlement, and on this general ground, being what he called a reasonable and sensible view of the matter, he decided in the widow's favour. In the absence of authority to the contrary, Lord *Watson*, even in opposition to his earlier doubts, came to regard that view as being in accordance with sound principle. He also considered that, as the testator had settled all his property on the members of his family, it could not be reasonably assumed, in the absence of any provision, either express or implied, that he intended to regulate the disposal of any part of his estate which might lapse into intestacy. His Lordship proceeds to point out that a man might by his will, either in express words or by necessary implication, make it clear that he was framing or contemplating a scheme by which, whether intestacy supervened or not, the widow's exclusion should form a part of it, and he says (1) that " the exclusion would certainly operate in favour of all those beneficiaries who took *provisione* of the deceased, and it would also operate in favour of those taking *ab intestato* if it were reasonably apparent that denying effect to it would disturb the scheme which the deceased contemplated."

The case is consequently quite in line with those already referred to, and considerably supports the views I have based upon them.

I therefore am of the opinion that the decision of *Street* J. was correct, and that this appeal should be dismissed.

> *Appeal dismissed. Costs of both parties, by agreement, to come out of the estate.*

Solicitor, for the appellants, *R. G. C. Roberts.*
Solicitors, for the respondents, *Read & Read; Curtiss & Barry.*

C. A. W.

(1) (1899) A.C., 495, at p. 502.

[HIGH COURT OF AUSTRALIA.]

HODGE AND OTHERS　.　.　.　.　.　APPELLANTS;

AND

THE KING (ON THE RELATION OF O'SULLIVAN AND OTHERS).　.　.　.　.　.　.　} RESPONDENT.

ON APPEAL FROM THE SUPREME COURT OF QUEENSLAND.

Local Authorities Act 1902 *(Queensland) (No.* 19 *of* 1902*), 3rd Schedule, rule* 11— *Election of councillors for shire—Extraordinary vacancy—No election held at time prescribed—Expiration of time for giving notice of election—Meaning of election—Ouster.*

H. C. of A.
1907.

SYDNEY,
Dec. 16, 17.

Griffith C.J.,
Barton and
Isaacs JJ.

Rule 4 of the 3rd Schedule to the *Local Authorities Act* 1902 (Qd.), provides that on the occurrence of an extraordinary vacancy in the Council of a Shire the Returning Officer shall within thirty days after the occurrence of the vacancy give public notice of an election to fill the vacancy, specifying a day not less than fourteen nor more than twenty-one days after the publication of the notice as the day of nomination. By rule 11, if at the time prescribed or appointed for holding an election no election is held, or no candidates are nominated, or the number of candidates nominated is less than the number of members to be elected, the Governor in Council may appoint a ratepayer or ratepayers to fill the vacancies which ought to have been filled at such election.

Held, that an election under the Act is not merely the taking a poll, but a continuous process consisting of several steps, notice of election, nomination of candidates, and taking a poll when a poll is necessary, and that as soon as the time prescribed by the Statute for the taking of any of these steps has expired without such steps having been taken, and it has thus become impossible to hold an election in accordance with the Statute, the power of appointment conferred upon the Governor comes into operation. It is not necessary that he should wait until the last day which could have been fixed for taking a poll has passed without a poll being taken.

Decision of the Supreme Court, *The King v. Hodge; Ex parte O'Sullivan,* 1906 St. R. Qd., 18, reversed.

H. C. of A. APPEAL from a decision of the Supreme Court of Queensland,
1907.   ousting the appellants from the office of councillors of a shire.

HODGE   The appellants were appointed by the Governor in Council,
v.   under rule 11 of the third Schedule to the *Local Authorities Act*
THE KING.   1902, to be members of the Council of the Shire of Rosewood, to
             fill four extraordinary vacancies that had occurred in that Shire.
             The relators applied to the Supreme Court under sec. 23 of the
             Act, to have the appellants ousted from office, on the ground that
             the circumstances had not arisen in which the Governor in
             Council had power to appoint councillors, and therefore the
             appellants were not duly elected. The appellants were called
             upon to show cause, and after argument the Supreme Court held
             that their appointment was invalid and ordered that they should
             be ousted: *The King* v. *Hodge* ; *Ex parte O'Sullivan* (1).

             The facts, and the material sections of the Act are fully set out
             in the judgments hereunder.

             O'Sullivan and *Douglas*, for the appellants. No election was
             held at the time prescribed, within the meaning of rule 11, Schedule
             3. "Election" is not merely the taking a poll, but consists of
             several steps: first, notice of election ; second, nomination ; and
             third, if more candidates are nominated than necessary to fill the
             vacancies, the polling. If any one of those steps is not taken at
             the time prescribed by the Act, there can be no election. By
             rule 4 the notice of election must be given within 30 days after
             the occurrence of the vacancy. That is the "time prescribed"
             intended by rule 11. It does not mean the time appointed by
             the Returning Officer for an election. As soon as the 30 days
             after the occurrence of the latest vacancy expired without any
             notice having been given, it became impossible to hold an election
             in accordance with the Statute in respect of any of the vacancies;
             in other words no election had been held. The notice is as
             essential to the validity of an election as any other step. There
             being no possibility of fixing a day for the election, it would have
             made no difference to the position if the Governor had waited
             until the expiration of the latest time that might have been
             fixed. [They referred to rules 2, 4 and 11 of the 3rd Schedule.]

             _____
             (1) 1908 St. R. Qd., 18.

The Governor had no power under rule 10 to extend the time for giving notice. He could only extend the duration of the notice after it was given. Even if he had such power, he was not bound to exercise it, but was entitled to exercise the power of appointment. Upon the relators' construction of rule 11, the Governor, if he had not the power when he purported to appoint the appellants, has no power now. Consequently no election of any kind can ever be held without fresh legislation, and the affairs of the shire will fall into chaos. A construction which has · such a result will not be adopted in an Act intended to provide for efficient local government unless no other construction is open. The construction contended for by the appellants is a reasonable one and should be adopted. It is in accordance with the obvious purpose of the legislature, that there should be no breach of continuity in the system of local government : *Widgee Shire Council* v. *Bonney* (1).

The section as to ouster, sec. 23, does not apply to the case of persons appointed by the Governor in Council. It applies only to persons elected, or purporting to have been elected, by the ordinary process. *Quo warranto*, therefore, is the proper remedy. That is a discretionary writ, and would not be granted under the circumstances. The appointment was, as the evidence showed, a salutary one, and the relators were not acting *bond fide*. There was also delay in making the application, and it would now be futile to put the appellants out of office, as the Governor could immediately re-appoint them. [They referred to *The King* v. *Venn King* ; *Ex parte Maloney* (2); *Shortt on Mandamus and Prohibition*, 1887 ed., p. 149.]

By sec. 368, sub-sec. (4), no Order shall be deemed invalid on account of any omission.

[GRIFFITH C.J.—That refers only to cases where certain prescribed preliminaries have been omitted, not to cases of total want of authority.]

McGregor (*Watson* with him), for the respondent. The Court, if it sees that no serious harm has been done, should rescind the special leave.

(1) 4 C.L.R., 977, at p. 983.   (2) 1903 St. R. Qd., 336.

H. C. of A.
1907.

HODGE
v.
THE KING.

[GRIFFITH C.J.—The ground for granting special leave to appeal was that, since the Governor should not interfere unnecessarily in elections for local authorities, it was important to know whether a case for his intervention arose under the actual circumstances.]

The whole question depends upon the construction of rule 11. According to the proper construction of that rule the Governor has no power to appoint members until a day has been appointed · by the Returning Officer for the election, and that day has passed without an election being held. The day of election would be the day of nomination where no more than the required number of candidates are nominated, or the day of polling where more than that number are nominated. No day having been appointed, the power conferred upon the Governor never came into operation. The day prescribed or appointed for an election means the day fixed by the Returning Officer in his notice. If, owing to the mistake or default of the Returning Officer, no day is appointed and the Statute provides no way of getting over the difficulty, then the legislature can make provision to meet the case.

[ISAACS J.—The main object of the legislature is not to be defeated merely because the draughtsman has used inexact words : *Salmon* v. *Duncombe* (1); *Maxwell on Interpretation of Statutes*, 3rd ed., p. 319; *The King* v. *Vasey* (2).]

" Election " should be construed in the same sense as in other parts of the Act. It is in general used to mean the polling, not the preliminary steps. [He referred to sec. 28; rules 38, &c.]

[ISAACS J.—I do not think there is much strictness in the use of words in the Act.]

It was not absolutely necessary that the notice should be given within the thirty days. That provision is merely directory to ensure that there will be no delay ; but if no notice is given within the time, one may be given later, and the Governor may validate it. The ousting of the appellants, therefore, need not interfere with the working of the system. [He referred to *Reg.* v. *Moffatt* (3); rule 15 (3); and the *Divisional Boards Act* 1887, sec. 53.]

(1) 11 App. Cas., 627.   (2) (1905) 2 K.B., 748.
                        (3) 5 Q.L.J., 79.

O'Sullivan in reply, referred to *The King* v. *O'Donahue and Sloane*; *Ex parte Grant* (1).

H. C. of A.
1907.

Hodge
v.
The King.

Dec. 17.

Cur. adv. vult.

GRIFFITH C.J. This is an appeal from an order of the Supreme Court of Queensland making absolute an order *nisi* for the ouster of four members of the Council of the Shire of Rosewood. The four members in question were appointed by the Governor in Council, and the point taken by the relators was that the Governor had no authority in law to appoint them.

The law as to local government in Queensland is contained in the *Local Authorities Act* 1902. The Council of the shire in question consists of seven members, of whom three form a quorum. The manner of election of councillors is prescribed by the rules of the third Schedule of the Act. It will be necessary therefore to refer to some of the provisions of that Schedule. Rule 2 provides that :—" At every election the Chairman or other person appointed by the Local Authority ; or, if there is no Local Authority, or no person is appointed by the Local Authority, then such person as the Governor in Council appoints, shall be the Returning Officer." Rule 4 provides that :—" In every year, on or before the tenth day of January, the Returning Officer of every shire shall give public notice of the annual election by advertisement in some newspaper," which is to specify a day, "not less than fourteen nor more than twenty-one days after the publication of the notice, as the day of nomination," and to fix the place of nomination. Paragraph 4 of that rule provides that:—"On the occurrence of an extraordinary vacancy, a like notice shall be given within thirty days after the occurrence of the vacancy," that is to say, a notice specifying a day not less than fourteen days nor more than twenty-one days after the publication of the notice, as the day of nomination. Rule 10 provides that the time prescribed for the length of the notice of the day of nomination or of the day for taking or closing the poll may be extended by the Governor in Council. Rule 11 provides that " if at the time prescribed or appointed for holding an election no election is held, or no candidates are nominated, or the number of candidates

(1) 1907 St. R. Qd., 16, at p. 20.

nominated is less than the number of members to be elected, the Governor in Council may appoint a ratepayer of the Area or a sufficient number of such ratepayers to be a member or members of the Local Authority to fill the vacancies which ought to be filled at such election, and the ratepayer or ratepayers so appointed shall be deemed to have been duly elected at such election." In the events that have happened five of the seven members of the Council of this shire resigned their seats, three on 23rd March, one on 30th March, and one on 4th April. The Chairman was not amongst those who resigned, but he was advised that he could not act as Returning Officer without a formal appointment by the Governor in Council, and as it was impossible to form a quorum, the local authority could not appoint any person to act in that capacity. It was therefore necessary, if an election was to be held at all, for the Governor in Council to appoint a Returning Officer. Accordingly that was done on 22nd April, but the gentleman appointed was not notified of his appointment until 24th April. The time prescribed by rule 4 for giving notice of the election to fill extraordinary vacancies is, as I have pointed out, thirty days after the occurrence of the vacancy, so that the notice for the election to fill the vacancies created by the resignations of the three councillors on 23rd March could not be given later than 22nd April, the day on which the Returning Officer was appointed. The last day for giving notice of an election to fill the vacancies created by the resignations of the other two Councillors would have been a few days later. But for some reason, to which it is not necessary to refer, as we are dealing with a dry point of law, the Returning Officer failed to give any notice of election within thirty days after the occurrence of any of the vacancies. The last day on which a notice could have been given for the latest of them was 4th May. No election, therefore, was held. In point of law none could be held. Thereupon the Governor in Council, on 13th May, appointed five ratepayers, including the four appellants, to fill the vacancies.

The objection now taken is that the Governor in Council, in the events which happened, had no authority to fill the vacancies. That depends wholly upon the meaning of rule 11, which pro-

H. C. OF A.
1907.
Hodge
v.
The King.
Griffith C.J.

vides that if at the time prescribed no election is held, or no candidates, or an insufficient number, are nominated, the Governor in Council may fill the vacancies. The learned Chief Justice, as I understand his judgment, was of opinion that that rule did not come into operation until some of the proceedings for holding an election had been taken. *Power* J. concurred in this view. *Noel* J.. on the other hand, was of opinion that the time appointed for holding an election meant the time appointed for taking the poll, and that as no time had been appointed for taking the poll, the occasion provided for by the section had not arisen.

Appeal is made by the relators to the literal words of the rule. Let us take that view and see what it means. There are three alternatives mentioned, one that no election is held within the time prescribed for holding the election; the second that no candidates are nominated; and the third that the number of candidates nominated is less than the number to be elected. Now the construction contended for by the relators assumes that a nomination is necessary. But, read literally, the rule itself shows that the case where no candidates are nominated does not fall within the scope of the words "no election is held." Supplying the words necessary to be supplied the rule would read: "If no election is held, or, although an election is held, no candidates are nominated." But the word election, it was said, must mean polling. No doubt polling is part of an election. So is nomination. The polling may perhaps be considered as an adjournment of the election from the day of nomination. But the election begins when the first step is taken that is prescribed by law as a necessary step in the process of holding an election. The term "election," in my opinion, includes the whole proceeding from the first step taken by the Returning Officer, in giving notice to the electors, to the day of the return of the candidates, if any are elected. The fact that the words if "no election is held" precede the words "or no candidates are nominated," shows, indeed, that the failure to hold an election may precede the time for the nomination of candidates. I think that, as soon as it becomes apparent that no election can be held, the jurisdiction of the Governor in Council comes into operation. The words are: "At the time prescribed or appointed for holding an election." Seeing,

H. C. of A. therefore, that an election consists of various steps, the giving
   1907.   notice of the election, the appointment of a day of nomination
  HODGE   and of a day for holding a poll, if a poll becomes necessary, and
    v.   that the rules fix limits of time for each step, when once the limit
THE KING.   of time for any particular step is passed, it becomes impossible to
Griffith C.J. do what the Act has prescribed. When a step prescribed has not
been taken and cannot be taken, it is, in my opinion, right to say
that an election has not been held. On 13th May it was impossible that there should be an election for the extraordinary
vacancies that had occurred. The case is therefore within the
plain meaning of the words. I think that the appointment by
the Governor in Council was warranted by the Statute, and
that the order for ouster should be discharged.

BARTON J. Sec. 23 of the *Local Authorities Act* 1902 provides
that " When any person declared duly elected to the office of
member has been elected unduly or contrary to this Act, . . .
the Supreme Court, or a Judge thereof, may, upon the application of any five ratepayers of the Area, grant an order calling
upon such person to show cause why he should not be ousted
from such office." That is the section under which the proceedings were taken that resulted in the Supreme Court of Queensland ousting the five persons, of whom four are now appellants,
and who became holders *de facto* of the office of councillor in this
way. The Shire of Rosewood should have seven councillors.
On 23rd March Councillors Lane, O'Donahue and Sloane resigned
from office, the first named being the person elected for division 1
of the shire, the second for division 2, and the third for division
3. Councillor Coulson, also a representative of division 1,
resigned his office on 30th March, and on 4th April Councillor
Just, a representative of the same division, also resigned. On
4th April, there being these five vacancies, there appears to have
been a consultation between the remaining members, as a result
of which the chairman offered himself for the appointment of
Returning Officer. By sec. 31, sub-sec. 1, a separate election must
be held to fill any vacancy arising from any cause except annual
retirement. Sec. 28 provides that the rules contained in the
third Schedule shall regulate the proceedings in relation to

elections under the Act. By rule 2 it is provided that at every election, if there is no local authority, or no person is appointed by the local authority (which were the conditions in the present case) then such person as the Governor in Council appoints shall be the Returning Officer. On 22nd April the Governor in Council by Order in Council appointed H. N. Stevens Returning Officer to conduct the election of five members to fill the vacancies. By sec. 31, sub-sec. 3, the election in a shire is to be held at the time appointed by the Returning Officer, and by rule 4, paragraphs 2 and 4, on the occurrence of an extraordinary vacancy, public notice of the election shall be given by that officer within thirty days after the occurrence of the vacancy, that is to say, a notice specifying a day of nomination not less than fourteen nor more than twenty-one days after the publication of the notice. By rule 8, if the number of persons nominated as candidates does not exceed the number of members to be elected, the persons nominated are to be declared duly elected by the Returning Officer, on the day of nomination ; and by rule 9, if the number of persons nominated as candidates exceeds the number of members to be elected, a poll must be taken on a day and at a place appointed by the Returning Officer, not more than thirty nor less than fourteen days from the day of nomination. Now, in the present case the Returning Officer, though appointed on 22nd April, did not receive notice of his appointment until 24th April. It is not necessary to inquire how it came about that it was so late, but the required thirty days had expired as to three of the vacancies, and the Returning Officer pointed that out to the Department. He expressed the opinion that under the circumstances it would be useless to conduct an election, and recommended the Minister to obtain an appointment by the Governor in Council to fill the vacancies, referring to the provisions of rule 11. Whether that advice was good or bad we need not now inquire. But the Governor in Council, finding that the means adopted to fill all the vacancies had been abortive, appointed the four appellants and another gentleman, all of whom were ousted by the Supreme Court of Queensland on the ground that no day had been appointed for the election. This action of the Governor was taken under rule 11. The real question is whether this was a valid exercise of the

H. C. of A.
1907.

HODGE
v.
THE KING.

Barton J.

statutory power given by the rule. I am of opinion that it was.
I think that the rule covers the case where steps have been taken
to hold an election, and those steps have been abortive or have
failed, so that without action by the Governor in Council there
would be no representation of the local authority at all. I think
that the prevention of such a state of affairs was the absolute
purpose and design of rule 11, and it was in view of that that the
appointments in question were made. The rule contemplates the
case in which there has been a miscarriage or blunder, because it
speaks of the vacancies which *ought* to be filled, as where duty
has not been done, where efforts to hold an election have failed,
so that no election has been held, or no candidates have been
nominated, or a less number has been nominated than the number
to be elected. There is in each of those cases a failure to fill a
vacancy that ought to have been filled. Rule 11 was devised in
order to enable the machinery of local government to go on
working. Without it there would be a necessity for passing
special legislation. The necessary consequence of Mr. *McGregor's*
argument would be to defeat the very purpose for which this rule
has been framed. It has been urged for the appellants that the
section as to ouster, sec. 23, does not apply to the case of an
appointment by the Governor in Council. It is true that the
section refers in terms to cases where members declared elected
have been elected unduly or contrary to the Act, and it may be
that there is some force in the argument that these words do not
apply to the cases of persons not declared elected within the
meaning of the section, or, rather, that the words do not cover
such cases as the present, but I will not go into that question.
In the view I take it is not necessary to decide it. But it
seems to me that the view of the Chief Justice of Queensland,
with reference to disqualification and the effect of irregularities
or disqualifications upon the election by force of rule 11, might
have been strongly tenable but for the concluding words of rule
11 from "at such election" down to the end. That puts such
persons, once appointed, upon the footing of persons duly elected,
and seems to me to obviate all questions of the kind raised as to
the validity of the proceeding taken by the Governor in Council
so long as at the time prescribed there have been no elections, or

no candidates, or a less number than the number to be elected has been nominated, and the Governor in Council has in due form appointed a ratepayer or ratepayers to fill the vacancy or vacancies. There is nothing in rule 11 which appears to me to be new, or indeed anything more than a transcript from the *Divisional Boards Act* 1887, sec. 50.

The meaning of the word "election" was the subject of considerable argument in this case, and Mr. *McGregor* pointed out certain sections and rules in which that word could only mean the poll.   In some cases it may mean nothing but the poll; but there are other cases in which it obviously means, or includes nomination, for instance, where the requisite number of candidates has been nominated, and none in excess. And there are cases where the word as obviously applies to the whole process adopted under this law for bringing about the result of an election.   Now, where the words " holding an election " are used as they are in this rule, it seems clear that they contemplate the whole process of election, so that full effect may be given to the rule by the construction that, when the means adopted for bringing about an election break down, and it becomes plain that the election cannot be held and the very consequence that must be provided against occurs, this rule may be brought into operation for the purpose of preventing the proceedings from being altogether futile.   I am therefore in accord with the view of the construction of rule 11 taken by the Chief Justice, and think it applies expressly and designedly to the present case, and that its provisions are sufficient for the purpose of preventing the deadlocks that would otherwise occur.   The construction contended for by Mr. *McGregor* has no doubt a good deal of support in the literal signification of the words used in this and other parts of the Act, but it is a construction which, if adopted, would result in there being a *casus omissus* in the Act.   That is a construction against which the Court will generally lean as strongly as it can within reason.   Because it is not lightly to be assumed that a provision, either by design or forgetfulness, has been left out which would be only an ordinary provision for securing the proper and continuous working of the machinery of local government. There is certainly that construction open, and

H. C. of A.
1907.

Hodge
v.
The King.

Barton J.

there is also a possible construction which gives at the same time effect to all the words now in question in the Act and in the rules, and provides against a *casus omissus* by giving this and other portions of the Act a meaning which ensures that the operation of the law shall be continuous, and not subject to a break down such as would be the consequence of adhering to a too literal construction of the mere words. If we follow the principle that, where you find a word used in one sense in a Statute you are to construe the word in the same sense whenever it appears throughout the Statute, there is a great deal in the respondent's contention. But there are parts of the Act where it is impossible to give the word the limited application contended for, because to do so would result in defeating the chief purpose aimed at by Parliament in the Act or the part of it in question. That is very frequently the case with Statutes. I think that this word has been used in various senses in the Act, and must be construed in the different sections in its relation to the subject with reference to which it is used. That being so, I am unable to take the view put forward by the respondent, but I think the construction of the other side is the reasonable one, giving fair force and effect to the various provisions of the Act, and, on that construction, what has taken place is well within the provisions of rule 11, and the gentlemen whose appointment is now in question have been duly appointed whether duly elected or not, and as such duly appointed persons are entitled to be deemed to have been duly elected, and to be continued in their office.

Isaacs J. The question this Court has to determine turns entirely upon the proper interpretation of rule 11 of the third Schedule of the *Local Authorities Act* 1902. The respondent's case depends entirely upon what may be called a rigid construction. Mr. *McGregor* contends, as *Noel* J. held in effect, that unless the date of an election has been fixed and that date has elapsed, and having elapsed it is found that no poll has been taken, or that no candidates are nominated, or that an insufficient number are nominated, the Governor in Council has no power to act. There is a serious difficulty on ordinary principles of con-

H. C. of A.
1907.

HODGE
v.
THE KING.

Isaacs J.

struction that bears against the adoption of that construction, because it would attribute no meaning whatever to the second and third elements or conditions, as they may be called, referred to in the rule. It is very plain that if it is sufficient to allow the time prescribed for taking the poll to pass, and no poll is held, if that is both sufficient and essential, it is perfectly immaterial whether the cause of the failure was or was not the absence of candidates or the absence of a sufficient number of candidates, and, therefore, that construction would assume that the legislature was using expressions that were immaterial, unnecessary, and meaningless. So that, for what I may call a comparatively unimportant reason, there is already a difficulty in the path. I say comparatively unimportant reason because there is behind a very much more important matter, namely, the question whether it is absolutely necessary that the scheme of local government shall in certain instances fail beyond any power of being retrieved so long as the law stands as it is. If the words mean what is contended for by the respondent, then in such a case as the present the Governor in Council has no power whatever to mend the matter at any time or under any circumstances, because, as I read rule 10, although His Excellency might in a proper case extend the length of the notice of the day of nomination or of the day for taking or concluding the poll, that would not give him the power, and there is no other power existent in the Act, to allow that notice to be given beyond the period of thirty days from the occurrence of the vacancies; it is made imperative by rule 4. So that, that time having passed without any notice being given by the Returning Officer, it means that, as far as the Shire of Rosewood is concerned, local government is at an end. That is a construction that a Court will not adopt if by any reasonable interpretation to be placed upon the words of the legislature another construction can be given to the rule. I have never yet seen a case where the rule in *Heydon's Case* (1) is more necessary to be applied than the present, the rule that it is the office of the Court, having ascertained the mischief and defect for which the law did not otherwise provide, and the remedy Parliament hath resolved and appointed, and the true reason of

(1) 3 Rep. 7a, at p. 7b.

H. C. of A.
1907.

HODGE
v.
THE KING.

Isaacs J.

the remedy, "to make such construction as shall suppress the mischief, and advance the remedy, and to suppress subtle inventions and evasions for continuance of the mischief, and *pro privato commodo*, and to add force and life to the cure and remedy, according to the true intent of the makers of the Act, *pro bono publico*." Now the intent of the legislature here is transparent, and sec. 31, sub-sec. 1, is in these terms: [His Honor read the sub-section.] There can be no shadow of doubt that the legislature meant a vacancy to be filled in some way, and made somewhat elaborate provisions for filling it, and we cannot assume that they intended that there should be a means by which that intent should be frustrated. The question is whether, therefore, the words of rule 11 are reasonably open to a construction which will effectuate the intention that has been declared by the legislature itself. The respondent's construction, of course, makes that intention fail utterly, as I have pointed out. During the argument I read a passage to which I will now only refer, from the case of *The King* v. *Vasey* (1), where Lord *Alverstone* C.J. adopted a passage from *Maxwell on Interpretation of Statutes*, 3rd ed., p. 319. But I will quote a few words from the judgment of *Fry* L.J. in *Curtis* v. *Stovin* (2):—"If the legislature have given a plain indication of this intention, it is our plain duty to endeavour to give effect to it, though, of course, if the words which they have used will not admit of such an interpretation, their intention must fail. Do the words which they have used in this case present any insuperable difficulty?" And then further on his Lordship, after explaining one possible construction, said:—"The only alternative construction offered to us would lead to this result, that the plain intention of the legislature has entirely failed by reason of a slight inexactitude in the language of the section. If we were to adopt that construction, we should be construing the Act in order to defeat its object rather than with a view to carry its object into effect." Now these are only some of the numerous authorities in which the Courts have not been merely careful but astute to see that the plain intention of the legislature did not fail by reason of some inexactitude, as it has been called, in the method of

(1) (1905) 2 K.B., 748, at p. 751.   (2) 22 Q.B.D., 513, at p. 519.

H. C. of A.
1907.

HODGE
v.
THE KING.

Isaacs J.

expression. Having already pointed out that the words " election held " would lead to a difficulty in intrinsic construction, having regard to the other words which I have already quoted, I turn to the Act to see whether there is anything in its object which is adverse to the more liberal construction.   I find in sec. 28, sub-sec. 2, the provision upon which the third Schedule depends, these words: [His Honor read the sub-section.]   Now I cannot, I do not think anyone could, say that the legislature by the phrase used there, " elections held," wished to confine itself to the taking of a poll.   I should think that there, as in other places in the Act, the legislature has referred to the whole of an election as a combined process, a continuous process, consisting of a number of steps ending in the election of some representatives for local Councils.   And that is borne out by other phrases frequently used, as for instance, in secs. 20, 29, 30 and 32, in which we find such expressions as " conclusion of an election," " conclusion of an annual election," " conclusion of such election," by which it is manifest that the legislature meant the final step, the taking of the poll, or declaration of election where no poll was taken, the conclusion of a combined process.   Once you arrive at that point, rule 11 may be well approached in order to see whether it is not, not only reasonably, but better open to the more liberal construction than to the rigid one which would defeat the intention of the legislature as manifested throughout the Act.   Turning to the rule again, it seems to me that it means this, that if the time prescribed or appointed for holding an election, that is, if the point of time has passed, by which the Act requires some definite and assigned step to be taken for the purpose of holding an election, or in other words, for the purpose of this combined process, and one or other of three things is found to exist, then, in my opinion, no election is held; that is to say, if no election at all is in course of being held, or if, though an election is in course of being held, no candidates are nominated when they ought to be nominated, or if, although some are nominated, an insufficient number is found to be nominated, then it is found that there is a failure, or that there must be a failure to have a valid election, and the Governor in Council may step in and appoint a ratepayer or ratepayers to make up the requisite number to fill the vacancies which ought to be filled at such election. What is the meaning of "such election"? If election is to be held to mean a poll, then it seems to me that there is a departure in the meaning, according to the respondent's argument, of the word "election," when we read the phrase "the ratepayer or ratepayers so appointed shall be deemed to have been duly elected at such election." That, according to the argument, must mean at the polling. The rule shows intrinsically that the legislature were using the expression "election" in the widest sense in which they have used it throughout the Act. There are some instances where "election" must from the context bear the narrower signification, but not in this instance. And where you find that in a regulation introduced for the purpose of preventing paralysis of the system of local government, words are used, which, construed in the narrower sense contended for, would produce that paralysis and lead to a result obviously not consistent with the purpose of the regulation itself, and utterly opposed to the intent of the Act, I think we are taking the right course in giving effect to the intent of the legislature and putting on their words the most reasonable construction that they are susceptible of in order to prevent the disastrous results that would otherwise follow.

For these reasons I agree with my learned brothers that the appeal should be allowed, and the rule for ouster discharged.

> *Appeal allowed. Order appealed from discharged. Rule nisi discharged with costs. Respondent to pay the costs of the appeal.*

Solicitor, for the appellants, *G. V. Hellicar*, Crown Solicitor for Queensland.

Solicitor, for the respondent, *J. A. Snow* for *W. H. Summerville.*

C. A. W.

[HIGH COURT OF AUSTRALIA.]

THE MASTER UNDERTAKERS' ASSOCI-
ATION OF NEW SOUTH WALES } . APPELLANTS;

AND

CROCKETT . . . . RESPONDENT.

ON APPEAL FROM THE SUPREME COURT OF
NEW SOUTH WALES.

Industrial Arbitration Act 1901 (*N.S. W.*), (*No.* 59 *of* 1901), *secs.* 12, 26—*Enforcement of Order of Court—Order for payment of fine payable under rules of Union —Attachment for non-payment—Power of Court—Prohibition.*

Sec. 12 of the *Industrial Arbitration Act* 1901 provides that the President of the Court of Arbitration may on application duly made order the payment by any member of an industrial union of any fine, penalty or subscription not exceeding £10, payable under the rules of the Union, and by sec. 26 the Court has power to make rules regulating the practice and procedure of the Court, with reference, *inter alia*, to the enforcement of its orders.

Held, that the Arbitration Court had no power under sec. 26 to enforce by attachment an order made by the President under sec. 12. The failure to obey an order for payment of money is not a contempt in the face of the Court, such as an inferior Court of record could punish by imprisonment, and there are no words in the *Industrial Arbitration Act* from which it can be inferred that the legislature, in giving the Court a general power to make rules for the enforcement of its orders, intended to confer upon it the power to compel obedience to its orders for the payment of money by imprisonment.

Decision of the Supreme Court : *Ex parte Crockett*, (1907) 7 S.R. (N.S.W.), 143, affirmed.

APPEAL from a decision of the Supreme Court of New South Wales making absolute a rule *nisi* for a prohibition to the Court of Industrial Arbitration.

H. C. OF A.
1907.

SYDNEY,
Dec. 9.

Griffith C.J.,
Barton and
Isaacs JJ.

H. C. of A.
1907.

The Master Under-takers' Association of N.S.W.
v.
Crockett.

The respondent, a member of the appellant Union, became liable under the rules of the Union to pay certain fines. On the application of the Union he was ordered by the Deputy-President to pay the fines in question. He failed to do so and the Deputy-President ordered writs of attachment to issue against him under rule 75. The Supreme Court granted a prohibition against the enforcement of the attachment: *Ex parte Crockett* (1), and from that decision the present appeal was brought by special leave.

Further reference to the facts, and a full statement of the rule in question and the material sections of the Act will be found in the judgments hereunder.

Gordon K.C. and *Windeyer*, for the appellant Union. Rule 76 authorizes the issue of a writ of attachment, and rule 75 provides for an application by summons to show cause why a writ should not issue. The power given by sec. 26 (*n*) of the *Industrial Arbitration Act* 1901 includes a power to attach for disobedience to an order of the Court. The words are general and unrestricted, and the Court has full discretion as to the method of enforcement. The order in this case was made under sec. 12. It is not suggested that this is a punishment for contempt of Court, it is merely a means of enforcing the Court's order for the payment of money. There is no reason why such a power as this should not be conferred upon the Court. The District Court can enforce payment of money under its orders in a similar way. The Deputy-President has the same powers in this connection as the President.

J. A. Browne, for the respondent. No doubt the order for payment is one which the Court has power to enforce under sec. 26 (*n*), but the powers of enforcement are limited to the methods provided in sec. 37. There is no warrant in the Act for interference with personal liberty for the purpose of compelling payment of money payable under an order of the Court. If the legislature had intended to confer power to imprison for debt, it would have done so by clear words. The general power of the Supreme Court to enforce judgments for the payment of moneys

(1) (1907) 7 S.R. (N.S.W.), 143.

by attachment was abolished by 10 Vict. No. 7, and limited to the cases expressly provided by the Statute. The power conferred upon the District Court, the Bankruptcy Courts, and the Probate Court are clearly defined by the Statutes, not left to inference. See *District Courts Act* (No. 4 of 1901); *Bankruptcy Act* (No. 25 of 1898), sec. 134 (6); *Probate Act* (No. 13 of 1898), sec. 149. [He referred also to *Small Debts Recovery Act* (No. 13 of 1899), secs. 34, 35; the *Companies Act* 1899, sec. 127; Equity Rule 211.] The Court will not hold that such power is conferred in the absence of clear and express provision.

Gordon K.C., in reply, referred to *In re Smith*; *Hands* v. *Andrews* (1); *Poyser* v. *Minors* (2); *In re Edgcome*; *Ex parte Edgcome* (3); *In re Gent*: *Gent-Davis* v. *Harris* (4).

[ISAACS J. referred to *Stonor* v. *Fowle* (5); and *In re Watson*; *Ex parte Johnston*; *Johnston* v. *Watson* (6).]

GRIFFITH C.J. The 12th section of the *Industrial Arbitration Act* provides that the President of the Arbitration Court, on the application of an industrial Union, may order payment by any member of the Union of any fine, penalty, or subscription payable in pursuance of the rules, provided that such subscription shall not exceed £10.

In the present case the respondent, who was a member of the appellant Union, committed breaches of the rules, for which several fines of £10 were inflicted upon him. Application was made to the Deputy-President of the Arbitration Court for an order for payment, and an order was duly made. The money was not paid. Thereupon the appellants applied to the Court on summons, for leave to issue writs of attachment against him for non-payment, relying upon rule 75 of the rules made under the Act, which provides that the Court, or President, on summons taken out by any person affected by such breach of non-payment, may order that a writ of attachment issue. The second paragraph provides that this shall apply " where a person fails to pay money ordered by the Court or President to be paid, and the Court or

Right margin:

H. C. OF A.
1907.

THE MASTER
UNDER-
TAKERS' AS-
SOCIATION OF
N.S.W.
v.
CROCKETT.

Dec. 9.

---

(1) (1893) 2 Ch., 1.
(2) 7 Q.B.D., 329, at p. 333.
(3) (1902) 2 K.B., 403.
(4) 40 Ch. D., 190.
(5) 13 App. Cas., 20.
(6) (1893) 1 Q.B., 21.

H. C. of A.
1907.

The Master
Under-
takers' As-
sociation of
N.S.W.
v.
Crockett.

President, as the case may be, is satisfied that he has means to pay such money, or is evading or attempting to evade payment."

The short result is that, if this summons can be granted and that rule is valid, the breach of the domestic rules of the Union may be enforced by imprisonment. That may be the law, but the person alleging it to be the law may fairly be asked to show where the legislature has indicated any such intention. It has been settled by this Court that the Industrial Arbitration Court is an inferior Court, and there are certain recognized rules applicable to inferior Courts. One settled rule is that a Court of inferior jurisdiction, although a Court of record, and therefore having power to punish for contempt, cannot commit for a contempt not committed in the face of the Court. That is clearly pointed out in the case of *The Queen* v. *Lefroy* (1).

But it is said that they have power to enforce non-payment of a judgment debt. Sec. 26, sub-sec. (*n*), is relied upon for that contention. That section enumerates all the powers of the Court. Sub-sec. (*c*) gives power, subject to the approval of the Governor, to make rules regulating the practice and procedure of the Court, and more especially but not so as to limit the generality of its powers in the premises with reference to:—(i.) the times and places of sitting; (ii.) the summoning of parties and witnesses; (iii.) the persons by whom and conditions upon which parties may be represented; (iv.) the rules of evidence; (v.) the enforcement of its orders; (vi.) allowances to witnesses, costs, court fees; (vii.) generally regulating the procedure of the Court; (viii.) appeals under this Act; (ix.) the reference of any matter.

It is contended that when a judgment or order of the Court is to be enforced it is merely a matter of form whether it should be enforced by execution against the goods or person of the debtor, and that, if it thinks fit to issue execution against the person of the judgment debtor, it is within its power to do so.

Is that so? The distinction between a superior and an inferior Court in this respect is pointed out in *The Queen* v. *Lefroy* (1), by *Cockburn* C.J., who, in drawing the distinction between superior and inferior Courts, and referring to the power claimed by an inferior Court to exercise jurisdiction to punish for contempt

(1) L.R. 8 Q.B., 134.

not committed in the face of the Court, said (1):—"No case is to
be found in which such a power has ever been exercised by an inferior Court of record, or, at all events, upheld by a decision of the Superior Courts. Finding, therefore, this distinction, that the Superior Courts have exercised the power from time immemorial, and that no such power has ever been known to be exercised by an inferior Court, that would be sufficient to dispose of this case."

I apply that to the present case. The power of enforcing judgments of the superior Courts for payment of money by execution against the person was exercised by Superior Courts in England from time immemorial, but not by any inferior Courts that I know of—certainly not in Australia. Sixty years ago the legislature of New South Wales abolished the right of execution against the person of a debtor, except in certain cases, and that has been the law of New South Wales ever since, and they have never conferred upon an inferior Court the right to enforce payment of a judgment debt by taking the person of the debtor except under carefully limited conditions.

Primâ facie, then, it is not likely that the legislature would entrust this newly created Court with a power which leaves it open to reintroduce a system that has been abolished for nearly 60 years, and which has never been exercised by any inferior Court. It would require very strong words to lead me to hold that the authority of the Court extends to the enforcement of its orders by imprisonment. If it does, what consequences would follow? Are the old laws relating to *ca. sa.* to be introduced? Is the debt taken to be discharged as soon as the debtor is arrested, or is he to be treated under some new system? How long is he to be kept in prison? Under the old system he might be kept there indefinitely. What is to be the rule? Is it to be supposed that the legislature intended to go back to the old law of 60 years before by such general words as are used here?

All probabilities are against it, and I think, taking into consideration the history of legislation, and what has been done in other cases, that the legislature cannot have intended to confer any such power upon an inferior Court.

(1) L.R. 8 Q.B., 134. at p. 137.

H. C. of A.   The particular process in this case is called a writ of attach-
1907.   ment, sometimes spoken of as a form of execution under the
THE MASTER *Judicature Act.*   But attachment is in reality a proceeding for
UNDER-   contempt of Court, and, regarded from that point of view, this
TAKERS' AS-
SOCIATION OF is an attachment for contempt for the non-payment of money,
N.S.W.   which is certainly not a contempt committed in the face of the
v.
CROCKETT.   Court.

Griffith C.J.   On all these grounds it seems to me that the authority contended for is not conferred upon the Court by the legislature.

BARTON J.   I concur, and adopt the reasons that the learned
Chief Justice has expressed.   Further, I wish to express my
agreement with the Chief Justice of the Supreme Court when
he says (1) that if it had been intended by the legislature that
the Arbitration Court should possess this enormous power of
committing a man to gaol because he has not paid a fine, or
obeyed the order of the President, or Deputy-President, that he
must pay a sum of money—a power of interfering with a man's
liberty and sending him to imprisonment for an indefinite period
—the power would have been given in express terms, and not
left to be inferred.   I think we are asked to draw too strong an
inference from the words used in the Act, having regard to the
legislative history of inferior Courts.

ISAACS J.   I agree with what has fallen from my learned
colleagues, but would like to say in addition how the matter
strikes me.

This Arbitration Court is a new tribunal, exercising a new
jurisdiction over new causes of quarrel.   The powers of that
Court must be found in the Statute either in express words or
by necessary implication.   The appellants' contention, which has
been very ably presented by Mr. *Gordon*, amounts to this : That
under sec. 26, sub-sec. (n), you find express words by which the
Court has jurisdiction and power to deal with all offences and to
enforce all orders under this Act.   And the argument is that
those words are plain, that the legislature has placed no limitation upon the method of enforcement, and therefore the Court is
at liberty to enforce any order in any manner it thinks fit.

(1) (1907) 7 S.R. (N.S.W.), 143, at p. 147.

H. C. OF A.
1907.

THE MASTER
UNDER-
TAKERS' AS-
SOCIATION OF
N.S.W.
v.
CROCKETT.

Isaacs J.

While there may be enactments in which the word "enforce" may be legitimately extended to that point, it all depends on the intention of the legislature, and on the whole Statute, and the question is, is that the meaning here ? There was a case before the Privy Council—*Buckley* v. *Edwards* (1) in which the question at issue was the meaning of words giving the Executive power to appoint Judges in New Zealand: "Such other Judges as His Excellency . . . . shall from time to time appoint." It was urged there that these words were unqualified. Lord *Herschell* in delivering the judgment of the Privy Council, after referring to certain weighty considerations that had been advanced why that power should not be unqualified, said (2):—"Nevertheless, weighty as these considerations are, if the natural meaning of the general words used be to confer the power contended for, and if there be no other provisions in the Act showing that this was not the intention of the legislature, effect must be given to the enactment without regard to the consequences. But it cannot be disputed that it is legitimate to read every part of an Act in order to see what construction ought to be put upon any particular provision contained in it."

Applying that rule to this case, what do we find ? That the Court is a Court to settle industrial disputes, and its powers must be taken to be ancillary to that object. It is not a Court of the ordinary type. It consists of a Judge and two laymen. If the powers are to be stretched to the extent contended for, then they are not only as great, but more absolute, than those of any other Court, for this reason—that by sec. 26, sub-sec. (*a*), its jurisdiction is to hear and determine according to equity and good conscience. Under sub-sec. (*p*) it has power to demand and "call for such evidence as in good conscience it thinks to be the best available whether strictly legal evidence or not."

By sec. 32 no power exists of appeal or review of its decisions, always supposing, of course, they are within its jurisdiction and not contrary to natural justice. When all those considerations are taken into account, is it not in the highest degree improbable that the legislature intended to incorporate in the powers that were expressly given to it the old doctrine of the Courts of

(1) (1892) A.C., 387.   (2) (1892) A.C., 387, at p. 397.

H. C. of A.
1907.

THE MASTER
UNDER-
TAKERS' AS-
SOCIATION OF
N.S.W.
v.
CROCKETT.

Isaacs J.

Westminster—that non-payment of money costs was a matter in the nature of a contempt to be met by imprisonment, by the arrest of the person?

I do not think it a fair conclusion to arrive at, and I think, looking at rule 75 along with rule 76 and Form 22, it was clearly intended that the process applicable to rule 75 was not one in the nature of contempt. Therefore I can find no indication, so far, that the meaning contended for was intended to be given to the word " enforce " by the legislature.

But I do find in the Act what seem to be indications to the contrary. I shall mention some of them. Wherever you find penalties mentioned in the Act the reference is to money penalties. There is nothing that has been pointed to, or that I can find, where the Court has power to impose a penalty, under any circumstances by way of imprisonment, except that which may be necessarily implied in the case of a breach of injunction. Injunction would be absolutely nugatory unless the Court had power of enforcing its orders in such a way.

Sec. 37 provided the mode of obtaining satisfaction for penalties and fines, but so far as I can see, there is nothing to be found on the face of that section beyond the power given to sue for the recovery of fines and penalties.

Sec. 40 provides that where an award or order of the Court, or an industrial agreement, binds specifically a corporation, &c., " any property . . . shall be available to answer such award, order, or agreement, and any process for enforcing the same," and then it provides for contribution by members, and limits the amount of personal contribution. No member is to be liable for more than £10, a very significant limitation protecting him from payment of a greater amount than £10. The same thing is to be found in sec. 12, under which this order is made. In sec. 45, where the Governor is given power to make regulations, sub-sec. (j) provides that penalties may be fixed by regulations, and the penalty for breach of them must not exceed £20, and that is to be recovered in a summary way in the Court of Petty Sessions, and nowhere can you find express power of imprisonment. I attach a great deal of importance to sec. 31 where power is given the Court, or on the written authority of the Court, to " enter any building," and so on, to inspect and inform the Court for the performance of its functions, and any person who hinders or obstructs—which is ordinarily looked upon as contempt of Court —is liable to a penalty.

That is the place where you might expect to find imprisonment. The legislature has said here that "any person who hinders, or obstructs the Court shall for every such offence," and then provides the prescribed punishment. He shall be liable to a penalty not exceeding £5. Well, if in a case of that kind, where there is a direct hindrance of the Court in the performance of its functions, and that hindrance or obstruction is stigmatized as an offence, there is no penalty of imprisonment, and you find in sec. 26, sub-sec. (n), that the legislature has contented itself with a monetary penalty, how can you, then, say that it is a legitimate deduction, or necessary implication in sec. 26, sub-sec. (n) that any person who simply fails to pay money, whether he is able to pay or not, may be punished with indefinite imprisonment? I cannot see that myself.

I, therefore, come to the conclusion—from the nature of the Court, the nature of its functions, the express provisions of the Act, contenting itself with references to penalties of a pecuniary nature, and the absence of express power of imprisonment—that imprisonment was not intended as a means of enforcing an order for payment of money. On those grounds, concurring as I do in what has fallen from my learned brothers, I agree that the judgment appealed from was right, and that this appeal should be dismissed.

Appeal dismissed with costs.

Solicitors, for the appellants, *Pigott & Stinson.*
Solicitor, for respondent, *R. J. M. Foord.*

C. A. W.

H. C. of A.
1907.

The Master
Under-
takers' As-
sociation of
N.S.W.
v.
Crockett.

Isaacs J.

[PRIVY COUNCIL.]

THE COMMISSIONERS OF TAXATION, } APPELLANTS;
NEW SOUTH WALES

AND

BAXTER . . . . RESPONDENT;

THE ATTORNEY-GENERAL FOR THE } INTERVENANT.
COMMONWEALTH OF AUSTRALIA

WEBB . . . . APPELLANT;

AND

FLINT . . . . RESPONDENT;

THE ATTORNEY-GENERAL FOR THE } INTERVENANT.
COMMONWEALTH OF AUSTRALIA

ON APPEAL FROM THE HIGH COURT OF
AUSTRALIA.

PRIVY
COUNCIL.*
1907.

November 28.

1908.
January 14.

Special leave to appeal from High Court—Reasons for refusing—Question not again raisable—Sum in dispute inconsiderable in amount.

Special leave to appeal from a decision of the High Court will not be granted by the Privy Council where the question in controversy cannot be raised again, and where the sums actually in dispute or indirectly affected are inconsiderable in amount.

Petitions for special leave to appeal from the judgments of the High Court in *Baxter* v. *Commissioners of Taxation, New South Wales*, 4 C.L.R., 1087, and *Flint* v. *Webb*, 4 C.L.R., 1178, dismissed.

---

* Present.—Lord Loreburn L.C. ; The Earl of Halsbury ; Lord Macnaghten ; Lord Robertson ; Lord Atkinson ; Lord Collins ; and Sir Arthur Wilson.

PETITIONS for special leave to appeal to His Majesty in Council from the decisions of the High Court: *Baxter* v. *Commissioners of Taxation, New South Wales* (1); *Flint* v. *Webb* (2).

The judgment of their Lordships was delivered by

LORD LOREBURN L.C.　Their Lordships intimated on 28th November last that they would state the reasons why they were unable to advise His Majesty to grant special leave to appeal.

The dispute between the parties was whether or not one of the Australian States could impose income tax upon a salary paid by the Commonwealth to its officers, or to a Member of the Commonwealth Parliament, resident in such State.　There had been decisions of State Courts in the affirmative.　The High Court of Australia overruled these decisions, and when the whole matter came before His Majesty in Council in the case of *Webb* v. *Outtrim* (3), this Board took the view that such taxation could be imposed, therein differing from the High Court.

Thereafter, in the present cases, the High Court entertained fresh appeals, and adhered to their former view.

The petitioners applied that special leave should be given to appeal to His Majesty in Council from that last determination of the High Court.

Before these petitions could be heard by their Lordships an Act of the Commonwealth was passed expressly authorizing States to impose taxation of the kind in question, so that the controversy cannot be raised again.

The sums actually in dispute or indirectly affected are inconsiderable in amount.

In these circumstances it would not be in accordance with the practice of this Board to advise His Majesty to grant special leave to appeal.

There will be no order as to the costs of these petitions.

PRIVY
COUNCIL.
1907.

COMMIS-
SIONERS OF
TAXATION
(N.S.W.)
v.
BAXTER.

WEBB
v.
FLINT.

(1) 4 C.L.R., 1087.　　　　　(2) 4 C.L.R., 1179.
　　　　(3) (1907) A.C., 81.

[HIGH COURT OF AUSTRALIA.]

UTICK   .   .   .   .   APPELLANT;
RESPONDENT,

AND

UTICK   .   .   .   .   RESPONDENT.
PETITIONER,

ON APPEAL FROM THE SUPREME COURT OF
NEW SOUTH WALES.

H. C. OF A.   *Petition for dissolution of marriage and permanent maintenance — Failure of*
1907.   *respondent to enter appearance in suit—Right to be heard on question of main-*
              tenance.
SYDNEY,
November 29.   In a suit for dissolution of marriage in which the petitioner asked for an
              order for permanent maintenance, the respondent failed to enter an appearance
Griffith C.J., in accordance with the rules of Court, but at the hearing asked to be allowed
Barton and   to be heard by his solicitor on the question of maintenance only. The Judge
Isaacs JJ.   refused to hear the solicitor, and made an order for the payment of permanent
              maintenance.

                 Held, that, notwithstanding the failure to enter an appearance in the suit,
              the respondent, in the absence of express provision to the contrary, was
              entitled to be heard, and the order for maintenance, having been made
              without hearing him, was bad.

                 Order of *Simpson* J. directing the payment of permanent maintenance set
              aside.

APPEAL from an order of *Simpson* J. in the Matrimonial Causes
Jurisdiction of the Supreme Court, directing that permanent
maintenance should be paid by the respondent to the petitioner
in a suit for dissolution of marriage.

The facts sufficiently appear in the judgments hereunder.

McManamey, for appellant.   It is a general principle of law that every person has an unassailable right to be heard if he desires it when it is sought to make an order against him : *Smith* v. *The Queen* (1).   It may be that failure to comply with rules as to appearance would subject him to the risk of having an order made against him, on the assumption that he does not desire to oppose it, but if, before an order is made, he asks to be allowed to appear, then, although the validity of what has already been done cannot be affected, he should be allowed to be heard, possibly upon terms.   Even in the suit on the main question, a respondent may be heard, though he has failed to enter an appearance : *Stow* v. *Stow* (2).   *A fortiori* he should be allowed to be heard on the subsidiary question of maintenance, although the main issues have gone against him by default.   Once the order is made the respondent is bound for all time unless he can show a change of circumstances.   [He referred to *Matrimonial Causes Act*, No. 14 of 1899, secs. 39, 40, and rules 12, 20, 108-116.]

Curtis, for the respondent.   The present case does not involve the general question of the right of a party who has not entered an appearance to be heard *vivâ voce*, but only the question whether under the particular circumstances of the case His Honor rightly exercised his discretion in refusing to hear the respondent.   A proper procedure is prescribed by the rules for the case of a respondent who has failed to enter an appearance in time, and wishes to do so later.   If that is not adopted the Judge has a discretion as to whether the party in default should be allowed to appear.   The respondent had not followed the procedure prescribed, and offered no valid excuse for not having done so.

[*Isaacs* J. referred to *Bradley* v. *Bradley* (3).]

Special leave should not have been granted.   There has been no denial of justice.   At any time within the year the respondent may apply to have the amount reduced.   He is merely paying for his remissness in not adopting the proper procedure.   The effect of the order was, not that the respondent must pay the

(1) 3 App. Cas., 614, at p. 623.   (2) 9 N.S.W. W.N., 52.
(3) 3 P.D., 47, at p. 50.

amount ordered for all time, but only until he took the steps open to him to have the amount reduced. It is a mere question of procedure : *Bagnall* v. *White* (1).

GRIFFITH C.J. This is an appeal from so much of an order made by *Simpson* J. in the divorce jurisdiction of the Supreme Court as directs that permanent maintenance be paid by the present appellant to his wife, the petitioner in a suit for dissolution of marriage. The appellant did not enter an appearance in the suit, but when the case came on for trial his solicitor asked to be allowed to enter an appearance, not for the purpose of being heard as to the merits of the suit, but only on the question of maintenance. The learned Judge, in the exercise of a discretion apparently conferred by the rules, refused to allow an appearance to be entered at that stage, and further refused to hear the solicitor on the question of maintenance. It is, to me at any rate, novel that on the trial of an action a party may not be heard in his defence either by himself or by his counsel, even though he has not entered an appearance. I referred in the course of the argument to the case of a writ of inquiry after judgment by default for want of appearance. It is novel to me that a defendant in a case of that kind cannot be heard simply because he has not entered an appearance. In the *Annual Practice*, 1907, p. 475, dealing with Order XXXVI., rule 56, under the head " Practice," it is stated that, where the defendant is in default of appearance, " Some notice, besides filing in default, should be given, because a defendant to an action for damages is entitled to let judgment go by default, and yet is also entitled to receive notice of the assessment of damages." There is no authority cited for that proposition—probably because none was necessary, the proposition being in accordance with obvious principles of justice. As was pointed out in the case cited by my learned brother *Isaacs*, an application for maintenance is a separate and independent application from the application for dissolution of marriage. Upon what principle of justice can it be suggested that a man, against whom an order for maintenance is sought, is not entitled to be heard on the issue of what is a proper amount

(1) 4 C.L.R., 89.

to order to be paid by him ? Is the Judge to take the uncontested version of the wife as to her husband's means or as to her own ? It seems to me that a refusal to hear a man under these circumstances is a violation of the rule *audi alteram partem*, and cannot be supported. The failure to enter an appearance in the office does not seem to me, in the absence of positive provision to the contrary, a sufficient reason for refusing to allow a man to defend himself by word of mouth. Even when a man has pleaded guilty to a criminal offence he is allowed to be heard before sentence is passed upon him. One of the consequences of the appellant's failure to enter an appearance in the suit was that he was liable to have an order made against him for maintenance. But for how much ? Surely according to every principle of justice he was entitled to be heard on that question. I think, therefore, that the order was wrong on that ground. It may have been a perfectly just order. But, to quote the well-known epigram of Seneca, "*quicunque aliquid statuerit, parte inaudita altera, aequum licet statuerit, haud aequus fuerit.*"

BARTON J. I concur.

ISAACS J. I think that, once you arrive at the position that is laid down by Lord *Westbury* in *Sidney* v. *Sidney* (1), referred to in *Bradley* v. *Bradley* (2), that the application for alimony or permanent maintenance is a totally distinct proceeding for a totally different object from the main question in the suit, the difficulty here is solved. And Lord *Westbury* said at the conclusion of the passage quoted by *Sir James Hannen* (3), " In fact, although it may not be so in terms, it is really an order pronounced upon an application to the discretionary power of the Court, which application can only be made after the other and more important jurisdiction has been exercised." Well, in the present case, in the petition, no doubt, notice was given that an application would be made for permanent alimony, and, apparently, the respondent not wishing to contest the main question, the case was allowed to go by default, and when the

(1) L.R., 1 P. & D., 78.　　　(2) 3 P.D., 47.
　　　(3) 3 P.D., 47, at p. 50.

H. C. OF A.
1907.

UTICK
v.
UTICK.

ISAACS J.

application for maintenance was made, the respondent said, in effect, "Now that that application has been made, I desire to be heard upon it." But he was not allowed to be heard. This Court is not in a position to say that the order was just any more than His Honor was. The very first principle of justice requires that, when one party comes into Court and asks for an order, the other side should be heard, and unless it is heard, no one can tell whether the order asked for or made is just or not. Under these circumstances there is no alternative but to set aside that portion of the decree which orders that permanent maintenance be paid by the appellant.

GRIFFITH C.J. The application for maintenance is still pending, as it has not been properly heard. The case must be remitted. It is left in the position of an application to *Simpson* J. not yet heard.

Appeal allowed. Order appealed from discharged. Case remitted to the Supreme Court.

Proctor, for the appellant: *R. W. Fraser.*
Proctor, for the respondent: *J. B. Frawley.*

C. A. W.

[HIGH COURT OF AUSTRALIA.]

MITCHELL　.　　　.　　　.　　.　　.　　.　　APPELLANT ;
COMPLAINANT,

AND

SCALES　.　　.　　.　　.　　.　　.　　.　　.　RESPONDENT.
DEFENDANT,

ON APPEAL FROM THE SUPREME COURT OF
NEW SOUTH WALES.

Applicability of English law in New South Wales—Vagrancy Act, 5 *Geo. IV. c.* 83 　H. C. OF A.
—*Effect of Ordinance,* 6 *Wm. IV. No.* 6 (*N.S.W.*)—*Repeal by implication*—　　1907.
9 *Geo. IV. c.* 83.

SYDNEY,

The provisions of the Imperial *Vagrancy Act*, 5 Geo. IV. c. 83, were never *Dec.* 9, 10, 11.
capable " of being applied in the administration of Justice " in New South
Wales, within the meaning of 9 Geo. 1V. c. 83, sec. 24.

Griffith C.J.,
Barton and
Isaacs JJ.

Even if any of its provisions were ever in force in New South Wales, the
Ordinance 6 Wm. IV. No. 6, which dealt comprehensively with the subject
of vagrancy in New South Wales, had the effect of either repealing by
implication those provisions of the English Statute which dealt with the same
subject matter, or of a legislative declaration that they were not in force.

Quan Yick v. Hinds, 2 C.L.R., 345, considered and approved.

Per Griffith C.J. and *Barton* J.—In considering whether an English Statute
was introduced into New South Wales by 9 Geo. IV. c. 83, regard must
be had to the suitability of the Statute as a whole to local conditions, and, so
regarded, 5 Geo. IV. c. 83 as a whole was inapplicable, and therefore
never in force in New South Wales.

Per Isaacs J.—*Quære,* whether before 6 Wm. IV. No. 6 was passed
such portions of 5 Geo. IV. c. 83, as dealt with offences against society
in general, were not in force in New South Wales by virtue of 9 Geo. IV.
c. 83.

Decision of *Sly* Acting J., 19th July 1907, affirmed.

APPEAL from a decision of *Sly* Acting J. on a special case stated under the *Justices Act* 1902.

The respondent, Mary Scales, was proceeded against by the appellant, before a magistrate, upon an information which alleged that she "did unlawfully pretend to one L.H.C. to tell the fortune of him the said L.H.C. by clairvoyancy to deceive and impose upon the said L.H.C.," &c. At the conclusion of the evidence the point was taken on behalf of the respondent that the acts alleged and proved in evidence did not constitute an offence, inasmuch as the Imperial *Vagrancy Act,* 5 Geo. IV. c. 83, which makes it an offence to pretend to tell fortunes, was not in force in New South Wales, and there was no local Act under which the respondent was liable to prosecution. It was contended for the prosecution, that, notwithstanding the decision of the High Court in *Quan Yick* v. *Hinds* (1), the Act 5 Geo. IV. c. 83 was in force in New South Wales, and that the evidence supported the charge stated in the information. The magistrate, following the decision of the High Court, dismissed the information, and stated a case for the opinion of the Supreme Court, whether his determination was erroneous in point of law.

The special case came on for hearing before *Sly* Acting J. sitting in Chambers, who held that he was bound to follow the decision in *Quan Yick* v. *Hinds* (1), and dismissed the appeal with costs, 19th July, 1907.

From this decision the present appeal was brought by special leave.

Piddington, for the appellant. The case of *Quan Yick* v. *Hinds* (1), if it rests upon the ground that, at the date of 9 Geo. IV. c.83, there were no Courts of Quarter Sessions in New South Wales, should be reconsidered. The Act 4 Geo. IV. c. 96, sec. 19 gave power to the Governor to establish Courts of Quarter Sessions in New South Wales, and the power was exercised by proclamation in 6 Geo. IV. No. 18. The first local Statute on the subject of rogues and vagabonds was 9 Geo. IV. No. 14, secs. 1, 2, by which persons found in unlicensed houses of entertainment were deemed to be rogues and vagabonds, but the punishment was under 5 Geo. IV.

(1) 2 C.L.R., 345.

H. C. of A.
1907.

MITCHELL
v.
SCALES.

c. 83. The law under 9 Geo. IV. No. 14 continued in force until 14 Vict. No. 23, which repealed and, in the main, re-enacted its provisions. The 14 Vict. No. 23 was consolidated by No. 26 of 1897. Some portions therefore of 5 Geo. IV. c. 83 have always been in force here. It was practically a consolidation of the law of vagrancy, and those portions of it which were not expressly repealed by subsequent local Statutes have remained in force to the present time. The 6 Wm. IV. No. 6, which was repealed by 15 Vict. No. 4, covered part of the same ground, but did not operate as a repeal of the provisions left untouched. It increased the punishment, but did not create new offences, and did not purport to be a codification. The English law of vagrancy with unimportant modifications, as to punishment and machinery, has always been in force in New South Wales. The adoption of a great part of it in 6 Wm. IV. No. 6 is some evidence that it was suitable to the conditions of the Colony, at any rate so far as the classification of offences is concerned. Fortune telling was held to be an offence here under sec. 4 of 9 Geo. II. c. 5, though the procedure and punishment were different: *R. v. Colan* (1). An offence may be within the general law and the provisions of the Poor Law also. The Vagrancy Acts are mainly directed to making offences punishable summarily which otherwise would require an indictment. [He referred to *R. v. Giles* (2); *Monck v. Hilton* (3).] The omission to provide for this offence in 6 Wm. IV. No. 6 is more consistent with its having been deemed unnecessary to do so owing to there being already adequate provision for it. [He referred to the preamble of 6 Wm. IV. No. 6.] It should not be read as impliedly repealing Statutes that create and provide for specific offences: *Attorney-General for New South Wales* v. *Edgley* (4); *Aarons v. Rees* (5). No reason can be suggested why fortune telling should not be treated as an offence in this country. Even if some of the provisions of 5 Geo. IV. c. 83 are unsuitable, the whole Statute should not be discarded. Fortune telling is in a different branch of the law from the offences dealt with in *Quan Yick* v. *Hinds* (6). There is, and always has been,

(1) 1 S.C.R. N.S. (N.S.W.), 1.
(2) 10 Cox Cr. Ca., 44.
(3) 2 Ex. D., 268.

(4) 9 N.S.W.L.R., 157.
(5) 15 N.S.W.W.N., 88.
(6) 2 C.L.R., 345.

H. C. of A.
1907.

MITCHELL
v.
SCALES.

adequate machinery for dealing with the offence here. [He referred to *Jex* v. *McKinney* (1); *MacDonald* v. *Levy* (2); 5 Wm. IV. No. 10; 4 Vict. No. 29; 30 Vict. No. 13; 15 Vict. No. 11, sec. 10; 17 Vict. No. 21, sec. 88; 31 Vict. No. 25, sec. 5.]

[GRIFFITH C.J. referred to *Michell* v. *Brown* (3); *Youle* v. *Mappin* (4).

ISAACS J. referred to *Fortescue* v. *Vestry of St. Matthew, Bethnal Green* (5).]

Hammond, for the respondent. 5 Geo. IV., c. 83 was a mere police provision and would not be introduced on the settlement of the Colony under the common rule law: 1 *Blac. Comm.*, p. 107; *Quan Yick* v. *Hinds* (6). Even if it had been a law capable of general application, it was not passed until 1824, *i.e.*, after the date of the settlement of the Colony. It was not introduced here by 9 Geo. IV. c. 83, sec. 24 because it was not capable of being applied here within the meaning of that section. Its provisions are in most cases dependent for their efficacy upon the English Poor Laws and the law as to gaols and houses of correction, which were never in force in New South Wales. The machinery for its enforcement never existed here. The local Statutes dealing with offences of a similar kind omit all reference to the machinery of the English Act, and establish machinery of their own. [He referred to 5 Geo. IV. c. 83, secs. 1-22; 4 Geo. IV. No. 28; 9 Geo. IV. No. 5, sec. 3; 4 Vict. No. 29; *Slapp* v. *Webb* (7); *Ryan* v. *Howell* (8); *Reg.* v. *Maloney* (9).]

Even if 5 Geo. IV. c. 83 was ever in force here, it was impliedly repealed by 6 Wm. IV. No. 6. The fact that that Act dealt with the subject of vagrancy in a comprehensive manner, and made provisions totally dissimilar to those of the English Statute, both as to machinery, classification of offences, and punishment, raises a strong presumption that the legislature either intended to repeal any existing Statutes that may have been in force, or deemed the English Statutes not to be in force

(1) 14 App. Cas., 77.
(2) 1 Legge, 39.
(3) 1 El. & E., 267.
(4) 30 L.J.M.C., 234, at p. 237.
(5) (1891) 2 Q.B., 170.

(6) 2 C.L.R., 345, at pp. 363, 372.
(7) 1 S.C.R. (N.S.W.), app. p. 54.
(8) 1 Legge, 470, at p. 473.
(9) 1 Legge, 74, at p. 80.

here as being unsuitable to local conditions, more especially when, as in this case, the local Statute was passed within seven years of 9 Geo. IV. c. 33, which is said to have introduced the English law to the Colony. This presumption is strengthened by the language of the preamble which recites that it is expedient "to make provision," not "to make better provision" for the subject of vagrancy. In 15 Vict. No. 4, which amends 6 Wm. IV. No. 6, the intention of the legislature is stated to be "to make more effectual provision" &c. [He referred to *Quan Yick* v. *Hinds* (1); *Rex* v. *Hilaire* (2); *Harris* v. *Davies* (3); *Glasson* v. *Egan* (4).]

Piddington in reply, referred to 1 Jac. I. c. 12 ; 9 Geo. II. c. 5, sec. 4 ; *Attorney-General for New South Wales* v. *Love* (5).

GRIFFITH C.J.　In this case the Court is invited to review the considered judgment of the Court in *Quan Yick* v. *Hinds* (6), delivered on 10th April 1905. In that case the Court held that the Act 5 Geo. IV. c. 83, passed in 1823, commonly called the *Vagrancy Act*, was not one of the laws introduced into New South Wales by the New South Wales Act, 9 Geo. IV. c. 83, which came into operation on 1st March 1829.

The reason why the Court held that the Act was not in force was that there were provisions in it, essential to its operation, which could not be applied at that time in New South Wales. The particular point upon which all the members of the Court were agreed was that the right of appeal to the Quarter Sessions, which was a right expressly given to a person convicted before justices under the Act, was not available. The Court was informed by counsel that at that time there was no law as to Courts of Quarter Sessions in force in New South Wales. Since then it has been discovered that that was a mistake, and that there was such a law in force. Therefore that particular reason for holding that the Act was not in force fails. We are asked now to come to the conclusion that the Act was in force.

H. C. of A.
1907.

MITCHELL
v.
SCALES.

---

(1) 2 C.L.R., 345, at pp. 362, 364, 372, 381.
(2) (1903) 3 S.R. (N.S.W.), 228.
(3) 10 App. Cas., 279.

(4) 6 S.C.R., (N.S.W.), 85.
(5) (1898) A.C., 679, at p. 686.
(6) 2 C.L.R., 345.

H. C. of A.
1907.

MITCHELL
v.
SCALES.

Griffith C.J.

For myself, I was of opinion that the Act was not a law which was introduced into New South Wales for other reasons also, which I will state. I was further of opinion that, if it had been introduced, it did not continue in force after 1835, but was repealed by implication in that year by the Ordinance 6 Wm. IV. No. 6, which was the first local law on the subject of vagrants.

The vagrancy laws of England date back to a very early period. I have before me a reference to a Statute of Henry VIII., by which a vagrant, after being whipped, was to take an oath that he would return to the place where he was born, and remain there for a period of three years, and there labour as a clean man ought to do. Persons found a second time in a state of vagrancy were not only to be whipped, but were to have the upper part of the gristle of their right ear cut off. For a third offence the penalty was death. From time to time after that many Acts were passed in England dealing with vagrants, amongst others the Act 17 Geo. II. c. 5 "to amend and make more effectual the laws relating to rogues, vagabonds, and other idle and disorderly persons," &c., the scheme of which was intimately connected with the administration of the Poor Laws. In sec. 2 amongst other persons mentioned were persons pretending to be gipsies, or "wandering in the habit or form of Egyptians," or pretending to have skill in palmistry, or pretending to tell fortunes. That Act was amended by others, and finally, in 1823, the Act 5 Geo. IV. c. 83 was passed, which repealed all existing laws as to rogues and vagabonds, and enacted a series of new provisions. The scheme of that Act was based entirely upon the existing state of things in England at that time—the County organisation and County funds, the organization of parishes and the burdens cast by the Poor Laws upon parishes. Throughout the Act continual reference was made to those provisions. It is true that the Act dealt with many matters that might have been dealt with as substantive parts of the criminal law, but the legislature thought fit to deal with them as part of the law of vagrancy. I referred to several of those provisions in the case of *Quan Yick* v. *Hinds* (1), and came to the conclusion that the Act was not suitable to the circumstances of New South Wales.

(1) 2 C.L.R., 345.

I said (1) what I will now repeat :—" That if the general provisions of a Statute were not unsuitable to the conditions of the
Colony, the mere fact that some minor or severable provisions
could not come into operation owing to local circumstances is not
a sufficient reason for denying the applicability of the Statute as
a whole.   On the other hand, if the general provisions of a
Statute were inapplicable, it would seem to follow that it is not
competent to select a particular provision of the Statute which if
it stood alone might be applicable, and to say that it is therefore
applicable."

I still think that a correct statement of the law. The question
to be considered is, not whether such a law might reasonably
have been then enacted in New South Wales, but whether the
provisions of the Statute, regarded as a whole, were so applicable
to New South Wales as to be incorporated in its law. You cannot select one isolated provision and say that that alone is such
as might have been made law in New South Wales. That is not
the correct doctrine. I adhere to the opinion that the whole
structure of the Act shows that it was not applicable to New
South Wales.

It was, however, contended that the subject matter of the Act
was of such a nature that it was suitable to the conditions of the
Colony, and that that was shown conclusively by the fact that
in 1835 the Ordinance 6 Wm. IV. No. 6 was passed by the
Governor and Legislative Council of New South Wales, which
dealt to a very large extent with the same subject. That, it was
said, shows that the law was suitable to be applied to New
South Wales. In my opinion it shows that the Governor and
Legislative Council were of opinion that this subject matter
needed to be dealt with by legislation, and, so far from showing
that the English law was in force, it seems to me to indicate
exactly to the contrary. As I pointed out in *Quan Yick* v.
Hinds (2), the Act or Ordinance 6 Wm. IV. No. 6 recited that
" it is expedient to make provision for the prevention of vagrancy
and for the punishment of idle and disorderly persons and rogues
and vagabonds in the Colony of New South Wales "—not that it
was expedient to make " better " provision for that purpose.

(1) 2 C.L.R., 345, at p. 364.   (2) 2 C.L.R., 345, at p. 363.

H. C. of A.
1907.

MITCHELL
v.
SCALES.

Griffith C.J.

H. C. of A.   That indicates, if anything, that the Governor and Legislative
   1907.   Council thought, not that the English law had been introduced
MITCHELL   into New South Wales, but that it had not.   Apart from that, I
   v.   think it is a very serious thing to ask this Court, after a lapse
SCALES.   of so many years—from 1829 to 1903 or 1904—during which
Griffith C.J. it has never occurred to anybody that this Act was in force, to
             say that it was.   I think that the opinion of the Governor and
             Legislative Council in 1835 on such a matter is entitled to very
             great weight.   One member was Sir Francis Forbes.   There is
             nothing to indicate that he thought that the Act was in force in
             New South Wales.   If he had, he would probably, as legal adviser
             to the Government, have caused the Ordinance 6 Wm. IV. No. 6,
             to be couched in very different language.   I adhere, therefore, to
             the opinion that the English Statute never became part of the
             law of New South Wales.

             In *Quan Yick* v. *Hinds* (1), I expressed the further opinion that
             the Ordinance 6 Wm. IV. No. 6 ought to be read either as a
             legislative declaration that it was not in force, or as a codifica-
             tion of the law on the subject, in exercise of the power conferred
             by sec. 24 of the Act 9 Geo. IV. c. 83 to declare whether a Statute
             was to "be deemed to extend to New South Wales, or to make
             and establish such limitations and modifications of its provisions
             as might be deemed expedient."

             It is contended that a law cannot be repealed by silence.   I
             concede that.   But it may be repealed by necessary implication,
             and I think that the cases of *Michell* v. *Brown* (2), *Youle* v.
             Mappin (3), and *Fortescue* v. *Vestry of St. Matthew, Bethnal Green*
             (4), establish this proposition, that when by a Statute the elements
             of an offence are re-stated, and a different punishment is indicated
             for it, that is a repeal by implication of the old law.   Both these
             conditions apply to the present case.

             For this purpose I will assume that the Act 5 Geo. IV. c. 83
             was in force in New South Wales.   The local legislature in 1835
             undertook to deal with the subject in the Ordinance which I
             have already cited.   The English Act dealt with three offences—
             being an idle and disorderly person, being a rogue and a vagabond,

             (1) 2 C.L.R., 345.   (3) 30 L.J.M.C., 234, at p. 237.
             (2) 1 El. & E., 267 ; 28 L.J.M.C., 53.   (4) (1891) 2 Q.B., 170.

and being an incorrigible rogue—and defined the elements which constituted each offence. The New South Wales Ordinance did the same, and defined the elements which constituted each offence, modifying the provisions of the English Act to suit the obvious conditions of a new country. The punishments inflicted in the English Statute were, respectively, one month, three months and six months imprisonment. The punishments inflicted by the local Ordinance were three months, six months and one year. One mode of committing the offence of being a rogue and a vagabond under the English Act was this (sec. 4):—" Every person wandering abroad and lodging in any barn or outhouse, or in any deserted or unoccupied building, or in the open air, or under a tent, or in any cart or wagon, not having any visible means of subsistence, and not giving a good account of himself or herself." This was obviously aimed at gipsies.

Such provisions, applied to New South Wales in 1829, would have been, I think, absurd. Persons of that sort in England might be called rogues and vagabonds. They were certainly vagabonds and generally rogues. They might be said to be vagabonds in New South Wales, but not necessarily rogues. But the local legislature in 6 Wm. IV. No. 6, sec. 2, gave a very different definition:—" Every person not being a black native or the child of any black native who being found lodging or wandering in company with any of the black natives of this Colony shall not being thereto required by any justice of the peace give a good account to the satisfaction of such justice that he or she hath a lawful fixed place of residence in this Colony and lawful means of support and that such lodging or wandering hath been for some temporary and lawful occasion only and hath not continued beyond such occasion," &c. And the person who fulfilled those conditions was not declared to be a rogue and vagabond, but to be an idle and disorderly person. I think I have said enough to show that in this Act the elements of the three offences were re-stated, and I have pointed out the difference in the punishment indicated. In my opinion, this is sufficient to establish that, if the Act in question was ever in force in New South Wales, it was repealed by the Ordinance 6 Wm. IV. No. 6.

The appeal, therefore, should be dismissed.

BARTON J.   In the case of *Quan Yick* v. *Hinds* (1), I had
grave doubts whether the Act 5 Geo. IV. c. 83 could apply to
New South Wales.   In the additional light which has been cast
upon the subject by the researches of Mr. *Hammond* and Mr.
Piddington I find my doubts entirely removed.   I think that, in
the first place, the enactment in itself was not applicable in this
Colony in a judicial sense.   That is to say, it is coupled with
machinery that could not well be put in motion in this State
without additional legislation, and it has required additional
legislation to make the provisions applicable at all.   In that
legislation the operation of the laws dealing with fortune telling
and vagrancy has been left out.

In neither of the Acts 6 Wm. IV. No. 6, and 15 Vict. No. 4, is
there any reference to the vagrant laws of England.   In these
circumstances I entirely agree with the Chief Justice in his
exhaustive judgment, to which I think it is quite unnecessary to
add anything more.   I therefore agree in the opinion that this
appeal must be dismissed.

ISAACS J.   I also think this appeal must be dismissed.   I desire
not to express any decided opinion as to whether the Act 5 Geo.
IV. c. 83 was in force as to some of its provisions.   As to others
it clearly never was.   But as to certain of its provisions—as, for
instance, those regulating certain conduct such as personal
indecency, exposing certain indecent pictures in public, public
betting, being on premises with burglarious instruments, intent
to commit a felony, and other matters which are offences against
society at large—if I had to consider that question, I should
desire further time in which to do so.

But I am quite clear that, from the moment Ordinance, or Act
6 Wm. IV. No. 6 was passed, there was no valid reason for saying
that any part of the Act 5 Geo. IV. c. 83 was in force in New
South Wales.   The Ordinance in question was passed very
shortly after the *Charter of Justice*, 1835.   By its title it
assumes to make provision which, in the absence of qualifying

(1) 2 C.L.R., 345.

words, I take to be ample provision—such as the New South
Wales legislature then thought proper for the circumstances of
the Colony. That legislature had before it the Act of Geo. IV.,
and followed it in most particulars, modifying those particulars
to suit existing circumstances, and deliberately omitting from
that Act any mention of fortune tellers. There is no doubt that
the omission was deliberate. There is no contention that it was
not deliberate, but it is urged for the appellant that the omission
was deliberate because it was desired to preserve the law in New
South Wales with regard to fortune tellers, which was then
conceived by the legislature to be already in force, and to leave
fortune tellers to the operation of the English Statute, although
every other instance of the several groups was dealt with subsequently by the legislature in New South Wales, and a different
punishment attached to the two first groups. But I think the
punishment of one year and whipping in the case of men was
adhered to in the case of incorrigible rogues.

Now, I think, as to the application of the maxim "*Expressio
unius est exclusio alterius*," this is a very proper instance
to apply it, and it is difficult to think otherwise looking at
the Ordinance, which not only enumerated the categories of
conduct which might constitute one or other of the three classes
of offences—idle and disorderly persons, rogues and vagabonds,
and incorrigible rogues,—but set out the charge, and provided a
full and complete manner for hearing a case, punishing offenders,
allocation of fines, &c., which would have been quite unnecessary
if the contention of the appellant was correct, namely, that all
that was desired to do was to alter the punishment.

Not only did the legislature assume to make provision—
not further provision, or additional provision, but provision—for
the class of cases indicated, but a later Act, 15 Vict. No. 4, was
passed which was called an Act for the more effectual prevention
of vagrancy and the punishment of rogues and vagabonds, &c., in
the Colony of New South Wales. It stated that the Act of 6
Wm. IV. No. 6, was repealed. Not a single word is found in that
Act about repealing, or altering, or changing the position of
fortune tellers in the Act of Geo. IV., and the argument of the
appellant, perforce, conveys that the legislature was still deter-

H. C. of A.
1907.

MITCHELL
r.
SCALES.

Isaacs J.

mining to leave fortune tellers under the operation of the English Statute, and for some reason, which has never been suggested, and I do not think could be suggested, the legislature intended to leave fortune tellers to the same punishment as was allowed by the English Act.

The new Act 15 Vict. No. 4 increased the punishment of idle and disorderly persons to a maximum of two years. That related to rogues and vagabonds; but when it came to deal with incorrigible rogues, it omitted to mention the whipping, so that thenceforth there was no power to administer a whipping as punishment for incorrigible rogues. Up to that point the argument must be that it was intended to be more lenient to fortune tellers than to others. Now the argument must be that it was intended to be more severe, because the legislature must have intended, if the argument was right, to leave them still open to be whipped if men, and to abolish that punishment altogether in other cases now called vagrancy. That seems to me to savour of inconsistency.

When the legislature of 1901 passed the *Vagrant Act* (No. 13) it entitled the Act " an Act to consolidate the Acts for the prevention of vagrancy," and one would imagine that meant the consolidation of the whole of the Statute law relating to vagrancy in force in New South Wales. No mention is made of fortune tellers, and yet the argument still continues that the legislature, as it did in 1835, and intermittently since, persevered in its original intention to leave fortune tellers to the Act 9 Geo. IV. Again, in 1902, in Act No. 74, the same thing was done.

I look upon the Act 6 Wm. IV. No. 6 as an indication by the legislature, then thoroughly well acquainted with the condition of the country, in their reference to the Act 9 Geo. IV. c. 83, either that they did not think that the English Act was in force at all, or that they had determined that it should not thenceforth be in operation here, but that the only law in regard to the subject matter they were dealing with should be their own law. Therefore, *quacunque via*, I should say that the Act 5 Geo. IV. c. 83 could not be said, after that period, to be in force.

It has been urged that there was no implied repeal. It is very hard to formulate a rule which will apply to every case of implied

repeal. Each Act which is relied upon as a repeal must be con-   H. C. of A.
sidered to see whether its necessary implication is to abrogate the   1907.
former law.   See the expressions used in the judgment in *Michell*   MITCHELL
v. *Brown* (1), and the cases there cited.   The principle is stated   SCALES.
very well in an American decision which I cite because it expresses
my own view perhaps better than I could express it myself.   Isaacs J.

In *Norris* v. *Crocker* (2), Mr. Justice *Catron* said :—" As a
general rule it is not open to controversy, that where a new Statute
covers the whole subject matter of an old one, adds offences, and
prescribes different penalties for those enumerated in the old law,
that then the former Statute is repealed by implication ; as the
provisions of both cannot stand together."

Now the subject matter of the Ordinance of 6 Wm. IV. was the
three offences, idle and disorderly persons, rogues and vagabonds,
and incorrigible rogues.   That subject matter was divided into
three groups, and what are called vagrancy offences were arranged
categorically under the various groups. The Ordinance therefore
dealt with precisely the same matter as the Act of 5 Geo. IV., but
it added offences and omitted offences, and prescribed different
penalties for some of those under the old law. Therefore, looking
at the two Acts, I should say that the necessary implication is that
one was intended to stand in the place of the other.

In my opinion the inevitable conclusion is, looking at the
Act 6 Wm. IV. No. 6, it was intended as a substitute for the provisions which prevailed in England under the Act 5 Geo. IV.,
and, whether that Act of 5 Geo. IV. c. 83 was to be taken as
being in force here or not, the result is the same.   It seems to
me, therefore, that—without my entering upon the question' of
the original operation of the Act of 5 Geo. IV. in this State, as to
which I offer no opinion, and do not dissent from the observations that have fallen from my learned brothers—this appeal
must be dismissed.

Appeal dismissed with costs.

Solicitor, for the appellant, *The Crown Solicitor for New South
Wales.*

Solicitors, for the respondent, *Aitken & Aitken.*

C. A. W.

(1) 1 El. & E., 267.   (2) 13 Howard, 429, at p. 438.

[HIGH COURT OF AUSTRALIA.]

SPENCER . . . . APPELLANT

PLAINTIFF,

AND

THE COMMONWEALTH OF AUSTRALIA   RESPONDENT.

DEFENDANT,

ON APPEAL FROM A JUDGE EXERCISING THE ORIGINAL
JURISDICTION OF THE HIGH COURT.

H. C. OF A.
1906.

PERTH.

Nov. 13, 14,
15, 16, 22.

Higgins J.

1907.

PERTH,

Oct. 23, 24,
25, 29.

Griffith C.J.,
Barton and
Isaacs JJ.

Resumption of land—Valuation—Weight of evidence—Procedure—Pleading—Plea of Payment into Court—Admission of value pro tanto—Costs—Property for Public Purposes Acquisition Act 1901, (*No.* 13 *of* 1901), *secs.* 14, 15, 16, 17—*Rules of High Court, Order XVII., r.* 3; *Order XVIII., r.* 5.

Where, in an action for compensation under the *Property for Public Purposes Acquisition Act* 1901, issue has been joined upon a plea of payment into Court without denial of liability, the only issue is whether the amount paid in is sufficient, and the plaintiff is entitled to that sum in any event.

In assessing the value of land resumed under the Act, the basis of valuation should be the price that a willing purchaser would at the date in question have had to pay to a vendor not unwilling, but not anxious, to sell.

APPEAL from the judgment of *Higgins* J. exercising the original jurisdiction of the High Court.

The Commonwealth in 1905 resumed the plaintiff's land by proclamation under the *Property for Public Purposes Acquisition Act* 1901, secs. 6, 7, for the purpose of erecting a fort for the defence of Fremantle harbour, and offered £2,641 in compensation, with a formal notice of valuation under the Act. The plaintiff brought an action in the High Court under sec. 15 of the Act claiming £10,000 as compensation. The Common-

wealth paid into Court without denial of liability £3,000 with
interest, and issue was joined whether that sum was enough to
satisfy the plaintiff's claim.   At the trial the only contest was as
to the true value of the land, and it was not suggested by the
plaintiff that he was entitled to receive at the least the amount
paid into Court.   Counsel for the plaintiff admitted that the
Court had power to order the payment out of Court to the
defendant of any excess over the amount which might be awarded.

The action was heard before *Higgins* J.

Pilkington K.C. and *Stawell*, for the plaintiff.

Keenan A.G., and *Northmore*, for the defendant.

HIGGINS J. read the following judgment.   This is a claim for
£10,000 compensation for land taken by the Commonwealth for
defence purposes on the 22nd July 1905, under the *Property for
Public Purposes Acquisition Act* 1901.   The land is situated
at North Fremantle, about 10 miles from Perth, and contains
6 acres 1 rood and 2 perches.   There are no improvements,
except a picket fence on the boundary, and a rude building
to which no one attaches any money value.   The plaintiff is
entitled to receive an amount equivalent to the value of the
premises as on 1st January 1905.   The land consists of sand-
hummocks overlooking the Indian Ocean.   It has no grass; and
it is useless in its present condition for any purpose of production.
The owner is entitled to the benefit of any value attributable to
the view and to the breezes of the ocean; and he is entitled also
to any value which has been added to the site by the growth of
population, by the erection of buildings in the neighbourhood,
and by the enterprise of the Government and of the municipality.
Roads have been made around the land; there are railway lines
and conveniences within a short distance; and the harbour has
been made and deepened, and wharves constructed.   Under sec.
19 of the Act it is my duty not to have regard to any alteration
in value " arising from the proposal to carry out the public purpose for which the land is taken;" but I agree with Mr. *Pilkington* that I should take into account all the prospects and potenti-

H. C. OF A.
1907.

SPENCER
v.
THE COM-
MONWEALTH.

Nov. 22, 1906.

alities of the land as on 1st January 1905, including the fact that, by reason of the position of the land, the Defence Department might possibly become a competitor for it, and thus increase its value in competition (*Browne and Allan on Compensation*, 2nd ed., p. 718 ; *Ripley* v. *Great Northern Railway Co.* (1); *In re Gough and Aspatria, Silloth and District Joint Water Board* (2)).

Now, I have heard the evidence and the arguments ; and, with the assistance of counsel for the plaintiff and for the defendant, I have inspected the land. As a result, I entertain a very strong view that the claim for compensation is most excessive. Even the valuations made by the defendant's valuers are liberal. The truth is that, in such cases as this generally, no land agent or valuer has any tangible interest in straining the value unduly downwards, whereas most have a tangible interest in the opposite direction. I do not at all imply, however, that the gentlemen who have given evidence have not given their opinion honestly, on *data* which they frankly state. Yet in this case I am face to face with valuations varying so widely as £8,400 and £2,066. The plaintiff's witnesses assume that the Clifton Street frontage is required for factory or storage purposes, and that the Railway Commissioner will be able and willing to run a siding across Clifton Street into the buildings. As one of the witnesses said to me, his valuation of this frontage—£5,296 or £8 per foot—is the price which a manufacturer would give if *he needed this part of the land*; and another admitted that there is no advantage in having the railway so near unless one can get the private siding. While desiring to give ample weight to the possibilities of this land, I refuse to treat these contingencies as if they were certainties. I believe the evidence of the defendant's witnesses that there is not, and was not on 1st January 1905, any demand for land for factory or storage purposes, and that, if such a demand should arise, there is other land available. I accept the evidence also of those who state that the land is not suitable for villa residences, but only for workingmen's dwellings. I do not think anything is to be gained by an exhaustive statement of the evidence submitted, or of the relative qualifications of the experts. Some of the transactions deposed to with regard to lands in the

(1) L.R. 10 Ch., 435.   (2) (1903) 1 K.B., 574.

H. C. of A.
1907.

SPENCER
v.
THE COM-
MONWEALTH.

Higgins J.

vicinity I cannot regard as being of much use in enabling me to ascertain the fair value of this land. Indeed, there are so many factors which may operate as an inducement to any particular dealing in land, that it is unsafe for the Court, which cannot have full knowledge of all the circumstances, to rest its decision on any one transaction. Some of the land in John Street opposite this land was sold with difficulty at various times, chiefly from 1896 to 1902, when land values were higher than on 1st January 1905, at prices averaging about £45 per lot, and on terms, without interest. Some of the lots have not yet been sold, and are for sale at the best terms obtainable. Each lot has 33 feet frontage with a right of way at the rear. This would mean about £1 6s. 8d. per foot frontage. These frontages are admitted by the plaintiff's witnesses to be of the same value as the plaintiff's land facing John Street, except that the plaintiff's frontages would have greater depth; and yet the plaintiff's witnesses claim £3 per foot for the plaintiff's frontages to John Street. There are other standards of comparison of more or less weight. In 1904 the half interest of the late Mr. George Leake in similar land, of nearly the same area (over 6 acres), but not quite so near the wharves, was sold to the owner of the other half interest for £937 10s. This would mean about £1,875 for over six acres, even if we assume that the owner of the other half interest would not be willing to give more than an ordinary purchaser. Moreover, in December 1901, before the great fall in values in Fremantle, the Shell Oil Company bought three sections (about 5 acres) at the rate of £480 per acre, and these sections Mr. Learmonth regards as being very much more valuable than the plaintiff's land. Personally I should have felt much doubt, if I were to rely on my own judgment, as to the possibility of getting even the prices which the defendant's witnesses mention. But I have to remember that the land available for sites in and around Perth and Fremantle is all, or nearly all, of a sandy character, and I am not justified in refusing to give credence to expert witnesses who say that they could find purchasers as stated. If it is not invidious to make a selection among competent and honourable witnesses, I should prefer to rely on the opinion of Mr. Learmonth, and he is the witness who fixes the value at the lowest—£2,066 or £330 per acre.

H. C. of A.
1907.

Spencer
v.
The Com-
monwealth.

Higgins J.

There is no claim made by the plaintiff for damage under secs.
13, 14, 19 in addition to the value of the land taken. But the
plaintiff's counsel urge that it is incumbent on the Court to allow
10 per cent. more than the true value in consideration of the
land being compulsorily taken; and I have been referred to
certain Victorian cases: *Leslie* v. *Board of Land and Works*(1);
and *In re Wildman*; *Ex parte Lilydale and Warburton Railway Construction Trust* (2) in support of this contention. I am
unable to see how a consideration of this kind enters into the
question of value, at all events, in the case of land held merely as
a speculation, land which the owner does not want for its own
sake, land as to which he is not an additional competitor; and it
is only on the question of value, not of damage, that the point is
pressed. Besides, even if it is a grievance to suffer compulsion,
it must be remembered that the owner is saved the expense of
surveying and levelling, and preparing the land for sale, of
advertising, of agent's commission, &c. I do not quite appreciate
some of the expressions used by the learned Judges in the cases
cited. But, without taking it upon me either to condemn or to
endorse these expressions, it is enough for me to say that there
is phraseology used in the Victorian Acts referred to in *Leslie's
Case* (1) which are not found in the Federal Act, and that the
Federal Act seems to be sufficiently clear and .definite as to my
present duty. Having regard to all the potentialities of the site,
and to all the other circumstances, I think that I am giving to
the plaintiff all that he can justly claim if I determine the amount
of compensation at £2,250. This amount is less than that offered
to him—£2,640 19s. 10d. on 18th December, 1905; and it is still
less than the amount paid into Court (including interest) £3,086
1s. 2d. I determine the amount of compensation at £2,250 and
direct judgment to be entered accordingly. I order that the
money in Court be paid out to the defendant after the payment
to the plaintiff of the £2,250 with interest thereon as prescribed
by sec. 20. No costs. I have had great doubt whether I should
not make the plaintiff pay all the costs; but, inasmuch as the
plaintiff was probably misled by the amount of possible purchase

(1) 2 V.L.R. (L.), 21.   (2) 27 V.L.R., 43; 22 A.L.T., 199.

money, £6,400, which appeared provisionally in the papers presented to Parliament by the Federal Treasurer, I think it a fair
thing, on the whole, to let each party abide his own costs.
Liberty to apply.

This order, in so far as it involves the repayment to the defendant of the difference between the amount awarded and· the
amount paid into Court, seems to be justified on the authority of
Gray v. *Bartholomew* (1), and Mr. *Pilkington*, on behalf of the
plaintiff, has intimated that he does not dispute my power to
order the repayment.

H. C. of A.
1907.

SPENCER
v.
THE COM-
MONWEALTH.

Higgins J.

The plaintiff moved the High Court for a new trial on the
ground that the finding as to value was against evidence and the
weight of evidence.

Pilkington K.C. and *Stawell*, for the appellant.　Upon the
evidence that was given the value assessed was too small.　*Higgins*
J. considered all the witnesses fair and honest and equally
credible; yet out of the ten expert witnesses, five on each side,
who testified as to the value, he chose the evidence of the lowest
valuator on the Commonwealth side, contrary to the opinion of
nine others equally competent and credible.　Also the Public
Works Department of Western Australia had made an independent
valuation, which the Commonwealth used in its Estimates in
1904, assessing this land at £6,400.

It is admitted that, by sec. 16, the Judge is not to be bound in
any way by the amount of the valuation notified to the claimant,
which was £2,641 ; and, by sec. 19, the land cannot gain any
value arising from the proposal to carry out the public purposes
for which the land was taken.　But the Act does not refer in any
way to payment of money into Court, which was an admission of
liability to the extent of the money paid in : *Hennell* v. *Davies*
(2); *Berdan* v. *Greenwood* (3); *Dunn* v. *Devon and Exeter Constitutional Newspaper Co.* (4); *Langridge* v. *Campbell* (5);
Dumbleton v. *Williams, Torrey & Field Ltd.* (6); *Hobson* v.

(1) (1895) 1 Q.B., 209.　　　(4) (1895) 1 Q.B., 211n.
(2) (1893) 1 Q.B., 367.　　　(5) 2 Ex. D., 281.
(3) 3 Ex. D., 251.　　　　　(6) 76 L.T., 81.

H. C. of A. *Stoneham* (1); *Chitty's Archbold*, 12th ed., p. 1366; *Elliott* v.
1907.   *Callow* (2). The plaintiff is not to blame for not taking that
Spencer   money out of Court, because, under Order XVIII., r. 5, it must
v.   be taken in satisfaction of the whole claim. If there was juris-
The Com-
monwealth. diction to award plaintiff a less amount than was paid into Court,
            the balance could be paid out to defendant: *Gray* v. *Bartholo-
            mew* (3); but there was not such jurisdiction.

The assessment of the value was arrived at on a false basis. It
was treated as though at the time of the resumption the land must
necessarily be realized as if at a forced sale, and in the shape of
a subdivision into small workingmen's allotments. The weight
of the evidence was that the most advantageous sale would be as
a factory site; the Judge was not entitled to follow his own
opinion: *London General Omnibus Co.* v. *Lavell* (4). The
awarded value being against the evidence, it is open to the Court
to fix the value. The proper basis for a valuation is, what would
a willing purchaser be reasonably expected to have to pay to an
owner willing, but not anxious, to sell; the plaintiff is not bound
to produce immediately a willing purchaser; he is entitled to
wait a reasonable time for a purchaser for that purpose for which
the land can reasonably be expected to have most value: *In re
Ossalinsky (Countess) and Mayor &c. of Manchester* (5); *In
re Gough and Aspatria, Silloth and District Water Board* (6);
Leslie v. *Board of Land and Works* (7); *In re Wildman; Ex
parte Lilydale and Warburton Railway Construction Trust* (8);
Russell v. *Minister of Lands* (9); *Housing of Working Classes
Act* 1890 (Eng.), (53 & 54 Vict. c. 70), sec. 21.

Keenan A.G. and *Northmore*, for the respondent. There was
power to award less than the amount paid in. This being a
resumption case, there could not be any denial of liability in the
plea, unless the Commonwealth had desired to deny the plaintiff's
title to the land. The money paid in was therefore not an
admission of liability to that extent, but a deposit of so much to

(1) 13 V.L.R., 738.   sation, 2nd ed., App. p. 659, at p. 622.
(2) 2 Salk., 597.   (6) (1903) 1 K.B., 574.
(3) (1895) 1 Q.B., 209.   (7) 2 V.L.R. (L.), 21.
(4) (1901) 1 Ch., 135.   (8) 27 V.L.R., 43; 22 A.L.T., 199.
(5) Browne and Allan on Compen-   (9) 17 N.Z.L.R., 241, 780.

be available against whatever the Court might award; the balance to be refunded, on the authority of *Gray* v. *Bartholomew* (1). The High Court Rule, Order XVIII., r. 1, materially differs from English Rule, Order XXII., r. 1, in containing the additional words "unless otherwise stated." The question for the Judge was not the bare issue whether the money paid into Court was enough; sec. 16 of the Act requires him to find what damage the plaintiff has suffered. Once the plaintiff has declined to take out the money paid into Court, but on the contrary has pleaded an issue which goes to trial, he has no indefeasible title to the money. Payment into Court is only in continuation of the notification of valuation to the plaintiff: secs. 13, 15; and under sec. 17 the Judge is empowered to award less than that amount. The pleadings cannot affect the procedure prescribed by the Act, which affords the sole remedy between the parties; and sec. 16 binds the Judge to ignore any admissions as to value made in the pleadings and to assess the true value.

With regard to finding the value of the land, the Court is bound to consider only reasonably immediate probabilities and potentialities, legitimate expectations, not barely possible contingencies. There was no evidence that there was any reasonable prospect of the land being required for factory and storage sites; the only positive evidence given was the other way, that the land was saleable only as workingmen's lots; a buyer would considerably abate his offer if buying to realize on less proximate probabilities of demand for other special purposes. Defendant's witnesses valued the land properly, at the price that ordinary prudent buyers would give, not on the basis of a forced sale, but in an open bargain with a prudent seller. The fact that the land was specially adapted for a fort might introduce the Commonwealth Government as an additional competitor, but not at fancy prices. The discretion of the Judge in these resumption cases, as in the analogous awards in salvage cases, should not be disturbed: *The " Alice "* (2). The pleadings did not raise the issue whether the money paid in was enough to satisfy the plaintiff's claim, but really whether it was not more than enough, *i.e.*, whether

(1) (1895) 1 Q.B., 209.   (2) 5 Moo. P.C.C. N.S., 300, at p. 303.

plaintiff's claim was excessive : *Hennell* v. *Davies* (1) ; *Dumbleton* v. *Williams, Torrey & Field Ltd.* (2). In *Gray* v. *Bartholomew* (3) the order was made in that way because, under Order XXII., r. 5, the plaintiff was entitled to the whole money paid in, " unless the Court otherwise orders," which words are not in the High Court Rules ; that judgment did not decide the effect of a plea of payment in on the rights of a plaintiff.

[ISAACS J.—*Langridge* v. *Campbell* (4) is very plain that payment in irrevocably admits that so much is due, and leaves only one issue to decide, whether a greater, not a less, amount is owing.]

The whole case was conducted upon a different understanding, and defendant should therefore have leave to amend in order to raise the true issue requisite under the Act.

[GRIFFITH C.J.—Apparently no direct rule for payment out was put in the High Court Rules because of the old rule at law that money once paid in was thenceforward the plaintiff's property. It would prejudice the plaintiff, after conducting his case on that basis, to allow such an amendment.]

If the plaintiff is declared entitled to the amount paid in, and no more, the defendant is entitled to costs since the date of payment in.

Pilkington in reply. There is no doubt that plaintiff's land was " fit " for industrial purposes ; the only element of futurity in its value was the finding of an actual purchaser ; and plaintiff was not bound to produce him. The special " adaptability " spoken of in *In re Ossalinsky (Countess) and Mayor of Manchester* (5), referred to peculiar purposes such as quarry and reservoir sites, not to ordinary purposes such as industrial sites. The plaintiff is entitled to have the Judge's misdirection of himself corrected, so that the land may be valued at its present value having regard to the reasonable probabilities of sale at the most advantageous price : *Montgomerie* v *Wallace-James* (6).

The plaintiff should get all the costs if he gets the full amount

(1) (1893) 1 Q.B., 267.
(2) 76 L.T., 81.
(3) (1895) 1 Q.B., 209.
(4) 2 Ex. D., 281.

(5) Browne and Allan on Compensation, 2nd ed., App., p. 659.
(6) (1904) A.C., 73.

paid into Court: sec. 17 of the Act; or, at any rate, should not have to pay costs.

Cur. adv. vult.

H. C. of A.
1907.

SPENCER
v.
THE COM-
MONWEALTH.

Oct. 29, 1907.

The following judgments were read :—

GRIFFITH C J. This is an action brought under the provisions of the *Property for Public Purposes Acquisition Act* 1901 (No. 13 of 1901) to recover compensation for land taken by the defendant for public purposes. The land was in fact taken as a site for a fort. By sec. 6 of that Act land might be acquired by the publication of a notice in the *Gazette*. Persons claiming compensation in respect of any land so acquired were within a prescribed time to serve a notice on the Minister of the Department concerned and the Attorney-General (sec. 13). If a *primâ facie* case for compensation was disclosed, the Minister was required to cause a valuation to be made of the land, and to inform the claimant of the amount of the valuation (sec. 14 (2)). If the claimant and the Minister did not agree as to the amount, the claimant might institute proceedings in the High Court in the form of an action for compensation against the Commonwealth (sec. 15), which was to be tried by a single Justice without a jury (sec. 16). In determining the amount of compensation the Justice was not to be bound by the amount of the valuation notified to the claimant (*Ib.*). If judgment were given for a sum equal to or less than the amount of the valuation notified to the claimant, he was to pay the costs of the action unless the Justice otherwise ordered, but, if the judgment were for a sum one third less than that amount, the claimant was to pay the costs in any event (sec. 17). Either party might move for a new trial or to set aside the finding in accordance with the practice of the High Court (*Ib.*). The Act did not contain any other special provisions as to procedure. In my opinion the direction that the proceedings were to be by action incorporated the general practice of the Court relating to actions, so far as no other practice is substituted.

The plaintiff by his statement of claim, after setting out the necessary facts showing his title to sue, claimed £10,000. The defendants' defence was in the following words :—" The defend-

H. C. of A.
1907.

SPENCER
v.
THE COM-
MONWEALTH.

Griffith C.J.

ants bring into Court the sum of £3,086 1s. 2d. and say that it is enough to satisfy the plaintiff's claim." Accompanying particulars showed that that sum was made up of £3,000 for the value of the land and £86 1s. 2d. for interest at 3% from the date of acquisition to the date of payment, which was the rate prescribed by sec. 20 of the Act.   The plaintiff simply joined issue.

Upon these pleadings the action was set down for trial before *Higgins* J., who, after hearing much conflicting evidence, found that the value of the land at the relevant date (1st January 1905) was £2,250 only.   He thereupon ordered that that sum with interest at the rate prescribed by the Statute should be paid out to the plaintiff, and that the residue should be paid to the defendant, and directed that judgment should be entered without costs.   From this judgment the plaintiff appeals.

Two distinct questions are raised upon the appeal : (1) whether the plaintiff is entitled in any event to the whole of the money paid into Court, and (2) whether the learned Judge was wrong in assessing the value of the land at a sum not exceeding £3,000. The first question depends upon the effect of the Rules of Court; the second depends partly upon the principles to be applied in estimating the value of the land, and partly upon the evidence in the case.

I have already pointed out that the ordinary practice of the Court is applicable to the action.   By Order XVIII., Rule 1, a defendant in an action to recover a debt or damages may before or at the time of delivering his defence (or later by leave of the Court or a Justice) pay into Court a sum of money by way of satisfaction, "which shall, unless otherwise stated, be taken to admit the cause of action in respect of which the payment is made."   Or he may pay money into Court with respect to any cause of action with a defence denying liability, in which case the money is subject to the specific provisions contained in Rule 6, one of which is that, if the plaintiff does not accept it in satisfaction, it remains in Court until the determination of the action, and is subject to the orders of the Court.   If the defendant succeeds in the action the whole amount is to be repaid to him, and if the plaintiff recovers less than the amount paid in the balance is to be repaid to the defendant.

H. C. of A.
1907.

SPENCER
v.
THE COM-
MONWEALTH.

Griffith C.J.

Rule 5 provides that when money is paid into Court the plaintiff may before joining issue accept it in satisfaction, in which case he may tax his costs up to that date, and if they are not paid within four days may sign judgment for them. The Rules do not contain any express direction as to the payment out to the plaintiff of money paid into Court either with or without denial of liability, but under Order XVII., Rule 3, which provides that when admissions of fact are made on the pleadings any party may at any stage of the cause apply to the Court or a Justice for such judgment or order as upon the admissions he is entitled to, it is clear that the plaintiff is entitled to ask for payment out to him at any time. If a formal order is necessary it is little more than formal, although, no doubt, the Court or a Justice might allow a defendant in a proper case to amend his defence or withdraw his notice of payment, but in the absence of such amendment I think that the plaintiff's right to the money paid into Court without denial of the cause of action is absolute, whatever may be the result of the action. This is in accordance with the view that was always accepted as to the effect of payment into Court before the statutory provisions of the Common Law Procedure Acts (see *Archbold's Practice*, ed. 1866, vol. 2, p. 1366).

In the present case the defence contained nothing to limit the effect of the payment into Court. It follows that the plaintiff's cause of action in respect of which the payment was made was admitted. No case was cited to us in which it has been expressly decided that the admission involved in a plea of payment into Court is an admission of liability to the full amount paid in, but in all the cases cited this seems to have been taken for granted. In any view the plaintiff became entitled to receive the money as soon as it was paid in, and nothing has since occurred to disentitle him to it, unless the finding of the learned Judge has that effect. The only issue for trial raised by the joinder of issue was whether the sum paid into Court was or was not enough to satisfy the plaintiff's claim. It was, therefore, not material to consider whether it was more than enough. If it was not enough, the plaintiff would be entitled to damages *ultra*, if it was, he was entitled to no more than he already had. It was suggested that the direction that the Justice should not be bound by the

H. C. of A.
1907.

SPENCER
v.
THE COM-
MONWEALTH.

Griffith C.J.

valuation notified to the claimant implies that he should not be bound by an admission on the record, but I am unable to accept this suggestion. I am, therefore, of opinion that the plaintiff is entitled to recover at least the amount paid into Court. In an ordinary case, if a plaintiff does not recover more than the sum paid into Court, judgment is given for the defendant, but the Statute appears to contemplate that there must be a formal judgment for the plaintiff in every case. I think, therefore, that the plaintiff is entitled to judgment for the sum paid into Court in any event.

I proceed to consider whether he is entitled to anything more. The evidence, as I have said, was conflicting, but the divergence was not so much with regard to facts as with regard to the point of view from which the question of value was regarded.

The land is situated at North Fremantle, within 100 yards of the ocean, and at a very short distance from the harbour. The area is more than six acres, and there is a railway line separated from it only by a road. Fremantle is the principal port of the State of Western Australia, and some persons naturally entertain a high opinion of its future prospects. The plaintiff's witnesses thought that the land in question, by reason of its situation, its height, and its exceptionally large area amongst a number of small subdivisions, had a prospective value as a site for a factory or some other enterprise requiring a considerable space. It was also one of a very small number of suitable sites for a fort. The defendants' witnesses on the other hand thought that the land was not fit for anything except subdivision into small allotments for workmen's dwellings, of which there were several in the immediate neighbourhood, and they estimated the value on the basis of the sum which they thought could have been realized for it in January 1905, if so subdivided. The learned Justice, in effect, accepted the view of the defendants' witnesses, or rather of those of them who put the lowest valuation on the land, and, if I rightly understand his judgment, applied his mind to the question of what the plaintiff could have realized by a sale of the land in January 1905, if he had then sold it.

It has often been pointed out that, when a cause has been heard by a Judge on oral evidence, a Court of Appeal is very

reluctant to differ from him on a question of fact, especially when
there is a conflict of evidence. And the same considerations
apply whether the conflict is as to the actual facts, or as to a
matter of opinion as to which it is material to weigh the relative
values of the opinions of different witnesses. So far, therefore,
as *Higgins* J. founded his judgment on the weight to be given to
the opinion of the different witnesses as to relevant facts, I am
not prepared to differ from him. I therefore accept the conclusion (though I doubt whether I should have arrived at it
myself) that, if the land had been cut up and sold in small allotments in January 1905, it would not have realized more than
£2,250. I will assume also that he thought that at that date it
would have realized more if sold in that mode than in any other.
But I do not think that these facts conclude the question of value,
although they are very relevant to the question.

In the case of chattels it is often, though not always, easy to
ascertain the value. In order that any article may have an
exchange value, there must be presupposed a person willing to
give the article in exchange for money and another willing to
give money in exchange for the article. When there is a large
or considerable number of articles of the same kind which are
the subject of daily or frequent sale and purchase, the value of
the articles is taken to be their current price. Thus, in the *Sale
of Goods Act*, the measure of damages for wrongful refusal to
deliver goods is to be ascertained with reference to " the market
or current price of the goods." The foundation of this doctrine
is that a man desiring to sell such articles can readily find a
purchaser at a price which is fairly certain, and conversely that
a man desiring to buy can find a seller at about the same price.
But these considerations are not necessarily equally applicable to
land. There is, no doubt, much land in many places the value of
which per acre is as definitely fixed as the price of wheat or
sugar. But in the case of a new port, in a new State, where the
area of land is limited, and each piece differs in many of its
characteristics from the rest, it is impossible to apply any such
rule. Bearing in mind that value implies the existence of a
willing buyer as well as of a willing seller, some modification of
the rule must be made in order to make it applicable to the case

H. C. of A.
1907.

SPENCER
v.
THE COM-
MONWEALTH.

Griffith C.J.

H. C. of A.
1907.

SPENCER
v.
THE COM-
MONWEALTH.

Griffith C.J.

of a piece of land which has any unique value. It may be that the land is fit for many purposes, and will in all probability be soon required for some of them, but there may be no one actually willing at the moment to buy it at any price. Still it does not follow that the land has no value. In my judgment the test of value of land is to be determined, not by inquiring what price a man desiring to sell could actually have obtained for it on a given day, *i.e.*, whether there was in fact on that day a willing buyer, but by inquiring " What would a man desiring to buy the land have had to pay for it on that day to a vendor willing to sell it for a fair price but not desirous to sell ? " It is, no doubt, very difficult to answer such a question, and any answer must be to some extent conjectural. The necessary mental process is to put yourself as far as possible in the position of persons conversant with the subject at the relevant time, and from that point of view to ascertain what, according to the then current opinion of land values, a purchaser would have had to offer for the land to induce such a willing vendor to sell it, or, in other words, to inquire at what point a desirous purchaser and a not unwilling vendor would come together. This is not, as I understand the evidence and the decision of the learned Justice, the test which was applied by him or by the witnesses upon whose testimony he relied. On this ground I think that his assessment of the value is open to be reviewed.

But, applying what I conceive to be the true test, I am unable to come to the conclusion upon the whole evidence that the plaintiff has satisfied the onus, which is upon him, of showing that such an owner would not in January 1905 have accepted an offer of £3,000 cash, although I am not prepared to say that he would have accepted a smaller sum. In coming to this conclusion I have given much weight to the opinion of the learned Justice, as I understand it, as to the value of the testimony of the respective witnesses so far as regards their accuracy and the soundness of the basis of their opinion. I am, therefore, of opinion that on this ground, as well as on that already dealt with, the plaintiff was entitled to recover £3,000. But the result, so far as regards the issue for trial, is the same, namely, that the sum paid into Court was enough to satisfy the plaintiff's claim.

H. C. OF A.
1907.

SPENCER
v.
THE COM-
MONWEALTH.

Griffith C.J.

If the action had been triable, and tried, with a jury, the result would have been that the plaintiff would have had to pay the costs of the issue on which he failed. And I do not see any sufficient reason for departing from this rule in the present case. *Higgins* J., in the exercise of his discretion under sec. 17 of the Act, relieved the plaintiff from payment of costs although he recovered less than the amount of the valuation, and the Court could not review that exercise of discretion if it applied to the case as now determined. But I do not think that he applied his mind at all to the question of costs on the basis that the plaintiff was entitled to the £3,000 paid into Court. We must, therefore, exercise our own discretion, which I think will be best done by following the ordinary rule.

Counsel for the defendant asked for leave to amend the defence by stating that the liability for the full sum paid in was not admitted. Assuming that such an amendment could be made, it would, in the view which I take of the facts, be prejudicial and not beneficial to the defendant, for it would entail payment by it of the costs of the action. But, even if I took a different view of the facts, I do not think that any sufficient ground was shown for allowing so unusual an amendment.

The judgment appealed from should therefore be varied by directing judgment for plaintiff for £3,081 1s. 2d., with costs up to the time of payment into Court. The plaintiff must pay the defendant's costs of action after payment. The respondent should pay the costs of this appeal.

BARTON J. The amount of the valuation being £2,640 19s. 10d., and the defendant having paid £3,000 into Court without any denial of liability, the first question is whether the plaintiff is not entitled to have at least the whole £3,000, and I think he is. Sec. 17 of the *Property for Public Purposes Acquisition Act* 1901 provides that in determining the amount of compensation the Justice who tries the case shall not be bound by the amount of the valuation notified to the claimant. But I do not see how the defendant can have the benefit of that section after paying into Court, irrespectively of the valuation, a sum exceeding it in

H. C. of A.
1907.

SPENCER
v.
THE COM-
MONWEALTH.

Barton J.

amount and tendering issue on the bare averment that the sum
so paid in was enough. The plaintiff was entitled to join issue on
the plea as filed, and to prove, if he could, that £3,000 was not
enough, and thus the contest invoked by the defendant was
solely on the sufficiency of that sum. The plea deliberately
abandoned the valuation as the subject of contest, and by offering
£3,000 without denying liability, disabled the defendant, in my
opinion, from contending that a less sum should be assessed as
compensation. Any contention that a less sum was enough
became irrelevant to the issue raised by the defendant, by whose
own pleading the sole question was, £3,000, or how much more?
It is true that the Statute does not expressly authorize the plea of
payment into Court, but it does not exclude it even by implication (although in some circumstances it may be rather an
imprudent plea to an action under the Statute). The authority
given to the claimant by sec. 15 to proceed for compensation refers
only to an action, and if an action is brought, it is reasonable to
conclude that the practice and procedure in ordinary actions
are to be applied as far as may be. Now as to their application.
In the first place, keeping in mind that the payment into Court
was unaccompanied with any denial of liability, it must be taken
to admit the plaintiff's cause of action to the extent of £3,000,
and the interest, £86 1s. 2d., follows as of course under sec. 20 of
the Act: *Hennell* v. *Davies* (1). The Chief Justice has made a
close analysis of the Rules under Order XVIII. which are
relevant to this case, and I cannot add to that; further, I think
it impossible to resist the construction of Order XXVII., Rule 3,
which lays it open to a plaintiff to treat such an admission of fact
as this plea as the foundation for an application, at any stage of
the cause, to the Court or a Justice, for the payment out to him
of the amends tendered with the plea. From that construction
it follows, not only that the refusal of such an order is scarcely
to be thought of, but also that the right to it is not dependent on
the result of the action. The comprehensive Rule in question, so
construed by its framers, is probably the reason why it has not
been thought necessary to provide specially for payment out of
Court, as in England is done by Order XXII., r. 5. I am, there-

(1) (1893) 1 Q.B., 367.

H. C. OF A.
1907.

SPENCER
v.
THE COM-
MONWEALTH.

Barton J.

fore, of opinion that the plaintiff was and is entitled to the whole of the money paid into Court.

The remaining question is whether the plaintiff has shown a right to compensation exceeding the sum paid in. For it is on him to show it, and he undertook to do so. As in most cases of the kind, the witnesses, called as experts in land values, presented a view for each side difficult to reconcile with that for the other. The differences were upon a matter in which the worth of opinion, and not the degree of truthfulness, was in question. Still, the matter was one of credibility in that sense, and the conflict was strong. In such a case a Judge who sees and hears the witnesses has a distinct advantage over others who are asked to review his decision. Therefore I am very loath to attempt such a process in this case, and can only do so on the ground of necessity. But, after giving my best attention to the judgment of *Higgins* J., I am unable to find that he has applied certain principles which, as it appears to me, should be applied to a question of this kind. I am unable to say that the bare market value of the land for workingmen's residences on a particular day would be a value constituting a real compensation for this taking. The Court must take into consideration all the circumstances, and, to quote the admirable judgment of the Supreme Court of New Zealand in *Russell* v. *The Minister of Lands* (1), must "see what sum of money will place the dispossessed man in a position as nearly similar as possible to that he was in before." His loss is to be tested by the value of the thing to him : *Stebbing* v. *Metropolitan Board of Works* (2), and the loss he has sustained is not necessarily to be gauged by what the land would realize if peremptorily brought into the market on a day named. True, it is "value" which is to be assessed, but the value to the loser of land compulsorily taken is not necessarily the mere saleable value. See *Russell* v. *The Minister of Lands* (No. 2), (3). I make these observations without losing sight of the fact that, in arriving at the market or saleable value of £2,250 for workingmen's cottage sites, which is the only value that I think he found, *Higgins* J. was perfectly entitled to follow, as he did, that one of

(1) 17 N.Z.L.R., 241, at p. 253. *burn* C.J.
(2) 40 L.J.Q.B., 1, at p. 5, *per Cock-* (3) 17 N.Z.L.R., 780.

H. C. of A.
1907.

SPENCER
v.
THE COM-
MONWEALTH.

Barton J.

the defendants' witnesses who gave the lowest estimate of market value, and I should not be at all disposed to disturb his conclusion on that element of the case, as an element.

The plaintiff's witnesses attributed considerable value to this land, or a great part of it, as a site for a factory—one of them said a freezing-house. One cannot shut one's eyes to the fact of the importance of Fremantle as a port, or refuse to see that Australian ports generally are growing in trade and consequence. It may be that commerce and manufactures will for years be concentrated on the part of the port south of the river, but probably that will in a reasonable time cease to be the case with this the chief port of this State. A man is perfectly entitled, so long as he escapes government resumptions, to hold his land, in view of such progress as he sees going on, in the hope and belief that it will realize its best return to him before many years as a site for some manufacture or the like. And its value to him in that regard, though often called prospective, may even be a very present one if he exercises due care and does not exhibit too great anxiety to sell. The plaintiff's witnesses have attributed such a value to the land, and though I do not doubt that they have been sanguine as to amounts, I still think that something should have been allowed the plaintiff in this regard, that is, that it was a factor of the value which *Higgins* J. left out of consideration, but which the plaintiff was entitled to have estimated : See *In re Gough and Aspatria, Silloth and District Joint Water Board* (1), and *In re Ossalinsky (Countess) and Mayor &c. of Manchester* (2). All "reasonably fair contingencies," as *Grove* J. put it in that case, are to be considered ; and then he uses these words :—" What it would sell to a willing purchaser for in consequence of its having these additional advantages."

Of course, the price for which land would sell to a willing purchaser is there intended by *Grove* J. to be the test, whether there are special advantages or contingencies to be valued or not. And I should say, in view of the many authorities cited and upon the sense of the matter, that a claimant is entitled to have for his land what it is worth to a man of ordinary prudence and fore-

(1) (1903) 1 K.B., 574.
(2) *Browne and Allan on Compensation*, 2nd ed., App. p. 659, at p. 661.

H. C. of A.
1907.

SPENCER
v.
THE COM-
MONWEALTH.

Barton J.

sight, not holding his land for merely speculative purposes, nor, on the other hand, anxious to sell for any compelling or private reason, but willing to sell as a business man would be to another such person, both of them alike uninfluenced by any consideration of sentiment or need.

But while I think with great respect that His Honor did not take into consideration all the factors that he might have done, or apply principles as broad as such a case required, I am still not satisfied that the plaintiff has proved himself entitled to more than the £3,000 paid into Court. As it is now for this Court to name the sum which will really compensate the plaintiff, I am bound to say that, taking all things into consideration, I think the fair value of this land to such a vendor as I have described exceeded on 1st January 1905 (sec. 19), the sum found by the learned Justice, but that it did not exceed the sum of £3,000 paid into Court. Ordinarily that conclusion would mean a verdict for the defendant, but in view of secs. 17 to 20 of the Act I agree with the Chief Justice that the proper form of judgment is for the plaintiff for £3,086 1s. 2d., being the whole amount, including interest, paid into Court.

As this is a finding that the sum paid in was enough, it is a result which on an ordinary trial by jury would involve the payment of the costs by the plaintiff from the time of payment in. Though *Higgins* J. ordered the sum of only £2,250 to be paid out to the plaintiff, he did not order him to pay costs. But, as we have been unable to agree with his judgment, we cannot say how he would have treated the costs after deciding the compensation on the principles now applied, and as we cannot possibly say how he would then have exercised his discretion, we must use our own. For my part I cannot see any reason why, awarding the plaintiff the £3,086 in Court, we should exempt him from the normal consequence of such a result in costs; while the costs up to payment into Court should be paid by the defendant. I think the respondent should pay the costs of the appeal, as the appellant has succeeded in having the amount awarded to him increased by £750.

As to the question of amendment, I do not see how we could

H. C. of A. possibly allow so radical an alteration in these pleadings at such a
1907.   stage.

SPENCER
v.   ISAACS J.   I agree with the order proposed by the learned Chief
THE COM- Justice.   The only issue raised by the pleadings was whether
MONWEALTH.
          the sum of £3,086 1s. 2d. brought into Court without any denial
Isaacs J. of liability was enough to satisfy the plaintiff's claim. His
          claim for compensation was solely for the value of the land itself,
          and did not include any claim for damage otherwise. The
          particulars of the sum paid into Court showed that the money
          was in respect of the identical claim made, and consisted of an
          amount representing the valuation of the land together with
          interest at 3% from the date of acquisition of the land until the
          date of payment into Court.

          The amount found by the learned primary Justice as the true
          value of the land was £2,250, and His Honor directed that judg-
          ment should be entered for that sum.

          The first question is, whether the plaintiff, notwithstanding the
          finding that £2,250 was the actual value, is entitled to judgment
          for the amount of £3,086 1s. 2d. paid into Court.

          Section 15 of the *Property for Public Purposes Acquisition
          Act* 1901, which was in force when this action was tried and
          until July 1st 1907, prescribed that, in the absence of an agreement
          as to the amount of compensation, proceedings might be instituted
          in the High Court in the form of an action for compensation.
          This brings into application the principle enunciated by *James
          L.J.* in *Dale's Case* (1). " It was strongly urged that this was a new
          jurisdiction and a new procedure. According to my view of the
          case, that is not material, because if a new jurisdiction is given
          to an existing Court—that is to say, a jurisdiction to deal with
          some new matters in a different mode and with a different pro-
          cedure—if that jurisdiction be so given to a well-known Court,
          with well-known modes of procedure, with well-known modes of
          enforcing its orders, it must, unless the contrary be expressed
          or plainly implied, be given to that Court to be exercised *according*
          to its general inherent powers of dealing with the matters which
          are within its cognizance."

                        (1) 6 Q.B.D., 376, at p. 450.

H. C. of A.
1907.

SPENCER
v.
THE COM-
MONWEALTH.

Isaacs J.

Subject, therefore, to any special provision contained in the Act itself, the ordinary rules and practice of the Court apply; and in the absence of any express rules or practice governing the procedure, the Court must *pro hac vice* act on its own views of justice and convenience. There is nothing in the Act which in any degree interferes with the constant rule that the Court tries the issues raised, and does not treat as still in contention any matters admitted between the parties on the pleadings as they stand.

What then is the effect to be attributed to the payment of £3,086 1s. 2d. into Court upon the only item of claim made by the plaintiff? Clearly, that the defendant has expressly admitted the value of the land to be at all events £3,000, and that so much in any event ought to be paid to the plaintiff.

Money paid in on a plea not denying liability, so long as the pleading so stands, is, as it always has been, a formal admission that the sum paid in is due.

In the words of Lord *Denman* C.J. in *Steavenson* v. *Berwick Corporation* (1), the defendants say "We do not choose to dispute so much of the demand." The cases are uniform as to this.

Whether in any particular case such a payment has any further effect may depend on the form of the action and of the payment itself. But money paid in simply and without denial of liability is, in the absence of permitted amendment, the money of the plaintiff if he chooses to take it; but if he determines to proceed for more, then he runs the risk of the money, which is his money, being dealt with by the Court so as to protect the defendant from some possible injustice. Apart from that contingency, the unqualified payment into Court is for him, and leaves the money at his disposal.

There having been no amendment of the pleadings, it was not, in my opinion, competent for the defendant to dispute the right of the plaintiff to a judgment for at least £3,000 with interest.

It appears, however, that this view was, by inadvertence, not placed before *Higgins* J., and that it was admitted before him by plaintiff's counsel that under the authority of *Gray* v. *Bartholomew* (2) there was power to order the repayment to the defendant

(1) 1 Q.B., 154, at 159.   (2) (1895) 1 Q.B., 209.

H. C. of A.
1907.

Spencer
v.
The Com-
monwealth.

Isaacs J.
of the difference between £2,250 and £3,086 1s. 2d. Assuming there was power to limit the amount recoverable by the plaintiff to £2,250, there was also power to order the balance to be refunded; and, in any event, if costs were payable to the defendant, there was equally power to order them to be first paid out of the sum in Court before payment out to the plaintiff.

There were no costs so payable; and though the learned Justice was quite justified in asking himself, and indeed bound to ask himself, the true value of the land irrespective of the amount paid in, yet when that was once ascertained to be below the amount paid in, the answer only enabled the Court to determine in favour of the defendant the issue as to sufficiency of the amount paid in. It did not alter the admission of the pleadings up to that amount, or the plaintiff's right to receive the sum paid in. In an ordinary action final judgment would in such a case be given on the issue for the defendant, but here the language of the Act contemplates a judgment for the plaintiff, and in the circumstances the judgment must be for at least the sum paid in.

The plaintiff, however, was not content to accept that sum as sufficient; he denied its sufficiency, and has further contended on the appeal that the learned Justice ought to have given more. Invited to state the minimum amount that would meet the legal requirements of the evidence, learned counsel for the appellant candidly admitted it would be impossible to do so.

It would be profitless to examine the evidence in close detail, but there are some broad considerations to which reference may be directed.

In the first place the ultimate question is, what was the value of the land on 1st January 1905?

All circumstances subsequently arising are to be ignored. Whether the land becomes more valuable or less valuable afterwards is immaterial. Its value is fixed by Statute as on that day. Prosperity unexpected, or depression which no man would ever have anticipated, if happening after the date named, must be alike disregarded. The facts existing on 1st January 1905 are the only relevant facts, and the all important fact on that day is the opinion regarding the fair price of the land, which a hypothetical prudent purchaser would entertain, if he desired to

H. C. OF A.
1907.

SPENCER
v.
THE COM-
MONWEALTH.

Isaacs J.

purchase it for the most advantageous purpose for which it was adapted. The plaintiff is to be compensated; therefore he is to receive the money equivalent to the loss he has sustained by deprivation of his land, and that loss, apart from special damage not here claimed, cannot exceed what such a prudent purchaser would be prepared to give him. To arrive at the value of the land at that date, we have, as I conceive, to suppose it sold then, not by means of a forced sale, but by voluntary bargaining between the plaintiff and a purchaser, willing to trade, but neither of them so anxious to do so that he would overlook any ordinary business consideration. We must further suppose both to be perfectly acquainted with the land, and cognizant of all circumstances which might affect its value, either advantageously or prejudicially, including its situation, character, quality, proximity to conveniences or inconveniences, its surrounding features, the then present demand for land, and the likelihood, as then appearing to persons best capable of forming an opinion, of a rise or fall for what reason soever in the amount which one would otherwise be willing to fix as the value of the property.

In *The Queen* v. *Brown* (1) *Cockburn* C.J. said :—"A jury, whether the dispute be as to the value of land required to be taken by the company, or as to the compensation for damages by severance, in assessing the amount to which the landowner is entitled, have to consider the real value of the land, and may take into account not only the present purpose to which the land is applied, but also any other more beneficial purpose to which in the course of events at no remote period it may be applied, just as an owner might do if he were bargaining with a purchaser in the market. That is the mode in which the land would be valued." Having mentally placed itself in the position of the bargaining parties as on the critical date, 1st January 1905, the question for the tribunal is, what is the point at which the parties would meet; what is the sum the one would be willing to give and the other to take? That is practically the same as asking what is the highest sum such a purchaser would give, because we must assume the owner would be willing to take the best he can get. The best he can get in those circumstances is the test of

(1) L.R. 2 Q.B., 630, at p. 631.

H. C. OF A.   what he loses, and it is his loss which must be replaced. It is
1907.   not, as it seems to me, proper for this purpose to assume that the
SPENCER   owner retains his land unsold indefinitely because such an
v.   assumption could only be for the purpose of getting an improved
THE COM-
MONWEALTH.   value, arising from more favourable circumstances than those
existing in January 1905, which is the very thing forbidden by
Isaacs J.   the Statute. If permissible in his favour, it would also be
permissible against him, and it would be palpably unjust to him
to diminish the price he could actually have got in January 1905
because some time after he could not have obtained so much.
What is to be avoided is the supposition that on the specified
date there is to be a forced sale, and that is completely guarded
against by the considerations I have enumerated. That being so,
how has the plaintiff satisfied the onus he undertook in asserting
the insufficiency of the amount paid into Court ? The value of
the land for workmen's cottages as determined by the learned
Justice cannot, on the materials present here, be disturbed on the
ordinary principles upon which an appellate tribunal acts. It is
urged, however, that His Honor was wrong in not accepting the
estimates of the plaintiff's witnesses on the basis of a business
site. But apart from balancing their relative competency as
compared with the gentlemen called for the defendant, by reason
of varying personal professional experience of this particular
locality, there is ample material to justify the primary tribunal
to disregard this aspect of their testimony without being charge-
able with error which the appellate Court would correct. As
the Privy Council said in *Secretary of State for Foreign Affairs*
v. *Charlesworth, Pilling & Co.* (1) :—" It is quite true that in all
valuations, judicial or other, there must be room for inferences
and inclinations of opinion which, being more or less conjectural,
are difficult to reduce to exact reasoning or to explain to others.
Everyone who has gone through the process is aware of this lack
of demonstrative proof in his own mind, and knows that every
expert witness called before him has had his own set of con-
jectures, of more or less weight according to his experience and
personal sagacity. In such an inquiry as the present, relating to
subjects abounding with uncertainties and on which there is little

(1) (1901) A.C., 373, at p. 391.

experience, there is more than ordinary room for such guesswork ; H. C. of A.
1907.

SPENCER
v.
THE COM-
MONWEALTH.

Isaacs J.
and it would be very unfair to require an exact exposition of
reasons for the conclusions arrived at."

The suitability of the land for a factory site is incontestable.
But its inherent suitability, and its money value, for a factory
site are two very different matters. No demand for factory sites
there existed on 1st January 1905, and therefore no special value
could be placed on it for that purpose, unless the hypothetical
prudent purchaser would then take into his calculation the future
prospects of the land being wanted for such a site. As to this
not a single concrete fact leading to such a probability, or likely
to influence a would-be purchaser, is adduced. Indeed, one
witness for the plaintiff, James Morrison, although his valuation
is on the basis of a factory site, says :—" Owing to the neighbourhood, I think of no value except for workmen's cottages."

The evidence for the defendant, equally honest and capable,
was precise and clear that the highest price obtainable for the
land was for cottage property. There was a general agreement
of opinion among the witnesses that for some years past prices
of land have come down in the locality and are still on the
decline. Reading the judgment as a whole, I understand the
learned Justice practically to arrive at a special finding that on
1st January 1905, whatever the property might have fetched as
a future factory site, the highest value of the land was for
workmen's cottages. This conclusion was founded on conflicting
opinions of equally honest competent and confident experts. I
entertain no doubt that such a finding cannot be reversed by a
Court who do not see the witnesses, and are not in so favourable
a position as the learned primary Justice to form what after all
is only a judicial opinion of the relative weight to be attached to
the opinion of witnesses regarding the estimate they think a
hypothetical purchaser would form of the probable use to which
the land might in the indefinite future be most beneficially
applied. This is altogether too unsubstantial for an appellate
Court to act upon in such a case. Unless some error of principle
is established, or the evidence on one side so far preponderates
over that on the other, by reason of its character, force or quality,
as to distinctly outweigh the disadvantages of not seeing and

H. C. of A. hearing the witnesses, it is almost impossible to disturb a finding
1907.   of the nature now under consideration.

Spencer   In the result then the special adaptability of the land for
v.   factory sites is immaterial, and the general value of the land as
The Com-
monwealth. workmen's residences prevails, at a sum not exceeding the
Isaacs J.   amount paid into Court.

The question of costs is all that remains. Ordinarily that is
also a matter for the discretion of the primary tribunal. But
here the plaintiff invokes the general practice of the Court to
escape from the specific finding of the learned Justice limiting
him to £2,250, and he is entitled to do so ; but the same general
practice also says that in such a case the ordinary rule is that
the plaintiff should get his costs up to payment into Court, and
should, if he fail on the issue as to sufficiency, pay them to the
other side.   That is only the complete statement of the one rule.

As a new feature operating to his advantage has been introduced into the judgment at the instance of the plaintiff to secure
a benefit, it is only just to apply it in its entirety unless special
circumstances, not appearing here, make it more just to order
otherwise.   In this sense the order varying the provision of the
judgment as to costs is no departure from the well established
rule of non-interference with the discretion of the primary Court
as to costs.   It is not improbable that, if the principle we are
acting upon had been urged before *Higgins* J., he would have
accompanied its application with the same order as to costs that
this Court now makes.

> *Judgment appealed from varied by direct-*
> *ing judgment for plaintiff for* £3,082
> 1*s.* 2*d., being the amount paid into*
> *Court. Plaintiff to pay defendant's*
> *costs of action after payment in. Re-*
> *spondent to pay costs of appeal, includ-*
> *ing cost of printing.*

Solicitors, for the appellant, *James & Darbyshire.*
Solicitor, for the respondent, *Barker* (Crown Solicitor).

N. G. P.

[HIGH COURT OF AUSTRALIA.]

HAZELTON . . . . APPELLANT;
PLAINTIFF,

AND

POTTER . . . . RESPONDENT.
DEFENDANT,

ON APPEAL FROM THE SUPREME COURT OF
NEW SOUTH WALES.

*Action for false imprisonment—Arrest by police officers on foreign warrant—Justi-
fication—Reasonable belief of defendant—Mistake of law—Notice of action—
Act done under authority of law honestly believed to be in force—Law of British
possession—Pacific Order in Council 1893, Articles 112, 139.*

H. C. of A.
1907.

SYDNEY,
Nov. 26, 27,
28.
Dec. 9.

Griffith C.J.,
Barton and
Isaacs JJ

The Pacific Order in Council 1893 established a High Commissioner's Court
with jurisdiction over the Pacific Ocean, and the islands and places therein
which were British settlements or under British protection or were under no
civilized government, but exclusive of any part of the British dominions or
territorial waters within the jurisdiction of any British
possession. The jurisdiction of the Court was vested in a High Commissioner
and Deputy Commissioners. Article 112 of the Order in Council provides
that where a person is to be removed for trial or for the execution of a sentence
the Judge of the High Commissioner's Court shall issue a warrant (in a prescribed form) under which the person may be put on board a British warship,
or some other fit ship, and conveyed to the place named in the warrant and
pending removal detained in custody, and that the warrant shall be sufficient
authority to the person to whom the warrant is directed and every person
acting under it or in aid of the person to whom it is directed, to take and
keep the person named in it.

The appellant was convicted at Gizo in the Solomon Islands before a
Deputy Commissioner and sentenced to a term of imprisonment at Fiji. The
ship on which the appellant was put for the purpose of being conveyed to Fiji
ended her voyage at Sydney, and while there the appellant was taken into

custody by a Sydney police officer under a warrant purporting to have been made by the Deputy Commissioner at Gizo, but actually signed in Brisbane, directed to the supercargo of the ship by name, who was commanded to convey the appellant to Sydney, and "there to deliver him to the magistrate gaoler or other officer to whom it may appertain to give effect to any sentence passed by the Court there exercising criminal jurisdiction &c., that the said sentence may be carried into effect."

In an action in the Supreme Court of New South Wales by the appellant against the police officer for damages for false imprisonment :

Held, that the warrant, even if valid, afforded no justification for the arrest inasmuch as it did not authorize the conveyance of the appellant to Fiji but to Sydney, and whatever authority for the detention of the appellant it purported to confer terminated on the delivery of the appellant to the keeper of the prison in Sydney, and consequently his detention there was not a necessary act in aid of the execution of the warrant.

Held, further, that, although under a warrant duly addressed to the gaoler at Fiji, a temporary detention of the appellant by a Sydney officer for the purpose of aiding the execution of the warrant might be justified on the ground of necessity, the High Commissioner had no authority to address a warrant to the keeper of a prison in Sydney or to authorize a detention by him, and the warrant was therefore invalid on the face of it.

Leonard Watson's Case, 9 A. & E., 731, distinguished.

Article 139 provides that any suit or proceeding shall not be commenced " in any of Her Majesty's Courts " for anything done or omitted in pursuance of execution or intended execution of the Order in Council unless a month's notice of action in writing is given by the plaintiff to the defendant.

Held, that the defendant was not entitled to the benefit of this provision, because, even if it applied to actions brought in the Courts of New South Wales, which was doubtful, the arrest was not anything that could be done under the Order in Council. Article 112, under which the defendant assumed to act, was not in force in that State, and in order that advantage may be taken of such a provision, the defendant must establish that he honestly believed in a state of facts which, if it had existed, would have afforded him a justification under the *lex fori.*

Roberts v. *Orchard,* 2 H. & C., 769 ; 33 L. J. Ex., 65, applied.

Decision of the majority of the Supreme Court, *Hazelton* v. *Potter,* (1907) 7 S. R. (N.S.W.), 270 reversed.

APPEAL from a decision of the Supreme Court of New South Wales making absolute a rule *nisi* for entering a nonsuit.

The appellant had recovered a verdict for £229 damages against the respondent, an officer of the police force in Sydney, New South

Wales, in an action for false imprisonment. This verdict was set aside by the Full Court (consisting of *Simpson, Pring* and *Rogers* JJ.) by a majority, and a nonsuit ordered to be entered, on the grounds, that the defendant had acted under a warrant, good on its face, in the honest belief that it was a valid warrant, and that the defendant was entitled to notice of action under Article 139 of the Pacific Order in Council 1893. On both points *Pring* J. dissented from the majority of the Court: *Hazelton* v. *Potter* (1).

From this decision the present appeal was brought by special leave.

The facts and the material portions of the Order in Council sufficiently appear in the judgments hereunder.

D. G. Ferguson (*Windeyer* with him), for the appellant. The warrant was bad. The Deputy Commissioner had no jurisdiction to authorize a Sydney police officer to detain the appellant in Sydney. His jurisdiction is limited by the Pacific Order in Council 1893 to the islands and other places in the Pacific outside the limits of self-governing Colonies of the Empire. Moreover the warrant was not in the form prescribed by the Order in Council, Schedule Form C. 17. It should have specified Fiji as the place to which the appellant was to be removed. It was no warrant for anything after the conveyance to Sydney. (See Article 112 of the Order in Council.) These defects appeared on the face of the warrant, and consequently the person who acted under it was not protected. [He referred to *Pollock on Torts*, 5th ed., p. 112; *The Marshalsea* (2); *Clark* v. *Woods* (3); *Clerk and Lindsell on Torts*, 2nd ed., p. 643; *Andrews* v. *Marris* (4); *Carratt* v. *Morley* (5); *Watson* v. *Bodell* (6); *Dews* v. *Riley* (7).

[ISAACS J. referred to *Hill* v. *Bateman* (8); *Shergold* v. *Holloway* (9).]

Even if the warrant were good on its face but really bad, it would afford no protection to a person acting under it.

(1) (1907) 7 S.R. (N.S.W.), 270.
(2) 10 Rep., 69, at p. 76a.
(3) 2 Ex., 395; 17 L.J.M.C., 189.
(4) 1 Q.B., 3.
(5) 1 Q.B., 18.
(6) 14 M. & W., 57.
(7) 11 C.B., 434; 20 L.J.C.P., 264.
(8) 1 Stra., 710.
(9) 2 Stra., 1002.

H. C. of A.
1907.

HAZELTON
v.
POTTER.

No notice of action was necessary. The warrant being bad on its face, the respondent had no reason to believe in the existence of a state of facts which would justify him in acting upon it. Even assuming the warrant to have been good on its face, Article 139 does not protect the respondent, because it has no application to proceedings in Courts of New South Wales, nor does it apply to acts done outside the territorial limits of the jurisdiction of the Western Pacific Court. If it had purported to apply to these Courts it would be *ultra vires* : see Articles 4, 7, 14, 19, 49. The meaning of the words "any of Her Majesty's Courts" may be gathered from a reference to Articles 109, 110. They may fairly be construed as referring to the High Commissioner's Court and Courts established under sec. 2 of the *British Settlements Act* 1887. The *lex fori* is to be applied in matters of procedure such as this. [He referred to *Macleod* v. *Attorney-General for New South Wales* (1); *British Settlements Act* 1887, secs. 2, 6 ; Preamble to Pacific Order in Council 1893.]

[GRIFFITH C.J. referred to *Leroux* v. *Brown* (2); *Scott* v. *Lord Seymour* (3).

ISAACS J. referred to *Westlake on International Law*, 3rd ed., pars. 238, 239.]

The British legislature has dealt with the same subject in sec. 13 of the *Foreign Jurisdiction Act* 1890, which renders Article 139 *ultra vires*: *Bentham* v. *Hoyle* (4); *Ferrier* v. *Wilson* (5). Even if Article 139 applies to an action in these Courts, the respondent is not entitled to the benefit of it, because the arrest was not made under the Order in Council within the meaning of that Article, but in pursuance of a warrant issued under the Order: *Shatwell* v. *Hall* (6), cited in *McLaughlin* v. *Fosbery* (7). Nor was there anything in the warrant that could lead the respondent to reasonably believe that he was acting under the Order. The warrant did not purport to direct the conveyance of the appellant to Fiji. Detention in Sydney could only be authorized by Imperial or New South Wales legislation, not by a warrant out

(1) (1891) A.C., 455, at p. 458.
(2) 12 C.B., 801 ; 22 L.J. C.P., 1.
(3) 1 H. & C., 219 ; 32 L.J. Ex., 61.
(4) 3 Q.B.D., 289, at p. 295.
(5) 4 C.L.R., 785.
(6) 10 M. & W., 523.
(7) 1 C.L.R., 546, at p. 565.

of the High Commissioner's Court. Article 112 is not law in this State. The respondent's belief that it was is immaterial.

Scholes and *Piddington*, for the respondent. The warrant was good on its face, as a warrant for the conveyance of a prisoner from Gizo to Fiji by an officer of the Court, signed at Gizo by a person who had jurisdiction to sign it. The ordinary and natural route between those places is through Sydney by transhipment, and the detention of the appellant in Sydney was ancillary to the execution of the warrant. Article 112 authorizes any person to aid in the execution. [They referred to *Leonard Watson's Case* (1)].

[GRIFFITH C.J. referred to *Attorney-General for Canada* v. *Cain and Gilhula* (2).]

The Order in Council takes effect in all parts of His Majesty's dominions, wherever it may be necessary that some act should be done for the purpose of carrying it out. Article 112 may be read as an express exception from the exclusion in Article 4. " Expressly provided " merely means clearly provided : *In re England* (3), and includes necessary implications.

It is a necessary implication in Article 112 that the conveyance of prisoners may be through the territory of other British legislatures when the only practicable route lies that way : *Robtelmes* v. *Brenan* (4). The warrant in this case, even if it cannot be read as a warrant to convey from Gizo to Fiji, could be read as a warrant to the respondent to assist in the conveyance by taking custody of the appellant in Sydney, and the respondent was entitled to assume that there was another warrant in existence for the complete journey. The warrant need not be in the exact Form C. 17.

If the warrant was good on its face the respondent could justify, under Article 112, being an officer of the law, acting as such in aid of the person who had the execution of the warrant. He knew nothing of the defect in Robertson's authority, and was not bound to inquire into that or into the validity of the warrant.

[They referred to *Carratt* v. *Morley* (5) ; *Painter* v. *Liverpool*

(1) 9 A. & E., 731.
(2) (1906) A.C., 542.
(3) 13 N.S.W.L.R., 121, at p. 122.
(4) 4 C.L.R., 395.
(5) 1 Q.B., 18.

Oil Gas Light Co. (1); *Henderson* v. *Preston* (2); *Demer* v. *Cook* (3); *Webb* v. *Batchelour* (4); *The Marshalsea* (5).]

[GRIFFITH C.J. referred to *Grant* v. *Bagge* (6).]

The appellant by his conduct before and after arriving in Sydney submitted to the jurisdiction of the High Commissioner's Court and to the detention by the respondent in furtherance of that Court's order, and is estopped from now denying the authority of the respondent to detain him in Sydney. This defence is open to the respondent under the plea of not guilty: *Heane* v. *Rogers* (7); *Pickard* v. *Sears* (8); *Goff's Case* (9).

[GRIFFITH C.J.—The representation, if any, made by the appellant was on a matter of law, as to which there can be no estoppel.]

The respondent was entitled to notice of action. The words "in any of Her Majesty's Courts" include the Courts of this State. They are not used elsewhere in the Order in Council, and must therefore be intended to mean something different from the High Commissioner's Court, which is always called "the Court." [They referred to Articles 25, 137 and 139.] The action for trespass is a personal one, and may be brought wherever the defendant happens to be. There is no reason why notice should be considered necessary in one Court and not in another. The defendant honestly and upon reasonable grounds believed that the warrant was valid and had been duly issued.

[GRIFFITH C.J.—But if Article 112 had no effect in New South Wales, it was immaterial whether the respondent thought that it had, or believed in a state of facts which, if it had, would have justified him.]

The Order as a whole is in force in New South Wales for the purpose of protecting persons acting under it, if the Order cannot reasonably be carried out without doing some act in New South Wales.

[ISAACS J.—Assuming that Article 139 purports to control the Courts of New South Wales, what authority had the Queen in Council to make such an Order ?]

(1) 3 A. & E., 433.
(2) 21 Q.B.D., 362.
(3) 88 L.T., 629.
(4) Vent., 273.
(5) 10 Rep., 69, at 76a.

(6) 3 East., 128.
(7) 9 B. & C., 577, at p. 586.
(8) 6 A. & E., 469.
(9) 3 M. & S., 203.

The power conferred by the *Pacific Islanders Act* 1875, sec. 6. It was necessary for the administration of the islands that there should be such a provision.   If the Article is in force here, then the respondent was justified in believing that he was acting lawfully.   The Court should presume in his favour that his interpretation of the warrant was reasonable : *Crowley* v. *Glissan* (1).   The facts, as they appeared to him, warranted him in believing that he was justified in detaining the appellant. [They referred to *Cook* v. *Leonard* (2); *Mason* v. *Newland* (3); *Roberts* v. *Orchard* (4); *Selmes* v. *Judge* (5); *Graves* v. *Arnold* (6).]

Ferguson in reply.   In *Leonard Watson's Case* (7) the defendant justified under an Act which was in force in England where the action was brought.   But there is no law in force in New South Wales under which the defendant could justify even if the warrant were valid.   Detention in New South Wales is not justifiable under the Order in Council unless it is absolutely necessary for the purpose of carrying out the Order.   There is no evidence of such necessity in this case.

Cur. adv. vult.

GRIFFITH C.J.   This is an appeal from a judgment of the Full Court of New South Wales entering a nonsuit in an action brought by the appellant against the respondent, in which at the trial he had recovered a verdict for £229 damages.   The action was for assault and false imprisonment.   The defendant was an officer of the police in New South Wales, and the alleged wrongs were committed in Sydney.

The defendant sets up two defences.   First, he justifies under the Pacific Order in Council of 1893, and says that under the authority of that Order he did the acts complained of in the action.   His other defence is that under that Order in Council notice of action is necessary before any action can be brought for anything done or intended to be done under the Order in Council. He says he intended to act under the Order in Council.

(1) 2 C.L.R., 744.
(2) 6 B. & C., 351.
(3) 9 C. & P., 575, note *a*.
(4) 2 H. & C., 769; 33 L.J. Ex., 65.

(5) L.R. 6 Q.B., 724.
(6) 3 Camp., 242.
(7) 9 A. & E., 731.

H. C. of A.
1907.

HAZELTON
v.
POTTER.

Griffith C.J.

Before referring in detail to the facts of the case, which are in
some respects remarkable—although their singularity, as it
happens, is not relevant to the decision—I will refer to some of
the provisions of the Order in Council. It was passed on 15th
March 1893, and recites the *British Settlements Act* 1887, by
which the Sovereign in Council is authorized to establish laws and
Courts for the peace, order and good government of Her Majesty's
subjects and others within any British possession. It recites also
the *Pacific Islanders Protection Act* 1872, which authorized Her
Majesty to exercise jurisdiction over her subjects in every part of
the Pacific Ocean and any parts or places, &c., not within the
jurisdiction of any civilized power. The Order further authorized
establishment of Courts of Justice, and, moreover, provided that
Her Majesty might by Order in Council direct that those powers
and that jurisdiction might be vested in and exercised by the
Court so to be established, and might also be exercised by the Court
of any British Colony designated by the Order.

The 4th Article of the Order prescribes what are called the
limits of the Order, which are thus defined :—" The limits of this
Order shall be the Pacific Ocean and the islands and places
therein, including (*a*) islands and places which are for the time
being British Settlements; (*b*) islands and places which are for
the time being under the protection of Her Majesty ; (*c*) islands
and places which are for the time being under no civilized
government, but exclusive (except as in this Order expressly
provided in relation to any particular matter) of (1) Any place
within any part of Her Majesty's dominions, or the territorial
waters thereof, which is for the time being within the jurisdiction of the legislature of any British possession ; (2) Any place
for the time being within the jurisdiction or protectorate of any
civilized power."

The Order in Council, therefore, does not take effect within
His Majesty's dominions in general, unless so expressly provided
in relation to any particular matter. The Order in Council established a Court called the High Commissioner's Court, and by
Article 60 that Court had authority to try persons subject to
the jurisdiction of the Court who are charged with having committed any crime triable by the Court.

H. C. of A.
1907.

HAZELTON
v.
POTTER.

Griffith C.J.

Article 78 provides that sentence of imprisonment shall be carried into effect "in such prisons and in such manner as the High Commissioner from time to time directs," and "if there be no such prison, or by reason of the condition of any such prison, or the state of health of the prisoner, or on any other ground, the Court thinks that the sentence ought not to be carried into effect in such prison, the prisoner shall, by warrant, be removed in custody to Fiji, there to undergo his sentence."

Article 112 provides for carrying the prisoner for the purpose of undergoing his sentence. I will read the first four paragraphs :—

"Where a person is to be removed either for trial or for the execution of a sentence, or under an order of deportation, a warrant for the purpose shall be issued by the Judge of the Court under his hand and seal, and the person may, under such warrant, be taken to and put on board of one of Her Majesty's ships or some other fit ship, and shall be conveyed in such ship or otherwise to the place named in the warrant.

"Pending removal, the person shall, if the Court so orders by endorsement on the warrant, be arrested and detained in custody or in prison until an opportunity for removal occurs.

"On arrival at the place named in the warrant, the person, if removed under an order of deportation, shall be discharged, or otherwise shall be handed over to the proper gaoler, constable, magistrate, or officer.

"A warrant of removal is sufficient authority to the person to whom it is directed or delivered for execution, and to the person in command of any ship, and to every person acting under the warrant or in aid of any such person, to take, receive, detain, convey, and deliver the person named therein in the manner thereby directed, and generally is sufficient authority for anything done in execution or intended execution of the warrant."

The form of warrant is given in the Schedule of the Order in Council, Form C. 17, as follows :—

"To X.Y. and other officers of the Court.

"The above-named A.B. having been on the .   .   . day of .   . convicted before this Court for that, &c.

"The Court did thereupon sentence the said A.B. for his said offence   .   .   .   to be imprisoned for, &c.

" You are hereby commanded, with proper assistance to convey the said A.B. to [   ] that the said sentence may there be carried into effect and you are there to deliver him to a magistrate, gaoler, or other officer to whom it may appertain to give effect to any sentence passed by the Court there exercising criminal jurisdiction, together with this warrant or a duplicate thereof.

(Seal) "

In the case of a person committed to Suva, that would be a warrant to take the man to Suva, and there " deliver him to the magistrate, gaoler, or other officer to whom it may appertain to give effect to any sentence passed by the Court." Those words are taken from Article 112, and they are words of general import, meaning, in substance, the person in charge of the gaol. There is one other provision of the Order in Council to which I must call attention, which is relied upon for the contention that notice of action should have been given.

Article 139 says :—" Any suit or proceeding shall not be commenced in any of Her Majesty's Courts against any person for anything done or omitted in pursuance or execution or intended execution of this Order, or of any regulation or rule made under it, unless notice in writing is given by the intending plaintiff or prosecutor to the intended defendant one clear month before the commencement of the suit or proceeding, nor unless it is commenced within three months," &c.

Now as to the facts. The plaintiff, it is alleged, was sentenced at Gizo, a place in the Solomon Islands, to be imprisoned for three months at Suva for an offence. For the purpose of taking him from Gizo to Suva, he was brought by a steamer trading between the Solomon Islands and Sydney to Sydney, that being, it is alleged, the necessary mode of transport to Suva, and when in Sydney, the officer of the High Commissioner's Court handed the plaintiff over to the defendant, who was, *pro hac vice*, acting as an officer in charge of a gaol. The defendant's pleas are justification and want of necessary notice of action. Now those defences depend upon whether the provisions of Articles 112 and 139 are part of the law of New South Wales. It is contended for the respondent that they are—that is to say, that the warrant, issued in one part of the Western Pacific to be executed by taking the person named in it to another part of the Western Pacific, runs in New South Wales so as to authorize the detention of that person in New South Wales, for, I suppose, a definite period, for the purpose of transhipment. With respect to the other Article, the contention is that the Order in Council for the Western Pacific was intended to establish a rule of procedure to be followed by the Australian Courts and English Courts, or for that matter, all the Courts of Her Majesty's possessions.

I will first say a few words with respect to that contention. To begin with, it is exceedingly improbable that under the Order of 1893, or at the time when these Acts were passed, in the seventies, eighties, and nineties, it should have been intended by the Imperial legislature to authorize the Sovereign in Council to legislate for the internal affairs of self-governing communities. No doubt the Imperial legislature might have conferred such a power, but, *primâ facie*, it is highly improbable that they would. The improbability is confirmed by the manner in which they did pass enactments when they desired to interfere with the internal powers of self-governing communities.

For instance, the *Fugitive Offenders Act*, passed in 1881, relates to offenders going from one part of Her Majesty's dominions to another. In that Act careful provision is made for the detention of a person in a possession not under the authority of another. Sec. 25 got over any difficulty such as that which had been suggested, that the warrant of one possession did not extend beyond its own territorial boundary, not even at sea, or in transit between parts of its own possession. [His Honor read sec. 27 and continued.] I think it highly improbable, when the legislature were in the habit of dealing with such matters in such a way, that a general warrant issued in one part of the Western Pacific should be intended to have legal force in a part of Australia. The improbability is made further clear in the *Colonial Prisoners Removal Act* 1884, providing for the removal of prisoners and criminal lunatics from Her Majesty's possessions out of the United Kingdom. That Act provides that this can only, be done under a warrant of the Governor, or Secretary of State.

These considerations lead me to the conclusion that it is

H. C. of A.
1907.

HAZELTON
v.
POTTER.

Griffith C.J.

extremely improbable that it was intended by the legislature
which had passed the Acts recited in the Order in Council, to
confer on the Sovereign in Council authority to enact a law
affecting the liberty of persons within a self-governing possession.
The extreme improbability that it was intended that the Order
in Council itself should embody such a law appears still greater
on reference to Article 111, which provides for the case of persons
who are deported from the Western Pacific. In that case they
may be taken to a British possession and landed there, but only if
the Government of that possession has consented to the reception
of persons deported under the Order.

The contention of the respondent in this case is that, although
a person may not be brought and set free on shore without
consent of the Government of the possession, yet a person in
custody may be brought and detained, and no Court here has
power to release him. That is extremely improbable. The only
serious argument addressed to us in respect to this contention
was that it was necessary in order to give effect to the provision
for removal from one part of the Pacific to another, and reliance
was placed on *Leonard Watson's Case* (1).

Supposing that case was in point—I do not think it is—still it
would be necessary to establish that it was necessary, in order to
convey a person from the Solomon Islands to Suva, to imprison
him in Sydney while in transit. To anyone acquainted with
the geography of the Western Pacific, that is absurd. It is
only lately that there have been steamers running between the
Solomon Islands and Sydney. At present it is probably the
most comfortable and convenient way to Suva to come by steamer
to Sydney, but to suggest that a person may be brought two or
three thousand miles for the sake of convenience, not absolute
necessity, seems to be a straining of words. In my opinion there
was no necessity to bring him by way of Sydney. In one year
it might be convenient to go by way of New Caledonia, in
another year perhaps by way of New Guinea. It seems to me
for these reasons improbable that the section gives the powers
contended for.

I turn to Article 139, which, it is said, imposes a rule binding

(1) 9 A. & E., 731.

on Courts of Justice in all Her Majesty's possessions. True the
words of the Act are vague. The words are "any of Her Majesty's
Courts," and the literal meaning of those words undoubtedly
includes Courts of New South Wales, or any of Her Majesty's
Courts. But, again, it seems improbable that the legislature
intended that provision to apply to an action in Australia. My
brother *Barton* pointed out that by the Pacific Order in Council
the Supreme Court of any of the Australian Colonies might have
jurisdiction conferred upon it co-extensive with that of the High
Court, under the *Pacific Islanders Protection Act* 1875. In
such a case the Australian Court would be a Court having
jurisdiction over all British subjects within the Western Pacific,
and in that case might very well be said to come within the
terms "any of Her Majesty's Courts" in Article 139. I think
that is very probable, and it gets rid of the argument that the
legislature intended to interfere with the freedom of government
of the Australasian Colonies. I do not think it necessary to
formally decide the point, but for the reasons I have given I
think it very improbable that the legislature had any such
intention.

I return to the actual facts of this case. The warrant,
instead of being signed in the Western Pacific, was signed in the
Brisbane River, outside the limits of the Order, and at a place
where the person who signed it, Mr. Oliphant, clearly had no
jurisdiction. It is entitled:—" In His Britannic Majesty's High
Commissioner's Court for the Western Pacific at Gizo, British
Solomon Islands, Criminal Jurisdiction. Held at Gizo on the
15th day of June 1905," &c.

It is addressed to "George Robertson, and other officers of the
Court." Robertson was the supercargo on the steamship which
was on its way from the British Solomon Islands to Sydney.
The warrant was "to convey the said Hazelton to Sydney, New
South Wales, and . . . there to deliver him to the magistrate,
gaoler, or other officer to whom it may appertain to give effect
to any sentence passed by the Court there exercising criminal
jurisdiction, together with this warrant, or a duplicate thereof,
that the said sentence" (of imprisonment) "may be duly carried
into effect."

There is no date, except the date at the head. The person receiving that document might, perhaps, suppose it was signed at Gizo on 15th June, and was within the jurisdiction of the person who signed it. Robertson, who wrote it out himself in the Brisbane River, knew that that place was not within the Western Pacific, and that he was not an officer of the Court, and I suppose he knew that Oliphant had no power there to appoint him an officer of the Court. Perhaps such a warrant might operate as a justification to another person acting under it, but it is not necessary to determine that question.

I will assume, then, without so deciding, that a warrant of removal signed within the limits of the Order in Council, addressed to an officer of the High Commissioner's Court, and directing him to remove a prisoner to Suva to serve a sentence of imprisonment, would authorize that officer to detain the prisoner in custody on shore in Australia in transit from the place where the warrant was issued, if it should become necessary, in order to give effect to the particular route lawfully chosen for removal, to detain him in Australia awaiting the departure of another vessel bound to Suva. The foundation of such an authority would be the necessity of the case. Now, the authority to remove conferred by Article 112, whatever its extent, is conferred only upon the officer to whom the warrant is addressed, and in the case supposed the prisoner would be still in his custody, and the detention on shore in Australia would be by him or by his authority. I will assume also, without so deciding, that such a warrant would authorize any subject of His Majesty in Australia to assist the officer for the purpose of such detention. I will assume further that a warrant in the Form C. 17, although not in terms addressed to the keeper (as is usual in English and Australian warrants), would be sufficient authority to the keeper of the prison at Suva to receive and detain the prisoner. Making these assumptions, how does the case stand?

The warrant in question was not signed within the limits of the Order in Council, but this fact may, perhaps, be disregarded. It was addressed to a person who was not an officer of the Court, and could not lawfully be appointed as such officer at the place where the appointment, which was made, if at all, by the warrant, purported to be made. This fact also may, perhaps, be disregarded. But the warrant does not purport to authorize, and cannot on any reasonable construction be read as authorizing, Robertson, the person to whom it was directed, to remove the appellant to Suva. Whatever authority it purported to confer on him terminated on his delivery of the appellant to the keeper of the prison in Sydney. Any detention of the appellant, therefore, in Sydney was not a detention by Robertson, and could not be justified as such under the terms of the warrant. Again, assuming that a warrant in Form C. 17 would, if Suva were mentioned as the place of imprisonment, justify the reception and detention of the prisoner at Suva by the keeper of the prison there, the warrant in question was not addressed to him, and it is manifest that the High Commissioner's Court has no authority to address a warrant to the keeper of a prison in Australia. The argument from necessity, which alone would justify the detention by the officer in Australian territory, has no application, and the detention by the keeper of an Australian prison is wholly unauthorized by the warrant. The defence of justification under the warrant therefore fails.

With regard to the defence of want of notice of action, very similar considerations apply. I will assume, but without so deciding, that Article 139 applies to an action in the Supreme Court of New South Wales. In order that advantage may be taken of this provision, the defendant must show, to begin with, that at the place where the act complained of was done there was some law in force under which it might under some circumstances have been lawful. It is quite immaterial that he thought there was such a law, if in fact there was none. And the law must be a law of the place where the act was done. If the provisions of a law of a foreign country are binding in a State, they are binding, not as the law of the foreign country, but because the law of the State or of a paramount authority has made them part of the State law. The furthest extent to which it can be suggested that the Order in Council has effect in the present case is that *ex necessitate* the person to whose custody a prisoner is committed for removal to Suva may himself detain him in custody in Australia. There is no pretence that any other person in Australia can be

authorized (except in aid of that person) to detain the prisoner
independently. From every point of view, therefore, it is plain
that there was no law in force in New South Wales under which
the detention of the appellant by the respondent under the circumstances alleged could have been lawful. Now, the test whether
notice of action is required is, as stated in *Roberts* v. *Orchard* (1),
whether the defendant honestly believed in the existence of a
state of facts which, if it had existed, would have afforded a
justification under the Statute invoked. The reasonableness of the
defendant's belief, if he honestly entertained it, is not to be inquired
into, except as an element in determining the honesty : *Chamberlain* v. *King* (2). Nor is a mistake in the construction of the
Statute fatal to the defendant : *Selmes* v. *Judge* (3). But there
must be some Statute in force under which the act complained of
could under some circumstances have been lawful. A mistake by
the defendant as to the existence of a law cannot be brought
within these principles.

In the present case there was no law in force in New South
Wales which authorized the High Commissioner's Court to
address a warrant to a keeper of a prison in that State or which
authorized a keeper of a prison to detain of his own authority
a person in course of removal to Suva. The mistake of the
respondent was neither as to a matter of fact nor as to the
construction of a law of New South Wales, but as to the existence of such a law. In the words of *Bayley* J., in *Cook* v.
Leonard (4) there was no colour for supposing that the act done
was authorized. It is unnecessary to consider whether a mistaken interpretation of a warrant could afford ground for notice
of action, for in the present case the language, so far as regards
the respondent, was plain and unambiguous. He thought that
such a direction was valid under some law in force in New South
Wales, and there was no such law.

For these reasons I think that notice of action was not necessary, and that the appellant is entitled to retain his verdict.

It was suggested that the acts done by respondent did not

(1) 2 H. & C., 769 ; 33 L.J. Ex., 65.   (3) L.R. 6 Q.B., 724.
(2) L.R. 6 C.P., 474.   (4) 6 B. & C., 351 ; at p. 353.

H. C. OF A.
1907.

HAZELTON
v.
POTTER.

Barton J.

amount to an imprisonment. But that point was practically aban-doned, and I do not think it necessary to say anything about it.

BARTON J.   In the way in which this case has shaped itself the defence is narrowed down to the general plea of justification under the Order in Council and as to the warrant that was issued, and as to the question of notice.   I pass over the second plea, because it relates to a document called the warrant, which is not in evidence, but which, upon the evidence taken, was not in the hands of the respondent at the time when the acts com-plained of were committed, and of which he knew nothing at that time. Speaking, then, to the third plea, which is justification under the warrant actually in evidence, and throughout the case was known as Exhibit B, I am of opinion that, upon the face of it, that warrant was no authority to Robertson, to whom it was given, to remove the plaintiff to Suva.   Robertson was the supercargo of the steamer, the *Moresby*, on which both plaintiff and Oliphant came from Gizo on the journey from the Solomon Islands to Sydney, at which port the *Moresby* ended her voyage. Looking at the words of the warrant, they are addressed to "George Robertson and other officers of the Court."   Robertson was not an officer of the Court when he left Gizo, and was not even colourably an officer of the Court, unless the appointment of him made at Brisbane River in Australia made him an officer, as to which it is not necessary to express an opinion. "Robertson and other officers " were commanded to convey Hazelton to Sydney, and " there to deliver him to the magis-trate, gaoler, or other officer to whom it may appertain to give effect to any sentence passed by the Court there exercising criminal jurisdiction, together with this warrant, or a duplicate thereof."

Now it will be observed that, so far as Robertson is concerned, he did nothing in execution of this warrant.   His function ceased when he had delivered Hazelton to "the magistrate, gaoler, or other officer to whom it may appertain to give effect to any sentence passed by the Court there exercising criminal jurisdic-tion." The delivery was to the Superintendent of Police by Robertson, unless it is held that the delivery was to the two detectives who came down to see about the matter. None of the persons concerned in the detention of the plaintiff were either a "magistrate, gaoler or other officer" of the kind who could give effect to the sentence passed by a Court exercising criminal jurisdiction in Sydney. Therefore, in the first place, Robertson did something wrongfully. He ignored the authority given him by the document. He handed Hazelton over to Potter, who seemed to have assumed the functions of "magistrate, gaoler or other officer" described in the warrant, but without authority. A moment's reflection would have shown Potter that he was not an officer charged with the execution of sentences of the local criminal Courts. There is nothing in the warrant authorizing the doing of anything with the plaintiff after he should be handed over to somebody in Sydney. The matter rests with his reception in Sydney. There is nothing to show what is to be done with him after he is taken into the hands of some person, really or assumedly under the warrant, in Sydney. Certainly we have the words at the end of the document: "that the said sentence of imprisonment may be duly carried into effect"; but it is impossible to argue that such words give authority to any person to take him beyond Sydney, or to keep him there for an hour. What, then, can be the meaning of such a warrant? Can it be a warrant fulfilling the requirements of Article 112 of the Order in Council, even supposing Article 112 applies? Is it a warrant for the removal—and it can only be a good warrant if it is this— of the person arrested and sentenced in order that he may be detained in Suva, Fiji? Obviously there is not a word in it which makes a direction to that effect, and it is impossible to suppose it to be a good warrant for such a purpose. But its badness in that respect is not a mere matter of argument. The hiatus which is constituted by want of any direction to take him beyond Sydney gapes on the face of the document, and it could not possibly be assumed by Potter, exercising his intelligence, that he was authorized by this document—or that anybody was authorized by this document—to take the prisoner beyond Sydney. If it was not a warrant to remove the prisoner beyond Sydney it was palpably bad. How could anyone, then, taking him there, justify keeping him?

Robertson had finished his share of the matter when he relinquished the custody of the appellant to Potter. Potter was not within the terms of the persons described in the warrant, and the warrant was not, upon any possible construction, a warrant for the removal of the plaintiff to Suva or beyond Sydney. If he was not to be in Sydney indefinitely, which goes without saying, in whose custody was he to be taken to Suva ? In my opinion, the whole thing was visibly and radically bad. I consider, therefore, that the warrant set forth in this plea is no justification of the conduct pursued towards the appellant. In truth its face was almost a warning against interference with the liberty of the person named in it.

Now as to the plea that there was no notice of action. Speaking to the law on that subject generally, apart from the terms of the Order in Council, I will first refer to the case of *Cook v. Leonard* (1). *Bayley* J., in giving judgment, referring to cases of arrest under the supposed authority of a Statute, said :—" These cases fall within the general rule applicable to this subject, viz., that where an Act of Parliament requires notice before action brought in respect of anything done in pursuance or in execution of its provisions, those latter words are not confined to acts done strictly in pursuance of the Act of Parliament, but extend to all acts done *bonâ fide*, which may reasonably be supposed to be done in pursuance of the Act." That is an assertion that the person acting should have some fair reason for acting, and if it appears that he has acted *bonâ fide* he will be justified. *Bayley* J. went on to add (2):—" Where an Act of Parliament says, that in the case of an action brought against any person for anything done in pursuance or in execution of the Act, the defendant shall be entitled to certain privileges, the meaning is, that the act done must be of that nature and description that the party doing it may reasonably suppose that the Act of Parliament gave him authority to do it." *Holroyd* J. and *Littledale* J. gave judgment in the same direction.

In the case of *Cann* v. *Clipperton* (3), the necessity for there being a reasonable ground for belief is again emphasized. Lord

(1) 6 B. & C., 351, at p. 354.　　　(2) 6 B. & C., 351, at p. 356.
　　　　(3) 10 A. & E , 582, at p. 588.

H. C. of A.
1907.

HAZELTON
v.
POTTER.
——
Barton J.

Denman C.J. there said :—" Else I am unwilling to say that, if a party acts *bonâ fide* as in execution of a Statute, he is justified at all events, merely because he thinks he is doing what the Statute authorizes, if he has not some ground in reason to connect his own act with the statutory provision." *Williams* J. says in the same case (1):—" It would be wild work if a party might give himself protection by merely saying that he believed himself acting in pursuance of a Statute; for no one can say what may possibly come into an individual's mind on such a subject. Still, protecting clauses, like that before us, would be useless if it were necessary that the person claiming their benefit should have acted quite rightly. The case to which they refer must lie between a mere foolish imagination and a perfect observance of the Statute." Obviously, if there were no show of observance of the Statute, there would be no necessity for notice.

I have referred to those cases in order to show that the law goes now a little further as to the protection of persons acting in pursuance, or intended pursuance, of an authority under a Statute. There is the case of *Read* v. *Coker* (2) on that subject, where *Jervis* C.J. said :—" The defendant does not want to establish a full and complete justification for the plaintiff's apprehension ; to entitle him to a notice of action, it is enough to show that he *bonâ fide* believed he was acting in pursuance of the Statute, for the protection of his property."

The law seems to have relaxed a little the strictness of earlier cases, in which it was necessary not only to have *bonâ fide* belief, but to have reasonable ground for such belief. It seems now to have been laid down that the existence of *bonâ fide* belief is sufficient, and it is only where the question of the *bona fides* itself is to be tested that it will depend upon the reasonableness of the belief. At the same time, as His Honor has pointed out, there must be some ground for entertaining that belief, and if the person thinks that he has been acting in pursuance of the Statute, or the law, there must, at any rate, be some law which may be capable of constituting a defence when his conduct is impeached.

(1) 10 A. & E., 582, at p. 589.   (2) 13 C.B., 850, at p. 861.

In *Roberts* v. *Orchard* (1), *Williams* J. said:—"Most of the cases on this subject have been cited, and the result of them is, that where the question is whether a defendant is entitled to notice of action under an Act of Parliament of this nature, the proper way of leaving the question to the jury is thus :—' Did the defendant honestly believe in the existence of those facts which, if they had existed, would have afforded a justification under the Statute ? ' The law was so laid down by *Erle* C.J. and myself in the case of *Herman* v. *Seneschal* (2) and that appears to me good law and the result of the authorities."

That case supports what His Honor has said, that there must be in existence some law to which the person whose conduct is impeached could appeal in bar of the action if the facts were as he honestly thought they were.

Well, now, putting the matter on that basis—all the cases pre-suppose the existence of some law as to which such a belief could be at least colourably held. What law, then, was it ? None has been suggested, whether as a law of New South Wales itself, or a law of some other community made binding here by our legislature or that of the mother country. If the plaintiff lawfully reached Potter's hands in Sydney, how could he take him to Suva ? What colour was there for supposing that the act done was authorized ? It seems to me that it is impossible to urge that there was any real colour.

With reference to Article 139, upon which respondent strongly relies, it has been broadly and strongly argued that the words "in any of Her Majesty's Courts," make the giving of such a notice necessary even in Courts of the King outside the limits of the Order. The limits of the Order are defined in that Article. [His Honor read the Article].

Of course the State of New South Wales, or any State in Australia would be excepted by the terms of that Article, unless it is otherwise expressly provided, in relation to any particular matter, and the question is, therefore, whether Article 139, by using the words "any of Her Majesty's Courts," expressly provides for the inclusion of the Courts of any autonomous self-governing community such as this. We are not deciding this

H. C. of A.
1907.

HAZELTON
v.
POTTER.

Barton J.

(1) 2 H. & C., 769, at p. 774.   (2) 18 C.B.N.S., 392.

question to-day, but I should like to say that it would take a vast deal more argument than I have heard yet to persuade me to affirm the proposition that the Imperial Statute under which the Order in Council was made ever authorized the extension by this kind of legislation of a rule of procedure—because it is nothing but a rule of procedure—to Courts outside the limits of this Order, and the Courts of countries which are accustomed to manage their own business for themselves.

And looking at the terms of sec. 6 of the *Pacific Islanders Protection Act* 1875, it occurred to me that the explanation of the term "any of Her Majesty's Courts" might be found in the second and third paragraphs of the section, because the second paragraph empowers the Sovereign under Order in Council to create a "Court of justice," and so on, "and Her Majesty may by Order in Council from time to time direct that all powers and jurisdiction aforesaid, or any part thereof, shall be vested in and may be exercised by the Court of any British Colony designated in such Order, concurrently with the High Commissioner's Court or otherwise." It is clear that that provision might account for the use of the words "in any of Her Majesty's Courts," because, if we assume it was the intention not only to create the Court, but to designate other Courts in the British Colonies under this Order, then there would be reason for the Order, and for the term "in any of Her Majesty's Courts," being Courts created or designated as having jurisdiction in that behalf, and that is probably the reason for the use of the term. It should be added that the Supreme Court of New South Wales has not been "designated" in that behalf.

At any rate, it is a matter of ambiguity whether the term "any of Her Majesty's Courts" was intended to include any Court outside the limits of the Order, especially in view of the strictness with which Article 4 of the Order recognizes the existence, and, as far as possible, the exception, of self-governing communities. Where there is an ambiguity we are at liberty to adopt the more reasonable of two constructions open, and it seems to me that the construction to which we lean is more reasonable than that which would give this Article of the Order in Council an operation co-extensive with the whole judicial

H. C. OF A.
1907.

HAZELTON
v.
POTTER.

Barton J.

system of the British Empire. If I had to decide whether Article 139 bore the construction that respondent's counsel places upon it, I should have to say that they had not convinced me of that construction.

As it happens, we are not driven to pronounce a decided opinion upon that question now, because the defendant, even assuming that the term "any of Her Majesty's Courts" is co-extensive with the judicial system of the Empire, did not establish that he was entitled to notice of action. On the question whether the provision as to notice of action under Article 139 could be held to apply to an action brought in a Court of New South Wales, I think the case of *Scott* v. *Lord Seymour* (1) is worthy of attention. That case is cited by *Sir Frederick Pollock* in his book on *Torts* (7th ed., p. 201), as authority for the proposition that "Nothing less than justification of the law will do. Conditions of the *lex fori* suspending or delaying the remedy in the local Courts will not be a bar to the remedy in an English Court in an otherwise proper case. And our Courts would possibly make an exception to the rule if it appeared that by the local law there was no remedy at all for a manifest wrong, such as assault and battery committed without any special justification or excuse."

It is not necessary, either, to decide specifically the questions which arose under Article 112, which provides :—" On arrival at the place named in the warrant, the person if removed under an order of deportation, shall be discharged or otherwise handed over to the proper gaoler, constable, magistrate, or officer." That Article intensifies other criticism that has been uttered this morning upon the warrant as framed, because it shows how vitally necessary it was that the final place should be named in the warrant, and direction given for the conveyance of the prisoner thither by some person designated.

It has been urged that under Article 112 there was authority in case of necessity to bring the person in custody to Sydney on his way to Fiji. To that I would only say that necessity has not been shown in this case. We have had only vague evidence as to the time which might be occupied in taking him one way or the

(1) 1 H. & C., 219.

other, but not to justify his being brought to Sydney; and more than that, to justify any transference or delegation of his custody, it would have to be shown that a strict necessity existed, such as the absence of reasonable means of communication, and of that we have no evidence.

I shall not say more as to the meaning of Article 112, because the whole case for the defendant has so broken down upon other grounds that it is not necessary to discuss these points. I agree with the learned Chief Justice that the appeal should be dismissed.

ISAACS J. read the following judgment:—The first defence ultimately persisted in is that the acts complained of were justified in law, that is, so far as the defendant is concerned. The justification alleged is shortly this: That the plaintiff was sentenced by a competent Court at Gizo to be imprisoned for three months at Suva, that a warrant was in fact, or appeared on its face to have been, duly issued to remove him from Gizo to Suva, that the plaintiff was brought to Sydney under the warrant on his way to Suva, and that all the defendant did was to receive and detain the plaintiff in aid of the person acting under the warrant, and in the manner thereby directed, and in the execution and intended execution of the warrant; and for the authority in law to do this, Article 112 of the Pacific Order in Council 1893 is relied on.

The acts complained of being *primâ facie* illegal in New South Wales, they cannot be justified except under some law having force within that State. See for instance, *The Queen* v. *Lesley* (1).

There is no law of New South Wales to protect the defendant, even assuming all the facts to be as alleged, and, therefore, unless he can point to some Imperial law empowering him to seize and imprison the plaintiff in New South Wales, his acts were unlawful. The defendant contends that Article 112 of the Order in Council is in force in New South Wales, and being made by virtue of an Imperial Statute is paramount to any law of that State. The Order in Council recites three enactments under the powers of which it is made, and adds the not uncommon expression as to powers, "or otherwise in Her Majesty vested." I pass by this additional phrase with the observation that no further power

(1) 29 L.J.M.C., 97.

has been suggested, and it would have to be one couched in the clearest terms to authorize an Order in Council conflicting with the Constitution and laws of New South Wales.

H. C. of A.
1907.

HAZELTON
v.
POTTER.

Isaacs J.

The legislative enactments referred to are the *British Settlements Act* 1887, the *Pacific Islanders Protection Acts* 1872 to 1875, and the *Foreign Jurisdiction Act* 1890.

The first named Act enables the Sovereign in Council to make laws and constitute Courts for the peace, order and good government of British subjects and others within any British settlement, that is, within certain British possessions not under a legislature constituted otherwise than by virtue of that Act or an Act repealed by it. New South Wales could not be affected by that provision.

The same Act also gives power to confer on any Court in any British possession—which, of course, includes New South Wales —any such jurisdiction, civil or criminal, in respect of matters arising in a British settlement as could be conferred on a Court in the settlement itself.

This power has not been exercised so far as New South Wales is concerned, and even if it had been, the jurisdiction conferred would not, in view of the express terms of the section, include an act done in that State.

The Statute may therefore be laid aside as immaterial to the matter in hand.

The *Pacific Islanders Protection Act* 1872 contains nothing relevant, and has not been referred to in argument.

The *Pacific Islanders Protection Act* 1875, by sec. 6, empowers the Sovereign to exercise jurisdiction over British subjects within any islands and places in the Pacific Ocean, not being within the British Dominions, nor within the jurisdiction of any civilized power, to create a High Commissioner—" in, over, and for such islands and places, or some of them," and by Order in Council to confer on the High Commissioner power to make regulations for the government of British subjects "in such islands and places."

So far there is no power conferred by the section to infringe on the autonomy of the State of New South Wales.

Then the same section proceeds to enact that the Sovereign may: (1) By Order in Council create a Court of Justice with

H. C. of A.
1907.

HAZELTON
v.
POTTER.

Isaacs J.

jurisdiction over British subjects within the islands and places to which the authority of the High Commissioner shall extend, with power to take cognizance of offences on the sea or within jurisdiction of the Admiralty ; and (2) by Order in Council direct that *such jurisdiction* may be vested and exercised by the Court of any British Colony designated in such Order ; and provide for the transmission of offenders to such Colony for trial and punishment, for the admission of certain evidence on the trial, and for all other matters for carrying out such Order in Council ; (3) by Order in Council ordain laws for the government of British subjects, *being within such islands and places.*

I am unable to find a word in the enactments referred to which directly empowers the Crown to legislate by Order in Council for the government of British subjects in New South Wales ; nor, apart from the power to invest a Court in that State with jurisdiction to decide, and having decided, to enforce its judgments, in what may be shortly termed "Pacific Island Causes," and apart from the power to provide for matters auxiliary thereto, is there to be found a syllable enabling the Crown to legalize any act committed in the State which would otherwise, and according to the law of New South Wales, be unlawful.

The last Act specifically referred to as the source of authority for the Order in Council is the *Foreign Jurisdiction Act* 1890. But that Statute has no bearing on this case. It may be shortly described as an Act to provide for the exercise of British Courts outside the British Dominions, and by British Courts within the Dominion, over matters occurring outside the Dominions.

None of these legislative provisions directly gives power to authorize the imprisonment in New South Wales of a person who has been tried and convicted at Gizo, even though he be in course of removal to Suva.

Authority, however, to do so is claimed to rest on the necessity of the case, and reliance is placed on two cases, *Leonard Watson's Case* (1), and *Attorney-General for Canada* v. *Cain and Gilhula* (2). Neither of these cases supports the contention. In *Leonard Watson's Case* (1), the Court determined that, in pursuance of legislation in Upper Canada held to be valid apparently because

(1) 9 A. & E., 731.   (2) (1906) A.C., 542.

an Imperial Act recognized the power to authorize transportation, the applicant could and did in Upper Canada bind himself to submit to transportation from Upper Canada to Van Diemen's Land as a condition of pardon, and that the Crown was entitled to carry out the bargain so made, in the only way in which it could practically be performed. Lord *Denman* C.J. said (1) that the matter for consideration was " whether, under the circumstances of this prisoner, he can justly complain that he is injured and has a right to be set free." And his Lordship further said (2):—" As soon as the conditional pardon has been granted on the prisoner's petition, the Crown had a right to enforce the condition, and to take all necessary steps for that purpose. The circumstances confer the authority; and no warrant could enlarge it. . . . . As it is physically impossible to embark at once for Van Diemen's Land from Upper Canada, in every intermediate territory where the prisoner was confined in the necessary performance of the *condition to which he had lawfully bound himself* he was lawfully confined." Then the learned Lord Chief Justice adds:—" And Statute 5 Geo. IV. c. 84, (an Imperial Statute) in the section before quoted, shows that transports from the Colony on commuted sentences had been habitually received in England in their passage to the penal settlements."

The reasons for the decision seem to me to completely differentiate this case from the one cited. Here everything of which the plaintiff complains was done *in adversum*; the only thing in the nature of consent being to apologize to the High Commissioner in order to escape imprisonment of any kind; there is no Imperial Statute or State Statute recognizing interim imprisonment in New South Wales *en route* from one part of the geographical limits of the Western Pacific region to another, and consequently I fail to see how *Leonard Watson's case* (3) can be regarded as an authority for the defendant.

The Attorney General of Canada v. *Cain and Gilhula* (4), decides in accordance with a well established principle that when a power is granted everything necessary to effectuate it is impliedly granted with it unless expressly forbidden. Lord

(1) 9 A. & E., 731, at p. 782.
(2) 9 A. & E., 731, at p. 786.

(3) 9 A. & E., 731.
(4) (1906) A.C., 542.

H. C. of A.
1907.

Hazelton
v.
Potter.

Isaacs J.

Atkinson said (1) that since a State had power to expel aliens "it necessarily follows that the State has the power to do those things which must be done in the very act of expulsion, if the right to expel is to be exercised effectively at all."

But the obvious limitation of the rule of necessary implication is the necessity itself. As Lord *Selborne* said in *Burton* v. *Taylor* (2), "The principle on which the implied power is given confines it within the limits of what is required by the assumed necessity."

I do not understand that a voyage from Gizo to Sydney and thence to Suva is a necessary part of a prisoner's removal from Gizo to Suva, in the sense in which the constraint on the person of the alien outside Canada was held to be a necessary part of the act of his deportation in the case cited. It might be very convenient to make Sydney a resting place, but that is no inherent part of the act of the authorized removal.

Equally with the former case, the decision last cited fails to lend any support to the respondent's cause.

I am, therefore, not prepared, as at present advised, to assent to the proposition that, under the various Acts referred to, it is in any circumstances justifiable by virtue of the doctrine of necessity to authorize the imprisonment in New South Wales of malefactors sentenced in one part of the Western Pacific to punishment in another, and removed there by lawful warrant. It is, however, unnecessary to decide that point definitely in this case, because I am satisfied that the facts do not raise it.

But if there is power to enact by Order in Council such an authority, the respondent must show that it has been so enacted. It is no easy task to read Article 112 in conjunction with the rest of the Order so as to protect a person committing an act in New South Wales.

However general the expressions used throughout the body of the Order, they must in all cases be understood with reference to the 4th Article, defining at the outset the possible limits within which the Order may operate.

That Article begins by declaring that the limits of the Order shall be the Pacific Ocean and the islands and places therein.

(1) (1906) A.C. 542, at p. 546.   (2) 11 App. Cas. 197, at p. 204.

These are the extreme possible limits of the operation of the Order and consequently of every provision in it.

But from these possible limits of operation, there is an express exclusion. Unless otherwise expressly provided by the Order itself in relation to any particular matter, two descriptions of places are wholly excluded namely :—(1) British possessions having a legislature ; (2) Places having a foreign jurisdiction or protection.

The respondent's construction of Article 112 might with equal accuracy be extended to bring in the second (foreign) class of excluded places as the first (British) ; and it is no answer to say that we cannot presume the Imperial legislature would invade the rights of foreign powers, because Article 4 expressly includes the Pacific Ocean and the islands and places therein, except the two classes specifically mentioned, and the mere fact of exclusion sufficiently indicates the extent of the earlier words if left unqualified. And yet it would scarcely be argued that if Honolulu, for instance, had a more convenient line of vessels from Sydney, the 112th Article would authorize removal via Honolulu.

I have used the expression "possible limits" because the actual working limits of the Order are made still narrower.

While it was evidently felt that the policing of the Western Pacific might in time require further proportions of space, it was thought sufficient in the meantime to specify a restricted part of the vast region described in Article 4 as the area within which—in the absence of directions from a Secretary of State—the jurisdiction should be exercised.

Accordingly Article 6 carefully cuts down the actual sphere of jurisdiction to an area within certain meridians and parallels. The boundaries of the area so limited are fully described in Article 6, and I need not repeat them. But a glance at the map shows that area to include, besides the islands mentioned in the sub-clause (1) of Article 6, a vast number of other islands and places " which are not excluded by the 4th Article of this Order," these latter words being carefully inserted in the 6th Article.

Within the area are territories some of which then belonged and still belong to other nations, and others have since become foreign territory, as American, French and German possessions.

H. C. of A.
1907.

HAZELTON
v.
POTTER.

Isaacs J.

Within that area, too, is situated practically the whole of Queens-
land, and a substantial strip of New South Wales.   And the 6th
Article provides:—" Until otherwise directed by a Secretary of
State as hereinafter provided " (that is, by instructions to the
High Commissioner) "jurisdiction under this Order shall be exer-
cised only in relation to the following parts of the limits of this
Order," that is, the specific parts I have referred to.

It is necessarily part of the defendant's case, that the 112th
Article confers whatever jurisdiction exists—express or implied
—to remove a prisoner, and to aid in that removal.   But, if so,
how escape from the precise words of the 4th and 6th Articles,
the one delimiting the extreme possible sphere of jurisdiction, and
the other more definitely restricting the working area of the
jurisdiction ?

The argument of implication resorted to in this case—an argument which entirely sets aside the actual language of the two
Articles designedly inserted to control the interpretation of the
whole Order—would equally well, in conceivable circumstances,
subject the whole of Queensland, except a narrow strip on the
West, and also no inconsiderable part of New South Wales, to the
jurisdiction of the High Commissioner.

Indeed, the same argument, if valid to extend Article 4, might
be pressed on still further, so as to override the explicit terms of
the 6th Article, and to include all the rest of New South Wales,
and the whole of Victoria, Tasmania, and New Zealand, all of
which are within the extreme possible sphere, but beyond the
actual working area of the High Commissioner's jurisdiction.
These considerations appear to me to place the contention of the
respondent outside the pale of probability.   This is more evident
when one looks also at the delimited area of the 6th Article, and
sees the relative positions and distances of, say, the Solomon
Islands and the Fiji Islands, on the one hand, and those of the
same islands in respect of Sydney.   New South Wales is not
within Article 111 (2) of the Order, because its government has
not consented to the reception of persons deported, and, even if
there had been such consent, this is not a case of deportation. In
short, therefore, there has been no express inclusion of New South
Wales within the possible sphere of the 4th Article ; nor if there

were, has there been any inclusion of the State in manner provided by the 6th Article, so as to get over what I may term the
double exclusion ; and lastly, an inclusion by implication is both
contrary to the words of the 4th and 6th Articles, and in this
case, at all events, unsupported by the facts.

But even this is far from constituting the full weakness of the
defendant's case, which must fail even if he could succeed in
establishing that Article 112 was part of the law in New South
Wales. For even supposing that that Article would in appropriate
circumstances apply, the elements of fact necessary to its application are wholly wanting. There has been no warrant of removal
such as is contemplated by the Article. The only document in
the nature of a warrant was one prepared and signed by Mr.
Oliphant in Brisbane, outside his jurisdictional limits, and in contravention of Article 14, and, indeed, quite outside the limits of
the Order. The warrant was consequently invalid in law (see
Perkin v. *Proctor* (1)). The principle affirmed in such cases as
Hill v. *Bateman* (2) and *Shergold* v. *Holloway* (3) was, however,
invoked in aid of the respondent. It was argued on his behalf
that, as the warrant was on its face a good warrrant, he was
protected in any action he took in executing it. But, in my
opinion, it was properly answered that, the warrant being invalid,
and Potter not being an officer of the Court out of which it issued,
and therefore not under any duty to execute it, was at best a
mere volunteer *qud* the warrant, and not within the principles of
protection.

With equal force, it was also answered, that the warrant on its
face was not a warrant of removal within the terms of the 112th
Article because its terminus was Sydney. The fact that it
authorized Robertson or some other officer of the Court to deliver
the plaintiff and the warrant itself to some person in Sydney
shows conclusively, to my mind, that it could not reasonably be
read as containing authority to Robertson or any other person to
convey Hazelton to Suva. Possibly it was intended to supple-
ment it by some other warrant ; but no other warrant appears, or
was relied on. It was that warrant and that only on which this

(1) 2 Wils., 382, at p. 384.　　　　(2) 2 Stra., 710.
　　　　　(3) 2 Stra., 1002.

defence is rested. Its concluding words, "that the said sentence of imprisonment may be duly carried into effect," discloses not an authority, but an object; and applies not to authorize the conveyance of the appellant from Sydney to Suva, but to indicate the purpose of imprisoning him at Suva on his arrival there. On its face the intended effect of that particular warrant was unmistakeably exhausted in Sydney.

There is consequently no ground upon which Potter can obtain the benefit of the principles of the cases cited, and in the result he fails to show any legal exoneration for imprisoning the appellant.

Then Mr. *Scholes* relied, and ultimately founded his chief reliance, on Article 139 of the Order in Council. He contended that the phrase " Any of Her Majesty's Courts " includes the Supreme Court of New South Wales. So it does if read alone. But still there is the constantly speaking limitation of Articles 4 and 6, always reminding us that, however wide the language of any particular Article may be, nothing short of some express provision is to include the territory of any ordinary self-governing Colony. If under sec. 6 of the *Pacific Islanders Protection Act* 1875 the Court of a self-governing Colony be designated, it may, as suggested by my learned brother *Barton*, be the subject of an Order in Council. But such an Order in Council, conferring jurisdiction on Courts in British Colonies, would have to be made wider than the present, and, as required by the words of the Statute, would have to designate the Colony. The insuperable difficulty in the way of the defendant's construction, even with the aid of sec. 6 of the Act of 1875, is that the present Order in Council has fixed its utmost possible limits, " the Pacific Ocean and the islands and places therein," and apparently no extension whatever of this limitation is contemplated by the Order, though restrictions within the limits are provided for. The 139th Article could not, therefore, as the present Order in Council is framed, apply for instance to the Supreme Court of Western Australia or the Supreme Courts of England or Canada. Then why to that of New South Wales ?

There is what I may term internal evidence contained in the Order which runs contrary to the respondent's contention. When

the frame of the Order is looked at, it is found that Part XVI. is
headed " Official," that is, official for the purposes of the Order ;
and it contains three Articles.   Article 137 has a heading
"general official powers," that is certainly within the limits.   It
uses equally large terms with those found in Article 139.   It
speaks of " Any of Her Majesty's Officers "—clearly referring to
officers performing duties within the specified limits, and not to
officers all over the Dominion, or rather all over the world.
Article 138 relates to cases heard by Acting Commissioners
which must always be within the same limits.   The only other
Article of the Part is Article 139, and it prescribes procedure and
practice for " Her Majesty's Courts," and speaks later on of
" the Court."   Why should not the same principle be applied to
this Article as to the two preceding Articles of the same group ?

Neither is it to be overlooked that, though the only Court
constituted is the High Commissioner's Court, yet that tribunal
is subdivided into what are frequently called " Courts " in
various Articles of the Order, and are regarded as separate
tribunals for many purposes.   Moreover, much of the jurisdiction
conferred by the Order is personal only, and within limits where
foreign tribunals co-exist.   These are expressly referred to in
Article 110, and on the whole it seems to me that the phrase
" any of Her Majesty's Courts " was not used with the intention
of including every British Court throughout the world.   If
the unlimited meaning contended for is to be allowed to this
expression, then I see no reason why in Article 110 the same
method of interpretation should not be applied to the equally
wide phrases " foreign Court " and " foreign officer," and " Court
of any State in amity with Her Majesty " so as to empower the
High Commissioner's Court to order any person within its
jurisdictional limits to go to San Francisco or St. Petersburg and
attend and give evidence before the Courts there.

If then the 139th Article does not operate in New South Wales,
so as to govern and control the tribunals there, it cannot have
any application to the case.   It was indeed said by *Rogers* J.
that, though it did not bind the Courts, it bound the parties.   It
could not bind the parties in respect of any act done in New South
Wales unless it operated as part of the law in force in that State,

H. C. of A.
1907.

HAZELTON
v.
POTTER.

Isaacs J.

and, if that be so, it would equally bind the Courts. But if it is not part of the law of New South Wales it binds no one, whether Court or individual, within the State territory. Finally, assuming once more that Article 139 is in full force in New South Wales, for it is not essential to definitely determine that question one way or the other, though I entertain no doubt upon it, still, in the circumstances of this case the principle of *Roberts* v. *Orchard* (1), followed in *Chamberlain* v. *King* (2), and *Rochfort* v. *Rynd* (3), and affirmed in *McLaughlin* v. *Fosbery* (4), would, by reason of the undisputed facts, place the respondent outside the shelter of the Article. In the Irish case cited the defendants, who were justices, were sued in trespass for a seizure under a distress warrant, and they pleaded the 8th section of an Act which prohibited any action against a justice of the peace for anything done by him in the execution of his office, unless commenced within six months. The action was commenced after the period, and the defendants moved on affidavit to set aside the action. The applicability of the 8th section was in question, and the decision turned on whether the signing of the distress warrant was an act done by the defendants in the execution of their office.

Palles C.B. said (5):—"The true rule is that the protection of the 8th section is afforded in every case in which the Justice *bonâ fide* believes in the existence of a state of facts which would have entitled him to act as he did" (citing *Chamberlain* v. *King*) (2); and he adds also supported by that case, "If the belief be *bonâ fide*, the protection is not lost by it not being reasonable, but the fact of its being unreasonable is, of course, an element in the determination of the *bona fides.*"

After reciting the facts, the learned Chief Baron proceeeds to recognize and apply a rule which is very material in this case. He says (6):—"These being the facts, and the onus of proving the defence lying on the defendants, they should have affirmatively shown a *bonâ fide* belief, not that they had authority to do as they did, but that facts existed which would have so authorized them. Neither is the existence of this belief sworn to, nor are

(1) 2 H. & C., 769.
(2) L.R. 6 C.P., 474.
(3) 8 L.R Ir., 204.

(4) 1 C.L.R., 546, at p. 566.
(5) 8 L.R. Ir., 204, at p. 208.
(6) 8 L.R. Ir., 204, at p. 209.

facts alleged which would show that such a belief might have been entertained."

The motion was accordingly refused, and the whole facts were left to be determined on the trial. Here in like manner the defendant had the onus of proving the defence, yet he does not say he had any belief in facts which would have justified him, and if he had said so, the evidence incontrovertibly establishes that he could not as a reasonable man have believed, and therefore could not have *bonâ fide* believed, that the warrant he assisted to execute was a warrant of removal from Gizo to Suva. That consideration is at once fatal in any aspect to his claim to succeed under the 139th Article.

I am therefore of opinion that this appeal must be allowed.

> *Appeal allowed. Order appealed from discharged, and rule nisi for nonsuit discharged with costs. Judgment for plaintiff restored, respondent to pay costs of appeal and of motion to rescind leave.*

Solicitors, for the appellant, *McEvilly & McEvilly.*

Solicitor, for the respondent, *The Crown Solicitor of New South Wales.*

C. A. W.

[HIGH COURT OF AUSTRALIA.]

McKELL AND ANOTHER   .   .   .   . APPELLANTS;
DEFENDANTS,

AND .

RIDER   .   .   .´   .   .   .   .   . RESPONDENT.
INFORMANT,

ON APPEAL FROM THE SUPREME COURT OF VICTORIA.

H. C. OF A. *Health Act* 1890 (*Vict*) (*No.* 1098) *secs.* 216*, 222—Nuisance—Common nuisance—
1908.   *Chimney sending forth smoke—Defence—Fireplace or furnace constructed to*
⌣⌣   *consume smoke as far as practicable.*

MELBOURNE,   On a prosecution under sec. 222 of the *Health Act* 1890 (Vict.) charging
March 23, 24.   that by the sufferance of the defendants a nuisance within the meaning of sec.

Griffith C.J.,   216 of the Act arose, viz., a chimney (not being the chimney of a private
O'Connor and   dwelling-house) sending forth smoke in such quantity as to be a nuisance, it
Higgins JJ.   is not a defence that the fireplace or furnace connected with such chimney is
constructed in such manner as to consume as far as practicable, having regard
to the nature of the manufacture or trade, all smoke arising therefrom, and

---

* Sec. 216 of the *Health Act* 1890, so
far as material, is as follows :—

" For the purposes of this Part of
this Act.—

.   .   .   .   .

"(7) Any fireplace or furnace whether
constructed before or after the passing
of this Act which does not as far as
practicable consume the smoke arising
from the combustible used therein, and
which is used for working engines by
steam, or in any mill factory dyehouse brewery bakehouse or gaswork,
or in any manufacturing or trade process whatsoever ; and any chimney (not
being the chimney of a private dwelling-
house) sending forth smoke in such
quantity as to be a nuisance :

.   .   .   .   .

" Shall be deemed to be a nuisance
and shall be liable to be dealt with in

manner provided by this Part of this
Act. Provided—

.   .   .   .   .

" Secondly.   That where a person is
summoned before any court in respect
of a nuisance arising from a fireplace
or furnace which does not consume the
smoke arising from the combustible
used in such fireplace or furnace, the
court shall hold that no nuisance is
created within the meaning of this Part
of this Act, and dismiss the complaint,
if it be satisfied that such fireplace or
furnace is constructed in such manner
as to consume as far as practicable,
having regard to the nature of the
manufacture or trade, all smoke arising
therefrom, and that such fireplace or
furnace has for that purpose been carefully attended to by the person having
the charge thereof."

H. C. of A.
1908.

McKell
v.
Rider.

that such fireplace or furnace has for that purpose been carefully attended to by the person having the charge thereof.

The word "nuisance" in the phrase "sending forth smoke in such quantity as to be a nuisance," in sec. 216 (7) means a common nuisance.

Judgment of *Hood J.*, (*Rider* v. *McKell*, (1908) V.L.R., 110 ; 29 A.L.T., 77), affirmed.

APPEAL from the Supreme Court of Victoria.

At the Court of Petty Sessions at Prahran an information was heard whereby Henry Rider, City Inspector of the City of Prahran, proceeded against John McKell and Abraham Baxter, trading as the Australian Gas Retort and Firebrick Manufacturing Company, for that, between 13th June 1907 and the date of the information, at Toorak Road in the municipal district of Prahran, by the sufferance of the defendants a nuisance within the meaning of sec. 216 of the *Health Act* 1890 arose, such nuisance being a chimney (not being a chimney of a private dwelling-house) sending forth smoke in such quantity as to be a nuisance.

From the evidence it appeared that the defendants carried on the business of brick manufacturers in a neighbourhood which was thickly populated; and that during the period in question large volumes of smoke were every day emitted from a chimney of their factory. Several residents near the factory deposed that linen hung out to dry was soiled and damaged, that it was consequently often necessary to wash linen two or three times, that their houses inside and outside were fouled with smuts, that they had sometimes to keep their houses shut and could not get fresh air, and that the smoke was worse at night than in the day time. This evidence was corroborated by the informant who also said that the smoke on certain days was so thick that "you could scarcely walk through it."

At the close of the evidence for the prosecution, counsel for the defendants tendered evidence that the fireplaces or furnaces were properly constructed so as to consume as far as practicable the smoke, and that the fireplaces or furnaces had been carefully attended to. This evidence was objected to by counsel for the informant, and the magistrates refused to receive it. No evidence

H. C. of A.
1908.
⌣
McKELL
v.
RIDER.
——

was given by the defendants. The magistrates having convicted the defendants, they obtained an order nisi to review, which was discharged by *Hood* J.: *Rider* v. *McKell* (1).

From this decision the defendants now by special leave appealed to the High Court.

Mitchell K.C. and *Schutt*, for the appellants. The evidence was properly admissible under the second proviso to sec. 216 of the *Health Act* 1890. That proviso is intended to relate to a prosecution for a nuisance consisting of a chimney sending forth smoke, as well as to a nuisance consisting of a fireplace or furnace which does not as far as practicable consume its smoke. A great majority of the chimneys there referred to are connected with, and carry the smoke away from, the fireplaces and furnaces there mentioned. And the protection given by the proviso should be available to persons charged in respect of chimneys just as to persons charged in respect of fireplaces and furnaces. They referred to *Ex parte Schofield* (2); *Cooper* v. *Woolley* (3); 38 & 39 Vict. c. 55, sec. 91. The word "nuisance" in the clause "sending forth smoke in such quantity as to be a nuisance," means a common nuisance, and not a private nuisance. If that be so, there is no evidence here of a common nuisance, but merely of a private nuisance. *Harris's Principles of Criminal Law*, p. 155; *Stephen's Digest of Criminal Law*, 5th ed., p. 140; *R.* v. *Lloyd* (4). The smoke must be injurious to the general health of the public to constitute a common nuisance: *R.* v. *Davey* (5); *Great Western Railway Co.* v. *Bishop* (6).

[GRIFFITH C.J. referred to the *Criminal Code* (Qd.) sec. 230, as to the meaning of a common nuisance.]

The decision in *Weekes* v. *King* (7), that the second proviso only applies to the nuisance consisting of a fireplace or furnace which does not as far as practicable consume its smoke, is distinguishable by reason of the differences between sec. 91 of the English *Public Health Act* 1875 (38 & 39 Vict. c. 55), on which it was decided, and sec. 216 of the *Health Act* 1890.

(1) (1908) V.L.R., 110; 29 A.L.T., 77.
(2) (1891) 2 Q.B., 428.
(3) L.R. 2 Ex., 88.
(4) 4 Esp., 200.

(5) 5 Esp., 217.
(6) L.R. 7 Q.B., 550.
(7) 15 Cox., Cr. Ca., 723.

The nuisance consisting of a chimney (not being the chimney of a private dwelling-house) sending forth smoke in such quantity as to be a nuisance, should be limited to chimneys not being chimneys "used for working engines by steam, or in any mill, factory, dyehouse, brewery, bakehouse, or gaswork, or in any manufacturing or trade process whatsoever."

Starke (with him *MacFarlan*), for the respondent. The word "nuisance" in the phrase "sending forth smoke in such quantity as to be a nuisance," no doubt means a common nuisance. But it is not necessary that it should be injurious to the public health : *Gaskell* v. *Bayley* (1); it is sufficient that it should interfere with the comfort of persons living in the neighbourhood : *Banbury Urban Sanitary Authority* v. *Page* (2) ; *Bishop Auckland Local Board* v. *Bishop Auckland Iron and Steel Co.* (3). A nuisance created by Parliament might be the subject of indictment ; *R.* v. *Neil* (4); *Archbold's Criminal Pleadings*, 22nd ed., p. 1121.

[O'CONNOR J. referred to *R.* v. *Crawshaw* (5).

GRIFFITH C.J. referred to *R.* v. *Gregory* (6).]

The clause relating to fireplaces and furnaces may be for the benefit of persons employed in factories. The second proviso is a definition of what the words "as far as practicable" mean.

GRIFFITH C.J. Sec. 216 of the *Health Act* 1890 provides that for the purpose of Part X. of the Act certain things shall be deemed to be nuisances. The 7th category is :—" Any fireplace or furnace whether constructed before or after the passing of this Act which does not as far as practicable consume the smoke arising from the combustible used therein, and which is used for working engines by steam, or in any mill factory dyehouse brewery bakehouse or gaswork, or in any manufacturing or trade process whatsoever ; and any chimney (not being the chimney of a private dwelling-house) sending forth smoke in such quantity as to be a nuisance." There are two provisoes to that section, the second of which is :—" That where a person is

(1) 30 L.T., N.S., 516.	(4) 2 C. & P., 485.
(2) 8 Q.B.D., 97.	(5) Bell C.C., 303.
(3) 10 Q.B.D., 138.	(6) 5 B. & Ad., 555.

summoned before any Court in respect of a nuisance arising from a fireplace or furnace which does not consume the smoke arising from the combustible used in such fireplace or furnace, the Court shall hold that no nuisance is created within the meaning of this Part of this Act, and dismiss the complaint, if it be satisfied that such fireplace or furnace is constructed in such manner as to consume as far as practicable, having regard to the nature of the manufacture or trade, all smoke arising therefrom, and that such fireplace or furnace has for that purpose been carefully attended to by the person having the charge thereof." The section is taken from sec. 91 of the English *Public Health Act* 1875 (38 & 39 Vict. c. 55) with slight variations, the only variations, so far as now material, being that in the clause, "any chimney (not being the chimney of a private dwelling-house) sending forth smoke in such quantity as to be a nuisance," the word "black" is inserted in the English Act before the word "smoke," and that that clause is in the English Act printed as a separate paragraph instead of running on after the preceding words. It was suggested before us that the change in the collocation made the concluding words "sending forth smoke in such quantity as to be a nuisance" operate as a qualification of the whole category, but the grammatical construction precludes the adoption of that argument.

The appellants were charged with the offence, which is created by sec. 222, of being persons by whose sufferance a nuisance within the meaning of sec. 216 arose and continued, the nuisance being a chimney (not being a chimney of a private dwelling-house) sending forth smoke in such quantity as to be a nuisance.

Before the magistrates there was evidence sufficient to warrant the conclusion that the appellants had committed a nuisance at common law by sending out smoke from their chimney, but they claimed to be entitled to the benefit of the second proviso, and to show that they had used in their works a fireplace constructed in such a manner as to consume as far as possible, having regard to the nature of their manufacture or trade, all smoke arising therefrom, and that their fireplace had been for that purpose carefully attended to by the person having charge thereof. The

H. C. or A.
1908.

McKELL
v.
RIDER.

Griffith C.J.

evidence was rejected, and, upon appeal to the Supreme Court, *Hood* J. held that it was rightly rejected.

The main contention of the appellants is that that proviso should be held to apply to a charge of suffering the nuisance consisting of a chimney sending forth smoke in such quantity as to be a nuisance as well as to a charge of suffering the other nuisance. A similar question was raised in England in the case of *Weekes* v. *King* (1), and the Court was of opinion that the offence of keeping a fireplace which does not as far as practicable consume the smoke, and the offence of keeping a chimney, which sends forth black smoke in such quantity as to be a nuisance, are two separate offences. The construction of the language is not altered by the omission of the word "black." That decision, given in 1885, has never since been reviewed, although it is said that an ineffective attempt was made to review it. I can see no reason to doubt the correctness of that decision.

The Court pointed out that there were really two distinct offences, one that of committing a nuisance by means of a chimney sending forth smoke, and the other failing to consume smoke as far as practicable. The word "nuisance" in the Act must, I think, be read as meaning a nuisance according to the definition of that term at common law—an indictable nuisance. In this case, as I have said, there was ample evidence to show that the smoke constituted such a nuisance.

The second proviso is carefully framed to deal with the first part of clause (7), which in constituting the offence uses the words "as far as practicable." Now those words are ambiguous. It may be contended—as I have known it held by a Judge—that they mean as far as is mechanically practicable, or that they mean practicable having regard to the nature of the purpose for which the fireplace or furnace is used—that is, practicable for carrying on the business. The legislature, in order to prevent any difficulty of that sort from arising, laid down that besides the two elements which obviously go to constitute practicability—that is, the construction of the fireplace and proper attention being paid to it—there should also be taken into consideration a third element, namely, the purpose for which it was used; and that is

(1) 15 Cox Cr. Ca., 723.

all they did by the proviso. That proviso has no reference to an act such as that complained of here, which is itself a nuisance at common law. There was no reason to protect a person who had offended against the common law. He might have been indicted for the offence. But this Act purported to give more complete and summary methods of suppressing nuisances. The English Statute law at first only contained provisions for the abatement of nuisances. Afterwards summary proceedings for that purpose were added. In the *Health Act* 1890 both those results are provided for in the same Statute. The effect of the provision for summary punishment is not to alter the character of an act which is a nuisance, but is to provide a more summary remedy. In this case it was necessary for the prosecution to establish that the emission of smoke was a nuisance at common law. Having done so, the Act declares that the defendants, in suffering that omission to take place, were suffering a nuisance for the purpose of the Act, and were liable to be dealt with in a summary way. The failure to consume smoke as far as practicable is also declared to be a nuisance for the purpose of the Act. That might or might not be a nuisance at common law, but whether it was or not, is immaterial for the purpose of the Act provided it comes within the language of the section. A similar provision is to be found in sub-sec. (2) of the section which provides that:—"any cesspool or other receptacle for night-soil which is not perfectly watertight shall be deemed to be a nuisance."

For these reasons it appears to me that the appellants were not entitled to rely on the proviso, and that the evidence which they offered was properly rejected. The conviction was therefore right, and the appeal should be dismissed.

O'CONNOR J. I am of the same opinion. I do not think it necessary to add anything.

HIGGINS J. I concur.

Appeal dismissed.

Solicitors, for the appellants, *Upton & Plant.*
Solicitor, for the respondent, *D. H. Herald.*

B. L.

[HIGH COURT OF AUSTRALIA.]

ELIZA BROWN . . . . APPELLANT;
PLAINTIFF,

AND

DAVID ABBOTT AND OTHERS . . . RESPONDENTS.
DEFENDANTS,

ON APPEAL FROM THE SUPREME COURT OF
VICTORIA.

Will—Settlement—Annuity—Charge, whether on corpus or income—Order of Court —Transfer of Land Statute 1866 (Vict.) (No. 301), sec. 86.

H. C. OF A.
1908.

MELBOURNE,
March 16, 17,
23.

Griffith C.J.,
O'Connor and
Isaacs JJ.

By a marriage settlement made in 1887 the settlor, the intended husband, gave a term of 99 years in certain land to his trustees who were directed "out of the rents and profits" thereof to raise the annual sum of £500 and pay it to the intended wife during her life. The settlor subsequently by his will devised the land to certain beneficiaries subject to the charge created by the settlement. After the settlor's death, viz., in 1882, by order of the Supreme Court, an instrument of charge under the *Transfer of Land Statute* 1866 (Vict.) to secure the annuity was executed, which had the effect of rendering the corpus as well as the income of the land liable to satisfy the accruing payments of the annuity. The land was subsequently sold pursuant to an order of Court and the proceeds of sale were invested. An order of Court was afterwards made directing the trustees of the settlor's will to set aside a certain sum to answer the "rent charge" on the land and to pay the residue of the proceeds of sale to the beneficiaries entitled thereto. This order was never carried into effect, as the income from the investments representing the proceeds of sale had become insufficient to pay the annuity, which fell into arrear.

Held that, whether under the settlement the annuity was or was not a charge upon the corpus as well as the income of the land, it became so by virtue of the instrument of charge under the *Transfer of Land Statute* 1866; that it was too late to have that charge corrected, if it had been inadvertently made; that that charge equally attached to the proceeds of the sale of the land;

H. C. of A.
1908.

BROWN
v.
ABBOTT.

that nothing which had subsequently happened diminished the extent of that charge ; and therefore that the annuitant was entitled to an order for payment of arrears of the annuity out of the corpus of the investments representing the proceeds of the sale of the land.

Judgment of *Hood* J. affirmed.

APPEAL from the Supreme Court of Victoria.

On 3rd November 1880 a bill in equity was filed in which Eliza Brown, who sued on behalf of herself and all other the residuary devisees under the will of Edwin Trenerry, deceased, was plaintiff, and the defendants were David Abbott, and Frederick Trenerry Brown, trustees of the will of Edwin Trenerry ; Joseph Trenerry and his eldest son William Trenerry, Thomas Trenerry and his eldest son William Trenerry, and William Martyn Trenerry and his eldest son William Martyn Trenerry the younger, specific devisees under the will of Edwin Trenerry ; and Louisa Trenerry (now Louisa Wilkinson) widow of Edwin Trenerry. The Equity Trustees Executors and Agency Co. Ltd., who had subsequently been appointed to act in place of the trustees of the will, were afterwards added as defendants, and Thomas Trenerry and William Martyn Trenerry the elder had since died.

The facts, the nature of the suit, and the various proceedings and orders in it are sufficiently stated in the judgment hereunder.

On 25th April 1907 a motion was made in the suit on behalf of the defendant Louisa Wilkinson " that so much of the principal moneys and securities representing the proceeds of the sale of Tregothnan Estate in the hands or under the control of the defendants the Equity Trustees Executors and Agency Co. Ltd. as may be necessary may be applied or sold or otherwise realized and appropriated to provide for the payment of the arrears of annuity now due to the applicant and to provide for the due payment in future of the full amount of the annuity payable to her. And that all necessary directions for the immediate payment of the said arrears and for the future payments of the said annuity be given. And that the costs of this application be then dealt with."

The motion was heard by *Hood* J. who made an order declaring that Louisa Wilkinson was entitled to a charge upon the

principal moneys and securities representing the proceeds of the
sale of Tregothnan Estate to secure the annuity of £500 payable
to her, and that the sum of £550 and upwards was then due in
respect of arrears of such annuity, and further ordering the
Equity Trustees and Agency Co. Ltd. to sell a certain piece of
land, being one of the securities before mentioned, and out of the
proceeds to pay £250 in part satisfaction of the arrears of the
annuity, and to pay the balance into Court to be invested and
the income applied in accordance with prior orders of the Court.

From this order the plaintiff now appealed to the High Court.

Arguments were adduced by counsel for the appellant upon
the question whether under the deed of settlement the annuity
was a charge upon the corpus as well as upon the income of
Tregothnan Estate, but in the view the High Court took this
question became immaterial, and the question was not argued by
counsel for the respondents. Therefore only the authorities
cited on this question are set out in this report.

Irvine K.C. (with him *H. I. Cohen*), for the appellant.
Although when the instrument of charge under the *Transfer
of Land Statute* 1866 was executed the annuitant had the rights
of a mortgagee and might have the land sold to pay arrears of the
annuity and to satisfy accruing payments of the annuity, yet,
when under the subsequent order of the Court the land was sold
and that instrument of charge was discharged, the original
settlement revived, and any subsequent orders of Court dealing
with the proceeds of that sale dealt with them strictly in accordance with the settlement.

[As to the question of the nature of the charge created by the
settlement, the following authorities were referred to :—*Birch* v.
Sherratt (1) ; *Stelfox* v. *Sugden* (2) ; *In re Boden* ; *Boden* v.
Boden (3) ; *Wormald* v. *Muzeen* (4) ; *In re Moore's Estate* (5) ;
In re Bigge ; *Granville* v. *Moore* (6) ; *Baker* v. *Baker* (7) ; *In re
West's Estate* (8) ; *In re Tyndall* (9) ; *Booth* v. *Coulton* (10) ;
Theobald on Wills, 5th ed., p. 451.]

(1) L.R. 2 Ch., 644.   (6) (1907) 1 Ch., 714.
(2) John., 234.   (7) 6 H.L.C., 616.
(3) (1907) 1 Ch., 132.   (8) (1898) 1 I.R., 75.
(4) 17 Ch. D., 167 ; 50 L.J. Ch., 482.   (9) 7 Ir. Ch. R., 181.
(5) 19 L.R. Ir., 365.   (10) L.R. 5 Ch., 684.

H. C. of A.   *Miller*, for the respondents, William Trenerry, son of Joseph
1908.   Trenerry, and William Martyn Trenerry the younger, adopted
———   the arguments on behalf of the appellant.
BROWN
v.
ABBOTT.
———   *Weigall* K.C. (with him *Richardson*), for the respondent
Louisa Wilkinson. When the instrument of charge under the
Transfer of Land Statute 1866 was executed, Mrs. Wilkinson
had the rights of a mortgagee over the land.

[GRIFFITH C.J.—If the decree had been drawn up so as to
make it appear that something was decided which never was
decided, the Court could amend the decree: *Ivanhoe Gold Corporation Ltd.* v. *Symonds* (1); *In re Swire*; *Mellor* v. *Swire* (2).]

A further stage was reached, for the annuitant became in effect
mortgagee of the land. When that land was sold with the
approval of Mrs. Wilkinson and of everyone concerned, she was
entitled to the same security over the proceeds as she had over
the land itself. There is nothing in any order of the Court which
is inconsistent with that view, and much in those orders recognizes
that view. One of the objects of the original suit was to have
the rights of Mrs. Wilkinson defined, and they were defined as
being such that she was entitled to have a legal charge upon the
corpus as well as the income, and that it would be proper to give
her an instrument of charge: *Brown* v. *Abbott* (3). That
having been obtained, the settlement was to that extent gone,
and the instrument of charge was substituted for it. Under the
order of 2nd May 1891, if the £15,000 had been set aside the
annuitant would undoubtedly have been entitled to resort to the
corpus of the fund set apart: *Harbin* v. *Masterman* (4).

[ISAACS J. referred to *Carmichael* v. *Gee* (5).]

And as that fund was not set aside the annuitant is in no
worse position than if the order had never been made.

[He also referred to *Phillips* v. *Gutteridge* (6).]

Vasey, for the respondents the Equity Trustees Executors and
Agency Co. Ltd.

———

(1) 4 C.L.R., 642.   (4) (1896) 1 Ch., 351.
(2) 30 Ch. D., 239.   (5) 5 App. Cas., 588.
(3) 7 V.L.R. (E.), 121 ; 3 A.L.T., (6) 3 D. J. & S., 332.
47.

Irvine K.C. in reply.

Cur. adv. vult.

GRIFFITH C.J. delivered the judgment of the Court.

This is an appeal from an order made by *Hood* J. in the course of a suit instituted in November 1880. The circumstances which gave rise to the suit and the present inquiry may be stated briefly. On 26th September 1877 a marriage settlement was executed upon the marriage of Edwin Trenerry and Louisa Rich, now Louisa Richardson, which purported to convey a certain property in Victoria called Tregothnan to trustees for the benefit of, amongst others, the intended wife. The only trust to which I need refer is a trust for the term of 99 years, during which the trustees were, during the life of the wife, out of the rents and profits of the land to raise the annual sum of £500, and pay it to the wife during her life ; and subject to the said annual sum the trustees were to permit the rents and profits of the land to be received by the persons entitled under the settlement to the land in reversion immediately expectant upon the term of 99 years. Then, following the term of 99 years, and subject to the trusts thereof and to the annual sum of £500 thereby secured, was a term of 1,000 years for the purpose of raising portions for the children of the marriage. The land comprised in the settlement was held under the *Transfer of Land Statute* 1866, but the settlement, which was executed in England, was not in the form required by that Statute, and therefore did not operate to convey the legal estate to the trustees. The annual income from the land was at that time between £800 and £900, and there was no reason to suppose that the income would fall short of the £500 intended to be secured to the wife.

In November 1887 Edwin Trenerry made his will, by which he specifically devised the property called Tregothnan, subject to the charges created by the settlement. He also made a specific devise of certain other lands, known as Doctor's Creek and the Ballarat property, to certain other devisees, and he made a residuary devise to the persons represented by the present appellant. Edwin Trenerry died on 21st April 1880.

In the interval between the execution of the settlement and

the death of the settlor he had deposited the deeds of the three properties specifically devised with the Commercial Bank of Australia Ltd. to secure an overdraft, and at the time of his death he was indebted to the Bank in the sum of about £10,000, which was secured by the equitable mortgages over those three properties. The trustees after his death sold the residuary real estate and out of the proceeds paid off the Bank. The appellant in her representative capacity then claimed to be entitled to have the debt secured by the equitable mortgages paid out of the properties mortgaged, and that, at any rate, she and the other devisees represented by her were entitled to have a charge upon those properties until they were recouped. Thereupon this suit was instituted by the appellant on 3rd November 1880. The main object of the suit was that the residuary devisees might have recouped to them out of the specifically devised properties the amount of the mortgages which had been discharged by the trustees out of the proceeds of the residuary estate. The bill being framed in that view, for the purpose of apportioning the payments it was necessary to ascertain the values of Tregothnan, Doctor's Creek, and the Ballarat property. The appellant alleged in the bill that the testator was the registered proprietor of Tregothnan under the provisions of the *Transfer of Land Statute* 1866, and that the indenture of settlement was not registered and could not be registered as an instrument under the *Transfer of Land Statute* 1866, and therefore was not a valid legal disposition under that Statute, but that " the plaintiff and all other parties hereto admit that the same was and is operative in equity as a valid charge of £500 a year for the life of the said Louisa Trenerry upon Tregothnan and that " the trustees of the will " should at the request of the trustees of the indenture execute any instrument under the *Transfer of Land Statute* which may be required for the purpose of making the said annuity a valid first charge upon Tregothnan in accordance with the trusts of the said indenture."

The defendants practically accepted that view of the case. What was the precise meaning of the terms of the indenture does not appear to have been the subject of contention, as the income from Tregothnan was much more than sufficient to pay the annuity of £500, and the construction of the settlement does not appear to have been debated in the course of the suit.

By the decree, which was made on 20th October 1881, it was referred to the Master in Equity to inquire and report as to the value of Tregothnan "subject to the charge which subsisted thereon at the testator's death under the indenture of settlement."

Those words are repeated afterwards, and then came this declaration :—" This Court doth declare that the said indenture of settlement dated 26th September 1877 was operative in equity as a valid first charge of £500 a year for the life of the said Louisa Trenerry And this Court doth order that the" trustees of the will " and all other necessary parties do execute an instrument under the *Transfer of Land Statute* for the purpose of making the said annuity a valid first charge upon Tregothnan aforesaid in such manner and form and with such trustee or trustees whether named in the said indenture of settlement or not as the " trustees of the will "and the defendant Louisa Trenerry may agree upon And doth order that the said Master do settle such instrument and appoint a trustee or trustees in case the said parties differ about the same." In accordance with that decree— which seems to have been made in the presence and with the concurrence of all parties, and, again, without special regard to the meaning of the settlement—an instrument of charge was drawn up which was registered on 5th July 1882. By that instrument the land was charged for the benefit of the trustees appointed by the widow with an annuity of £500 during and throughout the life of the widow, with all the rights and remedies given to an annuitant by the *Transfer of Land Statute.*

I turn to the *Transfer of Land Statute* 1866 to see what those rights were. In the event of default in payment of the annuity charged upon the land, the annuitant, or in this case the trustees for the annuitant, might sell the land and apply the purchase money :—" first in payment of the expenses of and incidental to such sale and consequent on such default ; then in payment of the moneys which may be due or owing to the annuitant or his transferrees ; and the residue shall be deposited . . . at interest in the savings bank or in some other bank in Melbourne in the joint names of the annuitant or his transferrees and of the registrar, to satisfy the accruing payments of the charge, and subject thereto for the benefit of the parties who may be or become entitled to the residue of the deposited money" (sec. 86). As soon, therefore, as the charge was registered the annuitant became entitled to those rights. That is to say, that if any default in payment of the annuity occurred, the property could be sold, the proceeds applied in payment of the moneys due and owing to the annuitant, and the corpus as well as the income would be liable to satisfy the accruing payments of the annuity.

After this a favourable opportunity for the sale of Tregothnan occurred, and it was sold under an order of Court in the present suit. It could not, of course, be sold so as to give a clear title without the consent of the widow. She was not formally a party to the proceedings on that occasion, but with her tacit, if not express, consent the property was sold and the purchase money was ordered to be paid into Court. Now it is clear that, when property subject to a charge is sold by the Court, the charge attaches just as much to the proceeds of the sale as it attached to the land, and the Court will give effect to the charge, and will not diminish the right of the person entitled to the charge unless the other facts warrant such a diminution.

So matters continued for many years. Then, by reason of the depreciation in the value of real estate, the income from Tregothnan fell short of £500, and after some time application was made to the Court for an order to make up to the annuitant the arrears of the annuity.

In the meantime, on 2nd May 1891, after the order for the sale of Tregothnan had been made, the Court ordered that the defendants, the trustees of the will, should, out of the proceeds of the sale, set aside and keep invested the sum of £15,000 to answer the "rent charge" on Tregothnan; and, with the consent of the widow, the Court further ordered that the residue of the proceeds of sale should be paid to the residuary devisees, in part recoupment of the charge upon Tregothnan to which they were entitled for principal and interest in respect of the payment out of the residuary estate of the debt secured by the mortgages to the Bank. The Court went on to order "that the income to arise from the investment of the said sum of £15,000 be applied

H. C. of A.
1908.

Brown
v.
Abbott.

first in payment of the said 'rent charge' and then in or towards payment of such principal and interest as aforesaid."

The appellant contends that the original charge, or what was called a charge, upon Tregothnan was only a charge upon the income, and not upon the corpus of the estate. She further contends that, that being the true construction of the deed of settlement, the construction of the deed has never been investigated or disputed, and that none of the orders since made has prevented the Court from now inquiring and giving effect to the deed. On the other hand, it is said that that is not the true effect of the deed, that it did create a charge upon the corpus, and that, even if it did not, yet under the subsequent orders of Court, the widow became entitled to a charge upon the corpus which has never been taken away from her.

The appellant further contends that the order of the Court of 2nd May 1891 had the effect of taking away from the widow any right of recourse to the corpus which she might have had accidentally acquired by the charge under the *Transfer of Land Statute* 1866.

The first question, as to the construction of the deed of settlement, is a matter of very great difficulty, and there is a great deal to be said on both sides. *Hood* J. was of opinion that the case fell within the principle of *Birch* v. *Sherratt* (1), and not that of *Stelfox* v. *Sugden* (2). In the view we take of the case it is not necessary to determine that question, for we are of opinion that, whatever the rights of the parties might have been under the original deed of settlement, they passed into *res judicata* by the decree in the suit and what was subsequently done under it, when the instrument of charge was executed and the widow became in point of law entitled under it to a charge on the estate. If the order for the execution of an instrument of charge was made inadvertently, an application might have been made to have the charge corrected. But, considering that more than twenty-five years have elapsed since the instrument was executed, it is now too late to make such an application. The widow having acquired the right and having enjoyed it for so many years, the charge which attached to the fund paid into

(1) L.R. 2 Ch., 644.   (2) John, 234

Court continued at the time when the order of 2nd May 1891 was made. When that order was made the condition of things was that a fund was supposed to be in Court to the whole of which, corpus as well as income, the widow was entitled to have recourse for the payment of her annuity. The Court ordered £15,000 to be set aside, which was supposed to be sufficient to give effect to her rights, and the rest of the fund was available for the residuary devisees. Is there anything upon the face of this order to show that the Court intended to deprive the widow of any right she had at law ? We can find nothing. The charge is described as a "rent charge," but that is merely an error of description. What was meant by it was the charge the widow had on Tregothnan, whatever that was, by reason of the instrument of charge under the *Transfer of Land Statute* 1866. It was intended to diminish her right to the extent indicated, but it would require very plain words to show that the Court intended to deprive her of her rights to any greater extent. The Court, in ordering £15,000 to be set aside, and the balance to be applied for the benefit of the residuary devisees, intended to diminish her rights to that extent. Whether that sum was actually set aside or not, we think, makes no difference. The Court clearly did not intend to diminish the widow's rights in respect of the £15,000, and, as these rights would have extended to the corpus as well as the income, the widow's rights to the fund were not affected.

We therefore think that the order made by *Hood* J. is right, and that the appeal should be dismissed. As no objection is offered, the costs of all parties may be paid out of the fund.

Appeal dismissed.

Solicitors, for the appellant, *Lamrick, Brown & Hall.*

Solicitors, for the respondents, *Moule, Hamilton & Kiddle;* *Eales.*

B. L.

[HIGH COURT OF AUSTRALIA.]

BAYNE AND ANOTHER .　.　.　.　.　APPELLANTS ;
PLAINTIFFS,

AND

BLAKE AND ANOTHER .　.　.　.　. RESPONDENTS.
DEFENDANTS,

ON APPEAL FROM THE SUPREME COURT OF
VICTORIA.

*Practice—Appeal to High Court from Supreme Court of State—Cause remitted to
Supreme Court—Postponement of proceedings by Supreme Court—Duty of
Supreme Court—Relation of High Court to Supreme Court—Judiciary Act
1903 (No. 6 of 1903), sec. 37—Commonwealth of Australia Constitution Act
1900 (63 & 64 Vict. c. 12), sec. V.—The Constitution, secs. 51 (xxxix.), 73.*

H. C. OF A.
1903.

MELBOURNE,
March 19.

Griffith C.J.,
Barton and
O'Connor JJ.

Sec. 37 of the *Judiciary Act* 1903, in so far as it authorizes the High Court
in the exercise of its appellate jurisdiction to remit a cause to the Supreme
Court of a State for the execution of the judgment of the High Court, and
imposes upon the Supreme Court the duty of executing the judgment of the
High Court in the same manner as if that judgment were the judgment of the
Supreme Court, is a valid exercise by the Parliament of the power conferred
by sec. 51 (xxxix.), of the Constitution.

On an appeal from the Supreme Court of a State to the High Court, the
High Court, in allowing the appeal, ordered the judgment appealed from to
be discharged, and that in lieu thereof there should be substituted a declaration that the plaintiffs were entitled to recover a sum to be thereafter
ascertained, and further ordered that the cause " be remitted to the Supreme
Court to do therein what is right in pursuance of the judgment." Leave to
appeal to the Privy Council from the judgment of the High Court having
been obtained by the defendants, and a stay of proceedings having been
granted by the High Court and subsequently removed, an application to the
Supreme Court to proceed with the inquiry directed by the High Court was
made by the plaintiff.

H. C. of A.
1908.
⌣
BAYNE
v.
BLAKE.

Held, that an order made by the Supreme Court, that the matter should be deferred until the decision of the Privy Council should be made known, was a stay of proceedings, and therefore was an order which the Supreme Court had no authority to make.

Peacock v. *D. M. Osborne & Co.*, 4 C.L.R., 1564, applied.

The High Court may directly order an officer of the Supreme Court of a State to obey a judgment of the High Court.

Judgment of the Supreme Court reversed.

APPEAL from the Supreme Court of Victoria.

In an action upon an administration bond, brought in the Supreme Court of Victoria by Lila Elizabeth Bayne and Mary Bayne against Arthur Palmer Blake and William Riggall, judgment was given for the defendants. An appeal to the High Court from this judgment was on 17th September 1906, allowed: *Bayne* v. *Blake* (1); and the Court ordered that the judgment appealed from should be discharged and that in lieu thereof the following declaration and judgment should be substituted :—" It is hereby adjudged and declared that the deed of 20th May 1886 in the pleadings mentioned is void as against persons beneficially interested in the estate of the deceased and that the plaintiffs as representing such persons other than the administratrix are entitled to recover from the defendants such sum not exceeding £5,000 as represents the amount by which the shares of such persons in distribution were diminished by reason of the failure of the administratrix to duly administer the said estate but so that no sum shall be recoverable in respect of any diminution of the share of any such person by reason of any failure in which such person concurred and acquiesced. And it is further ordered that the defendants do pay to the plaintiffs their costs of the action up to and including the hearing thereof but not including the cost of the reference of a certain question of law referred by Mr. Justice *Holroyd* to the Full Court. And let the further consideration of this action be adjourned and all parties are to be at liberty to apply as they may be advised." The High Court further ordered " that this cause be remitted to the Supreme Court to do therein what is right in pursuance of the judgment."

(1) 4 C.L.R., 1.

On 2nd November 1906 the Privy Council granted leave to appeal from the judgment of the High Court, but refused an application for a stay of execution. In November 1906 the case appeared in the list of cases for hearing in the Supreme Court before a Judge, and on 13th November 1906, the case coming on for hearing before *Hodges* J., his Honor made an order adjourning the case until the determination of the appeal before the Privy Council, or until further order.

On 14th December 1906, on the application of the defendants, *Griffith* C.J. in Chambers ordered a stay of all proceedings under the judgment of the High Court until further order on payment into Court by the defendants of the plaintiffs' taxed costs of the appeal to the High Court. Those taxed costs amounting to £388 11s. 4d. were subsequently paid into Court by the defendants.

On 6th March 1907 an application was made by the plaintiffs to *Griffith* C.J. in Chambers to remove the stay, but the application was on 15th March refused : *Bayne* v. *Blake* (1).

On 27th March 1907 the application of the defendants to remove the stay was renewed, and *Griffith* C.J. ordered that the stay granted on 14th December 1906 should be removed so far as might be necessary to enable the Supreme Court to proceed with the inquiries directed by the judgment of the High Court.

In July 1907 the case was in the list of cases for hearing in the Supreme Court before a Judge, and on 22nd July 1907 the matter came on for hearing before *Hodges* J., who adjourned the case *sine die* on the ground of the pending appeal to the Privy Council.

On 27th September 1907, on the application of the plaintiffs, *Griffith* C.J. in Chambers made an order that the stay of 14th December 1906 should be wholly removed, and that the sum of £388 11s. 4d. paid into Court by the defendants be paid out to the plaintiffs upon the plaintiffs giving their personal undertaking to repay such sum if ordered to do so.

On 24th October 1907 the plaintiffs applied to *Madden* C.J. to proceed with the inquiries directed by the High Court, but an order was made that the matter should be deferred until the result of the decision of the Privy Council had been made known.

(1) 4 C.L.R., 944.

H. C. of A.
1908.
⌣
BAYNE
v.
BLAKE.
——

The plaintiffs now by special leave appealed to the High Court from the order of *Madden* C.J.

During the arguments it was intimated by counsel that the appeal to the Privy Council had been heard, and that judgment had been reserved.

Agg (with him *Ah Ket*), for the appellants. Under sec. 37 of the *Judiciary Act* 1903 it was clearly the duty of the Supreme Court to carry out the judgment of the High Court of 17th September 1906 so far as it could : *Peacock* v. *D. M. Osborne & Co.* (1). It was even more imperative that the Supreme Court should have had the inquiry made after the order of this Court of 27th September 1907.

[GRIFFITH C.J.—Having heard all that had happened I made that order considering that the defendants were in contempt in asking the Supreme Court not to proceed with inquiry, and were not entitled to any privilege whatsoever.]

If the Supreme Court will not direct its officer to make the inquiry ordered by the High Court, the High Court may make an order directing that officer to make the inquiry : *Martin* v. *Hunter's Lessee* (2). The order of *Madden* C.J. was an order thwarting the order of the High Court. This Court should either direct the Chief Clerk of the Supreme Court to make the inquiry, or should direct one of its own officers to make it.

Irvine K.C. and *Weigall* K.C., for the respondents. The leave to appeal should be rescinded as the matter is not an appealable one. The order of *Madden* C.J. was under the circumstances a right and proper order to be made. The order made by *Hodges* J. on 13th November 1906, adjourning the matter until the determination of the appeal by the Privy Council, was made without complaint as to the jurisdiction to make it or as to the propriety of making it. The main question turns on the meaning of the order of this Court of 14th December 1906 removing the stay so far as to enable the inquiry to be made. That order was either a mere removal of the stay so as to enable the Supreme Court to proceed with the inquiry, or was a direction to the Supreme Court to proceed at once with the inquiry.

(1) 4·C.L.R., 1564, at p. 1566.   (2) 1 Wheat., 304.

H. C. of A.
1908.

BAYNE
v.
BLAKE.

[GRIFFITH C.J.—The only direction to the Supreme Court was in the original order of this Court of 17th September 1906.]

That raises the question of the precise relation between this Court and the Supreme Court. It is a relation which does not permit this Court to direct or order the Supreme Court to do anything. This Court is to hear appeals from the Supreme Court, and the Commonwealth Parliament has no power to impose any duty upon the Supreme Court in relation to such appeals. The Supreme Court is responsible only to the Parliament of the State. If this Court remits a cause to the Supreme Court, the Supreme Court is charged with the cause, and may deal with that cause as it would with any other cause that came before it. That is quite consistent with orders made by the Supreme Court being subject to appeal to this Court.

[GRIFFITH C.J.—A denial of justice is appealable.]

That is a generally admitted principle. But in the interests of justice this appeal should not be allowed. A cause being remitted by this Court to the Supreme Court, a Judge of that Court has a discretion as to when the cause will be heard, and he is bound to exercise that discretion : See *Rules of Supreme Court* 1906, Order XXXVI., r. 34. The power to postpone the hearing of a cause is discretionary, and an appellate Court will not review the exercise of that discretion : *Boucicault* v. *Boucicault* (1). Unless the effect of the partial removal of the stay, taken in conjunction with the original order of this Court, amounts to a command which is directly enforceable by this Court, there is nothing improper in a Judge of the Supreme Court exercising his discretion. The order of this Court removing the stay altogether indicates that this Court acted upon the view that there is a direct duty of official obedience imposed on the Supreme Court.

[GRIFFITH C.J.—The duty of obedience may be upon the parties and not upon the Supreme Court.]

There is no ground for saying that the defendants were in contempt. The defendants disclaim any intention to flout this Court, but they are entitled by all lawful means to resist an inquiry being entered upon which they believe will be rendered

(1) 4 T.L.R., 195.

H. C. of A. useless by the result of the appeal to the Privy Council, and
1908.   which will involve them in expense which they have no hope of
Bayne   ever recovering.   If the Supreme Court had jurisdiction to deal
v.   with the matter and may go wrong, it is not contempt for a
Blake.   party to ask the Supreme Court to act in a way which this Court
afterwards decides to be wrong.

[Griffith C.J.—I used the words "in contempt" in the sense
in which they were formerly used in the Court of Chancery.]

That would not justify an order having the effect of allowing
the plaintiffs to take out of Court a large sum of money belonging to the defendants which, if the appeal to the Privy Council
is successful, the defendants have no hope of recovering.   If sec.
37 of the *Judiciary Act* 1903 has the effect of making the
Supreme Court an official means of carrying out the orders of the
High Court, then that section is *ultra vires.*   Under sec. 73 of
the Constitution this Court has in relation to the Supreme Court
only an appellate jurisdiction.

[Griffith C.J.—Sec. 51 (xxxix.) of the Constitution gives the
Parliament authority to make laws as to matters incidental to the
execution of any power vested in the Federal Judicature.   It is
incidental to the powers of this Court that it should have power
to give effect to its decrees.]

Sec. 51 (xxxix.) gives the Commonwealth Parliament no power
to regulate the Supreme Court.   The power which is authorized
by that section is limited to the execution of the powers expressly
given by sec. 73.   Unless mandamus should go to the Supreme
Court there is no substance in this appeal.   It is neither desirable
that the expense of the inquiry should be incurred, nor is it in
the interest of justice that the inquiry should proceed.

Agg in reply.   The applications made by the plaintiffs have
been for the purpose of executing the judgment of this Court
under sec. 37 of the *Judiciary Act* 1903.   The orders of the
Supreme Court are obstructive of the judgment of this Court.
There is no difference between this case and *Peacock v. D. M.
Osborne & Co.* (1), and that case was brought under the notice of
Madden C.J.

(1) 4 C.L.R., 1564.

H. C. OF A.
1908.

BAYNE
v.
BLAKE.

GRIFFITH C.J. delivered the judgment of the Court. This case raises a question which from one point of view is of very great importance as appertaining to the relations between the High Court and the Courts of the States, and from another point of view has become of trivial importance. It is necessary to refer to the facts in some detail. On 17th September 1906, upon the hearing of an appeal from a decision of the Supreme Court of Victoria, the High Court held (1) that the defence set up by the defendants in the suit was invalid, and declared that the plaintiffs were entitled to recover from the defendants a sum of money the amount of which was not then ascertained, but which was such a sum, not exceeding £5,000, as represented the amount by which the shares of the beneficiaries were diminished by failure of the administratrix to duly administer, but so that no sum should be recoverable in respect of any diminution of the share of any beneficiary by reason of any such failure in which such beneficiary had concurred or acquiesced. The Court adjourned further consideration of the action with liberty to apply, and further ordered that the cause should be remitted to the Supreme Court to do therein what was right in pursuance of the judgment. The order was made in pursuance of sec. 37 of the *Judiciary Act* 1903 which provides that the High Court in the exercise of its appellate jurisdiction may " remit the cause to the Court from which the appeal was brought for the execution of the judgment of the High Court; and in the latter case it shall be the duty of that Court to execute the judgment of the High Court in the same manner as if it were its own judgment." The validity of that order was impeached by Mr. *Irvine,* but it is obviously authorized by the powers conferred by sec. 51 of the Constitution, which authorizes the Parliament to make laws as to matters incidental to the execution of any power vested in the Federal Judicature. The power of an appellate Court has always in practice in the British dominions been held to imply a power to remit the judgment for execution to the Court from which the appeal is brought. Moreover, if that were not so, it would be necessary to appoint a number of officers in the several States for the purpose of executing the

(1) 4 C.L.R., 1.

H. C. of A.
1908.

BAYNE
v.
BLAKE.

judgments of this Court, if anything remained to be done before final justice was done between the parties. We have no doubt as to the validity of the provision in sec. 37 of the *Judiciary Act* 1903, and the only question is as to its interpretation. In the case of *Peacock* v. *D. M. Osborne & Co.* (1), decided in September last by the Full Bench, this Court said :—" Now, there is no doubt that the Supreme Court has jurisdiction to make any order consequent on an order of this Court for the purpose of executing the latter order, but the Supreme Court has no power to make any order for the purpose of preventing its execution." It was then pointed out that the Supreme Court might formally make such an order, but that it would be invalid. The Court then went on to say :—" An order staying proceedings until further order is not an order in execution of a judgment of this Court, but is an order thwarting or obstructing the execution of that judgment. Therefore, whatever the merits may be, it is an order that ought not to be made, and must be set aside on appeal." With these preliminary observations I proceed to state the facts of this case.

· After the judgment of this Court was given in September 1906, His Majesty with the advice of the Privy Council was pleased in November 1906 to grant special leave to appeal from the order then made. Thereupon application was made to a Judge of this Court, and the Judge thought it fit that such a stay should be granted, except in one particular which it is not necessary to further mention. Subsequently another application was made on behalf of the plaintiffs to allow some of the proceedings to go on notwithstanding the stay. That application was at first refused: *Bayne* v. *Blake* (2). It was pointed out that, as a general rule, proceedings should be stayed when an appeal to the Privy Council was pending, but that there might be circumstances which would justify some of the proceedings going on notwithstanding the pendency of the appeal. That application was adjourned, and was subsequently brought on again upon materials which were then debated, and, rightly or wrongly, the Judge to whom the application was made came to the conclusion that, under the circumstances, it was right that the inquiry which was

(1) 4 C. L. R., 1564, at pp. 1567, 1568.   (2) 4 C. L. R., 944.

directed by the original order of this Court should be made at once, and the stay was to that extent withdrawn. Thereupon the original judgment of this Court came, to that extent, into full operation, and it was, in the words of sec. 37 of the *Judiciary Act* 1903, the duty of the Supreme Court " to execute the judgment of the High Court in the same manner as if it were its own judgment." I have already pointed out that, according to the opinion of this Court, an order staying proceedings is not an order in execution of a judgment of this Court. The plaintiffs, having obtained a withdrawal of the stay granted by this Court, made an application in July 1907 to *Hodges* J., and counsel for the defendants asked that the hearing of the case should be adjourned until the decision of the Privy Council was given. That was, in effect, asking a stay of proceedings. The learned Judge is reported to have said:—" The matter is now before the final Court of Appeal, and I think it would be a wicked waste of public time and a wicked waste of the private moneys of the parties to conduct the inquiry whilst that appeal is pending." Upon that I will only say that the language is somewhat unusual to use in reference to a judgment of an appellate Court. The learned Judge then adjourned the matter indefinitely. Subsequently the case of *Peacock* v. *D. M. Osborne & Co.* (1) came before this Court in which, as I have said, it was laid down by the Full Bench that the Supreme Court could not grant a stay of proceedings. Fortified by that decision, the plaintiffs made an application to *Madden* C.J. to proceed with the inquiries directed by this Court. That application came on for hearing in December 1907, and the learned Chief Justice, to whom *Peacock* v. *D. M. Osborne & Co.* (1) was cited, ordered that the matter be deferred until the result of the decision of the Privy Council should be made known, and he further ordered that the plaintiffs should pay the costs of their application which had been made to him in order that the order of this Court might be carried out. The learned Chief Justice is reported to have said :—" The High Court cannot direct the Chief Clerk of the Supreme Court to proceed with these inquiries; and I am not the servant of the High Court, so that anything I do must be as a Judge of the Supreme Court, according to the procedure of this Court, and there is no authority for the present

H. C. of A.
1908.

BAYNE
v.
BLAKE.

(1) 4 C.L.R., 1564.

H. C. of A.
1908.

BAYNE
v.
BLAKE.

application in the Rules of this Court." I do not know what the
last remark refers to. It probably refers to some formal matter.
Although the learned Chief Justice is not a servant of this Court,
yet he is a citizen, and he is a member of a Court of the Commonwealth, and, by the express language of sec. V. of the *Commonwealth of Australia Constitution Act*, " all laws made by the
Parliament of the Commonwealth under the Constitution, shall
be binding on the Courts, Judges, and people of every State, and
of every part of the Commonwealth, notwithstanding anything in
the laws of any State." The learned Chief Justice is therefore
bound by the *Judiciary Act* 1903 just as is any private person,
and sec. 37 of that Act expressly says that it shall be the duty of
the Court to which a cause is remitted to execute the judgment
of the High Court in the same manner as if it were its own
judgment. So that the learned Chief Justice, although he is not
a servant of this Court, is an officer of the law required by law to
execute the orders of this Court. Under these circumstances it
is manifest that the order he made is wrong; he had no right to
order that the inquiries directed by this Court should be adjourned
until the decision of the Privy Council was made known. That
was a stay of proceedings which this Court had shortly before
declared the Supreme Court had no authority to make. It
follows that the plaintiffs were entitled to an order. Whether
proceedings should now be stayed on grounds which show a
change of circumstances, is a matter irrelevant to the present
discussion.

In the result the defendants, notwithstanding the order of this
Court, and the withdrawal of the stay by this Court, have
obtained a delay of about twelve months. Under those circumstances they are not entitled to any consideration. We were very
glad to hear the disclaimer on behalf of the defendants of any
intention to act in defiance of the High Court. But it is manifest
that any attempt of that sort must be futile. The High Court is
not only a Court having federal jurisdiction, but it is also a Court
of Appeal for every State, and as much respect is due to it as if
it were a Court of Appeal from the Supreme Court in the State.

We should like to add a word as to the observation of the learned
Chief Justice that " the High Court cannot direct the Chief Clerk

H. C. of A.
1908.

BAYNE
v.
BLAKE.

of the Supreme Court to proceed with these inquiries." It is not necessary, for reasons I will give directly, to discuss that statement, but I may remark that this Court can make any order that the Supreme Court ought to have made, and, if it was the duty of the Supreme Court to direct its Chief Clerk to make the inquiries, this Court also can make that order. We will not contemplate the case of an officer of the Supreme Court refusing to obey an order of this Court. It is sufficient to say that in the United States it is the practice for the Supreme Court to make a direct order on a State officer to obey its judgment. For these reasons we are of opinion that the order appealed from is wrong and must be discharged.

It would follow in the ordinary course that this Court should direct an inquiry by the Chief Clerk of the Supreme Court. But for certain reasons there is apparently no necessity to make that order at the present moment. It will be sufficient to allow the appeal, to discharge the order appealed from, and to order the defendants to pay the costs of the appeal.

The costs of the application to the Supreme Court should be costs in the cause.

Appeal allowed with costs. Order appealed from discharged.

Solicitor, for the appellants, *J. L. Clarke.*
Solicitors, for the respondents, *Blake & Riggall.*

B. L.

[HIGH COURT OF AUSTRALIA.]

In re REGINALD STANLEY'S APPLICATION FOR A TRADE MARK.

H. C. of A.   *Practice—Patent—Application to Court for indulgence—Attendance of Commissioner*
1908.   *of Patents—Costs.*

MELBOURNE,   Where an applicant for a patent applies to the High Court for an indulgence
April 28.   on notice to the Commissioner of Patents it is the duty of the Commissioner
     to attend the hearing, and the applicant, whether he is or is not successful,
Isaacs J.   must pay the costs of the Commissioner.

In Chambers.   MOTION.

On 11th January 1905 an application was made by Reginald
Stanley, who resides in England, by his agents, Collison & Co.,
for a patent for an invention entitled " Improvements in combined
apparatus for grinding or crushing, washing and separating ores."
The complete specifications were lodged on 9th October 1905,
and accepted on 18th October 1905. On 20th October 1905 the
agents were informed by the Commissioner of the acceptance, and
were requested to forward five additional copies of the specification.

On 3rd January 1906 the acceptance fee of £2 was paid. On
11th May 1906 the time for sealing the letters patent expired,
and on 22nd May 1906 an advertisement was published in the
Gazette to the effect that the application had lapsed. On 22nd
August 1906 the agents for the applicant were informed that the
application had lapsed. On 4th December 1906 an application
was made to the Commissioner to revive the application, but was
on 12th December refused.

An application was now made to the High Court by motion on
behalf of the applicant and on notice to the Commissioner for an

order extending the time for sealing letters patent under the application, and for such other order as to the Court should seem fit.

H. C. of A.
1908.

Re
Stanley's
Application
for a Trade
Mark.

Mann, for the applicant.

Schutt, for the Commissioner.

Isaacs J., by consent, ordered that the applicant should within seven days lodge five additional copies of the specification, and that thereupon the time for sealing the letters patent should be extended until the expiration of six months from the date of the order.

Mann. The Commissioner should not be allowed costs. He was informed that counsel for the applicant would place before the Court any matters which he should desire, and that his attendance by counsel was unnecessary.

Isaacs J. I think the applicant should pay the costs. The application is for an extension of time by way of an indulgence. The Commissioner has acted in discharge of his public duty and strictly under the terms of the Regulation. That is not now challenged as being illegal, and I have not now to decide that. The applicant has allowed a considerable period of time to elapse since he admittedly had knowledge of the lapsing of his application—if it ever did in law lapse. Now, when he comes here, the Court cannot do its duty to the public and protect public interests in respect of the desired monopoly without the presence of the officer who is charged by law with the administration of the Patents Office. I do not think he would do his duty to the Court if he stayed away from the Court. A question might arise at any moment as to which his assistance would be desired. He himself might not see it, and the parties might not, but when the affidavits were read the Court might see it, and desire the Commissioner to give some information or to obtain it for the Court. Therefore I think the Commissioner should attend under all circumstances, and his costs of coming here are

H. C. of A.
1908.

Re
STANLEY'S
APPLICATION
FOR A TRADE
MARK.

part of the necessary expenses of the applicant. Under these circumstances I think I should not be doing right if the public officer were not allowed his costs, not as a penalty on the applicant, but as part of his expenses of obtaining the necessary attendance of the public officer. I therefore order the applicant to pay the costs of the Commissioner, which I fix at £5 5s.

Application granted. Applicant to pay costs of Commissioner.

Solicitors, for applicant, *Waters & Crespin.*

Solicitor, for Commissioner, *C. Powers,* Commonwealth Crown Solicitor.

B. L.

[HIGH COURT OF AUSTRALIA.]

LEVER BROS. LTD. . . . . . APPELLANTS;

AND

G. MOWLING & SON . . . : . RESPONDENT.

H. C. of A.
1908.

MELBOURNE,
Feb. 27.

Griffith C.J.

IN CHAMBERS.

Practice—Appeal from Supreme Court of State—Extension of time for giving notice —Rules of the High Court 1903, Part I., Order XLV., r. 6; Part II., Section I., r. 4, Section III., r. 4.

Semble, Rules of the High Court 1903, Part I., Order XLV., r. 6, does not apply to an appeal from the Supreme Court of a State, and the High Court has no jurisdiction to extend the time for giving notice of such an appeal.

SUMMONS.

This was an application by Lever Brothers Ltd., who proposed to appeal from a decision of the Supreme Court of Victoria, in a matter in which they and G. Mowling & Son were parties (*In re* Application of G. Mowling & Son, Ex parte Lever Brothers Ltd.) (1) for an extension of the time within which to give notice of appeal and to file the affidavit required by r. 7A of Section III. of Part II. of the *Rules of the High Court* 1903.

H. C. of A.
1907.
LEVER BROS.
LTD.
v.
G. MOWLING
& SON.

Sproule, for the appellants, in support, referred to *Rules of the High Court*, Part I., Order XLV., r. 6 ; Part II., Section I., r. 4, and Section III., r. 4.

Levinson, for the respondents, *contrá*, was not called upon.

GRIFFITH C.J.   I have grave doubts whether Order XLV., r. 6, has any application to such a matter as this.   I am disposed to think that I have no jurisdiction to extend the time for giving notice of appeal.   If the power exists, I think it is one that ought not to be exercised.

Summons dismissed, with costs.

Solicitor, for appellants, *E. Hart* for *A. De Lissa*, Sydney.
Solicitors, for respondents, *Braham & Pirani.*

B. L.

(1) (1908) V.L.R., 123 ; 29 A.L.T., 169.

A'BECKETT AND ANOTHER .   .   .   . APPELLANTS;
DEFENDANTS,

AND

THE TRUSTEES EXECUTORS AND AGENCY⎫ RESPONDENTS.
Co. LTD. AND OTHERS   .   .   .⎭
PLAINTIFFS AND DEFENDANTS,

ON APPEAL FROM THE SUPREME COURT OF
VICTORIA.

H. C. OF A. *Settlement—Trustee and cestui que trust—Appointment—Gifts out of specific fund—*
1908.   *Gift of residue—Abatement—Proceeds of sale—Rescission—New appointment—*
‿‿‿   *Revocation—Substituted gifts—Construction.*

MELBOURNE,
1907,   In execution of the powers reserved by a marriage settlement, a revocable
Sept. 26.   appointment was made by deed whereby the appointors, the husband and
———   wife, directed the trustees to hold the net purchase money already received
1908,   and to be received in respect of a certain contract of sale upon trust, on the
Feb. 24, 25, death of the survivor of the appointors, as to three several sums of £15,000
26 ;   for each of three of their daughters, and as to £12,500 for their fourth
March 27.   daughter (to whom had already been advanced £2,500), and as to the
———   "remainder" one moiety to each of their two sons. The contract of sale
Griffith C.J., referred to was of certain land subject to the settlement, and was for a sum
Barton and   of £100,000, of which £20,000 had already been paid. The deed also con-
Isaacs J.J.   tained appointments of two pieces of land, which had been bought out of the
             £20,000, one to a daughter and the other to a son. The contract of sale was
             subsequently rescinded on the purchaser paying a further sum of £20,000.

             Held, by *Griffith* C.J. and *Barton* J., that, in the events which had hap-
             pened, the principle that, where a person disposing of a sum among different
             persons acts on the assumption that he is dealing with a fund of specific
             amount, and gives part of the fund to one or more persons and the residue to
             another, if the fund falls short, all the gifts abate proportionately, would not
             apply, and therefore the sons would get nothing under the gift of the
             "remainder."

H. C. of A.
1908.

àBeckett
v.
Trustees
Executors
and Agency
Co. Ltd.

Page v. *Leapingwell*, 18 Ves., 463, distinguished.

By *Isaacs* J. That principle would have applied to the appointment as it stood before the rescission of the contract of sale, and what happened afterwards would not alter the construction of the appointment.

Out of the balance of the £40,000 paid in respect of the contract of sale, other lands were afterwards purchased, and certain advances were made to one of the appointors and to some of the beneficiaries, leaving a balance of £7,600. The appointors then made a new appointment whereby they revoked the appointments of the prior deed as to the net purchase money therein referred to, " but so far only as may be necessary to the validity of the directions and appointments hereinafter contained and not further or otherwise." They then appointed the land the subject of the contract of sale to their four daughters equally as tenants in common ; they appointed a sum of £1,000 (part of the £40,000) to one daughter ; they revoked the appointment of the land appointed to one daughter and appointed it to one of the sons ; they revoked the residuary appointment, "but so far only," (as before) ; they appointed two other pieces of land to a son and daughter respectively ; they appointed all debts due by one of the settlors to one of the sons with a gift over to the other ; they appointed all debts owing by either son to that son ; and they appointed that the trustees should stand possessed of the moneys in their possession or under their control subject to the trusts of the settlement " of which no other appointment is made " by the first deed " or by these presents " upon trust as to two-thirds to one son and as to one-third to the other. Each of these appointments was to take effect on the death of the survivor of the appointors.

Held, by *Griffith* C.J. and *Barton* J. (*Isaacs* J. dissenting), that, having regard to the known state of the trust fund, under the second deed the appointment to the two sons of the moneys in the hands or under the control of the trustees &c. could only apply to the £7,600, that no other appointment of that sum was made by either deed, or within the meaning of the second deed, and therefore that the two sons were entitled to it in the proportions of two-thirds and one-third to the exclusion of the daughters.

Judgment of *Hood* J. reversed.

APPEAL from the Supreme Court of Victoria (*Hood* J.).

The Trustees Executors and Agency Co. Ltd., who sued as trustees of the marriage settlement of William Arthur Callander àBeckett, deceased, and his wife Emma àBeckett, deceased, and of two deeds of appointment dated respectively 10th September 1889 and 9th February 1900, made by Mr. and Mrs. W. A. C. àBeckett, instituted proceedings by originating summons to obtain the opinion of the Supreme Court on certain questions arising under such settlement and deeds of appointment. The defendants were William Gilbert àBeckett and Arthur Heywood St. Thomas

àBeckett, sons of Mr. and Mrs. W. A. C. àBeckett, and Emily
àBeckett Backhouse, Emma Minnie Boyd, Constance Matilda
Brett, and Ethel Beatrice Ysobel Chomley, daughters of Mr. and
Mrs. W. A. C. àBeckett.   The questions asked by the summons
were as follow :—

"1. (Generally). Upon what trust or trusts should the fund
consisting of the sum of £7,600 together with interest accrued
thereon and representing so much of the sum of £37,500 received
under the contract of sale to the General Land and Savings Co.
Ltd. as is not represented by other properties or funds specifically
appointed by the said deeds be held ? "

(This question was at the hearing amended by striking out the
words " consisting of the sum of £7,600.")

" 2. (In particular). Does the appointment of the lands in the
said contract of sale comprised which appointment is by the said
deed dated 9th February 1900 made to the defendants the
daughters of the said deceased namely E. àB. Backhouse, E. M.
Boyd, C. M. Brett and E. B. Y. Chomley entirely take the place
of and stand in substitution for the appointment of £57,500 by
the said deed dated 10th September 1889 made to the said
defendants the said daughters ?

" 3. (In particular). Are the defendants (both sons and
daughters) in respect of the said fund consisting as aforesaid
entitled to share proportionately according to their interests in
the purchase moneys under the said contract of sale as set forth
and determined by the said deed dated 10th September 1889 and
if so what is the amount of each proportionate share ?

" 4. (In particular). Should the said fund consisting as aforesaid be held in trust for the defendants the said daughters only
and in proportions corresponding to the proportions in which the
sum of £57,500 was appointed to them by the said deed dated
10th September 1889 ? "

The provisions of the two deeds and the other material facts
are sufficiently set out in the judgments hereunder.

The summons was heard by *Hood* J., who ordered and declared
that the four daughters were, to the exclusion of the two sons,
entitled to the fund together with interest accrued thereon,
representing so much of the sum of £37,500 received under the

contract of sale to the General Land and Savings Co. Ltd. as was not represented by other properties or funds specifically appointed by the deeds of 10th September 1889 and 9th February 1900, and that the daughters as between themselves were entitled to share in the said fund and interest in proportions corresponding to the proportions in which the sum of £57,500 was appointed to them by the deed dated 10th September 1889.

The two sons W. G. àBeckett and A. H. St. T. àBeckett now by special leave, (*àBeckett* v. *Backhouse* (1)), appealed to the High Court.

H. C. of A.
1908.

àBeckett
v.
Trustees
Executors
and Agency
Co. Ltd.

Mitchell K.C. and *Guest*, for the appellants. The insertion in the deed of 9th February 1900 of the words " but so far only as may be necessary to the validity of the several directions and appointments hereinbefore and hereinafter contained and not otherwise or further" was for the purpose of preserving the validity of advances made on the assumption that the deed of 10th September 1889 was effectual. Whatever was the object of those words, the appointment of all moneys in the hands or under the control of the trustees and of which no other appointment was made is an appointment " hereinafter contained." That appointment can only refer to the uninvested and unappointed balance of the money received under the contract of sale, for the trustees never had, nor could they have, any other money in their hands, inasmuch as money received by them in respect of sales of land by them was subject to the same directions as the land itself. The money received as deposit on a purchase is not purchase money if the sale is not completed ; therefore, the sale to the General Land and Savings Co. having fallen through, there was no purchase money to which the deed of 10th September 1889 could apply. Assuming the moneys in question are subject to the deed of 10th September 1889, the appellants are entitled to have an abatement all round. The case falls within the principle of *Page* v. *Leapingwell* (2), viz., that where a settlor, in dealing with an ascertained sum, makes a gift of part of the fund to one or more persons, and gives the residue to another, all the gifts

(1) 4 C.L R., 1334.　　　　(2) 18 Ves., 463.

will be treated as specific and, if the fund falls short, all the gifts will abate proportionately. See *Walpole* v. *Apthorpe* (1).

[Isaacs J. referred to *In re Tunno*; *Raikes* v. *Raikes* (2).]

In that case there was no division into fractions or aliquot parts, but there is here. See also *Wilson* v. *Kenrick* (3); *Baker* v. *Farmer* (4); *Wright* v. *Weston* (5); *Ashburner* v. *Macguire* (6).

[Isaacs J. referred to *Higgins* v. *Dawson* (7); *Robertson* v. *Broadbent* (8); *In re Maddock*; *Llewelyn* v. *Washington* (9).]

Pigott, for the respondent trustees.

Weigall K.C. (with him *Arthur*), for the other respondents. By the deed of 10th September 1889 the gift of the residue of the proceeds of sale was not a specific legacy. The appointors were not then dealing with a fund of a specified amount. It was not known what the amount would be, for there would be deductions in respect of commission &c., from the amount of the purchase money. The appellants were only intended to have what should be left after payment of the legacies to the daughters. There was no division into aliquot parts: *De Lisle* v. *Hodges* (10); *In re Tunno*; *Raikes* v. *Raikes* (11).

[Isaacs J.—The facts in *In re Phillips*; *Eddowes* v. *Phillips* (12) are very similar to those in regard to the deed of 10th September 1889, and it was held that, though there was a gift of residue, the division was into aliquot parts.]

The intention to divide a fund into aliquot parts must be clearly manifest on the face of the document itself, and that is not so in the present case. That being so, and the fund being by reason of the sale falling through reduced to £40,000, which is less than the total amounts specifically given to the daughters, the appellants are not entitled under the deed of 10th September 1889 to any of the fund. The deed of 9th February 1900 made no difference in this respect. The intention expressed by that deed was that everything specifically dealt with by it should go

(1) L.R. 4 Eq., 37.
(2) 45 Ch. D., 66.
(3) 31 Ch. D., 658, at p. 661.
(4) L.R. 3 Ch., 537, at p. 540.
(5) 26 Beav., 429.
(6) 2 Wh. & T.L.C., 6th ed., p. 106.

(7) (1902) A.C., 1.
(8) 8 App. Cas., 812.
(9) (1902) 2 Ch., 220, at p. 228.
(10) L.R. 17 Eq., 440.
(11) 45 Ch. D., 66, at p. 69.
(12) 66 L.J. Ch., 714.

as it directed, but that everything not specifically dealt with
should go as directed by the deed of 10th September 1889. In
other words, the deed of 9th February 1900 relieved from the
trusts of the deed of 10th September 1889 all the things which
were specified in the later deed, but otherwise left the earlier
deed to operate. In any event the Court should make it a
condition that the appellants should not seek to recover any
money paid away by the trustees in reliance upon the judgment
appealed from.

Mitchell K.C. in reply.

[GRIFFITH C.J. referred to *In re Walpole's Marriage Settlement*; *Thomson* v. *Walpole* (1); *Reresby* v. *Newland* (2).]

Cur. adv. vult.

The following judgments were read :—

GRIFFITH C.J. The question for determination in this case
arises upon the construction of a deed of appointment dated 9th
February 1900, made in execution of the powers reserved by a
settlement dated 11th August 1859 executed in pursuance of ante-
nuptial articles entered into on the marriage of Mr. and Mrs. W. A.
C. àBeckett, by which real and personal property was conveyed to
trustees upon trust, *inter alia*, after the death of Mr. and Mrs.
àBeckett, for such uses for the benefit of the children of the
marriage as they should by deed jointly appoint. The parties,
other than the respondent company, are the children of the
marriage. The deed contained a covenant to bring after-acquired
property into settlement, but, so far as appears, no property
ever became subject to the covenant.

By a revocable deed of appointment dated 10th September
1889 reciting a previous revocable deed of 29th October 1884,
and further reciting that under the provisions of the original
settlement a sum of £2,500 had been applied by the trustees of
the settlement for the benefit of the respondent Mrs. Brett, all
the appointments made under the former deed were revoked " so
far as the same are by law revocable having regard to the here-
before recited advancement " to Mrs. Brett. The deed then

(1) (1903) 1 Ch., 928.   (2) 2 P. Wms., 93.

proceeded to appoint various portions of the trust estate. The first appointment was of lands to the appellants as tenants in common in fee, with gifts over in certain contingencies. The second was as follows:—" The trustees or trustee for the time being of the said settlement shall from and immediately after the decease of the survivor of them the said W. A. C. àBeckett and Emma àBeckett stand possessed of the net purchase moneys already received and to be hereafter received in respect of the contract of sale dated 30th June 1888 to the General Land and Savings Co. Ltd. of allotment 3 of section 4 City and Parish of Melbourne upon the trusts following that is to say—As to the sum of £15,000 part thereof Upon trust for E. àB. Backhouse her executors administrators and assigns As to the sum of £15,000 other part thereof Upon trust for E. M. Boyd her executors administrators and assigns As to the sum of £12,500 other part thereof Upon trust for C. M. Brett her executors administrators and assigns such last mentioned sum to be in addition to the sum of £2,500 already applied for her benefit as hereinbefore mentioned As to the sum of £15,000 Upon trust for the said E. B. Y. àBeckett her executors administrators and assigns As to one moiety of the remainder of the said purchase moneys Upon trust for the said W. G. àBeckett his executors administrators and assigns And as to the other moiety thereof Upon trust for the said A. H. St. T. àBeckett his executors administrators and assigns But in case either of them the said W. G. àBeckett and A. H. St. T. àBeckett shall predecease the survivor of them the said W. A. C. àBeckett and Emma àBeckett without leaving issue then the moiety to which the son so dying would have been entitled had he survived both his parents shall be held in trust for the other of such sons."

The third appointment was to the appellants and the respondent Mrs. Brett as tenants in common of so much of two parcels of land as might be found to be subject to the trusts of the settlement. The fourth appointment was of a piece of land at Gembrook to the appellant W. G. àBeckett; the fifth of a piece of land at Prahran to the respondent Mrs. Backhouse, if living at the death of the survivor of the appointors, with a gift over to the appellant W. G. àBeckett. Then followed a residuary

appointment of the residue of the trust premises, whether consisting of real or personal estate, to the appellants as tenants in
common.   All the appointments were revocable.

The purchase money payable under the contract of 30th June
1888, and intended to be dealt with by the second appointment,
was £100,000, of which £20,000 had been received at the date of
the deed of 1889, leaving £80,000 outstanding less incidental
charges.   Both the Gembrook and the Prahran land had been
purchased out of the £20,000, whilst other portions of the money
had been applied in advances to beneficiaries in accordance with
the terms of the settlement.   There was, however, a conflict
between the appointments of the whole fund and the appointment of those lands which represented part of it.   The whole of
the settled property was in fact comprised in these appointments.
The third appointment did not take effect, as the land to which
it applied was found not to be subject to the trusts of the settlement.

In June 1891 a further sum of £20,000 was paid by the purchasers under the contract of June 1888, but in July 1893 the
contract was rescinded by mutual consent, upon the terms that
the vendors, the trustees of the settlement, should retain the
£40,000 already received by them as well as retaining the land.
The effect was that the land was unappointed otherwise than by
the residuary appointment.   It may be open to discussion
whether under these altered circumstances the appointment of
the fund of about £100,000 still subsisted as to so much of the
£40,000 actually received as had not been expended in the purchase of land appointed by the same deed.   Assuming that it did,
the question would arise whether the shares of the several beneficiaries should abate in accordance with the principle followed
by *Sir William Grant* M.R., in the case of *Page* v. *Leapingwell*
(1), or whether the gifts to the daughters (amounting to £57,500),
which would more than exhaust the actual fund, should be first
satisfied subject to abatement amongst themselves, but leaving no
part of it to the appellants, who, however, would obtain the land
under the residuary appointment.

In one view of the present case it is necessary to determine

(1) 18 Ves., 465.

this question, and as its determination will throw considerable light upon the construction of the deed of February 1900, I will deal with it at this stage. The principle underlying the decision of *Sir William Grant* M.R. is that, when a person, disposing of a fund amongst different persons, acts upon the assumption that he is dealing with a fund of specific amount, and then makes a gift of part of the fund to one or more persons, and gives the residue to another, then, if the fund falls short, all the gifts must abate proportionally. In that case the word used to describe the rest of the fund was "overplus." In the present case the word used is "remainder." It is sometimes said that in such a case the gift of the residue is regarded as a "specific" gift. But there is no magic in these words. The rule is a rule of common sense applied in order to give effect to the intention of the donor, and only applies to demonstrative legacies. It cannot be pressed to purposes for which it is not designed, or so as to defeat the intention of the donor, or, I think, if the diminution of the fund is the donor's own act. In the present case I cannot doubt that the intention of the appointors was to distribute the specific fund, which, as was expected, would represent the land contracted to be sold, amongst all their children in definitely allotted proportions, and not to give any preference to the daughters over the sons. And if, by reason of subsequent events, the sum representing the expected fund had fallen short—if, for instance, the trustees had taken a mortgage upon the land for the balance of the purchase money and had afterwards sold it at a price insufficient to make up the whole £100,000—the gift to the sons and daughters would, in order to give effect to the intention of the settlor, have had to abate proportionally. But I think that this intention was contingent upon the whole fund, whatever its actual amount might be, being got in and becoming available for distribution. When that contingency failed it is impossible to say that an intention to be inferred from one state of facts ought to be inferred as applicable to facts essentially different, or to hold that the donors intended that the sons should still share in the fund which represented part of the purchase money, and should also take the whole of the land under the residuary appointment. In my opinion, therefore, if

H. C. of A.
1908.

àBECKETT
v.
TRUSTEES
EXECUTORS
AND AGENCY
Co. LTD.

Griffith C.J.

the appointment of the fund contained in the deed of 1889 continued in force at all after the rescission of the contract of sale, the gifts to the daughters would have had to abate proportionally, but the gift to the sons would have been treated as residuary for all purposes, and would have failed.

The application of this doctrine would not, in the actual facts, have brought about equality in abatement even between the daughters, since Mrs. Brett had already received £2,500 in full, which she was not required to bring into account, and the Gembrook land and the Prahran land, bought out of the fund, had been appointed to the appellant W. G. àBeckett and the respondent Mrs Backhouse respectively. But any argument to be derived from these circumstances would seem rather to negative the continued efficacy of the appointment than to exclude the application of the rule.

In order to determine the amount of the residue of the fund originally intended to be divided between the appellants some deductions would have had to be made from the full sum of £100,000 in respect of the amounts expended in buying the Gembrook and Prahran lands, as well as in respect of any sum paid out of the purchase money for commission and expenses, and the actual aliquot shares of the several beneficiaries in the diminished fund would depend on the total so ascertained. If the whole sum of £100,000 had been available, the distribution would have been in 80ths, 12 parts going to each of three daughters, 10 to the fourth, and 17 to each of the sons. In the actual circumstances the proportionate share of the daughters would have been somewhat larger and those of the sons somewhat smaller, but for convenience we may speak of the division as into 80ths. Under the altered circumstances the division among the daughters would have been in 23rds.

This being the state of affairs, and the deed of September 1889 no longer operating to give effect to the intention of the appointors when they executed it, the deed of 9th February 1900 was executed. In the meantime other land had been bought out of the fund, and some payments had been made out of it by way of loans or advances to W. A. C. àBeckett and to beneficiaries. The balance of the fund, represented by cash and government securities, amounted to about £7,600.

This deed, which purports to be indorsed upon or annexed to the deed of September 1889, first recited that since the execution of that deed the contract of sale of 30th June 1888 had been rescinded and the lands comprised in it had become re-vested in the trustees of the settlement and were held upon the trusts of the settlement subject to the terms of the prior appointment "so far as applicable thereto," and that the appointors were desirous of revoking and altering "in manner and to the extent hereinafter appearing" the appointments made under the former deed of appointment, and subject thereto of finally releasing the power of appointment. The appointors then revoked, "but so far only as may be necessary to the validity of the directions and appointments hereinafter contained and not further or otherwise," the directions and appointments in the deed of September 1889 contained as to the net purchase money then already received and to be thereafter received under the contract of sale of 30th June 1888, and made eight several appointments, which, so far as material, were as follows :—

First : They appointed the lands which had been the subject matter of the contract of sale to the four daughters (respondents) in equal shares as tenants in common in fee without liability to give credit for or bring into account the amount of any advances theretofore made to them or for their benefit.

Second : They appointed a sum of £1,000 (which was in fact part of the £40,000) to the respondent Mrs. Chomley.

Third : They revoked the appointment of the Prahran land to the respondent Mrs. Backhouse, and appointed it to the appellant W. G. àBeckett.

Next came, introduced by the words "and these presents further witness," a revocation of the residuary appointment in the deed of September 1889 "but so far only as may be necessary to the validity of the several directions and appointments hereinbefore or hereinafter contained and not further or otherwise," immediately followed by five other appointments, as if intended to be in substitution for it. They were as follows :—

Fourth : The appointors appointed another piece of land at

H. C. or A.
1908.

àBeckett
v.
Trustees
Executors
and Agency
Co. Ltd.

Griffith C.J.

Prahran, which had in the interval been bought out of the £40,000, to the respondent Mrs. Backhouse in fee.

Fifth : They appointed other lands, which had also in the interval been bought out of the same money, to the appellant A. H. St. T. àBeckett in fee.

Sixth : They appointed all moneys, which at the death of the survivor of them might be due to the trustees of the settlement by W. A. C. àBeckett (being other part of the same £40,000), to the appellant W. G. àBeckett if then living, but otherwise to the appellant A. H. St. T. àBeckett.

Seventh : They appointed all moneys, which at the death of the survivor of the appointors might be due to the trustees of the settlement by the appellants or either of them, to those appellants respectively so that such appointment should operate as a release.

Eighth : They appointed that from the decease of the survivor the trustees should stand possessed of the moneys then in their possession or under their control subject to the trusts of the settlement " of which no other appointment is made by the said within written deed of appointment of the 10th September 1889 or by these presents" upon trust as to two-thirds for the appellant W. G. àBeckett and as to one-third for the appellant A. H. St. T. àBeckett.

It is upon this last appointment that the question now arises for our determination.   The appellants contend that it governs the fund of £7,600 already referred to, together with any other moneys which might by any chance be recovered for the trust in respect of expenditure (if any) improperly made by the trustees.

The respondents (other than the company who merely submit the matter for decision) contend that, as these sums form part of the £40,000, the appointment of the purchase moneys contained in the deed of September 1889 still governs them, and that they are entitled to the whole, or, alternatively, to a share bearing the same proportion to the whole as the £57,500 intended to be appointed by the deed bears to the whole sum intended to be appointed.

It is not in dispute that there was in fact no residuary trust fund upon which the eighth appointment could operate unless it applied to these moneys.   As a matter of construction, I am of opinion that the appointment of February 1900 was not intended to, and did not in law, operate as an appointment of any funds not then actually subject to the settlement. But it was intended to be a complete disposition of all the funds so subject, and the investments representing them.

The appointors must, I think, be taken to have known of what the trust estate consisted, and *primâ facie*, some effect must be given to every part of the deed. If, however, the eighth appointment does not extend to these moneys it is altogether inoperative, since the deed in fact specifically appointed all the rest of the trust estate not included in unrevoked appointments made by the deed of 1889.

We can only ascertain the intention of the appointors from the words they have used, paying due regard to the subject matter. If we place ourselves in the position of the appointors under the circumstances already stated, and look at the matter from their point of view, there can be no doubt that the dominant intention was to make a fresh distribution of that asset of the settled property which at the time of the first appointment consisted of a sum of £20,000 and an expected further sum of £80,000, and at the time of the second deed consisted of the land which had been contracted to be sold, and a sum of £40,000 or investments representing it. The appointors did not, however, desire to disturb anything that had been lawfully done in accordance with the terms of the first deed while it subsisted in force. I do not stop to inquire whether they could do so. They accordingly appointed the land to the daughters to the exclusion of the sons, appointed specifically so much of the property in question as was represented by land or by debts owing to the trust estate, and then appointed to the sons the moneys which might "then," *i.e.*, at the death of the survivor, be in their hands. The word "then" shows that they contemplated that at the decease of the survivor the trustees would, or at least might, have some such moneys in their hands. They evidently, therefore, intended by those words to deal with an actual asset of the estate. In order to give effect to this disposition as well as the others, they revoked all the appointments in the first deed so far as was necessary. Now, in order that this final appointment should have any effect, it was necessary that the appointments of the sums of £12,500 and the three sums of £15,000 (if they still subsisted) should, so far as they continued to affect the sum of £7,600, be revoked. Is there, then, anything in the language of the appointment of the moneys inconsistent with this view?

The first and second deeds contained specific appointments of land which represented part of the £40,000, and of moneys representing all the rest of it except the sum of £7,600. It seems to have been contemplated that this sum might be still further reduced before the death of the survivor by loans to W. A. C. àBeckett or the sons. Whether this could or could not be done without a breach of trust is not material to the present question.

The words "of which no other appointment is made" must mean "no appointment operating as an appointment of these moneys, *i.e.*, of moneys to be at the death of the survivor in the hands of the trustees." Upon a strictly literal construction this disposition is meaningless, for the first deed appointed the whole of the settled estate, either specifically or as a residue. The literal construction must then be rejected if any other is possible without doing violence to the words. I think another construction is fairly open. It was clearly intended that this new appointment should at any rate supersede the former residuary appointment so far as regarded moneys in the hands of trustees. There was no residuary real estate, and there could not be any other residuary moneys. The residue of moneys was given to the same persons, but in different proportions. We are thus one step advanced towards finding a meaning for the word "other," which must, if it is to have any effect at all, mean "inconsistent with giving effect to this present appointment." It cannot, therefore, include the residuary appointment in the first deed so far as that related to moneys. We are forced thus to the conclusion that the words "no other appointment" mean "no specific appointment inconsistent," &c. The word "specific" is not in the deed, and I use it in the sense of "descriptive" or "demonstrative." Is, then, the suggested continued appointment of the fund of £7,600, more or less, in 23rds, such a descriptive or demonstrative appointment as to fall within the words "other appointment" in the sense intended by the appointors? I think not. The continuance of that appointment was, as I have shown, just as inconsistent with giving effect to the new appointment of "moneys" "then" in the hands of the trustees as the old residuary appointment was. I think that the meaning of the words "other appointment" is an appointment which, in the events that had happened, (*i.e.* at the date of the deed), operated as an appointment of property definitely earmarked by actual description of the property itself in its existing conditions. These attributes no longer attached to the appointment of money to the daughters by the first deed. In the events that had happened that appointment had come to operate, if at all, merely as an appointment of a small residue of a fund of which the greater part, and possibly the whole, was specifically appointed by the second deed.

In the light of these facts, and bearing in mind that, unless the appellants' view is accepted, the residuary appointment of moneys was, and must have been known to the appointors to be, wholly inoperative, I am compelled, as a matter of construction, to the conclusion that the appointment of the purchase money by the first deed does not fall within the words "other appointment" in the sense in which they were used by the appointors in the second. This is the only construction which will give full effect to the whole deed, including the residuary appointment, and is, indeed, the only one which will give any effect at all to that appointment. For these reasons I think that the funds now in question were appointed by the second deed to the appellants to the exclusion of the daughters.

BARTON J. I have had the advantage of reading and considering the judgment which the Chief Justice has delivered. To my mind the course of reasoning therein followed is clear and convincing. The consequent construction of the two deeds of appointment brings the words of the donors in their true meaning into harmony with their intentions so far as the subject matter, the dealings with the funds, and the purchases of lands thereout in the interval between the two deeds, the consequent changes in the trust estate, and the surrounding circumstances assist us in the ascertainment of those intentions.

I therefore agree in the conclusions at which His Honor has arrived.

H. C. of A.
1908.

àBeckett
v.
Trustees
Executors
and Agency
Co. Ltd.

Isaacs J.

Isaacs J. The first contention of the appellants, namely, that the moneys, representing the purchase money fund and not otherwise specifically appointed, belong to the sons exclusively, cannot in my opinion be supported. The words relied on in the deed of 1900 do not, in my judgment, amount to a revocation of the appointment in the earlier deed. In the deed of 1889 there is an express appointment of these moneys, the appointment purporting to deal with the whole of them; of this there is no express absolute revocation, but it is argued that the appointment in the later deed supersedes that in the first as being inconsistent with it. The second appointment, however, is couched in language that cannot, as I conceive, bear the suggested interpretation. It speaks of moneys "of which no other appointment is made by the said within written deed of appointment of 10th September 1889 or by these presents." If these moneys are specifically appointed by either deed, they do not fall within the terms of this particular appointment. In fact, as I have already said, they were originally specifically appointed by the deed of 1889, and although I appreciate much of the argument as to the fairness of the suggested disposition and the probable desires of the settlors, I am unable to bend their language so as practically to reverse its plain ordinary meaning. In *Roddy* v. *Fitzgerald* (1), Lord *Wensleydale* said of a will:—"The first duty of the Court expounding the will is to ascertain what is the meaning of the words used by the testator. It is very often said that the intention of the testator is to be the guide, but the expression is capable of being misunderstood, and may lead to a speculation as to what the testator may be supposed to have intended to write, whereas the only and proper inquiry is, what is the meaning of that which he has actually written? That which he has written is to be construed by every part being taken into consideration according to its grammatical construction and the ordinary acceptance of the words used, with the assistance of such parol evidence of the surrounding circumstances as is admissible, to place the Court in the position of the testator."

(1) 6 H.L.C., 823, at p. 876.

That I take to be the guiding rule in this case. Unless the later appointment is inconsistent with the first, there is no revocation of the earlier appointment, that being explicitly saved except so far as is necessary to effectuate the later appointments, and the moneys received as for purchase money being by the very words of the second deed recognized as still having their original character.

I do not stop to investigate what I may call the collateral arguments, based on extrinsic circumstances, such as, on the one side the depreciation in value of the land, and on the other the probable reasons—such as advances to the sons—for not revoking out and out the first appointment, because, whatever the motive, it was not done, and that appointment was left to stand except so far as it might be inconsistent with the new appointments; and as the language of the new appointment relied on cannot, in my judgment, be held to comprise the moneys now in controversy, it does not confer the right claimed by the sons. This view, if correct, would end the first contention. Now the words of the appointment, moneys " of which no other appointment is made by the said within written deed of appointment of 10th September 1889 or by these presents," are in themselves clear. If moneys as such are at the designated time in the hands of the trustees, and are not found to be specifically appointed by either deed, then this appointment operates. I think I may appropriately quote the words of Lord *Halsbury* L.C. in *Higgins* v. *Dawson* (1):—
" One does not doubt that, where you are construing either a will or any other instrument, it is perfectly legitimate to look at the whole instrument—and, indeed, you must look at the whole instrument—to see the meaning of the whole instrument, and you cannot rely upon one particular passage in it to the exclusion of what is relevant to the explanation of the particular clause that you are expounding. That is perfectly true as a general proposition; but I ask myself here what other words— what part of the will, what provision other than the one I am construing, reflects any light on, or gives the smallest interpretation to, the particular words which I am called upon to expound."

I should refer to what is urged in opposition to this view,

(1) (1902) A.C., 1, at p. 3.

H. C. of A.
1908.

aBeckett
v.
Trustees
Executors
and Agency
Co. Ltd.

Isaacs J.

namely, that it gives no meaning to the words of the appointment relied on by the appellants. In the first place, I think such a meaning may be given, this particular appointment is of moneys which the trustees for the time being shall after the decease of the surviving appointor *then* have in their hands or under their control.

In the marriage settlement there was a covenant by W. A. C. àBeckett that, if his wife or he in her right should become entitled to any real or personal property of the value of £20 or upwards, it should be conveyed or assigned to the trustees upon the trusts of the settlement. This might have happened; but further, if it were the case that no other meaning than the one suggested by the appellants could be given to the words, that meaning appears to me too contradictory to the words to be the true one. I again apply the words of Lord *Halsbury* L.C. in *Hunter* v. *Attorney General* (1) quoted by him in *Higgins* v. *Dawson* (2):—" That certainly would be a strange mode of construing a will, that because you cannot find what else he must have intended to be done with his money except something of that nature, although it is admitted that there are no words in the will to convey the intention which it is suggested he had in his mind, you can invent provisions and impose conditions which the testator himself has not introduced." As Lord *Davey* said in the same case (3) that would be making a will for the testator and not interpreting the words he had used. That is what I feel here.

Looking at the frame of the second deed, I find it is broken up into sections. First, the recital of the rescission of the contract of sale, and of the desire to revoke, and alter in manner and to the extent thereinafter appearing, the appointments made by the first deed, and subject thereto of extinguishing the power of revocation, and then a series of provisions of distinct subject matters each introduced by the words " and these presents witness."

The first of the series is the limited revocation of the purchase money fund, followed by an appointment of the lands which have

(1) (1899) A.C., 309, at p. 317.   (2) (1902) A.C., 1, at p. 6.
          (3) (1899) A.C., 309, at p. 322.

revested, these apparently being treated as cash, and the
daughters not being required to give credit for advances, and as
part of the same subject matter £1,000 given to Mrs Chomley.
Up to this point there is no revocation respecting the purchase
money actually received. Then follow a number of specific
appointments each introduced by the words referred to.   Again,
as a separate matter with the same verbal introduction, is the
limited revocation of the residuary appointment in the first deed.
Needless to say the purchase money fund did not come within
the original residuary appointment, and the second deed treats it
as still not within that appointment. But immediately after
that limited revocation, and apparently consequent thereon, are
a number of directions and appointments of land and money.
Doubtless the moneys, like some of the lands which were
specifically appointed by these deeds, represent part of the
original purchase money fund, but just as the Gembrook land,
for instance, though bought out of that fund was treated
separately, so apparently the moneys lent, though coming out of
that fund too, were for this purpose and rightly or wrongly
treated separately and were specifically appointed as if they
would have otherwise fallen under the residuary claim. At
all events the appointors were explicitly stating what properties
represented by the purchase money fund were to be disposed of
differently from the original disposition.   Following upon these
appointments comes the particular provision relied on by the
appellants treating these moneys on the same footing. These
considerations seem to me material when considering the
intention of the appointors as discoverable from the deed itself.

Looking back to the express recognition in the second deed of
the continued appointment of the purchase money fund except
as modified by the appointment of the later deed, and looking
also to the severance of the various subject matters dealt with
by the later deed as well as to the unambiguous words of the
appointment relied on by the appellants, I am not able to yield
to the argument that the first appointment is entirely revoked,
and the whole of the existing purchase money given to the sons
exclusively. I ought not to overlook the view presented that
the absence of an express total revocation is due to the

appointors' desire to protect advances already made. The answer to that I conceive to be twofold. First, it would have been easy to say so; and next, the appointors, when they did intend to protect such advances notwithstanding a revocation, have expressly said so, as where in the earlier deed they so provided with regard to the advancement to Mrs. Brett.

Then comes the other extreme question whether the daughters are exclusively entitled. Now I am clearly of opinion that the case originally fell within *Page* v. *Leapingwell* (1). The principle is stated by *Chitty* L.J. in *In re Phillips* ; *Eddowes* v. *Phillips* (2) ; in these terms :—" Where a settlor is dealing with a sum which is ascertained or fixed, or, having the control of a fund, he treats it as a fund of that character, and there is an apportionment, then the principle of *Page* v. *Leapingwell* (1) applies."

With regard to the apportionment, no distinction in principle could have been made between the present case and *Page* v. *Leapingwell* (1). As to the definiteness of the fund, the language of the settlors leads me to the conclusion that they were then dealing with the sum as being of £100,000—knowing there would be deductions for the commission of £2,500, and the necessary ordinary expenses, and perhaps the amount invested in property afterwards specifically appointed—as a fixed and ascertained sum ; and they obviously proceeded to apportion it as on that basis. It was suggested that they contemplated a possibility of the actual receipts falling short of the agreed sum, and therefore regarded the fund as indefinite.

I cannot read their words in that way, and if such an eventuality had been present to their minds, I should have expected some further and contingent provision in the event of the purchaser for any reason failing to pay the full amount of purchase money.

The original intention still stands good unless altered by the second deed. I do not think the partial failure of the fund, arising even from an external act of the appointors, could alter what would otherwise be the legal construction of the deed ; and the second deed only limits the extent of the fund, which is to be

(1) 18 Ves., 463.　　　　(2) 66 L. J. Ch., 714, at p. 716.

subject to the appointment. Within those limits *Page v. Leapingwell* (1) applies in my opinion. If, however, it does not, it seems to me, in the absence of complete revocation, the daughters should get the whole existing portion of the fund exclusively.

GRIFFITH C.J. The order appealed from will be varied by substituting a declaration that the appellants are entitled, to the exclusion of the respondent daughters, to the fund in question. When special leave to appeal was given we were told that the appellants would not have desired to appeal but for the fact that they were led to believe that the trustees were under the judgment making large claims against them in respect of moneys said to have been paid to them by the trustees, and they asked for leave to appeal in order to protect themselves to that extent. So far as the judgment related to £7,600 they were content. In the meantime, however, the greater part of that sum had been divided amongst the daughters in accordance with the order of the Supreme Court. When leave to appeal was given the appellants undertook not to claim a refund of any moneys paid over by the trustees to any of the daughters after 7th March 1907 and before the notice of motion for special leave was given to them, if this Court on the hearing of the appeal should think it just that such moneys should not be refunded, and also to indemnify the trustees against any payments properly made by them under the order: *àBeckett* v. *Backhouse* (2). The Court think it is just that these moneys should not be refunded, and that the undertaking should be given. The appellants must indemnify the trustees in accordance with their undertaking. The costs of all parties must be paid out of the fund, as between solicitor and client.

Appeal allowed. Order appealed from varied.

Solicitors, for the appellants, *Snowden, Neave & Demaine.*
Solicitors, for the respondents, *Hamilton, Wynne & Riddell; Blake & Riggall.*

B. L.

(1) 18 Ves. 463.   (2) 4 C.L.R., 1334, at p. 1337.

[HIGH COURT OF AUSTRALIA.]

THE WESTERN AUSTRALIAN BANK   .   APPELLANTS;
PLAINTIFFS,

AND

THE ROYAL INSURANCE CO.   .   .   .   RESPONDENTS.
DEFENDANTS,

ON APPEAL FROM THE SUPREME COURT OF
WESTERN AUSTRALIA.

Fire insurance—Assignment of policy to mortgagee—Insurable interest of mortgagee—New contract with mortgagee—Conditions precedent to action—Subsequent insurance by mortgagor—Notice of loss—Suspension of right of action.

A mortgagee, whether legal or equitable, has an insurable interest in the mortgaged property.

The owners of certain property effected a policy of fire insurance No. 7213012 for £650 over the property, and being indebted to their bank, they, in addition to depositing the deeds of the property and the policy with the bank, executed a memorandum indorsed upon the policy by which they purported to assign all their right, title and interest in and to the policy and every renewal thereof and the moneys thereby assured unto the bank for and on behalf of the bank to the extent of their then present and future indebtedness to the bank, and subject thereto for the benefit of themselves. The insurance company also executed a memorandum indorsed on the policy to the effect that the transfer by the owners to the bank conferred on the bank whatever rights might accrue to the owners under the policy subject nevertheless to all the obligations and conditions of the policy. The next renewal premium was not paid when due, and according to its terms the policy thereupon expired. Subsequently the premium was paid and the agent of the insurance company executed a document whereby he acknowledged that he had received from the owners and the bank as mortgagees the sum of —— for premium deposit for the insurance of £650 " on property as per proposal in consideration of which such insurance is held in force for a period not exceeding fourteen days from issue of this receipt subject to the terms and conditions of

H. C. OF A.
1908.

MELBOURNE,
Feb. 28;
March 2, 3, 4,
27.

Griffith C.J.,
Barton,
O'Connor and
Higgins JJ.

H. C. OF A.
1908.

WESTERN
AUSTRALIAN
BANK
v.
ROYAL
INSURANCE
CO.

the company's policies and to the condition that the company reserves the right of rejection or alteration in the terms of the insurance by notice to that effect delivered or posted but the insurance is held in force pending any such notice." This receipt was followed by another by which the agent of the insurance company acknowledged that he had received the premium for "continuance of policy No. 7213012 of this company in the name of" the bank, and a similar receipt was given for the premium due the next year.

Held, that a new contract of insurance was created between the bank and the insurance company upon the terms of the original policy so far as applicable, and upon which the bank was entitled to sue in its own name.

One of the conditions of the policy was :—" The insured must give notice to the company of any insurance or insurances made elsewhere on the property hereby insured or on any part thereof the particulars of which must be indorsed on the policy and unless such notice be given and indorsement be made the insured will not be entitled to any benefit under this policy." After the assignment of the policy to the bank, and after the receipts hereinbefore mentioned had been given, the owners insured the property with another company. In an action by the bank against the first mentioned insurance company :

Held, that the bank was not bound to give notice of the second insurance to the company as a condition precedent to recovery.

By *Griffith* C.J., *Barton* and *O'Connor* JJ., on the ground that the second insurance was not "on the property" insured by the bank.

By *Higgins* J., on the ground that the condition required notice to be given only of insurances effected by the insured.

By *Griffith* C.J. on both grounds.

Another condition of the policy provided that :—" On the happening of any loss or damage by fire to any of the property insured by this policy the insured must forthwith give notice in writing thereof to the company or its agents and within fifteen days at the latest deliver to the company or its agents at his own expense as particular a statement and account as may be reasonably practicable of the property and the several articles and matters damaged or destroyed by fire . . . and in default of compliance with the terms of this condition or any of them no claim in respect of any such loss or damage shall be payable or sustainable unless and until such notice statement account proofs and explanations and evidence respectively shall have been delivered produced and given as aforesaid and such statutory declaration if required shall have been made."

Held, that there was no obligation on the insured to give the notice, statement and account, &c., therein referred to within 15 days, but that the condition merely suspended the right of action until the notice, statement and account, &c., had been given.

Comments by *Higgins* J. on the maxim *Verba chartarum fortius accipiuntur contra proferentem.*

APPE
An
trali
ance
"§
"1
the
ing
"2
made
that
calle
insur
the p
situa
hotel
agre
back
polic
fire a
(in c
the
defer
make
or tl
excee
the i
happ
"3
of th
so in

"4.

H. C. of A.
1908.

Western
Australian
Bank
v.
Royal
Insurance
Co.

the company's policies and to the condition that the company reserves the right of rejection or alteration in the terms of the insurance by notice to that effect delivered or posted but the insurance is held in force pending any such notice." This receipt was followed by another by which the agent of the insurance company acknowledged that he had received the premium for "continuance of policy No. 7213012 of this company in the name of" the bank, and a similar receipt was given for the premium due the next year.

Held, that a new contract of insurance was created between the bank and the insurance company upon the terms of the original policy so far as applicable, and upon which the bank was entitled to sue in its own name.

One of the conditions of the policy was:—"The insured must give notice to the company of any insurance or insurances made elsewhere on the property hereby insured or on any part thereof the particulars of which must be indorsed on the policy and unless such notice be given and indorsement be made the insured will not be entitled to any benefit under this policy." After the assignment of the policy to the bank, and after the receipts hereinbefore mentioned had been given, the owners insured the property with another company.   In an action by the bank against the first mentioned insurance company :

Held, that the bank was not bound to give notice of the second insurance to the company as a condition precedent to recovery.

By *Griffith* C.J., *Barton* and *O'Connor* JJ., on the ground that the second insurance was not "on the property" insured by the bank.

By *Higgins* J., on the ground that the condition required notice to be given only of insurances effected by the insured.

By *Griffith* C.J. on both grounds.

Another condition of the policy provided that :—"On the happening of any loss or damage by fire to any of the property insured by this policy the insured must forthwith give notice in writing thereof to the company or its agents and within fifteen days at the latest deliver to the company or its agents at his own expense as particular a statement and account as may be reasonably practicable of the property and the several articles and matters damaged or destroyed by fire   .   .   .   and in default of compliance with the terms of this condition or any of them no claim in respect of any such loss or damage shall be payable or sustainable unless and until such notice statement account proofs and explanations and evidence respectively shall have been delivered produced and given as aforesaid and such statutory declaration if required shall have been made."

Held, that there was no obligation on the insured to give the notice, statement and account, &c., therein referred to within 15 days, but that the condition merely suspended the right of action until the notice, statement and account. &c., had been given.

Comments by *Higgins* J. on the maxim *Verba chartarum fortius accipiuntur contra preferentem.*

H. C. of A.
1908.

WESTERN
AUSTRALIAN
BANK
v.
ROYAL
INSURANCE
Co.

Decision of Supreme Court (*The West Australian Bank* v. *The Royal Insurance Co.*, 9 W.A.L.R., 78), reversed.

APPEAL from the Supreme Court of Western Australia.

An action was brought in the Supreme Court of Western Australia by the Western Australian Bank against the Royal Insurance Co., in which the pleadings were as follow:—

"STATEMENT OF CLAIM.

"1. The plaintiffs are an incorporated banking company and the defendants are an incorporated fire insurance company carrying on business in Western Australia and elsewhere.

"2. By a policy of insurance bearing date the 10th April 1899 made by the defendants and numbered 7213012 it was witnessed that Henry William Taylor and Patrick Connolly (hereinafter called the insured) having paid the defendants £32 10s. for insuring against loss or damage by fire as thereinafter mentioned the property therein described that is to say the Tasmanian Hotel situate at South Boulder in the sum of £650 (subject to the said hotel being used and kept open as a licensed hotel) the defendants agreed with the insured (but subject to the conditions on the back of the said policy which were to be taken as part of the policy) that if the property should be destroyed or damaged by fire at any time between 10th April 1899 and 10th April 1900 or (in case of a renewal of the policy) at any subsequent date during the period for which the same should have been renewed the defendants would out of their capital stock and funds pay or make good to the insured the value of the property so destroyed or the amount of such damage thereto to an amount not exceeding £650 and also not exceeding in any case the amount of the insurable interest therein of the insured at the time of the happening of such fire.

"3. The said H. W. Taylor and P. Connolly were at the time of the making of the said policy interested in the said property so insured as aforesaid to the amount insured thereon.

"Further particulars.—The said H. W. Taylor and P. Connolly were interested in the said property as owners thereof.

"4. The said policy was duly renewed from year to year by

H. C. of A.
1908.

WESTERN
AUSTRALIAN
BANK
v.
ROYAL
INSURANCE
Co.

the payment to the defendants of the said premium of £32 10s. to 10th April 1902.

" Further particulars.—The said premium was paid by the cheques of the said H. W. Taylor and P. Connolly drawn on the plaintiff bank by the said H. W. Taylor and P. Connolly to the agent of the defendant company at Kalgoorlie on the following dates:—On or about 10th April 1900; on 18th April 1901.

" 5. On or about 13th November 1901 the said H. W. Taylor and P. Connolly duly assigned the said policy by indorsement thereon to the plaintiffs as mortgagees as security for their then present and future indebtedness to the plaintiffs.

" Further particulars.—The then present indebtedness of the said H. W. Taylor and P. Connolly to the plaintiffs was the sum of £1863 13s. 9d.

" 6. Due notice of the date and purport of such assignment was afterwards given to the defendants and on 25th February 1902 the defendants noted the said transfer on the back of the said policy.

" Further particulars.—Notice of the said assignment was given by lodging with the agent of the defendants the said assignment indorsed on the said policy between 13th November 1901 and 25th February 1902. The plaintiffs cannot now say whether the said notice was given to the defendants' agent at Kalgoorlie or at Perth.

" 7. The plaintiffs duly renewed the said policy from 10th April 1902 for one year and again from 10th April 1903 for one year expiring 10th April 1904 by paying to the defendants the said annual premium of £32 10s.

" Further particulars.—The said premium was paid by the cheques of the said H. W. Taylor and P. Connolly drawn on the plaintiffs. It was paid by the said H. W. Taylor and P. Connolly on behalf of the plaintiffs at Kalgoorlie on the following dates:—On 27th May 1902; on 21st April 1903.

" 8. On or about 16th December 1903 whilst the said policy was in full force and effect and whilst the said hotel was being used and kept open as a licensed hotel the same so insured as aforesaid was burnt down and destroyed.

"9. The plaintiffs were at the time of the said assignment to them and thence until and at the time of the said loss interested in the said property so insured as aforesaid as mortgagees to an extent beyond the sum insured thereon.

"Further particulars.—The plaintiffs were interested to the extent of £1,863 13s. 9d. at the time of the said assignment and to the extent of £1,542 6s. 5d. at the time of the said loss the said amounts being the indebtedness of the said H. W. Taylor and P. Connolly to the plaintiffs at the said respective times.

"10. By reason of the said fire the plaintiffs suffered loss on the said property to the amount insured thereon as aforesaid.

"Further particulars.—The loss sustained by the plaintiffs was in the total destruction by fire of the Tasmanian Hotel and the amount of such loss was £1,000.

"11. The plaintiffs gave notice in writing of the said loss to the defendants and delivered to them a statement and account of the property destroyed with the estimated value thereof at the time of the said fire and also the actual amount of loss occasioned by the fire to the said property estimated with reference to the state and condition and value thereof immediately before the happening of the said fire after making proper deductions for depreciation in the value of such property from use or otherwise and also a statement of the interest of the plaintiffs therein.

"Further particulars.—The said notice was given and the said statement delivered by the plaintiffs to the defendants on 17th December 1904—

"(a) The actual loss to the said property was £1,000 and over.

"(b) The interest of the plaintiffs was that at the time of the said fire the plaintiffs had a lien over the said building and policy as mortgagees of the said H. W. Taylor and P. Connolly.

"12. A difference having arisen between the defendants and the plaintiffs as to the amount of the alleged loss by fire the same was referred to arbitration as provided by the 14th condition of

H. C. of A.
1908.

WESTERN
AUSTRALIAN
BANK
v.
ROYAL
INSURANCE
Co.

H. C. of A.
1908.

WESTERN
AUSTRALIAN
BANK
v.
ROYAL
INSURANCE
Co.

the said policy and by an award of the arbitrators duly appointed by the parties dated 4th December 1905 the said loss was ascertained and awarded to be the sum of £700.

"13. All conditions have been performed and all things have happened and all times elapsed necessary to entitle the plaintiffs to be paid the sum insured on the said policy but the defendants have not paid the same or any part thereof.

"Further particulars.—The conditions performed things happened and times elapsed are as follow :—

"The premium payable under the said policy was from time to time actually paid and the receipts therefor issued from the defendants' office as provided by condition 4 indorsed on the said policy.

"Notice of the assignment of the said policy from the said H. W. Taylor and P. Connolly to the plaintiffs was given to the defendants and the subsistence of the said policy in favour of the plaintiffs was declared by a memorandum indorsed thereon and signed by a duly authorized person on behalf of the defendants as required by condition 5 indorsed on the said policy.

"The said hotel was burnt down and destroyed while the said policy was in full force and effect and while the said hotel was being used and kept open as a licensed hotel.

"On the happening of the loss by fire notice thereof in writing was given and a statement and account of the property destroyed by fire was delivered to the defendants or their agents as required by condition 6 indorsed on the said policy.

"A difference having arisen between the defendants and the plaintiffs as to the amount of the loss by fire such difference was referred to arbitration as provided by condition 14 of the said policy. Arbitrators were duly appointed and the amount of the said loss was ascertained and this action was commenced within six calendar months next after the delivery of the award.

H. C. of A.
1908.

Western
Australian
Bank
v.
Royal
Insurance
Co.

" The plaintiffs claim £478 18s. 11d. (being thirteen-nineteenths of £700) under the said policy and interest thereon from 14th December 1904 to judgment at the rate of £8 per centum per annum."

" Statement of Defence.

" 1. The defendants admit paragraphs 1, 2 and 4 of the statement of claim.

" 2. The defendants do not admit the allegations contained in paragraph 3 of the statement of claim.

" 3. The defendants deny :—

"(*a*) That on or about 13th November 1901 H. W. Taylor and P. Connolly assigned the policy by indorsement thereon to the plaintiffs as mortgagees as security for their then present and future indebtedness to the plaintiffs or at all.

"(*b*) That due notice of the date and purport of such alleged assignment was afterwards given to the defendants and that on 25th February 1902 or on any other day the defendants noted the said transfer on the back of the policy.

"(*c*) That the plaintiffs duly renewed the policy from 10th April 1902 for one year and again from 10th April 1903 for one year expiring 10th April 1904 by paying to the defendants the annual premium of £32 10s. The defendants say that if the said policy was renewed (which is not admitted) it was renewed by the said H. W. Taylor and P. Connolly only.

"(*d*) That the plaintiffs were at the time of the alleged assignment of the policy to them and until and at the time of the said alleged loss interested in the property insured as mortgagees or at all to an extent beyond the sum insured thereon or in any other sum.

"(*e*) That by reason of the alleged fire the plaintiffs suffered loss on the said property to the amount insured thereon or to any other amount or at all.

"(*f*) That the plaintiffs gave notice in writing of the said alleged loss to the defendants and delivered to them a statement and account of the property alleged to

H. C. of A.
1908.

Western
Australian
Bank
v.
Royal
Insurance
Co.

have been destroyed with the estimated value thereof at the time of the alleged fire and also the actual amount of the loss occasioned by the fire to the said property and also a statement of the interest therein of the plaintiffs.

" (g) That a difference having arisen between the defendants and the plaintiffs as to the amount of the alleged loss by fire the same was referred to arbitration as provided by the 14th condition of the policy and that by an award of the arbitrators the loss was ascertained and awarded to be the sum of £700.

" (h) That all conditions have been performed and all things have happened and all times elapsed necessary to entitle the plaintiffs to be paid the sum insured on the said policy or any other sum.

" (i) That the defendants are indebted to the plaintiffs in the sum of £478 8s. 11d. or any part thereof or in any other sum at all.

" 4. The defendants do not admit the allegations contained in paragraph 8 of the statement of claim.

" 5. The defendants say that the plaintiffs were not the insured under the said policy and that the plaintiffs were not insured against loss or damage under the said policy or at all.

" 6. If the policy was assigned by H. W. Taylor and P. Connolly to the plaintiffs (which is denied) the defendants did not agree to any such assignment.

" 7. The plaintiffs had not at the time of the alleged fire and have not now an insurable interest in the subject matter of the said insurance or in the said policy.

" 8. The plaintiffs did not sustain any loss or damage by the alleged damage or destruction of the property by fire.

" 9. The plaintiffs are not entitled to institute or maintain any action or claim against the defendants in respect of the said policy.

" 10. The plaintiffs were not and are not claimants entitled to call upon the defendants to proceed to arbitration under condition 14 indorsed on the said policy nor has any arbitration been held nor the amount of alleged loss or damage been referred to

H. C. or A.
1908.

WESTERN
AUSTRALIAN
BANK
v.
ROYAL
INSURANCE
Co.

arbitration in accordance with the said condition 14 which is a condition precedent to the commencement or maintenance of any action against the defendants.

"11. The policy was subject to conditions precedent (numbered 6) that upon the happening of any loss or damage by fire to the property insured the insured must forthwith give notice in writing thereof to the defendants and within fifteen days at the latest deliver to the company at the expense of the insured as particular a statement and account as might be reasonably practicable of the property damaged or destroyed by fire and of the actual amount of loss or damage occasioned by fire. These conditions were not complied with.

"12. The policy was subject to a condition (numbered 11) that the insured must give notice to the defendants of any insurance made elsewhere on the property insured the particulars of which must be indorsed on the policy and that unless such notice be given and indorsement be made the insured would not be entitled to any benefit under the policy. The insured under the said policy or alternatively H. W. Taylor and P. Connolly made an additional insurance on the property insured with the Commercial Union Assurance Company Ltd. in the sum of £300 but no notice thereof was given to the defendants nor were the particulars of such additional insurance indorsed on the policy. The plaintiffs are by reason of the said condition and the matters aforesaid not entitled to any benefit under the said policy.

"13. Alternatively the defendants say that if the plaintiffs are entitled to any benefit under the policy (which is denied) or to bring or maintain this action in respect thereof (which is denied) the defendants claim instead of paying the sum of £478 18s. 11d. to the plaintiffs in money the right to exercise the option to reinstate or replace the property alleged to have been damaged or destroyed or any part thereof pursuant to the condition 9 indorsed on the said policy."

"REPLY.

"The plaintiffs say that—

"1. Except as to paragraphs 11, 12 and 13 of the defence they join issue thereon save in so far as the same contains admissions of the plaintiffs' statement of claim.

H. C. of A.
1908.

WESTERN
AUSTRALIAN
BANK
v.
ROYAL
INSURANCE
Co.

" 2. As to paragraph 11 of the defence the conditions (numbered 6) indorsed on the said policy are not conditions precedent and they complied therewith before bringing this action. They will contend that the effect of the said conditions (only portions whereof are set out in paragraph 11 of the defence) is merely to postpone the right of payment until complied with.

" 3. As to paragraph 12 of the defence they were the insured under the said policy and deny that as such insured they made any additional insurance on the same property within the meaning of condition 11 indorsed on the said policy.

" 4. As to paragraph 13—(*a*) The defendants never elected to reinstate the said property and the same has been rebuilt by the said H. W. Taylor and P. Connolly.

" (*b*) The defendants ought not now to be admitted to claim the right to exercise the option to reinstate the property destroyed or any part thereof pursuant to condition 9 indorsed on the said policy because they always wrongfully denied their liability and wrongfully refused to admit any claim in respect of the said loss.

(*c*) The defendants abandoned their right to reinstate the property by repudiating all liability under the said policy.

" Further particulars.—The present building is of brick. Re-building commenced 14th July and finished 29th September 1904."

In addition to the conditions set out in the judgment of *Griffith* C.J. hereunder, there were indorsed on the policy the following conditions (*inter alia*):—

" 1. Any material misdescription of any of the property proposed to be hereby insured or of any building or place in which property to be so insured is contained or any omission to disclose the existence of any hazardous trade or of any apparatus in such building or place in or by which heat is produced other than grates in common domestic fire-places with brick or stone chimneys and any mis-statement of or omission to state any fact material to be known for estimating the risk whether at the time of effecting the insurance or afterwards renders this policy void as to the property affected by such misdescription mis-statement or omission respectively and any matter referred to in the proposal form shall be deemed material and such proposal

H. C. of A.
1908.

WESTERN
AUSTRALIAN
BANK
v.
ROYAL
INSURANCE
Co.

shall in all cases be deemed to be made by the insured and throughout these conditions the stipulations provisions and requirements applicable to loss on property shall also be deemed to apply in the case of any insurance on rent.

" 4. No insurance proposed to the company is to be considered in force until the premium be actually paid. No receipts for any premiums of insurance shall be valid or available for any purpose except such as are printed and issued from the company's office and signed by one of the clerks or duly authorized agents of the company and any condition or proviso contained in indorsed upon or referred to in any such receipt shall be taken as part of this policy.

" 5. This policy ceases to be in force as to any property hereby insured which shall pass from the insured to any other person otherwise than by will unless notice thereof be given to the company and the subsistence of the insurance in favour of such other person be declared by a memorandum indorsed hereon and signed by some duly authorized person on behalf of the company or if the same become the subject of a contract of sale or if there may be any change in the nature of the interest of the insured in such property.

" 12. If at the time of any loss or damage by fire happening to any property hereby insured there be any other subsisting insurance or insurances whether effected by the insured or by any other person covering the same property this company shall not be liable to pay or contribute in respect of such loss or damage more than its proportion rateably with the amount of such other insurance of such loss or damage.

" 13. In all cases where any other subsisting insurance or insurances whether effected by the insured or by any other person on any property hereby insured either exclusively or together with any other property shall be subject to average the insurance on such property under this policy shall be subject to average in like manner."

The other material facts are sufficiently set out in the judgments hereunder.

The action was tried before *Parker* C.J. who gave judgment

H. C. of A.
1908.

WESTERN
AUSTRALIAN
BANK
v.
ROYAL
INSURANCE
Co.

for the plaintiffs for £478 18s. 11d., and interest thereon at 8 per cent. per annum to 8th December 1905, with costs.

From this judgment the defendants appealed to the Full Court, which allowed the appeal, directed the judgment for the plaintiffs to be set aside and judgment to be entered for the defendants with costs: *West Australian Bank* v. *Royal Insurance Co.* (1).

From this judgment the plaintiffs now appealed to the High Court.

Irvine K.C. (with him *Coldham*), for the appellants. Either the appellants were the insured under the original policy or there was a novation. The appellants were to get the policy money if a fire occurred, and were responsible for the premiums. The appellants have an insurable interest. Although this is a contract of indemnity, the appellants, as mortgagees who had insured, are entitled to be compensated in respect of the whole property insured, and not merely in respect of their interest in it as mortgagees: See *North British and Mercantile Insurance Co.* v. *London, Liverpool, and Globe Insurance Co.* (2); *Castellain* v. *Preston* (3); *Irving* v. *Richardson* (4). The mortgagee, mortgagor, and insurer may agree to any contract they like as to insurance. The indorsement on the policy is an assent by the respondents to the assignment, and not merely a promise by the respondents to pay to the appellants the insurance moneys that may become due under it, and the appellants became the insured: *Ellis* v. *Insurance Company of North America* (5). The receipts for premiums show that there was a new contract of insurance. Each of those receipts shows a renewal of a policy as to which the appellants are the insured. The policy will be read most strongly against the respondents: *North British and Mercantile Insurance Co.* v. *London, Liverpool, and Globe Insurance Co.* (6); *Broom's Legal Maxims*, 7th ed., p. 444; *Fowkes* v. *Manchester and London Assurance and Loan Association* (7); *Braunstein* v. *Accidental Death Insurance Co.* (8).

(1) 9 W.A.L.R., 78.　　　　　　　(5) 32 Fed. Rep., 646.
(2) 5 Ch. D., 569, at p. 583.　　　(6) 5 Ch. D., 569.
(3) 11 Q.B.D., 380, at p. 397.　　(7) 3 B. & S., 917.
(4) 1 Moo. & R., 153; 2 B. & Ad.,　(8) 1 B. & S., 782.
193.

H. C. OF A.
1908.

WESTERN
AUSTRALIAN
BANK
v.
ROYAL
INSURANCE
Co.

[HIGGINS J. referred to *Norton on Deeds*, p. 118.]

The Court will struggle against a general and literal meaning of such words as are in clause 11 of the conditions of the policy: *Anderson* v. *Fitzgerald* (1). That clause refers to insurances effected by the insured, and not to those effected by anyone else. At any rate, it does not refer to insurances of which the insured has no notice. As to clause 6, the respondents cannot now rely on it because they repudiated any liability before the time when notice was to be given, and the clause is too uncertain in its meaning for the respondents to gain any advantage from it. See *Bunyon on Fire Insurance*, 5th ed., p. 216; *Weir* v. *Northern Counties of England Insurance Co.* (2). It is sufficient under that clause if the particulars required by it are given before trial: *Grau* v. *Colonial Insurance Co. of New Zealand* (3); *Davis* v. *National Fire and Marine Insurance Office of New Zealand* (4).

Mitchell K.C. (with him *Downing*), for the respondents. The effect of the assignment was not to assign the policy but to assign certain rights Taylor and Connolly had under it, and that is all that the respondents assented to.

[HIGGINS J. referred to *Crossley* v. *Glasgow Life Assurance Co* (5); *Ettershank* v. *Dunne* (6).]

The appellants had only an equitable mortgage and their insurable interest was limited to the amount from time to time due from the mortgagors. If the fire had occurred while the mortgagors' account was in credit, the appellants would have had no insurable interest. What the parties intended was that the appellants should get a security to the extent of their debt, but, subject to that, the insurance was to be for the benefit of the mortgagors. There was no novation, for there is no evidence of consent of all the parties. The policy after the assignment was not a new contract. An acceptance in the form used here is a renewal only. If this had been a new contract a higher stamp duty would have been payable: *Stamp Act* 1882 (46 Vict. No. 6,) secs. 5, 13, 60; *Stamp Act Amendment Act*

---

(1) 4 H.L.C., 484.
(2) 4 L.R. Ir., 689.
(3) 2 Q.L.J., 53.

(4) 10 N.S.W.L.R. (L.), 90.
(5) 4 Ch. D., 421.
(6) 5 V.L.R. (E.), 99.

H. C. of A.
1908.

WESTERN
AUSTRALIAN
BANK
v.
ROYAL
INSURANCE
Co.

1902 (2 Ed. VII. No. 21). There was no evidence that the payment of premiums by Taylor and Connolly was with the authority of the appellants or was ratified by them. See *Buffalo Steam Engine Works* v. *Sun Mutual Insurance Co.* (1); *State Mutual Fire Insurance Co.* v. *Roberts* (2). Whether the appellants became the insured or not, Taylor and Connolly did not cease to be the insured, for the person who can sue in law is not the only person who can be the insured.

Assuming the appellants are the insured and not Taylor and Connolly, then under clause 11 the applicants should have given notice of the second insurance. The reason for that clause is to enable the respondents to get out of the risk if they think fit: *Sinnamon* v. *New Zealand Insurance Co.* (3). That reason would apply in the case of a second insurance by the mortgagor when the first was by the mortgagee.

[GRIFFITH C.J.—That clause may refer to policies already existing.]

That case is covered by clause 1.

[GRIFFITH C.J. referred to *Queen Insurance Co.* v. *Parsons* (4).]

Clause 11 requires notice of all policies of which the insured knows: *Harris* v. *Ohio Insurance Co.* (5); *Stacey* v. *Franklin Fire Insurance Co.* (6).

[HIGGINS J. referred to *Ætna Fire Insurance Co.* v. *Tyler* (7).]

The appellants knew of this second policy and had control over it, for it was entered in their securities book and they had a lien over it. See also *Carpenter* v. *Providence Washington Insurance Co.* (8); *Ebsworth* v. *Alliance Marine Insurance Co.* (9); *Bunyon on Fire Insurance*, 5th ed., p. 383. The policy of which the insured must give notice is one of which they have knowledge and which effects the danger against which clause 11 is intended to guard.

[GRIFFITH C.J. referred to *Foster* v. *Equitable Mutual Fire Insurance Co.* (10).]

(1) 17 N.Y. St. R., 401.
(2) 31 Pa. St. R., 438.
(3) 8 Q.L.T., 144.
(4) 7 App. Cas., 96.
(5) 5 Ohio St. R., 467.
(6) 2 Watts & Sergeant (Pa.), 506.

(7) 16 Wendell (N.Y.), 385; 30 Amer. Dec., 90.
(8) 16 Peters, 495.
(9) L.R. 8 C.P., 596.
(10) 2 Gray (Mass.), 216.

As to clause 6 no amendment to raise a plea of waiver should
now be allowed.   The clause must be interpreted *reddendo*
singula singulis.   The fact that the respondents said they would
not pay does not excuse the appellants from complying with the
clause.   Compliance with the clause within 15 days of the fire is
a condition precedent to recovery under the policy.   See *Trask*
v. *State Fire and Marine Insurance Co. of Pennsylvania* (1);
Friemansdorf v. *Watertown Insurance Co.* (2).

Irvine K.C., in reply, referred to *Lazarus* v. *Commonwealth*
Insurance Co. (3); *Bunyon on Fire Insurance*, 5th ed., p. 375.

H. C. of A.
1908.

WESTERN
AUSTRALIAN
BANK
v.
ROYAL
INSURANCE
Co.

Cur. adv. vult.

The following judgments were read :—

GRIFFITH C.J. This action in its original form was an action
by the appellants claiming to be assignees of a policy of fire
insurance effected in April 1899 by H. W. Taylor and P. Connolly
with the respondents.   During the progress of the case, however,
it became apparent that the real nature of the plaintiffs' claim,
if any, was in respect of a contract of insurance between
themselves and the defendants, the terms of which were to be
found by reference to Taylor and Connolly's policy.   No formal
amendment of the pleadings was asked for, but the case was
contested, and evidence was adduced, upon this footing.

Various defences were set up.   The defendants denied the
plaintiffs' right to sue as assignees of the policy, and denied that
any fresh contract had been established.   They also denied the
existence of any insurable interest in the plaintiffs at the time
of the loss.   They also alleged failure to comply with two
conditions of the policy, viz., condition 6, relating to notice and
proof of loss, and condition 11, requiring the insured to give
notice to the defendants of "any insurance made elsewhere on
the property."

The facts of the case, except on one point, appear to be free
from doubt.   The policy, which was for £650 upon a building at

March 27.

(1) 29 Pa. St. R., 198.   (3) 2 Hare and Wallace's American
(2) 1 Fed. Rep., 68.   Leading Cases, 797, at p. 825.

H. C. of A.
1908.

WESTERN
AUSTRALIAN
BANK
v.
ROYAL
INSURANCE
Co.

Griffith C.J.

Kalgoorlie, was effected by Taylor and Connolly, the insured, on 10th April 1899, and was to continue in force till 10th April 1900, and so from year to year so long as the annual premium was paid. In 1901 the plaintiffs were Taylor and Connolly's bankers. On 1st February and 23rd August in that year they executed in favour of the plaintiffs two instruments called "general liens," by which they charged to the extent of their indebtedness, *inter alia*, all fire policies and all property real and personal evidenced by any documents which had been or might be deposited with the plaintiffs by them, or which belonging to them might come into the custody of the plaintiffs. On 13th November 1901 Taylor and Connolly executed a memorandum (indorsed upon the policy of April 1889) in the following terms:—

> "For valuable consideration we hereby assign all our right title and interest in and to the within policy and every renewal thereof and the moneys thereby assured unto the Western Australian Bank for and on behalf of the said Bank to the extent of our present and future indebtedness to the said Bank and subject thereto for the benefit of us the transferors. The receipt of the said Bank to be a full discharge for the said moneys.

"Dated at Kalgoorlie the 13th day of November 1901."

The policy had apparently been previously deposited with the plaintiffs. On 25th February 1902 the defendants by their agent executed a memorandum (also indorsed on the policy) as follows:—

> "Perth 25th February 1902. The transfer of the 13th November 1901 confers on the Western Australian Bank whatever rights may accrue to Henry William Taylor and Patrick Connolly under this policy subject nevertheless to all the obligations and conditions of this policy."

At this time the premium for the year ending 10th April 1902 had been duly paid. The plaintiffs' claim as assignees was founded upon these two documents. The Supreme Court were of opinion that they did not operate to confer on the bank a right to sue in their own name, and this view was not contested before us.

The renewal premium due on 10th April 1902 was not paid,

and the policy, according to its terms, thereupon expired. On 22nd May 1902 the defendants' agent at Kalgoorlie signed a document in the following form :—

H. C. of A.
1908.

WESTERN
AUSTRALIAN
BANK
v.
ROYAL
INSURANCE
Co.

Griffith C.J.

"ROYAL INSURANCE COMPANY

(Western Australian Branch)

253 St. George's Terrace, Perth.

Kalgoorlie (c) Agency, 22nd May 1902.

"No. 533.

"Received from Connolly and Taylor and the W.A. Bank as mortgagees on account of the Royal Insurance Company the sum of——for premium deposit for the insurance against fire of six hundred and fifty pounds on property as per proposal in consideration of which such insurance is held in force for a period not exceeding fourteen days from issue of this receipt subject to the terms and conditions of the company's policies and to the condition that the company reserves the right of rejection or alteration in the terms of the insurance by notice to that effect delivered or posted but the insurance is held in force pending such notice. Further acceptance of the proposal will be notified by the issue of receipt by the Perth office.

"Premium £32 10s.　　　　　　　G. W. A. Cross, Agent."

It is to be noted that this document is not in the form used for a receipt for a premium upon an existing policy, but is a form apt for a receipt given by an agent for money paid upon a proposal to effect a new insurance, which proposal may or may not be accepted by the principal—which, indeed, was in law the real nature of the transaction. This provisional receipt was followed on 27th May 1902 by another in these words :—

"Received the undermentioned premium for the continuance of policy No. 7213012 of this company in the name of Western Australian Bank insuring the sum of £650 for 12 months from 10th April 1902 to 10th April 1903 at four o'clock in the afternoon.

"This receipt shall not be valid until countersigned by the duly authorized agent of the company at Kalgoorlie.

"Premium £32 10s.　　　　　　A. W. Pike, Local Manager.

　　　　　　　　　　　　　　per W. E. H.

H. C. of A.
1908.

Western
Australian
Bank
v.
Royal
Insurance
Co.

Griffith C.J.

" Countersigned at Kalgoorlie this twenty-seventh day of May 1902.   G. W. A. Cross, Agent."

A receipt in similar terms was given for the premium due in April 1903.

The plaintiffs contend that the effect of these documents was to create a new contract of insurance between them and the defendants upon the terms of the original policy so far as applicable. The Supreme Court rejected this argument on the ground, as I understand them, that this was not the intention of the parties. There was no evidence beyond the documents themselves to show the intention of the parties. Such evidence,. indeed, if given, could only be used to show that the documents were not intended to have a contractual effect at all—not to qualify the nature of the contract, if any, disclosed by them.

In my opinion these receipts, properly construed, establish a new contract between the plaintiffs and the defendants upon which the former are entitled to sue in their own name. It was contended before us that from this point of view the receipt of May 1902 ought under the Western Australian *Stamp Act* to have been stamped as a policy. Probably this is so, but, if the point had been taken before the trial Judge, he could under the Act have allowed it to be stamped then and there, and it is too late now to raise such an objection.

I turn to the other defences, as to which we have not the advantage of knowing the view of the learned Judges of the Full Court.

The objection that the plaintiffs had no insurable interest cannot be sustained. There is, I think, no doubt that under English law a mortgagee has an insurable interest in the mortgaged property, whether the mortgage is legal or equitable. (See *per Bowen* L.J. in *Castellain* v. *Preston* (1)).

Difficult questions, not solved by any English decision, may arise with respect to the extent of his insurable interest, whether it is co-extensive with the value of the property or only with the amount due on the mortgage at the date of the loss, or even a less sum. It is sufficient to say that they do not arise in the present case, since the debtors, Taylor and Connolly, were

(1) 11 Q.B.D., 380, at p. 398.

indebted to the plaintiffs at the time of the fire in a sum exceeding the amount of the policy.

H. C. of A.
1908.

Western
Australian
Bank
v.
Royal
Insurance
Co.

Griffith C.J.

I will deal next with the defence raised under condition 11, which is as follows:—" The insured must give notice to the company of any insurance or insurances made elsewhere on the property hereby insured or on any part thereof the particulars of which must be indorsed on the policy and unless such notice be given and indorsement be made the insured will not be entitled to any benefit under this policy."

It appears that on 18th June 1903 Taylor and Connolly effected a policy in their own name upon the same property with the Commercial Union Assurance Company for £300, and that no notice of this policy was given by the bank to the defendants, nor were the particulars of it indorsed on the policy of April 1899. The defendants contend that this was a breach of the condition, the plaintiffs that the condition does not apply to such a case. On the one hand, it is said that the words "the property hereby insured" mean the building; on the other, that they refer to the interest insured. No doubt, under the contract between Taylor and Connolly and the defendants evidenced by the policy alone they have the former meaning. But it does not follow that in the new contract between the plaintiffs and the defendants evidenced by the receipts they have the same meaning. It may be, indeed, that as between plaintiffs and defendants they would have that meaning in other parts of the policy, and that this may be one of the rare cases in which the same words have different meanings in different parts of the same instrument. But, having regard to the subject matter of the insurance, that is, the bank's interest as mortgagees, I am disposed to think that the words "the property hereby insured" were intended to refer to that interest, and not to the interest of the mortgagors, or to the property regarded as a physical object. If, however, they have the latter meaning, I think that the condition refers only to insurances effected by the insured, and not to insurances effected by other persons.

It is open to argument whether condition 11 applies at all to insurances effected after the date of the principal policy, but I express no opinion on this point.

H. C. of A.
1908.

Western
Australian
Bank
v.
Royal
Insurance
Co.

Griffith C.J.

In this regard I will cite a very cogent argument contained in the judgment of Chancellor Walworth of New York in the case of *Ætna Fire Insurance Co.* v. *Tyler* (1) when a similar condition as to prior insurances was under consideration. " No one can suppose for a moment that these underwriters intended to be so unreasonable as to require a person insuring with them, under the penalty of a forfeiture of his policy, to give notice of every insurance which any former owner of the property might have made thereon, although he had no interest in that insurance, and the rights of the company could not in any way be affected thereby; that if there was any such insurance, even in those cases where the fact was notified to the underwriters, the person insured with them should only recover a part of his loss from them, although he had no interest in and could not be benefited by the other insurance. To suppose the underwriters intended that such a construction should be given to this part of the policy, would be to suppose that they intended to entrap those who insured with them. The plain and obvious meaning of the whole clause is, that if the assured has any other policy or insurance upon the property, by assignment or otherwise, by which the interest intended to be insured is already either wholly or partially protected, he shall disclose that fact and have it indorsed on the policy, or the insurance shall be void; and the same where he shall make any subsequent insurance; also, that in case of any such prior or subsequent insurance, although it is notified to the company and indorsed on the policy, the underwriters in the two policies shall contribute rateably to his loss, so that in no event he can recover more than the amount of his actual loss."

The case of *Foster* v. *Equitable Mutual Fire Insurance Co.* (2) is to the same effect.

I think, therefore, that this defence fails.

I pass now to the defence raised under condition 6, which so far as material is as follows:—" On the happening of any loss or damage by fire to any of the property insured by this policy the insured must forthwith give notice in writing thereof to the

(1) 16 Wendell, 385 ; 30 Amer. Dec., 90, at p. 97.
(2) 2 Gray (Mass.), 216.

company or its agents and within fifteen days at the latest deliver to the company or its agents at his own expense as particular a statement and account as may be reasonably practicable of the property . . . . . and in support of such statement and account shall produce and give all such invoices vouchers proofs and explanations and other evidence as may be reasonably required by or on behalf of the company . . . and in default of compliance with the terms of this condition or any of them no claim in respect of any such loss or damage shall be payable or sustainable unless and until such notice statement account proofs and explanations and evidence respectively shall have been delivered produced and given as aforesaid and such statutory declaration if required shall have been made."

It appears that when the loss occurred Taylor and Connolly's solicitor, who was also the plaintiffs' solicitor, endeavoured to comply with this condition by giving notice of the loss, nominally on behalf of Taylor and Connolly. It appears also that the defendants thereupon repudiated all liability either to Taylor and Connolly or to the plaintiffs. But it does not appear whether this repudiation took place within fifteen days from the loss or not.

The defendants contend that the obligation to deliver the statement within fifteen days at the latest is absolute, or, if not absolute, that there is no evidence of waiver of it by them. The plaintiffs contend that the concluding words of the condition beginning with "unless and until" preclude this construction, which, they say, would give no effect to the latter words.

There is no doubt that, in order to give an intelligent and consistent construction to the condition, it is necessary either to reject the words "at the latest" or else to read the word "until" as not applying (except for fifteen days) to the words "statement and account" which immediately follow it. In the case of *Weir* v. *Northern Counties of England Insurance Co.* (1) a condition substantially the same as that now in question, except that the word "unless" was not used, was held to require only that the statement and account should be made before action, and that the words "at the latest" must be rejected. *Parker* C.J.,

H. C. of A.
1908.

WESTERN
AUSTRALIAN
BANK
v.
ROYAL
INSURANCE
Co.

Griffith C.J.

(1) 4 L.R. Ir., 689.

H. C. of A. who tried the present case, followed this decision.   In the case
1908. of *Grau* v. *Colonial Insurance Co. of New Zealand* (1), in which

WESTERN *Weir's Case* (2) was not cited, the Supreme Court of Queensland
AUSTRALIAN arrived at a contrary conclusion on a similar condition. The Full
BANK
v. Court of Western Australia expressed no opinion on this point.
ROYAL
INSURANCE The text writers who have written since *Weir's Case* (2) was
Co. decided have referred to it as establishing that such a condition

Griffith C.J. when the word " until " alone is used merely suspends the right
of action, so that the failure to render the statement and account
within the prescribed time is not fatal.

At the trial, as already said, the actual facts relating to the
claim made on behalf of Taylor and Connolly were not fully
gone into, and I cannot help thinking that the rights of the
parties so far as they depended on this condition were not really
considered.

If I felt compelled to adopt the construction contended for by
the respondents I should be disposed to think that the case ought
to be remitted, on proper terms, for further investigation on this
point.   But I understand that my learned brothers are all of the
opinion that the effect of condition 6 is merely to suspend the
right of action.   I confess to entertaining some doubt, but I am
disposed to take the same view for reasons which I will state
very briefly.   The sentence beginning " and in default " does not
come into operation at all until there has been a failure to comply
with the preceding provisions of the condition.   In the absence of
this sentence the failure would be an absolute bar, and the object
of the sentence is to make the bar qualified and not absolute.
The words " unless and until " are often used together as words
of futurity, and might reasonably be so interpreted by an insurer.
The doctrine *verba chartarum fortius accipiuntur contra
proferentem*, although seldom to be resorted to, rests on a solid
foundation of justice.   If one party to a transaction uses, verbally
or in writing, language reasonably susceptible of two constructions, the party to whom they are used may fairly say that he
understood them in the sense most favourable to his contention:
Ireland v. *Livingston* (3) (a case of principal and agent).

(1) 2 Q.L.J., 53.   (2) 4 L.R. Ir., 689.
                     (3) L.R. 5 H.L., 395.

So far, therefore, from dissenting from the conclusion of my brethren on this point, I am prepared to assent to it.

In my judgment the respondents have failed to establish any of the defences set up, and the appellants are entitled to succeed.

BARTON J. Having regard to the conduct of the case at the trial, the first and the principal question for decision is whether at the time of the loss there was a contract of fire insurance between the plaintiff bank, the appellants, and the defendant company, the respondents. The answer to that question depends, (1) on the fact that the renewal premium for the year beginning 10th April 1902 was not duly paid, and remained unpaid at the time of the alleged new contract, so that in law the policy to Taylor and Connolly had before that time ceased to be in force : *Bunyon*, 5th ed., pp. 174-178; and (2) on two receipts dated respectively 22nd and 27th May 1902. These receipts have already been read. The first of them is undoubtedly in the form appropriate to the inception of a new proposal, provisionally accepted by an agent. That this is so is made more apparent by a comparison of it with the last previous receipt for a premium accepted to renew the original policy from 10th April 1901 to 10th April 1902, which is in the ordinary form of a renewal receipt. The receipt of 22nd May 1902 shows that the premium *deposit* was accepted " from Taylor and Connolly, and the W.A. Bank as mortgagees," not for " continuance," but for " insurance against fire." In consideration of it, " such " insurance—*i.e.*, that proposed—is held in force for a period not exceeding 14 days from the issue of the receipt, " subject to the terms and conditions of the company's policies," &c., clearly as if it were then first written on one of their usual proposal forms ; and "further *acceptance* of the *proposal*" is to be notified by the issue of the receipt by the Perth office. This is signed by the respondents' Kalgoorlie agent. This was followed by another receipt given by the local manager at Perth for the premium of £32 10s. on the form adopted by the respondents for the continuance of policies, but describing the policy as " in the name of Western Australian Bank." It was countersigned by the Kalgoorlie agent and dated 27th May 1902. The next year's renewal premium was in the like form. That

H. C. OF A.
1908.

WESTERN
AUSTRALIAN
BANK
v.
ROYAL
INSURANCE
Co.

Barton J.

H. C. of A.
1908.

WESTERN
AUSTRALIAN
BANK
v.
ROYAL
INSURANCE
Co.

Barton J.

was the last receipt, for the hotel was burnt down before another premium became due. The documents, namely those mentioned together with the two indorsements on the policy, to which the Chief Justice has referred, constitute, together with the fact of the failure in due payment of the renewal premium due 10th April 1901, the whole of the evidence to support the appellants' contention that a new contract was made between them and the respondents. The two indorsements on the policy were antecedent to the due date of the 1902 renewal, as they were made in November 1901 and February 1902.

I think there was sufficient evidence to establish a new contract with the appellants in substitution for or in succession to that which the respondents had granted to Taylor and Connolly: *Thompson* v. *Adams* (1). It was argued that the fact that the premiums of May 1902 and April 1903 were paid by Taylor and Connolly, like any other mortgagors, was some evidence that they continued to be the insured. To my mind it is quite immaterial who it was that actually paid them. They were received by the respondents as consideration for an " insurance " (not to call it a contract) which they acknowledged to be in the name of the bank.

It is not necessary to rely on the case of *Ellis* v. *The Insurance Co. of North America* (2), though it might be strongly argued that that case and the present one rest on the same principle. Here, at any rate, the central fact that the original policy had lapsed gave the bank, the assignees under it, sufficient reason to propose to substitute a new contract ; and that lapse together with the terms of the receipts in my judgment afford material supporting the inference that a contract, in substitution for the assigned policy and embodying the same terms, was concluded, and that this was the intention both of the appellants and the respondents. I think, therefore, that the plaintiffs were entitled to sue in their own name, being the insured.

The next question is whether the appellants, as the insured, had an insurable interest. They were equitable mortgagees of the insured premises under their liens and the deposit of securities. *Bunyon on Fire Insurance*, 5th ed., at p. 42, summarizes insurable interests as " any legal or equitable estate, or right which

(1) 23 Q.B.D., 361. (2) 32 Fed. Rep., 646.

H. C. of A.
1908.

Western
Australian
Bank
v.
Royal
Insurance
Co.

Barton J.

may be prejudicially affected, or any responsibility which may be brought into operation by a fire." Of the case of a mortgagee, *Bowen* L.J., says in *Castellain* v. *Preston* (1):—"If he has the legal ownership, he is entitled to insure for the whole value, but even supposing he is not entitled to the legal ownership he is entitled to insure *primâ facie* for all. If he intends to cover only his mortgage and is only insuring his own interest, he can only in the event of a loss hold the amount to which he has been damnified. If he has intended to cover other persons besides himself, he can hold the surplus for those whom he has intended to cover. But one thing he cannot do, that is, having intended only to cover himself and being a person whose interest is only limited, he cannot hold anything beyond the amount of the loss caused to his own particular interest." And his Lordship points out that the whole matter is regulated by the doctrine of indemnity. As the Chief Justice has pointed out, the debtors owed the appellants more than the amount of the policy at the time of the loss, so that there can be no problem to solve as to the extent of the mortgagees' insurable interest. They can recover at any rate to the amount of the debt due to them when the fire took place, upon proof and within the value insured. A further defence was raised under condition 6 of the policy, which, if there is a new contract such as I have endeavoured to show, is a condition of that contract. It will be observed that it is almost *totidem verbis* with the condition which was the subject of the decision in *Weir* v. *Northern Counties of England Insurance Co.* (2). The only difference on which counsel placed serious reliance was that in the present case the words "unless and" are inserted, and precede "until" in the last sentence of the condition. Notice, with a statement and account under this condition, was not sent to the insurers until 17th December, a year after the fire, and as we are told, after the buildings had been reinstated. It was argued that the delivery of the statement, and within fifteen days after the happening of the loss, was a condition precedent to the right to recover. I think *Weir's Case* (2), so far as it goes, ought to be followed by us. It is now more than 28 years old, and so far as I can learn, has not been challenged during that time, although

(1) 11 Q.B.D., 380, at p. 398.　　　(2) 4 L.R. Ir., 689.

H. C. of A.   there must have been many opportunities of raising the question
1908.   in British Courts. The decision has, no doubt, been followed in the

WESTERN   transaction of insurance business throughout the interval, and we
AUSTRALIAN should do nothing to disturb it now. Moreover I am strongly
BANK
v.   disposed to think it correct. For very many years the clause
ROYAL
INSURANCE existed without the addition of the words beginning "and in
Co.   default thereof," and in that state it was repeatedly construed as

Barton J. imposing a condition precedent on the right to recover. No
doubt its very plain terms justified that interpretation, which it
received in the several instances cited in *Weir's Case* (1). The
distinct inference from the words was that if the fifteen days had
elapsed without delivery of the notice, account, &c., on the part
of the insured, he could not afterwards be allowed to sustain his
claim. But *expressum facit cessare tacitum*, and in *Weir's Case*
(2), it was held that the added words "have the effect of only
deferring the right to payment until the notice and account are
given, and thus enlarging the time." The Court thought that
the words had been added with the purpose of defining what
should be the consequence of failure to comply with the requirements within the time limited. Instead of saying (as tacitly it
had said) that in default no action shall be brought or payment
made, it says that no claim shall be payable until such notice
and account &c. are given. "Besides," added the Court (3), "the
words are those of the company's own form, and the maxim
applies, *fortius contra preferentem*." It was held, therefore,
that the delivery of the notice, account, &c., within fifteen days
was not a condition precedent.

We have now to inquire what difference is made by the
insertion of the words "unless and" before the word "until." I
am not disposed to hold that there is any alteration in the sense.
The important words are "in default thereof." On failure to
deliver the notice, account &c., within the fifteen days, the
insured shall have no claim unless he afterwards gives the notice
and account and until he gives them. These two things are about
equal to one another if we consider their effect after default. It
is presupposed that the fifteen days have elapsed without com-

(1) 4 L.R. Ir., 689, at pp. 691, 692.   (2) 4 L.R. Ir., 689, at p. 692.
(3) 4 L.R. Ir., 689, at p. 693.

H. C. of A.
1908.

WESTERN
AUSTRALIAN
BANK
v.
ROYAL
INSURANCE
Co.

Barton J.

pliance with the requirement. After that time, no claim is to prevail unless and until, &c. Given the end of the fifteen days as the starting point, I doubt whether the addition of " unless " adds to the stringency of the clause. There is, no doubt, an ambiguity, and when we consider also the prior words " at the latest," I do not see how that ambiguity is solved by the application of the ordinary rules of construction. But if that point of intractability is reached we are entitled to apply the maxim *verba chartarum fortius accipiuntur contra proferentem*: *Lindus* v. *Melrose* (1). Lord *St. Leonards*, in *Anderson* v. *Fitzgerald* (2), said :—" A policy ought to be so framed, that he who runs can read. It ought to be framed with such deliberate care, that no form of expression by which, on the one hand, the party assured can be caught, or by which, on the other, the company can be cheated, shall be found upon the face of it : nothing ought to be wanting in it, the absence of which may lead to such results." And this passage affords the strongest reason for his having said a little earlier, speaking of the policy (3) :—" It is of course prepared by the company, and if therefore there should be any ambiguity in it, must be taken, according to law, more strongly against the person who prepared it." I am therefore content to hold that the clause does not impose a condition precedent as to the fifteen days, and that sufficient notice has been given, there being no other objection taken to it and the accompanying documents.

The remaining question is that raised under condition 11, exacting notice of insurances made " elsewhere " on the property insured, and any such insurance must also be indorsed on the policy.

It is not disputed that the appellants have never given the respondents notice of a certain other policy granted to Taylor and Connolly by the Commercial Union Company for £300 on the same building that their old policy covered, with £50 on furniture. It is equally clear that the original policy bears no indorsement of it. In clause 11, as applied to the new contract, I think the interest (or " property ") meant is not such an interest

(1) 3 H. & N., 177, at p. 182.   (2) 4 H.L.C., 484, at p. 510.
                    (3) 4 H.L.C., 484, at p. 507.

H. C. of A.
1908.

WESTERN
AUSTRALIAN
BANK
v.
ROYAL
INSURANCE
Co.

Barton J.

as is the subject of Taylor and Connolly's second policy. The parties have treated the bank's mortgage interest as "the property insured," and it is quite capable of that meaning in its relation to the receipts, from which and from the expiration of the original policy I have held that a new contract of insurance is deducible. It is only the interest of the appellants that can be the subject of that insurance, and although that may be described as property, it remains only the kind of interest which they as mortgagees can insure, and that is not the kind of interest or "property" which Taylor and Connolly have insured. There has been no other insurance of the appellants' interest or of any part of it.

Further, I have grave doubts whether the words "made elsewhere" are so comprehensive as to include insurances of which "the insured" have no knowledge. But it is not necessary to give an actual opinion on that point. As to condition 11, therefore, the respondent company fails as it does on the other questions. On the whole case I think *Parker* C.J. was right in his judgment at the trial. That judgment should be restored and the appeal be allowed.

O'CONNOR J. The Supreme Court of Western Australia disposed of this case on one only of the various grounds that were argued before us. They came to the conclusion that Taylor and Connolly remained "the insured" within the meaning of the policy, thereby reversing the finding of *Parker* C.J. on that question. If they were right in that conclusion it would follow that there had been a breach of the 11th condition of the policy which would prevent the plaintiffs from succeeding in the action. But that, in my opinion, was not the right conclusion to draw from the evidence and documents.

The transaction between Taylor and Connolly, the bank, and the insurance company, may be regarded in either of two ways. Either there was an assignment to the bank by consent of the insurance company of Taylor's and Connolly's rights to any moneys which might become payable under the policy, Taylor and Connolly remaining the contracting parties with the insurance company, or there was an arrangement by which a

H. C. of A.
1908.

WESTERN
AUSTRALIAN
BANK
v.
ROYAL
INSURANCE
Co.

O'Connor J.

new contract between the bank and the insurance company was entered into by which the bank became the contracting party under the policy instead of Taylor and Connolly. The arrangement between these three parties was in all its essentials reduced into writing.

It is to be found in the receipts given by the insurance company and the memorandum indorsed on the policy in pursuance of clause 5, and the relation of the parties depends really upon the proper interpretation to be put on these writings.

The policy, it will be noted, covered fire risks for a year from the 10th April in one year to 10th April in the following year; and on its renewal in each year it was open to the parties to continue it in any form they thought fit. There might be, I think, good ground for interpreting the assignment of Taylor and Connolly of 13th November 1901 and the respondents' assent of 25th February following, taken together, as amounting merely to an assignment, with the assent of the insurance company, of Taylor's and Connolly's right to receive the policy moneys in the event of their becoming due. The insurance under that agreement expired in April 1902. The renewal took place on the 22nd May 1902, over a month afterwards; and it will be noted that the receipt given by the insurance company's local agent at Kalgoorlie acknowledges payment of the premium by Taylor and Connolly and the bank as mortgagees as on an original proposal for insurance which would begin at the date of the receipt. That document gave an interim cover for fourteen days only.

A receipt was issued by the Perth office of the insurance company in pursuance of the interim cover, and was countersigned on 27th May 1902 by their agent at Kalgoorlie, and the latter document it seems to me must be taken to embody the terms of the contract as finally agreed to. The policy was renewed in precisely similar terms in the following year, the receipt of the Perth office being countersigned at Kalgoorlie on 21st April 1903. It was that insurance which was current when the fire occurred.

According to the interim receipt of 22nd May 1902 the premium had been paid by Taylor and Connolly and the Western

H. C. of A.
1908.

Western
Australian
Bank
v.
Royal
Insurance
Co.

O'Connor J.

Australian Bank as mortgagees. The Perth office's receipt, countersigned on 27th May, embodying the terms of the 12 months' insurance, declares that the premium was received for the continuance of the old policy from 10th April 1902 to 10th April 1903, in the name of the Western Australian Bank. The plain inference to be drawn from these documents, in my opinion, is that the premium was paid by the original policy holders and the bank jointly as the consideration for the making of a new contract by which the insurance company were to hold the Western Australian Bank assured under the terms and conditions of the old policy. In other words, the agreement was that there was to be a new contract under which the person insured was to be the Western Australian Bank instead of Taylor and Connolly. The Western Australian Bank having become the "insured," it follows that the insurance effected by Taylor and Connolly with the Commercial Union Assurance Company was not made by "the insured" within the meaning of the 11th condition. The ground, therefore, upon which the Supreme Court decided against the claim of the appellant bank must fail. But the respondents further contend that, even if the bank are to be taken to be "the insured" within the meaning of the 11th condition, the appellants were bound under that condition to give notice to the insurance company of the second policy although it was effected by Taylor and Connolly.

There are two answers to that objection. In the first place, the condition does not require a notice where the second insurance has been effected by a person other than "the insured." Having regard to the terms of the 12th and 13th conditions, which must be read with the 11th, the latter does not, in my opinion, put the insured under an obligation to notify insurance on the property effected by other parties. If the second insurance were effected by some other person by direction of the insured or for his benefit, or with the knowledge of the insured and in his interest, different considerations would of course arise.

In connection with this aspect of the matter a question of fact was raised as to whether the appellant bank had any knowledge of the second insurance. There was no evidence before the Judge at the trial of any such knowledge. The Supreme Court had before it some additional evidence from which, perhaps, an inference of knowledge on the part of the bank might have been drawn, but it became unnecessary from the course the case took before that tribunal that any conclusion upon that question should be arrived at. So also the bank's knowledge of the second insurance becomes immaterial in view of the second answer to this ground of objection, namely, that the second insurance was not on the same property within the meaning of the condition.

The condition provides that the insured must give notice to the company of any insurance or insurances made elsewhere on "the property hereby insured," and the material question to be determined is whether the second insurance effected by Taylor and Connolly was an insurance "on the property insured." Taking the words in their literal sense no doubt it was an insurance "on the property hereby insured" because the insurance covered the risk of fire on the same building. But the question is in what sense have the words been used in this condition. They must be interpreted in view of the context, and the nature and effect of the contract of insurance. Some observations of *Sir George Jessel* M.R. in construing a somewhat similar condition in the *North British and Mercantile Insurance Co.* v. *London, Liverpool, and Globe Insurance Co.* (1) are worthy of consideration :—

"The word 'property,'" he says, "as used in several of the conditions, means, not the actual chattel, but the interest of the assured therein. What is the meaning of the words 'covering the same property' in the 9th condition ? They cannot mean the actual chattel. The most absurd consequences would follow if you read those words in that sense. I am satisfied that this condition was put in to apply to cases where it is the same property that is the subject-matter of the insurance, and the interests are the same. It never could have been meant to apply, for example, to the cases of a tenant for life and remainderman, or a first mortgagee and second mortgagee, both insuring the same goods."

Mortgagor and mortgagee may each have an insurable interest

(1) 5 Ch. D., 569, at p. 577.

H. C. of A.
1908.

Western Australian Bank
v.
Royal Insurance Co.

O'Connor J.

H. C. or A. in the same building, just as a remainderman, a tenant for life,
1908.   or a tenant for years, may have.   Each may take out a separate

Western   and independent insurance on his own interest.   In each case
Australian the "property insured" is the particular interest of the insured
Bank   in the building covered by the policy, and, on settlement in the
v.   event of fire, none of them could receive for his benefit more
Royal
Insurance than the amount of loss sustained by him in respect of his interest.
Co.

O'Connor J. In America similar words in similar clauses have been for many
years interpreted on the same principle as that enunciated by
Sir George Jessel.   A number of cases in which the meaning of a
condition similarly worded was discussed are referred to in the
second volume of *Hare and Wallace's American Leading Cases,*
and in a passage at page 899 the result of them appears to be
correctly summarized as follows :—" A subsequent will not avoid
a prior insurance, unless the parties are the same, nor when the
interest covered by the policy is different.   *Nichols* v. *Fayette
Insurance Co.* (1); *Cox* v. *Phœnix Insurance Co.* (2); *Tyler* v.
The Ætna Insurance Co. (3); *Mutual Insurance Co.* v. *Hall* (4).
Hence a mortgagee may enforce an insurance effected for his
benefit, notwithstanding a subsequent insurance of the premises
by the mortgagor.   *Foster* v. *Equitable Insurance Co.* (5); *Wood-
bury Bank* v. *The Charter Oak Insurance Co.* (6); and a policy
obtained on the freight of the vessel by the consignee, will not
preclude the consignor from enforcing a prior policy containing a
warranty that there is no other insurance."   Applying these
principles to the words of this policy, I am of opinion that the
second insurance was not " on the property insured " within the
meaning of the 11th condition, and that it was not necessary,
therefore, for the appellant bank to give notice of it to the
respondent company.

It was also contended that the appellant bank have not complied with the 6th condition of the policy, and, therefore, cannot
recover.   For the purposes of my decision I assume that they
did not give notice of the fire " forthwith," and that they did not
deliver particulars of their claim within fifteen days, although

(1) 1 Allen 63.   (4) 2 Comstock 35.
(2) 52 Maine 355.   (5) 2 Gray 216.
(3) 16 Wend. 385.   (6) 31 Conn. 517.

the questions of facts as to this and the alleged waiver of the condition do not seem to have been really inquired into. It follows that, if compliance with these requirements is a condition precedent to their right to sue, they cannot succeed in the action. The contest between the parties is as to the proper interpretation of the condition. A condition to that effect, though not always in that form, is to be found in practically all fire policies, and, if it were not for the qualifying words of the last three lines, it would come within the class of conditions which have been always interpreted by the Courts as conditions precedent.

The last sentence of the condition is in these words: "and in default of compliance with the terms of this condition or any of them no claim in respect of any such loss or damage shall be payable or sustainable unless and until such notice statement account proofs and explanations and evidence respectively shall have been delivered produced and given as aforesaid and such statutory declaration if required shall have been made." It is the last few words of qualification beginning "unless and until such notice," &c., that create the difficulty. If the qualifying words were omitted, compliance with the requirements in question would be clearly a condition precedent. On the other hand, if the words "unless and" were omitted, there is direct authority for the position that failure to give the notice forthwith, or to deliver the particulars and account within the time named, would not deprive the plaintiffs of their right of action, but would suspend it until the condition was in these respects complied with. The qualifying words of the condition in *Weir* v. *The Northern Counties of England Insurance Co.* (1) were substantially identical with those of the condition now under consideration, except for the occurrence in the latter of the words "unless and" before "until." The decision in that case has never been questioned, and is quoted as settled law in all the text books on insurance. *Lawson* J., in delivering the judgment, says (2):—"Why then are those words added, without which the clause would have had the stringent operation of a condition precedent? Is it not for the purpose of defining what shall be the consequence of failure to comply with the requirements of

(1) 4 L.R. Ir., 689.　　　　(2) 4 L.R. Ir., 689, at p. 692.

H. C. of A.
1908.

Western
Australian
Bank
v.
Royal
Insurance
Co.

O'Connor J.

H. C. of A.
1908.

WESTERN
AUSTRALIAN
BANK
v.
ROYAL
INSURANCE
Co.

O'Connor J.

giving notice and account within the time limited ; and instead of saying that in default no action shall be brought or payment made, it says, that no claim shall be payable *until* such notice and account, etc., are given, thus giving an enlarged time for doing it, provided it is done before the claim is payable ? This is the ordinary grammatical construction of the words, and it may well be that those words were added in order to get over in favour of the assured the stringency of the prior words, as interpreted by the cases to which I have referred."

That argument is unanswerable in reference to the condition with which the learned Judge was then dealing, and the same line of reasoning seems to me to be applicable to the condition now under consideration, notwithstanding the words "unless and."

I was at first impressed by Mr. *Mitchell's* argument that these words made it necessary to construe the qualifying sentence distributively, " unless " being taken in connection with the direction to give notice of the fire forthwith, and to deliver the particulars of loss ; " until " being taken as applying to the proofs, explanations, and evidence, which are to be furnished on request. But when the whole clause is examined it will appear that, if that is the meaning of the condition, the qualifying words are surplusage, because without them the different consequences set forth would follow the neglect to comply with the different requirements of the condition respectively.

On the other hand, it is clear that the full meaning cannot be given to the expressions " forthwith " and " within fifteen days at the latest " if the requirements as to notice of the fire and delivery of particulars of loss within fifteen days are not conditions precedent. Indeed, the only way a substantial meaning of any kind can be given to the condition as a whole is to treat its terms as being requirements which the assured undertakes to comply with, the consequence of failure to comply being, not loss, but postponement of the right of action until they have been complied with.

It cannot, however, be denied that such a construction fails to give effect to every word of the condition. It is in fact impossible to find any construction which will give full effect to every word. The case is just one of those in which, by reason of the

H. C. OF A.
1908.

WESTERN
AUSTRALIAN
BANK
v.
ROYAL
INSURANCE
Co.

O'Connor J.

obscurity of the language used by the parties, a fair adjustment can be made only by the application of the principle of construction embodied in the maxim *Verba chartarum fortius accipiuntur contra proferentem* which was adopted by *Lawson* J. in *Weir* v. *The Northern Counties of England Insurance Co.* (1).

We were referred to some observations of *Sir George Jessel* M.R., in which he appears to have expressed a doubt as to whether the maxim could be considered as having any force at the present day. But it is now too firmly established as a rule of interpretation to be seriously questioned, and it has since those observations been judicially recognized and applied in *Burton & Co.* v. *English & Co.* (2), by *Brett* M.R. In the interpretation of insurance policies the maxim has been frequently used in cases where the application of the ordinary rules of interpretation have failed to elucidate the meaning of some obscurely worded condition. In *Notman* v. *The Anchor Assurance Co.* (3) the terms of a memorandum indorsed on the back of a life policy giving the assured leave to reside abroad were under discussion. In delivering judgment *Cockburn* C.J. said (4):—" Nothing could be more easy than to express that in plain terms in the instrument itself: the permission might be granted for a residence from a given day to another given day. They have not, however, done so here : the permission is given simply for a twelve months' residence at Belize, without specifying any period from which that residence is to date. This instrument being the language of the company, must, if there be any ambiguity in it, be taken most strongly against them."

In *Fitton* v. *The Accidental Death Insurance Co.* (5), *Willes* J. applied the same principle, although he did not refer to it in express terms. He says :—" It is extremely important with reference to insurance, that there should be a tendency rather to hold for the assured than for the company, where any ambiguity arises upon the face of the policy."

In *Braunstein* v. *Accidental Death Insurance Co.* (6), the meaning of a condition in an accident policy was under con-

(1) 4 L.R. Ir., 689.   (4) 4 C.B.N.S., 476, at p. 481.
(2) 12 Q.B.D., 218, at p. 220. (5) 17 C.B.N.S., 122, at p. 134.
(3) 4 C.B.N S., 476.   (6) 1 B. & S., 782.

H. C. of A.
1908.
~
WESTERN
AUSTRALIAN
BANK
v.
ROYAL
INSURANCE
Co.

O'Connor J.
sideration. *Blackburn* J. in delivering judgment said (1):—" I quite admit that parties may make what they please a condition precedent, but it must be shewn that they so intended. Here the stipulation is the language of one party, the Company, and ' *verba fortius accipiuntur contra proferentem*.' No doubt they might have stipulated that no money should be payable under a policy unless the directors obtained any evidence they chose to ask for, but it would require very distinct language, and much stronger than any used here, to show that the parties so intended."

It is abundantly clear from these instances that, in dealing with obscure conditions in policies where, notwithstanding the application of all ordinary rules of interpretation, the meaning of the condition still remains doubtful, the Courts have adopted the governing rule of resolving the doubt by holding against the insurance company, which sought to gain advantage from the condition.

The question of construction may, therefore, be narrowed down to this. The insurance company's interpretation does not give any substantial effect to the qualifying words of the condition. The bank's interpretation, although not giving full effect to the earlier words of the condition, gives some substantial effect to every part of it. Without applying the maxim which I have been discussing, I should have felt bound to follow the latter interpretation. But applying the maxim, as it has been applied in the cases I have cited, I have no doubt that the condition must be construed against the insurance company which prepared the condition, and now puts it forward as a defence against a claim made under the policy. I am, therefore, of opinion that the condition does not make compliance with the requirements in question a condition precedent, and that on that ground of objection also the respondents must fail.

On the whole case, therefore, the objections against the judgment of the learned Chief Justice in the Court below are untenable. In my opinion his judgment was right and the judgment of the Supreme Court of West Australia setting it aside must be reversed, and the appeal upheld.

(1) 1 B. & S., 782, at p. 799.

HIGGINS J. The Full Court of Western Australia reversed the
judgment of *Parker* C.J. on appeal, on the ground of condition
11 of the policy :—" The insured must give notice to the company
of any insurance or insurances made elsewhere on the property
hereby insured or on any part hereof the particulars of which
must be indorsed on the policy and unless such notice be given
and indorsement be made the insured will not be entitled to any
benefit under this policy."   It appears that in 1903, after the
policy, the original insured, Messrs Taylor and Connolly, effected
another insurance with another company, and that no notice
was given to the defendant company. The position at the time
was that Taylor and Connolly had borrowed money from the
bank, had lodged the policy with the bank, had given a general
lien over this policy and other documents, and had, on 13th of
November 1901 by indorsement on the policy, made an equitable
assignment to the bank expressly by way of security. The local
manager of the defendant company had signed another indorsement stating that the assignment conferred on the bank whatever
rights might accrue to Taylor and Connolly under the policy.
The Full Court has held that these two indorsements did not
pass to the bank the legal title to the policy moneys, and did not
make the bank " the insured" within the meaning of condition
11 ; and if Taylor and Connolly were " the insured " when the
second policy was effected, they did not comply with the condition, and they could not, nor could their assigns, recover the
policy moneys. I concur with the Full Court in the view that
the two indorsements did not of themselves pass the legal title,
and did not make the bank "the insured": *Buffalo Steam
Engine Works* v. *Sun Mutual Insurance Co.* (1); *State Mutual
Fire Insurance Co.* v. *Roberts* (2).   I concur with *McMillan* J.
in his view of the case of *Ellis* v. *Insurance Company of North
America* (3).   There, the interest of the insured was assigned
absolutely—not by way of mortgage. The insured ceased
thereby to have any insurable interest ; and the Court came to
the conclusion that the consent of the company could have no
meaning unless the intention was to create a new contract on

H. C. of A.
1908.

WESTERN
AUSTRALIAN
BANK
v.
ROYAL
INSURANCE
Co.

Higgins J.

(1) 17 N.Y., 401.   (2) 31 Pa., 438.
                    (3) 32 Fed. Rep., 646.

H. C. of A.   the same terms as the old (1). But the bank relies on certain
1908.   subsequent receipts for premiums as showing a new contract
Western   between the bank and the company, whereby the bank became
Australian   "the insured." There is a receipt of the company dated 27th
Bank
v.   May 1902 as follows :—"Received the undermentioned premium
Royal   for the continuance of policy No. 7213012 of this company in
Insurance
Co.   the name of *Western Australian Bank* insuring the sum of
               £650 for twelve months from 10th April 1902 to 10th April
Higgins J.   1903." It will be noticed that this premium was received after
               the due date, and dated back to it. There was a similar receipt
               given on 21st April 1903 for the year 10th April 1903 to 10th
               April 1904. The fire occurred on 16th of December 1903. Now,
               I can give no other meaning to these receipts than that the
               defendant company insure the bank as they had insured Taylor
               and Connolly ; and on the conditions which appear in the policy.
               The name of the bank is to be substituted for the names of
               Taylor and Connolly ; but the terms of the contract are to be the
               same as in the expired policy. This is the substantial effect of
               the receipt. The bank becomes the contracting party with the
               company. The bank becomes "the insured." There was no
               need for a novation in the strict sense. The contract of
               insurance made with Taylor and Connolly had expired, and the
               bank was now insured on the same terms. It is true that the
               premiums for which these receipts were given were paid out of
               rents which Cross—agent for the defendant company and also
               for Taylor and Connolly—collected for Taylor and Connolly.
               It does not appear whether the rents were collected from
               properties subject to the bank's general lien ; nor does the reason
               appear for the substitution of the bank as the insured. But the
               payment of the premium was made on behalf of the bank ; and
               the bank has ratified the transaction. It is also true that the
               statement of claim does not treat the receipts as being fresh
               contracts with the bank, and speaks of the plaintiff as "renewing"
               the policy by paying the premiums for April 1902 and April
               1903. But the receipts are in evidence ; there has been no
               surprise on the defendants ; the case of new contract was fully
               discussed in Perth before and by the Full Court ; and it would

                        (1) See 17 N.Y., 401, at p. 407.

be a ridiculous technicality, as well as unjust, to refuse now to give to the receipts their full effect.

But the defendant company urges that, under condition 11, the bank, even if it is to be treated as the insured, is under a duty to give notice of any insurance effected by anybody, at all events if it knows the particulars. I cannot find any sufficient evidence that the bank knew the particulars of the second policy ; and indeed the learned Chief Justice at the trial found expressly that it did not know. But I am prepared also to hold that condition 11 does not apply to policies effected by others than the insured. In the next succeeding conditions, where the parties refer to other insurances, they expressly add the words " whether effected by the insured, or by any other person ;" and the fair inference is that condition 11 refers to insurances effected by the insured. No explanation whatever has been suggested of the difference in language in these conditions on the defendants' interpretation. Cases can easily be suggested of extreme injustice should an insured lose his right to policy moneys because of some other person effecting an assurance without his knowledge ; and it is laid down that we are to avoid a construction which will produce injustice " if another and more reasonable interpretation is present in the Statute :" *Knowlton* v. *Moore* (1). Mr. *Mitchell*, indeed, felt the force of this consideration, and suggested a limitation of the section to the case of another policy effected with the knowledge of the insured. But the context does not refer to knowledge, and does not warrant the insertion of any such words of limitation. The condition must, in my opinion, mean either all policies by whomsoever effected, or policies effected by the insured ; and, as *Jessel* M.R. says in *North British and Mercantile Insurance Co.* v. *London, Liverpool, and Globe Insurance Co.* (2), it is our duty, if the words admit of a reasonable construction to adopt it, rather than a construction equally admissible but absurd or unlikely. " You must read the condition in a sensible way, and not assume that these great companies intended to entrap their policy-holders and to destroy the value of the contract of indemnity by reason of the accidental contract of somebody else,

H. C. of A.
1908.

WESTERN
AUSTRALIAN
BANK
v.
ROYAL
INSURANCE
Co.

Higgins J.

(1) 178 U.S., 41 at p. 77.   (2) 5 Ch. D., 569, at p. 577.

H. C. of A.   which had no connection with the subject-matter of the contract,
1908.   or with the price paid for the insurance."

Western   As to condition 11, I think I ought to say that I do not rely
Australian   for my judgment on the view that "the property insured" means
Bank
v.   the interest of the mortgagee in the property, and that the
Royal   second insurance effected by Taylor and Connolly was therefore
Insurance
Co.   not within the terms of the condition. The words of *Jessel* M.R.

Higgins J.   just quoted were directed to a peculiar policy in which it was
clear that in several of the other conditions the word "property"
meant, not the actual chattel, but the interest of the assured
therein; and he came to the conclusion that this same meaning
was carried on into condition 9. But in this policy, contract
and conditions, there is not to be found any instance of such a
meaning. The "property" is always the iron building—"The
Tasmanian Hotel"; and, so far as I can find, there is no place in
the policy or conditions in which the word is used as referring
to a mere interest (see policy and conditions 1, 2, 3, 5, 6, 8, 9, 10).
In short, the meaning of the word "property" in the London
and Liverpool policy is not a guide to the meaning in this policy.
Of course, each policy has to be construed according to its own
language. As for the new contract made with the bank, the
word "property" is not used in the final official receipt—
the document that binds the parties; but, as it provides for the
" continuance " of the former policy, it must be read as applying to
the same property.

There appeared to be a formidable objection to the bank's
claim in paragraph 11 of the defence—that the bank had not
forthwith after the fire given notice thereof to the defendant
company, or within 15 days delivered to the company a statement and account, as prescribed by condition 6. The evidence is
not very distinct as to notice, but there is no doubt that the
statement and account were not given within 15 days after the
fire. Condition 6 is very long, and in parts very obscure. But,
for the present purpose, it is sufficient to say that it prescribes
notice " forthwith," and a statement and account within 15 days,
showing the property destroyed, the value, the loss, the interest
of the insured, &c.; and the insured is to give such proofs, explanations and evidence as may be required, and, if required, a

statutory declaration as to truth. If condition 6 had stopped
here, there is little doubt that the delivery of the statement and
account within the 15 days would be a condition precedent to
the right to recover : *Roper* v. *Lendon* (1). But the words which
follow state the consequences of failure to comply with the course
prescribed : —

> "And in default of compliance with the terms of this con-
> dition or any of them no claim in respect of any such
> loss or damage shall be payable or sustainable unless
> and until such notice statement account proofs and
> explanations and evidence respectively shall have been
> delivered produced and given as aforesaid and such
> statutory declaration if required shall have been made."

It is urged that by force of such a condition the insured must
within fifteen days give all the particulars prescribed, or lose all
right to the policy moneys—even if he happen to be in England
when the fire occurs in Kalgoorlie. If such is the meaning,
the subordinate sentence beginning "unless and until," and indeed
all the words beginning with "and in default" are unnecessary.
The previous words made the policy useless, unenforceable ; what
more do these words effect? To give effect to all the words of
the condition, it seems to me that the claim is not payable or
sustainable *unless and until* the notice, statement, &c., be
delivered. The policy is useless only until the notice, statement,
&c., have been supplied. No action can be brought until they
have been supplied. The position of the words "as aforesaid"
certainly tend to show that they relate to the verbs "delivered
produced and given," and not merely to the nouns "notice statement," &c. But there is no necessary inference that "as aforesaid"
relates to the time prescribed for giving the notice, &c., as well as
to the description of and the manner of giving the notice. It is
purely a question of construction of the conditions of this particular policy, and I do not place much reliance on any decision
under a policy which contains conditions similar but not the
same ; but the decision and the reasoning in *Weir* v. *Northern
Counties of England Insurance Co.* (2) are favourable to the
view that the notice, statement, &c., may be given after the time

(1) 1 El. & E., 825.   (2) 4 L.R. Ir., 689.

H. C. of A.
1908.

WESTERN
AUSTRALIAN
BANK
v.
ROYAL
INSURANCE
Co.

Higgins J.

specified, but before action. Personally I do not attach much practical importance to the maxim, *verba chartarum fortius accipiuntur contra proferentem.* I think that contracts ought to be construed in the same way whether they are framed or put in evidence or relied on by one party or the other. In many cases the verb *proferentem* seems to be treated as if it referred to the drafting or framing of an instrument: *Broom's Legal Maxims*, 7th ed., pp. 441, &c. I do not know on what grounds. I confess that I am in sympathy with the words of *Jessel* M.R. in *Taylor* v. *St. Helen's Corporation* (1) on the subject of this rule of construction. The maxim is taken from a bundle of maxims collected in *Coke Litt.*, 36*a*; and it is followed by a maxim equally sound, no doubt, and equally valuable: *Generalia verba sunt generaliter intelligenda.* If the maxim in question means merely that a document written by A. is to be read as outsiders would read it, and not as A. would read it, the doctrine is true, but trite, and not warranted by the words used. Yet if the maxim is applicable as the last resort in construction, it certainly ought to be applied to such a condition as this in a policy, inasmuch as the insurance company frames the language of the conditions in its own way and in its own interest. I am of opinion that the defendants fail as to this defence also.

A further defence might possibly have been raised under condition 3—that the bank was not the legal owner of the land and buildings—that it held only a general lien; and that it did not expressly describe its position. But this defence has not been raised by the pleadings or urged by the company at the bar; and I pronounce no opinion with regard thereto. On these grounds I concur in the judgment.

> *Appeal allowed. Order appealed from discharged. Respondents to pay costs of appeal.*

Solicitors, for the appellants, *Stone & Burt.*
Solicitors, for the respondents, *Downing & Downing.*

B. L.

(1) 6 Ch. D., 264.

[HIGH COURT OF AUSTRALIA.]

GANDER . . . . APPELLANT ;
DEFENDANT,

AND

MURRAY . . . . RESPONDENT.
PLAINTIFF,

ZOBEL . . . . APPELLANT ;
DEFENDANT,

AND

MURRAY . . . . RESPONDENT.
DEFENDANT,

ON APPEAL FROM THE SUPREME COURT OF
NEW SOUTH WALES.

Vendor and purchaser—Contract for sale of mining property—Vendor only entitled to limited interest—Enforcement—Rights of purchaser against subsequently acquired interests of vendor—Equitable estoppel—Authority to enter—Mining on Private Lands Acts (N.S.W.)—Partnership Act (N.S.W.), (55 Vict. No. 12), sec. 31.

H. C. OF A.
1907.
～～～
SYDNEY,
Dec. 4, 5, 6,
16.
───
Griffith C.J.,
Barton and
Isaacs JJ.

G. and Z. were carrying on mining operations in partnership upon 20 acres of land, under an authority issued to G. under the Mining on Private Lands Acts. The authority conferred no interest in the land, but merely the right to enter and search for minerals upon a certain area for one year, in anticipation of a title to be subsequently acquired by lease from the Crown of the minerals contained in the area. G., believing himself to have authority from Z. to sell Z.'s share, though he had not such authority in fact, agreed to sell to M. the whole interest of the partners in the land, mining machinery, effects and ore, &c., upon the land. Before the expiration of G.'s authority to enter, M. made an unsuccessful application for an authority to enter an area of 33 acres including the 20 included in G.'s authority, and later, G.'s

H. C. of A.   authority having expired, Z., on his own behalf, obtained an authority to
1907.   enter the 33 acres, having previously agreed to take G. in as a partner in
               the new adventure, and the two proceeded to work the area on the same
GANDER   terms as before.
v.
MURRAY.   In a suit by M. against G. and Z., to have Z. declared a trustee for him of
               the authority to enter and the benefits attaching to it, and for an injunction
ZOBEL   and account, with consequential relief :—
v.
MURRAY.   *Held*, on the evidence that Z. acquired the authority free of all equities as
               far as M. was concerned ; and that, as the contract of sale, if it could take
               effect at all, could only take effect as to G.'s limited interest in the original
               undertaking, and that undertaking had terminated on the expiration of
               G.'s authority to enter, there was a complete break of title between G.'s first
               and second interests, and there was no equitable estoppel arising out of the
               contract by which G.'s subsequently acquired interest could be affected so as
               to entitle M. to have Z. declared a trustee for him of G.'s half share.

                  Held, further, that even if G.'s subsequently acquired interest could be
               regarded in equity as an accretion to or in substitution for his interest in the
               original undertaking, the interest which he had at his disposal on that
               assumption was so substantially different from what he contracted to sell
               that, whatever remedy M. might have by way of damages, he was not
               entitled in equity to have the contract enforced even to the extent of G.'s
               limited interest.

                  Principle stated by *Jessel* M.R. in *Cato* v. *Thompson*, 9 Q.B.D., 616, at p.
               618, and adopted by *Farwell* J. in *Rudd* v. *Lascelles*, (1900) 1 Ch., 815,
               applied.

                  Held, also, that the contract operated as an assignment by G. of his share
               in a partnership, and, therefore, by sec. 31 of the *Partnership Act* 1892 could
               not be enforced as against Z. the other partner.

                  Decision of *A. H. Simpson* C.J. in Equity : *Murray* v. *Zobel*, (1908)
               8 S.R. (N.S.W.), 81, reversed.

APPEAL from a decision of *A. H. Simpson*, C.J. in Equity.

This was a suit by the respondent against the appellant and
one Zobel, in which the plaintiff sought to have it declared that
Zobel was a trustee for him of the benefits attaching to what is
termed an authority to enter under the Mining on Private Lands
Acts. He also asked for an injunction restraining the defendants
from dealing with certain machinery and other chattels alleged
to have been sold by the defendants to him, for an account of
profits derived from the working of the land included in the
authority to enter, and for the appointment of a receiver, and for
other consequential relief.

H. C. of A.
1907.

GANDER
v.
MURRAY.

ZOBEL
v.
MURRAY.

Upon the suit coming on for hearing *A. H. Simpson* C.J. in Equity made a decree declaring the defendant Zobel a trustee of the lands comprised in the authority to enter, upon trust as to one moiety for the plaintiff and as to the other moiety for himself, and ordered accounts to be taken of the receipts and expenses of the mine under the working of the defendants. No order was made as to Zobel's costs of suit : *Murray* v. *Zobel* (1).

From this decision the present appeal was brought by the defendant Gander. An application by Zobel for special leave to appeal on the question of costs was allowed to stand over to the hearing of the main appeal.

The facts appear sufficiently in the judgments hereunder.

Cullen K.C. (*Maughan* with him), for the appellant. On the evidence Zobel acquired his authority free of all equities so far as Murray was concerned. He was a purchaser for value from the Crown, and as he owed no duty to any person but himself, he was at liberty to dispose of a share in the benefit of the authority, and could give Gander a good title thereto: *Harrison* v. *Forth* (2).

[ISAACS J. referred to *Barrow's Case* : *In re Stapleford Colliery Co.* (3)].

The appellant's interest in the undertaking carried on under Zobel's authority was not affected by any equities created by his contract with Murray. It was wholly distinct from his interest in the original enterprise. There was a complete break of title, and in the interval the land was open to the world. There was no continuity whatever between the interest of the holder of the second authority and that of the holder of the original one. It was a new authority granted to a new person in respect of a different area of land. [He referred to Acts 57 Vict. No. 32, secs. 8, 9, 11, 12; and 60 Vict. No. 40 ; *Hanrick* v. *Patrick* (4).] The appellant was not estopped in equity from enjoying the newly acquired interest as his own. The only interest that could be affected by the contract of sale had come to an end by force of law. This is not a case of the estate feeding the estoppel:

(1) (1908) 8 S.R. (N.S.W.), 81.　　(3) 14 Ch. D., 432.
(2) Pre. Ch., 51.　　　　　　　　(4) 119 U.S., 156, at p. 175.

H. C. of A.
1907.

GANDER
v.
MURRAY.

ZOBEL
v.
MURRAY.

Smith v. *Osborne* (1); *Williams on Vendor and Purchaser*, p. 1056. The appellant was not in a fiduciary position towards Murray so as to be bound as to any rights he might subsequently acquire. He only sold his right, title and interest in the property at the date of the sale.

[ISAACS J. referred to *Watts* v. *Driscoll* (2)].

It was an assignment of a share in a partnership within sec. 31 of the *Partnership Act* 1892, and the suit should have been dismissed on that ground.

In any case the claim is barred by laches and acquiescence on the part of Murray: *Clarke* v. *Hart* (3); *Moore* v. *Morgan* (4) *Rowe* v. *Oades* (5).

Langer Owen K.C. (*Charles Manning* with him), for the respondent Zobel, having asked for special leave to appeal from the decision of *A. H. Simpson* C.J. in Equity as to Zobel's costs of suit, was heard on the question of costs.

Zobel should not have been deprived of his costs of suit merely because he admitted that he only claimed to be a trustee as to half the property for the appellant. He was altogether successful as to the half which he claimed for himself. Even if the appellant does not succeed on this appeal Zobel should be allowed his costs of suit: *Westgate* v. *Crowe* (6).

If the appellant is successful, it follows that Zobel was right in claiming to be a trustee for the appellant, and should have his costs.

The appellant should succeed. The benefit of the authority granted to Zobel was free of all equities. He was in no fiduciary position towards Murray: *In re Biss*; *Biss* v. *Biss* (7); *Kennedy* v. *De Trafford* (8). The appellant's interest in the new undertaking was not affected by the contract of sale: *Smith* v. *Osborne* (1).

Harvey, for the respondent Murray. The appellant when he made the contract with Murray honestly and rightly believed he

(1) 6 H.L.C., 375.
(2) (1901) 1 Ch., 294.
(3) 6 H.L.C., 633, at p. 656.
(4) 21 N.S.W.L.R. Eq., 158.

(5) 3 C.L.R., 73, at p. 78.
(6) 24 T.L.R., 14.
(7) (1903) 2 Ch., 40, at pp. 55, 57, 58.
(8) (1897) A.C., 180.

H. C. of A.
1907.

GANDER
v.
MURRAY.

ZOBEL
r.
MURRAY.

had authority to sell Zobel's interest. The partnership, therefore, was not dissolved : *Hooper* v. *Herts* (1). The contract was for the sale of the mining property, not merely of the benefit of the authority to enter, and the method by which Murray was to get the property was a mere matter of conveyancing. The appellant was estopped from saying that he had no authority from Zobel, or from saying that his subsequently acquired interest is not the same as that which he sold to Murray. He should be compelled to carry out the contract to the extent of his interest at least. He is estopped as between himself and Murray from contending that Zobel's authority to enter *quâ* the appellant's interest is not an accretion to his original interest. The authority obtained by Zobel must be taken to have been obtained for the partnership : *Featherstonhaugh* v. *Fenwick* (2); and Zobel stood in such a relation to Gander that, if he refused to ratify the sale to Murray, the partnership still continued, and, Murray having stepped into Gander's shoes, Zobel became a trustee for Murray, at any rate, to the extent of Gander's interest. On the evidence his Honor was in error in holding that Gander had no ostensible authority from Zobel to sell the whole property. There was no laches or acquiescence on Murray's part. In any event, if the suit is dismissed it should be without any order as to Gander's costs, as he misled the plaintiff.

Cullen K.C. in reply. The plaintiff failed to establish that there was any fiduciary relationship between Zobel and himself, or that he had placed Zobel in a better position than he was in himself with regard to obtaining an authority.

Cur. adv. vult.

GRIFFITH C.J. The subject matter of this suit may be described   Dec. 14. as an interest in a mining adventure carried on upon private lands under the provisions of the Mining on Private Property Acts. Mining operations seem to have been carried on intermittently upon the land in question for some years, at a place known as the Mount Bulga mine, the mineral sought for being copper. The nature of the title or interest conferred by the

(1) (1906) 1 Ch., 549.   (2) 17 Ves., 298.

H. C. of A.
1907.

GANDER
v.
MURRAY.

ZOBEL
v.
MURRAY.

Griffith C.J.

Acts I have mentioned depends upon a document called an
authority to enter, which may be granted by the Warden to the
holder of a miner's right or business licence. The authority continues in force for one year, and authorizes the holder of it to
enter upon the particular area of private land described in it,
to prospect for the mineral or minerals specified, and to carry on
mining operations subject to certain prescribed conditions. But
it does not confer any title to the land itself; it is not transfer-
able; it may be renewed; and it is regarded as being merely
anticipatory to a title to be afterwards acquired by lease from the
Crown of the minerals contained in the private land. So much
for the nature of the property. The appellant Gander held an
authority of this kind for an area of about twenty acres of land,
which was granted on 2nd August 1904, and consequently expired on 1st August 1905. It is alleged in the statement of
claim that the authority was held by Gander on behalf of himself and the defendant Zobel in equal shares, and it may be taken
to have been established that, although the authority was in the
name of Gander, he and Zobel were equally interested in the adventure. I use the neutral term "adventure" advisedly. In July
1905, very shortly before the authority expired, the respondent
Murray entered into negotiations with Gander for the purchase
of the adventure. At that time Gander represented, probably
honestly, that he had authority from his co-adventurer Zobel to
sell his share, and was consequently in a position to dispose of
the whole adventure. On 1st August 1905 an agreement in writing was drawn up between Gander and Murray, by which Gander
agreed to sell to Murray for £200 all the machinery, fittings,
chattels, property, and effects used in connection with the adventure on the land, also the copper ore that had been mined and
was lying upon the land. No one was then in possession of the
land. The agreement was silent as to any title or interest in the
land itself. With a view to carrying out the bargain between
Gander and Murray, which was made in the first instance verbally, it was arranged between them that, in order to give effect
to it, Murray should apply for an authority to enter the land in
his own name. He, however, desired to have a larger area, viz.,
33 acres, including the 20 acres comprised in the authority held

by Gander.   Accordingly, on 20th July, before the execution of
the written agreement of 1st August, Murray lodged an application with the Warden for authority to enter the 33 acres, and
on 1st August, the day on which the agreement was signed,
Gander notified the Warden that he had abandoned the 20 acres
held by him under his authority.   It seems to have been supposed
that upon that intimation a fresh authority would be granted to
Murray by the Warden for the 33 acres.   The Warden, however, took a different view, and held, in effect, that as Gander's
authority was still in force, it was a bar to Murray's application,
and on 10th August he refused it.   On the same day, 10th
August, Zobel applied for authority to enter the 33 acres, and
on 12th August Murray made a second application which was
also refused.   Then he lodged an objection to the authority being
granted to Zobel.   There followed what may be called a quasi-
litigation between Murray and Zobel.   The parties appeared
before the Warden, Zobel pressing his application and Murray
opposing it.   Gander, loyally endeavouring to carry out his
agreement with Murray, assisted him in trying to defeat Zobel's
application.   The result was that early in 1906 it was understood
that the Warden would grant Zobel's application, and on 12th
March in that year Zobel received a formal authority to enter
the 33 acres.   Shortly before 12th March, when it was known
what the Warden's decision would be, Zobel had agreed to take
in Gander as a partner with him in the new adventure, which
was intended to be carried out under the new authority.

These being the facts, this suit was brought by Murray.   His
claim was put in this way : That the property being a mining
adventure ought to be treated as one which may be properly the
subject of specific performance ; that Zobel by his agent agreed to
sell his share, so that the whole adventure was really sold to
Murray ; that Zobel, having immediately afterwards taken up the
land himself, was acting in fraud of the agreement ; and that an
equity attached to the whole property, by virtue of which the
plaintiff, Murray, was entitled to claim the benefit of the new
adventure.   There were some legal difficulties in the frame of
the suit as it was brought, but they were not pressed before us,
and it was assumed that they could be got over.   The suit was

H. C. of A.
1907.

GANDER
v.
MURRAY.

ZOBEL
v.
MURRAY.

Griffith C.J.

H. C. of A. founded on the doctrine in *Keech* v. *Sandford* (1), applicable to
1907.   the renewal of a lease by a trustee in his own name.

GANDER   As I have already pointed out, the adventure was the joint
v.   adventure of Zobel and Gander. Before further dealing with
MURRAY.   the facts of the case, it is important to consider what was the
ZOBEL   nature of their joint interest in the mining adventure. There
v.   was clearly no estate in the land itself. Whatever right the
MURRAY.   partnership had with regard to the land was not in the nature of
Griffith C.J. partnership assets, but a mere right to work it, belonging to
            Gander, to the benefit of which both partners were entitled so
            long as the partnership existed. In his statement of defence
            Zobel denied Gander's authority to sell his interest in the partner-
            ship, and the learned Judge has found that Gander had no such
            authority, so that the attempted sale of the whole adventure
            failed. The defendant Gander in his statement of defence alleged
            that the only authority he had held from Zobel was contained
            in three letters to which he craved leave to refer. He further
            alleged that he informed Murray that that was all the authority
            he had, and that Murray understood that, except so far as these
            letters conferred authority, he had none. The facts being, as the
            learned Judge found, that Gander had no authority to sell Zobel's
            interest, the transaction could not be carried out in the form
            originally intended. The plaintiff did not make any alternative
            claim, or ask for an amendment claiming that he was entitled to
            a half share in the mine, as in *Price* v. *Griffith* (2), if he could
            not get it all; but it seems to have been assumed that there was
            no difficulty in giving the plaintiff the same relief with respect
            to the half share as he would presumably have been entitled to
            with respect to the whole. The learned Judge in his judgment
            declared that Zobel held the land, with respect to which he had
            received the new authority to enter, upon trust, as to one moiety
            for the plaintiff and as to the other moiety for himself, and he
            directed that there should be a reference to the Master to take an
            account of the receipts and expenses in respect of the mine as
            between the defendants and the new partner Murray from 1st
            February 1906, with some other directions.

                It is obvious that this decree is founded on two propositions

            (1) Sel. Ch. Ca., 61.   (2) 1 D.M. & G., 80.

that were assumed to be established: (1) that the contract regarded as applying to the half share was one of which specific performance could be granted; and (2) that the substituted property, that is to say, the share which Gander acquired in Zobel's new adventure of March 1906, ought to be regarded in equity as an accretion to, or in substitution for, the subject matter of the original contract, or rather for the half share which is now assumed to be the subject matter of the original contract. The second proposition proceeds upon what is sometimes called equitable estoppel.

These being the two propositions upon which the plaintiff's claim rests, in my opinion he fails on both points. In *Thomas* v. *Dering* (1), before Lord *Langdale* M.R. in 1837, the plaintiff brought a suit for specific performance of a contract of sale. It appeared that the defendant could not give the plaintiff what he had contracted to give him, as he was only partially interested in the property. The plaintiff thereupon claimed that he was entitled to a decree that the defendant should give him as much as he could give him. I quote from the judgment (2):—"Though the vendor cannot be heard to suggest the difficulties which he has occasioned, the Court cannot avoid them. It is impossible not to see that the *cyprès* execution of the contract which is given in these cases is in fact the execution of a new contract which the parties did not enter into, in which there is no mutuality, and in which there are no adequate means of ascertaining the just price. . . . I therefore apprehend it to be clear that the Court will not, in all cases, afford the sort of relief which is here asked." And again (3):—"But without derogation, in any respect, from the jurisdiction, it is apparent that the Court will not, in every case, compel the vendor to convey such estate as he can: and omitting on this occasion those cases in which the purchaser, at the time of the contract, knew of the limited interest of the vendor, or in which an attempt has been made to commit a fraud on a power, which have no application to the present case, I apprehend that, upon the general principle that the Court will not execute a contract, the performance of which is unreasonable, or would be prejudicial to persons interested in the property, but

H. C. of A.
1907.

GANDER
v.
MURRAY.

ZOBEL
v.
MURRAY.

Griffith C.J.

(1) 1 Keen, 729.   (2) 1 Keen, 729, at p. 746.   (3) 1 Keen, 729, at p. 747.

H. C. of A.   not parties to the contract, the Court, before directing the
1907.   partial execution of the contract by ordering the limited interest
GANDER   of the vendor to be conveyed, ought to consider how that pro-
v.   ceeding may affect the interests of those who are entitled to the
MURRAY.   estate, subject to the limited interest of the vendor." In *Lumley* v.
ZOBEL   *Ravenscroft* (1) the same question was discussed by the Court of
v.   Appeal. In that case there were two vendors, one of whom was
MURRAY.   an infant, so that the contract as far as he was concerned
Griffith C.J.   could not be enforced. *Lindley* L.J. said (2):—"What is the law?
Specific performance is out of the question. You cannot get
specific performance against an infant, and upon the evidence
before us no case is made out for specific performance against
the other defendant either. This case is not within the exception
as to misrepresentation or misconduct stated in *Price* v. *Griffith* (3)
and *Thomas* v. *Dering* (4), but comes within the general rule
that where a person is jointly interested in an estate with
another person and purports to deal with the entirety specific
performance will not be granted against him as to his share. The
plaintiff's only remedy is by way of damages. As to that I say
nothing. But if it would be wrong to grant specific performance,
it follows that it would be wrong to grant an injunction." I
will also refer to *Rudd* v. *Lascelles* (5) decided by *Farwell* J.,
which also was a case in which the vendor could not give all that
he had contracted to sell. *Farwell* J. said (6):—"But in this
case, if I grant specific performance I shall decree specific performance not of the contract made by the parties, but of a new
contract made for them by the Court." He then quoted the
passage which I have just read from the judgment of Lord
Langdale in *Thomas* v. *Dering* (7), and continued:—"In the
present case the bargain between the parties contains no provision for compensation, such as is now common in conditions of
sale. Cases where there is such a provision do not present so
much difficulty because compensation is part of the bargain.
But here nothing of the sort was contemplated, and if I enforce
the contract with compensation I am compelling the vendor to

(1) (1895) 1 Q.B., 683.   (5) (1900) 1 Ch., 815.
(2) (1895) 1 Q.B., 683, at p. 684.   (6) (1900) 1 Ch., 815, at p. 818.
(3) 1 D.M. & G., 80.   (7) 1 Keen, 729, at p. 746.
(4) 1 Keen, 729, at p. 744.

H. C. of A.
1907.

GANDER
v.
MURRAY.
____
ZOBEL
v.
MURRAY.

Griffith C.J.

perform a contract into which she did not enter." Then he referred to the fact that the case rested upon equitable estoppel, and he went on (1)—" But I am not compelled to decide the case on that ground alone ; there is a further ground which depends on a dictum of *Jessel* M.R. in *Cato* v. *Thompson* (2), a dictum, I need not say, of very great weight. One ground for refusing specific performance with compensation is the great difficulty of properly assessing the compensation, and in *Cato* v. *Thompson* (3), in which there were restrictive covenants like those in the present case, and the purchaser brought an action to recover his deposit, *Jessel* M.R. said in answer to an argument that the purchaser ought to complete with compensation :—'Now, in the first place, this is not a case for enforcing specific performance on a purchaser with compensation. It is almost impossible to assess compensation for covenants of this nature. I think that cases of specific performance with compensation ought not to be extended. In many of them a bargain substantially different from that which the parties entered into has been substituted for it and enforced, which is not right. I think this not a case for compensation.' " There is no question of compensation here, because the plaintiff is willing to pay the whole price for the half share, but I think the general observations made in the judgment are applicable to this case. There was another case before *Farwell* J. in the same year, relating to the sale of a partnership, where it was sought to carry the doctrine to this extent—that in no case would specific performance be granted of the sale of a share in a mine, but the learned Judge said that he could see no reason why the contract should not be enforced to the extent of a half share where there had been a sale of the whole. (*Hexter* v. *Pearce* (4)). But that is a very different thing from the case where all that the vendor can do in pursuance of his part of the agreement is to give a share in a partnership. Applying this doctrine to the present case, it is clear that the contract cannot take effect as it was intended to take effect. The Court is really therefore asked to make a new bargain between the parties. Supposing the authority, instead of terminating almost immediately after the contract

(1) (1900) 1 Ch., 815, at p. 819.   (3) 9 Q.B.D., 616.
(2) 9 Q.B.D., 616, at p. 618.   (4) (1900) 1 Ch., 341.

H. C. of A.
1907.

GANDER
v.
MURRAY.
——
ZOBEL
v.
MURRAY.

Griffith C.J.

was made, had had nine months to run, and under these
circumstances Gander had agreed to sell to Murray the whole
interest in the mining adventure, and the plaintiff had sought to
enforce that bargain as to the half share, the plaintiff would not
be asking for specific performance of a contract for sale of
property but of a contract for the sale of a share in the partnership and that as against the other partner. The *Partnership
Act* (55 Vict. No. 12) forbids such a suit. Sec. **31** provides
that :—" An assignment by any partner of his share in the
partnership, either absolute or by way of mortgage or redeem-
able charge, does not, as against the other partners, entitle the
assignee during the continuance of the partnership, to interfere
in the management or administration of the partnership business
or affairs, or to require any account of the partnership transactions, or to inspect the partnership books, but entitles the
assignee only to receive the share of profits to which the assigning
partner would otherwise be entitled, and the assignee must accept
the account of profits agreed to by the partners." It is therefore
clear that as between Murray and Zobel, so long as the adventure
was carried on under the existing authority, Murray would have
acquired no rights against Zobel to be treated as a partner, nor
could he have compelled Zobel to take out a new authority
for his benefit. He could not claim any share in the land itself.
For these reasons it seems to me that, if the case had not been
complicated by the termination of the original authority and the
substitution of the new one, it would have been clear that the
plaintiff could not have obtained any relief in equity against
Zobel, though he might have had a remedy in damages against
Gander.

Turning now to the other assumption, that there is a substantial identity between the old adventure and the new one:
What are the facts ? At the expiration of Gander's authority
on 1st August 1905 he had no further right to the land, or in
any way connected with the land. Zobel, whose share in the
partnership had been ineffectually sold, was, when that authority
expired, perfectly free to obtain authority for himself to enter
the land. There was no privity between him and Murray. Zobel
only did what he was entitled to do when he got his authority

to enter the land, and it cannot be disputed that he acquired that authority free from all equities as far as Murray was concerned; consequently any rights which the plaintiff could acquire in the new adventure did not accrue until Gander became a member of the new partnership with Zobel. His only claim as against Zobel was founded on the supposition that Gander before entering into the·new partnership had agreed to sell him his rights in that partnership. Under these circumstances, as I have pointed out, he was not entitled to any ruling as against Zobel; certainly not to have Zobel declared a trustee for him. Again: As against Gander the plaintiff cannot have any greater rights *quoad* the property than he would have had if, instead of relying upon an equitable estoppel, he had relied on a legal estoppel, such as is created by a conveyance in the case of a property capable of being conveyed. If he had relied upon anything of that kind the case of *Smith* v. *Osborne* (1) is conclusive to show that such an estoppel would not have applied to an interest arising under a new and distinct title. There is no doctrine that I am aware of under which a general right can exist, as one might say *in gremio*, to any interest which another man may acquire in property, at any future time, or by any means. A contract to that effect may be made, but there is no equitable doctrine that lays down that it may be enforced specifically, or otherwise than by a claim for damages for breach of contract. *A fortiori* there is no doctrine that, because a man has made an ineffectual contract to buy the share of a partner in a partnership which has since terminated, he is entitled to claim that partner's share in another partnership entered into six months afterwards relating only in part to the same property. For these reasons I am of opinion that the plaintiff's case entirely fails on both grounds, and that the appeal should be allowed.

BARTON J. As to the enforcement of specific performance on a vendor with compensation for defects, in *Rudd* v. *Lascelles* (2), *Farwell* J. expressed the opinion that relief should be confined to cases where the actual subject matter is substantially the same as that stated in the contract, and should not be extended to cases

H. C. OF A.
1907.

GANDER
v.
MURRAY.

ZOBEL
v.
MURRAY.

Griffith C.J.

(1) 6 H.L.C., 375.   (2) (1900) 1 Ch., 815.

H. C. of A.
1907.

GANDER
v.
MURRAY.
——
ZOBEL
v.
MURRAY.

Barton J.

where the subject matter is essentially different. That is surely right. The property here (if it can be called property) is not in substance identical. The original authority granted to Gander was for 20 acres, and that was the interest which was the subject of the agreement between Gander and Murray, as to which Gander appears to have assumed authority to dispose of Zobel's interest as well as his own. That area of 20 acres was the subject of Gander's application. Gander's authority to enter had expired, but it could have been regranted or renewed in certain circumstances, in pursuance of the agreement. Gander appears to have done his utmost to see that Murray obtained a fresh authority. These authorities are personal rights, and they do not seem to stand on anything like the same footing as ordinary estates the subject of contracts which may be ordered to be specifically performed. At any rate we find that, notwithstanding the efforts of Gander in his support, Murray failed to obtain an authority to enter and search the 20 acres, or the 33 acres which included the 20 acres. It appears to me, that when the authority to Gander ran out, there was, as Dr. *Cullen* contended, an entirely fresh departure in title (if title it can be called), and that there was nothing which could for a moment be successfully contended to be the identical subject matter upon which the application of Gander originally had been granted. It seems impossible to contend that what Murray applied for was the same subject matter respecting which Gander held authority to enter. The fact that the same acreage was applied for by Zobel afterwards, cannot possibly be held to make it the same right in respect of which the contract or agreement between Gander and Murray was entered into. The title against which specific performance is sought is an entirely new one. Gander had abandoned, but he had done so in assisting Murray to obtain a new authority. By applying at the wrong time, Murray failed, and he repeated his failure for the same cause. In these failures Gander was in no sense concerned, nor was he responsible for either of them. Gander had done all that was demanded of him. He had done his best in assistance of Murray's application. Gander cannot be said to have broken his contract. Murray's failures were not the fault of Gander. They were due to his too hasty application in the first instance,

and his too tardy application in the second, in competition with
Zobel, who seems to me to have been under no obligation whatever to him to abstain from applying or to give him any of the
fruit of his application.   He was free to do as he did.   Between
him and Murray there were no transactions whatever out of
which a trust in him in Murray's favour could arise.   As to the
alleged estoppel, my learned brother the Chief Justice has pointed
out that the case of *Smith* v. *Osborne* (1) completely disposes of
the plaintiff's contention.   For these reasons I am of opinion
that the appeal should be allowed.

H. C. of A.
1907.

GANDER
v.
MURRAY.

ZOBEL
v.
MURRAY.

Barton J.

ISAACS J. My judgment is based on the view I take of the
nature of an authority under the Mining on Private Property
Acts, and of the effect of the contract between Murray and
Gander.

An authority under those Acts is nothing more than a permission to enter on another man's land, and to prospect for whatever
metal is mentioned in the authority, for such a time, consistent
with the provisions of the Acts, as will give a proper opportunity
to the holder of determining whether he will apply for a lease or
not.   The authority holder obtains no interest in the land itself.
He has rights and obligations with respect to the land; rights of
prospecting and, if he wishes, of applying for a lease, and obligations to observe statutory conditions on pain of losing all his
rights.   But the rights, like the obligations, are purely personal,
and no provision exists to transfer any of them.   The landowner
retains his full estate and interest in the land, qualified only by
the right of entry for the purpose of prospecting and discovery,
by the possibility or option of the authority holder applying for
a lease, and of the Government choosing to grant it to him.   But
with the termination of the authority itself all the attendant
rights and obligations come to an end.   A succeeding authority
holder, whether the predecessor's authority is abandoned voluntarily or is cancelled, no more inherits the rights of the predecessor than his obligations, say, to pay rent in arrear, that is
rent not paid within one month after it falls due.   Each authority
is a new departure, and all the provisions of the Act must be

(1) 6 H.L.C., 375.

H. C. of A.
1907.

GANDER
v.
MURRAY.

ZOBEL
v.
MURRAY.

Isaacs J.

observed with regard to it, irrespective of anything that has occurred under a previously existing authority. It is simply a statutory licence. It is not in any sense a grant. Although there is involved in it the permission to take away and appropriate metals found, yet that is only because it is a necessary, though subsidiary, part of prospecting which is the direct and real object of the enlarged powers granted by the Act of 1896. Now assuming, as has been assumed throughout the argument, that Gander's oral promise to assist Murray in his new application was a binding. term of their agreement, though not inserted in the written document, the effect, and the necessary effect, of carrying out the bargain was to entirely put an end to the authority under which Gander was working, and having extinguished that authority, to throw the land again open to the world, so that whoever got it would get it under a new, distinct and independent authority, quite unconnected with Gander's old authority, not flowing from or consequent upon it in any shape or form, and therefore in no sense an adjunct to or a renewal or continuation of the old right under which Gander operated for the benefit of himself and Zobel. The agreement, shortly put then, may be summarized thus:—Sale of chattels, abandonment and extinction of existing authority which was for copper, agreement to leave the ground open to Murray's application to the Warden whether for copper or any other mineral, and not to compete with him but to assist him to get an authority to himself. That ended when Murray got delivery of the chattels, and when his application, which was for both copper and iron, failed. There was nothing further on which the agreement could operate. He had had his chance, the chance bargained and paid for. Thenceforth Gander was free so far as anything remained to be done under the contract. Zobel was always free because he had never authorized the sale of his interest. When he found himself improperly deprived by the cancellation of Gander's authority of all rights to prospect the land, he applied for and got a new authority for himself, again for copper. In this Murray had no interest; it was not only independent of but adverse to him, and if Zobel had chosen to remain solely interested in it, Murray could not have asserted any rights in it. But if so, where was Gander's disability to receive from Zobel any interest Zobel chose to give him ?

H. C. of A.
1907.

GANDER
v.
MURRAY.

ZOBEL
v.
MURRAY.

Isaacs J.

The bargain between Murray and Gander raised no fiduciary relations between them except as to Gander's interest in the chattels sold, and, possibly, in the then existing authority until its extinction ; but only in the sense in which the vendor is regarded as a trustee for the purchaser with respect to the property sold. There was nothing of a continuously fiduciary character in their relations which would extend beyond that, and attach to any other property, and convert Gander into a trustee for Murray of whatever interest in the land he might at any future time become possessed of.

Their relations were contractual, and for any breach of the contract or of warranty of Zobel's authority, Murray may or may not have a legal cause of complaint. But I see no reason for importing into the matter the doctrine of trusteeship, and the case must therefore fail.

For distinctness of principle I have so far treated the case as if the authority which Gander agreed to assist Murray in obtaining was for the original area of 20 acres. But the fact that Murray applied for a much larger area, 33 acres, though including the former 20 acres, the authority being indivisible, leads to one of two results : either the promise to assist was not binding in relation to an application for 33 acres, or if it was, it bound Gander only, inasmuch as Zobel's alleged authority to sell the partnership property could not be supposed to cover a personal undertaking by him with respect to a matter known to be altogether outside the partnership business.

The 33 acres too, being outside that business and beyond the ambit of the original authority, cannot by any process of reasoning be regarded as appertaining to the property sold, or in any way connected with it.

My judgment would be the same if there were no extension of area, but in face of that extension, the hopelessness of Murray's case is clear to demonstration.

I would add with regard to acquiescence, it is unnecessary, taking the views I have already expressed, to determine it ; but I feel bound to say that Murray's conduct impressed me as lacking

H. C. of A.
1907.

GANDER
v.
MURRAY.

ZOBEL
v.
MURRAY.

Isaacs J.

that promptitude which is so important a feature when a man is asserting an equitable right to interests in a speculative enterprise.

For the reasons I have given I agree that this appeal should be allowed.

> *Appeal allowed. Judgment appealed from discharged. Suit dismissed, against Zobel with costs, against Gander with costs subsequent to the statement of defence. Respondent, Murray, to pay the costs of the appeal and in the Supreme Court.*

Solicitors, for the appellants, *McLachlan & Murray.*
Solicitors, for the respondent, *Robson & Cowlishaw.*

C. A. W.

[HIGH COURT OF AUSTRALIA.]

MANN . . . . APPELLANT;
COMPLAINANT,

AND

DOO WEE . . , ... RESPONDENT.
DEFENDANT,

ON APPEAL FROM THE SUPREME COURT OF WESTERN
AUSTRALIA EXERCISING FEDERAL JURISDICTION.

H. C. of A.
1907.

PERTH,
Nov. 5.

Griffith C.J.,
Barton and
Isaacs JJ.

Justices Act 1902 (*W.A.*), (2 *Edw. VII. No.* 11), *secs.* 135, 137, 191—*Criminal Code* 1903 (*W.A.*), (1 & 2 *Edw. VII. No.* 14), *secs.* 553, 614—*Appeal from justices— Order for rehearing—Abandonment of appeal—Proof of charge de novo —Absence of accused.*

Where an appeal from a summary conviction is heard by way of rehearing, the fact that the appellant at the outset abandons his appeal and absents himself from the Court is no ground for allowing the appeal and quashing the conviction.

An order that an appeal shall be heard by way of rehearing does not operate to quash the conviction appealed against.

AN appeal from the order of *Rooth* J. exercising federal jurisdiction in a matter under the *Immigration Restriction Acts* 1901-05. The respondent was arrested and charged before a Police Magistrate at Perth with being a prohibited immigrant, and after due hearing was convicted and sentenced to imprisonment for two months. He lodged an appeal to the Supreme Court of Western Australia on the ground that he could bring evidence, which he did not previously know was necessary on his part, to prove that he had been resident in the Commonwealth more than a year.

On the respondent's application *Parker* C.J. made an order that the appeal should be by way of rehearing, in pursuance of sec. 191 of the *Justices Act* 1902. The appeal came on for rehearing before *Rooth* J., and counsel for respondent (the then appellant) thereupon informed the Court that he desired to withdraw the appeal. This was not allowed, His Honor ruling that, as an order for rehearing had been made, this was equivalent to a quashing of the conviction, and the prosecution must proceed to prove the charge *de novo*. After protest, counsel for the prosecution opened the case and proceeded to call witnesses ; but, it being pointed out that the accused person was absent, *Rooth* J. ruled that the procedure was governed by the *Criminal Code* (1 & 2 Edw. VII. No. 14), sec. 614, and the charge could not be proved in the absence of the accused. His Honor refused to issue a bench warrant to compel the attendance of the accused, and made an order allowing the appeal and quashing the conviction. The complainant appealed to the High Court.

Thomas, for the appellant. The offence of being a prohibited immigrant is a summary, not an indictable, offence ; the procedure therefore was governed by the *Justices Act* 1902, and not by the *Criminal Code* 1903, sec. 553. That being so, the absence of the accused person was immaterial ; the accused was represented by his counsel, and therefore present before the Court : *Justices Act* 1902, sec. 137 ; and under sec. 135 the Judge could have proceeded *ex parte*.

But in any event the order that the appeal should be by way of rehearing did not require the proof of the whole case over again; that order was only a step in the procedure of hearing the appeal, to allow the appellant to adduce fresh evidence in support of his appeal. The conviction stands until it is properly reversed; and the accused having expressly abandoned his appeal, there was nothing to do but affirm the conviction.

No appearance for the respondent.

GRIFFITH C.J. I think that where the learned Judge fell into error was in treating the order of the Chief Justice that the appeal should be by way of rehearing as a substantive order disposing of the appeal *pro tanto*, instead of, as it really was, a mere step in the hearing of the appeal itself. The application to the Chief Justice for that order, the order' itself, and the subsequent hearing of the appeal before *Rooth* J. were all parts of a single proceeding, that is, the appeal. The case came properly before the Court of Appeal, and thereupon the appellant asked to withdraw his appeal and declined to proceed with it. At that time the conviction stood. The learned Judge, instead of dismissing the appeal when the appellant abandoned it, entered upon the hearing, and then allowed the appeal on the ground that no evidence could be given in the absence of the appellant. In the first place, I am of opinion that he ought to have dismissed the appeal as soon as the appellant abandoned it. In the second place, I have no doubt that the appellant was present in contemplation of law all through the proceedings, since he was there when they began. It was quite immaterial that he went out of Court while they were going on. If it had been necessary under the circumstances to hear evidence, I have no doubt that it was competent for the Court to do so; but, if it had then been necessary, I think it would now be necessary to remit the case for rehearing. But in the actual circumstances it was not necessary. A conviction stands until it is quashed. If an appellant when the appeal comes on abandons it, there is an end of the appeal, and the conviction remains in force. For these reasons I think that the learned Judge was wrong and that this appeal should be allowed.

BARTON J.　Sec. 614 of the Criminal Code appears to relate only to the trial of indictable offences, and I do not think there can be any application of it in this case.　The appellant, being present by his counsel at the calling on of the appeal, and having through his counsel abandoned the appeal, made the most cogent admission of the propriety of the original conviction which could be made in a Court of Justice, and therefore this appeal should be sustained.

ISAACS J.　I am of the same opinion.　The respondent was summarily convicted, and sec. 183 of the *Justices Act* gave him an absolute right to appeal on complying with certain conditions. Those conditions were complied with, and he therefore was an appellant.　Sec. 187, in prescribing the security for his appearance, directs that he should enter into a recognizance to appear before the Court to which the appeal is made, and to submit to the judgment of the Court.　He cannot, in my opinion, by breaking the requirements of the Statute, put himself in a better position than if he complied with them.　Then the Act goes on to provide for the hearing of the appeal, and sec. 191 provides that there may be a rehearing in either of two cases : If the parties agree, or if the Court to which the appeal is made so orders.　But that is only, as has already been put by the Chief Justice, a matter of procedure ; it is not the main order in the case ; and if the appellant chooses to abandon his whole appeal he abandons it altogether, including any agreement for rehearing or any incidental order for rehearing which may have happened to be made.　I think, therefore, that the view taken by his Honor Mr. Justice *Rooth*, that the order for a rehearing was the main order, was not correct ; and that is shown very distinctly by this, that secs. 192 and 193 provide for cases where a decision is not affirmed by the appellate Court, and where the decision of the justice is affirmed by the appellate Court.　If the decision is affirmed, then the order made by the justice, embodied in that decision, has to be carried out ; the conviction stands, in other words, until it is set aside.　It never was set aside, and although the appellant was enabled to take steps to challenge it, and did take steps to challenge it, he abandoned his right to do so ; and the only consequence

H. C. OF A.
1907.
MANN
v.
DOO WEE.
——
Isaacs J.

is that, having formally abandoned it, the original conviction stands. I agree therefore that the appeal should be allowed.

Appeal allowed. Order appealed from discharged. Conviction restored.

Solicitor, for appellant, *Barker* (Crown Solicitor).

N. G. P.

[HIGH COURT OF AUSTRALIA.]

MAURICE MYERSON . . . . . APPELLANT;

AND

THE KING . . . . RESPONDENT.

ON APPEAL FROM THE SUPREME COURT OF
NEW SOUTH WALES.

H. C. OF A.
1908.
——
SYDNEY,
April 22.
——
Griffith C.J.,
Barton,
O'Connor and
Isaacs JJ.

Criminal Law—Verdict—Recommendation to mercy—Ambiguous expression in rider—Meaning of jury's finding.

Where the jury in a criminal trial add to a verdict of guilty, and objection is taken to the conviction on the ground that the rider is a rider finding special facts which are alleged to be inconsistent with guilt, the Court must look at the whole finding including the rider, and if it then appears reasonably doubtful whether the jury have found the facts necessary to establish the offence charged, the accused is entitled to the benefit of the doubt and the conviction should be quashed ; but the effect of a clear finding of guilty is not cut down by a rider stating facts which, considered in the light of the circumstances of the case and the nature of the offence charged, are consistent with guilt.

Held, also, that, where there has been a verdict of guilty on several counts, some of which are subsequently held bad on demurrer, the nature of the material allegations in the defective counts and the fact that the jury have found them to be proved are relevant in ascertaining the meaning of a rider applicable to the verdict upon all the counts.

To a verdict of guilty upon three counts of an indictment against two persons for conspiracy the jury added a rider recommending one of the accused to mercy on the ground that he was an "unsuspecting tool" of the other.

Held, that, in view of the circumstances of the case, the nature of the offence, and the findings on other counts, the rider could not be regarded as equivalent to a verdict of not guilty as regards the accused to whom it referred.

Quære, whether special leave to appeal should have been granted.

Decision of the Supreme Court : *Rex.* v. *Myerson* (1907) 7 S.R. (N.S.W.), 748, affirmed.

APPEAL from a decision of the Supreme Court of New South Wales upon a Crown case reserved under the *Crimes Act* 1900.

The appellant and his brother were convicted upon an indictment containing three counts for conspiracy to defraud. The jury added a rider recommending the appellant to mercy on the ground that he was the "unsuspecting tool" of the other accused. On a Crown case reserved the Supreme Court held that the second and third counts of the indictment were bad, and that a demurrer to them should have been allowed, but that the first count was good. Objection was then taken for the appellant that the rider was equivalent to a verdict of not guilty as regards the appellant. The Supreme Court decided against him and affirmed the conviction : *Rex* v. *Myerson* (1).

From that decision the present appeal was brought by special leave.

The facts are fully stated in the judgment of *Griffith* C.J.

G. H. Reid K.C. and *Garland,* for the appellant. The Court should look at the recommendation as well as the verdict. It is really part of the finding, and if it shows that the jury have

(1) (1907) 7 S.R. (N.S.W.), 748.

H. C. of A.
1908.

MYERSON
v.
THE KING.

H. C. of A.   found certain facts inconsistent with the guilt of the accused,
   1908.   the whole finding should be treated as equivalent to a verdict of
MYERSON   not guilty : *Reg.* v. *Dickson* (1); *Reg.* v. *Gray* (2); *Reg.* v.
   v.   *Crawshaw* (3). The dictum of Lord *Campbell* C.J. in *R.* v.
THE KING.   *Trebilcock* (4), to the effect that the rider forms no part of the
            verdict is not supported by later cases on the subject. The rider
            is of equal weight with the verdict strictly so called in showing
            the conclusion at which the jury arrived on the facts. It is
            not necessary that the rider should clearly contradict the rest of
            the finding in order to avoid the conviction. It is sufficient if
            the result is to render it uncertain whether the jury really have
            found the facts necessary to support a conviction of the offence
            charged. If the words used by the jury are reasonably capable
            of a construction which will have that result the conviction
            should be quashed. The defect might have been cured by the
            Judge refusing to accept the verdict, but, that not having been
            done, it has become impossible to say that the jury have really
            found the accused guilty. The Supreme Court were in error in
            dealing with the finding in two parts ; they thought that,
            because the first part was clear and the latter part ambiguous,
            they should disregard all but the mere finding of guilty.

            The words used by the jury should be construed in their
            ordinary popular sense, not in any technical sense, and the Court
            should consider the words themselves and not speculate as to
            what the jury might or should have meant. [They referred to
            Stewart and Walker v. *White* (5).] So regarded, the words
            "unsuspecting tool" not merely render the finding uncertain,
            they plainly negative guilt. An intent to defraud was an
            essential element of the offence charged. The conspiracy alleged
            was an agreement to defraud creditors. It is impossible to
            conceive a person agreeing to defraud his creditors in the way
            alleged here without suspecting that the result of the agreement
            would be to defraud. The rider is equivalent to finding that the
            accused was unknowingly guilty. A "tool" may be guilty or
            not guilty, but an "unsuspecting tool" is an innocent tool.

(1) 4 S.C.R. (N.S.W.), 298.   (4) 1 Dears. & B., 453; 27 L.J.M.C.,
(2) 17 Cox Cr. Ca., 299.   103.
(3) 8 Cox Cr. Ca., 375; Bell C.C., 303.   (5) 5 C.L.R., 110, at p. 119.

[They referred to *Reg.* v. *Moore* (1); *Mulcahy* v. *The Queen* (2); *Reg.* v. *Beirne* (3); *Hardgrave* v. *The King* (4).]

Pilcher K.C. (*Pollock* with him), for the Crown. Although the Court is entitled to consider all that the jury have said, the actual verdict and the rider do not stand on exactly the same footing. The verdict should be upheld if the rider is capable of any reasonable construction upon which the whole finding can stand together. The Court will endeavour to make sense of what the jury has said, and should construe the finding reasonably and in the light of the facts proved in the case: *Reg.* v. *Trebilcock* (5). In *Reg.* v. *Dickson* (6) the words of the rider were absolutely inconsistent with the verdict of guilty, and could not be construed otherwise. There were three counts here and the appellant was found guilty on all of them, and, though two of them were held bad on demurrer, the facts alleged must be taken to have been proved, as there is no suggestion that the evidence was insufficient to support the information. Looking at the allegations in the several counts, it is clear from the nature of the case that there are many senses in which the appellant may have been an " unsuspecting tool " and yet have been guilty. The jury may have meant that he did not realize the wrong he was doing, or that he was influenced by the stronger mind of his brother, without realizing where he was being led. But it is no excuse that a man did not know that he was doing wrong. [He referred to *Rex* v. *Esop* (7); *Bank of New South Wales* v. *Piper* (8).] The onus is on the appellant of showing that, under the circumstances of this case, an unsuspecting tool must have been an innocent tool. In other words, he must show that the jury really made a mistake when they found him guilty. At the most he has only shown that " unsuspecting tool " is capable of a construction consistent with innocence. He has not shown that those words necessarily negative guilt. [He referred to *Reg.* v. *Morce* (9).]

(1) 2 N.S.W.W.N., 6.
(2) L.R. 3 H.L., 306.
(3) 14 S.C.R. (N.S.W.), 351.
(4) 4 C.L.R., 232, at p. 239.
(5) 1 Dears. & B., 453 ; 27 L.J.M.C., 103.
(6) 4 S.C.R. (N.S.W.), 298.
(7) 7 C. & P., 456.
(8) (1897) A.C., 383.
(9) 13 A.L.T., 262, at p. 263.

H. C. of A.
1908.

MYERSON
v.
THE KING.

Griffith C.J.

G. H. Reid K.C., in reply, referred to *Reg.* v. *Sleep* (1).

[GRIFFITH C.J. referred to *Reg.* v. *Orman* (2).]

GRIFFITH C.J.   Special leave was granted in this case to appeal from an order of the Supreme Court affirming the conviction of the appellant upon a charge of conspiracy.   The information presented against him, which was in somewhat vague terms, contained three counts.   The first alleged that the appellant and another conspired together to cheat and defraud certain named creditors and others of "divers large quantities of goods and merchandise and divers large sums of money the property of the creditors aforesaid."   The second count alleged that the accused were on 7th June 1907 made bankrupt, and that on 1st June in that year they, with intent to defraud the same creditors, conspired and agreed together that they should within four months before the sequestration order dispose of otherwise than in the ordinary way of trade certain goods and merchandise which they had obtained on credit from the creditors mentioned, and for which they had not paid.   The third count I need not refer to.   The jury found the accused guilty on all three counts and added :—" We strongly recommend the accused Maurice Myerson to mercy on account of ill-health, and because we believe that he was a tool, an unsuspecting tool, of Abraham, his brother," the other accused.   The learned Judge before whom the case was heard reserved three points for the consideration of the Full Court.   The first two related to a demurrer.   The third, which is the only one for our consideration, is that the rider to the verdict of the jury was equivalent to a verdict of not guilty against Maurice Myerson, the appellant.   When the case came before the Full Court they held that the demurrer to the second and third counts ought to have been allowed, and, considering the matter with reference to the first count, came to the conclusion that, under the circumstances, they were unable to say that the rider was equivalent to a verdict of not guilty.   The matter cannot be put better than in the language of *Cohen* J.   He pointed out that the question was what did the jury mean, and, after referring to the similarity of the meaning of the word " tool " to that of the word " dupe," which

(1) Le. & Ca., 44.   (2) 14 Cox Cr. Ca., 381.

H. C. of A.
1908.

MYERSON
v.
THE KING.

Griffith C.J.

had been the subject of decision in the Supreme Court of New South Wales, in *Reg.* v. *Beirne* (1), went on to say (2) :—" Apart from that it is difficult to see what the jury had in their mind. Unsuspecting as to what ? The jury came to a conclusion which, taken by itself, admits of no doubt that the accused were guilty. The Court must see that that part of the finding of the jury, which fixed the accused with guilt, is so affected by the subsequent recommendation, that the Court can see that the recommendation, taken with the verdict of guilty, cannot stand." It is contended for the appellant that the finding that the appellant was the unsuspecting tool of his brother is inconsistent with the finding of guilty.

As I have pointed out, the only question that now arises is as to the first count, and the question is, what is the meaning of the rider added by the jury ? But, in considering that, we must not reject what was meant by the jury in finding a verdict of guilty. They found the accused guilty on the second count as well as on the first, and the fact that they found the material allegations in the second count proved is very relevant to the question what they meant by their finding, despite the circumstance that that count was subsequently found not to disclose an offence. The jury therefore found, in effect, not only that, in the language of the first count, the accused conspired together to cheat and defraud the creditors of large quantities of goods and merchandise and large sums of money, but also that they had conspired together to dispose of, otherwise than in the ordinary way of trade, goods and merchandise which they had obtained on credit from those creditors and for which they had not paid, with intent to defraud. Reference was made in argument to the case of *Reg.* v. *Trebilcock* (3), in which Lord *Campbell* C.J. expressed a doubt whether a rider of the jury recommending the prisoner to mercy ought to be referred to in order to ascertain what the jury meant, as it was not part of their finding. But subsequent cases go to show that that doubt cannot be supported, and that it is the duty of the Court, where a jury has found a prisoner

(1) 14 S.C.R. (N.S.W.), 351.　　　　(3) 1 Dears. & B., 453 ; 27 L.J.M.C.,
(2) (1907) 7 S.R. (N.S.W.), 748, at　　103.
p. 760.

guilty and added a rider to their verdict, to look at the whole
of the finding, and that if it appears reasonably doubtful, taking
the whole finding together, whether the jury have found the
facts necessary to establish the offence charged, the accused is
entitled to the benefit of the doubt. The question is how is the
rule to be applied in the present case. The main contention for
the appellant is this : that in a charge of conspiracy to defraud
intent is an essential element of the offence, and that there cannot be an intent to defraud on the part of one who is the unsuspecting tool of another. That, however, depends upon the
meaning of those words, and the sense in which they are used.
A conspiracy to defraud may be proved in various ways, and the
means of carrying out the conspiracy may also be very varied.
In the present case the jury have found that one part of the
agreement between the accused was that they should dispose of,
otherwise than in the ordinary way of trade, goods for which
they had not paid. It is obvious that one person might agree
with another to assist in an enterprise of that kind and yet
truthfully be called the unsuspecting tool of the other. The
words seem to me to be capable of various significations. They
may mean that the person spoken of did not suspect that the
enterprise was unlawful. But *ignorantia juris haud excusat.*
The words must be taken with reference to the circumstances of
the particular case. If the nature of the offence in the present
case were such that a person, who could be fairly described in the
ordinary meaning of the words as an unsuspecting tool, could not
be guilty of the offence, I think that the conviction could not be
supported. But it is impossible to come to that conclusion, having
regard to the nature of the offence charged and the facts found.
One meaning that the words are capable of bearing is that the
accused did not know that there was any harm in what he was
doing, or did not know that he was exposing himself to criminal
liability, and it is extremely probable that that was what the
jury meant. Having, then, a clear finding that the accused was
guilty of conspiring with the other accused to defraud his creditors,
and having only this ambiguous expression in the rider to qualify
it, I think it is a case for the application of this principle that a
clear statement or finding of fact is not to be cut down by the

subsequent use of ambiguous words.   For my own part, I am H. C. of A.
disposed to think that we ought not to have granted special leave 1908.
to appeal in this case, and I had grave doubt on the point at the MYERSON
time.   But there has been no application to rescind the special v.
THE KING.
leave, and I have expressed my opinion on the merits.   The only
question really involved is not one of general interest or import- Griffith C.J.
ance in the administration of the criminal law, as to the right of
an accused person to get the benefit of an uncertainty in the
conviction, but is rather a question of the meaning of the
particular words used by the jury in this case.   That is not a
matter of general importance.

When we granted special leave to appeal we had not the
advantage of seeing the reasons of their Honors of the Supreme
Court. If we had, it is still more doubtful whether we should
have granted it.

BARTON J., O'CONNOR J., and ISAACS J. concurred.

Appeal dismissed.

Solicitor, for the appellant, *E. R. Abigail.*
Solicitor, for the respondent, *The Crown Solicitor for New
South Wales.*

C. A. W.

THE KING (ON THE PROSECUTION OF WATERS) .   PLAINTIFF;

AND

THE REGISTRAR OF TRADE MARKS   .   DEFENDANT.

H. C. OF A.   *Trade Marks Act* 1905 (*No.* 20 *of* 1905), *secs.* 33, 37, 41, 46, 94, 105—*Trade Marks*
1908.   *Regulations* 1906, *regs.* 27, 28—*Application for registration—Notice by Registrar*
                     —*Failure of applicant to reply —Abandonment of application —Validity of*
MELBOURNE,   *regulation—Extension of time for reply—Power of Registrar.*
March 25, 26,
27.   Regulation 28 of the *Trade Marks Regulations* 1906, in so far as it provides
                 for an application being deemed to be abandoned in a certain event, is a lawful
Griffith C.J.,   exercise of the power conferred by sec. 94 of the *Trade Marks Act* 1905, and
O'Connor,   is not inconsistent with sec. 37.
Isaacs and
Higgins JJ.
                     So held by the Court, *Higgins* J. doubting.

                     If the Registrar is satisfied that the failure of an applicant to answer the
                 notice referred to in regulations 27 and 28 arises from circumstances for
                 which the applicant should be excused, he may under sec. 105 of the Act
                 extend the time for so answering, and, in considering whether he should or
                 should not extend the time, the Registrar is bound to exercise his discretion.

ORDER *nisi* for mandamus.

On 12th December 1907, upon the application of Edward Need-
ham Waters, an order *nisi* was granted by *Higgins* J. calling
upon the Registrar of Trade Marks to proceed with application
No. 3036 for registration of a trade mark, or, alternatively, to
give notice under or in pursuance of sec. 37 of the *Trade Marks
Act* 1905 in respect of the said application, or show cause why
such other order with regard to the said application be not made
as to the Full Court should seem fit.

From the affidavits it appeared that on 20th November 1906
one Downman Miles, agent for Fromy Rogee & Co., brandy

growers, of St. Jean d'Angely, Cognac, France, applied on behalf of that firm for the registration of a certain trade mark, and gave as his address for service, 369·Collins St., Melbourne.

H. C. OF A.
1908.
THE KING
v.
THE REGIS-
TRAR OF
TRADE
MARKS.

On 30th July 1907 the Registrar of Trade Marks wrote a letter to Downward Miles stating that the examiner had made a certain report, and that he (the Registrar) might have to refuse the application on the grounds forming the subject of the examiner's report.   The letter then continued :—" 3. Before taking such definite action, adverse to the applicant firm, I am prepared to hear you upon the matter.   4. Notification of your intention to be heard must be lodged at this office, on Form E, within 30 days from date of this letter."   This letter was addressed to " Downman Miles Esq., 369 Collins St., Melbourne," and was posted.

The letter, however, was not delivered, but was returned through the dead-letter office to the Registrar.

On 4th October 1907 a notification appeared in the Australian Official Journal of Trade Marks that the application No. 3036 had been abandoned.

On 17th October 1907 a letter was sent to the Registrar written on behalf of Downman Miles & Co., which was as follows :—

" Immediately after our return to Melbourne from Europe we called at the Trades Marks Office to inquire whether the registration of the above mark had been completed, to hear to our surprise that the application had been advertised abandoned.

" Whilst thanking you for your explanation of the circumstances which lead to this, we cannot, however, accept the responsibility for the irregularity which has unfortunately transpired for the reason that the Act specifically stipulates that the applicant must furnish you with an address.   This we obviously did, but we have not received any communications whatsoever from you on the subject, therefore our view is that having carried out our contract the matter should proceed.

" For your guidance we may mention that 369 Collins street has been our address since July 1906, and we constantly received letters addressed to Mr. Downman Miles, in substantiation of which we enclose a communication so addressed posted in Portsmouth on September 13th and received here by last mail.

H. C. OF A.
1908.

THE KING
v.
THE REGIS-
TRAR OF
TRADE
MARKS.

" The serious error of the postal authorities cannot surely be advanced as a plea for disposal of this important application.

" We quite understand that we can make a fresh application, which would not only be an injustice, but is most unsatisfactory to us, and we contend that we have not done anything to necessitate this, and as we have faultlessly observed the regulations we now apply to have the original application reinstated."

The Registrar, however, decided that he was bound by regulation 28 of the *Trade Marks Regulations* 1906 to hold that the application had been abandoned.

Schutt, for the prosecutor. The notice which was sent by the Registrar was never received by the applicant within the meaning of regulation 28, and therefore there was no default and no abandonment within that regulation. Although the notice may have been properly given or served under secs. 106 and 107 of the *Trade Marks Act* 1905, regulation 28 contemplates an actual receipt by the applicant. The Registrar should therefore have proceeded with the application and then should either have accepted or refused it. See sec. 33 (3). The provision in regulation 28 as to abandonment is *ultra vires*. It is not authorized by sec. 94 of the Act, and is inconsistent with sec. 37, under which abandonment cannot be assumed to have taken place until twelve months after the application.

[He referred to *Jackson & Co.* v. *Napper*; *In re Schmidt's Trade Mark* (1); *Kerly on Trade Marks*, 2nd ed., p. 76 ; *Sebastian on Trade Marks*, 4th ed., p. 330.]

McArthur, for the defendant. Regulation 28 is not *ultra vires*. It is a provision which is necessary and convenient for giving effect to the Act within the meaning of sec. 94. Sec. 37 does not apply to a case of this kind. It contemplates that everything has been done which is necessary for registration except some act on the part of the applicant, for doing which fourteen days will be ample time, and which having been done registration will follow as a matter of course. Sec. 41 is another case in which abandonment is to be presumed.

(1) 35 Ch. D., 162.

[HIGGINS J. referred to *James* v. *Stevenson* (1) as showing that abandonment is a question of intention.

GRIFFITH C.J.—Under sec. 105 the Registrar can extend the time for replying to the notice.]

Schutt in reply.

Cur. adv. vult.

H. C. OF A.
1908.

THE KING
v.
THE REGIS-
TRAR OF
TRADE
MARKS.

March 27.

GRIFFITH C.J. This is a rule *nisi* for a mandamus to the Registrar of Trade Marks to command him to proceed with application No. 3036 for the registration of a trade mark, or, alternatively, to give notice under sec. 37 of the *Trade Marks Act* 1905 in respect of that application.   An application was made for the registration of the trade mark.   The Registrar applied to the applicant for certain information, but did not get it, and after the lapse of fourteen days he treated the application as abandoned. Then, nearly a year after the application was made, the Registrar was asked to proceed upon it, but he regarded himself as precluded by the regulations from doing so.

The *Trade Marks Act* 1905 makes general provisions as to the mode of dealing with applications for trade marks. By sec. 33 (3) it is provided that :—" Subject to this Act the Registrar may either accept the application, with or without modifications or conditions, or refuse it."   I take that to mean that he must do one or other of the two things, and may do either.   An appeal lies from the Registrar to the law officer and to the Court. Sec. 37 provides that :—" If, by reason of default on the part of the applicant, the registration of a trade mark has not been com-pleted within twelve months from the date of the lodging of the application, the Registrar shall give notice of the non-completion to the applicant, and if, at the expiration of fourteen days from that notice or such further time as the Registrar in special cases permits, the registration is not completed, the application shall be deemed to be abandoned."   If the application is accepted it is required to be advertised for three months, during which time notice of opposition may be lodged, and, if there is opposition, further steps may be taken, so that the whole process of obtaining

(1) (1893) A.C., 162.

H. C. of A.
1908.

THE KING
v.
THE REGIS-
TRAR OF
TRADE
MARKS.

Griffith C.J.

the registration of a trade mark must occupy a period more than three months after acceptance of the application.

Sec. 94 authorizes the Governor-General to make regulations prescribing all matters " which are necessary or convenient to be prescribed for giving effect to this Act or for the conduct of any business relating to the Trade Marks Office."

Now, it is an incident of every application for the grant of a privilege, just as it is of the prosecution of every enterprise, that the person making the application or prosecuting the enterprise may abandon it if he does not think it worth his while to go on. In all Courts provision is made for bringing proceedings to an end if the plaintiff or petitioner does not prosecute them with diligence. In the case of an office like the Trade Marks Office or the Patents Office, where a great deal of business is transacted, it is certainly at least convenient that there should be some provision whereby it may be known whether applicants intend to go on with their applications, so that the office may not be encumbered by an accumulation of applications with which there is no intention to proceed.

In professed exercise of the powers conferred by sec. 94, regulations were made on 28th December 1906, of which I will read regulations 27, 28, and 29 :—

" 27. If the Registrar is of opinion that the trade mark is not in compliance with the Act or that some bar to its registration exists he shall give notice thereof to the applicant. The notice shall state the grounds of the Registrar's opinion and shall inform the applicant that he is entitled to be heard personally or by his agent before the Registrar deals with the application.

" 28. Within fourteen days from the receipt of the notice or such further time as is fixed by the notice, the applicant shall notify to the Registrar whether or not he desires to be heard upon the matter, and in default of his doing so the application shall be deemed to be abandoned.

" 29. If the applicant notifies the Registrar that he desires to be heard the Registrar shall fix a time for the hearing, and shall give to the applicant not less than ten days' notice of the time so fixed, and if the applicant fails to appear personally, or by his

agent, at the time fixed for the hearing, the application shall be deemed to be abandoned."

H. C. of A
1906.

THE KING
v.
THE REGIS-
TRAR OF
TRADE
MARKS.

Griffith C.J.

These regulations on their face are in accordance with the usual method of regulating proceedings to be taken before a tribunal or person entrusted with discretionary powers, viz., that, if the person invoking action fails, when called upon, to take some necessary steps within a reasonable time, his case shall be treated as at an end.

It is contended that these regulations are *ultra vires.* I confess I have some difficulty in following the argument. The main point urged is that they are inconsistent with sec. 37, which I have already read. But the fact that an application is to be deemed to be abandoned at the end of twelve months does not prevent the applicant from abandoning it sooner. Moreover, sec. 37 appears to me to have been enacted *alio intuitu.* I doubt whether it applies at all to such a default as that in the present case. It seems to contemplate that the default is such that it is still possible for the registration to be completed within 14 days, which is impossible if the application is not yet accepted. Nor is there any inconsistency. Sec. 37 does not contain negative words. It provides for a particular contingency. I can see no inconsistency between that section and the regulations I have read. I think therefore that the regulations are *intra vires.*

What actually happened was this. The Registrar gave notice to the applicant under regulation 27, informing him that he was entitled to be heard personally or by his agent. Owing to circumstances to which it is not necessary to refer in detail the applicant did not receive that notice, and consequently took no action, and at the expiration of the time mentioned the Registrar conceived that he was bound to act under regulation 28, and accordingly published in the Journal of Trade Marks a notice that the application had been abandoned. When this came to the knowledge of the applicant, he asked the Registrar, in substance, to revive the matter. The Registrar answered that there was no provision in the Act or regulations providing for such a contingency, that is, the non-receipt of the notice by the applicant, being taken into consideration in the case of an application abandoned under regulation 28. He thought that he had no power to

H. C. of A.
1908.

THE KING
v.
THE REGIS-
TRAR OF
TRADE
MARKS.

Griffith C.J.

reinstate the application. Apparently he lost sight of the provisions of sec. 105, which provides that:—"Where by this Act
any time is specified within which any act or thing is to be done,
the Registrar may, unless otherwise expressly provided, extend
the time either before or after its expiration." It was therefore
competent for the Registrar, if satisfied that the failure to answer
the notice had arisen from circumstances for which the applicant
might be excused, and which were such as to show that he had
not really abandoned his application, to allow an extension of the
time to answer the notice and then to proceed with the matter
in the ordinary way. In my opinion the Registrar was bound to
exercise his discretion as to granting such an extension. It is
not necessary to express any opinion on the question whether he
ought to have extended the time, since Mr. *McArthur* has stated
on behalf of the Registrar that he will do so.

The order should be made absolute for a mandamus directing
the Registrar to entertain and determine the application by the
applicant that the application No. 3036 may be reinstated and
proceeded with, and that for that purpose the time for answering
the notice may be extended.

O'CONNOR J. The Registrar has declined to further entertain
this application on the ground that the applicant is in default
under regulation 28. That regulation provides that, if within
fourteen days from the receipt of a notice under regulation 27,
the applicant does not notify the Registrar whether he desires to
be heard or not, the application shall be deemed to be abandoned.
It is quite evident that in fact the applicant never received that
notice under regulation 27. It is also clear that he never had
any intention of abandoning his application. But the Registrar,
thinking himself constrained to hold, as a matter of law, that
under regulation 28 there had been a receipt of the notice under
regulation 27 and an abandonment of the application under
regulation 28, declined to entertain an application for any purpose
whatsoever. On that refusal the applicant has come to this Court
to obtain a mandamus commanding the Registrar to discharge
whatever may be his legal duty as to the application.

The first question is whether regulation 28 is or is not *ultra*

vires. I have no doubt at all that it is within the powers
conferred by the Act. Sec. 94 enables the Governor-General to
make regulations not inconsistent with the Act in respect of all
matters necessary or convenient to be prescribed for giving effect
to the Act. Having regard to the nature of the work to be done
under the Act, it is essential that the business of the Registrar's
office should be carried out on some system, and that applications filed should be dealt with in accordance with some regular
order of procedure. Above all things it is necessary that the
administration of the office should not be choked by a number of
pending applications in regard to which the Registrar is uncertain whether they are going on to completion or not. I agree
with the learned Chief Justice that the right of making an application involves the right to abandon it, and it equally follows
that abandonment may be evidenced in other ways than by a
statement of the applicant himself. He may show by his conduct
that he has abandoned his application, and a regulation, which
enables the Department to ascertain whether a man has acted
in such a way as to reasonably lead to the inference that he has
abandoned his application, is certainly necessary and convenient
for the administration of the Act.

But it is said that the regulation is *ultra vires* because it is
inconsistent with the Act. The Act provides in three instances
for abandonment on failure to comply with certain provisions.
One of them is in sec. 37, to which I shall refer later. The others
are in secs. 41 and 46. Sec. 41 (2) provides that, if the applicant
fails to lodge a counter-statement to a statement made in opposition within a certain time, he shall be deemed to have abandoned his application. Sec. 46 provides that an order may be
made in certain circumstances for security for costs by a person
giving notice of opposition or appeal and that, if that order is not
complied with, the opposition or appeal shall be deemed to be
abandoned. It is said that the only circumstances in which
abandonment can be inferred are those thus expressly mentioned
in these sections and those set out in sec. 37. I am of opinion
that that is not so. None of the sections referred to in any way
hamper the Governor-General in making regulations for the convenient administration of the Act. There is nothing in secs. 41

H. C. of A.
1908.

THE KING
v.
THE REGIS-
TRAR OF
TRADE
MARKS.

O'Connor J.

H. C. of A.
1908.

The King
v.
The Regis-
trar of
Trade
Marks.

O'Connor J.

and 46 inconsistent with regulation 28.   But it is said that that regulation is inconsistent with sec. 37.   I take the object of that section to be the prevention of undue delay from any cause in the prosecution of an application.   It is assumed in sec. 37 that, within twelve months from the date of the application, the registration of the trade mark ought to be completed, and the section empowers the Registrar at any time to give notice of noncompletion, whether there has been failure to comply with any other provision of the Act or not.   He is thus empowered to look into the position of every trade mark application which may not be completed within twelve months, and, if he finds that it has not been completed by reason of some default of the applicant, he may give the notice.   That is quite a different thing from regulation 28, which is simply a provision of procedure.   I am, therefore, of opinion that regulation 28, being merely a regulation of procedure in a matter which is necessary and convenient for carrying out the Act, is not inconsistent with any provision of the Act, and is *intra vires*.

The other question of law, that is to say, whether there has been a receipt of the notice, it is not necessary to consider, because I agree with the learned Chief Justice that the Registrar had power under sec. 105, if he had applied his mind to that particular view of the matter, to extend the time for making this application.   In other words, the Registrar might have exercised his power of reviving the application.   He evidently was of opinion that he had not the power, and I think the mandamus ought to go directing him to consider whether the application ought or ought not to be revived.   I therefore think that the mandamus should go in the terms stated by the learned Chief Justice.

Isaacs J. read the following judgment.   I agree with the order proposed by the learned Chief Justice.   In my opinion, regulation 28 is within the powers conferred by sec. 94. Having regard to the vast territory operated upon by the Act, and the desirability of clearing the ground of futile applications so as to enable substantial applications to be promptly dealt with, I have no doubt that the regulation is one which, in the words

H. C. of A.
1908.

THE KING
v.
THE REGIS-
TRAR OF
TRADE
MARKS.

Isaacs J.

of sec. 94, is "necessary or convenient to be prescribed
. . . . . for the conduct of any business relating to the
Trade Marks Office." It takes away no right of the applicant,
it does not prevent him being heard if he chooses; it merely
operates so as to enable him to indicate by silence and without
expense that he does not intend to persevere in an application,
which the Registrar thinks should fail, for reasons furnished
to the applicant. If, notwithstanding those reasons, he desires
to proceed, he has only to say so; then by regulation 29 he
is to be fully heard. His silence in the circumstances amounts
to an intimation that he does not desire to proceed, in other
words, that he desires to yield to the objections, and abandon
his application. He cannot, therefore, as I conceive, be heard
to complain if his application is thenceforth treated as abandoned.
The Act expressly enacts that in some other circumstances an
application is to be deemed abandoned, but that is quite
consistent with an abandonment by the assent, express or
implied, of the applicant himself. The regulation, therefore, is
perfectly valid. Whether it was complied with here is a question
of fact depending on the peculiar circumstances of this case, and
in view of the order agreed to is a matter unnecessary now to
determine.

HIGGINS J. read the following judgment. I concur with the
order proposed to be made, on the assumption that regulation 28
is valid. The distance of the applicants from the registry, the
absence from Australia of their agent, and the mistake of the
postman in not leaving the Registrar's letters at the Melbourne
address, are circumstances to which the Registrar may attach
importance in exercising his discretion as to extending time under
sec. 105 of the Act; and the Registrar has not yet exercised his
discretion.

But it is my duty to say that I am by no means satisfied of
the validity of Regulation 28. Briefly, I regard secs. 32-34 as
giving each applicant a right to a decision from the Registrar—
either acceptance (absolute or conditional), or refusal; and also a
right of appeal to the law officer or the Court if there be a refusal
or only a conditional acceptance. The regulation cannot take

H. C. of A.
1908.

THE KING
v.
THE REGIS-
TRAR OF
TRADE
MARKS.

Higgins J.

away these rights: the regulations must be "not inconsistent with the Act" (sec. 94). The Act itself, indeed, makes an exception to these rights in the case of twelve months elapsing before registration by reason of default of the applicant. After that period the Registrar can give notice to the applicant, and if within fourteen days (or some longer time) the registration is not completed, the "application shall be deemed to be abandoned." But under regulation 28 the Registrar may give a notice on the very day that the application is lodged; and unless the applicant notify to the Registrar within fourteen days from receipt of the notice that he desires to be heard, "the application shall be deemed to be abandoned." The regulation, in effect, makes sec. 37 superfluous; it strikes out the condition that twelve months must elapse before notice. I assume that an applicant may voluntarily abandon his application at any time; but the abandonment must be his abandonment, an abandonment in fact, an intentional abandonment—however evidenced, by words or by conduct—even by silence. "Abandonment" is a question of intention: see *James v. Stevenson* (1); and I cannot, I confess, see how the regulation making power can foist upon the applicant an intention which he never entertained, to declare an application abandoned which has not been abandoned in fact, and thereby enable the Registrar to avoid giving his decision, and to avoid an appeal. The fact that a regulation is "necessary or convenient to be prescribed" does not settle its validity. It may be convenient for the Registrar to get rid of an application on the expiration of fourteen days from the lodging of the application by sending a notice to the applicant, even if he is in France. But the Governor in Council has no right to make the applicant's silence for fourteen days conclusive evidence of abandonment. Whichever view of the regulation is correct, I am glad to see that the order proposed is likely to do substantial justice in this present case.

> Order absolute for mandamus to the
> Registrar to determine an application
> by the prosecutor that application
> No. 3036 may be reinstated and pro-

(1) (1893) A.C., 162.

ceeded with, and that for that purpose the time for notifying to the Registrar his desire to be heard upon the matter of the Registrar's notice of 30th July 1907 may be extended.

Solicitors, for the prosecutor, *Waters & Crespin.*

Solicitor, for defendant, *Charles Powers,* Commonwealth Crown Solicitor.

B. L.

H. C. of A.
1908.

THE KING
v.
THE REGIS-
TRAR OF
TRADE
MARKS.

THE AUSTRALIAN MUTUAL PROVIDENT } APPELLANTS;
SOCIETY AND OTHERS . . .
DEFENDANTS,

AND

ARTHUR JAMES GREGORY AND OTHERS. RESPONDENTS.
PLAINTIFFS AND DEFENDANTS,

ON APPEAL FROM THE SUPREME COURT OF
TASMANIA.

Private international law—Distinction between immoveables and moveables— Incorporeal right with respect to immoveable—Interest in trust estate—Trust to sell—Insolvency—Notice to trustees—Effect of foreign insolvency—Subsequent assignment—Priorities—Bankruptcy Act 1870 (Tas.) (34 Vict. No. 32), sec. 16 —Law No. 47 of 1887 (Natal), secs. 51, 52, 53.

A right enforceable with respect to an immoveable is, for the purposes of private international law, an immoveable.

A person claiming in Tasmania under an assignment of an equitable chose in action executed by a bankrupt after sequestration, who took his assignment without notice of the bankruptcy and has given notice of his assignment to the trustee of the property to which the chose in action attached, is entitled to priority over the trustee in bankruptcy who has not given notice.

H. C. of A.
1908.

HOBART,
Feb. 19, 20,
21.

MELBOURNE,
March 23.

Griffith C.J.,
Barton and
Isaacs JJ.

The recognition offered by the rules of private international law to an assignment to creditors of the moveables of a debtor under the law of a foreign country extends only to recognizing it as having the same validity as an assignment made in accordance with the laws of the situs of the moveables.

A testator by his will devised land in Tasmania to trustees to pay his widow out of the income a certain annuity, and to pay the residue of the income to his sons in equal shares, and he directed that upon the death of his widow the trustees should sell the land (with a discretionary power to postpone the sale for seven years) and divide the proceeds equally among the sons. One of the sons having gone to the Colony of Natal, in South Africa, before the death of his mother, became insolvent there, and according to the law of Natal his trustee in insolvency would have priority over subsequent incumbrancers of the insolvent's choses in action without the necessity of giving notice. The insolvent, having returned to Tasmania, executed an assignment of his interest in his father's estate to an assignee who had no notice of the insolvency and who gave notice to the trustee of the property.

Held, that from the date of the testator's death until the date of the sale of the land the interest of each son was an immoveable within the principle of private international law, and therefore that the insolvency in Natal did not operate in Tasmania as an assignment of the insolvent's interest in his father's estate.

Held, further, that even if the insolvent's interest were a moveable, the assignee in Tasmania had priority over the Natal trustee in insolvency.

Decision of the Supreme Court reversed.

APPEAL from the Supreme Court of Tasmania.

By his will, dated 23rd July 1900, and two codicils dated respectively 19th November 1903 and 31st December 1903, James Gregory of Queenborough in Tasmania, who died on 7th January 1904, gave, devised and bequeathed all his property real and personal to his trustees, his two sons Arthur James Gregory and Frank Gregory, upon trust to pay to his wife an annuity of £200, the payment of which he charged upon all his real estate, except a certain property at Parattah, with a direction not to sell such real estate during the life of his wife. Subject to the payment of such annuity he directed the trustees to pay and divide the net rents and profits of such real estate equally amongst his eight named children, including George William Gregory, described in the will as " of South Africa," and the widow of a deceased son, for their own several and respective use and benefit. The second

H. C. or A.
1908.

AUSTRALIAN
MUTUAL
PROVIDENT
SOCIETY
v.
GREGORY.

codicil contained the following clause :—" And I declare that my trustees shall upon the decease of my said wife sell all my real estate (excepting my said property at Parattah) by public auction or private contract and with power to postpone the sale for not exceeding seven years after my wife's decease and to sell at their discretion   And after payment of all expenses to stand possessed of the net proceeds upon trust to pay and divide the same equally between and amongst my said eight children and my said daughter-in-law Harriet Gregory for their own absolute use as tenants in common." Probate was granted on 23rd January 1904 to Arthur James Gregory, reserving the right of Frank Gregory to come in and prove.

The testator's son George William Gregory was on 21st June 1904 adjudicated insolvent by the Supreme Court of the Colony of Natal, in South Africa, and Thomas Herbert Green of Durban in South Africa was duly appointed trustee of the insolvent estate.   Shortly afterwards George William Gregory returned to Tasmania, and on 17th February 1905 he assigned his interest under his father's will to the Australian Mutual Provident Society to secure the payment of certain advances, and on the same day notice of the assignment was given to the trustees of the will. Other assignments of his interest were made to other persons, among them to Frederick Henry Crisp and Frederick Rolfe Stops, to secure advances by them, and notice of all of the assignments were given to the trustees. All the notices except one were given before the death of the testator's widow, that one being given on 4th November 1905. Mary Ann Gregory, widow of the testator, died on 16th October 1905.   On 6th November 1905 the trustees of the will received notice of the insolvency in Natal of George William Gregory.

On the 10th March 1906 an originating summons was taken out on behalf of the trustees of the will to obtain the opinion of the Supreme Court of Tasmania on the following questions (*inter alia*):—

1. Is the trustee of the insolvent estate of George William Gregory, one of the beneficiaries of the will of the said James Gregory, entitled to the one-ninth share of the said George William Gregory or any portion thereof and, if so, what portion ?

2. Will the claim of the trustee in insolvency be postponed to
bonâ fide mortgagees of the share of the said George William
Gregory, notices of which mortgages were given to the trustees
prior to notices of insolvency having reached them ?

5. To whom and in what proportions will the trustees of the
will of the said James Gregory deceased be justified in handing
over an equal one-ninth part of a certain sum of £2,860 12s. 3d.
representing the net proceeds of a sale of portion of the real
estate of the said James Gregory deceased and also all future net
proceeds arising from the sale of the real estate of the said James
Gregory deceased? How the costs of and incidental to this
application are to be provided for ?

The matter having been referred to the Full Court, that Court
held that the title of the Natal trustee in insolvency prevailed
over the titles of the several mortgagees, and ordered that the
share of George William Gregory in the capital moneys and
annual income should be paid to T. H. Green, and that the costs
of all parties other than T. H. Green should be paid out of that
share.

From this judgment the Australian Mutual Provident Society,
Frederick Henry Crisp and Frederick Rolfe Stops appealed to
the High Court.

Bavin, for the appellants the Australian Mutual Provident
Society. In the case of a person made bankrupt under the
Tasmanian *Bankruptcy Act* 1870, which in this respect follows
the English *Bankruptcy Act* 1869, it is necessary for the trustee
in bankruptcy to give notice of the bankruptcy to a trustee who
holds a fund in trust for the insolvent in order to perfect his
title and give him priority over a subsequent encumbrancer who
has given notice: *Palmer* v. *Locke* (1); *In re Barr's Trusts* (2);
In re Atkinson (3); *In re Jakeman's Trusts* (4); *Mercer* v.
Vans Colina (5); *In re Stone's Will* (6); *Lloyd* v. *Banks* (7); *In
re London and Provincial Telegraph Co.*(8); *In re Beall; Ex parte*

(1) 18 Ch. D., 381.
(2) 4 K. & J., 219.
(3) 2 D.M. & G., 140.
(4) 23 Ch. D., 344.

(5) (1900) 1 Q.B., 130 (n).
(6) (1893) W.N., 50.
(7) L.R. 3 Ch., 488.
(8) L.R. 9 Eq., 653.

H. C. OF A.
1908.

AUSTRALIAN
MUTUAL
PROVIDENT
SOCIETY
v.
GREGORY.

Official Receiver (1); *Wace on Bankruptcy*, p. 260; *Ryall* v. *Rowles* (2); *Dearle* v. *Hall* (3).

[ISAACS J. referred to *Jameson & Co.* v. *Brick and Stone Co.* (4); *In re Lake; Ex parte Cavendish* (5); *Montefiore* v. *Guedalla* (6).] Under Law No. 47 of 1887 (Natal), secs. 51, 52, 53, which is similar in this respect to the English *Bankruptcy Act* 1849, sec. 141, no such notice is necessary : *In re Bright's Settlement* (7). But a foreign trustee in insolvency has no higher right in Tasmania than a trustee under a Tasmanian bankruptcy, and, whether the interest of this insolvent under the will is a moveable or an immoveable, the Natal trustee must perfect his title according to the law of Tasmania, and priorities will be adjusted according to that law. In *Ex parte Rogers ; In re Boustead* (8) it was said that the Imperial *Bankruptcy Act* 1869 only passed immoveables in a Colony according to the law of the Colony. See also *Cullender, Sykes & Co.* v. *Colonial Secretary of Lagos* (9); *Dicey's Conflict of Laws*, p. 334; *Westlake's Private International Law*, 4th ed., p. 165. There is no reason for any distinction in this respect between moveables and immoveables : *Story's Conflict of Laws*, 8th ed., p. 766. The law of the State where moveables are as to perfecting title must be observed : *Dulaney* v. *Merry & Son* (10); *In re Queensland Mercantile and Agency Co.; Ex parte Australasian Investment Co.; Ex parte Union Bank of Australia* (11); *Kelly* v. *Selwyn* (12); *Foote's Private International Jurisprudence*, 3rd ed., p. 327; *Westlake's Private International Law*, 4th ed., p. 404 ; *Jeffery* v. *M'Taggart* (13).

[Counsel also referred to *Story's Conflict of Laws*, 8th ed., p. 456; *Harrison* v. *Sterry* (14); *Sill* v. *Worswick* (15); *Westlake's Private International Law*, 4th ed., p. 173.]

Nicholls, for the appellants F. H. Crisp and F. R. Stops. The interest of the insolvent in his father's estate is an immoveable,

(1) (1899) 1 Q.B., 688.
(2) 2 Wh. & T. L.C., 6th ed., 799, at p. 853.
(3) 3 Russ., 1.
(4) 4 Q.B.D., 208.
(5) (1903) 1 K.B., 151.
(6) (1903) 2 Ch., 26.
(7) 13 Ch. D., 413.
(8) 16 Ch. D., 665.

(9) (1891) A.C., 460.
(10) (1901) 1 K.B., 536.
(11) (1891) 1 Ch., 536 ; (1892) 1 Ch., 219.
(12) (1905) 2 Ch., 117.
(13) 6 M. & S., 126.
(14) 5 Cranch., 289.
. (15) 1 H. Bl., 665, at p. 691.

and, if so, there is no doubt that the Tasmanian law applies. That interest, although it may not be an estate in land, is an interest in land. It arises out of the land and carries with it the right of the insolvent to have the land sold, and may be lost if the land is lost. The fact that the land is for certain purposes, e.g., succession and taxation, deemed to have been converted does not change the interest of the insolvent from an immoveable into a moveable. The doctrine of notional conversion does not apply to private international law: *Westlake's Private International Law*, 4th ed., p. 203 ; *Dicey's Conflict of Laws*, pp. 312, 72, 73. Until the land is actually sold the interest remains an immoveable: *In re Piercy* ; *Whitwham v. Piercy* (1). The insolvent's interest is a chattel real, just as is a leasehold interest in land, and is governed by the *lex loci*: *Freke v. Lord Carbery* (2); *Duncan v. Lawson* (3) ; *Foote's International Jurisprudence*, 3rd ed., pp. 202, 213, 308. See also *Pepin v. Bruyère* (4); *In the Goods of Gentili* (5); *de Fogassieras v. Duport* (6).

There was no privity between Green and the trustees of the testator's estate so as to give a Court of Equity jurisdiction.

[ISAACS J. referred to *British South Africa Co. v. Companhia de Moçambique* (7); *Lewin on Trusts*, 11th ed., p. 48.]

Butler, for the respondents the trustees of the estate of James Gregory.

Lodge, for the respondent T. H. Green. The interest of the insolvent is a moveable. It is in its essence money and nothing else in the eye of the law of Tasmania, according to which the nature of the interest must be decided: *Viner v. Vaughan* (8); *Foote's Private International Jurisprudence*, 3rd ed., p. 238. The interest was intended to be divorced from the land. All that the insolvent has is a right to a definite share of the proceeds of the sale of the land. The only class of property included in personalty which is not included in moveables is chattels real. The doctrine of equitable or notional conversion applies. That is a

(1) (1895) 1 Ch., 83.
(2) L.R. 16 Eq., 461.
(3) 41 Ch. D., 394.
(4) (1900) 2 Ch., 504 ; (1902) 1 Ch., 24.

(5) Ir. R., 9 Eq., 541.
(6) 11 L.R. Ir., 123.
(7) (1893) A.C., 602, at p. 626.
(8) 2 Beav., 466.

doctrine which is known to other countries than the British Dominions and is a fit doctrine to be applied in international law : *Buchanan* v. *Angus* (1).

[GRIFFITH C.J.—Before the *Judicature Act* it was held that the doctrine of equitable conversion would not give the Court jurisdiction over a will limited to real property : *In the Goods of Barden* (2).]

So far as the trustees of the estate are concerned the land remains realty, but the insolvent's interest in it is for the purposes of succession and assignment personalty. If the insolvent were domiciled abroad the interest would pass according to the law of his domicil. The appellants themselves treat it as personalty for the purpose of their title to it. The equitable conversion operates from the death of the testator : *Clarke* v. *Franklin* (3), but only as to so much of the land as is afterwards sold : *Fitzgerald* v. *Jervoise* (4); *Stead* v. *Newdigate* (5). The only kind of personalty which is immoveable is chattels real, and the insolvent's interest in this estate is not a chattel real. See *Dicey's Conflict of Laws*, pp. 73, 514.

[ISAACS J.—A partner's interest in land of the partnership appears to be personalty : *Attorney-General* v. *Hubbuck* (6); *Attorney-General* v. *Marquis of Ailesbury* (7).

GRIFFITH C.J. referred to *Chatfield* v. *Berchtoldt* (8).]

The passage in *Dicey's Conflict of Laws*, p. 312, only means that in the hands of the trustee the interest is an immoveable. If it means more, the authorities there cited do not support it. See *Forbes* v. *Steven* (9); *In the Goods of Gunn* (10).

[GRIFFITH C.J.—Apart from municipal law, is not this interest an incumbrance upon the land just as a real charge is ?]

No. The trustee could give a good legal and beneficial title to the land without the intervention of the beneficiaries. What the insolvent is entitled to is a debt: *Lord Sudeley* v. *Attorney-General* (11). The equitabe conversion enured to the benefit of

H. C. OF A.
1908.

AUSTRALIAN
MUTUAL
PROVIDENT
SOCIETY
v.
GREGORY.

(1) 4 MacQ. H.L. Cas., 374.
(2) L.R. 1 P. & M., 325.
(3) 4 Kay & J., 257.
(4) 5 Madd., 25.
(5) 2 Mer., 521.
(6) 13 Q.B.D., 275.
(7) 16 Q.B.D., 408.
(8) L.R. 7 Ch., 192.
(9) L.R. 10 Eq., 178.
(10) 9 P.D., 242.
(11) (1897) A.C., 11.

H. C. of A.   the insolvent while he was in South Africa.   Why should it not
1908.   enure to the benefit of his trustee in insolvency there?

AUSTRALIAN   [GRIFFITH C.J.—Can a trust of land be administered anywhere
MUTUAL   else than in the country where the land is?]
PROVIDENT
SOCIETY   The answer to that question does not affect the nature of the
v.   beneficiaries' interests in the land.
GREGORY.
              [ISAACS J. referred to *In re De Nicols*; *De Nicols* v. *Curlier*
        (1); *Gray* v. *Smith* (2).]

          Assuming this interest to be a moveable, then on the authority
        of *Palmer* v. *Locke* (3), the necessity under the Tasmanian law
        for notice to the trustee of the estate by a Tasmanian trustee in
        insolvency is not disputed.

          [ISAACS J. referred to *In re Brown's Trust* (4); *Ex parte Agra
        Bank*; *In re Worcester* (5); *Sturt* v. *Cockerell* (6).]

          But the question of assignability must in this case be
        determined according to the law of Natal.   This was a moveable
        in Natal which passed to the trustee by virtue of the Natal law,
        and, if it so passed, the Tasmanian Courts will recognize the
        assignment with all the incidents of the law of Natal, and if it
        appears that something happened in Natal which destroyed for
        ever the right of the insolvent to deal with this property, the
        Tasmanian Courts will recognize that provision of the Natal law.
        See *Selkrig* v. *Davis* (7); *McEntire* v. *Potter & Co.* (8); *In re
        Coombe* (9); *Thompson* v. *Bell* (10).

          Nicholls, in reply, referred to *Foote's Private International
        Jurisprudence*, 3rd ed., p. 298; *Dicey's Conflict of Laws*, pp. 781,
        789 (n1); *In re Stokes*; *Stokes* v. *Ducroz* (11); *In re Davidson's
        Settlement Trusts* (12).

                                                   Cur. adv. vult.

          The following judgments were read:—

March 23.   GRIFFITH C.J.   James Gregory by his will and codicil devised
        land in Tasmania to trustees to pay to his widow out of the
        income an annuity of £200, and to pay the residue of the income

(1) (1900) 2 Ch., 410.   (7) 2 Rose, 291, at p. 315.
(2) 43 Ch. D., 208.   (8) 22 Q.B.D., 438.
(3) 18 Ch. D., 381.   (9) 1 Giff., 91.
(4) L.R., 5 Eq., 88.   (10) 23 L.J.Q.B., 159.
(5) L.R., 3 Ch., 555.   (11) 62 L.T., 176.
(6) L.R. 8 Eq., 607.   (12) L.R., 15 Eq., 383.

to his eight sons and the widow of a son in equal shares. The
testator directed that upon the death of his widow the trustees
should sell the land (with a discretionary power to postpone the
sale for seven years), and divide the proceeds equally among the
same nine persons, of whom G. W. Gregory was one.

The testator died on 7th January 1904. It is not in controversy
that G. W. Gregory's interest in the proceeds of the land so
directed to be sold became a vested interest at the testator's death,
or that by the municipal law of Tasmania that interest was for
the purpose of succession to be regarded as personalty. It was
further contended that the notional conversion took effect from
the testator's death.

On 21st June 1904 G. W. Gregory's estate was placed under
sequestration by the Supreme Court of the British Colony of
Natal upon his own petition, and the respondent Green was
appointed trustee of his estate. The insolvent subsequently
returned to Tasmania, and executed successive assignments of his
interest under the testator's will to the appellants and other
persons for valuable consideration, the first being dated 17th
February 1905, and the others being all antecedent in date to the
death of the widow, which occurred on 16th October 1905.
Notice of all these assignments was duly given to the trustees of
the will before that date. On 6th November 1905 Green gave
them notice that he claimed the interest by virtue of the
sequestration. The jurisdiction of the Supreme Court of Natal
to make the order of sequestration was not disputed.

Both parties appealed to the recognized rule of private international law that the assignment of a bankrupt's property to the
representatives of his creditors under the law of a foreign country
which has jurisdiction over the bankrupt's person operates as an
assignment of the moveables of the bankrupt wherever locally
situated, but not of his immoveables: *Dicey*, Rules 107, 108;
Westlake, secs. 134-140.

The rules of what is called international law are, after all,
only general principles which, by the comity of nations, are
adopted by civilized States as part of their own municipal law,
and effect is given to them, not as laws paramount, but as part

H. C. of A.
1908.

AUSTRALIAN
MUTUAL
PROVIDENT
SOCIETY
v.
GREGORY.

Griffith C.J.

H. C. of A.   of the municipal law.   The rule just stated is accepted as part of
1908.   the law of England and of Tasmania.

AUSTRALIAN   The appellants contend that G. W. Gregory's interest was an
MUTUAL
PROVIDENT   immoveable, the respondents that it was a moveable, within the
SOCIETY   meaning of this rule.   The appellants further contend that, even
v.
GREGORY.   if it was a moveable, notice to the trustees of the will was

Griffith C.J. necessary to complete the respondent Green's title as against the
              other assignees.   The Supreme Court decided in favour of that
              respondent on both points.

                  The distinction between moveables and immovables is
              primarily, as the words themselves denote, a distinction of fact.

                  It is generally possible by the use of the senses to say whether
              in rerum naturâ an object is moveable or immoveable.   This
              question of fact is not affected by the municipal laws of the place
              where the object is situated.   With advancing civilization there
              come into existence incorporeal rights of property with respect
              to both moveables and immoveables.   No one doubts that
              incorporeal rights with respect to moveables are themselves
              regarded as moveables.   And I am unable to see any reason why in
              the case of immoveables also the incorporeal right should not
              follow the character of the thing to which it is an accessory.
              The circumstance that the municipal law of a country thinks fit
              to treat some kinds of immoveable property as having for certain
              purposes some of the qualities or incidents of personal property
              seems to be quite irrelevant to this question of fact.   Thus, a
              leasehold estate in land is an immoveable, because the land is in
              fact immoveable, and the circumstance that English law regards
              such an estate as what it calls "personal property" does not alter
              the fact.   For the purposes of international law the fact, and not
              the epithet, is regarded : *Freke* v. *Lord Carbery* (1).   So a rent-
              charge, which is an incorporeal right accessory to land, is an
              immoveable, although some rent-charges are by the *Wills Act*
              treated for certain purposes as personal property : *Chatfield* v.
              Berchtoldt (2).   Some confusion has been caused in discussion on
              this point by reference to the analogous division of property into
              realty and personalty under English law.   The analogy no doubt
              exists, and, but for some positive rules of that law, might be

(1) L.R., 16 Eq., 461.   (2) L.R., 7 Ch., 192.

H. C. of A.
1908.

AUSTRALIAN
MUTUAL
PROVIDENT
SOCIETY
v.
GREGORY.

Griffith C.J.

complete. But it is a mistake to argue that, because the English technical distinctions between real and personal estate no longer depend entirely upon physical facts, the distinction between immoveables and moveables in the application of the rule of international law has been equally qualified. So far as I am aware, such a doctrine has never been suggested by any English judicial authority.

Law, as has often been pointed out, deals with rights and not with things. But, so far as regards property, the rights with which it deals are rights with respect to things, that is, physical objects capable of being apprehended by the senses. International law deals with things as they are, and not with words as they may chance to be defined in dictionaries of municipal law.

In my opinion the question whether a particular right is to be regarded as a moveable or an immoveable for the purposes of international law depends upon the nature of the thing with respect to which the right is asserted, and not upon the municipal law of the country in which it is locally situate.

No doubt the law may treat as an immoveable a thing which in its apparent form is moveable, if it is so closely connected with an immoveable as to be a mere accessory to it, as, for instance, in the case of title deeds. But this is not a real exception, for the deed, except so far as the material on which it is written is concerned, is a mere record of a right to a physical object.

What, then, was the subject matter of G. W. Gregory's interest at the date of sequestration ? Plainly the subject matter was land in Tasmania. Gregory's interest was a right (which could not be enforced for seven years) to have the trusts of the will administered and, for that purpose, to have the land sold. If authority were needed to support the proposition that this right could only be enforced in the country of the situs of the land, it is afforded by the cases of *Whitaker* v. *Forbes* (1), and *British South Africa Company* v. *Companhia de Moçambique* (2). In my judgment, this right followed the nature of the land to which it related, and was in law as well as in fact an interest in land (see per Lord *Cairns* L.C. in *Brook* v. *Badley* (3)), although

(1) 1 C.P.D., 51.   (2) (1893) A.C., 602.
          (3) L.R., 3 Ch., 672, at p 674.

for some municipal purposes treated as if it were personal property. It was therefore an immoveable. No authority, nor even an expression of opinion, was cited to us to the contrary effect. Mr. *Dicey*, indeed, treats this view as so obvious as not to require elucidation. Dealing with the term "personal property" as used in English municipal law, he says (page 312):—"Personal property includes land (immoveables) of two different descriptions. In the first place, it includes . . . chattel real. It includes, in the second place, land which, though not a chattel real, is by any rule of law treated as personalty, or, in other words, made subject to the incidents of personal property. Such, for example, is land which under a rule of equity is, as the expression goes, 'converted into personalty.'" In other words, land which under a rule of equity is deemed to be converted into money is, although included in the term personalty, an immoveable. No doubt, he says (page 72) that "'immoveables' are equivalent to realty, with the addition of chattels real or leaseholds; 'moveables' are equivalent to personalty, with the omission of chattels real." But that this general statement was not intended to contradict the other is shown by the passage on page 73:—"Immoveable property includes all rights over things which cannot be moved, whatever be the nature of such rights or interests."

In my opinion, therefore, the respondent Green never acquired any right to Gregory's interest by virtue of the sequestration. I will, however, proceed to deal with the second point, on the assumption that that interest was a moveable and not an immoveable. It appears to be accepted as the law of England that under the *Bankruptcy Act* of 1869, as well as the Act of 1883, the rule in *Dearle* v. *Hall* (1) applies to assignees in bankruptcy as well as to assignees under assignments by act of parties, so that a person claiming under an assignment of an equitable chose in action executed by a bankrupt after sequestration, who took his assignment without notice of the bankruptcy, and has given notice of it to the trustee of the property, is entitled to priority over the trustee in bankruptcy who has not given notice. The doubt suggested by Lord *Selborne* L.C. in *Palmer* v. *Locke* (2) seems not to have been regarded as

(1) 3 Russ., 1.   (2) 18 Ch D., 381.

diminishing the authority of the cases of *In re Barr's Trust* (1); and *In re Atkinson* (2):   See *In re Stone's Will* (3).   The law of Tasmania is in this respect the same as the law of England.   It is said, however, that by the law of Natal the rule is otherwise, and I will assume this to be so.   It was then contended that the law of Natal governs the case.   But I think it is clear in principle that the recognition afforded by the rules of private international law to an assignment to creditors under the law of a foreign country extends only to recognizing it as having the same validity as an assignment made in accordance with the laws of the situs of the moveable.   The law of one country can never have effect *per se* as law in another country.   Whatever effect it has is given it by the law of the country whose jurisdiction is invoked.   If that country for reasons of international comity gives effect to such a law, it is because it adopts the rule of the foreign law as part of its own law *quoad illud*.   No authority was cited to us to show that the provisions of a foreign law as to the perfecting of a title to local property have ever been so adopted.   The authorities, such as these are, all point the other way. *Dicey* (page 334) says:—" When, further, a bankruptcy in one country is an assignment of property situate in another, it passes the property subject, speaking generally, to any charge acquired thereon prior to the bankruptcy under the laws of the country where the property is situate, and subject also to the requirements, if any, of the local law as to the conditions necessary to effect a transfer of such property "; citing, amongst other authorities, the dictum of *Jessel* M.R. in *Ex parte Rogers* (4), and adding that this dictum applies apparently to moveable property as well as to immoveables.

Story (*Conflict of Laws*, sec. 550) says :—" Although moveables are for many purposes to be deemed to have no situs, except that of the domicil of the owner, yet this being but a legal fiction, it yields whenever it is necessary for the purpose of justice that the actual situs of the thing should be examined.   A nation within whose territory any personal property is actually situate has as entire dominion over it while therein, in point of sovereignty and

H. C. of A.
1908.

AUSTRALIAN
MUTUAL
PROVIDENT
SOCIETY
v.
GREGORY.

Griffith C.J.

(1) 4 K. & J., 219.
(2) 2 D. M. & G., 140.

(3) (1893) W.N., 50.
(4) 16 Ch. D., 665, at p. 666.

H. C. of A.
1908.

AUSTRALIAN
MUTUAL
PROVIDENT
SOCIETY
v.
GREGORY.

Griffith C.J.

jurisdiction, as it has over immoveable property situate there.
It may regulate its transfer, and subject it to process and
execution, and provide for and control the uses and disposition
of it, to the same extent that it may exert its authority over
immoveable property. One of the grounds upon which, as we
have seen, jurisdiction is assumed over non-residents, is through
the instrumentality of their personal property, as well as of their
real property, within the local sovereignty. Hence it is that,
whenever personal property is taken by arrest, attachment, or
execution within a State, the title so acquired under the laws of
the State is held valid in every other State; and the same rule is
applied to debts due to non-residents, which are subjected to the
like process under the local laws of a State."

The recent case of *Kelly* v. *Selwyn* (1) before *Warrington J.*
is to the same effect. The Supreme Court thought that the law
of Natal governed the case on this point. For the reasons I have
given I am unable to agree with them. I think, therefore, that in
either view of the nature of Gregory's interest the respondent
Green has failed to establish any title to it, and that the
appellants are entitled to succeed.

BARTON J. It is not disputed that if the interest which is the
subject of the assignments to the several appellants is an immoveable that conclusion is fatal to the claim of Mr Green, the
respondent trustee of the estate of G. W. Gregory under *The
Insolvency Act* of 1867, a law of Natal. See *Dicey's Conflict of
Laws*, Rules 107, 108.

In the exercise of international comity the Courts will apply
the maxim "*mobilia sequuntur personam*," in favour of the
trustee or assignee under a foreign bankruptcy or insolvency.
But nations in self-protection refrain from allowing foreign laws
either to accomplish or to regulate the transfer of land and other
immoveables within the domestic bounds. The Natal insolvency
is a foreign one in respect of its relation to the laws and the
Courts of Tasmania. For the purposes of the argument the
direction to the trustees of James Gregory, by his will, to sell the
realty within 7 years of the death of the widow, which happened

(1) (1905) 2 Ch., 117.

in October 1905, was taken to have operated as a conversion on and H. C. of A.
1908.
from the testator's death in January 1904, a few months before
the adjudication in Natal and the appointment of the respondent Australian
Green as trustee thereunder, and for the same purposes G. W. Mutual
Provident
Gregory was taken to have acquired domicil in Natal before his Society
insolvency. Was then G. W. Gregory's interest under the will, v.
Gregory.
the land having been, in equity, converted into personalty in Barton J.
January 1904, from that time a moveable or an immoveable ?

Under the head of "Interpretation of Terms," Mr. *Dicey*, in
his book already referred to, says, at p. 72 :—"The division of the
subjects of property into immoveables and moveables does not
square with the distinction known to English lawyers between
things real, or real property, and *things personal*, or personal
property. For though all things real are, with certain exceptions,
included under immoveables, yet some immoveables are not
included under things real; since chattels 'real,' or, speaking
generally, leaseholds, are included under immoveables, whilst
they do not, for most purposes, come within the class of realty,
or things real. On the other hand, while all moveables are with
certain exceptions included under things personal, or personalty,
there are things personal, viz., chattels real, or, speaking generally,
leaseholds, which are immoveables, and are in no way affected by
the rules hereafter laid down as to moveables. To put the same
thing in other words, 'immoveables' are equivalent to realty, with
the addition of chattels real or leaseholds; 'moveables' are
equivalent to personalty, with the omission of chattels real."

But this eminent jurist, later in the same book, expands his
view of the subjects of personal property included among
immoveables. At p. 312 he says :—" Personal property includes
land (immoveables) of two different descriptions. In the first
place, it includes land in which a person has less than a freehold
interest, e.g., a leasehold. . . . . . It includes, in the second
place, land which, though not a chattel real, is by any rule of law
treated as personalty, or, in other words, made subject to the
incidents of personal property. Such, for example, is land which
under a rule of equity is, as the expression goes, 'converted into
personalty,' as where freehold property is under a settlement
conveyed to trustees in trust to sell the same, and after the death

of A to stand possessed of the proceeds of the sale for the purposes of the trust."

If this is correct, the interest of G. W. Gregory under his father's will, which for the purpose of succession has become personal property, is nevertheless an immoveable. And it must be remembered that the author is speaking of immoveables in the character which, in the view of English jurists, they maintain as subjects of private international law. If that interest is an immoveable then the assignment of G. W. Gregory's property to the respondent Green, under the *Insolvency Act* of Natal, does not pass the interest to him, as that law does not affect an immoveable of the insolvent situate in Tasmania.

Then is the view taken by Mr. *Dicey* justified in law?

Let me put the question thus. In considering the effect of a foreign bankruptcy on property physically within the domestic bounds, that is, in applying the principles of private international law, does the law of England, which for this purpose is the law of Tasmania, keep in mind the substance of the thing, or the rules and methods which dictate its treatment for certain municipal purposes? I am of opinion that it is the substance alone that is to be considered. One may leave aside mere accessories, which follow the substance of necessity. Title deeds, for instance, must go with the land because without the former the right to the latter could not be proved, and the law will not give the property in the land to the owner, say, in Tasmania, and the property in the means of proof to another person, who may take them anywhere. But take the case of chattels real, or leasehold lands. They are personal property for all purposes of devolution. The physical possession, or the right to the possession of them, must be proved in order to sustain an action for trespass upon them. And no such action can be brought except in the country which includes them. So as to lands held in trust for conversion and deemed in equity to be personalty. The trustees must still defend the possession or the title when either is assailed, and no law of a foreign country can force them to defend anywhere but in the *locus rei sitæ*. But then, it is said, these considerations do not apply to a mere reversionary interest in the trust property directed to be sold. I think they

H. C. of A.
1908.

AUSTRALIAN
MUTUAL
PROVIDENT
SOCIETY
v.
GREGORY.

Barton J.

still apply, for whatever affects the right of the testator or the trustee to the unsold land, by consequence affects the right to receive the proceeds. As to the land itself, from the inception of the trust it is in equity merely money for the limited purposes of the trust, but only so far as those purposes extend. Apart from those purposes it remains land, and as an immoveable is in relation to international law governed by the doctrines applied by the *lex situs* in administering that law. Similar considerations have prevailed in the case of a rent-charge *pur autre vie* issuing out of English land, which was held liable to legacy duty as personal estate under the English Statutes, 14 Geo. II. c. 20, and 1 Vict. c. 26 : *Chatfield* v. *Berchtoldt* (1). These Statutes make estates *pur autre vie* applicable as personal estate in the hands of personal representatives. In the case just cited the testatrix was domiciled in Hungary, and it was argued that the English Statutes had so completely impressed the interest with the character of personalty, notwithstanding its original character of reality, that it was not liable to legacy duty because *mobilia sequuntur personam*. The decision (on appeal) was that it was only made personal property for the limited purpose of charging it with legacy duty, to which the Court held it liable, and that, apart from that purpose, it was English real estate, and subject to English law. Of this decision Mr. *Foote*, in his work on Private International Jurisprudence, 1st ed., p. 219, says:—"Had it been the law of the testator's domicil that assumed to declare English realty to be personal estate, the case would have been too clear for argument ; but in the actual circumstances the *lex situs* was given much stronger effect, being allowed to change the nature of realty into personalty for its own purposes, without exposing it as such to the law of the foreign domicil." Here is a strong illustration of the truth that, notwithstanding any rule or method of treatment applied for limited purposes municipally, yet so far as those purposes do not extend, there is no change in the substance of the thing as between nations and their laws. This again is clearly the *ratio decidendi* of the case of *Freke* v. *Lord Carbery* (2). There the question was of leaseholds in England devised by a testator, whose domicil was Irish, on trust to sell and to accumulate the

1) L.R., 7 Ch., 192.   (2) L.R., 16 Eq., 461.

H. C. of A.
1908.

AUSTRALIAN
MUTUAL
PROVIDENT
SOCIETY
v.
GREGORY.

Barton J.

proceeds for certain trust purposes for a period prohibited by the *Thellusson Act.* That Act has no force in Ireland. The argument rejected was that all questions as to personal property of the testator must be determined by the law of his domicil; that this was personal property, for leaseholds are such by English law; and, therefore, that the trusts were good. Lord *Selborne* L.C. on the contrary held that the trusts, though good as to certain other and purely personal estate, were void as to the leaseholds. These, he held, though for some purposes regarded by English law as chattels, were land, and land, whether held for a freehold or for a chattel interest, is *as a matter of fact,* and in the nature of things, immoveable, and therefore untouched by the rule which the Roman law expresses in the maxim *mobilia sequuntur personam.* It is the idea that "personal property" and "moveables" are co-extensive terms that causes confusion on this subject. To use Mr. *Foote's* words again, 1st ed., at p. 170, chattels real are personal property "merely in name, and only in the contemplation of the English law." That law, however, when it turns its attention to that branch of it which is called international jurisprudence, does not class these as moveables, because in the nature of things they are not such. It is not prompted to set the nature of things at nought by "the deference which, for the sake of international comity, the law of England pays to the law of the civilized world generally" (Lord *Selborne* L.C. in *Freke v. Lord Carbery* (1). Now, as the interests in land known as chattels real and as estates *pur autre vie* are, as above shown, dealt with according to their substance and the nature of things, is there any reason why an interest in land subject to a trust for conversion should fare differently? I have not heard any such reason from the bar. Certainly it was urged that chattels real were the only immoveables included in personal property, but upon what reason could they be so included, and such an interest in land as we are now dealing with excluded? Though they are both personal property for some purposes, what is there to make the one *interest* a moveable when the other is an immoveable? In my opinion they stand or fall together. If it is contended that, because such an interest as that of G. W. Gregory is for

(1) L.R. 16 Eq., 461, at p. 466.

H. C. of A.
1908.

AUSTRALIAN
MUTUAL
PROVIDENT
SOCIETY
v.
GREGORY.

Barton J.

some purposes personal property, it is so for all purposes, and therefore a moveable, the cases of *Brook* v. *Badley* (1), *Ashworth* v. *Munn* (2), and *In re Watts*; *Cornford* v. *Elliott* (3), show that it is an interest in land. And in the case of *Murray* v. *Champernowne* (4), *Andrews* J. expressly held that real estate, vested in trustees upon trust to sell and to hold the proceeds upon certain trusts, was while it remained unsold an immoveable, notwithstanding the direction to sell.

For these reasons I am of opinion that G. W. Gregory's Tasmanian interest was at the time of the Natal adjudication an immoveable, and, therefore, the Natal adjudication and the appointment of Mr Green as trustee did not operate to vest the interest in that respondent.

This conclusion is sufficient to dispose of the case in favour of the appellants.

But in view of possible further proceedings it is perhaps desirable that we should give an opinion on the second question debated at the bar, which can be dealt with only on the assumption that G. W. Gregory's interest is a moveable. On that assumption the respondent Green affirms that an assignment of an insolvent's property to the representative of his creditors under the Insolvents Act of Natal is, or operates as, an assignment of the moveables of the insolvent situate in Tasmania, at least if he is domiciled in Natal. So much may be granted, but the matter does not end there. And first, it is convenient to clear the question of any contention founded on such cases as *In re Bright's Settlement* (5) and later cases on the same point. The present claim arises under an insolvency which, as I have pointed out, is a foreign one in its relation to the laws and the Courts of Tasmania. Though by the comity of nations the law of Tasmania will give effect to that as an assignment of the moveables, applying the maxim so often quoted, it will not also favour the foreign creditors by giving effect to special conditions for their protection, such as are contained in the negative words at the end of sec. 51 of the Natal Statute, to the detriment of Tasmanian claimants under Tasmanian

(1) L.R., 3 Ch., 672.   (4) (1901) 2 I.R., 233.
(2) 15 Ch. D., 363.   (5) 13 Ch. D., 413.
(3) 29 Ch. D., 947.

H. C. or A.
1908.

AUSTRALIAN
MUTUAL
PROVIDENT
SOCIETY
v.
GREGORY.

Barton J.

transfers otherwise good.　Internationally, the law of that State will recognize the universal effect of the assignment on moveables, but as an assignment only.　It gives no more extensive operation to the assignment than could be claimed for it if made in Tasmania.

But, further, the assignee, appealing to the Tasmanian law to give effect to his claim on international principles, will not be allowed to dispense with the ordinary requirements of that law in respect of priorities acquired by reason of acts done for the perfection of title, where such requirements have been complied with by local assignees.　The Natal assignee takes the Tasmanian moveables subject to any equities administered in the local Courts: *In re Barr's Trusts* (1).

What then are the equities in this case ?　The rule in *Dearle* v. *Hall* (2) is thus clearly expressed in *White and Tudor's Equity Cases*, 17th ed., p. 116, in the notes to *Ryall* v. *Rowles* (3).　"If the assignee of a chose in action, or a trust estate of personalty, does not perfect his title by giving notice of the assignment to the debtor or trustees, a subsequent purchaser or incumbrancer without notice of the former assignment giving notice of his assignment will thereby acquire priority."　*Sir Thos. Plumer* M.R., in deciding *Dearle* v. *Hall* (2), put it that the assignee of a thing which does not admit of actual tangible possession must do that which is tantamount to obtaining possession by placing every person who has an equitable or legal interest in the matter under an obligation to treat it as the assignee's property.　He said (4):—" Possession, or what is tantamount to possession, is the criterion of perfect title to personal chattels, and he who does not obtain such possession must take his chance."　After notice, the trustees of the fund become trustees for the assignee who has given them notice.　See also *In re Atkinson* (5) as to insolvency, and *In re Barr's Trusts* (6), where Lord *Hatherley*, then *Page-Wood* V.C., held that the reasoning of the Master of the Rolls in *Dearle* v. *Hall* (2) applies as fully and as forcibly to an assignee in bankruptcy (or in insolvency) as to an assignee for valuable consideration. And on the whole I do not think that the authority of either of the

H. C. of A.
1908.

Australian
Mutual
Provident
Society
v.
Gregory.

Barton J.

last-mentioned cases is impeached by *Palmer* v. *Locke* (1). The rule in *Dearle* v. *Hall* (2), in its application to equitable interests, was exhaustively considered by the House of Lords in *Ward* v. *Duncombe* (3), where it was stated by Lord *Macnaghten* to be :— "That an assignee of an equitable interest in personal estate without notice of an existing prior assignment may gain priority simply by the act of giving notice to the person who has legal dominion over the fund before notice is given by the earlier assignee." In the Court of Appeal *Stirling* J. quoted these words as a final expression of the law, in *In re Dallas* (4). And to come closer to the case of a foreign assignment, *Warrington* J., in *Kelly* v. *Selwyn* (5), held that where an English Court is administering an English trust fund settled by the will of an English testator, the rights of the claimants to that fund must be regulated by English law. Accordingly he decided that the plaintiff, who held a second assignment but had given the first notice to the trustees, was entitled to priority over the defendant, who held an assignment prior in point of time, executed in the State of New York, where the assignor was at that time domiciled, although the law of that State did not exact notice to the trustees to render perfect an assignment of a chose in action or a reversionary interest in personalty. The question, in the opinion of the learned Judge, was, not whether the assignment in New York was valid, but in what order English law was to treat claimants with charges on the fund ; and until notice was given to the trustees the assignee of a share in the fund was not completely constituted a *cestui que trust* by English law. This case seems to me to apply completely to the present on the assumption that the interest in dispute is a moveable. On grounds, then, both of principle and of authority, I am of opinion that, on the assumption stated, the claim of the trustee in the Natal insolvency is postponed to those of the several local assignees, for valuable consideration and without notice of the insolvency, who anticipated him by giving prior notice to the trustees under the will of James Gregory. But, apart from that assumption,

(1) 18 Ch. D., 381.　　　　　(4) (1904) 2 Ch., 385, at p. 415.
(2) 3 Russ., 1.　　　　　　　(5) (1905) 2 Ch., 117.
(3) (1893) A.C., 369, at p. 384.

the claim, in my opinion, fails completely on the ground that the interest of G. W. Gregory did not pass to the claimant, because it is an immoveable.

ISAACS J.   The first question is as to the nature of the property claimed by the Natal trustee in bankruptcy, that is to say, the nature of the property to which George William Gregory was entitled under his father's will.

That question must, in my opinion, be determined by the law of the situs. Before the maxim *mobilia sequuntur personam* can be applied it is obviously requisite to determine whether a given property is a moveable or an immoveable.   In the absence of any specific rule by the *lex loci rei sitæ* the actual nature of the thing itself is taken as the criterion to determine the matter. But if the *lex situs* lays down any specific rule with regard to any property actually situate within its jurisdiction—whether as to mobility, immobility, assignability, mode of transfer, &c.—there is no principle, so far as I know, requiring or permitting the Courts of that jurisdiction to apply any other rule.   It is really not necessary here to determine how the Courts of a foreign jurisdiction would for the purposes of their own causes regard such a rule if differing from the inherent nature of the property, but, if it were necessary, I should think the canons of international law as understood in British Courts would lead them to recognize and respect the sovereignty of the country where the thing is situate, and to accept the legal quality which the law of that country has impressed upon property under its exclusive jurisdiction.

Thus in *Ex parte Rucker* (1), reversed on another point in 2 *Mont. & Ayr.*, 398, an English Court of Bankruptcy held slaves to be realty because the *lex situs*—in that case Antigua—pronounced them so.

Dicey on the Conflict of Laws, Ch. 21, on the Nature of Property, formulates a rule in accordance with this view, though with doubt.   *Story*, in sec. 447, says :—" For every nation having authority to prescribe rules for the disposition and arrangement of all the property within its own territory, may impress upon it

(1) 3 Deac & Ch., 704.

H. C. OF A.
1908.

AUSTRALIAN
MUTUAL
PROVIDENT
SOCIETY
v.
GREGORY.

Isaacs J.

any character which it shall choose; and no other nation can impugn or vary that character. So that the question, in all these cases, is not so much what are or ought to be deemed, *ex sua natura,* moveables or not, *as what are deemed so by the law of the place where they are situated.* If they are there deemed part of the land, or annexed (as the common law would say) to the soil or freehold, they must be so treated in every place in which any controversy shall arise respecting their nature and character. In other words, in order to ascertain what is immoveable or real property, or not, we must resort to the *lex loci rei sitæ.*"

In the case quoted by *Story, Chapman* v. *Robertson* (1), *Wallworth* C. says:—"And it has been decided that the *lex loci rei sitæ* must also be resorted to for the purpose of determining what is or is not to be considered as real or heritable property, so as to have locality within the intent and meaning of this latter principle." The principle the learned Chancellor is referring to is that the creation of a trust must be made according to the *lex situs.*

The Courts of the *lex situs* at all events must be bound by the law of that place, and though the general rule of actual nature, *primâ facie,* applies, it can be overridden by special rules of law, however arising, whether out of Statute or common law. In *Chatfield* v. *Berchtoldt* (2), a case as to a rent-charge out of English lands, the Court of Appeal decided against the respondent's contention that the property was personalty. But the ground of decision was clear. *James* L.J. said (3):—"The statutory provision is not that it shall be personal estate, but that in certain circumstances, and certain circumstances only, it shall be applicable as personal estate. *Simile non est idem.* It lay on the respondent to show that by the law of England estates *pur autre vie* in land had been converted into pure personalty or moveables; and we are of opinion that he has not discharged this burthen by showing that by some statutory provisions in some cases they are to be applied in the same manner as personal estate."

(1) 6 Paige (N.Y.), 627, at p. 630.   (2) L.R. 7 Ch., 192.
(3) L.R. 7 Ch., 192, at p. 198.

Therefore the law of Tasmania must govern the question as to
the nature of the property.   There is no difference in this respect
between the law of Tasmania and that of England.   I proceed
to consider what is that law.   The trustees of the will contend
that the property is by that law pure personalty, and must be so
regarded.

Reliance is placed upon the principle of *Fletcher* v. *Ashburner*
(1) by which land, directed to be sold and the proceeds disposed
of, is considered in equity as personal estate and passes to
personal representatives.   Undoubtedly many cases may be
found lending great support to the contention.   In *Buchanan* v.
Angus (2) Lord *Westbury* L.C. said:—"If real or heritable property
be vested in trustees upon an absolute and unconditional trust
for sale, either declared or necessarily implied, and the proceeds
of such sale are disposed of, there is (in the quaint phrase of the
English law) an out and out conversion for the purposes of that
disposition; and the interest of every beneficiary taking under
the disposition is of the nature of personal or moveable property."

In *Bolling* v. *Hobday* (3) *Chitty* J., speaking of the interest of
two beneficiaries under a will devising land in trust to sell and
divide the proceeds, said :—"They were not equitable tenants in
common of an estate under the will; they were only entitled to
the one-fourth share each of the proceeds of the sale of the real
estate, and in that sense—but in that sense only—had they any
equitable interest in the land."

Perhaps the strongest case in this direction is that of
Du Hourmelin v. *Sheldon* (4), where Lord *Langdale* M.R. was
pressed with an argument very much resembling the argument
of the trustees of the will in this case.   Land in England was by
will of a testatrix who died in 1829 appointed to trustees to sell,
and after certain payments to invest the proceeds in trust for
certain persons some of whom were aliens.   It was contended
that the aliens had an interest in the realty.   The Master of the
Rolls said (5):—"But it is argued, that taking the case as it
stood at the death of the testatrix, and as it must remain until

(1) 1 Bro. C.C., 497.   (4) 1 Beav., 79.
(2) 4 Macq. H.L. Cas., 374, at p. 379.   (5) 1 Beav., 79, at p. 89.
(3) 31 W.R., 9, at p. 11.

H. C. of A.
1908.

AUSTRALIAN
MUTUAL
PROVIDENT
SOCIETY
v.
GREGORY.

Isaacs J.

the conversion shall be completely made, the land is the source, from which the money, or stock, in the shares of which the aliens are to be interested, is to be realized; and that, in that respect, the aliens have an interest in the land." His Honor proceeds to advert to the distinction between the case in which land is given to a trustee to be held by him in trust for an alien—in which case the alien takes in the land, a permanent equitable interest—and the case in which no interest in land was ever intended to vest in the alien, and his right, if right he has, is only to have the land converted into money, and is so far of a transitory nature that it endures only till the purposes of the donor can be performed by the due execution of the trusts he has created. Further on in his judgment Lord *Langdale* describes more specifically the interest which the alien has in the last mentioned case. He said (1) :—" During the time which may elapse, before the conversion can be completed, the alien is, by the peculiar doctrine of this Court, considered to have an interest in the land which is to be converted : *i.e.*, an interest that the land should be sold to persons that can legally hold it, in order to raise the money, which he, the alien, can legally hold." That decision was affirmed on appeal by Lord *Cottenham* L.C. (2). I shall quote only one passage from the Lord Chancellor's judgment which sufficiently shows how he regarded the point. He said (3) :—" Decisions, that aliens cannot enjoy, against the Crown, trusts of land, any more than the land itself, leave untouched the present question."

In accordance with this too is *Craig* v. *Leslie* (4), where the Supreme Court of the United States previously came to the same conclusion on the same question.

In *Tyrrell* v. *Painton* (5), a case to which we have been referred since the argument, it was held that a similar interest is personalty, and not an interest in land, that is so as to be subject to an elegit under a particular Statute.

But however general the expressions in some of the cases, they were not, in my opinion, intended to lay down a universal rule that

(1) 1 Beav., 79, at p. 91.
(2) 4 My. & C., 525.
(3) 4 My. & C., 525, at p. 533.

(4) 3 Wheat., 563.
(5) (1895) 1 Q.B., 202.

H. C. of A.   such property was to be deemed in English law to be personalty
1908.   for all purposes and under all circumstances.   For purposes of
AUSTRALIAN   succession, and certain fiscal purposes, it is so considered.   Again,
MUTUAL   for determining the question as to the right of the Crown to take
PROVIDENT
SOCIETY   the interest of the alien, the law was declared to be that the
v.   alien's interest in the land was too slight and transitory—at all
GREGORY.   events until he validly elected to take the land itself—to come
Isaacs J.   within the rule by which an alien's realty could be claimed by
the Crown.

But, even in some of the cases already mentioned, the Court
refers to the interest in the land.   In *Du Hourmelin* v. *Sheldon*
(1) the Master of the Rolls declares the nature of that interest to
be that the beneficiary has an interest that the land should be
sold in order to raise the money.   But though transitory it is
real, and though slight it is essential.   Without that interest in
the land itself, the benefit of the trust might be lost.   In short,
equity, while for purposes of substance it looks rather at the
ultimate benefit intended to be conferred, does not obliterate the
interest in the land itself, which is the link, slender but indis-
pensable, to the attainment of the real bounty conferred.

In *Pearson* v. *Lane* (2) *Sir William Grant* M.R., said:—
" Where land is given upon a trust to sell, and to pay the produce
to A., though no interest in the land is expressly given to him, in
equity he is the owner ; and the trustee must convey, as he shall
direct.   If there are also other purposes, for which it is to be sold,
still he is entitled to the surplus of the price as the equitable
owner subject to those purposes ; and, if he provides for them, he
may keep the estates unsold."

It will be seen presently that the principle remains the same
where there are more than one beneficiary.

A number of cases decided under the *Mortmain Act*, not cited
in argument but which I have since examined, illustrate this
doctrine very strongly.   In *Attorney-General* v. *Harley* (3), *Sir
John Leach* V.C. said :—" That money to arise from the sale of
land is an interest in land, admits of no doubt."

Brook v. *Badley* (4) is most distinct.   The Act enacted by the

(1) 1 Beav., 79.   (3) 5 Madd., 321, at p. 327.
(2) 17 Ves., 101, at p. 104.   (4) L. R. 3 Ch., 672.

3rd section that, *inter alia*, any gift of lands or of any estate or interest therein to a charitable use should be void. Lord *Cairns* L.C. had to determine whether the bequest by a beneficiary under a will of a legacy, payable out of personalty and the proceeds of sale of real estate, was a gift of an interest in land within the meaning of the Act. The Act itself provided no definition, and the Court was consequently thrown back on general principles. The Lord Chancellor was very decided that the interest of the legatee which she bequeathed to the charity was an interest in the land. He said (1):—" If a testator devises his land to be sold, and the proceeds given, not to one person, but to four persons in shares, and if one of those four persons afterwards makes his will, and gives either his share of the proceeds or all his property to charity, the position of that second testator with regard to the estate which is to be sold is in substance that of a person who has a direct and distinct interest in land. The estate is in the hands of trustees, not for the benefit of those trustees, but for the benefit of the four persons between whom the proceeds of the estate are to be divided when the sale takes place. It may very well be that no one of those four persons could insist upon entering on the land, or taking the land, or enjoying the land *quà* land, and it may very well be that the only method for each one of them to make his enjoyment of the land productive, is by coming to the Court and applying to have the sale carried into execution, but nevertheless the interest of each one of them is, in my opinion, an interest in land ; and it would be right to say in equity that the land does not belong to the trustees, but to the four persons between whom the proceeds are to be divided." His Lordship then proceeds to practically overrule two cases so far as they are at variance with his own views.

Two Courts of Appeal have since approved of Lord *Cairns'* view, viz., in *Ashworth* v. *Munn* (2) and *In re Watts ; Cornford* v. *Elliott* (3).

In the result, it cannot, as I conceive, be regarded as a principle or rule of English or Tasmanian law that property of the nature

H. C. of A.
1908.

AUSTRALIAN
MUTUAL
PROVIDENT
SOCIETY
v.
GREGORY.

Isaacs J.

(1) L.R. 3 Ch., 672, at pp. 674.　　　(2) 15 Ch. D., 363.
　　　　　　(3) 29 Ch. D., 947.

given to the bankrupt under his father's will is pure personalty—
i.e., with no element of immobility—and therefore such as would,
by the law of the situs, be considered simply as *mobilia* and as
passing under a universal assignment by the law of a foreign
domicil. The case of the Natal trustee therefore must fail
independently of any consideration of notice of assignment.
But as this further and important question has been agitated,
and has, indeed, formed the basis of the decision of the Full Court
of Tasmania, it is desirable to deal with it. Assuming the
interest of the bankrupt is pure personalty, and in the nature of
a chose in action, the right of his trustee in bankruptcy is
challenged on the ground that the particular assignees gave
prior notice to the trustees of the will. It is admitted that in a
controversy arising out of a Tasmanian bankruptcy this
argument would prevail.

The contention is advanced, on the part of the trustee in
bankruptcy, that the ordinary rules of equity are inapplicable to
a case of international competition, and it is said that the title of
the trustee under the law of Natal where the bankrupt was
domiciled is complete there under the Natal Statute, and independent of any formalities or requirements which would have
been necessary to give a perfect title to a Tasmanian assignment,
and will therefore be respected and enforced in Tasmania. On
this ground it was urged that the principle of such cases as
Palmer v. *Locke* (1), *per Jessel* M.R. (not overruled); *Stuart* v.
Cockerell (2); *In re Barr's Trusts* (3); and *In re Atkinson* (4)
is not applicable.

The argument is presented, and the Supreme Court of Tasmania has determined that, inasmuch as sec. 51 of the Natal
Statute (No. 47 of 1887), not only vests all property of every
kind in the Master of the Supreme Court in the first instance
and subsequently in the trustee, but goes on to say that after the
order for sequestration has been made " neither the insolvent nor
any person claiming through or under him shall have power to
alienate, give, cede, deliver, mortgage, pledge, or recover, or to
release or discharge the same or any part thereof " the ordinary

(1) 18 Ch. D., 381.   (3) 4 K. & J., 219.
(2) L.R. 8 Eq., 607.   (4) 2 D.M. & G., 140.

H. C. or A.
1908.

AUSTRALIAN
MUTUAL
PROVIDENT
SOCIETY
v.
GREGORY.

Isaacs J.

rule of equity as laid down in *Dearle* v. *Hall* (1) is displaced, and the bankrupt is incompetent even in Tasmania of making an assignment which can on the doctrine of that case, under any circumstances, confer a right to the property.

Reliance is placed on *In re Bright's Settlement* (2), and *In re Coombe's Trusts* (3), where similar negative words were held to protect the assignee in bankruptcy. But the point of these cases is that the Court was giving effect to an Act of Parliament in force in England, prohibiting, and therefore nullifying, any attempted subsequent assignment by the bankrupt. It is plain that these and similar cases are irrelevant to the matter in hand. That prohibition was no part of the assignment to the assignee, and no part of his title, but a separate and independent enactment of a legislature whose determinations bound the tribunals. The fallacy on this branch of the argument of the trustee in bankruptcy is in treating the prohibitory words in sec. 51 of the Natal Act as part of and completing the trustee's title. They are simply a law operating in Natal and not beyond it, and having no force or effect in Tasmania on transactions entered into in that State. Had Gregory after bankruptcy assumed while in Natal to mortgage his interest, it might be that the act, being forbidden in the place where done, would be disregarded in Tasmania. That is possible, I do not say more of it, but that is not the present case. The trustee's contention amounts to importing into Tasmania, by way of appeal to international law, and for the benefit of the foreign trustee in the bankrupt's domicil, the binding force of the Natal prohibition as such, and to say it supersedes in his favour the Tasmanian requirement of notice of assignment.

He does this directly by invoking the maxim of international law *mobilia sequuntur personam*, by which he fictionally transfers to Natal both the property and the assignment by the bankrupt to the appellants, and assumes a contest before the Natal Court and the decision of that Court that the assignment was contrary to the Statute there in force, and then contends that the Tasmanian Court is bound to give the same decision.

(1) 3 Russ., 1.　　　(2) 13 Ch. D., 413.　　　(3) 1 Gif., 91.

H. C. of A.
1908.

AUSTRALIAN
MUTUAL
PROVIDENT
SOCIETY
v.
GREGORY.

Isaacs J

In my opinion the fiction *mobilia sequuntur personam* cannot be pushed so far.   Unless the trustee establishes one of two things he must fail.   These are either that the negative words in the Statute are part of his title, and not merely a prohibition against the bankrupt doing an act which, notwithstanding the trustee's title, he might otherwise have lawfully done ; or that the prohibition is in force as a law in Tasmania.   But neither of these positions can be sustained.

The property in fact being in Tasmania, and the assignment to the appellants in fact taking place there, it is the law of Tasmania which must decide the matter and not the law of Natal : See *Turner* V.C. in *Caldwell* v. *Vanvlissingen* (1).

Lord *Stowell's* observations in a Scotch marriage case *Dalrymple* v. *Dalrymple* (2) before him are in point :—" Being entertained in an English Court, it (the cause) must be adjudicated according to the principles of English law, applicable to such a case."   The words "applicable to such a case" are in the highest degree important.   In some cases the English law enforces one set of rules as appropriate, and in others quite different rules.   Thus, in determining the validity of a marriage ceremony, it depends (with certain exceptions) upon the law of the place of celebration. The law is taken as the test of validity, not because it is in force *ex proprio vigore* in England, but because English law says it is appropriate to such a case.   But is it appropriate in such a case as the present that the Tasmanian rule of priority according to notice should be set aside in favour of the Natal prohibition ?

There are two considerations which limit the application—*ex comitate, ob reciprocam utilitatem*—of foreign law.

They are shortly stated in *Wheaton's International Law*, 4th ed., at p. 131, as follows :—"In modern times, all States have adopted, as a principle, the application within their territories of foreign laws; subject, however, to the restrictions which the rights of sovereignty and the interests of their own subjects require.   This is the doctrine professed by all the publicists who have written on the subject."   See also Lord *Wensleydale's* speech in *Fenton* v. *Livingstone* (3).

(1) 9 Ha., 415, at p. 425.   (2) 2 Hag. Con., 54, at p. 58.
               (3) 3 Macq. H.L. Cas., 497, at p. 548.

H. C. of A.
1908.

AUSTRALIAN
MUTUAL
PROVIDENT
SOCIETY
v.
GREGORY.

Isaacs J.

Both these considerations, viz., that of the right of sovereignty, and that of the interests of the citizens of Tasmania, are involved in the present case. As to the first, it is a distinct part of the law of Tasmania—and it is I apprehend quite immaterial how it has become the law whether by Statute or common law—that the title of the assignee of such a right as that now in question is not perfect until notice to the trustee of the fund: *Lloyd's Bank* v. *Pearson* (1); *Foster* v. *Cockerell* (2); *In re Lake*; *Ex parte Cavendish* (3); *Ward* v. *Duncombe* (4). In *Montefiore* v. *Guedalla* (5) *Cozens-Hardy* L.J. says :—" The rule laid down in *Dearle* v. *Hall* (6) is now part of the law of the land." Starting with that position, why should it be disregarded in favour of the Natal trustee ? Why should he be held to have perfected his title without complying with the special mode of transfer appropriate by Tasmanian law to the particular class of property dealt with ?

In Mr. *Dicey's* work, at p. 334, it is stated that bankruptcy in one country is an assignment of property in another, but subject (*inter alia*) to the requirements, if any, of the local law as to the conditions necessary to effect a transfer of such property, and the learned author, after quoting the authority of *Ex parte Rogers* (7) for this position as to realty, adds :—"And this dictum, though confined to immoveable property and to property in the Colonies, applies apparently to moveable property and to property situate in any foreign country."

It is in accordance with Scottish law as appears from *Erskine's Institute of the Laws of Scotland*, ed. of 1871, pp. 717 and 718, where it is said :—" On a similar principle, where a foreign ground of debt, perfected *secundum legem domicilii*, is sustained by our Supreme Court, the diligence which is to proceed upon it, and the other judicial steps necessary for giving it full effect, must be governed by the law of Scotland ; because these previous steps are required to deeds of the same kind, even supposing them perfected in the Scottish form ; and that Judge within whose territory the debt is situated, and under whose authority it is to

(1) (1901) 1 Ch., 865.   (5) (1903) 2 Ch., 26, at p. 37.
(2) 3 Cl. & F., 456.   (6) 3 Russ., 1.
(3) (1903) 1 K.B., 151.   (7) 16 Ch. D., 665.
(4) (1893) A.C., 369.

H. C. of A.
1908.

AUSTRALIAN
MUTUAL
PROVIDENT
SOCIETY
r.
GREGORY.

Isaacs J.

be recovered, must necessarily determine all questions of diligence
and competition concerning it, according to the laws of his own
country, and not according to those of a foreign state, which may
be utterly unknown to him, and which have no authority, nor were
ever designed to bind the Judges of any State which is not subject
to the legislature who enacted them. Thus because no assignation
is, by the law of Scotland, effectual against an arrester, if it has
not been intimated previously to the arrestment; neither is a
foreign assignment, not intimated, effectual against him, though
the *lex loci* should not require assignations to be intimated."

The second consideration to which, as stated in the passage
from *Wheaton*, the application of foreign law is subject here is
the interests of Tasmanian subjects. Whatever else may have
formed the ground of judgment in *Dearle* v. *Hall* (1) there was
certainly involved in the decision the prevention of fraud against
future assignees. The appellant society resident in Tasmania
would undoubtedly have been protected if the assignor had
become bankrupt in Tasmania where it might more easily have
learnt the fact of bankruptcy, and why should it lose its protection
when his bankruptcy occurred so far from its probable means of
knowledge? On the ground also that the principle of *Dearle* v.
Hall (1) would apply to this case if the bankrupt's interest were
a moveable, notwithstanding a Natal assignment in bankruptcy,
I am of the opinion the appeal should be allowed.

GRIFFITH C.J. The order of the Court will be as follows:—
Appeal allowed. Order appealed from discharged. The first
question will be answered—" The respondent Green is not entitled
to any portion of the share." The fifth question will be answered
—" The one-ninth part is payable to the other assignees thereof
from G. W. Gregory who have given notice of their assignments
to the trustees of the will to the extent of their respective charges
thereon, and in priority according to the dates of their respective
notices." Costs of the trustees of the will in the Supreme Court
to be paid out of the fund. All other parties except the respondent
Green to be at liberty to add their costs in the Supreme Court
to their securities. The respondent Green to pay the appellants'

(1) 3 Russ., 1.

costs of the appeal.   The appellants to be at liberty to add their
costs to their respective securities so far as they are not recovered
from the respondent Green.   The appellants to pay the costs of
appeal of the trustees of the will and recover them from the
respondent Green, and to be at liberty to add them to their
respective securities as far as they are not recovered from him.
The trustees' costs to be taxed as between solicitor and client.

H. C. of A.
1908.
~~~
Australian
Mutual
Provident
Society
v.
Gregory.

Griffith C.J.
</div>

<p align="center"><i>Appeal allowed.</i></p>

Solicitors, for appellants, *J. B. Walker, Wolfhagen & Walch*;
*Nicholls & Stops*.

Solicitors for respondents, *Perkins & Dear*.

<p align="right">B. L.</p>

---

<p align="center">[HIGH COURT OF AUSTRALIA.]</p>

## BARRIER WHARFS LIMITED   .   .   . Appellants;
### Plaintiffs,

<p align="center">AND</p>

## W. SCOTT FELL & COMPANY LIMITED   . Respondents.
### Defendants,

<p align="center">ON APPEAL FROM A JUSTICE OF THE HIGH COURT.</p>

*Contract—Absence of formal contract—Contract contained in letters—Subsequent
correspondence, effect of.*

The plaintiffs, who were wharf owners, were negotiating with the defendants, who were shipowners, for the use by the defendants' ships of the
plaintiffs' wharf.   The plaintiffs wrote :—" I beg to state that I am prepared
to find accommodation for your steamers at our wharf, you to be charged sixpence per ton on all coal and coke landed there, provided you undertake to do all
your business other than that with the B. Co. with us.   I understand your
coal contracts provide for approximately 50,000 tons exclusive of the B. Co.
Tonnage dues as per printed schedule handed you to be charged.   I undertake to provide a berth for your steamers at all times on the understanding

<div align="right">
H. C. of A.
1907.
~~~
Melbourne,
August 19, 20,
21, 22;
September 2.

Higgins J.

1908.
~~~
Melbourne,
March 18, 19,
20.

Griffith C.J.,
Barton,
O'Connor and
Isaacs JJ.
</div>

H. C. of A.
1908.

BARRIER
WHARFS LTD.
v.
W. SCOTT
FELL & Co.
LTD.

that reasonable notice, say two days, be given to our manager at Port Pirie of expected arrivals.   If this arrangement is acceptable to you I suggest that it be for a term of two years from 1st March next." The defendants replied :— " We are anxious to do business with you if possible, and will endeavour to come to your figure provided you agree to waive tonnage dues on all our steamers loading and discharging at your wharf." Plaintiffs replied :—" I hope we shall be able to fix up our wharfage arrangements . . . . I could not entertain the suggestion to waive the tonnage dues on your steamers visiting our wharf . . . . . Of course you are aware that a steamer paying at one wharf has not to pay at another ; this could all be arranged to your satisfaction, I am sure." Defendants replied :—" We are willing to conclude with you for wharfage on the basis of sixpence per ton and will be glad if you will make a contract for our approval and signature." Plaintiffs replied :—" I note with pleasure that you have decided to accept the wharfage rate of sixpence per ton as per correspondence which has passed, and I will arrange a contract accordingly."

Held, that these letters did not constitute a binding contract between the parties.

Held, also, that, if the letters could be construed on their face as a contract, the subsequent correspondence and conduct of the parties showed that no binding contract was intended.

Judgment of *Higgins* J. affirmed.

APPEAL from judgment of *Higgins* J.

An action was brought in the High Court by the Barrier Wharfs Limited, a Victorian company owning a wharf at Port Pirie, South Australia, known as the Barrier Wharf, against W. Scott Fell & Co. Ltd., a New South Wales company carrying on business there as shipowners and merchants, claiming £2,540 damages for breach of contract. Paragraph 4 of the statement of claim was as follows :—" By a contract made between the plaintiffs and the defendants about the month of February 1906 (which said contract is partly verbal and partly contained in letters passing between the plaintiffs and the defendants dated respectively 24th January 1906, 25th January 1906, 29th January 1906, 31st January 1906, 2nd February 1906, 6th February 1906) it was agreed as follows :— .

" That the plaintiffs find accommodation and berthing for the defendants' steamers at the said Barrier Wharf at all times on the understanding that reasonable notice, say two days, be given to the plaintiffs' manager at Port Pirie of expected arrivals ; that

the defendants do all their business at Port Pirie with the plaintiffs other than business with the Broken Hill Proprietary Co.
Ltd.; that the defendants pay the plaintiffs for such accommodation and berthing sixpence per ton on all coal and coke landed at
the said wharf and also tonnage dues as per printed schedule of
tonnage dues payable at wharves at Port Pirie; that the said
agreement be for a term of two years from 1st March 1906."

The main defences were that no contract was entered into
between the parties, and a contention that as a matter of law the
letters and verbal communications referred to did not constitute
the contract alleged or any binding contract between the parties,
inasmuch as no final agreement is thereby arrived at between the
parties.

The facts and the correspondence between the parties, so far as
material, are set out in the judgments hereunder.

The action was heard before *Higgins* J.

Starke, for the plaintiffs.

Coldham and *Kilpatrick*, for the defendants.

HIGGINS J. read the following judgment. This is an action for
breach of contract. The plaintiff company has a wharf at Port
Pirie in South Australia. The defendants, shipowners and merchants of Sydney, had secured contracts with seven mining companies of Broken Hill for the supply of coal to them, for two
years from 1st March 1906. The plaintiffs allege that there was
about February 1906 a contract, partly verbal, partly contained
in letters dated 24th, 25th, 29th, 31st January, and 2nd and 6th
February to this effect—that the plaintiffs find accommodation
and berthing for the defendants' steamers at the said Barrier
Wharf at all times, on the understanding that reasonable notice,
say two days, be given to the plaintiffs' manager at Port Pirie of
expected arrivals,—that the defendants do all their business at
Port Pirie with the plaintiffs, other than business with the Broken
Hill Proprietary Co. Ltd. That the defendants pay to the plaintiffs
for such accommodation and berthing sixpence per ton on all
coal and coke landed at the said wharf, and also tonnage dues as

H. C. OF A.
1908.

BARRIER
WHARFS LTD.
v.
W. SCOTT
FELL & CO.
LTD.

September 2,
1907.

H. C. of A.
1908.

BARRIER
WHARFS LTD.
v.
W. SCOTT
FELL & CO.
LTD.

Higgins J.

per printed schedule of tonnage dues payable at wharves at Port Pirie. That the said agreement be for the term of two years from 1st March 1906. It is admitted that, if there were such a contract, it has not been carried out by the defendants, who have berthed and discharged steamers at other wharves. The question is, was there such a contract?

Now, the burden of proof lies, of course, on the plaintiffs. If there was not a complete contract, the plaintiffs must fail. The law knows no gradations in the contractual relation. It knows nothing of virtual agreements, or honourable understandings. Even if the defendants were shown to have disappointed the legitimate expectations of the plaintiffs for some unworthy reason—to have meanly backed out of almost completed negotiations—the action must fail. There is no contract unless the two parties mutually consented to be bound one to the other by one agreement. Moreover—though it ought to be superfluous to say it—it is one thing for two parties to settle what are to be the terms of an agreement, if it should be made; and quite another thing to make the agreement. I have found, in my experience, that the two processes are frequently confounded; and, if I may judge from some of the cases to which I have been referred by Mr. *Starke*, the confusion has not always been avoided even in the Courts.

The conversations on which the plaintiffs rely took place in or near Adelaide and Port Pirie between Mr. Howard, managing director of the plaintiff company, and Mr. Scott Fell, managing director of the defendant company. It is not disputed that these gentlemen had each authority to bind his company. The objection as to the want of a seal is abandoned by Mr. *Coldham*. No objection has been raised by the defendants on the ground of the want of a writing sufficient to satisfy the *Statute of Frauds* (sec. 4). There is a conflict of evidence as between Fell on the one side, and Howard on the other. In one point Howard is corroborated by his brother—the wharfinger. Both the Howards say that the schedule of rates for Port Pirie wharves with regulations attached was handed to Fell. I accept their statement. I think that Fell must be mistaken, especially as the handing of the schedule is referred to in the plaintiffs' first letter,

H. C. of A.
1908.

BARRIER
WHARFS LTD.
v.
W. SCOTT
FELL & Co.
LTD.

Higgins J.

and is not denied. But I see no reason for disbelieving Mr. Fell on other points, or for even giving the palm for accuracy to Mr. Howard—as I find that he made mistakes also, as hereinafter mentioned. So far as the conversations are concerned, in January 1906 I find that the berthing of steamers at the plaintiffs' wharf was keenly discussed; that Howard offered finally to berth them at sixpence per ton; that Fell said he was ready to give the plaintiffs the preference at sixpence, all things being equal, if he eventually decided to make a contract; and that he added in effect—" Whatever you have to propose, place it in writing so that I may submit it to my Board on my return to Sydney." I should add that, even on Howard's version, the contract now alleged by the plaintiffs was not concluded when the conversations ceased. I am all the more inclined to treat Mr. Fell's account as the more accurate, when I find that it accords with Mr. Howard's account to the secretary of this company, and to his brother, in the letters of the 19th of January 1906—written when the facts were fresh in his memory, and when no dispute had occurred.

" The Secretary,　　　　　　　　　　19th January 1906.
　　Melbourne.

Port Pirie. I returned here this morning after having been at Port Pirie and Broken Hill. I had a battle royal with Mr. Fell extending over most of two days, and do not think that I ever had such a task before. However, I consider I beat him in the end, and I have fixed up with him to do his business at the rate allowed me by the committee of the Combination—sixpence. I tried very hard to do better than this, but I think that we have got an excellent arrangement. The matter is not finally closed up because I have to write him the terms that I intend to propose, but the thing is virtually settled." Howard writes to the same effect to his brother on the same date, and says—" This is not absolutely definitely settled, but I think there is no fear of the business not being completed." I prefer to accept the evidence of these contemporaneous letters to Mr. Howard's present statement from memory—that the matter was absolutely concluded before Fell left—that, so far as agreement was concerned, the thing was absolutely concluded—absolutely definitely settled.

H. C. of A.
1908.

BARRIER
WHARFS LTD.
v.
W. SCOTT
FELL & Co.
LTD.

Higgins J.

All the evidence points to the fact that the main matter—the wharfage rate—was practically arranged; but that the defendants' directors were to have all the terms, minor as well as major, put before them, so as to enable them to decide as to accepting or rejecting a contract of a rather delicate and complex nature.

Now, as to the correspondence in which the contract is said to have been " partly contained." The defendants wrote a letter on 24th January 1906 from Sydney; and this crossed a letter from the plaintiffs of 25th January from Adelaide. The defendants' letter says:—" Referring to the writer's interview with you in connection with the wharfage at Port Pirie, kindly let us have, as promised, your lowest quotation for wharfage on coal, landed over your wharves, which we understand will not exceed sixpence per ton. In your offer it will be necessary to stipulate that the wharf will be available when required by us, and if you will allow our steamers to be free of tonnage dues, we will endeavour to meet you to the extent of sixpence per ton. Your prompt reply will be appreciated."

This letter bears no indication of a completed agreement. The plaintiffs' letter of 25th January 1906 says:—" Referring to our recent interviews on the subject of wharfage at Port Pirie, I beg to state that I am prepared to find accommodation for your steamers at our wharf, you to be charged sixpence (6d.) per ton on all coal and coke landed there, provided you undertake to do all your business other than that with the Broken Hill Proprietary Co. with us—I understand your coal contracts provide for approximately 50,000 tons exclusive of the Proprietary Company. Tonnage dues as per printed schedule handed you to be charged. I undertake to provide a berth for your steamers at all times on the understanding that reasonable notice, say two days, be given to our manager at Port Pirie of expected arrivals. If this arrangement is acceptable to you I suggest that it be for a term of two years from 1st March next. Every facility will be given your business on our wharf so that quick despatch may be obtained."

So far as form is concerned, this is an offer; notice of arrival is for the first time mentioned; and the term of two years from 1st March is merely suggested, " if this arrangement is acceptable."

The question now is, has the offer contained in that letter of 25th January 1906 been accepted?   The next letter of the defendants is dated 29th January 1906.

" We are in receipt of your letter of the 25th inst., which has evidently crossed ours in reference to the same subject.   We are anxious to do business with you if possible, and will endeavour to come to your figure, provided you agree to waive tonnage dues on all our steamers loading and discharging at your wharf.   Please let us have an early reply, as the representative of this office leaves for Port Pirie in a few days should necessity for so doing then exist."

It will be noticed that in this letter no reference is made to any of the terms mentioned in the letter of 25th January 1906 except the wharfage rate and tonnage dues.   The defendants are merely anxious to do business with the plaintiffs and inclined to consent to the wharfage rate (not necessarily to conclude the agreement) if tonnage dues are waived.   I cannot find, so far, any definite agreement, or anything but commercial higgling as to tonnage dues before deciding as to making the proposed contract.

On 31st January 1906, the plaintiffs write to the defendants: —" I have to thank you for your favour of the 29th inst. duly received, and I note all you say.   I hope we shall be able to fix up our wharfage arrangements, and I shall be happy to see your representative as he comes through on his way to Port Pirie.   If I can be of any assistance please command me.   I could not entertain the suggestion to waive the tonnage dues on your steamers visiting our wharf.   It would be quite contrary to the wharf agreement and the custom.   Of course you are aware that a steamer paying at one wharf has not to pay at another; this could all be arranged to your satisfaction I feel sure."

At this stage the plaintiffs have declined to waive the tonnage dues; and the defendants have said nothing with regard to any of the proposed stipulations except as to wharfage rates and dues; have said nothing as to accepting or rejecting the contract. Then comes the defendants' letter of the 2nd February, on which Mr *Starke* has so much relied for the plaintiffs.   " We thank you for your favour of the 31st ulto. contents of which are noted.   We are willing to conclude with you for wharfage

H. C. of A.
1908.

BARRIER
WHARFS LTD.
v.
W. SCOTT
FELL & Co.
LTD.

Higgins J.

H. C. of A
1908.

BARRIER
WHARFS LTD.
v.
W. SCOTT
FELL & Co.
LTD.

Higgins J.

on the basis of sixpence per ton and will be glad if you will make a contract for our approval and signature. We must have permission to store what necessary plant we may have for use in connection with working while alongside your wharf, free of charge. We take it you will grant us this as customary, and as offered by others. We thank you for your kind offer of assistance should we require any in Adelaide, and we will not fail to avail ourselves of such should an opportunity occur."

To my mind this letter merely expresses contentment with sixpence per ton as wharfage, a willingness to conclude on that basis; and a request for a contract to be submitted for approval as well as signature—approval, not of solicitors, but of the Board of Directors. In effect, the defendants say : "The rate for wharfage is the central factor. Now that we have settled that, let us see the whole proposal in the form of a contract, so that we may decide whether we will yield on the minor question of tonnage dues. We have not consented to pay tonnage dues; but we may consent when we see that all the other terms are satisfactory." There are cases in which silence gives consent; but I cannot infer consent from the silence of the letter. Indeed, the plaintiffs seem to me to have come to the same conclusion, for on the 6th of February Howard writes the following letter :—

"I am obliged for your favour of the 2nd inst. to hand this morning, and I note with pleasure that you have decided to accept the wharfage rate of sixpence per ton as per correspondence which has passed, and I will arrange a contract accordingly. We will arrange to store your plant on the wharf free of charge."

Howard does not say in that letter that the defendants have decided to accept his offer as detailed in the letter of 25th January, but that the defendants have decided to accept the wharfage rate of 6d. per ton; and he will proceed to "arrange a contract accordingly."

There is now a pause in the correspondence. The letter of 6th February is the last of the letters on which the plaintiffs rely as containing the alleged contract. So far, I am clearly of opinion that no contract has been shown. But the plaintiffs also rely on the subsequent correspondence and acts of the parties as evidence that there was a concluded contract in the conversation and letters up to 6th February. I shall assume—as there is no argument to the contrary—that this position is open to the plaintiffs notwithstanding the pleadings and particulars delivered. Mr. Fell left for Europe about the middle of February; 1st March came, and the defendants' steamers began to come with their coal for the mines at Port Pirie, and berthed at other wharves. The plaintiffs knew of this fact from the first, and made no complaint to the defendants. Mr. Howard happened to be in Sydney on other business, and called on Mr. Dawson, a director of the defendant company, at their office on about 15th March. If I have to decide between the account of the conversation given by Mr. Howard, and the account given by Mr. Dawson, I should accept the latter. It is more circumstantial and probable; and it agrees with what was written by the plaintiffs shortly afterwards. Howard was a director of the Broken Hill South Mining Co.; and he expressed to Dawson his anxiety to get the stock of coal increased for that company. Dawson said he had sent 500 tons by the Pocohontas. Howard asked—incidentally—" When are you going to send your steamers to our wharf? We are all ready for you." Dawson said "I am waiting for the promised ageement." Howard, "Haven't you got that yet? I will send it along." Howard, on cross-examination, says he does not recollect any arrangement to send the draft agreement to Dawson —says he thought it had been sent; and yet, on 21st March, he writes to the defendants :—" You will receive by this mail from the Barrier Wharf Company's solicitors in Melbourne a draft form of agreement as arranged by myself with you last week, which I trust will be found in order."

The plaintiffs' solicitors, Messrs Bruce and Robinson, sent the draft agreement on 23rd March. This draft went beyond what the plaintiffs can claim on their own evidence; for it purports to bind the defendants as to all vessels loading or unloading at Port Pirie—even vessels loading for export. It should have been confined to vessels with coal or coke. It also purports to bind the defendants by all the numerous rules and regulations in the schedule—an obligation which had not previously been suggested. These variances and others of a minor character tend to show that the parties were not yet *ad idem*; although I

H. C. of A.
1908.

BARRIER
WHARFS LTD.
v.
W. SCOTT
FELL & CO.
LTD.

Higgins J.

H. C. of A.
1908.

BARRIER
WHARFS LTD.
v.
W. SCOTT
FELL. & CO.
LTD.

Higgins J.

do not treat such variances as conclusive, for it is not uncommon for solicitors in drawing formal agreements to try to vary and improve informal agreements in the interests of their principals. On 28th March the defendants write to the plaintiffs acknowledging the draft agreement and adding :—

" We would like, however, to have a little further information in reference to the proposed agreement, as now that we have had the actual working with several steamers we see very grave difficulties presenting themselves.　As you are doubtless aware, all the coal from our vessels is now being discharged at the Proprietary Wharf, as under the old conditions the lead is also loaded there.　We understand all concentrates and ore are or will be loaded at the Barrier Wharf ; it seems apparent to us that if we agree to the conditions of the agreement now under consideration, it will mean that we shall have to discharge part of our inward coal cargo at the Proprietary Wharf, shift berths to the Barrier Wharf to discharge the balance, and return to the Proprietary Wharf to load the lead.　These operations will necessarily be attended with the loss of time and much expense. In addition to this it will entail the erection of a separate discharging plant, entailing an additional outlay of at least £1,000. We shall, however, be pleased to have your views on this matter, and we can assure you that we are willing to enter into any contract for the benefit of our mutual interests, provided that we are not asked to make any agreement that will operate against us, and we feel sure that you would not ask nor expect us to do this. We are perfectly willing to discharge any vessels at your wharf that have no cargo on board for the Broken Hill Proprietary (conditionally that your plant is used), but we see many obstacles if we are expected to move from wharf to wharf."

The difficulties indicated in this letter would strike one as genuine ; but, whether they were genuine or not, the defendants write as being unconscious of having made any agreement yet. The letter speaks of " the proposed agreement," and of willingness to enter into any contract for the parties' mutual interests, and of perfect willingness to discharge vessels at the plaintiffs' wharf if there be no cargo on board for the Broken Hill Proprietary.　The reply of the plaintiffs dated 2nd April is significant.

H. C. of A.
1908.

BARRIER
WHARFS LTD.
r.
W. SCOTT
FELL & Co.
LTD.

Higgins J.

The plaintiffs do not assert : "But the agreement is actually made, it is not merely proposed." The plaintiffs minimise the alleged difficulties; suggest that, with so much business, the vessels with coal for the Proprietary could be kept separate from the vessels with coal for the other companies ; and speak of the agreement as "suggested." The letter winds up with vague expressions of hope and good will, thus :—" I hope that you can see your way to arrange for your steamers to come to our wharf at an as early date as possible, and I can assure you on our part that we are ready and willing to carry out our part of the contract to facilitate your business in every way."

Mr *Starke* has laid great stress on the use of the word "contract" as showing that the contract alleged in the statement of claim had been made. I cannot so read the letter. The words which follow indicate, to my mind, that the words "our part of the contract" are used in the loose popular sense, and refer to some friendly understanding as to helping the defendants in the business. For the defendants were not in the coal ring or in the shipping ring, and might need friendly assistance. On 6th April, the defendants write that the matter is being placed before the Board of Directors. "Meanwhile we have to thank you sincerely for your kind offers of assistance to facilitate our business in connection with the carrying out of the contract. As before explained there are several matters in connection with the subject under discussion that require serious consideration, meantime we can assure you that it is our desire to work in with you as much as possible ; and we shall feel obliged if you will inform us, in the event of our being able to arrange as you suggest for some of the steamers to discharge the whole of the cargoes (outside the Broken Hill Proprietary Co.) at your wharf at what price you would be prepared to do the stevedoring, that is, the discharging of the coal and the loading of the concentrates."

This letter clearly treats the agreement as not yet made. It seeks information as to the price of stevedoring " in the event of our being able to arrange as you suggest for some of the steamers to discharge the whole of the cargoes (outside the Broken Hill Proprietary Co.) " at the plaintiffs' wharf. It echoes, but inaccurately, the phraseology of the final clause of the letter of

H. C. of A.
1908.

BARRIER
WHARFS LTD.
v.
W. SCOTT
FELL & CO.
LTD.

Higgins J.

2nd April :—" Your kind offers of assistance to facilitate our business in connection with the carrying out of the contract." Here again the word " contract " is used ; but, if it refer to the alleged contract between the plaintiffs and the defendants, the sentence is almost unmeaning. I rather think that the defendants refer to the seven contracts to supply the Broken Hill mines, all of which were in the same terms and covering the same period, under the name " the contract." But even if it refer to a contract between the plaintiffs and the defendants, it is clear from the rest of the letter that it must mean the contract projected, not the contract made. In any case, nothing was further from the defendants' mind than to admit that there was a binding contract as now alleged ; for the letter speaks of the sending of vessels to the plaintiffs' wharf as if it were a matter contingent, not obligatory. The defendants then make inquiries as to stevedoring, and on 11th April the defendants telegraph :—" If can arrange steamer your wharf what rate can you discharge her coal only you find plant." The plaintiffs telegraph " Fourteen pence stevedoring, but company hope give us lower quote when secretary returns from Pirie," and defendants telegraph on 12th April, " Have instructed Pirie office discharge Pocohontas Barrier Wharf you find necessary plant sails eighteenth give us best rate possible."

On the 17th April the defendants write to the plaintiffs :—" A suitable opportunity presented itself in the case of the S.S. Pocohontas which could have been discharged at your wharf, as she had no coal outside of the Proprietary Co." (evidently a mistake for " no coal for the Proprietary Co. ")' and we wired you accordingly. We are in receipt of a telegram from our Port Pirie office this morning informing us that you were unable to accommodate this vessel. We shall not fail to advise you when arrangements will permit of us sending vessels to your wharf, and we regret that you were unable to avail yourself of the opportunity in the case of the Pocohontas."

This letter obviously treats the defendants as still free to send or not to send their vessels to the plaintiffs' wharf. It shows an intention to experiment as to the plaintiffs' wharf in the case of vessels not containing any cargo for the Proprietary. It

H. C. OF A.
1908.

BARRIER
WHARFS LTD.
v.
W. SCOTT
FELL & CO.
LTD.

Higgins J.

certainly shows no consciousness of an obligation dating back to 1st March, such as the plaintiffs claim to exist. The plaintiffs' explain that the defendants' agent at Port Pirie has misinformed the defendants, and the Pocohontas is therefore discharged at the plaintiffs' wharf and pays sixpence per ton wharfage, and the usual tonnage dues. On 23rd April the defendants write :—" We cannot quite reconcile the difference of opinion that apparently exists concerning the adaptability of your wharf for the discharge of this vessel's cargo, but as we have your assurance that everything is in order, we have instructed our Port Pirie office that our arrangements with you must be respected and the vessel must discharge there. Please have your wharfinger wire us when work is commenced, when we shall instruct him whether it is necessary to incur any overtime."

The statement here, that "arrangements with you must be respected," does not show that the contract proposed had been made. Arrangements had been made to have the Pocohontas discharged at the plaintiffs' wharf, and these "arrangements" must be carried out. Meanwhile, the draft agreement was not returned by the defendants, and on 29th May Messrs. Bruce and Robinson write for it to Sydney. Mr. Dawson was at Broken Hill at the time; and Mr. Fell was still away from Australia. The latter returned in August 1906; and on 27th August Messrs. Bruce and Robinson write again complaining of the delay. The expressions used are significant: "As you are aware the *preliminary arrangements* were made by letter in February last and on 23rd March a draft of the *proposed* formal contract was sent to you for perusal . . . At the same time we have also to point out that the contract is not being complied with inasmuch as certain business which should have been transacted with our client has been done elsewhere." This is the first indication of an assertion on the part of the plaintiffs of anything of the nature of breach of contract; and it comes from the solicitors, not from the plaintiffs or Howard. It seems to be rather inconsistent also with treating the letters of February as mere "preliminary arrangements." But probably the explanation is that the contract was to come into operation as from 1st March; and if it should be signed, the obligation would have to relate back

H. C. of A.
1908.

BARRIER
WHARFS LTD.
v.
W. SCOTT
FELL & CO.
LTD.

Higgins J.

to that date. The defendants promise that Mr. Fell will go into the matter. All this time the defendants' vessels are coming to Port Pirie, and discharging at the Proprietary wharf; but in December the defendants write, as to the Cape Corrientes, that the defendant company "are endeavouring to make arrangements to discharge the whole of her coal cargo at your wharf"; and ask for bedrock quotation for stevedoring. The defendants add:—"It is our intention as far as possible to send these steamers to your wharf when the occasion will permit." The plaintiffs do not write insisting that the carrying out of this intention "when the occasion will permit" is not a satisfaction of the alleged contract; but make arrangements for prompt discharge at 13d. per ton. On 7th February 1907 Messrs. Bruce and Robinson again demand the return of the agreement, and claim damages for breach. On 11th February the defendants write denying knowledge of any contract.

I am of opinion that there was no contract concluded in the conversations and letters referred to in par. 4 of the statement of claim, and in the particulars given thereunder; and that the subsequent facts and correspondence in no way establish the fact that there was such a contract. It is true that the schedule rate for wharfage was 9d. per ton; and that the defendants paid, in respect of the Pocohontas and the Cape Corrientes, only 6d. per ton—being the rate specified in the proposed agreement. But, in my opinion, this reduced rate was accepted in the hope that the contract would be made, which was not made. The business which the defendants could bring to the Port Pirie wharves was so considerable that the plaintiffs were only too glad to take the defendants' steamers at the lower rate—a rate which, according to the evidence, was the same as that payable by the defendants at the Proprietary wharf. Moreover this is not an action for short payment of wharfage rates—not an action for the difference between sixpence and ninepence per ton.

I have been referred to a multitude of cases on the question of contract or no contract; but I think the law, so far as applicable to this case, is clearly enough settled. The difficulty lies in firmly grasping the essential facts, and in applying well known legal principles thereto. Was there a "final mutual assent" of the parties to this alleged agreement ?　This is the phrase used by Lord *Westbury* L.C. in *Chinnock* v. *Marchioness of Ely* (1), and adopted by Lord *Cairns* L.C. in *Rossiter* v. *Miller* (2).　I was much impressed at first with the candid admission of Mr. Fell, in answer to a question put by myself, as to the letter of the 2nd February 1906.　He said that, unless that letter leaves open the question of tonnage dues, there is nothing left to be settled (leaving aside the question of a written contract).　But, on examining closely that letter, one sees that it says neither yes nor no to the small item of the tonnage dues.　It leaves that matter open until the board of the defendant company could see all the conditions of the proposed contract set forth in one document.　From first to last there is nothing to indicate acceptance of any of the terms of the proposed agreement, except that as to the wharfage rate ; and there is nothing to indicate that the defendants at any time gave their final assent to the terms proposed in the letter of 25th January.　This is not the case of an acceptance coupled with the request for a formal document—not such a case as that referred to in *Rossiter* v. *Miller* (3) or in *Crossley* v. *Maycock* (4).　This is a case in which there has been no acceptance of the proposed terms at all.　No one disputes, of course, that parties may make a binding contract by letters or otherwise, although they intend to have a complete formal agreement drawn up.　It is all a question of intention ; and in this case I find that the defendants did not mean to bind themselves until they had an opportunity of considering the whole of the terms in a formal agreement.　It is also significant that the first suggestion that there was already a binding agreement came to the defendants, not from the plaintiffs, but from the plaintiffs' solicitors, after the letters had been submitted to the ingenious scrutiny of lawyers.　It was urged strongly on me that the silence of the defendants in the letter of 2nd February with regard to the tonnage dues, and indeed with regard to the other terms proposed, was evidence of assent to all the terms ; and reference was made to some remarks by Lord *Esher* M.R. in *Wiedemann* v. *Walpole* (5).　But there is no such legal principle

H. C. of A.
1908.

BARRIER
WHARFS LTD.
v.
W. SCOTT
FELL & Co.
LTD.

Higgins J.

(1) 4 D.J. & S., 638, at p. 645.　　(4) L.R. 18 Eq., 180.
(2) 3 App. Cas., 1124, at p. 1139.　(5) (1891) 2 Q.B., 534, at pp. 537, 538.
(3) 3 App. Cas., 1124.

H. C. of A.
1908.

BARRIER
WHARFS LTD.
v.
W. SCOTT
FELL & Co.
LTD.

Higgins J.

as to silence. In each the inference from silence, if any, must depend on the facts of the case and on common sense. As *Kay* L.J. puts it (1):—" The only fair way of stating the rule of law is that in every case you must look at all the circumstances under which the letter was written, and you must determine for yourself whether the circumstances are such that the refusal to reply alone amounts to an admission." In other words, there is no rule of law on the subject at all. In this case the defendants merely express willingness to conclude a contract " *on the basis* " of 6d. wharfage, and a desire to see a contract with all the terms. But even if the letters from that of 24th January to that of 2nd February inclusive could be treated as sufficient, if there were nothing else, to show a contract, the defendants are entitled to have the whole of the correspondence, and the whole of the facts examined: *Hussey* v. *Horne-Payne* (2); and when these are examined, it is, to my mind, clear that there was not any contract. It is a case in which, as *Lindley* L.J. said in *May* v. *Thomson* (3):—" the parties corresponded intending to come to an agreement, fully expecting that they would come to an agreement, knowing perfectly well that the subject-matter of the sale was such that a formal agreement was absolutely essential, and that certain things of very great importance in matters of this kind . . . would have to be discussed and finally settled when they signed the final contract." In that case it was held that there was no agreement, although " the parties thought that they had agreed to all the more material terms "; as they did not intend to be bound until the final agreement was signed.

I accept also the view put by Lord *Cranworth* in the case of *Ridgway* v. *Wharton* (4) that the fact of the parties contemplating a subsequent document of agreement is strong evidence to show that they did not intend the previous negotiations to amount to an agreement.

As for the question of damages, I was disposed to make an assessment so as to save the parties the expense of a new trial in the event of my decision being reversed. But I do not think that I have proper material for a satisfactory assessment; and it

(1) (1891) 2 Q.B., 534, at p. 541.   (3) 20 Ch. D., 705, at p. 722.
(2) 4 App. Cas., 311, at p. 316.   (4) 6 H.L. C., 238, at pp. 263, 268.

seems better that I should leave the question of damages open for further consideration, if necessary, of both parties, and probably for further evidence.

I direct judgment for the defendants, with costs. Certify for discovery.

H. C. of A.
1908.

BARRIER
WHARFS LTD.
v.
W. SCOTT
FELL & Co.
LTD.

From this judgment the plaintiffs now appealed to the Full Court.

Starke, for the appellants. The appellants do not now rely on any verbal negotiations as forming part of the contract. By the letters ending with that of 6th February 1906 there was a concluded contract. The drawing up of a formal contract was not intended to be a condition precedent to the parties being bound. Such an intention must be shown by distinct words : *Bonnewell v. Jenkins* (1). The mere expression of a desire to have the arrangement put into formal terms where there has been an acceptance of an offer does not prevent there being a binding contract : *Crossley* v. *Maycock* (2) ; *Fry on Specific Performance* 4th ed., pp. 122, 227.

[BARTON J. referred to *Lewis* v. *Brass* (3).]

ISAACS J. referred to *Pollock on Contracts*, 7th ed., p. 40. The sending of a document to a solicitor is cogent evidence that the parties did not intend to be bound until a formal contract is signed : *Ridgeway* v. *Wharton* (4).]

If a formal document is drawn up and signed it may be concluded that the preceding transactions were negotiations leading up to the contract. There is a great difference between contracts for the sale of land and ordinary mercantile contracts. In the former case it is the usual thing to have a formal contract drawn up, but in the latter case it is quite exceptional.

[GRIFFITH C.J.—The surrounding circumstances, including the subsequent conduct of the parties, may be looked at to see whether the parties intended to be bound : *Howard Smith & Co. Ltd.* v. *Varawa* (5).

(1) 8 Ch. D., 70.
(2) L.R., 18 Eq., 180, at p. 181.
(3) 3 Q.B.D., 667.

(4) 6 H.L.C., 238.
(5) 5 C.L.R., 68.

H. C. of A.
1908.

BARRIER
WHARFS LTD.
v.
W. SCOTT
FELL & Co.
LTD.

ISAACS J.—Where there are a number of important details left to be discussed and agreed upon the parties will not be held to be bound: *Page* v. *Norfolk* (1).]

There were no essentials which had not been agreed upon on 6th February.

[ISAACS J.—After a contract has apparently been made the parties may go on negotiating. Then neither of them can go back and say a contract has been made: *Brauer* v. *Shaw* (2).]

There would then be a re-opening of the matter, but it has never been pleaded or contended that that happened here. There is nothing ambiguous in the contract, and therefore the subsequent correspondence cannot be looked at to see what the parties thought the contract meant: *Marshall* v. *Berridge* (3). Unless there is something in the subsequent correspondence which breaks down the *primâ facie* agreement, that agreement stands: *Hussey* v. *Horne-Payne* (4). Where there is a clear contract by letters, a subsequent proposal to add a new term does not affect the existence of the contract: *Bristol, Cardiff, and Swansea Aërated Bread Co.* v. *Maggs* (5); *Bellamy* v. *Debenham* (6).

Schutt (*Coldham* with him), for the respondents. Up to 6th February all the terms of the contract had not been agreed upon. There were many other and important matters to be arranged for besides those mentioned up to that time. See *Brogden* v. *Metropolitan Railway Co.* (7). The parties intended not to be bound until a formal contract was entered into, and their subsequent conduct shows that they were waiting for that formal contract to be prepared. Even if the letters taken together did settle the terms of the contract, they were never intended to be operative as they stood.

[He also referred to *May* v. *Thomson* (8).]

Starke in reply referred to *Austin* v. *Austin* (9); *Bruner* v. *Moore* (10); *May* v. *Thomson* (11); *Wiedemann* v. *Walpole* (12).

(1) 70 L.T., 781.
(2) 168 Mass., 198.
(3) 19 Ch. D., 233, at p. 241.
(4) 4 App. Cas., 311, at p. 317.
(5) 44 Ch. D., 616, at p. 625.
(6) 45 Ch. D., 481, at p. 486.

(7) 2 App. Cas., 666, at p. 674.
(8) 20 Ch. D., 705, at p 716.
(9) (1905), V.L.R. 564; 27 A.L.T., 43.
(10) (1904), 1 Ch., 305, at p. 312.
(11) 20 Ch. D., 705, at p. 723.
(12) (1891), 2 Q.B., 534.

H. C. of A.
1908.

BARRIER
WHARFS LTD.
v.
W. SCOTT
FELL & CO.
LTD.

Griffith C.J.

GRIFFITH C.J. The matter has been very fully discussed, and nothing would be gained by reserving our judgment. The plaintiffs are the owners of a wharf at Port Pirie, and the defendants are a company carrying on the business of coal carriers from New South Wales to Port Pirie. They carry a large quantity of coal to that port, and take away from it cargoes of ores and metals, and it appears that a very large portion of the coal they carry is for the Broken Hill Proprietary Co. Ltd. The defendants were anxious to make a contract with the plaintiffs for the use of the plaintiffs' wharf for discharging their cargoes. Negotiations took place between the representatives of the plaintiffs and the defendants with the view of arranging for berthing the defendants' ships at the plaintiffs' wharf, except when those ships were engaged in carrying coal solely for the Broken Hill Proprietary Co., that company's coal being delivered at its own wharf. In negotiating a contract of that kind many things must necessarily be taken into consideration, amongst others the price to be paid for the accommodation, and it appears that the price was discussed on the basis of a certain rate per ton on all coal landed. After some discussion the rate was fixed, more or less definitely, at sixpence per ton. The ordinary price at Port Pirie was ninepence per ton, although the defendants paid only sixpence to the Broken Hill Proprietary Co. After negotiations had gone on for some time the plaintiffs' manager was asked to make an offer in writing to be submitted to the board of directors of the defendant company, and on 25th January 1906 the plaintiffs' manager wrote to the defendants as follows :—" I beg to state that I am prepared to find accommodation for your steamers at our wharf, you to be charged sixpence (6d.) per ton on all coal and coke landed there, provided you undertake to do all your business other than that with the Broken Hill Proprietary Co. with us. I understand your coal contracts provide for approximately 50,000 tons exclusive of the Proprietary Co. Tonnage dues as per printed schedule handed you to be charged. I undertake to provide a berth for your steamers at all times on the understanding that reasonable notice, say two days, be given to our manager at Port Pirie of

H. C. of A.
1908.

BARRIER
WHARFS LTD.
v.
W. SCOTT
FELL & Co.
LTD.

Griffith C.J.

expected arrivals. If this arrangement is acceptable to you I suggest that it be for a term of two years from 1st March next."

That letter referred to five distinct conditions or terms of the proposed contract :—

(1) The price, sixpence per ton on all coal and coke landed at the wharf :

(2) That the defendants should undertake to do all their business other than that with the Proprietary Co. with the plaintiffs :

(3) Tonnage dues to be charged as per printed schedule handed to the defendants' manager :

(4) That a berth should be provided for the defendants' steamers at all times on reasonable notice, say two days, being given :

(5) That the arrangement should be for a term of two years.

I pause here to remark that, although those were the principal things to be determined in a contract of this kind, necessarily a great many other things had to be settled. When the ship is berthed alongside of the wharf, what is to be done there? Are the shipowners to provide their own trucks? Are they to be allowed to keep their coal on the wharf for an indefinite time? What other use may they make of the wharf? There are a great number of details incident to a contract of that sort, and it might be anticipated that the parties would come to some understanding about them before a formal agreement was entered into. They were matters of detail as to which there would probably be little or no difficulty, but still they were matters to be settled, and not left at large to be determined from time to time as occasion might arise. I mention this point because it is very relevant to the inquiry whether the matters referred to in the correspondence were regarded by the parties as the only matters to be dealt with in the contract. The learned Judge below pointed out—and I entirely adopt what he said—that "it is one thing for two parties to settle what are to be the terms of an agreement, if it should be made ; and quite another thing to make the agreement."

The letter of 25th January 1906 was replied to by the defendants on 29th January as follows :—" We are anxious to do business with you if possible and will endeavour to come to your

H. C. of A.
1908.

BARRIER
WHARFS LTD.
v.
W. SCOTT
FELL & Co.
LTD.

Griffith C.J.

figure provided you agree to waive tonnage dues on all our steamers loading and discharging at your wharf." That is the only one of the five terms to which any reference is made. In reply to that the plaintiffs' manager wrote on 31st January :— " I hope we shall be able to fix up our wharfage arrangements. . . . I could not entertain the suggestion to waive the tonnage dues on your steamers visiting our wharf. It would be quite contrary to the wharf agreement and the custom. Of course you are aware that a steamer paying at one wharf has not to pay at another ; this could all be arranged to your satisfaction, I am sure." That, in my opinion, shows that there were then some conditions still to be arranged between the parties.

Then on 2nd February the defendants wrote a letter which the plaintiffs say amounts to an acceptance of a definite offer. They wrote :—" We are willing to conclude with you for wharfage on the basis of 6d. per ton and will be glad if you will make a contract for our approval and signature."

They then added another term, viz., that they must have permission to store their plant free of charge, to which the plaintiffs afterwards agreed. Do, then, the words I have quoted amount to the conclusion of an agreement on the terms mentioned in the letter of 25th January ? I cannot see how those words can reasonably be held to have that meaning, especially when the matters referred to in the letter of 31st January had still to be arranged to the defendants' satisfaction. Sixpence per ton had been the basis of the discussion between the plaintiffs and the defendants, and the defendants were willing to enter into a contract on that basis. When the defendants said " we will be glad if you will make a contract for our approval and signature," they evidently intended a contract that would contain provisions for all that might be necessary in carrying out a bargain of that kind, including the terms that " could be arranged," and not a contract containing only the terms mentioned in the correspondence.

The plaintiffs replied on 6th February :—" I note with pleasure that you have decided to accept the wharfage rate of sixpence per ton as per correspondence which has passed, and I will arrange a contract accordingly." It appears to me that the words both of the letter of 2nd February and of that of 6th Febuary are

H. C. of A.   words of futurity relating to a contract to be made thereafter in
1908.   conformity with the terms which had been arranged preliminarily

Barrier   in the correspondence.

Wharfs Ltd.   I agree, therefore, with the conclusion of the learned Judge
v.   below that up to that time there was no concluded contract. It

W. Scott
Fell & Co.   appears to me that what the defendants did was to intimate
Ltd.   their willingness to enter into a contract upon the basis of

Griffith C.J.   the terms as to which there had been a provisional agreement,
but that a formal contract must be drawn up, which was to be
approved by them, and that that approval was to be given
before a concluded contract should come into existence.

It is said for the plaintiffs that, even if that were so *primâ
facie*, yet the subsequent correspondence showed that in fact
there was a contract entered into on 6th February ; and that, if
there was any ambiguity in the terms of that contract, the
subsequent correspondence showed what the real intention of the
parties was. For the defendants it is said that, even if the
documents up to 6th February on their face disclosed *primâ
facie* a concluded contract, the subsequent correspondence was in
the nature of continued negotiation, and showed that a concluded
contract had not been entered into. I do not think it is necessary
to refer in detail to that correspondence. It is sufficient to refer
to one or two of the letters. The plaintiffs prepared a draft
agreement, in which were inserted various conditions certainly not
to be found in the correspondence, and some of which are inconsistent with the correspondence. The defendants replied, pointing
out objections to these proposals, and, amongst other things,
they pointed out that, in the event of their carrying coal for the
Broken Hill Proprietary Co. as well as for other companies, their
ships would be obliged to go first to the Proprietary wharf to
discharge the coal for that company, then to go to the plaintiffs'
wharf to discharge the balance, and then go back to the
Proprietary wharf to load ore. In reply to that the plaintiffs
endeavoured to meet the arguments of the defendants and
suggested a way in which that difficulty could be avoided. The
plaintiffs further referred to what had taken place as " the agreement suggested," and spoke of the defendants' manager as having
" agreed to enter into the contract with this company." The

defendants then pointed out that there were "several matters in connection with the subject under discussion that require serious consideration, meantime we can assure you that it is our desire to work in with you as much as possible, and we shall feel obliged if you will inform us, in the event of our being able to arrange as you suggest for some of the steamers to discharge the whole cargoes (outside the Broken Hill Proprietary) at your wharf, at what price you would be prepared to do the stevedoring." The plaintiffs' manager in reply writes: "I note that the matter of your business at Port Pirie is receiving the attention of your board." This, to my mind, negatives the idea of an existing concluded contract.

In my judgment the learned Judge below was right in his conclusion that there was no concluded contract in fact; that the letters did not on their face disclose a contract. I think further that, if *primâ facie* they disclosed a contract, the subsequent correspondence shows that it was not in the contemplation of either party that they were to be bound until all the essential preliminaries had been agreed to, nor until a formal contract had been drawn up embodying all the matters incidental to a transaction of such a nature.

BARTON J.　Although this case presents some difficulties, I have come to the same conclusion, upon the ground that what was done by way of correspondence between the parties does not evidence their intention to make that correspondence the actual contract. It is not necessary to enter into any further analysis of the correspondence until we come to the letters of 2nd and 6th February 1906. If the plaintiffs' case is based upon the alleged offer and acceptance contained in those two letters, it is not clear to me that on those letters there was nothing further to be done and that the parties were to be finally bound. It may have been that each of them required for their own protection a formal contract, or that the desire for self protection was exclusively on the part of the defendants. All that is material is that there was to be no contract until the formal contract was approved and signed. The term "We are willing to conclude with you for wharfage" is in itself, perhaps, a little ambiguous. It may be

H. C. OF A.
1908.

BARRIER
WHARFS LTD.
v.
W. SCOTT
FELL & Co.
LTD.

Griffith C.J.

H. C. of A.
1908.

BARRIER
WHARFS LTD.
v.
W. SCOTT
FELL & CO.
LTD.

Barton J.

that the writer did not intend to strike the bargain there and then, or it may be that the interpretation put on the expression by the letter of 6th February—" I note with pleasure that you have decided to accept the wharfage rate of sixpence per ton "—is the correct one, but that is not, I think, reasonably clear. "Wharfage on the basis of sixpence per ton " is a phrase which presents still further difficulty. What is meant by "the basis of sixpence per ton "? Does it mean that an agreement embodying the terms of the correspondence dealing with sixpence per ton is the whole matter to be dealt with as the subject of agreement? That, of course, cannot be entertained for a moment. It must be that there were other terms. If there were, are all those terms contained in the correspondence prior to 6th February? If they are, then does not the demand of a contract for approval and signature evidence that, even, though they appear to be so contained, there were other matters that would have to be included in the contract when it was fully expressive of the desire of the parties? It seems to me that would clearly be so when we look at the terms of the contract which was prepared by the plaintiffs themselves for the defendants' approval. Some of its terms are inconsistent with those in the correspondence, and others are new. The plaintiffs themselves by the draft contract which they tendered seem to admit that there were some other terms to be arranged before finality was reached. Then the expression in the plaintiffs' letter of 6th February, " I will arrange a contract accordingly," seems further to elucidate the matter. It seems a rather clear inference from the defendants' letter of 2nd February that the written document must be submitted for the approval by the defendants of its terms before it would be allowed to bind the defendants, and the answer "I will arrange a contract accordingly" contains no negation of that inference, but rather a more or less clear consent on the part of the plaintiffs to submit such a document, and they in fact did submit a draft of it.

On the whole, whatever opinion one may hold about the consensus on the terms contained in the correspondence, I think that the parties said for themselves that the binding contract must be contained in the final document. That document,

H. C. of A.
1908.

BARRIER
WHARFS LTD.
v.
W. SCOTT
FELL & Co.
LTD.

Barton J.

as submitted in draft, contained more than the terms mentioned in the correspondence.

Further, seeing that the final document was required by the defendants for their own protection, and that their desire for such a document was assented to by the plaintiffs, I think that it cannot be successfully contended that an action could be brought independently of a tender and final settlement of that document. For, after all, the request for a written contract and the fact that that request seemed to be assented to, must mean that the discussion was still open. I think that *Higgins* J. was right in holding that the plaintiffs had not made out their case, and therefore the appeal should be dismissed.

O'CONNOR J. I agree with the conclusion arrived at by the learned Judge of the Court below. I do not think it is necessary to add anything to what has already been said. I think the appeal should be dismissed.

ISAACS J. I am of the same opinion. I base my judgment upon the necessity for a written contract. The question whether such a contract is a condition precedent to the obligation arising depends upon the question whether the written contract was intended by the parties to be a mere record for their convenience and for future reference, or whether it was insisted upon as a *sine quâ non* of the obligation arising at all. In this case I think that, if the appellants' view were acceded to, it would give no meaning to some of the words in the letter of 2nd February. I take the second sentence of that letter to mean that the defendants intimated that they were prepared to enter into a bargain, and that they required for that purpose a contract to be made out for their approval and signature. Merely to say that formal reduction into writing of the arrangement already made was necessary would, I think, not give effect to the words " for our approval and signature." It was not a request to make out a contract which should represent the arrangements of the parties already expressed, but it was a request for a document which the defendants were to see and consider and approve and sign, as a condition of the obligation existing at all.

H. C. of A.
1908.

Barrier
Wharfs Ltd.
v.
W. Scott
Fell & Co.
Ltd.

Isaacs J.

I think this question may very fairly be put:—Suppose the document on being submitted to the defendants was not approved by them, did the parties mean that nevertheless a contractual obligation should exist? I do not think they did.

It is not necessary to go further and say that by the subsequent correspondence and by the terms of the draft agreement the precise conditions in the letters of 2nd and 6th February were departed from. If it were necessary, I think the conduct of the parties subsequent to 6th February shows that it was not understood that they were bound down contractually to the exact terms which had already been set out in the letters. Such a view would be inconsistent with the numerous departures from the terms in those letters. For these reasons I agree that the appeal should be dismissed.

Appeal dismissed with costs.

Solicitor, for the appellants, *Arthur Robinson.*
Solicitors, for the respondents, *Gillott, Bates & Moir.*

B. L.

[HIGH COURT OF AUSTRALIA.]

RALPH HENRY REIS AND ALBERT REIS⎫
(TRADING AS REIS BROS.)　　　　　 ⎬　APPELLANTS ;
PLAINTIFFS,　　　　　　　　　　　　⎭

AND

EDMUND　WILLIAM　CARLING　AND ⎫
COURTNEY CARLING (TRADING AS E. ⎬　RESPONDENTS.
W. CARLING AND CO.)　　　　　　　 ⎭
DEFENDANTS,

ON APPEAL FROM THE SUPREME COURT OF
QUEENSLAND.

Interest on Judgments—Practice—Judgment with costs—Interest—Judicature Act
1900 (Qd.), (64 Vict. No. 6), sec. 3—Judicature Rules 1900—Order XLVII.,
Rule 17, Schedule I., Part VI.

H. C. OF A.
1908.

BRISBANE,
April 30, 31.

SYDNEY,
May 21.

Griffith C.J.,
Barton and
O'Connor JJ.

The English Act 1 & 2 Vict. c. 110, sec. 17, has not been adopted in
Queensland.

Order XLI., Rule 14, of the Rules contained in the Schedule to the
Judicature Act of 1876 provided that every writ of execution for the
recovery of money should be indorsed with a direction to levy interest on
the money sought to be recovered from the time when the judgment or order
was entered or made. Under the Forms prescribed for giving effect to that
Rule interest on costs was to be computed from the date of the certificate
of taxation. Under the Rules of 1900 and the Forms prescribed for writs
of execution interest upon costs is to be computed from the date of entry of
judgment, and not from the date of the certificate of taxation.

Held : (1) The Rules and Forms of 1900 are *intra vires*, being only such a
modification or amendment of the former Rule as was authorized by sec. 3 of
the *Judicature Act* 1900. But—

(2) The Rule does not confer any independent right to recover interest on a
judgment debt. In the absence of any statutory provision conferring such
right, the right to interest is incident to the right to issue execution; and,
therefore, where the judgment debtor by reason of prompt payment of the
debt prevents the issue of a writ of execution, no right to interest accrues.

Decision of the Supreme Court : (*Reis Bros.* v. *Carling & Co.*, 1908 St. R.
Qd., 76), reversed.

APPEAL by special leave from a decision of the Full Court of
Queensland dismissing a motion for a stay of proceedings.

An action between the parties was tried in May and June
1905, and judgment was entered on 11th August in the same
year. The costs under this judgment were not taxed for some
time, and it was not until 29th August 1907 that the taxing
officer, after review, gave his certificate.

On 3rd September 1907 Reis Bros. paid a cheque for the
amount certified to Carling & Co., who gave a receipt expressly
reserving to themselves the right to claim interest on costs
and to issue execution for the same if necessary. The defendants
subsequently demanded interest from the date of judgment until
payment. The plaintiffs refused to comply with this demand, and
took out a summons in Chambers to stay further proceedings.
The application coming on before *Cooper* C.J., he referred it for
hearing to the Full Court, who dismissed the application : *Reis
Bros.* v. *Carling & Co.* (1).

Shand and *Graham*, for the appellants. The respondents
claim under Order XLVII., rr. 13 and 17 and the Forms in
Schedule I., Part VI. It is not now pressed that these rules
are *ultra vires* (*Judicature Act* 1900, 64 Vict. No. 6, sec. 3.) At
common law interest was only allowed on a judgment debt when
an action was brought on the judgment : *Gaunt* v. *Taylor* (2).
1 & 2 Vict. c. 110, sec. 17, declared that every judgment debt
should carry interest from the time of entering up the judgment.
This section, though adopted in other States of the Commonwealth, was not adopted in Queensland. On the common law
side after the passing of this Act interest was held to run from
the time of the entry of the incipitur, and not merely from the
final completion of the judgment after taxation of costs : *Newton*
v. *Grand Junction Railway Co.* (3). A contrary practice obtained in equity : *Attorney-General* v. *Lord Carrington* (4).

(1) 1908 St. R. Qd., 76.   (3) 16 M. & W., 139.
(2) 3 Myl. & K., 302.   (4) 6 Beav., 454.

But, whatever the rules as now made under sec. 3 of the *Judica-* H. C. of A.
ture Act 1900 may mean, and they certainly are very ambiguous, 1908.
there can be no doubt that interest will only run when a writ Reis
of execution has been issued; and even when such a writ has *v.*
been issued the time from which it runs is very doubtful. See Carling.
Order XLII., r. 16, of the English Rules of 1883, and Appendix
H., Form 1, and *Pyman & Co.* v. *Burt* (1). The form of the writ
of *fieri facias* (Schedule I., Part VI., Form 3) shows that the
judgment debt is to be treated separately from the costs upon
which interest is to run from the —— day of ——. The ambiguity which appears in that Form again occurs in Forms Nos. 7
and 11 (writ of elegit) as to the meaning of "date aforesaid."
On general equitable grounds it would be hard on a party, who
is ready and willing to pay the costs as soon as he is informed
of the amount, to have to pay interest thereon for a long period
because taxation has been delayed.

[They referred to 24 Vict. No. 8 (N.S.W.); No. 9 of 1845 (S.A.);
31 Vict. No. 8 (W.A.); *Supreme Court Act* 1890 (Vict.), 54 Vict.
No. 1142; *Payne and Woolcock's Queensland Statutes*, p. 1837;
Rules of Court of 26th May 1863 (Qd.); *Harding's Supreme
Court Practice*, p. 698; English Rules 1883, Order XLII., r. 16;
Queensland Rules 1900, Order XLIV., r. 2; Order LXVII., rr.
46, 47 and 48; *In re North Sydney Investment and Tramway
Co. Limited* (2); *Rolfe and the Bank of Australasia* v. *Flower,
Salting & Co.* (3).]

Macgregor, for the respondents. 1 & 2 Vict. c. 110, sec. 17, has
admittedly never been adopted in Queensland, but there is no
ambiguity in the words "from the date aforesaid" in Form 3 of
Part VI., Schedule I. to the Rules of 1900. If the appellants'
contention as to the construction to be put upon Form 3 is
correct, then no provision has been made for the case where a
fixed sum is allowed for costs. On the other hand, a reading
of the "date aforesaid," as meaning the date of judgment
covers that case as well as the case where costs are left to be
taxed. Forms 3, 7, 9 and 11 in the Schedule show a clear

(1) 1884 W.N., 100; Cab. & E., 207.   N.S.W. L.R. (Eq.), 50.
(2) 7 B.C. (N.S.W.), 18, 53; 18   (3) L.R. 1 P.C., 27.

intention to make interest run from date of judgment. Since the *Judicature Act* costs have become part of the judgment. [He referred to *Boswell* v. *Coaks* (1); *The Jones Brothers* (2); *Pyman & Co.* v. *Burt* (3); *Taylor* v. *Roe* (4); *Garnett* v. *Bradley* (5); *Schroeder* v. *Clough* (6); *Landowners West of England and South Wales Land Drainage and Inclosure Co.* v. *Ashford* (7); *In re London Wharfage and Warehousing Co.* (8); *Ashworth* v. *English Card Clothing Co. Ltd.* (*No.* 2) (9).]

Shand, in reply. The cases cited for the respondents are of no assistance, inasmuch as they are either decided on the Act 1 & 2 Vict. c. 110, sec. 17, or after the English Rules of 1883 had come into force.

Cur. adv. vult.

May 21.   The following judgments were read:—

GRIFFITH C.J. At common law a judgment did not carry interest: *Gaunt* v. *Taylor* (10). By the English Act, 1 & 2 Vict. c. 110, it was provided (sec. 17) that "every judgment debt shall carry interest at the rate of £4 per centum per annum from the time of entering up the judgment . . . until the same shall be satisfied, and such interest may be levied under a writ of execution on such judgment." Sec. 18 provided that decrees and orders of Courts of Equity, rules of Courts of Common Law, and orders in Bankruptcy and Lunacy, whereby any money or costs should be made payable to any person should have the effect of judgments at common law, that the person to whom the same should be payable should be deemed a judgment creditor, and should have all the remedies of a judgment creditor. Upon the construction of this Act it was held by the Court of Common Pleas that interest on costs ran from the entry of the incipitur of judgment: *Fisher* v. *Dudding* (11). This decision was approved and followed by the Court of Exchequer in the case of *Newton*

(1) 57 L.J. Ch., 101; 36 W.R., 65.
(2) 37 L.T., 164, note (b).
(3) 1884 W.N., 100; Cab. & E., 207.
(4) (1894) 1 Ch., 413.
(5) 3 App. Cas., 944.
(6) 46 L.J.C.P., 365; 35 L.T., 850.
(7) 16 Ch. D., 411.
(8) 54 L.J. Ch., 1137; 33 W.R., 836.
(9) (1904) 1 Ch., 704.
(10) 3 Myl. & K., 302.
(11) 3 Scott N.R., 516; 3 M. & G., 238; 10 L.J. N.S., 323.

v. *The Grand Junction Railway Co.* (1). In the Court of Chancery, on the other hand, it was held that interest did not run on costs until the amount had been ascertained by taxation: *Attorney-General* v. *Lord Carrington* (2), a case in which *Fisher* v. *Dudding* (3) was not cited.

From this time the practice of the Court of Chancery and that of the Courts of Common Law appear to have been divergent. Accordingly the forms of *fieri facias* prescribed by the *Regulæ Generales* of Hilary Term 1853 directed the sheriff to levy the sum of " £ (*the amount of all the moneys recovered by the judgment*) . . . together with interest upon the said sum at the rate of £4 per centum per annum from the . . . day of . . . on which day the judgment aforesaid was entered up." The Consolidated General Orders in Chancery of 1860 (Order XXIX., Rule 6) prescribed forms of writs of *fieri facias*, of which the writ appropriate to the recovery of costs directed that interest should be levied from the date of the certificate of taxation. Both these forms were prescribed in order to give effect to the provisions of the Act 1 & 2 Vict. c. 119, sec. 17, as they had been interpreted by the Courts of Common Law and Chancery respectively.

In the year 1863 similar provisions were made by Rules of Court in Queensland. By *Regulæ Generales* of 26th May 1863 the form of writ of *fieri facias* on an execution upon a judgment was prescribed in the same form as by the English Rules of Hilary Term 1853, except that the rate of interest was directed to be £8 per cent. By the General Orders in Equity of 21st August 1863 (Order XXVIII., Rule 6) the form of *fieri facias* was prescribed in terms corresponding to that in the English Consolidated General Order of 1860, except that the rate of interest was left blank. It was evidently assumed that in Queensland, as in England, a judgment debt carried costs. In fact, however, the provisions of the Act 1 & 2 Vict. c. 110, sec. 17, have never been adopted in Queensland, although some provisions of that Act, including secs. 14, 15, 16 and 18, were adopted by the *Common Law Practice Act* 1867, secs. 49, 50, 48, 19.

(1) 16 M. & W., 139.
(2) 6 Beav., 454.

(3) 3 Scott N.R., 516 ; 3 M. & G., 238 ; 10 L.J. N.S., 323.

Apparently, therefore, the Rules of Court and General Orders of 1863, so far as they purported to authorize the recovery under a writ of *fieri facias* of interest on a judgment debt and costs, were *ultra vires*.

Thus matters stood till the passing of the *Judicature Act* 1876 40 Vict. No. 6, which contained a Schedule of Rules and Forms. Order XLI., Rule 14 was as follows: " Every writ of execution for the recovery of money shall be indorsed with a direction to the sheriff . . . to levy the money really due and payable and sought to be recovered under the judgment, stating the amount, and also to levy interest thereon, if sought to be recovered, at the rate of £8 per cent. per annum from the time when the judgment was entered up."

The form of writ of *fieri facias* was also given, which corresponded with that prescribed by the General Orders of 1863 as to the date at which interest on costs was to be levied. A similar form was contained in the Schedule to the English *Judicature Act* 1875 (Appendix F, Form 1).

Under this rule and the Form interest on costs ran from the date of the certificate of taxation: *Schroeder v. Clough* (1). As the rule and Form were incorporated in the Statute, no objection could be taken to the validity of the direction to levy interest, whatever might have been said as to the Rules and Orders of 1863. By the English Rules of 1883 a new form of writ of *fieri facias* was substituted, the effect of which was that interest on costs ran from the date of the judgment: *Pyman & Co. v. Burt* (2). In *Boswell v. Coaks* (3) it was held by the Court of Appeal that this new rule applied to a case in which judgment was given before, but the costs were not taxed till after, the Rules of 1883 came into operation. The Court treated the change as relating to a matter of practice or procedure, and not of substantive right, so that the alteration applied to pending cases. The right to interest on the costs having been given by the Statute of 1 & 2 Vict. c. 110, the substantive effect of the alteration in the Form was to direct that a judgment for costs should in all cases be entered *nunc pro tunc* notwithstanding

(1) 35 L.T., 850.   (2) (1884) W.N., 100.
        (3) 36 W.R., 65; 57 L.J. Ch., 101.

delay in taxation.   This might reasonably be regarded as a
matter of practice.

By the Act 64 Vict. No. 6 (Queensland, 1900) it was declared
that the authority of the Judges of the Supreme Court to make
Rules of Court under the *Judicature Act* extended to making
by way of re-enactment or amendment, any rule to the same
purport and effect as any rule contained in the Schedule to that
Act, with or without modifications or amendments.   Applying
this general provision to the particular case of Order XLI., r. 14,
the Judges were authorized to re-enact that rule with or without
modifications or amendments.   By the Rules of the Supreme
Court 1900, Order XLI., r. 14 was re-enacted (Order XLVII.,
r. 17), with the alteration of the rate on interest from 8 per cent.
to 5 per cent. The forms of writ of *fieri facias* were also altered.
The new form for use by a plaintiff (Schedule I., Part VI.,
Form 3) first directed the sheriff to levy the judgment debt " and
also interest thereon at the rate of £   per cent. per annum
from the (*date of judgment or order*) which said sum and
interest were lately . . . by a judgment . . . bearing
date . . . adjudged . . . to be paid . . . together
with certain costs in the said judgment . . . mentioned and
which costs have been taxed and allowed at the sum of £   as
appears by the Certificate of the Taxing Officer . . . filed
the . . . day of . . .: And further to levy the said sum
of £   " (the costs) " together with interest thereon at the rate
of £   per cent. per annum from the date aforesaid."

It may be noted in passing that the recital that the interest on
the judgment debt was awarded by the judgment itself appears
to be erroneous, and to be founded upon a notion that interest
ran by law upon a judgment debt.

The form of *fieri facias* for costs only (Form 1) was in
substantially the same terms.

The appellants contend that under this Form interest on costs
is to be calculated from the date of the certificate and not from
the date of the entry of judgment.   The utmost that can be said
for the contention is that the words are capable of that construction.   In two other forms of writs of execution, however (9 and
11) in the same Schedule interest on costs is directed in plain

H. C. of A.
1908.

REIS
v.
CARLING.

Griffith C.J.

H. C. of A.
1908.

REIS
v.
CARLING.

Griffith C.J.

terms to be computed from the date of the judgment or order. No reason can be suggested why a different rule should apply to different writs of execution. I think, therefore, that the writs, Forms 3 and 7, should be construed as contended for by the respondents and as held by the Supreme Court.

It was at first contended that, so construed, the rule prescribing the Forms was *ultra vires*, as imposing a new pecuniary liability upon individuals. In my opinion, however, the alteration was a modification or amendment authorized by the Act of 1900, since, as already pointed out, its only substantial effect was to make the addition of a memorandum of the amount of costs upon a judgment already entered equivalent to an entry of judgment for the costs *nunc pro tunc*, which might well be justified under the rule that a suitor is not to be prejudiced by delay on the part of the Court. These appear to have been the only points pressed before the Supreme Court, and I agree with their conclusions upon all of them.

But there is another aspect of the case arising upon the language of Order XLVII., r. 17, which Rule is the sole foundation of the respondents' right to recover interest. Mr. *Shand* contended that in the circumstances of this case that Rule has no application. The costs in question are costs which were awarded upon a judgment for the defendants in an action, but were not taxed until more than two years had elapsed from the judgment. A few days after taxation the appellants paid the amount as certified by the taxing officer, and the respondents' solicitors gave a receipt containing the following passage: "The defendants' claim for interest on costs and their right to issue execution for the same if necessary are hereby expressly reserved." The appellants contend that the only effect of the Rule is to authorize interest to be levied by execution in cases where the party can and does have recourse to that remedy, and that it has not the effect of making the judgment itself carry interest, so that if the judgment creditor, by reason of prompt payment of the judgment debt, has no occasion to issue execution, no right to interest accrues. It is, I think, clear that if an action were brought on the judgment interest could not be claimed as a debt founded upon the Rule. In England, on the other hand, it could be claimed as a debt founded upon the Statute. The question seems, then, to resolve itself into this : Were the appellants entitled to tender the amount of the judgment debt without interest before execution actually issued ?　I can find no ground for answering this question in the negative.　I think, therefore, that the respondents were never entitled to issue execution, and that on this ground, which does not appear to have been presented to the Supreme Court, the appellants were entitled to the stay of proceedings asked for.

BARTON J.　I concur.

O'CONNOR J.　In this case the defendants had a judgment which carried costs.　For reasons which are immaterial in the present appeal the taxation was delayed, and the date of the Taxing Officer's Certificate was over a year later than the date of entry of judgment.　It is to be taken for the purposes of our decision that the judgment was duly entered in accordance with the Rules and Forms now in force in the Supreme Court of Queensland so as to have entitled the defendants to issue a writ of execution under Rule 17 of Order XLVII. if the plaintiffs had failed to pay the amount adjudged to be due.　Before the issue of execution the plaintiffs paid to the defendants the amount of taxed costs appearing by the judgment to have been certified by the Taxing Officer together with interest from the date of the certificate to the date of payment.　The defendants received the amount without prejudice to their rights under the judgment, but contended that, in addition to interest from date of certificate, they were entitled to interest on the costs from the date of entry of judgment, and, as they threatened to issue execution for that amount, the plaintiffs, denying any further liability, applied to the Court for a stay of proceedings.

It is admitted that, if the defendants' contention is good, the application properly failed, and that, if it is not, the application should have been granted.　The Supreme Court, upholding the defendants' contention, refused the application.　It is against that decision that the plaintiffs have appealed, and they base their case on three grounds.　The first is that the writ of *fieri facias*

H. C. of A.
1908.

REIS
v.
CARLING.

O'Connor J.

in the form prescribed under the Rules (Schedule I., Part VI.,
Form 3) on the face of it authorizes levy for interest on costs
from the date of the certificate and not from the date of entry of
judgment. The question turns on the meaning of the words
" date aforesaid " in the seventh last line of the Form. Does
" date aforesaid " refer to the date of the certificate, which is the
date last mentioned, or does it refer to the " date of judgment "
described in those words in the earlier part of the form ?

No doubt the expression " date aforesaid," having regard to its
context, is ambiguous. It is capable of being interpreted either
as the plaintiffs or as the defendants contend. The real meaning
must be ascertained by a consideration of the rest of the Form
and by a comparison of its provisions with the other forms of
writ in the Schedule. It is, I think, quite clear that in Forms 7,
9 and 11 authority is given to levy for interest on costs from
the date of entering judgment. It would appear unlikely that
the Judges intended by these Rules to authorize the levy of
interest for different periods according as the judgment was
executed by writ of *fieri facias*, or by one or other of the forms
of writ referred to. A construction which would bring all forms
into conformity in this respect would be certainly more likely to
give effect to the intention of the makers of the Rules.

In view of these considerations I think that the interpretation
suggested by Mr. *Macgregor* in argument may well be adopted.
He contends that in the form of *fieri facias* writ the date mentioned
in connection with the Taxing Master's certificate is not the date
when the certificate was given, but the date on which it was
filed with the sheriff, which may or may not coincide, and that it
is referred to in the form merely for the purposes of identification,
in the same way as in Judge's orders, documents referred to are
usually identified, and that the expression " date aforesaid "
should not be taken as referring to the date of filing the certificate
when it may with equal correctness grammatically be referred to
date of entry of judgment, particularly as the Form is framed for
the purpose of exercising the power given by Rule 17 of Order
XLVII., which authorizes the indorsement of a writ to levy
interest " from the time when the judgment was entered." This
construction is not only reasonable, but it brings the four forms

of writ which I have mentioned into harmony. For these reasons
I have come to the conclusion that effect will be best given to the
true meaning of the Form and Rules by reading the form of writ
of *fieri facias* as authorizing the levy of interest from the date
of entry of judgment and not from the date of the certificate.

The second objection involves the interpretation of sec. 3 of the
Judicature Act 1900. There is embodied in the *Judicature Act*
1876, as a Schedule, a system of Rules of Procedure with Forms.
In the form of writ of *fieri facias* interest upon costs under a
judgment runs from the date of the Taxing Officer's certificate.
Section 17 empowers the Judges to make further or additional
Rules, and the *Judicature Act* 1900 enlarges that power by
declaring that the authority of the Judges to make Rules of
Court under the original Act "extends to making by way of
re-enactment or otherwise any rule to the same purport and
effect as any rule contained in the Schedule to the Act with or
without modification or amendment." · The matter to be determined is whether it is within the powers of the Judges as so
extended to alter the form of writ of *fieri facias* from being a
direction to levy interest on costs from the date of the Taxing
Officer's certificate into a direction to levy such interest from
the date of entry of judgment in the action.

Rule 14 of the rules in the Schedule to the *Judicature Act*
1876 provides that every writ of execution for the recovery of
money shall be indorsed with a direction to the Sheriff to levy
for interest on the judgment from the time when the judgment
was entered up ; judgment in that connection including the judgment for costs. Within the limits of that direction a form of
writ might have been framed dating the interest on costs from
the entering of judgment. The form actually prescribed in the
Schedule did not go to the full extent of that power. It directed
interest for the purposes of the levy to run from the date of the
Taxing Officer's certificate. In the new rules, prepared by the
Judges under the authority of the *Judicature Act* 1900, the rule
under the 1876 Act, Rule 17 of Order XLVII., reproduces verbatim
the rule of 1876 to which I have referred, but in the form for
carrying it into effect the directions to levy go to the full extent

H. C. of A.
1908.

REIS
v.
CARLING.

O'Connor J.

of the rule and authorize the levy for interest upon costs from the date of entering judgment. Thus, while altering the form of the writ, not going beyond the limits of the direction contained in the statutory rule.

I am of opinion that the alteration of the Form amounts to no more than a re-enactment of the old rule " with a modification," to quote the words of the Statute, which is well within the power conferred. The judgment of *Cotton* L.J. in *Boswell* v. *Coaks* (1) supports the view that such a change of form may well be regarded as only a change in the mode of procedure by which the Court directs its judgment to be made effective.

These were the only grounds argued before the Queensland Supreme Court, and if there had been no other grounds taken I should have come to the conclusion that the appellants' application had been properly refused. But the third objection to the respondents' further proceeding raises an important question. At common law a judgment debt did not carry interest, and the only way of recovering interest on such a debt was by action on the judgment. In England that defect was remedied by 1 & 2 Vict. c. 110, s. 17, which provided that every judgment debt should carry interest at the rate named in the Statute from the time of entering up judgment, and that there might be a levy for the recovery of such interest under a writ of execution on the judgment. The Act also authorized all Courts to frame writs in such forms as they should think fit for carrying that provision of the Statute into effect. In pursuance of that Act the Courts of Common Law issued a form of writ directing levy of all interest recoverable on the judgment debt, including interest on costs, from date of entry of judgment, but the Court of Chancery, acting under the same provisions, issued a writ in the form of a writ of *fieri facias* directing that the interest on costs should run from the date of the Taxing Master's certificate. "That is how it happened," says *Lindley* L.J. in *Boswell* v. *Coaks* (2), "that interest on costs ran in the Court of Chancery from the allocatur and not from date of entry of the incipitur." Such continued to be the practice in

(1) 57 L.J. Ch., 101 ; 36 W.R., 65.   (2) 36 W.R., 65, at p. 66.

the Courts of Common Law and Chancery respectively until the
passing of the first English *Judicature Act*.   In Queensland no
Statute was ever passed making interest payable on a judgment
debt, so that the old rules of practice in the Supreme Court of that
State authorizing the issue of writs at Common Law and in Equity
as in the English Common Law and Chancery Courts respectively,
do not appear to have had any statutory foundation.   In 1876 the
Queensland *Judicature Act* was passed, and then, for the first
time, a statutory right was given to a successful suitor in respect
of interest on a judgment.   The right, however, was not given as
in the English Act, 1 & 2 Vict. c. 110, which enacts that the judgment shall carry interest.   The sole provision relating to the
recovery of interest is that contained in Order XLI., r. 14 of the
Schedule, and the forms of writ for carrying that rule into effect.
No right of action is given in respect of interest on the judgment,
and interest becomes part of the judgment under one set of circumstances only, that is, when a writ of execution to recover the
moneys due on the judgment is issued.   Then the writ may be
indorsed with the claim to recover interest on the judgment, and
the amount levied may include interest accordingly.   As the
form of judgment included the costs, interest on the latter is by
this procedure recoverable.   The Rules and Form now under
consideration follow the same procedure with the exception of
the modification of the writ of *fieri facias* already alluded to.

Such being the only provision in force for the recovery of the
interest in question, the appellants contend that, as the whole
amount of the judgment debt in this case has been paid and
execution cannot be issued except to recover moneys due on a
judgment, the writ cannot issue.   In my opinion, that contention
must prevail.   The intention of the legislature of Queensland as
expressed by their enactment clearly was not to make interest
on a judgment a judgment debt payable by the judgment debtor
as part of that debt, but to make it recoverable only in cases
where the creditor was driven to put in force his remedy by
execution and as incidental to the exercise of that remedy.

As the respondents were not entitled to issue the writ or to
proceed further upon the judgment, it follows that proceedings
on the judgment ought to have been stayed as asked by the

H. C. of A.
1908.

Reis
v.
Carling.

O'Connor J.

H. C. of A.   appellants.   In my opinion, therefore, the appeal must be allowed
1908.   and all further proceedings on the judgment must be stayed.

REIS
v.   *Appeal allowed.*
CARLING.

O'Connor J.   Solicitors, for the appellants, *Atthow & McGregor.*
Solicitors, for the respondents, *Flower & Hart.*

H. V. J.

[HIGH COURT OF AUSTRALIA.]

DWYER . . . . APPELLANT;
PLAINTIFF,

AND

THE RAILWAY COMMISSIONERS OF NEW ⎱ RESPONDENTS.
SOUTH WALES . . . . . ⎰
DEFENDANTS,

ON APPEAL FROM THE SUPREME COURT OF
NEW SOUTH WALES.

H. C. of A.   *Practice—New Trial—Memorandum not signed by counsel who appeared at the*
1908.   *trial—Plaintiff applying in person for rule nisi—Regulæ Generales of the*
Supreme Court (N.S.W.), rr. 150, 151.

SYDNEY,   Rule 150 of the Supreme Court of New South Wales provides that any
May 5.   party who intends to move for a new trial must within a certain time after
the trial file a memorandum of such intention, which by Rule 151 must state,
Griffith C.J.,   *inter alia,* the grounds of the application, and, where the party had counsel
Barton and   at the trial, must be signed by one of such counsel.
O'Connor JJ.

A plaintiff, who appeared at the trial by counsel, was nonsuited.   Counsel's
retainer being then withdrawn, the plaintiff, intending to apply for a new
trial, filed a memorandum for a rule *nisi,* which was not signed by counsel,
and appeared in person in support of his application.   The Supreme Court
refused to entertain the application on the ground that the memorandum did
not comply with Rule 151.

H. C. of A.
1908.

Dwyer
v.
The Rail-
way Commis-
sioners of
New South
Wales.

Held, that as the right of a party to apply for a new trial existed at common law independently of the Rules of Court, and as Rule 151, which imposed a condition upon the exercise of that right, should be, and always had been construed by the Supreme Court, not as an absolute rule, but as a rule of convenience, to be relaxed on good cause being shown, the plaintiff should under the circumstances have been heard on his application for a rule *nisi*.

Decision of the Supreme Court on this point : *Dwyer* v. *Railway Commissioners*, 24 N.S.W. W.N., 72, reversed.

Motion for rule *nisi* refused on the merits.

APPEAL from a decision of the Supreme Court of New South Wales on an application for a rule *nisi* for a new trial.

The appellant, a solicitor, plaintiff in an action for damages against the respondents, was nonsuited. At the trial he was represented by counsel, but after the trial counsel's retainer was withdrawn, by consent. The plaintiff, desiring to apply for a new trial, filed a memorandum for a rule *nisi*, but, as he intended to move in person, did not obtain the signature of counsel as required by Rule 151 of the Rules of the Supreme Court. It appeared that he had shown the memorandum to counsel who had appeared for him, but had not obtained his signature to it. Plaintiff then appeared in person before the Full Court in support of his application, but the Court, on the ground that the memorandum was not in accordance with Rule 151, refused to entertain the application and ordered the appeal to be struck out : *Dwyer* v. *Railway Commissioners* (1).

From that decision the present appeal was brought to the High Court.

Appellant in person. Rule 151 has on several occasions been construed by the Supreme Court as one which may be relaxed, where the circumstances render it inequitable or oppressive to enforce it. If it is not an inflexible rule, the present case is one in which it should be relaxed. To enforce it would result in depriving the plaintiff of his right of appeal, for the retainer of counsel had been withdrawn and his signature could not be obtained. The Rule does not provide for signature by any other

(1) 24 N.S.W. W.N. 72.

H. C. of A.
1908.

Dwyer
v.
The Rail-
way Commis-
sioners of
New South
Wales.

counsel. [He referred to *Quigley* v. *King* (1); *Wentworth* v. *Hill* (2).]

[GRIFFITH C.J.—I should like to know whether the right to move for a new trial is given by Statute, by common law, or by rule of Court.]

Garland, for the respondents.   The right existed in the Queen's Bench at common law; and the Supreme Court has by the Charter of Justice, 9 Geo. IV. c. 83, the same powers in this respect as the Court of Queen's Bench in England.   Undoubtedly Rule 151 is not inflexible, but it is very important in the interests of convenience that the Court should have the authority of counsel who appeared at the trial, for the correctness of the grounds taken, and the substantial nature of the point to be argued.   If the Court is satisfied that the circumstances are such as to justify them in relaxing the Rule they will relax it, but that is a matter for their discretion.   They were not so satisfied in the present case.   According to the plaintiff's own statement, that he submitted the grounds of the memorandum to his counsel and did not obtain his approval, this is an instance of the very thing that the Rule was intended to prevent.   The respondents, however, do not oppose the hearing of the plaintiff's appeal on its merits.

[GRIFFITH C.J.—We are asked to review the decision of the Supreme Court.   We can scarcely do that by consent unless we think they were wrong in refusing to hear the application.   We think that we should hear the appeal on its merits and give our reasons afterwards.]

The *Appellant* entered upon his argument as to the merits of the application, but as this turned wholly upon the particular facts of the case and involved no general principle, it is not necessary to report it in detail.   The main grounds argued were that certain evidence tendered by the plaintiff in reply was rejected, and that the learned Judge who presided, in stating to the jury that a certain written statement given by one of the plaintiff's witnesses, which was contended by the plaintiff to be inconsistent with the evidence given by the witness at the trial, was really not incon-

(1) (1904) 4 S.R. (N.S.W.), 204.   (2) 7 N.S.W. W.N., 4.

sistent with it, had in effect misdirected the jury.   The appellant
also asked for permission to file affidavits as to fresh evidence
discovered by him since the trial.

H. C. of A.
1908.

Dwyer
v.
The Rail-
way Commis-
sioners of
New South
Wales.

Griffith C.J.

Garland, for the respondents, was not called upon.

GRIFFITH C.J.   The first point raised in this case is whether
Rule 151 of the Rules of the Supreme Court is so far imperative
that the Full Court were justified in the circumstances of the
present case in refusing to entertain an application by the plaintiff
for a rule *nisi* for a new trial.   Now, so far as I understand, it has
been the unvarying practice of the Supreme Court that a party,
after a trial by a jury, has a right to apply for a new trial, on
complying with certain conditions as to time, procedure, and so on.
It has also always been the right of a party to appear in person
or by counsel, or by his solicitor, when a solicitor is allowed to
appear.   If that were a privilege given by a rule of Court and
not a right given by law, it might be hedged in by any conditions
that the Court thought fit to impose, as, for instance, when a
person is applying for leave to sue *in forma pauperis* the Court
imposes as a condition in some cases that an opinion must be given
by counsel, in order to show that it is a fit case for such leave.
Rule 150, so far as is material, provides that when either party
intends to move for a nonsuit, or for a new trial, he shall within a
certain time after the trial file a memorandum of such intention ;
and by Rule 151 the memorandum is to state the day or days on
which the cause was tried, the verdict or other termination of
the trial, the motion intended to be made, and the grounds, and
" where the party had counsel at the trial, shall be signed by one
of such counsel."   That is to say, in effect, that if a party employs
counsel at the trial he shall not be afterwards allowed to exercise
this right in person.   If that were imperative it might give rise
to serious questions as to whether the Court can by such a Rule of
Court deprive a suitor of his right to be heard.   But the Rule has
always been construed by the Supreme Court itself as one which
may be relaxed on occasion ; not as an absolute rule, but as a rule
of convenience.   In the present case the ground of relaxation put
forward on behalf of the appellant is that the retainer of the

H. C. of A.
1908.

Dwyer
v.
The Rail-
way Commis-
sioners of
New South
Wales.

Griffith C.J.

counsel who appeared for him at the trial had come to an end, and he, therefore, had no counsel. He, therefore, was in this position, that he was under the necessity either of retaining new counsel or abandoning his right to apply for a new trial. Under these circumstances we thought that the rule, construed as the Supreme Court has always applied it, should have been relaxed, and the plaintiff should have been heard on his application for a rule *nisi*, and for these reasons we allowed him to be heard on the merits of the application.

As to the merits, it is clear that the plaintiff has none. There was a conflict of evidence and the jury found a verdict for the defendants. Two of the grounds of the plaintiff's application for a new trial are that the verdict was against evidence, and that it was against the weight of evidence. As to those grounds nothing is now said. The third ground was that the learned Judge who presided made some observations as to the effect of a certain document shown to a witness in cross-examination by counsel for the plaintiff. All that that amounted to was a comment by the learned Judge on the weight of the evidence, and that is not a ground for granting a new trial. The fourth ground was the wrongful rejection of evidence. But upon the issue presented to the jury that evidence was altogether irrelevant, and was therefore rightly rejected, if it was formally tendered, as to which there is some doubt.

It is suggested by the plaintiff that, when the memorandum was filed and before the case came before the Supreme Court, he discovered fresh evidence, and that he had affidavits on the point ready to be filed if he had been allowed to be heard, and that he would have then asked for leave to amend the memorandum, if necessary, and the Court might have granted him leave to do so. We asked him to state the reason of his not having discovered the evidence earlier and the nature of the evidence. For it is not enough to have discovered fresh evidence; it must also be shown to the satisfaction of the Court that the party could not by reasonable diligence have discovered it earlier. But it appears that whatever he may have discovered would have been quite irrelevant. In my opinion, therefore, if the application had been heard by the Supreme Court, the rule *nisi* ought to have been refused.

BARTON and O'CONNOR JJ. concurred.

Appeal dismissed.

Solicitor, for the respondents, *J. S. Cargill.*

C. A. W.

H. C. of A.
1908.

DWYER
v.
THE RAILWAY COMMISSIONERS OF
NEW SOUTH
WALES.

[HIGH COURT OF AUSTRALIA.]

PARKER . . . . APPELLANT;
PETITIONER,

AND

PARKER . . . . RESPONDENT.
RESPONDENT,

ON APPEAL FROM THE SUPREME COURT OF
NEW SOUTH WALES.

Husband and wife—Divorce—Domicil of origin—Change of domicil—Jurisdiction.

H. C. of A.
1908.

SYDNEY,
May 5.

Griffith C.J.,
Barton and
O'Connor JJ.

The respondent, whose domicil of origin was in Victoria, where he resided and carried on business, was married in that State, but never lived there openly with his wife. He had a branch office in Sydney; and a few years after his marriage he brought his wife and child from Melbourne to Sydney, and there made a home for them at which he lived with them for a few months and then deserted them. From that time, though in the course of his business he was frequently in New South Wales for considerable periods, he never had any fixed residence there.

In a suit brought by the wife in the Supreme Court of New South Wales for dissolution of marriage on the ground of desertion;

Held, on the evidence, that the respondent had not acquired a domicil in New South Wales, and therefore the Supreme Court had no jurisdiction to entertain the suit.

H. C. of A.
1908.
⌣
PARKER
v.
PARKER.

In order to establish a change of domicil in such a case there must be clear evidence of an intention by the husband to abandon his domicil of origin and to make a new permanent home in the State to which he has removed.

Decision of the Supreme Court : *Parker* v. *Parker*, (1907) 7 S. R. (N.S.W.), 384, affirmed.

APPEAL from a decision of the Supreme Court of New South Wales affirming the judgment of *Simpson* J. in a suit for dissolution of marriage.

The appellant filed a petition in the Supreme Court for divorce on the ground of desertion. The issues of marriage and desertion were found in favour of the petitioner, but the learned Judge was of opinion, on the evidence, that the respondent was never domiciled in New South Wales, and, therefore, that the petitioner was not domiciled in that State, and the Supreme Court had no jurisdiction to entertain the suit.

The evidence upon which the petitioner relied to establish domicil was, shortly, as follows :—The respondent was born in Victoria and was domiciled there at the date of his marriage in 1899. At that time, and up to the date of the petition, he carried on business in Melbourne as proprietor of a newspaper called *The Mining Standard*, having a branch office in Sydney. The petitioner, at the desire of the respondent, did not take the name of Parker, and the marriage was kept secret from his relatives. A child was born and the petitioner was sent to Sydney by the respondent. He visited her there but never lived with her. After about eighteen months she returned to Victoria where the respondent lived with her for some time. In August 1901 the respondent brought the petitioner with the child and household furniture to Sydney, where he took and furnished a house for her and lived openly with her as his wife for a time. In that and other houses taken by the respondent they lived together for short periods at intervals until October of that year, when the respondent left the petitioner and never lived with her afterwards, though he occasionally wrote to her and sent her money. Since that time the respondent has never had any fixed residence in New South Wales, but in the conduct of his business travelled a great deal from one State to another and at other times went as far as South Africa.

In August 1906 the petitioner instituted this suit for dissolution of marriage on the ground of desertion commencing in
October 1901. The suit having been dismissed by *Simpson* J.,
the petitioner appealed to the Supreme Court. That appeal
having been dismissed : *Parker* v. *Parker* (1), the petitioner now
appealed to the High Court.

Bradburn, for the appellant. The evidence establishes that
the respondent had abandoned his domicil of origin in Victoria
and acquired a domicil of choice in New South Wales. He
"made a home" for his wife and child in Sydney, and that
implies a home for himself, for he began to live with them at
the house he had taken and furnished. [He referred to the evidence at length.] That showed an *animus manendi*. It is
immaterial that the residence is of short duration so long as that
intention is proved. *Brook* v. *Brook* (2), upon which *Simpson* J.
relied, is distinguishable. In that case there was no satisfactory
evidence of intention to change the domicil ; the husband had
never lived in New South Wales at all. The facts that the
respondent made a home there, stayed there for business purposes,
and lived with his wife and child under the circumstances proved
in evidence are such strong evidence of intention to remain that,
in the absence of evidence to the contrary, that intention should
be presumed. To establish a change of domicil from one State
to another does not require such strong evidence as to establish
a change of nationality. [He referred to *Udny* v. *Udny* (3);
Wilson v. *Wilson* (4) ; *Platt* v. *Attorney-General of New South
Wales* (5); *Bell* v. *Kennedy* (6) ; *Webb* v. *Webb* (7) ; *Whitehouse*
v. *Whitehouse* (8); *Davies & Jones* v. *State of Western Australia* (9).]

No appearance for the respondent.

GRIFFITH C.J.   For my part I share the regret expressed by one

(1) (1907) 7 S.R. (N.S.W.), 384.
(2) 13 N.S.W. L.R. (Div.), 9.
(3) L.R. 1 H.L. Sc., 441, at p. 451.
(4) L.R. 2 P. & M., 435, at pp. 441,
443.
(5) 3 App. Cas., 336.
(6) L.R. 1 H.L. Sc., 307.
(7) (1901) 1 S.R. (N.S.W.) (Div.), 32.
(8) 21 N.S.W. L.R. (Div.), 16.
(9) 2 C.L.R., 29.

H. C. of A.
1908.

PARKER
v.
PARKER.

Griffith C.J.

of the learned Judges of the Supreme Court that the petitioner in this case is unable to get the relief which she is certainly entitled to get from some Court or other. The question for determination is entirely one of fact. The learned Judge of first instance declined to draw the inference that the respondent had changed his domicil from Victoria to New South Wales, and the learned Judges of the Full Court were of the same opinion. *Street* J. summed up his view of the facts in a few words, with which I quite agree (1) :—" The impression which it "—that is the evidence—" leaves upon my mind and the conclusion which I draw from it is that, though the respondent intended to settle his wife and child in a home of their own in Sydney, and though he probably intended at that time to provide for their support, he did not intend to make his home with them, but intended to continue to live apart in the future as he had done in the past." That state of facts makes this case very different from those in which the question of domicil usually arises. In most cases the definition in the code quoted by this Court in *Davies and Jones* v. *The State of Western Australia* (2) is applicable :—" It is not in doubt that every man has his domicil in the place where he sets up his household shrine and his principal establishment, whence he has no intention of again departing, unless something should call him away, so that when he goes thence he regards himself as a wanderer, whereas when he returns his wandering is ended." There are no facts in the present case to indicate that any such home as that was formed by the respondent in New South Wales. Nothing remains except the domicil of origin in Victoria, and the fact that the respondent came to New South Wales with his wife and child in 1901 and lived here for some time afterwards. That is not sufficient, in my opinion, to warrant the conclusion that he had lost his domicil of origin and acquired a new one in New South Wales.

A circumstance that should be borne in mind in all cases of this kind, in which the Court is asked to exercise a most important jurisdiction, is that in an undefended suit it hears only one version of the facts, and, unless my experience misleads me, it generally only hears a very small part of the material facts.

(1) (1907) 7 S.R. (N.S.W.), 384, at p. 396.   (2) 2 C.L.R., 29, at p. 41.

Under such circumstances it would be very dangerous for this Court to reverse the finding of two Courts on a pure question of fact.

BARTON J. I am of the same opinion. I think that it is totally unnecessary to add anything to the conclusive reasons given by *Cohen* J. in the Court below.

O'CONNOR J. I am of the same opinion, and have nothing to add.

Bradburn, for the appellant, asked for costs.

GRIFFITH C.J. I have never heard of an order for costs against a successful respondent. I doubt very much whether we have power to make such an order.

Appeal dismissed.

Proctor for the appellant, *S. Bloomfield.*

C. A. W,

H. C. OF A.
1908.

PARKER
v.
PARKER.

[HIGH COURT OF AUSTRALIA.]

THE COUNCIL OF THE CITY OF BRISBANE   APPELLANTS;
DEFENDANTS,

AND

HIS MAJESTY'S ATTORNEY-GENERAL FOR THE STATE OF QUEENSLAND (AT THE RELATION OF JAMES THOMAS ISLES, A RATE-PAYER OF THE CITY OF BRISBANE)   RESPONDENT.
PLAINTIFF,

ON APPEAL FROM THE SUPREME COURT OF QUEENSLAND.

Local Authorities Act 1902 (*Qd.*) (1902, *No.* 19), *secs.* 191, 192, 209, 210, 261-265— *Local Authority whose area is divided into Divisions—Expenditure on works in one Division—Accounts—Declaration and Injunction.*

H. C. OF A.
1908.

MELBOURNE,
Feb. 26, 27, 28 ;
March 23.

Griffith C.J.,
Barton,
O'Connor,
Isaacs and
Higgins JJ.

H. C. of A.
1908.
~
Brisbane
City Council
v.
Attorney-
General for
Queensland.
───

Sec. 265 of the *Local Authorities Act* 1902 (Qd.), which requires a separate
and distinct account to be kept of all moneys received in respect of General
Rates levied upon the rateable land in each of the several Divisions of the
area of a Local Authority and of any moneys received by way of endowment
in respect of such rates, does not cut down the absolute discretion of the
Local Authority as to expenditure from the Local Fund given in express
terms by sec. 192.

So *held* by the Court, *Isaacs* J. dissenting.

The account so required to be kept should not be debited with a proportional
part of the expenditure of the Local Authority for purposes other than works
within the limits of the particular Division.

Decision of the Supreme Court : *Attorney-General, at the relation of Isles* v.
Council of the City of Brisbane, 1907 St. R. Qd., 1, reversed.

Appeal from the Supreme Court of Queensland.

An action was brought in the Supreme Court by the Attorney-
General for Queensland, at the relation of James Thomas Isles a
ratepayer of the City of Brisbane, against the Council of the
City of Brisbane, in which the statement of claim was as
follows :—

1. The plaintiff is the Attorney-General for the State of
Queensland. The relator J. T. Isles is a ratepayer of the West
Ward of the City of Brisbane and the President of the Central
Ratepayers Association of Brisbane an association of upwards of
one hundred ratepayers of the East and West Wards of the said
City and as such President represents the ratepayers who are
members of the said Association.

2. The defendants are the Council of the City of Brisbane a
duly constituted Local Authority whose area is divided into
seven divisions known respectively as East Ward, West Ward,
North Ward, Valley Ward, Kangaroo Point Ward, Merthyr Ward,
and Cintra Ward.

3. The defendants have in every year since 31st December
1902 made and levied general rates equally upon all the rateable
lands within their area and have received large sums of money
in respect of such general rates.

4. The defendants have in each year since 31st December 1902
made and levied a cleansing rate upon all lands in actual occupation within their area and have received moneys in respect of
such cleansing rates but have not accounted for the same.

H. C. of A.
1908.

BRISBANE
CITY COUNCIL
v.
ATTORNEY-
GENERAL FOR
QUEENSLAND.

5. The defendants have not since 31st March 1903 by resolution passed at a meeting specially summoned for that purpose nor at all declared any work within their area to be a "general work" within the meaning of sec. 265 of the *Local Authorities Act* 1902 nor by any such resolution nor at all directed that the cost of the construction or maintenance of any work in their area should be defrayed out of the general revenues and should not be debited to the separate account of any division or ward.

6. The defendants have not expended the moneys received by them since 31st March 1903 in respect of general rates levied upon the rateable lands in the several divisions or wards of their area respectively upon works within the respective limits of the said several divisions or wards and have not kept separate accounts of the said several divisions or wards respectively showing the amounts standing to the credit or debit of the said several divisions or wards respectively but on the contrary have expended moneys which should be standing to the credit of the East and West Divisions or Wards respectively upon works within the limits of divisions or wards of their area other than the said East and West Wards.

7. The defendants refuse to account for the moneys received by them since 31st March 1903 in respect of general rates levied for the years 1903, 1904 and 1905 upon the rateable lands in the several divisions or wards respectively of their area particularly in the East and West Divisions or Wards respectively in accordance with the *Local Authorities Act* 1902 and particularly refuse in such accounts of such moneys as aforesaid to show the amounts standing to the credit or debit of the several divisions or wards respectively.

8. The defendants threaten and intend to expend the moneys hereafter to be respectively received by them in respect of general rates levied upon the rateable lands in the several divisions or wards of their area after all just deductions therefrom for salaries allowances and the management of the defendants' office and for such other expenditure as the defendants may hereafter from time to time by resolution properly direct otherwise than solely upon works within the respective limits of the several divisions or wards in respect of the rateable lands of which such

H. C. of A.
1908.

BRISBANE
CITY COUNCIL
v.
ATTORNEY-
GENERAL FOR
QUEENSLAND.

general rates shall be respectively received and threaten and intend to keep the accounts of the said several divisions otherwise than separate and distinct from each other and otherwise than to show the amounts from time to time standing to the credit or debit of the said divisions respectively.

The plaintiff claims :—

1. A declaration that all moneys received in respect of general rates levied upon the rateable lands in the several divisions or wards of the defendants' area and all moneys received by way of endowment upon such rates after all just deductions for expenditure in respect of salaries allowances and the management of the defendants' office and for such other expenditure as the defendants may by resolution from time to time properly direct to be paid out of general revenues shall be expended solely upon works within the respective limits of the several divisions or wards in respect of the rateable lands of which such general rates have been received.

2. An injunction restraining the defendants from expending or directing or permitting to be expended any general rates received in respect of the rateable lands in the several divisions or wards or their area otherwise than in accordance with the terms of the declaration hereinbefore claimed.

5. And for such further or other relief as the nature of the case may require.

[The third and fourth claims were abandoned in consequence of the decision of the High Court: *Brisbane City Council v. Attorney-General for Queensland* (1).]

The defence so far as material was as follows :—

1. The general rate made and levied by the defendants for the year 1903 upon the rateable lands situated within the Cintra and Merthyr Wards respectively was $2\frac{1}{2}$d. in the pound, whereas the general rate so made and levied for the same year upon the rateable lands situated within the East, West, North, Valley, and Kangaroo Point Wards was $1\frac{3}{4}$d. in the pound. Save as aforesaid the defendants admit the allegations in paragraph 3 of the statement of claim.

2. The defendants deny that they have not accounted for

(1) 4 C.L.R., 241.

the moneys received in respect of cleansing rates levied by them in each or any year since 31st December 1902 and say that they have in each year duly kept a separate and distinct account of all moneys received by them in respect of such rates. Save as aforesaid the defendants admit the allegations in paragraph 4 of the statement of claim.

3. All the moneys comprising the defendants' ordinary or general revenues and consisting of the general rates received as aforesaid ferry dues market charges rents fees and all other the moneys which the defendants have from time to time received under and in pursuance of the *Local Authorities Act* 1902 have been duly carried to the account of the City Fund and that the said City Fund has from time to time been duly applied by the defendants in and towards the payment of all expenses necessarily incurred in carrying the said Act into execution and in doing and performing all acts and things which the defendants were and are by law empowered and required to do and perform and in and towards the payment of sums due from time to time by the defendants under agreements lawfully made and of all such other sums as became payable by the defendants from time to time in respect of their loan indebtedness and in pursuance of lawful orders precepts and directions and not otherwise howsoever. The said City Fund consisting of the defendants' ordinary or general revenues as aforesaid has been so applied as aforesaid by the defendants under the authority of resolutions of the defendants in that behalf and in particular the cost of the construction maintenance and management of all local works and undertakings within the defendants' area has under the authority of such resolutions been defrayed out of the said City Fund. Save as aforesaid the defendants deny the allegations in paragraph 5 of the statement of claim.

4. The defendants have from time to time expended so much of the moneys received by them since 31st March 1903 in respect of general rates levied upon the rateable lands in the several divisions or wards as in their judgment and discretion they considered were necessary to be expended upon works within the respective limits of the said several divisions or wards. All the moneys so expended have been defrayed out of the said City Fund.

H. C. of A.
1908.

BRISBANE
CITY COUNCIL
v.
ATTORNEY-
GENERAL FOR
QUEENSLAND.

5. The defendants have at all material times kept separate and distinct accounts of all moneys received in respect of general rates in the said several divisions or wards and all the moneys expended as aforesaid upon works within the respective limits of the said divisions or wards have been duly debited to the respective accounts of the said divisions or wards and the said accounts respectively disclose the relation between the amount of general rates received and the amount of moneys expended upon works in respect of each such division or ward. The defendants contend that they are not authorized or required by law to keep any separate account of the said several divisions or wards other than as aforesaid.

6. The defendants contend that they are authorized and empowered by law as and when in their judgment and discretion they deem it to be necessary to expend the moneys received by them from time to time in respect of general rates upon any works within any division or ward of their area without regard to the actual amount of the said general rates 'which has been received by them in respect of any of the said divisions or wards and the defendants have from time to time duly expended the said moneys accordingly.

7. Save as aforesaid the defendants deny the allegations in paragraphs 6, 7 and 8 of the statement of claim.

8. The ratepayers of the defendants' area have not at any time appealed to the Minister charged with the administration of the *Local Authorities Act* 1902 against any resolution of the defendants directing how the cost of the construction and maintenance of any work or how any other expenditure of the defendants shall be paid or defrayed.

9. The accounts of the defendants in respect of the years 1903, 1904 and 1905 have been duly balanced and audited and have been duly allowed by the auditor authorized by the Auditor-General of Queensland to audit the said accounts and having been finally examined and settled by the defendants have been duly allowed and have accordingly been duly certified and signed and the defendants contend that each and every of the said accounts is final against all persons whomsoever.

Upon this defence there was a joinder of issue.

The material facts are set out in the judgments hereunder.

The action was heard by *Cooper* C.J. who gave judgment by which it was declared that all moneys received since 20th April 1906 in respect of general rates levied upon the rateable lands in the several divisions or wards of the defendants' area, and all moneys received by way of endowment upon such rates after all just deductions for expenditure in respect of salaries, allowances and the management of the defendants' office, and for such other expenditure as the said defendants may by resolution from time to time properly direct to be paid out of general revenues, ought to be expended solely upon works within the respective limits of the several divisions or wards in respect of the rateable lands of which such general rates should have been received; and the defendants were directed to keep separate and distinct accounts for each division of their area in accordance with the *Local Authorities Act* 1902 so as to show the amounts from time to time standing to the credit or debit of the said divisions respectively; and it was ordered that the defendants should be restrained from expending any general rates so received in respect of the rateable land in the several divisions or wards of their area otherwise than in accordance with the terms of the above declaration:. *Attorney-General, at the relation of Isles* v. *Council of the City of Brisbane* (1). From this judgment the defendants now appealed to the High Court.

The nature of the arguments sufficiently appears in the judgments.

Lilley & Shand, for the appellants.

Graham, for the respondent.

The following sections of the *Local Authorities Act* 1902 were referred to during argument :—Secs. 191, 192, 209, 210, 257, 261 to 265. Counsel also referred to :—*Queensland Rules of Court* 1900, Order XCI., r. 1 ; *Andrews* v. *Barnes* (2) ; *Valuation and Rating Act* 1890, sec. 34.

　　　　　　　　　　　　　　　　　Cur. adv. vult.

H. C. of A.
1908.

BRISBANE
CITY COUNCIL
v.
ATTORNEY-
GENERAL FOR
QUEENSLAND.

(1) 1907 St. R., Qd., 1.　　　　(2) 39 Ch. D., 133.

H. C. of A.
1908.

BRISBANE
CITY COUNCIL
v.
ATTORNEY-
GENERAL FOR
QUEENSLAND.

Griffith C.J.

The following judgments were read :—

GRIFFITH C.J. This is an action by the Attorney-General for the State of Queensland at the relation of a ratepayer of the City of Brisbane against the municipal council of that city claiming (in effect) a declaration that moneys raised by general rates in the several wards into which the city is divided ought to be expended solely upon works within the respective wards, and an injunction to restrain any infringement of the declaration. *Cooper* C.J. made a declaration in the terms asked for, to which it will afterwards be necessary to refer more particularly.

The question arises upon the *Local Authorities Act* 1902 (Queensland), which was a consolidation with amendments of the previous law relating to Local Authorities.

Sec. 191 provides that :—" The ordinary revenue of an area (which means the district in which the Local Authority has jurisdiction) shall consist of the moneys following, that is to say :—

> " Rates (not being Special Rates or Tramway Rates), ferry dues, market charges, and other dues, fees, and charges authorized by this Act, and rents ;
>
> " Moneys received by the Council under any grant or appropriation by any Act not containing any provision to the contrary, or in pursuance of any Act requiring moneys received by a Local Authority to be paid into the Local Fund ;
>
> " All other moneys which the Council may receive under or in pursuance of this Act not being the proceeds of a loan."

Sec. 192 is as follows :—

> " (1.) All such moneys shall be carried to the account of a Fund to be called, in the case of a Town the ' Town Fund,' in the case of a City the ' City Fund,' and in the case of a Shire the ' Shire Fund.' " (By section 7 the term " Local Fund " means each of these funds as the case may be).
>
> " (2.) The Local Fund shall be applied by the Local Authority towards the payment of all expenses necessarily incurred in carrying this Act into execution, and in doing and performing any acts and things which the Local

Authority is by this or any other Act empowered or
required to do or perform, unless this or such Act contains express provision charging such expenses to any
particular Fund or Account.

"(3) The Local Authority may pay out of the Local Fund
any sum due under any agreement lawfully made for
the purposes of this or any other Act, and any sum
recovered against the Local Authority by process of law,
and any sum which by any order made or purporting
to be made under this or any other Act the Local
Authority is directed to pay by way of compensation,
damages, costs, fines, penalties, or otherwise, unless this
or such other Act contains express provision charging
such sums to any particular Fund or Account."

The Local Fund, then, is a single fund applicable to the payment of all expenses incurred in the discharge of any obligations
lawfully incurred by the Council unless "this or some other Act"
contains *express* provision charging such expenses to any particular fund or account. The burden, therefore, of showing that
any particular expense is not to be defrayed out of the Local
Fund lies upon the party making that contention. The analogy
of the Local Fund to the Consolidated Revenue Fund is very
obvious. I will directly refer to the provisions in the Act
referred to by the words "any particular Fund or Account."

Part XII. of the Act deals with Rates.

Sec. 209 provides for two kinds of rates, general and special,
of which the former only form part of the Local Fund. The
amount of the general rates is not to exceed 3d. in the £.

Section 210 provides (par. 3) that when an area is divided, *i.e.*,
divided into wards or subdivisions (in the Act spoken of as
Divisions), the amount of the general rates made in respect of
rateable land in the several divisions need not be the same.
Secs. 213, 214, 216, 217, 220, 222, authorize the levying of special
rates for certain specified purposes.

Part XIII. of the Act deals with Accounts and Audit. Subdivision 2 of this Part, which comprises secs. 261-265, is headed
"Separate Accounts."

Sec. 261 is as follows :—

H. C. of A
1908.

BRISBANE
CITY COUNCIL
v.
ATTORNEY-
GENERAL FOR
QUEENSLAND.

Griffith C.J.

H. C. of A.
1908.

BRISBANE
CITY COUNCIL
v.
ATTORNEY-
GENERAL FOR
QUEENSLAND.

Griffith C.J.

" The Local Authority shall keep a separate and distinct account of—

(i.) All moneys received in respect of every Separate or Special Rate levied under this Act, and all moneys received by the Local Authority by way of endowment upon such rates respectively, so that the moneys so received shall be credited to the same accounts as the Rates in respect of which they were respectively received ; and

(ii.) All moneys disbursed in respect of the purposes for which such Rates are levied, including in such disbursements such reasonable part of the expenditure in respect of salaries, allowances, and management of the office as the Local Authority may direct;

and shall apply the moneys standing to the credit of such account for the purposes for which such Rates are levied and no other."

Sec. 262 requires a "separate and distinct account" to be kept " of all moneys raised by Special Rates for constructing and maintaining works for the manufacture or conservation and supply of gas or electricity or hydraulic or other power, and all moneys received from such undertaking, which are charged—

Firstly—with the principal money and interest required from time to time to be paid in respect of the loan (if any) raised for the establishment of the undertaking; and

Secondly—with the cost of maintaining the undertaking in good repair, and of paying the actual working expenses thereof," and provision for depreciation, renewal, and extension and incidental obligations.

If at any time the undertaking becomes so profitable that the revenue (*i.e.* the annual revenue) is more than sufficient to defray all the expenses and also the moneys payable in respect of principal and interest, the surplus is to be first applied in liquidation of the loan (if any), and thereafter at the discretion of the Local Authority is either to be applied in establishing a Reserve Fund or to be placed to the credit of the Local Fund. It will be observed that in each of the cases dealt with by these two sections the revenue, being derived from special rates, is not to

be paid into the Local Fund.   Although, therefore, the direction
is only to keep a separate and distinct account of the moneys
raised, the effect is to establish distinct funds, which, whether
mingled in a common banking account with other moneys or
not, are impressed with an exclusive trust for the purposes
specified.

H. C. of A.
1908.

BRISBANE
CITY COUNCIL
v.
ATTORNEY-
GENERAL FOR
QUEENSLAND.

Griffith C.J.

A third case is dealt with by sec. 263, which requires the Local
Authority to keep a separate and distinct account of all revenue
derived from waterworks, which is to be applied, firstly, in payment of the actual working expenses of the waterworks, and,
secondly, in repayment of instalments due in respect of moneys
borrowed for their construction.   The balance may, at the discretion of the Local Authority, be applied in defraying the cost
of maintenance, repair and extension of the works, or in reduction
of the loan, and not otherwise.

In this case the balance would appear to fall within the terms
of sec. 191, as being " other moneys which the Council may
receive under or in pursuance of this Act not being the proceeds
of a loan."   But they are nevertheless specifically appropriated
to the purposes mentioned.   Substantially, therefore, they form a
fund, which, though called an " account," and though not formally
segregated from the Loan Fund, is to be treated as if it were a
distinct fund.

A fourth case is dealt with by sec. 264, which requires the
Local Authority to keep a separate account in some bank of any
loan incurred by it, and the money raised by the loan is to be
applied solely to the purposes for which it was borrowed.   In
this case it is contemplated that there should be a separate
banking account, and consequently a separate fund.

In all four cases the moneys placed to the credit of the
separate account might not inaccurately be described as a
"particular Fund or Account," which are the words used in
sec. 192.

Sec. 265 provides that when an area is divided the Local
Authority must keep a separate and distinct account of all
moneys received in respect of general rates levied upon the
rateable land in the several Divisions, and of any moneys
received by the Local Authority by way of endowment on such

H. C. of A.
1908.

BRISBANE
CITY COUNCIL
v.
ATTORNEY-
GENERAL FOR
QUEENSLAND.

Griffith C.J.

rates, the endowment being credited in proportion to the rates. This provision is an extension of sec. 34 of the *Valuation and Rating Act* of 1890, in which a similar provision was applied to cases where the amounts of rates levied in different divisions were not the same. In that Act it was apparently intended for statistical purposes or purposes of information and record only.

In sec. 265, however, the provision is of general application. The section goes on to make further provisions, upon which the question now under consideration arises. They are as follows:—" And save as hereinafter provided all moneys expended upon works within the limits of the Division shall be debited to the account of that Division:

" Provided that when a work is of such importance to the whole of the area that the cost of its construction and maintenance may reasonably be a charge upon the general revenue of the Local Authority, the Local Authority may from time to time, by resolution passed at a meeting specially summoned for the purpose, declare such work to be a 'general work,' and direct that the cost of its construction and maintenance shall be defrayed out of the general revenues, and shall not be debited to the separate account of any Division, and such expenditure shall be so defrayed accordingly:

" Provided also that unless the Local Authority has directed that any part of the expenditure in respect of salaries, allowances, or management of the office should be debited to any separate account as hereinbefore provided, the expenditure in respect of all salaries and allowances and the management of the office of the Local Authority, together with any other expenditure as to which the Local Authority may from time to time by resolution so direct, shall be paid out of the general revenues, and shall not be debited to the separate account of any Division."

This concluding provision seems to refer to the resolution mentioned in the preceding paragraph. It is conceded that the words " as hereinbefore provided " refer to sec. 261 (par. ii.).

The contention of the relator is, in substance, that these provisions require that the financial affairs of the several Divisions shall be kept entirely distinct, that the general rates raised in each Division shall be treated as a separate earmarked fund, out of which the cost of all "works within the limits of the Divisions" which have not been declared general works under the first proviso is to be paid, with the consequence that the money expended upon such works cannot exceed the amount of those rates and the endowment upon them, and that the general expenditure of the Local Authority shall be apportioned among the several Divisions and debited to these funds, thus further reducing the amount available for works within the limits of the Divisions. He goes still further, and claims that each Division is entitled to have any balance to the credit of its fund expended upon works within the limits of the Division. The formal claim made and allowed by the judgment appealed from is a declaration " that all moneys received since 20th April 1906 in respect of general rates levied upon the rateable lands in the several Divisions or wards of the defendants' area, and all moneys received by way of endowment upon such rates, after all just deductions for expenditure in respect of salaries, allowances and the management of the defendants' office, and for such other expenditure as the said defendants may by resolution from time to time properly direct to be paid out of general revenues, shall be expended solely upon works within the respective limits of the several Divisions or wards in respect of the rateable lands of which such general rates shall have been received." I do not stop to inquire what is meant by "all just deductions," but I assume that it means some apportioned share of general expenses. I may say, in passing, that I doubt whether the judgment as drawn up correctly represents the opinion of the learned Chief Justice as expressed by him when delivering judgment.

Although this declaration is in form affirmative, it is in substance negative. The Court has, of course, no jurisdiction to compel a Local Authority to expend money upon works which it does not think necessary. So read, it is a declaration that the Council ought not to apply such parts of the Local Fund as have been derived from general rates to any purposes but those specified. Such a declaration is, *primâ facie*, inconsistent with sec. 192, which makes the whole Local Fund available for payment of all expenses incurred in carrying the Act into execution. It is,

H. C. of A.
1908.

BRISBANE
CITY COUNCIL
v.
ATTORNEY-
GENERAL FOR
QUEENSLAND.

Griffith C.J.

H. C. of A.
1908.

BRISBANE
CITY COUNCIL
v.
ATTORNEY-
GENERAL FOR
QUEENSLAND.

Griffith C.J.

however, contended that it is justified by sec. 265. The argument
is put in this way :—The section says that "save as hereinafter
provided" all moneys expended upon works within the limits of
a Division shall be debited to the account of that Division. It
then says that the Local Authority may at a specially summoned
meeting declare such a work to be a "general work," and direct
that the cost of its construction and maintenance shall be
"defrayed" out of the "general revenues" and shall not be
"debited" to the separate account of any Division, and that such
expenditure shall be so defrayed accordingly. These latter words,
it is said, import that "defraying" expenditure out of a fund and
"debiting" it to the fund are regarded as interchangeable expressions, and consequently that there is a direction that the cost of
such works shall be defrayed out of the separate accounts, which,
it is said, implies a prohibition against expending upon works in
a Division which have not been declared "general works" (and
which I will call "ward works") any greater sum than is standing to the credit of the account of the Division in respect of
general rates and endowment upon them. A change of language
in the same context does not, however, primarily suggest that the
words are synonymous, but rather the contrary. Then it is said
that the direction to "defray" the cost of "general works" out
of the general revenues would on any other construction be idle,
because sec. 192 has already made the same provision. This is,
perhaps, true, but it is not unusual in a Statute to find a provision repeated by way of emphasis or antithesis.

At the first argument of this case I was strongly disposed to
assent to this contention, and to think that the relator was
entitled to a declaration that the moneys expended upon works
within the several Divisions should not, in the absence of such a
resolution as is prescribed in the first proviso to sec. 265, exceed
the amounts standing to the credit of the accounts of the respective Divisions. Before further dealing with the case from this
point of view, I will refer to the other, and, indeed, the main
point of the relator's contention, which is that the "separate and
distinct accounts" of the moneys received in respect of general
rates and endowments upon them should be debited with a proportional part of the expenditure of the Local Authority for

purposes other than ward works.   In the first place, this contention is in direct conflict with the express enactment of the second
proviso that unless the Local Authority has directed any part of
the expenditure in respect of salaries, allowances, or management
to be "debited to any separate account as hereinbefore provided"
such expenditure, together with any other expenditure as to
which the Local Authority by resolution so directs, shall be paid
out of the general revenues and "shall *not* be debited to the
separate account of any Division."   The words "hereinbefore
provided" refer, as already pointed out, to sec. 261.   The words
"any separate account" used in that context must therefore refer
to the accounts mentioned in that section, which are accounts of
moneys raised by special rates.   They may possibly also refer to
the separate accounts of the Divisions, but I do not think so—
possibly also to the accounts referred to in secs. 263 and 264.
But, in the absence of such a direction, no part of these general
expenses can be debited to the accounts of the Divisions, nor does
the Act contain any provisions as to the proportions in which
they should be charged to them.   When, however, the legislature
intended that any particular expense or share of expenses should
be debited to particular accounts they knew how to express
themselves clearly, as is shown by secs. 261, 264, and also by
Part XVII. of the Act, which contains elaborate provisions for
distributing the burden of general expenses of Joint Local
Authorities among the several constituent authorities.   Under
these circumstances it is impossible to say that the Act contains
"express provision" charging any part of what may be called
general expenses to the separate accounts of the Divisions.   Moreover, if the separate accounts of the Divisions were intended to
be debited with a share of the general expenses, it would manifestly be necessary that the general receipts of the Local
Authority from sources other than general rates should also be
credited to the same accounts.   The Act is absolutely silent on
this point.   I am therefore compelled to the conclusion that this
contention fails.

I return to the contention that, at any rate, sec. 265 limits the
maximum expenditure upon ward works to the amount standing
to the credit of the Division in respect of general rates and

H. C. of A.
1908.

Brisbane
City Council
v.
Attorney
General for
Queensland.

Griffith C.J.

H. C. of A.
1908.

Brisbane
City Council
v.
Attorney-
General for
Queensland.

Griffith C.J.
endowment. In this connection reference was made to sec. 210, par. 4, which provides that if the Local Authority has, at the beginning of any year, to the credit of the Local Fund sufficient money to defray all its probable and reasonable expenses for the year, the Governor in Council may excuse the making of any general rate for the year either in respect of the whole area or any Division, or may reduce the maximum amount of any rate to be levied during that year; and it is suggested that the power to excuse from making a general rate in respect of a Division indicates an intention that the accounts of each Division should be kept separate at least to the extent contended for. The provision would, no doubt, be consistent with such an intention if it were shown by other provisions of the Act, but the general effect of the whole paragraph seems to me to tend in a contrary direction. For, if such a separation had been intended, we should expect the condition of the exercise of the excusing power in respect of a Division to be that there was sufficient money at the credit of the account of the Division to defray all proper and reasonable expenditure charged to that account, whereas the condition relates to the Local Fund as a whole, to which fund all such expenses are to be charged under sec. 192.

It is clear that upon any reasonable construction of sec. 265 it does not prohibit the expenditure upon ward works of revenue received from sources other than general rates. This was not, indeed, disputed.

Such a declaration as suggested would therefore be wrong. At most the declaration could be only to the effect that the expenditure upon ward works in any Division should not exceed the amount received in respect of general rates upon land in the Division (with endowment on them) together with such further amount as did not exceed the residue of the Local Fund after deducting the amounts raised by general rates in other Divisions, or, to put it in other words, that the Local Authority is not entitled to expend out of the Local Fund upon ward works in any Division such a sum that the residue of the Local Fund will be less than the total amount of the general rates raised in the other Divisions. In the case of the appellants the revenue from sources other than rates is itself more than the total amount spent

H. C. of A.
1908.

BRISBANE
CITY COUNCIL
v.
ATTORNEY-
GENERAL FOR
QUEENSLAND.

Griffith C.J.

on ward works in all the Divisions, so that such a declaration would be idle—a declaration "in the air," as used to be said.

It was suggested that the declaration might be in the form that the appellants are not entitled to expend upon ward works in any Division any moneys which are the proceeds of general rates in any other Division. But, as already shown, the general rates form part of a common fund, and it is impossible to say that any particular expenditure is defrayed out of them rather than out of any other part of the fund. The second declaration, which I have described as idle, would therefore be the only one not inconsistent with the express provisions of the Statute. It is not that asked for by the relator, and there is no suggestion that the defendants have proposed to do anything inconsistent with it. In my opinion it ought not to be made in this action, even if it would correctly declare the law.

It was contended that the concluding part of sec. 265, which allows an appeal to the Governor in Council against a resolution of the Local Authority declaring a ward work a general work, shows that the provisions of the section were intended to have some greater effect than the mere keeping of records of ward receipts and expenditure. It certainly suggests that idea, and it may be that the whole section indicates that its framers had an idea of establishing a system of separate ward funds. But, if they had, they have not expressed their intentions in such a manner that effect can be given to them. It is, however, by no means clear that they had any such intention. They may have deliberately stopped short at making provision for records of divisional receipts and expenditure. On the whole, I cannot at present find any sure ground on which to rest the conclusion that sec. 265 cuts down the absolute discretion of the Local Authority as to expenditure from the Local Fund given in express terms by sec. 192.

I think, therefore, that the appeal must be allowed.

BARTON J.   During the argument and re-argument of this appeal I have paid close attention to all that has been advanced in support of the plaintiff's contentions as to the meaning of the several enactments relied on, and as to the bearing of the facts.

H. C. of A.   The case is a difficult one, but I have not been convinced, as I
   1908.   must be before agreeing to any declaration in his favour, that
BRISBANE   the plaintiff has made out a case of breach of the requirements
CITY COUNCIL imposed by the *Local Authorities Act* 1902 upon the defendant
   v.
ATTORNEY-   Council. I do not think that the evidence proves that the
GENERAL OF
QUEENSLAND. Council have failed to keep a separate and distinct account of

Barton J.   the moneys received in the several Divisions for general rates
             and endowments, or that they have failed to debit to each such
             account the moneys spent on works within the Division the
             subject of the account. Nor is it established, although in one
             instance the facts were consistent with the assumption, that in
             the period under review they have expended on works within
             any Division more than the amount of the general rates received
             by them in respect of that Division. They may not have
             expended all moneys received in each Division for general rates
             and endowments solely in works within the Division in respect
             of which they have been received, and I do not see what part of
             the Act it is that binds them to do so. But the declaration,
             which, by the way, orders them to expend moneys in a certain
             way on works within the several Divisions, requires *inter alia*
             that, before doing so, all just deductions shall be made for
             expenditure on salaries, allowances and the management of the
             Council's office. It is here that a serious flaw in the plaintiff's
             contention appears. If it were possible within the terms of the
             Act to make the declaration in question with any prospect of
             its proving workable, it is plain that the "just deductions"
             directed must be made from the several divisional accounts.
             But then how are they to be made? The section, in the second
             proviso, prohibits such deductions except on a direction of the
             Local Authority, which has not been given. Even if they could
             be made, the Act is silent as to any principle on which the sums
             deducted could be apportioned to the several divisional accounts.
             I turn to the claim in its relation to the first proviso. In order
             that the plaintiff's contention may admit of the keeping of a
             series of divisional accounts which would represent actual
             financial facts, it is necessary that, where works are declared
             general (see first proviso to sec. 265), as the cost of their construc-
             tion and maintenance is to be defrayed out of the federal

H. C. of A.
1908.

Brisbane
City Council
v.
Attorney-
General for
Queensland.

Barton J.

revenues, a corresponding sum should be deducted, or a transfer made, from the amounts at credit of the divisional accounts. Otherwise those accounts will show sums to credit far exceeding the actual money balances. And unless such deductions could be made from the divisional accounts and credited to the Local Fund or general account, that fund could not stand the stress of the continual debits for construction and maintenance without corresponding credits to meet them. If the general rates received are to be imprisoned in the divisional accounts, and the Local Fund is not to be replenished out of them, how can that fund remain solvent ? The proviso says that " the cost of its construction and maintenance . . . . shall not be debited to the separate account of any Division " in such cases. In such a state of the law the passing of resolutions within the proviso would lead either to an entire disorganization of accounts or to financial disaster, yet the section and the rest of the Act are alike destitute of any provision to obviate such a result, easy as it was to have devised it if desired.

It appears to me that this consideration alone shows that if the legislature intended the complete " financial separation " contended for at the bar, which is open to doubt, they have not created the machinery necessary to make such a system practicable, and it is not the office of the Court to legislate by way of supplying the machinery. Nor could we possibly say what machinery the legislature would itself have created.

The whole section appears to be unworkable as a means of carrying out actual financial transactions. The framers must have had in view as a minimum the giving of information to ratepayers, and they seem to have meant more. But the section itself as it stands does not seem to be capable of being used even for accurate book-keeping, if I may dare venture on such ground. It is not unintelligible, but, in my judgment, it lacks the machinery which alone could make it the vehicle of an effective declaration. It seems to follow that the section does not operate to cut down the effect of sec. 192.

It has been suggested that the plaintiff is entitled to some relief to be founded on the defendants' admission and contention in paragraph 6 of the statement of defence. Even if the position

H. C. of A.
1908.

BRISBANE
CITY COUNCIL
v.
ATTORNEY-
GENERAL FOR
QUEENSLAND.

O'Connor J.

they assert were untenable, it has no real relation to the plaintiff's claim of relief as it stands, and I do not see that it gives any basis for a declaration within that claim.

I am of opinion that the appeal must be allowed.

O'CONNOR J. The substantial question raised by this appeal is whether the Brisbane City Council are prohibited by the Statute under which they carry on their functions from expending any portion of the general rates collected in a Division on any works other than those within that Division. The learned Chief Justice in the Court below held that they were so prohibited, and made an order declaring that all moneys received by the Council since 20th April 1906, in respect of general rates levied upon the rateable lands in the several Divisions of the area under their control, and all moneys received by way of endowment on such rates should (after certain deductions to which I shall refer later on) be expended solely upon works within the respective limits of the several Divisions in respect of the rateable lands of which such general rates shall have been received. The order goes on to direct that the defendants shall from the date mentioned keep separate and distinct accounts for each Division in accordance with the provisions of the *Local Authorities Act* 1902, so as to show the amounts from time to time standing to the credit or debit of the said Divisions respectively. Finally, there is an injunction restraining the Council from expending or directing or permitting to be expended any of the rates before described contrary to their duty as stated in the declaration. The powers and duties of the Council are all to be found within the four corners of the *Local Authorities Act* 1902, and the question for our consideration is whether, on the true construction of that Statute, there is any justification for the order or for any part of it.

Before entering upon the main question I wish to refer to some subsidiary matters which it is necessary to deal with. The attempt to prove that the accounts were not kept in accordance with the Act has, I think, entirely failed. The obligation to keep the accounts is imposed by sec. 265. All the particulars required by that section are contained in the accounts in evidence

H. C. of A.
1908.

Brisbane
City Council
v.
Attorney-
General for
Queensland.

O'Connor J.

before us. The accounts of each year have been completed and
closed in pursuance of the audit sections of the Act. The relator
complains that they are insufficient because they do not in each
year's accounts carry on the balance from previous years, so as to
make the account continuous. I can find in the Act no direction,
express or implied, that the accounts are to be so kept. In the
absence of express direction to the contrary, the Council were, in
my opinion, justified in treating the account as a record to be
made and completed separately of each year's transactions, and,
in so far as the judgment appealed from directs more than this
to be done, it cannot be supported. It seems to have been
assumed in the Court below that the appellants had expended
and intended to go on expending, unless restrained by order of
the Court, the proceeds of general rates on any object within the
scope of the Act without recognizing any such limitations of
their powers as are laid down in the judgment now under appeal.
There was, it appears to me, no satisfactory evidence before the
Court that the appellants had ever in fact exceeded their powers
even as so limited. But the Council undoubtedly did take up
the position in their sixth ground of defence, and they have
maintained it up to the time of their coming before this Court,
that they were authorized and empowered by law, as and when
in their judgment they deemed it necessary, to expend the
moneys received by them from time to time in receipt of general
rates upon any works within any Division of their area without
regard to the actual amount of general rates which had been
received by them in respect of any of the said Divisions, and
that they had from time to time duly expended the moneys
accordingly. On the argument before us Mr. *Lilley* did not
abandon that position, although he contended that the Council
had not in fact expended out of the general rates on works
within any Division more than the amount raised by general
rates in that Division. It seems to me, therefore, that we cannot
decide this appeal on the mere question of fact to which I have
alluded, but that we must adjudicate on the issue of law raised
by the defence, namely, whether the Council does or does not
possess the powers which it has claimed all through the suit the
right to exercise.

H. C. of A.
1908.

BRISBANE
CITY COUNCIL
v.
ATTORNEY-
GENERAL FOR
QUEENSLAND.

O'Connor J.

Before entering upon a consideration of the several sections which must be referred to, it is well to note that the Act took over a system of municipal administration authorized under a long series of Statutes, and which had been in operation for many years. The principle of that system was not the union for general purposes of Divisions which for divisional purposes were financially self-contained; on the contrary it was the establishment of the municipal area as one administrative and legal entity, with power, if necessary, to apply the financial strength of the whole area in carrying out necessary works in any portion of it. For purposes of elections and of convenient administration it was subdivided into Divisions, but, except in the case of the exercise of special powers or in the administration of special rates, the Division was not a "separate financial unit" in the sense in which that phrase has been used by the learned Chief Justice in the Court below.

It was, of course, open to the legislature, in passing the comprehensive enactment under consideration, to have altered the old system so materially as to have erected the Divisions into "separate financial units." Whether they have done so or not can only be gathered from a careful consideration of the Act.

Sec. 191 establishes the City Fund, or, as it is called in the Act, the "Local Fund," which consists of (i.) Rates (not being Special Rates or Tramway Rates), ferry dues, market charges, and other dues, fees, and charges authorized by the Act, also rents; (ii.) Moneys received by the Council under any grant or appropriation of public moneys, unless the appropriating Act expresses a contrary intention; (iii.) all other moneys which the Council may receive under or in pursuance of the Act not being the proceeds of a loan. The general rates thus become part of the Local Fund mixed with revenues of the Council from many other sources. In marked contrast to the elaborate provisions for the collection and administration of special rates, there is no provision for keeping a separate account of general rates as distinguished from the other items that go to make up the Local Fund. Much less is there any provision by which the general rates of one Division are to be earmarked as distinguishing them from the general rates of another Division.

By sec. 192 (2) it is enacted that "the Local Fund shall be applied by the Local Authority towards the payment of all expenses necessarily incurred in carrying this Act into execution, and in doing and performing any acts and things which the Local Authority is by this or by any other Act empowered or required to do or perform, unless this or such Act contains express provision charging such expenses to any particular Fund or Account."   In other words, the Local Fund is the general fund of the area containing its general revenues and applicable to its general purposes except in cases where there is express statutory provision to the contrary.   Expenditure on municipal works in any Division of the area clearly comes within the words "expenses necessarily incurred in carrying this Act into execution," and by the terms of the section the Local Fund into which the general rates have been paid may be applied in payment of such expenses unless there is express statutory provision "charging such expenses to any particular Fund or Account." There is no Statute other than that under consideration which bears on this particular question, and it is in that Act, therefore, if anywhere, that such express statutory provision is to be found.

Before the respondent can succeed he must show that the Statute contains some express provision charging the expenditure in question upon some Fund or Account which contains only the general rates of the Division in which the works to be carried out are situated, or upon some fund containing such general rates, and kept on a system which will earmark the general rates of each Division.   It must be admitted that there is no provision expressly directing the expenditure on works in each Division to be defrayed out of the proceeds of the general rates collected in that Division.   But the respondent contends that sec. 265, when properly construed, has that effect.   The appellants, on the other hand, ask us to view that section as merely a direction in the keeping of accounts, and contend that it in no way cuts down the authority conferred by sec. 192 to apply the proceeds of general rates forming part of the Local Fund to works in any Division indiscriminately.   On the face of it sec. 265 deals merely with accountancy.   It directs that an account shall be kept of the general rates raised in each Division,

H. C. of A.
1908.

BRISBANE
CITY COUNCIL
v.
ATTORNEY-
GENERAL FOR
QUEENSLAND.

O'Connor J.

H. C. of A.
1908.

BRISBANE
CITY COUNCIL
v.
ATTORNEY-
GENERAL FOR
QUEENSLAND.

O'Connor J.

and that all moneys expended on works within a Division shall be debited to the account of the Division. Then follow the two provisos upon which the respondent relies. The first enacts that, " when a work is of such importance to the whole of an area that the cost of its construction and maintenance may reasonably be a charge on the general revenue of the Local Authority, the Local Authority may from time to time, by resolution passed at a meeting specially summoned for the purpose, declare such work to be a general work," and direct that the cost of its construction and maintenance shall be defrayed out of the general revenues, and shall not be debited to the separate account of any Division, and that such expenditure shall be so defrayed accordingly. The second proviso, dealing with expenditure for salaries, allowances, and office management, enacts that unless the Local Authority has directed that any part of such expenditure should be debited to any separate account " as hereinbefore provided " (referring to the power conferred by sec. 261 to make an apportionment of office expenses as part of the cost of works constructed out of special rates) the expenditure in respect of salaries, allowances, and management of the office of the Local Authority, together with any other expenditure as to which the Local Authority may from time to time by resolution so direct, shall be paid out of the general revenues, and shall not be debited to the separate account of any Division.

The history of the clause may be usefully considered. The *Valuation and Rating Act* 1890 is one of many Acts whose provisions have been repealed by, and in a modified form embodied in, the *Local Authorities Act* 1902. Sec. 34 of the former Act provides that, where the amounts of general rates levied in the several sub-divisions of a District are not the same, an account shall be kept in each such sub-division of the general rates raised in that sub-division and of endowments received in respect of such rates. That section effected nothing beyond compelling the keeping of the credit side of a separate account of the general rates raised in each Division, and it applied to a limited class of cases only. The provisions of sec. 265 not only extend the obligation to keep the account to the Divisions of every area, but establish also a debit side of each such account in which the

H. C. of A.
1908.

BRISBANE
CITY COUNCIL.
v.
ATTORNEY-
GENERAL FOR
QUEENSLAND.

O'Connor J.

moneys expended on works in each Division are to be charged to the general rates account of that Division. On the face of the section up to that point there is nothing more than accountancy. But the addition of the debit side to the account made it necessary to make some provision for the matters which are dealt with in the provisos respectively. It would be obviously unfair that the general rates of a Division should have placed to their debit the cost of a work which, although situated within the limits of the Division, was for the general benefit of the whole area.

Again, from a business point of view a proportion of office expenses would be properly debited to a Division as part of the cost of each work; in the case of works paid for out of special rates that is authorized to be done under the provisions of sec. 261. If it were not for the second proviso an ambiguity would have arisen as to whether the debits to be charged against a Division were to include a proportion of office expenses, and, if so, what proportion, or, if not specified in the Act, to be fixed by what authority. The proviso makes the intention of the legislature plain by enacting that, except where the expenditure is out of special rates within the terms of sec. 261, all salaries, allowances, and expenses of office management shall be paid out of general revenues and shall not be debited to the separate account of any Division. In my opinion, therefore, the provisos deal with the keeping of accounts only, and in no way cut down the power given by sec. 192 of applying the general rates as part of the Local Fund in the general administration of the Act. Indeed, that view of the provisos could not, I think, be questioned were it not that in both of them the expressions are used "defrayed out of the general revenues" and "paid out of the general revenues" as correlative to the expression "debited to the separate account of any Division." The argument is that the phrase "debited to," having been used in the provisos in the sense, as it is contended, of "paid out of" or "defrayed from," must be taken to have the same meaning in the earlier part of the section, and that the second paragraph of the section must therefore be read as if the words were "all moneys expended upon works within the limits of a Division shall be defrayed out of the funds of that Division."

H. C. of A.
1908.

BRISBANE
CITY COUNCIL
v.
ATTORNEY-
GENERAL FOR
QUEENSLAND.

O'Connor J.

The provisos are no doubt clumsily drawn. There was no necessity to direct that the cost of the general works referred to in the first proviso, or of the office expenses mentioned in the second proviso, should be defrayed out of general revenues. That direction had already been given by sec. 192, and such a provision would ordinarily be out of place in a section which is concerned with account keeping. It may be it was deemed necessary for more abundant caution to repeat the direction so as to remove any ambiguity that might arise on a comparison of the sections relating to the general accounts kept for "special rates" and "separate rates" with that under consideration. Or it may be that the expressions to which I am referring were mere surplusage.

The general rule of interpretation, no doubt, is that a meaning must be given, if possible, to every word of a Statute. As Lord *Brougham* said in *Auchterarder, Presbytery of* v. *Lord Kinnoull* (1) in a passage quoted in *Hardcastle (Craies) on Statutory Law*, 4th ed., at p. 102:—"A Statute is never supposed to use words without a meaning." Courts will, however, when necessary, take cognizance of the fact that the legislature does sometimes repeat itself, and does not always convey its meaning in the style of literary perfection. Some expressions of judicial opinion collected on page 101 of *Hardcastle's* work from which I have just quoted are worthy of consideration in this connection:—
"'It may not always be possible,' said *Jessel* M.R., in *Yorkshire Insurance Co.* v. *Clayton* (2) 'to give a meaning to every word used in an Act of Parliament,' and many instances may be found of provisions put into Statutes merely by way of precaution. 'Nor is surplusage, or even tautology, wholly unknown in the language of the legislature.' (*Income Tax Commissioners* v. *Pemsel* (3)). 'A Statute,' said Lord *Brougham* in *Auchterarder* v. *Lord Kinnoull* (1) 'is always allowed the privilege of using words not absolutely necessary.' And in *Income Tax Commissioners* v. *Pemsel* (4), Lord *Macnaghten* pointed out (3) that 'it is not so very uncommon in an Act of Parliament to find special

(1) 6 Cl. & F., 646, at p. 686.   Lord *Macnaghten.*
(2) 8 Q. B. D., 421, at p. 424.   (4) (1891) A.C., 532.
(3) (1891) A.C., 532, at p. 589, *per*

exemptions which are already covered by a general exemption.' And Lord *Herschell* pointed out (1) that 'such specific exemptions are often introduced *ex majori cauteld* to quiet the fears of those whose interests are engaged or sympathies aroused in favour of some particular institution, and who are apprehensive that it may not be held to fall within a general exemption '."

It may be admitted that the expressions relied on by the respondent are capable of the meaning he seeks to attach to them, and that it is grammatically possible to construe the whole section as he contends it should be construed. But, putting the argument most strongly in his favour, the utmost that can be said is that the expressions relied on by him are ambiguous. Under the circumstances the Court must ascertain the sense in which the legislature intended to use them by a consideration of the context in which they are found, the other sections of the Act, its scope and purpose as gathered from its provisions.

In addition to the provisos already referred to, the respondent relies upon two other portions of the Act—sub-sec. 4 of sec. 210 and the concluding paragraph of sec. 265. The former of these makes, in my opinion, against his contention. It provides that if the Local Authority has at the beginning of any year to the credit of the Local Fund sufficient money to defray "all its probable and reasonable expenses for that year" the Governor in Council may excuse it from making any general rate during that year in respect of the whole area or any Division thereof. The argument is that, because the Governor is empowered to excuse the making of a general rate for the year in respect of any Division, it indicates that within the contemplation of the section Divisions are intended to be financially independent. If the condition precedent necessary for calling the power into operation were that there should be to the credit of the Local Fund in respect of any Division sufficient money to defray all the probable and reasonable expenses of that Division for the year, there would be some force in the argument. But the condition precedent is not that: it is necessary that there should be sufficient money to the credit of

(1) (1891) A.C., 532, at p. 574.

H. C. of A.
1908.

BRISBANE
CITY COUNCIL
v.
ATTORNEY-
GENERAL FOR
QUEENSLAND.

O'Connor J.

H. C. of A.
1908.

BRISBANE
CITY COUNCIL
v.
ATTORNEY-
GENERAL FOR
QUEENSLAND.

O'Connor J.

the Local Fund to defray the year's expenses of the whole
area before any Division of it can be relieved from a year's rates
by action of the Governor in Council, which would rather tend
to show that the financial unity of the whole area, rather than
the financial independence of any Division, was within the contemplation of the legislature when the section was passed.   The
respondent's contention gets more aid from the last paragraph of
sec. 265.   It certainly does seem to create somewhat weighty
machinery for dealing with what is merely a matter of accounts.
On the other hand, on its face it is quite consistent with the rest
of the section regarded as an accountancy section only, and is
entirely in aid of a vigilant control of the accounts of each
Division by the ratepayers interested.   After a careful
examination of the respondent's contention in the light of all
these considerations, I find myself unable to arrive at the
conclusion that sec. 265 does anything more than direct the
keeping of accounts for each Division showing on the credit side
the amount of general rates levied in each Division, and the
endowments received by the Local Authority in respect thereof,
and showing on the debit side all moneys expended on works
within the Division which do not come within the exception of
the first proviso.

    In stating my reasons for that conclusion I do not think it
necessary to do more than refer in general terms to the sections
bearing on the questions which I have already dealt with in
detail. The Act lays down in outline a complete system of
finance, a prominent feature of which is the difference between
the collection, expenditure, and accounting for, general rates and
special rates. The former, as I have already pointed out, are
paid into the general fund of the Local Authority where they
become mixed indistinguishably with revenue from other sources,
there being no direction to separate, or machinery provided for
separating them from any other form of revenue in the Local
Fund. Further, there is no provision of the Act, unless sec. 265
may be so construed, which recognizes the existence of the
general rates of the area, much less the general rates of a
Division, as a separate fund, or as a separate account in the
general fund, out of which any particular class of payments are

to be made. As to special rates, on the contrary, there are a number of provisions from sec. 261 onward dealing with every kind of special rate, and there are others placing the financial administration of such services as gas, electricity, and water supply, on the same footing. In all these cases there are express directions that a special account shall be kept of the proceeds of the rate or special service, that all expenditure for the special purpose for which the rate has been raised shall be defrayed out of and charged to that account, and, what is more important to the question now under consideration, there is in every case a provision that the proceeds of the special rate shall be applied to the purposes for which the rate has been raised, and to no other purposes.

One might reasonably anticipate that, if the legislature had intended to constitute the general rates levied in each Division as a separate fund available only for expenditure on the works of that Division, it would have used language express and definite to bring about so important a change in the law, and that, having regard to the elaborate provisions as to the administration of the separate funds created for the purposes of special rates, it would have provided, at least in outline, the necessary machinery for carrying the change into effect.

Consider also the impossibility of carrying out effectively a system of Divisions financially independent under the scheme of administration which the Act has provided. It is admitted by the respondent that the financial independence of the Division extends only to the proceeds of general rates. There is nothing to prevent the general revenues of the Local Fund from other sources from being expended on any Division, and to any amount which the Local Authority thinks fit to authorize. But where a divisional work is paid for out of the Local Fund there is no method expressly or impliedly directed to be followed which would enable the proportion of the payment which comes from general rates to be separated from the proportion which comes from other sources of general revenue; much less are there means provided by which the proportion of the payment which came from the general rates levied in the Division in which the work

H. C. of A.
1908.

BRISBANE
CITY COUNCIL
v.
ATTORNEY-
GENERAL FOR
QUEENSLAND.

O'Connor J.

H. C. of A. was being carried out could be separated from the proportion
1908. which came from the general rates of other Divisions.

BRISBANE   Again, it must be admitted that, if the cost of a work is to be
CITY COUNCIL charged against the funds of a Division, it would be fair and in
v.
ATTORNEY- accordance with ordinary business methods to debit the fund
GENERAL FOR
QUEENSLAND. with a proportion of general office expenses in respect of the

O'Connor J. work.   Indeed the relator's claim and the judgment under appeal
following the form of the claim purport to apportion a share of
the expenses to each Division.   It is expressly provided that that
apportionment may be made by the Local Authority in the case
of work charged to a special fund.   But in regard to general
rates, not only is there no power to make any such apportionment, but sec. 265 expressly prohibits it in any case except where
the apportionment has been made under sec. 261 in the case of.
expenditure out of special rates.   Having regard to these considerations I have come to the conclusion that the interpretation
which the respondent seeks to put upon sec. 265 is inconsistent
with many sections of the Act, and with its whole scheme of
financial administration.   The appellants' interpretation, on the
other hand, treating the section as dealing with accountancy only,
is consistent with every provision of the Act, and is that which I
think must be adopted.   That being so, there is nothing in sec.
265 which cuts down the power given to the Council by sec. 192
of applying general rates as part of the Local Fund in the carrying out according to their own discretion of any works which the
Act authorizes.   I am, therefore, of opinion that the Act on its
true construction does not support the view of the law taken by
the learned Chief Justice in the Court below, and that this appeal
must be allowed and the judgment appealed against set aside.

ISAACS J.   I regret to find myself unable to concur in the
opinion of my learned brethren upon the main question of this
case, but, although sec. 265 of the *Local Authorities Act* 1902 is
not so clearly and definitely expressed as it might have been, I
cannot say I have any real doubt as to its meaning.   The matter
becomes even plainer to me when the course of previous legislation is followed.

In 1878 a *Local Government Act* was passed which related to

Municipalities; and in 1887 a further Act was passed, the *Divisional Boards Act*, which dealt with local government of Districts outside the boundaries of Municipalities. Under both Acts provision was made which enabled a local governing body to receive ordinary revenue and other revenue, or, in other words, special revenue.

Ordinary revenue was defined by sec. 175 of the first Statute, and sec. 189 of the second, and included general rates. The ordinary revenue, and therefore the general rates, were in each case carried to a fund, called respectively the Municipal Fund, and the Divisional Fund, and out of this fund the local body could pay everything in the nature of expense it incurred, whether the expense so incurred was for the general benefit, or for the special or exclusive benefit of some particular portion of the area.

All rate revenues were treated as general revenues of the local body, that is, they were the contributions to and the property of the Corporation as a whole; and once contributed, no separateness of interest in these rates was recognized as between various parts of the area.

This unity of interest was preserved even as to the making of the rates, because, by sec. 187 of the first Act and sec. 191 of the second, the general rates were to be made equally upon all rateable property within the municipal district or the Division as the case might be. Up to 1890 no separate account for any portions of the area in respect of general rates was required to be kept under either Act whether the area was divided or not.

In 1890 there was passed the *Valuation and Rating Act* which commenced to recognize some diversity of treatment between parts of a divided area. Sec. 31 provided as follows :—
" When a District is subdivided the amounts of the General Rates made and levied upon the rateable land in the several subdivisions need not be the same, but every General Rate made and levied in respect of a subdivision shall be made and levied equally upon all rateable land within the subdivision." Sec. 34 was in the following terms :—" When the amounts of the General Rates levied upon the rateable land in the several subdivisions of a District are not the same, the Local Authority shall keep a separate and

H. C. of A.
1908.

BRISBANE
CITY COUNCIL
v.
ATTORNEY-
GENERAL FOR
QUEENSLAND.

Isaacs J.

H. C. of A.   distinct account of all moneys received in respect of such Rates
  1908.   for each subdivision, and of all moneys received by the Local
BRISBANE   Authority by way of endowment upon such Rates respectively, so
CITY COUNCIL that the moneys so received shall be credited to the same accounts
   v.   as the Rates in respect of which they were respectively received."
ATTORNEY-
GENERAL FOR
QUEENSLAND. So that it was not in every case of a subdivided area that this

Isaacs J.   separate and distinct account of general rates was required, but
             only where a differentiation of rates took place. There was no
             consequence expressly declared to follow from the credit given to
             the subdivisional account.   Sec. 175 of the one Act and sec. 189
             of the other still remained unqualified, and under these, notwith-
             standing the 1890 Act, all expenditure for works was still
             payable indiscriminately out of the ordinary revenue and without
             reference to its source. Sec. 34 of the 1890 Act seems to have
             been inserted merely to ensure a standing record of actual
             differentiation and the result of it.

             The legislature by the Act of 1890, apparently seeing that the
             invariable uniformity in rating up to that time led sometimes to
             unfairness or hardship, sought to remedy it by giving the local
             body power to correct it by differential rating where necessary,
             and compelling it to record the result of the differentiation so as
             to leave it always open to consideration with reference to its
             retention, modification or abolition. The possible difference in
             rating was thought sufficient to meet inequalities of situation or
             requirements.

             So the matter stood between 1878 and 1902. In the last
             mentioned year, however, a marked change was adopted by Par-
             liament in the language of its legislation.

             It then gave express directions the nature and effect of which
             we have now to determine. They appear to me to be unmistake-
             able, and to amount to a plain departure in policy and principle.

             The *Local Authorities Act* 1902 is entitled "An Act to consoli-
             date and amend the laws relating to Local Authorities." It
             repealed the Acts of 1878, 1887, and 1890, with others, and
             brought all Local Authorities under the same enactment.

             Sec. 191 defines ordinary revenue of a municipality very much
             as before. Sec. 192 provides that ordinary revenue (which
             includes general rates) "shall be carried to the account of a

H. C. of A.
1908.

BRISBANE
CITY COUNCIL
v.
ATTORNEY-
GENERAL FOR
QUEENSLAND.

Isaacs J.

Fund," which, speaking generally, is the Local Fund. The Local Fund is nothing more than the sum total of the ordinary revenues of the municipality, and these are to be carried to an account, called in this case the "City Fund."

Sec. 192 goes on to provide that the Local Fund is to be applied, briefly speaking, towards the payment of all lawful expenses incurred by the Local Authority, of every description, but subject to the all important qualification expressed in the words " *unless this or such other (that is, another) Act contains express provision charging such sums to any particular Fund or Account.*"

This was an inroad for the first time in the history of municipal legislation made into the universality of the power of the Local Authority to pay expenditure indiscriminately out of the ordinary revenues.

We have, therefore, to see what this Act contains whereby express provision is made charging expenditure to some particular fund or account, because *what is so directed to be charged cannot be paid under the authority of sec.* 192, and, if payable out of the ordinary revenue at all, must be so payable under and in accordance with some *other* statutory provision.

Secs. 261 to 265 are a cluster of sections dealing with separate accounts, and under the heading " Separate Accounts." Before examining these sections, attention may be drawn to sec. 251, in the same part of the Act, which concerns Accounts and Audit. That section provides that books are to be kept, and true and regular accounts are to be entered therein of all sums of money received and paid on account of the Local Authority, and of the several purposes for which they are received and paid. It directs that " every Local Authority shall cause the accounts to be balanced once at least in every month." The accounts then are to be true, they are to be regular, that is, the necessary entries are to be regularly made, and they are to be balanced at least once a month so that the exact state of each account may appear on inspection.

Turning now to the cluster referred to, one general observation is desirable. Substituting the appropriate heading, the words of Lord *Collins* in delivering the judgment of the Privy Council in

H. C. of A.
1908.

Brisbane
City Council
v.
Attorney-
General for
Queensland.

Isaacs J.

the *Toronto Corporation* v. *Toronto Railway* (1) are exactly in point with reference to sec. 265. His Lordship said:—"This clause is the last of a fasciculus, of which the heading is 'Track, &c., and Railways,' and, as was held in *Hammersmith Railway Co.* v. *Brand* (2), such a heading is to be regarded as giving the key to the interpretation of the clauses ranged under it, unless the wording is inconsistent with such interpretation."

This leads to the *primâ facie* presumption that the account mentioned in sec. 265 is a separate account in the same sense as those mentioned in the other sections of the group, though the restrictions on the application of the moneys in each account are different.

Reading the enactment itself, sec. 261 requires a separate and distinct account of special and separate rates &c., and the exclusive application of the moneys raised by them to the proper purposes. Sec. 262 provides specifically as to special rates for gas, electricity and power works. Sec. 263 requires a separate and distinct account of revenue for waterworks, although, where not the produce of a separate rate, that revenue is, by sec. 191, part of the Local Fund; and sec. 264 provides for separate accounts as to loans. The last of the series is sec. 265. The first paragraph of this section is based upon sec. 34 of the Act of 1890, but with important and striking differences. Its opening words make the section applicable to all cases where an area is divided, and, unlike its prototype, it applies in such cases without exception to all general rates, whether equal or differential. In every case, that is, in every case of a divided area, a separate and distinct account is to be kept of general rates levied in the several divisions. There cannot be any doubt that this is a "particular account" within the meaning of sec. 192. The main problem is, does sec. 265 make provision charging the expense of divisional works to that separate account?

Not only is the first paragraph of sec. 265 enlarged in its operation, but the remainder of the section is entirely novel. The second paragraph is in these terms:—"And save as hereinafter provided all moneys *expended* upon works within the limits of a Division shall be *debited* to the *account* of that Division."

(1) (1907) A.C., 315, at p. 324.   (2) L.R. 4 H.L., 171.

Much of the present controversy turns on the true meaning of that provision. The appellants contend that it is a mere book-keeping provision—that it has no practical effect, and is not intended to have any. They say, in short, that the Council has only to enter on the credit side of the account of the Division the amount received from it for the general rates, and on the debit side the sum, whether exceeding that amount or not, spent on works in that Division, and then the provision is fully complied with. They maintain, too, that general rates can be lawfully spent on divisional works exceeding the amount to the credit of the Division, even without the resolution and direction mentioned in the next paragraph of the section. Of course that reduces the rest of the section to a nullity, and the provision just quoted is at best a useless formality.

The other construction is that given to it by one branch—the main branch—of the argument of counsel for the respondent. He says, in effect, that the second paragraph of sec. 265 is one of the cases referred to in the qualifying passage beginning "unless" in sec. 192, and therefore there is no power under sec. 192 to pay for works within the limit of the Division. This view is, to my mind, supported by the words of the second paragraph of sec. 365 even without more. There is no difference between the expression "charged to" an account in sec. 192 and "debited to" the account in sec. 265, and therefore it appears to me that this particular class of expenditure is in any case outside the authority of sec. 192. If so, where is the authority to pay for divisional works out of general rates not being the general rates contributed by that Division? As far as I can see, that authority is contained in sec. 265, and only in compliance with the conditions there laid down.

Whatever doubt I might otherwise entertain as to the true meaning of the second paragraph, if the section ended there, is set at rest by the first proviso, which reads thus:—"Provided that when a work is of such importance to the whole of the area that the cost of its construction and maintenance may reasonably be a *charge* upon the general revenue of the Local Authority, the Local Authority may from time to time, by resolution passed at a meeting specially summoned for the

H. C. of A.
1908.

BRISBANE
CITY COUNCIL
v.
ATTORNEY-
GENERAL FOR
QUEENSLAND.

Isaacs J.

H. C. of A.
1908.

BRISBANE
CITY COUNCIL
v.
ATTORNEY-
GENERAL FOR
QUEENSLAND.

Isaacs J.

purpose, declare such work to be a 'general work,' and direct that the cost of its construction and maintenance shall be defrayed out of the general revenues, and shall not be debited to the separate account of any Division, and such expenditure shall be so defrayed accordingly."

My first observation on this proviso is that the expression "general revenues" mean the revenues of the Corporation generally and irrespective of what Division they come from. Read in connection with the phrase "general work" no hesitation need be felt as to this. Now, the first proviso applies only when, notwithstanding the local situation of the works within a particular Division, they are declared by the Council to be so important to the whole of the area that they ought properly to be declared to be "general works," and that their cost of construction and maintenance should be defrayed out of the general revenues, and not debited to the separate account of the Division. In such case—and as I read the enactment, in such case only—the cost of these works is to be defrayed out of the "general revenues."

The legislature, it will be noticed, does not say anything whatever about debiting to a Local Fund, but speaks of defraying out of general revenues in contradistinction to debiting the divisional account. In other words, when once the resolution and direction are arrived at, the burden of the paying for the works, so far as it is necessary to resort to the general rates, is expressly transferred from the Division to the area, that is, from the moneys contributed by the Division to the whole of the general rates in the common purse. I should have thought it would be accepted as clear that, unless the resolution is passed and the direction is given, the cost of these works is not to be borne by "general revenue" so far as it consists of general rates. Otherwise what effect is to be given to the proviso? Passing by for a moment the next proviso, let us consider for this purpose the provisions as to appeal to the Minister. Suppose the Council passes the resolution and gives the direction already referred to, thereby making the payment lawful out of general revenues, what, if the Minister reverses the decision, is to be the consequence? Is the expense to be nevertheless met out of general revenue including

H. C. of A.
1908.

BRISBANE
CITY COUNCIL
v.
ATTORNEY-
GENERAL FOR
QUEENSLAND.

Isaacs J.

general rates, or, what is the same thing, out of any of the moneys said to constitute the combined and undistinguishable Local Fund? If so, it is hard to discern any practical virtue in the section at all, and quite impossible to attribute any force to the first proviso. On this assumption the precise stipulations as to a resolution and direction, and a subsequent appeal to the Minister were inserted as mere empty phrases, and to comply with them is so much expensive but utterly idle amusement. The second proviso appears to me to support the view I have already expressed, and shows what expenditure is to be paid out of general revenues without a resolution, in contradistinction to divisional works which are not to be so paid.

Looking at the various sections already referred to as a whole, they seem to me, however, to deliberately enact a policy as to the burden of works upon the general rates which varies according to the nature of the municipality.

Sec. 191 applies without variation to all municipalities and defines ordinary revenue. This is, of course, subject to any subsequent provision.

Sec. 192, except as modified by sec. 265, also applies to all municipalities whether divided or not. It applies without qualification to an undivided area, and, therefore, general rates may by mere force of the section be applied in the same way and to the same extent as any other part of the ordinary revenue. They remain in the "account" mentioned in that section, namely, the Local Fund account, and are credited there only and may be applied generally, as there is no special direction to the contrary. There is every reason for them, in that case, to be credited in the general account and applied generally, and none for crediting them to any other account, or for creating any exception to their application. But in the case of a divided area, though as to the rest of the ordinary revenue—except waterworks—sec. 192 continues to operate, sec. 263 makes a specific and inconsistent provision as to revenue from waterworks, and sec. 265 makes a new, distinct and inconsistent provision with respect to the application of general rates to divisional works. General rates, by force of the inherent exception expressly made by sec. 192, and the specific mandate of sec. 265, are not to be carried to the Local Fund

H. C. of A. account in the form of an indistinguishable bulk sum, as if the
1908. area were a unified area, but are to be carried to the several
BRISBANE Divisions, and the powers of application in sec. 192 do not extend
CITY COUNCIL to them at all.
v.
ATTORNEY-   No authority to pay a shilling of general rates therefore exists
GENERAL FOR
QUEENSLAND. in such case under sec. 192, and sec. 265 recognizes this by
Isaacs J.   expressly providing the requisite authority, wherever such pay-
ment is proper by a local authority whose area is divided.

Shortly stated, the position is that no Division is to be bound
to contribute general rates to pay for works in which it has no
concern, but must contribute to all general expenditure. The
tentative discretionary provisions intended to some extent to promote by voluntary action the same end, introduced by the Act of
1890, were replaced by a more stringent scheme, which leaves the
operations of local government as free as before, but subject to
the rule of permitting no exclusive benefit to some members of
the corporation at the expense of their fellow. corporators, as far
as relates to contributions for general rates.

This interpretation of sec. 265 seems to me not only supported
by the terms of the section, but the only one consistent with its
language. The view presented by the appellants, that the section
is merely book-keeping, attributes so much futility to the
deliberate words of the legislature that, except as a construction
of extremity, it ought not to be adopted. It is not at all necessary to extend the strict language in order to give it the meaning
I have placed upon it, but if it were I should be prepared to do
so in order to effectuate the obvious design of Parliament. As
Lord *Hobhouse* said for the Privy Council in *Salmon* v.
Duncombe (1):—" It is, however, a very serious matter to hold
that when the main object of a Statute is clear, it shall be
reduced to a nullity by the draftsman's unskilfulness or ignor-
ance of law." See also on this point, *per* Lord *Alverstone* C.J.
in *Rex* v. *Vasey* (2).

So far, I am entirely with the construction put upon the section
by the respondent, which is that, in the absence of a resolution
and direction within the meaning of the first proviso—or, in other
words, so long as works in a Division are not shown to be of

(1) 11 App. Cas., 627, at p. 634.   (2) (1905) 2 K.B. 748, at p. 750.

general importance, so that their cost may reasonably be a charge on the general revenues, no matter from what source arising— then, so far as general rates are concerned, no other Division can be called upon to pay for them. Works exclusively for the benefit of one Division are not to be paid for out of general rates contributed by other Divisions, and the Local Fund, so far as it consists of general rates, is not applicable to the payment of such works.

H. C. of A.
1908.

Brisbane
City Council
v.
Attorney-
General for
Queensland.

Isaacs J.

I am, therefore, of opinion that on the main point the learned Chief Justice of Queensland was right.

But the respondent goes further in his argument and claims also that expenditure of general rates for general purposes in a divided area should be apportioned in some equitable manner amongst the various Divisions so as to enable each Division to see how much of the money, representing general rates and still actually remaining in the common purse, belongs to that Division. He contends, too, that beyond the sum so properly appearing to the credit of any Division for general rates on accounts taken upon that basis, no works should be done in the Division, in the absence of a resolution and direction.

On this branch I am quite unable to follow him. There is nothing in the language of the Statute which will support that view. It would require some direction in the Act to debit not only the Division in which the works are done, but every other Division with proportion of the cost. Not a word can be found which justifies the debiting of any Division separately with the cost of works done in another Division. And no standard is suggested by the Act by which the apportionment could be made. It might be proportionate to contributions which, in case of a differential rate, would vary as to the rating value of property, or to the relative benefit each Division received from local works declared to be general. But no hint of any standard of appor- tionment is given, and I can see no justification in law for the contention, and I agree as to this with the majority of the Court.

The judgment of *Cooper* C.J. is therefore, in my opinion, erroneous to this extent. To put the matter concretely ; my view is that, if an area consists of three Divisions, A, B, and C, of which A contributes £2,000 in general rates, B £3,000, and

H. C. of A.
1908.

BRISBANE
CITY COUNCIL
v.
ATTORNEY-
GENERAL FOR
QUEENSLAND.

Isaacs J.

C £4,000, then, in the absence of a resolution and direction, no moneys being general rates can be spent in any Division above the amount of general rates contributed by the Division; but £7,000 could be spent in general works, even though located in A; and still £2,000 could be spent in A in local works; whether before or after the expenditure in the general works.

The appellants' view, on the contrary, is that the whole £9,000, even if it is the only money belonging to the municipality, can be spent on purely local works in A without the resolution and direction; and it is this which I cannot think to be the intention and effect of the Act.

But the question then arises, what should the order be? Should the action be dismissed outright, or should the judgment be varied in accordance with the law? I think the materials before the Court show that both branches of the respondent's case as argued before this Court were raised and fought between the parties, both on the pleadings and in the Court below. The writ undoubtedly raised specifically and separately the first and main branch. The statement of claim also contains it though in a more involved form, since the pleader has included it in the larger claim. Paragraphs 5 and 6, as I read them, allege, *inter alia*, that without the necessary resolution and direction general rates contributed by the East and West Divisions have been spent on local works in other Divisions. The plaintiff must have included this method of dealing with the general rates in the charges contained in paragraph 8, and although that paragraph taken by itself is somewhat ambiguous, it appears to me to be quite open to the view that the "just deductions" referred to include, if necessary, all amounts properly expendible otherwise than for works. The defendants clearly so understood it. Paragraphs 4 and 6 are really an admission of all the facts necessary to raise the plaintiff's contention in either aspect, and are a distinct declaration of intention to do all that is complained of, and a clear challenge as to the validity of that course in the future as well as in the past. I do not see why the law as stated by *Chitty* J. in *Shafto* v. *Bolckow, Vaughan & Co.* (1) should not apply. Both parties understood

(1) 34 Ch. D., 725, at pp. 728-729.

the ground they were fighting upon, and though there is some confusion of the two branches in the judgment of the learned Chief Justice of Queensland, that arises from the fact that his Honor was in favour of the plaintiff on both points and did not find it necessary to separate them. But the reference to general rates in the concluding passage of his reasons shows that the judgment was not going beyond the question of general rates and extending to absolute financial separation in every sense.

The point was openly fought out in both Courts, it is of great importance to the citizens of Brisbane, and the difficulty of proving a contravention of the Act should be no bar to forbidding it—rather the contrary, particularly when the difficulty of finding an appropriate remedy for actual contravention is considered—and the importance of the case extends even more strongly to many municipalities in Queensland whose Local Funds consist mainly of general rates. I think the Attorney-General is entitled ·to a declaration and injunction to the extent I have mentioned. The amplitude of his claim does not prevent him from obtaining such relief as, in the facts raised and admissions made, he is in law entitled to. This was the law as stated by the Privy Council in *Cockerell* v. *Dickens* (1) where the rule laid down by Lord *Eldon* L.C. in *Hiern* v. *Mill* (2) was followed. The Privy Council held that the Calcutta Court, while rightly refusing the particular relief asked for, was wrong in dismissing the bill, and their Lordships under the general prayer granted an injunction which gave relief of the same description as that specifically prayed for, being only a different qualification or modification of the specific relief prayed. For the reasons I have given I think that Lord *Eldon's* rule applies to this case also.

There should accordingly, in my opinion, be a declaration that the defendants are not entitled to spend, and an injunction restraining them from spending, general rates raised in any Division upon works constructed in another Division, in the absence of the resolution and direction prescribed by sec. 265.

HIGGINS J. I have had the advantage of reading the judg-

H. C. OF A.
1908.

BRISBANE
CITY COUNCIL
v.
ATTORNEY-
GENERAL FOR
QUEENSLAND.

Isaacs J.

(1) 1 Mont. D. & De G., 45.　　　　(2) 13 Ves., 114, at p. 120.

H. C. of A.
1908.

BRISBANE
CITY COUNCIL.
v.
ATTORNEY-
GENERAL FOR
QUEENSLAND.

Higgins J.

ment of the Chief Justice, and as it fully expresses my views, I have decided to withdraw the judgment which I had written to the same effect. As for the possible declaration to which the Chief Justice has adverted—possible in another case and in other circumstances—I should like to say, as the matter has been referred to, that I see nothing sufficient in the Act to encourage litigation against the municipalities for the purpose of obtaining such a declaration.

I shall only add this, that sec. 265 is the only section in which the book-keeping word " debit " is used ; that there is not in sec. 265, as there is in the analogous sections 261-264, any provision as to the application or payment or defraying or charging of the general rates received in each Division ; that, but for the form of the provisos in sec. 265, the case for the relator would not even be arguable ; that, at the most, these provisos raise inferences in favour of the relator ; that the absence of provisions for apportionment of general expenses as between the wards, and for other necessary matters, raises counter inferences ; and finally, that, although argument by inference may aid in explaining what is ambiguous, it cannot be used to contradict or subtract from what is plain—especially in face of the distinct language of sec. 192 (2).

> *Appeal allowed. Judgment appealed from*
> *discharged. Judgment to be entered*
> *for the defendants with costs. Respon-*
> *dent to pay costs of appeal.*

Solicitors, for the appellants, *Macpherson, Macdonald-Paterson & Co.*

Solicitors, for the respondent, *Atthow & McGregor.*

B. L.

[HIGH COURT OF AUSTRALIA.]

THE MERCHANT SERVICE GUILD OF ⎱ CLAIMANTS;
AUSTRALASIA . . . . . ⎰

AND

ARCHIBALD CURRIE & CO., AND ARCHI- ⎱
BALD CURRIE & CO. PROPRIETARY ⎰ RESPONDENTS.
LIMITED . . . . . .

Operation of the Constitution and laws of the Commonwealth—Commonwealth Con-   H. C. OF A.
ciliation and Arbitration Act 1904 *(No.* 13 *of* 1904)—*Jurisdiction of Common-*   1908.
wealth Court of Conciliation and Arbitration—Industrial dispute—" Ships   ⌣
whose first port of clearance and whose port of destination are in the Common-   SYDNEY,
wealth"—Commonwealth of Australia Constitution Act (63 & 64 *Vict.c.*12), *sec.* V.   *April* 13, 14,
                                                 15.

A joint stock company registered in Victoria were owners of a line of ships   Griffith C.J.,
registered in Melbourne and engaged in trade between Australia, Calcutta,   Barton,
and South Africa. The officers of the company's ships resided in Australia   O'Connor,
   Isaacs and
and were engaged there, but the ships' articles were filled in and signed in   Higgins JJ.
Calcutta. The officers, though not entitled to be discharged in Australian
ports, were allowed to leave at such ports if they wished, with the consent of
the master. The ships did no inter-state trade, but occasionally made short
trips from Calcutta to other Indian ports.

The organization of employés to which the officers belonged filed a claim in
the Commonwealth Court of Conciliation and Arbitration for the settlement
of a dispute between the officers and their employers as to the wages, hours
and conditions of labour during the voyages of their ships.

Held, that the Court had no jurisdiction to settle the dispute. Ships
engaged in such a trade are not ships " whose first port of clearance and whose
port of destination are in the Commonwealth " within the meaning of sec. V.
of the *Commonwealth of Australia Constitution Act.*

SPECIAL case stated by *Higgins* J., President of the Commonwealth Court of Conciliation and Arbitration, for the opinion of

H. C. of A.
1908.

Merchant
Service
Guild of
Australasia
v.
Archibald
Currie & Co.
Proprietary
Ltd.

the High Court, under sec. 31 of the *Commonwealth Conciliation and Arbitration Act* 1904.

This was an industrial dispute filed in the Commonwealth Court of Conciliation and Arbitration by the claimants, an organization of employés registered under the Act, against the respondents Archibald Currie & Co., as to the wages, hours and conditions of labour of the officers employed on the respondents' ships. At the hearing *Higgins* J., President of the Court, added the respondent proprietary company as respondents, on it appearing that before the initiation of the dispute in the Court that company had acquired the property in the line of ships in question from the other respondents.

The learned President, after hearing evidence to establish jurisdiction, stated a special case for the opinion of the High Court on the question whether:—" Having regard to sec. V. (covering section) of the *Constitution Act*, has this Court of Conciliation and Arbitration jurisdiction to settle the dispute ? "

The facts sufficiently appear in the judgment of *Griffith* C.J.

D. F. Ferguson and *Flannery*, for the claimants. All that it is necessary to show in order to establish jurisdiction is that there is a dispute within the Commonwealth extending beyond the limits of any one State.

[HIGGINS J.—The question whether the dispute extends beyond the limits of any one State was not intended to be raised on this special case.]

Assuming that requirement to be satisfied, the Court has, in any view, jurisdiction as to a certain part of the relationship between the parties. A large portion of the work of the employés is performed within the Commonwealth. As to the conditions of that labour an award may be made, and it will not be presumed that the Court will exceed its jurisdiction. Such an award, if made, would not only be valid, but could be effectively enforced. But further than that, there is evidence upon which the President could find that the respondents' ships come within the meaning of the second part of sec. V. of the *Constitution Act*, so that the Court would have power to make an award extending to the whole voyage. The first port of clearance is in Australia. That

H. C. OF A.
1908.
~
MERCHANT
SERVICE
GUILD OF
AUSTRALASIA
v.
ARCHIBALD
CURRIE & Co.
PROPRIETARY
LTD.

is a question of fact, not of law. The port of clearance is the port at which a ship gets authority from the Customs to leave on a voyage. The first port of clearance, therefore, is the beginning of the voyage. It must be admitted that it would be open to the Court to find that the voyage began at Calcutta, but the evidence points more strongly the other way. The proper inference is that the ships take a round voyage from Australia through Calcutta back to Australia. The port of destination means the end of the voyage, not necessarily the most distant port on the voyage. As far as the freight is concerned, the voyage may be shown by the bill of lading to be from Australia to Calcutta, or *vice versâ*, but the ship's voyage is to be determined upon other considerations. The test is : Where is she owned, in whose interests is she sailed, and where are her movements directed ? The ship's articles are not conclusive one way or the other. It should be assumed, unless the contrary is shown, that the ship's vogage begins and ends at her " home." [They referred to *Chartered Mercantile Bank of India, London, and China* v. *Netherlands India Steam Navigation Co. Ltd.* (1)]. The articles are signed at Calcutta merely for the purpose of getting the benefit of sec. 125 of the *Merchant Shipping Act.*

In construing the words of the latter part of sec. V. regard should be had to the provision as it originally appeared in sec. 20 of the *Federal Council Act.* They should be construed so as to include all British ships doing the round voyage from Australia to Calcutta and back. Otherwise they are restricted to Australian ships engaged in coasting trade. Secs. 735 and 736 of the *Merchant Shipping Act* had already given power to a Colony to regulate that trade ; it should, therefore, be inferred that sec. V. was intended to go further.

But the first part of the section is wide enough to include the case, even if the latter part is not sufficient of itself. The laws of the Commonwealth govern the people of the Commonwealth, and may be enforced against them here in respect of things done on these ships beyond the territorial jurisdiction. The award would be made against persons who are citizens of the Commonwealth. Both employer and employé are resident here. The

(1) 10 Q.B.D., 521, at p. 534.

H. C. of A.
1908.

Merchant
Service
Guild of
Australasia
v.
Archibald
Currie & Co.
Proprietary
Ltd.

difficulty of enforcing the law in foreign parts is no objection to the validity of the award.

[Griffith C.J.—But the contention of the respondents is that the whole award would be in such a form as to extend beyond the jurisdiction of the Court. If that were so. the award would be bad unless it were severable.]

It is open to Parliament to provide that disputes that arise between the people of the Commonwealth in the Commonwealth as to the terms and conditions of labour are to be dealt with according to the law of the Commonwealth, not only in Australia, but wherever the parties may be. They are subject to the legislative jurisdiction of the Commonwealth. Parliament may control all their contracts. The contracts may only be enforceable while the parties are here, but breaches of them committed abroad might be dealt with here by means of some provision similar to that in the *Customs Act* 1901, which imposes a penalty for entering port with broken seals. [They referred to *Ashbury* v. *Ellis* (1).]

[Griffith C.J.—The State or Commonwealth could prescribe a rule of duty to be observed within its territory, but not beyond it. A sovereign State has a jurisdiction extending to its subjects in every part of the world, but a subordinate State has never been considered to have such power.]

That is as regards criminal matters, but it does not apply to civil jurisdiction. If the question arose in a foreign Court it would be for that Court to say whether it would apply the law of the Commonwealth or not.

[Higgins J. referred to *Peillon* v. *Brooking* (2).]

Knox K.C. (*Piddington* with him), for the respondents, reserving the right to either of the respondents to object to the jurisdiction of *Higgins* J. to add the respondent proprietary company as a respondent in the arbitration proceedings.

The objects of the *Commonwealth Conciliation and Arbitration Act* 1904 as stated in sec. 2, sub-secs. v., vi., and vii., and the definitions in sec. 4 must be read subject to the ordinary rule of construction that they refer only to matters within the

(1) (1893) A.C., 339.   (2) 25 Beav., 218.

territorial limits of the legislature : *Jefferys* v. *Boosey* (1) ; D'*Emden* v. *Pedder* (2) ; *Macleod* v. *Attorney-General for New South Wales* (3). That rule applies, except so far as it is cut down by sec. V. of the covering Act. An award can only apply to an industry carried on in the Commonwealth, or so far as it is carried on in the Commonwealth.

[HIGGINS J.—But the meaning of " industry " must be extended as far as sec. V. allows, if that section applies.]

Sec. V. was only intended to make Commonwealth laws prevail over all the States, notwithstanding the laws of the States.

[BARTON J.—And to prevent conflict with English law.]

Clearly the first part of the section has that object only, and does not purport to make the people of the Commonwealth subject to Commonwealth laws when they are beyond its limits. As to the latter part of the section, first port of clearance and port of destination must relate to one voyage. The first port of clearance is that port on a particular voyage at which the ship is empty and takes in passengers and cargo and gets a clearance. The port of destination is the last port on the particular voyage, whether it is a round voyage or a voyage outwards to some port from which a return journey may or may not be made. Assuming, without conceding, that a round voyage from Sydney to Calcutta and back is within sec. V., the claimants have not shown that the voyages of these ships come within that description. They must show that when the ships leave the first port of clearance, assuming that to be in the Commonwealth, there is some binding agreement, arrangement, understanding or intention that that voyage is to end in the Commonwealth. There must be some way of determining at the beginning of the voyage whether the ship's destination is in the Commonwealth or not, in order to know what law governs it on the voyage. The claimants have failed to establish any such case. There is more reason for regarding Calcutta than any Commonwealth port as the first port of clearance on a round voyage, if it is such a voyage. When a ship leaves the Commonwealth it cannot be said that she is on her way to the Commonwealth *via* Calcutta.

H. C. OF A.
1908.

MERCHANT
SERVICE
GUILD OF
AUSTRALASIA
v.
ARCHIBALD
CURRIE & Co.
PROPRIETARY
LTD.

(1) 4 H.L.C., 815, at p. 939.   (2) 1 C.L.R., 91, at p. 119.
                    (3) (1891) A.C., 455.

H. C. of A.
1908.

MERCHANT
SERVICE
GUILD OF
AUSTRALASIA
v.
ARCHIBALD
CURRIE & Co.
PROPRIETARY
LTD.

Primâ facie, the voyage, if it is a round voyage, begins and ends at Calcutta.

This Court has not to consider whether upon some claim properly made an award could validly be made to bind those ships in Commonwealth waters. The claim is general, applying to the whole trade, and there is no question of splitting the claim or limiting the award.

[ISAACS J.—But supposing that the President has jurisdiction to make an award as to work in Commonwealth waters, and, that being all that was claimed, made such an award, would sec. V. apply it of itself to this industry?]

No, because it is not a Commonwealth industry.

The *Commonwealth Conciliation and Arbitration Act* being highly penal, the jurisdiction of the Court should be jealously scrutinized in every case that comes before it.

[O'CONNOR J. referred to *In re Wellington Cooks and Stewards Award* (1).]

Ferguson, in reply, referred to *Merchant Shipping Act* 1894, sec. 265.

April 15. GRIFFITH C.J. This is a case which has been referred for the opinion of this Court by the President of the Commonwealth Court of Conciliation and Arbitration. The claim is preferred by the Merchant Service Guild of Australasia, an organization of employés registered under the *Commonwealth Conciliation and Arbitration Act* 1904, claiming an award as between themselves and the respondents as to the wages, hours and conditions of labour of the respondents' officers at sea. The respondents are Archibald Currie & Co., individuals residing in Melbourne, and Archibald Currie and Co. Proprietary Limited, a joint stock company registered in Victoria. The ships in question are registered in Victoria, and are engaged in trade between Calcutta and the neighbouring ports and Australia, sometimes going to South Africa. They carry cargo and passengers to and from Asia, Australia and South Africa.

The ships' articles are always signed in Calcutta, not in Aus-

(1) 26 N.Z.L.R., 394.

tralia. The officers are all domiciled in Australia and are always
engaged in Australia, although, as I have said, the articles are
signed in Calcutta ; and, although not entitled to be discharged at
Australian ports, they are usually allowed to leave at such ports
if they wish, with the consent of the master. The ships often
make short trips from Calcutta to other Indian ports, but do no
inter-State trade in Australia.

H. C. of A.
1908.

MERCHANT
SERVICE
GUILD OF
AUSTRALASIA
v.
ARCHIBALD
CURRIE & Co.
PROPRIETARY
LTD.

Griffith C.J.

The claimants claim that under these circumstances the
Commonwealth Court has jurisdiction to make an award which
will govern the wages, hours and conditions of labour of the
officers on those ships engaged in that trade.

Of course, the jurisdiction of the Commonwealth Courts and
the operation of the Commonwealth laws extend only to places
within the Commonwealth, except so far as a larger jurisdiction
or operation is given to them by law. Sec. V. of the covering
Act of the Constitution of the Commonwealth is as follows :—
"This Act, and all laws made by the Parliament of the Commonwealth under the Constitution, shall be binding on the Courts,
Judges, and people of every State, and of every part of the
Commonwealth, notwithstanding anything in the laws of any
State ; and the laws of the Commonwealth shall be in force on
all British Ships, the Queen's Ships of war excepted, whose first
port of clearance and whose port of destination are in the
Commonwealth." If reliance is placed on that provision, as,
indeed, it must be, when the jurisdiction of the Commonwealth
Court of Arbitration is invoked in this case, the question is
whether these ships, while engaged in the trade I have described,
are ships whose first port of clearance and whose port of
destination are in the Commonwealth. The terms "first port of
clearance" and "port of destination" are terms well known in
shipping law. Every ship, before starting on a voyage, must
obtain a clearance. The first port of clearance is the port where
she gets her clearance on beginning a voyage. The port of
destination obviously means the end of that voyage. So that
the Act applies only to cases where the beginning and the end
of a voyage are both in the Commonwealth.

Under these circumstances, it seems to me impossible to say
that these ships, while engaged in the trade I have described, are

H. C. or A.   ships " whose first port of clearance and whose port of destination
1908.   are in the Commonwealth." The most favourable view that can

MERCHANT   be taken in favour of the claimants is to assume that their port
SERVICE   of departure or first port of clearance is an Australian port,
GUILD OF
AUSTRALASIA   which is extremely doubtful. Regarding the case from that
v.   point of view, it is impossible to say that the port of destination
ARCHIBALD
CURRIE & Co.   is also in the Commonwealth. The question, therefore, must, in
PROPRIETARY
LTD.   my opinion, be answered in the negative.

Griffith C.J.   Numerous other questions were raised incidentally in the
course of the argument as to what may be a voyage within the
words of section 5, but on these I express no opinion.

BARTON J. I concur.

O'CONNOR J. read the following judgment :—I shall confine my
judgment to the one really substantial question upon which the
opinion of this Court is sought, and I take it to be this :—Has
the Commonwealth Court of Conciliation and Arbitration jurisdiction to settle this dispute, involving, as it does, the fixing of
rates of wages and conditions of employment on the respondents'
ships whilst voyaging on the High Seas to ports outside
Australia ?

The jurisdiction of that Court, as of any other Commonwealth
Court, must, of course, be confined within the territorial limits
over which the laws of the Commonwealth extend, and it is
conceded that, apart from the provisions of section V. of the
covering clauses of the Constitution, those laws can have no
operation beyond the three miles sea limit around Commonwealth
territory. The matter, therefore, for consideration is whether,
under the circumstances set forth in the case, the voyage of the
respondents' ships is such as to bring them within the meaning
of the latter part of section V. That involves two questions. In
the first place, what is the true interpretation of the words
" whose first port of clearance and whose port of destination are
in the Commonwealth ? " Secondly, is there sufficient evidence
before the Court that the voyage in which the ships are engaged
is of the class to which the section, when rightly interpreted,
applies ?

H. C. of A.
1908.

Merchant
Service
Guild of
Australasia
v.
Archibald
Currie & Co.
Proprietary
Ltd.

O'Connor J.

The expressions " first port of clearance " and " port of destination " are clearly intended to describe the beginning and the end of one continuous voyage. There is no difficulty about the expression " first port of clearance." The Merchant Shipping Acts, all Custom Acts, and many Port Acts, require compliance with various requirements before a ship is permitted to go to sea. The certificate of the officer authorized by law to determine that the requirements have been complied with, is known as the " clearance certificate " or the " clearance." The first port of clearance would, therefore, ordinarily be the port from which the voyage begins. The expression " port of destination," which describes the other terminal point is not so free from ambiguity. It might be said, although Mr. *Knox* did not raise that contention, that the voyage intended to be described was merely from port to port within the Commonwealth. But that interpretation is not consistent with the whole provision. There can be only one " first port of clearance " on each voyage, and, in the case of a ship making an inter-State voyage round Australia, if the words " port of destination " were read as meaning the first port of call the section would apply only between the commencement of the voyage and that port, for the rest of the voyage it would have no operation. The only interpretation which will give any effective operation to the section is to take the port of destination as meaning port of " final destination " or last port of the voyage. The words of sec. V. would then be taken to describe a round voyage beginning and ending within the Commonwealth. That is the class of voyage to which, in my opinion, the section was intended to apply.

In coming to that conclusion I have, in accordance with a well known rule applicable to the interpretation of ambiguous expressions in a Statute, considered the state of facts which must be taken to have been within the knowledge of the British legislature at the time these covering clauses were passed. It was well known that a shipping trade carried on by ships owned and registered in Australia, and manned and officered by Australian citizens, had for many years existed in Australia and was rapidly increasing, and that it extended to New Zealand and the Islands of the Pacific and Indian ports, and that in the natural

H. C. of A.
1908.

MERCHANT
SERVICE
GUILD OF
AUSTRALASIA
v.
ARCHIBALD
CURRIE & Co.
PROPRIETARY
LTD.

O'Connor J.

expansion of that trade Australia was destined to be the home
port of a very extensive shipping trade with the East and the
Islands of the Pacific. It was in recognition of the requirements
of Australia in that respect that sec. 20 of the *Federal Council
Act* 1885 was enacted, giving a much more extended operation
to Australian laws passed under the authority of that Statute than
is given to Commonwealth laws by the section now under
consideration in its widest interpretation.

Under these circumstances it would appear not unreasonable
to impute to the British legislature an intention to place the ships
engaged on round voyages in such a trade in the same position as
regards Australian laws as the ordinary British ship holds in
regard to British laws, namely, that, while on a voyage coming
within the meaning of the section, the Australian ship should be
for the purposes of Commonwealth laws a floating portion of
Commonwealth territory.   That being the meaning of the
section, it appears to me that, when once it is established
that the voyage is of that description, it is immaterial to what
part of the world it may extend. So that, if it were established
that the voyage of the respondents' ships was a round voyage
beginning at an Australian port, calling at Calcutta or any
other foreign port, and ending in an Australian port, the
ships during the whole of the voyage would be under the Commonwealth laws and under the jurisdiction of Commonwealth
Courts. In the interpretation of the section, therefore, I see no
reason to depart from the conclusion at which I arrived in
delivering my award in the case of the *Merchant Service Guild
of Australasia* v. *The Commonwealth Steamship Owners'
Association* (1). Whether, however, a voyage does or does not
come within the section must always be a question of fact. It is
upon this part of the case that the claimants must fail.

The proof of any fact necessary for jurisdiction must be on the
claimants, and where jurisdiction depends upon the fact of the
respondents' ships being engaged in a particular class of voyage,
they must establish that fact before they can claim that jurisdiction exists. On the documents and evidence before us I can
see nothing to show that the first port of clearance of the voyages

(1) 1 Commonwealth Arbitration Rep., 1.

of these ships is a port in Australia. The facts upon which Mr. *Ferguson* has relied, that the ships are owned, registered, repaired, and, as far as the officers are concerned, manned, by persons domiciled in Australia, are at most as consistent with the first port of clearance being in India as being in Australia. Indeed, the ship's articles, although in no way conclusive, would, in the absence of other evidence, appear to indicate that the commencement and end of the voyage was Calcutta rather than some Australian port. But even if the articles are to be left out of consideration in determining that question, it is clear to my mind that the claimants have not brought before the Court any evidence to show what are the terminal points of the voyage in which their ships are engaged, and have failed, therefore, to establish that their voyage is such as to bring them within that class in respect of which a specially extended jurisdiction is given to the laws and Courts of the Commonwealth under the section now under consideration.

I agree, therefore, that our answer to the question submitted in this case must be that the Commonwealth Court of Conciliation and Arbitration has, under the circumstances, no jurisdiction to settle the dispute.

ISAACS J. I agree, on the ground that there are no facts upon which the learned President could conclude that there was an industrial dispute extending beyond the limits of any one State, or that the first port of clearance and port of destination of any of these voyages are both in the Commonwealth.

HIGGINS J. I agree in the judgment pronounced by the Chief Justice, and desire to withhold all opinion as to the other matters that have been discussed, as they are matters which, in my opinion, do not really arise for decision in this case. I advisedly confined my question to the effect of sec. V. of the Constitution, and stopped all evidence as to the nature of the industrial dispute until that question should be settled. It was to be assumed for the purpose of this special case, that the claimants could show that the dispute extended beyond the limits of any one State. When the case came before me I could not see any evidence upon which

H. C. OF A.
1908.

MERCHANT
SERVICE
GUILD OF
AUSTRALASIA
v.
ARCHIBALD
CURRIE & Co.
PROPRIETARY
LTD.

O'Connor J.

H. C. of A.
1908.

MERCHANT
SERVICE
GUILD OF
AUSTRALASIA
v.
ARCHIBALD
CURRIE & Co.
PROPRIETARY
LTD.

O'Connor J.

I could find that these ships had their first port of clearance and port of destination in the Commonwealth. But I thought that some principle might possibly be found which would enable me to bind employers and employés as to wages, hours and conditions of labour beyond the limits mentioned, if, as here, the parties were resident in Australia and the employés were engaged in Australia; and I did not wish to preclude the claimants from establishing such a principle if they could do so. After the parties had had full opportunity for consideration of the matter, the claimants have failed to show me that there is any jurisdiction to settle the dispute.

Knox K.C., for the respondents, asked for costs of the special case in the High Court: *Commonwealth Conciliation and Arbitration Act* 1904, sec. 31 (3). If such costs are not allowed in this case there is no reason why they should ever be allowed in a special case, as the reference is always by the President. The claimants are responsible for the litigation, having invoked a Court which had no jurisdiction.

Ferguson, for the claimants. The claimants are not responsible for the High Court proceedings. They invoked a Court in which costs are not usually allowed, and which was not intended by Parliament to entail heavy costs: sec. 38 (1).

GRIFFITH C.J. There will be no order as to costs.

Question answered in the negative.

Solicitors, for the claimants, *W. C. Moseley.*
Solicitors, for the respondents, *Sly & Russell.*

C. A. W.

[HIGH COURT OF AUSTRALIA.]

DAVID . . . . APPELLANT ;
RESPONDENT,

AND

MALOUF AND ANOTHER . . . RESPONDENTS.
PETITIONERS,

ON APPEAL FROM THE SUPREME COURT OF
VICTORIA.

Insolvency Act 1890 (*Vict.*) (*No.* 1102), *sec.* 37—*Insolvency Act* 1897 (*Vict.*) (*No.*
1513), *sec.* 106 (2)—*Sequestration—Petitioning creditor's debt—Current promissory note.*

   Sec. 37 of the *Insolvency Act* 1890 (Vict.), as amended by sec. 106 (2) of
the *Insolvency Act* 1897 (Vict.), provides, in reference to a petition for the
sequestration of a debtor's estate, that " the debt of the petitioning creditor
must be a liquidated sum due at law or in equity, payable either immediately
or at some certain future time."

   Held, that a debt in respect of a current promissory note made by the
debtor and of which the creditor was the holder at the date of the petition
was a good petitioning creditor's debt.

   Judgment of Supreme Court affirmed.

H. C. of A.
1908.

MELBOURNE,
June 11, 12.

Griffith C.J.,
Barton,
O'Connor,
Isaacs and
Higgins JJ.

APPEAL from the Supreme Court of Victoria.

Charles Malouf and Mary Malouf petitioned for the sequestration of the estate of Joseph David.

The order *nisi* thereon, dated 3rd April 1908, was as follows,
so far as is material :—

"Upon reading the petition . . . . alleging and setting
forth that . . . . Joseph David . . . . is now justly
and truly indebted to the petitioners in the sum of £151 12s. 7d.

on six promissory notes signed by the said Joseph David in
favour of the petitioners and of which promissory notes the
petitioners are the holders that the whole of such sum is owing
to the petitioners that such promissory notes are all dated 1st
April 1907 and are as follows :—One for £26 12s. 10d. due 4th
April 1908 one for £26 7s. 3d. due 4th July 1908 one for £26
7s. 7d. due 4th October 1908 one for £25 15s. 11d. due 4th
January 1909 one for £25 10s. 4d. due 4th April 1909 one for
£21 4s. 8d. due 4th July 1909 and that the said debt is a
liquidated sum due at law to the petitioners payable at the times
aforesaid and is wholly unsecured and that the said Joseph
David has committed an act of insolvency within six months
before the presentation of the said petition namely on 23rd
March 1908 and that the act of insolvency committed by him
was that the said Joseph David made an assignment of his
property to a trustee for the benefit of his creditors generally and
praying that the estate of the said Joseph David might be
sequestrated for the benefit of his creditors . . . .   I do by
this order under my hand place the estate of the said Joseph
David under sequestration . . . .   until this order shall be
made absolute or discharged. . . ."

On the return of the order *nisi, Hood* J. made it absolute,
holding that he was bound by the finding of *àBeckett* J., who
made the order *nisi,* that the debt set forth in the order *nisi*
was a good petitioning creditor's debt.

From the decision of *Hood* J. the respondent now appealed.

Ah Ket (with him *Lowe*), for the appellant. A promissory
note not yet due cannot be made the foundation of a petition for
sequestration. Under the *Insolvency Act* 1890, sec. 37, it was
necessary that the petitioning creditor's debt should be a debt
presently due and payable. But that section is amended by sec.
106 (2) of the *Insolvency Act* 1897, so that the debt must be "a
liquidated sum due at law or in equity, payable either immediately or at some certain future time." When a man takes a
promissory note for his debt, the original debt is suspended and
is not due until the due date of the promissory note. The effect
of sec. 106 (2) of the *Insolvency Act* 1897 is that the original

debt may be a good petitioning creditor's debt notwithstanding such suspension, but the section has not the effect of making the debt on a promissory note which is not yet due a good petitioning creditor's debt. It is quite consistent with the facts here that the promissory notes were given for a debt of £20 with a money lender's rate of interest.

[BARTON J.—The interest might be apportioned : *In re Barr* ; *Ex parte Wolfe* (1).]

In *In re Raatz* ; *Ex parte Raatz* (2) it was held that where a bill of exchange was given for the price of goods, and the bill of exchange was still current, there was a good petitioning creditor's debt, but it was the original debt for the price of the goods.

[O'CONNOR J.—Could not the Judge have amended the order *nisi* ?

ISAACS J.—There is ample power under sec. 10 (2) of the *Insolvency Act* 1897.]

There has never been any application to amend. A promissory note cannot be said to be "due" until it is payable. It is only evidence of a debt which is not due and payable until the last of the days of grace.

[ISAACS J.—A debt "due" *primâ facie* includes all sums certain which any person is legally liable to pay whether those sums have become actually payable or not : *Ex parte Kemp* ; *In re Fastnedge* (3).]

In sec. 37 of the *Insolvency Act* 1890 "due" means "presently payable." In *Pyne* v. *Kinna* (4) it was held that a promissory note not yet due was not a debt which could be attached to answer a judgment debt.

[HIGGINS J.—*Tapp* v. *Jones* (5) is to the contrary.

GRIFFITH C.J.—In *Brett* v. *Levett* (6) a bill of exchange was held to constitute a good petitioning creditor's debt.]

In that case the bill of exchange was due at the time of the petition. See also *Sarrat* v. *Austin* (7).

[GRIFFITH C.J. referred to *In re Douthat* (8).]

(1) (1896) 1 Q.B., 616.
(2) (1897) 2 Q.B., 80.
(3) L.R. 9 Ch., 383, at p. 387.
(4) 11 I.R.C.L., 40.
(5) L.R. 10 Q.B., 591.
(6) 1 Rose, 102.
(7) 2 Rose, 112.
(8) 4 B. & A., 67.

There there was an antecedent debt for which the bill of exchange was given, and that was a good petitioning creditor's debt.

[Counsel also referred to *Encyclopædia of the Laws of England* (2nd ed.), vol. II., p. 4; 7 Geo. I. c. 31, secs. 1, 3; 5 Geo. II. c. 30, s. 22; 6 Geo. IV. c. 16, sec. 50.]

Goldsmith K.C. and *Agg*, for the respondents were not heard.

GRIFFITH C.J. The petitioning creditors' debt in this case is described as "the sum of £151 12s. 7d. on six promissory notes signed by the said Joseph David in favour of the petitioners and of which promissory notes the petitioners are the holders." The dates of the promissory notes are then given, showing that none of them had fallen due at the date of the petition. The objection is taken that that is not a good petitioning creditor's debt. Whether it is or is not depends entirely upon the Insolvency Acts. Sec. 37 of the *Insolvency Act* 1890 provides that "the debt of the petitioning creditor must be a liquidated sum due at law or in equity;" and it was held in Victoria in *In re Taylor*; *Ex parte Young Bros.* (1), following the decision of *Sir James Bacon* C.J. in *Ex parte Sturt & Co.*; *In re Pearcy* (2), that those words did not include the case of a debt in respect of which credit, which was unexpired at the time of the presentation of the petition, had been given. That case, which was not a case of a promissory note, but of credit given for goods sold, was decided in 1871, shortly after the English *Bankruptcy Act* 1869 was passed. That view does not appear to have been disputed, although much might possibly have been said against it.

The English *Bankruptcy Act* 1883, by sec. 6, substituted a new definition of a petitioning creditor's debt, viz., "a liquidated sum payable either immediately or at some certain future time," leaving out the word "due." Under that provision there have been many petitions in England founded upon debts not payable until a future time. It is suggested that in all of them, even if a promissory note or a bill of exchange had been

(1) 17 V.L.R., 121; 12 A.L.T., 158.   (2) L.R. 13 Eq., 309.

given, the petition was founded on the original debt. That may be so. Sec. 37 of the Victorian Act of 1890 was amended by the Act of 1897, which added after the words "in equity" the words "payable either immediately or at some certain future time." The question for our determination is whether under the definition now given in the Victorian Acts the holder of a current promissory note of sufficient amount can present a petition. That depends upon whether it is such a debt as can be described as "a liquidated sum due at law or in equity, payable either immediately or at some certain future time."

It was not disputed that in this case, if there was an original debt in respect of which the promissory notes were given, and that fact had been set out, the petition would be good. If it were only a question of fact the matter could probably be cured by amendment. The other point is of considerable importance, because, if the objection is good, an indorsee could not become a petitioning creditor for the sequestration of the estate of the maker of a current promissory note.

It seems to me that the relation between the maker and the holder of a promissory note is that of debtor and creditor—certainly for the purposes of the Insolvency Acts. There can be no doubt that, if a man in insolvent circumstances deliberately preferred one person in that position to another, it might be a fraudulent preference. Again, if he made a preferential payment with a view to defeat or delay such persons, they would be creditors who would be defeated or delayed. Again, if it became necessary to inquire whether a debtor was able to pay his debts as they became due out of his own moneys, certainly his obligations on promissory notes falling due on subsequent dates would be regarded as debts which he might be unable to pay out of his own moneys. So that, unless the words of the Acts compel us to hold the contrary, we are bound to decide that the holder of a current promissory note is a creditor of the maker and has a good petitioning creditor's debt.

Under sec. 37 of the Act of 1890 before its amendment the word "due" was capable of meaning "presently payable"; it was also capable of meaning "owing"; and a third meaning was that the debt was a sum due either at law or in equity, regarded as a debt, without reference to the time of payment. *Sir James Bacon* C.J. took the view that it meant " presently payable."

Assuming that that was the meaning of the word " due " in sec. 37 of the Act of 1890, when sec. 106 of the Act of 1897 added other words the context became different, and the meaning of the word " due " may, therefore, have become different. If we substitute in the phrase as amended the words " presently payable " for the word " due," and add the other words " payable either immediately or at some certain future time," we get " a liquidated sum presently payable at law or in equity, payable either immediately or at some certain future time." But that clearly would not be giving effect to the intention of the legislature. It seems then that, whatever the word " due " meant in its original context, it can no longer have reference to the time of payment, but must now refer to the nature of the obligation.

Another argument was that, although that view might apply to an obligation arising under a covenant or goods sold on credit, it does not apply to negotiable instruments, because the words " due " and " payable " are used as synonymous terms in the *Instruments Act* of 1890. That is, no doubt, the meaning of the word " due," as used in that Act. But it does not follow that in an other Act, in an entirely different context, the word " due " has the same meaning, nor that, if it once had that meaning in the Act of 1890, it can any longer have it after the Act of 1897. I think, therefore, that the petition is good on its face without amendment.

BARTON J. I am of the same opinion.

O'CONNOR J. I concur.

ISAACS J. I concur.

HIGGINS J. I concur.

Appeal dismissed with costs.

Solicitor, for the appellant, *R. L. Cross.*
Solicitor, for the respondents, *W. H. L. Roberts.*

B. L.

[HIGH COURT OF AUSTRALIA.]

HUGHES . . . . APPELLANT ;
COMPLAINANT,

AND

STEEL . . . . RESPONDENT.
DEFENDANT,

ON APPEAL FROM THE SUPREME COURT OF
NEW SOUTH WALES.

Public Health Act 1902 (*N.S.W.*) (*No.* 30 *of* 1902), *secs.* 81, 82—*Sale of adulter-*
ated liquor—Analysis of article sold—Certificate of analyst—Evidence of com-
pliance with statutory directions.

    Sec. 82 of the *Public Health Act* 1902 provides that a certificate may be
given by an analyst of the result of his analysis of any food or drug submitted to him for analysis in pursuance of the provisions of the Act ; and
that in any proceedings before any Court the production of a certificate purporting to be signed by the analyst shall be sufficient evidence of the identity
of the food or drug analysed and of the result of the analysis without further
proof of its authenticity.

    Held, that on a prosecution for selling food which is not of the nature,
substance, or quality demanded by the purchaser, where the certificate of an
analyst is admitted in evidence under this section, it is not necessary for the
prosecutor to prove that the analyst divided the food submitted to him by
the purchaser into two parts as required by sec. 81.

    Decision of *Sly* Acting-J. : *Hughes* v. *Steel*, 24 N.S.W. W.N., 146,
reversed.

H. C. of A.
1908.
⌣
SYDNEY,
May 14, 15.
———
Griffith C.J.,
O'Connor and
Isaacs JJ.

APPEAL from a decision of *Sly* Acting-J. on a special case stated
under the *Justices Act* 1902.

    The respondent, a hotel keeper, was proceeded against by the
appellant under sec. 88 of the *Public Health Act* 1902, upon an

H. C. of A.   information charging him with having, to the prejudice of the
  1908.   purchaser thereof, sold certain articles of food, namely, brandy
HUGHES   and rum, which were not of the nature, substance, or quality of
  v.   the foods demanded by the purchaser. It was proved that
STEEL.   the appellant, an Inspector of Police and District Licensing
            Inspector, went to the hotel kept by the respondent, and there
            purchased some liquor. After the purchase the Inspector gave
            notice to the seller that he intended to submit the liquor pur-
            chased to the government analyst for analysis, and, as required
            by sec. 80 of the Act, offered to divide the liquor into three parts,
            to be separately sealed and labelled, and to leave one of the parts
            with the seller. This offer being refused, he labelled and sealed
            the bottles there and then, and afterwards handed them to the
            government analyst. This evidence having been given, a certifi-
            cate purporting to be signed by the government analyst and to
            show the result of his analysis of the liquor in question was put
            in evidence without objection. The evidence for the prosecution
            being closed the point was taken for the defendant that, as there
            was no evidence that the analyst had divided the samples given
            to him in accordance with sec. 81 of the Act, the information
            should be dismissed. The magistrate upheld the objection and
            dismissed the information.

            A special case was stated by the magistrate for the opinion of
            the Supreme Court whether his decision was erroneous in point
            of law. *Sly* Acting-J., before whom the case was argued, held
            that the magistrate was right: *Hughes* v. *Steel* (1), and from that
            decision the present appeal was brought by special leave.

            The material sections of the *Public Health Act* 1902, are suffi-
            ciently set out in the judgments hereunder.

            Watt, for the appellant. *Ex parte Kilby* (2), upon which the
            Judge relied, does not apply to the present case. That was a
            decision as to the requirements of sec. 80. It may well be that
            the purchaser is bound to comply with that section as a condition
            precedent to a prosecution. But sec. 81 merely imposes certain
            duties on the analyst, for a breach of which he may perhaps be
            liable as a public officer under the general law or under sec. 106

            (1) 24 N.S.W. W.N., 146.   (2) (1901) 1 S.R. (N.S.W.), 228.

of the Act. Even if those requirements were conditions precedent, they would only affect the admissibility of the certificate,
and objection should have been taken on that ground. But they
are not an essential part of the case for the prosecution. The
prosecutor proved that he had done all that the Act required
him to do, and the certificate, being in the proper form, was
admissible on its mere production, under sec. 82. That section is
intended to obviate the necessity of calling the analyst, but, if
the construction put upon it by the Supreme Court is correct, the
analyst must be called in every case. There is no necessity to
make use of the certificate at all : *Bennett* v. *Bell* (1). An
analyst may be called to prove the result of his analysis. If that
is not convenient, sec. 82 provides an alternative method of
proving the same thing. It could not have been intended that
proof of performance of the analyst's duty was a condition precedent either to the admissibility of the certificate or to obtaining
a conviction. The part not analysed is retained to be produced
if the defendant requires it. If he does not call for it he cannot
complain. (See *Gettings* v. *Brian* (2)). The onus of proof
would rest on the defendant, and in the absence of evidence to
the contrary, *omnia præsumuntur rite et solenniter esse acta* :
Ex parte Kauter (3); *Motteram* v. *Eastern Counties Railway
Co.* (4); *Hill* v. *Hennigan* (5). The English decisions as to the
requirements of an analyst's certificate are not applicable here,
as the scheme of the English Act is altogether different. Under
it there can be no prosecution unless an analyst's certificate is
produced. [He referred to *Sale of Food and Drugs Act*, 38 &
39 Vict. c. 63, secs. 6, 9-15, 28, 29, and 62 & 63 Vict. c. 51, sec.
51; *Suckling* v. *Parker* (6).]

Blacket, for the respondent. Secs. 80 and 81 are alternative
sections. If the procedure under sec. 80 is carried out, sec. 81
does not apply. It only applies where the vendor does not
accept the offer of the purchaser to divide the article. There is
no reason why the two sections should be treated upon a different
footing as regards their legal effect. If, where sec. 80 applies, it is

(1) 23 N.S.W. W.N., 1.   (4) 29 L.J.M.C., 57.
(2) 21 N.S.W. W.N., 52.   (5) I.R. 11 C.L., 522.
(3) (1904) 4 S.R. (N.S.W.), 209.   (6) (1906) 1 K.B., 527.

a condition precedent to a conviction that its requirements should be complied with, then where sec. 81 applies it should be regarded as equally imperative, and the certificate provided for by the section should not be deemed valid unless the conditions have been fulfilled. It is established by a long line of cases that the provisions of sec. 80 must be strictly carried out. [He referred to *Barnes* v. *Chipp* (1); *Smart & Son* v. *Watts* (2); *Lowery* v. *Hallard* (3); *Suckling* v. *Parker* (4).] Sec. 82 only makes the certificate evidence of the identity of the article analysed and the result of the analysis. But it is not proof of a division by the analyst or of the retaining of one part for production. This is a provision for the benefit of the defendant and should be strictly enforced. The part retained should be ready for production, just as under sec. 80 one of the three parts must be kept by the purchaser. The object is to enable the defendant to check the *primâ facie* evidence of the certificate by having an analysis of the part retained. The suggested distinction between the English Act and this Act does not exist, for there may be a prosecution without any certificate at all : *Buckler* v. *Wilson* (5). Moreover in England the defendant has an advantage that he has not here. He may require that the analyst be called as a witness: [See 38 & 39 Vict. c. 63, sec. 21.] The facts to be proved under sec. 81 are facts solely in the knowledge of the prosecution and can only be proved by a witness on that side. The defendant should not be compelled to call a witness from the side of the prosecution in order to prove that the Act has not been complied with. The onus is on the prosecution to prove the fulfilment of all statutory conditions. If the legislature had intended to make the certificate evidence of the fulfilment of all those conditions it would have clearly said so. It would be a great extension of the maxim *omnia præsumuntur rite esse acta* to make it apply to conditions of this kind. No such presumption is made as to the requirements of sec. 80. Why should there be any presumption as to sec. 81 ? The directions in the two sections are much alike. The illustrations given in *Broom's Legal Maxims* are different in

(1) 3 Ex. D., 176.
(2) (1895) 1 Q.B., 219.
(3) (1906) 1 K.B., 398.
(4) (1906) 1 K.B., 527.
(5) (1896) 1 Q.B., 83, at p. 90.

kind from this case. *Hill* v. *Hennigan* (1) stretches the maxim too far. No presumption should be made as to acts which are collateral to the certificate and are not embodied in it or essential to it.

[ISAACS J. referred to *Waddington* v. *Roberts* (2).]

Even if this appeal is allowed costs should not be given against the respondent. The case, though of importance to the Crown as involving a principle, is not of great importance otherwise, as only a small amount is involved.

GRIFFITH C.J. We have had the opportunity of considering this case since the argument yesterday, and there is no reason why we should reserve our judgment.

The question arises under sec. 81 of the *Public Health Act* 1902. Sec. 80 provides that the purchaser or officer obtaining any food or drug with the intention of submitting it to analysis shall notify the seller of his intention to have it so submitted for analysis and offer to divide it into three parts, which, if the offer is accepted, are to be separately labelled or marked. Sec. 81 provides that, if that offer is not accepted by the seller or person dealing in the food or drug or his agent or servant, the analyst receiving the article from the purchaser for analysis shall divide it into two parts, and seal or fasten up one of them and retain it for production in the event of further proceedings being taken in the matter. Sec. 82 provides that the analyst who analyses any food or drug submitted to him in pursuance of the Act may give a certificate of the result of the analysis in a prescribed form, " and in any proceedings before any Court or justices the production of a certificate, purporting to be signed by the analyst, shall be sufficient evidence of the identity of the food or drug analysed, and of the result of the analysis without proof of the signature of the person appearing to have signed the same." The point taken is that in this case, in which the seller did not require the article to be divided into three parts, there was no evidence that the analyst divided the drug submitted to him into two parts and sealed one of them up and retained it for production as prescribed by sec. 81. The objection is well founded in fact. There was no such evidence.

(1) L.R. 11 C.L., 522.   (2) L.R. 3 Q.B., 579.

All that was proved was the purchase of the article, that the purchaser offered to divide it into three parts, that the seller did not accept the offer, and that the article was then sent to the analyst, and the analyst's certificate was produced. Reliance was placed by the defendant upon some English decisions, and one of the Supreme Court of New South Wales, as to the effect of the directions in sec. 80. No case was cited before us as to the effect of the provisions of sec. 81. It is to be remarked that the scheme of the English Act is very different from that of the New South Wales Act. Under the English Act there can be no prosecution at all by the purchaser until he has received a certificate from the analyst. That is not the scheme of the New South Wales Act. The certificate of the analyst in New South Wales is merely a mode of proving the committing of the offence. If reliance is placed upon the certificate, then the statutory directions, whatever they are, must be proved to have been complied with. No assistance, therefore, can be derived from these decisions. Moreover the provision in the English Act corresponding to sec. 83 is different. There is first a direction that the goods may be sent by registered letter to the analyst. Then there is a direction that the analyst, not only shall divide the article into two parts, but shall deliver one of the parts which was not analysed to the purchaser or officer either when he receives the sample or at the time when he supplies the certificate. So that if an article of food or drug is sent to an analyst for analysis the prosecutor will have in his possession, not later than the date of receiving the certificate, the half not analysed by the analyst. Sec. 81 of the New South Wales Act, on the other hand, provides merely that the analyst shall " retain such part for production in the event of proceedings being afterwards taken in the matter." " For production " must mean either to be produced if required by the defendant or by the prosecutor or to be produced in all cases. Now, the scheme of the Act is clearly that the analyst need not be called as a witness. That is the main purpose of sec. 82; and in a country like New South Wales the reason for such a provision is obvious. There is not likely to be an analyst in every town, at any rate not a competent one, though there may be prosecutions for offences against the Act wherever there are sellers of food or drugs. It seems to me, therefore, clearly to have been intended that the calling of the analyst should not be necessary. If the contention put forward by the respondent were correct it would be necessary to call the analyst in every case, so that the advantage intended to be given by the section would be gone. This provision, it seems to me, was inserted for the benefit of the defendant, but the defendant is entitled to take advantage of it only to the extent to which it was intended that he should be benefited, that is to say, if he desires to have this part produced he may ask for it. If he does not get it, or if any difficulty is placed by the magistrate in the way of his getting it, which I should think highly unlikely to occur, then a somewhat difficult question may arise, as to which I do not at present express any definite opinion. In my opinion it is not necessary for the purpose of obtaining a conviction under this Act to do any more than prove the purchase of the article, with the prescribed notification and offer, delivery to the analyst, and the result of the analysis. If the analyst fails to comply with the directions in sec. 81, that is a matter which may possibly afford a defence if it is established by the defendant, but it is not necessary for the prosecution to prove affirmatively that the analyst has complied with them. As for the suggestion that the maxim *omnia præsumuntur rite esse acta* applies, I would remark that that is a maxim to be applied with very great caution. The doctrine is applied by the Statute to the extent of making the certificate sufficient proof of the identity of the goods mentioned in it with the goods received by the analyst from the purchaser, but I should hesitate to extend it further. It was, as I have said, the obvious purpose of the enactment to render it unnecessary to call the analyst as a witness.

For these reasons I think that the learned Judge was in error in thinking that proceedings under this section were subject to the rules laid down in the English cases and in New South Wales with respect to the provisions of sec. 80.

O'CONNOR J. I am of the same opinion. The charge before the magistrate was laid under sec. 88, sub-sec. 2 of the *Public Health Act* 1902. It is necessary, in order to substantiate that offence, to prove that the article in question was not of the nature, substance, and quality demanded by the purchaser. In proof of that allegation the certificate of an analyst was put in evidence. Sec. 82 enables the analyst's certificate as to the result of the analysis to be put in evidence without calling the analyst, and there is nothing in that section which makes it necessary to prove that there has been a division of the sample into two parts as provided in sec. 81. In order to establish his contention, therefore, it was necessary for Mr. *Blacket* to satisfy the Court that from reading these sections of the Act together there can be deduced an expression of the intention of the legislature that the division of the samples under sec. 81 must be proved before the certificate can be allowed to be effective in evidence. Now, I am unable to find in these sections anything from which that deduction as to the intention of the legislature can be drawn. There is a very great difference between the position and duties of the analyst under the New South Wales Act and that of the analyst under the English Act. Under the English Act of 1875 (sec. 21) the party accused has the opportunity of having the analyst called as a matter of right by giving notice of his desire to have him called. After such notice, the analyst will then have to be called as a witness, bringing with him the portions of the articles which are directed to be sealed up and retained for production. With regard to the analyst and his duties under the New South Wales Act there is no such provision. The analyst there is a public officer. "Analyst" is by sec. 76 defined to be the government analyst, and to include any person appointed an analyst by the Board for the purposes of the Act. Power is given by the Act to appoint an analyst, in sec. 81 the analyst is treated as a public officer, and it becomes his duty to divide the sample received for analysis into two parts only in the event of the seller not accepting the offer of the purchaser or officer to divide the drug or food into parts as required by the Act. The analyst is not present when the offer is made, and therefore he must get information in some form from the purchaser as to whether the seller has or has not accepted the offer. This seems to me to clearly indicate that the communication of this information is to be regarded as a communication between one officer of the department and another, and under some circumstances it may become the duty of the magistrate to see that the part not analysed is produced. No doubt it was the intention of the legislature that this division should be carried out for the protection of the person charged, but it is merely a departmental matter, the failure to carry out which may be a contravention of the Act, possibly subjecting the analyst to punishment under sec. 107. However that may be, I have no doubt that the proof of that having been carried out is not a condition precedent to the putting in evidence of the certificate. If it were not for the cases cited as to the effect of sec. 80 and as to the corresponding sections of the English Act, I do not see how there could be any question that the meaning of the Act is what I have stated. But the argument has been raised by reason of the supposed analogy between the provision of sec. 80 and those of secs. 81 and 82. I do not see any such analogy. The position of the prosecutor, with whom sec. 80 deals, is altogether different from the position of the public officer, the analyst whose duty is set out in secs. 81 and 82.

I wish to rest my judgment entirely upon the Act itself. I think that the maxim *omnia præsumuntur rite esse acta* must be applied with a great degree of care. If it was the duty of the analyst to make this division, I am not at all certain that we should assume that it had been made from the mere fact of the certificate being produced. In my opinion, the matter should be decided entirely apart from any consideration of that kind. I rest my judgment, therefore, on the ground that it is not a condition precedent to the production and efficacy of the certificate that the division of the sample specified in sec. 81 should be proved to have been made.

ISAACS J. I am of the same opinion. The question here is, what is the intention of the legislature? As to whether the requirements of sec. 81 should be affirmatively proved before there can be a conviction, there is nothing in the Act which says that the omission to carry out those requirements shall invalidate the certificate. The intention of the legislature must be gathered from the Act itself and from a comparison of its various parts.

H. C. of A.
1908.

HUGHES
v.
STEEL.

Isaacs J.

Now Mr. *Blacket*, in a very able argument, has endeavoured to place sec. 81 upon the same footing as sec. 80. But there is one great difference between the two, as it seems to me. Sec. 80 provides that the purchaser shall do certain things. There is no provision in the Act as to any special mode of proving these things. The law therefore necessarily implies that he must be called to prove that these things have been done. Sec. 81 requires the analyst to do certain things, but sec. 82 definitely provides that he need not be called. When I say definitely provides, the section does not say that in so many words, but it provides that his certificate shall be evidence of the analysis, &c., which amounts to the same thing. It would be inconsistent with sec. 81 that any of the matters there directed to be done should go unproved, but it is not inconsistent with sec. 81 that the matters there mentioned should not be proved affirmatively. It would be inconsistent, on the other hand, with sec. 82 for affirmative proof to be required in respect of the matters prescribed in sec. 81. It would make sec. 81 qualify sec. 82. The learned Chief Justice has pointed out the inconvenience of such a requirement, and the reasons why the legislature of the State has provided that documentary evidence should be sufficient. There is nothing to prevent the defendant from proving, if he can, that the provisions of sec. 81 were not complied with. But that was not done in this case.

I rest my judgment upon the Act itself. I gather the intention of the legislature from reading secs. 81 and 82 together, and unless one is prepared to nullify the provisions of sec. 82, I do not see how you can give effect to the argument of the respondent here, that affirmative evidence must be given of the matters in sec. 81.

With regard to the maxim *omnia præsumuntur rite esse acta,* I do not think any English case goes the full length required for the appellant's argument here. There is an Irish case, *Hill* v. *Hennigan* (1), as to which I shall only say this, that I agree with Mr. *Blacket* that the decision goes to an extraordinary length, and I desire to reserve my opinion whether it can be justified or not.

(1) I.R. 11 C.L., 522.

Per Curiam. It is not the practice of the Court to grant costs of the appeal in such a case. It may be of great importance to the appellant to have the matter decided, but it is not of such importance to the other side.

H. C. or A.
1908.

HUGHES
v.
STEEL.

Isaacs J.

> *Appeal allowed. Order appealed from dis-*
> *charged. Case remitted to the magis-*
> *trate for determination. Respondent*
> *to pay the costs in the Supreme Court.*

Solicitor, for the appellant, *The Crown Solicitor of New South Wales.*

Solicitor, for the respondent, *J. W. Abigail.*

C. A. W.

[HIGH COURT OF AUSTRALIA.]

SWAN AND ANOTHER . . . . . APPELLANTS;
DEFENDANTS,

AND

RAWSTHORNE . . . . . . RESPONDENT.
PLAINTIFF,

ON APPEAL FROM THE SUPREME COURT OF
NEW SOUTH WALES.

H. C. or A.
1908.

SYDNEY,
April 24;
May 12, 18.

Griffith C.J.,
Barton,
O'Connor and
Isaacs JJ.

Vendor and purchaser—Assignment of leasehold—Agreement by purchaser to allow vendor to retain portion under sub-lease—Agreement by vendor to erect improvements—Delay on part of vendor—Right of vendor to specific performance—Compensation—Action by purchaser against vendor for trespass—Injunction.

The holder of a Crown lease agreed in writing to assign the leasehold and stock thereon subject to a condition that he should be entitled to retain a portion of the area on lease from the purchaser, who was to give him a sub-lease at law of that portion. The purchase was to be completed by a day fixed, failing which the purchaser was to be entitled to take possession as tenant to the vendor pending completion, paying interest on the purchase money. Before the date fixed for completion it appeared that certain improvements necessary for the working of the property were situated on the portion to be retained by the vendor, and a further agreement was then entered into in writing that the sub-lease should not be executed until certain improvements were erected on the rest of the area by the vendor. According to the vendor there was also a verbal agreement, though this was disputed by the purchaser, that the purchaser should have the right in the meantime to use the improvements on the portion to be retained by the vendor. On the day fixed the purchase was completed by transfer of land and delivery of stock, but, the improvements not having been erected, the purchaser claimed the legal and equitable title to the whole area free from any obligation to grant the sub-lease. The vendor thereupon excluded the purchaser's stock from the use of the improvements on the portion in question. The purchaser brought an action at law against the vendor claiming damages for trespass to land and wrongful impounding of stock. The vendor brought a suit in equity, claiming an injunction to restrain the action at law and specific performance of the agreement to grant him a sub-lease. On an interlocutory application the purchaser was given liberty to sign judgment in the action at law, but was restrained by injunction until the hearing from proceeding to assessment of damages.

Held, that the delay in completion of the improvements did not go to the substance of the transaction, but was a matter for compensation, and the vendor, having completed the improvements before the hearing of the suit, was entitled to a decree for specific performance ; but was not entitled to the injunction claimed.

Per Griffith C.J., Barton and *O'Connor JJ.*—The purchaser had never acquired a right to the exclusive possession of the portion to be retained by the vendor, and the vendor had, therefore, a good defence in law to the action for trespass to land, but, as the vendor had verbally agreed to the purchaser having the use of the improvements on that portion, and, as there had been part-performance of the main agreement to which that agreement was ancillary, he had no defence in equity, whether he had or had not at law, to the claim for damages for wrongful impounding, and, as the purchaser did not ask for an inquiry as to damages, but was content to rest on his judgment at law, it was not a case for the exercise by the Court of Equity of its discretionary power to grant an injunction for the purpose of doing complete justice between the parties.

Per Isaacs J.—The verbal agreement should not, in view of the issues raised at the trial and the conflict of evidence, be taken to have been proved, and upon the documentary evidence the legal title in the whole area passed to the purchaser by virtue of the transfer, and having entered into possession under the terms of the contract, and no sub-lease having been executed, he was in possession of the whole area, and the vendor became a trespasser and had no defence in law or in equity to the action at law, and was, therefore, not entitled to an injunction.

Judgment of *A. H. Simpson* C.J. in Equity varied and affirmed as varied.

APPEAL from a decision of *A. H. Simpson* C.J. in Equity of the Supreme Court of New South Wales in a suit for specific performance and an injunction.

The following statement of the facts is taken from the judgment of *Griffith* C.J.:—

The plaintiff, respondent, who was the owner of a pastoral property of about 100,000 acres, of which the greater part was held under lease from the Crown, arranged to sell it with the stock to the defendant Swan, with the exception of 10,240 acres which he proposed to retain for himself. As a Crown lease cannot be assigned in part, it was arranged that the whole lease should be assigned to the defendant Swan, and that that defendant should execute a sub-lease of the 10,240 acres to the plaintiff at the same average rental as would be payable by that defendant on the whole lease. Accordingly on 24th October 1905 a written contract of sale was drawn up and signed by the parties. The 12th condition was as follows :—" As to the 10,240 acres . . . part of lands above referred to the vendor is to be entitled to retain same on lease at the same average rental as the whole lease subject to compliance by him with the provisions of the *Western Lands Act* in respect thereof and to the provisions of the Crown Lands Acts and the fences round the said 10,240 acres are to be put in order by the vendor. As the said 10,240 acres are included in the total area of the lease of 100,680 acres the purchaser shall give the vendor a lease of same at law." The 9th condition provided that the purchase should be completed on 1st December following, and that if for any reason the matter was not then ready for completion the purchaser should be entitled to take possession as tenant to the vendor at a nominal rent pending completion, paying interest on the purchase money at 5 per cent. until completion.

After the contract was signed, the defendant Swan inspected the property, and found that the improvements, necessary for

H. C. OF A. working so large an estate, were all situated in the 10,240 acres, and
1908. not, as he alleged to have been represented to him by the vendor,
SWAN upon the other part of the estate. It is immaterial to inquire
v. how far his complaint was justified, or what rights he had under
RAWS- the circumstances, for he elected to go on with the purchase sub-
THORNE. ject to the terms of a further agreement dated 28th November,
by which it was agreed that the lease to the vendor of the
10,240 acres should not be executed by the purchaser until the
vendor should have erected certain improvements on specified
parts of the other 90,000 acres. This agreement contained also a
minor stipulation as to the rent to be paid by the vendor in
respect of the 10,240 acres, but contained nothing to qualify the
vendor's right to retain possession of that area on lease.

The plaintiff in his evidence said that it was agreed at the
time of signing the agreement of 28th November that the purchaser was to have the right of using certain improvements on
the 10,240 acres until the new improvements were completed.
The purchase was completed in January 1906 by transfer of the
land and delivery of the stock, plaintiff remaining in possession
of the 10,240 acres. Some delay occurred in the erection of the
improvements stipulated for by the agreement of 28th November.
The purchaser became dissatisfied at this delay and claimed to fix
a time for the completion of the improvements, at the expiration
of which time he claimed to have not only the legal but the
equitable title to the whole of the 100,000 acres, free from any
obligation to grant a sub-lease of the 10,240 acres. The vendor
thereupon interfered with the purchaser's stock, and excluded
them from the use of the improvements upon the 10,240 acres.
In respect of this interference the purchaser (with whom the
other appellant, Wheatley, was then associated) brought an action
against the vendor described in the statement of claim as an
" action for trespass and for wrongful impounding." The plaintiff
thereupon brought this suit, claiming specific performance of the
agreement to grant him a lease of the 10,240 acres, and an injunction to restrain the action. On an interlocutory motion the
Court ordered that the defendants should be at liberty to sign
judgment in the action, but should be restrained from proceeding
to assessment of damages. The defendants by their defence

denied the plaintiff's right to specific performance altogether, contending that he had lost it by delay in performing the agreement of 28th November. They further contended that the improvements stipulated for in that agreement were not completed, so that the suit was in any view premature. On the latter point the learned Judge of first instance found the facts against them, and his judgment on this point is not contested.

Upon the main point he was of opinion that in substance, though not in terms, the 10,240 acres were exempted from the sale, and that the plaintiff was entitled to retain possession of that area, and that any delay in the completion of the improvements stipulated for by the latter agreement did not go to the substance of the transaction and was no answer to the claim (see *Oxford* v. *Provand* (1).) He therefore decreed specific performance. He also granted a perpetual injunction against the action at law, thinking that the defendants had no right at all over the 10,240 acres, but without prejudice to any right of action that they might have against the plaintiff in respect of delay in completion of the improvements.

From this decision the present appeal was brought.

Dr. Cullen K.C. (*Brissenden* with him), for the appellants. The injunction was wrongly granted. The agreement gave the right of possession to the appellants, and the transfer put them in possession. The right to retain the 10,240 acres given by the agreement did not leave the vendor in possession of that area. The condition must be construed in the light of the rest of the agreement and the circumstances, and it will not be assumed that the parties intended to do what the law will not allow, *i.e.*, to divide the leasehold. The right of the vendor was a right to have a lease under certain circumstances, but in order to give a lease the appellants must be deemed to have possession. The second agreement postponed the vendor's right to have a lease and made it conditional upon improvements being erected. Those improvements were to be erected within a certain time, and time was of the essence of the contract, because the improvements were necessary for the working of the station. The words "lease shall not

(1) L.R. 2 P.C., 135.

H. C. of A.
1908.

Swan
v.
Raws-
thorne.

be executed" are ambiguous. They may refer either to the mere sealing and signing of a document or to the granting of the lease. Extrinsic evidence may be given to show what the parties meant: *Friary Holroyd and Healey's Breweries Ltd.* v. *Singleton* (1); *Tatham, Bromage & Co.* v. *Burr*; *The " Engineer "* (2); *Southland Frozen Meat and Produce Export Co.* v. *Nelson Bros. Ltd.* (3). The Judge excluded from consideration the circumstances under which the agreement was made, and looked at the documents alone. Even if under the first agreement the vendor was entitled to retain possession of the 10,240 acres, which the appellants do not admit, that agreement was displaced by the agreement of November, under which the vendor had no right to possession until he erected the improvements and obtained the sub-lease. The action was therefore rightly framed in trespass and the vendor had no defence in law; and had no defence in equity because he had not done that upon which his right to a lease depended. At the highest the vendor's right to the 10,240 acres would be that of a joint owner, which would not give him any right to interfere with the purchaser's use of the land. [He referred to *Roscoe, Nisi Prius Evidence*, 16th ed., p. 939.]

Having failed to erect the improvements in time the purchaser had disentitled himself to specific performance of the agreement for a sub-lease.

[Griffith C.J.—We are all of opinion that the plaintiff is entitled to a lease of the 10,240 acres. The only question is whether any terms should be imposed on him.]

Lingen (*Hammond* with him), for the respondent. The evidence shows that the appellants are entitled to little or nothing in the way of damages. If they were asking for an inquiry they would have to show that there was some damage. The respondent never surrendered possession of the 10,240 acres. The only right the appellants had to go upon that area was under a licence from the respondent. The property sold did not include that area, as appears from the word " retain " in the con-

(1) (1899) 2 Ch., 261.   (2) (1898) A.C., 382.
(3) (1898) A.C., 442.

dition. In its natural meaning that word imports a continuing in possession. The physical possession was never changed. The second agreement did not cut down the respondent's rights in this connection. If it had been intended by that agreement to deprive the vendor of his rights of property as to the 10,240 acres it should have been clearly stated. The respondent was not bound to plead this defence at law. Having a contract enforceable only in equity, he was entitled to assert any legal rights he might have in the same suit. As the Court had to deal with the matter in part it should deal with the whole. The respondent was therefore entitled to an injunction restraining the action at law. [He referred to *Equity Act*, No. 24 of 1901, sec. 8; *Rich, Newham, and Harvey, Eq. Practice*, p. 6; *Birmingham Estates Co.* v. *Smith* (1); *Duke of Beaufort* v. *Glynn* (2).] Any right that the appellants might have to compensation or indemnity could be dealt with in the suit. [He referred to *Oxford* v. *Provand* (3).]

The question as to the injunction is only subsidiary to the question of the right to specific performance, and if the Court is against the respondent as to the injunction, the order as to costs should be in favour of the respondent, except so far as they have been increased by the unsuccessful issues: *Jenkins* v. *Jackson* (4).

Cullen K.C., in reply. If the respondent has a defence at law he should not have an injunction. The injunction was only granted on his admission that he had no defence at law.

There was no issue as to damages in the equity suit and consequently it was not necessary to prove any, except so far as to show how the respondent had treated the appellants.

As to costs, the matter most seriously contested was the question of injunction, and whoever succeeds on that should have the main costs of the appeal.

Cur. adv. vult.

The following judgments were read :—

GRIFFITH C.J. [Having stated the facts up to 24th October

H. C. OF A.
1908.

SWAN
v.
RAWS-
THORNE.

MAY 13.

(1) 13 Ch. D., 506.
(2) 3 Sm. & G., 213.
(3) L.R. 2 P.C., 135.
(4) (1891) 1 Ch., 89.

H. C. of A.
1908.

Swan
v.
Raws-
thorne.

Griffith C.J.

1905 and referred to the 9th and 12th conditions of the agreement of that date, continued:] Under this agreement it was clearly the intention of the parties that the vendor should continue in possession of the 10,240 acres, although he would no longer be a tenant to the Crown, but a tenant to Swan. It was also their intention that the vendor should have a formal lease. These, in my opinion, were two distinct and independent stipulations, for breach of either of which an action could have been brought. Having regard to the nature of the property, the stipulation as to possession was obviously of much greater immediate importance to the vendor than that as to title, which was in one sense subsidiary only. It is, therefore, impossible to hold that the right to possession was dependent upon the execution of the sub-lease. [His Honor then stated the terms of the agreement of 28th November as already reported and continued:] Although Swan would not accept the plaintiff's version of the facts as to the verbal agreement of 28th November it must be taken upon the evidence that such an agreement was in fact made and was in fact partly performed. [His Honor then stated the rest of the facts, as already reported, and continued:]

So far as regards specific performance, I think that the learned Judge was clearly right. The only effect of the second agreement was to postpone the plaintiff's right to a formal title, but, as already said, it contained nothing to qualify his right to possession. Nor am I able to find on the face of it anything to qualify the nature of his possession.

But with respect to the injunction other questions arise. The contemporaneous verbal agreement qualified the nature of that possession to this extent—that the defendants were to be entitled to use certain improvements on the 10,240 acres until the new improvements were completed. An interesting question arises (which was not debated before us) whether this agreement was an agreement relating to an interest in land. (See the cases cited and commented on in *Harris* v. *The Sydney Glass and Tile Co.* (1).) A breach of that agreement, if it was valid at law, would give rise to an action, which might, perhaps, take the form of an action for trespass to the stock lawfully

(1) 2 C. L. R., 227, at pp. 237, 238.

using the land of which the plaintiff retained possession. But H. C. of A.
the agreement, whether valid at law or not, had been in part   1908.
performed, and was incident to a contract of which the Court   SWAN
could grant specific performance.   The Court could therefore   v.
give damages for breach of the agreement.   It follows that,   RAWS-
while the defendants could not maintain the action for trespass THORNE.
to the land—an action which is founded upon possession—they   Griffith C.J.
were entitled in some form of proceeding to claim damages for
the unlawful impounding, either by an action at law, founded
(whatever its form) upon acts done in contravention of an agreement valid at law, or by proceedings in equity founded upon
breach of a verbal agreement which had been partly performed.
In either view they ought not to be precluded from asserting
that claim in appropriate proceedings.   Now, the right to an
injunction is founded either upon the ground that the plaintiff
had no legal defence but had a good equitable defence to the
action, or upon the ground that the Court of Equity, having
assumed jurisdiction over the matter, would do complete justice
between the parties : *Duke of Beaufort* v. *Glynn* (1).

In the present case, upon the facts as they appear in evidence,
the plaintiff had a good defence at law to the action for trespass
to land, and had no defence in equity, whether or not he had at
law, to the claim for damages for wrongful impounding.   The
injunction, therefore, can only be justified on the second ground.
The exercise of this jurisdiction is, however, discretionary.   In
the present case it might have been invoked by the defendants
on the ground that a plaintiff seeking equity must do equity,
and that they, perhaps, will not be entitled to recover in the
action all that the Court of Equity would give them on an inquiry
as to damages.   The defendants, however, are content with their
judgment, and do not desire to have an inquiry before the Master
substituted for it.   Under these circumstances I think that the
decree must be varied by omitting the direction for an injunction.
The order for costs should be varied by giving the plaintiff the
costs of suit, except so far as they have been increased by the
claim for an injunction.

(1) 3 Sm. & G., 213, at p. 226.

H. C. of A.
1908.

SWAN
v.
RAWS-
THORNE.

Barton J.

BARTON J. As to the meaning of the two written contracts between the parties, I am entirely in accord with the Chief Judge in Equity. The agreement of 24th October 1905 does not purport to include what is called M. E. Rawsthorne's block in the sale, although it includes it in the mere transfer. But the respondent held the whole of "Dine Dine" under one lease from the Crown. Under the Statutes applicable, the leasehold itself could not be divided so as to exclude the Crown lease of Rawsthorne's block of 10,240 acres for the respondent. It was necessary, therefore, to put the legal estate in the appellant Swan as to the entire holding of 100,680 acres, and the only practical way of ensuring that the legal estate in Rawsthorne's block should in effect not pass from the respondent at all was to provide that he should have a sub-lease back from Swan, and that, simultaneously with the transfer of the whole to Swan, Rawsthorne was to retain, *i.e.*, keep, the block, but on lease, *i.e.*, sub-lease; in other words, he was not to lose possession of it, but was to have his title evidenced by a formal sub-lease from his purchaser. And there was no conceivable reason, at that stage, why the two formal evidences of title, Rawsthorne to Swan and Swan to Rawsthorne, should not be completed *uno ictu*, so that the execution of the sub-lease should immediately follow that of the assignment. That, in fact, was under the circumstances the natural way of giving effect to the two expressions, "retain," and "on lease." I may here observe that this agreement uses the word "retain" in precisely the same sense of keeping possession, in the only other place where it occurs—the schedule. Speaking of the cattle, it is there agreed that "the vendor may at his option *retain* these on allowing the purchaser £3 per head for same." Further illustrations of its use and meaning—if illustration be needed—are found in the contract of sale by the appellants to Rogers of August 1906, paragraph 18. I am not able, then, to adopt the view that the mere insertion of the words "on lease" alters the meaning of the phrase so as to take away the respondent's existing right of possession, (which, on the facts, I think he exercised continuously after as well as before the contracts), and vest it in his purchaser Swan until a lease should in fact be executed. But it is contended that some such effect is produced by the second agree-

H. C. of A.
1908.

Swan
v.
Raws-
thorne.

Barton J.

ment, that of 28th November 1905. This document was executed as a settlement of differences between the parties to the first agreement. The appellant Swan charged the respondent with having before the sale represented certain improvements as being on the leasehold sold to him, the truth being that they were on Rawsthorne's block. We have not to determine who was in the right in this dispute, since it is common ground that the agreement of November 1905 was made in settlement of it. We are left to infer, however, that the respondent deemed it to his interest to make some concession to the appellant Swan, for he agrees with him that the sub-lease to the respondent of Rawsthorne's block shall not be executed by the purchaser (Swan) until the vendor shall have placed certain improvements on the freehold (transferred to Swan) surrounding a tank known as Mackenzie's, and these improvements are no doubt to be in substitution for those which were found to be on Rawsthorne's block, and which, therefore, had not passed to the appellant Swan. Upon this document the appellants contended that, read with the first agreement, as it of course must be, it postponed not only the respondent's right to claim the legal estate by way of the sub-lease until the completion of the agreed improvements, but also postponed his right of possession until that time. I am quite unable to agree with that contention. It does not appear to be supported by any part of the agreement of November. On the completion of the original contract and the execution of the transfer of the leasehold, the respondent, already in possession of the block he had retained, would have been entitled *eo instanti* to his sub-lease. There is no word in either agreement to interfere with his possession or his right to it, and I cannot see anything from which an intention to interfere with it should be inferred. He agreed to the postponement of the execution of his sub-lease as a security to Swan that he would make the improvements, and until their completion he was to submit to a very real detriment by suspending his claim to the evidence of his legal right. Upon the original sale and transfer, Swan, the purchaser of 90,440 acres of leasehold and other lands, became also trustee for Rawsthorne, the vendor of these lands, in respect of this block of 10,240 acres, included in the legal transfer, but not in the substantive sale. The creation

H. C. of A.
1908.

SWAN
v.
RAWS-
THORNE.

Barton J.

of the trust did nothing in impairment of his possession or his beneficial ownership, and as for the legal estate, that was at his call, under the first agreement as soon as the assignment of "Dine Dine" should be executed, and under the second agreement, as soon as the improvements should be completed.

The learned Chief Judge has found that the improvements were completed before the institution of this suit, but whether within a reasonable time or not, he did not determine, nor was it necessary for him to do so. It appears to me that there is no answer to the respondent's claim to an order for specific performance of the agreement for a sub-lease, without prejudice to any right of the appellants to bring an action for damages for delay as to the improvements.

Now, as to the appellants' action for trespass to land and for wrongful impounding of their stock by the respondent. As the appellants never acquired a right to the exclusive possession of Rawsthorne's block, they cannot successfully sue the respondent for interfering with a possession which was not theirs, and an injunction was so far unnecessary. But as to the wrongful impounding, the case may be otherwise. The respondent in his evidence says :—"The day that I signed the last agreement" (28th November 1905) "the defendants were to have the right to use my yards in M. E. Rawsthorne's block until the new ones were made." Speaking of the same date, and of Wheatley's suggestion that he should remove the improvements from Rawsthorne's block to Mackenzie's freehold, he says :—" I agreed to remove them . . . I also agreed that he could have the use of the sheep-yards on M. E. Rawsthorne's portion." This verbal agreement was contemporaneous with the agreement of 28th November, and seems to have been received in evidence without objection. Although it is difficult to say that an agreement by the respondent to allow the appellants to use his yards, &c., pending the construction of the new improvements, is to be inferred from the writings, still the evidence quoted goes to show that the stock impounded were on the respondent's land by his own leave, so far at least as the user of his yards, &c., but not necessarily of his pasture, was concerned.

As far as we can now see, therefore, while the respondent is not liable at all for trespass to land, yet probably he is without defence at law to the action for wrongful impounding, and he could not set up any defence at all in equity.

The appellants' counsel is satisfied to keep his judgment at common law, which he can only maintain as to the impounding, and does not wish an inquiry in equity as to damages on that score. He prefers a dissolution of the injunction.

In these circumstances, I agree that the variations proposed by the Chief Justice should be made in the decree both substantively and as to costs.

O'CONNOR J. As to that portion of the decree which directs specific performance of the original contract, I entirely concur in the view taken by the Chief Judge in Equity. As soon as the agreement of 28th November 1905 was performed the respondent was entitled to have a sub-lease of the 10,240 acres executed and handed over to him by the appellant Swan. The learned Judge, having found as a fact that before the commencement of the suit all the work contracted to be performed under the agreement had been completed, was bound to decree, as he did, specific performance of the original contract.

The portion of the decree, however, by which the appellants were restrained from further proceeding on their common law judgment, stands upon a different footing. We have before us no more particular information about the form of the common law action than that it was for trespass and wrongful impounding, but I gather from the pleadings and evidence in this suit that it claimed damages for trespass to land and also for the respondent's wrongful interference with the appellants' sheep. The learned Chief Judge treated the action as being for trespass to land, and founded that part of his decree on the view which he took of the respondent's right to possession of the 10,240 acres having regard to the terms of the original contract. In my opinion, the matter cannot be disposed of in that way. Apart altogether from his rights under the original contract, the verbal agreement made contemporaneously with the contract of the 28th November 1905, which I agree with my learned brother the Chief Justice must be taken to have been established in evidence, gave the appel-

H. C. of A.
1908.

SWAN
v.
RAWS-
THORNE.

Barton J.

lants certain rights over the stock-yards, paddocks and other
conveniences on the 10,240 acres necessary for the working of
the station, and secured those rights to them until the improvements contracted to be made under the second agreement were
completed.

Questions might have been raised under the *Statute of Frauds*
as to whether we can give effect to the verbal agreement. No
such questions have been raised, but if they had been, I agree
that, having regard to the facts in this case, the Court would be
entitled to treat the agreement as being good by reason of part
performance. The alleged interference with the appellants' sheep
in violation of that agreement would give the appellants a right
of action for wrongful impounding and trespass to goods which
appears to be unanswerable. As to that part of the action the
respondent would seem to have no more defence in equity than
at law, and I can therefore see no ground upon the documents or
evidence which would justify the Court of Equity in preventing
the appellants from proceeding for that cause of action. But
apart from that aspect of the case, I am of opinion that the
original contract and that of the 28th November, interpreted
in the light of the circumstances which arose, gave the appellant Swan certain rights of possession over portion of the 10,240
acres, and that, in the events that happened, he was entitled to
sue the respondent at law for a disturbance of those rights.
Under the original agreement the whole 10,240 acres are included in the description of the property sold. Clause 9 expressly provides that "if from any cause the matter is not ready
for completion on the date named the purchaser shall be entitled
to take possession as tenant to the vendor at a nominal rent
pending completion. And the purchaser from the date of taking
possession shall pay interest to the vendor on the unpaid purchase
money at the rate of five pounds per centum per annum." That
clause, except so far as it may be modified by clause 12, applies as
well to the 10,240 acres as to the rest of the lands purchased.
Clause 12 in its opening words also treats the 10,240 acres as part
of the lands sold, but stipulates that, in so far as that part is concerned, the vendor is to be entitled to retain the same on lease at
a rental proportional to the average rental of the whole lease sub-

H. C. or A.
1908.
~~~~
SWAN
v.
RAWS-
THORNE.
———
O'Connor J.

ject to compliance with certain provisions of the *Western Lands Act*. Later on it provides that the purchaser shall give the vendor a lease of the 10,240 acres at a rental proportionate to the rental of the whole government lease, and for the same term. It is also material to observe that the terms of payment are a cash deposit on signing the contract and the balance by cash on completion.

Following the ordinary rule of interpretation, effect must be given as far as possible to each clause of the contract. To my mind it is quite clear that the 12th clause gives the respondent a right to remain in actual possession of the 10,240 acres, and that his possession is not to be disturbed except in so far as may be necessary to give effect to the other portions of the contract. On the other hand, the provisions of the 9th clause cannot be ignored. They clearly give the purchaser a right of possession in the event of any delay in completion over the whole of the property, including the 10,240 acres. Effect can be given to both clauses by reading clause 9 as giving the purchaser a formal right of possession to the 10,240 acres on 1st December 1905 for the purposes of vesting a title by sub-lease to the vendor, such possession to be divested immediately on completion when the sub-lease was to be executed, and contemporaneously with taking possession handed over to the respondent.

But then arose a position which made it essential, if the purchase was to be gone on with, that both parties should be in possession of at least a portion of the 10,240 acres, because, without the use of the yard and other working conveniences on the 10,240 acres, it would be impossible for the appellants to carry on the property. Then the agreement of 28th November was entered into postponing the date for conferring title on the respondent until after he had carried out the work necessary to make the property workable as under the original contract. That agreement, in deferring the time for conferring title on the respondent by sub-lease, was intended by the parties, in my opinion, to extend the purchaser's merely formal legal possession into an actual and effective possession for the purposes referred to until the time arrived when the respondent by completion of the work was entitled to have the sub-lease handed over to him. Both parties, therefore, were entitled to a qualified possession at the

H. C. of A.
1908.

Swan
v.
Raws-
thorne.

O'Connor J.

same time, and to that extent the respondent's rights of possession were modified by the agreement of 28th November. The appellants therefore being entitled to the undisturbed possession of so much of the 10,240 acres as might be necessary for the working of the property purchased, they were entitled to claim damages in an action for the respondent's interference with that possession. And although the form of the action in trespass may not have been appropriate, I can see no ground on which the Court of Equity was justified in preventing the appellants from enforcing their claim at common law in some form for these damages. I agree that it would have been within the power of the Court, in the exercise of its discretion to decree specific performance, to make its order dependent upon the vendor's compensating the purchaser for any delay of which he might have been guilty in the carrying out of the second agreement. But the appellants could not be allowed to retain their judgment at common law and also to have the benefit of that condition.

As they prefer to rest on their judgment, it becomes unnecessary to further consider that aspect of the case.

In the result, therefore, I agree in the conclusion at which my learned brother the Chief Justice has arrived, that the decree must be varied in so far as it enjoins the appellants from further proceeding in their action at law, and also as to the costs as mentioned in his judgment.

Isaacs J. I agree in the conclusions stated by my learned brothers, but I arrive at them for somewhat different reasons. This case does not appear to me to present any serious difficulties either of construction or of law. Mr. Rawsthorne, the respondent, was the owner of a station called " Dine Dine " consisting of 960 acres of freehold and 100,680 acres of leasehold under a Western Lands lease issued to him under the Act of 1901, No. 70. The appellants, Messrs. Swan and Wheatley, were also pastoralists, and on 24th October 1905 entered into a written contract with the respondent for the sale and purchase of the station. The first question is as to the respective rights of the parties immediately that contract was signed. In view of the arguments of the respondent, I find it necessary to make one or two preliminary observations. The first is, that the only intention of the parties which the Court can ever find and enforce is that embodied in the language which the parties themselves have used. The other is, that—though surrounding circumstances may be looked at in order to understand the subject matter of the contract and the situation of the parties so as, in the words of *Wigram* V.C., quoted by *Lindley* L.J. in *Dashwood* v. *Magniac* (1), to give to "the reader of any instrument the same light which the writer enjoyed," and so as to understand the application of the words used—yet they cannot be regarded for the purpose of altering the plain meaning and effect of ordinary unambiguous words which the parties have chosen to employ. There are few propositions which the Courts of highest authority have more strongly emphasized. See *per* Lord *Hatherley* and Lord *Blackburn* in *Inglis* v. *Buttery* (2); *per* Lord *Davey* for the Judicial Committee in *Bank of New Zealand* v. *Simpson* (3), and again by the same learned Lord in *Higgins* v. *Dawson* (4). With these guiding principles I turn to the contract itself.

There are no technical terms to be construed, and we know without any controversy the subject matter of the contract and the position of the parties. The contract is headed "Conditions and Terms of Sale for the undermentioned property." The property is described below as "Property known as Dine Dine . . . . area 960 acres freehold land 100,680 acres lease land under the *Western Crown Lands Act* of 1901. Also 7,800 sheep, 50 cattle, horse, dray and harness," &c. That is the property sold. When the 100,680 acres are mentioned, it does not, of course, mean the fee simple of those lands, but it means the whole Western Lands lease is to be bodily transferred by Rawsthorne to Swan without excepting any land whatever comprised in it. That is the first important point to bear in mind. Clause 9 of the contract has been substantially set forth by the learned Chief Justice. The meaning of that is not a matter of doubt. 1st December 1905 was the day fixed for completion, and time is stated to be of the essence of the contract. That might have had serious consequences in the event of any inability to complete by the day named

H. C. of A.
1908.
⌣
Swan
v.
Raws-
thorne.

Isaacs J.

H. C. of A.
1908.

SWAN
v.
RAWS-
THORNE.

Isaacs J.

and so the clause went on to provide an interim status for a
possible difficulty, viz., that if the matter were not ready for
completion on the day fixed the purchaser should be admitted as
tenant to the vendor *pending completion*, and the purchaser
should from the time of admission pay interest on the unpaid
purchase money at 5 per cent. This clause, though providing for
a possible tenancy of purchaser to vendor, has no bearing on the
present dispute, its effect not extending beyond the time of completion, nor extending beyond the portions of the land which the
contract intended should be permanently in possession of the
purchaser. Clause 12 is the field of controversy. Notwithstanding the complete change of ownership as Crown leaseholder
of the whole 100,680 acres, this clause makes specific provision as
to the 10,240 acres of Homestead lease, as it is called, that is M.
E. Rawsthorne's block, and, as the fight has largely centred around
the words of the clause, it is desirable, I think, to draw special
attention to some of its very distinct terms. It states the bare
fact in describing the 10,240 as " part of the lands above referred
to," that is, part of the lands described as property known as " Dine
Dine," and lower down it repeats that " the said 10,240 acres are
included in the total area of the lease of 100,680 acres." I should
have thought that no form of language could possibly make
clearer the fact that the 10,240 acres were included in the
property sold, and were not excepted from the sale, and that a
conclusion that the 10,240 acres were excepted from sale was
utterly inconsistent with the unambiguous words of the written
agreement.

But because the 10,240 acres were by the terms of the contract
sold by Rawsthorne, and as he evidently desired not to part with
possession of that block, he agreed by the 12th clause that he,
the vendor, should be entitled to " retain same on lease " at the
same average rental as the whole lease. Even this was " subject
to compliance " with the Act. The clause declares that " the
purchaser shall give the vendor a lease of same at a rental," &c.,
" such lease to contain all the covenants," and so forth.

Every syllable appears to me to strengthen the view that,
except for any rights the respondent was to have as lessee, he
had no further interest in the 10,240 acres. He is styled the

vendor and the appellant Swan is called the purchaser of that portion no less than of any other; Rawsthorne was "entitled," but not bound, to retain it on lease; and if he for any reason chose not to accept it, who could doubt that the purchaser would retain it unfettered?

H. C. of A.
1908.

SWAN
v.
RAWS-
THORNE.

Isaacs J.

What then was the legal effect of this document immediately it was signed?

I diverge for a moment from the consideration of this contract to inquire as to the nature of the Western Lands lease. The lease itself is not in evidence, but the terms and conditions of the lease may be gathered generally from sec. 18 of the Act, and Schedule A. The law does not allow such a lease to be split up as between the Crown and the lessee, but the regulations 31 and following made under the Act permit of a complete transfer, which brings the transferee into direct relation with the Crown as to the whole land comprised in the lease, and entirely eliminates the original lessee. A simple transfer without condition would have destroyed every right of the respondent to and in respect of the land. And therefore assuming, as we must assume from the contract itself, that his desire and intention were still to remain in possession of the 10,240 acres, there was only one way known to the law which would enable him to effect his object. But that very method necessitated his parting absolutely and forever with his then existing title to the land, and ceasing to be the owner of the whole lease. He was forced to this by stress of circumstances it is true, but that fact does not alter the legal effect of what was done. Instead of his independent title to the land direct from the Crown, he agreed to surrender that title to Swan, and then to take a new and altogether different title to the land—namely, a lease, or properly speaking a sub-lease, from the purchaser, the new owner of the lease. That sub-lease was to be henceforth his only title to the land. He was to "retain" an interest in the land, because that is what I think is meant by retaining the land on lease; "retain on lease" being equivalent to "hold without interruption on lease." Nothing was said about the right of possession because that would follow the interest, and could not have been intended to exist independently of it. The respondent has argued on the basis—fallaciously

H. C. of A.
1908.

SWAN
v.
RAWS-
THORNE.

Isaacs J.

as I think—that retaining on lease includes retention of possession independently of any interest. As the original contract stood he was safe enough. The transfer of his lease was to be synchronous with the giving of the sub-lease, so that there never would be an appreciable period of time when he would be without some sufficient title to remain; in other words, he would retain the land, but retain it on the only terms consistent with the contract, namely "on lease from the purchaser." The lease was to be immediate; and unless the purchaser was prepared to give it at once, the vendor would refuse to part with his full ownership. One feature may be specially adverted to at this juncture. His retention of the Homestead lease necessarily connoted exclusive possession, it was inconsistent with any joint possession, or any possession other than his own. Unless the subsequent agreement altered the nature of that possession, it must necessarily, so long as it lasted, preserve that exclusive character throughout. Had no subsequent friction arisen, the original arrangement would have worked out well enough.

Unfortunately, before 1st December, the date of completion, disputes arose, and as the learned primary Judge has found, the appellants threatened to rescind for alleged misrepresentations with respect to the improvements on the lands, and so on 28th November 1905 a second agreement was entered into which modified the first in relation to the 10,240 acres. That agreement has been read. I doubt extremely, but decide nothing as to whether Rawsthorne was bound to execute improvements any more than he was bound to take the lease; but he was no longer "*entitled*" to the sub-lease immediately on executing the transfer of the lease, nor until he had effected the stated improvements. He nevertheless insists that he had a right to *retain* the paddock of 10,240 acres. By what title? Not that of owner, for he had parted with it. Not that of lessee, because his right to it was postponed. He says, however, it was by reason of the contract alone, and notwithstanding he had then no title and no right to have a title. To enable him to stand in this anomalous situation he must needs divorce the words "on lease" from the word "retain," and then contend that to retain the land meant to retain, not an interest in it, but mere possession, and then

argue further that, although he might considerably delay the
improvements, in other words delay making good his alleged
representations, which nearly caused the rescission of the whole
contract, he could, at least in the meantime, still retain the land,
without a title and without a lease, without any obligation to
pay rent, and without any implied duty to pay for use or occupation. Indeed, if the contention of learned counsel for the
respondent be sound that the right to the lease was immaterial
to the right to possession, the latter standing independently, I
see no reason why his client would not be entitled to retain the
land even though, by wilful and protracted delay, he had lost
all right to specific performance of the agreement by the appellants to give a lease. In such case he would refrain from seeking specific performance and simply go on without a lease and
enjoy possession of the land without a title. He could never be
turned out if his contention be correct, because he had received an
irrevocable licence to remain. The situation, if correct, is extraordinary. The appellants would, of course, in the meantime be
bound to pay to the Crown the rent for the whole area, and be
liable to all the conditions of the lease, and their only satisfaction, and perhaps their only remedy, would be to delay the
actual signature of the sub-lease, which, to a man desiring, as the
plaintiff's whole case assumes he desired, not to leave the place
was of no serious moment, and some pecuniary gain. The
contention seems to me unreasonable and unbusinesslike; but in
addition it is, in my opinion, legally unsound. Without the lease
Rawsthorne was for the time an utter stranger to the land, and
with nothing more than a personal contract, entitling him in a
certain event, and in that event only, to get an interest in the
land. By the first agreement his occupation would have been
continuous, because, giving full force to the word "retain," and
to the words "on lease," he would have stepped instantly from
one title to the other.

The new agreement however deferred the commencement of
his leasehold title, leaving a gap between the old title and the
new, and thus breaking the legal chain of right to have possession
of the land. At law clearly he had no right to be there; equity
could not relieve him because his contract unfulfilled debarred

H. C. of A.
1908.

Swan
v.
Raws-
thorne.

Isaacs J.

H. C. of A.
1908.

Swan
v.
Raws-
thorne.

Isaacs J.

him claiming any legal title. If the consequences proved inconvenient to himself, his own conduct was the cause of it.

I agree with Dr. *Cullen* that, not only had the respondent no
exclusive right of possession, but that he had no concurrent right.
In my opinion, one or other of the parties had the right to be in
possession of the land, but not both. Either the appellants could
remain by reason of their legal title, unaffected by any equity
giving Rawsthorne the right to immediately enter and exclude
them ; or else Rawsthorne had his old right to retain the land
unimpaired, having only to wait for his former legal title in the
shape of a lease, and this original right was, as I have said,
clearly exclusive. There cannot, as I apprehend the matter, be
any *via media*. Neither party apparently thought there was.
There is nothing in the second agreement to alter the original
meaning of the word "retain." The respondent's own argument
is that the postponement of the execution of the lease did not
affect the question of possession, and if so, it left that matter just
where it was under the first agreement. In other words, the
possession remained exclusive. If, however, it did alter the
question of possession, why did it alter it ? Only because title or
no title made all the difference, and that simply affirms the
appellants' view. To give an intermediate effect to the transaction might be very reasonable or unreasonable—I do not know—
but it would, in my opinion, be making a new bargain for the
parties, and not interpreting the one they made for themselves.

Possession in fact was given generally to Swan in January
1906—after transfer and payment—though Rawsthorne kept
some stock in the disputed paddock all the time. But in August
1906 and some time later, but before Rawsthorne by completing
the improvements had become entitled to his sub-lease, he
asserted a right to exclusive occupation by turning the appellants' cattle out and threatening the servant in charge of them.

For this the appellants brought an action of trespass. Their
right to do so must be judged of as at the moment the acts complained of were committed, and at that instant Rawsthorne had
no title at law or in equity to possession. Where two rival
claimants for possession are on the land together, actual possession
is considered in law to vest in him who has the legal title. The

other is a trespasser. (Per *Maule* J. in *Jones* v. *Chapman* (1); per Lord *Selborne* in *Lows* v. *Telford* (2)). This is, of course, subject to any contractual variation, and if he had had an immediate right to a lease equity would treat him as being in upon the terms of it: *Walsh* v. *Lonsdale* (3). But only in that case. Here, as I have endeavoured to point out, the essence of both the old and the new contract is to make possession depend on title.

I am, therefore, of opinion, looking at the written contracts, that the respondent had no right whatever to stay the action at law for damages. There are some passages in the evidence which, independently of the documentary agreements, might appear to expose the plaintiff to an action—not for trespass to land, but either for trespass to sheep, or for breach of agreement to allow the sheep to remain on M. E. Rawsthorne's block. The main passage is that in the plaintiff's own evidence in which he alleges that on the day he signed the last contract the defendants were to have the right to use his yards in M. E. Rawsthorne's block until the new ones were made. If that were all, and if it were clear that the sheep were impounded because they were put into the yards referred to and nothing beyond, some action would undoubtedly lie on the plaintiff's own admission, and quite apart from any difficulty either as to the construction of the written contract, or as to staying the action at law because of the matter of title to land being submitted to a Court of Equity.

But the parties did not refer to this phase of the case, and I do not feel safe in basing any judgment upon it for the following reasons :—First, the defendant Swan in his evidence point-blank denies it. He says " It is not true that the day the contract was signed it was agreed that we were to have the right to use the plaintiff's yards on M. E. Rawsthorne's block until the new ones were made." After that he could scarcely be allowed to set up such a contract. Next the plaintiff says that after the verbal agreement as to the use of the yards, Wheatley asked his son to " draw up an agreement to that effect," and he continues " Leslie Wheatley then left the room and returned with the contract.

H. C. or A.
1908.

SWAN
v.
RAWS-
THORNE.

Isaacs J.

(1) 2 Ex., 802, at p. 821.   (2) 1 App. Cas., 414, at p. 426.
          (3) 21 Ch. D., 9.

H. C. of A. Leslie Wheatley read it over and I signed it and then Swan
1908.   signed it."

SWAN
v.
RAWS-
THORNE.

ISAAC J.

It seems to me, therefore, that everything merged in the
written document, and the conversation as to the use of the
yards must, in the absence of any claim to rectify the document,
be treated as mere negotiation.   But, further, the block consisted
of three paddocks—Tallebung, the Well paddock and Bald Hill
paddock.   It is not at all clear to me where the sheep were
impounded from, whether because they used the yards or because
they were using the Well paddock apart from the yards.   Reading Collett's evidence and Leslie Swan's evidence in addition to
that of the plaintiff's, I incline to think they were impounded
because of the defendants' insistence upon using the Well paddock.
I do not know sufficient of the facts to say definitely, because the
parties were not contesting that with a view to elucidate the
precise features of the alleged trespass.   They were only incidental to the suit, and I rest my judgment on the meaning and
effect of the documents.

With regard to specific performance I think that, having
effected the improvements under the circumstances related in the
evidence and found by the learned primary Judge, the respondent
is entitled to get his sub-lease : see *Oxford* v. *Provand* (1).
Though that right came too late to justify his trespass, he has it
now, and it should be given effect to.   The Court of Equity can
do complete justice with regard to loss occasioned by delay, and
can adjust the rights of the parties by means of compensation
and otherwise so as to place them in as good a position relatively
as if the contract had been properly carried out, according to its
very terms ; but the trespass already spoken of is quite outside
this sphere of consideration, and cannot, as I think, be dealt with
in the suit for specific performance.

Decree varied.

Solicitors, for the appellants, *Houston & Moses.*
Solicitors, for the respondent, *Whelan & Gilcreest* by *Russell
& Russell.*

C. A. W.

(1) L. R. 2 P.C., 135.

[HIGH COURT OF AUSTRALIA.]

THE KING AND MINISTER OF STATE
   FOR THE COMMONWEALTH AD-   }   PLAINTIFFS;
   MINISTERING THE CUSTOMS   .

AND

EDWIN FREDERICK SUTTON   .   .   .   DEFENDANT.

Exclusive powers of Commonwealth—Control of Customs—Rule as to legislation   H. C. OF A.
binding Crown—How far State Governments subject to Commonwealth legis-   1908.
lation—Goods imported by State Government—Removal from Customs control—
Customs Act 1901 (No. 6 of 1901), secs. 30, 33, 236—The Constitution (63 & 64   SYDNEY,
Vict. c. 12), secs. 52 (ii.), 86, 90.   *April* 14, 15.
   May 22.

The rule that the Crown is not bound by a Statute except by express   Griffith C.J.,
words or necessary implication applies only to those representatives of the   Barton,
Crown who have executive authority in the place where the Statute applies,   O'Connor,
and as to matters to which that executive authority extends. The Con-   Isaacs and
stitution binds the Crown as represented by the various States, and takes no   Higgins JJ.
account of the States and State Governments in relation to Commonwealth
legislation on matters within the exclusive control of the Commonwealth
Government, and, therefore, in the construction of Commonwealth Statutes
dealing with such matters, the rule applies to the Sovereign as head of that
Government, but not to the Sovereign as head of the State Governments.

The *Customs Act* 1901, being a valid exercise by the Commonwealth of the
exclusive power to impose, collect and control duties of Customs and Excise
conferred by secs. 52 (ii.), 86, and 90 of the Constitution, applies to goods
imported by the Government of a State as well as to those imported by
private persons ; and, therefore, goods imported by a State, whether dutiable
or not, are by sec. 30 of the Act subject to the control of the Customs, and
the authority of the State Executive is no justification for their removal from
that control contrary to the provisions of the Act.

A quantity of wire netting, which had been purchased in England and
imported into the Commonwealth by the Government of New South Wales,

was landed at the port of Sydney. Without any entry having been made or passed, and without the authority of the Customs officers, the defendant, acting under the authority of the Executive Government of the State, removed the goods from the place where they were stored.

Held, that the defendant had committed a breach of secs. 33 and 236 of the *Customs Act*.

Judgment entered for the plaintiffs for a penalty.

SPECIAL CASE stated for the opinion of the High Court under Order XXIX., r. 1 of the Rules of the High Court.

This was a proceeding by the Customs for the recovery from the defendant of pecuniary penalties for breaches of secs. 33 and 236 of the *Customs Act* 1901. The defendant was a carrier who at the time of the alleged offences held the contract from the Government of New South Wales for the carriage of its goods from the Sydney wharves. In August 1907 a large quantity of wire netting, which had been purchased in England by the State of New South Wales and imported into the Commonwealth at the port of Sydney, was landed from the steamship in which it had been brought there by the ship's hands with the consent of the Customs officers, and stacked near the wharf. A demand was made on behalf of the State Executive on the Collector of Customs that he should admit the wire netting duty free as being the property of the Crown, but the Collector refused to comply with the demand, and required that an entry should be passed and duty paid or deposited before the delivery of the goods. A few days afterwards, before any entry had been tendered, made, delivered or passed for the goods, the defendant, acting under an order issued by the Premier of the State in pursuance of a minute by the Governor in Council, removed a portion of the wire netting from the place where it had been deposited, without the authority and against the objections of the Customs officers, and delivered it to the officers of the State Government.

This case was stated by the parties for the opinion of the High Court upon the questions set out in the judgments hereunder, judgment to be entered for the plaintiffs or the defendant in accordance with the decision of the Court.

Gordon K.C. (*Cullen* K.C., and *Blacket* with him), for the
plaintiffs. Assuming for the purposes of this argument that the
State Government was not liable to pay duty on the goods in
question, the goods were nevertheless subject to the control of the
Customs until released in accordance with the provisions of the
Customs Act. All goods imported into the Commonwealth,
whether dutiable or not, are subject to Customs control by sec. 30
of the *Customs Act.* The defendant is therefore liable to a
penalty for a breach of sec. 33 or sec. 236 unless the State
Government, under whose authority he justified, is not bound by
the Act. As regards matters which were placed within the
exclusive control of the Commonwealth, the Crown as represented
by the States was bound once for all by the Constitution. The
Commonwealth has exclusive powers of legislation as to trade
and commerce with other countries, sec. 51 (i.), and as to Customs
and Excise, secs. 52 (ii.), 85-90, since the imposition of a uniform
tariff. There is nothing in the Constitution express or implied
exempting State Governments from the control of the Commonwealth in these matters. To exclude them from that control
would render nugatory the whole scheme of the Constitution in
this respect. The existence of an exclusive power in the Commonwealth is altogether inconsistent with the exemption of State
Governments. The only ground on which such exemption could
be claimed is the rule that the Crown is not bound by Statute
except by express words or necessary implication. Even if that
rule could apply in considering the question whether a State
Government is bound by Commonwealth legislation, there is quite
sufficient ground for holding that there is necessary implication
here. The Constitution may be said to have divided up the prerogative of the Crown and allotted different portions to different
individuals. *Quoad* the Customs power, the whole prerogative is
vested in the Crown as represented by the Commonwealth, and
the Crown as represented by the State is left with nothing. The
State is in a sense non-existent for that purpose. The power to
control goods imported is incidental to the Customs power, and,
therefore, the States must be deemed to have given it over wholly
to the Commonwealth. Whether the goods were dutiable in fact
or not is a question to be decided by the Customs, not by the

importer. The defendant, therefore, must contend that the State Government is altogether outside the operation of the *Customs Act*, because it is not mentioned. But there was no necessity for express words to bind the States. The Customs laws of the Commonwealth operate on all the people of the Commonwealth. On the one side is the Crown as represented by the Commonwealth, and on the other the people. The States are merely groups of subjects in the ambit of the sovereignty of the Commonwealth. General words in legislation under the exclusive powers are sufficient to bind the State Governments equally with private individuals. The Crown, which under the rule of construction may or may not be bound, according to the words used, is the Commonwealth Government, not the State. The State was, therefore, bound to comply with the *Customs Act* in order to obtain the goods, and the defendant had no justification for removing them.

Pilcher K.C., *Knox* K.C., and *Lamb*, for the defendant. The goods were not subject to the control of the Customs and were never lawfully in the custody of the Commonwealth. The *Customs Act* does not bind the Government of the State. A Statute is presumed to be intended to apply to subjects unless it appears on the face of the Statute that the Crown was intended to be bound: *Attorney-General* v. *Donaldson* (1); *Roberts* v. *Ahern* (2); *Weymouth, Mayor of* v. *Nugent* (3); *The King* v. *Cook* (4). There is no reason why that rule should not apply to the Crown as represented by the State as well as to the Crown as represented by the Commonwealth. [They referred to *The Commonwealth* v. *State of New South Wales* (5); *Federated Amalgamated Government Railway and Tramway Service Association* v. *New South Wales Railway Traffic Employés Association* (6).] The King is the same throughout the Empire, as was pointed out in *Williams* v. *Howarth* (7). The prerogative right of the Crown to immunity is not cut down by the fact that in the particular instance only part of the Crown's functions are

(1) 10 M. &. W., 117, at p. 123.
(2) 1 C.L.R., 406, at p. 417.
(3) 6 B. & S., 22 ; 34 L.J.M.C., 81.
(4) 3 T.R., 519.

(5) 3 C.L.R., 807, at p. 819.
(6) 4 C.L.R., 488.
(7) (1905) A.C., 551.

exercised by the authority representing the Crown. [They H. C. of A.
referred to *Young* v. *s.s. "Scotia"* (1).]   1908.

[O'CONNOR J.—Surely the whole scheme of distribution of   THE KING
powers between Commonwealth and State under the Constitu-   *v.*
tion presupposes the distinction between the King as represented   SUTTON.
by the Commonwealth and the King as represented by the State:
Municipal Council of Sydney v. *The Commonwealth* (2).]

The Act neither purports to bind the Crown nor does it by
necessary implication. Full power and effect can be given to it
without affecting the prerogative of the Crown, by making it
apply only to subjects.

[ISAACS J.—But if it is the King who is keeping the goods,
what cause of action is there ?

HIGGINS J.—Can the rule as to the King not being bound
apply in actions between the King in one capacity and the King
in another ?]

The prerogative is invoked on one side only. The power
claimed by the Commonwealth is a statutory one, and the
question is how far it extends. [See *Attorney-General of British
Columbia* v. *Attorney-General of Canada* (3).] The whole Act
should be looked at, and, if as a whole it is inapplicable to the
Crown, none of it is binding upon the Crown. The rule is as
applicable here as it was in the circumstances of *Roberts* v.
Ahern (4).

If the *Customs Act* purports to bind the Crown or attempts to
do so it is so far invalid, because under the Constitution the
Commonwealth has no power to do so. Such a power must be
expressly given. It will not be implied. The power depends
upon sec. 90.

[GRIFFITH C.J.—The trade and commerce power has always
been held to include the power of prohibiting importation.]

Possibly it may as regards importation by subjects, but not
importation by States, which represent the Crown. It is not a
necessary implication of that power or of the Customs power
that the Commonwealth can exclude State property. The
States have power to carry on their government in their own

(1) (1903) A.C., 501.   (3) 14 App. Cas., 295.
(2) 1 C.L.R., 208.   (4) 1 C.L.R., 406.

H. C. of A.   way free from interference by the Commonwealth unless that
1908.   interference is clearly authorized.   The Constitution should be
The King   construed in such a way as to preserve the rights of the States
v.   just as much as those of the Commonwealth.   Neither has a
Sutton.
greater claim to consideration than the other.   If the Commonwealth can prohibit the importation of goods by the State
Governments it can prevent them from importing things
necessary for carrying on State agencies and thereby practically
cripple them.   [They referred to *M'Culloch* v. *State of Maryland* (1); *South Carolina* v. *United States* (2).]

Even if the defendant's act was unlawful, he acted under the
authority of the Crown and in the *bonâ fide* belief that the
Crown had power to authorize his act: *Reg.* v. *James* (3).

[GRIFFITH C.J.—The intention with which the act was done is
immaterial.   A man who violates the specific provisions of the
law is liable, whatever his motive or reason for doing so.]

Gordon K.C., in reply.   The rule in *M'Culloch* v. *State of
Maryland* (1) has no application to this case.   The question
there was as to the extent to which powers admittedly possessed
by the States could be exercised so as to infringe upon powers of
the Commonwealth.   Here the question is what is the power
given to the Commonwealth by the Constitution ?   The Constitution gives exclusive power to the Commonwealth to make laws
as to trade and commerce with other countries.   The Commonwealth, therefore, *ex necessitate rei*, has power to do what would
amount to an infringment upon the powers possessed by the
States before federation.   A State cannot do by an executive act
what it has no power to do by legislation.

The rule, that the King is not bound except by express words
or necessary implication from the words of the Statute, would
apply if it were a question whether the Commonwealth Government were bound.   For the purposes of such an inquiry the
King means the King as represented by the authority which
passes the Statute.

                                        Cur. adv. vult.

(1) 4 Wheat., 316.   (2) 199 U.S., 437.
                   (3) 8 C. & P., 131.

The following judgments were read :—

GRIFFITH C.J.　This is an action for penalties for a breach of sec. 33 of the *Customs Act* 1901, which provides that no goods subject to the control of the Customs shall be moved, altered, or interfered with except by authority and in accordance with the Act.　The defendant, by authority of the Executive Government of New South Wales, took from the control of the Customs a quantity of wire netting recently landed from an oversea ship upon which Customs duties were claimed by the Commonwealth authorities.　The Government of New South Wales claimed that the goods were not liable to duty, and that they were entitled to take possession of them as soon as they were landed.　Three questions are formally submitted for the opinion of the Court :—

(a) Do the provisions of the *Customs Act* 1901 bind the Crown as representing the community of New South Wales ?

(b) Were the said 1,313 rolls of wire netting at the time of their removal by the defendant subject to the control of the Customs ?

(c) Was the defendant lawfully entitled to remove the said 1,313 rolls ?

The rule that the Crown is not bound by a Statute unless expressly mentioned, or unless it appears by necessary implication that it was intended to bind the Crown, is a rule of construction, the object of which, as of other rules of construction, is to give effect to the intention of the legislature.　If it appears clearly that the intention was that the Crown should be bound, effect is given to this rule by so holding.　The rule was expounded by this Court in the case of *Roberts* v. *Ahern* (1).　In that case, I said, in delivering the judgment of the Court :—" It is a general rule that the Crown is not bound by a Statute unless it appears on the face of the Statute that it was intended that the Crown should be bound by it.　The rule has commonly been based on the Royal prerogative.　Perhaps, however, having regard to modern developments of constitutional law, a more satisfactory basis is to be found in the words of *Alderson* B., delivering the judgment of the Court of Exchequer in *Attorney-General* v. *Donaldson* (2): ' It is a well established rule, generally speak-

(1) 1 C.L.R., 406, at p. 417.　　　　(2) 10 M. & W., 117, at p. 124.

ing, in the construction of Acts of Parliament that the King is
not included unless there be words to that effect; for it is
inferred *primâ facie* that the law made by the Crown with the
assent of the Lords and Commons is made for subjects and not
for the Crown.' The modern sense of the rule, at any rate, is
that the Executive Government of the State is not bound by
Statute unless that intention was apparent. The doctrine is
well settled in this sense in the United States of America. In
the language of *Story* J.: 'Where the Government is not
expressly or by necessary implication included, it ought to be
clear from the nature of the mischief to be redressed, or the
language used, that the Government itself was in contemplation
of the legislature, before a court of law would be authorized to
put such a construction upon any Statute. In general, Acts of
the legislature are meant to regulate and direct the acts and
rights of citizens, and in most cases the meaning applicable
to them applies with very different and often contrary force to
the Government itself. It appears to me, therefore, to be a safe
rule founded on the principle of the common law that the general
words of a Statute ought not to include the Government unless
that construction be clear and indisputable upon the text of the
Act: *United States* v. *Hoar* (1).' "

This being the meaning of the rule, it follows that it does not
apply to every person who in any part of the world represents
the Crown, but only to those representatives of the Sovereign
who have executive authority in the place where the law applies,
and, even there, only as to matters to which that executive
authority extends. The limits of the authority of a Governor
were pointed out by the Judicial Committee in the case of
Musgrave v. *Pulido* (2). " It is apparent from these authorities
that the Governor of a Colony (in ordinary cases) cannot be
regarded as a Viceroy; nor can it be assumed that he possesses
general sovereign power. His authority is derived from his
commission, and limited to the powers thereby expressly or
impliedly entrusted to him. Let it be granted that, for acts of
power done by a Governor under and within the limits of his
commission, he is protected, because in doing them he is the

(1) 2 Mason (U.S. Circuit Court), 311.   (2) 5 App. Cas., 102, at p. 111.

servant of the Crown, and is exercising its sovereign authority ; the like protection cannot be extended to acts which are wholly beyond the authority confided to him. Such acts, though the Governor may assume to do them as Governor, cannot be considered as done on behalf of the Crown, nor to be in any proper sense acts of state. When questions of this kind arise it must necessarily be within the province of Municipal Courts to determine the true character of the acts done by a Governor, though it may be that, when it is established that the particular act in question is really an act of state policy done under the authority of the Crown, the defence is complete, and the Courts can take no further cognizance of it."

The limits of the authority of the Executive Government of an Australian State are not merely geographical. Under the Constitution there are many matters with respect to which the Commonwealth Government has exclusive authority, and the State Governments have no concern whatever. The Crown, as the head of the Commonwealth Government, is for many, if not all, purposes a separate juristic person from the Crown as head of a State Government, as was pointed out in *The Municipal Council of Sydney* v. *The Commonwealth* (1).

In matters under the exclusive control of the Commonwealth Government the doctrine applies to the Sovereign as head of that Government, but has no application to the Sovereign as head of the State Governments.

What concern then has the State Government with the administration of Customs laws ? In my judgment, none. By sec. 86 of the Constitution the collection and control of duties of Customs passed to the Executive Government of the Commonwealth from its establishment, and by sec. 52 the power of the Parliament with respect to all matters relating to that Department of the Public Service became exclusive. It follows that for the purposes of Customs administration the State Governments are in no better position than private persons. For these purposes there is one territory only, and all goods imported into that territory are subject to the law of the Commonwealth.

It is suggested that, although this may be so, yet if the goods

(1) 1 C.L.R., 208.

H. C. or A.
1908.

The King
v.
Sutton.

Griffith C.J.

were in fact not dutiable the State Authorities were justified in taking them out of the control of the Customs. In the case of a private individual who imports non-dutiable goods, this argument will not bear statement. The Customs Authorities are not bound to accept the assertions of the importer as to the character of the goods imported, of which the importation may be altogether prohibited. The nature of the case renders it necessary —as has always been done in practice—that imported goods should be retained under the control of the Customs for a sufficient time to discover (1) whether they may be lawfully imported, and (2) whether they are dutiable, and if so at what rate. In my opinion, this law applies to goods the property of a State Government as well as to those of private persons, and it is quite immaterial whether the goods are in law dutiable or not.

The result of the contrary view would be extraordinary. Notwithstanding the paramount control as to external trade given in express words to the Commonwealth, the States would retain concurrent power to introduce goods the introduction of which is prohibited by the Commonwealth law. Moreover, Customs laws have always been regarded as a mode of exercising this power of control. If, however, the States have a concurrent power, that of the Commonwealth would be neither exclusive nor paramount.

If the suggested right of the Crown as representing the State Government exists at all, it must be capable of being exercised in any other part of the Commonwealth, a view which is, of course, inconsistent with the geographical limits of the authority of the State Executive.

For these reasons I am of opinion that the *Customs Act* 1901 applies to goods imported by the Government of a State.

It was not disputed that, apart from any question depending upon their being the property of the State, the goods in question were at the time of their removal subject to the control of the Customs.

It follows that the defendant was not lawfully entitled to remove the goods in question, and that there is no defence to this action.

BARTON J. The questions for our opinion are :—

(a) Do the provisions of the *Customs Act* 1901 bind the Crown, as representing the community of New South Wales ?

(b) Were the 1,313 rolls of wire netting at the time of their removal by the defendant subject to the control of the Customs ?

(c) Was the defendant lawfully entitled to remove the said 1,313 rolls ?

The case was argued on the assumption that the goods were not dutiable, although demand had been made for their admission duty-free, and the Collector for New South Wales had refused to comply with that demand, and had required that an entry should be passed and duty paid or deposited (sec. 167) before the delivery of the goods. Let us assume then that the Collector was wrong in insisting on duty ; the real question is whether the defendant, acting on the authority of the Executive Government of the State, was justified in removing even non-dutiable goods in respect of which the conditions of Part III. of the Act had not been complied with, or whether by removing them in such circumstances he has not rendered himself liable in this action to pay a penalty under sec. 33. His liability depends upon the answers of the Court to the questions stated in the special case. Unless the defendant is protected by the authority of the Government of New South Wales he has clearly no defence. Sec. 167 of the *Customs Act* provides a means of deciding disputes as to the liability of goods to duty. In this case the means provided were not adopted, but the goods were removed in face of the opposition or objection of the Customs Authorities, and if the protection claimed is not valid in law, the penalty has been incurred.

The question whether the goods were instrumental in carrying on the Government of the State was faintly suggested at the bar, but has not been seriously raised in this case. There is nothing in the case stated on which such a defence could be rested. The question will, however, demand close consideration in connection with the case of *The Attorney-General of New South Wales* v. *The Collector of Customs* (1), on which judgment stands reserved.

It is necessary now to inquire on what grounds the defendant

H. C. of A.
1908.

THE KING
v.
SUTTON.

Barton J.

(1) *Post.*

H. C. of A.
1908.

THE KING
v.
SUTTON.

Barton J.

relies on his authority from the Government of this State as a defence. They are two—I think in effect only one—namely, that the goods were the King's property, and that the *Customs Act* does not bind the Crown. The terms "the King" and "the Crown," are of course used respectively to denote the Executive Head of the State. The first proposition was based, broadly, on the rule of construction stated by *Alderson* B. in *Attorney-General* v. *Donaldson* (1). But I take the two propositions— that these goods were not subject to Customs control because they were the King's property, and that the *Customs Act* does not bind the Crown—as invocations of one and the same principle with a difference of form. To say, as *Alderson* B. said, that " it is inferred *primâ facie* that the law made by the Crown, with the assent of Lords and Commons, is made for subjects and not for the Crown," is only to say in other words, with *Story* J. in *United States* v. *Hoar* (2), that it appears to be "a safe rule founded on the principles of the common law that the general words of a Statute ought not to include the Government unless that construction be clear and indisputable upon the text of the Act." But, indeed, whether the matter is considered from the side of prerogative or from that of statutory construction matters little, since, if the words or the clear inference from words show that the Government of the legislating authority was intended to be included, the result is in either case the same, and the intention of the legislature will prevail. Let us turn then to the Act in question and examine a few of its provisions on this subject of Customs control. Sec. 30 provides that " Goods shall be subject to the control of the Customs . . . (*a*) As to *all* goods imported—from the time of importation until delivery for home comsumption," &c. By sec. 31, "All goods on board any ship or boat from parts beyond the seas shall also be subject to the control of the Customs whilst the ship or boat is within the limits of any port in Australia." ("Australia" includes the whole of the Commonwealth, see *Acts Interpretation Act* 1901, sec. 17). "The control of the Customs especially includes the right of the Customs to examine all goods subject to such control " (sec. 32). Is it possible to overrate the degree of

(1) 10 M. & W., 117, at p. 124.   (2) 2 Mason, 311.

H. C. of A.
1908.

The King
v.
Sutton.

Barton J.

confusion and inconvenience that would result to the administration of the Customs over this Continent and Tasmania, if provisions such as these were not of general application? Is it possible to suppose that the intention of Parliament was to license the wholesale importation of goods by States the sum of whose operations extends to every port and throughout this vast area; an importation unchecked not merely in extent, not merely in respect of duties, but even in respect of the most casual inspection? But what doubt remains when we look at sec. 33? " No goods subject to the control of the Customs shall be moved altered or interfered with except by authority and in accordance with this Act." Remembering that the absence of all check in respect of duty or otherwise would enable any State (for such is the real extent of the authority claimed) to be its own judge of what and how much it will import, and to set to such importation no bounds but those which the extent of its projects, or its relations with the Australian Government, might dictate; if every movement or treatment of every part of the enormous bulk to which such importations would soon grow is to be free of all regulation or control by the fiscal authority of any port, can one well conceive the state of affairs which would speedily arise if such uncontrolled importations and movements were licensed to proceed side by side with the work of ordered administration on the part of the Customs Department? It is not possible that Parliament has given its sanction to a state of the law which, once it reached its full operation, could only be productive of chaotic conditions and ruined revenue. In my opinion the Statute excludes the supposition.

But happily there is no danger of such results, for the federal power is strong to avoid them. In the first place the doctrines invoked by the defendant do not sustain the assumed authority on which he relies. They are correctly stated, but they fail completely in their application. It is *its own* Executive Government, in this case that of the Commonwealth, that the Parliament is deemed not to include by general words "unless that construction be clear and indisputable upon the text of the Act." A State Executive cannot claim the protection of the doctrine where it is not the King's agent. The Federal Executive is the King's

H. C. of A.
1908.

The King
v.
Sutton.

Barton J.

only agent in cases where the federal power is exclusive. When that power wholly occupies the field, as in the case of the control of the Customs, the State Governments are *ex necessitate* out of that field, which knows as occupants one Government and one people, the Australian Government, and the Australian people who give it life. So in the domain of exclusively national legislation there is no room for State Parliaments or Executives. They have great powers, which this Court has guarded, and will guard. But as far as the law of the Constitution is concerned, State Governments are supreme in their sphere and powerless beyond it. And this is also true of the Australian Government in its turn. In a note to the case of *Stockton* v. *Baltimore and New York Railway &c. Co.* (1), a very instructive case, Dr. *Thayer*, Weld Professor of Law at Harvard University, a high authority, says at p. 2,068 of his *Cases on Constitutional Law*, in relation to the power to regulate commerce with foreign nations, and among the several States, &c. :—" We think that the power of Congress is supreme over the whole subject, unimpeded and unembarrassed by State lines or State laws; that, in this matter, the country is one, and the work to be accomplished is national; and that State interests, State jealousies, and State prejudices do not require to be consulted. In matters of foreign and interstate commerce there are no States." That these words truly express the nature and extent of the commerce power, as interpreted by the Supreme Court of the United States, there can not be a doubt. So long as the legislative exercise of the power is kept within its ambit, that is, so long as the federal grantee does not attempt to regulate the purely internal and domestic commerce of a State, such exercise and its executive consequences cannot be hindered or nullified in any part by any legislative or executive act on the part of a State. A Statute of a State—the highest exercise of power of which it is capable—would be void so far as it purported to authorize such an act; and there is no constitutional authority in the Executive of the State to do that which no Statute of its Parliament could make lawful. It follows that in such a case no citizen can justify under an authority purporting to be granted him by a State Executive, for that is no authority at

(1) 32 Fed. Rep., 9.

all. Now, the case against interference by a State becomes
stronger when the subject matter is the control of the Customs.
The power of the Federal Parliament to impose duties of Customs
did not, it is true, become exclusive until the passage of the first
tariff (sec. 90 of the Constitution). But the collection and control
of Customs duties passed to the Executive Government of the
Commonwealth on its establishment (sec. 86). And, subject to
the Constitution, the Parliament has from the beginning had
exclusive power to make laws with respect to " Matters relating
to any department of the public service the control of which is
by this Constitution transferred to the Executive Government of
the Commonwealth " (sec. 52 (II.)). It is this power, indeed, that
the Parliament exercised when, in anticipation of the tariff, it
passed the *Customs Act* 1901 in its first session, and in the Constitution I find nothing that limits the operation of that Statute
further than its own terms disclose. But the terms which are
employed in secs. 52, 86 and 90 to secure the constitutional
powers with respect to the Customs, leave no doubt of their
plenary and exclusive character. Hence in the matter of the
control of the Customs and the imposition of import duties it
may be said that " there is no State " as emphatically, if not
more so, than it was said of matters of foreign and inter-
state commerce. In this matter, if in any, " the country is
one, and the work . . . is national," so purely national
(using the word in the limited sense properly imposed by the
Imperial connection), that the Constitution has made it the
exclusive concern of the Federal Parliament. *Bradley* J., in
the case of *Robbins* v. *Shelly County Taxing District* (1),
said :—" It seems to be forgotten in argument that the people
of this country are citizens of the United States, as well as of
the individual States, and that they have some rights under the
Constitution and laws of the former, independent of the latter,
and free from any interference or restraint from them." What
Bradley J. said of the citizens of the United States is equally
true of the people of Australia.

In my view, then, the answer to the first question must be in the
affirmative, but with strict remembrance that in exclusively Com-

(1) 120 U.S. 489, at p. 496.

H. C. of A.
1908.
⌣
THE KING
v.
SUTTON.
⎯
Barton J.
monwealth matters there are not seven Executive Governments,
but only one, that of the Commonwealth itself. It follows that
the second question must be answered in the affirmative, and the
third in the negative.

Judgment must therefore be for the plaintiffs, for such penalty
as may now be fixed.

O'CONNOR J. The *Customs Act* 1901 subjects all goods
imported into Australia to Customs control from the time of
importation until an entry passed in the proper form gives the
importer authority to move them, and the passing of such an
entry is as necessary in the case of goods duty free as in the case
of those liable to duty. It is therefore abundantly clear that, if
the goods, which are the subject of this action, and the persons
whose conduct is complained of, are subject to the *Customs Act*,
there can be no answer to the claim for penalties. The
defendant, however, rests his defence upon the legal ground raised
by the special case, which is that the Crown, as representing the
community of New South Wales, is not bound by the *Customs
Act*, and that the goods are its property.

The whole controversy turns upon the proper interpretation to
be placed upon the Constitution and upon the *Customs Act*.
The words of both Acts are wide enough to cover the facts of the
case and must be held to cover them unless for some reason their
meaning is to be restricted so as not to apply to the Crown in the
sense in which that expression is used in the case. The principle
relied on is entirely one of construction.

Before considering in what form it should be stated and in
what way it is applicable in the construction of the two Statutes
I have mentioned, it is necessary to advert to the position of the
King as executive head of each of the States and of the Commonwealth respectively. For some purposes the King, as representing the executive power of the Empire, is the same juristic person
throughout the whole of his Dominions. The enlistment and
control of his army is one of those purposes, as was held in
Williams v. *Howarth* (1). But, except for those purposes, he is
not the same juristic person throughout the whole of his

(1) (1905) A.C., 551.

Dominions. In the case of the *Municipal Council of Sydney v. The Commonwealth* (1) it became necessary to consider the matter, and the following statement of the Chief Justice, concurred in as it was by Mr. Justice *Barton* and myself, represents the opinion of the Court. "It is manifest from the whole scope of the Constitution that, just as the Commonwealth and State are regarded as distinct and separate sovereign bodies, with sovereign powers limited only by the ambit of their authority under the Constitution, so the Crown, as representing those several bodies, is to be regarded not as one, but as several juristic persons, to use a phrase which well expresses the idea. No better illustration can be given than is afforded by the lands now sought to be rated, which, having originally been 'property of the State,' *i.e.* lands of the Crown in New South Wales, have become 'vested in the Commonwealth,' *i.e.* vested in the Crown in right of the Commonwealth."

The King's representative in the Commonwealth and in each of the States cannot, as was pointed out in *Musgrave v. Pulido* (2), be regarded as Viceroy, or as possessing sovereign power. His powers are limited by his instructions and are also necessarily limited by the Constitution of the State or the Commonwealth as the case may be. In anything outside the exercise of the powers so limited he is in law no more than an individual subject of the King. A Federal Constitution in its very nature presupposes the separate and independent existence of the King as representing the community in each State and in the Commonwealth respectively, the King in that representative capacity as head of the Executive being in a position in each case to assert and maintain the rights of the political entity he represents.

Now, the rule of construction upon which the defendant relies was fully considered in *Roberts v. Ahern* (3), and I take it that the statement of the principle contained in the judgment in that case is that which must now be adopted by the Court :—

"It is a general rule that the Crown is not bound by a Statute unless it appears on the face of the Statute that it was intended that the Crown should be bound by it. This rule has commonly

H. C. of A.
1908.

THE KING
v.
SUTTON.

O'Connor J.

(1) 1 C.L.R., 208, at p. 231.　　　(2) 5 App. Cas., 102, at p. 111.
　　　(3) 1 C.L.R., 406, at p. 417.

H. C. of A.
1908.

Thᴇ Kɪɴɢ
v.
Sᴜᴛᴛᴏɴ.

O'Connor J.

been based on the Royal prerogative. Perhaps, however, having regard to modern developments of constitutional law, a more satisfactory basis is to be found in the words of *Alderson* B., delivering the judgment of the Court of Exchequer in *Attorney-General* v. *Donaldson* (1): ' it is a well established rule, generally speaking, in the construction of Acts of Parliament that the King is not included unless there be words to that effect ; for it is inferred *primâ facie* that the law made by the Crown with the assent of Lords and Commons is made for subjects and not for the Crown.' The modern sense of the rule, at any rate, is that the Executive Government of the State is not bound by Statute unless that intention is apparent. The doctrine is well settled in this sense in the United States of America. In the language of *Story* J.: ' Where the Government is not expressly or by necessary implication included, it ought to be clear from the nature of the mischief to be redressed, or the language used, that the Government itself was in contemplation of the legislature, before a Court of law would be authorized to put such a construction upon any Statute. In general, Acts of the legislature are meant to regulate and direct the acts and rights of citizens, and in most cases the meaning applicable to them applies with very different and often contrary force to the Government itself. It appears to me, therefore, to be a safe rule founded on the principles of the common law that the general words of a Statute ought not to include the Government unless that construction be clear and indisputable upon the text of the Act ': *United States* v. *Hoar* (2)."

Such being the principle upon which the rule of construction rests, it is obviously applicable only in the determination of the question whether the King, as representing the community whose legislation is under consideration, is or is not bound by enactment. It cannot be applied to determine whether the enactment binds the King as representing some other community. It is applicable in the inquiry whether a Commonwealth Act binds the King as representing the Commonwealth. But where the inquiry is whether the Commonwealth Act binds the King as representing one of the States it can have no relevancy.

(1) 10 M. & W., 117, at p. 124.   (2) 2 Mason (U.S. Circuit Court), 311.

Coming now to the application of the principle of construction to the enactments in question, it would follow that, although that principle may be used to ascertain whether the King, as representing the Commonwealth, is bound by the *Customs Act*, it cannot be used in the inquiry whether the King, as representing the community of New South Wales, is bound by the Constitution or by the *Customs Act*. In such a case the obligation of the Crown as representing the community of New South Wales to obey the Constitution and laws, such as the *Customs Act* passed under its authority, depends upon entirely different considerations.

It is, of course, conceded that the British Parliament in enacting the Constitution could confer on the Commonwealth the power of controlling the State Executives, and therefore the King as representing the community in any State, and it is beyond question that that power has been conferred in cases where the limitation of State powers is necessary for the effective exercise of Commonwealth powers. The main purpose of the Constitution is the distribution between the Commonwealth and the States of all the governmental powers of the people of Australia. The States, in the exercise of the powers exclusively reserved to them, are confined as before Federation within the jurisdiction of their territorial limits. But in the exercise of the exclusive powers of the Commonwealth, State boundaries disappear, and the whole of Australia becomes one territory. The laws of the Commonwealth are, to use the words of sec. V. of the covering clauses of the Constitution, " binding on the Courts, Judges, and people of every State, and of every part of the Commonwealth, notwithstanding anything in the laws of any State." Such laws have operation on all Australian citizens irrespective of their division into State communities, and any Commonwealth law may also expressly bind or except from its operation States or Executive Governments of States. In determining, therefore, whether the King, as representing the community of a State, is bound by a Commonwealth law, the only questions that can arise are whether its language includes the subject matter in question, whether the law is within the powers of the Commonwealth, and whether it has excepted the King as representing the community of the

H. C. of A.
1908.

THE KING
v.
SUTTON.

O'Connor J.

State, State itself, the State Executive, or the goods of the State from its operation.

Coming now to the Commonwealth law under consideration, it may also be an exercise of the power to regulate commerce, but it is primarily an exercise of the exclusive power of the Commonwealth to impose duties of Customs and Excise. Neither the King, as representing the community in each State, nor the State Executives have been excepted from its provisions—on the contrary it is plain that the effective operation of the Act would be impossible if the exemption now claimed were allowed. In my opinion, the goods of the State of New South Wales are under the *Customs Act* in the same position as the goods of any citizen of New South Wales, and the individuals constituting the executive authority of New South Wales are under that Act in the same position as any other individuals in New South Wales, and equally bound to obey the provisions of the Customs laws.

For these reasons I am of opinion that the legal ground of defence set up by the State of New South Wales must fail, and the questions put in the case must be answered in favour of the plaintiffs.

ISAACS J. No question of taxation is raised in this case. It was assumed that wire netting was free from Customs duty, and strictly speaking the only point for decision is as to the legality of the forcible seizure of the wire by the defendant. The following case (1), however, fully raises for judicial determination larger questions argued in both, and consequently it will be convenient to consider them at once so far as they are common to both cases. I leave out of consideration in this judgment the force and effect of sec. 114 of the Constitution. Apart, then, from that section, the issue is clear cut ; whether the States can import into Australia any goods they desire, of whatsoever nature and condition, free from the operation of the Commonwealth laws, and free from any Commonwealth supervision or examination ; or, if that proposition be not universally true, then with this limitation only, that the goods must be intended for utilization in some governmental function. When the power of legislation with respect to trade and commerce with foreign countries was granted

(1) 1 *Post*, p. 818.

to the Commonwealth, it was a surrender, not partial, but complete, of the supreme authority to control the introduction into Australia of goods from abroad.   How far any specified articles of merchandise might be the subject of that trade and commerce and intermingled with the common stock of property in the Commonwealth was not to be dependent on the single will of any State, nor on the separately declared will of all the States, but was to be determinable by the united action of the whole Commonwealth speaking for all the people, regarded as one community undivided by State lines.   The grant of the trade and commerce power was not intended to be illusory; but if the States had the rights contended for of bringing in whatsoever goods they please, even in antagonism to Commonwealth regulation of the subject, the grant would be altogether illusory.   By sec. 92, inter-state trade is declared to be absolutely free, and foreign goods once incorporated into the common stock are subject only to State regulation of trade, and consequently any federal regulation of foreign commerce would be nugatory if by means of State agency merchants could evade or overcome it.   On the plea that the goods were the King's property, the whole power of the trade and commerce clause could be rendered futile, and in this simple fashion one of the prime essentials of the federal system could be nullified.   A construction of the Constitution leading to so absurd and destructive a result is impossible of acceptance.

The argument is rested on the doctrine that the King is not bound by a Statute unless referred to expressly or by necessary implication.   So far as this argument is addressed to the Constitution, the instant answer is that the very essence of that instrument is to bind the Crown.   True, in a sense, the Crown is one and indivisible throughout the Empire, but its power is not one and indivisible: it acts by different agents with varying authority in different localities or for different purposes in the same locality.   The Constitution redistributed the Royal power over the territory of Australia.   Formerly, and subject only in the last resort to the will of the Imperial Parliament, the Sovereign exerted his authority over his subjects in each separate Colony solely by his local representatives and advisers there, and with regard to all matters of legislative and executive

H. C. of A.
1908.

THE KING
v.
SUTTON.

Isaacs J.

control. The distribution of power effected by the Constitution has produced this change in the position of the King : that his sovereign power is no longer exercised by means of those representatives and advisers over so large a field of subject matters or, in some cases, with the same finality. His Commonwealth representatives and advisers in all matters committed to them are now either the exclusive or the dominant depositaries of the Royal authority. Trade and commerce with foreign countries is one of those matters. Customs taxation is another. The States are still His Majesty's agents—so far, for instance, as the general construction and management of railways are concerned, and for the purpose of acquiring the ownership of property destined for use in connection with the railways in their respective territories—but they are not his agents to exercise his sovereign jurisdiction with regard to the introduction of articles of commerce into this continent contrary to the declared will of the Federal Parliament. That would be in plain repugnance to the supremacy of Commonwealth law expressly established by the Constitution. If the Commonwealth Parliament cannot bind the King at all because the Constitution gives it no power to do so, that inability on the part of the Parliament must exist with respect to the Sovereign as the head of every part of his Dominions alike. Under cover of this immunity—and learned counsel avowedly pressed the matter so far—the Governments of Canada, Jamaica, India, or Hong Kong could equally compel the Commonwealth to receive their property in opposition to its own laws because His Majesty is in law the owner, and once the goods come within the territory as part of the common stock, federal regulation of trade does not exist. The contention must logically carry with it the power of every State Government to introduce labour for its public works, from any country, of any description, and in any quantity, and in derogation of whatever prohibition upon the entrance of undesirable immigrants the Federal Parliament might think fit to adopt, for the argument if valid cannot stop at any class of Statute. A State might at any moment deem it advantageous to adopt an internal policy that would involve utter conflict between its ideas of public welfare and those declared by the Commonwealth Parliament, and if this argument for the defendant were to prevail, the way would be open for the State to disregard every federal law upon the subject of foreign trade and commerce, immigration, and almost every other subject enumerated in the Constitution, and so make that document practically worthless as an instrument of government, and reduce federation to a shadow.

The modified contention alternatively presented is said to be involved in previous decisions of this Court that Commonwealth law is incapable of impeding State instrumentalities, or, in other words, the means employed by the State to carry out its governmental functions. In this argument a distinction is made between sovereignty and trading, and reference was made to *South Carolina* v. *United States* (1). A possible distinction between the King as a Sovereign and as a trader was adverted to by Lord *Stowell* in the case of *The Swift* (2). But no decision to be found anywhere carries with it such a position as the defendant here contends for. The governmental authority of the State is limited to its own territory, and this branch of the argument is therefore answered by the fact of the fundamental difference between exercising sovereign power over property within the territorial limits, and insisting upon a right to bring property there from abroad, notwithstanding the prohibition by a lawful authority declared by the paramount law of the Empire to be in that regard supreme. I am, therefore, unable to agree with the contention that the Constitution leaves the Commonwealth powerless as against the States to regulate foreign trade and commerce ; or phrasing it differently, that the King, as representing the Executive of the States, was not intended to be affected by the transference or creation of the powers enumerated in the Constitution ; and I entertain no doubt that the Federal Parliament is authorized by appropriate legislation to prohibit the importation of goods by the State Governments.

This, however, does not conclude the controversy. The defendant took up the further position, that, assuming the power to control State importation, the Parliament had not exercised it, because, on the proper construction of the *Customs Act* itself according to acknowledged canons, the King is not bound. So

(1) 199 U.S., 437.　　　　(2) 1 Dods., 320, at p. 339.

far as the facts of this particular case are concerned, it appears
that the defendant, without entry made or tendered, seized the
goods *vi et armis* while in the control of the Customs within the
meaning of the Act.

It would be sufficient to say that, whether or not the general
provisions of the Statute as to prohibition and taxation were
intended to apply to goods of the State or to goods intended
for governmental use, the Commonwealth must at least have
control of goods imported to the extent of ascertaining the
ownership or the purpose of importation, and to test the assertion
of the person actually introducing them into the country. Once
that position is reached, it would obviously reduce the public
administration of the Customs law to a chaotic condition if
individual importers could under any pretence whatever legitimately use physical force in asserting their claims of unlawful
detention, leaving the officers of the Crown no alternative but
either to submit, which would be equivalent to the abandonment
of all government, or else to employ countervailing force in order
to overcome resistance. Still more serious would it be and more
destructive of public peace and order if States, attempting as in
this case to clothe their action with outward but futile forms of
lawful authority, were permitted to enter into open conflict with
the executive officers of the Commonwealth in the *bona fide*
discharge of their ordinary functions. If the rights of States or
individuals are infringed, the Constitution has provided a method
of redress, and any other would inaugurate a reign of disorder.
Such a state of affairs as would justify the defendant's action is
entirely outside the limits of legal contemplation, and can form
no basis of argument in a Court of law. Even on the assumption,
therefore, that the State had a right to demand possession of the
goods without payment of duty, and that this right was wrongfully denied by a refusal to restore possession, it was still a
wrongful step in forcibly seizing them from the Customs, and the
plaintiffs would be entitled to judgment. But, as I have said, the
broader question is involved in this and the next case taken
together as to whether the State is bound by the terms of the
Customs Act 1901. The liability of the State to taxation may
depend ultimately upon quite another consideration, but to

determine the applicability of this Act as such to the Crown I propose to regard it from the standpoint of dutiability as well as prohibition. Prohibition of imports is enacted in secs. 50 to 57 inclusive. The prohibition is perfectly general. It is immaterial to whom the goods belong. The goods themselves are prohibited imports. I need not repeat what I have already said as to the impossibility of maintaining this prohibition with any effect if six entrances are provided whereby free and unchecked access is permissible. This clearly could not have been the intention of the legislature. Nevertheless, says the defendant, however unreasonable it may be, however inconvenient it may prove, the Parliament has omitted technically to close up those entrances by express or necessarily implied references to the State Governments, and so they exist in law. I reserve my opinion as to whether this objection may not receive an equally technical answer by the combined effect of the *Acts Interpretation Act* 1901, secs. 2 and 32, aided by the *Magdalen College Case* (1). I do not enter upon that question because the question may be resolved by recourse to more enlarged principles.

In *The Municipal Council of Sydney* v. *The Commonwealth* (2) the learned Chief Justice said :—" It is manifest from the whole scope of the Constitution that, just as the Commonwealth and States are regarded as distinct and separate sovereign bodies, with sovereign powers limited only by the ambit of their authority under the Constitution, so the Crown, as representing these bodies, is to be regarded not as one, but as several juristic persons, to use a phrase which well expresses the idea."

I agree with those observations, which must govern, not only the construction of the Constitution itself, but also the laws made under it. The Constitution, in apportioning and distributing political powers, rights and duties, between Commonwealth and States, regards them as distinct and separate organisms for their several functions. This was necessary to the scheme of government it introduced, for operating as these several authorities do, at the same time, on the same territory, the same persons, and the same property, any other conception would produce confusion. No doctrine of law, however applicable to the purely unitary form of

(1) 11 Rep., 66.   (2) 1 C.L.R., 208, at p. 231.

H. C. of A. government, can, if inconsistent with the great, essential and
1908.   dominant purpose of the Federal Constitution, be allowed to
The King   prevail.
v.
Sutton.   Any theory, therefore, is inadmissible which would permit the
             the States, merely because allegiance is owed to the same Crown,
Isaacs J.   to claim entire exemption from the general operation of a federal
             law, regulating a matter of national concern, and made by virtue
             of a granted power of such a nature that the exemption would
             or might either utterly frustrate the legislation or render it
             practically ineffective.

             The regulation of foreign trade and commerce and the
             imposition of Customs duties are necessarily powers of that
             character.

             In *Pensacola Telegraph Co.* v. *Western Union Telegraph Co.*
             (1), *Waite* C.J. in words singularly appropriate to the present
             occasion said of the Government of the United States :—" It
             legislates for the whole nation, and is not embarrassed by State
             lines. Its peculiar duty is to protect one part of the country
             from the encroachments by another upon the national rights
             which belong to all."

             If, then, State lines are not to be observed in the field of
             national regulation of external trade and commerce and duties of
             Customs, there can be no room for the contention that the Crown,
             as representing the States, is not bound without express words or
             necessary implication, and the argument must consequently fail
             through its want of relevancy.

             For these reasons the acts of the defendant were, in my
             opinion, contrary to the law, and he is liable to the penalty
             imposed by the Customs Acts.

             Higgins J. It is unquestionable that, if this wire netting had
             belonged to a private person, it was subject to the control of the
             Customs, and that the defendant was liable to a penalty for
             removing it without passing a Customs entry, even if it was free
             from duty : *Customs Act* 1901, secs. 30, 33, 36. The defendant's
             counsel have wisely refrained from pressing the untenable point
             which was suggested in the case—that the wire netting was no

             (1) 96 U.S., 1, at p. 10.

longer in the control of the Customs after it had been placed on land vested in the Commissioner for Railways.

The question is, does the fact that the goods were removed by the order of the Governor of New South Wales in Council justify the removal? It is urged for the defendant that the *Customs Act* does not mention the King; that the King cannot be bound except by express words or by necessary implication; that even if the Commonwealth Parliament could by express words bind the King, it has not done so by the *Customs Act* 1901; and that therefore the State Government, as the King's agent, can ignore all the provisions of the *Customs Act*, can take goods without passing an entry, without even giving the Customs officials an opportunity of examining into the facts, and of ascertaining whether the goods are dutiable or not.

The goods in this case are in fact dutiable if imported by private persons; but for the purpose of dealing with the precise difficulty submitted in this special case, freed from other considerations, I shall assume that they are not dutiable. It would, indeed, be an extraordinary result if a lighter may take goods from a ship before it comes to the wharf, giving the Customs officials no information, leaving them in the dark as to the facts, and without any materials wherewith to decide whether the goods are liable to duty, or are prohibited as noxious to health or to morals, or as being made by prison labour, or even to decide whether they belong to the State. For ordinary imports the Customs officials have full power of examination (secs. 32, 49, 186), and of interrogation (secs. 234, 274). If the defendant is right, the State Government can loftily ignore a prohibition or regulation of the importation of opium, of Kanakas, of goods or persons from an infected port; and the powers of the Commonwealth Parliament, designed for the good of the people of Australia, will be rendered futile and illusory. According to the argument for the defendant, if the Canadian Government or the New Zealand Government claim an exemption from Customs entry and from examination, as to goods belonging to it and sent to Australia, the claim should be allowed; for the goods are in law the King's goods. Moreover, if New South Wales imported goods to be landed in Adelaide, in another State,—say, for a Broken Hill railway—the goods must

—as admitted in the argument—be landed without entry and without inspection.

Now, what are the limits to the doctrine by virtue of which the State Government claims a right to ignore the Customs machinery? The King, it is said, is not to be treated as bound unless the Statute says so, expressly or by necessary implication. But the State Government is not the King; nor is it an agent of the King so far as regards the function of regulating trade and commerce with other countries. The State Government is an agent of limited powers; the Commonwealth Government is also an agent of limited powers; and the question here is, not as between the King and any of his subjects, but between two agents of the King. One agent—the Commonwealth Parliament —has the exclusive power of regulating importation and of imposing Customs taxation; the other agent—the State Parliament or the State Government—has nothing to do with these subjects. The State does not enjoy the benefit of the King's prerogative rights except as to matters to which its agency extends; just as the Governor of a State is not protected as to matters beyond the authority confided to him: *Musgrave* v. *Pulido* (1). Even if the State Parliament passed a law on the subject of importation, it would be void; and even if it passed a law on some subject properly pertaining to the State—such as the State railways—that law is invalid in so far as it is inconsistent with the laws of the Commonwealth as to Customs; for the Commonwealth law is paramount (Constitution, sec. 109). Moreover, the King is at the back of the Commonwealth as well as at the back of each State; and His Majesty is as much interested in the due execution of the powers of the Commonwealth, so that he may get revenue for Commonwealth purposes, as he is in the due execution of the powers of the State for the purposes of the administration of the railways and the lands of New South Wales. No English case has been cited to us, or is to me conceivable, in which this doctrine, as to the implied exception of the King's property and agencies, has been applied as between one agent of the King and another agent of the King, each of whom has a separate power for separate purposes

(1) 5 App. Cas., 102, at p. 111.

of the King. The case is quite different when (*a*) the same Royal purse would take money for taxation as would pay, or when (*b*) the contest is between the King and his subjects. The doctrine is a mere rule of construction, and as such it gives way to necessary intendment. A local authority is in the same position as a subject for the purposes of the doctrine; for the moneys collected by the local authority are not to be spent by the King: *Weymouth, Mayor of* v. *Nugent* (1). The King is entitled to take the benefit of Statutes which do not name him, if they are for his advantage, or for the public benefit; and the Commonwealth is entitled to the benefit of this principle, as much as the State Government is to the benefit of the converse principle, as to the burden of a Statute. The defendant argues as if the King were behind the State only, and not behind the Commonwealth—as if he were the King of the State and not of the Commonwealth. The case of *R.* v. *Wright* (2) shows sufficiently that, where the King's interest is as much on one side as on the other, the maxim of construction pressed on us for the defendant does not apply. It seems to me to be also correct to say that the doctrine of construction applies to the Government of the State in State Acts, to the Government of the Commonwealth in Federal Acts. In other words, the Crown to be considered in applying the doctrine to a *Customs Act* is the Crown of the Commonwealth—the separate "juristic person" referred to in *Municipal Council of Sydney* v. *The Commonwealth* (3). To my mind, indeed, if secs. 106-109 of the Constitution be rightly considered, most of the difficulties as to the conflict of powers will vanish. The States' laws, and the States' powers to make laws, are all "subject to the Constitution"; and the Commonwealth laws made under the Constitution override any conflicting State laws made within the States' powers; and, so far as regards Customs machinery provided by the Commonwealth Parliament, the State officials must submit to it as if they were private persons. They are not servants of the King so far as regards importation; and the burden lies upon them, as it lies on other subjects of the King, of showing that they are

(1) 6 B. & S., 22, at pp. 32-33.   (2) 1 A. & E., 434, at p. 441.
(3) 1 C.L.R., 208, at p. 231.

H. C. of A.
1908.

The King
v.
Sutton.

Higgins J.

exempted, without express words to that effect, from the obligations created by a Federal Act.

I ought to add that I feel no doubt as to the power of the Commonwealth Parliament, as well as of a State Parliament, to expressly bind the Crown by its acts.

Judgment for the plaintiffs.

Solicitor, for the plaintiffs, *The Crown Solicitor for the Commonwealth.*

Solicitor, for the defendant, *The Crown Solicitor for New South Wales.*

C. A. W.

[HIGH COURT OF AUSTRALIA.]

THE ATTORNEY-GENERAL OF NEW SOUTH WALES . . . . } PLAINTIFF;

AND

THE COLLECTOR OF CUSTOMS FOR NEW SOUTH WALES . . . } DEFENDANT.

H. C. of A.
1908.

SYDNEY,
April 15, 16 ;
May 6, 8, 23.

Griffith C.J.,
Barton,
O'Connor,
Isaacs and
Higgins JJ.

Powers of Commonwealth Parliament—Duties of Customs—Importation of goods by State Government—Instrumentality of State—Liability to duty—Construction —The Constitution (63 & 64 Vict. c. 12), secs. 51 (i.), (ii.), 52 (ii.), 86, 90, 114.

The rule laid down in *D'Emden* v. *Pedder*, 1 C.L.R., 91, at p. 111, and applied to the case of interference by the Commonwealth with State instrumentalities in the *Federated Amalgamated Government Railway and Tramway Service Association* v. *New South Wales Railway Traffic Employés Association*, 4 C.L.R., 488, has no application to powers which are conferred upon the Commonwealth in express terms and which by their nature manifestly involve control of some operation of the State Governments, such as the power to make laws with respect to trade and commerce with other countries and with respect to taxation. It must be assumed that the legislature intended that, so far

H. C. of A.
1908.

ATTORNEY-
GENERAL OF
N.S.W.
v.
COLLECTOR OF
CUSTOMS FOR
N.S.W.

as is necessary for the effective exercise of these powers, the rights of State Governments should be restricted. The imposition of Customs duties being a mode of regulating trade and commerce with other countries as well as an exercise of the taxing power, the right of State Governments to import goods is subject to the Customs laws of the Commonwealth.

Further, the rule has reference only to the performance of the functions of Government within the Commonwealth, and, therefore, cannot be applied to the importation by a State Government of goods to be afterwards used in connection with one of its instrumentalities.

The levying of duties of Customs is not the imposition of a tax upon property within the meaning of sec. 114 of the Constitution.

Even if the words of the section are capable of that meaning, it is not the only or necessary meaning, and should be rejected as inconsistent with the plain provisions of the Constitution conferring upon the Commonwealth exclusive power to impose duties of Customs and to regulate trade and commerce.

Per Griffith C.J., Barton J., O'Connor J., and Higgins J.—Customs duties, whether capable or not of being included in the word "tax," are not a tax upon property in the sense in which that expression is used in sec. 114, being imposed upon the act of importation, not upon the goods themselves in their character as property.

Per Isaacs J.—Duties of Customs, as ordinarily understood and as enacted in the *Customs Act*, are imposed on the goods themselves, and, therefore, "on property" within the meaning of sec. 114, but do not come within the meaning of the word "tax" as used in that section and the Constitution generally.

Held, therefore, following *The King v. Sutton*, 5 C.L.R., 789, that the Government of the State of New South Wales was liable to pay Customs duty on steel rails imported by the State for use in connection with the Government railways of the State.

SPECIAL case stated for the opinion of the High Court under Order XXIX., rule 1, of the Rules of the High Court.

This was an action brought to recover from the defendant the sum of £539 18s. 1d. being the amount of duties of Customs demanded by the defendant upon the importation into the Commonwealth of certain steel rails, and paid under protest by the Government of the State of New South Wales. The rails in question, which had been purchased by the State in England for use in the construction of the railways of the State, were shipped from London to Sydney, consigned to the Secretary for Public Works of the State. On their arrival at the port of Sydney the

H. C. of A.
1908.

ATTORNEY-
GENERAL OF
N.S.W.
v.
COLLECTOR OF
CUSTOMS FOR
N.S.W.

defendant claimed that they were liable to Customs duties to the amount stated. The State disputed its liability to pay duty, and deposited the amount claimed, under protest.

This case was stated for the opinion of the Court upon the questions:—(1) Whether the provisions of the *Customs Act* 1901, and the *Customs Tariff* 1902, affect the Crown as representing the community of New South Wales in the sense that those provisions require the Crown to pay duties of Customs under the circumstances stated in the case ; (2) whether the steel rails were exempt from duty by virtue of sec. 114 of the Constitution ; and (3) whether the rails were liable to pay duty.

Judgment was to be entered by the Court for the plaintiff or defendant in accordance with its decision on the questions submitted.

Pilcher K.C. and *Knox* K.C. (*Lamb* with them), for the plaintiff. The duty is an interference with an instrumentality of the State, and as such comes within the rule laid down in *D'Emden* v. *Pedder* (1), and applied in *Federated Amalgamated Government Railway and Tramway Service Association* v. *New South Wales Railway Traffic Employés Association* (2). The railways are an instrumentality, on the authority of the latter case, and the means of carrying it on should be equally protected. The State might absolutely require to import rails for the purpose of constructing railways. Even if it were not necessary to import them, the State, according to the decision in *M'Culloch* v. *Maryland* (3), has the right to select its own means, and any impediment to the means selected is within the prohibition. [See *The Commonwealth* v. *The State of New South Wales* (4).]

[GRIFFITH C.J.—Those cases relate to transactions taking place wholly within the Commonwealth. Nobody disputes that the Commonwealth cannot interfere with the State's management of its railways within the limits of the State. Does it follow that it cannot interfere with what the State does in England by an agent ?]

The tax is just as much an interference with the exercise of

(1) 1 C.L.R., 91.   (3) 4 Wheat., 316.
(2) 4 C.L.R., 488.   (4) 3 C.L.R., 807, at pp. 820, 822.

the State function as a tax stamp upon a contract made in the Commonwealth. It is not the form of the tax, but the substance that is to be looked at: *Almy* v. *State of California* (1). Nor does it matter at what stage the interference takes place. To tax the goods in the process of acquisition is just as serious a hindrance as to tax them after they are acquired. If the Commonwealth has the power to tax the means of the State to any extent, it has power to do so to the fullest extent, and thereby to practically prevent the exercise of the State function.

[GRIFFITH C.J.—Is the mere intention to use the rails for State railways sufficient to exempt them ? They may not be used for that purpose at all.]

That objection would apply equally to the case of the stamp on the transfer in *The Commonwealth* v. *The State of New South Wales* (2). The Commonwealth might change its mind as to the use to which it would put the land it acquired.

[GRIFFITH C.J.—The principle of the cases cited is that the State may use, without interference, any instruments lawfully at its hand in the State. It must not be assumed that a proposition laid down in a particular case is absolutely and universally true. The limitation I have stated is, I think, implied.]

But if the rails are not in New South Wales they are not in the Commonwealth, and therefore they are not in the control of the Commonwealth. The duties do not attach until the goods are in the State. [They referred to *Young* v. *s.s.* " *Scotia* " (3).] There is nothing in the Constitution expressly giving the Commonwealth power to impose a tax upon goods of the States, or excluding the implication of the rule in *D'Emden* v. *Pedder* (4) in regard to such taxation. The power of taxation and regulation of trade and commerce are identical in the Australian and American Constitutions: *Baker, Annotated Constitution*, pp. 16, 19, and the limitation of State powers of taxation is the same: Art. 112. Sec. 90 of the Constitution does not confer any power. It merely fixes the time at which the power arises. The case of *South Carolina* v. *United States* (5) is, therefore, an

H. C. OF A.
1908.

ATTORNEY-
GENERAL OF
N.S.W.
v.
COLLECTOR OF
CUSTOMS FOR
N.S.W.

(1) 24 How., 169.
(2) 3 C.L.R., 807.
(3) (1903) A.C., 501.

(4) 1 C.L.R., 91.
(5) 199 U.S., 437.

H. C. of A.
1908.

ATTORNEY-
GENERAL OF
N.S.W.
v.
COLLECTOR OF
CUSTOMS FOR
N.S.W.

authority for the proposition that the Constitution does not warrant the imposition by the Commonwealth of any duty on articles
imported by a State for use in State agencies.

Sec. 114 expressly prohibits the Commonwealth from taxation
of the property of a State. Goods imported by a State are
property of the State in the ordinary sense of the word, and
there is nothing in the context to alter or restrict that meaning.
Sec. 131 of the *Customs Act* adopts that sense of the word in
providing that no goods the property of the Commonwealth
shall be subject to Customs duties. The tax on the goods
is a tax on the State with respect to the goods. It is immaterial
how it is described. The question is what is the substance.
In *Brown* v. *Maryland* (1), it was held that a tax on importers
was within the prohibition of the Constitution because it was
in substance a tax on imports, that is on the goods imported.
The goods are charged with the tax and all the means of
enforcement are with respect to the goods. The whole com-
putation of the tax is based on the nature and quantity of the
the goods. [They referred to *Customs Act* 1901, secs. 4, 131, 142,
145, 153; *Customs Tariff* 1902, sec. 5.] The intention of the
legislature is to be gathered from the words they have used, not
from some imagined consequences that might flow from the
ordinary construction. If it is said that the States could defeat
the Commonwealth provisions for raising revenue through the
Customs by importing goods of all kinds, it may be answered
that that is highly improbable, and in all probability never presented itself to the minds of the legislature as reasonably possible,
or there may be an implied limitation of the protection given by
the section to property used by the State in the ordinary and
usual exercise of State functions. The word "tax" must include
Customs duty. The only power to impose duties of Customs is the
power of taxation given by sec. 51 (II.). Until the imposition of
an uniform tariff the States could have imposed Customs duties:
Colonial Sugar Refining Company Ltd. v. *Irving* (2); secs. 107,
108 of the Constitution. If sec. 114 does not refer to Customs
duties the States could have crippled the Commonwealth by
duties in the interval. Sec. 55 of the Constitution speaks

(1) 12 Wheat., 419, at p. 437.   (2) 1902 St. R. Qd., 261, at p. 271.

of Customs duties as taxation. If the words are ambiguous, the
section being one that confers an exemption should be construed
liberally in favour of the exemption.

ATTORNEY-
GENERAL OF
N.S.W.
v.
COLLECTOR OF
CUSTOMS FOR
N.S.W.

[HIGGINS J. referred to *Armytage* v. *Wilkinson* (1).]   ·

On the question whether the Crown was bound by the *Customs Act*, counsel adopted the argument used in *The King* v. *Sutton* (2).

Gordon K.C. and *Cullen* K.C. (*Bavin* with them), for the defendant. If the rule in *D'Emden* v. *Pedder* (3) is applicable to this case, it cannot be limited to the case of railways. It must logically be extended to all State functions, so as to render inoperative all Commonwealth legislation so far as it affects goods imported for any of those services. The State alone is entitled to say whether a particular thing is necessary for the performance of any State function. Even the quarantine and immigration laws would be subject to an exception in favour of State Governments. The fallacy lies in assuming that the rule applies before considering the nature of the powers in question. If exclusive, or paramount power is given to the Commonwealth in respect of any subject matter, that subject matter is thereby wholly withdrawn from the power of the State. If that power cannot be effectively exercised to the extent to which it has been conferred without in some degree trenching upon the powers that the State Governments previously enjoyed, then it must be taken that the legislature intended that the Commonwealth should have power to interfere to that extent with the State powers, and, therefore, there can be no implied prohibition of interference. It may be conceded that the acquisition of steel rails by the States is a necessary means for carrying on its railways, which are admittedly one of its instrumentalities within the meaning of the authorities. It may also be conceded that Customs duties are an interference with the acquisition of the rails, and to that extent an interference with the free exercise of the State function. But such an interference is necessarily included in the exercise by the Commonwealth of its Customs power. The grant of the power to the Common-

(1) 3 App. Cas., 355.   (2) 5 C.L.R., 789.   (3) 1 C.L.R., 91.

H. C. of A.
1908.

ATTORNEY-
GENERAL OF
N.S.W.
v.
COLLECTOR OF
CUSTOMS FOR
N.S.W.

wealth necessarily implies a limitation of the State power. *M'Culloch* v. *Maryland* (1), has, therefore, no application. The power of taxation through the Customs is not dependent upon the power conferred by sec. 51 (II.). It also falls under the trade and commerce power, sec. 51 (I.). The existence of the federal power to regulate trade and commerce with other countries is wholly inconsistent with the existence of any power at all in the States with regard to such matters. The rule in *D'Emden* v. *Pedder* (2) can only apply in cases where both State and Commonwealth have some power, and the question is how far the power of each extends. It is a mere rule of construction. It does not apply to prevent the exercise of what is clearly intended to be an exclusive or paramount power in the Commonwealth. If such a power is clearly conferred then everything necessary to make it effective is conferred with it. *South Carolina* v. *United States* (3) merely decided that the federal power of taxation did not extend to certain objects; it has no application to the exercise of the power given by sec. 51 (I.). The prime object of the Constitution was that the whole Commonwealth should speak with one voice on questions of trade and commerce with other countries and between the States. Uniformity would be impossible if the Commonwealth legislation could be deranged by the operations of the State Governments.

As to the meaning of sec. 114, the only authority is the dictum of *Stephen* J. in *Attorney-General* v. *Collector of Customs* (4), to the effect that the section does not apply to Customs duties. " Tax on any kind of property " means a tax in respect of the ownership, possession or enjoyment of property. A Customs duty is not such a tax, if it can be called a tax at all. It is a tax upon the operation of bringing goods into the country. It is indirect taxation, whereas a tax on property in the ordinary sense is a direct tax. It may be that sec. 114 does not refer to duties of Excise, which are not taxes on property, but it is not necessary to argue that in this case. Customs duties are imposed wholly irrespective of ownership, possession or enjoyment. The fact that the *Customs Act* and the *Customs Tariff* speak of duties

(1) 4 Wheat., 316.
(2) 1 C.L.R., 91.

(3) 199 U.S., 437.
(4) (1903) 3 S.R. (N.S.W.), 115.

being imposed on the goods is not conclusive as to the interpretation of sec. 114. For the purpose of those Acts the expression
is sufficiently accurate. There is a clear distinction between a Attorney-
tax on property and a tax on dealings with property : *Knowlton* General of
N.S.W.
v. *Moore* (1); *Snyder* v. *Bettmann* (2); *Magoun* v. *Illinois Trust* v.
Collector of
and Savings Bank (3); *Commonwealth* v. *State of New South* Customs for
N.S.W.
Wales* (4).

[GRIFFITH C.J. referred to *United States* v. *Perkins* (5).]

Such taxes are regarded rather as conditions imposed by the
legislating authority upon the right to deal in certain ways with
property. So the payment of Customs duty is a condition imposed by the Commonwealth upon the right to bring in the
goods. *Brown* v. *Maryland* (6) merely decided that the licence
fee was an infringement of the prohibition against taxing imports, it did not decide that it was a tax upon property. [They
referred also to *Welton* v. *Missouri* (7); *Sutherland, Notes on
the United States' Constitution*, p. 86.]

[ISAACS J. referred to *Hamel on Law of Customs*, p. 29 ; *Western Union Telegraph Company* v. *Texas* (8); *Marriott* v. *Brune*
(9); *Algoma Central Railway Co.* v. *The King* (10).]

Even if the words "tax on property" in sec. 114 considered
alone are capable of the wider meaning so as to include duties of
Customs, they are capable of a narrower construction which is
more consistent with the context in which they are used. If
they are construed in the wider sense they come into direct conflict with the provisions of sec. 51 (I.) and 51 (II.). If possible,
they should be construed so as to harmonize with the rest of the
Constitution. The narrower meaning "tax on property as property" avoids that conflict and should be adopted, as better
carrying out the intention of the legislature. [They referred
to *D'Emden* v. *Pedder* (11); *Municipal Council of Sydney* v.
The Commonwealth (12).] The weakness of the plaintiff's argument is that he has to admit a limitation of the operation of sec.
114 to property of the States used in connection with State

(1) 178 U.S., 41.
(2) 190 U.S., 249.
(3) 170 U.S., 283.
(4) 3 C.L.R., 807.
(5) 163 U.S., 625.
(6) 12 Wheat., 419.

(7) 91 U.S., 275.
(8) 105 U.S., 460, at p. 465.
(9) 9 How., 619, at p. 631.
(10) (1903) A.C., 478.
(11) 1 C.L.R., 91, at p. 108.
(12) 1 C.L.R., 208, at p. 231.

H. C. OF A.
1908.

ATTORNEY-
GENERAL OF
N.S.W.
v.
COLLECTOR OF
CUSTOMS FOR
N.S.W.

functions. [They referred also to *Head Money Cases* (1); *Case of the State Tax on Railway Gross Receipts* (2); *Coe* v. *Town of Errol* (3); *Quick & Gurran, Constitution of the Commonwealth*, p. 539; *Story on the Constitution*, 5th ed., p. 35.]

[BARTON J. referred to *Case of the State Freight Tax* (4).

ISAACS J. referred to *Story on the Constitution*, p. 949.]

Pilcher K.C., in reply. The powers conferred by the Constitution are to be gathered from all the sections which refer to those powers, not only from that which confers the power in general terms. It may be assumed that sec. 114 was intended to prohibit some form of taxation included in sec. 51; otherwise it would not have been necessary. The nature of the power is shown by both sections together. No part of the Constitution is stronger than another. The prohibition of a tax should be construed in the wider sense unless there is very strong reason to the contrary. Customs duties are universally regarded as taxes on the goods. The importation is the occasion of paying them, but, on the only reasonable construction, they are "upon" the goods, *i.e.*, upon the person in respect of the goods. [He referred to *Encyclopædia of Law of Procedure U.S.*, 2nd ed., vol. XII., p. 1108, "Customs Duties"; *Story on the Constitution*, p. 949; 1 *Blac. Comm.*, p. 313; *Bank of Toronto* v. *Lambe* (5); *Municipal Council of Sydney* v. *Commonwealth* (6); *Customs Act* 1901, secs. 131, 133, 153; *Customs Tariff*, sec. 5; *Baker, Annotated Constitution*, pp. 16, 19.]

[ISAACS J. referred to *Quinn* v. *Leathem* (7); *Bates' Case* (8); *Broom Constitutional Law* (1866), p. 247; *Acts Interpretation Act* 1901, secs. 2, 22; *Magdalen College Case* (9).]

As to the rule in *D'Emden* v. *Pedder* (10), the power to impose stamp duty, which was in question in *Commonwealth* v. *State of New South Wales* (11), was given to the State in terms no less general than those which confer the taxation powers on the Commonwealth. There is no substantial distinction between the

(1) 112 U.S., 580.
(2) 15 Wall., 284.
(3) 116 U.S., 517.
(4) 15 Wall., 232.
(5) 12 App. Cas., 575.
(6) 1 C.L.R., 208, at p. 230.

(7) (1901) A.C., 495.
(8) 2 St. Tri., 371.
(9) 11 Rep., 66.
(10) 1 C.L.R., 91.
(11) 3 C.L.R., 807.

cases as regards the applicability of the rule. If Customs duties can be levied on State property so can Excise. Each is an exercise of the taxing power, and each is opposed to the principle of *D'Emden* v. *Pedder* (1). The one is as great an interference as the other, and is equally withdrawn from the taxing power. [They referred to *South Carolina* v. *United States* (2); *Deakin* v. *Webb* (3); *Van Brocklin* v. *Tennessee* (4); *Master Retailers' Association of N.S.W.* v. *Shop Assistants Union of N.S.W.* (5).

[Isaacs J. referred to *United States* v. *Lutz* (6).]

H. C. of A.
1908.

ATTORNEY-
GENERAL OF
N.S.W.
v.
COLLECTOR OF
CUSTOMS FOR
N.S.W.

Cur. adv. vult.

The following judgments were read:—

GRIFFITH C.J. The plaintiff contends that the steel rails in question, which were purchased in England and imported into New South Wales for the use of the State in the construction of State railways, are not liable to Customs duties. The grounds taken in the special case are:—(1) That the rails were the property of His Majesty, and that the Sovereign is not bound by the Customs Acts; and (2) That the rails were exempt from duty by virtue of sec. 114 of the Constitution.

May 23.

The first ground has been sufficiently dealt with in the case of *The King* v. *Sutton* (7), and I do not think it necessary to add anything on this point.

The point raised under sec. 114 is a more difficult one. That section provides that "A State shall not . . . impose any tax on property of any kind belonging to the Commonwealth, nor shall the Commonwealth impose any tax on property of any kind belonging to a State." The Attorney-General says that the rails in question are property of the State of New South Wales, that duties of Customs are a tax on property, and that the rails are therefore exempt. The defendant answers that duties of Customs are not a tax imposed on property in the sense in which those words are used in that section, and, further, that the section applies only to property already within the limits of

(1) 1 C.L.R., 91.
(2) 199 U.S., 437, at pp. 453, 459.
(3) 1 C.L.R., 585, at p. 611.
(4) 117 U.S., 151.

(5) 2 C.L.R., 94, at p. 107.
(6) 2 Blatchford, 383.
(7) 5 C.L.R., 789.

H. C. of A.
1908.

ATTORNEY-
GENERAL OF
N.S.W.
v.
COLLECTOR OF
CUSTOMS FOR
N.S.W.

Griffith C.J.

the Commonwealth, and not to goods in process of coming within those limits. It is pointed out that, if full effect were given to the Attorney-General's contention, it would be in the power of the States by becoming general importers of goods seriously to impair, and indeed practically destroy, the Customs revenue of the Commonwealth, and, further, that the power of the Commonwealth with regard to external trade would, so far as it is exercised by means of duties of Customs, be in reality, although declared to be paramount, subject to unlimited interference from the States. Reference was made on both sides to the case of *South Carolina* v. *United States* (1) in which the extent of the prohibition of taxation by Congress of the property of the States, which is held to be implied by the Constitution, was much debated. Counsel for the Attorney-General were disposed to concede that the express prohibition of sec. 114 must be limited, as the majority of the Supreme Court of the United States held in the case just cited with regard to the implied prohibition, to property employed in the ordinary affairs of government as understood at the date of the establishment of the Commonwealth. There are, however, difficulties in the way of implying any such limitation upon the terms of sec. 114, just as there are (as was pointed out in the *Federated Amalgamated Government Railway and Tramway Service Association* v. *New South Wales Railway Traffic Employés Association* (2)) in the way of saying that any function which a Sovereign Government assumes to exercise within the limits of its powers is not an ordinary function of government. But, even with this limitation, the prohibition of the section would extend to duties upon goods imported for the purposes of government departments, such as the Public Works and Education Departments, the Printing Office, Gaols, Police, Asylums, and many others, and this, whether the goods were directly imported into the State itself or through another State, as for instance, through Port Pirie in South Australia in transit to Broken Hill in New South Wales, or through Brisbane in Queensland in transit to the Northern Districts of New South Wales.

The defendant points out that the power to impose taxation con-

(1) 199 U.S., 437.   (2) 4 C.L.R., 488, at p. 539.

ferred by sec. 51 (II.), as well as the power to regulate importation conferred by sec. 51 (I.), are paramount, and are in form unlimited, and that they apply as well to the Governments of the States as to private persons (as was held in *The King* v. *Sutton* (1)). If, then, the construction sought to be put upon sec. 114 by the Attorney-General is correct, there is an apparent contradiction of a very serious character. If, however, the words of sec. 114 are capable of a construction consistent with giving full effect to the plain intention of sec. 51 (I., II.), that construction should be preferred.

Sec. 114 must, no doubt, be construed as an exception from sec. 51 (II.), but the extent of the exception is the point to be determined.

Are then the words of sec. 114 capable of two constructions? There is no doubt that in some contexts the words "impose any tax" might be capable of application to duties of Customs. Nor is there any doubt that the word "taxation" in sec. 51 (II.) includes the levying of duties of Customs. But these duties are nowhere in the Constitution described as a "tax," unless the use of the word "taxation" in sec. 51 (I.) is such a description of them; nor is the levying of them ever spoken of as the imposition of a tax on property. Sec. 86 speaks of "the collection and control of duties of Customs and of Excise." Secs. 88, 89, 90, 92, 93, 94, 95, all speak of the "imposition" of duties of Customs. Such duties are imposed in respect of "goods" and in one sense, no doubt, "upon" goods, which is only another way of saying that the word "upon" is sometimes used as synonymous with "in respect of." In the same way the word "upon" or "on" is used colloquially in speaking of stamp duties, succession duties, and other forms of indirect taxation, as taxes on deeds, &c., or on real and personal property. Yet it is recognized that these forms of taxation are not really taxation upon property but upon operations or movements of property. See, for instance, the cases of *The Attorney-General for Quebec* v. *Queen Insurance Co.* (2), and *United States* v. *Perkins* (3). In the last mentioned case it was held

H. C. of A.
1908.

ATTORNEY-
GENERAL OF
N.S.W.
v.
COLLECTOR OF
CUSTOMS FOR
N.S.W.

Griffith C.J.

(1) 5 C.L.R., 789.　　　　　(2) 3 App. Cas., 1090.
　　　　　　　　(3) 163 U.S., 625.

H. C. of A.
1908.

ATTORNEY-
GENERAL OF
N.S.W.
v.
COLLECTOR OF
CUSTOMS FOR
N.S.W.

Griffith C.J.

that a succession duty is not, in substance, a tax upon property, and consequently that the imposition by a State of such a duty in respect of property bequeathed to the United States was not obnoxious to the rule, implied under the Constitution, that a State cannot tax the property of the United States. After referring to some decisions of State Courts to the same effect the judgment of the Court proceeded (1):—" Such a tax was also held by this Court to be free from any constitutional objection in *Mager* v. *Grima* (2), Mr. Chief Justice *Taney* remarking that ' the law in question is nothing more than an exercise of the power which every State and sovereignty possesses, of regulating the manner and terms within which property, real and personal, within its dominions may be transferred by last will and testament, or by inheritance ; and of prescribing who shall and who shall not be capable of taking it. . . . If a State may deny the privilege altogether, it follows that when it grants it, it may annex to the grant any conditions which it supposes to be required by its interests or policy.' To the same effect is *United States* v. *Fox* (3). We think that it follows from this that the Act in question is not open to the objection that it is an attempt to tax the property of the United States, since the tax is imposed upon the legacy before it reaches the hands of the government. The legacy becomes the property of the United States only after it has suffered a diminution to the amount of the tax, and it is only upon this condition that the legislature assents to a bequest of it."

So far there seems no reason to suppose that the word "tax" was used, inexactly, in sec. 114 to denote duties of Customs.

The distinction between direct and indirect taxation is well enough known. Direct taxation is taxation by way of pecuniary payments directly imposed in respect of persons or things subject to the jurisdiction of the taxing authority, and the burden of which is designed to fall upon the taxpayer himself. Such taxes in respect of things are frequently, and not inaccurately, called property taxes, or taxes " on " property. Common instances are land tax and municipal rates. Similar taxes levied *ad valorem*

---

(1) 163 U.S., 625, at p. 629.   (2) 8 How., 490, 493.
                     (3) 94 U.S., 315.

upon the value of personal property were for many years imposed
in New Zealand and in many of the States of the American Union.
The Canadian Constitution (*British North America Act*, sec. 125)
provides that no lands or property belonging to Canada or any Province shall be liable to taxation. The powers of the Provinces being
limited to imposing direct taxation, the meaning of the prohibition
as regards them is not open to controversy.   With regard to the
power of the Dominion, however, it might have been contended
that the prohibition extended to indirect taxation through the
Customs of goods belonging to the Provinces.   We are informed
that it is the universal practice in Canada to levy Customs duties
on such goods.   Several Statutes of the United States were also
referred to, in which a remission of Customs duties upon State
property is expressly authorized. These instances appear to show
that in the United States and Canada, at all events, the prohibition
(in one case implied and in the other express) of the taxation of
State or Provincial property has never been understood as applying
to duties of Customs.

Again, the words " property belonging to the Commonwealth,"
" property belonging to a State," seem, *primâ facie*, to import
property lying and being within the Commonwealth. Neither the
Commonwealth nor a State can impose a tax upon property which
is not within the geographical limits of its jurisdiction.   Even if
they can impose a tax upon a resident in respect of property situated elsewhere, such a tax is a personal tax, and cannot be properly
regarded as a tax upon his property. It was contended, however,
that duties of Customs are a tax upon property within the Commonwealth, since the goods must have been imported before the
liability to duty can arise.   But this, although true in one sense,
is not true in any relevant sense.   The payment of the Customs
duty is an obligation or condition which must be fulfilled before
the goods can lawfully form part of the stock or mass of goods
in the country, although for convenience they are allowed to be
retained in bond in a King's warehouse until payment. Adapting
the words of Chief Justice *Taney*, cited in *Perkin's Case* (1),
I say that a Customs law from this point of view is nothing more
than an exercise of the power the Commonwealth possesses of

(1) 163 U.S., 625, at p. 629.

H. C. of A.   regulating the manner and terms on which goods may be brought
1908.   into the Commonwealth.

ATTORNEY-   For these reasons I am of opinion that the levying of duties of
GENERAL OF   Customs on importation is not the imposition of a tax upon
N.S.W.
v.   property within the primary and literal meaning of sec. 114,
COLLECTOR OF
CUSTOMS FOR   standing alone. I am further of opinion that, even if it is an
N.S.W.   imposition of a tax on property within the primary and literal

Griffith C.J.   meaning of that section, yet that meaning is not the only or the
necessary meaning, and that, for the reasons already given, it
must be rejected as being inconsistent with other plain provisions
of the Constitution. I think, therefore, that sec. 114 does not
apply to duties of Customs. This was the view taken by
Stephen Acting C.J. in the case of *Attorney-General* v. *Collector
of Customs* (1).

A further argument was addressed to us based upon the
doctrine laid down by this Court in the case of *D'Emden* v.
Pedder (2) and re-affirmed in *Baxter* v. *Commissioner of Taxation
(N.S.W.)* (3), " that when a State attempts to give to its legislative
or executive authority an operation which, if valid, would fetter,
control, or interfere with, the free exercise of the legislative or
executive power of the Commonwealth, the attempt, unless
expressly authorized by the Constitution, is to that extent
invalid and inoperative," which was applied by this Court in the
*Federated Amalgamated Government Railway Service Associa-
tion* v. *New South Wales Railway Traffic Employés Association*
(4) to the case of interference by the Commonwealth with State
instrumentalities. It was contended that the importation of
railway material from beyond the Commonwealth is, or may be
(as to which the State is the sole judge), necessary for the efficient
construction and carrying on of State railways, and that the
imposition of duties of Customs upon such importation is consequently a control of, or interference with, a State function.
This argument, if valid, applies, as already pointed out, to all
goods which any State may think fit to import into any part of
the Commonwealth for the purposes of any department of the
State.

(1) (1903) 3 S.R. (N.S.W.), 115.   (3) 4 C.L.R., 1087, at p. 1132.
(2) 1 C.L.R., 91.   (4) 4 C.L.R., 488.

H. C. of A.
1908.

ATTORNEY-
GENERAL OF
N.S.W.
v.
COLLECTOR OF
CUSTOMS FOR
N.S.W.

Griffith C.J.

The doctrine relied upon is, as has several times been pointed out by this Court, a rule of construction founded upon necessity. In one aspect it is analogous to the rule that the Crown is not bound by a Statute unless it appears on the face of the Statute that it was intended that the Crown should be bound. The word " expressly," as used in the rule, does not, of course, mean that the power to be interfered with must be mentioned *eo nomine*. If a power conferred upon the Commonwealth in express terms is of such a nature that its effective exercise manifestly involves a control of some operation of a State Government the doctrine has no application to that operation. Sec. 51 of the Constitution confers upon the Parliament many powers of this nature, *e.g.*, the power to control quarantine (IX.), weights and measures (XV.), immigration (XXVII.). The power to make laws respecting trade and commerce with other countries and among the States (I.) is of the same kind, and necessarily involves the power to interfere with the operations of the State Governments so far as to make effectual any condition or prohibition imposed by the Commonwealth upon importation. Taxation by means of Customs duties is in law, as well as in fact, a mode of regulating trade with other countries. It follows that it was the intention of the legislature that the right of State Governments to import goods should be subject to the control of the Commonwealth, so that the rule in *D'Emden* v. *Pedder* (1) has no application.

Moreover, the rule, as hitherto stated, has reference only to the performance of the functions of government within the Commonwealth, beyond which the functions of a State Government, *quâ* Government, do not extend. Although, therefore, the rule prohibits the Commonwealth in certain cases from interfering with the free exercise of the executive powers of a State within the State in making use of any means or instrumentalities lawfully at its command, it has nothing to say to the question whether any specific thing may be brought within the State so as to become such a means or instrumentality. The interference complained of in the *Federated Amalgamated Government Railway Service Association* v. *New South Wales Railway Traffic Employés Association* (2) related to a function performed wholly

(1) 1 C.L.R., 91.   (2) 4 C.L.R., 488.

H. C. of A.
1908.

ATTORNEY-
GENERAL OF
N.S.W.
v.
COLLECTOR OF
CUSTOMS FOR
N.S.W.

Barton J.

within the State, and as to which the Court thought that no power to interfere was given either expressly or by necessary implication. That case, therefore, has no application to the present.

For these reasons I think that our judgment must be for the defendant.

BARTON J. In the case of *The King* v. *Sutton* (1) judgments were delivered yesterday by the several members of this Court which relieve us from giving extended reasons for our opinion that in this case question 1, (paragraph 11 of the special case) must be answered in the affirmative. I desire, however, to add a few words before passing to the other questions. In addition to the power of taxation, exclusive as to the Customs (sec. 90), the power of regulating commerce with other countries and among the States is conferred on the Commonwealth. That power is inherently exclusive so far at the least that it cannot be exercised by any single State so as to operate generally. Its exercise, therefore, as regards the conditions on which trade with other countries may be regulated, on even terms as to all parts of the Commonwealth, must be exclusive. For this position authority is unnecessary, although it abounds. The commerce power, indeed, is the real authority for the prohibition of any particular importation, and is largely interwoven with the sole power to impose import duties in the practical regulation of importation. Now, taking the two powers together, with the light thrown on them by sec. 112, it clearly appears to have been the intention of the Constitution to place under the control of one Parliament the entire subject of imports, (I restrict this statement to the mere necessity of the occasion) and the decision, what should be admitted or excluded, and what should be the terms of admission. That being so, and bearing in mind that every grant of power carries with it all necessary protection for its effective exercise, can it be supposed that concurrently with such granted control a licence was given to the Executive of each State to nullify the prohibitions or defeat the exercise of the regulative discretion of the Federal Parliament ? Consider the effect

(1) 5 C.L.R., 789.

of such a constructive licence. With what approach to uniformity or consistency—the very objects of their existence—could the express and exclusive powers of the Australian union be exercised? Without attempting to discuss the inevitable results in the case of other federal powers, can it be said that a fiscal or a commercial policy of common value to the whole people could be even framed—much less carried into effect—by any Federal Government or Parliament? The slightest consideration must convince the impartial mind that the construction under which it would be, not only possible, but easy to paralyse the most vital of federal powers, is not within the bounds of reason.

If the right claimed were once conceded, it would be in the hand of one State to establish a discrimination between other States and herself with the object of discouraging commerce with one neighbour or encouraging it with another, or of gaining an advantage over her sisters by importing free the raw material of an internal industry of her own, to the defeat of that equality of unhampered interchange between the States which was one of the first objects of the people in federating. And the prohibition imposed on the federal power by sub-sec. (II.) of sec. 51 could be nullified at the will of every State in turn Moreover, the chief use of the power of Customs regulation, and one of the chief uses of the commerce power— namely, the raising of a revenue for the support of the general government—would be frustrated by the exercise of the licence claimed, to the maiming if not the ruin of that revenue. This Court stated the principle truly when it said, in *D'Emden* v. *Pedder* (1):—" With respect, however, to matters within the exclusive competence of the Federal Parliament no question of conflict can arise, inasmuch as from the point at which the quality of exclusiveness attaches to the federal power the competency of the States is altogether extinguished." And, inasmuch as this principle in its fulness is an essential condition of the safety of the Constitution, the reasons for its maintenance are in my judgment as applicable to the claim put forward in question 1, as to the question of instrumentalities of government, when once the field of action is granted to the federation *exclusively*.

(1) 1 C.L.R., 91, at p. 111.

H. C. of A.
1908.

ATTORNEY-
GENERAL OF
N.S.W.
v.
COLLECTOR OF
CUSTOMS FOR
N.S.W.

Barton J.

H. C. of A.
1908.

ATTORNEY-
GENERAL OF
N.S.W.
v.
COLLECTOR OF
CUSTOMS FOR
N.S.W.

Barton J.

I pass now to consider the contention that State railways have become, as was decided by this Court in the case of the *Federated Amalgamated Government Railway and Tramway Service Association* v. *New South Wales Railway Traffic Employés Association* (1), instruments in the carrying on of State governmental functions; that the acquisition of rails for the purposes of such railroads is a means of performing that function; that the exaction of Customs duty on the import of rails intended for such roads is an interference with the performance of the function, and that there is no express or necessarily implied power in the Constitution warranting the interference. Mr. *Knox* truly said that, unless the power were found, the interference, if there is one, is unconstitutional. The following words in the judgment of the Supreme Court of the United States, spoken by *Brewer* J., exactly apply. In a dual system of government, "There are certain matters over which the national government has absolute control, and no action of the State can interfere therewith, and there are others in which the State is supreme, and in respect to them the national government is powerless": *South Carolina* v. *United States* (2). Where a grant of power is made, this leading principle dictates its scope. If the grant is exclusive the control is absolute. Any action by the State, such as the attempted importation of goods, without observance of the condition which the grantee of the absolute control has imposed, is itself an interference with the exercise of the control. In this case the condition is the payment of the duty prescribed.

Further, I am of opinion that the State has not made out its claim to have these rails considered an instrument of its governing functions. It cannot be contended that the Government of New South Wales has any extra-territorial powers. But to sustain the claim made, the very purchase of the rails in England, or perhaps Belgium, and their transmission, would have to be considered as exercises of governing power. At what stage before their incorporation in the railroad itself they would begin to be a means of Government it is difficult to see. The railways themselves, including their rolling stock, are such; but can we go further? I for one find it hard to say at what earlier point

(1) 4 C.L.R., 488   (2) 199 U.S., 437, at p. 448.

the instrumentality begins, unless we go to the quite unwarranted length of determining that its starting point is the purchase abroad. But, however that may be, the doctrine of State instrumentality cannot be held to cut down by implication a federal power where that power is by the terms of its grant exclusive.

H. C. of A.
1908.

ATTORNEY-
GENERAL OF
N.S.W.
v.
COLLECTOR OF
CUSTOMS FOR
N.S.W.

Barton J.

Now as to sec. 114 of the Constitution. I must first guard myself against being supposed to agree with Mr. *Pilcher* that the prohibition applies only to property of Commonwealth or State which is a means or agency of Government as ordinarily understood. That position may be correct. On the other hand, it may be that the framers of the Constitution intended to protect all such property as either power might have or acquire, whether used or not in the ordinary essential functions of Government. There is this difficulty in the way of that construction. As their respective Constitutions stand it is open to the States to acquire and hold property for purposes without number. That is not so in the case of the Commonwealth, and in that aspect sec. 114 would scarcely seem to be a compact fair to the Commonwealth. On the other hand, as Mr. *Gordon* urged, if the prohibition in sec. 114 is co-extensive with the effect of the " instrumentality " doctrine, there does not appear to have been much reason for its insertion, inasmuch as the doctrine itself involves the implication of such a prohibition to the extent of the property used for governmental purposes. If then there was reason for the express provision, as *primâ facie* one would suppose, should it be limited in the way suggested ?

It is not necessary to decide that question in the present case, so I leave it open as far as I am concerned.

The effect which the plaintiff seeks to give sec. 114 is that a " tax on property " within the meaning of that section includes duties of Customs, and hence that these rails were exempt. To sustain this position it is necessary to show more than that the words of the section are capable of including Customs duties. It must be shown that the words do include such duties, so as to form an exception from the Customs power elsewhere expressed to be exclusive. First, there is the obstacle that the Constitution will primarily be taken to mean different expressions in different senses. Where import duties have been indicated the Constitution

H. C. of A.
1908.

Attorney
General of
N.S.W.
v.
Collector of
Customs for
N.S.W.

Barton J.

has elsewhere uniformly used the term "duties of Customs."
There is but one exception, and that is clearly by way of distinction.
It is in sec. 112. There, after describing the federal import duties
as "uniform duties of Customs"—an oft-recurring expression in
this document—a State is authorized to levy, subject to annul-
ment by the Federal Parliament, "on imports or exports, or on
goods passing into or out of the State"—that is by inter-state
traffic—"such *charges* as may be necessary for executing the
inspection laws of the State," and the net produce of "all charges
so levied" is to be for the use of the Commonwealth. Observe
that what would before Federation have been a Customs duty
imposed by a State becomes, in contradistinction to a Customs
duty imposed by the Commonwealth, a charge levied by a State
on imports or on goods passing into the State. There is
here a close attention to the change of conditions, and with it a
strict distinction between the federal duty on imports—the
"duty of Customs imposed"—and the limited State impost,—
the charge on imports, &c., levied. It seems, in view of
such nicety of distinction, more reasonable to infer that the
terms, "duties of Customs" and "tax on property" were
intentionally differentiated, than to infer that in the section next
but one following that marked by such careful distinctions, a
clumsy blunder in drafting should have been made. It is true
that the general power in sec. 51 (II.) is conferred in the word
"taxation." But that is probably the only word which would
include the four classes of burdens which the corresponding
power in the United States Constitution has categorically
termed "taxes, duties, imposts and excises." But where the
generic term is abandoned for a specific one, the Australian
Constitution carefully and distinctively points to the specific
class of burden that it permits or forbids. Sec. 55 is an instance
of the use of both the generic and the specific in their places;
and sec 53 is an instance of the generic only.

If, however, the words "tax on property of any kind" in sec.
114 raise an ambiguity, then that is solvable according to
ordinary principles. Looking at the fact that the powers to
impose Customs duties and to regulate commerce with other
countries are exclusive, to construe sec. 114 in the way contended

H. C. of A.
1908.

ATTORNEY-
GENERAL OF
N.S.W.
v.
COLLECTOR OF
CUSTOMS FOR
N.S.W.

Barton J.

for would be to cut down in that section what the exclusive grant in itself involves, namely, the absolute power to select the subjects and prescribe the quantum of Customs duty. This is so improbable a construction that I think the words must be construed in a sense at least more usual and more ordinary than that which the plaintiff attributes to them. Although the Customs duty may be in fact imposed " on " the article itself, as contended on an elaborate analysis of the judgment of *Marshall* C.J. in *Brown* v. *Maryland* (1), and although the goods which pass the Customs after entry may be " property," yet it is not usual to call a duty of Customs a tax on property, or indeed to call a tax on property a duty of Customs, when one finds either term standing by itself in a document. But when one finds the two terms in the same document he is the less likely to use them interchangeably, unless indeed he finds them so used in the context, or unless the context supplies some other good reason for inferring a looseness of expression.

I will not further deal with sec. 114, of which my learned brother the Chief Justice has given so full an exposition. My observations on it would have been briefer had not this case demanded our closest attention, both from its present importance and from its necessary bearing on the future government of Australia.

I am of opinion that our answers should be : To the first question, yes, observing that the expression " the Crown " there used is really a misnomer for the State, which is in substance the plaintiff: to the second question, no : and to the third question, yes : and that judgment should be for the defendant on the whole case.

O'CONNOR J. The matter in controversy is whether the Commonwealth Customs Department are entitled to charge the Government of New South Wales with Customs duties on certain steel rails the property of and imported by that Government for use on the railways of the State. The parties have agreed that their rights are to be determined in accordance with the view which the Court may take of the following questions of law submitted for decision in the special case :—

(1) 12 Wheat., 419.

H. C. OF A.
1908.

ATTORNEY-
GENERAL OF
N.S.W.
v.
COLLECTOR OF
CUSTOMS FOR
N.S.W.

O'Connor J.

(1) Do the provisions of the *Customs Act* 1901, and the *Customs Tariff* 1902, affect the Crown as representing the community of New South Wales in the sense that those provisions require the Crown to pay duties of Customs under the circumstances stated above?

(2) Were the steel rails exempt from duties of Customs by virtue of sec. 114 of the Constitution?

(3) Were the said steel rails liable to duties of Customs?

The first question is answered by the judgment of the Court in *The King* v. *Sutton* (1), delivered by this Court at its present sittings. For the reasons there stated that question must be answered in the affirmative.

The considerations involved in the third question make it convenient for the purposes of my judgment to deal next with that. In putting it in the broad form adopted the parties have asked the Court to view the matter apart from the provisions of sec. 114 of the Constitution. The plaintiff rests his case upon the principle expounded by this Court in *D'Emden* v. *Pedder* (2), and applied in several cases since then, notably in that of the *Federated Amalgamated Government Railway and Tramway Service Association* v. *The New South Wales Railway Traffic Employés Association* (3). In the case last named the principle is thus stated in the judgment of the Court, quoting *D'Emden* v. *Pedder* (4), as follows (5): — "It follows that when a State attempts to give to its legislative or executive authority an operation which, if valid, would fetter, control, or interfere with, the free exercise of the legislative or executive power of the Commonwealth, the attempt, unless expressly authorized by the Constitution, is to that extent invalid and inoperative. And this appears to be the true test to be applied in determining the validity of State laws and their applicability to federal transactions."

The judgment goes on to point out that, although in *D'Emden* v. *Pedder* (1) the question was as to an attempted invasion of the ambit of Commonwealth authority by a State authority, the

---

(1) 5 C.L.R., 789.   (4) 1 C.L.R., 91, at p. 111.
(2) 1 C.L.R., 91.   (5) 4 C.L.R., 488, at p. 537.
(3) 4 C.L.R., 488.

doctrine was equally applicable in the converse case where there was an attempt by the Commonwealth to invade the ambit of the State authority. Taking that principle as applicable, the plaintiff's contention is that the Government railway system is an instrumentality employed in the carrying out of one of the functions of the State Government, and that the imposition of a Customs duty on the rails required in the working of that system is such an interference with the exercise of the function as must be taken to have been impliedly prohibited by the Constitution. Since the judgment of this Court in the case of the *Federated Amalgamated Government Railway and Tramway Service Association* v. *The New South Wales Traffic Employés Association* (1) it must be taken as authoritatively settled that the systems of State railways in each State are governmental functions of the State, recognized as such by the Constitution. It may also be conceded for the purposes of the argument that the imposition of Customs duties on the importation by the State of rails the property of the State amounts to an interference with the unfettered exercise of the State's power of purchasing rails outside Australia. But before the principle can be applied we must ascertain by a consideration of the Constitution as a whole the extent of the Commonwealth power to impose duties on importation. In this connection must be borne in mind the maxim referred to in the judgment in *D'Emden* v. *Pedder* (2):—
" It is only necessary to mention the maxim, *quando lex aliquid concedit, concedere videtur et illud sine quo res ipsa valere non potest.* In other words, where any power or control is expressly granted, there is included in the grant, to the full extent of the capacity of the grantor, and without special mention, every power and every control the denial of which would render the grant itself ineffective."

The power to levy duties of Customs is conferred by two subsections of sec. 51 of the Constitution. It is included in the word " Taxation " in sub-sec. (II.), construing that word in its widest sense. It is also an exercise of the power to make laws relating to trade and commerce with other countries (sub-sec. (I.)). The language of these sub-sections is certainly wide enough to

H. C. of A.
1908.

ATTORNEY-
GENERAL OF
N.S.W.
v.
COLLECTOR OF
CUSTOMS FOR
N.S.W.

O'Connor J.

(1) 4 C.L.R., 488.   (2) 1 C.L.R., 91, at p. 109.

H. C. of A.
1908.

ATTORNEY-
GENERAL OF
N.S.W.
v.
COLLECTOR OF
CUSTOMS FOR
N.S.W.

O'Connor J.

cover the imposition of duties on the property of a State even on property necessary for the carrying out of the governmental functions of a State.

But it is urged that the interpretation of the general words used in their wider sense will bring about such an interference with the right reserved to the State to manage its own railways that the Court, applying the doctrine in *D'Emden* v. *Pedder* (1), will read the words in a sense sufficiently restricted as to preserve the uninterrupted exercise of the State power as it was before the inauguration of the Commonwealth. In my opinion, that contention cannot be maintained. In the distribution which the Constitution effects of all the governmental powers of the Australian people between the Commonwealth and the States some powers are left to the States complete and uncontrolled, and some are transferred to the Commonwealth, but amongst those powers left to the States some must necessarily be reserved in a restricted form. Wherever it is necessary for the effective exercise of a Commonwealth power that a State power should be restricted, it must be taken that the Constitution intended that it was to be reserved to the State in that restricted form. In such case the general words conferring the Commonwealth power will be interpreted in the wider and not in the narrower sense. It is therefore essential at the outset to see what is necessary for the effective exercise of the Commonwealth power to impose Customs duties and to regulate trade and commerce with foreign countries. In this connection the other powers expressly conferred on the Commonwealth may be considered, and, taken as a whole, they vest in the Commonwealth the power of controlling in every respect Australia's relations with the outside world. The control of trade and commerce with other countries, the imposition of Customs duties, immigration, quarantine, and external affairs, are all different aspects of Australia's relations with other countries. The manifold and varied activities which are recognized as functions of the State in Australia were well known to the framers of the Constitution, and it cannot be supposed that it was intended that the Commonwealth control of Australia's relations with other countries should be subject to the exception

(1) 1 C.L.R., 91.

H. C. of A.
1908.

ATTORNEY-
GENERAL OF
N.S.W.
v.
COLLECTOR OF
CUSTOMS FOR
N.S.W.

O'Connor J.

that it should have no operation in so far as State Governments in the exercise of their governmental functions were concerned. If the power of the Commonwealth were to be taken as so restricted, then, in regard to any goods which a State deemed necessary for the carrying out of its governmental functions, not only would the importation be free of duty, but the Customs control and examination of the goods would be at an end, general prohibitions on importation could not be applied, and, on the same reasoning, neither quarantine laws nor immigration laws could be allowed to stand in the way of the State. If the exercise of Commonwealth power were to be so restricted, it is difficult to see how Commonwealth control could be comprehensive and effective, how it could ever frame or carry out any general policy in respect of the finances, the industry, the health, or the trade of the whole Commonwealth. In other words, the power conferred could not be effectively exercised unless State dealings with countries outside Australia were within the control of the Commonwealth.

It being necessary, therefore, for the effective exercise of the Commonwealth power that the importation of the goods of a State by a State should not be exempt from the control of the Commonwealth, it follows that the Commonwealth power must be taken to include the right of restricting to that extent the rights which the State had previously exercised, and it must be taken that to that extent the State control of its railways has in the distribution of powers under the Constitution been restricted.

As to the third ground, therefore, I have come to the conclusion that, apart from sec. 114, the Constitution authorized the enactment of the *Customs Act* 1901 imposing duties on steel rails imported by the Government of a State.

The question remains, were the steel rails exempt from duty by virtue of sec. 114 of the Constitution? On this part of the case I shall add very little to what has been said by my learned brother the Chief Justice, whose judgment I have had the opportunity of reading, and in which I entirely concur. In the interpretation of sec. 114 I base my judgment on this ground. In the widest sense of the word no doubt a Customs duty is a tax, but in the circumstances under consideration it is in its nature and

H. C. of A. essence more properly a charge made in respect of the landing of
1908.   the goods in Australia.   But, used in relation to property and in
ATTORNEY- the expression " tax on property," there is a narrower meaning of
GENERAL of the word well known and recognized.   A tax on property in the
N.S.W.
v.   strict and narrower meaning is an exaction made in respect of
COLLECTOR OF
CUSTOMS FOR the holding or ownership of property.   That meaning would not
N.S.W.   include Customs duty on goods imported.   Whether the word
O'Connor J. " tax," being a general word and capable of the wider or of the
narrower meaning, is to be interpreted in its wider or in its
narrower sense, is a question to be determined as in all other cases
where a legislature has used an ambiguous expression, namely, by
a consideration of the context, of the other sections of the Constitution, and of its whole scope and purpose.   On that view I
have come to the conclusion that to construe the expression " tax
on property " in the wider sense as including Customs duties
would be to restrict, in the manner I explained in the earlier part
of my judgment, the effective exercise of the power clearly given
to the Commonwealth of the exclusive control of all importation
into Australia.

For these reasons, in my opinion, the second question must be
answered in the negative, and on the whole case judgment must
be entered for the defendant.

ISAACS J.   With every question discussed, except one, I have
already dealt in the previous case : *The King* v. *Sutton* (1).   But
this additional question gives rise to by far the most difficult of
all the problems we have had to solve.   It is whether sec. 114 of
the Constitution prohibits the Commonwealth from levying
Customs duties upon goods imported by the States for governmental purposes.   The prohibition is not expressly claimed for any
goods other than those intended for governmental purposes, but
there is no such constitutional limitation express or implied as to
the property protected.   If the concluding passage of the section
applies to Customs duties at all, it must apply without restriction
to State property of every description that is imported from
abroad.   The phrase that gives rise to the doubt is the expression
" any tax on property of any kind belonging to a State," and it is

(1) 5 C.L.R., 789.

urged with considerable force that these words, taken in the literal sense, include a Customs duty, and that the duty is a tax, and the goods upon which it is imposed are property, and that this sense should not be departed from. If a Customs duty falls within the meaning of the word "tax" in sec. 114, I am of opinion that the plaintiff's argument is made good. I see no escape from the contention that a Customs duty, as ordinarily understood and as enacted in the Commonwealth Acts, is a duty upon property, and if the goods belong to the State, the prohibition would apply. I am unable to accede to the view presented that a Customs duty is merely a tax on an operation, namely, the act of importation, and nothing more.

H. C. of A.
1908.

ATTORNEY-
GENERAL OF
N.S.W.
v.
COLLECTOR OF
CUSTOMS FOR
N.S.W.

Isaacs J.

A Statute might doubtless be so penned as to apply the tax to the act of importation only, and not to operate directly on the goods, but that, besides affording room for argument even then as to the substance of the enactment, would not be an ordinary *Customs Act*, nor is the Statute now in question of that nature.

The *Customs Tariff* 1902 in terms imposes the duties on goods imported. It is nevertheless urged that the goods considered as property are not the subject of taxation, but only the subject of importation, and that the importation and nothing more is the subject of taxation. This a fundamental argument, and as it affects indefinitely the constitutional relations of Commonwealth and States, it renders necessary a careful examination into the nature of Customs legislation as understood in England for some centuries.

The whole course of English precedent and authority appears to me to support the view that the tax is intended to fall, and does fall, on the goods in the same sense as is ordinarily understood by a tax on goods, and not on the mere act of importation.

It is true that importation is essential to the claim for duty, but nowhere do we find that it is the intangible act of importation which is the subject of taxation, but always the concrete property imported. The duty is on imports. *McCulloch's Commercial Dictionary* defines Customs as:—"Customs are duties charged upon commodities on their being imported into or exported from a country." Importation is an event or occasion which renders the property liable to taxation, just as if land were taxable if and

H. C. of A.
1908.

ATTORNEY-
GENERAL OF
N.S.W.
v.
COLLECTOR OF
CUSTOMS FOR
N.S.W.

Isaacs J.

when used for business purposes. In such case it might in an
unprecise and familiar way be said the use for business operations
was taxed, but the real subject of taxation would be the land.
Hamel on the Law of Customs, at p. 29, says :—" The Customs
duties are supposed to have been, at the commencement, small
sums paid by the merchant for the use of the King's Warehouses,
weights, and measures. But these were extended in course of
time and commuted into an *impost upon merchandise itself*, the
consideration given by the Crown being permission to its own
subjects, to travel out of the realm with their merchandise, and
to foreign merchants, to import goods into the kingdom," &c.
The same learned author speaking of drawbacks says, at p. 160 :—
" It is scarcely necessary to explain, that the familiar term ' draw-
back ' is applied to repayments of duties or taxes previously
charged on commodities, but from which they are relieved on
exportation, that they might be disposed of in the foreign market
on the same terms, *as if they had not been taxed at all.*"

Bates Case (1), a prosecution for not paying an import duty on
currants, ultimately led in 1610, as pointed out by *Broom on
Constitutional Law* (at p. 302 and following pages), to the
Petition of Grievances addressed to James I., which referred to
" taxing or imposing upon the subject's goods or merchandizes "
and to " impositions either within the land, or upon commodities
either exported or imported by the merchants."

The petition requested " that a law may be made during this
Session of Parliament, to declare, that all impositions set, or to be
set upon your people, *their goods or merchandizes*, save only by
common assent of Parliament, are and shall be void," &c. *Broom*,
also, at p. 371, quotes *Hargraves* as remarking " James I. claimed
the right of imposing duties on imported and exported merchandize by prerogative," and in discussing the question, states it
thus " May the Sovereign *jure coronæ tax our imports*" ? In
the course of a learned discussion he quotes the Statute 16 Car. I.
c. 8, granting tonnage and poundage to the King, and declaring
and enacting that " it is and hath been the ancient right of the
subjects of this realm that no subsidy custom impost or other
charge whatsoever ought to or may be laid or imposed *upon any*

(1) 2 St. Tri., 371.

H. C. of A.
1908.

ATTORNEY-
GENERAL OF
N.S.W.
v.
COLLECTOR OF
CUSTOMS FOR
N.S.W.

Isaacs J.

merchandize exported or imported by subjects denizens or aliens without common·consent in Parliament." Similarly was it so recited in sec. 6 of the Act 12 Car. II. c. 4. In *Sheppard* v. *Gosnold* (1) it is said that Queen Mary laid an imposition upon cloth, and James I. laid an imposition upon currants, "and so (upon the supposition that by the Common Law merchandize might be charged with Custom) possibly like impositions might be laid on Wax or any other Merchandize." That case, as it seems to me, places the matter in a very clear light. The Court thus summarizes the grounds of dutiability (2):—"From those words (*i.e.*, words of the Act of Car. II.) I observe, that wines liable to pay tonnage by the Act, must have these properties:— 1. They must be wines which shall come or be brought into the ports or places of the Kingdom. 2. They must come or be brought into such ports or places as merchandize, that is, for sale and to that end," &c., and then follow other grounds peculiar to the Act itself. It can scarcely be doubted that the Court were of opinion the duty was on the property itself.

I pass from these early expressions of the nature of the tax to one that is perhaps the most recent. In *Algoma Central Railway Co.* v. *The King* (3) Lord *Macnaghten*, speaking for the Privy Council, and dealing with a Customs Act of Canada, says:—"The duty is a duty imposed on goods imported." His *Lordship* does not say on the act of importation, but on the goods that are imported. The conception. therefore, of English law as to a Customs duty has for centuries been that of a tax upon goods, that is, upon the property.

Turning to the Constitution itself, though the language is not invariable, I read secs. 93 and 95 as contemplating that Customs duties are imposed on the goods themselves.

The framers of the American Constitution had before them the history of Customs duties and the enactments imposing the duties, and they correctly and tersely framed the prohibition to the States against imposing duties upon imports. I can see no distinction between duties imposed on " Merchandize . . . imported" as in the Act of Car. I., or "rates imposed upon

---

(1) Vaugh., 159, at p. 163.   (2) Vaugh., 159, at p. 165.
    (3) (1903) A.C., 478, at p. 481.

H. C. of A.
1908.

ATTORNEY-
GENERAL OF
N.S.W.
v.
COLLECTOR OF
CUSTOMS FOR
N.S.W.

Isaacs J.

merchandize imported" as in the Act of Car. II., on the one hand, and "duties on imports" in the United States Constitution on the other. One of the Imperial Statutes which caused dissatisfaction in America was 4 Geo. III. c. 15, and that enacted there should be raised certain rates and duties "for and upon all white and clayed sugars . . . which shall be imported or brought into any Colony or Plantation in America." The phrase "duties on imports" was only a concise mode of expressing the ordinary operation of Customs Acts as to goods imported.

In *Brown* v. *Maryland* (1) *Marshall* C.J. declared that a duty on imports meant more than a duty on importation, it extended to a duty on the thing imported. It is to be observed, if it be material, that he even went further and determined that a State Act requiring a licence upon the operation of selling imports was equivalent to imposing a tax on the imports themselves and was repugnant to the Federal Constitution. In *Almy* v. *California* (2), which followed *Brown* v. *Maryland* (1), *Taney* C.J. speaking of the earlier case said :—" the Court decided that the State law was a tax on imports." Here the property protected is defined in the widest possible terms, and includes goods whether in the character of imports or not.

I am, therefore, clearly of opinion that Customs duty is imposed upon the goods themselves, and if this were all, I should hold the case came within sec. 114.

But is a Customs duty a "tax" within the true meaning of the section ? In the broadest sense a tax it undoubtedly is, and if the word "tax" stood alone it would be impossible to deny its inclusion of Customs duties as well as of a direct tax on property after incorporation in the general stock of the country. But the word "tax" and its plural "taxes" are not words of invariable signification indicating any exercise whatever of the power of taxation; they are not infrequently used to denote a particular species of imposition, in contra-distinction to duties, and to duties of various kinds. The word "taxation," when used to confer a governmental power, carries the amplest meaning; but "tax" may or may not be as wide. The word must be looked at in relation to its surroundings,

(1) 12 Wheat., 419.   (2) 24 How., 169, at p. 173.

it must be considered with respect to the object of the
clause in which it stands, and the results which would flow from
one construction or the other; in short, its meaning must, like
any other word not of invariable signification found in a document, be ascertained by interpreting it by the light of the whole
instrument. There are many Statutes in which "taxes" may be
found differentiated from "duties." Some of these enactments
are of special value in this connection because they refer to constitutional powers. The Act 6 Geo. III. recited that several of
the Houses of Representatives in the American Colonies had
claimed the sole and exclusive right of "imposing duties and
taxes" and thereupon declared Imperial paramountcy. The Act
14 Geo. III. c. 83, making provision for the Government of the
Province of Quebec, while enacting that a Legislative Council
might be appointed with power to make Ordinances for the
peace welfare and good government of the Province, prohibited
the Council from laying "any taxes and duties" within the
Province except certain "rates and taxes" within Towns and
Districts. By a later Statute, 14 Geo. III. c. 88, the British
Parliament itself, for the purpose of defraying part of the
cost of Government in Quebec, imposed certain "rates and
duties" of Customs upon goods therein mentioned. They were
not called taxes. Without attempting, for I have no opportunity,
to make any extensive enumeration of Statutes which present
the distinction between the words referred to, I may mention two
others far removed in time and character from those just referred
to. They indicate, however, how the legislature sometimes
recognizes the restricted meaning of the word "tax." The Act
called the *Taxes Management Act* 1880 (43 & 44 Vict. c. 19) used
the word "taxes" in two different senses. In its short title, as is
seen, the word is employed in a comprehensive sense; but in the
full title to the Act a narrower sense is found. It styles itself
"An Act to consolidate enactments relating to certain Taxes and
Duties," &c. Customs duties are not included, others are. The
other Act is called the *Revenue Act* 1889 (52 & 53 Vict. c. 42),
and is an Act to amend the law relating to the Customs and Inland
Revenue, &c. Part I. is headed "Customs," and under this Part,
sec. 6 refers to a "duty of Customs." Part II. is headed "Taxes,"

H. C. of A.
1908.

ATTORNEY-
GENERAL OF
N.S.W.
v.
COLLECTOR OF
CUSTOMS FOR
N.S.W.

Isaacs J.

and refers to Land Tax, Income Tax, and Inhabited House Duties, a good instance of the accommodating meaning of the term as including some duties while excluding others. Part III. deals with Stamps. Part IV. with Excise. It is therefore evident that no invariable signification can be claimed for the word "tax," and not being unambiguous it is necessary for the purposes of construction to have regard to those circumstances to which I have already adverted. In approaching the construction of sec. 114 it must first be borne in mind that to constitutionally exempt a State from any obligation to pay Customs duty, leaving it free therefore at its own will to supply, not only its own sovereign needs, but also its own citizens, and through them the whole continent, with goods otherwise dutiable, might not merely weaken, but utterly frustrate the most cherished endeavours of the Federal Parliament to regulate the foreign trade and commerce of Australia, and seriously impair the revenues of other States. This would not merely leave to the several States the same power over the introduction of goods into Australia, which they had before Federation, but would vastly increase it, because the owners of goods never previously had the right which they now have of crossing State lines with their merchandise free of duty. This is a result certainly not to be courted, and is in clear antagonism to the primary intention of the Constitution gathered from the grant of exclusive powers over foreign commerce, and over that class of taxation which is inseparable from its effectual regulation. It could scarcely have been the object of the framers of the Constitution to render it so easily and mortally vulnerable. If, therefore, another meaning, less destructive of the main purpose of the grants of power affected, and yet affording substantial protection to the States, can with proper regard for the language of the section be placed on the word "tax," that more limited meaning should, in my opinion, be given to it. Sec. 114, is, I believe, the only clause of the Constitution where the word "tax" is found. "Taxation," the generic term, is frequently employed and, as in sec. 55, includes Customs and Excise duties. But there are a great number of sections in which the particular class of taxation now under consideration is referred to, and constantly as "duties of Customs." Nowhere is that species of

taxation called a "tax." Even in sec. 112 the same phraseology is H. C. of A.
1908.
retained. Then comes sec. 114, the structure of which is important.
It forbids a State to raise forces except with Commonwealth Attorney-
consent, and then forbids it to "impose any tax on property of General of
N.S.W.
any kind belonging to the Commonwealth." Stopping there for a v.
Collector of
moment it is of course clear that, treating the provision necessarily Customs for
as one of permanency, no Customs duty could be comprehended N.S.W.
in the prohibition to tax Commonwealth property. The suc- Isaacs J.
ceeding paragraph " nor shall the Commonwealth impose any tax
on property of any kind belonging to a State " is a reciprocal
inhibition relating to the same class of taxation.   To make so
serious an inroad into Commonwealth control of external commerce as the plaintiff's contention involves, would require the
clearest expression of intention, and the mere use of a word not
uncommonly employed in a limited sense, and indeed, in connection with the word " property " more often and more appropriately
used in a limited sense, combined with the marked omission of the
word " duties," convinces me that Customs duties are not within
the object and intention of sec. 114.

Mr. *Pilcher* urged the view that if Customs duties were
entirely outside the section, and completely within the control of
the Federal Parliament, so must Excise duties be in all cases open
to the Parliament to impose on the States.   It is not necessary to
determine this, but it may well be indicated that as the doctrine
of State instrumentalities, as it is called, or in plainer English,
the doctrine of the exercise of governmental functions, cannot be
applied outside the territory of the State but only within that
territory, its application, quite apart from sec. 114, may avert at
least some of the consequences feared by learned counsel.   Upon
that subject I say nothing further.

For the reasons I have stated, my opinion is that the defendant
ought to succeed.

HIGGINS J.   The case for the State has been well put and
forcibly, mainly on the grounds (1) that, according to the
principles laid down by this Court in *D'Emden* v. *Pedder* (1)
and in subsequent cases, the State agencies and functions are

(1) 1 C.L.R., 91.

case, therefore, must assume that these doctrines are, in their
application hitherto, unimpeachable. But the doctrine as to the
exemption of State agencies from Commonwealth taxation has
never yet been applied to Customs taxation, taxation of the act
of importation, as distinguished from internal taxation. It has
never yet been applied so as to make an exception to the
exclusive and paramount power of the Commonwealth Parliament
to make laws with respect to trade and commerce with other
countries, and with respect to Customs taxation (sec. 51 (I.) (II.);
sec. 90). For the reasons which I have stated in *The King* v.
Sutton (1) I regard the doctrine as to the King not being bound
save by express words, as being inapplicable as between the
States and the Commonwealth, at all events in the exercise of an
exclusive power of the Commonwealth; and I regard State laws
and State powers in respect of the railways as subordinated to
the Commonwealth powers with regard to trade and commerce,
and with regard to Customs taxation.

But the interpretation of sec. 114 of the Constitution raises
another difficulty. The section itself mixes up two distinct subjects. It forbids a State to raise a naval or military force
without the consent of the Commonwealth Parliament; and it
forbids a State to impose a tax on property of any kind belonging to the•Commonwealth. Then, apparently, it occurred to
the draughtsman that a similar prohibition should be inserted
against the Commonwealth taxing State property. The prohibition as to State taxation was, no doubt, suggested by the *British
North America Act*, sec. 125. But by substituting the word
" property " for " lands or property," the intention—if it was the
intention—to confine the prohibition to what are known as
" property taxes " has been somewhat obscured. Property is, by
the Constitution, subject to be taxed at the instance of the State
as well as of the Commonwealth; Customs taxation is solely a
matter for the Commonwealth (sec. 90). Taxes of retaliation, as
between the States and the Commonwealth, are possible as to
property taxes; but are impossible as to Customs taxes. But
whatever may have been the motive which led to this express
prohibition, in addition to the prohibition which this Court has

H. C. OF A.
1908.

ATTORNEY-
GENERAL OF
N.S.W.
v.
COLLECTOR OF
CUSTOMS FOR
N.S.W.

Higgins J.

(1) 5 C.L.R., 789.

H. C. of A.
1908.

ATTORNEY-
GENERAL OF
N.S.W.
v.
COLLECTOR OF
CUSTOMS FOR
N.S.W.

Higgins J.

held to be implied from the nature of the Constitution as to the taxation of State or Commonwealth agents, the phraseology is such as to point to taxation of property *as property* as being the subject of this express prohibition. "A State shall not, without the consent of the Parliament or the Commonwealth, . . . impose any tax on *property* of any kind *belonging* to the Commonwealth, nor shall the Commonwealth impose any tax on *property* of any kind *belonging* to a State." But is a Customs tax a tax on property *as such* ? The *Customs Tariff* 1902 speaks of "duties . . . on . . . goods," and the expression is roughly accurate, although, probably, if fully expressed it would be a tax on persons in respect of the importation of goods ; just as a property tax is usually, though not necessarily, a tax on persons in respect of their property. A Customs tax is a tax, not on property as such, but on persons in respect of the act of importation. There is a fundamental difference between taxing men for having property, and taxing men for moving property—and, in particular, for moving property into the country from over seas. A turnpike toll, or an *octroi* tax, is not, properly speaking, taxation "imposed on property," although the person who moves the animals or goods through the gate or into the city has to make a payment based on the number or character or value of the things which enter. Unless they enter, there is no tax ; if they enter, there is a tax—which has to be paid by the person who brings them in, whether he is the owner or not. In other words, it is not a "property tax." The case of succession taxes in the United States is analogous. Congress cannot, according to the doctrine of *M'Culloch* v. *Maryland* (1), tax State agencies ; but it can tax a bequest of money or a devise of land to the State. It can tax the movement from the dead hand into the hand of the State: *Snyder* v. *Bettmann* (2). Another analogy may be found in the distinction between taxation by a State of United States bonds, the property of a corporation, and taxation levied on the franchise or business of the corporation ; although the amount of the tax may depend on the value of the bonds in each case : *Home Insurance Co.* v. *New York* (3).

(1) 4 Wheat., 316.   (2) 190 U.S., 249.
                       (3) 119 U.S., 129.

H. C. of A.
1908.

ATTORNEY-
GENERAL OF
N.S.W.
v.
COLLECTOR OF
CUSTOMS FOR
N.S.W.

Higgins J.

Again, if the Commonwealth were to impose a property tax on Australian residents everywhere, based on the value of their property everywhere (for the present purpose I may assume—without deciding it—that such a tax would be valid), the tax would fall on them in respect of goods even in London. But when the Commonwealth imposes a Customs duty, the duty is not payable unless it be attempted to move the goods from London to Australia.

I prefer to base my judgment on this ground which I have stated. I cannot, confidently, take the ground that a Customs duty cannot be a tax within the meaning of the word " tax " in sec. 114. It is true that " duties of Customs " and " duties of Excise " are the usual expressions; but phraseology, such as is used in sec. 55, shows that the Constitution treats the imposing of such duties as being the imposing of taxes: " Laws imposing taxation, except laws imposing duties of Customs or of Excise, shall deal with one subject of taxation only." However, the fact that sec. 114 uses the mere word " tax "—not " tax *of any kind,*" although it speaks of " property *of any kind* "—strengthens the view that the framers of the section could not have had Customs duties in their minds at the time. They lay the emphasis on the thought on ownership—"*property of any kind belonging,*" &c.

I have based my reasoning on the words and the scheme of our own Australian Constitution. But it is a fact not to be ignored, that the plaintiff's counsel have not been able to point to any indication (to say the least) that in the United States or in Canada the separate States, or Provinces, are exempted from Customs taxation; although it is from the United States that this Court has adopted the doctrine as to the exemption of State agencies, and although the Canadian Constitution contains the section from which our sec. 114 is derived.

For the reasons which I have stated, I concur in the opinion that the States of Australia are liable to the payment of duties of Customs; that sec. 114 of the Constitution does not exempt them; that the duty was properly paid on the steel rails in question; and that judgment should be entered for the defendant with costs.

H. C. OF A.
1908.

ATTORNEY-
GENERAL OF
N.S.W.
v.
COLLECTOR OF
CUSTOMS FOR
N.S.W.

Questions answered accordingly.

Solicitor, for the plaintiff, *The Crown Solicitor for the Com-monwealth.*

Solicitor, for the defendant, *The Crown Solicitor for New South Wales.*

C. A. W.

[HIGH COURT OF AUSTRALIA.]

CAMERON . . . . APPELLANT;
PLAINTIFF,

AND

IRWIN AND OTHERS . . . . . RESPONDENTS.
DEFENDANTS,

ON APPEAL FROM THE SUPREME COURT OF
WESTERN AUSTRALIA.

H. C. OF A.
1908.

MELBOURNE,
February 24.

Griffith C.J.,
Barton,
O'Connor,
Isaacs and
Higgins JJ.

Appeal to High Court—Special leave.

In an action in the Supreme Court of Western Australia the jury found a verdict for the plaintiff for £200, and judgment was entered accordingly. On application to the Full Court to set aside the judgment on the ground of absence of evidence, the Full Court reversed the judgment below and entered judgment for the defendants.

Special leave to appeal to the High Court was refused.

APPLICATION for special leave to appeal.

An action was tried in the Supreme Court of Western Australia at Kalgoorlie, by *Burnside* J. and a jury, by which the plaintiff Robert Miles Fletcher Cameron, a legally qualified

medical practitioner, sought to recover from the defendants
Henry Offley Irwin and three others, who were also legally
qualified medical practitioners, damages for injury sustained by
reason of the defendants having combined to injure him in
his profession. The jury found a verdict for the plaintiff for
£200 damages, and judgment was entered accordingly.

The defendants applied to the Full Court to set aside the
judgment on the ground that there was no evidence that the
object of the defendants was to injure the plaintiff. On 23rd
December 1907 the judgment was reversed and judgment was
entered for the defendants with costs.

The plaintiff now applied to the High Court for special leave
to appeal from the judgment of the Full Court.

Starke, for the appellant. The Full Court has entered judgment for the defendants without setting aside the verdict of the
jury and without any motion to set it aside, and there were
no grounds for setting it aside. There is no authority for such a
course being taken.

[GRIFFITH C.J.—Special leave to appeal is never granted on a
technical error.]

It is very important that the principle of not interfering with
the verdict of a jury should be upheld.

[*Villeneuve Smith* referred to *Rules of Supreme Court*, Order
XXXVI. No. 10; *National Mutual Life Association of Australasia Ltd.* v. *Kidman* (1).]

There there was a motion for a new trial.

[ISAACS J. referred to *Scown* v. *Howarth* (2); *Ogilvie* v. *West
Australian Mortgage and Agency Corporation* (3).]

There was evidence from which reasonable men could find that
the combination of the respondents, however well formed, was
used to oppress the appellant and did injure him. [Counsel also ·
referred to *Martell* v. *Victorian Coal Miners' Association* (4);
Dublin, Wicklow and Wexford Railway Co. v. *Slattery* (5);
Wakelin v. *London and South Western Railway Co.* (6).]

(1) 3 C.L.R., 160.
(2) 25 V.L.R., 88; 21 A.L.T., 36.
(3) (1896) A.C., 257.
(4) 29 V.L.R., 475, at p. 496; 25

A.L.T., 120.
(5) 3 App. Cas., 1155.
(6) 12 App. Cas., 41.

H. C. OF A.
1908.

CAMERON
v.
IRWIN.

Villeneuve Smith for the respondents, was not heard.

GRIFFITH C.J. The question is entirely one of fact. Special leave will be refused, and the motion will be dismissed with costs.

Special leave refused.

Solicitors, for the appellant, *Gillott, Bates & Moir* for *Haynes, Robinson & Cox*, Perth, for *Keenan & Randall*, Kalgoorlie.

Solicitor, for the respondents, *Horace B. Joseph.*

B. L.

[HIGH COURT OF AUSTRALIA.]

McLAUGHLIN . . . . . . APPELLANT;
DEFENDANT,

AND

FREEHILL . . . . RESPONDENT.
PLAINTIFF,

ON APPEAL FROM THE SUPREME COURT OF
NEW SOUTH WALES.

H. C. OF A.
1908.

SYDNEY,
April 22, 23.

Griffith C.J.,
Barton and
Isaacs JJ.

Solicitor and client—Retainer by lunatic—Costs of proceedings to set aside lunacy order—Necessaries—Action by solicitor for costs—Pleadings—Res judicata—Amendment.

M. who had been declared insane by the Supreme Court, retained a solicitor to act for him in an application to have the lunacy order set aside. Before making the application the solicitor obtained an order from the Court directing that his costs of the application should in any event be paid by the committee out of M.'s estate. The application was then made and dismissed, and the previous order as to the solicitor's costs was embodied in the order dismissing the application. Before the costs had been paid M. recovered his sanity, and having been declared sane by the Court and having had the management of his estate restored to him, refused to pay the costs.

H. C. of A.
1908.
~~~~
McLaughlin
v.
Freehill.

The solicitor brought an action against M. to recover the costs, and, the only material defence being a plea of never indebted, obtained a verdict for the amount claimed.

Held, that the costs were necessaries, and that the solicitor was entitled to recover them from M. The fact that he had obtained an order for the payment of the costs out of M.'s estate did not show that in doing the work he had not relied upon the implied common law obligation of the lunatic to pay for necessaries supplied to him, nor did the order operate as *res judicata* as between him and M., not having been made in a proceeding in which they were independent parties.

Held, further, that the latter defence was not open on the pleadings, and, the sole question at the trial having been whether the costs were necessaries or not, an amendment should not be allowed after trial.

Decision of the Supreme Court: *Freehill* v. *McLaughlin*, (1907) 7 S.R. (N.S.W.), 253, affirmed.

APPEAL from a decision of the Supreme Court of New South Wales.

The appellant was on 7th August 1902 declared by the Supreme Court in its lunacy jurisdiction to be an insane person and incapable of managing his affairs, and a committee of his estate was appointed. He, thereupon retained the respondent as his solicitor to make an application to the Court to have the order declaring him insane set aside, on various grounds. Before making the application the solicitor applied for and obtained an order that his costs of the application should in any event be paid by the committee out of M.'s estate. The application was dismissed with costs on 18th November 1902, and the Court ordered that the costs of all parties to the application be taxed by the Master in Lunacy as between solicitor and client and certified, and that the costs of the applicant so certified be paid by the committee of the appellant's estate to the respondent. The appellant subsequently recovered his sanity, and was declared by the Court to be sane, and the management of his estate was restored to him. The costs not having been paid by the committee, the respondent called upon the appellant to pay them, but as he refused to pay them, the respondent brought an action to recover them. The only material plea was never indebted.

The case came on for trial before *Pring* J. and a jury, who found a verdict for the plaintiff.

H. C. of A.   The appellant moved the Full Court to set aside the verdict on
1908.   the ground that any claim the respondent had against his estate
McLaughlin   for work done as solicitor had merged in the order of the Court,
v.   which had the effect of a decree of the Court of Equity, and
Freehill.   that there was no evidence of any necessaries supplied by the
             respondent, and even if the services rendered were necessaries,
             they were not rendered so as to create any legal obligation on
             the part of the appellant to pay them.

             The Full Court refused the application: *Freehill* v. *McLaugh-
             lin* (1), and from their decision the present appeal was brought.

             After the institution of the appeal the respondent died, and on
             the application of the appellant the High Court allowed the
             names of the executors of the respondent's estate to be substituted
             for that of the respondent.

             [Reference was made to *High Court Procedure Act* 1903, sec.
             39; *Quick & Groom, Judicial Power*, p. 268; Order XI., r. 2, of
             the High Court Rules; sec. 5, r. 1, of the rules of December 1907;
             Stamp Act (N.S.W.), No. 27 of 1898, sec. 54.]

             Cullen K.C. and *Watt*, for the appellant.   Assuming that the
             work done was necessaries, as the jury found, the circumstances
             under which it was done exclude any liability on the part of the
             appellant to pay for it.   The respondent never looked to the
             appellant for payment.   He relied, not upon the implied obliga-
             tion of a lunatic to pay for necessaries supplied to him, but went
             to the Court and obtained an order that the costs should be paid
             out of the estate.

             [GRIFFITH C.J.—Was not the existence of the obligation the
             foundation of the order of the Court?   Otherwise what justifica-
             tion was there for ordering that the costs be paid out of the
             estate?]

             The foundation is the protection of the lunatic.   The Court is
             empowered by the *Lunacy Act* 1898, sec. 113, to make such an
             order so that the lunatic may not lack legal assistance in any
             necessary proceedings.   But it is quite distinct from the legal
             liability for necessaries.   That arises after the services are
             rendered, whereas the order is made before.   It is not open to

             (1) (1907) 7 S.R. (N.S.W.), 253.

the solicitor to say afterwards that he relied upon the implied contractual obligation. The costs were taxed under the order and the respondent still has his rights against the committee. [They referred to *In re Rhodes*; *Rhodes* v. *Rhodes* (1); *Beall* v. *Smith* (2); *Erskine* v. *Erskine* (3).]

H. C. of A.
.1908.

McLAUGHLIN
v.
FREEHILL.

[ISAACS J. referred to *In re Meares* (4); *In re Cumming* (5).]

Even if there would otherwise have been a liability on the part of the appellant it is merged in the order of the Court.

[GRIFFITH C.J.—That is, transmuted into *rem judicatam.* What possible foundation is there for such a defence ? There was no decision in a *lis* between the appellant and the respondent.]

The order is equivalent to a judgment between the parties. It is to have the same effect as an order in the Court of Equity for the payment of money. It was a substitution of the liability of the committee for that of the lunatic himself.

[ISAACS J. referred to *Howard* v. *Earl Digby* (6).]

Gordon K.C., *Harvey* and *Carlos*, for the respondent, were not called upon.

GRIFFITH C.J. This is an action by a solicitor for recovery of costs due to him, as he alleges, as solicitor for the appellant. The appellant had been declared by the Supreme Court of New South Wales to be an insane person. He naturally desired to have that order set aside, and consulted the respondent for that purpose. Now, it is settled that work done for the benefit of an insane person, although he is incompetent technically to make a contract, may nevertheless be regarded as something in the nature of necessaries. Consequently an action will lie against him, as it will in some other cases, for necessaries. The only plea to the action was never indebted, but there was a counterclaim for negligence, on which nothing turns, as it was abandoned. The only question left to the jury was whether the work done by the plaintiff for the defendant was necessaries, and the jury found a verdict for the plaintiff. Application was then made to the Supreme Court for a new trial, or nonsuit, and a rule

August 23.

(1) 44 Ch. D., 94.
(2) L.R. 9 Ch., 85.
(3) 21 N.S.W. L.R. (Div.), 1.

(4) 10 Ch. D., 552.
(5) 1 D.M. & G., 537.
(6) 2 C. & F., 634.

nisi was granted and afterwards discharged. The Court thought that the only question was whether the jury were justified in coming to the conclusion that the work was in the nature of necessaries. It is not contested here now that they were justified in doing so, and that the respondent is consequently entitled to succeed in the action, unless, although the work was of such a nature as to be necessaries, the other circumstances of the case negative the idea of any contractual or quasi-contractual obligation between the parties.

Let us consider for a moment what was the relative position of the parties. The application to set aside the order, which is alleged by the plaintiff to have been necessary, might have been successful or unsuccessful, and the question whether the work done was or was not necessary might possibly have depended on the result of the application. The application was successful, and this work was necessary. The plaintiff is therefore entitled to recover the money in some way. If the lunacy had continued he would not have been entitled to recover the money directly against the lunatic's estate, because that was in the hands of a committee, and the only course open to him would have been to invoke the aid of the Court, through the committee, and he might or might not have been successful in obtaining an order for payment of the debt. Under those circumstances the solicitor very sensibly made application to the Court, with the knowledge of the committee, for an order that any costs he might incur in the contemplated proceeding might be paid out of the estate, and the Court made that order, which was, in effect, an intimation or assurance from the Court that, whatever might be the result of the application, when the time came to consider whether the costs incurred ought to be paid out of the estate, the Court would consider that they should be granted. I fail to see how that can alter the character of the transaction as between the plaintiff and the defendant. It seems to me to be quite a collateral matter.

Dr. *Cullen* contends that there was no intention on the part of the solicitor that the costs should constitute a debt due by the defendant to him. There was no direct evidence on the point, and it does not appear to have been considered by the jury

I agree with what was said by *Lopes* L.J., *In re Rhodes* ; *Rhodes* H. C. of A.
1908.

McLaughlin
v.
Freehill.
___
Griffith C.J.
v. *Rhodes* (1):—"I do not think that unless the intention of the
party making the payment was that it should constitute a
debt, any obligation could be implied against a person under
disability." But the obligation implied against a person under
disability is *obligatio quasi ex contractu.* Here there was
prima facie an implied obligation or contract. There is nothing
to show that there was any intention on the part of the solicitor
—when he did the work—that he would not look to the defendant
for payment. If the defendant continued insane, of course
he would have to look to the estate, but if he recovered he
would look to him. The first application was unsuccessful.
Subsequently another application for a declaration that the
appellant was sane was granted, and the Court ordered, amongst
other things, that the present appellant's taxed costs should be
paid by the committee of the estate to his solicitor, the plaintiff
in the action. It is suggested that that amounts to an order of
the Court as between the appellant and his solicitor that the
debt should not be paid by the appellant to his solicitor, and
that any previous contractual obligation was merged in that
order.

We are all familiar with the rule that an obligation may be
merged in a judgment. That is purely a technical rule, but the
application of the rule implies litigation between parties. The
order in this case is an order made on the defendant's application
that his costs should be paid out of his estate to his solicitor. In
my opinion, that did not affect any contractual obligation between
the appellant and his solicitor any more than an order made in
an action for the administration of a trust, or of the estate of a
deceased person, that the plaintiff's costs shall be paid out of the
estate. The order may be to pay them to the plaintiff, or it may
be that they are to be paid to his solicitor. In either case the
direction operates as an authority to pay the money to the
person designated, but it does not operate as a judgment between
the plaintiff and his solicitor. The doctrine advanced, therefore,
seems to me to have no application at all to the present case.
Moreover, no such defence is pleaded. Application was made to

(1) 44 Ch. D., 94, at pp. 103, 104.

H. C. of A.
1908.
McLAUGHLIN
v.
FREEMILL.
Griffith C.J.

the Full Court, and removed to this Court, to be allowed to plead
res judicata, but that application was refused.   In this case it
would be most unreasonable to allow such an amendment.   The
debt is not denied, and the objection taken is purely formal.
Therefore I think the appeal should be dismissed.

BARTON J.   I agree with what has fallen from the learned
Chief Justice, and I do not think it necessary to add anything
further.

ISAACS J.   I agree that this appeal should be dismissed.   It is
not disputed that the claim of the respondent was for necessaries.
It also is not denied that the appellant did receive, and had full
benefit of, the work done and the money that has been expended,
and which forms part of the respondent's claim.   In *In re Meares*
(1) *James* L.J. said—and the same applies to money expended and
work done of which a lunatic has had the benefit :—" In *Williams*
v. *Wentworth* (2) the Court held that in the case of money
expended for the necessary protection of the person and estate of
a lunatic, the law would raise an implied contract, and give
a valid demand against the lunatic or his estate."   That seems to
me to be quite applicable to this case.   Here the respondent did
what is described in *In re Cumming* (3).   He applied to the
Court and obtained security for reimbursement of his costs from
the defendant, a lunatic.   The Court acceded to the application,
because the costs incurred in defending the interests of the
lunatic would be as described in *Howard* v. *Earl Digby* (4),
where Lord *Brougham* L.C. said :—" In the eye of that Court, be
it a Court of Law, or a Court of Equity, or the Chancellor sitting
in lunacy, they are valid debts incurred by the insane person,
and are discharged by the justice of the Court."

Therefore, his plea of never indebted fails absolutely.   The
only other plea was negligence, causing damages, pleaded by way
of a set-off, or counterclaim.   That, too, has failed, and is not
now urged.   That is an end of the case it seems to me.

The question of merger, so-called, has been raised.   I do not

(1) 10 Ch. D., 552, at p. 553.   (3) 1 D. M. & G., 537.
(2) 5 Beav., 325.   (4) 2 C. & F., 634, at p. 663.

understand how it applies exactly in the way of merger, but it has not been raised properly in the pleadings. Leave to add it was refused, and, in my opinion, properly refused. But I am also of opinion that if it had been raised formally it would not, for the reasons given by the learned Chief Justice, have been successful. On these grounds I think the appeal should be dismissed.

H. C. of A.
1908.

McLAUGHLIN
v.
FREEHILL.

Isaacs J.

Appeal dismissed with costs.

Solicitor, for the appellant, *J. H. McLaughlin.*
Solicitors, for the respondent, *Freehill & Donovan.*

C. A. W.

[HIGH COURT OF AUSTRALIA.]

ROBERT MYLNE GOW AND EBENEZER CHARLES CHAMBERS (TRADING AS R. M. Gow & Co.)   APPELLANTS ;

AND

THOMAS EDWARD WHITE .   .   .   RESPONDENT.

ON APPEAL FROM THE SUPREME COURT OF QUEENSLAND.

Insolvency—Fraudulent preference—Payment—Good faith—Insolvency Act 1874 (Qd.) (38 Vict. No. 5), secs. 107, 108.

H. C. of A.
1908.

BRISBANE,
April 29, 30;
May 2.

Griffith C.J.,
Barton and
O'Connor JJ.

The mere fact that a debtor, who is unable for the moment to pay all his debts as they become due, makes a payment to a creditor, is not conclusive evidence that the payment is a fraudulent preference within sec. 107 of the *Insolvency Act* 1874 (Qd.).

Stewart & Walker v. *White,* 5 C. L. R., 110, explained.

Payments by a debtor within six months of his insolvency of fortnightly sums of money in pursuance of a prior valid agreement with his creditor for the compromise of an existing debt :

H. C. of A.
1908.

Gow
v.
White.

Held, upon the evidence, to have been received in good faith by the creditor, and, therefore, that the payments were not fraudulent preferences.

A creditor bought £800 worth of butter from his debtor for cash, there being at the time a debt of £25 due and owing to the creditor by the debtor. The creditor paid the debtor by cheque £775.

Held, that there was not a delivery of butter by the debtor to the creditor in discharge of a past debt within the meaning of sec. 108 of the *Insolvency Act* 1874 (Qd.)

Decision of Supreme Court of Queensland, *In re Springall*; *Ex parte White*, 1908 St. R. Qd., 60, reversed, and judgment of *Cooper* C.J. restored.

APPEAL by special leave from a judgment of the Full Court of Queensland (1) reversing a decision of *Cooper* C.J., who dismissed a motion by the trustee in the insolvent state of A. F. Springall asking for a declaration that certain payments by the insolvent to the appellants were fraudulent and void as against the trustee, and for consequent relief. *Cooper* C.J., who heard the case mostly on oral evidence, found that the transactions did not come within the fraudulent preference clause of the *Insolvency Act* 1874 (Qd.) (38 Vict. No. 5) sec. 107, but were *bonâ fide* and valid.

The facts are fully stated in the judgments hereunder.

Stumm and *Graham*, for the appellants. *Real* and *Chubb* JJ. came to the conclusion that the appellants should have known that Springall was in insolvent circumstances. The evidence is, however, the other way, as it was proved that Springall got credit for £5,000 worth of butter from Brisbane merchants shortly before the adjudication in insolvency, and that the appellants also made full and satisfactory inquiries as to the insolvent's financial position. It cannot be said that Springall was insolvent in October when the arrangement for refunding was entered into.

[They referred to *Bills* v. *Smith* (2); *In re Vautin*; *Ex parte Saffery* (3); *Ex parte Mackenzie*; *In re Bent* (4); *New, Prance & Gerrard's Trustee* v. *Hunting* (5); *Sharp* v. *Jackson* (6); *Williams' Bankruptcy*, 8th ed., pp. 250 *et seq.*

(1) 1908 St. R. Qd., 60.   (4) 42 L.J. Bk., 25.
(2) 6 B. & S., 314 ; 34 L.J.Q.B., 68.   (5) (1897) 2 Q.B., 19, at p. 29.
(3) (1900) 2 Q.B., 325.   (6) (1899) A.C., 419, at pp. 421, 423.

The *Insolvency Act* 1874 strikes at the intention and not at the mere acts of parties : *Ex parte Taylor* ; *In re Goldsmid* (1). The arrangement was not made with a view of giving the creditor a preference but to enable the debtor to reap the advantage of a highly beneficial contract which he had entered into with another exporter. It was therefore not a fraudulent preference : *Ex parte Hill* ; *In re Bird* (2). The learned Judges of the Full Court refused to consider whether any excuse existed for the arrangement between the creditors and debtor, and overlooked the decision of the High Court in *Bank of Australasia* v. *Hall* (3). The present case is clearly distinguishable from *Stewart & Walker* v. *White* (4) in that the creditors in that case knew that the insolvent's business affairs were in a bad state, whilst in the present case the appellants were not aware of such instability. " Good faith " is defined in *Butcher* v. *Stead* ; *In re Meldrum* (5). The transaction as to the £25 worth of butter was in the ordinary course of mutual dealings ; and the deduction of £25 was merely to save the trouble of drawing two cheques, and is governed by the decision in *Spargo's Case* ; *In re Harmony & Montague Tin & Copper Mining Co.* (6). A Court of Appeal is always loth to disturb the findings of a presiding Judge who has the advantage of seeing and hearing the witnesses : *Coghlan* v. *Cumberland* (7); *Colonial Securities Trust Co.* v. *Massey* (8).

[O'CONNOR J. referred to *McLaughlin* v. *Daily Telegraph Newspaper Co. Ltd.* (9).]

Feez and *O'Sullivan*, for the respondent. This case is on all fours with *Stewart and Walker* v. *White* (4), the High Court decision in which had not been given when *Cooper* C.J. heard the case now under notice. No facts are in dispute in the present case, and the only difference between the judgment of *Cooper* C.J., and the State Full Court is as to the proper inferences to be drawn. *Coghlan* v. *Cumberland* (7), and *Colonial Securities*

(1) 18 Q.B.D., 295.
(2) 23 Ch. D., 695.
(3) 4 C.L.R., 1514.
(4) 5 C.L.R., 110.
(5) L.R., 7 H.L., 839, at pp. 847, 849.

(6) L.R., 8 Ch., 407.
(7) (1898) 1 Ch., 704.
(8) (1896) 1 Q.B., 38.
(9) 1 C.L.R., 243.

GRIFFITH J. This is an appeal from a decision (
Court reversing the decision of the learned Chief
Queensland on a motion by the trustee of a debtor
certain payments to the appellants to be fraudulent]
The payments in question were a series of sums of £
intervals of about a fortnight during the six months
the insolvency, which occurred in May 1907. Th
facts of the case lie within a very small compass.
was a butter buyer and manufacturer, selling the
other persons for export. The appellants were :
English buyers, and bought butter for export from
and others. They had been dealing with the debtor
years. In May 1906 their accounts nearly balance
month the appellants agreed to buy from the debtor :
worth of butter to be delivered at short dates, and a
£500 before delivery. The debtor's business, consist
ing from creameries and dairymen, naturally requir
mand of capital, and there is nothing very surprising
that he occasionally obtained payment in advance f
to whom he was selling to enable him to pay for the
bought it. Persons are at liberty to carry on busi
way if they like, and it appears that it is not un
butter trade, as, indeed, might naturally be expec
advancing this large sum of money, however, the ap
the precaution of inquiring as to the debtor's financ
from his bankers and received satisfactory answers
made other inquiries, the nature of which may not b
but, at any rate, they were sufficiently satisfied of hi
advance the £500. The debtor did not deliver £5
butter, and made excuses for not delivering it. Tl
did not ask for their money back, but they asked fo
This went on for some time, and in October it w
that the debtor should repay the £500 with intere
ments. The reason that he gave to the appellants fo
ing the butter, and for asking to be allowed to repay
was that he had entered into a contract to supply 1
of butter a month to another exporter, which was e:
very much more profitable to him than the contra

preferences, and that there was an absence of good fa
part of the appellants.

The learned Judges in the Full Court considered
bound by the decision of this Court in the case of
Walker v. *White* (1). In that case this Court had
express its dissent in part from a dictum attributed
Court in a previous case: *Russell, Wilkins & Sons* J
ridge Printing Co. Ltd. (2), as to the effect under sec.
Insolvency Act 1874 of pressure exercised by a cre
debtor, and my learned brothers *Barton* and *Isaacs*
the point at considerable length, and expressed th
from the view which was attributed in the report to
Judges of the Full Court. The learned Judges in
case, *Real* J. more especially, have explained that th
was not correctly apprehended, either through a de
report or from some other reason, and have corrected
they intended at that time to lay it down. I do r
necessary to refer further to that point, except to
the rule is now stated by them, there is not much
any, between the opinion expressed by my learned b
that expressed in his judgment by *Real* J. With re:
statement in that learned Judge's judgment (3), that
did not, and I certainly did not, intend to hold that
any way rendered invalid anything that would, but
be valid," I understand him to mean "anything which
of pressure would be valid." That is very much the
as this Court expressed in *Stewart & Walker* v. *Wh*
it relates only to the question of pressure, which in
case is absent.

Real J., after quoting from my judgment in *Stewo*
v. *White* (1), said (4):—" It would seem from the wo
judgment of the High Court, as stated in the Brist
report, that in attacking a payment on the ground
made with a view to prefer, all that is necessary to
from the question of good faith, is that the debtor v
pay his debts as they became due from his own mor

(1) 5 C.L.R., 110.   (3) 1908 St. R. Qd.
(2) 1906 St. R. Qd., 182.   (4) 1908 St. R. Qd

was aware of that fact; and, being aware of that fact, and intending the consequences of his act, using the word 'intention' in the same sense as it is used in the *Criminal Code*, sec. 302, sub-sec. 3, he made the payment otherwise than in the ordinary course of business."

I apprehend that the learned Judge referred to this passage in my judgment in *Stewart & Walker* v. *White* (1):—"I think that when a debtor, knowing that he cannot pay all his creditors in full, deliberately pays one of them, he intends the necessary consequences of his action, *i.e.*, he intends to give him a preference· And I think that under such circumstances he makes the payment with a view of giving the creditor a preference within the meaning of sec. 107." In the passage I have just read, the important words are, "Knowing that he cannot pay all his creditors in full, deliberately pays one of them." Now, it does not follow, from the mere fact that a debtor is unable at a particular moment to pay all his debts as they become due from his own moneys, that he cannot pay all his creditors in full, if time is allowed him. For certain purposes of the Insolvency Law that state of things is made conclusive evidence of insolvency. Failure to meet a promissory note is ordinarily sufficient evidence of such inability. But it is notorious that such a state of things does not necessarily lead to insolvency, nor does the payment of the debt due to one creditor necessarily have the effect of preferring him to the others. It may, on the contrary, be the best and only way of ensuring the ultimate payment of the others. In such a case it would be improper to infer an intention to prefer that creditor, because such a result is not probable. If the rule were as suggested, any debtor, who falls for a moment within the artificial rule of the section, has only two alternatives, to suspend payment or make a fraudulent preference of some creditor or creditors. Business could not be carried on under such conditions. If that is the principle which the learned Judges of the Full Court thought that we laid down, they were under a misapprehension.

The learned Judge of first instance found that, at the time the agreement of October was made, the debtor was in insolvent cir-

(1) 5 C. L. R., 110, at pp. 116, 117.

in prosperous circumstances and the payments were otherwise in the ordinary course of business. That cannot be the rule. The agreement of October being unimpeachable, payments made in accordance with it were made in the ordinary course of business in the sense in which I used those words in *Stewart & Walker* v. *White* (1). They were made in pursuance of a valid agreement. Whether the agreement itself was an unusual or a usual one is a matter of no consequence. It was a perfectly valid agreement, and, as I have said, unimpeachable, and the payments impeached were simply payments made in pursuance of a lawful, binding obligation, by a debtor who was apparently in prosperous circumstances and carrying on a large business. The fact that he happened six months before to be in temporary difficulties (as happens in the history of a very large number of prosperous mercantile concerns) is not conclusive. If, because a man has been once in difficulties, a creditor is not to be allowed to give him time to get out of his difficulties, I am afraid business could hardly be carried on. In my opinion, the conclusions of the learned Chief Justice were correct, and the motion of the trustee ought to have been dismissed.

There was another point raised with respect to one of the instalments—what was called the delivery of butter in satisfaction of a past debt. In the period during which the instalments were being paid, the appellants bought from the debtor about £800 worth of butter. It was a cash transaction, and when the time came for paying the £800 it happened that one of the instalments of £25 was due. Instead, therefore, of giving the debtor a cheque for £800, and taking a cheque from him for £25, they gave him a cheque for £775. That transaction is impeached on the ground that it was a delivery of butter in discharge of a past debt. The first answer is that that was not the transaction. There was no delivery of butter in satisfaction of a past debt. The appellants had bought £800 worth of butter, to be paid for in cash, and, instead of two cheques being passed, one cheque was given for £775. Suppose the appellants in the present case had only given him the £775, and the debtor had become insolvent, the trustee in his estate would have been

(1) 5 C.L.R., 110.

entitled to sue them for
titled to set off against h
promised to pay them on
got nothing. Why then
present case? I am of o
provisions of sec. 108 to
intended, if we were to h
that nature. For these r
allowed.

BARTON J. The learned
in which we intended th
& Walker v. White (1) to
to say that if our observat
must be sorry for that, but
again, I see no necessity f
I entirely concur in the c
has come to; and even wi
the case, it seems to me t
State, who sat in this
absolutely right in his co
appeal, therefore, should b

O'CONNOR J. The tran
must, I think, all be reg
with my learned brother
has taken of the transacti
substantial matter, theref
ments of the instalments
of the *Insolvency Act* 187
I do not propose to refe
of Queensland took as to
White (1), because, as the
was substantially that wl
to convey. *Stewart & W*
First, the meaning of tl
preference," in sec. 107, a

(

H. C. of A.
1908.

SYDNEY
HARBOUR
TRUST COM-
MISSIONERS
v.
WAILES.

Sec. 27 of the *Sydney Harbour Trust Act* 1900 vests in the Sydney Harbour Trust Commissioners certain lands enumerated, and provides that the Governor may at any time vest in the Commissioner any further lands the property of the Crown deemed to be necessary for the purpose of carrying out the provisions of the Act.

Held, that under that section the Governor had power to vest lands the property of the Crown in the Commissioners by Order in Council, and, that a proclamation by the Governor in Council declaring that land which had been resumed by the Crown under the *Public Works Act* 1900 was deemed to be necessary and should be thereby vested in the Commissioners for the purposes of the Act was sufficient evidence that the land had become vested in the Commissioners without any grant or further conveyance.

Decision of the Supreme Court: *Sydney Harbour Trust Commissioners* v. *Wailes*, (1907) 7 S.R. (N.S.W.), 567, reversed.

APPEAL from a decision of the Supreme Court of New South Wales.

The appellants were plaintiffs in an action of ejectment against the respondents. At the trial the presiding Judge directed the jury to find a verdict for the plaintiffs. The respondents then moved the Full Court to set aside the verdict and enter a nonsuit on the grounds that, the land claimed having become the property of the Crown by resumption, there was no evidence that the title of the Crown to the land was conveyed to or vested in the appellants, and that there was no evidence that the land was deemed to be necessary for the purpose of carrying out the provisions of the *Sydney Harbour Trust Act* 1900. The Full Court set aside the verdict and ordered a nonsuit to be entered: *Sydney Harbor Trust Commissioners* v. *Wailes* (1), and from that decision the present appeal was brought.

The facts and the material sections of the Acts are set out in the judgment of *Griffith* C.J.

Knox K.C. (*Garland* with him), for the appellants. The only point taken at the trial was that there was no evidence that the lands were deemed to be necessary. The Full Court granted a nonsuit on a point not taken at the trial. [He referred to *Mutual Life Insurance Co. of New York* v. *Moss* (2).]

(1) (1907) 7 S.R. (N.S.W.), 567.　　(2) 4 C.L.R., 311, at p. 322.

H. C. OF A.
1908.

SYDNEY
HARBOUR
TRUST COM-
MISSIONERS
v.
WAILES.

Sec. 27 of the *Sydney Harbour Trust Act* 1900 vests in the Sydney
Trust Commissioners certain lands enumerated, and provides that the (
may at any time vest in the Commissioner any further lands the pr(
the Crown deemed to be necessary for the purpose of carrying out
visions of the Act.

Held, that under that section the Governor had power to vest 1
property of the Crown in the Commissioners by Order in Council, a
proclamation by the Governor in Council declaring that land which
resumed by the Crown under the *Public Works Act* 1900 was dee
necessary and should be thereby vested in the Commissioners for th
of the Act was sufficient evidence that the land had become vest
Commissioners without any grant or further conveyance.

Decision of the Supreme Court: *Sydney Harbour Trust Commi*
Wailes, (1907) 7 S. R. (N.S. W.), 567, reversed.

APPEAL from a decision of the Supreme Court of Ne
Wales.

The appellants were plaintiffs in an action of ejectmen
the respondents. At the trial the presiding Judge dir(
jury to find a verdict for the plaintiffs. The responde
moved the Full Court to set aside the verdict and ente
suit on the grounds that, the land claimed having be
property of the Crown by resumption, there was no
that the title of the Crown to the land was conveyed to
in the appellants, and that there was no evidence that
was deemed to be necessary for the purpose of carryin
provisions of the *Sydney Harbour Trust Act* 1900.
Court set aside the verdict and ordered a nonsuit to b
Sydney Harbor Trust Commissioners v. *Wailes* (1),
that decision the present appeal was brought.

The facts and the material sections of the Acts are
the judgment of *Griffith* C.J.

Knox K.C. (*Garland* with him), for the appellants.
point taken at the trial was that there was no evidenc
lands were deemed to be necessary. The Full Court
nonsuit on a point not taken at the trial. [He r
Mutual Life Insurance Co. of New York v. *Moss* (2).]

(1) (1907) 7 S. R. (N.S.W.), 567.   (2) 4 C. L. R., 311, at p.

H. C. of A.
1908.

SYDNEY
HARBOUR
TRUST COM-
MISSIONERS
v.
WAILES.

[GRIFFITH C.J.—The words "shall vest" mean, *primâ facie*, that the legal estate shall vest.]

The section does not say that the land shall become vested, but that the Governor may vest them, and this he can do only by adopting the appropriate method of conveyance. The legal estate cannot come to the Commissioners without a grant. It does not follow that, because proclamation is expressly provided in sec. 28 for the case of withdrawal, it is intended to be the method for vesting under sec. 27. This may be a *casus omissus*, but that is a matter for the legislature. As it stands, sec. 27 merely empowers the Governor to "vest" the land in the Commissioners; it does not mention the method of vesting. [He referred to *Heydon v. Lillis* (1).]

[GRIFFITH C.J. referred to *Trustees Act* 1898, No. 4, sec. 29.]

Under that Act the Court has power to make a vesting order. The Governor is not empowered by sec. 27 to make such an order. He must take the steps required by law for the purpose of vesting. Though the Commissioners are an agency of the Crown, they are a corporation capable of holding property in the same way as an individual. [He referred also to *Chitty Prerog. of Crown*, c. xvi., sec. 2, p. 389; and the *Public Works Act* 1900, sec. 37.]

GRIFFITH C.J. This is an action for ejectment in which the plaintiffs, who are the appellants, had to prove their title. The title they set up is this:—The land in question had been resumed under the *Public Works Act* 1900 by the Governor by a proceeding called a notification of resumption. The notification was in the form of a proclamation which set out that the lands resumed shall be vested in the Minister for Works as trustee for the Crown, by virtue of sec. 27 of that Act. The *Sydney Harbour Trust Act* 1900 provides by sec. 27 that certain lands enumerated "shall be vested in the Commissioners upon trust for the purposes of this Act." Then follows a proviso that the Governor "may at any time vest in the Commissioners any further lands the property of the Crown, deemed to be necessary, and may remove from the Commissioners such lands as may be found unnecessary for the purpose of carrying out the provisions of this Act."

(1) 4 C.L.R., 1223.

H. C. of A.
1908.

SYDNEY
HARBOUR
TRUST COM-
MISSIONERS
v.
WAILES.

Solicitor, for the appellants, *The Crown Solicitor for New South Wales.*

Solicitor, for the respondents, *A. H. Delohery.*

C. A. W.

END OF VOL. V.

——Fra
Good fait
Vict. No

LEGISLATIVE POWERS—Exclusive powers of Commonwealth—Control of Customs—Rule as to legislation binding Crown—How far State Governments subject to Commonwealth legislation—Goods imported by State Government—Removal from Customs control—Customs Act 1901 (No. 6 of 1901), secs. 30, 33, 236—The Constitution (63 & 64 Vict. c. 12), secs. 52 (ii.) 86, 90.]—The rule that the Crown is not bound by a Statute except by express words or necessary implication applies only to those representatives of the Crown who have executive authority in the place where the Statute applies, and as to matters to which that executive authority extends. The Constitution binds the Crown as represented by the various States, and takes no account of the States and State Governments in relation to Commonwealth legislation on matters within the exclusive control of the Commonwealth Government, and, therefore, in the construction of Commonwealth Statutes dealing with such matters, the rule applies to the Sovereign as head of that Government, but not to the Sovereign as head of the State Governments. The *Customs Act* 1901, being a valid exercise by the Commonwealth of the exclusive power to impose, collect and control duties of Customs and Excise conferred by secs. 52 (ii.), 86, and 90 of the Constitution, applies to goods imported by the Government of a State as well as to those imported by private persons; and, therefore, goods imported by a State, whether dutiable or not, are by sec. 30 of the Act subject to the control of the Customs, and the authority of the State Executive is no justification for their removal from that control contrary to the provisions of the Act. A quantity of wire netting, which had been purchased in England and imported into the Commonwealth by the Government of New South Wales, was landed at the port of Sydney. Without any entry having been made or passed, and without the authority of the Customs officers, the defendant, acting under the authority of the Executive Government of the State, removed the goods from the place

LEGISLATIVE)
where they
defendant ha:
and 236 of
entered for th
King v. *Sutto:*

————Power:
—Duties of Ci
State Govern:
—Liability to
stitution (63
(ii.), 52 (ii.), 8
in *D'Emden*
111, and appli
the Common\
alities in the .
ment Railway
tion v. *New*
Employé: A:s
application to
upon the Col
and which by
control of som:
ments, such as
respect to tra
countries and
must be assu
tended that, :
effective exerc
of State Gove
The impositio
mode of regul
other countrie
taxing power,
to import goo
laws of the C
rule has refere:
the functions o
monwealth, an
to the importa
goods to be a
with one of it:
ing of duties of
of a tax upon :
sec. 114 of th
words of the se:
ing, it is not t
and should be
the plain provi:
ferring upon
power to imp:
regulate trade
C.J., *Barton* J
—Customs dut
being included
tax upon prop:
expression is
upon the act
goods themse!
perty. *Per I*
ordinarily un:
Customs Act,
selves, and, t
the meaning

7

certain improvements necessary for the working of the property were situated on the portion to be retained by the vendor, and a further agreement was then entered into in writing that the sub-lease should not be executed until certain improvements were erected on the rest of the area by the vendor. According to the vendor there was also a verbal agreement, though this was disputed by the purchaser, that the purchaser should have the right in the meantime to use the improvements on the portion to be retained by the vendor. On the day fixed the purchase was completed by transfer of land and delivery of stock, but, the improvements not having been erected, the purchaser claimed the legal and equitable title to the whole area free from any obligation to grant the sub-lease. The vendor thereupon excluded the purchaser's stock from the use of the improvements on the portion in question. The purchaser brought an action at law against the vendor claiming damages for trespass to land and wrongful impounding of stock. The vendor brought a suit in equity, claiming an injunction to restrain the action at law and specific performance of the agreement to grant him a sub-lease. On an interlocutory application the purchaser was given liberty to sign judgment in the action at law, but was restrained by injunction until the hearing from proceeding to assessment of damages. *Held*, that the delay in completion of the improvements did not go to the substance of the transaction, but was a matter for compensation, and the vendor, having completed the improvements before the hearing of the suit, was entitled to a decree for specific performance; but was not entitled to the injunction claimed. *Per Griffith* C.J., *Barton* and *O'Connor* JJ.—The purchaser had never acquired a right to the exclusive possession of the portion to be retained by the vendor, and the vendor had, therefore, a good defence in law to the action for trespass to land, but, as the vendor had verbally agreed to the purchaser having the use of the improvements on that portion, and, as there had been part-performance of the main agreement to which that agreement was ancillary, he had no defence in equity, whether he had or had not at law, to the claim for damages for wrongful impounding, and, as the purchaser did not ask for an inquiry as to damages, but was content to rest on his judgment at law, it was not a case for the exercise by the Court of Equity of its discretionary power to grant an injunction for the purpose of doing complete justice between the parties. *Per Isaacs* J.—The verbal agreement should not, in view of the issues raised at the trial and the conflict of evidence, be taken to have been proved, and upon the documentary evidence the legal title in the whole area passed to the purchaser by virtue

of the transfer, and having entered into possession under the terms of the contract, and no sub-lease having been executed, he was in possession of the whole area, and the vendor became a trespasser and had no defence in law or in equity to the action at law, and was, therefore, not entitled to an injunction. Judgment of *A. H. Simpson* C.J. in Equity varied and affirmed as varied. *Swan v. Rawsthorne* - - - - 765

G. and Z. were carrying on mining operations in partnership upon 20 acres of land, under an authority issued to G. under the Mining on Private Lands Acts. The authority conferred no interest in the land, but merely the right to enter and search for minerals upon a certain area for one year, in anticipation of a title to be subsequently acquired by lease from the Crown of the minerals contained in the area. G., believing himself to have authority from Z. to sell Z.'s share, though he had not such authority in fact, agreed to sell to M. the whole interest of the partners in the land, mining machinery, effects and ore, &c., upon the land. Before the expiration of G.'s authority to enter, M. made an unsuccessful application for an authority to enter an area of 33 acres including the 20 included in G.'s authority, and later, G.'s authority having expired, Z., on his own behalf, obtained an authority to enter the 33 acres, having previously agreed to take G. in as a partner in the new adventure, and the two proceeded to work the area on the same terms as before. In a suit by M. against G. and Z., to have Z. declared a trustee for him of the authority to enter and the benefits attaching to it, and for an injunction and account, with consequential relief :—*Held*, on the evidence, that Z. acquired the authority free of all equities as far as M. was concerned ; and that, as the contract of sale, if it could take effect at all, could only take effect as to G.'s limited interest in the original undertaking, and that undertaking had terminated on the expiration of G.'s authority to enter, there was a complete break of title between G.'s first and second interests, and there was no equitable estoppel arising out of the contract by which G.'s subsequently acquired interest could be affected so as to entitle M. to have Z. declared a trustee for him of G.'s half share. *Held*, further, that even if G.'s subsequently acquired interest could be regarded in equity as an accretion to or in substitution for his interest in the original undertaking,

Melbourne:
Harston, Partridge & Co., Printers,
452-454 Chancery Lane.

www.ingramcontent.com/pod-product-compliance
Lightning Source LLC
LaVergne TN
LVHW012209040326
832903LV00003B/217